ALAN RYAN

On Politics

PENGUIN BOOKS

PENGUIN BOOKS

Published by the Penguin Group
Penguin Books Ltd, 80 Strand, London WC2R 0RL, England
Penguin Group (USA) Inc., 375 Hudson Street, New York, New York 10014, USA
Penguin Group (Canada), 90 Eglinton Avenue East, Suite 700, Toronto, Ontario, Canada M4P 2Y3
(a division of Pearson Penguin Canada Inc.)
Penguin Ireland, 25 St Stephen's Green, Dublin 2, Ireland (a division of Penguin Books Ltd)
Penguin Group (Australia), 707 Collins Street, Melbourne, Victoria 3008, Australia
(a division of Pearson Australia Group Pty Ltd)
Penguin Books India Pvt Ltd, 11 Community Centre, Panchsheel Park, New Delhi – 110 017, India
Penguin Group (NZ), 67 Apollo Drive, Rosedale, Auckland 0632, New Zealand
(a division of Pearson New Zealand Ltd)
Penguin Books (South Africa) (Pty) Ltd, Block D, Rosebank Office Park,
181 Jan Smuts Avenue, Parktown North, Gauteng 2193, South Africa

Penguin Books Ltd, Registered Offices: 80 Strand, London WC2R 0RL, England

www.penguin.com

First published in the United States of America by Liveright Publishing Corporation,
a division of W. W. Norton & Company 2012
First published in Great Britain by Allen Lane 2012
Published in Penguin Books 2013

001

Copyright © Alan Ryan, 2012

ISBN: 978–0–140–28518–5

www.greenpenguin.co.uk

BOOK ONE

HERODOTUS TO MACHIAVELLI

FOR YURI RYAN SIMONOVICH

CONTENTS

INTRODUCTION: Thinking about Politics   xi

BOOK ONE: Herodotus to Machiavelli

Part I: The Classical Conception

Chapter 1: Why Herodotus?   5
Chapter 2: Plato and Antipolitics   31
Chapter 3: Aristotle: Politics Is Not Philosophy   71
Chapter 4: Roman Insights: Polybius and Cicero   111
Chapter 5: Augustine's Two Cities   149

Part II: The Christian World

Preface to Part II   187
Chapter 6: Between Augustine and Aquinas   193
Chapter 7: Aquinas and Synthesis   224
Chapter 8: The Fourteenth-Century Interregnum   257
Chapter 9: Humanism   291
Chapter 10: The Reformation   321
Chapter 11: Machiavelli   354

NOTES TO BOOK ONE   391

BOOK TWO: Hobbes to the Present

Preface to Book Two   403

Part I: Modernity

Chapter 12: Thomas Hobbes   411
Chapter 13: John Locke and Revolution   453
Chapter 14: Republicanism   497
Chapter 15: Rousseau   532
Chapter 16: The American Founding   577
Chapter 17: The French Revolution and Its Critics   616
Chapter 18: Hegel: The Modern State as the
   Work of Spirit   652
Chapter 19: Utilitarianism: Jeremy Bentham and
   James and John Stuart Mill   695
Chapter 20: Tocqueville and Democracy   729
Chapter 21: Karl Marx   770

Part II: The World after Marx

Preface to Part II   809
Chapter 22: The Twentieth Century and Beyond   815
Chapter 23: Empire and Imperialism   843
Chapter 24: Socialisms   879
Chapter 25: Marxism, Fascism, Dictatorship   911
Chapter 26: Democracy in the Modern World   946
Chapter 27: Global Peace and the Human Future   978

ACKNOWLEDGMENTS   1013
NOTES TO BOOK TWO   1015
BIBLIOGRAPHY   1029
FURTHER READING   1041
INDEX   1053

Introduction: Thinking about Politics

THIS IS A LONG BOOK, and a long time in the making. At first, I was reluctant to embark on it at all, knowing how long such projects take. In 1892 the brothers R. W. and A. J. Carlyle began to write an account of medieval political theory. The six volumes appeared between 1903 and 1936; by the time the final volume of *A History of Mediaeval Political Theory in the West* appeared, Sir Robert Carlyle had been dead two years; he did not die young, but at the age of seventy-five in retirement from a long career in the India Office. It remains an indispensable source for students of the subject, but today it would be the work of a team of authors and research assistants. When a publishing friend suggested thirty-five years ago that I might write a successor to George Sabine's *History of Political Theory*, I thought of the Carlyles and demurred. It was not merely that I had no brothers to help me—Robert Carlyle was fully employed in managing the affairs of India; most of the work fell to his brother, a historian at Oxford. More importantly, I was not sure what would give a long book its intellectual unity. If history is, as Henry Ford inelegantly put it, one damn' thing after another, was the history of thinking about politics merely one damn' thinker or one damn' idea after another? Was it even, as Macbeth more elegantly but more despairingly might have feared, a tale full of sound and fury signifying nothing, a chronicle of verbal fisticuffs at the end of which we were no wiser than at the beginning? But a flood of interesting work then appeared on particular writers and particular historical periods—Quentin Skinner's *Foundations of Modern Political Thought*, for instance, or John Pocock's work on the history of republican thought, *The Machiavellian Moment*. The plot formulated itself behind my back.

I start with Herodotus because the question turned out to be whether the Persians had defeated the Greeks, and we could do nothing about it. Perhaps the modern world, modern politics, and the modern state were the delayed revenge of the Persian Empire on the victors of Marathon and Salamis. The Greeks, and particularly the Athenians, fought to protect a distinctive and distinctively political way of life. In their view, the subjects of the great king of Persia were to all intents and purposes slaves even when not literally of a servile status. As Hegel later said, under an oriental despotism, one man alone was free. Yet Persia was an effective state, gathering taxes, administering justice, fielding armies; its subjects were more prosperous than the Greeks. It is not too fanciful to see Persia as the prototype of the modern nation-state, and not only because the U.S. Post Office is so deeply attached to Herodotus's description of the great king's messengers of whom he wrote, "Neither rain, nor snow, nor heat nor gloom of night stays these couriers from the swift completion of their appointed rounds." The essence of a modern state is centralized authority, bureaucratic management, the efficient delivery of the public services that only a state can provide; Persia provided fewer services than a modern state and "outsourced" much of the work to officials in semiautonomous political dependencies, but the principle was there. As to the early modern states to which our own political systems are the heirs, Louis XIV may have said, "L'état, c'est moi," but he knew what a state was: a legal person rather than a physical one. It was the state's all-encompassing authority that he embodied in his own majestic person. It was on the state's behalf that he was obsessed with the need to know whatever could be known about the resources of his kingdom and the lives of his subjects so that he could better manage their lives and resources for their own welfare.

The contrast between the Persian state—and by the same token the late Imperial Roman, Bismarckian, or modern European state—and the Greek polis is far from the only theme that dominates this story. A familiar contrast is between Athenian and Roman notions of freedom and citizenship. The Athenians practiced a form of unfiltered direct democracy that the Romans thought a recipe for chaos; the Romans gave ordinary free and male persons a role in politics, but a carefully structured and controlled one. Roman freedom was most basically a matter of not being a slave; secondarily, it was the possession of a legal status, being able to secure one's rights in court; thirdly, it carried political rights and duties, carefully graded accorded to one's financial status. It was also a status that exposed any free individual to taxation and military service, again according to financial capacity. As Rome grew, citizenship was extended to conquered cities, initially without extending the voting rights that the Romans had; the *civis sine suffragio*—a citizen without a vote—was nonetheless a free man. He could say, *civis Romanus sum*—"I am a Roman citizen"—and it meant something real, particularly if he was facing a court, or afraid that an official might be about to have him scourged, or detained without the prospect of a fair trial. The Athenian obsession with the right to speak and vote in the Assembly ruled out the thought that a *civis sine suffragio* was fully a free man; it ruled out also the thought that a citizen who was entitled to vote but not to hold any sort of judicial position was fully a free man. The Athenians associated freedom with unvarnished political equality, *isegoria*, or equal rights in the Assembly, and they would have regarded the Roman restrictions on access to judicial and political office as oligarchical. Variations on the argument between Athens and Rome have dominated European and American political thought since the English Civil War of the 1640s. How far we can, indeed how far we should be tempted to try to, follow the Athenians in securing the political equality of all citizens in the face of differences in wealth, education, civic-mindedness, competence, or public spirit is an unanswered question.

Much of the time, the question goes unasked in prosperous liberal democracies like Britain or the United States, because most of us see political equality as exhausted by "one person, one vote" and dig no deeper; we know that one person, one vote coexists with the better-off and better-organized buying influence through lobbying, campaign contributions, and use of the mass media, but we find ourselves puzzled to balance a belief that everyone has the right to use his or her resources to influence government—which is certainly one form of political equality—with our sense that excessive inequality of political resources undermines democracy. We must not sentimentalize the distant past when we wonder whether the better-off have too much political power. Although they often turned on them and dismissed them at a moment's notice, the Athenians were led by men of "good family." Nor should we think that the only source of political inequality in the modern world is the ability of the well-off to convert money into influence by buying politicians' loyalty. If the economically less well-off organize themselves, perhaps by piggybacking on trade union membership, or ethnic or religious identity, they may be equally formidable. The discrepancy in political effectiveness in modern industrial societies is between the unorganized and the organized; money is the life blood of organization, but not money alone. Can democracies protect the public at large—unorganized individuals—against well-organized special interests? The question plagues all modern democracies. Neither intellectually nor institutionally have we advanced very far beyond Rousseau's identification of the problem two and a half centuries ago in the *Social Contract*.

Although the Romans disavowed Athenian democracy, there are many "Roman" arguments for involving the citizenry in political life as deeply as possible. Machiavelli had no taste for Athenian democracy, but preferred citizen armies to mercenary troops, and like Roman writers before him and innumerable writers after him thought that, given the right arrangements, the uncorrupted ordinary people could check the tendency of the rich to subvert republican institutions. That was a commonplace of antiaristocratic republican thinking in eighteenth- and nineteenth-century Europe; it is a standing theme of American populism. Many writers on the left have taken a simpler view of the need for popular participation. It is an old thought that unless the less well-off use their numerical strength to offset the advantages of the better-off, they will lose out in the distribution of the economic benefits that a modern industrial society can provide. It is the most obvious of the instrumental arguments for universal suffrage; unless the worse-off have an adequate say in the rules that regulate the economy in which they earn their living, they will find themselves exploited. The history of trade union legislation in Britain and the United States is a textbook example of that simple point. Not all arguments for widespread participation are instrumental, however. Many writers, across the whole political spectrum, have thought that it is morally better to be an active citizen than a mere consumer of whatever benefits accrue in virtue of being an ordinary, economically productive member of one's society. All republicans, whether Athenian or Roman, agreed on that, even when they had grave doubts about just who could be an active citizen: certainly not women, but ordinary workingmen?

The modern anxiety about popular participation in political life has a long history, but has taken a distinctive form. Greek city-states were plagued by civil war between oligarchs and democrats; the last hundred years of the Roman Republic were marked by conflicts between *populares* and *optimates*, the (proclaimed) defenders of the interests of the people and the upper classes. For the past two centuries, the argument has focused on the political roles of elites and masses. "The masses" is a relatively modern term, whether applied optimistically, in looking to the awakened proletarian masses to make the revolution that ushers in the socialist millennium, contemptuously in belittling the low tastes of the uncultivated masses, good-naturedly when we welcome the huddled masses yearning to be free, or merely descriptively, as meaning simply a lot of people. The term emerged during the industrial revolution at a time of rapid population growth and rapid urbanization; but the contrast between the elite and the rank and file is ancient. The thought that astute practitioners of the political arts can do almost anything they like with the masses is as old as the critics of Athenian democracy, and so is its relatively benign counterpart, the Platonic vision of the statesman as a shepherd, no more expecting to be second-guessed by the ordinary man than the shepherd expects to be second-guessed by his sheep.

From Machiavelli to the present, thinkers have distinguished between the adept elite and the incompetent many. We may think that anyone who draws such a distinction and in such terms can be no friend to democracy; that is not true. If we are persuaded that in all societies only a small number of people will actually play a role in governing the society, it makes all the difference just *how* the elite secures and retains the allegiance of the many. A totalitarian elite employs the secret police; a democratic elite employs pollsters and advertising agencies. Totalitarian elites, military juntas, and the like intend to hold power for life; democratic elites allow themselves to be thrown out by the electorate. They may do their very best to cajole, persuade, or even bamboozle the voter, but they do not corrupt the courts, politicize the army, or send the secret police to the polling booth. Unillusioned commentators on modern democracies describe democracy as rule by *competing* elites. The competition produces better government than elite rule without competition and better government than rule by mass meeting, or whatever direct democracy might involve. We are destined to be ruled by elites, but "the circulation of elites" will ensure that incompetent elites are replaced by more-competent elites. The people may only get to choose between one elite and another, but open competition and free elections produce good government. Nonetheless, just who gets to be a member of the political elite, or elites, and how that person gets there remains a contentious issue; even in Western liberal democracies there might be a fierce competition between politicians, but a restrictive system of recruitment to the ranks of the competitors. The American system of primary elections was established to counter just that problem; its success has been only partial.

So-called elite democracy, or government by competing elites who gain power through the ballot box, is also often described as "rule by professional politicians." We should not be too quick to disparage professional politicians; there are many worse political systems than contemporary liberal democracies. The fact that professional politicians are in interesting ways not very like the population they represent is not in itself a source of anxiety; physicians are not very like the majority of the patients they care for, either. If politicians do a poor job of promoting the best interests of the people they represent, this may be less a matter of simple incompetence than of the conflicting pressures upon them, on the one hand, and the near-impossibility of the tasks they are asked to perform, on the other. All the same, those who hanker after something more Athenian than rule by professional politicians may wonder whether the role of the professional politician could be diminished and the ordinary citizen given more work to do. That is a question that runs through what follows.

Another way of framing the question was provided by the French political thinker Benjamin Constant early in the nineteenth century. His lecture on the difference between classical and modern conceptions of freedom is a liberal sacred text. Freedom for the citizens of ancient republics like Sparta or Athens was a matter of having a share of the sovereign authority; it was essentially public and political. It came at a high price; not only did such societies depend on the existence of slaves in order to free the citizens to do their citizen duties, but they were societies of mutual surveillance, in which everyone was under the scrutiny of everyone else. Modern freedom in contrast was essentially private; it was the ability to pursue our private economic, literary, or religious concerns without having to answer to anyone else. It was freedom *from* the political sphere rather than freedom *in* the political sphere. The subject of a modern liberal democracy benefits from its liberal aspect by having a full measure of modern freedom: occupational, educational, religious. Indeed, when most people talk of democracy today, they have these liberties much more clearly in their minds than any particular system of voting rights; that is hardly surprising when barely half of them exercise their right to vote in important national elections, and far fewer in local elections. Skeptics about participation will insist that what matters is accountability rather than mass participation; voting for any particular party or candidate matters less than the ability to vote against them. That is the democratic aspect of "liberal democracy," and it is impossible to achieve in the absence of the liberal freedoms. In what used to be called "people's democracies"—otherwise one-party communist states—or "guided democracies"—otherwise dictatorships—there was a very high level of participation, along with frequent opportunities to register enthusiasm for the ruling party and its policies. What there was not was the opportunity to canvass alternatives, to press for different policies or a different political leadership without risking imprisonment, torture, or death. Imperfect as liberal democracy is, it yields a measure of accountability to the public that the experience of the past hundred years suggests is indispensable to decent government and the rule of law.

Turning our gaze away from politics momentarily, we should also reflect that when we talk of democracy we very often mean something social rather than political, what Alexis de Tocqueville called equality of condition. I do not in what follows say very much in celebration of the modern Western world's commitment to forms of inclusiveness that would have astonished our ancestors, not least because they are so obviously worthy of celebration that adding my voice to the chorus seems otiose. Societies that think of themselves as unusually "democratic" do so because they pride themselves on an absence of snobbery, or because women occupy large numbers of senior positions in business or government, or because they have been successful in integrating large numbers of immigrants, or in diminishing race-based economic and other forms of inequality. They are democratic in the sense that they have removed many, if not all, previously acceptable grounds for claiming advantage: race, birth, gender in particular. To call this "social democracy" invites confusion, because the Marxist and post-Marxist socialist parties of western Europe called, and still call, themselves Social Democrats, and democracy in the sense described in this paragraph is very much at home with capitalism and free markets: if the claims of race, birth, and gender are rejected, what is left are the claims based on the contribution we make to the welfare of other individuals or society at large. Those contributions may range very widely, from simple manual labor to whatever it is that celebrities add to our lives, and the obvious way to discover what our contributions are worth is to see how they fare in the marketplace. Of course, all actual societies realize such values only very imperfectly, and markets are notoriously imperfect, too. Nonetheless, the thought that the core values of modern liberal democracies are social rather than political is far from foolish.

A presupposition of what follows is that the project of entering into the thoughts of the long dead and rethinking them for our own purposes is both possible and useful. That raises the question whether I am committed to the view that there is nothing new under the sun, or more guardedly to the view of Thucydides and Machiavelli, among many others, that since human nature is the same at all times and in all places, we can draw morals about what is likely to happen to us from what our predecessors have thought and done. The answer is "not exactly." The last fifth of this book takes very seriously the thought that over the past two and a half centuries several revolutions dramatically changed the world that politics tries to master. In no particular order, and without assigning priority to one aspect of an interconnected process, the industrial revolution, the demographic revolution, the literacy and communications revolution, and the political revolutions of the late eighteenth century and more recently have created a world that is in innumerable ways quite unlike the ancient, medieval, and early modern worlds. The most important of these ways reflect our greatly enhanced technological capacities. To put it brutally, we can keep vastly more people alive than ever before, and we can kill vastly more people than ever before.

Advances in agriculture allow us to feed ourselves healthily and reliably, the availability of clean water and efficient sewerage means we suffer fewer infections, medical advances allow us to treat previously untreatable diseases and injuries; and during the twentieth century two world wars showed how effective we were at killing millions of one another. To put it less brutally, our ability to produce so much more than our predecessors means that along with the useful things we produce, we produce much we wish we did not, pollution of all kinds with all its destructive impacts on our environment. Because all this happens on a global scale, the tasks that modern governments must grapple with not only are more numerous and more complex than our predecessors could have imagined but threaten evils on a larger scale than they could have imagined. So I end with some anxious reflections on the politics of an interconnected and increasingly crowded planet. Demography may not be destiny, but managing the problems of a planet of more than seven billion people is a very different enterprise from ensuring that a city-state of two or three hundred thousand could feed itself, protect itself from its enemies, and cultivate the rich civic life that even now we contemplate with envy.

Thinking about Politics

There are many people who, like me, have spent a working lifetime teaching and writing about what is commonly called "political thought" or "political theory." Yet there is surprisingly little agreement on what "political thought" is. It is not exactly history, although it engages with the ideas of long-dead thinkers; it is not exactly philosophy, although it engages with the arguments of thinkers both living and dead. It is not exactly sociology, although it is a valid complaint against anyone writing about politics that he is sociologically naïve. A colleague once described political theorists as people who were obsessed with two dozen books; after half a century of grappling with Mill's essay *On Liberty*, or Hobbes's *Leviathan*, I have sometimes thought two dozen might be a little on the high side. Even if they are hard put to it to explain themselves to one another, political theorists have no doubt that they are engaged in productive, if sometimes frustrating, conversations across the centuries with their long-dead predecessors, as well as their contemporaries. They want anyone who might be interested to overhear these conversations and join in. We are eavesdropping in the Elysian Fields, hoping to catch the cynical Machiavelli taunting Socrates for his otherworldliness, or hear Jefferson admit that Alexander Hamilton foresaw the American future more accurately than he.

There is no way to do this without running the risk of foisting our own views on the unresisting dead. It is the obvious danger of attempting to have a conversation with great, but absent, thinkers who cannot tell us we are talking nonsense. I am a great admirer of Isaiah Berlin, whose essays in the history of ideas provide one model for what I do here; nonetheless, there are moments in his work that make the reader wonder whether it is Montesquieu speaking or Berlin, or whether Machiavelli would have recognized the causes for which Berlin recruited him. The early twentieth-century philosopher and historian R. G. Collingwood claimed that historical explanation was a matter of rethinking past thoughts, and that thought was reflected in Berlin's work as it is in what follows. As to not foisting my ideas on the unresisting dead, I can only say that I have tried to keep the critical voices of my colleagues in my head as I wrote. One further element that gives Berlin's writings their extraordinary vividness is an almost uncanny ability to engage with the temperament of the thinkers he wrote about. The difficulties that beset the attempt to know just what someone thought equally beset the attempt to know just what it would have been like to meet him or her in the flesh, perhaps even more so. Nonetheless, if we are to see our predecessors in the round we must take the risk.

Like many contemporary commentators who bemoan the decline of the "public intellectual," I am uncomfortable with the thought that serious thinkers about politics may retire into the ivory tower and write difficult—if often very interesting—essays and books for their colleagues alone, leaving debates over the prospects of modern political life to the punditry of contributors to the op-ed pages, or the shouting matches that pass for political debate on some television channels. I am not particularly gloomy; the fact that a book such as Allan Bloom's lugubrious essay called *The Closing of the American Mind* could become a best seller suggests that the American mind was much less closed than he thought, and although I did not greatly admire Francis Fukuyama's book *The End of History and the Last Man*, its success demonstrated that there were public intellectuals in the marketplace, and a substantial audience for their ideas. History and biography have always had a wide popular appeal, and we are all richer for the work of Simon Schama or Gordon Wood, to name just two. But some accounts of the history of philosophy have secured an enviably wide audience. Bertrand Russell's *History of Western Philosophy*, which I read avidly at the age of fifteen, was one. Together with Mill's *On Liberty*, it changed my life, but reading it again years later was a salutary experience; questions of inaccuracy aside, it was spectacularly prejudiced—though very funny. I have taken Russell's lucidity as a benchmark, though the ability to write so transparently and easily, which rightly earned him a Nobel Prize in Literature, is a gift I can only envy. As to his prejudices, I share some of them, but have done my best to leave them out. One respect in which he is not a model is that he was too often dismissive, even contemptuous, of thinkers with whom he disagreed. Here I am sometimes sharp with thinkers whose greatness is indisputable: Plato and Marx, to take two obvious examples. I am neither contemptuous nor dismissive of them. My sharpness is addressed only to their arguments about how we may best govern ourselves; Plato's metaphysical speculation is deep, rich, inexhaustibly interesting, but his remedy for political chaos is not. Marx's thoughts about economic analysis and his historical sociology are endlessly fascinating, but his evasiveness about just how one might manage a socialist economy is unforgivable. Mockery of either is unthinkable; criticism is not.

As that suggests, I am a political enthusiast; I am fascinated by politics in all its forms, and avidly devour newspapers and current affairs programs. I am also a skeptic: like most people, a skeptic about the motives, intelligence, and competence of politicians; but unlike most people, skeptical about the way we talk about politics. Many ideas that governments, politicians, commentators, and ordinary citizens appeal to when they talk about politics have little substance; others made sense long ago, but not in the modern world. Notoriously, almost every modern government calls itself a democracy; but self-described democracies do not much resemble one another, and none resemble the political system for which Athenians fought and died two and a half thousand years ago. Are modern democracies really democracies, or something else? (The answer is "strictly speaking, something else," as we shall see.) We may wonder why we give them a misleading name, and whether it matters. It may not; many people share my surname, but we are rarely confused with each other.

On the other hand, it may be a mistake to operate new institutions under old labels, arousing impossible expectations and causing needless disappointment. It may have worse effects, perhaps enabling a plutocracy to exploit a political system for its own benefit, with "bread and circuses" pacifying the worse-off, who are flattered and cajoled but exploited nonetheless. We may be less deceived than self-deceived, knowing in our hearts that we are subjects, not citizens, that the world is divided between the givers of orders and the takers of orders, and that we are among the latter, but pretending to ourselves that we might make it all the way from the log cabin to the White House. The coins and armors of imperial Rome carried the legend "Senatus Populusque Romanus"; but "the Senate and people of Rome" lived under a military and bureaucratic dictatorship.

Raising such questions is not to condemn modern politics—life is vastly safer in most modern societies than in the ancient world; the politics of modern "democracies" are usually more rational than the politics of Athens, and less brutal than the politics of Rome; they are much less chaotic and less dangerous than the politics of Renaissance Italy and Reformation Germany. In the modern Western world, individuals have a host of rights—to free speech, to worship as they choose, to occupational freedom, to live where they like—that earlier ages never dreamed of conferring on ordinary people; the poor have votes, and women play a role in politics that would once have been thought impossible, dangerous, wicked, or unnatural, if not all four at once. But we should at least wonder *what* we are praising when we praise democracy; and when we pledge our commitment to liberty and justice for all, we should wonder whether these are the liberty and justice of the American founders, let alone the liberty and justice that Cicero or Marsilius said we could achieve only when the common good was pursued by selfless rulers. The best way to explore such questions is by contrasting our ideas and allegiances with those of thinkers from other places and other ages. Rome and Athens held very different views about freedom from one another and ourselves; yet we have acquired our vocabulary and its buried assumptions from both, while many of our institutions come from other sources entirely. It is perhaps surprising that we are not more confused than we are about democracy, freedom, justice, and citizenship.

This is a book about the answers that historians, philosophers, theologians, practicing politicians, and would-be revolutionaries have given to one question. How can human beings best govern themselves? That question raises innumerable others: can we manage our own affairs at all? Many writers have thought we are not the masters of our destinies, but the playthings of a malicious fate, or the unwitting agents of divine providence. Perhaps prayer rather than politics is the answer to the human condition. If we can control some of what happens, there is little agreement on how much and what. Many writers have thought that only some people were morally entitled or intellectually able to control their fates, for example, men but not women, Greeks but not Persians, property owners but not the laboring poor, Christian Europeans but not pagan Amerindians, free Americans but not slaves. Answers to our question over two and a half millennia form the subject of this book: they include "give yourselves over to the unfettered discretion of the wisest," "try to make sure that neither the rich nor the poor can dominate decision making," "find a godly ruler and give him absolute authority," and "do not ask; accept the powers that be and think of your immortal soul." Such answers are both ancient and contemporary. They raise more questions in turn: religious, philosophical, historical, biological, and sociological—what kind of justice the state should seek, whether there is a pattern to history, whether we are doomed by our biology to fight endless wars; ultimately, what the point may be of human existence. Different convictions may lead us to think the goal of politics is physical survival, the good life, glory, liberty, salvation in the afterlife, the liberation of human nature by the revolutionary overthrow of capitalism. All these answers have influenced political thinking and practice.

I follow the deeper questions only as far as they illuminate ideas about how we should govern ourselves. With philosophers such as Plato or Hobbes, this is a long way; with a skeptic like Machiavelli, only to explain why he eschewed deep questions. This is a book about politics, and only secondarily about philosophy, religion, biology, or sociology. It is also a book about books: what our forebears wrote. They wrote historical narratives, marshaled philosophical arguments, compiled handbooks of political advice, and often all these at once, but always trying to persuade their readers to follow one political path or another. Their readers took much for granted that we do not, and recognized the local implications of what they read as we cannot do without assistance, and sometimes not at all.

I hope what follows will inspire a taste for what they wrote and make comprehensible what might otherwise be hard going; but although there is a good deal of plot summary here, this book is no substitute for reading the originals. My hope is that readers will be moved to wrestle with these authors and their work for themselves. I have footnoted only sparsely, to give readers the chance to check up on my accuracy, but not to engage in battles with other interpretations; for that reason, I have also suggested further readings for each chapter, so that anyone interested can dig deeper than space permits here. Although this is a book about texts as well as their authors, it is not a textbook so much as a context book and a pretext book, concerned with settings and motives as well as the works themselves. Its success will be measured by the readers who pick up Plato's *Republic*, Hobbes's *Leviathan*, Hegel's *Phenomenology of Spirit*, and find themselves engrossed rather than baffled—and even when they are baffled, are happy to go on reading, interrogating, and arguing with their authors for themselves.

BOOK ONE

HERODOTUS TO MACHIAVELLI

PART I

THE CLASSICAL CONCEPTION

CHAPTER 1

Why Herodotus?

Talking Greek (and Latin) about Politics

WE HAVE INHERITED FROM the Greeks of twenty-five hundred years ago the words they used to talk about their political arrangements: "politics," "democracy," "aristocracy," and "tyranny" are all direct borrowings. We share many of their political ideals: most importantly, a passion for freedom, independence, and self-government. They were acutely aware that the Greek polis, the city-state of Greek antiquity, was an unusual political form, whose survival was always at risk from civil war, or from conquest by powerful foreign states, or neighboring city-states. The origins of the polis are obscure, but it flourished from around 600 BCE until the conquest of the Greek world in the middle of the fourth century by Philip of Macedon and his son Alexander the Great. Even after the failure of the Athenians' final attempt to recover their independence after Alexander's death in 322 BCE, the polis did not disappear. Greek cities practiced limited self-government under the Hellenistic monarchies until the middle of the second century BCE, and thereafter under the umbrella of the Roman Republic and Empire. It was a sadly diminished self-rule; they had lost what they most valued, the freedom of action in military and interstate affairs that they had successfully defended against the Persian Empire in the first two decades of the fifth century BCE.

We are very attached to describing ourselves as the Greeks described themselves; try persuading a friend that the United States is not really a democracy. But it is not clear that their ideals, and ambitions, and the assumptions embodied in that vocabulary, or the views on the best way to govern ourselves of those who created that vocabulary, make much sense in a world as different as ours. Think, first, of the demographic differences: democratic Athens at the beginning of the Peloponnesian War (431 BCE) contained perhaps 50,000 adult male citizens, 200,000 free native inhabitants, and perhaps 300,000 inhabitants in all, including slaves and foreigners. Athens and the countryside of Attica covered seven hundred square miles, about half the area of Rhode Island. A quarter of the population lived in the city, the rest in the countryside, and many city dwellers were farmers who walked to their nearby farms. Athens was much larger than other Greek city-states. We think about modern states with up to a billion inhabitants in terms bequeathed to us by people who lived in very different conditions. If this is not as surprising as it seems at first sight, it should make for caution when reading newspaper editorials or listening to politicians and commentators demanding "democracy" and meaning many very different things.

The tradition this book explores began when Greek thinkers saw that they governed themselves in a way their Asiatic neighbors did not, and concluded that they practiced *political* government while the Persians did not. *Politics*, they thought, could exist only in self-governing city-states—in a polis or republic, and under the rule of law.[1] There was no politics in Persia because the great king was the master of slaves, not the ruler of citizens. The point is beautifully made by Herodotus, the father of history and our own starting point. The exiled Spartan king, Demaratus, had taken refuge at the court of the great king of Persia, Darius I, in 491 BCE. Darius made him the ruler of Pergamum and some other cities. In 480 Darius's son and successor, Xerxes, took him to see the enormous army he had assembled to avenge his father's humiliation by the Athenians in an earlier attempt to conquer Greece. "Surely," he said to Demaratus, "the Greeks will not fight against such odds." He was displeased when Demaratus assured him that they certainly would. "How is it possible that a thousand men—or ten thousand, or fifty thousand, should stand up to an army as big as mine, especially if they were not under a single master but all perfectly free to do as they pleased?" He could understand that they might feign courage if they were whipped into battle as his Persian troops would be, but it was absurd to suppose that they would fight against such odds. Not a bit of it, said Demaratus. They would fight and die to preserve their freedom. He added, "They are free—yes—but they are not wholly free; for they have a master, and that master is Law, which they fear much more than your subjects fear you. Whatever this master commands they do; and his command never varies: it is never to retreat in battle, however great the odds, but always to remain in formation and to conquer or die."[2] They were citizens, not subjects, and free men, not slaves; they were disciplined but self-disciplined. Free men were not whipped into battle. A "republic" could be ruled by kings or aristocrats or democratic assemblies; but its independence was of the essence. So was the idea that its active members were citizens. Democracy—the idea that "the many" should rule—was far from a defining feature of politics. The Spartans lived under a system admired for millennia, and an influence on the American founding, which mixed monarchical, aristocratic, and democratic elements; but the Spartans were socially repressive, obsessively religious, and dependent on the manual labor of the so-called helots, neighboring peoples they had enslaved. Even under a democracy "the many" did not mean all. In Athens, only a proportion of the resident population was politically active; foreigners and slaves could not participate, and women were wholly excluded from public life. Still, the Athenians discovered that once citizenship is extended to the lower classes, the genie is out of the bottle, and nobody can govern without the consent of the citizens.

Political thought as we understand it began in Athens because the Athenians were a trading people who looked at their contemporaries and saw how differently they organized themselves. If they had not lived where they did and organized their economic lives as they did, they could not have seen the contrast. Given the opportunity, they might not have paid attention to it. The Israelites of the Old Testament narrative were very conscious of their neighbors, Egyptian, Babylonian, and other, not least because they were often reduced to slavery or near-slavery by them. That narrative makes nothing of the fact that Egypt was a bureaucratic theocracy; it emphasizes that the Egyptians did not worship Yahweh. The history of Old Testament politics is the history of a people who did their best to have *no* politics. They saw themselves as under the direct government of God, with little room to decide their own fate except by obeying or disobeying God's commandments. Only when God took them at their word and allowed them to choose a king did they become a political society, with familiar problems of competition for office and issues of succession. For the Jews, politics was a fall from grace. For the Greeks, it was an achievement. Many besides Plato thought it a flawed achievement; when historians and philosophers began to articulate its flaws, the history of political thought began among the argumentative Athenians.

The Birth of the Polis

The Athenians of the fifth century had a very fragmentary knowledge of the history of their own institutions and were not attentive to the modern line between "real" *history* and "mere" *myth*. Because the origins of the polis were obscure to them, they are obscure to us. Aristotle in the middle of the fourth century BCE set his students to compile an account of 158 Greek constitutions, of which only that of Athens has come down to us. It is unreliable on arrangements much earlier than the date of its compilation. There were two views of how a polis was formed. The first was military: a scattered group of people came to live in one city behind a set of protective walls. The other was political: a group of people agreed to live under one authority, with or without the protection of a walled city. *Synoikismos*, or "living together," embraces both. Any political entity implies a population that recognizes a common authority, but the first "city-states" were not always based on a city. Sparta makes the point. We think of Sparta as a *city*, but the Spartans were proud of the fact that they lived in villages without protective walls: their army was their wall and "every man a brick." Nonetheless, they belonged to one political entity.

There was no uniform pattern of political organization. In most cases, power and even citizenship were initially confined to a small group of aristocrats; some are described as having "kings."

The division of society into rich and poor was unquestioned, and in every society, including democratic Athens, the leading families, the *eupatridae*, or "wellborn," supplied political leaders. Nonetheless, class warfare was a constant threat. The poor feared they would be reduced to slavery by their betters; and the rich feared they would have their land and wealth seized by the poor. In many cities, tyrants were able to seize power by offering to protect the poorer citizens against the rich or vice versa. "Tyrant" is a word with an unlovely ring to it, but did not inevitably imply that a ruler was brutal or self-seeking, only that he had acquired power unconstitutionally, and governed as a sole ruler. Some tyrants governed moderately and rationally. The Peisistratids, father and sons, who ruled Athens in the late sixth century BCE, were such. Athens had been a democracy in the early sixth century, but even after the reforms of Solon, conflict between rich and poor, and between leading families, was uncontrollable. The tyranny of the Peisistratids averted civil war and was largely unbrutal. Still, although Athens prospered, they were not loved—aristocratic families thought it was their birthright to rule, and the poor wanted a guaranteed voice in public affairs. In 510 the tyranny was overthrown by a domestic insurrection assisted by Sparta.

Athenian Democracy

The replacement of the tyranny by an increasingly radical democracy was a Spartan achievement and wholly unintended. Sparta's policy was to install friendly oligarchies in other Greek city-states. In Athens they were disappointed. The radical Athenian democracy endured with interruptions for almost two centuries as the constitution of an independent state; for more than two millennia it stood as an inspiration to radicals and the poor, a warning to conservatives and the rich, and as a landmark in the history of political inventiveness, alongside the Roman

Republic and the United States. An aristocrat started the process. From 508 onward, Athenian politics were dominated by Cleisthenes, whose reforms aimed at military preparedness and at keeping social peace by opening political life to the poorer citizens. These things were connected; the lowest enfranchised class, the *thetes*, supplied the rowers of the Athenian fleet.

"The poorer citizen" was not just anyone dwelling within the boundaries of Athens. Athenian society rested on slavery, and its political morality rested on two sharp contrasts: between free and servile, and Athenian and alien. The boundary between free and servile was sacrosanct; no marriage between a free Athenian and a slave was countenanced, and the children of such an illicit union were slaves. There was no naturalization process; foreigners could not become citizens by long residence, and only with great difficulty and at great expense by specific legislation. It was a weakness of Greek cities that they were so ethnically exclusive, and it was one way in which the Athenians were less politically astute than the Romans, who made new Romans of the peoples they conquered. Athenian citizenship was by descent; a citizen had to be born to citizen parents. These fiercely binary oppositions extended to the contrast between male and female. In the fifth century Athens combined inventiveness in politics, trade, and warfare with a restrictive attitude to women that was not universal in Greece. This was not sexual puritanism; Athenian men were unabashed about frequenting prostitutes, and same-sex relationships between men and boys were commonplace. Nonetheless, high-status Athenian women were veiled in public and, apart from those who played a part in the religious life of the city, were expected to stay at home and to retire to the women's quarters if a male visitor arrived at the house. Working women were less restricted. As Athens became the dominant trading state in the eastern Mediterranean, it became a cosmopolitan city with a large foreign population. Plato's *Republic* grumbles about it. Athens developed a mercantile economy and systems of banking and insurance; Plato and Aristotle both complain about moneymaking. But rich foreigners remained foreigners; and women were citizens only in the sense that they were the daughters, sisters, mothers, and wives of citizens. They had no political role.

The key to Athenian democracy was the Assembly, or *ecclesia*. It was in modern terms legislature, judiciary, and executive, and there was no appeal against its decisions except to a later meeting of itself, or a court that was part of itself. Although its potential membership was 40,000, it operated through many smaller bodies, through courts of 500 members, and in particular through the 500 members of the governing council, or boule, whose members formed the Athenian administration for a year, and the *prytany*, the 30-strong body whose members formed the managing committee of the boule for a month at a time. Both bodies were chosen by lottery, after a careful scrutiny of the eligibility of those whose names went into the lottery. The next two centuries saw experiments with new committees and new courts, whose effect was to take power out of the hands of old aristocratic institutions and give it to the Assembly. To a modern eye, the fact that the Assembly was a court as much as a legislature seems strange, but it was an important aspect of the Athenians' suspicion of power. Anyone could be accused of misusing public office and be dismissed by the Assembly. There were no public prosecutors; all cases were brought by individuals, and very complicated rules governed the right to prosecute. Since the prosecutor was entitled to a share of whatever fines were imposed, it is unsurprising that the Athenians had a reputation for litigiousness. The system was wide open to abuse and nonetheless mostly remarkably effective.

Cleisthenes rationalized citizenship and membership of the Assembly and put the finances of the fleet and army onto a regular basis. The cost fell heavily on the better-off, because most of the population lived barely above subsistence level, but the expense was inescapable, and Athens was fortunate to have substantial silver mines and slaves to work them. Greek city-states existed on a permanent war footing; when not at war they soon might be, and when not actually fighting they were often in a state of armed truce. Cleisthenes solved the worst problems of internal conflict by organizing the citizens into ten "tribes"; these were geographical groupings, not class or kin groups, and they determined the political rights of their members no matter where they might live. The geographical units were the demes, or villages, of Attica. An Athenian would always identify himself as *so and so, from such and such a deme.* Each tribe supplied fifty members of the boule. The work of the boule was crucial because it prepared legislation for the Assembly and supervised the conduct of officials. Nobody could serve on it for longer than a year at a time, and eventually the rules were tightened so that nobody could serve more than twice in a lifetime. Given the small number of citizens and the large number of posts to be filled, ordinary Athenians had a good chance of being the equivalent of president of Athens for at least one day in a lifetime, and a member of the "cabinet" for a month. This reflected the Athenian passion for equalizing the political influence of every citizen; what we moderns would have to do if we shared that passion with the same intensity is an intriguing question, but it is doubtful we could keep many of our present political arrangements.

The ten tribes also supplied the ten *strategoi*, or generals. These positions were elective and could be held repeatedly. Some ceremonial offices were held for life, but they were either inherited or gained by lot, not election, and there was a permanent administration, inevitable in a city that sustained a substantial naval force and spent vast sums on beautifying the city. Military leadership was where Cleisthenes and his successors drew the line where democratic equality stopped, although even then a *strategos* could be dismissed on the spot by the Assembly. It is a crucial difference between the Athenians and ourselves that we rely on elected representatives whereas they took a random sample of the citizenry. It was a lottery only among the eligible; but as Athenian democracy grew more confident, restrictions on eligibility based on birth and wealth were removed. In the case of the *strategoi*, and other administrative positions, democratic principle was sacrificed to experience, expertise, and reliability. The most famous *strategos*, Pericles, who led Athens before the Peloponnesian War and during its early stages, was repeatedly reelected and exercised the authority of a modern president. Commenting on his career, Thucydides observed that "what was in name a democracy, became in actuality rule by the first man."[3] From the conservative aristocrat Thucydides this was praise. Modern commentators have noted that most leaders came from upper-class families and have suggested that Athens resembled modern democracies in being a de facto oligarchy; but Thucydides was not complaining. When he called Pericles "the first man," he meant he was the wisest and most honorable of the Athenians.

Pericles's hold over the Assembly was that of a demagogue, a leader of the demos, or common people. Those who thought ill of him, including Plato, did not hesitate to call him a demagogue, in the modern, abusive sense, meaning someone who cajoled the foolish many into doing whatever he wanted. Cleisthenes's creation was unlike a modern democracy not only in being a direct not a representative democracy. It was not a *liberal* democracy; there were no constitutional restrictions on what the Assembly could do, no boundaries between public and private life it could not transgress. The Athenians treated choice by lot as self-evidently the most egalitarian way of distributing power, where we use random selection for little beyond jury service. Athenian equality was narrowly political; the *eupatridae*, or wellborn families, had no doubt of their social superiority; men had no doubt of their superiority over women, nor did Athenians doubt their superiority to foreigners; a slave was at the bottom of the heap. Nonetheless, the Assembly's power was very real. It did not hesitate to dismiss Pericles, or other generals, and sometimes did so in a fit of ill temper and regardless of merit. Its sovereignty was absolute, and its members knew it. The consequences were predictable; unless the Assembly was on its best behavior, it could be seduced by flatterers, bamboozled by crooks, and led by the nose by the glib and quick-witted. If it lost its temper, it could behave atrociously.

The Glories and Failures of Democracy

It was astonishing that Cleisthenes's democracy survived its first three decades. Almost at once, Athens was fighting for its life. The fifth century was dominated by two great wars, the first a collective Greek triumph, the second an Athenian disaster. The Persian Wars lasted with interludes from 500 to 479 and at a lower level of intensity for twenty years more; the Peloponnesian War, between Athens and its allies on one side and Sparta, Corinth, and their allies on the other, broke out in 431 and ended in 404 with the utter defeat of Athens. After 479 Athens was the chief maritime power of Greece and the center of a maritime empire that embraced the Aegean and the western shore of Asia Minor. Fear of its growing power, especially in Corinth and Sparta, provoked the alliance that fought Athens in the Peloponnesian War. Even after its crushing defeat, Athens revived during its final three-quarters of a century as an independent state, and twice tried to re-create its Aegean empire. Only the decisive defeat of the allied Greek forces by Philip of Macedon at Chaeronea in 338 and a final defeat of the Athenian fleet by the forces of Macedon in the sea battle of Amorgos in 322 put an end to democratic Athens as an independent state.

The Persian and Peloponnesian wars called out the talents of two of the ancient world's greatest historians. Both were acute political commentators. Herodotus, the chronicler of the Persian Wars, was called both "the father of history" and "the father of lies." He has a reputation for swallowing tall stories, though later research suggests that where he had a chance of being right he usually was, and that many of his conjectures about what had happened centuries earlier were well founded. Thucydides, the chronicler of the Peloponnesian War, has never been accused of credulity and is one of the greatest political analysts of all time. Their histories are not evenhanded. Thucydides and Herodotus had aristocratic sympathies and thought democracies were vulnerable to dissension, inconstancy, and the wiles of ambitious scoundrels. Herodotus was sufficiently impressed by the effectiveness of the Persian monarchy to attract the accusation of being a *philobarbarian.* Herodotus leaves the reader surprised that Athenian democracy found the coherence to defeat the Persians, while Thucydides leaves the reader unsurprised that the Athenian Assembly could be self-destructive. Thucydides's history ends in 411, seven years before the defeat of Athens, but its inevitability stalks the narrative.

Herodotus wrote his *Histories* to explain why Greeks and Persians were doomed to fight one another; he never gave a definite answer, though one can be inferred. The wars began with the revolt of Miletus and other Greek cities on the western shores of Asia Minor in 500. They had succumbed to Persian invasion earlier in the sixth century and were subjects of the Persian monarchy for half a century before they revolted. The reason for the revolt is obscure. Their lives had not been much affected by subjection: they had to pay tribute, and intercity relations were controlled by the Persians, but internal government, religious ritual, and economic activity were their own affair, the pattern subsequently under the Hellenistic monarchies and the Roman Empire. Persian suzerainty had not become more oppressive at the end of the century, and the cities that revolted were prosperous. It may indeed have been a revolt of the prosperous and confident, not a lashing out by the downtrodden and wretched.

Asked for help, Athens sent twenty triremes. Its motives for putting itself in danger's way are obscure. The Athenians cited ties to former colonies, and "Ionian" loyalties, but such ties were usually treated lightly. Herodotus thought the conflict between despotic Persia and democratic Athens inevitable. Many writers after World War II followed Herodotus in thinking that autocracies and democracies cannot live quietly side by side; the visible presence of democratic governments inspires subjugated peoples to think of freedom, and oppressive regimes are tempted to expand their frontiers to prevent their democratic neighbors from subverting their subjects. In reality, tensions were never so great. Persians allied with Greeks and vice versa for their own ends, as the Peloponnesian War proved.

The revolt in Asia Minor was snuffed out in 494, and the Athenians realized that they had acquired a dangerous enemy. Darius I's first attempt at invasion in 492 was abortive: a huge storm wrecked his fleet. In 491 the Persians demanded "earth and water"—signs of submission—from the Aegean islands and mainland cities. Many submitted. Athens and Sparta not only stood firm but murdered the Persian ambassadors. The Athenians put them on trial and killed both the ambassadors and their translator for offenses against the Greek language; the Spartans simply threw them down a well. Darius invaded in 490, but his campaign ended on the seashore at Marathon, when an Athenian hoplite army routed a much larger Persian force. It was a wholly unexpected victory; the Athenians had no reputation as fighters on land, and the Spartans had failed to answer their pleas for assistance against the "barbarians" because they were engaged in a religious festival. Plataea unexpectedly sent its entire army of a thousand hoplites, which may well have been decisive. Marathon showed the Persians what they had to reckon with; and the fact that the Athenians and their allies achieved the victory without Sparta showed the Spartans—who arrived on the scene after the battle had been won—that their military supremacy was no longer unchallengeable. The Athenians began to aspire to become an imperial power in the Aegean. Hubris threatened.

Marathon did not mark the end of the Persian threat. Under Darius's son and successor, Xerxes, the Persians returned a decade later in greater strength; in the summer of 480 the Persian navy was checked but not defeated by an allied Greek fleet off Euboea, and the Persian army met the Greeks on land at the pass of Thermopylae. The narrowness of the space between the mountains and the sea gave a defending army the advantage over much larger forces, and without the treachery of Ephialtes, who showed the Persians a mountain path that ran behind the Greek positions, the seven thousand Greeks might have held their ground long enough to dissuade the Persians from going farther. Once their position was turned, the Spartan king Leonidas sent all but a small rearguard away, and three hundred Spartans made up for their hesitation ten years earlier by holding the pass long enough to let the main Greek force escape to more favorable positions; they died to the last man, together with seven hundred Thespians and several hundred Thebans and others. Their epitaph is legendary: "Go tell the Spartans, passerby, that here, obedient to their laws, we lie."[4] Demaratus was there with Xerxes's army.

Thermopylae was a triumph for Spartan values, but a military defeat; the Persian army could now march through Boeotia to Athens. The Athenian leader Themistocles persuaded the Athenians to abandon the city, sent a message to the Persian fleet suggesting he might be willing to change sides, and in September 480 lured the Persian fleet into the straits of Salamis, where it was comprehensively destroyed. After the Battle of Salamis, Xerxes returned to Persia, leaving his army under his general Mardonius to finish off the Greeks in the next campaigning season. Things went equally badly for the Persians in 479. A defeat on land at Plataea in which Mardonius was killed—this time the Greek forces were led by the Spartans—persuaded the Persians to abandon the attempt to conquer mainland Greece. It was not the end of conflict; there were battles in the eastern Aegean for many years. It was the end of a serious threat of invasion.

The next seventy-five years saw the rise and fall of radical Athenian democracy. Political writers for two thousand years and more saw in this history an object lesson in, variously, the dangers of hubris—overweening self-confidence—the folly of allowing the lower classes to dominate politics, the corrupting effects of power, and much else. The dominant lesson drawn thereafter was the impossibility of combining democratic politics and ordinary prudence. The problem was in essence simple; Athens turned itself into an empire and overreached. At the end of the Persian Wars, Athens was the dominant maritime power, and established an alliance of Aegean island states, whose purpose was to take advantage of Persian weakness to deplete Persian naval power and to loot Persian possessions by way of compensation for the war. This was the Delian League; it was based on the island of Delos, where its treasury was established. It swiftly turned into an Athenian empire. The members of the league became tributary states of Athens, and their taxes went to beautify the city and subsidize the political life of the Athenian lower classes; to run their form of democracy, the Athenians had to pay a subsidy to allow their lower-class citizens to take time off from earning a living, and they were not scrupulous about where the money came from. The Athenians did not moralize about this. They took it for granted that states tried to maximize their power; the more powerful would exploit the less powerful, even if they might keep exploitation within limits, in the hope of more willing assistance in the event of war.

The check on Athenian conduct was self-interest. If Sparta had kept its military and political leadership after the Second Persian War, the Athenians would have been more cautious; resistance from their island allies might have persuaded them that tribute seeking was not worth the candle. Neither obstacle stood in their way; Sparta was indecisive, and the tributary states were weak. Athens embarked on an extension of its democratic institutions. Ceremonial offices alone were reserved for the better-born. As power gravitated to the boule and the Assembly, no provisions were put in place to ensure the good behavior of the Assembly or the council; neither the modern idea of the separation of powers nor the modern view that a constitution should provide a check on the exercise of power made any headway. Both ideas are prefigured in Aristotle's *Politics* a century and a half later, and after the Peloponnesian War the constitution was modified in that direction, but mid-fifth-century Athenian practice was not. Athens was a radical democracy; the constitution placed absolute power in the hands of "the people," and on the good sense of the people the safety of the individual and the wise management of affairs depended.

The practice of ostracism illustrates the Athenian readiness to empower the common people. Ostracism allowed the citizens to expel whomever they wished, especially the eminent, for any reason or none. (The term "ostracism" was taken from the pieces of pottery on which citizens could scratch the name of the person they wished to expel.) A famous story was told about the ostracism of Aristides, a leading statesman and a hero of the Battle of Salamis. He was approached by an illiterate citizen who asked him to write the name of Aristides on his potsherd; inquiring whether the man had ever met Aristides, he was told no, but the man was fed up with hearing Aristides constantly described as "the just." Aristides wrote his name. The penalty was mild: it was notionally exile for ten years, but with no loss of property and with the right to return without question. Many victims left rather briefly. Aristides was exiled in 482 and recalled two years later, and this was common. Lesser mortals might be expelled because they were immoral, unneighborly, or excessively disagreeable.

Thucydides and His History

Athenian expansionism brought intermittent, low-level conflict with other Greek states over many years; but in 431 a war broke out that set Athens and its maritime allies against an alliance led by Corinth and Sparta. The alliance should have been swiftly victorious, given its overwhelming military superiority. Even without that disparity, Athens might without disgrace have sued for peace in the face of the plague that struck the city in the following year, or immediately afterward on the death of Pericles, the one man who could preserve unity in the face of disaster.

In fact, the war lasted twenty-seven years. Athens's ability to hold off the Peloponnesian League for so long reflected extraordinary ingenuity and energy, as well as an ability to raise money, equip fleets and armies, and appoint competent generals who remained loyal to the city in spite of the Assembly's habit of suddenly turning against them. Two and a half thousand years later, commentators still fall into the trap of thinking that we must choose between democratic politics and effective administration; Athens showed that this is a false dilemma. On the other hand, aspects of Athens's conduct of the war reflect quite badly enough, either on democracy, on the Athenians, or more generally on human nature itself.

The Peloponnesian War is better known than any before Caesar's campaigns because it was chronicled by Thucydides. Thucydides is much admired by political theorists who draw from the war the morals that he imposed on his account without always remembering that his history is a wonderful commentary on the shortcomings of democracy, because Thucydides wrote it as such. He was an aristocrat and a general who was dismissed and exiled by the Assembly in 424 when he failed to reach Amphipolis, in northern Greece, in time to stop the city from surrendering to the Spartans. Exile had its uses to the historian; he could see the war from the Peloponnesian side as easily as from the Athenian, but exile did not endear Athens to him. Three passages from his history stick in every reader's mind. The first is the funeral oration at the end of the first year of the war, in which Pericles praised the Athenian dead, celebrated Athens as "the teacher of Hellas," and defended the democratic way of life in terms that resonate today. Pericles's defense of Athenian courage, versatility, and intelligence forms a counterpoint to the debates between the Corinthians and their reluctant Spartan allies earlier in Thucydides's account. The Corinthians urge the Spartans to make war on Athens; the Spartans are not sure they can win. Both fear that Athens will wrongfoot them by sheer cleverness; their anxiety was a deeply sincere tribute.

The second episode is the Athenian massacre and enslavement of the inhabitants of the island of Melos; and the last, the disastrous expedition against Syracuse. Today we think a government is not "democratic" if it violates human rights. Contemplating the unabashed wickedness of the Athenian treatment of Melos should give us pause; Athens was unequivocally democratic and frequently wicked. We do not know what future generations will think of the way the democratic powers fought the Second World War, but firebombing civilian populations and the use of nuclear weapons against Japan may give our successors pause. We have also become convinced that democracies do not go to war against one another; during the twentieth century, the liberal democracies of North America, Europe, and the British Commonwealth were invariably allies. Democratic Athens made war on democratic Syracuse during the Peloponnesian War. Thucydides thought the Athenian democracy was addicted to war. The reason, equally true of the Romans later, was that ancient war could be profitable; looting paid better than agriculture, and the poor, who lived at the level of a bare subsistence, stood to benefit, if not on the scale of the rich. Thucydides thought that the aggressiveness of democracies was a universal trait. He told his readers that he had written his history "for ever"; human nature was the same at all times and places, and the political passions and ambitions of mankind were ineradicable, so any persons concerned with the politics of their own time could read Thucydides's account of the Peloponnesian War and derive instruction. A historically minded Plains Indian of the nineteenth century might have shared Thucydides's view of the aggressive and expansive habits of democracies. Certainly, international relations scholars in the twenty-first century read Thucydides for pleasure and instruction.

Pericles's Funeral Oration

Thucydides describes his literary technique beguilingly. *The Peloponnesian War* proceeds by a series of set-piece speeches that carry the action forward and reveal the characters of the participants in these great events. To the obvious question whether this is really what was said, Thucydides replies that where he knows what a man said, he quotes it; where he does not, he puts in his mouth what he ought to have said, given the occasion and its demands. Pericles's Funeral Oration is longer than Lincoln's Gettysburg Address and is two and a half millennia older, but they are widely regarded as the two greatest defenses ever written, not only of democratic government but of the ethos of a democratic society. Whether Lincoln modeled his address on Pericles's is unknown, but they feature a common rhetoric: the speaker insists that his words can do nothing to enhance the glory of the fallen, because their deeds speak for themselves; they praise their country's founders as well as the dead; and they praise the society and polity for which they died; grief at the loss of the dead must not undermine the determination that a unique polity and its way of life should survive. It does not diminish either speech that it was politically important to remind the audience what they were fighting for. Lincoln's Union was war weary. Pericles's Athenians were suffering far worse than they had expected. He had persuaded them to abandon the countryside and move into the city, knowing that the Athenian army could not prevent the Spartans and their allies from ravaging the countryside of Attica, and relying on the Athenian navy to secure food and supplies. It was an intelligent strategy, but it bore hard on everyone; the better-off faced the destruction of their houses and estates, and no farmer could bear the destruction wreaked by the Spartans and their allies. Military stalemate and plague disillusioned the Athenians; soon after, Pericles was fined and dismissed, then recalled, only to die of plague at the end of 429.

Athenian state funerals were an old tradition; the dead were commemorated and their remains interred in the Keramaikos cemetery. Pericles's speech, whether the words were his, Thucydides's, or a combination, represented a break with the usual pattern. He starts by saying that there should be no such speeches; the glory of the dead should not be imperiled by the clumsiness of commemorative speeches. He turns to honor the ancestors. These moves were probably conventional. Then he less conventionally turns to praise the city for which they died. "[Our form of government] is called a democracy on account of being administered in the interest not of the few but the many; yet even though there are equal rights for all in private disputes in accordance with the laws, wherever each man has earned recognition he is singled out for public service in accordance with the claims of distinction, not by rotation but by merit, nor when it comes to poverty, if a man has real ability to benefit the city, is he prevented by obscure renown."[5]

Pericles did not stop at extolling the virtues of appointment on merit and of holding rulers to account in a lawful way. He emphasized the liveliness of a free and open society. "In public life we conduct ourselves with freedom and also, regarding that suspicion of others because of their everyday habits, without getting angry at a neighbor if he does something so as to suit himself, and without wearing expressions of vexation, that inflict no punishment yet cause distress."[6] Still, it was a politically charged society of which he was speaking. "We do not say that a man who takes no notice of politics is a man who minds his own business; we say that he has no business here at all." This picture of a participatory democracy and a society in which political commitment was all but universal is one to which the twentieth century turned to measure its own success and failure in instituting democracy. Reformers in the late twentieth century disagreed about how far we can re-create the vivid, participatory world of ancient Athens in a modern industrial society, but few turned their back on the ideal.

Two moments in Pericles's oration give a modern reader pause. His peroration on the virtues of the Athenian dead includes the well-known line, "The whole earth is the tomb of famous men." He was praising the Athenians for valor in war; they can boast courage in war, stead-fastness in defeat, and unwavering loyalty to their fellow soldiers and sailors. Their fame was bound up with the military expansion that had provoked the conflict in which they had died. Some readers may think Athens would have been better-off with a more peaceful idea of fame; Thucydides thought they should at least have been more moderate. The moment that makes the modern reader's heart sink comes when Pericles turns to the women in his audience. He tells them that they should mourn their dead heroes, but that is the limit of their public role. "Your renown is great through keeping to the standard of your basic nature, and if your reputation has the least circulation among men, whether for virtue or in blame."[7] This is not the modern democratic ideal.

The "Melian Dialogue"

Thucydides wrote his history around the speeches that participants in events either made or "were called for in the situation." This makes a long book strikingly lively. The most famous of these set-piece debates is between the Athenians and the Melians; in 416 Athens demanded that the Melians surrender their city and pay tribute to aid the Athenian war effort. The Melians claimed the right to remain neutral and would not yield. Athens meticulously carried out its threat to kill every man of arms-bearing age and to sell all the women and children into slavery. This act is famous as the worst atrocity committed by a usually decent society, but even more as the occasion of one of the most famous assertions in history of the rights of unbridled power. The Athenian insistence that "justice is what is decided when equal forces are opposed, while possibilities are what superiors impose and the weak acquiesce to"[8] has been discussed, both by practical people and by philosophers, ever since. Not everyone has rejected the Athenian case.

Thucydides's account of events implies that Melos wished only to continue to be neutral. This was not true. Melos was a Spartan colony; neutral in theory, Melos provided help to Sparta from early in the war. Moreover, the Melians knew what to expect. Athens had come close to slaughtering an entire city before. Mytilene, on the island of Lesbos, revolted at the beginning of the war and held out until 427 with the aid of Spartan hoplites and some naval assistance. When the city surrendered, the Athenians decided to kill the adult men and enslave the women and children. The ships sent to announce their distasteful task to the soldiers on Lesbos were in no hurry to get there, and soon after they left, the Assembly changed its mind and sent another fleet to countermand their murderous instructions. Happily for Mytilene, the second fleet overtook the first. Ten years later, with the war dragging on, the Athenians did not have second thoughts. They had Spartan precedents. When Sparta subdued the city of Plataea in 426, the Spartans had not hesitated. Thucydides says that it was at the instigation of the inhabitants of Thebes that the Spartans acted, and it was certainly the Thebans who completed the physical destruction of the city some years later. Still, it was the Spartans who carried out the massacre. Every Plataean male of fighting age was asked what he had done to assist Sparta; since Plataea was an obdurate foe, none had done anything to help their enemies, and all were executed. The women and children were sold into slavery, and Plataea ceased to exist. At the end of the Peloponnesian War, the Spartans seriously considered treating the Athenians in the same fashion.

The debate is artfully constructed. The Melians admit that their weakness leads them to search for whatever arguments may fend off the Athenians, but they stick tightly to the two most relevant points. One is Athenian self-interest, and the other the Athenians' sense of justice. They tell the Athenians that they will create opposition to their empire among the independent neutral states, but the Athenians shrug off the danger; the Melians tell the Athenians that the Spartans will surely come to their aid, but the Athenians know that Sparta will not hazard its forces at a distance, and shrug off that danger. The crux is thus the patent injustice of the Athenian attempt on the independence of a small and helpless power. The Athenian view has been described: it is the law of nature that the strong do what they can and that the weak do what they must. The Melians refused to give in, the Athenians invested the island, and after a long siege and spirited resistance, the inevitable occurred. The Melians were starved into surrender, their men of military age were killed, and their women and children were sold into slavery. Five hundred Athenian colonists replaced them. It was an event that should give pause to anyone who supposes that democracies are by their nature peace-loving, humane, and just. Their capacity for mass murder should not be underestimated.

After fifteen years of war, neither Athens nor Sparta had gained the upper hand. This amounted to an Athenian victory; Sparta's aim was the destruction of Athens and its empire, while Athens aimed only to hold what it had. At least, this had been the aim of Pericles. Although many Greek cities chafed under Athenian domination, Sparta was an unlikely friend of liberty and self-determination. Nobody needed to be reminded of the Spartan treatment of the helots. For all their self-discipline in battle, the Spartans invariably succumbed to corruption once they were away from Sparta itself, and because Spartan policy was based even more crudely on simple self-interest than that of Athens, Sparta was an unreliable ally. If the Athenians had been content with avoiding defeat, the Peloponnesian League would have had to settle for the frustration of its aims. It would have been a remarkable achievement and would have shown how formidable Athenian democratic institutions, economic resources, and military imagination really were.

Alcibiades and the Sicilian Disaster

Athens defeated itself. The downfall of Athens was caused by personal rivalries, internal dissension, and a fatal overestimation of its capacity. The disastrous expedition to Sicily sprang from the ambition of Alcibiades, one of the most brilliant, self-destructive, and wayward political entrepreneurs of all times. The ward of Pericles, and the favorite pupil of Socrates—who was enchanted both by Alcibiades's physical charms and his philosophical talent—Alcibiades grew up with a passion for fame and no inhibitions about attaining it. He betrayed Athens to Sparta after 415, then betrayed Sparta to Athens, and in middle age was dangerous enough for the Spartans to persuade the Persians to murder him in 404. He was astonishingly brave, a brilliant general, and an inspiring leader. He was by turn the hero of the rowers in the Athenian navy, and the strategist who showed the Persians how to help Sparta to defeat Athens by assisting the oligarchical party at Athens to undermine the democracy. He came to symbolize the way a clever, glamorous, and unscrupulous demagogue could play on the susceptibilities of gullible ordinary folk, with disastrous consequences all around.

After the death of Pericles, Athenian politics became unstable, with a handful of demagogues competing for the support of the *ecclesia*, while the war degenerated into an inconclusive stalemate. In 421 the Peace of Nicias, named after the Athenian statesman who negotiated it, provided for a five-year truce, although it was taken for granted that the two protagonists would spend the interlude reinforcing their positions for a resumption of hostilities. The Sicilian expedition of 415 to 413 was an

Athenian effort in this direction. Athens had no interest in the western Mediterranean; its empire was in the Aegean; but it had an interest in weakening the ability of Greek colonies in Sicily and southern Italy to assist Corinth and Sparta. Hence the expedition to Sicily. It was led by Lamachus, Alcibiades, and Nicias. Lamachus was an experienced and aggressive general; if his proposal to launch an immediate and all-out assault on Syracuse had been accepted, the expedition might well have succeeded. His two colleagues had long been enemies, however. Alcibiades mocked Nicias's peace treaty, which gave all sides five years' breathing space and advocated more aggressive policies against Sparta. They had united to defeat the demagogue Hyperbolos in 416–415; but they were ill assorted, Nicias being as cautious and elderly as Alcibiades was the reverse.

Thucydides says that the Athenians were uninformed about the size of Sicily and the resources of Syracuse, and recklessly committed themselves to a second war on the scale of the Peloponnesian War. This is unfair. An unwinnable war crept up on them. The Sicilian cities that Alcibiades hoped to recruit as allies feared that Athens meant to turn them into subject states, and formed an alliance to resist Athens. Athens devoted immense resources to the expedition; this was on the urging of Nicias, either because he feared defeat with fewer resources or because he hoped that when the Assembly saw the cost of the enterprise it would call it off. During the campaign, Alcibiades was recalled to answer a charge of blasphemy; on the night of the fleet's departure, the herms—phallic sculptures set up around the city—had been mutilated, and in his absence Alcibiades's enemies had accused him of orchestrating this blasphemous misbehavior. When he discovered that he had been sentenced to death in his absence, he deserted to the Spartans. Then Lamachus was killed in a skirmish, and the Athenian forces were left to the wavering leadership of Nicias. They failed to establish a siege of Syracuse, suffered a catastrophic naval defeat in the great harbor at Syracuse, were cut off from supplies, and faced a choice between surrender and starvation. They surrendered and were worked to death as slaves in the Syracusan quarries.

Astonishingly, this was not the end of the Athenian war effort. A crash shipbuilding program restored the fleet, although nothing could be done to prevent the further devastation of Attica by the Spartan army, which profited until 411 from the skill and advice of Alcibiades. The Sicilian disaster reinforced upper-class hatred of popular government and its burdens. In 411 there was a short-lived oligarchical coup, which aimed to abolish the voting rights of the *thetes*—the lowest of the citizen classes and the source of the rowers in the fleet—and restore what the supporters of the oligarchy claimed was the constitution of Solon and Cleisthenes. There was no uniformity of purpose among the oligarchs, and the reduction in the rights of the lower classes was watered down under threat from the rowers. Democracy was restored, and Alcibiades briefly recalled, although he had been instrumental in fomenting the coup in Athens by promising Persian assistance if an oligarchy could be installed. Two blunders led to the final defeat. The first was the refusal of a Spartan offer of peace after Alcibiades had secured an Athenian sea victory at Cyzicus. Small-scale victories in Asia Minor misled the war party as to Athenian strength. The second blunder was the refusal of a second Spartan offer of peace after the final Athenian naval victory, at Arginusae in 406. That victory was marked by a piece of self-destructive wickedness. After the battle, the victorious fleet failed to rescue some wounded survivors; the Assembly put the generals on trial—illegally, since capital trials were reserved to the council of the Areopagus; ten were sentenced to death and executed soon after. As a way of alienating the leaders of Athens from the ordinary people, it could hardly have done more damage if the Spartans had contrived it. It was the end; the Spartans and the Persians finally established an alliance; Persian money and the skill of the Spartan general Lysander enabled the Spartans to defeat the Athenian fleet at Aegospotami and install an unbreakable siege of the city. Capitulation in 404 saw the destruction of Athens's famous Long Walls, the reduction of the fleet to twelve ships, and the installation of a savage oligarchy, the Thirty Tyrants.

The importance of the Peloponnesian War for our purposes is obvious. First, it—on Thucydides's account of it—exemplifies the strengths and weaknesses of democracy in ways that every succeeding age has seized on. On the one side, the resourcefulness, patriotism, energy, and determination of Athens were astonishing; on the other, the fickleness, cruelty, and proneness to dissension were equally astonishing. Ever after, the friends of democracy could say that the common man was capable of courage and initiative in the highest degree, and that the institutions of democracy were capable of selecting talented generals, gifted organizers, and public-spirited politicians, while the enemies of democracy retorted that, without extraordinary good luck, democracy led to factionalism, chaos, and military disaster.

Second, it reveals one major reason for the ultimate failure of the Greek states to survive the rise of the Macedonian and Roman empires. Greek city-states were conscious both of being Greek and of their own narrower ethnicity: Athenian, Theban, Spartan. To us, it is obvious that the Greek states should have set aside their differences over borders and styles of politics and united against Macedon and Rome as they had united against Persia. Yet the ease with which Sparta allied with Persia to defeat Athens shows how readily enmity toward fellow Greeks overcame the fear of non-Greek powers. This was not a peculiarity of Sparta; in the fourth century an alliance of Persia and Athens destroyed Sparta's military hegemony. Nor is it true that the Greeks did not discern the solution to the problem of reconciling their intense localism with their need for a broader political and military unity. It was they who discovered the modern world's most successful political invention: the federal state. The founders of the American Republic cited the long-lived Lykian League—a grouping of city-states in the eastern Aegean—in defense of their new creation.[9] Nor is that the only comparison we might draw. The United States barely survived the bloody Civil War of the 1860s, so it is no surprise that the Greeks of the fourth century BCE failed to subordinate sectional interests to the greater interest of the Greek people.

The Trial of Socrates

At the end of the war in 404, a short-lived but violent oligarchy was installed, led by Critias and Theramenes. Theramenes was a moderate, who had been prominent in the oligarchy of 411 and done much to ensure a bloodless return to democracy. Critias was an extremist. The Thirty Tyrants, as they were later known, deprived all but some five hundred citizens of any say in Athenian politics, allowed only the wealthiest five thousand citizens the right to be tried before a jury, and murdered numerous opponents without the formality of a trial. Indeed, they turned on Theramenes and executed him along with their democratic opponents; to ensure his death, they stripped him of his citizenship so that he, too, could be executed without a trial. They lasted barely a year before being overthrown by Thrasybulus, a long-standing democrat and a distinguished general. Athenian democracy was restored in 403, on a more moderate basis than before: the franchise was restricted, and the powers of the Assembly were reduced. Thrasybulus was deservedly awarded an olive crown for refusing to execute the defeated oligarchs and allowing them to choose whether to stay in the city or leave unmolested. The regime he established flourished until the triumph of Philip of Macedon. But one of its earliest acts was to put Socrates on trial for impiety; the judicial murder of Socrates has always ranked alongside the destruction of Melos in indictments of Athenian democracy, even though some commentators—Hegel and Nietzsche among them—have admired Socrates while thinking that Athens was right to silence him.

With the trial of Socrates, the history of Western political thinking begins. Socrates's death sparked off Plato's astonishing philosophical career. Only five of Plato's dialogues are centrally concerned with politics, though many bear on the practice of Athenian democracy. Even if Plato had never been born, Socrates's death would have raised hard questions about the limits of state authority and the citizen's duty to obey the legally constituted authorities. He was condemned to death in 399 on a charge of impiety; the essence of the charge was that he had denied that the gods existed and had corrupted the young. Socrates was in fact strikingly, but unconventionally, pious. Since he wrote nothing, and disapproved of writing, we have only his memorialists' accounts to go on, however. He appears to have claimed that the gods could not be as human beings depicted them; the gods were all-wise and all-knowing, but the poets depicted them as adulterous, murderous, quick to anger and slow to forgive, vain, sentimental, and foolish. Homer's *Iliad* is the obvious target of this criticism; it is an epic, and a modern reader might read it as an adventure story. To the Greeks, it had a semisacred status, and mocking its depiction of gods and heroes was dangerous. More importantly, the Athenians were both urbane and superstitious; during the Peloponnesian War, the Assembly had passed new laws against blasphemy, thinking, as most ancient peoples did, that making light of the gods invited their displeasure. These were the laws under which Alcibiades had been sentenced to death, and under which Socrates was tried and sentenced.

Politics may also have lain behind the trial. Socrates's friendship with the opponents of the democracy, both in the recent past and earlier in the case of Alcibiades, had alienated his fellow citizens. They did not mean him to die. At his trial, he was offered the chance to stop teaching, but would not take it.[10] He had the chance to propose a lesser penalty than death in his speech in his own defense, but provoked the jury by asking for a reward for helping them to live virtuously. His view, as he explained, was that the only harm the jury could do a good man was to make him less virtuous, and merely dying would not diminish his virtue. In any event he was an old man, and dying sooner rather than later was, if anything, a blessing. It is unsurprising that he was convicted of blasphemy by a narrow majority of the 500-man jury, but sentenced to death by a much larger margin.

Even after he had been sentenced to death, he was encouraged to leave the city and go into exile. Socrates's response has been a source of astonishment ever since. He insisted that he was an Athenian, a citizen, a law-abiding member of society. It was worse for him to break the laws by which he had been sheltered all his life than to drink hemlock and die. He duly drank the hemlock and died.[11] He left behind questions that have puzzled mankind ever since, and a pupil of genius who pursued a vendetta against Athenian democracy and perhaps against all possible politics. That was Plato.

CHAPTER 2

Plato and Antipolitics

The Paradoxical Plato

ALMOST ALL ACCOUNTS OF the history of political thinking begin with Plato. This is a paradox, because Plato's political thought is *anti*political. Readers of his *Republic* see that in the polis of Plato's imagination, there is no politics, and are puzzled; but throughout European history there has been a current of thought that seeks the resolution of the conflicts that "ordinary politics" resolves in the creation of a such a degree of social harmony that the conflicts which everyday politics resolves have simply disappeared, and politics with them. The apolitical utopia was not first imagined in 1513 when Thomas More's *Utopia* was published. We may safely assume there will be no politics in the heavenly kingdom of the Judeo-Christian God, though the family feuds of Olympus and Valhalla are another matter. Utopian thinkers hope to maintain social order and meet the needs of the population without economic or political competition, and without rulers' having to justify their decisions to their peers or to the common people. The founder of European political thought is the founder of antipolitical thinking. One might think that the chaos of the Peloponnesian War makes explanation of Plato's antipathy to politics unnecessary; anyone might have despaired of Athenian politics. That is true, but not everyone disenchanted with

Athenian democracy provided an elaborate philosophical justification for giving up on politics as such; many wanted oligarchy, others a version of the Spartan constitution, others the moderate government described some decades later in Aristotle's *Politics*.

The treatment of Plato's political ideas here is brief and selective, and concentrates on two fascinating dialogues, *Gorgias* and *Republic*. The treatment is critical, but not dismissive. Plato was accused by some of his twentieth-century critics of racism, totalitarianism, fascism, and other political crimes with a very contemporary flavor. These accusations are too anachronistic to be taken seriously; whatever explains Hitler and Mussolini, it is not the dialogues of Plato. The more plausible complaint is that Plato does not take seriously the inescapability of politics in some form. Plato's metaphysics is fascinating; so is his conviction that the just man does better than the unjust man, *no matter what earthly fate befalls him*. His political thinking often amounts to an injunction to abolish the conflicts that politics exists to resolve and fantasies about how it might be done.[1] He is not the only writer against whom the charge can be leveled. More than two millennia later, Karl Marx refused to say anything in detail about the politics of a communist society, because he thought the abolition of capitalism would abolish economic conflict and with it the need for government and politics. Like their French predecessor Henri de Saint-Simon, Marx and Engels believed that coercive government would be replaced by technical management.[2] Their refusal to prescribe for an unknowable future was admirable; but their unwillingness to say more about how a communist society might operate, beyond saying that the first step was to establish the dictatorship of the proletariat, turned out to be disastrous.

Knowing why Plato took the short way he did is important, because philosophers, political theorists, and many rulers have been tempted to follow him; but, as Aristotle complained, Plato does not so much purify politics as purify it to death. There is, said Aristotle, a degree of unity in a state beyond which it is not a state at all.[3] Plato's impact on European political thought is not easy to describe. Plato's metaphysics was influential on Christian thinking almost from the beginning, especially by way of his *Timaeus*; but when the cultural renaissance of the twelfth century reinvigorated classical scholarship in western Europe, it was Aristotle's *Politics* rather than Plato's *Republic* that scholars turned to for political illumination. The revival of interest in Plato during the Renaissance was a revival of interest in his metaphysics; although *Republic* was translated into Latin, and could now be read in Greek by a substantial number of scholars, it was the metaphysical dialogues that were important. Quite when *Republic* acquired its present dominant status is hard to say; in part, it seems to have been an artifact of the Victorian obsession with educating young men for public life. Ever since, many commentators have thought of *Republic* as a treatise on education; its political message is the need to enlighten us so that we may become fit to live in *kallipolis*, the ideal city.

It is tempting to compare Plato with Marx; indeed, I have done so. Like Plato, Marx looked forward to a future in which the state, law, coercion, and competition for power had vanished and politics been replaced by rational organization. But we must not press the comparison. Marx looked to radical political action in the present to abolish the need for politics in future: a proletarian revolution requires political organization to bring it about. Marx's utopia is egalitarian: everyone can freely agree to the demands of rational organization; and Marx's utopia demands material abundance: communism is possible only in an affluent society where hard labor is unnecessary. Plato abolished politics by philosophical fiat; only philosophers rule, because only they have the wisdom freely to assent to what reason requires. As for affluence, Plato's ideal society is more Spartan than the historical Sparta, and although Plato scarcely discusses work in *Republic*—as distinct from *Laws*—the existence of slaves and common laborers is presupposed. As the myth of the three metals explains, the cosmos is hierarchical, and only a few have the golden souls of rulers.

To say that Plato has only one concern in his political writings is unfair to the dogged and detailed emphasis of *Laws* on how to organize a second-best state if the utopia of *Republic* cannot be achieved. *Laws* is rich in institutional detail; some of it reappears in Aristotle's work, although he was as critical of *Laws* as he was of *Republic*.[4] He complains that neither work says enough about the *constitution* of the state, and that is a reminder that the title *Republic* is misleading. The Greek is *politeia*. *Politeia* means "constitution," which for Aristotle was the theory of finding the proper balance between all the various legitimate forces that operated on a state. Plato does not tackle that subject; his subject is the ignorance of politicians. The thought that nothing will go well until kings are philosophers or philosophers are kings is the thought of a man who believed that knowledge was the root of salvation and ignorance the root of perdition. The obvious question is *knowledge of what*. What should politicians know that they do not; what do philosophers know that entitles them to rule? We may also wonder why Plato was convinced that lack of *knowledge* was the issue rather than greed, anger, or the other dangerous emotions to which we are prey. Alcibiades's ambition rather than his ignorance seems the more obvious place to start; he was an excellent student of philosophy but a political menace.

Plato's relationship to Socrates holds the answer. Of the historical Socrates we know as little as we know of Plato; he is mocked in Aristophanes's hilarious comedy *Clouds*, represented as a figure of superhuman wisdom in Plato's dialogues, and described admiringly but less hyperbolically by Xenophon.[5] Socrates believed he had been called to bring enlightenment to Athens; the Gods had told him to walk the streets and debate with young men their views on important matters. It is easy to see why he was unsettling. The uncertainty in which dialogues such as *Gorgias* end seems to reflect what discussions with Socrates were really like. He was famous for claiming to know nothing; when the oracle at Delphi called him the wisest man in Athens, he was puzzled, but came to think that the oracle was right because other men thought they knew a great deal, while he at any rate understood that he knew nothing.

He held at least some of the doctrines attributed to him and defended by Plato: that nobody does evil willingly; that wickedness is error; that it is better to suffer wrong than to do it; that the virtues are one as well as many. He did not share Plato's passion for mathematics. He was a moralist and a mystic. Nor was he interested in scientific speculation: one tradition held that he thought the natural world was too difficult to think about; more importantly, its workings were morally irrelevant. Socrates was uninterested in having his thoughts written down for posterity, and is said to have thought that the invention of writing had enfeebled the intellect. He has thus frustrated the attempts of later commentators to discover what he really thought, as distinct from what Plato puts in his mouth. This has not stopped them from trying, but it has prevented them from reaching a consensus.

The ideas that modern readers find least plausible in *Gorgias* and *Republic* are those with the clearest origin in Socrates's known doctrines, particularly the equation of virtue with knowledge and the doctrine that no one does evil willingly. Nobody knows how far Socrates shared the antidemocratic ideas of *Republic*. It is possible that he, like Plato, thought that democracy is the second-worst of all forms of government, one step better than tyranny, and often its precursor. His friends were aristocrats who felt threatened by democracy, and he may have been executed by the revived democracy at least partly because he was friendly with members of the oligarchy of the Thirty Tyrants. Absurdly enough, he had come close to being killed by those very oligarchs. He was ordered to help seize an innocent man whom the oligarchy wanted to murder, but he refused.[6] The point of sending him on an illegal mission was to implicate him in the oligarchy's misdeeds; his refusal was opposition they could hardly have tolerated. He seems to have been saved by the fall of the oligarchy, only to be executed by the regime that had saved him.

Plato's Life

As with Shakespeare's, the immensity of Plato's influence is matched by the paucity of reliable information about his life. He was born about 428 and died some eighty years later. He came from an upper-class Athenian family, and his relatives were members of the oligarchy that briefly replaced the Athenian democracy at the end of the Peloponnesian War. His mother's cousin Critias and her brother Charmides were two of the most extreme and violent leaders of the oligarchy of 404–403; both were killed during the overthrow of the regime. Plato says in the *Seventh Letter* that he was asked to join the regime, but was repelled by its violence. Subsequently he took no part in Athenian politics. He was an aristocrat who disliked democracy, but disliked murderous oligarchies more. He initially welcomed the restoration of democracy as the restoration of the rule of law, but was disillusioned by the judicial murder of Socrates.

The trial and execution of Socrates in 399 was a key moment in European thought; more immediately, it was a crisis in the lives of his students and disciples. Many of Socrates's followers went into voluntary exile elsewhere in Greece, Sicily, and Italy, Plato among them; he returned to Athens several years later, and founded the Academy in 387. He taught there for the rest of his life. The Academy has given its name to innumerable later centers for research and teaching, but itself took its name from a wooded grove in Athens. The Academy's motto "Let nobody approach who does not know geometry" suggests Plato's obsession with what could be *known* and not just *believed*, as well as his conviction that it was only in the abstract fields of geometry and mathematics that knowledge had been reached, and that other forms of knowledge must model themselves on them. The Academy was a novelty, but once founded, it continued its work, with interruptions caused by war, until it was suppressed 916 years later, in 529 CE, on the orders of the emperor Justinian as part of a general purge of non-Christian ideas. Its aim was to teach good ethical and intellectual habits to aristocratic young men. In Plato's philosophy, training the mind and training the character were one and the same. The assumption was that such young men would occupy important public positions.

There were competing schools, and others sprang up later, but there was an earlier tradition of individual teachers of rhetoric and philosophy giving instruction to ambitious young men who hoped to make a name in politics. They were the Sophists, who receive hostile treatment throughout Plato's *Dialogues*. Socrates himself was a Sophist of sorts; the term means only "a wise man," and the oracle said he was the wisest man in Athens. Prompted by the Gods, he offered to debate with any Athenian the issues on which they could receive instruction from a Sophist. There was one crucial difference: the Sophists took their clients' desire for worldly success as the starting point, and taught them what they needed for success in the lawcourts and in debate in the assembly, while Socrates subverted their worldly ambitions and taught them to think of the welfare of their immortal souls instead. They also charged for their services; he did not. Plato aimed to continue and regularize Socrates's work.

Plato's practical interventions in politics were limited, and they nearly cost him his life. During his exile, he was befriended by Dionysius I, the tyrant of Syracuse, who then became irritated with him, and may—if the story is true—have decided to sell him into slavery. He was grudgingly allowed to leave Sicily for Athens in 387 when he founded the Academy. In 366—again, if the *Seventh Letter* describing these visits is genuine—he was asked to teach his captor's son and successor, Dionysius II, how to be a philosopher-king. Things again went badly, and he escaped with difficulty. Some years later, he was cajoled into a third attempt to turn a tyrant into a philosopher-king, and again escaped with some difficulty after he fell out with Dionysius. A very long time afterward, the existentialist philosopher Martin Heidegger, who acquired an unhappy notoriety for defending the Nazis in the early 1930s, took the post of rector of the University of Marburg in the hope that he could teach Hitler how to be a philosopher-king. After ten months, he gave up and was met by a colleague with an apt greeting, "Hello, Martin, back from Syracuse?" These adventures aside, Plato spent his time teaching and conducting the affairs of his family. No propertied man would have been without practical anxieties in the litigious society of Athens; but Plato ignored Athenian political life as completely as he advised the philosopher to do in *Republic*. What he has left us is his dialogues. Attempts to date them precisely have been inconclusive; even the usual grouping of "early," "middle," and "late" is contentious. Although they are located at particular times and places, which is one element in their charm, Plato introduces characters who had in historical fact died before the apparent date of the discussion, or who are of quite the wrong age. They are works of art, not seminar reports. They are also inexhaustibly interesting.

Plato was an extraordinarily talented writer. His obsession with keeping the arts under political control and his proposal to expel the poets from the utopia of *Republic* suggest a belief in the impact of art that no untalented writer would have. Nonetheless, the literary pleasures of his dialogues are variable. Those in which Socrates is a vivid participant, in the thick of controversy and fighting for his philosophical life, are livelier than those where Socrates is only a mouthpiece for Plato's mature doctrines. This is not an invariable rule: the *Symposium* is late and full of drama. Of the distinctively "political" dialogues, however, *Gorgias* and *Protagoras* are more genuinely dialogical than *Republic* after book I, while *Republic* in turn is livelier than *Laws* and *Statesman*. Here I focus on *Gorgias* and *Republic* for reasons now to be explained.

Gorgias

There can be no thumbnail account of "what Plato thought." The attraction of the dialogue as a literary device is that it lets an author consider ideas in them from a variety of different angles without wholly committing himself, and in the most "Socratic" of the dialogues, Plato takes full advantage of this. Focusing on *Gorgias* and *Republic* is justified by Plato's own obsession: what our rulers should know; the nature of the justice that they should seek for themselves and for the polis that they govern; the training they must they have if they are to govern wisely; what happens when wise men are not in command.

Gorgias was probably written around 380, although it may have been written earlier, and takes its title from a noted orator, Gorgias, a Sicilian teaching in Athens. It divides into three parts: first, Socrates interrogates Gorgias about what he teaches young men when he teaches them rhetoric; there follows a long confrontation with Polus, a student of Gorgias, in which Socrates defends the proposition that the seemingly powerful are in fact powerless, because they do not achieve what they "really" want, which is to live a righteous life; this leads to the claim that doing justice is always better for us than committing injustice, the claim he makes good in a wonderfully rambunctious—and on Socrates's own admission entirely inconclusive—argument with Callicles. "Rhetoric" had few pejorative connotations at the time. We tend to characterize rhetoric as "mere rhetoric," as did Socrates, but this was a minority view in Socrates's Athens. There was no implication that it was a bag of tricks to fool the gullible; it was simply the art of instructive and persuasive speech. Teaching rhetoric in the Greek and Roman world was an important and honorable occupation. Before his conversion to Christianity, Saint Augustine briefly became a professor of rhetoric as a step to a career as an imperial administrator. The political arrangements of Athens and Rome were very different, but in both the ability to make a convincing case in public was vital to political success. The assemblies of classical antiquity were lawcourts as well as deliberative and legislative bodies. The modern distinction of legislature, judiciary, and executive was foreign to them. They were used to being addressed in the way in which a modern jury would be addressed by an advocate in an important case. A man's property, social standing, and his very life might hang on his own or his agent's rhetorical skills. Three hundred years later, Cicero followed Plato on many philosophical issues, but not on the value of rhetoric. Cicero thought that the great orator was greater than either the statesman or the philosopher, since he had to master the skills of both. He was biased by his own vanity, but he caught the sense of the ancient world, and not of the ancient world only.

Socrates began the contrary tradition of belittling rhetoric, and *Gorgias* undoubtedly represents his views. His contempt was on full display when he was tried by the Athenian Assembly on the charge of corrupting the morals of the young; he snubbed both the jurors and the rhetorical conventions of Athenian public life. He was expected to agree not to go into the streets and talk about dangerous subjects with impressionable young men; but he announced that if he was acquitted, discussing dangerous topics was exactly what he would go on doing, because it was his divinely imposed duty. The reader can infer the way speakers in the Assembly ingratiated themselves with their hearers, not only from Plato's complaints about the way demagogues flattered the Assembly while despising its members but also from Socrates's ironic treatment of the conventions.[7]

The most significant victims of Socrates's questioning in *Gorgias* are Polus and Callicles, especially the latter; he, too, was a student of Gorgias, and as with Polus, that is all that is known of him. Plato directs against them the arguments that he deploys against Thrasymachus in *Republic* some thirty years later—notably the argument that it is better to suffer injustice than to do it, and that the unjust man is unhappy, no

matter how much worldly success he may attain. Nonetheless, the dialogue rightly begins with the unraveling of Gorgias's claims as a teacher,
and the denunciation of rhetoric. Plato had to evict the rhetoricians from
the terrain of the philosopher, just as he had to evict the poets from the
polis he was constructing, where philosophers were to be kings and the
educational system required strict censorship. What young men must
learn was the nature of justice; only those who *knew* what justice was
could teach it; only philosophers knew what justice was. Everything else
was ancillary.

The upbringing of aristocratic young men mattered immensely to
the ancient world—even more than the upbringing of privileged young
people matters to ours. It was a commonplace that the sons of eminent
men often turned out a disappointment, and that talented young men
might be corrupted by fame and destroy themselves and their city. Alcibiades, the young man on whom Socrates doted, offers a leading example; his father was a good man, and Alcibiades was Pericles's ward, but
he was a menace. Pericles's biological sons were nonentities; they did not
inherit their father's wisdom or courage. If good fathers can have wicked
or merely useless sons, either the virtuous man knows something that
he cannot teach, or he acts well without knowing what he is doing. The
son of the virtuous father who becomes corrupt and dissolute must have
been ill trained; things would have gone better if he had been properly
educated. What must someone know before offering to teach young men
who will grow up to be statesmen; what must we be taught if we are to
behave justly and lead a good life?

Gorgias presents himself as a teacher who teaches upper-class
young men to be successful. Socrates pricks up his ears and wonders
what extraordinary skill Gorgias has for sale. He swiftly forces Gorgias to admit that he cannot teach any of the particular arts and crafts
on which we depend for everyday health and comfort, as it might be
shoemaking or husbandry. That remains to this day the first question
about the nature of philosophy and rhetoric. Philosophy seems to be
about nothing in particular—not like plumbing or car maintenance, for
instance—but it seems vitally important to its practitioners. Gorgias is
a teacher of rhetoric rather than philosophy, but he is vulnerable to the

same question: if he is not teaching a skill such as medicine or carpentry, nor a science such as astronomy, he needs to explain just *what* rhetoric is the knowledge of. The subtext to the question is that what it *should* be is the art of ensuring that justice is done.

Under cross-examination, rhetoric turns out to be the art of presenting a case to an audience so that it appears to them as you want it to appear, no matter its intrinsic merits or lack of them. In Aristophanes's comedy *The Clouds*, that is the accusation leveled against Socrates, who is not in the play distinguished from Sophists generally; the young man Pheidippides has run up enormous gambling debts, so his father, the elderly farmer Strepsiades, enrolls him in the *phrontisterion*—the "thinkery"—to learn from Socrates the art of bamboozling an Athenian jury by making the better look worse and the worse look better.[8] One can see that the historical Socrates might have wanted to put the record straight; his pupil Plato held that rhetoric was exactly the reverse of philosophy. The aim of philosophy is to understand things as they really are, no matter how they may appear; it is the deceptiveness of appearances that makes philosophy necessary. Philosophy is the art of seeing through appearances to discern the hidden reality. At the end of the discussion with Gorgias, Socrates says that rhetoric is not a skill at all; it serves no useful purpose and achieves nothing that assists human existence. Changing tack somewhat, he adds that if it is a skill, it belongs with the skills of the marketplace, among those that are bad for our health, such as the art of the pastry-cooks, and what Socrates dismisses generically as "pandering." The truth about Gorgias's trade shows what is wrong with democratic politics and the democratic politician; the politics of flattery and deceit drives out the politics of truth.[9]

Socrates does not say that Gorgias's students are unsuccessful in the lawcourts and the Assembly, any more than he says that pastrycooks fail to make a living. He says that the successes Gorgias's students achieve are bad for them and for their city. Their badness is always the same, which is that they are based on making the worse appear better; Gorgias's skills promote injustice. Socrates's treatment of Gorgias seems to a modern reader thoroughly insulting, but the criticism is not personal. Gorgias does not prostitute his talents because he is wicked; but in a democracy everything is based on show and appearance and not on truth. Gorgias does not sin against the light, but in ignorance. Ignorance is not incurable, but it is unlikely to be cured in a democracy, where ignorance pays off and knowledge does not.

The underlying target of Socrates's attack is the commonplace Greek view that the unbridled pursuit of self-interest constitutes success. Gorgias says that he has the same power as a tyrant, or perhaps even more, because he can persuade people to do what the tyrant must force them to do; Socrates insists that this, too, is an illusion. What appears to be the successful pursuit of self-interest is nothing of the sort. The only thing worth having is a just soul. To bring about the death of your enemies and the confiscation of their property by unjust means is not success, but inner death. A man who had behaved like that and knew his real interests would wish to be punished for his crimes, not to get away with them. Unsurprisingly, this meets with entire disbelief from Gorgias's student Polus, who laughs at Socrates and points out that he will not find anyone to agree with him. Socrates points out that neither mockery nor majority opinion are good guides to the truth, and he asks Polus to show him the error of his ways by argument.

Socrates then defends against Polus the extreme version of the view that the unjust man is always worse-off than the just man, no matter what happens to them by way of earthly success. As the pupil of Gorgias, Polus proceeds, one might say, rhetorically. He mocks Socrates for believing what nobody else believes; Socrates is unmoved. Polus adduces examples of successful villainy, citing Archelaus, the king of Macedonia who gained his throne by murdering his uncle, cousin, and young brother; surely nobody could think that someone who possessed absolute power, who could do just what he wanted, could kill his enemies, seize their property, take their wives and daughters, was unhappy. The idea was absurd. There are two issues here, both of them central to Plato's distaste for conventional politics. The simpler is what motives impel people to seek political power. Polus takes it for granted that these are selfish motives, and he appeals to what he, like most of us, takes to be a universal truth: we much prefer to boss others about than to be bossed about ourselves. Like most of us, he assumes that if we had absolute power, we would be unrestrained in gratifying our urges, whether sexual, financial, or a taste for celebrity. One might think that unless Polus was broadly right, we would not take so much care to create constitutional systems to keep our rulers in check. Lord Acton's dictum that power corrupts and absolute power corrupts absolutely expresses just that anxiety. The oddity for a modern reader is the extent to which Polus's sympathies are unabashedly with the holder of absolute power.

The second, deeper issue is philosophical. Socrates disputes Polus's understanding of power. To put it paradoxically, having power is being able to achieve what you want, but getting what you want in the sense in which Polus understands it is not getting what you want and therefore not an exercise of power. One can sympathize with the exasperation of Socrates's critics. Happily, there is a simple translation. Socrates is drawing the familiar distinction between doing what you want and doing what is in your best interests. "You don't really want to eat that worm," we say to a child who has it in mind to do just that. What we mean is "Eating that worm will make you ill." Socrates thought that the ambitions that drove most political leaders were a form of madness or a sickness of the soul. Gorgias and Polus lack power over themselves; because they cannot pursue the good life that they do not understand, they cannot have power over others either.

Beneath the attack on Gorgias and Polus lies the argument that underpins both *Gorgias* and *Republic*. Socrates claims that we must try to teach justice; justice is not based on appearance; knowing what justice is is essential for a successful life; most importantly, justice benefits its possessor and is not socially useful only. Justice is good for its possessor *no matter what* may happen to him or her. Everyone reading Plato has wanted to defend some elements of this doctrine even though, or perhaps even because, the task seems so obviously impossible in the extreme form in which Plato states it. Weaker versions of the claim are easy to defend; stronger versions are defensible up to a point; the extreme case set out in *Gorgias* and *Republic* is another matter. But it was the extreme case that Socrates died for. One prefatory note is needed; all translations of Plato observe that the Greek term *dike* is not very happily translated as "justice." Its range is wider than the English term, and in this context, at least, is best thought of as "all-in rightness." The English term "righteousness" has too many biblical connotations to be quite satisfactory, but an *adikos* is certainly an unrighteous man, and English translations of the Bible as often speak of the just as they do of the righteous.

With Gorgias routed, and Polus leaving the debate, Callicles takes up the argument. One of the pleasures of the dialogues that seem truest to the historical Socrates is that Plato gives a no-holds-barred philosophical brawler the arguments that Socrates has the hardest time refuting. In *Gorgias* it is Callicles and in *Republic* Thrasymachus; but they argue the same case, equally noisily. Both begin by telling Socrates that he is a driveling and mewling infant who should not be let out without his nurse. Socrates claims that it is better to suffer evil than to do it—and in both *Gorgias* and *Republic* goes on to say that a wicked man is better off if he is punished than if he escapes punishment. Being treated justly is best for us, and acting justly is always the best thing to do, *no matter the consequences*. Callicles defends the commonsense view put forward by Polus, that a good man who suffers misfortune is worse-off than a wicked man who gets away with his crimes; he also defends what seems to modern readers a much less commonsense view, but one that was popular among Homeric heroes and attractive to Homer's readers, namely, that the good life consists of gratifying our impulses whatever they may be, with no regard for the interests of anyone else. The gods of the *Iliad* do it, and everyone would like to live like a god. That view itself has two different interpretations; one is that the good life for the individual is an immoral, or at least an amoral and *non*-just, life, the other the counterintuitive view that *justice according to nature* is *whatever one can get away with*. That was what the Athenians told the Melians. Plato was committed to the doctrine that nature is on the side of justice as we ordinarily understand it; indeed, that the cosmos is itself made orderly by justice. It is, of course, possible to think that both Plato and the Athenians were wrong; in *Republic* Glaucon produces an explanation of the nature of justice that rests on that assumption.

Callicles makes a shrewd observation that Socrates readily accepts. Philosophers are terrible politicians. An everyday politician will run rings around the most astute philosopher when it comes to winning a debate or a case in court. Socrates agrees. In *Gorgias* Plato does not use the analogy he appeals to in *Republic*, where he says that the philosopher has been so dazzled by the sun of Truth that he can hardly see where he is going in the world of mere appearances; here he depicts Socrates as simply agreeing that, by the worldly-wise standards of the political prac-titioner, the philosopher cuts a sorry figure. So much for the worldly-wise. Indeed, here as elsewhere, Socrates claims to be one of a very small handful of true statesmen to be found in Athens. But a true statesman can do nothing useful in a corrupt environment.

Callicles is wrong. Wickedness is bad for you. Socrates's argument is similar in *Gorgias* and *Republic*. Both discussions raise the question of how far Socrates's argument can get without an appeal to the existence of an afterlife with a system of postmortem punishments and rewards; but in both discussions Socrates leaves consequences, whether in this life or in a future life, out of account until the end of the argument. It is *being just for its own sake* in the here and now that the wise man is committed to; he would be made unhappier by being unjust than by any earthly pains. Nonetheless, in both discussions, Plato also imagines an afterlife in which our souls will be inspected and our eternal happiness and misery proportioned to the quality of our souls. He speculates that not many of the world's rulers will have an agreeable time in the hereafter—Aristides "the Just" is one of the few whom Socrates expects to be at ease on the day of judgment. But the claim that postmortem punishments will outweigh the this-worldly benefits of wickedness is very different from the claim that even in the absence of such punishments the unjust man does worse than the just man here and now. It is that claim which Socrates defends.

Socrates shows that Callicles is mistaken about the nature of good and evil by teasing him with questions about what *counts* as being stron-ger or better or wiser, and showing that paradoxical results flow from what looks at first sight simple: "My belief is," says Callicles, "that natu-ral right consists in the better and wiser man ruling over his inferiors and having the lion's share."[10] The better and wiser man rules over his inferi-ors in his *own* interests, not theirs. Socrates asks whether the better and wiser man is to rule himself as well as others, and receives the scornful answer that he certainly is not. Being ruled is shameful, even if it is being ruled by oneself; controlling our desires is just feeble. This is a fatal slip; Callicles should have agreed that self-control is required for success in even wicked projects. Callicles returns to the claim that the man of large and immoderate appetite who is good at getting his own way is the man to admire. He is then lured into agreeing that satisfaction is good and dissatisfaction bad. Socrates springs the trap: the more insatiable our appetites, the greater our dissatisfaction. It is, says Socrates, like trying to fill an infinite number of leaky barrels.

Socrates does not stop at arguing that a person of moderate appetites is going to be less dissatisfied than the person of uncontrolled appetite. This is vulnerable to Callicles's retort that if the avoidance of dissatisfaction is the point of existence, sticks and stones do pretty well. Socrates takes Callicles through a series of questions which reveal that, like everyone else, Callicles distinguishes between good and bad pleasures. Callicles needs a test for being a good person because only the good person's pleasures are good; after all, Callicles thinks that the pleasures of the quiet and contemplative man are not worth having, because they are the pleasures of the wrong sort of person. This would not force a less impetuous philosopher than Callicles to renounce the doctrine that the right sort of person is the successful self-aggrandizer. But it would force him to agree that the self-aggrandizer needs some of the qualities of more conventionally good men.

In *Gorgias* Plato does not further explore the nature of the virtues, as he does in *Republic*. Instead, and what lends plausibility to the thought that the dialogue was written before 380 and perhaps not long after the execution of Socrates, Socrates embarks on a long excursus about the relationship between the statesman and the public. This returns the dialogue to the political realm where it began with the interrogation of Gorgias. Socrates insists that he—alone—has studied the true art of statesmanship and is the only true statesman in Athens. Given Socrates's aloofness from Athenian politics, this is richly paradoxical, but it leads to the final discussion not only of the relationship between philosophy and rhetoric but also of what the statesman and the public owe each other. So far from being entitled to "the lion's share," the true statesman serves for nothing. But the true statesman does not expect to persuade an

Athenian jury that reducing young men to baffled incomprehension is a public service. In which case, says Socrates, he will content himself with the thought that an innocent man who is persecuted by villains dies with cleaner hands than theirs.

Republic

Gorgias leaves readers struggling not only with the arguments but with the shape of the discussion. We want conclusions, but we are left with riddles. As an aid to teaching, nothing could be better, but in the absence of the teacher, we cannot guess what Plato's students and readers made of it. *Republic* is different. The first book is a self-contained discussion of the question whether we always do better to practice justice rather than injustice, written in the open-ended fashion of *Gorgias*, with several interlocutors given equal time. It leaves the subject so much up in the air that the search for a definition of justice has to begin all over again. From book 2 on, there are only three speakers, save for a brief reappearance by Thrasymachus and Polemarchus halfway through, as a rather lame literary device to make Socrates restart the discussion of the nature of the best state and tackle it in more depth. For long stretches, Socrates takes over the discussion, with occasional interjections from Glaucon and Adeimantus. The exposition of Plato's theory of justice and its political implications is far from straightforward, with the argument twisting and turning, and being held up for long periods by extended digressions into metaphysics and epistemology, but it is unequivocally an answer to the question how we should govern ourselves. It not only says that we must be governed by philosophers but says much about the education and way of life of the ruling elite; and it does what *Gorgias* does not, which is to provide an account of what justice *is* as well as a defense of the doctrine that the righteous man is happy no matter what.

The natures of a just society and a just political order are still central concerns of political theorists, who are as far as ever from being of one mind about the nature of justice or the institutions that a just society requires. It goes without saying that Plato did not provide a conclusive argument for government by philosopher-kings; it is perhaps less obvious that Plato had a different conception of justice from the understanding of justice current in twenty-first-century liberal democracies, even making allowances for the different nuances of the Greek *dike* and our "justice." Outside the realm of "criminal justice," we think of justice primarily in economic terms and think that a state committed to social justice is aiming to achieve some form of economic fairness; Plato was looking for the rule of the righteous, who can ensure that the polity as a whole practices justice and displays in its organization and behavior the qualities that the soul of the just individual displays. Nonetheless, much of what Plato says in criticism of the politics of Athenian democracy would be, and has been, echoed by critics of contemporary democracies, as would much of what he says of the psychological chaos that rules the souls of democratic citizens.

The subject of *Republic* is ostensibly the subject of the second half of *Gorgias*, whether it is always better to suffer evil than to do it. Plato says yes, but *Republic* is primarily a search for the just polis, it being assumed that justice in the individual and justice in the state are one and the same. To understand the just individual, we must consider the just society. Plato presents that argument as the claim that it is easier to see what justice is in the large rather than the small, so we should look for it in the polis before we seek it in the individual.[11] It is a bad argument, but a nice rhetorical device. To establish what justice in the polis really is, he takes a roundabout route, setting up *kallipolis*, the beautiful city or utopia, focusing on the education that the leaders of a perfectly just society must receive, and on the social and economic arrangements of a society that will be utterly unlike the febrile, inconstant, and thoroughly this-worldly Athenian democracy. Plato's emphasis on order and stability raises the question whether a state ruled by philosopher-kings will be wholly invulnerable to change. One might think the answer is yes, but Plato says not and provides an account of the cyclical historical process in which states move between their best and their worst conditions. He ends this account as he ends *Gorgias*, with a description of the wretched state of the tyrant's soul, before rehearsing once more the conflict between poetry and philosophy and the fate of us all in the hereafter.

Republic opens with Socrates meeting several friends in the street; there is some byplay as his friends insist that he should stay with them for the night so that they can go and see a newly established festival to a moon goddess. Athens was known as the city of festivals; the Athenians celebrated around 120 each year. His friends tempt him with the promise of a horseback relay race by moonlight, and the chance to talk with numerous young men. Socrates agrees, and the party goes into a nearby house to talk while waiting for the festival to start. There is piquancy both in the cast and in the location; the two characters who carry on the conversation for the bulk of the book are Plato's real-life brothers, Glaucon and Adeimantus. Polemarchus, in whose house the conversation takes place, is the son of Cephalus, a rich, elderly, and genuinely good man who represents both the possibility of unreflective traditional virtue and its incapacity to explain itself. In real life, Polemarchus was one of the victims of the Thirty Tyrants, and he is here entertaining the cousins and nephews of the men who were to kill him. The festival takes place at the temple of Bendis, which was the site of the battle in which the Thirty Tyrants were overthrown and Critias killed. One can only speculate about Plato's intentions in choosing the location and the cast. The wild man of the party, who plays the role Callicles played in *Gorgias*, is Thrasymachus of Chalcedon, a Sophist of whom little is known.

The discussion starts with Socrates asking Cephalus what he thinks of old age. Cephalus recalls Sophocles's remark that being liberated from sexual passion was like being liberated from a savage slave master, and says the tranquillity of age has much to be said for it. Socrates teases him by saying that other people might think that he is tranquil only because he is rich. Cephalus will have none of it: extreme poverty would be hard to bear, but a miserable person is miserable however rich. A good character is our most important possession, rich or poor. Socrates agrees, of course, but asks Cephalus what the value of wealth really is. This produces the first of many definitions of justice. All except the definition that Socrates arrives at much later are defective as *definitions*, but each illuminates just behavior under particular conditions—with the exception of Thrasymachus's view that justice consists in the rule of the stronger in his own interest. That is always wrong. Cephalus says that his wealth means he need never cheat or steal, and he can die knowing he told the truth and paid his debts. Those are two of the elements in the classical view of justice: "harm nobody, live honestly, give everyone his due."

Socrates asks the first seemingly foolish question. Cephalus defines justice as telling the truth and repaying our debts, but is it always good to return what we have borrowed? What if we have borrowed a knife and the owner has gone mad in the meantime and is likely to do himself harm? As to truth, should we tell our mad friend that he has gone mad? Cephalus hands the argument to his son, who offers a classical definition of justice: *to give every man his due.* Socrates's account of justice will eventually embrace that, but at this stage he asks another question. "Give each his due" is a *formal* principle; we need to know *what* is due to everyone, and Socrates wants Polemarchus to tell him. Polemarchus produces a traditionally Greek answer; justice means doing good to our friends and harm to our enemies. Benefits are due to friends and injuries are due to enemies. Riches and power are good because they allow us to benefit our friends and injure our enemies. When the Athenians were asked to account for their conduct during the Peloponnesian War, they were unabashed about saying that their power enabled them to help their friends and harm their enemies. Good is due to friends and harm to enemies; the principle holds for both states and individuals.

Socrates denies this. It is never right to injure anyone, which means, as he understands it, that it can never be right to make someone *worse than he is.* He reaches this conclusion by a detour that puzzles modern readers, whereas in *Gorgias* he had made the point directly that punishment does not injure the person who is justly punished. Here Socrates asks who will be good at practicing justice defined as benefiting friends and harming enemies. The question strikes us as odd because we do not think of "doing justice" as having much in common with, say, mending a car or plowing a field; we do not think of it as a *skill.* Plato does. The kind of skill matters because everyone should be just, and living justly must be something that everyone can do. Yet every practical activity seems to be the province of a particular skill, at which some people are better than others. That raises unanswerable questions about what skill the just man practices if all the various practical skills are allocated elsewhere. Sailors sail boats, surgeons perform operations, and so on; every activity has its own practitioners and its own expertise. What expertise does justice imply?

If every action is guided by its own *techné*, or "art" (which is to say a technique or practical skill), what room is left for morality? The answer, which Aristotle makes clearer than Plato, must be that morality controls the way we use the other "arts" or skills. Faced with the claim that justice requires us to do good to our friends and harm to our enemies, Socrates asks who will be best able to do this. Curing our friends and poisoning our enemies is best done by a doctor; if we are at sea, saving our friends and drowning our enemies is best done by a sailor. Where there is a task, there is an art devoted to it, such as medicine or seafaring. It is therefore obscure what justice is supposed to be concerned with; as Socrates jokingly says, it seems that justice is no use at all. It does not achieve anything, while all the various arts bring about particular useful results.

Plato would not say what a modern writer might, that "being just" or "doing justice" is not a skill at all. Justice does something to the souls of those who act justly and of those who are treated justly. His own view is left obscure until the definition of justice as "sticking to one's last" is eventually reached. One might wonder even then whether "sticking to one's last" is a skill of any kind, but the thought that putting our souls in their proper, harmonious order involves a sort of skill is less unpersuasive. His immediate aim is to undermine the claim that justice means doing good to friends and harm to enemies. Harming someone means making him worse, says Socrates, and the point of justice cannot be to make someone worse. Punishment may be disliked by the people who suffer it, but if it is justly imposed it does not harm them, because it does not make them worse. It makes them better, which is why it is their due. Socrates's hostility to the traditional Greek view that justice means doing good to one's friends and harm to one's enemies was a real breach with a moral position that Thucydides, for instance, thought the Athenians took for granted, but Socrates's view was not absolutely novel. There are premonitions of it in Sophocles. There are none in Homer.

By now, Thrasymachus is coming to the boil. Like Callicles in *Gorgias*, Thrasymachus enters the dialogue by accusing Socrates of talking drivel and ignoring how people behave. It is hard not to feel sorry for

Thrasymachus; Plato deals him a worse hand, philosophically speaking, than he dealt Callicles. He is first made to say that there are no moral standards at all and then made to defend a distinctive morality. It is a counterintuitive morality, but a morality nonetheless. Since the combination is incoherent, he is a sitting target. Thus Thrasymachus begins by claiming that when people make moral judgments, they are talking nonsense, and the intelligent man sees through the charade. The intelligent man acts to suit himself; if he feels kindly and generous, he will behave in a kindly and generous fashion; if not, not. What he will not do is clutter his mind with talk of morality, even if he decides to make concessions to the nonsense other people talk. That is the position of the philosophical amoralist. It is coherent and not difficult to defend, and was one of the views that Nietzsche popularized two millennia later.

Plato also imposes on Thrasymachus the much harder task of defending a very unusual morality. He is made to argue that we are *required* to engage in self-aggrandizing behavior. There were elements of this in Callicles's case. As soon as either argues that we are *wrong* in failing to act in accordance with nature and *wrong* to observe conventional moral standards, he is arguing for an alternative morality—even if one predicated on the thought that successful conduct consists in doing down everyone else and behaving as "badly" as we can. Once again, it is not impossible to argue for a variation on this: that *some* individuals, at least, great-souled, heroic, self-assertive figures such as Achilles, *ought* to live by a code that the rest of us could not and should not try to live by. The case requires some moral ruggedness: when those of us who are less great-souled than Achilles ask what is to happen to *us*, we learn that the heroic morality is not interested in us. We may provide the raw material for heroic projects, but what is interesting and important is the heroic project, not us. As Nietzsche observed, lambs dislike eagles, but so what?[12] It is not a view that appeals to humanitarians or the naturally timid; nonetheless, it is not incoherent.

Thrasymachus is made to tie himself in knots. Justice, he says firmly, is whatever is in the interest of the stronger. This may be understood as the claim that whoever gets the upper hand *defines* right and wrong to suit himself—the rich define it as preserving property; the poor define it as generosity to the hard up—or as the claim that justice is *really* what is *really* in the interest of the stronger. The first is amoralism and the second an unorthodox morality. Thrasymachus's premises suggest the first, but the argument thereafter makes sense only on the basis of the second. He begins by pointing out that once we know the form of government of a Greek city, we can work out in whose interest legislation will be framed—it will favor the poor in a democracy and the tyrant in a tyranny, and so on. That is the claim that people define justice to suit themselves. He is then tripped up by a patently unfair argument. Socrates gets him to agree first that subjects are obliged to obey their rulers, which is to say that they behave justly in doing so; he next gets him to agree that rulers sometimes make mistakes about their interests. Putting the two premises together yields the conclusion that it is sometimes just for subjects to do what is not in the interests of the stronger. In other words, it is just not to be just, which is simply incoherent.

As in *Gorgias*, Socrates takes the argument on a detour through the skills that minister to everyday life. The question is whose interests these skills promote. Medicine is about the interests of the patient, not the doctor; the captain of the ship superintends the sailors for the benefit of the whole crew and their passengers. If justice is a quality in rulers, they should be concerned with the welfare of their subjects rather than themselves; justice promotes the interest of the weaker, not the stronger. Like Callicles, Thrasymachus responds by suggesting that Socrates ought not to be let out without his nurse. Rulers may be shepherds, but shepherds tend their flocks so that the sheep can be fattened for the slaughter. Thrasymachus has made the fatal slip of accepting the ordinary notion of justice and abandoning his own. From now on, justice is understood as the familiar (if still undefined) value that leads men to keep promises, tell the truth, do their duty, and obey the laws. Thrasymachus has abandoned the project of redefining justice in novel ways. He must now stick to a simpler argument: doing justice (as ordinarily understood) is strictly for idiots. Nonetheless, the new argument continues to be couched in a way the modern reader will find odd, for Thrasymachus does not give up the attack on justice. If practicing justice is bad for us, justice is not a virtue.

So he plays his second card. Justice is for idiots. The unjust man will always get the better of the just man, and the just man will come to a bad end when he gets in the way of the ruthless and the clever. Thrasymachus still hankers after his earlier claim that justice is what is in the interests of the stronger, and he cannot resist observing that people who commit crimes on a sufficiently grand scale not only get away with them but end up being admired. The sneak thief is despised, but the looters of temples are glorified; behaving badly on a large enough scale is admirable. Some years later, a pirate brought before Alexander the Great made himself famous by telling Alexander that the difference between them lay in the scale of the crimes they committed. His small-scale theft was piracy; Alexander's large-scale looting of empires was glorious. The usual modern view is that Thrasymachus's best hope would be to accept the conventional notion of justice, and then say that because we have no selfish reason to be just, justice is for the softhearted and softheaded. We know that Thrasymachus disagrees with the conventional view, since he refuses Socrates's offer to "argue the matter along conventional lines." He holds that if injustice pays off, it is a virtue, and if justice does not pay, it is not. This is not the skeptical position that there is no such thing as justice, nor the conventional view that justice is a virtue, but at odds with self-interest. It is the view that if justice is at odds with self-interest it is not a virtue. Injustice is a virtue, and justice a vice. This would not have struck Plato's readers as oddly as it strikes us. The Greek conception of ethics was not ours; the "good life" must benefit the individual who leads it, which is why Socrates has to argue that the good man is happy no matter what.

Socrates repeats his response to Callicles in *Gorgias*. No matter his earthly fate, the soul of the just man is in a good state, and to have one's soul in a good state is what it is to be happy. This is the literal meaning of *eudaemonia*. Socrates also makes the more conventional observation that whatever the fate of the individual, justice is essential if a group is to achieve its goals. Thieves who rob one another do worse than thieves who practice justice among themselves in order to be more effective in robbing others. We now have Socrates's case in its full vulnerability. Justice must be in the interest of both individuals and the community.

Showing that the usual rules of justice enable individuals to cooperate, and that this means they will do better on average and on the whole, is not difficult. A community where everyone respects everyone else's rights will be more prosperous than one where everyone tries to cheat and steal. The difficulty is that from the point of view of any single individual, what *looks* like the option that is most in his interest as a single individual is to live in a community where everyone else takes justice seriously, and he gets away with behaving badly. There is an enormous modern literature on what is known as the "free-rider problem," which is to say the problem posed by the person who thinks along these lines, and wishes to "free-ride" on the back of everyone else's good behavior. (The term "free rider" comes from the homely example of a person who wants to use the train or bus without paying his fare. As long as others pay their fares, there will be a bus or train service, and he will get its benefits without paying his share of the cost.) Five minutes' reflection suggests that if we suspect one another of harboring such sentiments, mutual distrust will undermine all cooperation between us; it also suggests that we should police one another to ensure that anyone who does harbor such thoughts is deterred from acting on them.

Further reflection raises the specter of how to police those who do the policing: *quis custodet ipsos custodes?* We have good reason to hope that we can all be committed to acting justly for its own sake. Nonetheless, we also have good reason to fear that there will be many occasions when our best interests will be served by violating the precepts of justice. The problem is especially acute in the context of economic relationships, where everyone is assumed to be acting in a self-interested fashion; why should we assume that they will not cheat on their bargains? Anyone who wants to analyze politics on the assumption that we are rational actors who are out to maximize our own payoffs faces the problem in its most acute form. If we think that people interacting in the marketplace can be policed by the state, and *made* to do what justice demands, we must next explain how the agents of the state can be policed and kept honest. On the face of it, they have every incentive to rob the rest of us. The issue surfaced in the debate between Thrasymachus and Socrates; it cannot be said to have been resolved even now.

The Argument after Thrasymachus

Socrates takes up the task of showing that the conflict between justice and self-interest is only apparent. The creation of the most influential utopia in history is a surprising part of the undertaking. The opening discussion ends when Thrasymachus grumpily abandons the argument, and Socrates admits that although he has routed Thrasymachus, he does not think he has made much headway in defining justice. Glaucon restarts the discussion and poses the crucial question: *is* it always in the interests of the individual to be just? If we could get away with behaving badly, would we not have good reason to do it? If we possessed the "ring of Gyges" that could make us invisible, would we not use it to sleep with other men's wives, and to assassinate kings and rule in their stead? (In the myth, the ancestor of the Lycian king Gyges was a shepherd who found a magic ring and used it for just that purpose.) Glaucon sets Socrates the impossible task of showing that the just man is better-off than the unjust man, even if the unjust man is believed to be virtuous, and lives and dies prosperous and admired, while the just man is believed to be wicked, and dies a painful and despised death.

Plato's answer takes us through the creation of the perfect polis, and what it requires by way of the education of its leading members. First, Glaucon offers a commonsensical view about the origins of justice. Glaucon's view has been taken seriously by political thinkers ever since Thomas Hobbes's *Leviathan* in 1651. In *Republic* it falls flat. It is not entirely obvious why, since it was hardly news to a Greek audience that much of mankind was selfish, and a commercial people like the Athenians were well acquainted with contracts. Glaucon says that we are selfish creatures who prefer our own welfare to that of others. We would behave badly when it suited us if we could get away with it; but we are more eager to avoid suffering at the hands of others than we are to exploit them, and agree to restrain ourselves in order to secure the same forbearance from others. Morality, or moral conduct, is a form of insurance. Justice springs from an agreement "neither to do nor to suffer harm." Glaucon is philosophically deft. He agrees that this is not an actual agreement, but the agreement that we *would* have made. It embodies a negative Golden Rule; we "don't do as we would not be done by." Explaining justice in terms of a hypothetical contract has been a favored move among political theorists for several centuries and is popular today. Glaucon failed to start a tradition of such thinking; his views are ignored by Socrates and were lost in later natural law theories, which explained the rules of justice as dictates of nature.

It follows from Glaucon's view that *if* we were entirely immune to the threat of punishment, we would do well by behaving badly. This thought is less alarming than it seems; we do not possess Gyges's ring and are not immune; we are born as dependent infants who need to ingratiate ourselves with our parents, and other adults, and in the process get educated out of unrestrained selfishness. We acquire a conscience and are thereafter kept in check by it. This way of thinking about morality does not close the gap between *physis* and *nomos*, between nature and morality; it does not show that if we follow nature we shall be just. It therefore does not achieve what Plato seeks. On Glaucon's view, morality is artificial, and a human invention; it may well be the most important of all inventions, because it underpins other great inventions on which our safety and happiness depend—the institutions of politics, government, and law. Plato held that morality was inscribed in the natural order; he despised the Sophist view that nature was amoral, that men were selfish by nature, and that law—*nomos*—was a matter of convention. How far this view was common to the Sophists is unclear; it would be surprising if no Sophist had anticipated Aristotle's middle way by arguing that man was a creature whose nature was to live by conventions. The difficulty of resting justice on convention is evidently that we need some explanation of how it is that we are disposed to abide by conventions to which we have agreed. Modern writers[13] suggest that we have had a sense of fairness programmed into us by evolution, and point to the fact that most primates appear to react to "unfairness" much as we do. Evolutionary theory was two and a half millennia in the future when Plato wrote *Republic*. He tackles the Sophists head-on.

Socrates persuades Glaucon and Adeimantus that the nature of justice will be easier to see *en gros* if we look at justice in a polis, and they set out to describe a well-made polis. Society rests on the division of labor—an idea that Plato shares with Marx and many others, but that is at odds with the Stoic view that society springs from natural sociability and that we unite for the sake of one another's company. Plato's picture is more utilitarian, though it resonates with contemporary evolutionary theory. It also embodies his view of justice as "sticking to one's last." In the simplest society, each does what he is best at. We unite to get the benefits of specialization; if I am a good farmer and a terrible shoemaker, I shall walk more comfortably if I trade my wheat for the talented shoemaker's shoes. This suggests a more "consumerist" world than Plato is really looking for. He wants only minimal specialization, and his spartan, or Spartan, proclivities swiftly emerge; self-sufficiency is easier to attain if our tastes are frugal. Glaucon protests that the society that Socrates describes lives like pigs; Socrates retorts by arguing that societies inevitably move swiftly from the search for modest comfort to the greed and self-aggrandizement that brings endless wars for the acquisition of territory and wealth. Leaving this thought to do its work, Socrates switches the argument to the centerpiece of *Republic*. If prosperity means warfare and we must be ready to fight in self-defense, we need soldiers; if we need soldiers, we need good, well-trained soldiers. We need soldiers who protect their own people and attack only their enemies, and do not set up exploitative regimes at home. We need soldiers who *know* whom to protect and whom to attack. Good guard dogs know how to do that, says Socrates. Good guard dogs are therefore philosophers; their human equivalent must be philosophers. We are at the point where *Republic* becomes a treatise on education.

Guardians and Their Education

In two pages, Socrates launches the most famous of all defenses of meritocracy and the best-known discussion of political education: a well-ordered polis requires a division of labor that yields a ruling elite that provides military defense when its members are young and social management in their mature years, provided by those with the greatest aptitude for philosophical study who will have had ten years of mathematics and five of dialectics. It perhaps should be said in passing that Plato's Academy was attended by men who shared few or none of his political views and went off to govern states possessing a variety of political arrangements. There were a very few women students, too. In *kallipolis* all will specialize in what they are best suited to do. Their skills will be based on natural talent, but they need development, and the education of an elite based on natural talent is the most important task the state has to perform. Those who dislike Plato complain that almost his first move is to expel all poets and artists from his polis. Even those who do not dislike him flinch. Plato's case is simple; the first stage of education is what the Greeks called "music"—*mousike* is wider in scope than "music" and includes dance, poetry, and celebratory ritual. Like Socrates, Plato thought early training had a profound impact on the souls of children, and he wanted it to instill courage and a regard for truth. Socrates died for saying that traditional Greek poetry defamed the gods by depicting them as lecherous, deceitful, vain, and worse. Neither denied the beauty of Greek poetry, and Plato was himself a considerable poet, but he thought most art was a form of attractive lying. Lying has no place in the philosophical state—a proposition the critical reader might think comes awkwardly from the inventor of the idea of "the Golden Lie"—so the poets will be garlanded and loaded with honors, escorted to the city boundaries, and sent to ply their trade elsewhere. There will be poetry, drama, and dance in early education, but it will be on decidedly Spartan principles.

Plato's understanding of art is not our subject, except in this respect. Plato's theory of knowledge, on which the arguments of *Republic* depend, explained the empirical world of everyday appearance as a distorted picture of the world of Truth. True knowledge is knowledge of the world of the Forms, the essences that make things what they are; they are unchanging and eternal, in contrast to the transitory objects we find around us. This is explained in the Allegory of the Cave that features in Plato's explanation of why philosophers will not wish to rule, and why they cannot rule in states as they are actually constituted. Art is a double misrepresentation, since it paints deceitful pictures of what is already a deceitful picture. It is an engaging feature of Plato's argument that he uses all the artful devices of the poets and painters in arguing against their activities. It is not merely that he employs every rhetorical device he possesses in the course of denouncing rhetoric; he does it so blatantly that he leaves readers at a loss to know what to take literally and what to read as ironic. One deeply disconcerting issue is that Plato, like Socrates, thought that if we did attain knowledge of the True, the Good, and the Beautiful, we would not be able to *say* what we knew. It seems that we must inevitably rely on allegories, parables, devices that point us toward the truth, but do not literally say what it is. More than once, in other dialogues, Socrates says that it is not he who is speaking but a force beyond his control, and in *Republic* his discussion of philosophical truth is invariably allegorical and contrastive, emphasizing its difference from empirical conjecture. We know more about what it is *not* than about what it *is*.

So far as the education of the ruling class is concerned, Plato seems to be wholly in earnest in his proposals, especially in his proposal that women should receive exactly the same education as men. One reason for taking him quite literally lies in the instructions for training young Spartans ascribed to Lycurgus. That was a more militarized version of the subjection of the individual child to the needs of the state than Plato puts forward, but the thrust of the training was the same: the unceasing repetition of lessons in self-discipline for the sake of political unity. What Plato puts forward in *Republic* echoes what Lycurgus was credited with creating in Sparta; and it is not hard to believe that someone whose family was attached to the pro-Spartan oligarchy that emerged at the end of the Peloponnesian War would have been attracted to Sparta's educational practice—except, and it is a very large exception, that in *Republic* it culminates in an education in philosophy, not in the creation of a hoplite infantry happy to die where it stood. What Plato's readers made of *Republic* is unknown, and impossible to guess. On the face of it, he was rash to put forward ideas with such an unmistakably Spartan ring. Athens continued to fight Sparta on and off in the fourth century as it had done in the fifth, and no Athenian democrat would forget that Plato's relatives had been members of the savage oligarchy installed by Sparta in 404.

Nonetheless, Plato did not despise the arts. Because they have such a powerful effect, he tried to ensure that they preached the right message: that the gods are always good and always virtuous. Some of his injunctions seem ludicrous, such as the prohibition on allowing children to play the roles of cowards and weaklings for fear it will rot their characters; but these strictures are squarely Spartan in origin and in line with the views of Cato the Censor and Jean-Jacques Rousseau among later writers. We are asked to imagine an education that will first inculcate virtue through a tightly constrained syllabus of poetry and drama, and will then take the young men and women and train them in gymnastics and the arts of warfare. It is worth emphasizing that girls will receive the same training; that was another un-Athenian but not un-Spartan thought. What counted for Plato was *character*; a person's sex was immaterial, though the Spartans did not expect women to fight alongside men. Eventually, the most apt will receive the philosophical training that will enable them to rule wisely and justly in utopia.

In arguing for the necessity of training a virtuous elite, Plato presents two arguments. The first concerns the different kinds of soul that human beings possess, and sets out the "Golden Lie" that citizens will be taught as an allegorical account of the hierarchy of talent; the second argument draws on the first and eventually yields the answer to the questions of what justice *is*. We must think of souls as bronze, silver, and golden; the possessors of bronze souls are the workers, of silver the soldiers—what Plato calls auxiliaries—and of golden souls the guardians, the philosopher-kings. He imagines a flawlessly meritocratic system for selecting the elite and proposes elaborate mechanisms to ensure that elite parents breed elite children; but he also expects ordinary people to need a picture of its basis that they can readily grasp. Readers of Aldous Huxley's *Brave New World* will recognize the ambition; "I'm awfully glad I'm a Beta," says the antenatally conditioned worker, who thinks the Alphas are much too clever and work terribly hard.[14] Bertrand Russell thought that Huxley had stolen the idea of brave new world from him; Russell feared that modern science would enable mankind to destroy itself in a new and terminal world war, and he looked to eugenic science to produce a pacified population. Huxley produces a ghastly parody of utopia. It makes all the difference in the world that Plato did not think that his elite was conditioning the people into believing that they were naturally what they had been genetically engineered into being. Plato's myth is a "golden" lie because it contains a deep truth. So we shall tell the populace that we are born with various metals in our souls and that our social position reflects the preponderance of these metals. This is the Golden Lie, the necessary myth. Plato does not argue for the assumption that makes the Golden Lie a deeper truth: the existence of a cosmic symmetry between the order of the ideal society and the order of nature. He assumes as a premise that we are naturally suited to different sorts of social roles, and that one of many things wrong with democratic Athens is that the wrong people end up occupying positions of power.

What reconciles *physis* and *nomos* is the thought that we can create a society whose social structure mirrors the natural harmony of the universe. It is an axiom of Plato's philosophy that we can be happy and fulfilled when we occupy a social position that reflects, or encapsulates, the position that our innate character fits us to occupy. Absent this vision of a harmonious natural hierarchy, the argument of *Republic* loses its appeal. Meritocracy is attractive if we believe both that society will be properly led only when natural leaders are in charge and that the rank and file will be happier in a subordinate position than in positions of power and responsibility. This provided another reason for combating the views of Callicles and Thrasymachus; they assumed that everyone would wish to exercise power, because everyone would wish to enjoy the payoffs from doing so. The rowers in the fleet hoped to profit from successful wars on their neighbors and valued their political power in the Assembly because it enabled them to force a warlike policy on their leaders. They failed to display the virtue of temperance that Plato thinks especially appropriate to the working classes. Writing two thousand years later, in the aftermath of the English Civil War, Thomas Hobbes, who translated Thucydides and was himself deeply hostile to democracy, made the revolutionary claim that we are by nature equal, not unequal, that there is no natural aristocracy, no natural division into workers and rulers, and that *all* political hierarchy is a contrivance.[15] We should give unhesitating obedience to our rulers, for the sake of peace, not because they were given us by nature. But Plato's cosmology was shared by Aristotle and other classical writers; it subsequently reinforced Christian ideas about the divine ordering of the universe and was reinforced by them, with obvious implications for social and political order.

Plato's case could be made differently. It could be argued as a flatly sociological proposition that a polis—or a modern state—functions best when there is a clear class structure with powerless workers, a military caste that knows its business, and an educated governing class whose right to rule is taken for granted. It would not be impossible to present modern China as evidence in favor of the thought. This is a sociological claim that needs no philosophical backing beyond the empirical evidence. If it is true at all, it is a truth of social science. Conversely, such a perfectly structured society can be presented as a dystopia rather than a utopia, something to avoid at all costs. In *Brave New World* Aldous Huxley created just that.

Justice Defined

With our three class structure before us, we can now see justice itself. The cardinal virtues are temperance, courage, reason, and justice, and we know which class embodies which. The virtue appropriate to the workers is temperance; they are, as it were, the stomach of the society, looking after its fleshly aspect, keeping it in operation as a physical enterprise. Their virtue is self-control. The virtue appropriate to the auxiliaries is courage; they are the heart of the society, and must be brave hearts. The virtue appropriate to the guardians is wisdom; they are the society's mind, and the virtue of the mind is wisdom. The discovery of three classes and three virtues seems to have exhausted the discussion; where, then, is justice? The answer is that justice is the overarching virtue that governs the whole. When all are in their proper place and each person and each class does its proper job and no other, there is justice.

This strikes us—modern readers—as implausible, because we think of justice as one among several virtues, whereas Plato uses the term to mean something very like "overall rightness." We have already seen that the Greek *dike* embraces more than our idea of justice; Aristotle took pains to distinguish two kinds of justice, one embracing overall rightness and the other justice in the narrower and more usual sense. The view that there may be a conflict between justice and mercy, for example, involves the narrower sense and not the wider sense with which Plato is concerned. In the wider sense there cannot be a conflict between justice and mercy; the "right" outcome is the "just" outcome. Plato believed that the ultimate criterion of "rightness" is that our souls are in order, that we are acting as our nature requires, contributing as we should to the order of the universe and of society. Nothing could be more at odds with modern liberalism.

Socrates's case for a philosophically based dictatorship is not a defense of aristocratic rule in the ordinary sense. The rulers get no earthly rewards from ruling, and exercising power is an exercise in self-abnegation. Readers of *Republic* have always been struck by the details of the domestic lives of Plato's ruling elite and how bleak their lives appear. Plato's guardians have no property; they have no families. Their children are the children of the whole class; Plato argues that in the absence of money or private property they will see the whole polis as "theirs" and will think only in collective terms. There will be no "I" and "mine," only "we" and "ours." Their interests are subservient to the interests of the whole, not vice versa. Glaucon and Adeimantus wonder whether the guardians can be happy, and Socrates has to take two bites at the answer—first, that the happiness of the guardians is less significant than that of the whole society; second, that they will be happy because they will be fulfilling their natures in doing their duty. Aristotle thought neither answer would do.

This is the moment to emphasize again the *unpolitical* or *antipolitical* nature of these thoughts about justice. There are two crucial thoughts about justice that Plato refuses to entertain, the first about the rule of law, and the second about political competition. The first holds that a major reason for the existence of government is to ensure that individuals are treated justly: that they are not robbed or assaulted, that their property is secure, and that their lives are regulated by rules rather than the whims of the powerful. Law vanishes in Plato's *Republic*. Once philosopher-kings rule, the conflicts that law regulates vanish. So therefore does a central aspect of justice. A second and related sense of justice in political contexts concerns the fair allocation of power—whether the wellborn or the many should rule, for instance. That question is answered by Plato: philosophers must rule, and nobody can have any interest in having his affairs run by the ignorant and ill informed, even if that includes himself. The idea that "the many" might have a legitimate interest in running their own lives just because they wish to is not one Plato entertains. This is an *unpolitical* politics, because the idea of legitimate but conflicting interests has no place. The task of the rulers is to know what the correct allocation of tasks and rewards is, and to institute it.

Last Thoughts

Much of the last two-thirds of *Republic* is a fabulously interesting exposition of Plato's metaphysical convictions; these are not directly relevant here, and we must neglect them. But three later arguments concern us. The first is why philosophers can and must rule, the second why the perfect state cannot endure forever, and the third Plato's final attempt to show that the just man is always happier than the unjust man. The rule of the philosopher is required because Plato has turned the ordinary political argument in favor of stability into a philosophical argument about the need to create a polis that reflects the order of nature. Since it is a philosophical skill to discern the divine order, the polis can be perfected only when put under the aegis of philosophy. For unphilosophical readers, the interest of the argument lies less in the details of Plato's ideas about the natural order than in the similarity between his argument for the rule of the philosopher and later arguments in favor of assorted kinds of theocratic government.

If the premise is accepted that the crucial task of politics is to align the social, economic, and political order with a divinely appointed natural order, a central role must be found for whoever understands that order, if not as the day-to-day ruler of a society, then as a spiritual guardian of the day-to-day ruler. How that authority is to be exercised is a question that roiled medieval Christendom and remains unanswered in the Muslim world. In medieval Europe the question whether popes could depose kings was one aspect of it; in the modern world Iran is an avowed theocracy, while Israel is avowedly but uneasily not one. Britain has an established church but is strikingly more secular than the United States, whose Constitution prohibits any establishment of religion, but whose politicians compete assiduously for the votes of the devout. Plato's answer was that philosophers must be kings and kings must be philosophers. One major difficulty was that on his own showing, philosophers would be unwilling to do the job. In the Allegory of the Cave, Plato likens the human condition to that of men sitting in a dark cave able to see only directly ahead; on the wall in front of them are the flickering shadows cast by people walking behind them, and these shadows will be taken for reality. Out of the cave, the philosopher is first dazzled by the sun, then sees things as they are. Will the philosopher who has engaged in a long and arduous search for Truth and has finally found it really be willing to return to the world of illusion? Surely not. Such reluctance is highly desirable, because government is best entrusted to men who are not consumed by ambition. On the other hand, it suggests that, outside utopia, philosophers may not be successful rulers.

In utopia government will not be complicated. A defect of Plato's utopia in the eyes of critics, but a virtue in the eyes of Plato himself, is that nothing much happens. It is too poor to excite the greed of neighbors, and its soldiers are tough enough to deter them; because everyone is doing what nature fits him to do, nobody will have any desire to do anything different, and novel tastes will be unknown. The guardians will organize the breeding of the ruling elite in such a way that the right people are born into the right positions—just what the calculations are that they perform and how they do it, Plato sadly leaves mysterious, although he gestures toward some barely intelligible equations. So long as they get the calculations right, timeless tranquillity rules.

Two large questions about the common, or "bronze-souled," people remain. One is whether they live just lives. We may think that they cannot, because their souls are of bronze, and their guiding virtue is therefore temperance; we may equally think that they do, because if they occupy the right social position and do what persons like themselves are intended to do, they live rightly or justly. They stick to their lasts. With both thoughts in mind, we may suppose that they *share* in justice, but not as fully as the philosopher does; even this may strike some of us as a repulsive conclusion in suggesting that moral capacity is class related. The other large question is what the common people do. The answer appears to be that they live as they would anywhere else, but undisturbed by political uproar. They do not have to fight; they cannot take part in politics, not least because there is none to take part in. Presumably, they farm, engage in handicrafts, look after their families, and are uncomplicatedly happy because they are secure and not out of their depth. They are not the helots of Messenia kept down by the brutality of Spartan overlords, but an invisible laboring class.

Decaying States

If utopia could be created, surely it would endure forever. Not so, says Plato. Something will go wrong. The mathematics of procreation may be miscalculated, or some other cause may lead to the guardians' losing their skills or commitment, and a cycle of political change would begin. Decay follows a cyclical path. First, honor supersedes wisdom as the basis of authority; the wise elite will become a "timocracy," or an aristocracy based on honor; this in turn will degenerate into an oligarchy where rich men oppress their inferiors. The timocracy is Sparta, as the text itself makes clear; this is the second-best state, moving away from perfection rather than toward it. Just as our souls mirror the condition of utopia, so the soul of the timocratic man will mirror the values of the timocratic state. The same will be true of oligarchy and the oligarchs; they are degenerate timocrats who have replaced the search for honor with the search for wealth. The oligarchical state is not one state but two, the state of the rich and the state of the poor, at war with each other. The inevitable revolution ushers in democracy.

The principle of democracy is freedom, and Plato is unabashedly hostile to it. The Athenian concept of political or democratic freedom was *isegoria*, or the equal right of all qualified citizens to speak in the Assembly; the term *eleutheria* had the more general meaning of having no master, not being enslaved. It was *eleutheria* that the Greeks defended against the Persians, and *isegoria* that Athenian democrats thought they particularly possessed. Plato complains that democracy is the rule of pure license, where everyone does just what he pleases. Slaves are insolent, and donkeys jostle citizens on the sidewalks. Finally it leads to the lowest point of the cycle when its excesses alienate the better-off and powerful and lead to the rise of the tyrant. Tyranny, the worst of all forms of government, might be transcended if the tyrant was somehow to become a philosopher and begin the cycle anew. Other than in utopia, philosophers should keep clear of politics, but perhaps a philosopher might teach the child of a tyrant to be a philosopher-king. When Plato went to Syracuse to try the experiment, he barely escaped with his life.

The enthusiasm for cyclical theories of history is a recurrent feature of the history of political thinking. They have little to be said for them as contributions to the analysis of political change, but Plato's cyclical story served other purposes. His account of "timocracy" is a nod toward Sparta, as if Sparta is far from perfect but only in the first stage of degeneration; that timocracies degenerate when aristocrats become obsessed with money was true enough of Sparta, and the distinction between the rule of the better sort and the rule of the greedy rich needed little elaboration to a Greek audience. The description of democracy as a regime addicted to liberty, where everyone does exactly as he pleases is mostly simple abuse of Athens and wholly unfair; it was, however, common coin in upper-class complaints, with Plato's complaints sounding very like those of the author known as "the Old Oligarch." It is also an inadvertent tribute to Pericles's account of the city whose citizens did not feel that they had to mind everyone else's business because they had interesting lives of their own to get on with. Plato's assault also fails in the eyes of modern readers because it makes Athenian democracy sound like such fun. It is the account of tyranny that we must take most seriously; for it provides Plato with the final vital link in his case for preferring justice to injustice.

Plato's premise is that the souls of the citizens mirror the character of the state. Democratic citizens are half-crazy with a passion for novelties, never making up their minds what to do, and never sticking with a decision; hence the disasters of the Peloponnesian War, and hence the imprudent overreaching that led to the war in the first place. The tyrant is Thrasymachus's hero, the man who can do whatever he likes because nobody can stop him. Plato paints a wonderful picture of the true horror of his situation. He can ascend to power only by murder and deception; and the maintenance of his rule depends upon exciting fear in his subjects. That means that he also excites hatred. He is, and knows he is, an enemy to the world and the world is an enemy to him. He cannot have a moment's peace of mind. His food may be poisoned; he may be stabbed in the night; old friends he has not murdered on his way to the top may turn out to be the assassins he fears. His life is not worth living, and he will probably meet the fate he fears sooner rather than later. The tyrant's life is a bad bargain even in this-worldly terms. As always, the critical reader will complain that Plato paints an exaggerated picture, but that is hardly the main point.

Plato concludes, first with an oddly interpolated rehearsal of the quarrel between philosophy and poetry, and then, as at the end of *Gorgias,* with an account of the fate of the just and the unjust man in the afterlife, where their souls will finally be assessed and they will receive their eternal rewards. This is where the ultimate payoff for the just and unjust life is received. Cicero built on the passage for "Scipio's Dream" in book 6 of *De republica,* to suggest that the Roman statesman who serves his republic unswervingly will be blessed with immortality, and Scipio's Dream served as the launchpad for discussions of reincarnation and the compatibility of Christian and Platonic cosmology for many centuries. There is, however, little to be said about the bearing of the myth of Er in the narrow context of the ostensible argument of *Republic* other than that it shows that Plato fails to answer Thrasymachus's challenge, or that if he has met Thrasymachus's challenge, he has not met Glaucon's: he has failed to show that a cool, calm, and collected tyrant (supposing such a person to be psychologically possible) would do worse *in this world* than his victims. As Immanuel Kant observed, we hanker for an afterlife precisely because virtue and happiness are so poorly correlated in this life.

More to the point in political terms, perhaps, is that although Plato fails on that score, as he surely must, he is entirely persuasive on the worthlessness of the tyrant's life. Contemplating the lives of Hitler and Stalin, we are not moved by envy; and that is enough to defeat Thrasymachus, if not to prove Socrates's case, which in its own fashion is as extreme as Thrasymachus's.

The final thought that *Republic* inspires is that Plato's account of the ideal polity belongs to soul craft rather than to statecraft; it is not a picture of political life at all. There is no economic life to regulate, no crime to suppress, no conflicting interests to balance, no competing views on policy to reconcile, no conflicts of value to assuage, accommodate, or suppress. To the question "How can we live together in spite of not being of one mind about so many important matters?" Plato's answer is to deny the premise. "Let us always be of only one mind about all important questions" is the response. *Brave New World* is a parodic commentary on the corrupt form the Platonic utopia would take in the twentieth century; Hobbes's *Leviathan* is an exploration of how far we must *make* ourselves agree if there is to be peace. From Aristotle onward, it has been recognized that Plato did not so much solve the problem of establishing a just polity as dissolve it. Plato's genius was, in part, to show so clearly how far our hankering after harmony—and how could we not hanker after harmony?—is at odds with making everyday politics work more productively. Pursuing that point, Aristotle set out to show what sort of justice we might achieve in a nonutopian polity, and to him we now turn.

CHAPTER 3

Aristotle: Politics Is Not Philosophy

Life and Times

UNLIKE PLATO, ARISTOTLE WAS embroiled in the politics of his day; indeed, he died in exile because the Athenians suspected his loyalty when they revolted against Macedonian rule in 323 BCE. He tutored Alexander the Great and was the father-in-law of Antipater, the Macedonian general whom Alexander installed as regent to keep Greece in order when he left to conquer the Persian Empire in 334. The ancient historians do not suggest Aristotle was devoted to his former pupil; Plutarch credits him with supplying the poison that may or may not have been the cause of Alexander's untimely death. (It was rumored that Antipater feared that Alexander had turned against him and was likely to have him executed; so Antipater preempted him.) Aristotle was born in 384 in the small town of Stagira, on the borders of Greece and Macedon—slightly east of the modern Salonica. He came to Athens in 367 to join Plato's Academy and spent the next twenty years there. The forty-five years between his arrival in Athens and his death in 322 saw Athens's revival after the destruction of the Peloponnesian War, and then the extinction of the Greek city-states' political independence following their defeat by Macedonian forces, first at the Battle of Chaeronea in 338 and when the death of Alexander the Great in 323 prompted Athens to revolt, at the naval battle of Amorgos in 322.

Aristotle's career at the Academy suffered a hiatus after the death of Plato. He and his friend Xenocrates left Athens when the Academy fell under the leadership of men whom Aristotle disliked. He spent time on Lesbos, where he was supported by the tyrant Hermias, a former slave of great ability who had gone on to buy the rulership of the city of Atarneus from the king of Persia. Hermias had spent time at the Academy and was reputedly an excellent philosopher; Aristotle later married Hermias's niece, after her uncle had been tortured and executed on the orders of the great king on suspicion of plotting to assist a Macedonian invasion of Persia. Whether Hermias brought Aristotle to the attention of Philip of Macedon is unclear, but in 342 Aristotle was summoned to Pella to become tutor to the young Alexander, a position he filled until 336. It must soon have been a part-time post, since as early as 340 Alexander was governing Macedonia in his father's absence, while two years later he commanded part of his father's army at the Battle of Chaeronea.

In 335 Aristotle returned to Athens to found his own school, the Lyceum. This was in the immediate aftermath of the second unsuccessful revolt of the Athenians against Macedonian rule. Surprisingly, neither Philip nor Alexander meted out to the Athenians the punishment meted out to Thebes, which was razed to the ground. Demosthenes, the most intransigent leader of the anti-Macedonian elements, was allowed to remain in Athens and not forced into exile. Xenocrates was now head of the Academy, but there is no suggestion that Aristotle set up in competition with his friend. There was no disloyalty in establishing his own school, and his school had a distinctive character. It was marked by an enthusiasm for empirical investigation; among other things, Aristotle founded the empirical discipline of politics by setting his students to describe and analyze 158 Greek constitutions. The "naturalism" of Aristotle's philosophy struck a balance between what we would recognize as a scientific, empirical, experimental approach to understanding the world, and a more nearly religious approach that regarded nature as the source of a beauty and order that human contrivance could not match. One result is that his political analysis is an engrossing mixture of practical wisdom and an almost Platonic attempt to show that the best state is best "by nature."

Aristotle's life in Athens after his return was not tranquil. The majority of Athenians were bitterly hostile to the hegemony of Macedon. Athenian politics until Demosthenes's death by suicide in 322 was dominated by the question of whether and how far the hegemony of Macedon could be resisted. Antipater was as unpopular as the head of an army of occupation is likely to be; and Aristotle felt himself not only a foreigner but an unwelcome one. The awkwardness was for a time reduced by Aristotle's friendship with Lycurgus, a student of both Plato and Isocrates, and now in charge of the finances of Athens and the upkeep of the city; Lycurgus was a nominal democrat and an ally of Demosthenes, but was the sort of moderate aristocratic politician praised in his *Politics*, who safeguarded the economic interests of the propertied classes and ensured they were kept friendly to the democratic constitution. Nonetheless, Aristotle's position eventually became untenable. In June 323 Alexander's unexpected death in Babylon at the age of thirty-two, whether from malaria, liver failure, or poison, provoked open revolt. Aristotle retired to Chalcis, on Euboea. He died there a year later, just as Antipater's victory at Amorgos destroyed Athenian hopes of recovering political and military independence.

Aristotle's Political Prejudices

Modern readers find several of Aristotle's views deeply repugnant. The two most obvious are his views on slavery and his views on the intellectual and political capacity of women.[1] Unsurprisingly, these are connected. The relation of master to inferior—of the male head of household to wife and slaves—is a basic and natural human relationship. For Aristotle the household of a man qualified to be a citizen is a family unit where slaves do the menial work: menial work unfits a man for political life; slaves and common laborers liberate the citizen for political life. The head of a household governs his family partly politically and partly not. The relation of citizen to citizen is that of equal to equal. The relation of master to slave, husband to wife, or parent to child is not one between equals, although wives are certainly free persons, whereas slaves are not.[2] Fathers exercise "royal" rule over children and "constitutional" rule over wives, but there is no suggestion that husbands and wives take turns in governing the household as citizens do the polity. We shall see how Aristotle argues for the justice of these relationships. It is worth pausing to notice two things. The first is the alarming suggestion that the acquisition of slaves is a branch of the art of war or hunting.[3] The ancient world was heavily dependent on slavery; and there were states, or pirate kingdoms, that regarded "man hunting" as a legitimate business and their own distinctive way of making a living. For villagers living within reach of their raids or for anyone forced to travel a long distance by sea, the danger of being seized and sold into slavery was very real. Aristotle suggests ways of regulating the practice of seizing captives in war and selling them into slavery, but the practice itself he does not criticize. Since he admits that many writers think slavery is unjust and contrary to nature, he certainly had the chance to do so.

The second thing to notice is that when Aristotle seeks a justification in the natural order for the existence of slavery, he appeals to the gulf in the capacity for self-government that—in his view—separates natural slaves from their masters. What he made of Hermias, the former slave, who was one of his students as well as his protector, a man to whom he dedicated a memorial and whose niece he married after her uncle's untimely death, one can only imagine. Hermias's last words were said to have been "I have done nothing unworthy of a philosopher." Along the same lines, Aristotle maintains that women are rational enough to fulfill the subordinate role in the family that he assigns to them, but have too little rational capacity to give their own independent judgment in the political arena. Women, slaves, and children belong within the well-ordered household, not in the agora or *ecclesia*. It is worth considering why readers are so often outraged that Aristotle held views that were entirely commonplace in the ancient Greek world. It is surely because so much of what he writes is strikingly down-to-earth and shows an attention to how politics is in fact conducted that is quite absent from Plato's sweeping rejection of political life in toto. Aristotle talked to many intelligent women and had every chance to change his mind; he had every opportunity to reflect on what the existence of Hermias implied for the justice of slavery. In short, modern readers might think that the remedy for Aristotle's blind spots is a more diligent application of the empirical methods he himself advocated.

Teleology: Nature and Politics

Aristotle would have been unmoved by our anachronistic advice. His conception of "nature" was not like ours, and the search for the natural order of things was not straightforwardly empirical. Hermias was transparently not a "slave by nature," but that did not mean there were no slaves by nature. Aristotle famously wrote that "it is evident that the state is a creation of nature, and that man is by nature a political animal."[4] We must, therefore, start from Aristotle's idea of nature. Aristotle is known for the doctrine of the four causes: the matter of what is to be explained; its form; the efficient cause, or how it is produced; and its final cause. The behavior of entities such as plants, animals, persons, and institutions was explained by their telos, or "end"—their goal or purpose or point. This is teleological explanation, explanation in terms of goals or purposes. The scientific revolution of the seventeenth century expelled teleological explanation from the physical sciences. Our idea of a physical cause is essentially that of the antecedent conditions that make something happen; we do not think that there is some state of affairs "proper" to physical nature, and the modern conception of nature is thus very different from Aristotle's. We use the term "natural" to describe the way things are when not affected by human contrivance— think of "natural blonde"—but Aristotle included human contrivance among the things that had their "natural" and their "unnatural" forms. A society like our own, where women have equal political rights with men, is "unnatural." "Natural" forms of life were good because they fulfilled their natural purpose. Today this Aristotelian view survives in the teaching of the Roman Catholic Church, where it is underpinned by the thought that God is the author of nature and that natural law and divine law reinforce each other. Aristotle did not think in terms of a deity who authored nature; nature itself was divine. He is therefore very exposed to the skeptical view that "natural" and "unnatural" are synonyms for "usual" and "unusual," or for "morally good" and "morally bad."

Throughout his *Politics* it is taken for granted that nature is the ground of social norms. When Aristotle asks whether there are slaves "by nature," he wants to know whether there are persons whose proper place in the world is to serve as slaves to others. If there are, it explains *both* why there is slavery *and* why it is good for (natural) slaves to be slaves. Discovering what is "natural" uncovers both the way things are and how they should be. Moreover, nature is hierarchical; everything aims at some good, and the highest things aim at the highest good. Human beings are at the top of the hierarchy of living creatures, and we must understand human behavior in the light of how we are meant to pursue the highest good. Allowances made for his prejudices, Aristotle did not simply impose a model of the good polity upon the evidence; investigating the way people do govern themselves shows how they should govern themselves.

The way to discover what nature aims to achieve is to observe what nature actually does. Nature does not always achieve the good she aims at: there are stunted trees, sickly children, unhappy marriages, and states that collapse into civil war. But we discover the standards embodied in words such as "stunted" and "diseased" by looking at what happens when things turn out well. Political science is thus a form of natural history with a strongly normative flavor. Aristotle set out the standards that explanation has to meet in his *Physics*, and they remained canonical for two millennia. The four kinds of cause—form, matter, purpose, and origin—all have their place in political analysis. The form of a state is its constitution, its matter is its citizens, its purpose is to allow us to live the best life in common, the cause of its coming into being appears from the first chapters of *Politics* to be the search for self-sufficiency; and Aristotle's discussion of revolution in later books of *Politics* is both an account of the causes of a state's ceasing to be and an account of the causes of its persistence as a going concern.

Aristotle did not share Plato's belief that all real knowledge must resemble geometry or mathematics. Plato condemned the world of sense as a poor shadow of reality. Sufficiently fine measurement will show that no equilateral triangle drawn by human hands is *perfectly* equilateral; measured sufficiently precisely, one side will be greater than another and the angles of the sides unequal. For Plato the empirical world itself was a botched copy of a transempirical reality; geometry studies perfect geometrical figures. Aristotle did not impugn the world of observation. The world is as we perceive it, though our senses can sometimes deceive us; a man with jaundice will see things as yellow when they are not. Successful explanation should "save the appearances"; it must explain why the world we see, hear, feel, taste, and smell appears as it does. In the seventeenth century Galileo, among others, persuaded his contemporaries that the earth rotated about the sun. Although he overturned Aristotelian astronomy and physics, he professed himself a disciple of Aristotle and accepted the obligation to explain why it *looked* as though the sun moved around the earth. He rejected much of Aristotle's physics—Aristotle thought the earth was truly the center of the universe—but he accepted Aristotle's claim that a successful explanation must explain why things look the way they do.

The study of politics is a form of natural history. Thomas Hobbes loathed Aristotle's politics, and in *Leviathan* followed Plato in modeling politics on geometry; but he admired Aristotle's biology. One consequence of that "biological" style is important, not only because it was at odds with Hobbes's—and Plato's—hankering after political geometry. Aristotle claimed that political analysis should aim only "at as much precision as the subject matter permits." Political wisdom cannot aspire to the precision of geometry, and must not pretend to. Aboriculture suggests an analogy: most trees grow best in firm soil with a moderate water supply; a few thrive with their roots in mud and water. Scientists achieve deeper understanding by analyzing the differences between the trees that do the one and those that do the other. This may or may not assist the farmer, and Aristotle's writings on ethics and politics suggest that it is the farmer's needs—which is to say, in politics, the statesman's and citizen's needs—that are important. In ethics and politics we seek knowledge for the sake of action. Aristotle complains that Plato treated all knowledge as if it served the same goals, but in ethics and politics we seek the truth for the sake of knowing what to do. They are practical disciplines. We try to improve our ethical understanding by reflecting on the way we praise and blame certain actions and characters and ways of life; but we do it to live better, not to gratify curiosity.

One final aspect of this view of nature and science matters to us. Most of us today begin by thinking about the rights or the needs of individuals, and ask what sort of state has a legitimate claim on their allegiance or will best promote their welfare. That is, the individual is—to use Aristotle's terminology—"prior" to the state. Not for Aristotle. The individual is intended by nature to live and thrive in a polis, so the polis is "prior" to the individual. This has the consequence that politics is the master science or the master art, since it aims to discover the conditions under which the best state can come into being and flourish. Just as the hand is explained by its role in enabling its owner, a human person, to flourish, the qualities of citizens are explained by their role in enabling the state to flourish. An analogy might be taken from the theater. Any actor longs to play Lear or Hamlet, the first because Lear is one of the greatest tragic heroes in all drama, and the second because every skill an actor might possess is needed to display Hamlet's agonies of indecision. King Lear and Prince Hamlet are characters in Shakespeare's plays. We understand them by understanding the plays. We understand citizens by understanding the polis, and just as any actor wishes to play Hamlet or Lear, any autonomous and intelligent being would wish to play the part of a citizen in an Aristotelian polis.

Ethics and *The Politics*

Aristotle claimed that the polis existed "by nature" because nature means us to live a good life in common. We must therefore start with his view of the good life; and because the central virtue of the polis is justice, we must see how different Aristotle's views of justice and of our motives for being just are from Plato's. In *Politics* Aristotle relies on the account of justice he gave in the *Nicomachean Ethics*. Ethics is the study of "living well." To know how to live well, we need to know the goal of human life, since knowing how well any activity has gone is a matter of knowing how far it has achieved its goal. Human life, says Aristotle, goes well when we achieve happiness, but only happiness of a certain sort, namely, happiness approved by reason. Only then are we exercising the capacities that nature intends us to exercise, and "living well." If I am a Mafia boss, and I have just murdered the entire family of a rival, men, women, and children alike, I may be happy; but I am happy because I have a vile character. No reasonable man wants to be made happy by a massacre.

Nature intends us to enjoy the happiness of a good person. This argument seems circular: we ask what the good life is and are told it is a happy life; we ask what happiness is and are told it is pleasure achieved in the right way by the right sort of person; we ask what the right sort of person is and are told it is someone who lives a life of virtue according to reason; and when we ask about the virtues, we are told that they are those habits of thought and action whose practice gives happiness to the person who has acquired the right kind of character. The argument is indeed circular but not viciously circular. To make progress, we must examine the particular virtues—reason, temperance, fidelity, courage, justice, and so on—and discover how they contribute to the good life. This is what Aristotle does. The fact that practicing the virtues can be shown to fit together in a well-conducted life gives Aristotle confidence in the framework. Once again it is worth noticing that our notions of morality and Aristotle's ideas about ethics are not quite on all fours. Many excellences that he thinks a well-found polis would encourage are not ones that we would call moral: being well-educated, having good taste, knowing how to bear ourselves in public. They are important in cementing a certain sort of social life, which is in turn important in preserving the cohesion of the polis, but they are not in the modern sense moral qualities.

Aristotle agrees with Plato that a successful polis must be built on justice, but his understanding of justice is not Plato's. The *Nicomachean Ethics* criticizes Plato for collapsing all the virtues into justice; Aristotle contrasts the justice that is one virtue among others with "justice" conceived of as virtue in general. "All-in rightness" is one thing; but justice in the usual sense is concerned with the distribution of goods and bads according to merit, giving everyone what is due. In a political context, this means the distribution of authority and power according to political virtue. A just state must have just inhabitants; states are just only if their citizens lead just lives. It would be a defect in Plato's utopia if philosophers alone could be truly just. We must therefore be able to show that an ordinary reasonable person can practice justice and will wish to do so; but it is enough if such a person wishes to be just only under nonextraordinary conditions. *Republic* lost sight of the limits of argumentative possibility in defending the view that justice profits its practitioners *no matter what.* Plato's argument was heroic but unpersuasive because the conception of happiness to which he appealed in arguing that the just man is inevitably happier than the unjust man is too unlike ordinary happiness; Aristotle repairs the defects in Plato's case.

A just man will wish to be just as one aspect of living a good life. It is rational to be just and to acquire a just character, but there can be no guarantee that the just man will always do better than the unjust man. Nature means the just to flourish, but a given individual may be unlucky and be brought low by behaving well. A society of just persons will always do better than a society of unjust persons, and a rational man will wish to belong to such a society; but it cannot be guaranteed that every individual in such a society will thrive. Doing justice comes more easily when supported by the other virtues. A generous man will think of his family and friends and wish them to live in a just society, and that will make it easier for him to be just. Even the least-just person believes in justice to the extent of wanting everyone else to behave justly: the burglar does not wish to be burgled, nor the robber to be robbed. But a good person wants to be just for its own sake. He is made happy by being just, and being just is indispensable to the happiness he wants: he wants the trust of his friends and the respect of his peers, and these are logically connected with his being a just person, that is, the sort of person who rightly excites trust and respect.

It can be difficult to see how right Aristotle is. If we think that the deep truth about human beings is that they are self-centered "utility maximizers," it is hard to see how they can interact except by treating one another as a means to their own selfish happiness. This is the worldview of Polus, Callicles, and Thrasymachus. Aristotle did not think we are the maximizers of anything in particular. We pursue many goals, each with its own point. There is still a hierarchy of goals: a rational man subordinates the search for worldly goods to the search for excellence of character, for instance. He hopes to be honored as such, and he will care very much what others think of him; but he is not only just instrumentally. "Greed is good" is not consistent with Aristotle's view, but each genuine good has its place in a well-conducted life. There is no *general* problem of the form "Why should essentially selfish creatures care about justice, honesty, or any other virtue that benefits other people rather than themselves?" The premise of the question is false.

Human beings seek their own well-being, but not always effectively. When they fail, something has gone wrong. What is good for us is *connected* with what we want, inasmuch as the well-balanced man wants what is good for himself. But what is good for us is not *defined* as what we want, as it was by Thrasymachus; the wrong wants (think of addiction to drugs or alcohol or gambling) are disconnected from the good. Misguided wants undermine the pursuit of our good. So does simple error, as when I drink poison, believing it to be a tonic, and die when I mean to restore my health. We may make more elaborate mistakes, as when we think that harshness toward defeated enemies will make them more cooperative rather than less, or jump to conclusions, as when we succeed once in intimidating our enemies and conclude that we shall always so succeed. Other mistakes stem from deficiencies in character; a coward misreads situations as being more dangerous than they in fact are, *and* fails to see the point of courage.

Political Analysis

The correct mode of political analysis seems inescapable. We should inspect whatever political regimes we can, and determine what makes for success and failure; we can distinguish corrupt governments from good governments; we can ascertain which regimes promote good political character and which the reverse; we can discover why different peoples adopt different kinds of regimes, and why what we call "politics" flourishes in some but not all societies. Aristotle sent students to discover the constitutional arrangements of Greek cities, although only *The Constitution of Athens* survives; it is itself something of a jumble and may or may not have been written by Aristotle himself rather than a student, but is fascinating nonetheless.

Politics consists of eight books, the two last very unlike their predecessors. These provide a picture of the ideal state and its educational system, a task that earlier books seemed to dismiss as a waste of time. They are also very incomplete; the final book amounts to a handful of pages devoted to the education of the young. The first six books form a well-organized argument; the first book distinguishes political associations from all others, and distinguishes their organizing principles from those of the family and the domestic household; the second discusses ideal states in theory and in practice; books 3 and 4 tackle the connected topics of forms of constitution and qualification for citizenship; and books 5 and 6 cover the connected topics of revolutionary upheaval and the construction of constitutional arrangements that will prevent or divert or defuse such upheaval.

Nonetheless, *Politics* is a sprawling work, and many issues come up for discussion more than once. The nature of citizenship is a running theme, for instance. It is discussed in the context of forms of authority in the first book, when citizen–citizen relations are distinguished from master–slave, husband–wife, parent–children relations; that launches the repudiation of Plato's model of the polity in the second book. Qualifications for citizenship are the topic of the third and fourth books, and that subject recurs in books 5 and 6 in the context of rethinking what sorts of people should have access to political power. The pleasures of brooding on these recurrent discussions are to be had by reading *Politics* slowly. What follows here selects rather brutally, with an eye to the discussion of Plato's *Republic*, and to what others made of Aristotle in the next two millennia. My discussion does not follow Aristotle's own sequence; it initially skirts book 2, in order to end with Aristotle's attack on ideal state theory in that book, and his later ventures into that field.[5]

Political Man

Almost at the beginning of his *Politics* Aristotle declares that man is a creature intended by nature to live in a polis. Before he does so, he makes three only slightly less famous observations. First, he claims that all associations exist for a purpose and that, as the most inclusive association, the polis exists for the most inclusive purpose. It is the ultimate form of human organization and exists to satisfy the highest goals of social life. Second, other associations need the shelter of a polis, but it requires no other association above it; it is self-sufficient and sustains a complete life for its members. Third, the correct way of governing such an association is peculiar to it; it alone should be governed "politically." Aristotle criticizes writers who conflate the authority of "statesmen"—constitutional rulers—with that of conquerors, husbands, fathers, or owners of slaves. Plato is the target. Authority in a polis is specific to it, not to be confused with authority in other relationships. A state is not a large family, and a family is not a small state. States may have begun as monarchies because they grew out of patriarchally governed clans; but if they grew out of clans, their goals are not a clan's goals. An association is to be understood in terms of its purpose rather than its origin; the purpose of the state is not that of a family or clan. The polis, he says, "grows for the sake of mere life, but it *exists* for the sake of a good life."

Aristotle has in mind the Greek city-state. Much of what he writes seems to be applicable to any state, and surprisingly often is; what he himself was concerned with was the successful functioning of the kind of state that the Athenians had created in the late sixth century, and its Greek peers. When he goes on to say that man is meant by nature to live in a polis, he means that the polis provides the environment in which human beings can best fulfill their potential and in which they can live the good life to the full. This appears on its face to contradict what he says elsewhere (and even in *Politics* itself) when claiming that the best of human lives is the philosopher's life of contemplation.[6] Aristotle has two plausible ways of resolving this tension, and his students would very likely have invoked both.

The first is to notice that few people will wish to follow the route that the philosopher follows. It may be true that *if* one has the tastes and aptitudes that philosophy demands, the life of the philosopher is uniquely fulfilling, and that nobody who has followed the life of the philosopher would wish to follow any other. Not many people have those tastes and aptitudes, and most people will find that the polis provides the environment in which they can lead the best life for them. Nor is this to say that they are "inferior" people. Their lives display virtues such as courage, justice, fidelity, honesty, and temperance; they live the best possible active rather than the best contemplative life. Nor is it a simple truth that the *vita contemplativa* is better than the *vita activa*, if it is a truth at all. The second move is to observe that the fulfillment of the philosopher is slightly odd. Aristotle claims that the man who does not need the polis is either a beast or a god; animals cannot form political societies, since they lack speech and reason, while gods are individually self-sufficient and do not need political association.[7] The philosopher aims to think God's thoughts, and if he succeeds, he also is so self-sufficient that the assessment of the success of his life escapes the usual categories. Whether this is a condition one would wish to be in, unless so irresistibly called to it as to have no choice in the matter, is a deep question not to be tackled here. It suggests yet again a tension between philosophy's search for absolutes and the political search for the modus vivendi, for ways of living together.

Aristotle devotes the first book of his *Politics* to following out the implications of this approach. Since a polis is an association of villages—he may have had in mind the demes of Athens—and a village is an association of households, he first analyzes the nature of households, with an eye to the relationship between economic and political life, always looking to differentiate the kind of authority exercised in these different spheres from political authority. Within the family, a male head governs women and children. Aristotle did not say that women were imperfect men, but he thought they were less well governed by their own reason than an educated man would be. It is therefore good for them to be governed by their husbands, and it would be bad for them to live public lives as male citizens do. A man exercises domestic authority as the head of a household, over wife, children, and slaves. As husband/father his authority is not based on force or exercised in his own narrow interests; his authority over slaves, however, is literally despotic: *despotis* means "master." The aim of his rule is to ensure that the family flourishes as a family. Aristotle bequeaths to posterity the thought that the extent and the nature of the authority that sustains human associations are determined by the functions for which the association exists, that is, by the nature of the association. Locke's analysis of the authority of government in his *Second Treatise*, published in 1690, relies on just this thought two millennia later; whether through Locke's influence or by some other route, the thought itself is enshrined in the American Constitution with its commitment to limited government, and the measuring of authority by the goals to be sought.[8]

Slavery

The insistence that authority follows function extends to the relationship that most troubles Aristotle's readers, slavery. Aristotle assumed that if a man (and it is only men he has in mind) was to have leisure to play a role in the political life of his society, slaves must do the manual labor that is beneath the dignity of citizens. The defenders of slavery in the antebellum American South sometimes relied on that argument, though they were more likely to draw on biblical than on philosophical inspiration, or simply to point to the miseries of "free labor" in the North, an argumentative resource not available to Aristotle. He very bleakly describes slaves as "animated tools," instruments to be set to work to achieve what their owners require of them. Greek slavery was mostly, but not always, less horrible than the plantation slavery of the southern United States and the Roman latifundia. It was easy for men, women, and children alike to end up enslaved after military defeat, with the result that many slaves were better educated than their owners, and the condition of household slaves was often tolerable. We may recall

Plato's complaint that in Athens one could not distinguish slaves from citizens, or the depiction of cheerfully idle household slaves in any of Aristophanes's comedies. The same could not be said of slaves working in the silver mines at Laurium, on which Athenian prosperity depended and where miners died of overwork and lead poisoning; but the Athenians had been on the receiving end of the same treatment when they were defeated at Syracuse and set to work in the Sicilian quarries, and they neither complained on their own behalf nor softened their treatment of others. Broad humanitarianism was no more current in the classical Greek world than in the Roman world.

The view that the slave is a living implement did not imply that the owner could do with a slave anything that he might do with a plow or a spade. It was rather that *if* the relationship between master and slave is founded in nature, the disparity between the intelligence of the master and that of the slave should be of such a degree that the slave has intelligence enough only to follow instructions, and needs the master's intelligence to direct him. It would be good if masters and slaves were physically unlike as well. Nature, says Aristotle, intends slaves to have strong but unattractive bodies meant for manual labor and their masters to have attractive and athletic but less strong bodies. Sadly, nature often fails.[9] Aristotle half admits that slavery is for the most part "conventional" and that many slaves, perhaps even most, may be wrongly enslaved. He avoids undermining slavery: slavery was necessary, if politics as Aristotle understood it was to be possible. If all went well, there could even be a form of friendship between master and slave, since the master would treat the slave in ways that conduced to the slave's wellbeing. Unsurprisingly, when Aristotle draws up the design for an ideal state, he suggests a compromise. Greeks should not enslave Greeks, only non-Greeks, since they have servile natures, whereas Hellenes do not.[10] These remarks, which remain quite undeveloped, indicate the distance between Aristotle's casual assumption of the ethnic superiority of the Greeks over all their neighbors and modern racism, and how little intellectual pressure he was under to provide an elaborate justification of an institution that was taken for granted until the Enlightenment.

The oddity of Aristotle's views, which explains why readers so often hope that he might really be meaning to undermine the institution, is that he contradicts himself in a way he rarely does elsewhere. The thought that a slave is an animated tool suggests the slave's owner need take only the interest in the slave's welfare that he would take in the well-being of a spade. A spade needs cleaning and sharpening to be fit for digging; but nobody thinks we could be friendly with a spade. The recognition that masters and slaves often existed on good terms undermines the thought that slaves are merely tools. This is not the only contradiction; Aristotle holds, as he must, that for those who are slaves by nature, slavery is good. Yet when he discusses the ideal state, Aristotle argues that slaves should be offered the prospect of manumission, although this would not be doing them a good turn if they were suited only to slavery. Defenders of antebellum slavery were more consistent in arguing that the freed slaves would be unable to survive. If freedom would be good for them, only captives taken prisoner in a just war are rightly enslaved; and their enslavement is a punishment brought to an end by manumission. Aristotle has the same difficulties with slavery as with the authority of husband over wife. If the relationship is not arbitrary and based on brute force, the superior party must be more rational than the inferior; but not only is the inferior likely to be as rational as the superior; it is implicit in the theory that the inferior must be intelligent enough to be governed as a rational human being. If slaves and women are intellectually indistinguishable from their owners and husbands, Aristotle's framework is threatened. His mode of justification creates more problems than he can admit to. It may suggest some residual unease that he says that if, *per impossibile*, plows could act of themselves, slaves would be unnecessary.[11] It does not, of course, follow that everyone who could employ machinery in place of slaves would choose to do so; it took the American Civil War to persuade the southern states to give up their slaves. It was not obviously and indisputably irrational of the southern slave owners to make some sacrifice of economic efficiency for the sake of preserving what they saw as an aristocratic way of life.

One explanation of Aristotle's persistence in the face of difficulty lies in a different aspect of the nature of politics. When he turns to defining politics for a second time in book 7, he says that there are climatic and cultural-cum-economic reasons why only some peoples can practice politics. In the cold and barren country of the Scythians, life is so hard that it leaves no time for public debate and for the give-and-take of politics. Peoples whose energies are consumed by staying alive can practice nothing properly called politics. They live off the land, they do not form settled communities, and their tribal organization cannot sustain political life. Conversely, people who live in too hot and enervating a climate cannot sustain the vigorous debate that politics requires; they will find themselves living under a despotism. The Persians, for instance, do not govern themselves politically. They are doubly non-self-governing. They do not govern themselves, since their lives are managed by the satraps of the Persian king; and the process whereby the satraps decide how to manage the people under their control are not public processes of debate and discussion, but secret and unaccountable. Aristotle does not quite say that we cannot talk of the "politics" of the Persian monarchy; but he makes a sharp contrast between the ways events are controlled and initiated in Persia and among the Greeks. Unsurprisingly, in view of Aristotle's habit of looking for the proper course of action in the mean between two extremes, he finds the Greeks uniquely suited by nature, climate, and economy to practice politics. In Greece there is, or can be, freedom without anarchy, and order without tyranny.[12]

Economic Activity

The economic activities that permit political life to flourish can also threaten it. Aristotle considers what sort of production and consumption best sustains citizenship. As one might expect, he seeks the mean between excessive austerity and riotous moneymaking and consumerism. The Spartans were obsessed with the dangers posed by the helots whom they enslaved and kept down by murder and brutality, and with the danger of their own citizens' becoming corrupted by soft living; they kept foreign trade to a minimum and made their young men eat at military messes, so that commensality would maintain public spirit and prevent them from hankering after a comfortable private life. It worked only partially. Spartans were notoriously rapacious once away from the repressive discipline of their own city. Spartan education and militarism were not successful in internalizing the desired morality. The Spartans turned their city into a boot camp; it produced soldiers willing to die for good, bad, or indifferent reasons, but not an intelligent devotion to duty. Spartans were easy to bribe; they also lacked the cultural refinements of less militaristic states.

Aristotle shared the aims of Plato and the Spartans: to create public-spirited citizens and avoid the subversion of public spirit by private economic activity, but he hoped to achieve them by nondrastic measures. Plato admired the Spartan contempt for physical comfort; Aristotle did not. More importantly, he was skeptical of Plato's obsession with abolishing private property. He agreed that *use in common* in the context of public feasts and festivals encouraged public spirit, but he denied that production in common could be efficient. He mocked Plato's belief that the community of wives, children, and property would encourage people to transfer the sentiments ordinarily attached to "my family" and "my property" to "our" common family and property. He saw a truth that the state of much public space reinforces today; we do not think that what belongs to all of us belongs to each of us; we think it belongs to nobody, and we neglect it. For a man to have an incentive to provide for his family, he must think of it as *his* family; to have an incentive to look after his farm and crops in the most productive way, he must see them as his. Aristotle argues for private production and common use.

Even more deeply embedded is the thought that some work is intrinsically degrading and bad for the character of those who do it; and some kinds of economic activity are wrong in themselves. The basic thought is familiar. Nature tells us what we need: what food and drink, what shelter and clothing. We need enough but not too much food, drink, shelter, and comfort, as any properly brought-up person understands. We may not be able to give a very detailed account of these needs, but we do not have to. We know what work is degrading even if we cannot say exactly why; and we know that a decent person would engage in some occupations and not in others even if we cannot say exactly why. Modern economists do not ask, as Aristotle and medieval writers did, about the *proper* end or goal or purpose of economic activity; we do not talk as they did about the just price of things, though we do have a strong, if not very clear, sense that some prices and some incomes are unconscionably high or low. Trade unions have always been committed to a fair day's pay for a fair day's work, which is not so different from Aristotle's economics. Aristotle thought that our natural needs set the bounds of acceptability. We work to provide food, drink, clothing, and shelter; the aim of production is consumption. Money is therefore problematic. Official coinage was a fairly recent invention in Greek society, the oldest surviving coins dating from around 600 BCE, and was regarded with suspicion by conservative moralists such as Plato and Aristotle. The way money is "worth" things to which it bears no physical or other relationship is "unnatural." When one considers that a pair of shoes is worth or costs $175, and that this is what a hundred loaves cost or are worth, it is tempting to think that something must underpin their shared value. Whatever underpins it, it is not the fact that people will give us pieces of silver for shoes or bread; the value of money itself is what needs explanation.

Two plausible views have dominated purported explanations from that day to this. One relies on the thought that what we use requires human effort to make, catch, dig up, or find; the other relies instead on the fact that what we purchase reflects what we *want*. The first measures value by the efforts of the producers; the second measures value by the desires of the purchasers. Neither works well in all circumstances, and certainly not on its own, though they work well in combination; if I am a terrible shoemaker, my shoes will cost me much effort, but have little value in the marketplace since nobody will want to wear them. If I stumble across a diamond, it will sell for a great deal, but it will not have cost me much effort. The two thoughts together suggest that the price of anything measures its scarcity relative to the demand for it. We all need bread for survival and diamonds only when our hunger is sated; but bread is easy to produce in quantity and diamonds are not.

Aristotle began the tradition of thinking that behind the prices of goods in the marketplace there lies a true or natural value that should determine those prices. His discussion of money and usury had an enormous influence on later economic thought; most importantly, he inspired the medieval condemnation of moneylending and usury, though not of course its anti-Semitic aspects. Those flowed from the fact that Christians were supposedly prohibited from lending money at interest, and Jews were shut out of most economic activity, with the result that the Jews became moneylenders and loathed in consequence. Aristotle does not denounce gouging or excessively high interest rates; using the biological metaphors that came so easily to him, he argued that things really useful to life were organic and that their creation and use are part of the natural cycle of production and consumption. Money is helpful when it promotes that cycle. It itself is barren, mere metal that cannot produce offspring as trees and plants do. Usury is therefore unnatural. The man who made his living by lending money at interest was setting barren metal to breed. As an unnatural way of making a living, it was to be deplored.[13]

Aristotle might be thought to be attacking the nouveaux riches. His complaints are rather more than social polemics, however. Most productive activities have a natural cycle; first we create and then we consume what we have made. Making money has no such beginning and ending. It has no natural terminus. Banking and moneymaking are solvents of social order, a point made by poets, playwrights, and social theorists ever since money was invented, and one that is made today whenever the excesses of operators in the financial marketplace threaten to impoverish everyone else.

Given Aristotle's views about economic activity, and his praise of self-sufficiency, it is unsurprising that he thought the polis is best governed by moderately well-off men who draw their livelihood from farms on which they themselves do not do so much work, or work of the wrong sort, that they unfit themselves for public life. Speaking of a regime in which farmers and the moderately wealthy form the citizen body, he suggests that they should have some but not too much leisure; if they cannot spend too much time in the agora "politicking," they will have to rely on standing regulations, that is, on the rule of law. Aristotle is the first writer to wish for the "government of laws not of men." When Aristotle speaks of "farmers" in that context, he means small landowners or tenants, who owned a slave or two with whose assistance they worked their farms;[14] at other times he means by "farmers" those who actually labor in the fields, and in the ideal state they would be slaves, some owned by private individuals and some by the state.[15] Having distinguished the domestic arts from politics as the master art concerned to create the conditions of a good life in common, he turns aside in book 2 to discuss ideal states. But he has laid the foundations for what most concerns him: citizenship, constitutional order, and the avoidance of stasis, and we can follow that discussion before turning back to the ideal state.

Citizenship and Constitution

With the ground cleared of ideal states and utopian experiments, Aristotle advances on the topics that have kept his work alive for two and a half thousand years: the nature of citizenship, the qualities of good constitutions, the causes of revolution, and prophylactics against upheaval. Their connection is that constitutions distribute power among citizens; the rules governing the gaining and use of political power are the central element of any constitution; and whether the inhabitants of a political community are content with the allocation of political rights and obligations is decisive in whether the community is stable or conflict ridden. Ways of allocating rights, obligations, and power that are least likely to provoke discontent are what we are seeking.

The subject raises questions about the connection between the qualities of the citizen as a member of a community and his qualities as an individual: loyalty, for instance, is a virtue in individuals and in the members of groups, but if the group is devoted to bad purposes, loyalty to the group is less obviously a virtue, because it will help the group achieve its (bad) goals. Criminologists suggest that there is in fact rather little honor among thieves, but our belief that there must be reflects the obvious thought that thieves who were honorable among themselves could prey on the rest of us more effectively. Whether a man can be a good citizen only by being a good man was hotly debated for the next two millennia. Among writers who drew their inspiration from ancient ideals, Machiavelli insisted that the man who is loyal to his country must often behave in ways a good man would flinch from, while Rousseau feared that Machiavelli was right and followed Plato in urging the merits of a small, simple, isolated, and uncommercial republic whose near-isolation from its neighbors would prevent the military and other entanglements that lead us into the temptation to sacrifice humanity and a wider justice to a patriotism that amounts to individual selflessness and collective selfishness. The modern nation-state has not rendered these anxieties obsolete; we are all too familiar with the fact that we know how to train young men to serve in our armed forces but do not know how to retrain them for civilian life.

Aristotle's ideas about the qualities needed by citizens reflect the assumptions of well-off Athenians about the members of different social classes as well as a hardheaded view of the way economic interests affect political behavior. Citizenship for Aristotle is not the modern world's notion, which is that of an entitlement to benefit from the protection of a particular government, and to exercise such political rights as that system confers. In most modern states, resident aliens can be expelled for misconduct; citizens cannot. Greek city-states habitually exiled their own leading citizens. Conversely, Swiss women were until recently unable to vote, but they were Swiss citizens in the modern sense of the word, since they carried Swiss passports and enjoyed the usual legal rights of inhabitants of modern states. In Aristotle's terms, they were free—not slaves—but not fully citizens. It is the right of political (but not economic) equals *to rule and be ruled in turn* that constitutes citizenship as he discusses it. Mere membership of a polity is not his central concern; nor was it to Greeks generally, living as they did in a world devoid of passports, and without the welfare arrangements that raise questions about our identities and entitlements. That is not to say that membership was unimportant; when the Athenians murdered the male inhabitants of Melos and enslaved their wives and children, membership was no light matter.

Aristotle keeps his eye on the question of who can safely be given the right to rule and be ruled in turn; and to that question his predilection for finding virtue in a mean is relevant. Since men are neither beasts nor gods, their social arrangements must suit an existence lying in a mean between the invulnerable self-sufficiency of gods and the mindless self-sufficiency of beasts. Political existence rests on a form of equality (or inequality) among men. Thinking of the constitutional arrangements that determine citizenship, he is impelled toward a familiar position. *If there were such a difference between one man and all others as there is between God and men or between men and animals, that man should have absolute authority.*[16] There is no such difference. Conversely, if there were no difference between rich and poor, slave and free, men and women, adults and children, natives and foreigners, all could be citizens of whatever city they found themselves in. But there are important differences between them. The equality that citizenship implies is to be found in the mean position.

Aristotle did not argue that since everyone needs the protection of the laws, everyone should have the rights of (modern) citizenship. Slaves, foreigners, and women were entitled to much less than Athenian citizens, and Aristotle had no difficulties with that, even though he was himself only a resident alien in Athens. Indeed, the calmness with which he describes people in his own position is astonishing: "we call them citizens only in a qualified sense, as we might apply the term to children who are too young to be on the register, or to old men who have been relieved from state duties."[17] Nor did he suggest that human beings possess common attributes that should ground a human right to citizenship in whatever state one happened to be born in. The Stoics later argued something close to this, and it is a commonplace of liberal democratic theory, but Aristotle did not. He took it for granted that there are better and worse candidates for citizenship and that properly educated, economically independent, native-born, free men are the best. Nature meant women to be ruled by their husbands, so it would be against nature to admit women to citizenship. Men employed in repetitive manual labor where they did not exercise their own judgment were unfit to give their views on political matters. He did not argue, like later opponents of female suffrage, that women do not bear men's military burdens and therefore cannot claim the same political status; nor did he suggest that regardless of mental capacity and occupation, the fact that we are all at risk from the errors of government entitles us to a say in their activities. His test was whether a person was naturally "autonomous." Someone who was not self-governing domestically could not be part of the self-governing political community.

No Athenian believed that a Greek could be uninterested in politics. At the very least, self-defense demanded that a man keep a close eye on the holders of power; they understood what Trotsky observed twenty-five hundred years later. "You say you are not interested in politics; but politics is interested in you." The uninterest in politics and the ignorance about both politicians and political institutions displayed by British or American "citizens" of the present day would have been incomprehensible. It would also have been very surprising in such small, face-to-face communities. Within the polis politics was often class warfare; it was understood that the upper classes would try to restrict eligibility for citizenship to protect their wealth and status, and that the lower classes would try to extend their political power in self-defense. The prehistory of Athenian democracy was a long struggle to open the right to participate and hold office to those not already entitled by wealth and birth; once Athenian democracy was instituted, it remained a struggle in which the common people tried to extend their grip on the political process and the oligarchically minded tried to roll back the gains of their opponents. These struggles were sometimes conducted with a degree of savagery that no political system could readily contain; Thucydides's account of the massacres that took place all over Greece when the war between Athens and the Peloponnesian League sparked off civil wars elsewhere makes it clear that rich and poor were ready to bring in outsiders to settle local scores, and settle them violently.[18] The violence of the Thirty Tyrants during their short-lived regime was notorious, and they were violently overthrown in turn, but atrocities were commonplace all over Greece. Aristotle's obsession with political moderation is all the more compelling given the long history of immoderate behavior that constituted Greek political life. Unsurprisingly, he wants moderate persons to be citizens and institutional mechanisms to moderate conflict.

Who is to be a citizen is the obverse of the question of the best form of constitution. The nature of a constitution in Aristotle's understanding of it is very like the modern understanding: the set of rules adopted by a polis that allocates functions to institutions, and lays down who possesses the right to participate in political decision making, and how decisions affecting their polis are to be made. Aristotle felt, but resisted, the temptation to which Plato succumbed. If "the best" could rule, everyone would do well to obey them. If there was one best man, there should be a *panbasileus*, a single ruler with no check on his authority. Since by definition he would always do what was best, there could be no reason to hold him back. More plausibly, there might be a group of individuals who were "the best," and if so there should be an ideal aristocracy. Aristotle muddies the waters by assuming that "the best" would be intended by nature to form a *hereditary* ruling elite and that nature would try to ensure that the appropriate qualities would be passed down from one generation to the next. The difficulty, as the history of Athens and everywhere else attests, was that the genetic transmission of political wisdom and political flair cannot be relied on. The puzzle that obsessed Plato—why virtuous men have wicked sons—did not obsess Aristotle, but he noted the contrast between the heritability of desirable qualities that breeders could readily achieve in animals and the absence of any similar inheritance of good character in humans. To his credit, he also noticed that the "naturalness" of aristocratic rule was less obvious to nonaristocrats than to the upper classes themselves.

Aristotle came very close to the solution that would have resolved his anxieties. He had the right premises: the talent for political rule is not widely distributed, so politics is intrinsically "aristocratic"; the talent is not reliably inherited, so *hereditary* aristocracy is imperfect. Many people who do not possess political talent can recognize its presence in others; they can choose a nonhereditary aristocracy. This is modern representative government. The reason he did not suggest it is instructive. The premises were in place. Aristotle firmly believed that although the wearer of a pair of shoes may not know how to make a pair of shoes, he knows where the shoe pinches. He also went out of his way to point out that in many contexts many heads are wiser than one. He lived two millennia before the invention of modern representative government; but representative government essentially allows a democratic citizen base to choose its own rulers. It is, when it works as we hope, the device for producing an elective aristocracy that Aristotle needed in order to unite the common sense of the many with the talent of the few. James Madison and James Mill, writing within two decades of each other in the late eighteenth and early nineteenth centuries, thought that representation was the great discovery of the modern age. It allowed democratic, or more exactly popular, government on a large scale. Aristotle thought a state in which citizens did not know each other by sight was no state at all; a state was necessarily limited in size. If there were no more than a few thousand citizens, they did not need representative arrangements, and the only purpose of election would be, as at Athens, to choose the occupants of official positions. His discussion of the correct size of the citizen body implies that Athens is far too large. The idea of representative democracy did not come easily to modern thinkers; representative institutions existed centuries before they were seen as a way of creating a form of democracy, namely, "representative democracy." Rousseau proposed elective aristocracy as the best of all forms of government, but denounced the idea of representation on which the modern version of elective aristocracy rests. A few years later, Madison saw the modern argument clearly, as did Jefferson when he distinguished "pure" and "representative" forms of democracy.

Aristotle's Classification of Constitutions

Aristocracy is in principle the best form of government: there the best men rule because they possess judgment, courage, justice, and moderation in the highest degree. They display excellence as citizens, and a constitution that places power in their hands achieves excellence as a constitution. A true aristocracy is the constitutional regime in which the few best rule in the interest of the whole. Yet experience shows that aristocracies have a regrettable habit of becoming oligarchies in which class pride, not public spirit, rules the day, and in which moderation gives way to the oppression of other social classes. To see how Aristotle resolved the difficulties as he understood them, we must turn to what he is best remembered for, the sexpartite distinction between forms of government according to the numbers who participate in them, on the one hand, and their goodness or corruption, on the other.

The three virtuous forms of government are kingship, aristocracy, and *politeia*, in which one, a few, or many persons possess ultimate power, and employ it to govern for the sake of the common good; the corrupt forms are tyranny, oligarchy, and democracy, in which one man, a few men, or the poor many govern in their own narrow interests.[19] When "democracy" became the preferred label for modern representative government, the fashion sprang up to call the bad form of popular government "ochlocracy," or mob rule; Aristotle had no such qualms. The *demos* are the "poor many," and like all Greek thinkers he assumed that the poor many would use political power in their own interest. The problem in designing a constitution is to distribute power so as to give every incentive to those who have it to use it for the common good, not in their narrow class interest. Democrats believed that poverty and the practice of mean occupations should not disqualify a man from active citizenship; Aristotle thought them doubly wrong. Poor men and practitioners of the banausic trades cannot raise their heads to contemplate the good of the whole society; as a class, the poor resent the better-off and will try to seize their wealth by whatever means they can. The "narrow democracy" or "expanded aristocracy" of the well-balanced *politeia* is the remedy. A narrow democracy would be a more restrictive version of the democracy that Cleisthenes had instituted, where the lowest social class was not yet permitted to hold most offices; conversely, an expanded aristocracy would be a system in which the requirements of birth and wealth were not as onerous as oligarchical parties wanted to institute. The thought is not complicated: too restrictive a constitution arouses resentment; too broad a constitution also does so. Somewhere in the middle ground lies the answer.

It is now clear how Aristotle connects the excellence of citizens with the excellence of the constitutional form. Although some men are undeniably superior to others, nobody is so unequivocally superior to every other man that his fellows will obey him unquestioningly. A virtuous man is more likely to be corrupted by absolute power than to become wiser and more virtuous; and untrammeled monarchical rule will turn tyrannical. Unbridled democratic government will so frighten the better-off that it will cause civil war. If it does not, it may become a collective tyranny. What is needed is what later came to be called checks and balances, and a selection process for political office that secures the service of people whose characters are adequate to the task. Nonetheless, Aristotle's perspective is not ours. Modern political discussion is imbued with a concern for individual human rights; we look to institutions to hold accountable those who wield power over their fellows, so that the rights of individuals are respected. Aristotle does not. Because he sees the world in teleological terms, he asks—as Plato did—how we can ensure that the state functions as it should. The excellence of the citizenry and the excellence of the constitution are understood in that light. Hence, of course, Aristotle's focus on the collective intelligence and collective good sense of collectives; if "the many" are not to be trusted, it remains true that many heads are better than one.

One way in which Aristotle surprises modern readers whose conception of democracy is tied to the existence of representative institutions and occasional visits to the polling booth by around half the electorate is his acceptance of the radical democratic view that *the* democratic mode of choice is the lottery.[20] Something else that surprises modern readers who reflect a little is how right he is. *If* what we wish to achieve is equal influence for all, and an equal share in the governing authority, choosing the occupants of political positions by a random procedure—a lottery—is uniquely effective. The fact that most people flinch from that conclusion suggests that—like Aristotle—they do not wish for equality of political influence above all else. They wish to secure both the benefits of aristocracy and the benefits of democracy without the defects of either. If we achieve this, we shall have created a *politeia*, the state that Aristotle claims is "on the whole best" and most likely to survive the problems that beset a political community.

The Avoidance of Stasis

Aristotle seems to set his sights very high in arguing that the polis exists
to provide the best life in common for man. But his eyes were also firmly
fixed on the need to avoid revolution. The fact that *politeia* is the best
practicable state is not a small matter; practicality is a central virtue in
a state. Aristotle's theory of revolution, or perhaps one should say his
theory of the avoidance of revolution, is interesting for innumerable reasons, of which one is that it is intrinsically highly persuasive and makes
excellent sense two and a half millennia later. Aristotle's conception of
revolution has two parts. It refers, on the one hand, to what he termed
stasis, the situation in which political life simply could not go on any
longer, and, on the other, to the bloody civil war to which this kind of
breakdown could easily lead.

Stasis in the first sense is the antithesis of what every British civil
servant is trained to regard as his purpose in life: "keeping the show on
the road." Stasis occurs when the show is decisively off the road. But the
struggle for power does not stop when matters come to a grinding halt.
When an existing ruling elite, or single ruler, loses the confidence of the
populace and loses the capacity to hold their attention and to coerce dissenters into obedience, it is invariably replaced by another ruler or rulers,
immediately or after a period of civil war. So the other face of Aristotle's
interest is in what later theorists summarized as "an unconstitutional
change of constitution," not just matters coming to a grinding halt but
some new ruling group seizing power. This conception of revolution
embraces both what Marx and other thinkers have taught us to think
of as "real" revolutions, involving insurrection, bloodshed, and the mass
mobilization of the populace, and what Marx's disciples dismiss as mere
coups d'état, in which no mobilization occurs and one elite is displaced
by another, probably violently, but without popular involvement.

Aristotle was concerned with two situations above all, and about
them he was extremely acute. The first was the tension between democratic and oligarchical factions. His interest was unsurprising, since it

was this tension that marked Greek city-state politics and led to the most violent and prolonged bloodshed. He had an interesting, if schematic, view of what was at stake. His first insight was that revolution was provoked not only by a conflict of economic and social interests but also by a sense of injustice. Aristotle added the thought that two distinct conceptions of justice were at issue. The democratic conception of justice fueled the argument that men with equal political rights should be equal in their economic advantages. This suggests that revolution in democracies is essentially economic, driven by the needs of the poor or by a desire to be better-off. Unlike Marx, Aristotle did not think that the many are driven to revolt by sheer need. He thought it a brute fact about democracy that men who say to themselves that since they are equal in political status, they should be equal in everything, will turn to the elimination of economic inequality as their revolutionary project. Aristotle had no sympathy with an aspiration for economic equality. His politics is founded on the belief that nature provides for differences in intellectual and other virtues, and therefore in desert, and he did not doubt that the better-off were generally entitled to their wealth and social position. The point was to meet everyone's aspirations sufficiently to preserve political stability.

If the democratic conception of justice might lead to an economic revolution among people who have the same political rights as their economic superiors, an oligarchical revolution proceeds in exactly the opposite way. The oligarchical notion of justice was that men who were unequal in wealth ought to be unequal in everything, that they should remove the political rights of the many and monopolize power as well as wealth. The history of Athens would have seemed to Aristotle sufficient evidence for this thought; but he could have drawn on innumerable other examples. The Peloponnesian War had been marked by savage struggles between oligarchs and democrats all over Greece and throughout the Aegean, and city-states were torn apart as oligarchs in one city aided their counterparts in another and democrats came to the aid of democrats.

Aristotle's delicacy of touch comes out in his recipes for holding off the evils of stasis. Even relatively bad states can profit from the intelligent application of the rules of self-preservation. Aristotle was happy even to advise tyrannical regimes on preserving their power. His advice has been echoed through the ages, and makes a great deal of sense. It is simple enough, though hard to follow. Since what disables a tyrant is either the simple illegitimacy of his rule or the wickedness of his behavior, and the first of these is by definition irremediable, he must adopt a double strategy; on the one hand, he must keep his opponents divided, so that they do not unite against him, and on the other, try to behave as a decent monarch who had come to power by constitutional means would do: moderately and virtuously. Pre-echoing Machiavelli and other advisers to princes ever since, Aristotle advises against undue greed and self-indulgence; the rationally self-interested tyrant, to employ the idiom of a much later day, will sacrifice the pleasures of the flesh and the satisfaction of personal grudges, to protect his hold on power. In particular, he should be careful to eschew sexual advances to the wives and children of upper-class men. It is one thing to deprive others of their rightful share in the government of their society, quite another to affront their family pride and their honor by assaulting the chastity of their wives and daughters. The same advice evidently applies to seizing their property. The tyrant whom Polus imagines in *Gorgias* would be short-lived.

The advice suggests Aristotle's concern to analyze how a state could function smoothly rather than to moralize from the sidelines about the wickedness of tyrants. The modern tendency to restrict the term "tyrant" to murderous dictators in the mold of Idi Amin makes Aristotle's willingness to give advice to tyrants on how to preserve their position seem more shocking than it is. Aristotle's patron and father-in-law, Hermias, was a good man but technically a tyrant. Not everyone was as unlucky as Plato in Sicily. Moreover, in Aristotle's day there was no such disparity between rulers and ruled in their access to murderous military power as there is today. Tyrants were uneasier then than now and had to watch their step in a way their modern successors do not have to, as long as they can preserve the allegiance of their armed forces.

Given his advice to tyrants, it is easy to guess that Aristotle advises other regimes to look to their strengths and avoid their weaknesses. Democracies are in danger of provoking revolution if they add to the distress caused to the traditional ruling elite when it was forced to yield power to the poor; so attempts to create an equality of wealth as well as an equality of power should be eschewed. The temptation to load all the burdens of public life onto the backs of the well-off should be resisted. Moreover, the better-off ought to be allowed a proper place in the political system; the more democracy counterbalances itself with the characteristics of aristocracy, the safer and longer lasting the regime will be. The converse holds good for oligarchies; they must strengthen those features that will make them less repugnant to democrats, and should endeavor to avoid the risk of a revolution in which the poor many revolt against being reduced to near-slavery.

In offering this advice, Aristotle began a tradition of empirically minded constitutional theorizing often described as the theory of the mixed constitution; his place in that tradition, however, is not easy to characterize. Commonly, theories of the mixed constitution set out to provide a recipe for achieving the advantages of monarchy, aristocracy, and democracy within one "mixed" constitution. Two centuries later, Polybius praised the Romans for adopting the recipe. More recently, much self-congratulatory thinking about British politics has pointed to the mixture of crown, Lords, and Commons as such a mixed system, matched by American self-congratulation on the subject of the virtues of a separation of powers and the ability of executive, legislative, and judiciary to check and balance one another. Aristotle was interested in something different. His recipe for a stable governmental system relied on matching political power and economic interest, and it anticipated the findings of twentieth-century political science. A political system that gives political power to the majority of the citizens so long as they also possess the majority of society's wealth is uniquely likely to be stable. This requires what sociologists called a "lozenge-shaped" distribution of wealth; if there are few very poor people, few very rich people, and a substantial majority of "comfortably off" people in a society, the middling sort with much to lose will outvote the poor and not ally with them to expropriate the rich; conversely, they will be sufficiently numerous to deter the rich from trying to encroach upon the rights and wealth of their inferiors. American political sociologists explained the resilience of American democracy by noting the United States' achievement of this happy condition after World War II. This is not an account of a mixed constitution in the sense of a regime that combines elements of monarchy, aristocracy, and democracy, but an argument about the economic basis of political stability. Nonetheless, both it and the genuinely mixed regime reflect Aristotle's search for a mean between extremes, as he acknowledges. He admits that commentators praise the mixed regime; it certainly benefits from being a mixture, just as bronze is stronger than the metals of which it is an alloy, but Aristotle's interest is really in what to do if we cannot simply rely on "the best men."

One-man rule degenerates too easily into tyranny, and democracy into mob rule; dictators are proud and prone to run amok, and the poor are ignorant and prone to be misled by demagogues. One difficulty Aristotle faced in giving unequivocal assent to the virtues of the mixed regime in the strict sense was that the system was made famous by Sparta; and Sparta failed in the task of encouraging the widest range of excellences among its citizens because it was devoted to one excellence only, military prowess. Aristotle relies instead on the good sense and steadiness of the middling sort, and his *politeia* allows the middling sort to exercise a preponderance of power that should ensure that things never get out of hand. This is why the distribution of wealth and income must support the distribution of political power. In 1961 Seymour Martin Lipset published a justly famous account of the conditions for stable liberal democratic government, freely acknowledging his debts to Aristotle and entitling the volume in which his argument appeared *Political Man*.[21] Dante's description of Aristotle as "the master of the wise" holds up very well six centuries after Dante.

A modern treatment of the subject would emphasize that if the middle class outnumbers the poor, as it is said to do in most prosperous modern economies, there is little advantage to be had in reducing the poor to beggary; even if the poor have some resources to exploit, the payoff for each member of the middle classes is too small to provide an incentive for misbehavior. Aristotle does not argue in those terms; he focuses rather on the effects of occupying a middle-class position on the character of middle-class people. The moderate social and economic condition of their lives would create a corresponding moderation in their desires; they would not wish to tear down their betters or to oppress their inferiors. Once again, we have to remember the principle that in all subjects we should aim only at as much precision as the subject affords. Aristotle's views do not apply to all times and all places, or to all sorts of economy. The middle class in modern liberal democracies is not exactly the middle ranks of Greeks society, nor should we extrapolate from a small, poor agricultural economy to a modern industrial economy with an elaborate and extensive public sector. The panic-stricken middle class that has been accused of bringing Hitler to power, described by Marxists as the *wildgewordene Kleinbürger*, is not what Aristotle had in mind. While we may admire the ingenuity of Aristotle's analysis, we cannot simply "apply" it to ourselves. Nonetheless, it remains astonishingly suggestive.

Ideal States

Aristotle's genius was for showing the ways in which we might construct the "best practicable state." This was not *mere* practicality; the goals of political life are not wholly mundane. The polity comes into existence for the sake of mere life, but it continues to exist for the sake of the good life. The good life is richly characterized, involving as it does the pursuit of justice, the expansion of the human capacities used in political debate, and the development of all the public and private virtues that a successful state can shelter—military courage, marital fidelity, devotion to the physical and psychological welfare of our children, and so on indefinitely. For this project to be successful, the state must practice what Aristotle regarded as politics in its essence. This essence is the bringing together of a diversity of people with a diversity of interests—to the degree that a community of Greeks from the fourth century BCE is not anachronistically described in such terms.

One of Aristotle's most famous distinctions was the one he drew between the mere gregariousness of bees and cattle and the *political* character of human beings. Recent evolutionary theory suggests that he may have underestimated the complexity of the social lives of bees and ants, but the distinction he had in mind holds up well enough. Gregarious animals come together without speech; their need for one another brooks no discussion. People unite in a political society only by agreement on the *justice* of the terms on which they do so. This agreement invites a lot of discussion. This is a thought that Hobbes later twisted to his own ends, claiming, quite falsely, that Aristotle had described ants and bees as naturally political, and going on to argue that humans were not naturally political precisely because they had to establish political communities by agreement on principles of justice.[22] The power of Aristotle's argument is perhaps attested by Hobbes's need to misrepresent it while stealing it for his own purposes.

The fact that politics achieves unity out of a plurality of interests and beliefs without suppressing them is the moral that Aristotle draws from his glancing discussion of Plato's *Laws* and *Republic* in book 2. The book discusses the theory and practice of ideal communities, but Plato's picture of utopia receives the most attention. If it is really true that Aristotle had worked with Plato on the writing of *Laws* when he was a student in the Academy, it would explain the similarities between the ideal state that Aristotle sets out in books 7 and 8 and the polity of *Laws*. In book 2, however, Aristotle criticizes *Republic* and *Laws* very severely. Plato, says Aristotle, was obsessed with disunity. This was not unreasonable. Athens was always on the verge of civil war; social class was set against social class; and the city's self-esteem was fueled by constant wars with its neighbors. The attractions of social cohesion, and of a society that did not keep peace at home by waging war abroad, were obvious. Still, Plato's attempt to secure peace by making the polis an archetype of a unitary order is a mistake.

It is a mistake because it turns a city into something other than a city. It is of the essence of the city that it is a compound of parts that have to be kept in a constantly changing but orderly relation to one another. Aristotle was the first critic to level against Plato the charge that has a particular resonance today as a criticism both of a certain sort of overly rationalistic politics and of the totalitarian state to which that kind of politics can lead. Plato does not provide for a better politics but for a society with no politics. He has purified politics to death. Nonetheless, Aristotle felt the attraction of this mode of thinking. At the heart of the attraction was the impulse to self-sufficiency. The centrality of self-sufficiency to Aristotle's analysis is evident. The polis is logically prior to the individual as being the more self-sufficient of the two; individuals must live in a polis because they are not individually self-sufficient. This is not merely a matter of physical survival; it is a moral matter as well. Without mutual discipline, men become worse than animals. The being with no need of a city is either a God or a beast. The temptation is to think that the more complete the unity of the city, the greater the degree of self-sufficiency, and the greater its immunity to the ravages of time and conflict.

Both the larger claim that Plato abolishes politics by overemphasizing unity and Aristotle's particular criticisms of Plato's work are well taken. We have already seen his defense of the family, his acceptance of the need for private property, and his skepticism whether Plato's abolition of family life for the guardians would mean their loyalties were transferred to the city. No doubt, some sorts of moneymaking are unnatural, and property for use is more natural than property for exchange and acquisition, but that does not impugn the desirability of private property as such. Aristotle approved of the Spartan tradition of making their young men dine in common messes, without thinking that it implied the end of private ownership or that Spartan austerity was good for us. Aristotle finally produced a devastating objection to Plato's belief that the society described in *Republic* would be happy. Plato had said that in spite of the deprivation of property, family, and private life, the guardians would be happy serving the polis; but he backed away from that claim and argued that the *city* would be happy—implicitly admitting that many of the citizens would not be. To which Aristotle replied that happiness was not the sort of thing that could exist in the whole without existing in the parts. If the citizens were not happy, the polis was unhappy.

Yet Aristotle ends his *Politics* by setting up his own version of an ideal state. Exactly what is happening in books 7 and 8 is obscure, in the sense that, even more than elsewhere in *Politics*, Aristotle recurs to themes tackled elsewhere, in ways that threaten the consistency of the work. The dismissive treatment of the construction of utopias in book 2 casts doubt on whether the project of books 7 and 8 makes much sense. That book's insistence that politics is the art of constructing a setting for the good life against the background of difficulties that can be controlled but never eliminated suggests that constructing ideal states is a dubious undertaking, suffering the problems suggested by the famous joke against the economist on a desert island who responds to the absence of a can opener with which to open the canned food washed up with himself and his companions with the sentence "Let x be a can opener."

Nonetheless, the last two books of *Politics* have an interest as revealing what Aristotle thought perfection would look like. Like Plato, Aristotle turns a central problem of politics on its head; abandoning the question "Given the frailties and imperfections of human character, how does a statesman preserve order and pursue the common good?" to answer the question "How does a statesman ensure that the citizens are of good and amenable character?" Aristotle produces the town planner's ideal state. The ideal polis will have no more than ten thousand citizens, so that all citizens can know one another, and in this context Aristotle makes his famous observation that a state can be neither too little nor too large, and rashly appeals to the obviousness of the fact that a ship cannot be five feet long or five hundred. Readers may wonder what we should call supertankers or the Chinese state. The citizens will be supported by an agricultural economy in which slaves will supply the workers needed for the farms, and the citizens will be fed at common tables. The detail into which Aristotle goes when discussing where the common tables should be established and especially where the common tables sponsored by the officials of the city should be located is surprising in itself and an indicator of the grip that Sparta exercised on his imagination as well as Plato's. It may also reflect his friendship with Lycurgus, who was responsible for the organization of festivals and the like.

More importantly, it reminds us that Aristotle's emphasis on the plurality of legitimate interests that politics exists to reconcile is not the ancestor of the social, moral, and religious pluralism of modern political liberalism. For although Aristotle acknowledges that different elements in a community will have strong views about the justice of their share of the benefits and burdens of social and political life, he does not acknowledge that they might legitimately have different and irreconcilable views about the nature of justice or the nature of the good life. The perspective is authoritarian. One aspect of this is Aristotle's uninterest in any such concept as that of privacy. For Aristotle, it is perfectly proper for the state to regulate the sexual and family lives of its citizens; he sets down strict rules governing the ages at which men and women should have children, and provides for compulsory abortion where women become pregnant in a way that might imperil population policy or produce unhealthy children. In the process, he begins a long history of controversy by suggesting that when miscarriages are induced, it should be before the fetus has life and sense, which he puts at the time of quickening.

In short, Aristotle's conceptions of a free society, political freedom, and the free man are not wholly foreign to us, but they are not ours. One can see this vividly in his fragmentary remarks about education at the very end of *Politics*. Aristotle is perhaps the first author of a theory of liberal education, which is to say, an account of the value of an education devoted to knowing things that are worth knowing for their own sake, and calculated to make the young man who learns them a gentleman. The definition of a liberal education as a *gentleman*'s education persisted into modern times; when Cardinal Newman wrote *The Idea of a University* in the middle of the nineteenth century, he declared that the object of a university was to turn out "gentlemen." Conversely, Locke's more utilitarian and vocational account of education had made an impact a century and a half earlier precisely because it subverted the older Aristotelian picture. But "liberal" in this context has nothing to do with political liberalism. It means "nonvocational" or "suited to a free spirit," and its social connotations are unabashedly aristocratic.

A piece of advice that strikes oddly on the modern ear is that well-bred young people ought to learn to play a musical instrument but not with such skill that they might be mistaken for professional musicians. This was not simple snobbery, or a matter of urging that a violinist of good family ensure he was not mistaken for Menuhin or Heifetz. Professional musicians were in demand in places of ill repute, hired in for parties at which prostitutes provided the entertainment. Today we would not expect a stag party to hire both strippers and a string quartet. Nonetheless, Aristotle's enthusiasm for the preservation of social distinction and his emphasis on the social position of the "high-souled" man remind us that even in his favored *politeia*, with as many respectable and steady men of the middle class admitted to political participation as is possible, Aristotle hankered after the rule of true, that is, *natural* aristocrats. If that attitude is not unknown two and a half millennia later, his unconcern with those left out of this vision of the world—women, ordinary working people, foreigners, slaves—is happily rather less common. But we shall not see much sympathy for ordinary lives and ordinary happiness for many centuries yet, certainly not in the work of Cicero.

CHAPTER 4

Roman Insights: Polybius and Cicero

Polybius and Cicero

NEITHER OF THE SUBJECTS of this chapter was primarily a philosopher; Cicero was a statesman, although he was a more accomplished philosopher and a less accomplished statesman than he supposed. Polybius was a soldier, a diplomat, and the third of the great Greek historians after Herodotus and Thucydides. His intellectual successors as writers of political and military history are the Roman historians Tacitus and Livy. Polybius's work entitled *The Rise of the Roman Empire* has survived only in part; but his explanation of the extraordinary political and military success of the Romans provided Cicero and writers thereafter with their understanding of the Roman or "mixed" republican constitution, and the dangers to which such a mixed republic might succumb. Since the constitutions of modern republics owe more to Roman republican inspiration than to Athenian democracy, we are ourselves his heirs. Polybius was a highly educated Greek aristocrat from Achaea, in the northwestern Peloponnese, and as a young man was active in the military and political life of his homeland. He was born at the beginning of the second century, sometime after 200 BCE and before 190. Roman military power had by then reduced the kingdom of Macedon to client status, in spite of attempts by kings of Macedon to recover their independence. At the end of the last of these Macedonian Wars in 168, he was one of many upper-class Achaeans taken off to Italy for interrogation and to be kept as a hostage.

He was in exile for eighteen years, during which time he had the good fortune to become close friends with Scipio Africanus the Younger, whom he served as tutor and whose lifelong friend he remained. Scipio was the son of the Roman general who had won the decisive Battle of Pydna against the Macedonians, where the younger Scipio had also fought. Grandson by adoption of Scipio Africanus the conqueror of Hannibal, he was responsible for the final destruction of Carthage in 146. That is the terminus ad quem of Polybius's *Rise of the Roman Empire*. Scipio the Younger plays the central—fictional—role in Cicero's *De republica*, articulating the values of Roman republicanism in its final years of glory before the republic's institutions decayed and civil war overtook them. Polybius spent his exile in Rome, where he served his friend as secretary and learned all there was to know about the workings of the Roman republic. In 150 he was allowed home, although he remained close to Scipio, accompanied him during the Third Punic War, and witnessed the destruction of Carthage. Polybius later served his homeland well by acting as a mediator with the Romans after another ill-judged rebellion ended as badly as rebellions against Rome usually did: he did such an excellent job that after his death a remarkable number of statues was erected in his honor all over Greece. The fate of Carthage, sacked, put to the flames, and razed to the ground, suggests the value of his services. His last years are obscure, but he is said to have died after a fall from his horse at the age of eighty-two in 118. The tale attests to a temperament more friendly to soldiers and statesmen than to speculative philosophers.

Cicero was ninety years younger than Polybius. He was born in 106 in Arpinum, a city not far from Rome. His family were prosperous provincial aristocrats, but not members of the senatorial elite; they belonged to the class of the *equites*, the "knightly" rank that reflected a man's ability to provide himself with a horse as well as the other equipment of a soldier—as it later did in medieval Europe. By this time the label picked out people who were simply well-to-do. Membership of the Senate was confined to men who had occupied one of the magistracies—high judicial and administrative positions; membership entailed restrictions on the senators' economic activities, so persons who were well-off but not very wealthy might think twice about embarking on the *cursus honorum*, the prescribed path to high office. However, Cicero's father was ambitious for his son, and sent him to Rome to learn how to advance himself in a world where he was a *homo novus*—a "new man" and the first in his family to aspire to public office. At sixteen, he served as a soldier in the Social War of 90, the war between Rome and its Italian allies, or *socios*, but he always meant to make his name in the courts and politics. He learned rhetoric from the best orators in Rome, Athens, and Rhodes and met some notable philosophers, including the leading Stoic, Diodotus, whose old age he later made comfortable by taking him into his home. His passion for philosophy and his philosophical talent are indisputable, but he emphasized the way his training in philosophy made him a great forensic orator. Studying rhetoric in Athens in 79–77, he encountered the rival philosophical schools of the Peripatetics and Academics, and acquired the ability to refute any argument of either side. He drew the moral that in the absence of certainty we should defend whatever doctrine seemed most persuasive on any given occasion. It is easy to see why critics doubted his honesty.

Cicero was vain and self-regarding; he was immensely ambitious, saw himself as potentially the savior of the Roman Republic, wrote like an angel, and in private life was a generous friend and a devoted father, even if always on the lookout for ways of advancing himself politically. Initially, his political rise was meteoric; he secured the offices of quaestor in 75, praetor in 66, and consul in 63, on each occasion at the earliest permissible age; but the republic itself was already in its protracted death throes. By the time he became quaestor, Rome had experienced two bouts of civil war and the bloodletting that accompanied the dictatorship of the hugely successful general Cornelius Lucius Sulla in 82. Sulla had revived the office of dictatorship, which had lapsed after the defeat of Hannibal more than a century before; and he revived it in a form that presaged the principate of Caesar Augustus. Previously, the dictatorship was instituted for six months only. In 82 Sulla had himself

made dictator without time limit. Surprisingly, he stepped down voluntarily after instituting some short-lived constitutional reforms. They had
less effect than the example of his success in turning his troops against
the city they were pledged to serve.

Cicero was quaestor in Sicily, where he earned a reputation as a prudent administrator of the province's finances, and later became famous
when he prosecuted Verres, the governor of the island, for extortion. It
was typical of Cicero's career that he scored a triumph—Verres was so
unnerved by Cicero's prosecution that he went into exile before the case
was decided—and that his opponents claimed Cicero had been bribed
to ask for a smaller penalty than Verres deserved. In fact, it was unprecedented for such a prosecution to succeed at all; such cases were heard by
a jury composed of members of the senatorial class who were expected
to acquit one of their own.

Many equestrian families took several generations before one of
their members moved on from the office of quaestor; but Cicero became
praetor, in charge of a financial court, at the age of forty and consul at
the age of forty-three. As consul, he was faced with the attempted insurrection of Catiline and his coconspirators. Catiline was a man of great
personal bravery but politically, financially, and sexually rapacious, even
if most stories about him were urban myths. He had previously been
tried for the rape of a vestal virgin; this was the most shocking of crimes,
since the vestal virgins were the keepers of the sacred flame in the temple
of Vesta, the goddess of the hearth, and committed to lifelong chastity.
He had been acquitted; by paying a bribe, said his enemies. Catiline not
only planned to seize power and make himself dictator, but boasted
that he had planned the murder of senators and officials who opposed
him. When Cicero secured his condemnation by the Senate, Catiline
fled Rome and assembled an army. In his absence, Cicero persuaded the
Senate to agree to the summary execution of those conspirators they
could lay hands on. This was flagrantly and doubly illegal; the Senate
had no authority to try capital cases, and it was conviction and execution
without due process. Yet with civil war brewing, action was needed, and,
as Cicero said, *inter armas silent leges*—the laws are silent amid the clash of
weapons. Hailed by his supporters as the savior of the republic, he spent

the rest of his life reminding his readers and hearers of his triumph: *non sine causa, sed sine fine*, "not without cause, but without end," said Seneca.[1] Catiline himself fled, not out of cowardice, but to raise an army against the republic. He may have been a thoroughly bad character, but he was also a very brave man. When his militia confronted the army raised by Cicero, he died heroically on the battlefield, far in front of his own soldiers and surrounded by the bodies of the enemy.

He was mourned by the *populares*, the leaders of the poorer Romans whose support Catiline had secured by proposing the forgiveness of their debts. Cicero belonged to the party of the *optimates*, the defenders of the upper classes who were opposed to any measures of debt forgiveness or anything that smacked of the equalization of property. Cicero was not savagely reactionary, but a conservative who thought Rome's troubles had begun when the Gracchi—Tiberius and Gaius Gracchus—brought in agrarian reforms to benefit the poor. Cicero praised their assassins, but in none of his works does he show much understanding of the social and economic causes of the republic's collapse. He was a moralist for whom the personal qualities of statesmen and citizens were everything, not a sociologist concerned with the economic and cultural conditions of political stability.

The Senate was not united behind Cicero, and once he was no longer consul, his opponents gathered. When Caesar, Pompey, and Crassus established the triumvirate in 60, he refused to be the fourth member of their group; they looked for the support of the *populares*, and Cicero allied himself with Cato the Younger, the leader of the *optimates*. He was exiled by the tribune Clodius in 58 and his property confiscated but was almost immediately brought back by Pompey and his property restored. The triumvirate had little use for him. Leadership at Rome depended on the ability to mobilize armies against the city and assemble mobs within it to intimidate the Senate and leading politicians. Cicero's skills as an advocate were not very relevant, nor was his political judgment astute. Like many others, he consistently backed the losing side: he was a protégé of Pompey, with whom he sided against Julius Caesar during the civil war of the late 50s. Pompey was defeated in 48, and Cicero was pardoned by Caesar in 46. As a notable writer himself, Caesar greatly admired Cicero's literary abilities. Cicero was not reconciled; he was not one of the conspirators who assassinated Caesar in 44—the conspirators knew he could not keep a secret and would have betrayed the plot out of sheer garrulousness—but he approved of the deed.

Caesar's assassins intended to rescue the republic from one-man rule. They succeeded in destroying the republic instead, sparking a series of civil wars that ended only when Caesar's adopted heir, Octavian, defeated Mark Antony at the Battle of Actium in 31 BCE. That was the end of the struggle between Caesar's most notable supporters, Mark Antony, who had been his lieutenant for two decades, and the boy—Octavian was only eighteen when Caesar was murdered—he had named as his heir. As to his assassins, they had underestimated Caesar's popularity with the Roman poor and were themselves nearly killed at once in the disturbances that accompanied his funeral. Cicero was killed not long afterward. Seeing Mark Antony as the greatest continuing threat to the restoration of the republic, he made a series of violent speeches against him in the Senate; the *Philippics* were modeled on Demosthenes's polemics against Philip of Macedon, and they cost Cicero his life. Mark Antony formed a short-lived alliance with Octavian—the future Caesar Augustus—in 43, and each gave the other a free hand in murdering his enemies. They concluded, reasonably enough, that Caesar's leniency toward his enemies after the civil war had allowed them to conspire against him and in the end to kill him. They were not going to repeat the mistake. They also wanted to seize the property of wealthy men to reward their supporters, and the bloodletting was considerable. It is said that three hundred senators and two thousand *equites* were killed. In Cicero's case, Antony indulged himself in some notable brutality; he had Cicero's head and hands cut off and nailed to the speaker's rostrum in the Senate to remind everyone of the perils of speaking out against tyranny. Cicero died bravely; attempting to flee, he was overtaken by his enemies. He put his head out of the curtains of the litter in which he was being carried, stretched out his neck, and told his murderers to do their job quickly. As his life and death suggest, Cicero was addicted to Roman politics; he wrote beautifully about the pleasures of a quiet life in the countryside, but hankered for the hurly-burly of the Senate and the courts.[2] His political theory is reflective but far from dispassionate.

Politics for Statesmen, Not Philosophers

To turn from Plato and Aristotle to Polybius and Cicero is to turn to a different way of thinking about politics. Put much too simply, it is the move from philosophy to statecraft; it is much too simple, because Cicero takes more than the titles of his works from Plato—*De republica* and *De legibus*. He says that *De officiis*—on duty—is modeled on the work of the Greek philosopher Panaetius, and indeed there is great deal of moral philosophy in it. Nonetheless, Cicero is less interested in what philosophers care about, the foundations of their view of the world, than in the use that a statesman, or a Roman politician, can make of the ideas of Greek sages. Plato and Aristotle disagreed about the nature of politics, but they were unequivocally philosophers. To call them "career philosophers" is anachronistic, but they spent their lives teaching philosophy and thinking about its problems. When Plato gave advice to Dionysius I and Dionysius II in Sicily—if he did—he taught them philosophy. He was not concerned to impart the techniques of keeping the show on the road. The distinction is not absolute, as Aristotle's readiness to give advice on keeping imperfect shows on the road demonstrates; by the same token, when Cicero claims that the most important aspect of statecraft is to secure the good character of our leading citizens and embarks on an account of the virtues, he blurs the distinction.

If political theory is a mixture of philosophical analysis, moral judgment, constitutional speculation, and practical advice, it is the extreme cases that sharpen the distinction between statecraft and philosophy. Hobbes's *Leviathan*, like Plato's *Republic*, is an unusually pure work of political philosophy, Polybius's *Rise of the Roman Empire* and Machiavelli's *Prince* unusually insistent on practicality, history, experience; Plato and Hobbes offer to show us how to escape from the rough-and-ready solutions to problems that politicians provide. Neither suggests that we can learn only from experience, and neither suggests that all we can learn is rules of thumb. Statecraft, by contrast, is focused on the political practitioner, politician, statesman, or ruler, and on the viability of the constitutional arrangements within which he is supposed to operate; experience is all-important, and the wise man accepts that its lessons will be valid "more or less." Philosophy looks at the statesman to assess the morality of his actions, and at a constitution to assess the legitimacy of different forms of rule. Statecraft has a strongly empirical bias, because it teaches the lessons of experience. Machiavelli's *Prince* and *Discourses* mock philosophers and emphasize the teachings of experience; Polybius has no time for utopias that nobody has tried to put into practice. "As for Plato's celebrated republic," he observes, "I do not think it admissible that this should be brought into the argument about constitutions. For just as we do not allow artists or athletes who are not duly registered or have not been in training to take part in festivals or games, so we should not admit the Platonic constitution to this contest for the prize of merit unless some example can be provided of it in action."[3]

In this light, Plato's dialogue *Statesman* is an ironic commentary on statecraft, not a contribution to it. The participants in Plato's dialogue discuss the definition of the statesman, and what he must know to be the master of his art. But that art is not that of preserving the republic against its corruption by ambitious men such as Alcibiades or Sulla or Caesar; and the Socratic statesman's argumentative skills are not devoted to persuading the Roman Senate to agree to the execution of Catiline's fellow conspirators on the basis that *salus populi suprema lex est*—the preservation of the republic legitimates an otherwise illegal act. The statesman of Plato's imagination is the godlike superior of the human herd or flock that he superintends, and Socratic statecraft is the tending of souls. Socrates did not expect to carry conviction in *Gorgias* when he described himself as the only true statesman in Athens. In the sense at issue here, his craft is not statecraft at all, and he is not a statesman.[4]

Aristotle advised tyrants and oligarchs on how to preserve their position in the face of hostile public opinion; but the *Politics* was not a treatise on statecraft, and his advice is generally very unlike Machiavelli's unabashed recommendation of violence and deceit. *Politics* was a treatise on the nature of the Greek polis, framed by a philosophical account of the nature of the good life. It explained why the skills and temperament of the statesman were useful, but it does not discuss them in detail or encourage the reader to acquire them. Aristotle's ideal was, as he said, the rule of laws, not men.[5] He theorized the political life, not the skills of statecraft. He made a persuasive case for the autonomy of the political realm, and for more everyday and down-to-earth values than those that Plato cared for; he provided a philosophical justification for the existence of statesmen and an account of why we should not seek to replace political leaders with philosopher-kings. Once he had explained the deficiencies of Plato's attempted purification of political life, he needed no elaborate account of the role of philosophy in practical life, since his account of ethics and politics in the *Nicomachean Ethics* supplied it, along with a caution that such inquiries were not for young men but for those whose blood had cooled a little.[6] Unlike Plato, he did not dismiss rhetoric as the art of making a bad case look good, but he made nothing of it in the *Politics*. The writer who made oratory central was Cicero.

Cicero wished to teach his Roman compatriots what Plato and the Stoics had to say about justice, courage, temperance, and wisdom, but insisted that he was imparting Greek wisdom and that he was himself only a student and instructor. The purpose of imparting the philosophical wisdom of the Greeks to his Roman contemporaries was political. The young men he wanted to teach were to be statesmen, not philosophers, and the value of philosophy was its usefulness to the republic—a training in the best thought of the Greeks would improve the young men's characters, and they would not behave with the greed, cruelty, vanity, and shortsightedness that were bringing the Roman Republic to its knees. *De officiis* is addressed to his son, Marcus, a very ordinary young man from whom Cicero hoped for great things. This little treatise on the virtues was commended to Christians by Saint Ambrose and much copied and commented on in medieval Europe; both Erasmus's and Luther's great ally Philipp Melanchthon encouraged the creation of pocket editions of the work; and either in the original Latin or in translation it remained an influential educational handbook for upper-class young men until the nineteenth century. It confessedly borrowed from Plato, Aristotle, and

the Stoics, but its target was upper-class Romans; when European ruling elites centuries later modeled themselves on their Roman predecessors, they professed—whether or not they practiced—the virtues Cicero
taught. It helped that Cicero's Latin is both beautiful and readable, a
model for anyone studying the classics. The political treatises that share
the name of Plato's political tracts—*Republic* and *Laws*—are only fragmentary, but in the same way they are Greek in inspiration and Roman
in purpose, and their character is what that suggests.

The Originality of Polybius

To make better sense of Cicero's aims and beliefs, we must first consider
what was probably the first articulate account of Roman political institutions and their success, provided by Polybius in one short book of *The
Rise of the Roman Empire*;[7] then we should place Cicero's political writings in
the context of his own tumultuous and catastrophic career. The Romans
were the military superiors of their immediate neighbors. Nonetheless,
they were one small Italian tribe among many others, and their rise to
supremacy in the known—Mediterranean—world was initially slow.
Until the third century they were preoccupied with their own internal
struggles between the upper (patrician) and lower (plebeian) classes and
had their work cut out to handle the military problems posed by their
rivals on the Italian peninsula and by Gauls invading from the north.
Only in the third century did they secure a firm grip on Italy from the
Alps in the north to the Strait of Messina opposite Sicily in the south.
Anyone with a taste for speculation may wonder what might have happened if Alexander had turned his attention to western Europe rather
than Persia.

The Romans' arrival within a stone's throw of Sicily brought them
into conflict with Carthage, the most powerful state in the western Mediterranean. So comprehensive was Rome's destruction of Carthage in 146
that no Carthaginian account of its history survived. Polybius's history
of the rise of Rome to mastery of the known world is the history of the
118 years between the outbreak of the First Punic War in 264 and the

city's destruction in 146. Carthage was a maritime power and a great trading city, and at various times it controlled Sicily, Sardinia, Corsica, much of North Africa, and southern Spain. Its constitutional arrangements seem to have been not unlike those of Rome, which is to say an aristocratic oligarchy with a substantial, but carefully controlled, role for a popular assembly. In the Second Punic War (218–202), the Carthaginian Hannibal was a better general than any Roman, with the possible exception of Scipio Africanus; but he demonstrated, like Napoleon and Hitler much later, that fighting far from home with insecure supply lines is the road to ruin. Carthage was enfeebled, and Rome now controlled Spain and North Africa. The final destruction of Carthage took place long afterward, in 146, after a revolt against the relentless erosion of Carthage's independence. This was the Third Punic War. The First Punic War brought Rome into hostile contact with the Greek eastern Mediterranean, the Hellenistic kingdoms that divided the legacy of Alexander the Great after his death in 323 BCE. Carthage was in origin a colony from Greek Asia Minor; fighting Rome, Carthage allied with Philip V of Macedon, while Rome formed alliances with Greek states hostile to Macedon. After the last of a series of Macedonian Wars, in 168, Rome had an empire in the eastern Mediterranean, and the Greek kingdoms were shattered. Rome was an imperial power.

These events are the subject of Polybius's *Rise of the Roman Empire*; our concern is with book 6, where he explains why the Roman Republic is superior to all other forms of government. The explanation lies in a theory of mixed government that was anticipated but not developed by Aristotle, and that has influenced thinkers down to the framers of the American Constitution. John Adams was a particular admirer. The Constitution of the United States is the most impressive tribute to the theory that Polybius laid out, though not, of course, Polybius alone. Indeed, he is never mentioned in *The Federalist*. Polybius traced the principles of the mixed constitution to the establishment of the Spartan constitution in the eighth century, and treated Lycurgus as the creator both of the theory and of the first mixed constitution; Lycurgus's fame as the founding father of Spartan stability is only slightly diminished by the uncertainty whether he really existed. Aristotle refers to the virtues of Sparta's constitution: "Some, indeed, say that the best constitution is made up of all existing forms, and they praise the Lacedaemonian because it is made up of oligarchy, monarchy and democracy. . . ."[8] Absent in Aristotle's mention of the mixed constitution is an account of what its strengths stemmed from, and Aristotle himself had little reason to develop the theory, since his own ideal was the rule of the "best men," a genuine aristocracy, even if the best practicable state was a *politeia* in which citizenship was extended more widely than in a pure aristocracy.[9]

Aristotle did not elaborate as Polybius did on the view that mixed government is superior to any single form. The theory of the mixed republic, strictly speaking, holds that the best government incorporates elements of monarchy, aristocracy, and democracy within one set of constitutional arrangements. This was Polybius's theory, and Cicero's. Aristotle's favored system of government—*politeia*, or "polity"—is a widened aristocracy (or tightly restricted democracy) that allows more men from humble backgrounds into the circle of "the best men" than a pure aristocracy (but many fewer than in a more radical democracy). Aristotle's account of *politeia* was tailored to a Greek context. He was writing for a people whose conception of citizenship was entitlement to hold office, "ruling and being ruled in turn," and who set store by being treated as political equals. Excluding fewer competent and well-qualified citizens than an aristocracy, while admitting fewer incompetents than a pure democracy, avoids the class conflict that commonly leads to revolution. This is mixed only in the sense in which all constitutions are mixtures— monarchs have advisory councils, assemblies have executive committees and chairmen, and so on.

He wrote as though mixtures were commonly stronger than their pure constituents. The existence of bronze, an alloy that is a great deal tougher than its component tin and copper, provided a potent argument that mixtures were stronger than what they were mixtures of. This was true not only of metals: mules are much tougher than horses and donkeys. This raises two questions: first, what the strengths of the mixed constitution are and, second, why we should expect that a mixture of constitutional forms will combine the strengths of the pure forms rather than their weaknesses. One might suppose that the strength of monarchy lies in the decisiveness that one man can bring to the making of policy, while the strength of democracy lies in the variety of opinions that will be presented, and in the greater likelihood that good sense will emerge among them; Cicero argues just that. If all goes well, and the strengths of both are combined, the decisive decision maker will be assisted by the collective wisdom of the many. What if it goes badly? Might we not find the fickleness and fecklessness of the many exacerbated by the arrogance and ambition of the man who leads them, as Plato thought happened when democratic Athens fell for a demagogue; and if things go only somewhat badly, might not a decisive leader be rendered impotent by indecisive followers? Polybius asked exactly this question; the value of his account lies in the way he explains how the Roman mixture checked the defects of the pure forms without losing their virtues. He turned what might have been an account of the Romans' success in solving local problems into a general theory of stable government.

He made life more difficult for himself and his readers by placing the theory of mixed government within a cyclical theory of constitutional change such as Plato set out in *Republic*. The difficulty is this: one might content oneself with explaining why mixed governments, combining elements of monarchy, aristocracy, and democracy were especially stable—because they accommodated different interests and therefore helped keep the show on the road—or especially legitimate—because they allowed each element of society to contribute as justice suggested it should. It would be perfectly proper to leave matters at that and defer to another occasion questions about the conditions under which such a form of government can be established in the first place. However, Polybius inherited the classical view that change is decay. An inference that he and many successors drew was that no matter what constitution we establish, we must get it right at the outset. All political arrangements deteriorate over time, and if we begin with a botched job, we shall have nothing but trouble. We must seek a Lycurgus, or hope that one turns up. That is another trope that endures to this day, reflected in the popular American view that there was a "miracle in Philadelphia" and that the founders were men of superhuman wisdom.

Polybius mentions Plato's theory, but his picture of the transformation of good constitutions into bad is more Aristotelian: the good forms—monarchy, aristocracy, *politeia*—turn into their bad opposites—tyranny, oligarchy, mob rule. Polybius had no interest in the search for a philosopher-king and was not concerned to explain why perfection could not last forever. Utopia was uninteresting; since it never existed, it could teach no lessons. Polybius knew that the works of man are imperfect; sooner or later even the Roman Empire will decay, probably sooner rather than later. The destruction of Carthage brought tears to Scipio's eyes, even as he ordered its completion; and Virgil's *Aeneid* is surely a reflection on the theme of Troy, Carthage—and Rome? The question was how the Romans had thus far escaped what seemed to be their inevitable fate. They had begun with a botched constitution: they established elected kings with few checks. Nonetheless, their ancient kings had not become tyrants; they had been expelled. Even then a mixed constitution was not instituted by a Roman Lycurgus, and all of a piece, but evolved by trial and error. How had the Romans done it? Prompted by Livy, who himself was much in debt to Polybius, Machiavelli asked just that question.[10] The question remains important even after we reject cyclical (indeed any or all) theories of history; states can recover from unpromising beginnings, and it is worth knowing how they do it. It was obvious to Polybius that Rome had done it; his problem was to square the facts with the theory.

Like many writers charmed by the analogy between the human body and the body politic, Polybius officially held the view that a healthy start is indispensable. Sickly children did not make healthy adults. Lycurgus was famous for getting the Spartan constitution right once and for all: "Lycurgus's legislation and the foresight which he displayed were so admirable that one can only regard his wisdom as something divine rather than human."[11] Polybius was nonetheless an astute critic of the inadequacies of Sparta's economic arrangements. They could preserve social peace and support a formidable defensive army, but anyone looking for economic arrangements that allow expansion and the conquest of the known world would find the Roman hospitality to trade and the accumulation of wealth essential.[12] The Spartans won the Peloponnesian War with Persian money not their own.

The belief that the founding moment is decisive dies hard. When the framers of the Constitution of the United States set out to construct "a machine that would go of itself," they expressed the inherited conviction that their new country's constitution would determine its future, and the belief that a Polybian recipe was needed. Neither peace nor prosperity would be secure if the constitution gave the demos absolute power; but class warfare would be inevitable if a wealthy upper class monopolized political power and exploited the lower classes. As for leadership, one man must be the focus of allegiance and the source of leadership as George Washington had been during the war, or the country would be rudderless; but if Washington was tempted to rule as George III had tried to, the United States would become a tyranny for which a second revolution would be the only cure. Not everyone took the analogy between the body politic and the human body so seriously as to think that an ill-made constitution could not sustain a long-lived and healthy regime merely because a sickly baby was unlikely to become a healthy and long-lived adult human being. Still, a surprising number of people did, and do.

The Romans broke the rules and prospered; indeed, they conquered the whole (known) world. They did not institute the best constitution at the beginning, but reached it through trial and error and flirtations with civil war. Class conflict was endemic; only in the middle of the fourth century did the patricians give up their hereditary monopoly of the highest positions in the Roman state. Machiavelli dwelled on this point at length, because it was so striking an exception to the general rule that an ill-founded state cannot achieve greatness. Sparta was the great example of the benefits of initial perfection, invoked even by those who were unsure Lycurgus had even existed. Cicero argued both sides; with Scipio Africanus as his mouthpiece, he quotes Cato the Elder's observation that Rome "was not shaped by one man's talent but that of many, and not in one person's lifetime but over many generations,"[13] but he cannot resist suggesting that Romulus's original constitution had been the same mixed constitution as Lycurgus's. Elsewhere he ascribes the success of Lysander, who led Sparta to victory in the Peloponnesian War, to the constitution created by Lycurgus four centuries before. Sparta's institutions were invariably credited to Lycurgus's genius alone. Lycurgus set up constitutional arrangements that mingled monarchical, aristocratic, and democratic elements; a pair of hereditary kings were advised by a council of mature men—the *gerousia*—with their decisions subject to the assent of five ephors, and with ultimate authority lying in the hands of a popular assembly. Variations on that model appealed to the enemies of pure democracy on one side and to those of pure monarchy on the other for the next two millennia.

The Peculiarities of Rome Explained

Polybius was an excellent historian, Thucydidean in his determination to gets things right. He therefore approached the history of the Roman constitution with caution, half apologizing indeed to his readers for keeping them waiting for his explanation of the role of Rome's political arrangements in facilitating its rise to world domination. The *Histories* were forty-eight books long; most of them are lost to us, but it hardly seems a great unkindness to readers to keep them waiting until the sixth book of forty-eight. But Polybius was right to be hesitant; how Rome rose to glory is not clear, and what will happen next less clear. He begins by demurring at the usual division of constitutional types into kingship, aristocracy, and democracy, arguing like Aristotle that only good forms of one-man rule can be called kingship, while the others are tyranny or despotism; by the same token, rule by the best is aristocracy, and is otherwise mere minority rule or oligarchy, while rule by the whole people under law is democracy, but lawless and fickle popular government mob rule. That introduces the cycle of degeneration in which monarchy becomes tyranny, aristocracy mere oligarchy, and democracy mob rule. Polybius complicates his account by distinguishing between "monarchy" as a generic form of one-man rule dependent on the leader's personal qualities of strength and bravery and "kingship" as the specific form of one-man rule that depends on the voluntary assent of the community and is constrained by law, what we might call constitutional monarchy. It is a useful distinction and worth making, and becomes important when tribal forms of one-man rule give way to legally structured forms, but it is one we can overlook here.

Polybius's picture of the motors of political change is persuasive if not taken rigidly, and it provides a rationalization of Roman history: leaders who rise by their talents will (at least initially) live like their fellows and arouse no hostility, while those who inherit a throne will separate themselves from everyone else and arouse envy. They will be opposed by men of the upper class affronted by the insolence of their king—or kings, since Polybius knew that Sparta and Rome had been ruled by a collective monarchy. When they are overthrown, their aristocratic supplanters will rule in their stead. That aristocracies degenerate into oligarchies is the most common complaint against aristocratic governments, and often leveled at their modern descendants, the elected aristocrats who occupy the seats of power in the modern democratic world. Readers will find less persuasive Polybius's claim that when an oligarchy is overturned, democracy invariably follows. He says that the memory of the tyranny of kings will be too fresh in everyone's mind for there to be a reversal of the cycle from oligarchy to monarchy, but this is empirically unconvincing; it turns the unusual experience of Athens and Rome into a principle. We are all too familiar with situations in which a disgusted public turns to a dictator, though it has to be said in Polybius's favor that "oligarchy-democracy-dictatorship" is perhaps the most common cycle of all.

The spectacle of the populace's following a single leader in a way that appeared to contradict its democratic attachments was familiar long before Julius Caesar charmed the Roman populace. Nor was it always a bad thing. Thucydides said that Athens was a democracy in name but a monarchy in fact when Pericles was in charge of its affairs, and he was not complaining. When the Athenians fell for Alcibiades, the problem was not that the demos followed one man but that Alcibiades was a crook. At the end of the Peloponnesian War the Athenian Assembly would surely have agreed to save itself from a pro-Spartan oligarchy by handing power to one man, if a Solon or Cleisthenes or Pericles had been available. Sadly, there was not. It is plausible that the Romans accepted that outcome in the hope of putting a stop to murder and civil war when

Octavian established the principate in 27 BCE as Caesar Augustus. Nor is an example taken 120 years later irrelevant to Polybius's analysis. The danger to the republic that led to its extinction was visible much earlier. Rome's conquests in the eastern Mediterranean put enormous wealth in the hands of the political and social elite and raised the specter of a military leader's using that wealth to secure the backing of his army in the field and the mob in the city, and seize power by brute force. The possibility of a successful coup by a rich and bold leader—Julius Caesar, say—was obvious; and the Roman populace might well have thought it would be better off as the prey of one man than as the prey of a large class of aristocratic exploiters. The possibility of political predation of that kind alarmed Polybius; Cicero complained that it had been realized by the time he wrote *De officiis* in 44 BCE.

Roman Success

At the moment of its greatest glory, Rome briefly achieved equipoise. Its armies were the most formidable in the world; its upper classes were public-spirited and nonrapacious; its ordinary people were prosperous. This raises two questions: how the Roman system *in fact* operated, and how plausible the presentation of the Roman system by Polybius and others is. The answers to these questions overlap at the most important point: the Roman understanding of Roman liberty and its role in securing the legitimacy of the Roman state. We must take one step backward to recapitulate why. The mixed republic secured stability; but it was the stability of free institutions, not the stability of, say, the Persian Empire of three centuries earlier. In Rome, neither tyrants, nor oligarchs, nor mobs threatened the liberty of their fellows. Roman citizens were not slaves; they were ruled by law, not the whim of tyrants. Their freedom gave all Romans something they would fight to preserve, just as Demeratus had told Darius that the Spartans would die to preserve their freedom. It was freedom, not license, liberty under law, and both Rome and Sparta were fierce in instilling the self-discipline that free institutions required. Because Sparta and Rome were highly militarized societies, we might think that the discipline of the Romans was simply that of well-trained soldiers. Aristotle sometimes said as much of the Spartans. In principle, it was much more, a self-discipline that sustained the rule of law. The Roman conception of *libertas* as freedom under law became a model for republicans from the Renaissance onward; it animates Machiavelli's discussion of the greatness of Rome in his *Discorsi* and inspires his exhortation to the Medici to liberate Italy from the barbarians at the end of *The Prince*. The freedom he longs for the Italians to recapture is the freedom that the Romans lost when they lost their republic. It was invoked in the American and French revolutions and explains a good deal about modern republican institutions.

What freedom was not is quite as important as what it was; it was not the modern notion of individual liberty or the modern notion of laissez-faire, laissez-aller. Nor was it the freedom of Athenian democracy. Roman writers were sure that direct rule by the common people led to chaos; the Athenians classified their citizens by wealth, but the Romans carried the process to an extreme. Even the lowest class had some political rights, but beyond the formal right to vote for magistrates and laws, they were few. Eligibility for office was confined to the richest class, the *equites*. Moreover, the republic itself was free inasmuch as it was not subject to any other state; it was free of external domination, so its inhabitants were free citizens of a free state. The individual Roman was free from personal oppression by any other Roman; the story of Saint Paul's dealings with the Roman legal authorities in Acts of the Apostles suggests how important that was. Slaves were paradigmatically unfree, but their presence sharpened the importance of the fact that every free man could rely on immunity to arbitrary ill-treatment by anyone else. Even those citizens in the provinces who had no voting rights in Rome and were *cives sine suffragio* were free. In the modern, liberal, individualist sense, Roman society was far from free. The state's demands were not light. No sharp line protected the private realm from public demands, and the *censor morum* could deprive a Roman of office and even of citizenship for disgraceful conduct. But all free Romans possessed a form of what we have come to call *negative* liberty—they were not vulnerable to anything other than legally prescribed penalties for misconduct; and according to their

status they might have one form of *positive* liberty, namely, an entitlement
to occupy office and make the laws that governed the Roman state.[14] The
sovereignty of Rome with regard to other states was untouched when the
republic collapsed, but although many of the forms of republican government were preserved under the empire, they became dead letters. The
central distinction between slave and free remained as important as ever,
although many citizens were manumitted slaves.

Polybius held, and generations followed him, that within the Roman
constitution the consuls represented the monarchical element, the Senate the aristocratic element, and the popular assemblies the democratic
element in the constitution. A modern American reader will project the
U.S. Constitution back onto this account; but wariness is needed. Polybius was not thinking of the modern separation of powers into executive,
judicial, and legislative branches; he certainly thought in terms of the
checks and balances that the modern doctrine of the separation of powers is supposed to reinforce, but he had no thought that particular institutions should exercise distinct powers. Nor was the Roman constitution
organized along the lines of an executive that answered to a legislature
composed of an upper and a lower house, with a separate and independent judiciary. What was mixed were the monarchical, aristocratic, and
democratic elements within one untidy system; our notion of executive,
legislative, and judicial functions was not theirs—indeed, the idea of
the separation of powers as now understood was not clear until Montesquieu, and perhaps not quite clear even to him.

Even Polybius thought the Roman constitution was untidy. The consuls were elected for one year only; they were two in number; each could
veto the acts of the other; and their role was to command the Roman
armies in the field. They could also veto any of the acts of the magistrates subordinate to themselves. Becoming consul was the pinnacle of
Roman ambition, and one of the most contentious issues in the long
struggle between patricians and plebeians in the early days of the republic was the eligibility of plebeians for the consulship. It was an elective
office, so although few Romans were eligible for the office, they were to
an extent answerable to the common people. Regulating the contest for
the consulship was the *cursus honorum*, or permitted path to the highest

office; it required a man to hold the lower offices of quaestor and praetor before he could stand for the consulship, ensuring that there was orderly competition and that the holders of the highest office had proved themselves and were old enough to behave with some discretion. Nonetheless, there were more men of ambition than positions for them to fill, and behind-the-scenes negotiations between leading families to fix the elections were common.

The Senate was composed of members of the highest social rank who had held one or more of the magistracies; they were appointed, initially by the kings of Rome, then by the consuls. It began with a hundred members, but in the late republic, it was first expanded to three hundred and then to nine hundred members when Caesar was dictator. This last step was a sign of the contempt in which Julius Caesar held the Senate, since so large a body could not perform the executive duties that the Senate had performed throughout its history. Senators were unpaid and restricted in the economic activities they could undertake without losing their status; initially, this meant they had to be landowners, not merchants; later it meant that only rich men became senators. The Senate exercised complete executive power when the consuls were absent from Rome, supervised the raising and expenditure of taxes, and dealt with foreign relations; military and foreign relations were its main concern for most of its history. So recent is the modern understanding of the division of powers between different institutions that James Madison imagined that the Senate of the United States would exercise such executive functions as late as the early days of the Philadelphia convention of 1787 that created the U.S. Constitution.[15] A general in the field who was on bad terms with the Senate would grow short of supplies and reinforcements and find himself harassed at all points. In the last resort, the Senate could withdraw his command; but senators were vulnerable to charges of unpatriotic conduct if they did it without good reason. The Senate did not in theory possess either legislative or judicial power, although its advisory judgments—the senatus consulta—had the force of law unless overridden. The Senate proposed legislation to the popular assemblies that were summoned by the tribunes of the people, and whose assent was required before proposed legislation became law. Criminal cases were tried by the assembly, not the Senate: the Senate laid a decree requiring a trial in a capital case before the assembly, which had to agree to hear it. In narrowly legal terms, Polybius was right to say that the Roman people possessed ultimate authority and that this was part of their freedom. They elected the magistrates, approved the laws, and conducted criminal trials (civil cases were held before specially appointed juries of well-off citizens). Yet, the more important point, as Polybius emphasized, was that every element in the constitution needed the concurrence of the others to perform effectively. Consuls could not antagonize the Senate; the people had no spontaneous authority, but their choices in elections decided whose career advanced and whose did not; the Senate would cover itself in ignominy if it made life impossible for soldiers in the field, and so on. A balance between the elements was the constitution's most striking feature.

Citizens

Many modern readers will know Saint Paul's assertion of his citizenship "civis Romanus sum," when he was faced with scourging, and infer that the rights of citizens included immunity to brutality at the hands of soldiers enforcing law and order. Others will recall images of sturdy Roman legionaries from the cinema and innumerable historical paintings. The Roman citizen features prominently in the history of political ideas, usually with little regard to the intricacies of the various rights and duties attached to citizenship, or to the different statuses that citizens might enjoy. This is not surprising. Roman historians wrote about a tiny elite, and the ordinary citizen is almost invisible except as an anonymous soldier, farmer, member of an urban mob. Polybius was writing for readers who understood Roman citizenship, and no thumbnail sketch can do justice to a system that evolved over several centuries. Two or three key elements must be picked out, however. The Romans knew they had achieved what the Greek city-states failed to do; as they expanded their rule from Rome and its hinterland first to Italy and then to the whole known world, they incorporated conquered peoples into their system of citizen rights and duties. This achieved two things; negatively, it protected the incorporated from a degree of exploitation by the Roman state that would have led to resentment, tax evasion, even outright rebellion and insurrection; positively, it opened military and political careers to ambitious provincials ready to be loyal to Rome and possessed of talents that Rome could use.

Although the Romans understood the merits of the policy of offering citizenship to the inhabitants of conquered cities, they were cautious about it. Roman citizenship, like that of Greek city-states, was based in the state's military and financial needs. All male citizens between the ages of seventeen and sixty were liable for military service. Because Roman armies were citizen militias, not standing armies, and not mercenary armies, legions were raised as needed, but once conscripted, a man might find himself serving for as long as eighteen years. He was not a volunteer, although late in the life of the republic when manpower shortages were acute there was a call for volunteers; in an emergency even slaves were enrolled by their masters. Citizens were enumerated in periodic censuses.

Allowances made for changes over time, in outline there were three "orders" of citizens, or *ordines*: senatorial, equestrian, and popular. The senators and *equites* formed an aristocracy of wealth, education, and ambition; below them were the common people, or *populus*. The patricians had been a hereditary aristocracy monopolizing political power, but had been forced to concede to the formerly powerless plebeians the *ius suffragii* and the *ius honorum*, the rights to vote and to hold office. By the time of Cicero, few Romans could claim patrician origin, and it meant nothing politically. The *populus* was divided into five classes, reflecting financial standing, and taxable and military capacity. This was the task of the censors, whose ability to affect a Roman's status was considerable; a member of the *equites* might be demoted for any number of reasons, including cowardice, reluctance to meet his duties, or general bad character. It was very rare for a citizen to lose his citizenship entirely, but not unheard of. The censors also allocated citizens to the thirty-five tribes, which were the basis of the military draft, as well as of the electoral, legislative, and, for some purposes, the judicial systems. They were geographically based, and each was further divided into 10 centuries, by financial standing and by age. The senior centuries embraced those aged forty-six and older. To these 350 centuries were added 18 centuries of *equites*. The system combined popular and oligarchical features: each century voted as a unit, casting one vote according to a simple majority within the century. The best-off centuries had fewer members than the worse-off, so each well-to-do citizen's vote was worth more than that of a poorer citizen. His military burdens were much greater.

Soldiers provided their own armor and weapons and, in appropriate cases, horses. They were supposed to be self-sufficient, and although they received pay, their subsistence was deducted from it. Rome resembled Greek states in which the upper classes formed the hoplite, heavy-armed infantry. In a Roman legion the heavy-armed troops formed the front ranks of the infantry, and they needed the courage of a Spartan. The connection between military service and politics was very direct; to stand for office, a man had first to undertake military service. The military system also demonstrated Roman conservatism in ways that echo to this day. Most generals preferred to recruit their troops from the countryside rather than from the urban tribes; the image of the sturdy yeoman under arms was a legacy from Rome to Britain and thence to the United States. The "well-regulated militia" spoken of in the Second Amendment to the U.S. Constitution was a Roman militia; the modern army of professional soldiers recruited from the poorest members of society was what the Romans wished to escape, and until late in the second century BCE did. Of course, the fighting forces were accompanied by civilians engaged in every imaginable occupation, including that of the purchasers of the loot collected on a successful campaign.

The system of a carefully graduated citizenship survived until late in the second century BCE. In addition, cities that Rome subdued were often admitted at first *sine suffragio*, which is to say their inhabitants had the civil rights of citizens but no voting rights at Rome. This allowed Rome to assimilate its nearest neighbors first, and then extend citizenship to the rest of Italy. Some cities preserved many of their own institutions, and their inhabitants had a form of dual nationality, which worried some observers, much as "hyphenated Americans" worried some observers in the late nineteenth and early twentieth centuries. Others, including Cicero, thought it enhanced a citizen's sense of belonging to have two *patriae* rather than one to attach himself to. Cicero's native city of Arpinum was admitted *sine suffragio* in 316, and its inhabitants were admitted to full citizenship only in 188. This allowed Cicero's many enemies to mock him as a provincial and not a "real" Roman. Their mockery, though not to be taken seriously, reveals the depth of Roman conservatism, and the extent of the Roman obsession with the pedigree of laws, institutions, and individuals.

The system was radically changed as late as 212 CE, when the emperor Caracalla extended citizenship to every free person within the empire. His motive was surely to widen the tax base, rather than to emphasize the blessings of Roman citizenship or the liberality of the imperial administration. It mattered very much to be a citizen, not only in the sense of not being a slave but also in the sense of having the full range of civil and, until the principate, political rights of a citizen. Women had the same civil rights as male citizens, but could not vote or stand for office. They could own property in their own right and dispose of it according to law, by sale or by testament. Because Roman politics depended so heavily on personal connection, heiresses were important, and marriage—or divorce—for political and financial reasons was a prominent feature of Roman politics, along with the device of adoption.

A citizen's political rights were the right to vote and the right to hold office; citizens who had these rights were *optimo iure*—as one might say "first-class citizens." A citizen *sine suffragio* or *minore iure*—a second-class citizen—nonetheless had important rights: one especially valued was the *ius provocationis*, which was the right to appeal to the assembly against a magistrate's sentence in a criminal case. When Saint Paul asserted his citizenship and was told, "You have appealed to Caesar, to Caesar you shall go," it was his *ius provocationis* that he exercised. Among the other privileges that citizenship carried were the rights not to be subjected to crucifixion, not to be tortured when asked to be give evidence, and not to be scourged. One might, upon conviction and after the failure of an appeal, be beaten with rods and beheaded, but that was another matter.

Less dramatically, citizenship carried rights to engage in trade, to marry, to use the civil courts in litigation, and to bequeath property by will. If the concept of politics is Greek, the concept of a legal system is Roman.

All this must be set against the background of the feature of Roman life that we find most alien, the institution of the *patria potestas*, or the absolute authority of the male head of the household over its members. In law, this "paternal power" was held by a father over his unmarried children, no matter what age they were; it embraced power over both their persons and their property. A woman left the *manus*—literally the "hand"—of her father on marriage and was then under the authority of her husband, though divorce was not difficult. Her children were his, however. It goes without saying that the power of a paterfamilias over his slaves was unchallengeable. In principle, but not in practice, a father might sell his children into slavery, or kill them for any reason that seemed good to him. An interesting contrast with Athens was that women were not excluded from the social life of the wider society, and though they were used as pawns in political games, daughters were much loved—if we can trust the evidence of poets and orators. Accustomed as we are to living into our seventies and eighties, we find the thought of children and grandchildren remaining under the sway of their fathers and grandfathers into their middle age hard to grasp. Life expectancy in the ancient world meant that few fathers survived to tyrannize over middle-aged sons. The patriarchal character of family life was a natural accompaniment to the practice of "clientelage," whereby the less well-off attached themselves to well-off men who needed their services.

Cicero

Together with the histories of Polybius and Livy, Cicero's polemical speeches and writings, and his personal correspondence, form some of the most important historical resources for understanding the Roman legal and political system. Here we focus only on his political theory narrowly construed, part of his program to adapt Greek philosophy to Roman social and political purposes, bypassing even the extended defense of the role of oratory in political life that became something like a handbook for the study of rhetoric. *De republica* and *De legibus* were written during the 50s BCE when Cicero was sidelined by the triumvirate of Pompey, Crassus, and Caesar; *De officiis* is the product of the aftermath of the assassination of Caesar. These works had very different and, in the first two cases, complicated histories. The *Laws* was never finished, and found no audience in antiquity, but was well-known during the Middle Ages, when Cicero was a resource for the education of humanists and legal scholars. *De republica* was well-known in antiquity; then vanished. Fragments were rescued in the nineteenth century; they were recovered from a manuscript of a work by Saint Augustine. It was a remarkable early feat of recovering a text from a palimpsest, but the work itself was dismissed by the great Roman historian Theodor Mommsen as a work of no political judgment and no intellectual interest. What kept the audience that Cicero sought was *De officiis* (*On Duties*). Cicero's skill was to combine ideas about virtue from Stoic, Platonic, and Aristotelian sources while glossing over their differences, and to make them applicable not only to the Roman statesman but to the citizen of the world. The idea that human beings are citizens of the world, governed by the laws of nature and of peoples, as well as citizens of an earthly state, was Stoic in origin; but so appealing to Christian Europe was its formulation in Cicero's work that he all but became an honorary father of the church. Augustine credited Cicero with first turning his mind toward God.

Cicero bent Greek ideas to his vision of the idealized Roman Republic, and his understanding of the *mores*—the morality and social attachments—of the gentlemanly statesmen who would hold power in a just republic. Readers familiar with Machiavelli's *Prince* will hear curious echoes of that work in Cicero's advice; curious because the pieties of Cicero's advice to the would-be statesman were satirized by Machiavelli sixteen hundred years later. If his philosophy was Greek and eclectic, Cicero owed his constitutional theory to Polybius; he was born soon after Polybius died, and read his history. And Cicero greatly admired Polybius's friend and employer Scipio the Younger. There are obvious differences of tone. Polybius celebrated Rome's achievement of equipoise, while Cicero lamented the ruin of the republic. Cicero's account of republican politics veers between a "constitutional" emphasis on the way that good institutions allow a state to function by recruiting men of good but not superhuman character, and a "heroic" emphasis on the role of truly great men in reconstituting the state when it has come to ruin.

Cicero's vanity was so notorious that everyone knew he had himself in mind as this hero—had he not saved the republic before when he quelled the conspiracy of Catiline?

The rhetorical tension so visible in Cicero continued to mark the tradition. It emphasizes *both* heroic founders and refounders *and* stable, predictable government; heroic founders set up the mixed republic with its balanced constitution, but lesser mortals make it work. Republican writers were not obsessed with leadership in the modern sense. Many modern writers are convinced that politics exists in a state of continuous crisis, either because this is the natural condition of the political world, or because leaders engineer crises to justify their hold on power. Republican theorists were obsessed with foundation and persistence. In many accounts of the foundation of republics, particularly the numerous near-mythical ones, the founder vanishes from the scene as soon as affairs are settled, as if to emphasize that after a successful founding new founders are not required. Sulla had role models when he stepped down from the dictatorship.

De republica and *De legibus* are fragmentary and hard to read as consecutive texts. Their interest lies in the way Cicero unites Greek philosophy and Polybius's theory of the mixed constitution to formulate a recipe for stable republican government. In so doing, he does something that scores highly on bravado and poorly on persuasiveness by insisting that the Roman *mos maiorum*, "the custom of our ancestors," incorporates the wisdom of Plato, Aristotle, and the Stoics. Given the anti-intellectual character of the early Roman Republic, the ancestors whose wisdom he praises might not have liked the compliment, but it allows Cicero to slide gracefully away from his philosophical allegiances. Virtue having had her due, the maintenance of republican institutions can be looked at without preconceptions. In *De republica* he hands the chief speaker, Scipio Africanus the Younger, the task of providing a *histoire raisonnée* of the Roman Republic at its best. The focus switches from a philosophical concern with the ideal state to a historical account of the creation of the best actual state. In Scipio's account, Plato is rebuked, though not by name, for an obsession with building utopias; it is easy to believe that Scipio had as a matter of historical fact shared Polybius's prejudices against such speculation. Cicero does not say in his own voice that the subject of politics is not the ideal but the best practicable, and that the method is not philosophical first principles but the historical analysis of prudent conduct. His hero does. *De republica* ends, however, with an extraordinary passage, Scipio's Dream, in which Scipio imagines himself taken up to heaven by his grandfather Scipio Africanus. This is a reworking of the Myth of Er from Plato's *Republic*. In a very un-Platonic fashion, Scipio is encouraged to be brave, to devote himself to his country, and to win the glory that will come from the destruction of Carthage; but at the same time he is urged to remember that the earth is vast, that he is unknown to most of mankind, and that the only good really worth having is to be had in heaven amid the music of the spheres. It goes without saying that the theme of the vanity of earthly success resonated with Cicero's Christian readers; until the nineteenth century, Scipio's Dream was the only portion of *De republica* that survived from late antiquity. It did so for entirely unpolitical reasons; the pagan philosopher and anthologist Macrobius, a contemporary of Augustine, devoted a long commentary to the work that focuses on the numerological aspects of Platonic and Ciceronian cosmology. We shall shortly see what Augustine made of Cicero.

Cicero's claims regarding the nature of the republic and the aims of political life defined the republican tradition once and for all, which was no small achievement. His definition of the nature of a commonwealth became canonical. The *res publica* is the *res populi*. *Res publica* almost defies translation; "the public thing" is neither elegant nor self-explanatory, to say the least. In essence the *res publica* gestures toward the entire set of institutional arrangements and the *mores* that sustain them in the task of pursuing the good of everyone. That is why the *res publica* is the *res populi*—the people's state. Unless the people "own" the republic, there is no republic. Cicero goes further than Polybius in making justice the defining feature of a republic that is truly a republic at all, and anticipates Augustine's famous remark that without justice a state is simply a large gang of thieves: a corrupt state is no commonwealth at all. There can be no *res publica* if the institutions of government are perverted to serve private interests. This raises an obvious question, What conditions must be in place if there is to be a *res populi*, that is to say a common good that belongs to the whole people and whose promotion is the task of politics?

Following Aristotle, Cicero says the common good is the pursuit of happiness according to reason; politics must foster its social, economic, and political conditions. He rejects Plato's instrumental account of society and follows Aristotle and the Stoics in saying that human beings are sociable by nature and take pleasure in one another's company independently of the practical returns from cooperating with one another. We all share a common good and an interest in its pursuit. Nonetheless, we also have private interests that may be at odds with other individuals' interests and with the common interest. Good institutions protect the common interest against erosion by private interests and prevent conflicts of private interest from becoming destructive. What those institutions must be is the subject matter of political theory.

De republica is less concerned to provide a general theory than to celebrate the success of the Roman Republic at its best, which is to say down to 133, and what it celebrates are the virtues of the mixed constitution. It was in 133 BCE that Tiberius Gracchus's agrarian reforms, pushed through by none too scrupulous methods, led to Tiberius's assassination; this, the first serious violence in domestic politics for many decades, marked the beginning of the conflict that ended with the death of the republic itself. Cicero's account has strengths that Polybius's lacks. Because Scipio is given space to narrate the history of the expulsion of the Tarquin monarchy and the development of the institutions of the classical republic, Cicero can claim that Rome fared better than Sparta because Rome had the chance to learn by trial and error which institutions would best work for the Roman people. How this squares with Cicero's praise of Lycurgus is unclear. Nonetheless, Scipio makes an excellent case. One great man will achieve more than a squabbling and disorganized multitude, but an orderly process of experiment brings a variety of perspectives to bear on problems and reveals truths that a great man may overlook. This thought must have underlain Polybius's account, since he simultaneously declared himself puzzled by Rome's success and gave a perfectly plausible trial-and-error explanation of what he claimed not to understand. But, like Polybius and others who are obsessed with the work of the founding figure, Cicero was tempted to think the founder had to get things right at the moment of foundation if success was to be ensured.

Sentimental though he often is, Cicero provides a more hard-headed account of Roman politics than Polybius. Polybius's emphasis on the democratic element in the mixture of monarchy, aristocracy, and democracy exaggerated the real power of the ordinary Roman. Cicero's mouthpiece Scipio makes no bones about the way the first Roman census organized the voting units of the assembly—the so-called centuries. Individuals did not vote as individuals; votes were taken century by century; and each century cast one vote. The centuries were so organized that the small number of wealthy citizens were divided into a sufficient number of centuries to outvote the much more numerous poor citizens. Since voting stopped when a majority of the centuries had been achieved, the lower classes rarely voted. Rome was a plutocracy. Given his approval of this device, it is not surprising that Scipio repeatedly observes that he would think monarchy the best of all governments if it were not so difficult to ensure that kings did not turn into tyrants, but since monarchy is the most dangerous form of government, it is not a candidate for the best practicable form. How committed Cicero is to all the doctrines he puts in Scipio's mouth is obscure. In any event, plutocracy or no plutocracy, Cicero has Scipio claim that when the people desire liberty, which Cicero and Scipio certainly approve, they want not a good master but no master. Even if the ordinary Roman had less opportunity to participate in politics than the ordinary Athenian, Roman *libertas* required the people to be self-governing. That forbids the return of kings to Rome; and indeed, no Roman emperor dared call himself *rex*.

Cicero's other improvement on Polybius's account of the merits of mixed government is a more detailed explanation of its positive advantages. Polybius concentrated on its negative virtues, the way one element of the governmental mechanism can prevent another element from getting out of hand. Mixed governments avert—or slow—the cycle of degeneration. Kings who require the assent of an aristocratic council less readily turn into tyrants; a judicial council that may have its decisions vetoed by another institution, as did the Spartan ephorate, is less tempted to give arbitrary decisions or to act from spite; if the fundamental rules must be ratified by a popular assembly, the rich hesitate to fix the rules governing property (and particularly debt) in ways that oppress the common people and make insurrection likely. This is the theory of checks and balances, and not to be despised; without an account of checks and balances, neither the later theory of the separation of powers nor the traditional theory of mixed government make much sense.

Checks and balances do not include the positive component that Cicero adds. There are advantages to rule by one person—decisiveness and an absence of divided counsels; there are advantages to rule by a true aristocracy—discussion without indecision, and the opportunity to secure the services of an elite devoted to politics as a career; and there are advantages to rule by the many—all views can be canvassed, decisions will have the support of a majority of the active population, selfish interests will have less opportunity to pervert decisions. The question is whether we can secure the desirable elements of each of these forms of government, and not merely fend off their disadvantages. Cicero's view is that a well-constructed mixed government secures the decisiveness of the one, the expertise of the few, and the common sense and loyalty of the many. His view has been repeated for two millennia; but before concluding that it is a two-thousand-year-old cliché, we should remember that the modern version of the doctrine is strikingly more inclusive of "the many." Cicero's emphasis on keeping the many under the tutelage of the wealthy and wellborn has simply disappeared in the modern world. Our conception of a government in which a president or prime minister, assisted and checked by a cabinet, answers to a parliament or congress, which in turn represents and answers to the whole adult population, is infinitely more open to the ordinary person than Cicero could have imagined.

Good Law and the Good Citizen

If the best of all practicable governments is the Roman Republic before it was pulled apart by class war and the feuding of warlords, two issues need to be addressed. The nature of law and the rule of law is tackled in *De republica* and *De legibus*; who must play an active part in politics and what virtues he needs is answered in *De officiis*. The answers to "What is law?" and "Who should govern?" run seamlessly into each other, partly because they rest on Cicero's Stoic conception of natural law, and partly because of Cicero's expository skill. Cicero did not have the modern view of law. Although he is one of the originators of modern discussions of the relationship between the positive law of particular states and an overarching natural law (as well as the law of peoples, or jus gentium), and although he was a sharp critic of the chaotic and archaic quality of Roman jurisprudence, he did not work with the modern notion of legislative authority or with our sharp distinction between the work of the legislator and the work of the judge. Nor were his interests in *De legibus* quite what one would expect; the great bulk of what we have concerns the regulation of religious and ritual conduct.

Because *De legibus* is fragmentary, we cannot tell how conscious Cicero was of how different his enterprise was from the work on which it was modeled. Plato's *Laws* answers the question of how to create a second-best state if the ideal state of *Republic* cannot be had. Cicero's *De legibus* focuses on the relationship between the law of nature—which Cicero equates with moral law or divine law—and the law of a particular state. Even then, he never explains quite how the nature of law as such illuminates the detailed Roman regulations to which he adverts. His account of the nature of law is Stoic in origin and the basis of endless later analysis: law is the deliverance of right reason; it rests on the natural sociability of mankind; it treats everyone equally; the mere say-so of any particular group of people does not suffice to make their decrees law. This last claim is the crux of Cicero's natural law theory. Laws must be made properly and for the right reasons to be laws at all. It became the basis of one of the most important—and hotly disputed—claims of medieval and subsequent jurisprudence: *injusta lex nulla lex est*. A law that violates justice is not a law at all. It is the view that sustains the claim that Nazi legislation depriving Jews of all civil and political rights *could not* have been valid law, because it was too unjust to count as law at all, a view that contrasts very starkly with the so-called positivist view that whatever a recognized legal system accepts as law is law, no matter how wicked or misconceived. Disappointingly, Cicero seems not to have meant anything so far-reaching; it appears that he had in mind particular cases of bad law in a Roman context, not the general claim that bad law is no law at all.

Given the fragmentary quality of both *De republica* and *De legibus*, it is not surprising that later generations seized on *De officiis*. It induces mixed feelings in a modern reader. It is a crisply written and cogent statement of an eclectic, mostly Stoic vision of the virtues and their social and political purpose; but it is hard not to feel sorry for Cicero's son, Marcus, the avowed target of the moral instruction and political advice that Cicero offers. He must have found his father's boasting a frightful burden. The cogency of the work, however, explains why it was embraced so warmly by Christian writers. It relies on the view that Cicero often expresses: most disputes between philosophers are terminological, and we should attend to what their doctrines have in common because that is what is true in each of them. The notion of "one truth, many formulations" has an obvious value, not only for pre-Christian Romans conscious that they lived in a multiethnic empire but eventually for Christians conscious that they must coexist with non-Christians and with Christians who interpret their common faith with different nuances. It is a highly political work, because it presupposes throughout that the young man to whom advice is being given will be a public-spirited, upper-class citizen ready to serve the republic to the best of his abilities.

Cicero set out to give an account of our duties that keeps duty and self-interest sufficiently separate while acknowledging that morality must also have a nonmoral point for the individual. He was hostile to the Epicureans because—he thought—they failed to do this; they collapsed morality into self-interest and explained our duties as whatever we find useful to ourselves. The beneficial is not identical with the honorable; the commonsensical view that we do not always benefit ourselves by being just or brave is prima facie right. Nonetheless, there is no deep or irresolvable conflict between the useful and the honorable; the morally good life is naturally attractive to us. Cicero provides an account of the four cardinal virtues—wisdom, justice, "greatness of spirit" or courage, and moderation—an account of the legitimate acquisition of whatever we value for ourselves, and an account of how to handle conflicts between duty and inclination. It can never be in our *ultimate* interest to act unjustly, and the conflict of virtue and utility is in the very last resort only apparent. Nevertheless, he sufficiently respects the realities of everyday life to do much more than dismiss the conflict out of hand. That is the other face of his rejection of Plato's claim that philosophical contemplation is the ultimate blessedness. He concedes that one might accept it as a religious doctrine; but he never retreats from the view that wise action is better than theoretical knowledge and that wise action is action in a community.

The foundations of ethics are reason and natural sociability. Reason is unique to human beings. We alone inquire into the nature of things, and we alone can reflect on our own nature and on the duties that stem from it. Cicero is even more eloquent on the subject of sociability. We are not drawn to each other to compensate for our weaknesses, but because we want the company of friends for their own sake. Although Cicero thinks of duties as including duties to ourselves as well as to others, *De officiis* is interesting above all as an account of the demands of justice. The arguments that become so important to later writers first emerge in a distinctive shape in these pages. For instance, Cicero quotes Plato's observation that we are not born for ourselves alone, but turns it into the thought that we are born for our friends, our country, and humanity, which Plato would never have done. Where Plato sees us pulled toward the depths of philosophical truth, Cicero embeds us in concentric circles of social connection.

Justice is the desire to give each man his own, to preserve as common what is common, and to keep as private what is private; and Cicero raises all the still familiar questions about how we should distinguish between justice and benevolence—the line between giving people what they are entitled to as opposed to giving them what they are not entitled to but what we are prompted to give them out of generosity. Characteristically, he reminds us that we must not be generous with what is not our own, nor even so generous with what *is* our own that we imperil our future ability to do good. He writes always with an eye to the way in which the way we behave will look to other people, and the notion of what is honorable or decorous is constantly to the fore. We do not behave justly for merely selfish reasons, but we should remember that being just is one way to make sure that we are well thought of by everyone else. It is a very Ciceronian thought that being well thought of is something to aim at— as long as the people who think well of us are people who judge rightly. The praise of the misguided or eccentric we can do without.

Cicero once more assimilates the philosophical arguments of the Greeks to the *mos maiorum* of the Romans. Roman history and contemporary Roman politics are everywhere visible, with all the usual targets receiving the usual rebukes. In the same vein, when he engages in a lengthy discussion of the stringency of the demands of honesty, he cites cases he would have come across as praetor, and one gets glimpses of his talents as an advocate. The most strenuous defense of traditional Roman values comes, however, when Cicero discusses the fate of Regulus. Marcus Atilius Regulus was consul and a Roman general during the First Punic War; after several victories he was defeated and captured in 255. He was held for several years, and the story has it that in 250 he was sent to Rome by the Carthaginians to arrange an exchange of prisoners, having given his parole to return to Carthage if he was unsuccessful in arranging the exchange. At Rome he argued against the exchange and urged his compatriots to continue the fight against Carthage. He then returned to Carthage in accordance with his oath and was tortured to death, either by being put in a barrel with a spiked interior and rolled down a hill, or by having his eyelids cut off and being exposed to the light of the sun. Cicero rather alarmingly insists that he did no more than his duty; even promises made under duress to an enemy must be kept. Regulus was right to return to the Carthaginians and face martyrdom because he had promised the Carthaginians that he would do so; conversely, the hostages taken at Cannae were wrong to try to evade their duty to return to their captors. Indeed, says Cicero, Regulus does not deserve great praise for his actions, because it was the republic that made them possible and inevitable.[16] This sets the price at which we *might* be asked to do our duty very high. Not all the links between high principle and Roman practice demand such sacrifice. When Cicero considers generosity, he takes for granted Roman clientelage: we owe most to those who have done most for us in the past. His political anxieties make an appearance when he observes that unusual generosity to strangers suggests that the seemingly generous man may be moved by ulterior motives and may—for instance—be cultivating political support for an improper purpose.

Cicero's style is a key to the success of *De officiis*, and not just the literary style, but the political and intellectual style. Regulus aside, the demands of duty generally stretch only as far as the well-educated, well-to-do man is likely to follow. Thus, he insists, in a famous metaphor that Machiavelli later stood on its head, that courage is necessary but the courage of a human being is not the ferocity of the lion, just as wisdom is necessary but the intelligence of the human being is not the cunning of the fox.[17] Sulla was said to combine the cunning of the fox with the ferocity of the lion, and Machiavelli famously held that the prince must know how to do so.[18] Cicero held that we are not to model ourselves on the lesser animals, but to ask always what the distinctively human form of conduct must be. Although reason links us to the gods, these are not injunctions for philosophers but recipes for good—that is, decorous, honorable, and reputable—conduct on the part of men of good family who are conscious of their duties to friends, family, class, and locality. Compared with the philosophical heights of Plato, Cicero is parochial; but this is one of many reasons why he talks to us in ways we still find persuasive.

What he was not and could not be was the savior of the Roman Republic. There is a valedictory note about Cicero's reflections on Roman politics which reminds us that the future lay not with a revived republic but with the Roman Empire, and that the spiritual and moral future lay not with the *mos maiorum* and traditional Roman piety but with Christianity. Christians who initially lived in expectation of an imminent Second

Coming had little to say about the politics of a world that offered them no more than grudging toleration when they were lucky and martyrdom when they were not. Nor did the conversion of Constantine in 311 see a sudden flowering of a distinctive Christian political philosophy, not least because Christianity did not become the "official" religion of the empire until the emperor Theodosius outlawed pagan cults in 382. That makes it the more astonishing that the first sustained account of a Christian's attitude to earthly politics is a work whose vitality continues after sixteen centuries. Augustine's *City of God against the Pagans* is very much more than a masterpiece of Christian political theology; but it is that, and Cicero was one of its targets.

CHAPTER 5

Augustine's Two Cities

Augustine's Life and Times

AUGUSTINE'S IMPORTANCE TO THE subsequent history of Europe is impossible to exaggerate. His political theory, which is all we focus on here, was a very small part of what he wrote in some 113 books and innumerable letters and sermons. Nonetheless, it is pregnant with arguments that racked not only Christian Europe but the modern world: how seriously should a Christian with his eyes on eternity take the politics of this earthly life; is it the duty of the state to protect the church, repress heresy, and ensure that its citizens adhere to the one true faith; absent a Christian ruler, are we absolved of the duty to obey our rulers, or must we follow Saint Paul's injunction to "obey the powers that be"?[1] More generally, Augustine articulated distinctive and long-lived thoughts on matters that remain controversial: the nature of just war, the illegitimacy of the death penalty, the limits of earthly justice. The fact that his views on all these matters were embedded in a theology of some bleakness does not mean that they do not survive on their own merits. One needs only the barest sympathy with the thought that we are fallen creatures to find many of his views deeply appealing, far from cheerful as they may be.

Augustine was a Roman citizen, born at Thagaste, in North Africa, in 354. It is generally assumed that he was ethnically a Berber. His father was a minor official, a decurion; the rank was initially a military rank in the auxiliary forces with which Rome kept order in the provinces; the civilian equivalent was a town manager. The family's curial rank mattered less than that his parents were just prosperous enough to send Augustine to boarding school at the age of eleven. His mother, Monica, was a devout but uneducated Christian, his father a non-Christian who may or may not have converted on his deathbed. Catholic Christianity had recently become the official religion of the Roman Empire, the final great persecution of the Christians having taken place under Diocletian in 305–6. Augustine was not baptized as a child, but infant baptism was far from universal. He claimed that he had a wholly miserable childhood. In *The City of God* he says that he would rather die than live his childhood over again; but the claim comes in one of his many descriptions of human life as a long journey through a vale of suffering, and is not conclusive evidence that his childhood was more miserable than most childhoods or than his subsequent life. Indeed, he does not suggest that it was, since he asks rhetorically, "If anyone were offered the choice of suffering death or becoming a child again, who would not recoil from the second alternative and choose to die?"[2]

He claimed that as a child he disliked learning and preferred the pain of punishment for refusing to learn Greek to the pain of the lessons. He also says, perfectly sensibly, that Latin came easily because everyone around him spoke it, but Greek did not, because it was a foreign language. Many of us have thought as much about the languages we have tried to learn. He was certainly very clever and perhaps as willful as he claimed; how much Greek he learned is unclear, but it seems likely that he could read it without great difficulty but much preferred Latin. He initially intended to advance himself with a career in the imperial administration. This required a training in the skills of the orator, and at sixteen he went to Carthage to learn rhetoric. While there, he took a mistress by whom he had a son, Adeodatus. In retrospect, he was appalled by these youthful yieldings to the urgings of the flesh. Modern readers of his *Confessions* find them wholly forgivable and are much more appalled that he never tells us the name of his mistress, and that he abandoned her a dozen years later—as anyone of his class and upbringing would have done—when he was minded to marry an heiress to advance his career.[3]

He taught rhetoric in North Africa, then Rome, and when he was thirty secured a distinguished position as professor of rhetoric in Milan, which was a stepping-stone to a provincial governorship. By this time Rome was no longer the imperial capital. Early in the fourth century Diocletian had established his eastern capital at Byzantium and his western capital in Milan. Under Constantine the imperial capital was Byzantium, now renamed Constantinople, but late in the century the empire became de facto an eastern and western empire, with the western capital at Milan, and later at Ravenna. When teaching in Milan, Augustine arranged to make an advantageous marriage, essential to membership of the Roman aristocracy, but after much mental anguish he renounced these ambitions, was baptized as a Christian in 386, and devoted himself to the service of the church. He was baptized by Ambrose, bishop of Milan, the most intellectually and politically powerful churchman of his day, but it was devout lay friends who had done the work of conversion, or reconversion, since he had been brought up as a Christian as a child and had abandoned his faith in Carthage. He had by this time explored many of the religious and quasi-religious resources of the late classical world. He was for a time a Manichaean "hearer" or acolyte, but found Manichaeanism intellectually unpersuasive and littered with superstition and myth. He was then attracted by the austere Neoplatonism of the pagan philosopher Plotinus, which was a very plausible gateway to the Christian faith. Once he had become a Christian, he returned to North Africa, first to Thagaste, where he set up a little community of celibate Christians, and then to Hippo, where he was inducted as a priest in 391 and made bishop in 395, taking up office in 396. He spent the second half of his life as bishop of Hippo, in continual controversy with movements he thought heretical or otherwise a danger to the church, and writing a stream of books and pamphlets to defend his view of the true church and the true faith.

One of the first things he wrote as bishop was a book that defies categorization, the *Confessions*, written in 397–400 and read with passionate interest ever since. Although it is a record of the route by which he came to his Christian faith, it is not an autobiography in the modern, or even in the ancient, sense. It is more nearly a continuous prayer to the God who had saved him, accompanied by lengthy passages of self-recrimination based loosely on his recollection of particular episodes of wrongdoing. It is made unforgettable by Augustine's extended reflections on the sheer mysteriousness of human existence. The first ten books are a loosely chronological *apologia pro vita sua*; the last three discuss time, the Trinity, and the Creation. Even readers who find Augustine's emotional style overpowering find it deeply engrossing, atheists as much as Christians.[4]

A bishop was not a grand figure in the church of the late fourth century. There were seven hundred bishops in the African church alone. He was nonetheless a central figure in the ordinary secular administration of his region, called on to exercise judicial functions and much else. Although such a life was not entirely thankless, it was exhausting, and Augustine lived it against the background of a steady decline in the western Roman Empire's ability to defend itself and protect its subjects. In 410 came the shattering event that launched Augustine on the task that occupied him for much of the rest of his life: writing *The City of God against the Pagans*, begun in 413 and completed after many interruptions in 427. When Alaric and his Visigoths sacked Rome in 410, the Eternal City was revealed as the indefensible former capital of the crumbling, and less important, western portion of the Roman Empire. The event was less important militarily than symbolically, but its symbolic importance was vast. Although Augustine does not mention it, Roman rule was decaying in North Africa as it was elsewhere. Roman control was increasingly fragile away from the coastal cities, and the military units meant to keep the peace on Rome's behalf were decreasingly under the control of the imperial administration, adding another danger to the incursions of barbarian tribes. In the last years of Augustine's life, the Vandals who had seized Spain realized that the province of Africa was at their mercy, and crossed the narrow straits to seize their prey. Augustine died in 430, with Hippo a besieged city full of refugees from the surrounding country. It was sacked and burned the following year.

In spite of the innumerable Renaissance paintings of Augustine at his desk, his daily round as a bishop was not spent in the study. He spent most mornings giving judgment in litigation over land, inheritances, and the other business of everyday life. His pastoral mission involved keeping his clergy even more than the laity on the straight and narrow, and managing intense relationships with the most spiritually aware of his congregation. Through his writings, Augustine would be second only to Saint Paul in his impact on the history of Christianity, but not only could he not have guessed this might happen; it would have been incredible to anyone else. The intellectual life of the Christian churches was still more Greek than Roman; Ambrose and Augustine were among the first Latin fathers, but that retrospective status was not something they set out to acquire. Greek was the language of philosophy, and Augustine's knowledge of Greek philosophy was secondhand, acquired from Cicero and from Latin translations of the Neoplatonist Plotinus. The churches of Constantinople or Jerusalem would have seemed much more likely sources of a Christian theology with real intellectual power.

As a Roman of the western empire, Augustine was not a natural intellectual leader of the Catholic Church. As an African, he was a provincial; the African church was provincial, too. It had a more austere view of the demands of Christianity than did the church in Italy; it did not accept the aristocratic laissez-faire that allowed Roman families to be partly pagan and partly Christian in their practice, and it was intolerant of doctrinal looseness. Retrospectively, we can see Catholic doctrine crystallizing into an orthodoxy; Augustine's contemporaries would have thought it was an open question where Christianity would settle on issues such as the freedom of the will, predestination, original sin, and the requirements for salvation. Augustine's vast and unwieldy masterpiece, *The City of God*, takes such firm and uncompromising views on all these issues that we are not surprised they triumphed; they have an unmatched intellectual power. Yet the price—intellectual, emotional, and moral—that must be paid for holding Augustine's views is so high that it is equally surprising that they made any headway.

Augustine excoriated himself for ever holding his pre-Christian beliefs. Nonetheless, they greatly influenced his view of the world as a Christian. To say that he remained a Neoplatonist or a Manichee would be foolish; to say that in temperament and in intellectual style he remained the man who found Manichaeanism and Neoplatonism attractive is the bare truth. This was not only a matter of Augustine's temperament and intellect. Christian doctrine was much affected both by the mysticism of the oriental mystery religions and by the rationalism of Greek philosophy. We can find our way into, and perhaps out of, Augustine's *City of God* most readily if we start with the dilemmas that any devout Christian must face when contemplating earthly politics, wrestle first with Augustine's youthful opinions, and enter *The City of God* by way of his confrontation with Cicero's *De republica.* This will involve a perhaps surprising degree of attention to the doctrinal pressures on Augustine, but much as Plato thought that only the truth as he saw it could redeem earthly societies, so Augustine, who thought that nothing but the grace of God could redeem anything mortal, thought that the truth inherent in his Christian faith contained the key to the value, limited as it was, of our earthly politics, as well as the explanation of the chasm that separated those politics from the nonpolitics of the true kingdom of God. Where philosophers and theologians are convinced that their ideas stand or fall as a systematic whole, there is nothing for us to do but to explore the edifice they have constructed.

Politics and Religion

Between the death of Cicero in 43 BCE and the birth of Augustine four centuries later, enormous changes had occurred. The most immediately momentous was the collapse of the Roman Republic and its gradual transformation into an empire. No thumbnail sketch of the following four centuries is possible here; but the crucial transformations can be briefly outlined. After the civil wars that followed the assassination of Julius Caesar, Caesar's adoptive grandson, Octavian, emerged victorious and established the "principate" that was recognized as the institution of one-man rule. The Roman hostility to the concept of a "king" remained as intense as ever, and for a surprisingly long time the forms of republican institutions were preserved. What we now think of as the imperial structure of administration and government was very late in coming.

Only when the entire empire was threatened by military disasters and economic and administrative chaos during the third century was there a radical transformation of its political structure that kept the empire alive for another century in the west and another millennium in the east.

A succession of emperors who gained power by military prowess created the centralized, bureaucratic, and uniform system of administration that we think of as defining the imperial system. The empire's ambition to rule the known world remained, even if the western empire was increasingly a patchwork of local regimes whose subordination to the empire was a legal fiction. At a doctrinal level, the Roman ideology of consensus, honored in the breach as it had always been, yielded to an emphasis on obedience and order. In terms of the contrast we began with, citizens gave way to subjects, and as emperors were increasingly drawn from the eastern empire, a more "Persian" view of a ruler's status crystallized. Christian rulers could not receive divine honors, but their pagan predecessors did, and the elaborate ceremonial of the court at Constantinople under Christian emperors was scarcely different.

The transformation of the pagan empire into the Christian empire that Constantine began to create and that became solidly established when Theodosius, the last emperor to reign over both the eastern and the western empires, outlawed pagan cults late in the fourth century, was in the long run even more momentous. The Christianization of the regions and peoples that composed the Roman Empire survived the decay of the western empire and ensured that the "barbarian" kingdoms that succeeded the western empire were Christian societies, just as the Byzantine Empire was. Somewhat fortuitously the Christianization of barbarian Europe fostered the process by which the pope ceased to be one bishop among many and became the head of the entire western church. The only language of law and culture they possessed in common was Latin—the language of western but not Greek Christianity—and Latin thus became the universal language of Western culture and gave the western Catholic Church a distinct identity.

Until Pippin and Charlemagne established the kingdom of the Franks in the eighth century, the Catholic Church was the only institution whose authority aspired to the geographical reach of the western empire. This sustained the concept of the universality of Roman rule while spiritualizing it in a way republican Romans would have found strange. It need not have happened. In retrospect the preeminence of the pope as the heir of Saint Peter seems inevitable, but when Constantine made Christianity the religion of the empire, it was to his city that eyes turned rather than to Rome. Thereafter, Milan and Ravenna were as important as Rome. Looking back, we see the ingredients assembled for the creation of the distinctive institutions of church and state, cooperating but serving different ends, and always in danger of coming into conflict either over doctrine or over the privileges of the clergy or over the different loyalties they appealed to. But if the western and eastern halves of the Roman Empire had not gone their separate ways, the history of Christianity would have been very different, and our ideas about the naturalness of a division of labor between religious and secular institutions would have been very different, too.[5]

The theoretical analysis of the role of religion in politics or of the politics of religion in all its forms is made harder by the ambiguity of both concepts. Politics and religion resist simple definition; nor can we wish these ambiguities away. It is of the essence of both religion and politics that it is an open question what is and is not a religious consideration or a political one. Politics as a simple struggle for power is not politics as Aristotle conceived it—the citizens of a polis ruling and being ruled in turn; and the politics of a society that seeks to find a "godly ruler" is not like either. The boundaries of the concept of religion are so porous that we habitually distinguish between "organized religion" and a "religious" view of the world more generally, with many writers thinking the first an enemy of the second.[6] The crucial contrast for our immediate purposes is between Christian politics and pagan politics: between the political implications of a theologically complex, fiercely monotheistic Christianity and the political implications of the theologically casual, polytheistic, "civic" religions of the Greek and Roman world. The contrast sheds light on the difficulties that pagan rulers had with the unwillingness of Jews and Christians to sacrifice to the local deities and on the very thin sense in which their persecutions were "religious" in motivation, and it also illuminates the first and most important articulation of Christian political theology.[7]

The very idea of a Christian political theology is problematic. If human beings are only transitorily on earth, and earth is but a vale of tears through which we must pass on our way to paradise, earthly politics loses almost all value. Life in the polis cannot be the good life for man, since fulfillment lies in the hereafter; here below, we must prepare for eternity. Earthly happiness for rational persons consists in whatever confidence they may entertain about the life hereafter. This "abstentionist" vision is in some ways at odds with the involvement of Christ in the everyday life of the community in which he spent his short life. He may not have taken part in "politics," and he certainly insisted that his kingdom was "not of this world." But he healed the sick, preached to large crowds, and taught an ethical system that would have made a deep political impact on any society open to his teaching. Roman Judaea was not wholly deaf to it, which may well have been one reason for his execution. In the first two centuries after the death of Christ, Christianity might well have been thought un- or apolitical, however. The belief that Christ's return was imminent undermined a concern with earthly politics, and Christianity initially appealed mainly to the poor, to slaves, and to outsiders with no role in Roman political and public life. In the innumerable cities of the Greek east that preserved their earlier institutions by Roman concession, there was "local politics" still. There was also a great deal of public life both in the administration of justice and the provision of the usual services of government, and in semicompulsory public duties incumbent on the upper classes, such as laying on games and paying for sacrifices. As a religion of the poor, Christianity had nothing to offer public life.

Both in Rome and in the provinces, the civic life of the empire certainly impinged on Christians, however; they faced punishments up to and including hideous forms of death for refusing to sacrifice to the emperor of the day or to the Roman gods, and they might at any time be made scapegoats for a famine or some other misfortune. When persecutions became infrequent and when Christianity began to appeal to the higher social classes, who were bound to accept their share of public obligations, the question of how Christians should relate to the state became harder to evade. Finally, when the emperor Constantine converted to Christianity and the empire became Christian, all the questions so familiar to us about how the state should support religion, and how Christians should support a Christian or a non-Christian state, demanded answers. Christian thinkers had to form a view on vexed issues: how did God's law relate to civic law, and beyond that to the law of nature—*lex naturae*—and the law of peoples—the jus gentium? Could a Christian shed blood as a judge imposing the death penalty? Should Christians serve in an army? Early Christianity was overwhelmingly pacifist, but Constantine's Christianity was the reverse. What moral sacrifices, and how many, could a Christian make to be a good citizen? Augustine neither raised nor answered all these questions, but he provided the intellectual apparatus with which subsequent generations did.

Manichaeanism

The story is rich in paradox. Augustine was a fierce critic of pagan philosophy and adamant that only in Christianity could salvation be found; but he found his way to an intellectually cogent Christianity by way of Cicero's philosophical works and Neoplatonism. His conception of the two cities was foreshadowed in Scipio's Dream, with which Cicero's *De republica* concludes, just as Scipio's Dream was foreshadowed in Plato's contrast between the two realms in which the philosopher finds himself: the earthly republic and the reality revealed by philosophy. Initially, Augustine was tempted by Manichaeanism.

He began his search for faith as a Manichaean "hearer," a spiritual fellow traveler who served the adepts of the faith—the illuminati—and prepared their food. Manichaeanism was not then the reviled heresy it became; there was no unified and authoritative source of Christian belief, such as the papacy became in medieval western Europe, and no authority able to impose a single view of orthodoxy and heresy. This did not encourage toleration, and it did not reflect a belief in the separateness of secular and spiritual authority; no premodern society entertained such a view. Churches and secular authorities repressed ideas they did not like, in a sporadic and inconsistent fashion; where they either could not do it or had no particular reason to do it, they were tolerant by accident rather than design. Manichaeanism was the creation of a third-century Persian sage, Mani, who described himself as the apostle of Christ.[8] Its one, very important intellectual strength was its answer to the problem of evil. The problem is simply stated: if God is both loving and omnipotent, why is there suffering in the world? Augustine eventually held that suffering exists because humanity is sinful, an answer built on an unflinching acceptance of the doctrine of original sin and the heritability of the taint of Adam. Pagan polytheisms did not face the problem. Evil was a brute fact, and accepted as such, unclouded by any idea that the gods might have intended there to be less of it.

Manichaeanism relied on one non-Christian—and non-Judaic—premise. It was dualistic. The material world is evil, as is all matter; that is why the world we live in is a realm of pain and suffering. The God revealed in the Old Testament is good, and is pure spirit; but contrary to Genesis, the physical world is not his creation but the work of the devil. For this reason, Manichaeanism held a negative view of sexual passion, both human and other. The created world is evil, as is our physical nature and sexual reproduction. This was one reason for the Manichaean commitment to vegetarianism, although the Manichaeanism of Augustine's day was independently committed to the virtues of fruits such as melons, which were identified with the sun, the supposed dwelling place of God. Sun worship was Zoroastrian, and the Zoroastrian element in Manichaeanism swiftly alienated Augustine. Mani's writings also made claims about stars and planets and phenomena such as eclipses that were patently false. When Augustine found that pagan writers had made careful celestial observations of eclipses and similar phenomena, and that their predictions were invariably right and Mani's wrong, his faith gave way.[9]

Nonetheless, the attractions of Manichaeanism are powerful. It does not blame innocent suffering on God. Innocent suffering is the rock on which Christianity is always in danger of shipwreck; critics of the Christian belief that this imperfect world is the creation of a benign omnipotence always point to the painful deaths of little children as clinching evidence that it cannot be. Either God is not omnipotent or he is not benign; few wish to bite the bullet and accept the third possibility—that tiny children are sinful and merit their suffering. Augustine bit the bullet, eventually arguing that we all enter the world tainted with the sin of Adam and deserve what we suffer.[10] One might think that the Manichaean view that God is the source of goodness, but unable to make headway against the devil, is less alarming. The persistence of Manichaeanism into the late Middle Ages suggests that many people have thought so.

Augustine's mother, the devout Monica, forbade Augustine the house while he was a hearer. Nonetheless, Manichees and Christians had a lot in common; and that was not surprising in an age when pagan philosophers numbered Christ among the wonder-workers and magi they admired, while rejecting as absurd the idea that a human could be literally the son of God, and dismissing the doctrine of the resurrection of the body as preposterous. Manichees saw Christ as the Gnostic heretics did: Christ was a great teacher. Like others who embodied great doctrines, he emanated from God, but was not literally his son. Nor could he have suffered bodily torment on the cross; the appearance that he did so was an illusion. Christ was pure spirit, and the human body that observers saw was the appearance that the divine spirit wore for temporary purposes. The point of Christ's mission was to spread enlightenment, and his work as a teacher was central to his life. The Resurrection was the emancipation of Christ's spirit from its earthly appearance, and resurrection for anyone else would similarly be the escape of the spirit from the body.

Gnostic sects were innumerable and various, and Manichaeanism embraced many local varieties, so it is impossible to give a more precise account of what Augustine believed than the one he gave in his *Confessions*. There are no competing accounts to set against his. The triumph of Christianity everywhere west of Persia and the dislike that political rulers felt for the anarchist implications of Manichaeanism mean that the literary remains of Manichaeanism are sparse. Precision is not necessary; once Christian orthodoxy embraced the Incarnation and the Resurrection of the body, Gnosticism was at odds with the two central items of the faith. The struggles internal to Christianity between Trinitarian and non-Trinitarian accounts of the divine nature were violent; but they were between Christians who shared precisely the doctrines that Manichees and Gnostics rejected.

Most religious faith owes less to its intellectual coherence, narrowly considered, than to two other elements. One is its ability to provide a lightning rod for powerful emotions; the other, the persuasiveness of the picture of the human condition it offers. For Augustine, Manichaean-ism appealed to a powerful element in his character, his sense that he was full of bad desires. This was his personal "problem of evil"; his religious sensibility focused on that sense of sin with lasting political consequences. Only when he found inspiration in Saint Paul, who had a similar sensibility to his own, did he find a more satisfying answer than Manichaeanism provided.

A last persuasive feature of Manichaeanism was that it offered a "two-tier" doctrine of the spiritual life that could readily migrate to a Christian worldview. Manichaeanism seems on its face to demand a suicidal hostility to the material world. If the flesh is evil and the spirit good, then taking leave of the flesh by suicide seems to be the route to felicity, or at least to emancipation from earthly evil. In practice, it was held to be sufficient even for the most devout to reduce the fleshliness of existence—by sexual abstinence, eating a sparse vegetarian diet, drink-ing water, wearing linen garments, and avoiding the use of animal hides and fur. In the Middle Ages the Manichaean elite, the *perfecti*, followed this regime; only those who felt themselves to be particularly called to live such lives were under any obligation to do so. Most people could continue to live their usual lives: so long as we are trapped here on the material earth, we do not sin if we do not succumb unduly to greed, lust, anger, and the other sins of the flesh. Elements of this acceptance of the limits of the demands we may make on ordinary life recur throughout *The City of God.*

From Manichaeanism to Christianity

Augustine's account of his escape from Manichaeanism to Christianity gives Neoplatonic philosophy pride of place in making him seek non-superstitious intelligibility in the human predicament. It is not easy to distinguish the part played by Cicero from the part played by the Neoplatonists Plotinus and Porphyry. It is easy to believe that the deep impact of the latter was greater; they were obsessed with the same problems as Plato and reacted in the same intense, determined, and detailed way. Cicero's writings certainly had the greater impact on Augustine's ideas about politics. At nineteen he read a work of Cicero's that has long been lost and whose contents are unknown—*Hortensius*—but *The City of God* draws explicitly on Cicero's political writings: Augustine's criticism of Rome was that it suffered from the *libido dominationis*—a lust for power for its own sake that is inimical to the pursuit of even earthly justice, a complaint that comes straight from Cicero's *De republica*. In *The City of God*, the most "political" discussions come many books apart, and many years apart in their writing, when Augustine so to speak returns to the argument with Cicero that he begins in book 2 and concludes in book 21, but the argumentative method is the same: to hold Rome to Cicero's standards.

What Augustine learned from the Neoplatonists was how to reconcile the goodness of ultimate reality with the miseries of the world of everyday experience. This world is inevitably a vale of tears, for it is a shadow of the true world illuminated by the light of the divine mind. Stripped of Mani's absurd cosmogenic myths, the thought became acceptable that ultimate reality is one, perfect, indivisible, and unshakable, while the world in which we dwell is fragmentary and chaotic and incessantly shaken by disasters both natural and contrived by passionate and unwise humanity. Evil is privation, not a positive force in the world. The notion that the ultimate misfortune for humanity is separation from God is a thought of the same kind. There was room for a dialogue at least between adherents of the Christian and Jewish faith in a strongly personal God and Neoplatonists attached to the idea of a central Mind or Intelligence animating the world. Augustine himself observed that he found in his philosophical reading the insight that begins Saint John's gospel: "In the beginning was the Word, and the Word was with God, and the Word was God."[11]

Still, Augustine was converted—or reconverted—by reading Saint Paul. He had become increasingly unhappy and unsure of himself. He finally convinced himself that he had received a divine message to open the Bible and read what it commanded. He opened the book, read a passage from the Epistles, and took it as a direct injunction to arm himself with the Lord Jesus Christ. The sharpness of the break was greater at an emotional than an intellectual level, but at the emotional level it struck like a thunderbolt, which is just the impression his *Confessions* conveys. All the same, conversion implied nothing about whether Augustine should do something other than climb the career ladder to a provincial governorship. Most Christians were laymen and laywomen going about their ordinary lives; only a few became recluses or members of monastic communities. Augustine was initially inclined to become a recluse and adopt a Christian version of the quiet life led by Plotinus when he retired into the country to think. Nor did his return to Africa after the death of Monica lead immediately to the priesthood; he established a small community in Thagaste before being more or less strong-armed into the priesthood by the congregation at Hippo.

Practical Politics and Theoretical Politics: The Provocation for *The City of God*

His reluctance to give up the quiet life of the scholar was genuine. Augustine would happily have kept away from the world of politics. He was combative, and his work is polemical; but the fights he picked were with those who committed intellectual, moral, and spiritual errors. He was a warrior in the cause of theological truth. This means, inter alia, that although *The City of God* is an enormous book, "a loose, baggy monster," as it has been called,[12] it is not Augustine's "political theory." That is an intellectual construction of later ages, not something Augustine created. Most of *The City of God* is concerned with theological controversies and large philosophical issues. Some of it is historical controversy. Some things that the modern world would think part of a political theory, even things one would have thought central to a Christian political theory, such as an account of the right of the state to enforce religious uniformity, hardly feature in *The City of God*. They hardly feature, because Augustine takes it for granted that it is a good thing if an earthly ruler is imbued with the true faith and is willing to bring his people to that faith. He had scruples about the means used; he did not, for instance, wish to see torture employed against the Donatists, the North African sect that threatened his church in the early 400s, even though the Donatists were themselves physically violent. But he took it for granted that earthly rulers should bring their subjects to God if they could. What else were they to do?[13]

The provocation for writing *The City of God* was the sack of Rome in 410. This did not mark "the fall of the Roman Empire"; the western empire had been militarily on the defensive for two centuries, the last emperor, the sixteen-year-old Romulus Augustus, was deposed only in 476, and elements of Roman administration persisted for another century in the west. The Byzantine Empire endured until 1453. Nor was the physical damage done to Rome by Alaric and the Visigoths particularly severe; this was not the Romans sacking Carthage. The psychological shock was another matter. Moreover, it provoked the argument about the role of Christianity in the destruction of Rome that Augustine responded to. When Christians were persecuted in earlier centuries, before the emergence of Christianity as the official religion of the empire, the reason was that their unwillingness to sacrifice to the traditional gods imperiled the state. Pagan religion ascribed earthly misfortune to the malice of gods who had been insulted or slighted, so the Christian unwillingness to sacrifice to the gods was a literal threat to the well-being of their fellow citizens.[14] It was rarely suggested that they posed any other threat—although Nero, seeking a scapegoat for the burning of Rome, latched onto the Christians as an unpopular group on whom to pin responsibility, as others did thereafter in face of a variety of disasters.

Augustine was not quick to respond to the suggestion that Christian hostility to the old gods was the deathknell for Rome. He began to write *The City of God* in 413, three years after Alaric's invaders had ransacked Rome. Whatever his immediate purposes, it turned out to be a fruitful provocation. Augustine created a Christian political theology by turning Cicero inside out. At the end of *De republica*, Cicero placed the fantasy of Scipio's Dream, a few lyrical pages that purport to record the encounter of Scipio Africanus the Younger with the first Scipio Africanus in the heavens where his spirit now dwelled. The older Scipio gave an account of the afterlife very like that which Plato provides at the end of *Republic*, and rehearsed many of the ideas on which Stoics and Neoplatonists agreed—the vanity of earthly desire, the transitoriness of human glory, and the triviality of the life of the body, among them. The passage illuminates the tension that Augustine had to handle throughout *The City of God*, though he, like Macrobius, was interested in Scipio's Dream only as a source of reflection on such topics as the transmigration of souls. In *The City of God*, it is Scipio's account of the history of Rome and his account of a true *res publica* that Augustine criticizes. Scipio the Younger was the leading speaker in *De republica*; he sets out the standards for a true *res publica* and the conditions necessary if there is to be a true *populus*, a people whose common good is served by a republic practicing earthly justice. If there is no justice, there is no *res populi*, and therefore no *res republica*. The standards of justice are universal; they are given in natural law; and natural law is known to all mankind who consult their reason. The key ideas are justice and reason; the republic is founded on justice, and the requirements of justice are known to reason. Man is distinguished from the beasts by the possession of reason, and from other gregarious creatures by being able to found a community on the practice of justice rather than sociability alone.[15]

Augustine subverts these claims by accepting them. He does not deny that man possesses reason, but by the time he began to write *The City of God*, he had ceased to believe that reason was capable of motivating human beings to behave as they ought; we have only a very limited degree of free will, and in general, he says, reason merely assists us to choose one more or less sinful course over another. Nor does Augustine deny that Cicero's account of justice is an accurate account of the nature of justice:

a settled intention to give everyone his due is what justice is. What he denies is that *any* state on earth ever was, is now, or ever will be a true *res publica* in the Ciceronian sense, and therefore that any actual people can be a *populus* in the Ciceronian sense of a political community practicing real justice. *The City of God* makes two claims, one more difficult than the other. The simpler claim is that no pagan state practices Ciceronian justice, because no pagan state gives the one true God his due. By the same token, no pagan state can have a true common good, so no pagan state can be a true *res populi*. This seems an unfair and ad hoc argument, since justice between members of a political community hardly seems on all fours with justice toward God. Nonetheless, it is a useful part of a case against those who accused the Christians of bringing about the downfall of Rome by forbidding the worship of the old gods. Their complaint was that the Christian emperors who forbade the worship of the old gods had treated the old gods unjustly by depriving them of the worship that was their due; so the old gods had retaliated by withdrawing their protection from Rome. One of Augustine's best, and wholly effective, retorts was that the old gods had never kept their side of the bargain; they had never protected any state, however devotedly their adherents had kept up their cults. He lists the innumerable disasters that Rome suffered when most attached to the old cults; throughout *The City of God* he insists that good and bad fortune falls upon the just and the unjust alike.[16]

The more difficult claim is that it is not clear that even a Christian state can practice true justice, though it obviously clears the hurdle at which pagan states must, on this view, fall at once. It can give God his due by worshipping the one true God and no others. But since real justice is giving everyone what is really due to him or her, and the only being who knows what that is is God, true earthly justice is beyond us, or, at least, we cannot know whether we have achieved it. If justice is not the foundation of human affairs, what is? The reply is *love*, but love in a very difficult sense; it is tempting, though cowardly, to leave the word in Augustine's Latin, *libido*. Love, in Augustine's usage, embraces love in the ordinary sense of strong affection, and it certainly embraces sexual desire; but it also embraces the mathematician's desire to discover an elegant proof of a difficult theorem and the general's wish to win a victory. Nor is Augustine saying anything so banal as that we do what we do because we *want* to. That is true, but uninteresting. Love in Augustine's sense is an active force in the world, as we see when he claims that in any loving relationship between two people there are three agents in action: the lover, the beloved, and "love itself." *Libido,* or active desire, makes the world move, and especially the social and political world. It is important, too, that it is an active force that can take possession of us; the Rome whose misfortunes provoked the writing of *The City of God* was animated by a *libido dominandi*—a desire for conquest—that then dominated Rome herself. Just as sexual passion can become addictive, so can the desire for glory.

Augustine escaped the clutches of the Manichaean view that evil was an active force when he accepted Plotinus's view that evil is privation, a loss of good, and not a positive force. Understanding evil as estrangement from God and his grace was a Christian rendering of the Neoplatonists' claim that the world is the more evil and the more unreal the farther away it is from the One and the True. Nonetheless, Augustine did not empty the world of forces that would, if misdirected, get humanity into trouble. Love was the most important of them. Their existence did not undermine individual agency. Indeed, Augustine emphasized the individual will in ways the ancient world had not. For Augustine the problem of the will was central. He was a strong-willed person by anyone's standards; and he possessed an acute sense that he had when young deliberately willed to do wrong. This was a breach with the Platonic tradition every bit as great as identifying the impersonal "one" of Neoplatonism with the very personal God of the Old Testament. Socrates surprised his contemporaries by insisting that we do evil only in error and that it is a lack of knowledge of the good that explains human wickedness. Augustine articulated what is implicit in Saint Paul; we sin against the light because we have a will do evil.

Some commentators have been puzzled by one of the stories that Augustine retailed in his *Confessions*.[17] When he was a boy, he and some friends stole pears from a neighbor's orchard. It was a pointless theft. The pears were no good; he had no need of them; he and his companions gave them to the pigs. The misdemeanor was doubly symbolic. It was a willful crime, committed not to get the pears but out of sheer devilment;

he wanted to break the rules and committed a pointless theft to gratify that desire. Adam had no need of the apple; he said he was beguiled by Eve, but that was an evasion. He wanted to break the most important of the few rules that God had laid down for him. Why might we, or Adam, or Augustine want to behave like this? Two reasons occur to Augustine: first, simple pride. We are creatures who not only have wills but wish to make those wills effective. Why else does God afflict Job with all sorts of unmerited misfortune save to humble his pride? Not until Thomas Hobbes twelve centuries later does another thinker appear with the same eagle-eyed insight into the role of the will and the centrality of pride in our misfortunes.

The second reason is to keep company with others. Adam was not so much "beguiled" by Eve as ready to do whatever it took to remain in her good books. We cannot survive without company. Augustine wanted the approval of the local hoodlums and joined in their wickedness. He had a surer grasp of what motivates rioters and looters in the contemporary world than commentators looking for the deep causes of unrest. He is unflinching about the fact that he chose to do what he did and that he enjoyed it. This is non-Manichaean—it was *he*, not his body, who acted—and non-Platonic—it was not a mistake but willed misbehavior. Augustine's view of the freedom of the will is difficult, and its intricacies must be evaded here; but it is worth noting that true freedom of the will, that is, the ability to choose between good and evil at will, belonged to Adam, and only between the Creation and the Fall.[18] Fallen men can only choose between evils unless they receive divine grace, and that is the unearned gift of God. Nonetheless, we make choices, and it is we who make them.

Armed with these insights, Augustine can make short work of his opponents, though he allowed himself fourteen years, twenty-two books, and twelve hundred pages of text to do it. The fall of Rome is not to be laid at the door of the Christians; Rome did not fall because the Romans' neglect of the old gods led to the gods' rejection of Rome. Much of *The City of God* focuses on that issue, though the reader is hard put to it to remember the fact, when Augustine is pursuing Roman historians through the last recesses of their narratives of the glory of Rome. He ignores innumerable traditional issues. He nowhere bothers to discuss the merits of different forms of government; Polybian or Aristotelian classification does not interest him, and he is not interested in Aristotle's great concern, the prevention of stasis. One might have expected him to be, but Augustine's world was not the Athenian polis, with its restless citizenry, but the bureaucratic empire; the empire might come to grief at the hands of invading barbarians, but it would not succumb to anything resembling stasis. In any event, trying to build an eternal polity is futile. Peace is better than war, in general and with necessary exceptions; but the preservation of perpetual peace is beyond mortal men, and they must live with that fact. Indeed, they must look only for the consolation of knowing that, in the eternal scheme of things, it is of small account whether they perish this year or in a decade's time. This deflates Roman glory, and especially Roman *libertas*: "As far as this mortal life is concerned, which is spent and finished in a few days, what difference does it make under what rule a man lives who is soon to die, provided only that those who rule him do not compel him to what is impious and wicked?"[19] Rome may have done the peoples it subjugated no real harm by conquering them, but by the same token, the glory the Romans got did them no real good.

The Citizens of the City of God

We must, to make complete sense of all this, start with the most obvious question. What is the city of God and who are its citizens, and what is the earthly city and who are its citizens? Augustine's answer is that the citizens of the city of God are those whom God by his grace has admitted to the company of the saved. The earthly city is defined by exclusion as the company of all the rest. The "earthly city," as much as the "city of God," is a conceptual rather than a geographical entity; Old Testament saints are citizens of the heavenly city, and so are those yet unborn who will receive God's grace in future. The population of a physical earthly city contains both the elect and the nonelect, and earthly judgment cannot be sure which is which. Election is not something we can discern with mortal eyes, or something we can earn by good behavior. We are all sinners, and God might justly have condemned all of us to eternal punishment: Augustine uses an argument that the violently reactionary critic of the French Revolution Joseph de Maistre found invaluable fourteen centuries later. Voltaire had asked why God chose to destroy Lisbon in the earthquake of 1755; was there not dancing and misbehavior in Paris too? Maistre's reply is Augustine's. None of us is innocent of the sin of Adam. A godless pride is built into us at birth. We talk of childish innocence, but babies are not innocent. They are weak; the red-faced baby longing for its mother's breast and bawling fit to burst its lungs is powerless to wreak upon the world the violence it would like to wreak in its frustration.[20] The content of its desires is as bad as could be. When God saves some but allows many to suffer eternal punishment, it is not his sin but theirs that explains why they are punished. We should be grateful that he has spared some when he might in justice have punished all.

We mortal spectators here below cannot know who is a member of the city of God; not the least powerful of the implications is that political relationships cannot be based on distinguishing the saved and the elect. Augustine's insistence on the mixed nature of all human communities was a powerful argument in the local conflicts of his own day, but equally important in explaining the nature of Christian politics. In insisting that any ruler who provided the limited earthly goods that a state could provide was entitled to our obedience, Augustine provided the foundations of two famous arguments, both controversial. The first was the view of Aquinas that Christians must obey non-Christian rulers; the second was what became in seventeenth-century Europe the highly unpopular claim that a Christian commonwealth should be governed in the same way as any other commonwealth.[21] The local problems that provoked him were specific to his time and region. The great threat to the unity of the Catholic Church in Africa was posed by the so-called Donatists, named after a bishop of Carthage—Donatus the Great—who was their leader in the mid-fourth century. They were extreme rigorists, who wanted a church of the elect alone. Their standard of election was a person's conduct during the last of the persecutions. They denied that anyone who had succumbed to persecution was entitled to give the sacraments; and they insisted on rebaptizing members of their sect.

The Donatists were condemned many times by imperial edicts and church councils, became more extreme in the face of persecution, and by the end of the fourth century convinced themselves they were the only Christian church in all the world, and entitled to convert dissenters by force. They occupied twenty years of Augustine's time as bishop and were a sore trial to his spirit. They also made him more ready to employ the brute force of the state to bring heretics to obedience than when he first took office. They were not the only unamenable sect to plague Augustine; the Circumcellions—the name means simply "those who live in the neighboring villages"—were a still more violent offshoot of the Donatists. Their political interest is that they forced him to articulate clearly the view that it is the sacrament, not the minister, that is efficacious: what matters is the sacrament being administered and not the moral purity of the minister. This is not a directly political view, but it has clear political implications: if what matters is the law and its effects, we should not inquire into the character of political leaders but look to their impact on the lives of their subjects.

Augustine's doctrine of the mixed quality of all human communities— the Catholic Church included—meant that no earthly body could claim to be "the city of God on earth" and that although Christian asceticism was acceptable—he himself lived with a community of celibates from the moment he became a priest—it did nothing to lessen the contrast between the mixed earthly community and the city of the saved. A community of ascetics could not lay claim to be a community of the elect. This had large implications for the authority of the church vis-à-vis the state. Augustine had no doubt that it was the task of the church to warn rulers as well as their subjects when they were acting immorally; not to do so was to commit an injustice toward them, since admonition was their due.[22] In general, however, the church ought not to exercise earthly responsibilities. This did not mean that the functionaries of the church might not also have to perform secular administrative duties. Augustine knew that de facto the empire could not function unless bishops took responsibility for hearing civil cases in their dioceses, and since emperors had placed this burden upon them, they were obliged to discharge these duties to the extent consistent with the Christian faith. It meant that the church as an institution should attend primarily to its one unique function, caring for the souls of its members, although caring for the unfortunate and the destitute was a Christian duty, too.

Augustine had to steer a careful path. Christ told his followers to render unto Caesar the things that were Caesar's. They were to pay taxes and obey the civil authorities in everything not contrary to the direct injunctions of Christ; by the time of Augustine, the pacifism of the early church had been transcended, and it was agreed that if Christians were recruited to fight in the imperial armies, they must do so. Nonetheless, they were not to embroil themselves in politics. They were not to resist tyrants, nor were they to disobey their lawful rulers except under very extreme circumstances, and then only by passive disobedience. Only when they were given a command that in effect amounted to the requirement to deny Christ, might they refuse. Martyrdom occurred in all persecutions when those suspected of Christian attachments were required to sacrifice to the pagan Gods and eat the sacrificial meat, or required to swear allegiance to the cult of the emperor. Swearing allegiance to the emperor's cult was regarded by the civic authorities as the *least* demanding declaration of civic loyalty they could ask of a Roman subject, but it was a sticking point for both Jews and Christians. Augustine thought that if they were so required, they had to, if they had the strength, refuse and endure the consequences. On no account were they to engage in rebellion, incite tyrannicide, or disturb the earthly peace of the empire.[23]

One need only recall the way in which Cicero's writings are replete with praise for tyrannicides, including the murderers of the Gracchi, himself in the case of Catiline's followers, and subsequently the murderers of Julius Caesar, to see the gulf that has opened up between the classical and the Christian political universe. The reasons need no rehearsing, but vast as these differences are, we must not exaggerate their implications. Cicero's thinking is this-worldly, Augustine's other-worldly; Cicero's republic is worthy of respect, admiration, and loyalty, and its glory is a great good, but Augustine thinks all earthly states are the playgrounds of violent and self-deluded men, and earthly glory mere vanity. The temptation that we must resist is to conclude that Augustine has nothing good to say about earthly life and that the state is to be regarded with contempt.

Politics as a Limited Good

This is wrong. The world is God's creation. To despise it is blasphemous. Augustine did not follow classical philosophers in their wholesale contempt for the body. They elevated mind and, in so doing, deprecated body. Given his extraordinary intelligence, he had no need to do the first, and he was not tempted to do the second. He was certainly curious about the body. One of the things that has given rise to the belief that he was obsessed with sex is his recurrent discussion of the contrast between pre-Fall Adam, who would have had sexual intercourse with Eve for the sake of friendship and mutual affection, and would have had an erect penis when and only when he wanted one, and fallen man, who is driven by lust, has erections when he does not want them, and cannot have them when he wants them.[24] He was not in fact as concerned with sexual continence to anything like the extent to which he was concerned with deceit, malice, and plain brutality.

What the curious case of the male sexual organs demonstrates is the way in which *we*—that is, the fallen male we—cannot control what we very much want to control. The disunity of mind and body is a fact of deep significance. Nor did he confine these thoughts to the case of men. He made a point of arguing that the women who were raped by Alaric's Visigoths in the sack of Rome were not violated and not dishonored; there was all the difference in the world between being the victim of rape and the instigator of fornication. Even if some of them had found themselves sexually excited against their will, they were not to feel ashamed— this is one of the cases where the body acts of its own accord. As to the Roman heroine Lucretia, who committed suicide after being raped by Tarquin, Augustine claimed that she was doubly wrong—wrong to think herself dishonored by the rape and wrong to kill herself. Raped, she was an innocent victim of assault; in committing suicide, she had killed an innocent woman and was a real murderess. Augustine discussed Lucretia at what even he agreed was perhaps excessive length, but uses this, and many other examples where Roman historians and poets had praised a suicide, to argue that suicide was murder—not to be admired but deplored.[25]

The earthly kingdom exists to promote peace in this world. The goods of this world are as nothing to the ultimate good of union with God, but they are not to be despised. Peace on earth is as nothing to the peace we shall enjoy in the company of God, but peace is a very great good. We and the world we live in are God's creations. While we live here below, we must accommodate ourselves to its reality. One such reality is the impotence of religion to fend off earthly evil. The Christians were not responsible for the downfall of Rome, and Mars was not responsible for Rome's glory. Earthly success and failure have earthly causes. God's misfortunes rightly fall upon the just and the unjust alike, and to seek the proximate cause of disaster in local wickedness is an error. The larger claim, one to which Augustine recurs throughout *The City of God*, is that even the success of Rome was not something to glory in. States exist because we care for earthly things and require earthly arrangements to satisfy that desire. Property, to take the central worldly institution that the state protects, has a limited but real value. Without laws governing *meum et tuum*, there would be dissension and bloodshed, and starvation into the bargain. All the same, property has a relative value only, and its side effects are unattractive, including as they do greed and cupidity and opportunities for theft.[26] Without a state there could be no stable ownership, so the existence of political and legal arrangements of the minimal kind required to sustain the rule of law, and an economy adequate to keep us fed and sheltered, is desirable.

Such a regime cannot achieve *ultimate* justice; that is, it does not give to everyone what is really due to him or her, not least because that will not be known until the last judgment; but as institutions built on our love of earthly things and taking advantage of nothing more than our intelligence to coordinate our behavior in the interests of our long-run welfare rather than our short-run impulses, property and the legal institutions that maintain it are to be valued. If we may not kill ourselves, we ought not to neglect ourselves, either; so ordinary legal or conventional justice is to be valued and conscientiously pursued. Augustine makes life difficult for the reader because he moves back and forth between agreeing that "there was, of course, according to a more practicable definition, a commonwealth of a sort; and it was certainly better administered by the Romans of more ancient times than by those who have come after them,"[27] and reiterating his negative reply to the question "Whether there ever was a Roman commonwealth answering to the definitions proposed by Scipio in Cicero's dialogue."[28] The negative reply rests as always on the thought that no society can give a man his due if it takes him away from the worship of the one true God. A godless republic is no *res publica*. Since the only *res populi* that matters is the worship of the one true God, a polity devoted to the worship of demons has no *res populi*, and the multitude of whom it is composed is no true *populus*. Viewed in that light, the only true *populus* are the citizens of the city of God. Viewed more "practicably," earthly justice is self-evidently better than injustice.

Rome did not confine itself to the rational pursuit of earthly but not overrated interests; Rome conquered the world. Contrary to Polybius and Cicero, who thought the Roman Republic of the midsecond century BCE was the height of political success, Augustine almost invariably attacks the whole enterprise as driven by the *libido dominandi*, the lust for conquest. Like Plato, he thought imperial ambition was a self-destructive folly. If human beings had been rational, they would have created not empires but an enormous number of very small states—Augustine says *regna*, literally "kingdoms," but he means any set of political arrangements whatever. A multitude of tiny, harmless polities could have lived at peace among themselves and therefore at peace internally, just as a city contains innumerable households, none of which seeks to dominate the others, and all of which may be domestically at peace.[29] This was not the revival of Christian pacificism. Augustine freely admits that there are just wars and thinks it a grave sin not to fight them when we should. Nonetheless, it is a rather astonishing suggestion, even if one might think the example of the Greek city-states of antiquity suggests that large numbers of small states is not a reliable recipe for peaceful coexistence.

The State, Punishment, and Just War

The central feature of the state is that it wields coercive power. Private individuals can cajole and entreat; the state can issue orders and back up those orders by violence against the recalcitrant. Punishment serves two purposes. The threat of punishment gives bad people a motive to behave better. Their wills may only be amenable to earthly inducements, but against the attractions of misconduct we can set the dissuasion of earthly penalties and thereby promote peace. Since the Fall we have only limited free will, but Augustine does not underestimate the possibility that with appropriate aids we can avoid choosing the more obvious and antisocial evils. The ultimate cause of the existence of political societies is sin; absent the Fall, we might live in simple, egalitarian, communist communities with neither property, nor law, nor political authority. Our fallen nature needs regulation. Augustine's day-to-day conduct in his little celibate community certainly suggests that he thought that both reproof and encouragement could strengthen the wills of his fellows in the direction of good and away from evil, and that is what he argues in *The City of God*.[30] If threats fail, punishment may reform the criminal. Because Augustine hoped for the reformation of the criminal, he was hostile to the death penalty. He was unflinching about the brutality of the Roman state, but his understanding of the purpose of punishment made the death penalty simply wrong. The infliction of punishment is an educative process. Like the father chastising his son to get him into the good habits that will regulate his conduct without the need for further chastisement, the state that imposes successful punishment will train the criminal into better behavior. If the better behavior becomes habitual, there will be no need for further punishment. To kill a man deprives him of the possibility of repentance.[31]

Augustine's argument goes deeper than this, with regard both to the criminal and to the court and the executioner. The criminal is supposed to be brought to a state of repentance, but Augustine thinks it almost impossible for him to die in a good frame of mind. Given the barbarity of

Roman executions, that seems all too plausible. The argument is backed by other considerations. In Roman criminal procedure, accused persons were commonly "put to the question," which is to say tortured until they gave what were perceived by their interrogators as honest answers; and material witnesses could expect the same treatment. The privilege that a Roman citizen most valued was that a citizen was not tortured for his evidence. Augustine was passionate that nobody should be condemned unjustly. He thought the judge's task was hideous at the best of times. Since certainty was not to be had, the judge could never be sure that he had done (earthly) justice. Sentencing a man to flogging or execution for a crime he had not committed was something that Augustine shuddered at. The same reasoning applied to the criminal. An innocent man might endure torture without incriminating himself, only to die of the torture; or he might incriminate himself falsely to spare himself the pain of further torture. To kill an innocent man or to force an innocent man to perjure himself was an appalling evil. These evils lay squarely on the conscience of the judge, and Augustine is more appalled by the impact of sin on our souls than by the torments inflicted upon the body.

This is not the expression of a modern humanitarian impulse. The extent of modern humanitarianism is in any case debatable; we have more in common with Romans who enjoyed seeing criminals torn to pieces by wild beasts than we like to acknowledge. Augustine did not flinch from physical suffering; and hypocrisy was wholly foreign to him. He did not flinch from the *fact* of the hangman or the soldier or the civilian police. It no doubt took a peculiar temperament to earn a living by butchering one's fellow human beings, but it did not follow that the hangman was not God's instrument. In this vale of sorrows, he is. Nor should we, looking back from a safe distance, ignore the fact that corporal and capital punishments are almost inescapable in societies where the expense of housing and feeding prisoners would be intolerable, and where only the better-off would have had the resources to pay fines—as they frequently did. The violent poor would suffer violence at the hands of the state, as would poor robbers and housebreakers. Augustine's fear was not that they would suffer but that they would suffer for what they had not done.

Given such a view of punishment, it was possible to imagine the state acting like a stern father, compelling a reluctant offspring to toe the line. This view of punishment provides the premises for Augustine's account of just war, which has been immensely influential, even though it partly rests on an analogy between the state's right to punish its own members and its right to punish other states, an analogy that the modern world largely rejects. The most familiar parts of the case are very familiar indeed. Self-defense is always a legitimate ground for fighting, and nobody should hesitate to fight back when attacked; self-defense is always a valid casus belli. Nor need we wait until the enemy is literally at the gates before we resist; we may frustrate his preparations for attack as well. These claims became part of the standard account of just war doctrine in the later Middle Ages and are enshrined in modern doctrine, to the extent of featuring in the Charter of the United Nations. The less usual claim is that in a just war a state punishes the crimes of another state and its people. On the face of it, this seems to involve a notion of collective guilt otherwise foreign to Augustine and a willingness to see the innocent die that seems at odds with his condemnation of the death penalty. The state acts, so to speak, in the name of global justice—due precaution taken about the extent to which we can achieve here below anything properly called justice, and how far Augustine thought that there was a law of peoples that conferred such a right—or duty.

A just war is motivated by the intention to give to each what is his due, in this case the punishment due to an aggressor. The idea that a state should act to promote justice was not at odds with Roman ideas; it was at odds with what Augustine thought had in fact motivated Rome. There was an old Roman tradition of not going to war in the absence of a casus belli, a quasi-legal justification for an attack, which was in reality an equally old tradition of manufacturing situations to produce the necessary excuse. There is an obvious rhetorical awkwardness in Augustine's insisting on the inadequacy of earthly justice while defending what we cannot but call a "just war," much as there is an awkwardness when he emphasizes that there is no *real* justice here below at the same time that he insists that we must play our part in the institutions that administer "justice," such as the courts, police, and prisons. But Augustine is, after all, talking of both the city of God, the community of the saved that is here on earth only as a "pilgrim," as well as the earthly city, and he quite rightly reminds us that this world is not just as the heavenly city will be just and that our capacity to determine the deserts of states and individuals is limited.[32]

There is a further twist to Augustine's position. Unlike his predecessors such as Cicero and almost equally bleak successors such as Thomas Hobbes, Augustine believed that we are sinners. Cicero thought many Romans behaved badly, but he did not discuss this in terms of "sin." Hobbes thought we were provoked into harming one another in the absence of secure government and often behaved badly for reasons such as pride; but he expressly repudiated the idea of original sin. For Augustine original sin is the most important fact about us. Some are saved and some are not, but all are sinners. This puts a distinctive complexion on what would in the absence of the framework provided by the doctrine of original sin be a grim, pessimistic, this-worldly, and empirically wholly plausible outlook on political authority and political life. In the absence of government, with its attendant apparatus of law and law enforcement, we cannot help behaving badly because we are terrified of being robbed, assaulted, or murdered by other people; where there is no government and no law enforcement, we are rationally tempted to make a preemptive strike and attack them before they can attack us—the knowledge of which increases their fear of us and makes it more likely that they will attack us preemptively. That is Hobbes.

Absent original sin, this vicious circle is broken by the institution of government. We shall not be afraid of others if we know that they are afraid of the law; and they will not fear us when they know that we, too, are afraid of the law. We are a threat to one another because we fear one another; when that fear is removed, we can become peaceful and cooperative creatures. Augustine anticipates every step of this (Hobbesian) argument, but he cannot stop there. One could say that he pauses there when he admits that, "in a practicable sense," Rome at its best practiced (a sort of) earthly justice; but if he pauses, he does not stop there. If humanity was as coolly and self-controlledly rational as this argument suggests, our history would be infinitely less unhappy than it has been.

Our problem is that we suffer from what one might call surplus motivation toward theft and violence—namely, the wickedness that stems from original sin. The boy who stole pears out of devilment is a younger version of the men who rob their neighbors and invade other countries for loot and for glory. This is the sin that Augustine identifies as the sin that drove Adam to take the apple; the apple was neither here nor there. The self-will that led to its taking was. Augustine praises the state for quelling violence and robbery, but reminds us that the drive toward violence and robbery is still there—not cured, only counteracted.

For Augustine, then, the sense that the earthly city is the city of those driven by love of earthly things is pervasive; he had few reasons to explain at length which earthly cities are better than which others, and why, though it was clear that some were much better than others. It is obvious that peace and good order are good; obvious that chaos and war are bad. That almost exhausts the comparison. Relatively good earthly cities are not in the deepest sense just, but "well ordered." This is a powerful thought, and an elegant kidnapping of an idea usually more at home in the thinking of republicans. The "well-ordered" republic that Machiavelli and Rousseau longed for was an idealized version of the republic described by Cicero, and hankered after by the founders of the American Republic. In Augustine's discussion, mixed republics and well-founded states are at no particular advantage. Augustine thinks *any* state can be "well-ordered" so long as there is peace, agreements are kept, laws are observed, and affairs are predictable. Rousseau's claim that when an absolute monarchy achieves these things, we achieve the silence of the graveyard would have struck Augustine as romantic nonsense.

To the modern eye, one further disconcerting and interesting element in Augustine's accounts of just war, of punishment, and of the individual's relationship to the state is the insistence that the individual must leave politics to the powers that be. Augustine's grounds for insisting that we must not resist our rulers under (almost) any circumstances are interesting and, it must be said, dangerous. They are at odds with almost everything other writers have said on the subject. Hobbes insisted that we must obey our sovereign in anything that did not threaten our lives; in what did threaten our lives, we must do what we could to save ourselves. This is not a doctrine of *resistance*, as in Locke, let alone tyrannicide, as in Cicero. Locke allows us to resist the sovereign when he violates the compact that establishes his authority; Cicero think tyrants are criminals and should be killed. Hobbes held the wholly secular view that no state can survive if individuals are free to pick and choose which rules to obey, so we must obey our rulers unless our life is imperiled. Augustine anticipates the secular argument, but his conviction that it does not matter very much whether we die sooner or later means that he does not rely on the right of self-defense to uphold a "last-ditch" right to disobey our rulers. Augustine accepted the Pauline claim that the powers that be are ordained by God and that disobedience—save under the conditions spelled out earlier—is an affront to God.

Nonetheless, this is not a defense of the divine right of kings, and not a defense of theocracy—not an argument for giving priests political power. Augustine does not argue, as later writers did, that kings are the Lord's anointed and that their right to govern is *personal*; his argument is only that God has created rulers whose power is part of the providential order, and must be accepted as such. The bleakness of the argument is extreme. One can see how bleak it is by considering the famous tag in book 4 of *The City of God*: "if justice is absent, what is a state other than a large and successful band of robbers?" Augustine says that even robbers must observe some of the rules of justice in order to prosecute their schemes successfully; and robbers know as well as anyone else that robbery is wrong and unjust, since they themselves do not wish to be robbed. All this has led many commentators to draw the obvious inference that Augustine is following Cicero in arguing that what defines a true state is that it is based on justice. Since orderly coordination even for wicked purposes requires justice, how much more so an organization created for good purposes?

If Augustine had gone down that track, he would have been more plausible but less original and interesting than he was. Some states would have been nothing more than *magna latrocinia*—large and successful bands of robbers—and others would have been lawful regimes founded on justice. The Nazi regime would have been the former and Britain and the United States the latter. Augustine did not do the obvious thing. He quoted with pleasure the brave—or foolhardy—response of a captured pirate to Alexander the Great. Asked by the great conqueror what he meant by his piracy, he replied that he meant just the same as Alexander, and that he took it amiss that just because Alexander had many ships and he had only one, he was condemned as a pirate and Alexander was praised as a hero. Augustine's view seems rather to be that states are by nature *magna latrocinia*, but that under their protection the limited goods of this earthly life can be pursued.

In short, the authentic Augustinian note is that states are organizations built to allow the earthly passions of human beings to be satisfied without excessive disorder. These passions always tend toward disorder, and no amount of law will put an end to that. Punishment and the threat of punishment can bend men's wills in the right direction, even though it is only because we care so much for life, liberty, and property that we are amenable to threats of death, imprisonment, and fines. Generally speaking, states are indeed much the same as large bands of robbers; substantial states get into wars and are animated by the lust for domination. More sensible and less passionate creatures than we would have lived in innumerable small, self-centered, and self-satisfied states and would not have got into the fights we have. But just as cowardly bishops can administer the sacraments, and we are not to inquire into their characters but accept the sacraments at their hands, earthly rulers must be obeyed because they are rulers and not because they are good men. If we have benign and merciful rulers, we are lucky; if not, we cannot complain. The deficiency of this view is that it offers no defense against genocidal madmen such as Hitler and Stalin other than the reflection that they will in due course come to grief: little consolation to their victims.

If he does not encourage resistance when one wishes that he had, Augustine equally takes no advantage of the potential for toleration and religious liberty inherent in his own ideas. Consider the way in which his distaste for the death penalty owed so much to his wish that in struggles between the Catholic Church and its rivals—especially the Donatists in Africa—the losing party should come around to the opinion of the victors and should be brought back into the fold by love and by argument. At a personal level, he seems eventually to have become exasperated with the Donatists. Who would not have lost patience with people who resorted to violence and intimidation to make converts and reduce the ranks of the Catholics, and who denied the right of the secular authorities to regulate their affairs while constantly appealing to the imperial authorities for judgment in their favor and refusing to take condemnation for an answer? The Circumcellions were worse. It is not surprising that he urged the secular authorities to suppress them.

The personal element in Augustine's reactions is not important. More important is this: Augustine's account of the limited utility of the earthly city, taken in conjunction with everything he says about the mixed nature of all earthly associations, including the church, leads naturally and readily to the thought that the task of the state is to care for externals—to keep the peace, to regulate property, and to perform useful tasks such as providing lawcourts to settle disputes. Deep matters, questions of the meaning of life and the ultimate rewards of virtue, must be settled elsewhere. Coercion is the natural and proper instrument of the state, but force is not an argument. We can frighten people into behaving as we wish, but we cannot frighten them into an unforced belief in what we wish. Eventually, this was the soil that nourished the Protestant conception of toleration; the church is a voluntary organization for worship in common and the discussion of matters of faith, while the state is a coercive and nonvoluntary organization for the regulation of external matters.

Augustine would have found these conclusions almost unintelligible. He was heir to the pagans who feared that Christian hostility to the cults of the gods would bring disaster upon the Roman state. He drew the line at employing extreme measures of coercion, and especially at employing the death penalty because of its terminal quality. Nonetheless, although one might regard him as the very remote founder of Protestantism, he never contemplated the suggestion that religion was in any way "off-limits" to state control. This was hardly surprising. The modern idea of toleration was more than a thousand years away, and it made headway as much because of European exhaustion after the religious wars of the sixteenth and seventeenth centuries as because of the acceptance of a new principle. Roman emperors automatically protected religious institutions, and the church had now become the beneficiary rather than the victim of the policy.

The dangerous novelty was the extension of coercion from enforcing outward observance to the suppression of heresy; neither Socrates nor the victims of God's wrath in the Old Testament had been accused of heresy. One could be put to death for blasphemy, for outraging the gods, and for worshipping the wrong gods; but the concept of heresy was a distinctively Christian invention. The danger it posed was that it allowed Christians to persecute one another with a clear conscience. Augustine took it for granted that being coerced into receiving the truth was a benefit, not a burden; it was a view one might expect from a man who thought that corporal punishment might be administered lovingly and with the intention to bring the offender to his senses. Whether it was consistent with the sharp line he drew between body and soul when arguing that the women who had been raped by Alaric's soldiers remained unviolated, because accidents to the body did not impugn the integrity of the soul, is another matter. Whether, indeed, it was a plausible view, coming from the pen of the man who remembered that he had been more willing to receive a savage beating than to learn Greek, is also another matter. It became part of Christian orthodoxy. The acceptability of coerced orthodoxy to Christians relied almost entirely on Christ's injunction to "compel them to come in," and the Augustine who strained to read Christ's injunction to "turn the other cheek" in a metaphorical and spiritual sense, in order to permit Christians to serve in the military with a good conscience, now strained to read the *cogere intrare* of the parable of the reluctant wedding guests in the most literal sense to explain why earthly rulers might—indeed must—compel orthodoxy among their subjects. It was a dangerous legacy: not only did it place the Christian subject at the mercy of his ruler's ideas about what was and was not heresy; it made it inevitable that the church would claim to police the Christian ruler's orthodoxy, and inevitable that rulers would resist.

PART II

❦

THE CHRISTIAN
WORLD

Preface to Part II

GIVEN THE INFLUENCE OF Saint Augustine on subsequent Christian thinking, it may seem perverse to draw a line under classical political thinking with his death. Should we not rather begin a consideration of Christian political thinking with him? There is no conclusive response to this, but one fruitful way of looking at the history of political thinking runs as follows. Augustine's political world was that of the Roman Empire. The empire was undeniably in decline in the west, dismantled piecemeal by the incursions of innumerable "barbarian" warrior tribes. It was not yet in decline in the east, and under the sixth-century emperor Justinian it reconquered a good deal of the territory lost to the invaders: North Africa, Italy, Sicily, Spain, and Dalmatia. This was a short-lived triumph, however; Justinian was the last emperor whose first language was Latin rather than Greek, and after his death his territorial gains were soon lost. It was the western empire on which Augustine's gaze was fixed. His polemical target, as we saw, was Cicero's conception of a legitimate republic, and apart from his astute observation that the world might have been better-off without the imperial ambitions of Rome, with humanity living in a multitude of small kingdoms—*regna*—

which kept the peace and left each other alone, it was the Roman conception of politics that he criticized.

In the long-drawn-out aftermath of the dissolution of the western empire, the one unifying force in western Europe was Catholic Christianity. Politically, Europe was for several centuries a patchwork of kingdoms where authority rested with leaders whom the modern world would have called warlords. Ironically, the modern image of a state as an entity whose essence is unified authority, exercised through law and focused on one man or a group of men who embody that authority and wield it with the assistance of subordinate officials, was fostered by the church rather than by lay authorities. It was the papacy, rather than the barbarian kingdoms that inherited the territory of the empire, that inherited the imperial conception of a state. This was not merely a matter of the papacy's mimicking the outward trappings of imperial office, although it did so. It was rather that the church was the means by which Roman notions of a law-governed political community were transmitted to medieval Europe.

This is not to say that secular political development was unimportant. One reason behind the relative ease with which William the Conqueror secured his position after the invasion of Britain in 1066 was that there already existed a centralized state that was both militarily effective and capable of enforcing law and order, securing property and personal rights, and governing in a recognizably modern fashion. Certainly, kingship carried an obligation to lead one's soldiers into battle, but this was not a barbarian horde but a feudal levy. By this time, of course, the Merovingian and Carolingian kingdoms had come and gone; Charlemagne had been crowned emperor in 800, and the Ottonian empire, which is often thought of as the "real" beginning of the Holy Roman Empire, had come into existence with the coronation of Otto I as emperor in 962.

Political thinking in the eight centuries between Augustine and Aquinas is resistant to analysis. Thinkers saw society as a Christianized whole, and they did not view politics as a distinct activity with its own rules and purpose. Trying to allocate different modern ideas to their medieval sources is more like trying to unbake a cake than like unraveling a sweater into lengths of colored wool. Nonetheless, the difficulty is

not that the modern view of human nature is very different from that
of the early Middle Ages. It is easy to think that it must be, because it is
easy to think that if medieval political thinking was structured by religion, ours is defined by secularization, that the Middle Ages believed in
God and original sin and we do not. Or in the alternative, we think we
are obliged not to let our views about God and sin influence our views
about politics, public policy, and the structure of government, whereas
our medieval forebears could have made no sense of letting anything else
dictate their political views.

That is not the true line of cleavage; whether or not we believe in
original sin, everyone knows that the political arena tempts us to behave
exactly as original sin would prompt us to do: to engage in pointless
conflicts for the sheer pleasure of crushing opponents, to exploit our
fellow citizens for our own benefit, to ventilate malice and cruelty, and
to exhibit the *libido dominandi* that Augustine deplored. David Hume
was a religious skeptic and a central figure in the eighteenth-century
Enlightenment, but he insisted that it was "a just political maxim *that
every man must be supposed a knave.*"[1] Bertrand Russell, a committed atheist, claimed that nobody should run a school who didn't have a deep
conviction of the reality of original sin. He was not alluding to the
Fall; he meant that the desire to commit pointlessly unkind, unjust, and
treacherous acts is deeply ingrained in children and that teachers who do
not acknowledge this grim truth will have a hard time.[2] Sigmund Freud
shocked early twentieth-century readers by claiming that children were
racked with sexual desire and that an amorphous but all-consuming
need for sensual gratification was built into us at birth. Neither Russell
nor Freud shared Augustine's religious beliefs, but they shared his view
of human nature. Commentators often say that Augustine seems oddly
"modern," but he was simply unblinkered. Politics is as constrained by
dealing with fallen human nature as it ever was, and perhaps even more
so, given the rewards offered by the modern world to those who behave
badly and get away with it.

More alien is Augustine's belief that human nature properly speaking—the nature with which God endowed man at the creation—existed
only in the period between Adam's creation and his transgression. What

we ordinarily refer to as human nature without qualification is depraved, postlapsarian human nature. Fallen human nature is what politics has to deal with. The concept of a fall makes for a devaluation of earthly politics beyond anything that an acceptance that we often behave badly will do. The effect was that even when Christianity had become the established religion of the Roman Empire and Christians held office in the Roman administration, there was an arm's-length quality about the Christian insistence on the moral obligation to do such jobs and to do them conscientiously.

Christians take politics seriously as a realm in which imperfect but constructive motives check sinful and destructive motives, but as against the classical political philosophers and historians, Christianity devalues politics; if this life is merely a preface to our life elsewhere, politics is less important than religion, and the greatest service the state can render us is to help us live as good Christians. Modern liberalism may be contrasted with classical patriotism in the same way; if the ultimate values are those of the private realm of culture and personal relationships, the political realm is valuable only as a shelter for these private goods. The Christian devaluation of politics was never complete, however; after Aquinas had absorbed Aristotle's *Politics*, it was again possible to talk of the polity as the highest form of (secular) human association. Nonetheless, the Augustinian insistence that we are *peregrini*, pilgrims passing through the earthly life, undermines Aristotle's view that the political life is the life of the highest goodness. The earthly city is at best a pale reflection of the heavenly city to which the Christian's deepest allegiance is owed; when Augustine agrees that the Roman Republic admired by Polybius and Cicero exhibited a "certain goodness," he supposes that God intended it to show us how we should feel toward the true City of God.[3] In the early church the conviction that the Christian was a citizen of another city verged on antinomianism—the idea that Christians were not bound by the laws of the local state, because Christ had come to repeal the law—or anarchism—the idea that Christians should live in a Christian community and take no heed of the political world around them. During the Reformation the urge to recover the purity of the early church produced similar effects.

By then, however, the recovery of most of the literature and philosophy of the ancient world that we possess had occurred, the medieval revival of the classical city-state in the Italian republics had reached its apogee and was in decline, and the modern, bureaucratically managed monarchical state was emerging in northern Europe, delayed by religious conflict in the territories of the Holy Roman Empire, delayed in France by the aftermath of the Hundred Years' War and religious conflict, and in Britain by the dynastic conflict of the Wars of the Roses. But the direction of travel was clear enough. Whether the new monarchical regimes were to be more or less absolutist, whether they were to be Catholic or Protestant, only the balance of forces on the ground would decide. That this was the coming state form and all else peripheral was clear.

CHAPTER 6

Between Augustine and Aquinas

Did Medieval Political Theory Exist?

THIS CHAPTER IS ONE of four whose theme is the impact of religion, and of Christianity in particular, on ideas about politics. Unlike its immediate neighbors, it focuses less on individual thinkers than on issues that preoccupied secular and religious authorities: the authority of rulers and the obligations of subjects; the medieval view of law, property, and slavery; and relations between church and state. It ends with a short coda on what many commentators have seen as the rebirth of distinctively *political* thinking with John of Salibury's *Policraticus*, published in 1159. To talk of the rebirth of *political* thinking implies some doubt whether there was such a thing as medieval political thought. Some writers have indeed denied that there was, and every commentator agrees that what there was was unlike what went before and came after. This is not a terminological issue. The Greeks, like the Romans until the death of the republic, argued about the politics of city-states—*poleis* in the strict sense. Their citizens did not speak the modern language of individual human rights, but they had a strong sense of their entitlement to play a role in the political life of their cities and states, and to be the authors of the laws they lived under. There was room for argument about the virtues of monarchy, aristocracy, and democracy and the dangers of tyranny, oligarchy, and mob rule; indeed, argument was inescapable.

The replacement of the Roman Republic by the Roman Empire after the principate of Caesar Augustus, established in 27 BCE, left one political model in command of the field, intellectually or doctrinally speaking, namely monarchy. Moreover, the empire, like its Hellenistic predecessor monarchies, adopted the Persian habit of worshipping its rulers as quasi-divinities. From the fourth century onward, the Christian emperors who followed Constantine could not have themselves deified as their pagan predecessors did, but they did everything short of it. Far from the western church checking the practice, the papacy copied the thrones, tiaras, and robes of the Roman Empire, and in the course of time, the cardinals, who were originally the assistants of the pope in matters of liturgy and care of the poor, came to form a College of Cardinals that replicated the Roman Senate. In the eastern empire, secular and spiritual authority were united in the emperor, whose right to appoint the patriarch of Constantinople was unquestioned; in the west, there was no settled view of the proper mode of appointment of the pope until 1059, when a reforming papacy insisted that election by the College of Cardinals was the only legitimate route. The existence of the one transnational institution of the papacy alongside a patchwork quilt of kingdoms and smaller entities raised a question with no classical antecedents—the relationship of secular and spiritual power. Were kings to appoint bishops or popes to appoint kings, or at least to bless their appointment?

For intellectual resources, thinkers still drew on classical philosophy, even if at second hand and, until the twelfth century, with no direct knowledge of the political writings of Plato and Aristotle. One consequence is that the political institutions of modern western Europe and the countries of European settlement have their institutional roots in the European Middle Ages, but we think about them in ways borrowed from the Greeks and Romans. The roots of modern representative government lie in medieval systems of legal administration and military recruitment—often described as feudalism and with a prehistory in older forms of tribal organization—but we talk about them in the language of Greek democracy and Roman republicanism. Representative

government as we know it began in the Middle Ages with the representation of places and groups, and we still elect legislatures from geographical constituencies; but we now think of representation in terms of
individual citizenship. British parliamentary government evolved from a
monarchical "king and council" system, while the United States inserted
the English system of representation into a framework derived from a
very different tradition—a republic based on Ciceronian ideals and perhaps inspired in part by the example of the Lykian League. The paradox
is only apparent: classical ideas illuminate medieval institutions, no matter that the ideas originated elsewhere. The Polybian view of mixed government aligns easily with the medieval idea that a king should rule with
the advice of an aristocratic council and seek consent for taxation from
a body representing the "commons." The Greeks operated representative
institutions in the leagues for mutual defense they created in the fourth
and third centuries, and the Lykian League did so for much longer. If
the occasion had arisen, a fourth-century Athenian or a second-century
Roman could have explained the Greek or Roman concept of citizenship
to an Anglo-Saxon of the tenth century CE.

Medieval Conceptions of Authority

Some writers on medieval political ideas have made much of the distinction between *ascending* and *descending* theories of authority.[1] The ascending
view sees political authority as something with which a ruler is invested
by individuals, or groups, or "the people" in their entirety, while the
descending view sees authority as inherent in the ruler, or as something with which he is endowed by a superior, as it might be God. The
descending view seems more suited to monarchy and to a world in which
God is seen as the King of Kings. Yet the feudal institutions of early
medieval Europe combined ascending and descending conceptions in the
contractual relationship between lord and liege. Republican institutions
provide the paradigm case of an ascending model of authorization, but
even the most extensive assertion of absolute authority could in principle
derive that authority from a (once and for all) grant of authority from

the people, and the emperor Justinian did it in fact in the early sixth century. There is no paradox in imagining a situation in which the citizenry grants absolute authority to a leader for shorter or longer periods, although it raises difficult questions about the revocability of the grant.

Between the deposition in 476 of the last emperor of the western Roman Empire, the sixteen-year-old Romulus Augustus, and the end of World War II, some form of one-man rule was the most common form of government in Europe, government by kings, princes, dukes, counts, bishops, and popes. There were others. The city-states of Italy and the Adriatic were republics that Cicero would have recognized. None practiced Athenian democracy, though some came close; most were ruled by aristocratic families who saw their right to govern as an inheritance rather than a conditional gift from the people, and many existed on sufferance from royal or papal overlords. Most political units were small but in 800 Pope Leo III crowned Charlemagne, who had been king of the Franks since 768, as emperor of the Romans. This first iteration of the Holy Roman Empire was short-lived; in 962 the German Otto became emperor, and the continuous history of an institution mocked by Voltaire as "neither Holy nor Roman nor an Empire" began. Its basis was Germany, but the emperor's status was elective, and the geographical Germany contained a multitude of diverse political entities, ranging from prince-bishoprics to kingdoms to free cities, that were finally swept away only in the nineteenth century when Germany was forcibly unified by Prussia.

Subordinate institutions, such as universities, guilds, and communes all over Europe, practiced various forms of self-government from around the millennium onward; these institutions were not political oddities, but the strength of the descending view of authority is suggested by the way their rights of self-government were so often rationalized as gifts or concessions from a superior authority. Marsilius of Padua provided a clear formulation of the doctrine that rulers rule by the consent of their subjects only in the fourteenth century, and even he argued that what the people do is choose a wise and worthy single man to rule them. The descending theory of government, in which authority comes from God and descends to popes and kings, and thence to their dependants, and so on downward, suited medieval rulers and the Christian understanding of the world. The Christian worldview rested on a hierarchical and hierocratic conception of authority that transcended the merely political: all authority came from God and was divinely ordained. Christ was a King like no other, but he was King, not chairman for a day of a governing committee on the Athenian model.[2]

When Diocletian became the first emperor from east of the Adriatic, in 284, he established a non-Christian cult of the emperor and backed it up by persecuting his Christian subjects. That kind of deification of the emperor was impossible once Constantine converted to Christianity, and established Christianity as the imperial religion in 324; nonetheless, Constantine and his successors went to all lengths short of reestablishing the cult of the emperor. These eventually included the use of elaborate stage machinery in the imperial palace in Constantinople to heighten the impression that visitors were entering the presence of a more than merely human being. He was emperor *Dei gratia*—by the grace of God. The impact of the Byzantine Empire on the west was limited, even though the empire based on Constantinople called itself *Rhum* and thought of itself as the (only) Roman Empire. Until around 1050 there was a faint prospect that the Byzantines might invade Italy, or rather, the *rest* of Italy, since Byzantium had held Sicily until displaced by Arab conquest in the eighth to tenth centuries, and still held enclaves in the south. Justinian had reconquered Italy from the Goths in the sixth century, and it was not wholly impossible that his successors might do so again. But much of Italy had fallen to Lombard invasion within a few years of Justinian's death, and the two Roman empires drifted farther apart. The Byzantine Empire spoke Greek; and the lingua franca of the west was Latin. New Rome was Greek, and increasingly alien.

After the coronation of Charlemagne as Roman emperor on Christmas Day, 800, western Europe claimed the inheritance of Rome. As the Byzantine Empire was slowly dismembered by Slav and Muslim enemies, its claim to be the inheritor of the universal empire of Rome became weaker, and its influence was further diminished because liturgically and doctrinally, the eastern church became increasingly unlike the western Catholic Church. Doctrinal differences were sometimes greater, sometimes lesser: western Christianity was emphatically Trinitarian, for instance, while Greek Christianity did not regard the Holy Spirit as a third "person." The two churches' reactions to the main issues of church politics were very different, too: the location of final authority in church and state, the duties of subjects and rulers, the allocation of tasks between secular and spiritual authorities. The final breach between the Roman Catholic and the Greek Orthodox churches occurred only in 1054, but earlier rifts over the veneration of statues and images of saints and the authority, if any, of pope over patriarch and vice versa presaged the breach, unhealed to this day, even though the excommunications and anathemata of 1054 have been rescinded.

Politically, the eastern emperor's appointment of the patriarch of Constantinople exemplified what the papacy wished to avoid. There was never any doubt that the Byzantine emperor held supreme authority; the patriarch of Constantinople was his appointee. In the west there were periods when the pope was *in fact* installed and removed by German kings and later by French ones, but these were aberrations; royal power was exercised by bullying, not by fiat. Indeed, in the fourteenth century the French monarchy took bullying to novel lengths by removing the papal court to Avignon, where it could better be kept under supervision. The papacy's constant aim was to preserve its freedom of political action, and it was helped by the fact that western kingdoms were numerous, generally small, and their rulers always poorer than the papacy. The Byzantine unification of all authority in one pair of hands was neither attractive nor feasible. Nor did the patriarch of Constantinople possess the authority over all Orthodox churches that the pope claimed over all Catholic churches. From a Roman perspective, he was too much the servant of his emperor and too little the master of his own church.

Passive Obedience and Political Obligation: Who Judges?

The Christian view of political authority rests on Saint Paul's declaration in Romans that the powers that be are ordained of God. They are to be obeyed for conscience's sake and for fear of hell fire. Not all questions are answered by that peremptory injunction. One that is not is the relationship between God's general government of the universe and any given monarch's title to rule. For Augustine government was necessitated by mankind's fallen nature; governments discipline the earthly desires of mankind by taking advantage of those desires to threaten earthly penalties and promise earthly rewards. Local variations of form or personnel were unimportant when set against the larger issue: classical philosophy saw self-sufficiency as the great good, and the polis as the most perfect institution because the most self-sufficient; Christians knew that man could never be self-sufficient on earth and would find true peace and justice only in God's kingdom. Here we must simply obey the powers that be.[3] How a given ruler came to be in charge was neither here nor there. This might satisfy the provincial subjects of the Roman Empire; it was not always a satisfactory answer for the more powerful subjects of the new kings and princely rulers of western Europe. Any one of them might think he had a better title to the throne than whoever happened to occupy it, and take up arms to vindicate his claim.

The powers that be are ordained of God; and we must obey our rulers for conscience's sake as well as from fear of punishment. Damnation is the lot of the disobedient. Kings are God's vice-regents, and the office of kingship is divinely instituted. Even if a given king is a pagan or a heretic, obedience is due. That position mirrored in the political sphere Augustine's insistence that in religious practice we respect the office and the sacrament, not the person of the officeholder.[4] It did not answer the question whether an incumbent ruler ruled by right. Some kings were tyrants; others attained their thrones by murdering their predecessors; Byzantine emperors routinely murdered their relatives upon accession. The office was divinely instituted, but this did not answer the question how far obedience to the present occupant of any particular throne was due. There was surely some point at which we should disobey. The conventional view down to the sixteenth century was that if a ruler required his subjects to repudiate Christ, they did not have to comply; short of that, they had to obey. The obligation not to comply implied no positive right to overthrow one's lawful rulers; the counterpart to passive obedience was passive disobedience. How much readiness to court martyrdom this required was disputed even after the persecutions under the Roman Empire had stopped. Rigorists held that a readiness to embrace martyrdom was obligatory for all Christians; their opponents held that it could not be. God would consider what was in our hearts rather than what was on our lips; we could repudiate Christ in speech, but keep our allegiance to him in our hearts. Augustine was anxious to distinguish martyrdom from the pagan suicides that he deplored.[5] Roman authorities indeed appear to have thought their Christian subjects were much too ready to get themselves martyred.[6]

If a direct assault on Christianity destroys the obligation to obey, but does not license rebellion, there is the issue of our duty to kings who do not attack the true faith. It was not obvious whether God institutes all of them or only those that gain their thrones by a legitimate route; or where a lawful pedigree is not at issue, whether God institutes only those who govern for good ends and not for their own or their henchmen's advantage. If the important question is whether a ruler does what rulers exist to do, the tyrant who governs lawlessly, murders his people, seduces their wives, and steals their property seems to be so far from serving the purposes of government that we might properly conclude that he has forfeited God's commission.[7] This raises the famously difficult question of who is to judge that a ruler lacks God's warrant, and who has the power to absolve subjects from their obedience to their rulers. In due course, popes claimed that they could release the subjects of a king from their allegiance on grounds of heresy or moral turpitude, and that if they excommunicated a king, his subjects' duty of obedience was at an end. The English king John discovered how powerful a papal interdict could be in the early thirteenth century; others discovered they could safely defy the pope. After the sixteenth-century Reformation, the English church became Protestant; in 1570 the pope declared Queen Elizabeth deposed for heresy. It did no harm to the queen. Nonetheless, it stiffened the English dislike for the Catholic Church's interference in politics, and following the revolution of 1688–89 the coronation oath of an English monarch required her or him to denounce as "heretical and impious" the "damnable doctrine" that a pope can depose a monarch for heresy.[8]

The extraconstitutional defense against tyrants is tyrannicide: political murder. The classical Roman view that tyrannicide is the act of a virtuous man was unattractive to anyone who believed in passive obedience. In any case, tyrannicide does not answer the question whether we may resist our ruler's commands in particular cases without denying the authority of the office and, perhaps, without denying our ruler's legitimacy. We might think a king had no right to command his subjects to subscribe to any particular religious faith, and they might disobey his orders *in that sphere* as best they could, without thinking they were entitled to kill him as a tyrant, or entitled to disobey him except in the sphere in which he had exceeded his authority. If the federal government commanded us to attend Episcopalian churches on Sundays, we would be entitled to take no notice, irrespective of the command's unconstitutional status; but as to everything from paying taxes to observing traffic regulations, we should surely continue to obey meticulously. The conspirators plotting to kill Hitler in 1944 were no less obliged to obey the ordinary law of the land because they had determined to kill the head of state. A nontyrant may act ultra vires in some area without being tyrannical more generally; and we should cooperate with bad regimes to the extent that we thereby serve good ends. Nor does the defense of tyrannicide tell us whether any earthly tribunal can say with authority when a king has forfeited his right to rule. The one thing that seemed incontestable to most medieval writers was that private individuals were not to make that judgment for themselves; Locke's insistence in the late seventeenth century that they had no choice but to do so was a real breach with that tradition.[9]

"Who judges?" gave rise to enduring controversies. If a king is answerable to a lay body, we need to decide who constitutes it; and what happens when its views and his are at odds, as they surely will be. The possibility of such a body was a plausible inference from Roman history: consuls could act only with the assent of the Senate and indeed of each other. Later examples abounded. Germanic tribes elected their military leaders and deposed them for incompetence; those who shared in their commander's leadership in war were entitled to judge his military competence, and perhaps other aspects of his leadership. Once the feudal system of land tenure was established, the idea that the authority of rulers existed on terms and by consent took root. A tenant swore allegiance and owed military service in return for the secure occupancy of his land and impartial justice from his lord. At the apex of this hierarchy was the king; his actions could perhaps be judged by the leading figures of a feudal kingdom. If he refused to accept their judgment, it was not obvious how to enforce their views without civil war. Maybe the king's most eminent feudal tenants—such as the English "barons" who extracted Magna Carta from King John in 1215—could in the last resort declare the king deposed and his subjects freed from their allegiance. Everyone flinched from that conclusion: it came too close to inciting rebellion and letting anarchy loose on the world. Nonetheless, by the end of the fourteenth century, the idea that not only a king but the pope also could be judged by those with whose advice and consent he governed was defended by thinkers who wanted the pope to be answerable to a council of the church. Answerability to a body with a Roman precursor was not an idea applicable only to one institution.

Popes and Kings

Feudal aristocrats were not the only candidates for the task of judging royal legitimacy; if secular rulers might be deposed for wickedness, the church surely had a role. The gospels were read to imply that Christ had given to Saint Peter the power to bind and loose; whatsoever he bound on earth would be bound in heaven, and whatsoever he loosed on earth would be loosed in heaven.[10] That suggested that decisions on the moral fitness, if not the practical competence, of kings and other lay authorities are for the church to make. Augustine tasked bishops with reproving sovereigns but not with removing them from office; discussing Saint Ambrose's famous insistence that the emperor Theodosius confess and repent before he entered Ambrose's basilica in Milan, he emphasizes Theodosius's goodness of heart rather than Ambrose's authority.[11] It is easy to press the argument to dangerous extremes. If anyone knows the terms on which God institutes the powers that be, and the conditions under which obedience is suspended, it should surely be senior figures in the church. Implicitly, this gave the pope authority to depose kings *ratione peccati*—for reasons of their sinfulness—and popes in due course claimed that authority. A danger of doing so from their point of view was that the thought that *all* authority comes from God can cut the other way. Christ was both king and priest; kings were anointed during their coronations to symbolize the divine origin of their authority. If kings are ordained of God, this suggests that kings may possess authority over, or within, the church. If popes may depose kings, *ratione peccati*, it opens the way to kings' deposing popes for breaches of canon law or mismanagement of the church. If kings and popes are thought to exercise a shared authority over both secular and ecclesiastical institutions, there is room for conflict over the source and extent of the bishops' authority over their clergy and the pope's over his bishops. A diocese is a geographical entity, and like many governments today, rulers regarded the earthly institution of the church as being under their authority. They might not rule on doctrine, though they frequently did, but the church as a property-owning institution was another matter.

The possibility of contriving a constitutional mechanism whereby individuals could be deposed, by peaceful and lawful means, was ignored for several centuries, and is ignored today in much of the world where rulers hang on to their positions by brute force and bribery and are forced out only at gunpoint. Many popes and kings were wicked or incompetent or both, and many kings and a few popes were removed from office by fair means or foul—but rarely after due process and because they had forfeited their authority for constitutionally enshrined reasons. Where a constitutional case was made against an individual, it was commonly by impugning his *acquisition* of the office, not by impugning his *performance*, save to the extent that the latter shed light on the former. Nor is it surprising that the papacy presented quite unusual difficulties in that regard. The pope presented an image of absolute and unconstrained authority that seemed to rule out a constitutional process of deposition; it even appeared to rule out resignation. The theory of papal authority was that each pope received his authority directly from Christ; he was the heir of Saint Peter, not of his predecessor as pope. Each pope was absolute. No pope could bind his successor, and concessions made by one pope could not bind another. At election, each pope acquired the *plenitudo potestatis* of

Saint Peter, the power to bind and loose that Christ had conferred. The secular nobility, as distinct from the College of Cardinals, rejected the idea that concessions made by a king did not bind his heirs. They had an interest in constitutional rather than absolute monarchy. Cardinals hoped themselves to become pope and had different incentives.

Natural Law and Conventional Law

Medieval legal history is a vast and fascinating subject not to be entered on lightly, and here almost not at all. The evolution of law out of tribal custom and the edicts of Germanic kings, the discovery of the work of Justinian in the eleventh century, the establishment of institutions to train canon and civil lawyers that began in Bologna in the eleventh century, must all be ignored. The one question we cannot evade is the impact of Christian ideas on arguments about law and its authority. Whatever else the God of the Bible is, he is certainly a lawgiver, but the doctrine of the Fall poses an obvious problem for our relation to all forms of law, divine, natural, or conventional. It is not clear that fallen man can know what the law is; if he can, it is not clear that he will obey it rather than look for ways to avoid its requirements. Throughout the Christian era, the problem of reconciling earthly law and the law given by Christ has been exacerbated by the fact that Christ is reported both as urging punctilious obedience to "Caesar" and as holding seemingly antinomian views.[12] The easiest way to understand the medieval Christian view of law is through the problems posed by two central social and legal institutions—slavery and property. Christian thinkers inherited the classical question whether natural law lay behind conventional, local law, but understood that question both in classical terms, as the relation of the law of reason to local law, and in Christian terms, as the relation between divine commandment and local law. Plato and Aristotle had said that there was a natural law known to reason, antecedent to written law, and binding on all human beings. "Some say there is one justice, as fire burns here and in Persia," wrote Aristotle, and agreed.[13] Custom relates to natural law in complicated ways. Different marriage customs can fulfill similar tasks, but the welfare of children and the preservation of family property are morally desirable however achieved. Different customs can meet the universal demands of natural law. Not everyone who held that view shared the same conception of natural law, either in antiquity or later. Roman commentaries start with assertions of the natural equality of all mankind that Plato and Aristotle would have rejected, but that Stoics and Christians accepted.

The authority of local law poses problems with which we are still familiar. Is the law of a particular society law because it is the word of a local ruler, because it is local custom, or because it accords with natural law? When General Sir Charles Napier in the nineteenth century tried to prohibit the practice of suttee, or widow burning, in India, he was met with the reply that local custom demanded it; he responded by pointing out that British custom demanded the hanging of those who murdered women.[14] Augustine would doubtless have thought widows who willingly immolated themselves—if they did—were guilty of murder, too. The inherited tradition pointed medieval thinkers in the same directions as modern legal theory: on one view law is the word of a sovereign lawgiver, and on the other law follows the dictates of reason for the welfare of mankind. Justinian's *Corpus juris civilis* embodied the first view. His conception of authority, both his own and that of the law, was squarely "descending." He was the heir of Hellenistic conceptions of kingship: he was an autocrat—*autokrator* and *kosmokrator*, sole ruler of the world. Justinian's compilation described law as the reflection of the ruler's will; the validity of law was a matter of its pedigree in the will of the ruler. *Dicet rex et fiat lex*; when the king speaks, he makes law. That is the view that finds the lawfulness of law in the dictates of a sovereign legislator; and it is the view that most people today accept, with the necessary qualifications made for legal systems in which a written constitution constrains the legislature. The sovereign legislator may be a many-person sovereign legislature, but the thought that law gains its authority from the word of a person or body with authority to legislate is compelling.

However, the *Corpus* was a compilation based on the work of older authorities, and those authorities belonged to a different tradition. They were commentators from the second and third centuries. Although the

republic was long dead, they recorded what they believed to be the traditional Roman view of law. Like Cicero, they thought that behind local
law lay a law of nature (*lex naturae*) and a law of peoples (jus gentium)
that set a standard to which law should conform. Cicero complained of
the inscrutability and indeterminacy of the law that Roman officials had
to apply; but its indeterminacy reflected an openness to such standards,
and it gave judicial officials leeway in providing equitable relief where
there was no other way of achieving justice. If those who were subject to
the law were to have a moral as well as a legal obligation to obey it, the
law had to meet appropriate moral standards. The difference between
lex naturae and the jus gentium was not always made consistently, but the
distinction is substantially that between a law intelligible to all rational
creatures—the answer to the question "What rules would rational creatures agree to abide by for the sake of security, justice, and the better
pursuit of the common good?"—and the common law of the society of
nations, the answer to the question "What common principles regulate
human societies?" The *ius civile* was the law of one particular society,
Rome; it was the law that the *populus Romanus* had given to itself, and the
inhabitants of western Christendom in due course came to see themselves as after a fashion a new *populus Romanus*, employing the *ius civile* to
regulate their affairs.

The answer to the second question is not a flatly empirical "some
societies do this and some societies do that." It sifts diverse practice
in search of underlying rational principles, as does common law within
a single society. The law of nature would dictate that there must be
some rules governing the acquisition, use, and disposal of useful material
things—laws of property. Property rights are thus mandated by the law
of nature. The common practice of almost all societies acknowledges
private property, recognizes acquisition by labor and by purchase, and
makes specified members of an owner's family the heirs to his property
ahead of others. These would be the dictates of the jus gentium. The
closeness of fit of the laws of nature and the common law of peoples is
not always so complete. On the legitimacy of slavery, the law of nature,
understood as the Stoics understood it, declared that all men were equal
and that nobody is naturally a slave. However, slavery is licit as part of

the jus gentium; the law of peoples is law for people living in a state other than golden age innocence. The most detailed features of the jus gentium were those that nations adopted in their dealings with each other, such as the treatment of heralds and the return of prisoners of war, so that the jus gentium had features of an unwritten international law. This, too, would imply that slavery is part of the jus gentium, and not of the *lex naturae*, because so many accounts of slavery root it in the capture of prisoners in a just war.

What came down to medieval Europe was untidy, but philosophically provocative. Some commentators became interested in the question whether *all* creatures, irrational and rational, were governed by natural law. Aristotle had said that in a limited way they were; nonhuman animals followed instinctively the "laws" that led them to flourish in the way appointed for creatures of their kind. Since they did not understand the law they were following, they could not be said to be virtuous, but they did not break the law as humans did. A skeptic might think that the implication of Aristotle is that Adam's prelapsarian goodness was merely animal innocence. The more common view was that only creatures capable of recognizing the dictates of reason could follow natural law. On that view, the law of nature applies to rational creatures alone, thus only to human beings, since they alone can understand the law and follow or fail to follow it of their own volition. The Roman commentators whom Justinian's compilers exploited for the raw materials of his *Corpus juris civilis* were not of one mind. The most famous was the early third-century jurist and imperial adviser Ulpian; he had held that all creatures followed natural law, while human beings followed the jus gentium, the law of peoples. But the jus gentium so understood embraced much of what other writers described as natural law.

The Origins and Justification of Private Property

The earliest Christian communities expected an imminent Second Coming. They appear to have practiced a simple form of communism in which members put what they had into a common pool and took what they needed from it. If the Second Coming was indeed imminent, there was little room for a discussion of the nature of property. Once there were churches and monasteries, which received gifts and owned land and buildings, familiar questions about the nature of ownership needed to be answered. By the turn of the millennium, the papacy owned a great deal of property and was a powerful political institution. It was the most legally sophisticated institution in western Europe, and its administrative needs were a powerful force behind the revival of legal theorizing. The need for a secular theory of law is obvious. Whatever label such a theory wears is less important than that it should answer the questions that appeals to the laws of nature and the jus gentium answered. One of the most important was the nature of property and the justification of private ownership. To the modern eye, slavery, that is, property in human beings, is a particularly difficult issue, but slavery created less difficulty in early medieval thinking than private property generally. Before the Fall, slavery was impossible; at the other end of the historical process, in God's kingdom, there is neither Jew nor Gentile, slave nor free. In this vale of tears, slavery is one more unfortunate consequence of the Fall; the early churches employed slaves to till their fields. Monastic communities were forbidden to do so not because slavery was wrong but because labor was an essential part of monastic life. Little more was said than that slaves should obey their masters and masters should treat their slaves with kindness. Nor did criminal law pose the intellectual and political difficulties of civil law. It was debatable whether Christians should wield the sword of the executioner, and a Christian judge might wonder how sure he could be that he was not punishing the innocent. About the need for and the nature of the criminal law, there was no argument. When writers put the dictates of nature and the dictates of Christ together by assimilating natural law to the Golden Rule—"do as you would be done by, and do not do as you would not be done by"—it was easy to see that this ruled out physical assault, and equally easy to see that it ruled out theft *once there was private property*. It was not difficult to extract a view of punishment: we may defend ourselves against force and theft and exact from others what would appropriately be exacted from us. The deeper problem was to explain property rights in the first place.

The importance of property is obvious. People wish to know what is theirs and need to know how to acquire and transfer property, if they are to farm, to trade, and to leave property to their children or anyone else. Slightly less obviously, in societies that were never more than two bad harvests away from famine, an account of the duty of the haves to the have-nots is needed. I may own the corn in my granary, but if you are starving and I have plenty, do I own *all* of that corn; or do your rights diminish my ownership? Without a coherent account of the basis of property, it is hard to say what rights and what kind of rights owners and nonowners may have over the same things. For Christians, urged by Christ to sell all they had and give to the poor, it was and remained a problem to know what the proper limits of economic activity were; if nobody acquired anything, there would be nothing to dispose of charitably; but it was too easy for the greedy and the selfish to hide behind that platitude to accumulate wealth and never find the right moment to give even a small portion to the poor. As all students of Saint Paul remember, however, it is the *love* of money that is the root of all evil, not money itself; moderation in acquisition and generosity in charitable giving form the obvious basis for Christian economics.[15]

There was less agreement on the nature of ownership. Roman law distinguished sharply between *ius in rem* and *ius ad personam*, which is to say between rights in things and rights against persons. All rights are rights against persons in one sense, since only people can either respect or flout our rights; my ownership of my horse is a right *in rem*, but it takes another person to steal it, sell it fraudulently, ride it without my leave, and so on. Ownership is good against all the world. *Everyone* is obliged to respect my ownership. A right *in rem* and good against the world contrasts with rights that hold against particular other people. If I owe you money, it is only I whom you can sue for the debt, and you are the only person to whom I am obliged to repay it. The owner in Roman law is, so to speak, sovereign over the thing owned; its fate lies in his hands.

Under feudal arrangements, and the customary law that developed in northern and western Europe, ownership was less clear-cut. Some commentators have said that there was no such thing as ownership under feudalism, which is extreme. In one sense, the king owned all the territory he governed inasmuch as feudal tenures theoretically ran upward in such a way that the chain of tenant and lord terminated in the suzerain, the king who was the feudal superior of all. Tenants below the king had rights of possession and use over what they held of the king or of one of his tenants. Rights of disposal were another matter. In principle, they lay with the superior and could be exercised by his tenant only with his permission; in practice, this meant a payment in kind or in cash for his presumed acquiescence, his tenants paying a fee on disposal and the new tenant a fee on taking possession. Ownership thus embraced rights of use and occupation good against any other person's claims, but not the absolute right *in rem* of Roman law. In English law, this was true of free-hold ownership of real property until 1925, and it remains true even now of real estate held without a registered title. Ownership meant having a "better right" than a competitor.

Such a title was always vulnerable to someone's appearing with a better right—a long-lost relative might always appear and establish a claim to be the rightful heir of whoever had held the property in the past; innumerable English plays and novels rely on the device, and title insurance companies exist to make everyday life less dramatic. The importance of different images of ownership becomes visible when arguments erupt over the duty of the rich to share their resources with the poor during times of hardship; commentators sometimes say that the starving poor *own* the grain in the rich man's granary, and sometimes draw a sharp line between the rich man's *ownership* and the entitlement of the poor to *charity*. Locke later said that the poor had a "right" to the rich man's surplus, while Hume said it hardly mattered since in the event of famine the political authorities would always break open the granaries.[16] One contentious problem throughout the medieval period was the property owned by the church. In the beginning many Christians were attracted to a mendicant way of life, taking literally Christ's injunction to take no thought for the morrow and living in the expectation of an imminent Second Coming. The church became an institution, and institutions notoriously cost money to run, so churches became dependent on their members' taxing themselves for the churches' benefit; laymen began to make gifts to their local churches, and the aristocracy began to make substantial gifts to the church in Rome and in capital cities such as Milan and Ravenna.

Some pressing questions now arose: should the church own any-thing, and who was "the church" for such purposes? The bishop of a diocese could not own the charitable gifts as his personal property, so it must be the church as a corporate owner. The appropriate persons to exercise the corporate body's rights of disposal by sale or exchange were the bishop or a group of deacons, a committee to act as steward of what its members owned collectively but not individually. This corpo-rate model came to be the way the ownership of property by the church was thought of; the pope was the administrator of the church's property, not its owner. The classical world had been at ease with such arrange-ments in the case of publicly owned property. In a feudal setting the trouble that lay ahead was not conceptual but political. When laymen gave their property to the church, the gift deprived the layman's feudal superior of the "incidents" of ownership. When a lay tenant bequeathed his property to his heir, his heir inherited after a payment in cash or kind to the superior from whom he held his property. These payments were, in effect, payment for a lease, paid when the lease was renewed or a new lessee put into the lease.

The church was immortal; it had no heirs, its property never passed from one owner to another, and no feudal dues were paid. The landlord lost out; and the landlord most likely to take this amiss was the king. Moreover, there was a temptation to sharp practice; if someone gave his property to the church on the right terms, he could secure for his heirs an income and a substantial degree of control over the property, or a comfortable occupation in the church. This was not the only prob-lem posed by the church's ownership of property. Two other issues were tithes and the church's exemption from ordinary taxation. Tithes were a tax levied on lay property for the church's benefit. It was not clear how the church had come by the right to levy the tax, conversely, since the secular government provided protection for the church, it seemed plau-sible to many secular rulers that they should be able to levy taxes on the church as well as on the laity. The exemption of the property of charities from ordinary taxation was not an issue that arose for the first time in the twentieth-century United States.

These issues poisoned church–state relations for centuries. They are capable of causing a frisson of unease even today, as witness the surprise that American students feel when they discover that most Germans pay taxes to the government for church purposes. The history of property rights, and devices such as the Statute of Mortmain (1279) that the English crown employed to make gifts to religious establishments less attractive to both donors and recipients does not concern us. What does is that these developments forced thinkers to give an account of the moral justification of property rights. It became orthodox doctrine that property had at first been held in common—not the view of the Roman lawyers, but of the Stoic philosophers.[17] God gave the world to mankind in common; reason and natural law concurred in seeing the world as a gift to mankind collectively, and not to anyone in particular. For reasons spelled out by Aristotle, but available to the common sense of those who never read him, it was right to divide the inheritance of the human race among individuals; it gave each person an incentive to care for what he held personally and whose product would go to him and his family. Still, this would be acceptable only if there was some overarching notion of the common good that property institutions served. If we could not quite say that the starving man *owned* the grain in the rich man's granary, we could certainly say that a rich man who thought he could let the poor man starve was mistaken. His rights lapsed if his behavior was intolerable.

Outside (Non)Influences

The history of the collapse of the western Roman Empire was in large part the history of invasions by Germanic tribes; and much of the subsequent history of western Christendom is the history of the kingdoms that emerged when formerly nomadic and seminomadic peoples settled in what became France, Germany, and England. But one phenomenon whose physical impact was as great as its impact on political thinking was slight was the rise of Islam. The presence of Islamic states in North Africa and the Near East colored European politics from the eighth century all the way to the present, whether by way of the Crusades of the late eleventh to the thirteenth century, the Spanish *reconquista* of the eleventh century to the late fifteenth, or the rise and fall of the Ottoman Empire, and the instability of the successor states that emerged from its ruins. Islam as a creed could have no impact on Western political thought. Islamic scholars had much to say about the political organization of Islamic communities and about the relations of Muslims and unbelievers, but these ideas could have no purchase outside Islam. Even if any Western thinker had been willing to pay attention to them, the Western distinction between the sacred and the secular has no place in Islam, and the Western anxiety about relations between church and state finds no purchase in a faith without the Western conception of a church. Western philosophy, medicine, and technology were all deeply indebted to Arab scholars, not least for preserving and translating Greek texts that would have otherwise have been lost; but finding new ideas about how to govern ourselves more effectively in the work of Arab scholars would have been implausible even if there had been an incentive to look.

The impact of Islam was military; the first wave of Islamic conquest overran not only Spain but much of southern France. Moorish warriors got as far north as Tours, on the Loire, where they were defeated by Charles Martel at the Battle of Poitiers in 732. This was the battle that inspired Gibbon to claim that if Charles Martel had been defeated, "the Arabian fleet might have sailed without a naval combat into the mouth of the Thames. Perhaps the interpretation of the Koran would now be taught in the schools of Oxford, and her pulpits might demonstrate to a circumcised people the sanctity and truth of the revelation of Mahomet."[18] Their conquests in North Africa were not reversed as they were in Sicily in the eleventh century, and in Spain only over several hundred years; nor was the slow destruction of the Byzantine Empire, which ended with the fall of Constantinople in 1453 ever halted. Islam remained entrenched in Greece and the Balkans until the end of World War I.

In the conquered territories non-Jews and non-Christians were offered a stark choice between conversion to Islam or death. Jews and

Christians as "peoples of the book" were tolerated if they accepted the political authority of their Islamic rulers and paid extra taxes in recognition of their inferior status. The Islamic "solution" to the problem of accommodating a variety of creeds and cultures under one political umbrella—what became the millet system—had its virtues: Islamic rulers allowed their non-Muslim subjects a large measure of community autonomy. Jews were much safer under Islam than in Christian Europe. Nonetheless, Islamic pluralism did not generate political ideas that would mean anything to a Western reader until it sparked an interest many centuries later among those who contrasted Ottoman and Western forms of pluralism. The thinkers with whom we associate Islamic philosophy—al-Farabi, Avicenna, and Averroës—were interested in the metaphysics of Plato, Aristotle, and the Neoplatonists. Ibn Khaldun in the fourteenth century was perhaps the first Islamic political writer of a wider interest, and he depended on Aristotle for his moral and political views. He was, if the anachronism is permissible, an original political sociologist, among whose achievements was a persuasive account of what later became known as the theory of the circulation of elites, but not an original political thinker.[19]

Like their Arabic-speaking counterparts, Jewish scholars preserved, translated, and wrote commentaries on the masterpieces of classical Greek thinking, but had no reason to provide ideas about the authority of kings, bishops, popes, and nobility that Western thinkers could use. They transmitted medical and mathematical knowledge in advance of anything generated in western Europe before the end of the first millennium; they did not provide what their Christian neighbors could recognize as distinctive moral and political ideas. It would have been astonishing if they had, and more astonishing if they had done so and their Christian neighbors had made anything of them. The Jews of the diaspora had little need to think about secular authority. Doomed to live as barely tolerated outcasts under governments in which they had no say, they had much to say to themselves about their survival as a righteous community, and about such unnerving subjects as the moment at which it was laudable to escape persecution by suicide, but nothing relevant to the political dilemmas of their Christian persecutors.

Finally, we must remember something so obvious that it is easy to overlook. Medieval thinkers were almost always theologians first, philosophers second, and political speculators third and last. Augustine was a great political thinker, because he was a great thinker provoked by the political problems of the day, but it was the least of his achievements. One of the most influential figures in medieval thought was "Pseudo-Dionysius the Areopagite," a Syrian monk who lived shortly after Augustine; it was through him that Neoplatonic ideas came down to the twelfth and thirteenth centuries. Those ideas were eventually important for political theory because they reinforced the idea that the entire universe was hierarchically organized, and humanity part of a "great chain of being" that dictated the rights and duties of all creatures. These were ingredients in the synthesis of classical and Christian learning that Aquinas constructed in the third quarter of the thirteenth century. Nonetheless, the Pseudo-Dionysius belongs to the history of theology, and not to any but an unusually comprehensive history of political thought.[20]

Papal Absolutism and the Investiture Controversy

That said, one of the most important elements of the intellectual apparatus of early medieval political thinking was contributed by a late fifth-century pope in little more than two paragraphs of sharp prose. Gelasius I was pope for four years between 492 and 496, under conditions of extreme difficulty. The last Roman emperor in the west had abdicated sixteen years before; the Catholic Church was beset by heretics and pagans; Rome was stricken with plague; and the doctrinal authority of the pope over the patriarch of Constantinople was bitterly contested. The patriarch was protected by the emperor, whose appointee he was and who was naturally reluctant to concede papal authority over his appointee. The dispute provoked Gelasius's letter of 494 to the emperor Anastasius in which he laid down what became the doctrine of the two swords, and insisted on the superiority of the spiritual power to the secular. It was superior because in the last resort the pope answered to God for the morals of the emperor. The doctrine of the two swords is simple: God grants authority to both pope and emperor. Each is absolute in his own sphere. Each should sustain the other's authority. So far, so uncontentious. But the emperor in Constantinople thought his authority greater than either the patriarch's or the pope's. Gelasius held the opposite view.

The crucial passage of Gelasius's letter is two paragraphs in length. And the point on which so much turned was the second of two short opening sentences: "There are two powers, august Emperor, by which this world is chiefly ruled, namely, the sacred authority of the priests and the royal power. Of these that of the priests is the more weighty, since they have to render an account for even the kings of men in the divine judgment."[21] The letter went on to observe that there is a quid pro quo, with priests obeying the laws that the secular power made to preserve earthly peace and prosperity and the emperor being willing to acknowledge the authority of the pope in matters of faith. A later age sees this as the terms of a concordat between church and state; to Gelasius and popes down to the early thirteenth century, it meant something different. Certainly it was a statement of the division of labor that everyone accepted. More contentiously, it was a denial of the authority that the emperor unhesitatingly exercised in Constantinople, as well as an assertion of the autonomy of the papacy, and beyond that a claim by the pope to primacy over all other patriarchs—at Jerusalem, Antioch, and Constantinople. It was pregnant with trouble, since it claimed almost in passing the pope's right to judge the emperor's fitness for office, and by implication any other secular ruler's fitness, because one of the many juridical fictions that were half accepted until the late Middle Ages was that every ruler in Christendom was subordinate to the emperor, which later meant the elected Holy Roman Emperor.

The institutional conflict remained latent until it came to a head in the so-called investiture controversy in the mid-eleventh century. By this time, bishops were not only princes of the church; as the controllers of substantial territory and other property, they were also members of the feudal nobility. They were expected to provide military support to their secular overlords; some led their own forces into battle and died alongside them. Two practices grew up as the result of this meshing of roles; one was the creation of "proprietary churches," where the lay donor who had established a church and endowed it with property owned the church and installed as incumbent whomever he chose and on his own terms; the other practice was "lay investiture." A bishop was "invested" with his bishopric by a secular ruler in the same way that a feudal tenant received his fief from his lord. In effect, he did homage to the king for his diocese. Both devices made good sense for the secular authorities; when so many of the economic and military resources of troubled societies were in the hands of churchmen, their availability for secular purposes had to be guaranteed.

Pious nobles and princes founded or refounded monasteries and endowed them with land and buildings; but although these practices enhanced the authority of the church, they endangered its spiritual mission. A bishopric was a valuable piece of property, well worth purchasing— but buying ordination as a priest or bishop was the sin of simony and strenuously forbidden. It was also widely practiced. The papal tiara itself was frequently bought and sold. Simony became the target of reformers, as did the lifestyle of bishops who lived more like lay lords than priests. The reform movement built slowly, beginning with the reformation of monastic life in the tenth century and gathering momentum when a succession of reforming popes coincided with the accession of an underage emperor, Henry IV. Leo IX, pope from 1049 to 1054, Nicholas II, pope from 1059 to 1061, and Gregory VII, pope from 1073 to 1085, set out to achieve three things. The first was to ensure that popes were elected by the College of Cardinals and by nobody else. Leo IX laid the ground, and a Lateran Council called by Nicholas II decreed this mode of election in 1059. This was primarily aimed at reducing the influence of the Roman aristocracy, from whom the cardinals were largely recruited, but also at the influence of the emperor. The emperor was essentially a German king whose value to the papacy was his ability to control the Lombards, who periodically invaded northern and central Italy and threatened the territory of the papacy. The conflict of the 1070s between Gregory VII and Henry IV over lay investiture marked a paradoxical finale to a reform process that had begun when the emperor Henry III called a council to cure the scandal of the 1040s when three contenders claimed the title of pope. When the Council of Sutri in 1046 removed Benedict IX, Sylvester III, and Gregory VI, trouble was narrowly averted. The pious Henry III refused to receive his imperial crown from Gregory VI, because he had bought the papal tiara from Benedict IX and was therefore guilty of the sin of simony; but he installed his own choice as Clement II and was unwilling to give up the principle that just as the emperor in Constantinople appointed the patriarch, so the Holy Roman Emperor would nominate his choice for election as pope.

The second papal aim was to eliminate lay investiture. The object was to ensure that an archbishop or pope would invest a bishop with the regalia of his office, with no lay involvement. Henry IV resisted for the reasons suggested above. Gregory excommunicated him; there was near civil war in Italy and Germany. Gregory initially gained the upper hand, and in 1077 Henry had to humiliate himself, standing in the snow outside the pope's castle of Canossa to beg forgiveness. But Gregory overreached himself, was driven out of Rome, and died in exile. The dispute ended in the obvious compromise, enshrined in the Concordat of Worms of 1122 only after the deaths of both Gregory VII and Henry IV. The imperial side conceded the issue so far as investing the bishop with his office went, but ensured that the emperor or his representative would be present at the investing of bishops with their temporalities. The church secured control over the appointment of bishops, and the crown secured its rights over the land and property of the diocese. The concordat did not give either side all it wanted, but it established the papacy as a quasi-monarchical institution with the pope as the absolute head of the church in spiritual matters, and the papacy as a considerable secular power in central Italy. The papacy's third aim was to secure the primacy of the Catholic Church within Christendom. This met with total failure. Leo IX succeeded only in creating the breach with the church in Constantinople that remains unhealed to this day. In 1054, papal delegates traveled to Constantinople to secure the patriarch's acceptance of papal supremacy; when they did not get it, they excommunicated the patriarch Michael Cerularius, who anathematized them in turn. The papacy secured its political autonomy and its spiritual supremacy over a shrunken domain.

It is easy to represent medieval political thought as focused entirely on the conflicts of church and state, and generations of commentators have done so. This neglects the day-to-day evolution of political thinking forced upon both church and lay officials by the exigencies of their own institutional lives. Practicing lawyers in particular developed ideas about the ways in which superiors and inferiors related, and about the relationship between the will of a superior and the law. It was not from nowhere that institutions such as the English Parliament, which first met in 1265, developed, and not from nowhere that there arose in the church the so-called conciliar movement. Nonetheless, these developments belong more to the general historian than to the historian of ideas, precisely because they began as practical demands or responses to them. Conversely, one finds occasional outbreaks of intellectual originality that are hard to explain or to place and that have no impact as they occur, but are exploited long afterward.

John of Salisbury

One such was the writing of *Policraticus* by John of Salisbury. The fact that anyone could have written a work replete with ideas that we associate with the much later Middle Ages or with the modern world, as well as with the writings of classical political thinkers, suggests that similar ideas must have been in circulation from the end of antiquity without leaving any written evidence of their existence. Perhaps they were submerged by theological and ecclesiological discussion but remained part of an oral tradition. John was born in Salisbury around 1110 and ended his life as bishop of Chartres; he was a friend and confidant of Thomas à Becket and wrote a biography of the martyred archbishop. He was more than once exiled as a result of his ties to Becket and to Archbishop Theobald, Becket's predecessor as archbishop of Canterbury. He lived through one of the most intense periods of church–state conflict, but could take advantage of the new translations and epitomes of classical

philosophy that had sparked the so-called twelfth-century renaissance.[22]
He was not, however, a scholar in his own right, and relied very heavily
on florilegia, anthologies of extracts.

Policraticus, "the book of the statesman," is in part a work in a familiar
genre, a handbook addressed to rulers to remind them of their duty—
in flattering rather than admonitory tones. Like Christine de Pizan's
Book of the Body Politic, discussed in a later chapter, it relied heavily on
exempla, illustrative stories from Greek, Roman, and biblical history, that
emphasized the moral the author wanted to draw. The work became
famous because it resurrected, or found room for, the ancient doctrine
of tyrannicide. The argument was not complicated, but the conclusion
was bold; John discusses over and over the crucial differences between
the prince and the tyrant, and even introduces the novel category of the
ecclesiastical tyrant.[23] The book's fundamental premise was that of all
medieval thinkers. Political authority comes from God; the authority of
a true king is divine and is rejected at the peril of our souls as well as our
bodies. That this was not wholly a truism can be appreciated when it is
remembered that even Justinian's *Corpus* first insisted that the word of
the king is law, but went on to say that the law binds the king's subjects
because the king had been given that authority by the *populus*. The tension between the claim to wield authority *Dei gratia* and as the expression
of the vox populi is obvious, but was passed over by Justinian's compilers.
John of Salisbury has no notion of the king's authority being bestowed
on him by the people; it comes from God; that is why it is authority.
This remained the conventional wisdom; four centuries later, Sir John
Fortescue refers to England as a realm that is *regale et politicum*, "royal and
political," which is to say, governed by a monarch in a constitutional
fashion. Its laws are made with the assent of the people, and it is a body
politic, because the common will of the people for their common good is
what makes it a unity of which the king is the head. It is a *corpus mysticum*
rather than a physical body, but that is hardly different from Cicero's
insistence that a *res publica* is a "public thing" because it exists to secure a
common good. The crucial difference is that the king's subjects are subjects, not citizens; they have no independent power of action.[24]

John holds that God gives kings authority only in order that they shall conduct themselves in a law-abiding fashion, serve law and justice, and attend to the welfare of the people over whom God has seen fit to place them. This is not constitutionalism, but it opens the door to an important distinction that John made much of. There is a vast difference between a king and a tyrant. This in itself was uncontentious. As the Carlyles pointed out in their monumental history of medieval political thought, Augustine's evasiveness about whether an earthly king can give true justice to his people stirred no doubts in subsequent writers in the Middle Ages. They universally came down on the side of supposing that when Augustine said that a state without justice was simply a large gang of bandits, he meant that a lawfully constituted state was not a gang of bandits but a realm in which justice could be done and be seen to be done. That was John of Salisbury's view.[25] It makes Augustine less interesting but more usable.

A true king practices justice and is to be obeyed. We are to obey him as the agent of God, but the mark of his being God's agent is that he does justice. God's conferral of authority is conditional on the king's practicing justice and doing those things for whose sake God institutes kings in the first place. This is more sensible, less anarchic, and less grim an account of politics than Augustine's; it is also less intellectually interesting and less morally demanding. The consequence that John draws is on its face dramatic. A ruler, or rather a purported ruler, who does not do justice is not a king but a tyrant. Lawful rule is monarchy; unjust rule is tyranny. Tyrants do not have God's authority behind them, and—here is the crux—if they are resisted and killed by their people, they have no legitimate complaint and their people have done no wrong.[26] The question is how far this thought is to be pressed. The answer is not simple. Recall Cicero: for him, the killing of a tyrant was not simply excusable but morally and politically meritorious, and tyrannicide was the positive duty of those who were in a position to effect it. Cicero rightly suppressed the followers of Catiline, and Brutus and his friends rightly killed Caesar. John also says that the killing of a "public tyrant" is a meritorious act.

Nonetheless, he was not trying to resurrect Roman republican ideals. His examples come from the Old Testament rather than Roman republican history, and when he discusses Nero, Caligula, and the like, he suggests that Christians were obliged to endure their tyranny. Even in the case of the Old Testament, he comes down on the side of thinking that Saul was a deserved affliction for the rebellion of the people of Israel against the word of God. John was milder and more moderate than the Roman tyrannicides. The ruler's word is law but only when it is (really) law. The prince's whim is not law; that would be a license for wickedness, but when the prince is guided by equity and justice, what he lays down for the good of his society is law. This is not constitutionalism, since it implies nothing about the institutions we might erect to ensure that kings and popes are so guided, but it is a defense of the rule of law. The pope is *servus servorum Dei*, the servant of the servants of God; the king is the servant of the common good according to law. He possesses genuine authority and is *legibus absolutus*, exempted from the law he gives to his subjects, but only insofar as that exemption serves the public good. There is no conflict between governing *Dei gratia* and governing according to law. God rules the universe by law; the king who serves God serves the law by which God governs his universe.[27]

This leaves John's understanding of tyrannicide somewhat up in the air. It is one thing to say that a prince who becomes a tyrant forfeits his authority and cannot complain if his people resist him or kill him. It is another to say that if a prince becomes a tyrant, it is somebody's duty to kill him and that doing so is an act of political virtue. John is torn between the Christian tradition of passive obedience and the classical tradition of tyrannicide. There is no doubt that he approves of past slayings of tyrants; he quite rightly invokes the Old Testament as well as Roman history to make the point that tyrannicides have been praised for their deeds. He certainly thought that tyrants forfeited their immunity to deposition. Nonetheless, the Christian framework, if not that of the Old Testament, sits uneasily with the classical doctrine. Tyrants may, after all, and as Augustine suggested, be God's punishment for our sins, and we may be intended not to resist evil but to suffer it patiently. The astonishing thing, even so, is John's readiness to extrapolate an argument that comes from republican writers of many centuries earlier to the position of clerical leaders. If it is lawful to kill tyrants; it must be lawful to kill clerical tyrants if there are such. Old Testament stories about the killing of the priests of Baal show that the wicked exercise of power by priests is to be punished.

In short, a writer like John in the twelfth century could draw on a great variety of intellectual resources to make some striking points about the conditionality of both secular and ecclesiastical authority and about the limits beyond which ordinary people were not to be pushed. There is an obvious moral to be drawn: we should neither exaggerate the closeness of such thinkers to ourselves nor treat them as though they were so distant in space and time that their ideas need decoding as if they were Mayan hieroglyphs concerned with a wholly inscrutable way of life.

CHAPTER 7

Aquinas and Synthesis

The Revival of Philosophy

AQUINAS DOMINATES THIS CHAPTER, but its theme is the impact on Christian political thinking of the rediscovery of classical philosophy and classical legal and political thought. Aquinas's situation was the reverse of Augustine's. Augustine lived in a Roman Empire that had only recently been Christianized. Its intellectual resources were largely pagan. The Europe of Aquinas was Christendom; its identity was Christian, and the eight centuries between Augustine's death and Aquinas's birth had seen a decline into and recovery from the chaos of the fall of the western empire. The unity of Europe was spiritual—Christian—not political. Its intellectual unity rested on the universality of Latin as a legal, scholarly, and spiritual language and on the existence of the church universal. Reinserting classical philosophy into that environment was quite unlike fighting the superstitions of the pagans.

Aquinas's attempt to integrate the insights of pagan philosophy with a Christianity that a rational man could commit himself to was a heroic undertaking. The church authorities were at best anxious about the rediscovery of Aristotle and at worst entirely hostile; his writings were condemned yet again in 1270, a bare four years before Aquinas's death. Aquinas's work was therefore decidedly brave. It rarely looks like that to modern readers in search of Aquinas's political ideas. They know that Aquinas became the "official" philosopher of the Catholic Church and look for something astonishing; and they are disappointed. This is partly because his thoughts on politics form a very small part of the enormous corpus of his work but more because those thoughts are almost invariably sensible, but often read like diluted Aristotle, offering excitement only when an Aristotelian view is so at odds with Christian orthodoxy that reconciliation is especially hard. The contrast with Augustine, who is often unnerving but never dull, could not be sharper. That, however, is the point. Augustine is unflinching in associating politics and the state with our sinful, fallen natures. Aquinas never disputes that we are fallen creatures, but—following Aristotle—thinks that the state shelters forms of social life that are at least relatively good. Unlike Aristotle, he does not believe that we can perfect ourselves within the political community; nonetheless, we can lead virtuous, happy, and fruitful lives. He is unsurprising in part because he so successfully erased Augustine's relentlessly negative view of earthly existence from ethical and political debate. If he did not himself advance much beyond Aristotle, apart from setting him in a Christian framework, others soon did.

The difficulties posed for the modern reader are exacerbated by the literary style of the *Summa Theologiae*. Under no conditions would Aquinas have been a stylish writer. Given that he was writing so much and so rapidly, on occasion dictating to as many as five scribes at a time, the "angelic doctor" would have been supernaturally blessed if he had written elegant and attractive prose. Much more problematic for modern readers is the style imposed by medieval Scholasticism. In any translation true to the original text and its organization, Aquinas's views are set out as answers to questions, followed by subquestions provoked by the answers, answers to those subquestions, and so on. The style reflects the lecturing (and learning) habits of medieval universities, not the reading habits of the twenty-first century. It is the style of Scholastic treatises, and its destruction was a goal of the critics of Catholic theology and medieval philosophy from the fifteenth century to the seventeenth who made "Scholastic" a term of abuse. They succeeded so well that a twenty-first-century reader is disabled from finding Aquinas easy going by almost every aspect of present-day education, in style, content, and argumentative method.[1] We must step back and ask what the project was within which such sensible political opinions, however expounded, found their place—remembering always that a Dominican, even one from an aristocratic family, put himself at risk whenever he put forward ideas, however "sensible" we may think them, which his superiors did not care for.

Aquinas's Life and Times

Aquinas was not long-lived. He was born in 1224 or 1225 and died in 1274. His family were aristocrats from Aquino, north of Naples; they owned a castle, Roccasecca, in which he was born, and where his siblings held him captive for a year when he was twenty in the hope of persuading him not to join the Dominican order. For the first stages of his education, he was sent as a child to the Benedictine monastery at Monte Cassino, where his uncle was abbot, and in 1238 went to Naples to the newly founded university. There he discovered the Dominicans. In 1244 he decided to join the order. His family had their sights set on his entering Monte Cassino as a Benedictine. The abbot of Monte Cassino was a great man in thirteenth-century Italy, and the position one to be coveted. Thomas's obstinacy was greater than his family's; after a year, they allowed him to leave for the University of Paris.

He studied for his novitiate with Albertus Magnus, a German theologian of immense learning, first in Paris and then in Cologne. His lecture notes on Albertus's lectures on Aristotle's *Ethics* survive, along with his notes on Albertus's lectures on the works of the Pseudo-Dionysius. Aquinas was a substantial young man—in later life, the table at which he sat was scooped out to accommodate his girth—and was jokingly called "the ox" by his colleagues. They saw he was extraordinarily intelligent, and Albertus observed that "the bellowing of that ox will be heard throughout the world," though he could hardly have foreseen that Thomism would eventually become the official philosophy of the Catholic Church. In 1252 Aquinas returned to Paris to work for his *licentium docendi*, which he received in 1256. One of the requirements for the degree was a commentary on Peter Lombard's *Sentences* both in a written form and delivered as lectures. Once licensed, he lectured and took part in disputations; and he began the first of his two summae, the *Summa contra Gentiles*, intended for use by missionaries attempting to convert Muslims and Jews. In spite of the chaotic conclusion to the Fourth Crusade (1215), whose only achievement was the sacking of Constantinople, the effort to proselytize in the Islamic world intensified in the thirteenth century, and the Dominicans were a proselytizing order.

After three years, he went to the Dominican house in Naples, and then to the Dominican priory attached to the papal court in Orvieto. In 1265 he opened a *studium generale* in Rome, and there wrote *De regimine principum* and began the *Summa Theologiae*. During these years, he worked with William of Moerbeke, who had begun to translate Aristotle out of the original Greek, bypassing the inaccuracies and infelicities introduced by translators who had turned Aristotle's work into Arabic and thence into Latin. In 1269 he returned to Paris as professor and for a time rector of the university. After three years he returned to Naples and in December 1273 suffered a collapse in health that led him to declare that he could write no more. "All that I have written seems like straw to me," he is reputed to have said.[2] He seems to have suffered a stroke, but that did not stop his superiors from sending him on a mission to the Council of Lyons. On the way he suffered an accident that led to his death on March 7, 1274. He was canonized in 1323, but Thomism became the official Catholic philosophy very slowly. It was only when the Protestant Reformation persuaded the papacy that it needed all the intellectual resources it could lay its hands on that Thomism became identified with philosophically sophisticated Catholicism.

The Dominican order had been founded in 1216. Whereas the Franciscans emphasized poverty and simplicity of life, and a ministry to the poor, the Dominicans were from the first a learned order. A Dominican was *canis Domini*, a hound of the Lord, and the order was the intellectual arm of the church militant, initially created to defend the church against heretics such as the Albigensians in southern France. The sword of the secular authorities was not enough; the Church required educated men who would go out and proselytize on behalf of the faith, and the Order of Preachers did so with enormous energy. The Dominicans were especially employed by the papacy to be preachers of crusades—crusades against heresy, against the Saracens, and against the emperor Frederick II during the struggle between pope and emperor. The order required that when not engaged in religious duties Dominicans were to study; they were initially confined to scriptural and theological inquiry, but this restriction was soon eased. They were notable linguists: members of the order became fluent in the languages of wherever they went as missionaries, and were soon preaching in Arabic and Hebrew as well as Greek. Aquinas's decision to become a Dominican was right.

Intellectual Life in Thirteenth-Century Europe

Much of Aquinas's life was spent teaching at the University of Paris. The universities of medieval Europe were initially founded by kings who needed competent lawyers, and in the beginning their intellectual life focused on the study of Roman law. The church had its own system of law, canon law, and highly trained lawyers; the secular authorities required skilled lawyers of their own. Bologna, founded in the ninth century, was the ancestor of all other European universities, including Paris and Oxford. Gradually, universities became communities of scholars devoted not only to law, medicine, and theology but also to a syllabus including mathematics and "natural philosophy"—physics and astronomy. A pattern emerged of lower-level and higher-level inquiries in a system that admitted students to advanced studies once they had attained proficiency at the "bachelor" level. At that point they achieved a *licentium studendi*, permission to study the higher disciplines; they were awarded a *licentium docendi*, permission to teach, once they demonstrated proficiency at the "master of arts" level. Canon and civil law remained central, along with medicine, and by the thirteenth century science and mathematics were thriving. Nonetheless, this was Christian Europe, and theology was the queen of the sciences and the crowning discipline of the academy. As ever, there was turf warfare, and the ownership of ethics and politics was disputed between the lawyers—particularly canon lawyers—philosophers, and theologians. One thing that did not trouble medieval universities was a conflict between vocational and nonvocational education. All study was vocational.

Theology was the queen of the sciences, but speculation was dangerous and so were non-Christian sources of reflection. The authorities feared the effect on undisciplined young minds of exposure to pagan thought; the boundaries beyond which unorthodox ideas would not be tolerated were unclear, but condemnation for heresy meant imprisonment or worse. Nonetheless, the rise of a philosophically informed approach to the Christian faith was unstoppable because so much of the received doctrine of the Christian church had been thrashed out by church fathers who had themselves employed the resources of Greek philosophy. The period between the death of Augustine and the beginning of the second millennium has often been labeled the Dark Ages, but outside northern Europe this is a libel. The intellectual resources of students were never as scanty as later ages thought. They were, however, lopsided and gave a distorted sense of the full range of Greek and Roman thought.

The empirical, scientific aspect of Greek thought was initially lost. The more mystical parts of Greek philosophy that strike modern readers as proto-Christian were known in part and always congenial to Christian Europe. Neoplatonism was given a new lease on life by Augustine and the Pseudo-Dionysius in the fourth and fifth centuries; and although only three of Plato's dialogues circulated in Latin translation, they included the *Timaeus*, so students knew the authentically metaphysical Plato. They did not know Plato's political writings. The church fathers were anthologized and widely read in the *Sentences* of Peter Lombard; these and the encyclopedic works of Saint Isidore of Seville provided access to the philosophical resources of the early church and empire. After 1100 Arab scholars who translated his works into Latin brought Aristotle to Western notice, and he swiftly acquired the status of "the philosopher." Aristotle was somewhat "Platonized" by translators whose interests were more religious than political or scientific, and when they commented on Aristotle's politics and ethics, it was in ways that diminished the distance between him and Plato. This was not a disaster: the Neoplatonist

Aristotle of Avicenna and Averroës was more easily assimilated than he would have been if he had been encountered whole and in Greek. Even so, the study of Aristotle was periodically forbidden by the church.

The works of Aristotle made their way into the universities during the twelfth century. They initially arrived in Latin translations of Arabic translations from the Greek; few scholars in the west could read Greek. When translations were made directly from Greek into Latin, Aquinas insisted on working with them. Aristotle's *Politics* was one of the first works translated directly from the Greek by William of Moerbeke, the fellow Dominican whom Aquinas recruited for the purpose. It was another two centuries before the ability to read Greek was common enough in western Europe for the texts to be widely used in the original language.

Reason versus Revelation: Faith and Philosophy

The importance of metaphysical and religious questions to the practice of politics is a political choice. Theocracies make religious orthodoxy the basis of political legitimacy, while modern secular states insist that a variety of religious convictions is consistent with political loyalty and political legitimacy. Societies where it is thought that there is only one true faith find it hard to believe that dissent in matters of religion will not have dire political consequences. Relaxedly secular polities see no difficulty in diversity. Taking Aristotle's metaphysics seriously posed spiritual, intellectual, and political difficulties for a Christian. The problems begin at the very beginning. Aristotle believed that the world was eternal and infinite and its existence rationally necessary. Christianity rested on the Jewish creation story, in which the creation of the world is a matter of divine will, and the world is in its essence a historical entity with a beginning in God's first creation, a history that starts with the Fall and attains its end with the Second Coming, the Last Judgment, and the restoration of God's kingdom. Platonic and Neoplatonic myths were more congenial than Aristotle's science.

Aristotle's philosophy was indisputably philosophy; Christianity is indisputably not. Like Judaism and Islam, it is a historical, particularistic creed and rests on revelation. Truth is divinely revealed to particular groups and individuals at particular moments in history. For a philosopher, the providential story set out in the Bible poses obvious difficulties. To a rational inquirer unaided by revelation, it was not obvious *why* God had created a world at all; to suppose that God had *had* to do so limits God's freedom of action, which is blasphemous, but to suppose the Creation was arbitrary seems to insult the divine intelligence, too. Aristotle had argued that an uncaused first cause was necessitated to create the world; but the first cause was not personal in the sense in which Yahweh was. Understanding what Aristotle had in mind has puzzled philosophers, but it does not raise unanswerable questions about the *motivation* of the entity to which it ascribes the origin of the universe.

Aquinas set out to reconcile Aristotle's metaphysics with Christian faith. The nuanced view of the relationship between Christianity and philosophy he provided was greatly needed. Too much reliance on faith opened the door to irrationalism; too much reliance on reason opened the door to skepticism. Reason is the light of nature, but natural reason can take us only so far. One of Aquinas's best-known remarks is *gratia naturam non tollit sed perfecit*—grace does not destroy nature but perfects it.[3] Human reason cannot uncover *everything* we need to know; but human reason is a God-given instrument to be employed effectively within its own limits. Aquinas's confidence in the use of reason within its proper sphere contrasts very sharply with the more extreme attitude of Augustine. Augustine more than once claimed that reason was essentially delusive, providing an example of the philosopher who argues brilliantly against brilliance in argument.

Aquinas avoided the skepticism of Augustine and the much more extreme skepticism of later writers like Hobbes, who held that we simply *had no idea* what it might be like to see the world sub specie aeternitatis and who thus deprived reason of any role in religious matters. Aquinas held the claims of faith and reason in balance. We can have *some* but not an *adequate* idea of the matters that faith dealt with. Reason can lead us to acknowledge the need for faith, and make it plausible that what we believe on faith is true; but the full revelation of the final mysteries of existence must await our vision of God in the afterlife. Until that time, we can only reason by analogy to what the ultimate truth *might* be.

Within philosophy and within Aquinas's *Summa Theologiae*, ethics and politics have a doubly subordinate place. They form a fraction of the concerns of a thinker whose chief topic is the nature of God, the nature of creation, and the relation of all God's creations to each other and to God. Moreover, they are not part of philosophy in its higher reaches. Philosophy tries to set out what is necessarily true; it explains why things *must* be the way they are, and not some other way. It aims at demonstrative truth. Aquinas followed Aristotle in thinking that we should aim only at as much certainty as a subject admits of; ethics and politics seek practical rather than theoretical knowledge, and their conclusions are true on the whole or for the most part, not demonstratively certain. It is the realm of prudence and good sense, not the realm of the geometricians. Aquinas wrote commentaries on Aristotle's *Nicomachean Ethics* and on his *Politics* for the benefit of his students in Paris in the early 1270s, but no work entirely devoted to politics. *De regimine principum* (On royal government) would have been such; it was intended as a gift to the king of Cyprus, but Aquinas wrote only the first chapter and part of the second chapter of the work before abandoning it when its dedicatee died. The book was expanded and completed by Ptolemy of Lucca. Aside from a letter to the duchess of Brabant in answer to her query about how heavily she could tax her Jewish subjects, everything else of interest comes from the two summae, the *Summa contra Gentiles* and the *Summa Theologiae*.

The Political Background: Church and Empire

Although politics and political theory were not Aquinas's major concern, it is surprising that the hostilities between papacy and empire that provided an unsettled backdrop to his life do not surface in his work. Emperor Frederick II was a distant relative, and the Dominicans were preachers of crusades, one of which was launched against Frederick II by Pope Innocent IV. No short, coherent account of the conflict between the papacy and successive emperors is possible; indeed, it is not clear that a wholly coherent account can be given at all. The political theorist may be tempted to see the diplomatic and military conflict between a succession of popes and emperors as inevitably arising from the problem raised in the previous chapter: *who* possesses the ultimate authority that Christ conferred on earthly rulers?[4] This would seriously overstate the role of ideas in conflicts of interest. The major cause of conflict was territorial and financial. The papacy was a powerful secular political entity in central Italy; the Papal States formed until the reunification of Italy in 1871 an S-shaped band of territory that stretched from Ravenna to in the northeast to Rome in the southwest. Frederick II was king of Sicily and the feudal overlord of much of northern Italy. His interest lay in extending his authority over central Italy, and the pope's lay in preventing him from doing so. The allegiance of allies depended overwhelmingly on bribery and coercion, but contending views of legitimacy came into play, too. The agreement that pope and emperor were absolute, each in his own *ordo*, or sphere, which was implicit in the creation of the Holy Roman Empire in 800, could hold only on the basis of an agreed view about where the boundaries of the two spheres lay. None was to be had, and each claimed the authority to depose the other in extremis.

Some views of political and ecclesiastical authority were equally unattractive to popes and emperors alike, because they appealed to secular and "ascending" theories of authority. Republican and natural law theories represented authority as something generated within a community that might legitimately adopt many different constitutional arrangements for creating law, clarifying it, and enforcing it. This was a bad basis for absolutism, whether papal or royal. Cicero's works were popular with civil lawyers and provided the most familiar and durable version of such an ascending theory: natural law sets the standards of communal justice, a *populus* invests an elite with the authority to make law in accordance with natural law, and the form of government matters less than that the form of government should suit the people who live under it and unite justice with the pursuit of the common good. The *populus* would be wise to establish a monarchy as all medieval writers agreed; nonetheless, the source of authority was rather too visibly the people.

This view had particular resonance in the numerous Italian city-states that practiced some form of self-government from the twelfth century to the sixteenth, and sometimes longer; the Venetian Republic endured until it was extinguished by Napoleon. Popes and emperors alike denied that the Italian city-states were truly autonomous; both insisted that they had only such rights of self-government as their papal or imperial overlord granted. The vexed question was the extent of papal authority over the emperor and vice versa. The papacy had no choice but to argue the extreme case that since the Holy Roman Empire had been a papal creation at the time of Sylvester III's coronation of Charlemagne, the emperor was subordinate to the pope. How it came about that the pope could create an emperor was a question answered by the supposed Donation of Constantine. Constantine had given the empire to the pope, who had, so to speak, granted it back to Constantine and his heirs.[5] Once his help to protect the territory of the papacy against invasion by the Lombards was no longer needed, the emperor was a threat to the papacy's political independence. To the south the emperor held the Kingdom of Sicily, embracing the island and much of the mainland ("the Kingdom of the Two Sicilies"), and to the north he was overlord of much of northern Italy, as the feudal superior of many of the city-states of the region. An emperor in control of southern Italy who could bring armies over the Alps and down through northern Italy could evict a hostile pope and install a friendly one. Indeed, even without a secure hold on southern Italy, an invader could make his way down the west coast of Italy to Rome; if the pope was driven out of Rome, it would not be hard to bully or bribe the College of Cardinals to declare him deposed.

The situation seemed to favor the emperor. It did not. The emperor was elected, and the papacy's most powerful weapon was the internal dissensions of the German princes who were the electors. Nor was the emperor welcome in northern Italy; the city-states valued their autonomy and were ready to defend it against their notional overlord. The early thirteenth-century pope Innocent III was a master of political maneuver. He threw his weight behind a friendly candidate for the imperial title, then betrayed him by engineering an alliance to prevent his adding Sicily to his German possessions and securing Sicily for the future Frederick II, who became king as a child of three. By the time he was an adult,

Frederick was the most intelligent, best-educated, and most engaging of all medieval kings, fluent in half a dozen languages, and a formidable enemy. Innocent secured a moral advantage by agreeing to crown Frederick king on condition that he do homage to the pope as his feudal superior and renounce the Kingdom of Sicily if elected emperor. He also got Frederick to promise to launch a crusade at some unspecified date; his grandfather the emperor Frederick Barbarossa had, after all, died on the Third Crusade in 1190, after many years of battling the papacy of Alexander III, and even if Frederick II survived, he would be distracted from the affairs of Italy. Frederick had no intention of treating the pope as his superior; after Innocent III's death, he had himself elected and crowned emperor in 1220 and announced his intention to unify Italy from Sicily to the Alps. He spent almost no time in Germany, where his authority was tenuous outside the south, and he never returned after 1237, claiming that nobody could govern a country where they spoke a language that resembled the barking of dogs and the croaking of frogs. His ambition was to establish a secular, polyglot kingdom in Italy based on Sicily and incorporating the papal and northern states.[6]

Frederick died in 1250, having very narrowly failed in the attempt and after exhausting his own and much of the papacy's resources; the imperial throne remained vacant for almost a quarter of a century. Within half a century the king of France became a more potent threat to the papacy's independence than the emperor had been. This was less significant in political theory than in political practice; only with Jean Bodin's *Six Books of the Commonwealth* of 1576 did anyone articulate the modern concept of a sovereign state and theorize its unity in terms of the indivisible sovereignty that encouraged a king to say, "*L'état, c'est moi.*" The medieval world was the world of Christendom, not the nation-state. The papacy's problem in the late thirteenth and early fourteenth centuries lay with the success of the Capetian monarchy in France; from a position in which the kings of France were weaker than their most powerful feudal vassals, successive monarchs had established themselves as their undoubted superiors. By the late thirteenth century Philip IV—Philip the Fair—could launch military and diplomatic initiatives that the papacy could not counter. Papal edicts of excommunication and deposition were effective if a king was unloved, not in command of his great nobles, not adequately funded, and unable to put effective armies in the field for long campaigns. Philip IV was not much loved, but he was in command of his nobles, his finances, and his armies, and therefore of events. Frederick II was not in command of the same resources, so his attempt to create the first secular state in Europe was stillborn. Philip's contemporary Edward I of England was as effective a monarch as Philip and equally unwilling to respond to papal financial and political demands, but fortunately for the papacy, the English crown had no interest in Italy.

Aquinas's Political Theory

Aquinas's writings were dictated not by local politics but by his aim to produce a synthesis and summary of the findings of theology and philosophy. At the highest level, where the Christian conception of divine law encounters classical notions of the natural law, the question is how divine law and natural law are related, and what their relation is to positive law. Of the institutions that human beings regulate by law, property is one of the most important, and against the background of the Franciscan criticism of wealth and its misuse, the crucial question is whether private ownership is legitimate and natural, and what its limits are— for instance, whether property in human beings, slavery, is legitimate. Against the background of Aristotle and the Bible, Aquinas could not avoid the question of what forms of political authority men can legitimately institute, and whether any are more natural—more legitimate, or more prudentially desirable—than others; and, in terms of the behavior of rulers and subjects, what difference the truth of Christianity makes to the conduct of politics.

This last question is obviously not one that could be addressed to Aristotle; but although classical political philosophers rarely took a view about the literal truth of religious claims, they invariably emphasized the political importance of religion. Aristotle was much concerned with the arrangements for the priesthood in both actual and ideal states. Nobody before the sixteenth century would have thought that secular authority could be indifferent to the religious practices of its subjects; a defense of toleration on the grounds that private religious practice was no business of the law would have been unintelligible. The Roman Empire accepted a great variety of religious practices where they were consistent with political unity, and where their practitioners could plausibly be thought to be cementing their loyalty to the state; but the idea that religion was not the state's business would have been scoffed at. Even Frederick II, who was famous for insisting that Jews and Muslims should practice their faith freely in the Kingdom of Sicily, had heretics burned at the stake in Lombardy.

In discussing natural law, Aquinas had to defuse the tension between a Christian view that separated the social arrangements of post-Fall mankind from those that would have been appropriate if we had never fallen and the pagan view that saw the social and political world as continuous with the natural world. This contrast was somewhat blurred by the popular classical view that mankind had once lived more simply, more rationally, and more happily in a golden age of innocence. In the golden age men had been free and equal and innocent; the Stoic vision of their subsequent corruption overlapped with the Christian vision of the Fall, at least to the extent of identifying the growth of sophistication with a loss of virtue. Nonetheless, the dramatic fall from grace imagined in Judaism and Christianity has no classical counterpart. There is no Stoic equivalent to the thought that death comes into the world only with sin, and no thought that the essence of the Fall is a revolt against God. Given the Stoic vision of God as the soul of the world, immanent in every part of creation, there hardly could be. The idea that each of us has a personal relationship with an angry but loving God is wholly unclassical; and the idea that only divine intervention—that is, grace— can save us from ourselves equally so. Nor can Christianity do anything with the Stoic doctrine of *apatheia*, detachment from desire. *Apatheia* frees us from bondage to the flesh and its disorganized urges and ensures that we are immune to threats and cajoling, and open only to reason; a Christian might think *apatheia* good to the extent that it clears our minds and hearts of obstructions to the voice of God. It cannot be a solution. Grace is the only solution, and Stoicism has no room for grace.

If the redemptive element in Christianity is the most striking difference from its classical antecedents, the Christian picture is not at odds with all classical natural law theories, but is so with anything one can easily find in Aristotle. One crux is the (non)naturalness of inequality. Christianity drew a sharp distinction between natural equality and conventional inequality; in Aristotelian natural law, the hierarchies visible throughout the natural world include the hierarchy of better and worse in society; aristocrats are by nature better than the rank and file, even if nature sometimes makes mistakes and upper-class children turn out worse than the children of the lower orders. One of Aristotle's most extreme assertions of the doctrine of natural inequality is the claim that there are slaves by nature whose servile condition benefits them as well as their masters.[7] In that respect, Stoicism was much closer to Christianity inasmuch as its starting point is the natural equality of all mankind and the nonnaturalness but inescapability of slavery.

Aquinas could not simply take over Aristotle's conception of nature, but he could readily accommodate himself to Aristotle's approach to the relations of nature and convention. He accepted contra Aristotle the orthodox Christian claim that God had given the world to man in common, so that in the strictest sense, there was neither property nor slavery nor political authority by nature.[8] But he had no problems with Aristotle's defense of private property. Indeed, he took over Aristotle's naturalism with regard to earthly affairs with no visible strain. Like Aristotle, he thought that within their proper limits, observation and reflection can tell us almost all we need to know about the conduct of everyday life. He found Aristotleian teleology especially illuminating. Almost more enthusiastically than Aristotle, Aquinas argues that everything is created to achieve some good proper to the sort of thing it is; apples, for example, exist to provide food of a certain sort, but they are also intended to grow to a proper roundness and redness in the process. We describe plants as "flourishing" and thus show that we understand them as having a destiny as *good* specimens of their kind.

So although Aquinas agreed with Christian orthodoxy that if we had never fallen into sin, we would not have needed to live in a political state at all, he went on to agree with Aristotle that the polity exists in order that we can live as good a life as possible on earth.[9] The coercive state may be necessitated by sin, but a well-ordered state is more than a regrettable necessity. We cannot achieve what Aristotle regarded as the greatest good, which is absolute self-sufficiency; for that, we must wait until we encounter God. Nonetheless, the Aristotelian view that the polis was the highest form of human association is *almost* accepted by Aquinas. It cannot be accepted in its entirety, for the good and sufficient reason that the highest community is the community of the Christian faithful. However, we are not mere *peregrini*, as Augustine described us, waiting until our time of tribulation is over. We are here to lead good lives, and, as Aristotle said, the individual needs others with whom to live the good life in common, just as families need the support of larger communities, and villages need a legal system to regulate the behavior of their inhabitants and their relations with other villages. A political system is required to secure all these things and make the good life possible.[10]

In *De regimine* Aquinas is concerned to argue that the best form of government is monarchy; in a treatise addressed to a king he could hardly do otherwise. Still, he does it at a high level of abstraction; kingship is not particularly personal. Rather, one man embodies the unity of the common good and the coherence of its pursuit more effectively than the multitude or a numerous body.[11] In *Summa Theologiae* Aquinas discusses Aristotle's account of *politeia*, the constitutional state that keeps the peace by doing justice to both the better- and the worse-off by blending aristocracy and democracy. Curiously, he does so in the context of a discussion of God's provision for the government of the Jews of the Old Testament, but he accepts without anxiety Aristotle's preference for *politeia* as the best practicable state.[12] Generally, he thinks, as did Aristotle in the abstract, that if it can be had, aristocracy is even better than *politeia*; but he goes further than Aristotle in preferring monarchy to aristocracy on grounds of efficiency. In the light of Aristotle's division of good and bad governments, democracy is to be preferred to tyranny on grounds of *inefficiency*: misrule by the many is less effectively evil than one-man misrule. In all, what is notable is the extreme matter-of-factness of the discussion.

One might ask whether this means that after all the state does exist "by nature," as Aristotle claimed. Yes and no. It is natural in the sense that it suits humanity to organize itself in this fashion, there are genuine goods that political organization shelters and encourages, and virtues that are required for and elicited by living a political life. It is not natural, in the sense that mankind would not have lived in a political community in the absence of the Fall. The argument is delicately set out. Adam neither needed nor exercised coercive authority of the kind that sets the state apart from informal associations; but Adam posssessed something a little like property and something a little like political authority. He had the right to use lower forms of creation for his own benefit, and if he had not sinned, he would have had the authority of a father over his wife and children even in the Garden of Eden. He would have been a patriarch with authority over an extended family whose members would have acknowledged that authority. Coercive law would not have been needed and would not have existed. Aquinas quotes and dissents from Augustine's claim that "God did not intend that His rational creature, made in His own image, should have lordship over any but irrational creatures: not man over man, but man over the beasts."[13] In so doing, he accepts something very like Aristotle's picture of natural hierarchy: parents govern children, husbands govern wives.

The Varieties of Law

Aquinas was fascinated by the taxonomic issues that any discussion of the law raises. He begins by arguing that there is an eternal law, implicit in the fact that God constructed the universe on rationally intelligible principles and for rationally endorsable ends. To the objection that there cannot be an eternal law, because God is the giver of law and preexisted the world, he replies that law is a principle of practical reason in the lawgiver, not a set of instructions the lawgiver issues to those subject to the law. God is eternal, and the principles inherent in God's plans for the universe are eternal also. However, the eternal law of reason is not identical with natural law. *Natural law*, strictly, is something that only human beings can follow, because it requires reason to discern it; animals following principles of action that lead to their own welfare follow natural law only analogically. Aquinas is happy to say that nonrational animals are guided by or governed by natural law, but the law is not "in them," and they do not follow it as we can.[14] As to the content of natural law, Aquinas insists that its precepts are simple and universal, reducing in the last resort to "seek good and eschew evil," or in the alternative to some variant of the Golden Rule, that we should do unto others as we would have them do to us and more especially *not* do unto others what we would wish them *not* to do to us. The simplicity of ultimate principles does not carry over to their implications; here common sense must come in, and casuistry in the nonabusive sense of reasoning to the particular case. Thus, the prima facie obligation to restore to another the possessions we have borrowed from him, which is the general rule, will fail if we have borrowed a weapon from a man who proposes to use it to fight against his country. Such considerations affect the legitimacy of private property, where the legitimacy of the institution takes one only a limited distance in deciding the rights of an individual in a particular case.

Aquinas introduces a further distinction between different forms of law. Jews and Christians have been given laws by God in a more direct, localized way. This is divine positive law. That the Jews were given laws by God Aquinas did not doubt; this was the old law. The question he took more pains to answer was whether there was one divine positive law or several. The answer could go in two different directions. One might say that God rules all mankind, is lawgiver to all mankind, and gives one law only. On the other hand, Christ said that he came to give a new law, and that implies that the old law and the new are two. Aquinas finds his way deftly between the horns of the dilemma. The sense in which the law is one is that it is given by one God; this anticipates nineteenth-century philosophers of law who explained the unity of a legal system in terms of its issuing from a single sovereign authority. The sense in which the law is more than one is that it is addressed, sequentially, to more than one community. Much as a human being is one and the same person when a boy and a full-grown man, even though the boy and the man may look very different, so the law is one law when it is given partially to the Jews in the Old Testament and fully to Christians later.[15]

Explaining why there has to be both divine law and eternal law, Aquinas argues that the eternal law, which is underwritten by reason as well as God, serves as a standard for any rational creature, but is silent on many issues that divine positive law speaks to. The new law contained in the gospel therefore contains within itself the natural law, but not vice versa. The same considerations dictated Aquinas's treatment of the question whether natural law is capable of change; the pro and contra are clear enough: on the one hand, the immutable principles of reason are just that, but, on the other, God gave particular instructions in the Old Testament that contradicted natural law, and human law introduces institutions such as private property that are not known to natural law. The resolution once again is that natural law is immutable as to first principles and not as to secondary consequences; where something is to be added or subtracted for the achievement of the law's purpose, there is both change and immutability.

This brings us to familiar issues, such as whether we could live without law, and whether positive human law must conform to one or other of eternal law, natural law, or divine law to be law properly speaking, and to command our obedience. This demands an account of what gives human law authority over us, and how its authority is constrained by the other forms of law to which we are subject. The medieval view held two possibilities in tension. On the one hand, rulers issued law in virtue of the authority that God conferred on them as rulers. This is the "top-down," or descending, view of authority, and no other seems (to almost anyone other than Hobbes) to make sense where *God's* law is at issue. On that view, law is the command of the sovereign. On the other hand, it was often claimed that rulers had received their authority to make law by grant from the people, or by concession of the community; this is a "bottom-up," or ascending, conception of authority and makes good sense of the authority of constitutional rulers. On that view, law expresses the will of the political community. The authority of natural law, which Cicero and Aristotle took to set the standard for positive law, must be accounted for differently; if we have a duty to pursue our own and the common good, we have a duty to obey those rules which minister to that good.

This still leaves the question of how far natural law constrains the legitimacy of human law. Aquinas consistently tries to apply the ideas of Aristotle, to whom modern conceptions of political obligation were foreign, and who provided no clear-cut answer to the question whether a law that fails the test of compatibility with natural law fails the test of being a law at all. The obvious, commonsensical view is to recur to the distinction between general rules binding on all rational creatures and the specification of what those rules require in particular conditions; purported laws that violate all the most important considerations that natural law rests on cannot possess any (morally) binding force, but if the complaint against them is that they are good-faith but incompetent attempts to implement natural law, the considerations that favor obedience will have greater force.

Nonetheless, Aquinas's views are not Aristotle's. Like any Christian writer, he has an unclassical sense of the gulf between the political world of sinful men and the prelapsarian world that preceded it. There is, he says, an indispensable role for human law in the fallen world in which we live. It is at the very least *useful*—though he means "indispensable"—to institute human law to supplement the other laws by which we are governed.[16] Aquinas's understanding of usefulness does not turn him into an eighteenth- or nineteenth-century utilitarian; the value of law is not exhausted by its usefulness in promoting ordinary happiness. Aquinas's view of the good life is much closer to Aristotle's than to Jeremy Bentham's, allowance made for Aquinas's dependence on Christian rather than classical ideas of virtue and what "the good life according to virtue" entailed. The purpose of human law is to make men behave virtuously, not merely to organize their relations with one another in a tidy fashion. Narrowly utilitarian considerations are not absent, but they are not central.

Aquinas quotes the observation of Isidore of Seville—he might have quoted Augustine and numerous others—that many men can be made to behave properly only by being threatened with punishment, and Aquinas agrees that this is a good reason to institute coercive law. Still, he does not appeal to many of the considerations that a modern writer would. We are as impressed as he by the usefulness of the criminal law in repressing antisocial and wicked behavior, but most of us are even more impressed by the usefulness of the civil law in assisting economic activity. Aquinas was not very interested in economic activity; he takes an Aristotelian view of moneymaking, is hostile to exchange for the sake of monetary gain, and is especially critical of usury;[17] he thinks like a thirteenth-century Dominican not an eighteenth-century classical economist. Even when Aquinas accepts Aristotle's observations about the need for human beings to cooperate with one another because they are not self-sufficient, the self-sufficiency he immediately discusses is self-sufficiency in leading the life of virtue. The service men do one another is less importantly that of cooperating to satisfy each other's physical needs than that of fulfilling "the need to receive from one another the discipline by which they arrive at virtue."[18]

Laws lose their authority by being unjust: *lex injusta nulla lex*. They also lose their authority when they cease to serve the purpose for which they are properly made. Aquinas's treatment of property rights illustrates the point. He took the Stoic-Christian view that by nature there is no private property. God gave the earth to mankind in common for the benefit of life, and but for our sinful natures there need be no rules of mine and thine. Aquinas has no interest in economic growth or ever-increasing prosperity; as a good Aristotelian, he thinks that we should aim to have "enough," not as much as possible. Aristotle's advocacy of the mean is Aquinas's touchstone; ascetics who starve themselves to death are as misguided as gluttons who eat themselves to death. The assumption of utility maximization that underpins modern economics implies a psychology alien to Aquinas.

The Virtues of Private Property

The morality of private property concerned Aquinas for the reasons it concerns ourselves—the contrast between the poverty of those who have too little and the greed of those who have too much—as well as for reasons remote from us. Dominicans and Franciscans took opposed views about property; the Franciscans claimed that they owned nothing, either individually or as an order, while the Dominicans took the view that the order, though not its individual members, owned what it seemed to own. The Franciscans were from the beginning, officially at any rate, more ascetic and self-denying than the Dominicans; they insisted that their order owned nothing and merely used what the pope allowed them. The distinction was important. In a Christian context, where the *amor habendi*, or desire for possessions, was held to be the root of all evil, the prelapsarian condition was seen as a time when Adam could use God's bounty, but owned nothing in the sense in which an individual's ownership entitles him to exclude everyone else from what he owns. It is easy to see the propaganda advantage accruing to the Fransciscans.

When he argues for the legitimacy of the private ownership of goods and land, Aquinas argues that we can accept some famous criticisms of property without concluding that all ownership is illicit. The argument runs briskly and persuasively. God is the sole lord of the world, so one form of dominion over the external world—better understood as sovereignty than as ownership—is simply not available. Nonetheless, God gave the world to mankind to use and to improve; and he gave mankind dominion over inferior creatures. It follows that there must be a right to appropriate whatever in the external world is useful for human life. As to the merits of individual, private property, he invokes the Aristotelian view that it is more efficient than other sorts of property both because people care more for their own than for common property and because we each know which things are our responsibility to care for. Perhaps more interestingly, he also says that an equitable distribution of property among individuals so that each is content with his own portion makes for peace. Dissension is more common where property is held in common than where it is held as private property. He may have had peasant communities in mind, but more probably he meant only that, in the absence of agreed rules, people will try to grab what they can.[19]

Use, on the other hand, should be as far as possible use in common. Aquinas bends an Aristotelian thought to Christian purposes. "Private ownership and common use" was Aristotle's attempt to secure the virtues of Sparta without a Spartan existence. The Spartan institution of military messes, where all males were supposed to eat together, was what Aristotle had in mind; but it was not at all what Aquinas was thinking of. Aquinas starts from the idea that law aims at the common good; property depends on the law for its legitimacy, and therefore the distribution of property should serve the common good, not the selfish interest of the legal owner. His defense of common use is an account of charity; a man can use his property as he chooses so long as he is ready to share with others in times of need. Sitting tight on his legal ownership and denying others the means of subsistence invalidates his ownership. This is farther from the Spartan messes in which Plato and Aristotle were interested than from the morality of the modern welfare state.

Aquinas recurs to the issue in discussing theft. Theft is self-evidently wrong. The essence of property is to be under the control of its owner, and its use should depend upon his permission; there cannot be property without rules against theft, so theft is transparently wrong. Aquinas considers the degrees of wrongness of theft under different conditions, but the crucial question is what we are to say about someone who commits theft only at the point where he will otherwise simply starve? Here Aquinas boldly says that the rich man's superfluity belongs to the starving man and that he commits no theft in taking what is his by right of necessity.[20] The argument reappears verbatim three centuries later in Locke's *First Treatise* on government.[21] It is a striking claim, but it is significant that Aquinas phrases it the way he does. The poor can be required to abstain from taking what they need from the stores of the rich only if the security of the possessions of the better-off is essential to the welfare of the poor themselves. Saint Basil had said that the rich man was like a man who comes into the theater and takes a seat and thus ensures that there is no seat for the next comer. If Saint Basil was wrong, it must be because the possessions of the rich do not prevent the poor from acquiring possessions of their own, and the wealth of the rich ensures that the poor can thrive.[22]

When that condition fails, the argument falls. The poor man is no longer obliged to keep his hands off the rich man's stores. In time of famine, the poor are entitled to help themselves if nobody else helps them. Aquinas seems to go further in saying that the superfluities of the rich "belonged" to the starving poor; ordinary speech does not suggest that the poor *own* the rich man's superfluities any more than patients own the public hospital that is obliged to treat them. Aquinas may have thought that in extreme necessity mankind was plunged back into a state of nature, where all things are common, or he may simply not have drawn such a sharp distinction as we do between one and another sort of "belonging." The latter suggestion is, however, at odds with the emphasis the Dominicans and Franciscans placed on exactly the distinction between ownership strictly speaking and a right of use, and the former thought is probably the right one.

War

Property is unimaginable without law to sustain it, and that involves criminal courts and punishment. It is also hard to imagine property existing without a state to protect it; but states are many rather than one, and they frequently engage in war with one another. Aquinas is one of the most influential theorists of justice in war, and he treats the justice of warfare, very plausibly, as part of the larger question of what entitles us to cause the deaths of other human beings. Since politics exists to preserve peace and unity, the state of war is the polar opposite of a properly political condition, but it can to some degree be regulated. Aquinas follows Augustine's account of the just war step by step, citing his authority at every turn. For war to be lawful, three things are needed: first, it must be official, declared by a person or persons authorized to do it; private revenge and banditry are not war and cannot be justified; individuals have courts to turn to for the redress of injustice and neither need to resort to war nor have the authority to do so.[23] Second, the cause of the war must be just; wars should be fought only in self-defense, but self-defense extends in one temporal direction to a preemptive strike to prevent imminent attack, and in the other to taking belated measures, for instance, to recover territory that has been unjustly seized and not returned. Third, the war must be fought with the right intention, with the aim of restoring peace and punishing the wicked always before our minds.[24]

Common sense marks the discussion. Aquinas goes on to argue against the active participation of bishops and priests on the battlefield, but does not suggest that they can play no part whatever in warfare; they may encourage the combatants and comfort the wounded. It was a live issue in medieval Europe, where bishops exercised secular authority and might lead a feudal host or their own militia into battle. In cases like this, Aquinas's attempts to extract firm principles from Aristotelian premises require a good deal of supplementation from without; like Aristotle, he believed that persons primarily engaged in one task were not to engage in others at odds with it, but he does not so much rely on the thought that a bishop who sometimes goes into battle will be a significantly worse bishop during times of peace as on the thought that "warlike tasks have a greatly unquiet character, and hence much distract the mind from the contemplation of Divine things and from praising God and offering prayers for the people, which belong to the duties of clerics."[25] More obvious objections to bishops' fighting could be drawn from the gospels; but the injunction to turn the other cheek appears to forbid everyone to fight, not priests alone, and, following Augustine, Aquinas had defused that objection already.

The State and Christianity

For all his faith in Aristotle, Aquinas's account of politics is neither modern nor classical, but Christian and medieval. His Aristotelian resources fail him—as they must—at the point where he has to discuss the role of religion in politics in terms that make no sense outside a Christian setting: the secular authority of the pope, the allegiance we owe or do not owe to non-Christian rulers, the treatment of Jews, nonbelievers, and heretics. Aristotle did not advocate religious toleration, but the concept of heresy was foreign to him. The modern ideal of toleration, which is four centuries newer than Aquinas's ideas, requires the Christian obsession with heresy to give it purchase and to illuminate what the ideal requires. It is not merely that we—anyone likely to be reading this—think it better to tolerate heretics than to burn them, but that we are impressed by the conviction and commitment that leads heretics to prefer death at the stake to apostasy. It is because heretics care so passionately about their dissident ideas that we think their repression so evil.

Aquinas thought no such thing. The Christian polity can do what no pagan polity could do. It can bring its citizens to as much understanding of the truths of the Christian religion as mortal minds can possess, and it can make them comport themselves so as to have a hope of grace and life eternal. The Christian state cannot directly bring individuals to understanding or a proper moral outlook; that is for the church. The state can promote true religion by ensuring that the church is safeguarded against whatever evils assail it, and by following the guidance of the church in moral matters. That raises the question of the relation of secular and ecclesiastical authority. Aquinas's views are no more extreme here than elsewhere. He does not repudiate the papacy's claims of immunity for its clergy in criminal courts or its claim that church property may be taxed only with the church's agreement; but he does not suggest that the pope has any secular authority outside the Papal States.[26] Nonetheless, he claims that the church has secular authority over Jews and says that the church does not assert its rights over unbelievers as a concession.[27] In the everyday politics of a Christian polity, the church's authority is not in competition with that of the state; secular affairs must generally be left to the secular authorities. Where the pope has a standing in secular politics, it is *ratione peccati*, and the pope legitimately intervenes in politics when a moral issue of sufficient gravity arises. The commonest occasion is if a royal marriage must be dissolved and papal authorization is required. "Sin" is an elastic justification, and we might fear that *ratione peccati* could ground unbridled papal authority over secular princes; after all, most political controversies have a moral dimension. Aquinas was infinitely far from defending that sort of papalism; Boniface VIII asserted a sweeping jurisdiction over secular affairs thirty years after Aquinas's death and led the papacy to disaster. Aquinas provided no resources for such an expansion of the pope's role in secular affairs.

The reader may wonder why Aquinas did not press the point that the state exists to further our earthly interests, and the church to further our interest in the afterlife, and thus embrace the modern separation of the jurisdictions of church and state. One answer is that nobody did. Seventeenth-century ideas about toleration and the separation of church and state were not a thirteenth-century discovery. The thirteenth-century view was that there are distinguishable jurisdictions, but they are interlinked and overlapping. Americans deeply attached to the separation of church and state tolerate a lot of dubious jurisprudence to maintain the division; Aquinas took it for granted that states tried to foster virtue in their citizens. The nature of virtue is largely known by reason, but the Christian revelation has enlarged our understanding of it; a Christian ruler promotes virtue as understood by Christians. Moreover, it would be scandalous for a Christian ruler to allow Christian belief to loosen its hold on his subjects or allow confusion and disorder to seize the church within his domain. The doctrines around which he had to preserve unity were better understood by the church and its priests, including the bishop of Rome, than by the laity, so the secular ruler should generally accept the authority of the church in such matters. Things go better when everyone sticks to one job. A takeover of secular functions by the church made no more sense than monarchs setting themselves up as theological authorities; neither did a sharp line of separation between the spheres of authority of church and state. Kings should rule with the moral guidance of the church; the church should look to the salvation of souls with the earthly assistance of the state.

Aquinas took an equally moderate view regarding the right of unbelievers to exercise authority over Christians. De facto, Christians found themselves reliant on the protection of non-Christian governments if they traveled beyond the borders of western Europe; the interesting question was how far they were morally bound to obey non-Christian rulers, and on this Aquinas sided with the tradition that appealed to Christ's acceptance of the authority of the pagan Roman Empire. Aquinas did not share Augustine's relish for the thought that God places us under the dominion of wicked rulers to drive home the fact of our sinfulness, but he did note that the fathers of the church expected to deal with pagan emperors. Saint Peter lived under the mad and wicked Nero without suggesting that the power to bind and loose that he had received from Christ could be used to depose Nero.[28] The argument is simple: earthly rulers are to be obeyed when they perform the functions that earthly rulers are supposed to perform. When they do not, the situation becomes more complicated, but the fundamental duty to do justice and act lawfully implies that we must not resort to extralegal activity unless we shall do more good than harm. The one exception to this is the much discussed case where a ruler demands an action explicitly forbidden by Christian teaching. Augustine held that we should engage in purely passive disobedience under such conditions. Aquinas held a more complicated view; he says that such a ruler had forfeited his right to have us obey his orders, and that we had returned to a state of nature in which we could legitimately do whatever was morally acceptable to restore a stable, lawful, unoppressive regime. To see to the bottom of Aquinas's view, we should first turn to two other aspects of the role of Christian faith in secular politics and then to his discussion of the treatment of tyrants.

First, then, the question of heretics and, second, the treatment of the Jews. Aquinas observes that there are many arguments against compelling unbelievers to adopt the Christian faith.[29] Faith is something we must come to willingly, and forced professions are not faith. As often, he argues from the symbolic interpretation of gospel texts: thus, Christ's admonition to his disciples not to pull up the tares for fear of pulling up the wheat with them is to be understood as an injunction not to kill unbelievers for fear of killing potential Christians. The injunction *compelle intrare* is also given much weight. The parable of the man who gave a wedding feast and, lacking guests, told his servants to go out into the highways and byways and "compel them to come in" led to a lot of bloodshed over the centuries. It seems to enjoin Christians to force non-Christians into the church. Aquinas trod carefully. We should certainly stop unbelievers from subverting the faith of Christians. The Christian ruler of a state containing a minority of nonbelievers may limit the nonbelievers' freedom of speech and action to avoid unsettling the faith of the Christian majority.

It is not a license to kill unbelievers because they are unbelievers; killing the infidel is not good in itself. Nonetheless, Aquinas moves unnervingly from discussing the usefulness of mild coercion in bringing the unbeliever to a Christian faith to considering their execution. The argument for mild forms of coercion is neither complicated nor implausible, even if liberal readers will not much like it. Coercion works, and mild coercion works best. Savage persecution arouses resistance, but mild measures of coercion do not. Many people say that they are glad to have been made to observe the practices of the faith and that they regard themselves as having been kept on the straight and narrow by such means. To use a vulgar modern analogy, a man might be grateful that when he was intoxicated his friends took away his car keys, though he put up a fight at the time. The newly persuaded Christian will be grateful that he was enabled to see the light by being forced to look in the right direction.

Heretics are another matter; they are not mere unbelievers. They are backsliders and resilers from a faith they have adopted; they are in breach of obligations freely made and must be forced to meet them. This does not explain the savagery with which the church dealt with heresy, but Aquinas is unflinching. The heretic has committed a mortal sin and has condemned himself to eternal death; his crime is worse than that of the forger and counterfeiter who is executed for his crime. Summary execution is warranted, even though it never happens in fact because the church exercises a self-restraint and mercy appropriate to its mission, and never seeks the death of a heretic until he has had several chances to repent and return to the faith. Since heresy is so much worse than mere unbelief, it follows that although an unbeliever who has never been a Christian may exercise ordinary political authority over Christians, and Christians are obliged to obey him and treat his laws as binding, the heretic is another matter. He can be deposed for apostasy. Aquinas does not insist that he *must* be deposed, but he does say that Gregory VII's deposition of the emperor Henry IV was valid.[30] The pope was right to excommunicate him, and an excommunicated ruler has no authority over his subjects. One wonders what Aquinas thought of the fact that his distant relative Frederick II, the emperor during the first twenty-five years of Aquinas's life, was excommunicated no fewer than four times, including the time he was first excommunicated for failing to go on crusade as promised and again for going on crusade while still excommunicate.

Among unbelievers who have never been Christians, the Jews form a special case. Aquinas accepts the canon law claim that Jews are "the slaves of the church," even though the church never acted on that claim even in the Papal States where it had the physical capacity to do so, and it was a canon that was contradicted by other canons. His acceptance comes the more oddly because Aquinas was not interested in the conversion of the Jews, and did not suggest they committed any crime merely by being non-Christians. If they convert to Christianity, they can be held to what they have promised, and relapses into their former faith can be punished. Otherwise, they should be allowed to live as they traditionally have done, partly because it is more trouble than it is worth to do anything else, and partly because they may serve a useful purpose as exemplifying the old imperfect faith that Christianity has perfected. This was not a display of friendship toward the Jews and their faith: his discussion of the need to tolerate their religious rites is reinforced by an appeal to one of Augustine's more surprising suggestions—that we permit prostitution to avoid the whole world's being consumed by lust.[31]

These thoughts are elaborated in Aquinas's response to a question posed by the duchess of Brabant on the lawfulness of exacting a tribute from the Jews. He responded with a letter on the government of the Jews.[32] He says that since the Jews are perpetual slaves, their property is their ruler's, and all of it can be taken save a bare subsistence. The duchess may have been less happy with his response to her claim that everything which the Jews in her jurisdiction possessed had been acquired by the practice of usury, and that since usury was illicit, she could seize the property on which the profits of usury had been spent and use it for her own purposes. He replied that it could legitimately be taken from the Jews, but should be returned to those who had paid the usurious interest. If they could not be located, it must be spent on charity. It must not be taken as tax revenue. Aquinas was not by the standards of his day severe or superstitious; he was far from suggesting that Jews might be killed just because they were Jews, or because they inherited the taint of those who had killed Christ, which was what medieval anti-Semitism often amounted to. He did not suggest that their rulers might treat them absolutely as they liked. Nonetheless, as with his acceptance of slavery and the division of the world into the better- and the worse-off, Aquinas demonstrates how easy it is to reconcile the natural equality and freedom of all mankind with the inequalities of the world as we have it.

Politeia, Kingship, Tyranny

De regimine principum provides a simple defense of moderate monarchy. The polity exists for the sake of peace and unity, and it is best ruled by a king. The unity of the larger is mirrored in the unity of the smaller, and one-man rule suits most polities. What a polity is for is constant: it must preserve peace and unity by means of law, and law aims at a common good, which is not an additive sum of the various private goods of the members of the society but the good of living in common the life of virtue. Aristotle might wonder where his concern for balancing social forces to fend off revolution has gone to, and the answer is that Aquinas is drawing on the authorities known to him—biblical, Ciceronian, Aristotelian, and the traditions of canon law—not in order to write political sociology but to write a mirror of princes. The genre is moral exhortation, not political theory.

Nonetheless, he does something important. Aquinas finesses the contrast between descending and ascending theories of legitimate authority, with no sleight of hand. The unity of a polity is best encapsulated in kingly rule; but the authority of the king is the authority of the political community. He takes it for granted that a wise king governs with the advice and consent of his nobles, and in conformity to the teaching of the church. This is not the Polybian theory of the mixed constitution, for Polybius's discussion is in the "sociological" mode of Aristotle's discussions of the avoidance of revolution. Aquinas was making the moral point that it is not the personal will of the king that makes his laws laws, but what we might—though Aquinas does not—call his representative will. Arbitrary will has no place in a constitutional polity. If a ruler is a source of disunity and scandal rather than unity and peace, his title to govern is undermined. Christian morality provides resources for a theory of constitutionally limited authority and an account of government as essentially representative government.

For Aquinas this provides a solution to the question of the deposition of tyrants and the praiseworthiness of tyrannicides. That tyrants may be deposed he does not doubt. One-man rule is the best form of government when it conforms to its own proper principles, but one-man misrule or tyranny is the worst form of government. The instrumental view of government that permeates *De regimine principum* provides a simple but adequate principle to govern the deposition of tyrants; if they can be got rid of, they should be, and enduring tyrannical rule is defensible only on the grounds that attempting the overthrow of the tyrant will create still worse evils. There is no Augustinian insistence on passive obedience or passive disobedience, nor a Ciceronian enthusiasm for political murder. Since the king's authority rests on the consensus of the community, his removal from office must be an act of the community, not of a single individual. This eminently sensible view raises a question that Aquinas did not address but others did: who speaks for the community? When Locke came to discuss revolution in 1680, he termed it an "appeal to heaven"—as did many American revolutionaries a century after that. Appealing to heaven may be something that a single individual has to do to start the revolutionary process, but it is done *on behalf of* a whole political community. Not surprisingly, commentators have seen Locke as a disciple of Aquinas.

The tyrant has forfeited the trust placed in him and should demit the office he has disgraced; if he will not do so willingly, he must be made to do so. What is needed is an account of who in particular may launch this process, and what we shall find is that once an answer is given, it becomes difficult not to go further and argue that the body or bodies that can approve and disapprove the conduct of kings ought themselves to be sovereign. If defenders of royal absolutism could argue that it was absurd to suppose that a sovereign might have a sovereign set above him, and equally absurd to suppose a "lower" body could have the right to dismiss him, critics could accept those premises and conclude that the body that could dismiss the sovereign must be the source of the sovereign's powers and that he could govern only as its agent. Down that path lay the conciliar movement within the church, the revival of republican theory in the city-states of Italy, and, very much farther down the path and a long time later, the rise of modern representative democracy.

CHAPTER 8

The Fourteenth-Century Interregnum

Roads Not Taken—Until Later

THE CONCERNS OF THREE fourteenth-century thinkers dominate this chapter: Dante's advocacy of universal monarchy, Marsilius of Padua's claim that representative and constitutional arrangements should govern both state and church, and Bartolus of Sassoferrato's analysis and defense of the semiautonomous city republics of northern Italy. The conciliar movement for church reform provides a very brief coda, while William of Ockham receives all too brief a discussion, as do Nicholas of Cusa and Jean Gerson, the theorists of conciliarism. In terms of their impact on the immediate political scene, all wrote in vain. The attempt to unify Italy under imperial rule that exhausted previous emperors had been abandoned by the first Habsburgs in the late thirteenth century, and the attempts of Henry of Luxemburg and Ludwig of Bavaria early in the fourteenth century met with no success. Ludwig's successor, Charles IV, was concerned only with his native Bohemia, and in accordance with a promise to the pope, he spent only one day in Rome when he was crowned emperor, by the prefect of the city rather than the pope. The vision of a new Roman empire with the political and military reach of the western Roman Empire died.

The city-states on which Marsilius and Bartolus focused their attention were increasingly dominated by their aristocratic and autocratic rulers, who were themselves increasingly dependent on the favor of popes or foreign monarchs. Conciliarist pressures for a constitutionally governed church were briefly successful in the early fifteenth century, then failed. Thereafter they were overtaken by the Reformation of the sixteenth century, after which the Roman Catholic Church remained monarchical and hierarchical, while the Protestant churches exhibited an almost infinite variety of political forms—though none that much resembled that of the Roman Catholic Church.

Nonetheless, to dismiss the ideas discussed in this chapter merely as "roads not taken" would be a mistake. These are roads taken in surprising ways a very long time afterward; Napoleon first, and Hitler more terrifyingly, came close to establishing a European empire on the scale that fired the imagination of Frederick II and Dante; the European Union is sometimes accused of being on the way to doing so. Representative government as practiced throughout the Western world would not wholly surprise Marsilius; and if it is overly imaginative to say that the relationship between the individual states of the United States and the federal government, or that between the European Union and its constituent national states, would have been a fertile field of study for Bartolus of Sassoferrato and the jurists who thought about the legal status of semi-independent city-states, it is not wholly fanciful. Conciliarism was almost entirely concerned with church government, not with politics more broadly, but its advocates would not have been surprised by representative democracy in the twenty-first century, and the theoretical analysis of the voting systems we employ today (as well as some we do not) began with Nicholas of Cusa.

Church and State

The background to the development of political thought at the turn of the fourteenth century is the familiar conflict between church and state, especially between papacy and empire: the conflicts between Pope Boniface VIII and Philip the Fair, king of France, and then yet again between the papacy and the empire. Conflicts between successive popes and the kings of England, France, and Spain almost always had their origins in the desire of kings to tax the wealth of the church and were amenable to compromise. The conflict between papacy and empire was more nearly a zero-sum game. One or the other could dominate central Italy, but not both. Either the pope had a special role in the election of the emperor, or not; either the emperor had a special role with regard to the papacy, or not. This lent a sharper ideological, theoretical, and theological edge to disputes, which was one reason why they were drawn out and intractable. The Holy Roman Empire was a creation of the papacy, and the coronation of the emperor by the pope of the day was essential to the emperor's status as emperor, until Emperor Charles IV issued the so-called Golden Bull of 1356, which named the seven imperial electors and decreed that election by them was all that was required, and that a majority of the seven was sufficient for election.

Until that time, popes took the view that what they could confer they could take away; and they had some historical authority on their side; the election of Charlemagne's father, Pippin, as king of the Franks was preceded by a deputation of nobles to Rome to ask papal permission to depose Childeric, the last Merovingian king, not for sin or heresy but because he was "useless." The pope had concurred. One of Marsilius of Padua's many offenses in the eyes of the church was his tract *De translatione imperii* (On the transfer of power), which argued that the deposition of Childeric and the election of Pippin had been acknowledged by the pope, but was in itself legally valid and legitimate as the act of the appropriate members of the Frankish political society.[1] The doctrine of the two swords that Gelasius had laid down was much debated by both canon and civil lawyers, without a clear consensus emerging on the vexed question whether the superiority of the spiritual sword meant that its bearer could dictate to secular rulers and, if so, whether the pope could dictate to all, to the emperor in particular, and over what range of issues. It was never suggested that popes could supplant a secular ruler in his ordinary judicial and administrative roles; there were two swords, not one. Nor was it ever denied that the spiritual sword was "superior," in the same sense that the soul was superior to the body and heavenly concerns to

earthly concerns. That settled none of the disputes about the rights of
secular courts over the clergy, the coercive powers of ecclesiastical courts,
or taxation.

At the end of the thirteenth century and the beginning of the fourteenth, it became clear that the papacy was all but impotent in secular
politics outside Italy. It was a French king, not a German emperor, who
made it obvious. When Aquinas died in 1274, this could not have been
predicted; the imperial throne remained empty for two decades after
Frederick II died frustrated in 1250. A new emperor was elected only
in 1272. The papacy had won—or had drawn with the advantage on
its side—every contest with lay rulers. In 1209 Innocent III imposed a
papal interdict on England and forced King John to humiliate himself
by acknowledging the pope as his feudal overlord. In the second quarter
of the thirteenth century, Gregory IX and his successor Innocent IV had
frustrated Frederick II's hopes of creating a secular Italian state stretching from Sicily to the Alps. But in the last years of the thirteenth century
and the first years of the next, Philip IV of France decisively defeated
Pope Boniface VIII. Indeed, the French monarchy kidnapped the papacy,
physically and organizationally, relocating the papacy to Avignon and
beginning the so-called Babylonian Captivity, which ended only in 1378.
The territory of Avignon, the Comtat Venaissin, was, legally speaking,
part of the Papal States until the French Revolution, but practically, the
papal court was at the mercy of the French king. Whether this was worse
than being at the mercy of rival Roman aristocrats is another matter.

The papacy's success in frustrating the efforts of successive emperors to unite Italy and make the unity of Europe a reality was deceptive.
After King John had humbled himself before Innocent III, English kings
were unaffected by the terms on which the excommunication had been
lifted. The church was marginally more free to choose whom it wished
as bishops, but a royal veto on elections persisted, and in spite of Innocent's insistence that the clergy could be taxed only by papal permission,
the kings of both France and England continued to levy taxes on their
clergy without waiting for it. The Catholic Church was a formidable
force; it was wealthier than any single European state—owning perhaps
a quarter of all the land and movables in Europe—and had a firmer grip

on the loyalties of Christendom than most secular rulers. But these were wasting assets; bishops who lived like princes gave the lie to the claim that the church held its wealth in trust for the poor; and popes who spent taxes raised in France and England on fighting emperors in Italy ran into a growing sense of national identity and national loyalty. When Boniface VIII tried to emulate Innocent III and lay down the law to the kings of France and England, he violated the tacit compromise by which for eighty years the peace had been kept outside of the empire, and began a fight he could not win.

The weakness at the heart of the papacy was Rome itself. It was a city in incessant turmoil, where aristocratic families schemed, bribed, and fought each other to gain the papal tiara. The Gaetani and Colonna families were notorious for treating the papacy as a get-rich-quick scheme for themselves and their relatives. Popes had relied on the divisions of the German princes to undermine emperors from Henry IV to Frederick II. In the early 1300s, Philip IV played the same trick on the papacy, using the mutual loathing of the Colonna and the Gaetani to undermine the pope. Boniface VIII was a Gaetani. After his defeat the papacy continued to wield military and political power over the papal territories until the nineteenth-century reunification of Italy; but the ability of the pope to challenge secular rulers on their own territory ended with the defeat of Boniface's pretensions, and the papal states looked increasingly like all the other Italian princely states.

Philip IV inflicted the decisive defeat in 1303, a decade before Dante wrote *De monarchia*. In 1294 Boniface VIII was elected under bizarre circumstances. From 1292 to 1294 the papal throne was vacant because the cardinals could not agree on whom to elect; the scandal was resolved by the election of the aged Peter Murrone, a simple hermit who took the title of Celestine V. He could not handle the demands of office and resigned after a few months. He was placed under arrest by his successor, escaped, was recaptured, and died in captivity ten months later. Boniface was elected to succeed him. He was old, suffered from painful urinary ailments, and unsurprisingly had a vile temper; he was also astonishingly energetic and had extreme hierocratic views. The election was contentious. Celestine had no right to resign, and arguably there was no vacancy. To this day his is the only resignation in the history of the papacy. Dante placed Celestine in the lowest circle of hell for his cowardly refusal of the office ("che fece per viltate il gran rifiuto").[2] Dante's motive must surely have been that Celestine's abdication opened the way to the election of Boniface VIII, whose papacy saw the destruction of everything Dante cared for and brought about Dante's exile. Ever since then popes die miserably and uncomfortably in office rather than follow Celestine's example.

Boniface was immediately at odds with the English king Edward I and Philip IV over the taxation of the clergy. Each wished to raise the funds to make war on the other from their most prosperous subjects—the clergy. Whether motivated by a laudable desire to see peace restored or a less laudable desire to see the clergy's taxes in his own treasury, Boniface set out to starve the two monarchs of funds. He issued a papal bull, *Clericis laicos*, which restated Innocent III's claim that the clergy could be taxed only with papal permission and excommunicated clergy who paid taxes to lay authorities without permission. With the letter *Ausculta fili* addressed to Philip IV, and the subsequent bull *Unam sanctam*, it formed the clearest statement of Boniface's claim of legal authority over kings and emperors. Edward I ignored it. Philip went on the offensive and forbade the export of currency and precious metals from France. Fear of bankruptcy might have caused Boniface to retreat, but he had trouble close to home; the Colonna cardinals denied the validity of his election and in June 1297 accused him of having murdered his predecessor. Boniface backed down and agreed that in an emergency Philip could tax the clergy without papal permission. The papacy's finances were restored, and in 1300 a successful Jubilee was celebrated.

This may have made Boniface incautious when the next challenge occurred a year later. In 1301 Philip had the bishop of Pamiers arrested on charges of blasphemy, heresy, and treason, took him to Paris, tried him in a royal court, had him found guilty, and jailed him. This violated the long-standing "privilege of clergy" whereby clerics were tried only in church courts; to rub salt in the wound, Philip demanded that the pope endorse the proceedings. This reopened the old quarrel about the right of lay monarchs to appoint and depose bishops. The king was on solid ground in claiming that a secular ruler could not be impotent in the face of a bishop's treason, but the fact that the charges were both secular and religious seemed to imply that the king was assuming jurisdiction over spiritual offenses. As to the request for papal endorsement, it might in one light seem to accept that it was for the pope to press charges of heresy, but in another light suggest wholesale contempt for the pope's role within France.

Boniface was provoked to issue a papal bull, *Ausculta fili*. The literal translation "Listen, son" is infinitely too vulgar to catch the tone of pained regret with which Boniface tells the king that "although our merits are insufficient, God has set us over kings and kingdoms, and has imposed on us the yoke of apostolic service to root up and pull down, to waste and destroy, to build and to plant in his name and according to his teaching."[3] *Ausculta fili* did not in so many words assert that the pope had temporal jurisdiction over the king, but it came close enough to allow the king to claim that it did. He summoned a national council of clergy, nobles, and commons—an occasion of great importance as the first meeting of the Estates General—to repudiate the pope's claims and assert royal control over the church in France. He also engaged in a propaganda battle of extreme unscrupulousness, circulating forgeries of the pope's letters and a (forged) royal reply that addressed the pope as "your fatuity." A majority of the bishops and all the lay representatives supported the king. The pope insisted that he had well understood the doctrine of the two swords for more than forty years, and that the "fatuitas" and "insipientia" of claiming clerical jurisdiction over secular affairs had never crossed his mind.[4]

Matters did not immediately come to a head—the crushing defeat of the French forces in Flanders by the burghers of Courtrai in the summer of 1302 forced a pause. Then, in November, Boniface issued the bull *Unam sanctam*, in which he committed himself to the supremacy of the spiritual power in terms that could readily be misrepresented as a claim of lordship—though not the feudal suzerainty that Innocent III had forced Frederick II and John to acknowledge. It suited the king to pretend that the pope claimed to be his feudal overlord. Since *Unam Sanctam* drew on the writings of Aquinas among many others, it was inconceivable that the pope would have done so. What the pope claimed was the power to depose kings *ratione peccati*, for sin. This was the bottom line of Gelasius's claim for the spiritual authority of the papacy more than eight centuries before. The obvious difficulty with a claim to authority *ratione peccati* is that few actions of a government raise *no* moral questions; even such mundane enterprises as road traffic schemes may place unfair burdens on one or another group, and unfairness is a moral failing. The doctrine was generally held to apply only to monarchs of unusually vile character or blatantly heretical opinions. It was invoked in 1570 when Elizabeth I of England was declared deposed by Pope Pius V. She reigned for a further thirty-three years, but was provoked to judicially murder large numbers of her Catholic subjects by this seeming incitement to treason. Today the idea that a conservative pope might try to depose an American president *ratione peccati* is unthinkable, even if Catholic bishops may urge their flocks to vote against politicians who uphold abortion rights. *Unam sanctam* infuriated Philip, who promptly called another council; it declared Boniface's election invalid and the pope heretical; what its authority was in either case was unclear. On his side, the pope prepared to excommunicate the king.

Philip struck first. There were no French military forces near Rome, but mercenaries were easily hired for strong-arm tactics. When Boniface left Rome in the summer of 1303 for the Gaetani stronghold of Agnani, Philip's chief adviser, Guillaume de Nogaret, attacked the town with an army of mercenaries and Colonna troops. The assault brought about the pope's death. Boniface, very old and very ill, survived the terrifying experience for only a few weeks. Nogaret and Sciarra Colonna nearly lost their own lives, too: they were at a loss what to do after seizing the castle of Agnani with so little trouble, and spent a day quarreling over the next move. The outraged townspeople had time to organize an attack on the invaders, which they narrowly escaped. Nonetheless, Philip secured all he hoped. Boniface's immediate successor lived only a few months; and after his death, the cardinals elected Clement V, a Frenchman who never went to Rome but established the papal court at Avignon.

Papal weakness did not play into the hands of the emperor. French kings were old hands at stirring up trouble among the German princes who elected the emperor, so rendering an aggressive imperial policy impossible. For many years the electors could not agree on a candidate for emperor. After the death of Frederick II in 1250, there was an interregnum until Rudolph of Habsburg was elected in 1272; he had no Italian ambitions. The next emperor who did was Henry of Luxemburg (1308–13); he was the first emperor since Frederick II to be crowned in Rome—but not in St. Peter's and not by the pope. Henry's Italian expedition began well, but turned into a stalemate. His soldiers died of malaria or drifted away, and he fell sick and died. That expedition, on which Dante had hung his hopes for political change in Florence, was the inspiration of *De monarchia*.

Dante

Dante's place in European cultural history rests on his poetry, *La divina commedia*, above all.[5] Nonetheless, he was anything but apolitical. He was born in 1265, and as an ambitious young man joined one of the guilds that supplied candidates for civic office; in June 1300 he became one of the six "priors" who governed Florence—they held office for a year and presided for two months of it. In 1301 he went on a diplomatic mission to Rome; while he was away, a coup brought the so-called Black Guelphs to power; Dante was forced into exile on pain of death at the stake if he returned. Florence had always sided with the papacy against the empire and was thus Guelph, although the labels of Guelph and Ghibelline were loosely applied. With the election of Boniface VIII, the Florentine Guelphs split into factions; the White Guelphs—Dante's allies—were hostile to Boniface, while the Black Guelphs were papal clients.

Florentine politics were brutal, and Dante never forgave Boniface VIII his exile at the hands of the Black Guelphs. He found exile intolerable and safe haven hard to come by. His criticism of the papacy and its political meddling was public and savage, and giving him asylum was an invitation to revenge by the allies of the papacy. He was not impressed by his Florentine allies, nor they by him, and when peace was restored in Florence, he was never given honorable terms for a return, and died in exile in Verona in 1321. A tomb was later erected in Santa Croce in Florence, but Verona refused to return his body to his ungrateful mother city, and the tomb remains empty. The intensity of the description of the expulsion of Adam and Eve from paradise in the *Divine Comedy* is often said to reflect Dante's misery at his exile from Florence. *De monarchia* is his philosophical and political riposte to the theocratic ambitions that exiled him and a vision of the political world he longed for. *De monarchia* is divided into three books that argue the case for universal monarchy on three different bases: philosophy (that is to say, Aristotle), the history of Rome, and scripture. In argumentative terms, the first and third parts do the hard work; the middle portion adduces factual evidence in support of the arguments that precede and follow it.

About its merits commentators are divided. Dante scholars, for whom the *Divine Comedy* is Dante's great bequest to European culture, rarely have a good word to say for *De monarchia*, although their hostility has nothing to do with its politics. Dante wrote *De monarchia* in philosophical Latin, while in their eyes his achievement was to write great poetry in the Italian vernacular. Whatever language it was written in, it would resist sentence-by-sentence analysis, and it is hard to imagine that it can ever have seemed a very persuasive defense of the proposition that the only lawful political authority in the world was that of the emperor, and that all other powers, including the church, were subordinate to it. Dante's case was far from foolish, but it was utopian. His ultramonarchism did not mean that he thought that Henry of Luxemburg or his successors should conduct the day-to-day administration of Italian city-states such as Dante's native Florence, let alone the daily life of the church, and he had no thought that a universal monarch should aspire to govern the entire globe in detail. At the height of its power, Rome largely left the cities of the empire to attend to their own affairs in their own way, and Rome was the example that Dante had in mind. Nonetheless, Dante argued an extreme case: only a revived empire on the Roman model could provide the environment in which humanity could flourish. His negative target was the church's pretensions to secular authority, and unsurprisingly the book was loathed by the papacy; as soon as the Index of forbidden books was created in 1559, it was placed on it and removed only in 1891.

The extraordinary syllogistic form of the first book of *De monarchia* often misleads readers into thinking the tract is a theoretical exercise by an exiled poet, and a philosophical dream. Impractical it may be, and its treatment of the history of Rome in the second book is more akin to the elaboration of a myth than a rendition of Roman history; but the violence of the papal reaction shows that its enemies took it seriously. The first part justifies monarchy by the light of reason alone, and the third argues that there is no justification in scripture for papal supremacy over the temporal power. It is not the papacy's spiritual authority but its overreaching in secular matters that Dante condemns. Nor does he advocate the separation of church and state; even Marsilius's *Defensor pacis* does not go so far. As a good Christian, Dante thought the papacy should exercise an appropriate authority in secular matters, and gave a coherent account of it. What he repudiated was Boniface VIII's claim that the pope was the legal and political superior of the emperor and other earthly kings. The proper relationship was what Aquinas and innumerable others had spelled out: a morally upright monarch looked to a spiritually impressive pope for spiritual advice and used his own power to secure the church's earthly interests. The secular authority of the pope was the moral authority that an uncorrupt pope exercised over a righteous ruler. Endless misfortunes had fallen upon Italy in particular and the world more generally because the papacy had not kept within those limits.

Disentangled from the formality of its structure, Dante's argument is attractive. It contains ideas that five centuries later would underpin the philosophies of history of Kant, Hegel, and Marx. It seems astonishing that Dante derived them from an Aristotelian original to which the idea of historical development is wholly foreign, but the Christian conception of providence provided resources that Aristotle did not. Dante's premise is that the purpose of life in society is to allow the human species to manifest all distinctively human perfections; the two most important are the capacity of the individual to attain the life of reason and to govern himself by moral law. These perfections cannot be achieved in the absence of peace, and the preservation of peace is the fundamental duty of rulers. Like almost every thinker in that notably violent age, Dante longed for peace.[6] The supreme obligation of government is to govern justly so that the ruler's subjects can employ the blessings of peace to develop their abilities to the utmost. Peace and justice are the conditions of good government and a good life.

This is a deliberate echo of Aristotle's claim that the polity exists for the sake not of mere life but of the good life. The reader may wonder how Dante can extract a defense of the authority of the emperor from such premises; Aristotle held that the best life was led within the confines of the Greek city-state, and the best life was, in his view, available only to Greeks. Dante humanized the argument by adding a premise that was central to Kant's *Project for a Universal History with a Cosmopolitan Purpose* centuries later, and the works it influenced. The achievement of perfection cannot be the work of one person or group. It is the whole species that must accomplish it. We need each other's companionship and assistance to achieve anything, but when we aim at perfection we cannot stop with smaller and more limited associations. We must conceive of the whole of mankind as involved in the universal human striving after perfection. "There must needs be a vast number of individual people in the human race, through whom this potentiality can be actualised."[7] It is *universal* monarchy to which we owe our allegiance, not this or that king, count, or duke. One may wonder how Dante squared this thought with his all-consuming love of the city of Florence, but many thinkers have felt no tension between cosmopolitanism and deep affection for their own country.

The argument is encumbered by Dante's ostentatious logical demonstration of his case. Why he was so determined to show that he—almost alone—observed the rules of syllogistic inference, and committed none of the blunders that Aristotle had reproved, is hard to guess. It may simply reflect a passion for philosophy, which Dante had studied in depth in the 1290s. Having shown to his own satisfaction that universal monarchy is a demand of reason, Dante turns in the second book to showing that it was God's will that there should be a Roman Empire. The exercise induces unease; empirically considered, Dante's historical analysis is decidedly hit and miss. A caustic critic might complain that unreliable facts do little to support an intrinsically shaky conclusion. To understand what Dante was doing we must not complain that he was not a very good historian, but see him responding to anxieties about the role of providence in history.

Augustine's treatment of Rome in *The City of God* illuminates the project. Augustine argued that Rome had a place in God's providential scheme; the Roman Empire performed a limited service to fallen men, although at a high price in violence, while the rulers of Rome had themselves been dominated by their own lust for domination. Augustine did not think as his pagan contemporaries did: that the gods had favored Rome; and to the extent that a disbelief in a pagan providence admitted of degrees, he disbelieved even more strongly that Rome had benefited from the goodwill of particular gods. Like all political enterprises, Rome was a case of faute de mieux, a contrivance for making the lives of sinners less violent and painful than otherwise. Nonetheless, it was God's will that it existed, and the patriotism, courage, and honesty of the best of its citizens showed the virtues the citizens of the city of God should display.

Dante gave a much more positive role to government. He did not see Rome as only a large and successful example of doing the lesser evil to prevent the greater. Rather, he saw in Rome a manifestation of God's intention that humanity should develop all its capacities under the tutelage of a regime of peace and justice. The question was not whether *an* empire was a good; reason showed that it was. He had to argue that *this* empire was a good. Given the bloodiness and brutality that attended the rise of the Roman Empire, this was not easy for a squeamish thinker. Dante's boldest stroke was to claim that Rome had acquired power lawfully; it had done so by right of combat.[8] This was an oddly anachronistic argument: some historians say that trial by combat was not used during the Middle Ages, and is a literary invention, others that it was used occasionally; but classical history and mythology are full of occasions when two evenly matched armies decide not to hazard the lives of everyone but to allow two champions or two groups of champions to decide the matter. Dante combined the classical thought that the gods

smiled on the success of heroes with a more Christian and juristic idea—
not that might makes right, but that success under appropriate conditions is a mark of heaven's favor.

Since reason favored *an* imperial project and God acting through
history endorsed the *Roman* imperial project, it remained for Dante to
conclude his defense of the imperial project by demolishing the idea
that scripture gave authority to the pope rather than the emperor. He
did much more than this in the third book of *De monarchia*, however,
because he also assaulted the historical claims of the papacy, in particular the papal appeal to the so-called Donation of Constantine, a
notoriously implausible document concocted in the mid-eighth century
or perhaps a century later. It purported to be a charter of the fourth
century in which Constantine transferred authority over the western
Roman Empire to Pope Sylvester I and his successors. The donation was
widely taken to be a forgery, although the papacy defended its authenticity until the sixteenth century, by which time historical scholarship had
utterly destroyed its credibility. The papacy was on much firmer ground
in tracing its secular sovereignty over the papal states to grants by Pippin and Charlemagne, and subsequent confirmation by later emperors.
Dante emphasized not the inauthenticity of the donation but its legal
invalidity. In the *Divine Comedy*, he concentrates on its corrupting effect
on the church. Here he claims that it is invalid because an emperor cannot divest himself of imperial authority; the act is self-negating. This
is not the claim that an emperor cannot abdicate. An emperor could
certainly abdicate and a new emperor be elected in his place. If that happened, the emperor would have renounced his imperial authority, and
the process of election would transfer the imperial authority to a successor. What the emperor could not do by fiat was to alienate the imperial
authority and deprive himself and his successors of it: "nobody has the
right to do things because of an office he holds which are in conflict with
that office, otherwise one and the same thing would oppose itself in its
own nature, which is impossible." It is not an easy argument to assess;
emperors could choose their successors, and they could and did divide
the imperial authority between an eastern and a western emperor, and
even establish a quadrumvirate. On the other hand, there is something

incoherent about invoking imperial authority to validate the gift of that authority to a different institution.[9]

For the rest, Dante engages in standard New Testament exegesis; he insists that the passages adduced in defense of papal claims are reports of Jesus's attitude to political power and physical coercion, and cannot be read as deeply significant allegories. The famous "two swords" passage is flattened out: Christ had told his disciples that they should take steps to defend themselves in the face of his extreme unpopularity. That suggested that they should acquire a dozen swords, one apiece. When he asked how many they actually had, and they said "two," his reply, "it is enough," meant what it said: two swords would be enough to defend themselves if need be. Gelasius's contortion of the passage to argue that Christ had instituted both a secular and a spiritual power, and that the spiritual was superior, was ungrounded in the text. The conferral on Saint Peter of the power to bind and loose presents greater problems, but Dante dismisses them. Christ said to Peter that *whatsoever* he bound or loosed on earth was to be bound or loosed in heaven, which indeed sounds very like the gift of a *plenitudo potestatis*, or absolute authority. On the contrary, says Dante, all it means is that so far as all those things that he *could* do here on earth were concerned, his power was unlimited. There was much he could not do. Saint Peter could not even dissolve a validly contracted marriage by his simple say-so, and the idea that "whatsoever" included the deposition of emperors when it did not include the dissolution of a marriage was bizarre.[10] In any event, nobody at the time of Christ or at the time of the writing of the gospels had ever doubted that the emperor was in possession of freestanding political authority over the known world. Had Christ intended to deny it, he would have done so.

The sting in the tail from employing Aristotelian premises to defend royal authority against the pretensions of the papacy is that it implies that a political community is a good thing in its own right, and its preservation a duty. This diminishes the special position of monarchy. Nonetheless, it does not wholly undermine it. Neither Aristotle nor Aristotelianism was *anti*monarchical. Not only Aquinas but also John of Paris and most writers of the day assumed that one-man rule was generally better than any other. If Aristotle was right about the intrinsic value of political order, it remained true that its best form was monarchy. *All* constitutional regimes that consistently aimed at the common good were acceptable; one of them—monarchy—was best. *No* lawless regime that aimed only at the ruler's or rulers' private good was acceptable, and one of them—tyranny—was worst. Nonetheless, the thought was latent in Aristotle that the political community was prior to any particular form of constitution; and from this it seems with hindsight a short step to the thought that rulers should govern with the advice and consent of those they govern. Commentators have been surprised that the disciples of Aristotle discussed the communal governments of Italian city-states less often than monarchical government; but when the salient issue was the papacy's claims to secular authority, it is less surprising that it was the authority of secular monarchy they defended.

Marsilius of Padua

An attack on the pretensions of the papacy that caused even deeper outrage was that of Marsilius of Padua, set out at length in *Defensor pacis* (*The Defender of the Peace*) and more briefly in later works such as the *Defensor minor* (*The Shorter Defender*) and *De translatione imperii*. Marsilius was born in the late 1270s, in Padua. He belonged to a distinguished family of lawyers, the Mainardini, but himself studied medicine. His early years are obscure, but in 1313 he served as rector of the University of Paris for the usual three-month term, and thereafter he was frequently employed on the business of the Della Scala family of Verona and the Visconti of Milan. It is not clear when he began to write *Defensor pacis*; it is generally assumed that it must have been around 1315. It was published anonymously in 1324. When word of his authorship leaked out, Marsilius decided Paris was unsafe—with the pope and the French king reconciled to each other, he could look for no help from the secular authorities if the church took measures against him. He fled to the court of the emperor, Ludwig of Bavaria. He took part in Ludwig's inconclusive Italian expedition of 1327–28 and was briefly Ludwig's vice-gerent in Rome. He remained close to the royal court, without exercising much influence throughout the 1330s. Around 1340 he wrote the *Defensor minor*, to answer Ludwig's need for a defense of his actions in dissolving the marriage of the countess of Tyrol and remarrying her to his son, and to restate the main ideas of the *Defensor pacis*. He died soon afterward, probably in 1342.

The Defender of the Peace is a long book—some 500 pages in most translations. It was so fiercely antipapal that Pope John XXII declared it heretical on five counts even before reading it; it provided for the first time a theory of secular authority carefully distinguished from the account of spiritual authority by which it was accompanied; and the view of authority in both spheres rested on the doctrine of government by consent. Almost as important, the account of government by consent was backed by a theory of representation. As with most works of political theory, the question of *cui bono?*—for whose benefit was it written?—is an interesting one, but no easier to answer in this case than usually. Although Marsilius spent a long time in the service of Ludwig of Bavaria, and the treatise is dedicated to him, the work was written before Ludwig established himself as emperor in 1328. After the death of Henry of Luxemburg in 1313, it took a ten-year civil war to settle the succession. *De monarchia* was an antipapal and imperial tract; *Defensor pacis* is an antipapal tract, but not an imperial tract, although two later works, *Defensor minor* and *De translatione imperii*, certainly were.

The book makes a *negative* case, in that it argues *against* the absolute authority of the pope over the church, and against the papacy's role in secular politics. Marsilius's argument is not anticlerical or anti-ecclesiastical. His long and densely argued treatise set out to base secular authority on the consent of the governed; this consent was to be given through representative devices familiar in northern European cities as well as Italian city-states. Marsilius's bolder claim was that since this is the way to govern cities and kingdoms, it is also the way to govern the church. Heretical as this seemed to John XXII, it was not wholly groundbreaking. The early church held innumerable councils to resolve doctrinal and other issues, and some of them—such as the Council of Nicaea—became particularly famous as the occasion when the church settled deep and intractable questions—such as the nature of the Trinity. Most councils had been summoned by secular rulers, but the implications of that fact for church government were not agreed. The one indisputable fact was that accountability to a council and the suggestion that it was up to lay rulers to create such councils were unattractive to any pope.

The innovation was not the claim that a system of government that engaged numerous representatives could solve many practical problems. The novelty was Marsilius's use of the Aristotelian theory of government to claim that authority is morally legitimate only when founded on the consent of a people. He was perhaps the first writer to make that thought do some real work. The thought that hierarchical and populist theories of authority can be reconciled, intellectually at least, was familiar. Many writers held that authority was *generated* in the community and then *vested* in the ruler, much as Justinian had held that his authority had originated in the people and been transferred to the emperor without reservation and without the possibility of revocation. Justinian was an absolute sovereign, but the sovereignty had been the people's before they transferred it. On the theory embodied in the forged Donation of Constantine, sovereignty over the empire had been Constantine's; he had then transferred it to the pope; the pope had then charged him with the management of the empire's secular affairs. It was entirely possible to argue that authority had first been "in the people," became the emperor's by transfer from the people, then the pope's by transfer from the emperor, then the emperor's by delegation from the pope. Others had argued that God was the sole source of authority, but that God's grant to a ruler was valid only when a good man governed wisely and with the assent of his people. Election, which permeated that very hierarchical institution, the Catholic Church, could readily be understood as a process in which God made known his choice by inspiring the voices of those charged with the election: *vox populi, vox Dei.* It was God's authority even though we could discover where God bestowed it only through the voice of the people. Pure divine right theory, where God is not only the fount of authority but directly appoints the earthly ruler, is one of many possibilities.

Marsilius constructs the first of the three discourses that make up *Defensor pacis* by appealing to what he takes to be self-evident: men come together in a political community to live a self-sufficient life. The state—*regnum*—is the highest form of association because it is the only one that achieves self-sufficiency. This is pure Aristotle, as is his claim that we associate for the sake of life but practice politics for the sake of the good life. Aquinas had followed Aristotle so far. Marsilius goes further. *Ultimate* self-sufficiency is for the hereafter, but "civil happiness" is earthly self-sufficiency. What could have no roots in Aristotle and would have outraged Aquinas is Marsilius's claim that the great threat to peace and civil happiness is the papacy. The purpose of the book, he says at the outset, is to demonstrate a cause of strife and disorder that Aristotle could have known nothing of, because it came into the world so long after his time.[11] Marsilius also goes beyond Aristotle in analyzing the components of a polity in functional terms: the chief components, he says, are judicial, military, and religious. Book I of Aristotle's *Politics* analyzes the polity by distinguishing it from more-limited forms of association. This is an extension of that thought. Marsilius maintains that secular rule has a religious function because the secular ruler must secure the spiritual as well as the physical well-being of the citizenry. The priestly function is one of the functions of any well-conducted polity. This was not a surprising thought. Aristotle discussed the establishment of the priesthood in his design for an ideal polis, and Cicero, whom Marsilius cites, assumed that a properly constituted priesthood is needed by a successful polity. But the analysis of the functions of different sorts of authority and institutions is the beginning of institutional analysis as we understand it today.

Marsilius set out to defend what he termed "temperate" rule.[12] He says that the word "state" has several meanings, all of them in Aristotle, and he intends to discuss what is common to "temperate" regimes generally. There is no suggestion that a temperate monarchy is an implausible aspiration. Temperate government was not limited government in the modern sense. The modern conception of limited government holds both that there are things that no government is entitled to do and that there is a limited range of activities for which the coercive powers of the state are necessary and useful, beyond which its authority lapses. Medieval writers certainly thought there were things that governments were not entitled to do, but these were mostly defined by religion; a ruler who commanded his subjects to deny Christ must be disobeyed, and a ruler who led his people away from the true faith lost his title to rule. But the teleological framework within which medieval writers wrote after the recovery of Aristotle meant that they were disinclined to set the rights of subjects against the rights of rulers. The task of government was to do all the good it could. Controversialists often claimed that some particular ruler could not act in certain ways because his actions were contrary to the known and agreed custom and law of his polity; but the thought that subjects had rights that limited the authority of any government whatever was foreign to them. Marsilius argued that a "temperate monarchy" must act according to law, as Aristotle had done when defending the thought that "laws not men" should govern; but he did not hold the modern view that there are areas of life about which the law must be silent.

This difference affects Marsilius's explanation of representative institutions and systems of election. In the modern world they are devices to keep government within bounds, by holding government to account. This is not Marsilius's justification; he thinks the point is to ensure that the wisest rule. It is obvious upon reflection that there is no necessary connection between elections and limited government; *what* authority a person may wield is one thing, *how* they acquire it another. Popes were elected, but claimed a *plenitudo potestatis*, absolute authority. Marsilius wanted wise government, not limited government. Nineteenth- and twentieth-century dictators secured their authority in plebiscites. Marsilius wants not dictators but temperate rulers. The wise will be temperate, and the purpose of enlightened institutional arrangements is to secure wise rulers. What Marsilius discusses throughout the first part of *Defensor pacis* is how to secure government by the wise.

Nor is his idea of election quite the same as ours. Marsilius has struck many readers as very bold when he claimed that not only is popular consent the "efficient cause" of government—that government had originated in the agreement of a community to be governed—but that the community's continuing consent makes law law. In other formulations, that claim was not unprecedented, and with a little ingenuity could be extracted from Cicero; but it was unprecedented in the voluntaristic form that Marsilius gave it. He held that continuing consent was essential to legality. The thought that a well-conducted polity makes law for the common good, according to the will of the people, and with their consent is not surprising. It was a central element in the Roman self-image. It becomes bolder once Marsilius asks whose consent is to count, and replies that it is consent of everyone other than the vicious and undiscerning and those so poor they have no stake in the society at all. To the usual aristocratic and hierarchical claim that the multitude is vicious and undiscerning, he retorts that "most citizens are neither vicious nor undiscerning most of the time" and points out, as Aristotle had before him, that a citizen who cannot craft legislation himself can judge its merits when it is presented to him.[13]

If he recruits Aristotle to the cause of basing legitimacy on consent in a fashion that might have surprised him, Marsilius picks up Aristotle's argument for *politeia*—good government by many, but not "the many"—with perfect accuracy. Having begun boldly, he moves a very short distance toward a democratic conception of consent. Like others, he argues that many heads are better than one, that a wise ruler needs counsel, and that the best government involves many persons. To borrow a modern coinage, it is *polyarchy*.[14] This supports the governments found in Italian city-states such as Padua, and parliamentary or conciliar forms of government in other places, and is an argument for employing these forms of government in institutions other than secular states—such as the church. In any case, support for persons and policies will be greater the more directly it is based on the choice of the people. The "people" in this connection means enough people, and particularly enough of the more important people to provide a representative and powerful expression of public opinion. The term Marsilius uses as a synonym for enough of the right people is the *valentior pars*, literally the "more powerful part." It is not an argument that the will of the majority is binding on the whole people, but an argument for involving enough of the people who count. "Enough" can be a very small number; the imperial electors suffice to constitute the *valentior pars*, when the question is the legitimacy of the emperor. Marsilius was greatly indebted to Ludwig of Bavaria, Holy Roman Emperor by election. Nor would it be an implausible thought that Marsilius's influence was to be seen in the 1338 declaration by six of the imperial electors that the imperial title was conferred by a majority of the electors and needed no papal confirmation, the view enshrined in the Golden Bull of 1365.

The argument, then, is that the way to secure a "temperate" regime is by the rule of a lawful ruler over free citizens; citizens are those who play an active role in the affairs of their polity. This would be very like the Aristotelian theory of *politeia*, except that it is almost always couched in terms of securing moderate one-man rule. In Aristotle's *politeia* the citizens are engaged in "ruling and being ruled in turn," but Marsilius spends so much time discussing "temperate monarchy" that it often seems that the only question that concerns him is how to rest one-man rule on the consent of the better-off, wiser, and steadier members of the community.

He was, of course, primarily attacking his bête noire. What occupied more than three times as much space in *Defensor pacis* as the theory of legitimate state authority in general was his assault on the political power of the papacy. He was repetitive, savage, comprehensive, and persuasive. The unpersuaded were outraged; the hostility of the Catholic Church persists to this day. Marsilius began at the beginning by attacking the first step in the papacy's claim to authority, Christ's gift to Saint Peter of the power to bind and loose. He was not the first to argue that Christ gave no such power to Peter alone; others had argued that Christ's authority was given to the apostles equally. If the apostolic succession inhered in bishops and priests generally, authority within the church should be shared, and this was an argument for a conciliar form of church government.[15] Not content with undermining the papacy's claim to a plenitude of power, Marsilius went on to argue that the church was not entitled to the vast wealth it had acquired. Like the radical Franciscans, he argued that the apostles' reliance on their followers to provide shelter and support was the proper model for the fourteenth-century church.

The upshot was radical. The church had no legitimate coercive authority. Like almost everyone, Marsilius thought the power to coerce was the essential mark of legislative capacity; if the church had no right to coerce, it could not legislate. This meant that canon law was not strictly law at all. The church had a power over the faithful that all agreed on: the power to excommunicate. However, where others both before and after thought the church had the right to ask the secular arm to impose additional sanctions on the excommunicate, Marsilius did not. Even the limited sanction of excommunication belonged to the church rather than the pope. The final blow to the papacy's claims to secular power was decisive. Marsilius broke new ground by arguing that the power that Christ had conferred on the disciples was the power to teach and advise, not to rule. We are very close to the view of the nature of a church that John Locke argued for in his *Letter Concerning Toleration* 350 years later: a church is a voluntary association held together by the agreement of its members on articles of faith; its object is to allow its members to worship and encourage and instruct one another in the faith and its consequences for conduct. The demand for the commitment to poverty in the church, to which Locke paid no attention, is justified here by the thought that the moral authority of those who preach chastity, unworldliness, and contempt for the pleasures of the world, the flesh, and the devil is diminished by wealth.

Bartolus and the Italian City-State

Unlike freestanding kingdoms such as England or France, the states and cities of northern and central Italy were at least notionally dependencies of either the empire or the church. De facto, they resisted attempts by their nominal overlords to establish a tighter hold, especially attempts by successive emperors to assert their authority over the city-states of Lombardy. The political arrangements and legal status of the city-states of central and northern Italy were hard for contemporaries to analyze; their history and politics defy description. If the shifts by which the cities defended their independence against emperors with the help of the papacy, and against the papacy with the help of emperors, and against everyone with the help of outsiders hoping to profit by their meddling, are hard to describe, their predicament is not. The *regnum Italicum* covered the area conquered by the Lombards and liberated by German kings on the urging of the papacy in the ninth and tenth centuries. Technically, most of the cities and their inhabitants were subjects of the empire; those in the Papal States were subject to the papacy, strictly speaking as the result of a grant of suzerainty from empire to papacy, subsequently on the basis of direct rule, or rule by an agent installed by the papacy, a "papal vicar." For our purposes, the point is that the source of the legal competence of cities such as Milan, Pisa, Arezzo, or Perugia was the universal sovereignty of the emperor, but his actual authority was slight to nonexistent.

From the twelfth century most cities under nominal imperial over-lordship were not under the emperor's effective control and had no intention of being. Each cared for its own freedom of action; none cared about neighboring cities; they cooperated when threatened by an imperial expedition to enforce the emperor's authority, and otherwise acted with the mixture of rivalry and distrust that had marked the Greek city-states one and a half millennia before. In the following centuries, and aided by successive popes, they defeated the threats to their independence from Frederick Barbarossa, Frederick II, and their successors. The popes' interest was obvious; if the German emperor controlled the Kingdom of Sicily and the *regnum Italicum*, the Papal States were held in a vice. Nobody supposed that the independence of the city-states held any other appeal to the pope. More interesting was the ideology of the city-states themselves. They claimed to be defending their liberty, which they held to be the *libertas* that the Roman Republic had enjoyed, and Romans had lost when the republic became an empire. Minimally, it meant they were autonomous in the literal sense, that is, entitled to make laws for themselves. This meant legal independence of the empire and a capacity to make their own laws. We shall see how Bartolus of Sassoferrato argued that they were so entitled, but on the face of it, anyone who held a narrowly legalistic view of the right to make law could not have seen them as sovereign states, but as having only a devolved legal capacity by permission of the emperor pro tem.

If one adopts the perspective of Justinian's *Digest*, there was one legitimate lawmaker for the entire world, and that was the emperor. All other jurisdictions must in some fashion be legislating by tacit permission. The absurdity of insisting on such a narrow understanding—which implied among other things that France and England had their own legal systems either by dispensation from the emperor or by usurpation—made no difference when emperors wanted to insist on their authority over the Italian cities. But emperors had their own problems; they wanted the law on their side against the cities, but did not want canon lawyers claiming that the pope had a legal authority that trumped the emperor's. A canon lawyer might agree that city-states had no autonomous legislative capacity, but then argue that the emperor derived his legislative capacity only from his coronation as emperor by the pope; that was what Marsilius and Dante denied.

The cities needed a coherent account of their legal status and an affirmation of their sovereignty. They also needed forms of government that served their administrative and economic purposes. In the eleventh century they reinvented many features of the early Roman Republic, in particular the appointment of magistrates to very short periods of office as a defense against tyranny. When they evicted their kings, the Romans had elected consuls for a year at a time only, and consuls were what Pisa, Milan, and Arezzo began by giving themselves. These city-states were in many respects genuine revivals of the city-state of antiquity. An essential condition of their existence was that they controlled their rural hinterland; their *contadini* were not tenants of feudal landlords but small farmers who owned their own farms or were tenants of landowners from the city. Twelfth-century observers were struck by the absence of great lords, the feudal magnates of France, Germany, and England; when that changed, it undermined their political systems, as mercantile and banking wealth was converted into aristocratic status, and wealth and status into power. The cities faced problems familiar to their antique precursors: the prevention of tyranny, on the one hand, and the avoidance of class warfare and confiscatory projects, on the other. Their devices for preventing the rise of tyrants brought familiar negative effects: rapid turnover of leaders made consistency of policy hard to achieve, and competition for office led to extreme factionalism and zero-sum politics.

The solution devised for a lack of expertise was almost invariably a council, with whose assent the podesta ruled; a common pattern was a double council, one with many members that met in public and had few powers beyond the veto, and one with fewer members that met in secret and made policy. The problem of factionalism was rarely solved except at the cost of the liberty the city valued so much. The cities wanted, or late in the day discovered that they wanted, Roman *libertas*, which is to say stable constitutional government, the rule of law, independence of other authorities, and greatness for their city. Like Rome, they discovered that faction fights between aristocratic rivals for high office end in the exhausted or enthusiastic acceptance of one-man rule. With the exception of Venice, the greatest and most successful of all city-states, where the city established a hereditary mercantile aristocracy as early as 1279, their eventual fate was to be governed by hereditary dukes or counts, who were frequently themselves kept in power by powerful outside forces such as the papacy, the empire, or in due course the French or Spanish monarchy. The similarities with the Greek city-states and their fate at the hands of Macedon and Rome were not lost on observers.

Nonetheless, their fate was not so inevitable that an intelligent and passionate participant and thinker like Machiavelli was foolish to hope at the end of the fifteenth century that Florence could renew its populist energies and become a new Rome. Whatever one thinks of Machiavelli's hopes, for four centuries, from the eleventh to the early sixteenth, the city-state revived aspects of the political life of the ancient world, good and bad. Given their systems of government, it is unsurprising that Marsilius should have taken Aristotle's *Politics* as his guide in analyzing temperate government. Given, too, that he was fighting the papacy's pretensions to secular authority and its fondness for worldly wealth, it is not odd that he should have devoted so much effort to rebutting the scriptural interpretations of papal apologists. What puzzles modern readers rather more is the attention that writers in the fourteenth and fifteenth centuries devoted to the implications of civil law for the legitimacy of the city-states of Italy. It is less odd than it seems; modern American politics revolves around issues of legitimacy hardly less complicated. Not only the intersection of canon and civil law but the divergent practices of different cities needed legal resolution. The intellectual training of the most highly educated Italians took them into canon and civil law, and the practical needs of governments and merchants alike ensured a market for their services.

The most distinguished of legal theorists was Bartolus of Sassofer-rato. He was born in 1313 and died in 1357, and was, one might say, born to be a professor of law; he studied at Perugia and Bologna, taught at Pisa, and then at Perugia, where he died at the early age of forty-three. He wrote lengthy commentaries on most aspects of Roman law and most of Justinian's *Corpus juris civilis*. He is still thought of as the great founder of the study of the conflict of laws. Political theorists remember him mostly for a very brief but influential discussion of tyranny, but his views on the legal status of semiautonomous states are full of good sense and pregnant with ideas that become important centuries later. Bartolus's position was elegant and straightforward. The German emperor had lost de facto control over the cities of northern Italy. A true sovereign united in one pair of hands both de facto power and the de jure authority that entitled him to wield it. To assert de jure authority when a long period had elapsed in which those over whom it was asserted had taken no notice of the assertion was nugatory. This sounds very like what later ages knew as legal positivism; law in any particular place is whatever the accepted local process of law creation says it is, and what confers legitimacy on a lawmaking authority is effectiveness. Bartolus was more delicate than that; he was a Roman lawyer and could not easily reject the idea that the one lawmaking community was the heirs of the *populus Romanus* in whose name Roman law was made. The legal systems of Roman law countries, essentially most of Europe other than England, were indebted to him for centuries, until the codification of civil law at the end of the eighteenth century and after.

Although the claims of the emperor could largely be ignored, as a matter of political practice, not every city governed itself without owing (or admitting) allegiance to an overlord, including the emperor. Not all were what Bartolus elegantly called *civitas princeps suae*. By the time Bartolus wrote, many cities in the Romagna willingly or unwillingly acknowledged the pope as overlord; and the invasion of Henry of Luxemburg at the time of Bartolus's birth came close to putting the *regnum Italicum* back under the authority of the German emperor. It was no easy task to discuss divided sovereignty; civil law was built on Justinian's *Digest* and inhospitable to the thought that custom could be a source of law in its own right. The admiration of historians is wholly justified, though the technicalities of Bartolus's treatment are rebarbative.

His short essay on "the government of cities," *De regimine civitatis*, is interesting for two main reasons. The first is that it provides an Aristotelian account of politics that explains how a city can be an autonomous lawmaking entity: a city exists when a people gives itself laws. This echoed Cicero's claim that a *res publica* exists only when there is a *populus*, that is, a people whose good is pursued by constitutional means; from Cicero also came the definition of the justice that a good king must practice: "a constant and perpetual will which renders to each one his due." Like Aquinas and Marsilius, Bartolus reads Aristotle as saying that monarchical government is the absolutely best, where it can be instituted, and for much the same reason, that the unity of will of one man is a greater security for peace and good order than the precarious unity of a multitude. It is "monarchical" government that he defends; "kingship" covers numerous forms of one-man rule, ranging from the emperor who claims universal lordship to the duke or count who rules a city and its hinterland.

Bartolus says much that comes as no surprise to readers of Aristotle, but that served a distinctive purpose. He revived Aristotle's concept of *politeia*, under the label of *policratia*, to describe a government in which most of those who have the attributes of citizenship play an active role, and which is directed toward the common good. He had a commonsense enthusiasm for popular governments where they could be instituted, that is, governments where neither the magnates nor the indigent wielded absolute power, but men with a solid stake in the city did. Like Aristotle, he finds six forms of government, and a seventh, un-Aristotelian "monstrosity" to be discussed shortly, divided according to Aristotle's own principles. Good forms aim at the common good, bad forms at the interests of the ruling party; the best is monarchy and the worst is tyranny. Given that Italy was full of tyrants in the narrowest and most literal sense, single rulers who had acquired power by unconstitutional methods, the pressing issue was obviously how to avert tyranny, selfish and lawless rule by a single ruler.

Thinking like a lawyer about legitimacy, Bartolus argues that kingship by election is closest to what is divinely approved; behind that thought lies distaste for the way tyrants installed their nearest relatives to create hereditary ruling families. As to how a ruler is to live up to the high standards of wisdom and justice that he has laid down, Bartolus shelters behind the (rather persuasive) views of Giles of Rome (Egidius Colonna): what a single ruler needs is wise advice, sage counselors, an independent council to keep him wise and honest. Since a ruler must retain a constant and unalterable will to be governed by justice and legality, it is important that he can rely on collective wisdom, but the unity of the city requires a single focus of authority—nowhere more obviously than in an Italian city-state.

The most fascinating aspect of Bartolus's essay is his hostility toward the anarchic condition of contemporary Rome. Rome was not even badly governed; it was a monstrosity—all government supposed some degree of unity in the polity, but in Rome there was none. Whether a government was popular, aristocratic, or kingly, it required a head, a person or institution that answered the question of what the laws were and what policies were to be pursued. Rome was a chaos of competing tyrants, with an entirely ineffectual notional ruler or city prefect. Machiavelli made himself deeply unpopular in the early sixteenth century by ascribing the chaotic condition of Italian politics to the misdeeds of the papacy, but at this point in the fourteenth century, the pope himself was in Avignon, firmly under the control of the French monarchy, and governing the church with the assistance of a college of cardinals who were overwhelmingly French. It was less the presence than the absence of the pope and cardinals that was to blame.

Bartolus was appalled by the condition of Rome for some of the same reasons of historical nostalgia as Machiavelli; the great stabilizing force of the ancient Mediterranean world was now a source of weakness and disorder. Toward the papacy itself, Bartolus displayed no animus. In a tract on tyranny written shortly before he died, at a time when the papal legate Egidio Albornoz was engaged in a very deft operation to turn the tyrants of north and central Italy into "vicars of the church," Bartolus dwelled at length on the legal issues raised by tyrannical governments operating in the territories over which the papacy claimed lordship, and more briefly on the possibility of "legitimation after the event."

He anticipated Machiavelli in arguing that tyranny could be acceptable as a transitional government, as it was when pope or emperor later
made a regime lawful by turning a tyrant into a "vicar"—a vice-regent.
Discussing city government, Bartolus treated tyranny as the corruption of monarchy and condemned it, but this did not answer the practical question of how to regard the acts of a long-lasting tyrant. If a
tyrant—defined narrowly as someone who had acquired power without
a title—governed well for a substantial period, it would be absurd to
say that every agreement made under his power was de jure invalid. His
acts lacked complete legitimacy, but not all were illegitimate. Oppression, iniquitous and unjust taxation—with which Bartolus was much
concerned—and the unjust exile and ill-treatment of all opponents was
another matter; and those who had profited from extortion should not
benefit from legal amnesia.

He was not enthusiastic about the papal and imperial policy of converting tyrants into vicars, but, faute de mieux, it might be justified. "For
as a careful sailor throws overboard his less valuable cargo in order to
save the more precious, and as the prudent householder makes a choice
of his more valuable goods to rescue, so a just overlord comes to terms
with a tyrant and makes him his vicar in order to accomplish great and
pressing reforms." The welfare of a tyrant's subjects might require such a
measure, much as the doctor may prescribe life-threatening treatment to
avert certain death. The tone is disapproving; the ideal of the ruler who
secures office through proper procedures of election and governs for the
common good casts a glaring light on the defective title of tyrants. And
the insidiousness of tyranny is such that it might even be invisible; someone occupying no official position could exercise lawless power and be a
tyrant. Bartolus thought that the factionalism of Italian city politics—
he wrote a tract on the Guelphs and Ghibellines—meant that faction
leaders might have such a hold over the officials notionally in charge that
they were the true powers in the city and, if unjust, then tyrants. The
modern Mafia springs to mind.

The world to which Bartolus was speaking is easily imagined by
anyone who has seen Ambrogio Lorenzetti's allegories of good and bad
government, painted a few years before Bartolus wrote about city gov-

ernment. Under good government, Justice reigns, aided by the virtues: peace, courage, temperance, and magnanimity; above Justice seated on her throne floats wisdom; under bad government injustice rules in the form of the Tyrant, depicted as the devil himself, and the vices that assist tyranny are anger, avarice, divisiveness, treachery, and cruelty. The payoff of a just regime is prosperity, willing taxpayers, and a successful state respected by its neighbors; the payoff of an unjust regime is famine and death. When the frescoes were painted in 1338–39, the Sienese were congratulating themselves on having regained their liberties after a tyrannical interlude; to the political theorist, the interest of the frescoes lies in the way in which Christian, Aristotelian, Stoic, and Ciceronian ideas about the demands of stable and peaceful government are all invoked without any sense that they are embarrassingly disparate. But those were the fourteenth century's intellectual resources; naturally, they are all employed when they concur in what they commend and deplore. Trouble ensues only when one or the other loses credibility or one tradition leads in dramatically different directions from the others.

Conciliarism and Ockham

We have seen how readily one or another version of the doctrine of government by consent could be applied to the government of the church. In historical fact, the conciliar movement was the product of the appalling state into which the papacy fell at the end of its "Babylonian exile" in Avignon. The papacy's capacity to influence European politics was obviously undermined by its being so firmly under the thumb of the French monarchy. Thus, its ability to mitigate the horrors of the Hundred Years' War between France and England was almost nil when the English regarded the pope as a far from impartial mediator. The papacy was also unpopular because it was seen as increasingly authoritarian, centralized, and corrupt. When the papacy returned to Rome in 1377–78, at the end of the pontificate of Gregory XI, the city was in its usual turbulent state, and the aristocracy of the city aggressively hostile to the non-Italian cardinals. Most would happily have returned to Avignon, but Gregory XI died soon after the return to Rome, and his successor Urban VI refused to leave. This provoked a revolt by the French cardinals, who declared Urban's election invalid and elected Clement VII as antipope. They were driven out of Italy and returned to Avignon. There were now two popes. France, the Kingdom of Naples, and the Spanish kingdoms of Leon and Aragon adhered to Avignon; England, the empire, and northern Italy, to Rome.

The obvious way to heal the schism was to call a council of the whole church to restore peace and unity. In practice, it took the secular monarchies almost seven decades to achieve a final settlement; and a movement that might have established constitutional, representative government as the European norm ended by enhancing the power of bureaucratically organized absolute monarchies. The intellectual interest of the conciliar movement is greater than its practical (in)effectiveness. The urgent but unanswerable question that needed an immediate answer was who had the authority to call a council of the church. Neither the pope at Rome nor the antipope at Avignon wished to call a council that might declare him deposed; the emperor was parti pris. An account was needed of where authority lay in the church as a whole.

An obvious source was Marsilius. Indeed, he was *the* obvious source and widely appealed to. If a political community was by its nature a body that generated the authority that it delegated to rulers by some process of representation, it took little imagination to argue—as he had—that this was true of the church. The arguments needed were negative arguments to show that Christ had not conferred on Saint Peter and thereafter on successive popes an absolute authority that shut out the representative principle. If there was no obstacle to the church as a community exercising its innate authority by delegation, a council was the obvious device to overcome the scandal of schism. William of Ockham was an equally usable source, but although he was less intransigent than Marsilius in his hatred of the papacy, he was intellectually more radical. Ockham was English, born in the 1280s. He became a Franciscan friar, studied and taught in Oxford, but when he was summoned to account for his work before Pope John XXII in Avignon, he like Marsilius took refuge in the court of Ludwig of Bavaria, where he wrote antipapal tracts on Ludwig's behalf.[16] He was a philosophical empiricist and took a markedly skeptical view of the doctrine that the church (like any other corporation) was a *corpus mysticum*, or mystical body, arguing that in reality it is simply a collection of individual believers. Popes do not represent the mystical unity of the church; if there is to be representation, it must be by delegation from the individuals whom we call, collectively, the church.

Pressure to call a council to resolve the schism had very mixed results. The first council, held in Pisa in 1409, failed to persuade either of the rival popes to resign; it added to the confusion by electing a second antipope, Alexander V, who died soon afterward and was succeeded by John XXIII. A few years later, the Council of Constance (1414–18) succeeded in deposing all three popes and electing Martin V, eventually accepted as the one legitimate pope. The success of Constance was a tribute to Jean Gerson (1363–1429), who had spent almost twenty years arguing the moderates' case, which was not to assert the authority of the whole over the part, or the community over its head, as Marsilius and Ockham and all radicals did, but simply to recommend giving authority in emergency to a council of the whole. The council itself took the radical view, and in *Hanc sanctam* declared that it had its authority directly from Christ and not from a pope. In fact, it owed its efficacy to the support of the emperor Sigismund, who had many reasons for wanting to see unity in the church, of which not the least was the Hussite rebellion in his native Bohemia. Nonetheless, the council declared itself the supreme governing body of the church and insisted that councils meet frequently.

They did not. The successor to the Council of Constance was the Council of Basel (1431–49), and although it provoked an important tract from Nicholas of Cusa (1401–64), *De concordantia catholica*,[17] the council itself ended ignominiously by splitting in two. Nicholas's work attempted to balance the two competing principles at stake, the consent of all Christians and the pope's position as head of the church. It was not a "political" work, in that it did not try to set out institutional arrangements that might have satisfied all sides, a hopeless task in any case, but a philosophical reflection on the various ways in which individuals can represent persons, ideas, or principles. Theologically, Nicholas was a mystic, but he was technically adept enough to devise a voting system for the election of the Holy Roman Emperor that was rediscovered three hundred years later and is much used today, known as the "Borda count" method of weighing preferences. After the Council of Basel, the papacy returned to its autocratic and hierarchical style. Whether a different outcome would have headed off the Reformation of the sixteenth century is doubtful. Ockham and Marsilius wanted a reformed church, but at Constance, Gerson prosecuted Jan Hus, whose views on church reform prefigured those of the Reformation a century later, and Nicholas attended Basel to reinforce his claims to a bishopric. They wanted unity in the church, not dramatic change.

CHAPTER 9

Humanism

What Was Humanism?

THE NEXT THREE CHAPTERS consider from three different angles the political ideas of one period of time within a single, chaotic context. The late fifteenth and early sixteenth centuries are the last time we can talk of western Christendom as a single entity. After the middle of the sixteenth century, there was a confessional divide between Catholic and Protestant Europe that remains unclosed. The violence of earlier centuries has disappeared, though by no means all of the distrust. The political history and political aspirations of Catholic and Protestant Europe diverged, too, although the connection between the confessional and the political history was less close than Protestant propagandists claimed. Two of the themes pursued in these chapters are familiar; no account of the origins of our own political ideas could ignore Machiavelli on the one side and Luther and Calvin on the other. The third has been less explored until recently. We begin with it.

Analysis of humanism and its bearing on politics is not easy. Commentators divide. Some have detected a political movement they call "civic humanism," sparked by the reading of classical moral and political texts, and committed to a revival of republican virtue.[1] The revival was centered on Florence, and an aspect of Florence's self-image as a self-governing republic rather than a princely despotism or a papal or imperial client, as well as a reaction against the tightening grip of the Florentine merchant princes on the city's politics. Critics of the idea that humanism and republicanism were born twins have observed that most humanists were less interested in politics than in establishing reliable texts of Latin and Greek literature, identifying their authors, and distinguishing genuine writings from fakes. Forgeries were rife, and the textual criticism that revealed them as forgeries marked the beginning of modern historical scholarship. The connection with an enthusiasm for republican virtue is not obvious. A plausible "elective affinity" is that an interest in classical antiquity might reinforce the sense that Italian politics in the fourteenth and fifteenth centuries presented an embarrassing contrast with the politics of republican Rome. Still, the connection is tenuous; such a reaction was equally strong in Marsilius, who was attached to the Scholastic and syllogistic style of reasoning that humanists disliked, and Machiavelli, whose views on the "virtue"—or *virtù*—that a prince should display were shockingly at odds with conventional humanist views.[2] Humanist credentials were neither necessary nor sufficient to inspire an enthusiasm for republics; many humanists admired tradition and hierarchy, and the most characteristic political product of a humanist was a "mirror of princes," or a tract on princely education.[3]

Humanism originated in the need for educated lawyers. Technical and formal instruction in the law was not concerned with the literary graces; but the so-called *dictatores*, men who drafted documents, drew up contracts for merchants and others, and handled the governmental correspondence of the Italian cities, had to write well. They needed an education in humane letters, and such an education also became part of the prelegal education of lawyers. Familiarity with literary texts bred an interest in their quality as literature, and a more sophisticated historical and philological approach to authorship and interpretation rapidly followed. The possession of literary and linguistic skills became a source of pride even among aristocratic and royal families. Princes and princesses were forced to learn the Greek that Saint Augustine had balked at; Queen Elizabeth I, to take one famous instance, was a more than competent scholar.

A close analysis of humanism would draw distinctions ignored here—for instance, the differences between earlier Italian humanism and later northern European humanism—and would distinguish the very varied political allegiances of literary humanists. All we can do here is explore some ways in which humanist writers discussed political issues, not least by the use of novel literary forms. The playful use of political utopias was one novelty, as was the invention of the short polemical essay. While the Protestant Reformation gave new life to Augustine's conviction of the depth of original sin, and reform theologians were emphasizing that good works (let alone papal indulgences) could not secure salvation, other thinkers were inspired by the utopian speculations of the Greeks. Humanism also begat interestingly nonhumanist variants on its themes. Machiavelli did not share the humanists' views about how princes should behave, but he was capable of utopian speculation; his hopes for a revival in Florence of the civic virtue of the Roman Republic were utopian in both the abusive and the nonabusive senses of the term, while his essay *The Prince* bears a wonderfully ambiguous relationship to the "mirror of princes" tradition.

Humanism is conventionally described as a literary movement that originated with Petrarch. This emphasizes the place of poetry and literature in the humanist sensibility, but does not cast much light on humanist political thinking. Taking another tack, we may begin with its hostility to Scholasticism. The humanist desire to escape syllogistic formalism and the reduction of all moral and political questions to issues in theology did not express a desire to escape rational argument, or a hankering for paganism. Machiavelli wished modern thinkers to reflect on ancient practice and to draw some very un-Christian conclusions, but he was highly unusual; when humanists turned away from Aristotle, they frequently turned to a spiritualized Platonism. This was unorthodox to the degree that Plato's leanings toward mathematical mysticism were taken up and exaggerated, but not at odds with the age-old links between Neoplatonism and Christian theology.

Deciding who is and who is not a humanist is an ungrateful task: how much enthusiasm for which aspects of classical literature must someone display, and how much dislike for syllogistic inference? Pico della Mirandola, who was uninclined to reject any source of illumination, was undeniably a humanist but forgave the medieval Schoolmen their lack of Greek and their infelicities in Latin prose. A better test is simpler. Writers who lay out their ideas in the formulaic fashion common to Aquinas and Thomistic political theorists such as Francisco de Vitoria lie on one side of the divide and are late Scholastics; essayists, utopians, and poets lie on the other side. Machiavelli is anti-Scholastic and a dubious humanist. Uncontested members of the tradition include Coluccio Salutati, Leonardi Bruni—though he refused to translate Plato's *Republic* into Latin because he thought Plato's eugenicist defense of a community of wives too disgusting to be given wide circulation—Pico della Mirandola, the author of the oration *On the Dignity of Man*, Erasmus, and Montaigne; here I begin with Christine de Pizan and emphasize Thomas More, the former almost unique as an intelligent woman taken seriously by her contemporaries, and the latter because he was both a humanist, a powerful politician, and the author of the little book that gave Utopia its name.

Christine de Pizan

Christine de Pizan's rarity value as a well-regarded woman writer in the late Middle Ages—she was born around 1363 and died sometime after 1430—hardly needs emphasis. She astonished her contemporaries by making a living by her writing at a time when almost nobody, male or female, did so. This was out of necessity—her father was a royal employee and well liked at court, but of humble origins. She married at sixteen, but her husband and father both died soon thereafter, and at the age of twenty-four she was left a widow with three children and a widowed mother to care for. Since she had friends at court but no resources of her own, writing for royal and aristocratic patrons was a possibility. Her life spanned the worst period of the Hundred Years' War between France and England; she was born as Charles V (king from 1364 to 1380) began to restore French fortunes after the Battle of Poitiers in 1356 when the English destroyed the French army and captured Charles's father, King John. But Charles died prematurely and was succeeded by his son. Known both as Charles the Well-Beloved and Charles the Mad, Charles VI, who died in 1422, was a boy of twelve at his accession and was plagued from his midtwenties by bouts of insanity. Accounts of his symptoms suggest that he was schizophrenic. The resulting dynastic infighting made France ungovernable and would have left France defenseless if the English had not themselves been racked with dissension. As it was, Charles was forced to acknowledge Henry V of England as his heir following another catastrophic defeat, at Agincourt in 1415. Christine de Pizan died just as the French began to get the upper hand in the war, inspired by Joan of Arc; her last known work was a panegyric to Joan, written before Joan's betrayal by the duke of Burgundy and execution by the English.

Christine de Pizan has become famous as the author of *The Book of the City of Ladies* and *The Book of the Three Virtues*, sometimes called *The Treasury of the City of Ladies*. We focus, not on these, but on *The Book of the Body Politic*. The more famous books are feminist manifestos, but not political in focus or purpose. They belong, as does Mary Wollstonecraft's *Vindication of the Rights of Woman* four hundred years afterward (though not her *Vindication of the Rights of Man*), to the *genre* of *la querelle des femmes*. There was a medieval literary genre that belittled women's intelligence, prudence, self-restraint, and sense of justice, and depicted women as silly, flighty, selfish, and vain. *The City of Ladies* was in the countertradition of defenses against such foolishness. It exemplifies the humanist conviction that God and Reason are on the same side: in this case on the side of the view that women can be as virtuous as men, and for the most part consists of *exempla* illustrating the virtue of women and, occasionally, the wickedness of men such as Nero.[4] No political implications are drawn. Everyone knew that women had managed estates, organized the military defense of cities, and done everything a competent man could do, just as everyone also knew that the poor and unlettered often fought more bravely and displayed more initiative in battle than their superiors and often displayed better sense in the everyday conduct of their lives—but nobody other than Plato drew the conclusion that political capacity had nothing to do with birth and sex and that neither should political authority.

The Book of the Body Politic was written around 1407. It was an advice book to the then dauphin, Louis of Guyenne; it is, as it says, a book concerning the whole body politic, prince, nobility, and "the universal people," but not only is the section devoted to the prince twice as long as that devoted to the nobility and three times as long as that devoted to the ordinary people, most of the advice to the ordinary people concerns their duties to the prince. The dauphin died eight years later, five years before his father. The book was one of a flurry of works, including reflections on the changeability of human fortune, a biography of Charles V, the later *Lamentation on the Troubles of France*—urging the duc de Berry to prevent the horrors of civil war from overwhelming France—and *The Book of Peace*, addressed to the dauphin in the year before he died. There is no way of knowing what priority Christine attached to her works. She was writing for patrons, among whom the dauphin was a virtual prisoner of the duke of Burgundy at the time she wrote *The Book of Peace*. *The Book of the Body Politic* is short and slight, but not uninteresting. The imagery of the body politic went back into antiquity—Plato used it at length in the *Republic*—but it was not much employed in formal works of moral and political advice. Commonly, the use made of it was hardly more than observing that the head as the seat of wisdom gave direction to the whole body, and so a wise king could give direction to the whole community.

In Plato the imagery had done some contentious work; Plato's tripartite division of the soul and its virtues placed temperance in the belly and assigned it as the one virtue needed by the laboring classes; the chief characteristic of democracy was, on that view, greed.[5] Pizan made a use of the metaphor that was interestingly friendlier to the common people: the ruler is the head, the knights and nobles are the active element, the chest, arms, and hands, so to speak—and the common people are the belly, legs, and feet, devoted to creating the means of subsistence.[6] The inadvisability of pressing the metaphor very far is suggested by the fact that the clergy are placed with the common people, although one might expect them to be located somewhere above the waist, and in fact they sometimes seem to be associated with the head in providing wisdom. The third part of the book is an exhortation to the "three estates" of the French cities and Paris particularly to cooperate and preserve unity; here the clergy are the first of the estates "high noble and worthy of honour among the others," as the fount of good learning and piety.[7]

Any work that combines the Platonic formula of distributing the virtues around the body politic with the formulae of the mirror of princes will be concerned with the education of the prince. Christine was presenting the text to the dauphin, who was eleven years old at the time, so she begins with the education of a ruler's son before turning to the way the son should behave once grown up. The advice is not complicated: the prince should entrust his son to a good scholar, but to a virtuous man before a merely wise one. The wisdom the youth should learn is classical, and the virtues he should acquire are the usual combination of Christian and Ciceronian (or Stoic) virtues. None of that is surprising; it may seem more surprising that Christine treats classical, mainly Roman and republican, examples as so straightforwardly relevant to the conduct of a Christian prince, and treats Roman expectations for consuls, dictators, generals, and senators as guides for fifteenth-century Frenchmen. This is because she draws so heavily on a book of *exempla* by Valerius Maximus—the *Facta et dicta memorabilia*—that was widely used in the moral education of the upper classes. The importance of the cardinal virtues—justice, courage, temperance, and prudence—might seem obvious; good stories about those who flourished by possessing them make the point without belaboring it. She may have thought that as a woman she had need of their borrowed authority.[8] *Exempla* could reinforce more disconcerting morals, as they did in Machiavelli's *Prince* and *Discourses*.

There are perhaps four things to say about a short book that is both highly readable and intellectually undemanding. First, it has a human touch that many such works lack. Christine insists that the prince's teacher be sober, cleanly dressed, and not given to talking nonsense, but reminds him that the prince must be allowed to play children's games and must be given treats. He is not to be fed only grammar and logic. A second feature is how ferociously critical she is of the decayed state of the church in her time. It is no surprise that the prince is told to guide his conduct by the light of Christian virtue; and no surprise that he is told to look to the good of the whole people and not only to his own. Everyone relied on the distinction between the prince who pursued the good of his people and the prince who cared only for his own interests as the dividing line between the legitimate monarch and the illegitimate tyrant. The advice to choose wise councillors, levy moderate taxes, and be brave in battle and merciful in peacetime could be expected in any work of this sort. But the ferocity of her attack on the misconduct of clergy and bishops who have shamed themselves and their religion by turning their churches into something closer to stables than temples has the ring of real anger.[9] "They are truly devils and the infernal abyss, for as the mouth of Hell may never be filled nor satisfied no matter how much it receives or takes, neither can their desires be satisfied or filled since they have such great greed in them for money and luxuries, for which they do great evil to the people!" She was writing in the twenty-ninth year of the Great Schism, and her anger is not inexplicable.

A third unusual feature of the book is its sympathy with the common people. There is a strong sense that their lives matter, and their well-being should be the main concern of the ruling elite. "Of all the estates, they are the most necessary, those who are the cultivators of the earth which feed and nourish the human creature, without whom the earth would end in little time."[10] However, the section in which she discusses their political role is brief; it amounts to little more than an admonition to the members of the three estates—clergy, merchants, and artisans—to make their contribution to the well-being of the polity with due seriousness and deference to those set in authority. Her sympathy with their lot does not extend to thinking that ordinary folk should play a political role; given her origins, Christine is surprisingly insistent on the incapacity of ordinary people to govern themselves: they simply cannot do it, and Aristotle was right to say that one-man rule was best. Her account of the obedience the common people owe their rulers draws exclusively on the standard scriptural accounts of the nature and origins of political authority: the powers that be are ordained of God, and paying (moderate) taxes without complaint is the way to render unto Caesar the things that are Ceasar's.

The fourth feature of the book, conversely, is how un-Christian is her discussion of the virtues and obligations of the knightly class. Christine relies entirely on pagan and classical, largely Roman and republican, examples in urging appropriate behavior. They should obtain honor only by deserving it, and they should deserve it by displaying courage, perseverance, and an indifference to the financial payoff of victory, as the heroes of the Roman Republic did. Modern readers may eventually find the stream of stories lifted from Valerius wearying, but they are not without interest, and they were in any event part of the standard repertoire of didactic literature. Her ready acceptance of the savagery of Roman behavior in battle seems at odds with her pleas for peace in other works and her reflections a decade later on the sufferings of the women whose husbands had been killed or captured at Agincourt. And the cheerfulness with which she endorses Valerius's praise of the trickery and deception practiced by Roman heroes seems equally at odds with her insistence that honesty and keeping faith are indispensable virtues without which no honor can be gained. It would be wrong to think that *The Book of the Body Politic* was simply cobbled together, however. The tensions demonstrate the difficulty of writing readably and persuasively in several different genres at once. The Christian scriptures celebrate humility above prowess in war, pagan philosophers looked for self-sufficiency, but the Hundred Years' War still had many years to run before the English were expelled from everywhere but Calais.

Later Humanists: Pico's Oration

Pico della Mirandola died too young to write a mature work. He was born in 1463 and died in 1494. The oration is a very young man's work; Pico was twenty-four when he wrote it as part of his offer to prove nine hundred theses on every topic in logic, metaphysics, theology, physics, and natural history before the College of Cardinals. He was not an upstart show-off but an aristocrat who renounced his share of the family duchy to pursue a life of learning. He believed in eclecticism—that the truth could be elicited by bringing together all possible intellectual, spiritual, and religious traditions—and his range was breathtaking. We do not flinch at an enthusiasm for Plato and the Neoplatonists, but his belief in Hermes Trismegistus—a supposed Egyptian magus—may raise eyebrows, as might his faith (not uncommon at that day) in Chaldean theology and Jewish medieval kabbalistic learning. He was, nonetheless, a devout Christian; his interest in the kabbalah did not reflect respect for Judaism but the desire to refute "the stony-hearted Hebrews" out of their own works.

On the Dignity of Man was representative neither of Pico's oeuvre nor of humanist thinking generally, but it strikingly expresses some intellectual and stylistic commitments of humanism. What excites the enthusiasm of modern readers are the few paragraphs in which God tells Man to go and make of himself the highest and most intelligent thing that he can; it was the source of Walter Pater's notorious injunction that we should endeavor to "burn with a hard, gem-like flame." The idea that the task of humanity was self-creation verged on the heretical: neither Christianity nor classical thought had much room for the idea. Classical thought was too committed to the idea that everything had a fixed nature and that perfection was a matter of fulfilling it; Christianity was too committed to the idea of original sin. Pico was in fact condemned for heresy, but not because of these enthusiasms. It was for thirteen claims ranging over the nature of transubstantiation, eternal punishment, and whether Christ had really been present during the descent into hell. He defended himself energetically, but it is hard not to sympathize with his accusers.

The image Pico drew on was older than Plato and appears as a creation story in Plato's dialogue *Protagoras*: God gave all the other animals specific means of survival, such as wings, beaks, claws, armored scales, great speed. Human beings had none of these and had to rely on intelligence to flourish. More importantly, they had to invent political communities and practice justice.[11] The thought that humans needed to live in political communities just because they were not equipped with the same means of individual survival as animals was periodically rearticulated. Pico was not a romantic before his time; he did not think of self-perfection as a historical enterprise as the romantics did in the eighteenth and nineteenth centuries, and he did not see human perfection as something to be promoted politically. He was too caught up in the magical wisdom of the ancients and exotic mystics to see self-creation as something to be achieved only in the far future. The sense in which Pico is a "precursor" of later political utopians is that he inspired many thinkers who read him with pleasure. One of them was Sir Thomas More, the author of *Utopia*, who in 1510 translated the *Life* of Pico written by his nephew Francisco.

Orthodox readers in his own day—Pico was forbidden to engage in a public disputation over his nine hundred theses, and the *Oration* was published only in 1496, two years after his death—would have been startled by the claim that theology could bring us to the direct vision of the divine. It is usually thought to be a blessing of the afterlife. Pico held that we can make ourselves cherubim, one rank below the seraphim, but close enough to God to contemplate him. The political implications are obscure, and never explored by Pico; we might expect a Platonist to look to philosopher-kings, but a Christian Platonist is equally likely to turn away from politics and ask no more than space for a community of scholars intent on attaining the mystic vision of God as he truly is. This is not Montaigne's explicitly antipolitical defense of the quiet life. Montaigne did not expect the vision of blessedness to appear if we could keep perfectly still; he sought peace and disengagement for their own sake. Pico did. That attaining the blessed vision might require a strenuous engagement with Chaldean theology, the Hebrew kabbalah, and the theological speculations of Arab Neoplatonists did not unnerve Pico— those were his real interests.

Erasmus

Erasmus defines the humanist temper and the full humanist range, literary, political, and philosophical. He was born in 1469, the illegitimate son of a future priest and a physician's daughter. A native of the Netherlands, he got his classical training at the school in Deventer that produced Nicholas of Cusa and Thomas à Kempis. Without parents or money, he could not attend university and pursued his studies in a monastery. He had no spiritual vocation, but the contemplative life attracted him, and he knew that patience and self-control never hurt scholarship. Technically, he remained in monastic orders all his life, but he hankered after the wider world, and when he attached himself as a secretary to the bishop of Cambrai in 1492, he began a career in which the search for patrons bulked large. One of his main contributions to political thinking, *The Education of a Christian Prince*, which is always printed alongside a *Panegyric* for Archduke Philip of Austria, was part of a long campaign to advance himself economically. The *Panegyric* was written in 1504 and addressed to the father of the future emperor Charles V; it was therefore an apt companion for the instruction addressed to his sixteen-year-old son. Their financial motivation does not discredit either. To modern readers, the habit of laying on flattery with a trowel is unpersuasive; to early modern writers and readers, it was a literary trope with a certain ironical twist—the author told the dedicatee that he was virtuous, wise, brave, and a patron of learning, but presented him with a work that urged him to distinguish true praise from mere flattery and laid out an account of the virtuous prince that no one has ever lived up to.

The interest of *The Education of a Christian Prince* will become more obvious when we turn to Machiavelli's *Prince*. It was written three years after that work—in 1516 against 1513—and Erasmus was seeking employment, much as Machiavelli was. Erasmus played it straight, whereas Machiavelli did something with the genre that interpreters are still puzzled by. The striking feature of Erasmus's version of a mirror of princes was the insistence that peace was the highest good. Ironically, the future Charles V became a notable practitioner of war and coercive diplomacy; Erasmus subsequently made a gift of the work to Henry VIII of England, another monarch whose pacific inclinations were not obvious at the time or later. But Erasmus's defense of peace was sincere; his pacifism was deeply felt and underpinned by a great distaste for all forms of cruelty. His hatred of war was shared by his very good friend Sir Thomas More, but More was more than ready, if not positively happy, to see heretics taken out and burned at the stake; Erasmus insisted that religious differences were not a ground for quarrel of any sort, let alone for disgusting forms of execution.

The Education of a Christian Prince jolts the modern reader, not so much by its fulsome praise of Charles V as by invoking Xenophon to claim that "there is something beyond human nature, something wholly divine, in absolute rule over free and willing subjects."[12] We find the thought of absolutism on the one side and freedom and willingness on the other hard to embrace. It is in fact no different from the thought we found in Marsilius: popular consent *legitimates* government, but it does not *limit* it in the sense in which modern constitutions do. Good rulers display a divine quality that it would be absurd to restrain, but they can display it only by ruling over consenting subjects. This is not Justinian's claim that the Roman emperor held absolute legislative authority because it had been conferred on him by "the people" who had possessed it in the first place. Justinian's claim was an explanation of the pedigree of absolute authority; Erasmus gives us an account of its nature. The crucial contrast is Marsilius's: tyrants coerce the unwilling without regard to the common good, while absolute princes govern the willing in the general interest and not their own. Like Marsilius, but in a more Platonic mode, Erasmus links authority to wisdom and suggests that the good prince is a Platonic guardian, supreme not in wealth and power but in wisdom.[13]

This may be the first time since late antiquity that Plato's *Republic* makes itself felt in political theorizing. The full text had come into educated consciousness with Marsilio Ficino's translation of 1469. Erasmus thought the mark of an educated man was equal facility in Greek and Latin, which had become feasible when the Ottoman conquest of Constantinople in 1453 had driven the classical scholars and philosophers of the city to take refuge in the west, but it was still likely that an educated man would read Plato in Latin translation. Whether in Greek or in Latin translation, however, Plato's utopian scheme for a state in which kings would be philosophers and philosophers kings was now in the educational curriculum in a way it had not been. More's *Utopia*, published at the same time as *The Education of a Christian Prince*, was a jokily written but seriously intended reworking of Plato's ambitions. Like his friend, Erasmus wanted philosophically minded rulers to govern.

Erasmus imagines the prince's tutor disputing this point with "some idiot courtier," who objects that Erasmus's schemes for the education of the prince would create a philosopher and not a prince: "Do not think that it was an ill-considered thesis of Plato's, praised by the most laudable men, that the state will eventually be blessed if and when either the rulers take up philosophy or the philosophers take over the government."[14] Erasmus's gloss is important and reflects the hostility of the humanists toward the Scholastics: a philosopher is not "someone who is clever at dialectics or science" but someone who can distinguish reality and appearance, and unflinchingly cleave to the good. In fact, "being a philosopher is in practice the same as being a Christian; only the terminology is different." The insistence on the prince's ability to distinguish between appearance and reality is the great theme taken from Plato, and a main preoccupation of the educational program.

Thus, public opinion is not to be trusted, because the masses are in the grip of illusion, trussed up like the prisoners in Plato's famous cave, unable to see what is real and what is merely a shadow on the cave wall. Again, the prince is to be taught that true happiness is to be attained only by pursuing virtue; the pleasures of the flesh, the carnal amusements of sex and gluttony, are of no account compared with the unshakable happiness of the good man. This doctrine is in some respects overdetermined; the Stoic would have argued that only the virtuous man is free, since only he can spurn the temptations of the flesh and steer by the compass of his rational nature; and the Christian would have argued that the joys of the world are snares and delusions, traps set by the devil to lead us into the fiery pit and away from our heavenly destination. Erasmus knows all this; that is why the philosopher is a Christian—using different terminology.

The prince must learn early the dangers of flattery. True praise is good, for it encourages activity in the path of virtue. Flattery is a noxious drug. It gratifies the senses for a moment and undermines judgment. This thought has obvious implications for the importance of the prince's choosing his advisers wisely. Advisers who always tell him what he wants to hear and never remind him of the dangers into which he may run if he pursues a rash or thoughtless path are no use. Advisers who have an eye to their own profit and not that of their country are a danger to everyone. Although Erasmus's great friend Sir Thomas More had a sharply ironic view about the chances of the philosopher's being heeded—by this time, Plato's *Seventh Letter* was well known, and his narrow escape from death or slavery at the hands of Dionysius had become a familiar cautionary tale—Erasmus is, or appears to be, undaunted.

We once again see some familiar thoughts in novel terminology and with echoes of sources different from those encountered earlier. There are two crucial dichotomies on which everything turns. The first is the recurrent insistence on the difference between tyranny and legitimate rule. Because of what they became, we tend to think of the French and the Spanish monarchies in ways appropriate to the absolutism of Louis XIV and Louis XV, with their defenders resting on the doctrine of divine right. But whereas later defenders of absolute monarchy invoked divine right in opposition to the idea of government by consent, Erasmus adhered to the old view that the consent of the subject legitimates the ruler. Nor does he raise questions about one-man rule. He insists that the common opinion of philosophers is that monarchy is the best form of government, and does not suggest that Cicero, or Roman writers up to the time of Caesar, might not have agreed. He was not writing intellectual history; he was painting a picture. He encourages the prince's tutor to depict the tyrant in animal imagery to emphasize his full wickedness. On the one side is the picture of the legitimate ruler, full of wisdom and virtue, safe in the love of his people, and legitimated by their willing acceptance of his rule. On the other is the tyrant, a creature described as worse than the ravening bear, more dangerous than lion or poisonous snake. If the virtuous ruler partakes of the excellence of God, we know what the tyrant partakes of.

Tyrants, then, govern in their own interest and not that of the whole people, and they do not try to secure the consent of their subjects but force obedience on them as best they can. Although *The Education of a Christian Prince* is a moralistic work, it is not only that. When Erasmus urges moderation in the taxation that a prince imposes on his people, he makes the wholly practical point that a lightly taxed people will be more prosperous and provide greater resources for the government than a people who can barely keep themselves alive. He also points out, in the way familiar since Aristotle, that princes who have an eye to their own security and well-being will not render themselves objects of hatred to their subjects. Grinding them into the ground with excessive taxes inspires revolts.

Lawfulness is essential. Tyrants allow their friends to break the law, but enforce it cruelly against their enemies; a legitimate prince governs according to the law, making no exceptions save what clemency commends. What is no more present in Erasmus than in Christine de Pizan is praise of tyrannicide, and the thought that a man who kills a tyrant is a benefactor of mankind. Whatever impact Cicero had on humanism, it did not extend to his endlessly repeated praise of tyrannicide. But there is no explicit repudiation of a right of resistance, and no insistence that tyrannicide is forbidden no matter what evils the rulers may perpetrate. The reminder that rulers who alienate their subjects risk their own lives does not come with the qualification that subjects would be wicked to revolt. There is no hint of the Augustinian injunction to submit in patience to the brutalities of any system whereby a minimal peace is maintained.

The second great contrast that Erasmus insists on is between the prince who seeks peace and the prince intent on war. The most distinctive feature of the work—although we find something like it in More—is the elaborate discussion of how to pursue peace. Erasmus observes that the ancients divided the arts of statecraft into the arts of peace and the arts of war. This is an error. All of the arts of a statesman are the arts of peace, because "with them he must strive to his utmost for this end: that the devices of war may never be used."[15] The thought contains a twist we shall find again in Hobbes. Today we think of arguments against war in humanitarian terms, and there are humanitarian arguments in Erasmus. The central argument, however, is that civilization is a good in itself. A good society is prosperous and cheerful; people are not ground down by overwork, not burdened by taxation, not frightened of arbitrary and irrational laws; but what makes a society truly civilized is the level of learning it fosters; and what makes warfare so terrible is not only that it is inimical to learning—which is not the banal thought that lectures cannot be given while troops are quartered in the lecture room—but that the project of killing one's enemies is directly at odds with the project of living in a community governed by reason.

The prince needs the arts of peace. The details are familiar and classical; the prince should be generous, but not in ways that destroy the public credit, he should appoint unbribable magistrates, ensure that the law is stern but not harsh, and so, entirely plausibly, on. There are departures from the ordinary. One is Erasmus's discussion of punishments. He dislikes the whole subject, but his rule of thumb is that where there are two ways of securing compliance—more stick or more carrot—choose the gentler. Admonition and persuasion leave the chastised person a free agent, ready to act on what he now knows, whereas brutality leaves him a sullen and hostile animal. Another is when he turns to the ways in which the law can encourage work and repress idleness. Criticizing Plato's proposal to evict beggars from his republic, Erasmus observes that few people beg by preference; if old age and illness have taken a toll, the remedy is not expulsion but institutions to house the incapable. Conversely, we should not be hidebound in our view of what constitutes idleness. The inhabitants of Marseilles rightly refused to let into their town a gang of priests who wished to live in idleness by hawking relics.

By the same token, it would be right to limit the number of monasteries, since the monastic life is a kind of idleness. So is life in many universities; Erasmus had visited Cambridge and spent some years at the Sorbonne, with whose orthodox faculty he had come into conflict. Turning away from clerical idleness, he considers servants. People kept as retainers and servants merely for ostentation should be put to useful employment; that allows some sharp thoughts on soldiers: "Soldiering, too, is a very energetic kind of idleness, and much the most dangerous, since it causes the total destruction of everything worthwhile and opens up a cesspit of everything that is evil. And so, if the prince will banish from his realm all such seed-beds of crime, there will be much less for his laws to punish."[16]

The sixteenth century was not more bloody than the seventeenth, let alone the twentieth, but it was a century of continuous warfare. Dynastic alliances were formed and broken, cemented by marriage and torn apart when the marriage broke up—or the marriage was torn apart when one or other side wished to be rid of the encumbrances of the alliance. Through marital alliances the Habsburg family extended its reach to every part of Europe; Charles V's success in unifying Spain, keeping successive popes at bay, and becoming the most powerful monarch in Europe reflected his military and political talent. However, he also took care to marry Isabella of Portugal to reunite the Iberian kingdoms, and one of his last acts was to arrange the marriage of his son Philip to

Mary Tudor, queen of England. If they had produced children, a Catholic England would have become a dependency of Spain. It was thus bold of Erasmus to denounce the role of marital alliances in contemporary politics. Indeed, it was even bolder than it might seem. When he offered *The Education of a Christian Prince* to Henry VIII, Charles V had recently broken off—given his age one should say he had been got out of—an engagement to Henry VIII's sister, Mary. (Her subsequent marital career included a brief marriage to Charles's rival, Francis I of France, and a love match with the duke of Suffolk.) Erasmus's little book was written barely two years after those events reduced relations between Henry and the Habsburgs to frigid hostility.

The attack on marital alliances was nothing to the sheer ferocity of Erasmus's condemnation of war. The idea of a just war is swept aside; there may be just wars, but even if there are, we should do everything in our power not to fight them. Augustine's view that we might properly fight wars to punish nations for their wickedness is not directly controverted, but it is pointedly ignored. Christ was the Prince of Peace, and the Christian prince should do his utmost to secure a reputation as a prince of peace. Charles V's career, including as it did, the Battle of Pavia in 1525, where he captured Francis I, and the sack of Rome by imperial troops in 1527, was a wry commentary on Erasmus's hopes for the young man. Erasmus knew that he was seen as a peacemonger—he published *The Complaint of Peace* in 1512 and was part of the peace party that looked for reconciliation between the separatists of Flanders and their Spanish king. He also knew that any argument that princes should not stand on what they took to be their rights would be met with the retort that unless we are ready to stand on our rights, nobody's rights will be respected.

To this he makes the only possible response: in a world of continuous warfare, no rights are safe. A measure of give-and-take is essential; securing most of our rights through peaceful negotiation is better than trying to secure them all by war. Moreover, says Erasmus, "a prince cannot revenge himself upon his enemies without first opening hostilities against his own subjects."[17] Conscripting supplies and soldiers is painful; confining your citizens within walled cities to protect them from the enemy is scarcely better than being besieged. As to why we are so inclined to make war on each other, Erasmus offers two savage comments.

The clergy, who should be preaching peace, spend their time fomenting warfare. His condemnation was provoked by the wars in Italy that had been set off by the determination of Popes Julius II and Leo X to prevent a union of northern Italy and the Kingdom of Naples in imperial or any other hands. The Holy Roman Empire was now, effectively, the Habsburg dynastic empire; the Kingdom of Naples was in Spanish hands, and northern Italy a battleground between papal, French, and imperial (or Spanish) forces. Erasmus was unsparing in his criticism of popes and bishops who pursued worldly political interests. If Christians must fight, they should fight the Turks; but even that they ought not to be too hasty to do, seeing that there is no point in defeating the Turks if we cannot institute a Christian peace. One novelty was that Erasmus denounced, for what seems to be the first time, the hostility that stemmed from nationalism, one nation hating another for no reason beyond its otherness. "Nowadays, the Englishman generally hates the Frenchman for no better reason than that he is French. The Scot, simply because he is a Scot, hates the Englishman, the Italian hates the German, the Swabian hates the Swiss, and so on; province hates province, city hates city."[18]

When Erasmus ends by observing that people who behave like this are running into a storm with folly as their guide, he reminds us of one thing more. A feature of humanist thinking was new forms of literary expression that allowed serious arguments to be expressed in a nonserious literary form. Perhaps the most characteristic work that Erasmus wrote was his self-mocking, seriocomic tract *The Praise of Folly*. He said, probably not expecting to be believed, that he wrote it in a single week, while staying with Thomas More during 1509, recovering from illness after a journey from the Continent, and without his usual books. That is no doubt one reason why the mockery extends in the best humanist manner to citing the authority of every serious writer who had written a comic work. Its Latin title is *Encomium Moriae*, a pun uniting the Greek word for madness and his host's surname; its structure is an extended joke that keeps turning serious—it begins with Folly complaining that nobody ever makes speeches in her honor. As she says, this is very unfair, seeing how devotedly they follow her every whim, so she will make a speech in praise of herself.[19] This she does with the aid of her allies: intoxication, deep sleep, ignorance, and stupidity. This enables Erasmus to mock contemporary social, religious, and political life—while saying that since it is only Folly talking, it isn't to be taken too seriously.

No commentator has been able to decide just what he was up to. That surely would have given Erasmus pleasure. In part, he may simply have enjoyed the intellectual exercise of writing from the standpoint of sheer foolishness. It is difficult to do well; getting across a serious point in a way that requires the author to say exactly the reverse of what he intends is not easy, and Folly herself apologizes from time to time for getting carried away and speaking like a serious person. Although Erasmus was surprised at the book's popularity, getting students to emulate it was a popular pedagogical device in Tudor England, and forcing students to argue against their favorite beliefs remains a popular pedagogical device to this day. Folly becomes serious when attacking Erasmus's familiar targets, including a corrupt and spiritually bankrupt church, and she is only marginally less savage about the useless drones who lecture on logic in the universities. The peroration is a masterpiece of double meanings seriously meant; Folly takes the opportunity presented by the fact that she is only a foolish woman to set out some hair-raising theological views.[20]

The masses, she says, are trapped in the flesh, like the prisoners in Plato's allegory of the cave; they see only illusions, and they are at the mercy of the things of the flesh. Neoplatonism had inspired early Catholic theology; but appealing directly to Plato to send his readers a message about the ways in which the flesh is a prison to the spirit was unorthodox. In any event, the cause in which Erasmus wished to invoke Plato was calculated to cause offense. Using Folly as his mouthpiece allowed Erasmus to remind his readers that Christianity took a view of the world that common sense would think insane—and therefore that people who seemed insane to the world might see a deeper truth than any available to common sense. Erasmus had insurance against complaint; Saint Paul preached Christ crucified and said it was "foolishness" to the Greeks. For

Erasmus to say that Christian mysticism was insanity to the *homme moyen sensuel* was squarely in that tradition. But the argument was not wholly comfortable—either he meant that Christianity was a creed for madmen (which he did not) or that the truth of Christianity was the same truth that Plato had enunciated (which he might well have thought) and that, as he later said in *The Education of a Christian Prince*, "only the terminology is different."[21] In which case, the need for a church as well as an academy is not obvious. Certainly, a church filled with corrupt and greedy hangers-on was not needed. Erasmus never left the Catholic Church and had some quarrelsome exchanges with Luther on the subject of free will, but critics have always thought him an inspiration to Protestant as well as Catholic reformers, and for all that his patrons were absolute monarchs, he displays the modern liberal temper of mind in a very pure form.

Sir Thomas More

Erasmus's dearest friend, Thomas More, knight, lord chancellor, and Catholic martyr, perhaps went him one better with *Utopia*. More is an enigmatic figure. He was one of the cleverest men of his age, whose skill as a lawyer led him into politics and the dangerous world of the Tudor court during the reign of Henry VIII. He was Speaker of the House of Commons in the 1520s and became the most powerful of the king's ministers when he succeeded the disgraced Cardinal Wolsey as lord chancellor in 1529. It was not ambition that drove him; he combined a quick and mordant wit with a piety that almost took him into the cloister rather than the lawcourts. He was nearly ten years younger than Erasmus, born in 1474 and judicially murdered by Henry VIII in 1535, the year before Erasmus died. He was convicted of treason when he refused to swear the oath acknowledging the king's supremacy as head of the Church of England. The king, knowing how unpopular More's execution was, forbade him to make a speech on the scaffold in justification of his conduct. More obeyed to the last. "I die the King's good servant," he said, "but God's first."

What makes More an enigma is the contrast between his skepticism about the political and social life around him—in evidence throughout *Utopia*—and his readiness to accommodate himself to the brutality and duplicity of the world of Tudor politics until he took his final stand. If he had not died a martyr to the Catholic faith, he would have had the reputation of a man who could justify everything his royal master did. He may well have appreciated the irony that many years before they fell out, he had helped Henry VIII secure the title of "Defender of the Faith," bestowed on him by the pope in recognition of Henry's condemnation of Luther's view of the sacraments. This was in 1520 and, as usual in controversy with Luther, provoked a furious response, to which More wrote an anonymous reply that outdid Luther's in scatological invective. Ironically, More had at the time urged Henry to be less fulsome in acknowledging the authority of the pope; English feelings toward the papacy were decidedly cold: there was only one English cardinal in a college of fifty, no Englishman would ever become pope, and the English saw no reason to have the English church governed by Italians in the interests of the French or the Spanish.

Utopia is a very good read, but More's life makes it puzzling. The word "utopia" is More's coinage. He was an excellent classical scholar and translated several works of the Greek satirist Lucian into Latin as a joint project with Erasmus. One of Lucian's best-known works was a *True History*, a detailed account of events that never took place; and one of the tall stories the friends translated was *Menippus Goes to Hell*, in which a Cynic philosopher takes a tour of the underworld. "Utopia" read as *outopia* means "no place," and More exploits the punning ambiguity inherent in its similarity to *eutopia*, or "the good place." The main river of the island of Utopia is Anydrus—waterless—and the traveler who has returned to tell More and his Flemish friend Peter Gilles all about the place is called Raphael Hythlodaeus—*hythlodaeus* meaning something very like "absurd." So we have a tall story about a nonexistent island, told by a confessedly unreliable witness. The contrast with Plato's ponderous exposition of his plans for the ideal polity after the first book of *Republic* could not be more marked—which suggests that part of the point of the exercise was to write a *Republic* for a later age and provide both a defense and an internal critique of Plato's scheme. Raphael Hythlodaeus, who admires everything about Utopia, is in effect Plato's spokesman, and the fictional "More" the defender of common sense. Both are, of course, More with the two sides of his character conducting rhetorical warfare against each other.

How far *Utopia* reveals More's political ideals is not easy to say. The simple view is as plausible as any: that More felt a great distaste for the pomp and circumstance of the rich and powerful, and anger at the misery of the poor. No sentient creature in More's England could overlook the enormous gap between the rich and powerful at one end of the social spectrum and the starving poor at the other. Much of the wealth of England at this time depended on the wool trade, and although the overall benefit to the economy was great, the impact on poor laborers who were thrown off farms converted to pasture, or found the commons enclosed for sheep runs, was severe. Tudor governments responded to unemployment by savage penalties for theft and vagrancy. Although war on the Continent took able-bodied men out of England, it was no permanent help; wars came to an end, and unemployed soldiers were more effective criminals than unemployed laborers and spread even more fear.

More's *Utopia* is certainly a running critique of the ills that beset England in the early sixteenth century. The description of the island of Utopia occupies only the second book of *Utopia*, and the first book is a long prologue notable for More's denunciation of the way that sheep have consumed men, the injustice of executing unemployed men for theft—presenting them with the choice between a quick death by strangulation or a slow death from starvation—and the wickedness of the exactions of monarchs who rob their subjects to wage predatory wars on other nations. The first book also contains a long argument over the question whether More should retire to a life of study or commit himself to public service. More was debating just that question with himself at the time. The first book's complaints are echoed in the last few pages of book 2, when Raphael Hythlodaeus makes a long speech against the tyranny of wealth and the misery of poverty—while More affects to be sitting there thinking how terrible it would be to live in a world without pomp and circumstance and aristocrats.[22] It is clear that More was genuinely attracted to the main features of Utopian society, however little chance there was of any movement toward them in his own time and country.

What are these main features? The most obvious and the root of all others is the abolition of money. The joking aspect of More's mind appears when he tells us that the Utopians employ gold for making chamber pots; they allow children to play with precious stones but expect them to grow out of such play rather rapidly. William Morris used the same imagery in *News from Nowhere* three and a half centuries later, though his variation on the chamber pot story was to establish a huge dung hill on the site of Parliament. The Utopians run a communist economy, where everyone must work for six hours a day, and every family draws on the common stock for necessities. Modern readers flinch at forced labor, but More did not. For four years, he submitted voluntarily to the monastic discipline of the Carthusians and had no qualms about disciplined hard work. The underlying logic is anyway obvious. Mankind is forced to labor; nature is a benevolent mother only to those who make use of their own natural gifts—intelligence and energy—to acquire the gifts she provides in the fertility of the soil and the availability of plants and fruits and animals for our use.

Since labor is a necessity, there is nothing to complain of in doing it under the discipline of a state. The question is whether rewards allocated under the familiar system of a monetary economy and the vagaries of the marketplace are more generous and allocated more justly and securely than under Utopian communism. Once the question is asked in those terms, the answer is inescapable. In sixteenth-century England, willing workers were thrown out of work and hanged for stealing or whipped for vagrancy; meanwhile, hordes of useless servants were maintained for display by rich men, and thrown out of employment themselves when their master died or fell on hard times. As for the rich, it was bad for their characters to be underemployed and subject to no discipline. Critics reacted to Max Weber's wonderful essay *The Protestant Ethic and the Spirit of Capitalism* by observing that many Catholics had imbibed the Protestant ethic before Protestantism arrived on the scene. More was one.

Work is a discipline; substantial equality is a dictate of justice.

Human life cannot be wholly without fear and anxiety; we all die in the end, and we are all subject to ill health and to the miseries and disappointments of everyday life. But even if all flesh is as grass, starvation is a great evil, while an austere but decent standard of living—there is good wine in Utopia—secured by work while we are strong and given gratis when we can work no longer, is enough in itself and the foundation of a life of intelligent reflection. Against that background, More's belief that the security provided by a society like Utopia is a very good bargain becomes easy to understand. Indeed, it becomes impossible to resist.

More denounced capital punishment for theft as an evil and an absurdity; the starving vagrant can hardly be expected to be deterred by it, and like Erasmus, More thought excessive harshness brutalized both criminals and noncriminals. Modern readers are unlikely to find his alternative a model of humane treatment, but by the standards of the early sixteenth century, it was mild. In Utopia thieves became slaves; they serve a lifetime sentence of hard labor, though sentences are commuted for good behavior, which provides an incentive to reform. They do not suffer brutal ill-treatment, but whereas everyone else works only as long as needed, whence More's assumption that six hours a day was enough, slaves work a long day as part of their punishment. More began a long tradition of specifying in minute detail just how life in Utopia will operate; for a debased version of the same enthusiasm (or overenthusiasm) for detail one could turn to a modern utopia, Edward Bellamy's *Looking Backward* (1883), where we find the same desire for a world without money, an emphasis on work as social duty, though a more sophisticated view of how much of it we might do, and the same incautious assumption that a wise ruler could dictate the details of everyday life to universal satisfaction.[23]

Utopian institutions are of interest as a critique of the nationalism and commercial rivalries that were beginning to dominate European politics, as they continue to do. There is almost no central government in Utopia; there is a capital, but the towns are all of the same size and layout. In the capital there is a parliament, but the only details of Utopian government that Raphael Hythlodaeus offers concern local administration. Its most obvious feature is mathematical neatness: groups of households choose leaders and these form a council that chooses a mayor for the township. There are few laws, and no lawyers; there are many intellectuals, but they study the liberal arts and think about deep matters rather than how to rob their neighbors. To the extent that any state offered a framework for Utopia it would have been Venice, but More is only half-serious about filling in the institutional gaps that Plato's *Republic* notoriously left, for the good reason that in utopias of this sort politics in the ordinary sense is a casualty of consensus, and the institutions that express and control political attachments and rivalries are absent. Venice controlled these forces rather than abolishing them by literary fiat.

Religion is described in detail. Utopians are attached to a form of theism that seems to anticipate Unitarianism; the Utopians call their God Mythras without any suggestion that this is really his name. The common elements of belief are few: there is a God, the universe is divinely ordered for the benefit of human life and the attaining of eternal happiness, and a person who conducts herself or himself with a view to salvation will lead a good and happy life on earth. Death is not to be feared, because it is the gateway to communion with God. Different beliefs flourish, and the only absolute in Utopian religious life is an absolute ban on intolerance; one of More's sharp little jokes is the narrator's tale of a Christian convert exiled for denouncing other faiths as false.[24] More's classical allegiances are visible when he says that violent attempts at converting others are put down as breaches of the peace, not as blasphemy, a category that seems unavailable in Utopia. From a man who sent heretics to the stake, this is a powerful and dangerous doctrine, though it casts a curious light on his own career. Atheists are tolerated, but not trusted; they must not proselytize in public and cannot hold public office. They are encouraged to argue with the priesthood in the hope that they may see the light rather than to give the priests useful intellectual exercise. Nonetheless, *Utopia* ends with something of a surprise; Raphael says that the one defect of Utopia was its failure to heed the Christian message but that the good news is that it has been converted to Christianity. That may be, as many commentators suggest, an affirmation of More's distinctively Christian humanism. It may, on the other hand, lead readers to wonder whether conversion will be followed by dissension and sectarianism, and whether the Utopians might not have done better to stick to Mythraism. Utopia's founder, Utopos, conquered the island with no difficulty because it was riven with religious conflict.[25]

Services are musical, the prayers are for enlightenment, and priests are highly regarded, because they are well educated and the servants of peace. More gives the priests a substantial role in the conduct of war. More was ironic where Erasmus was passionate, but the underlying thought is common to them. Utopians despise war. They also despise hunting—an aristocratic sport always praised in handbooks for princes as good training for war—because hunting, like war, is a form of butchery. Unlike most nations, the Utopians would rather secure victory by deceit and bribery than by force. A bloody victory is as bad as a bloody defeat; ideally, they subvert their opponents by bribery—which is easily done, because they have a lot of gold and silver that they do not themselves need and can use to suborn their enemies. Twentieth-century observers of the United States' travails in Vietnam sometimes thought they could have undermined the Vietcong at a vastly lower cost in both blood and money had they followed the lead of More's Utopians. More breaks with conventional views of just war by describing the Utopians as happy to wage wars of national liberation to free other people from dictatorial governments; in this they go beyond the United Nations Charter, which forbids "regime change" as a legitimate reason for making war, and perhaps display a utopian overconfidence in the ease with which one people can liberate another from its homegrown tyrants. They do not wage war to advance their self-interest beyond the demands of self-defense. One way and another, they are strikingly unlike their European contemporaries, who were about to embark on a century and a half of religious conflict and five centuries of imperialism in the Americas, Asia, and Africa.

They use their priests to minimize destruction; a priest will prevent an army from killing defeated foes, will protect the fallen, and has the authority to bring a battle to an end by declaring it ended. In time of war, priests go with the army to preserve humanity and not to pray to the almighty to massacre their enemies. The Utopians' matter-of-fact approach to conflict extends to an unwillingness to have their citizens killed in battle; their wealth allows them to hire mercenaries and to secure their loyalty by offering colossal rates of pay. They have worked out that the high death rate among their hired soldiers means they will have to pay only a small proportion of them. More imagines that the Utopians employ for preference a distant people, the Zapoletes, who are not so much unaware of the dangers they run as utterly indifferent to them; they are greedy, violent, loyal to whoever employs them but willing to kill each other without compunction, and plainly possessed of a much greater taste for excitement than the sober Utopians. The Utopians despise them, but More is not inviting the reader to wonder whether they have other employment opportunities; he is condemning warfare.

Taken seriously, these passages suggest that More's distance from the politics and religion of his own day was more than a matter of psychological reserve. How best to take *Utopia* seriously, however, is not self-evident. Utopia building is useful for something other than providing blueprints. What have come to be called "dystopian" works, such as Huxley's *Brave New World*, do not suggest that the dystopian world is immediately around the corner, or that we must take immediate and dramatic steps to prevent its arrival; they serve to sharpen our self-consciousness about the implications of what we think of as progress. *Utopia* is not a blueprint for pacifism and the abolition of social ranks, or for religious disestablishment; its comic elements not only protect More from any accusation of being a dissident and a man to be carefully watched but also protect the text itself from being treated as a statement of the politically desirable. *Utopia* has an ironic distance from reality that Plato's *Republic* does not. But it certainly serves to raise questions: do we benefit from possessing ever more wealth while others starve; must states fight for prestige; can we not tolerate religious dissenters? And so indefinitely on.

How much of what such sketches teach us is intended by their authors is a biographical mystery. Almost every work escapes its author's control in some respects, and almost any work betrays its author's intentions in both meanings of the word "betray." The one thing we should try to do is curb the urge to infer from the text to what the author "must" have intended by it. A modern reader will see in *Utopia* a cautionary tale about the way the desire for a perfect society breeds totalitarianism: the inhabitants of Utopia cannot travel without permission; premarital sexual intercourse is penalized by a lifelong prohibition on marriage for either partner; and, as More says, everyone is acutely conscious of being always under the eye of everyone else.[26] We squirm; after Orwell's *1984*, mutual surveillance means to us Big Brother. It seems much too high a price to pay, even for the peace and security on offer. We should not assume that More would share our doubts. Writing from the little room in the Tower of London where he was awaiting trial and execution, he did not complain of his loss of liberty but expressed gratitude for the simplification of his existence. This was no doubt a gallant attempt to comfort his family; he had an enviably happy marriage and was greatly loved by his children. It also reflected the hankering after a life free of earthly concerns that an admirer of Plato should have felt.

Montaigne

Erasmus and More appeal to modern readers because of their skepticism. The sixteenth-century humanist who epitomizes the use of skepticism for moral and political purposes was Montaigne. This is paradoxical, because his *essais* touch only indirectly on political organization or the management of everyday affairs; they are investigations, "assays," of the self, attempts to investigate the human psyche from the evidence of the one person whom Montaigne knew best—that is, himself. Nor are they confessional like Augustine's *Confessions*. Montaigne was interested neither in confessing his weaknesses nor in praising God for his mercy in redeeming him from them. Like Augustine, Montaigne thought that man was a mystery to himself, but there is none of Augustine's deep anguish at that fact, rather an acceptance that patience, self-control, and caution in taking anything for granted are essential for self-understanding.

The political bearing and inspiration of this Stoic, skeptical introspective concern are direct, however. In translations other than English translations, his essays are described as "moral and political," as they are. Montaigne was born in 1533, and took part in the French civil wars of the midcentury, so his discussions of courage, betrayal, the dangers of negotiation, and much else have the voice of experience.[27] These were wars of religion exacerbated by conflicts in royal and aristocratic families, and by the underlying struggle between a centralizing monarchy and an aristocracy whose power and prestige was local or regional. Montaigne came from a noble family, studied law, and was a counselor in the Bordeaux *parlement*, but found public affairs distasteful. Selling his position in the *parlement* gave him an income, but leisure made him miserable. Although his *essais* are not a record of unhappiness, they were provoked by it. The injunctions on which happiness depended were Stoic in their concern that the world should not too much touch us, Christian in their moral basis, and modern in their fascination with the individual as an individual.

Politics is more to be feared for its dangers than enjoyed for its opportunities, rulers are essential, and monarchy is the best form of rule; but wise men eschew the search for military glory and try to build good public morals on the most tolerant possible version of Christianity. As to the rest, the greatest goods are friendship, a quiet mind, and the study of those things that philosophy and religion can teach us. One should resist the temptation to credit a writer with the invention of anything, but it is hard to resist the temptation to credit Montaigne with discovering both the modern sense of individuality and the modern concept of private life. Indeed, his essays, avowedly about the one subject he really knew, namely himself, can plausibly be said to be the first modern autobiography, that is, an autobiography in the modern sense of the term.

And here we begin to see the emergence of a new conflict between the private and the public: not the traditional tension between self-interest and public spirit, or the Christian tension between the concerns of the here and now and those of the hereafter, or the Platonic tension between the search for Truth and doing our duty to our fellows, but the distinctively modern conflict between the pleasures of intimate relationships, domestic happiness, the quiet contentment of living our own lives in our own way, and the pleasures—equally real but utterly different—of public life. The door opens to a new reading of the tension between man and citizen.

CHAPTER 10

The Reformation

The Reformation

L IKE "THE RENAISSANCE," "THE Reformation" is a loose term, but inescapable except at the price of appalling circumlocution. Neither geographically, nor temporally, nor doctrinally does the idea of a single, definable Reformation (or Renaissance, for that matter) bear scrutiny, but the fact remains that before 1500 there was no institutionalized confessional divide among western European Christians, and after 1550 there were several. The political consequences were enormous. Most of the doctrines of leading Protestant thinkers had first been articulated by Jan Hus and John Wyclif a century earlier; Luther drew heavily on the fiercest and most alarming ideas of Saint Augustine; and a return to the purity of the early church was widely demanded. But theological originality is not our topic. The impact of the new theology on the legitimation of political authority is. "How are we to govern ourselves?" takes on a new urgency when rulers and ruled are at odds over their religious allegiances.

Dramatic change in church governance might have occurred a century earlier during and after the Great Schism. It did not; the Reformation occurred not in the fifteenth century but in the early sixteenth. It broke out when and where it did because the *political* hostility to the papacy long felt by the rulers of western Europe, whose financial needs made the wealth of the church an irresistible target for cash-strapped monarchs fighting costly wars, found ideological backing in a widespread moral, spiritual, and theological hostility to the papacy. The *confessional* divide was an artifact of, and instrumental in accelerating, the long process by which churches became *national* churches. The inability of the papacy to preserve the unity of Christendom owed more to the political alliances the papacy had made to preserve its position in Italy than to any Europe-wide movement of opinion against the church as such. Neither the complaint against the worldliness of the papacy nor the wish for a more conciliar, or congregationalist, or in a broad sense democratic, form of church organization was novel. The decisive factor was the readiness of secular authorities to take control of the religious life of their own states.

The most spectacular example was English. Henry VIII broke with Rome because he wanted a male heir. He may have been convinced that his marriage to his sister-in-law Catherine of Aragon produced one daughter and several miscarriages because it violated the church's prohibition on marriage between near-relatives; then again, he may not. He was certainly pious, and took Mass five times a day when he was not hunting. The pope could not grant Henry an annulment; his predecessor had granted a dispensation to allow Henry's marriage to his dead brother's widow in the first place, and an annulment would have required him to condemn his predecessor's decision. The more decisive reason was the papacy's political weakness; Catherine was the aunt of Charles V, the Holy Roman Emperor, and the pope was virtually Charles's prisoner after Charles's sack of Rome in 1527. Henry VIII took the bold step of declaring himself head of the Church of England, and amenable bishops gave him his annulment. Henry, as distinct from his son Edward VI, was not attracted to Protestantism, whether in its Lutheran or its Calvinist form. After their acrimonious exchanges of 1520, the king was unlikely to take Luther as a spiritual mentor.[1] Until 1547 the Church of England was doctrinally and liturgically unchanged; the change, an enormous one, was that the king was the spiritual head of the church, and the church in England a creature of English law. The two swords had been put into the hands of one person.

Protestantism and Antinomianism

Because liberal democracy first took root in Protestant countries, there is a temptation to think that there is a natural affinity between the "congregationalist" style of governance of many Protestant churches and liberal democratic politics. The connection is not very close. Britain and the Netherlands became Protestant constitutional monarchies, while Denmark and Sweden became Protestant absolute monarchies; France passed through civil war and emerged as a Catholic absolute monarchy. Venice remained a Catholic republic. Spain was for a time almost a theocracy. How this happened is a matter for political and social historians, but the facts suggest that there is no very direct connection between the religious and political ideas of the reformers. The focus here is on the novelties and tensions in the political ideas of a few leading Protestant thinkers, with a brief glance at the ideas of the extremists. The immediate difficulty we face in talking about the *political* impact of Reformation thinkers is simple. Protestantism initially involved a turning away from institutions of all kinds. Once the role of priestly intercession in securing our salvation is denied, the idea of an institutional church is threatened; political institutions in their turn seem likely to be treated in the arm's-length fashion of Augustine's *City of God*. The state has greater institutional legitimacy than the church, since we need law and order in a way we do not need anyone to get between ourselves and the Bible and its author. That seems all we can say. But much more was said, and we must explore it.

The impetus for the late fifteenth-century attacks on prevailing institutions was not theological. The destruction of the monasteries in England and elsewhere was a consequence not of Protestantism but of princely ambitions encountering a shortage of cash; Catholic monarchs also raided church property. By the mid-seventeenth century only Italy and Spain had made no inroads into church property. Henry VIII's dissolution of the monasteries in the 1530s coincided with his decision to break with Rome and institute himself as head of the English church and was particularly violent and comprehensive, but the dissolution itself was the final episode in a prolonged budgetary crisis that had set Henry and the papacy at odds since 1515, and was not in essence different from Philip IV's assault on the fiscal privileges of the church two centuries before. What induced Henry to take the extraordinary step of making himself head of the church in England was the need to secure his divorce from Catherine of Aragon. Absent that, it is not clear that church reform would have taken the course it did in England.

The term "Protestant" itself emerged relatively late. The emperor Charles V called a meeting of the princes of the Holy Roman Empire—the Diet of Speyer of 1529—to reverse the existing policy that the local faith was a matter for local decision, and to bring the dissident principalities back into the Catholic fold. The rulers he was trying to discipline protested his decrees and took the label *protestant*. They had initially called themselves evangelicals: they based themselves on the gospels and held that the individual's conscience and the vernacular Bible were sufficient for Christian practice. This veneration of the vernacular Bible was almost the most important feature of the Reformation. The consequences for politics, science, and literature, as well as for religion narrowly conceived, were enormous. It put a premium on literacy, close reading, and thinking for oneself whose long-term effects we are living with.

The view that the Christian faith could be found in "the scriptures alone" undermined the importance of the church as a corporation. It is obvious enough that *extra ecclesia nulla salvatio* is not a Protestant doctrine; Protestantism is centrifugal rather than centripetal. The purest version of the Protestant conception of a church was articulated long after Luther, but is implicit in his first, most extreme views on the subject. Locke's *Letter Concerning Toleration* of 1698 distinguished church and commonwealth in the simplest fashion: The state is a nonvoluntary organization with the right to coerce men's behavior for the sake of the earthly well-being of a society only; a church is a voluntary society of individuals united for common and public worship of God.[2] The church comes into contact with the state only in the same way as nonreligious entities: its property will be regulated in the same way as secular property, and its rituals cannot require criminal acts. A state that tolerates all religious beliefs that are not subversive of good order, and that confines its activities to the protection of earthly security, property, and good order, need never come into conflict with a church. As to the authority that each institution wields, dissent from the (just) dictates of the state must be met with physical penalties; dissent from a church's articles of faith can be met only with separation, with no other penalties than those implicit in the separation itself.[3]

Locke felt no anxiety about the probable result: sects will multiply, and the distinction between a church and a sect will become vanishingly small. Such insouciance about the multiplication of sects was not widely shared. The Constitution of the United States explicitly rules out a federally established church, but the New England colonies persecuted dissenters from the majority faith, and Connecticut had an established church until 1818. Radical anti-establishmentarianism of the kind Locke articulated was rarely accepted by governments before the end of the eighteenth century. Put simply, Protestantism is vulnerable to antinomianism, the view that Christians have no need of law, whether the law of the state, conventional morality, or any other, for love of one another is the whole law.[4] Once governments have seen outbreaks of antinomian enthusiasm, they try to corral enthusiasm in socially manageable forms. The vulnerability of Protestantism to antinomianism stems from the thought that obedience to externally imposed law cannot secure salvation. Luther, following Saint Paul, insisted that salvation depends on God's grace and nothing else; neither indulgences nor penances nor outward performances will prevail.[5]

Inner certainty is evidence of salvation; but it may be delusive. It may be a manifestation of pride, or simple error. Nonetheless, many thinkers convinced of their own election have thought their salvation assured, irrespective of how far they obeyed the laws their earthly rulers have laid down, how far they followed or flouted the rules of conventional morality, indeed, no matter how they lived. At the end of this track lies pure antinomianism, where the elect feel so wholly saved that they preach indulgence in the sins of the flesh as a demonstration of their saved condition. Luther expressed that attitude when he wrote, though only in a private letter to Philipp Melanchthon, that we should sin bravely, confident in our redemption. As on other occasions, he later recoiled from what he had encouraged. Very small amounts of the behavior that antinomianism justifies (or even a handful of people preaching its acceptability) unsettle the respectable and unnerve the political authorities. When political authorities become unsettled, they seek order, and Protestant communities have been as ready as their Catholic counterparts to enforce order by whatever means seemed effective and no worse than the disease they were to cure.

The vulnerability of different societies to outbreaks of antinomian enthusiasm varied greatly. Societies where order was already fragile saw earlier and more extreme upsurges of religious and political radicalism: Germany suffered earlier and more strikingly, and England only mildly more than a century later during the English Civil War. A closely associated phenomenon was millenarianism; antinomianism and millenarianism are not the same entity but lead to the same conclusion: if the Second Coming is imminent, submission to local rulers seems pointless. Why entire societies are seized with a conviction that the end is nigh is mysterious, but once they are, the consequences can be appalling. The mass suicides and the like of our own day had many precursors in medieval history and later. The people to whom chiliastic myths appeal may damage other people, but they have throughout history suffered dreadful reprisals from the forces of law and order. All this occurred in full measure during the Peasants' War of the mid-1520s, when Thomas Müntzer and others launched an abortive attempt to radically democratize politics and equalize wealth, and again in a flare-up a dozen years later when Anabaptists under the leadership of John of Leiden took control of the city of Münster for several months; they were put down with extreme savagery by combined Catholic and Protestant forces. To see why these millenarian outbreaks not only ended in disaster and repression but provoked Luther to strikingly violent outbursts of indignation against all who would challenge law in any of its manifestations, we must turn to Luther's career and political ideas.

Luther: Life and Times; Theological Premises

Unsurprisingly, Luther has been written about at enormous length. The bare facts of his life nevertheless remain mysterious, not least because legends accreted around him long before his death. He contributed to the mythmaking, not because he was a fabulist but because he had a vivid imagination. A powerful sense of how things *must* have been when he was a young man led him to give different and inconsistent accounts of his early life. Most importantly, he gave conflicting accounts of his decision to embark on the monastic life, what he thought of that life at the time, what he thought of Rome on his first visit, and what made him take his famous stand on the ninety-five theses nailed to the Wittenberg church door. As with Augustine's *Confessions*, the detached observer is appalled and enthralled by the psychological spectacle. Fortunately, this does not make it impossible to give a rather brisk account of his political ideas. Luther's passions were theological and spiritual; his political ideas were less central, and detachable both from the events that provoked him to offer them to the public and from his theological commitments. Their style is unmistakably his, their content less so.

Luther was born in Eisleben, in Saxony, in 1483 and died in the same town in 1546. His father was a miner, and a man of extreme shortness of temper, who beat his son for any reason and none. Although Luther's aide and disciple Philipp Melanchthon describes Luther's mother as pious, modest, and prayerful, she seems to have been as violent as her husband, and one of Luther's several accounts of his decision to enter a monastery was that he did it to escape the cruelty of his parents. It is easy to see how such parents might have created the man whose career was marked by outbursts of uncontrollable fury against his friends as much as against his enemies. School was no respite; it was equally brutal. His secondary schooling took place at Magdeburg and Eisenach; at the age of eighteen he entered the University of Erfurt; his father intended him to be a lawyer. In 1505, however, he entered the Augustinian monastery of Erfurt. His own account of his reasons we have seen; an alternative explanation, which refers to the death of a friend and a narrow escape from death by lightning, appears to be mythmaking. The most likely explanation is that Luther suffered a spiritual crisis in his early twenties and thought the discipline of the monastic life would give coherence to his life and personality.

A dozen years later, on October 31, 1517, Luther posted on the door of the castle church at Wittenberg his ninety-five theses. They denounced an ecclesiastical scandal, the sale of indulgences to raise money for the construction of the new and magnificent St. Peter's. The theses were declared heretical in virtue of their (wholly unoriginal) insistence that no earthly power, not even that of the pope, can absolve us from our sins. This is the only conclusion one can draw from the Augustinian doctrine of salvation by grace alone. The doctrine had been watered down, and the sale of indulgences was one consequence. Indulgences were somewhere between a mere blessing and a certificate entitling one to remission of one's sins, sold to raise money for church purposes. They were believed, or half believed, to purchase a reduction of the time to be spent in purgatory postmortem. They were more importantly a form of church taxation and are morally dubious in much the same way as present-day state lotteries. The date of the posting of the theses conventionally marks the beginning of the Protestant Reformation, and the last Sunday in October is celebrated as Reformation Day. This was not a young man's outrage. Luther was thirty-four years old and well established; he was ordained priest in 1507, and steadily went through the steps for his doctorate in theology at the University of Wittenberg, where he became a professor of theology in 1511. He became district vicar of his order in 1515.

He was heavily overworked. Meeting the spiritual obligations of the order, keeping up with his intellectual work, and doing enough for three men as a monastic middle manager was too much. He was emotionally ill equipped to handle the strain; he suffered sudden collapses of energy, for which he compensated with bouts of overwork, or in the case of failures in his devotions, with bouts of self-mortification. His lectures were animated by the conviction of mankind's utter sinfulness and estrangement from God. They were at odds with the optimistic naturalism and

Aristotelianism of Aquinas's theology, and even more with the humanism of Erasmus. Nevertheless, Luther had no need to turn against the
church, any more than Augustine had seen such a need. The fact that our
wills are irremediably sinful, that God has destined some to be saved and
some to be damned, that God's reasons for doing so are inscrutable, and
that there is nothing we can do about it does not imply that the church
should be dissolved. A community of mutually concerned believers who
keep each other up to the mark serves a useful purpose, even if it cannot
guarantee salvation.

The external provocations of Luther's stand were clear; under Julius
II and Leo X the papacy launched an avalanche of indulgences, to finance
their wars on the one hand and the building of St. Peter's on the other.
Luther's local archbishop, the archbishop of Brandenburg, was embroiled
in the process. He was corrupt on his own account: enemies were trying
to have him deposed, so he was paying bribes to an agent in Rome and
recouping the cost by buying multiple benefices to receive their income,
thereby committing the sin of simony. For absolution from this sin, he
paid Julius II and Leo X for the necessary indulgences. Someone with a
much less fastidious conscience than Luther's might have drawn the line
at that. The effect was out of all proportion to the cause. Nailing theses
to a church door (it is not clear that Luther actually did it) and offering
to defend them was not a revolutionary gesture. Lecturers in universities
often posted theses and offered to defend them against all comers, as
Pico della Mirandola had tried to do with his nine hundred theses. It
was a way for a lecturer to make his name. What turned the event into
the beginning of a religious, social, and political revolution was the fact
that Luther had a secular protector who could ensure that Luther would
not suffer the fate of Jan Hus, who had been summoned to the Council
of Constance a century earlier with a promise of safe-conduct, and had
then been burned as a heretic.

Many German princes were, as often, at odds with their emperor,
and Luther's prince, Frederick the Wise, elector of Saxony, was in no
mood to defer to the seventeen-year-old emperor Charles V. Other
political factors worked in Luther's favor. Germany was on edge, and
the authorities hesitated to stir up unrest by taking a severe line. One

source of anxiety was the lesser nobility, sometimes called "the German knights," a social group that in other countries would have counted as minor gentry. They were suffering economic hardship as their military skills became obsolete; they felt oppressed by the princes of the church and the emerging patricians of the major towns and were natural allies of Luther, whose ideas they invoked when they broke into open revolt in 1522. Behind them were the "peasants" of the impending Peasants' War. "Peasants" is misleading. The unrest was urban as much as rural, and the leaders were articulate artisans. Some Marxist historians, though not Engels, who wrote a short history of the Peasants' War in his youth, see them as the first bourgeois revolutionaries. It is more plausible to see them as typical of social groups squeezed by economic change, who are socially or geographically uprooted. Engels was right when he said that the Lutherans were a nascent bourgeoisie; they were self-controlled, far-sighted, and careful, but the participants in the revolts that broke out between 1475 and 1525 were anything but; they were antinomian, utopian, and millenarian. Luther was a useful ally to Frederick the Wise; curbing him offered no benefits and might provoke trouble.

Luther's greatest weapon was the recently invented Gutenberg printing press with movable type. The Reformation was not "the Gutenberg revolution" but it was certainly a Gutenberg revolution.[6] Pamphlets, letters, manifestos, and denunciations could be produced in multiple copies at a hitherto impossible speed and disseminated far and wide. In six years 1,300 editions of various Lutheran pamphlets made their way across Europe. Luther had always advocated the translation of the Bible into the German vernacular, and its dissemination to all who could read it or have it read to them; the printing press made this practicable. There was nothing original about wanting to make the gospels available in the common language of ordinary people; Wyclif had urged it more than a hundred years earlier; his translation of the Bible became the basis of the King James Bible. Now vernacular Bibles could be disseminated cheaply on a scale that defeated attempts to prevent it. The use of print for propaganda purposes was a greater novelty; and both Luther's followers and his foes employed it to the best of their ability. Luther is the first writer we have thus far encountered who wrote for a mass audience, with every chance of reaching it.

The ninety-five theses marked a halfway point in the evolution of Luther's ideas and the origins of Protestant political thinking. After suffering agonies over the prospect of arbitrary salvation and damnation for several years, he was struck by the idea of justification by faith in 1513; once he had absorbed its implications, his later theological ideas and their political implications needed only to be brought into the light. The doctrine of justification by faith alone, not by works, and emphatically not by the purchase of indulgences, does not imply that ordinary sinful men can save themselves by willed belief. Faith is given by God, and our role in acquiring it is strictly a matter of opening ourselves to it *if* God should give it to us.[7] We can choose to stand where the lightning may strike; but only God can launch the lightning. To make ourselves receptive to God, we must reflect on the sacrifice made by Christ. This drove Luther's insistence on the priority of the New Testament over the Old. Nor was this the quietist mysticism of Meister Eckhart or Thomas à Kempis; they may have paved the way for an acceptance of Luther's views, but fierce though he was in denouncing excessive confidence in reason—"that pert prostitute"—he urged strenuous engagement, not quiet waiting. Moreover, to be "justified" was to be no less a sinner—as a strange novel, James Hogg's *Private Memoirs and Confessions of a Justified Sinner*, reminds us. The danger in emphasizing faith, as distinct from the grace by which faith is given to us, is that it encourages individuals to rely on their own conviction of salvation as a proof that they are saved. That done, sinning boldly becomes attractive, and antinomianism lurks. One response was that of the more severe Calvinists, to emphasize that the conviction itself might be a delusion and a mark of pride. Grace was truly inscrutable.

Political Theory

After the ninety-five theses, it was only a matter of time before the church tried to discipline Luther. He pressed ahead regardless. In 1520 fourteen

of the theses were declared heretical, and a papal bull, *Exsurge Domine*—
"Rise Up O Lord"—formally excommunicated him. Luther responded
by making a public bonfire of the papal bull and a number of other
documents, including volumes of canon law. In fact, he retaliated before
his enemies struck; some six months before his excommunication, he
published *An Address to the Christian Nobility of Germany*, a work that tells us
almost everything about Luther's conception of church–state relations.

He had by this time come to the view that the sacrament of ordination, like all but four of the sacraments of the Catholic Church, was
irrelevant to a Christian's ability to relate to Christ; the doctrine of
"the priesthood of all believers" was the positive face of this denial. We
acquire through baptism a relationship to Christ that gives us the ability to assist others in finding their way to him, and a duty so to assist.
Priests are those who have a particular vocation to do this. The church is
the congregation of the faithful, and more important as a church invisible than as a church visible. This is interestingly cruder than Augustine's
similar thought; for him, the city of God was the city of the saved, and
wholly invisible. The church was not the city of God, since the church
was an association that gathered together the saved and the damned, and
it was not for us to know which was which. An actual church nonetheless
played a role in human life of some value even to those who might turn
out to be damned.

The scything attack of *An Address* left little standing. For instance, the
idea that there were distinct estates of the realm, the clergy constituting
the spiritual estates and everyone else the secular estates, was declared
incoherent; in a Christian community, *everyone* belongs to the spiritual
estate. By the same token, the legal code embodied in canon law was a
chimera; the church was not a body politic that could exercise jurisdiction over some parts of a person's life while the state exercised jurisdiction over the rest, and canon law was not law. There was a good deal of
yearning for the simplicity of the primitive church, and Luther was as
careless as the church fathers about the separation of church and state.
Godly rulers had to provide for the everyday needs of the practitioners
of the faith; this implied a state-sponsored church or some other form of
official sponsorship of religious practice. Next year, Luther attacked the

monastic life; locking monks away breached the duty to evangelize, the emphasis on monastic devotions rested on the false belief in justification by works, and clerical celibacy was absurd. A decade later he drew the implications for his own life by marrying, very happily, and begetting six children.

The question is whether this provides any foundation for secular politics. The casualness of Luther's assumption that godly rulers would attend to the needs of the community of the faithful was not surprising, since there had been more than a millennium of professedly godly rulers claiming to do that. But Luther's negative views raise large questions in an acute form. The most obvious concerns the criteria for judging whether a ruler is a godly ruler; this takes us straight back to Pope Gelasius and the doctrine of the two swords. Luther held that there was only one sword and that the earthly ruler wielded it. What he was less consistently of one mind about was the consequential question whether any person or institution had the right to decide that a given ruler was so ungodly that he might lawfully be resisted. Resistance to unjust rulers was a persistent and difficult problem for Luther. In general, he defended the traditional doctrine of passive obedience. This allowed passive *disobedience* in the last resort, but it never justified rebellion; if it came to the point where the ruler commands us to do what is manifestly in contradiction of what Christ commanded, the ruler's command must be refused, but not violently resisted. Luther read Saint Paul in the orthodox fashion; the powers that be are ordained of God, even the bad and the brutal; the Christian's role is to suffer the consequences of disobedience, not to overthrow the local ruler. Rebellion even against a bad and un-Christian ruler is (with interesting exceptions) a rebellion against God as well.

An Address was an appeal to the princes and the emperor-elect; Charles V had been elected but not yet crowned in 1520. In that year, Luther had no expectation of a world in which the German states would have different confessional allegiances, nor any inkling of what would happen when Charles V remained a staunch Catholic and waged war on his Protestant subjects. For all his astuteness, Luther was blind to the alliances that had saved his own skin. *An Address* appealed for the reformation of the church by the secular authorities. It lamented the failure of the Hohenstaufen emperors to bring the papacy to heel in the twelfth and thirteenth centuries, though Luther agreed that Frederick Barbarossa and Frederick II had overreached themselves and had suffered divine chastisement for their arrogance. *An Address*'s technique, narrowly speaking, is polemic ad hoc rather than innovative political theorizing, but the results are radical. Luther observed that the papacy hid behind three lines of defense: that the secular power has no power over the church, although the church morally superintends the secular power; that the church alone is the interpreter of scripture; and that only a pope can summon a council and give it authority. The first line of defense is laid waste by Luther's insistence on the priesthood of all believers. Once the unique standing of the church is gone, then "benefit of clergy," the clergy's exemption from many of the usual legal restraints and duties, goes with it, and we have the simple view that in a community of Christians there is a division of labor but no division of authority. The second line of defense is plainly inconsistent with the thought that every man is to read the Bible for himself.

In spite of appearances, this does not mean that there is to be no church. Luther was radical in thought and conservative in temperament. He would happily have seen the pope forced to beg for his living in the highways and byways, and St. Peter's taken down and replaced by a simple country church. Nonetheless, when he offers twenty-seven proposals for things that the emperor or a council should do to reform the church, he expounds a vision of a church with a dozen cardinals, a tiny curia, and little infrastructure; he does not sweep away the entire apparatus. He does not even propose to abolish all monastic institutions, contenting himself with the admirably sensible advice that nobody should pledge himself to the celibate life before the age of thirty.

The church's third line of defense, the insistence that only a pope can call a council, is given an equally rough handling. This, says Luther, is the same thing as insisting that the pope is an earthly potentate, but unlike all others, one who is answerable to nobody. This was hardly a startling accusation, since popes had long claimed to govern by divine right. Luther's point is cleverer than that; the pope is his own confessor, judge of the faith, and the only judge of the rightness of his actions. Other rulers, however absolute, answer to God and their consciences, but the pope has absolved himself of that obligation. The point is simple and well taken. It is in fact two points, as emerges when Luther embarks on his twenty-seven propositions. The first is that any institution needs the means of its own reform, and both the history of the church and the exigencies of the case suggest councils as the only reliable means; the same history suggests that councils need the assistance of the secular authorities to succeed. The second is that it is preposterous for the papacy to hide behind its spiritual role to cover up the reality of its actions, namely, the extraction of funds from impoverished German parishes for ostentatious enterprises in Italy such as building St. Peter's. The church needs either complete decentralization, so that every priest is responsible to his own congregation, or devolution of authority to archbishops, so that hierarchy is minimized and people with the interests of their local church at heart can serve its needs.[8]

On Secular Authority

Luther followed up *An Address* some three years later with his only work expressly devoted to the question of the nature and extent of secular authority. It is not obvious why he wrote it; there was no immediate external provocation of the kind that explains his outbursts against "the murdering hordes of peasants" or his assaults on the "Romish pontiff." This may explain why it is markedly less polemical than most of his writing. Its lack of polemics is a matter of degree: Luther begins by observing that his *Address* had been intended to tell the German ruling elite its positive duty: what it should do. It had been a complete failure; the German princes were no better Christians and no more competent rulers than they had ever been. Now it was time to tell them what not to do, but doubtless that would have as little effect as anything else he wrote.[9] Heavy irony was one of Luther's stylistic trademarks, employed here in double measures.

Still, the line of thought Luther pursued makes eminently good sense, and one can see from the beginning both where the argument will lead and where it will run into difficulties. Luther starts from the radical claim that almost everyone has made a mistake about obedience. Princes think they are entitled to rule as they choose, and the plain man thinks he must obey them no matter what they command. The plain man's mistakes are more forgivable than his rulers' errors, since they are merely mistakes; the rulers' errors are grounded in hypocrisy. What Luther thought was clear: the local rulers of Germany justify their commands as "required by the emperor," as though absolute obedience was always due to the emperor. They do not mean it. Were the emperor to try to take possession of their land or occupy a castle or two, they would resist and make an end of the doctrine of absolute obedience. They also claim that their subjects owe them absolute obedience because they are the transmission belt between the authority of the emperor and the duties of the subject; but invoking the emperor and his authority is just an excuse for overtaxing their wretched subjects and subjecting them to the tyranny of the church. They get away with it because the common people believe that they must do whatever they are told by their rulers, and misunderstand both the gospels and their Christian duty.[10]

Luther does not doubt the need for secular authority; its emblem is the sword. The sword must be employed on behalf of earthly justice, but it is the executioner's sword rather than the judge's robes that is the true symbol of earthly authority. Saint Paul's words serve their usual purpose: the powers that be are ordained of God, to be a terror to the evildoer. Luther is fiercer than most; the sword is rightly employed not only by the agents of the law but by soldiers. Christians are not only to be obedient but to serve as enforcers. The rule that murderers are to be slain is coeval with Adam, was known to Cain, and reconfirmed by God after the flood. It is divinely commanded, and we must obey. Luther knew that recourse to the sword was thought by many radicals to be forbidden by Christ's injunction "resist not evil." How, then, can it be permissible to wield the sword to put down evil?[11]

Luther did not answer the conundrum head-on, but blunted the conflict by distinguishing first between Christians and non-Christians and then between the spiritual and secular law. True Christians, who are much scarcer than the presence of so many baptized people might suggest, have no need of secular law or the secular sword. They follow the paths of justice for righteousness' sake. This includes suffering evil *done to them alone* unresistingly, acting in obedience to the commandment to resist not evil. The unrighteous do what the law requires because they are coerced: "they need the law to teach, compel and urge them to act rightly."[12] However, we are all tempted to be unrighteous; so the law is rightly imposed on all. Really good men do not need it, but they are very few, and it would be absurd to prescribe for the many in the light of what is attainable only by the few. May Christians take part in making and enforcing the law, then? Certainly, says Luther. If there is a shortage of hangmen, court officers, judges, or police, a Christian who can do these jobs must offer his services. There would be mere chaos and bloodshed in the absence of law and its enforcement; the Christian owes it to his fellows to play his part in government and law enforcement with a good conscience. We should not look out for ourselves but serve others: "you satisfy the demands of God's kingdom and the world's at one and the same time, outwardly and inwardly; you both suffer evil and injustice and yet punish them; you do not resist evil and yet you do resist it."[13] As a piece of logic it is less than perfect, but it serves very well; a good man takes up the sword for the sake of others. It might be said that a society wholly composed of true Christians would be disabled even so, since the claim that we should take up the sword to protect other people is not wholly persuasive if those others are committed to nonresistance. That may be dismissed as a quibble, because in a society of true Christians, the occasion for nonresistance would never present itself, because nobody would offer violence to anyone else, and if the society were attacked from the outside, self-defense to teach the ungodly a lesson is permitted.

Luther is less eager to argue that government backed by brute force is essential if order is to be kept than to argue two further things: first, there is no place for coercion in matters of faith, and, second, we have no business following ungodly rulers even though we may not engage in rebellion against them. The view that there is no role for coercion in the spiritual life is defended on several grounds, but mostly with the division of labor argument of *An Address*, and the theology of *The Freedom of a Chris-*

tian. Within the one community, secular law and order is maintained by providing simple external incentives—such as the desire not to be executed—which restrain the unrighteous and remind the righteous of the existence of sin and its punishment. The spiritual law, and Luther is not comfortable with the idea that it is law at all, works in the heart by faith; it is God's business whether we are obedient to his law, and God (alone) sees into our hearts.

The secular authorities have no business trying to make us believe anything in particular; all they can exact is hypocritical expressions of what we do or more probably do not believe. This is close to the view that Hobbes later expressed, which suggests that it is not in itself a defense of toleration. Locke's argument that toleration requires a state to allow people to worship as they choose, publicly, and in the company of fellow believers, needs more than the observation that secular power can secure only an outward conformity. The state may want only an outward conformity; Hobbes considered it enough. Like Luther, Hobbes thought governments wasted their time trying to see into the hearts of their subjects; but he also thought that, for the sake of peace, governments must regulate what people publicly affirmed on contentious issues, and dictate the forms of public worship. For Hobbes's purposes, outward conformity sufficed, because the object was to stop dissension that would inevitably lead to violence, not to hinder thought. In the early 1520s Luther was unafraid of dissension, because he thought religious argument could be conducted without violence; so he swept straight past Hobbes's stopping point. In 1523 he still held that heresy was not to be repressed by force. "Here God's Word must strive; if that does not accomplish the end, it will remain unaccomplished through secular power, though it fill the world with blood."[14] The larger importance of Luther's argument is that here he holds diametrically un-Augustinian views. Augustine stood firm on *compelle intrare*—we should go into the highways and byways and compel them to come in, that is, to join the true church. Luther ordinarily followed Augustine; here he did not.

An Address was directed to Christian princes, but the Christian prince will be, as Luther says, "a very rare bird." What he will do, and how he will be animated, is not difficult to describe. His life will be one of ser-

vice and of love, not an insistence on his power and authority. His people
will not be his people as if they were his property to do with as he pleases,
but his to serve. Such a ruler would, says Luther, not be begrudged his
dances and his hunts and his games by God or his subjects; in any case,
he would be too busy to have much time for diversion, since the welfare
of his subjects would demand all his time and attention. Given the rarity
of such birds, Luther turns to the awkward topic of our duty to obey the
wicked. Where they do what is right, we must follow them for the sake
of the right; where they do wrong, we must refuse to assist them. If they
require us to deliver up a copy of Luther's New Testament that we have
in the house, we must refuse; if they come into our house and seize it,
we must not resist.[15] By the same token, rulers must not follow wicked
superiors into wicked courses, but must not resist when those superiors
behave badly toward them. It is an awkward resting place.

Luther's role in German politics thereafter was considerable,
but mostly not in ways that impact on the history of political thinking. Luther's tirades against the "murdering hordes of peasants" do not
amount to a theoretical explanation of why religious radicalism must not
be pushed to an extreme. Rather, he believed from the outset that the
peasant wars sprang from the disobedient lower classes hoping to profit
from unrest; he may also have been troubled by the fact that an essentially
anarchic movement claimed to have been inspired by him. "Let whoever
can, stab, smite, slay. If you die in doing it, good for you! . . . If anyone
thinks this too harsh, let him remember that rebellion is intolerable and
that the destruction of the world is to be expected every hour."[16] Subsequently, in "An Open Letter on the Harsh Book against the Peasants,"
he did something to lessen the offense he had given by emphasizing that
it was only active and obdurate rebels he had written against; but he
promptly went on to insist that the tract against the peasants had been
entirely right, and that whether the ruler of the state was Christian, Jew,
Turk, or pagan made no difference. The secular sword was to be wielded
to preserve order, and it was everyone's duty to aid its wielder.[17] He was
evenhanded in his denunciations; his "Open Letter" ends with the story
of a German noble attempting to rape the pregnant widow of Thomas
Müntzer, and although he was ferociously critical of Müntzer, Luther

relishes the thought of the would-be rapist burning in hell for all eternity. Although his rhetoric is violent in the extreme, his hatred of physical violence and his fear of disorder were genuine; argument was one thing, fighting another. Religious dissension was a sign of vitality, but permissible only if we could argue without fighting. Tongues might wag, but the fist must remain unclenched. Many of his works make no great contribution to political thinking, among them his denunciations of the Jews; they do not even illuminate the lamentable history of anti-Semitism, other than to demonstrate that a change of confessional allegiance did not improve Christian attitudes toward the Jews, while his views on usury showed only that theological inventiveness does not guarantee economic insight.

The Theory of Resistance

The one point on which Luther changed his mind significantly and influentially was on nonresistance. His use of the orthodox Pauline doctrine was initially at the extreme end of the spectrum; passive disobedience is all we are permitted. Indeed, we are not only permitted but obliged to engage in passive disobedience, since otherwise we would be aiding the unrighteous in their wickedness, and this was as unjust as resisting them. Luther's twentieth-century critics have complained that he undermined the possibility of a liberal Germany by so emphasizing the absolute wickedness of rebellion; a less passive attitude toward the powers that be would have helped prevent the rise of Hitler and assured a more spirited resistance to his rule. Given the enormous number of other explanations for German subservience to authority and the lack of resistance to the Nazi regime, a decent skepticism vis-à-vis Luther's responsibility for the horrors of the twentieth century is in order. Nonetheless, attending to the situation of sixteenth-century Germany alone, we might think that Luther's adherence to Augustine's views about nonresistance was ill judged by the late 1520s.

It became apparent in 1529–30 that adherence to a literal reading of Luther's doctrine of nonresistance might require the Protestant princes to face their Catholic enemies with their hands tied behind their backs. Charles V never reconciled himself to a Germany divided between Catholics and Evangelicals, but until the end of the decade of the 1520s he was embroiled elsewhere and could not devote himself to enforcing doctrinal and political unity. When it became clear that he proposed to return all of Germany to the Catholic Church, by brute force if need be, Luther's protector, the elector John of Saxony, asked Luther whether resistance to the emperor was lawful. Other Evangelicals had argued that it was; and Luther was not a believer in nonviolence. He had argued that good Christians should fight for their prince against foreign opponents and rebels, even if their prince was a Turk. But Charles V was not a foreign prince, even if he had until this moment been more concerned with his Spanish possessions and his French rivals in Italy than with Germany. Luther and his allies were hampered by several factors. Having declared the church to be only a congregation of the faithful, they had no institutional forum that could formally declare a ruler a tyrant and depose him. This was the effect of giving away one of Gelasius's two swords; if nobody held the spiritual sword, nobody could declare a king deposed *ratione peccati*. The Protestants were also hampered by their contempt for the traditions of natural and canon law, which provided ample jurisprudential arguments for the claim that Charles had become a tyrant and forfeited his authority. It was equally impossible for them to go back to Cicero's defense of tyrannicide, although Philipp Melanchthon wrote a commentary on Cicero's *De officiis* and held ideas about resistance to tyrants much more in line with traditional constitutionalist thinking than Luther's.

The emperor's opponents certainly could not renounce self-defense. Various views were canvassed. The most persuasive was that if the emperor attacked his Evangelical subjects, he was violating the law, and they would be upholding it in resisting him. This constitutionalist position had a good pedigree and is very like Locke's subsequent justification of revolution as the act of a people defending its constitution against a tyrannical ruler. There were many ways of reaching that result, and it is evidence of the depth of Luther's discomfort with any loosening of the bonds of obedience that the one he preferred relied so heavily on the claim—implausible as it might seem—that the *positive law* of the empire required the princes to resist notorious injustice. A modern reader might have difficulty seeing how this could save the day, since an emperor might hold himself to be *legibus solutus*, above the law and able to override positive law when it seemed good to him. Nor does it sit easily with the modern mind to combine the thought that earthly monarchs have been given absolute authority by God with the thought that it can be constitutionally limited. These were tensions that the late medieval mind had resources for handling. A properly constituted secular authority shared God's absolute authority, even if its constitution meant that the authority of the earthly ruler operated within stated limits. The constitution in its entirety bound prince and subject alike *jure divino*. One might resist unlawful authority in the name of lawful authority.

Once the door to a theory of resistance had been opened by the thought that imperial authority in general required disobedience to a particular holder of imperial authority, Luther could employ arguments that had a long history and would be much employed in future. Thus, a ruler who uses unjust force has ceased to be a ruler and is in the position of a private person who is attacking us; nobody doubts that a private person can be resisted on grounds of self-defense, and a ruler who has, morally speaking, abdicated by violating his trust is a private person. This is where the hoary example of the lawfulness of a private citizen killing the consul whom he finds in bed with his wife belongs. Mostly, Luther accepted the constitutionalist claim that if the emperor was the aggressor, he was in rebellion against the lawful order and might lawfully be resisted. What he was terrified of, and others to varying degrees were less fearful of, was any doctrine that gave a right of resistance to individual subjects. This is where comparisons with Locke and later constitutionalists collapse; the Lockean right of resistance inheres in "the people," who must use their best judgment about when the time for resistance has arrived; but Locke ignores the question of who is entitled to speak for the people. In rebelling on good grounds, each of us represents all of us.[18]

Luther confined the right to resist to "inferior magistrates," to those who ordinarily had authority under the law to make decisions with the force of law; in this context, that meant the princes of the empire. Most thinkers after Luther similarly confined the right to resist a ruler to a recognized body, if not to the "inferior magistrates" that the constitution of the Holy Roman Empire suggested, then to a body such as the Estates General in France, or the governing councils of Swiss city republics such as Zurich or Geneva. Nonetheless, however cautious Luther's response, and however driven by the needs of the moment, it inspired both an ideological change and a change of tone. A movement toward a more overtly constitutionalist view of politics took place, within which a much more nuanced view of authority and resistance to authority became possible. The Catholic view continued to be that the pope was an absolute monarch, holding the authority of the Roman emperor described in Justinian's *Digest*; but a countercurrent even within the church relied on the old legal tag *nemo dat quod non habet*—nobody can give what he has not himself possessed—"the people" could not give the right to exercise unresisted power to anyone, because they had never had such a right in the first place.

Even if all authority was held on terms, the avoidance of chaos required that any discussion of the question whether there had been a breach of those terms must be confined to the right body under the right conditions—perhaps a council of the church, perhaps the Estates General. In the German context, the issue was simpler. The electors of the emperor might well think they had elected the emperor on terms; if those terms were violated, the election was invalidated. The emperor Wenceslaus was deposed by the electors in 1400 on just those grounds; they elected him to keep the peace and preserve the unity of the empire, and he had failed hopelessly to do what he was pledged to do.

Luther died in 1546. He died when Protestantism most needed a political theory to sustain it as a church militant, and his death coincided with a counterattack on Protestantism that nearly erased it in its German heartlands. From 1543 Charles V had been assembling forces to confront the so-called Schmalkaldic League of Protestant German states; in 1546 he provoked them to armed conflict and in April 1547 crushed them at the Battle of Mühlberg. Their leaders, the electors John of Saxony and Philip of Hesse, were captured and kept in prison for the next five years. In 1548 Charles outlawed Lutheranism throughout the empire, sowing the seeds of the Thirty Years' War, which ravaged Germany in the next century. Five years later the Reformation was under threat in England, where Charles's daughter-in-law, the Catholic Queen Mary secured her place in history as "Bloody Mary" by approving the death by fire of over three hundred of her Protestant subjects. Before that, the French had assisted Catholic Scots to turn back the Protestant tide, and in France itself, Francis I abandoned his temporizing policies in favor of persecution in the late 1530s, and the persecution was intensified under his successor, Henry II. By the end of the 1550s, France was in the throes of religious civil war. If Mary Tudor had not been succeeded by her younger sister Elizabeth in 1558, no major European state would have been safe for the reformed churches. Switzerland was a different matter. It experienced much violence, but both Zurich and Geneva, self-governing cities with extensive rural hinterlands, were solidly if not securely Protestant, and they generated much of what we have come to think of as Protestant political thinking.

Jean Calvin

Protestants under attack could not fold their hands and await martyrdom, but their attachment to a Pauline theory of authority was a handicap in articulating a right of resistance. No more than their Catholic opponents and predecessors did they find it easy to convert their account of the distinction between spiritual and secular authority into an argument for the legitimacy of resistance. It was easy to argue, as Luther had, that the church as such wielded no coercive authority; but that gave the secular authorities in Catholic states a free hand in putting down their Protestant enemies. Passive disobedience would not secure the Protestant future from determined rulers who did not mind how many heretics they sent to the stake. It is often said that Calvin went further than Luther in providing a theory of resistance that would meet the exigencies of the situation. This contains some but not the whole truth. Calvin was a second-generation Protestant. He was born in 1509, by which time Luther was suffering agonies of doubt in Wittenberg. Like Luther, he was intended for the law by his father, but on the death of his father he abandoned the law for the life of a scholar. His opinions made France dangerous, and he went first to Basel, then in 1536 to Geneva, and after a period of exile, back to Geneva in 1541, where he remained for the last twenty-three years of his life. Geneva was a republic ruled by a city council, and that provided a context in which Calvin could reach beyond Luther.

Calvin has been praised as a political thinker, but his political views occupy only the last section of his *Institutes of the Christian Religion*; and this suggests the limited place of politics in his wider concerns. Calvin was no more eager than Luther to open the door to popular uprisings. Unlike Luther, he was actively involved in legislating for a city republic. Like Luther, he starts his discussion of the two governments that mankind is under by insisting that the freedom of the Christian is not a license to dispense with all laws and remodel all institutions; civil government is instituted by God and demands the allegiance of Christians. More straightforwardly than Luther, he insists that the first obligation of civil government is the duty to "foster and protect the external worship of God, defend pure doctrine and the good condition of the Church."[19] This accommodates the fact that churches are institutions; and it articulates what Luther took for granted, that the local state must look after the local church. The central point is Luther's: a Christian may not ignore the demands of secular government. If the kingdom of God were already on earth, there would be no need of civil government; but here below we are, as Augustine said, *pellegrini*, pilgrims on a journey toward that ultimate destination; while we are here, we need civil government for our peace and tranquillity; but we also need it to lead us toward righteousness.

Calvin's discussion of the two kingdoms to which we owe allegiance does not imply the separation of church and state. Nor did Calvin have in mind the easygoing approach of ancient Rome in welcoming the gods of its defeated subjects into the city. The church must have its mode of worship fixed by the state, individuals must be compelled to attend services, and the pastors of the church must judge the citizens' morals. Calvin was living in Geneva, and safe from the Catholic reaction, so he was fighting enemies on his radical, antinomian flank, not Catholics: there was to be no turning the world upside down, and no retreat into a hermetic existence. Orthodoxy in matters of faith was to be preserved. Notoriously, he had Michael Servetus burned as a heretic at the gates of Geneva because Servetus denied the doctrine of the Trinity. Nonetheless, Calvin was politically innovative in linking the concerns of an early modern constitutional lawyer with those of a theorist of the polis.

He imagined a political community that not only exhibited the top-down legislative and coercive capacity that constitutes the essence of the state in all modern analyses but also conferred authority on a recognized body of intermediate magistrates. His inspiration seems to have been the Spartan constitution, in a form modified by what Ulrich Zwingli had achieved in Zurich during his brief and tumultuous rule. Zwingli was more important to political practice because of his posthumous influence on the England of Elizabeth I than for his achievements in Zurich, but Zurich displayed the political possibilities of reformation theology beyond anything Luther had seen. Born in 1484, Zwingli was a devout Catholic until 1518; but when he became a pastor in Zurich, he experienced a conversion to Luther's view that the Gospels were all-sufficient. Until his death he epitomized the church militant. He led reform in Zurich and united in his own hands the governance of both church and state. He was literally an iconoclast: the physical purification of churches was the order of the day; paintings and organs were evicted from the local churches, though Zwingli was an accomplished musician and an accomplished Greek scholar who corresponded with Erasmus. In 1529 he and Luther conducted an inconclusive disputation over the Eucharist, with Zwingli taking the radical view that the sacrament was a commemoration of the Crucifixion and that no transformation of the bread into the body of Christ took place; Luther believed in consubstantiation. Zwingli's downfall was the result of the energy that had taken him so far; he urged the expulsion of Catholicism from the other Swiss cantons, if necessary by force. This was taken as a declaration of war by Zurich's neighbors. The result was war in 1531 and Zwingli's death in battle.

His impact on Protestant theology and political practice was considerable. Like Luther, he unloosed radical forces to his "left" that he could not easily control. Unlike Luther, he was unflinching in his belief that the church must employ the coercive force of the state to maintain doctrinal and political unity. He had no problem accepting *compelle intrare*. In Zurich he unhesitatingly persecuted Anabaptists. The fundamental tenet of Anabaptism was the wrongness of infant baptism: absent a full understanding of the purpose of the rite by the person baptized, baptism must be ineffacious. Debating the Anabaptists was an ungrateful business, because there is no scriptural warrant for infant baptism, and Zwingli fell back on physical coercion. He had the leaders of the Zurich Anabaptists drowned, relishing the unkind joke implicit in the manner of their death. This uncompromising understanding of the unity of church and state was transmitted to Elizabeth's England by Zwingli's follower Heinrich Bullinger; the death toll among Catholics in England was the highest in Europe.

Violence aside, the Protestant understanding of authority had been transformed in ways that came naturally to anyone with classical republican models in mind. Zwingli imagined classical republican government revived within a religiously purified city. Classical republics never contemplated the idea that the secular magistrate would ignore the religious practices of his people, and Zwingli's vision of a devout republic did not embrace the separation of church and state. It did allow everyone to think of orderly and constitutional ways to avert tyranny. That allowed the emergence of the view for which Calvin is famous, that it was the business of a middle layer of constituted authorities to ensure that the government did not become tyrannical. This opened new possibilities. For, if the authority of even a king was held conditionally, nobody was *legibus solutus*, and "inferior magistrates" could provide a mechanism for pronouncing that a ruler had gone too far, had become a tyrant, and was de jure no longer the ruler.

The point was this. To rely on the thought that a ruler who acts outside the bounds of his office was simply a private person and might be treated like any other private person was all very well when applied to the example of the adulterous consul. The majesty of rulers was the majesty of the office; committing adultery was not part of the office. The difficulty is obvious. A policy of religious persecution is ultra vires, if it is so, not because it is a sin committed in a private capacity. It is an assault on the people, not on an individual; or to put the matter the other way around, if individuals treated policies they deplored as private offenses in the way the ancient example imagines, anyone might think himself entitled to assassinate just about any ruler whatever. And although Calvin provides an account of legitimate resistance, he consistently repeated Augustine's and Luther's message that we must put up with bad rulers in accordance with the Pauline injunction.

Calvin set all this out in a tripartite discussion of civil government: the nature and purpose of law, the role of magistrates, and the duties of the people. However magistrates may be chosen, they are accountable to God; they must always bear in mind that they will be required to render an account of their conduct in the hereafter and should conduct themselves accordingly. He gives a very slight account of the virtues of different forms of government, but sufficient for his purpose: which is to insist that even if mixed governments are best, since kingship may become tyranny and democracy turn seditious and the balance the Spartans struck is attractive, it is not the business of private men to debate forms of government but to live peaceably under the regime it has pleased God to institute for them.

So the argument proceeds almost until the very end. Whenever the private citizen asks whether it is really necessary to put up with whatever our rulers inflict on us, the reply is that we must. The consolations for following this advice are few beyond the assurance that God uses wicked men as his unwitting tools for ends beyond their imagining. Then Calvin changes gear. Having insisted yet again, "Even if the punishment of unbridled tyranny is the Lord's vengeance, we are not to imagine that it is we ourselves who have been called upon to inflict it. All that has been assigned to us is to obey and suffer," he goes on to say, "Here as always, I am speaking about private persons." If magistrates have been appointed to restrain the willfulness of kings, as were the ephors of Sparta, the demarchs of Athens, and as "perhaps" the three estates are when they assemble as the Estates General, they are not merely permitted to restrain tyrants but would commit a grave sin if they omitted to do so.[20] In the Calvinist moral and political universe, little is permitted that is not also required, and this is not one of those cases. It was left to later Calvinists to unite the constitutional theory of resistance to which

Calvin had opened the door with the contractualism that implied that "private persons" could decide that a ruler had violated his trust and had lost his authority. When they did, they created the modern, liberal theory of revolution. To reach that point, one necessity was the conviction that "most men," as Locke put it, were too slow to rebel rather than too quick. That thought never occurred to Luther or Calvin; the evidence of the times was against it.

The Radicals

A reason for the fear of chaos alluded to throughout this chapter was the presence of what one might call the extreme wing of Protestantism, namely Anabaptism. A detailed account of the political ideas of the Anabaptists in all their variety is impossible in this short compass, and perhaps impossible *tout court*; the most notable characteristic of Anabaptism *after* the Peasants' War of 1524–26, and the Münster uprising of 1534 when Anabaptists were embroiled in violent insurrection, is that it became a pacifist and apolitical creed. Even in the few decades when Anabaptists had been ready to fight, they would do so only on their own terms and for their own reasons. They were the targets of Luther's and Calvin's denunciation of Christians who will not serve the state. When they were willing to fight, they fought to the death, usually their own.

The interest of their views is twofold. First, it is clear that what provoked the Peasants' War was economic distress. It was not a political revolution, but an insurrection provoked by economic distress. Whose economic distress mattered most is hard to say, since Germany had become a kaleidoscope of states and statelets with a great diversity of local political arrangements, and economic tensions existed between town and country, within towns, and between peasants and their landlords. Peasants wanting relief from oppressive landlords certainly provided the bulk of those who fought, and were killed in very large numbers. It was said that 300,000 rebels had taken part and that, by the time the imperial armies had suppressed the rebellion, 100,000 had been killed. The religious demands of the rebels caused as much offense as their economic demands, in particular, their demand for a reduction of tithes and a say in the choice of their own pastors. Second, it was Luther who much against his will gave the Peasants' War its character. Without a Lutheran Reformation, it is very likely that there would have been an insurrection in 1524–26; peasant revolts had been a feature of German life for a century. But the tensions between the Catholic and Evangelical princes of the empire suggested that some princes might side with the rebels, and undermine the unity of the empire. Because the religious demands of the rebels were Lutheran, he was widely thought to have instigated the revolt. That partly explains the ferocity of his attack on the rebels, just as Luther's contempt for the Anabaptists underlay the ferocity of Thomas Müntzer's attacks on Luther.

Müntzer was contemptuous of conventional politics, but his views had profound political implications. The chief characteristic of the radical reformers—as distinct from the "magistral" reformers, Luther, Zwingli, and Calvin—was their reliance on the spiritual sense of the community as the basis of authority. In such unsettled times, this was not likely to yield unanimity, but to the extent that the radical Protestants had any view of political authority, it was a theory of popular sovereignty. The authority of the godly prince was drawn from the community, not from divine institution; Müntzer held an uninhibitedly ascending theory of authority. Like Luther, Müntzer began by hoping that godly princes would reform the church; unlike Luther, he believed that he was living in the "last days" and that the reform of the church was not only a Reformation but the prefiguring of an apocalyptic transformation. Once millenarianism was added to the rejection of the sacraments, the ingredients for upheaval were in place.

Initially, Müntzer's radicalism did not imply violent insurrection. His followers' violence took the form of popular iconoclasm: direct action to smash statues and destroy stained glass, shouting down unpopular ministers, and instituting a very austere Lord's Supper in place of the traditional Mass. Müntzer was operating in the dark, but the political authorities saw where violence, even when ostensibly directed only against buildings and objects, might lead, and they tried to expel the religious extremists. The Anabaptists abandoned the churches and met in private houses, which gave the authorities further grounds for suspicion, and also allowed increasingly extreme views, economic and political as well as religious, to gain ground among the Anabaptists. Müntzer and his followers claimed that the violence to which they eventually resorted was more than justified self-defense, but they can hardly have expected anything other than the repression they encountered.

Events unrolled too fast and chaotically to allow any of the protagonists to develop a coherent vision of what the godly community's political arrangements should be. To the extent that they did so in the months after the military destruction of the peasants' insurrection in May 1525, they focused on the need to institute a simple republican constitution. It was politically radical in that the nobility was denied a hereditary right to govern, and economically radical in that a nobility with no political role had no right to impose taxes. It did not propose the equalization of property; the old church would be expropriated, but no lay person's property would be touched. The claim that the radicals were hell-bent on communism, free love, and the end of all authority came from the hysterical imagining of their opponents, or deliberately mendacious propaganda. Nonetheless, they were utopians and millenarians, believing that the communities they would institute prefigured the Second Coming and the end of days. After the defeat, the radicals did two things; they agreed on their common beliefs in the so-called Schleitheim Articles, and they divided on tactics.

They agreed that their kingdom was not of this world and that the true Christian must separate himself from the world. Müntzer's hopes for the establishment of more or less anarchic godly communities were given up in the face of reality, and the Schleitheim Articles provided some minimal guidelines for the organization of a church that could survive repression. Their fears were well founded: it was made a capital offense throughout the empire to preach or practice adult baptism—the central element in Anabaptism. The wing led by Michael Sattler, who drew up the Schleitheim Articles, espoused radical pacifism, exhorting their followers to refuse military service and political office and to live as strangers to the political and judicial arrangements of the society in which they found themselves. This was not what governments looking for conscripts for their armed forces would tolerate. Sattler's views look like a recipe for head-on conflict with the authorities, but by setting out the possibility of living a spiritual life in secret, they offered the prospect that Anabaptists might secure their existence as a saving remnant with no prospect of converting others. A family might transmit the faith generation by generation to its descendants, but scarcely anyone else.

The other wing, following Balthasar Hubmaier, turned back to the Lutheran theory of authority but continued to subscribe to the quietism that Luther eventually rejected. Its members agreed that Anabaptists could hold office and wield the sword, since godly rulers needed assistance and it was right to give it. Where the ruler was ungodly, they must simply endure. Taking up arms against an appointed ruler was at one with taking up arms against God. Hubmaier's position provided the basis of a peace treaty with the authorities; its appeal to Anabaptists was that they could live openly *if* they could find a prince who would tolerate them. The drawback, as many devout and harmless people discovered in the next two centuries, was that princes were prone to change their religious allegiances, and tolerant fathers were prone to leave fanatical sons who gave their dissenting subjects the choice between death and exile.

The famous epilogue to the radicalism of the 1520s was the short-lived reign of terror that John of Leiden and Bernhard Knipperdolling instituted in Münster in 1534–35. To hang these events on Anabaptism is wholly unfair, but the enemies of the Anabaptists succeeded in doing so. What happened in Münster has been much examined. During the 1950s the madness that seized the city was thought by sociologists to provide deep insights into the making of revolutions in the twentieth century.[21] Half a century later, it seems to belong more firmly to a category sui generis of events such as the mass suicide at Jonestown in Guiana, where an apocalyptic sect followed its leader's commands to the point of killing themselves and their children with a soft drink laced with cyanide. Münster was an imperial city in Westphalia, ruled by a prince-bishop with whom the inhabitants got on badly. It turned Lutheran in the early 1530s, at much the same time that a group of itinerant messianic preachers who had been expelled from Strassburg and then from the Netherlands were looking for converts.

In January 1534 Bernhard Knipperdolling went over to these Melchiorite missionaries, and with Jan Matthys and Jan Bockelson—John of Leiden—set out to turn Münster into their vision of the New Jerusalem. The Catholic prince-bishop besieged the city, assisted by Philip of Hesse, who was a Lutheran but who could recognize anarchy when he saw it. Within the besieged city, mayhem ruled; Matthys got himself killed by leading a sortie against the besiegers in response to what he took to be the direct tactical instructions of God; John of Leiden took over and eventually proclaimed himself king. Here for once, the stories about polygamy and communism became true; John took two dozen wives, arrayed himself in fine robes, and played out an Old Testament drama as the population gradually starved to death under the siege. Astonishingly, the defenders held out to the bitter end; they drove back the besieging forces in August 1534, and although local uprisings elsewhere failed to take the pressure off them, it was only in June 1535 that the city fell. Even then, it fell to betrayal. The inhabitants were massacred, men, women, and children alike; Knipperdolling and John of Leiden were tortured to death, and the authorities hunted down everyone who could be suspected of complicity in the uprising. The events had a sobering effect on the purveyors of apocalyptic visions that lasted a long time—though the man who began the whole business, Melchior Hoffman, survived it all. He had been thrown in jail in Strassburg, and remained there until he died a decade later.

CHAPTER 11

Machiavelli

Life and Times; the Political Context

MACHIAVELLI WAS BORN IN 1469 and died in 1527. His father was a notary, which tells us little more than that Machiavelli's father was literate, since there were more notaries in Renaissance Italy than available legal work required. A notary of low social standing might earn most of his living as a farmer or artisan. An upper-class notary would probably employ his legal skills in the affairs of his friends and allies, and perhaps in the political arena. One thing it tells us is that he had the humanist education that was a prelude to an education in law; it provided a training in eloquent and persuasive writing and in making suitable speeches to a court or a committee that Cicero, and the Sophists before him, had identified as crucial for the politician and the lawyer.

Little is known about Machiavelli's life before 1498, when he became second chancellor of the Florentine Republic that had been established after the overthrow of Savonarola. This was a "civil service" post. As in classical Athens, political office in the Florentine Republic was held on a brief tenure, and officeholders were either elected or chosen by lot. Without a permanent skilled bureaucracy, Florence would have been ungovernable; Machiavelli was part of that bureaucracy. A month later he was appointed secretary to the Ten of War, the committee that supervised foreign relations and military preparedness. He spent much of the next fourteen years on diplomatic missions to the papal court, to the court of Louis XII in France, and to the court of Emperor Maximilian. Because Florence was friendly to France, it took delicate maneuvering to retain the friendship of the French without incurring the hostility of the empire—to hunt with the Valois without being hounded by the Habsburgs.

In the course of these missions, Machiavelli spent a lot of time with Cesare Borgia in the Romagna and with Pope Julius II, the most warlike of Renaissance popes, whose financial exactions were one of the provocations of Luther's campaign of church reform. The stories that give piquancy to Machiavelli's advice in *The Prince* and the *Discourses on Livy* are often prefigured in his lively correspondence with his masters in Florence. One of Machiavelli's less remembered but important achievements as secretary of the Ten of War was the institution of a Florentine militia recruited from the *contado*, the countryside around Florence. He was hostile to mercenary troops, who, as he pointed out, would desert to the enemy for higher pay if the enemy could offer it, or else subvert the government of their employers. It was an innovation to treat the *contadini* as fit material for warfare; the right to bear arms had been confined to the *cittadini*, the citizen body of Florence itself. Florence's forces were no more of a match for the armies of France or the empire than those of any other Italian state of the day, but Machiavelli's reforms provided an effective militia for local hostilities. The army he created brought the interminable war with Pisa to a successful conclusion.

Machiavelli was not a great figure in the Florentine Republic, but he was well-known, and he took pleasure in doing an impossible job well. He also took pleasure in the fact that his intellect, wit, and erudition made him welcome in upper-class circles from which his origins would otherwise have excluded him. His career, but not these friendships, came to an end in 1512 when Florence's delicate balancing act between papacy, France, and empire proved impossible to sustain, and the republic surrendered to the forces of Ferdinand, the king of Spain, dedicatee of Erasmus's *Panegyric* and predecessor of the emperor Charles V. The Medici were installed as de facto hereditary dukes—though the title was not conferred for another thirty years, and republican forms were initially preserved. Machiavelli was immediately dismissed; it is not clear why, since many colleagues kept their posts, but he was closely associated with Piero Soderini, the foremost spirit of the republic, and Machiavelli's leading role in missions that would ordinarily have been entrusted to aristocrats rather than to bureaucrats reflected Soderini's confidence in him. Six months later an abortive plot to assassinate the new rulers was uncovered, and Machiavelli's name was found on a scrap of paper belonging to a conspirator. Arrested on suspicion, he was tortured and jailed, but his innocence was obvious, and he was released a few weeks later.

For the rest of his life, he lived on his farm at Percussina, seven miles from the city, writing and dreaming of a return to public life. Although he was married and had six children, he pined for the excitement of politics. Attempts to find employment with the Medici in Florence or Rome came to nothing, but he secured some writing commissions, and by the time he died was sufficiently in everyone's good graces to be buried in Santa Croce. Nonetheless, only his treatise on the creation and training of a militia, the *Arte della guerra*, was published in his lifetime. *The Prince* was written at breakneck speed in the last six months of 1513, after his release from prison, but published only in 1532. It was the first work to be put on the *Index auctorum et librorum prohibitorum* when that instrument of compulsory intellectual hygiene for adherents of the Catholic faith was created in 1559 by the pope and made permanent in 1564 by the Council of Trent; it was not removed from the Index until the twentieth century and was for many years thought to be so subversive that anyone wishing to read it for purposes of refutation had to ask permission of the pope. Permission was usually refused.

In this enforced retirement, Machiavelli remained a member of the group that met in the gardens of the Rucellai family palazzo in Florence. The *Discourses* was probably written at the request of Cosimo Rucellai, to whom it is dedicated. Like Cicero, Machiavelli thought writing a poor second best to playing an active part in politics; his famous account of the way he would settle down to write by dressing in his state robes and retiring to his study to commune with the immortal dead has a melancholy air. "For four hours I experience no boredom, I forget all my troubles and my fear of poverty, and death holds no more terrors for me."[1] It makes a great difference to what he wrote and how we should read it that Machiavelli was writing practically oriented books. They had to appeal to their dedicatee—*The Prince* was a failed job application—but they bore on one crucial question: how Florence and similar city-states could be governed. Machiavelli's answer was that everything depended on the circumstances. If it were possible to reinstate the Roman Republic, it should be done; if, as seems probable, it is not, we can only hope that a true master of the skills that enable a man to gain power and keep it will arise and establish order. This is not very distant from Bartolus's argument that tyranny may be a necessity in extreme conditions.

The Unplaceability of Machiavelli

Machiavelli has always been an elusive thinker because he was much more (and less) than a "political theorist." This is not because he longed to be active in politics; Cicero is far from unplaceable. It is because he had an astonishing impact on how Europe talked and wrote about politics after his death. Whether he made any impact on the way European politicians acted, as distinct from providing them with a target to criticize for their own hypocritical ends, is unanswerable. Frederick the Great, tongue in cheek, suggested that any ruler who was about to launch an unprovoked attack on his neighbors should first attack Machiavelli. Machiavelli's impact on political rhetoric is undeniable. "Hobbesian" is a term of art familiar to political theorists and political scientists; "Machiavellian" needs no explanation. Whereas "Hobbesian" or "Platonic" carry few pejorative overtones, "Machiavellian" is not a neutral term. The "murderous Machiavel" was a stock figure in Elizabethan drama; and high-minded denunciations of Machiavellianism are to this day part of the standard repertoire of duplicitous politicians who have never read a sentence of his work. On one occasion, President Eisenhower denounced what he took to be Machiavelli's doctrine that "the end justifies the means" without explaining just what might justify the means other than the end.

The popular image of Machiavelli as the "teacher of evil," who praised deceit and violence for their own sake is not the whole truth; most commentators think it is no part of the truth, and few scholars think it is much of the truth. Machiavelli outraged opinion because he took pains to insist that political success demands morally obnoxious acts from anyone seriously engaged in politics. This was not news; it was the lesson the Athenians taught the inhabitants of Melos. It was, however, denied by Stoicism, which was committed to the doctrine that there could be no ultimate conflict between justice and expediency, between the *honestum* and the *utile*.[2] Common sense and everyday political practice in Renaissance Italy suggested that whatever might be true once we take our fate in the hereafter into account, virtue and effectiveness were all too visibly at odds here and now. Our rulers are moved by "reason of state," which is to say the need minimally to "keep the show on the road," and where possible to maximize the state's capacity to enforce order internally and to compete effectively on the international stage. Nonetheless, the readiness to say that political success demanded an unflinching willingness to violate every moral precept appropriate to private life as sharply as Machiavelli did was novel in Christian Europe. Even more unnerving was his seeming uninterest in seeking a justification beyond political success; combating the thought that Romulus's murder of his twin, Remus, was an evil act, he admits that homicide is ordinarily a bad thing and goes on to say that once a city is founded, the freedom to commit such homicides should be denied our rulers. As to Romulus, the result justified the action. Still, "if the means accuse, the end must excuse" is not exactly a moral justification.[3]

Machiavelli's insistence on the tension between the demands of morality and the demands of political practice is more than plausible, but it is unnerving because he left that tension so visibly unresolved. What he intended his readers to feel about it is obscure. It is possible that Machiavelli suffered no more anguish about the tension between the demands of morality and the demands of *raison d'état* than did the Athenians threatening the Melians with massacre, and that he was concerned only to remind his readers of what they knew in their hearts: turning the other cheek may gain the kingdom of heaven but is likely to lose an earthly kingdom. He certainly thought that his fellow Florentines were much too willing to think they were under the peculiar protection of God, and were therefore lackadaisical about their political and military affairs. A sharp reminder of the conflict between Christian virtue and political common sense was what they needed, if not what they wanted.

More than most thinkers, Machiavelli suffers if taken too much out of context. The works we read today—*The Prince* and *Discourses on Livy*— were written to help their author realize his ambition to play a role in Florentine politics, preferably under a republic, but failing that, in any regime that would employ him. Unattractive though the advice offered in *The Prince* may be, Machiavelli's advice to a "new prince" who must stamp his authority on a republic that had prized its liberty had an obvious relevance to the restored Medici family, reinserted by a foreign army in the city that had expelled them eighteen years before.[4] The *Discourses* was written when the Medici were again unpopular, and although Machiavelli died before the short-lived restoration of the republic in 1527–30, a treatise on how the Roman Republic had gained and kept its liberty had obvious resonance. The question whether a state that has once been corrupted can regain its liberty, which preoccupies both works, has an obvious relevance both to the republics of 1494 and 1498 and to the republic of 1527–30. Most of Machiavelli's other works were written to order; *Mandragola*, his louche little play on the theme of foolish husbands, ingenious adulterers, and corrupt friars, was commissioned by Francesco Guicciardini when he was governing Modena on behalf of Leo X; Guicciardini had been Machiavelli's superior in Florence, and managed the transition to a new employer more successfully than he, though not without some personal risk. The *History of Florence* was commissioned by Leo X, the first Medici pope. Leo died before it was finished, and it was presented five years later to Clement VII, the second Medici pope, though published only in 1531. To see how Machiavelli may have expected his work to be read, we need some sense both of the constitutional arrangements and the practical politics of

Florence, Florentine relations with the papacy and with the Habsburg and Valois dynasties, the empire and France.

Florence

Florence was constitutionally a popular republic; but for most of the previous century it had been ruled de facto by the Medici family. This situation was not uncommon, but the contrast of republican institutions and more or less covert princely rule was particularly striking in Renaissance Florence. Florence was also a regional power, and its emphasis on *libertas* for citizens of Florence was not reflected in the treatment of the subordinate cities that it controlled. Florentine ideology was at odds with Florentine practice. The ideology held that *liberty* was so vital to the citizens of Florence that they would sooner die than be ruled by a tyrant; practice suggested that as long as the Medici did not *claim* to rule by hereditary right and were good managers, they would be accepted as the rulers of Florence. This is not very different from modern liberal democracies, where professional politicians beget professional politicians, or acquire them as sons- and daughters-in-law, much as law and medicine run in families. Many medieval theorists would have seen the tension between populist theory and monarchical practice as a small matter. As we have seen, the conventional wisdom was that the *regimen regale* was the best of all regimes so long as the "king"—who might be a duke or a count—governed justly, and in the common interest, not his own self-interest. The danger of a *regimen regale* was that it could degenerate into simple tyranny; but constitutional government by one temperate, wise, brave, and just man was best if it could be had. Devout republicans feared that one-man—or one-family—rule would inevitably become simple tyranny; less devout republicans thought that so long as they did not empty the state treasury or murder their rivals without recourse to law it was not truly tyranny. *Some*, but only a minority, of the citizens of Florence thought after the event that Lorenzo Magnifico had been a tyrant because he had paid himself out of the state coffers for the services he rendered the city; others might well have thought that he had neglected the family's banking business to devote himself to the greater glory of Florence and earned his pay.

During periods of acute stress, such as that of Machiavelli's employment in the chancellery, discussion turned more intensely to classical thinking about republican institutions, and during Machiavelli's lifetime with more sophistication than before. Florence was where political stress could have been expected to produce intelligent and original thought about politics. It was the center of Renaissance intellectual life. Along with Milan, Venice, and the Papal States, it was one of the dominant powers in northern and central Italy; to the south, the Kingdom of Naples was fought over by the French and Spanish crowns. Florence was a great trading state, linked to the trade routes and commercial fairs of northern Europe, and prospering on a luxury trade in textiles in particular. It was the first banking center in Europe, and the Medici had prospered by being exceptionally skilled merchants and bankers. Its prominence now made Florence vulnerable, too powerful to be ignored, too weak to act as it chose.

The Florentine constitution was a classical city-state constitution. It had been instituted in 1293 after a revolt against the incumbent nobility. The aim was to ensure that neither the nobility nor the urban poor could hold unchecked power. The city was ruled by the *signoria*, a committee of eight "priors" chaired by the *gonfaloniere* of justice. It met together with two other committees—the committee of "twelve good men" and the committee of the sixteen *gonfalonieri* of the city's sixteen districts. Legislation was considered, but not initiated, by two other councils, the Council of the People and the Council of the Commune, whose members, three hundred and two hundred, respectively, were chosen by the *signoria*; under the Medici, they were replaced by the Seventy and the Hundred. These bodies rotated membership at very frequent intervals—two to six months—and the main committees of the republic were selected by lot. The names of eligible persons were placed in bags and the names of those who were to serve were drawn out. It was common for many names to be disqualified because the persons named were in arrears with their taxes or otherwise ineligible; this gave a lot of power to the scrutinizing committee that pronounced on eligibility to be considered and to serve. In a city of perhaps eighty thousand inhabitants in Machiavelli's day, some three thousand citizens each year were called on to perform a governmental function. It is easy to imagine that the unambitious who wished to attend to their families' affairs would hope to avoid public office if someone competent would take their place, while the ambitious would think it intolerable to be reduced to guessing whether their allies would be drawn from the bags. Upper-class families spent much time and energy ensuring that their allies were in the right place to protect their interests.

Such a complex and intrinsically slow-moving system was doomed to be overturned or subverted. For a long time it was subverted in ways that kept up appearances. In the sixty years before the republic of 1494, the Medici family did not hold prominent public offices. Yet nobody doubted that they ruled Florence. Their ascent to power was far from untroubled. Cosimo de' Medici narrowly escaped death at the hands of the rival Albizzi family in 1433, when he was exiled for ten years and fined an enormous sum. The Albizzi instantly alienated their own supporters, and in 1434 Cosimo returned in triumph. He then ensured that the major bodies in the government were filled with his supporters. He achieved this partly within the constitution and partly without; an emergency council was assembled to reinstate him and remove his opponents, but he brought enough armed men to the meeting to secure his own safety and to ensure that the assembled citizens knew their duty. The Medici governed Florence within republican forms by controlling the personnel of government and ensuring that their friends were in control. The family suffered from hereditary uricemia, the disease underlying gout, and were short-lived, so their rule was never wholly secure. Because they died young, they inherited power young, and the success of any particular Medici ruler depended on temperament and innate capacity more than experience.

The two greatest Medici were Cosimo, who managed the affairs of Florence from 1434 to 1464, and Lorenzo the Magnificent, who took the reins in 1469 and died in 1492. Savonarola's Republic of Virtue came about partly because Lorenzo's successor, Piero di Lorenzo, was incompetent, but mostly for reasons outside anyone's control. In 1494

Lodovico Sforza of Milan persuaded the French king, Charles VIII, to revive his claim to the Kingdom of Naples. To everyone's surprise, Charles took up the idea and headed into Italy. Florence had for fifty years played off the papacy, the empire, and France against each other to preserve its freedom of movement. Now, the game was up. The price of avoiding a full-scale invasion and the sack of Florence was allowing the French armies free passage down the west coast of Italy and accepting French occupation of the main cities en route. Piero became the scapegoat for this disaster and was sent packing.

From 1494 to 1498, the government was in the hands of the partisans of Girolamo Savonarola, an ascetic and visionary Dominican friar, but he could achieve no more than Piero in foreign affairs, and his campaign against ecclesiastical corruption drew the hostility of the papacy. Florence had always been friendly to the papacy; if Florence resiled from its allegiance, it was vulnerable to the depredations of warlords like Cesare Borgia operating from the Papal States. The city was also vulnerable to the threat of papal interdict, which the city would lie under if Savonarola was excommunicated. By withdrawing the church's protection from the persons and property of the citizens of Florence, the papacy could threaten the city's trade throughout Europe; the goods of the excommunicated were fair game. Papal pressure and Florentine discontent resulted in Savonarola's removal from office, followed by his torture and execution for heresy. The end of the affair was the establishment of the reconstituted republic of 1498, of which Machiavelli was the servant.

Its chief novelty was the creation of the Grand Council, in imitation of that in Venice. The motive was the wish to keep a tight rein on the *grandi* or *nobili* who might be tempted to seize power for themselves; it was also a last flicker of the Florentine urge to return to what were conceived of as the most ancient institutions of the city. The rules of membership resulted in a council far larger than anyone anticipated, and over the next fourteen years attempts were made to make this unwieldy body less useless when quick decisions were needed. Whether the republic could have survived its constitutional infirmities, given reasonable luck, is anyone's guess. It did not have reasonable luck; Italy was in a state of continual upheaval; French, Spanish, German, and Swiss armies fought sporadic wars across the country, and the Italian cities and princely states made and broke alliances in a futile attempt to gain advantage from the chaos. The papacy under Alexander VI and Julius II was well to the fore in this, and its fate was typical; they were strikingly successful in cementing the papacy's control of the Papal States, but fifteen years after the fall of the Florentine Republic, Rome was sacked by mutinous imperial armies, against the wishes of their commander in chief, Emperor Charles V. The humiliation of the Medici pope Clement VII provoked the expulsion of the Medici from Florence in the summer of 1527. The republic that followed lasted only until the final restoration of the Medici three years later and Florence's transformation into a grand duchy.

The Prince

Machiavelli wrote *The Prince* following the failure of his beloved republic. What it is about is not hard to understand. The subject matter is one on which Machiavelli had often reflected during his career, as he watched Cesare Borgia imposing himself on cities whose government he had subverted, and as he contemplated the French conquest of Milan and the subsequent failure of the French to hang on to what they had taken. Machiavelli's topic is carefully specified: how a "new prince" is to take power and maintain himself in power. Nonetheless, although the topic is narrowly specified—Lorenzo de' Medici, to whom the book is dedicated, was preeminently a new prince to whose conduct chapter 5 of *The Prince* ("The Way to Govern Cities or Dominions That, Previous to Being Occupied, Lived under Their Own Laws") was all too glaringly relevant—the staying power of *The Prince* comes from its sweeping statements about human nature, the role of chance, or *fortuna*, in political life, and, above all, its insistence on the need for a clear-sighted appreciation of how men really *are* as distinct from the moralizing claptrap about how they *ought* to be that had brought so many princes and their states to ruin.

What made *The Prince* so timely emerges in the "Exhortation to Liberate Italy from the Barbarians," with which the book concludes. Lorenzo was the nephew of Pope Leo X; with the Medicis in power at

Rome and in Florence, the way was open for the two most substantial powers in central Italy to pursue an ambitious military policy: "There is no one in whom Italy can now place any hope except your illustrious family which (because it is successful and talented, and favoured by God and the Church of which it is now head) can take the lead in saving her."[5]

The Prince divides in two; the first eleven chapters consider different sorts of principalities and the way to acquire and hold them; fourteen of the remaining fifteen form a parodic mirror of princes, covering a variety of topics familiar in the literature from Cicero and Seneca down to not yet written works like Castiglione's *The Courtier*: military prowess, honesty, mercy, generosity, the avoidance of contempt and hatred. It ends with an exhortation to the Medici princes to unify Italy and evict the "barbarians"—the foreign forces that had rampaged through Italy since 1494, and would continue to do so for another three decades. Italian writers in the nineteenth century hailed Machiavelli as the prophet of the *risorgimento*, but the description of the transalpine invaders as barbarians was common enough, even on the part of popes and dukes who had rashly invited them in to promote some local quarrel. It is an anachronism to see Machiavelli as a nineteenth-century Italian nationalist, rather than someone inspired by the glories of ancient Rome.

Machiavelli begins *The Prince* by telling Lorenzo that he has reflected both on his own experience and on ancient history to provide genuinely new advice. That in itself represented a double change in thinking, first in departing from the Florentine desire to revert to the past—which is a trait that perhaps reappears in the *Discourses*—and second in using ancient history not as a moral guide as in collections of *exempla* but as a quarry for examples of successful practice. *The Prince* then runs straight into serious business, beginning with laying out its subject matter: newly acquired principalities and their retention. The single paragraph that constitutes the entire opening chapter buries a wealth of recent history when it separates out hereditary states from states that are not, states that are completely new to a family from those annexed to a state that has long been ruled by the same family, states that were formerly republics from states that were principalities, and—a wide-ranging gesture that took in both the astonishing luck of Cesare Borgia and the reinsertion of the Medici with the assistance of Spanish troops—those "acquired either with the arms of others or with one's own, either through luck or favour or else through ability."[6]

Hereditary principalities are of no interest; they present no challenge to the political skills of the prince. Long habits of obedience give the incumbent an advantage over rivals; anyone who loses a state of which he is the hereditary ruler deserves to do so, though Machiavelli well knew that misfortune makes the inhabitants of any state turn against their rulers, hereditary or not. The crucial discussion begins with chapter 3, as he first turns to the way to keep control of "mixed" principalities, by which he means states that the prince has conquered with the aim of annexing them to his present state, explains why some states remain quiet when conquered while others do not, and embarks on the contrast between states acquired by the prince's own ability and those acquired with help from others.[7] The chaos of recent events dominates the discussion, but the Roman treatment of Greece during the conquest of the early second century BCE is adduced to emphasize the point he makes several times, that the French had bungled the acquisition of power in Italy when they first captured Milan and were then driven out.

The argument is simple: an annexed state will be hard to hold if its people are culturally very different from the conqueror's own state. The French would inevitably have a harder time securing their power in Milan than in, say, Burgundy, where the inhabitants lived much as in the rest of France and spoke more or less the same language as other Frenchmen. It is, however, not impossible to retain power under such conditions; the Romans were strikingly effective in keeping a grip on conquered kingdoms. The underlying difficulty is the same in all new acquisitions: it is not hard to acquire a state, because human beings are quick to be discontented, ready to blame their present rulers for their miseries, and happy to see the back of them. Having done so, they will discover that the new rulers are no improvement on their predecessors, and very likely worse, because the costs of conquest fall heavily on the conquered population. In that case, they will, if they can, rebel against their new masters.

What is to be done? Two things: first, ensure that there are no partisans of the deposed ruler to cause trouble; second, go and live in the conquered territories. Machiavelli did not by this literally mean that Louis XII should have gone in person to live in Milan, as the instances of Turkish and Roman conquest make clear. The thought is rather that he should have installed an administration of his own that could see what was going on and nip trouble in the bud. The French could have kept hold of Milan by establishing colonies, as the Romans would have done, or by installing their own administrators throughout the region, as the Turks do. "Colonies" in this context means settlements of soldiers who are rewarded with farms rather than colonization in the imperialist sense of the next several centuries. Doing neither, they were evicted. What startles modern readers is the calmness with which Machiavelli observes, "Wanting to annex territory is indeed very natural and normal, and when capable men undertake it, they are always praised, or at least not criticised. But if men who are not capable of achieving it are bent on undertaking it at all costs, this is a blunder that deserves censure."[8] This is the voice of Greek and Roman imperialism, adjusted to the world of the Renaissance. He argues that colonies of the Roman kind are better than an army of occupation because it is cheaper to establish colonies that can support themselves than to quarter soldiers on the country; moreover, because soldiers need so many resources, paying for them arouses great irritation. The republic that Machiavelli served ground to a standstill because incessant warfare required decisions on taxation to pay for it that could not be arrived at within the unwieldy constitution; it is easy to see how much feeling hides behind these calm observations on military budgets.

The Machiavelli who was a scandal to European morality emerges in passing. As between soldiers and colonists, he says, colonists cause less anger because the only people injured are those whose land is seized for the benefit of the colonists. Since they will be few and scattered about the countryside, they do not pose a formidable problem. He then produces the underlying principle that governs the discussion: "It should be observed here that men should either be caressed or crushed; because they can avenge slight injuries, but not those that are very severe. Hence any injury done to a man must be such that there is no need to fear his revenge."[9] To a modern eye the assumption that the small farmers and other inhabitants in the countryside can safely be discounted because they are unorganized and unable to defend themselves against the evils visited upon them by the invaders is repulsive. Machiavelli accepts the assumptions of the Romans when they took over the territory of their neighbors; no Roman worried for long about the violation of their neighbors' human rights.

On the way to offering advice to princes who have taken over a republic that may not be glad to receive them, Machiavelli offers a nice vignette of the way in which a country that is used to being governed as a despotism will be easy to retain even by the not very skilled. His example is the empire of Alexander the Great. Alexander had no sooner conquered his empire than he died, sighing for new worlds to conquer, but because the subjects of Darius, king of Persia, were used to being governed in a centralized state, Alexander's heirs did not need to take extraordinary measures to preserve their power. He might have observed that Athens in contrast tried to recover its freedom and was defeated by the highly competent Antipater. In fact, he draws a contrast with the Roman experience in Gaul, where innumerable small, independent tribes had been used to liberty and did not take kindly to rule by outsiders. He expected the same would soon happen in France. Perhaps presciently in view of the wars that were to plague France in the second half of the sixteenth century, he observes that not only were Brittany and Burgundy recent enough acquisitions to remember their independence of the French crown, but the aristocracy in general was very local in its attachments and ready to revolt against a monarchy based in Paris if provoked. They are easy enough to manage if their existing way of life is not disturbed, but unlikely to acquiesce in any tighter control than that.[10]

A long tradition of genuine self-government poses problems for a new prince. In republics, "there is greater vitality, more hatred, and a stronger desire for revenge; they do not forget, indeed cannot forget, their lost liberties." That being so, there are three pieces of advice worth hewing to: a ruler should be prepared to live in the conquered state; he should utterly destroy all the old institutions; or he should leave as many as possible intact, so as to govern with the least irritation to old sentiments. Machiavelli draws his morals from the Romans and the Spartans: "The Spartans held Athens and Thebes by establishing oligarchies there; yet they eventually lost control of them. In order to hold Capua, Carthage and Numantia, the Romans destroyed them; and consequently never lost them." Initially, the Romans tried to emulate the Spartans in exercising only a loose suzerainty over Greece, but eventually had to destroy the Greek kingdoms to avoid incessant revolts. Polybius's picture of the Romans seducing their conquered subjects by offering them participation in the Roman state and its way of life is not directly contradicted, but where Polybius asked, "How did Rome acquire an empire whose peoples came to feel loyal to Rome?" Machiavelli poses a tougher question, "How does one ensure that a conquest will 'take'?" His answer boils down to the familiar binary opposition: kill or caress. Either show a respect for their institutions by governing behind the shield they provide and veil your authority; or stamp on opposition, exile or kill the previous elite, and make it clear that those who are not for you are as good as dead.

Although the first eleven chapters of *The Prince* constitute a unity, they are internally structured in an interesting fashion. Machiavelli was fascinated by the contrast between those who were astute and effective operators in the political world, and deserved congratulation, and those who were installed in power by the efforts of others or by simple good luck. *Fortuna*, or chance, is one of the most hotly debated of Machiavelli's terms, and we shall return to it. The role of chance in politics is obvious; and it is impossible not to feel that some political actors have had more than their share of good luck and others more than their share of bad. To observe that some people are thrust to prominence by chance is to say nothing startling. This understates Machiavelli's interest in the subject. Florence was superstitious almost as a matter of policy. An extravagant example soon after Machiavelli's death was that in 1527 the newly revived republic elected Christ as its king; more generally, the Florentines were unusually ready to believe that prayer and self-mortification would attract divine favor. Conversely, they seemed unable to deal with Cesare Borgia just because it seemed that fortune, along with his father, Pope Alexander VI, was on his side. Machiavelli was deeply hostile to anything that undermined the Florentines' ability to analyze the balance of forces they confronted.

He draws a crucial contrast between those who rely on their own political capacity—*virtù*—and those who rely on others or on luck. Plainly the first are less vulnerable to fortune's turning against them or to their allies' leaving them in the lurch. Cesare Borgia is a puzzle for this simple dichotomy, as we shall see. Those who display outstanding virtue and are therefore less dependent on fortune are the heroes one would expect, though the presence of Moses alongside Theseus, Cyrus, and Romulus may raise eyebrows, as Machiavelli admits. Machiavelli lets himself be distracted by his four heroes into a reflection on the fate of Savonarola that produces one of his best aphorisms. In the middle of his reflections on those who acquired a principality through their own arms, he says, "all armed prophets succeed, whereas unarmed ones fail." The figure of the armed prophet is a trope of twentieth-century political analysis. Machiavelli says, "If Moses, Cyrus, Theseus and Romulus had been unarmed, the new order which each of them established would not have been obeyed for very long. This is what happened in our own times to Fra' Girolamo Savonarola, who perished together with his new order as soon as the masses began to lose faith in him; and he lacked the means of keeping the support of those who had believed in him, as well as of making those who had never had any faith in him believe."[11] Behind Savonarola were innumerable prophetic figures who had frightened the authorities of their day but whose followers, with the exception of the militarily effective Hussites of Bohemia, lacked the capacity to overthrow their ungodly rulers.

The intellectual interest of these thoughts lies below the surface. Machiavelli had a strong sense that although there was much to be said in politics for a sudden, bold stroke, human beings were also creatures of habit, both good and bad, which argued for taking things slowly. The Florentines' ingratitude toward rulers who were devoted to the republic, but meeting with undeserved misfortune, was a long ingrained bad habit. Good habits need to be inculcated. The aid of religion was not to be scorned, nor its efficacy overestimated. Habits of obedience should be instilled by a mixture of fear and favor and backed up by whatever moral and spiritual resources came to hand; force mattered because once everyone could see that opposition was fatal, they would obey, and their beliefs would come into line with the habit of obedience. The *fact* of obedience would soon turn into a belief that they *ought* to obey. Most writers have tended to palliate the familiar fact that conquered populations come to subject themselves voluntarily in this fashion; Machiavelli did not. Force creates acceptance, reluctant at first, but willing in due course. Not to know this is to throw away the chance of success. The thought that if belief sustains authority, authority can reinforce the beliefs that then sustain it, is true enough; but it lacks the sharp edge that Machiavelli gives the observation. The fact that unarmed prophets invariably fail means that we may believe as firmly as we like that God is on our side, but it will do us no good if physical force is not on our side as well.

The Puzzle of Cesare Borgia

Ceasare Borgia is a major figure both in *The Prince* and in the *Discourses*. He presents a problem for Machiavelli. Was he, or was he not, unduly reliant on luck? Was he a skillful practitioner of the arts that new princes should possess and brought down in the end by pure bad luck; or was his success due only to luck, and was he brought down by a failure to take the measures he should have taken to ensure that bad luck could not destroy him? Of course, admirers of Machiavelli's cynical style can relish his discussion of Cesare Borgia's rise to power simply as a literary tour de force. Cesare, the brother of Lucrezia the famous poisoner,[12] was the son of the future Borgia pope Alexander VI. He was made a cardinal in his teens, but when Alexander became pope, the possibility beckoned of advancement in the secular realm. He renounced his cardinal's hat and was appointed captain general of the papal armies. Alexander's intention was to bring the Papal States firmly under the papacy's control, to enhance his son's prestige and power, and beyond that to unify the Italian states under his leadership.

This was what Machiavelli urged on Leo X and Lorenzo de' Medici in the final chapter of *The Prince*, and the policy itself was not one he deplored. What he deplored was the fact that the papacy was too weak to implement it, but too powerful to allow any other state to do so.[13] Alexander dismissed the so-called papal vicars, the agents who administered the Papal States, and left Cesare to secure the Romagna, which he did with astonishing energy and success. What would have happened if events had favored him is hard to say, but Alexander was pope for only half a dozen years (1497–1503), and Cesare himself was at death's door with malaria at the very moment his father died. He could not influence the papal succession, and his attempts to get on good terms with Julius II, who loathed the Borgias, got nowhere. Cesare fled to Naples, but was arrested, exiled, and imprisoned in Spain; he was killed in battle soon after being released in 1507. The question his career posed for Machiavelli was whether there was anything more that Cesare could have done to secure his position. Machiavelli inclines toward the view that there was not; perhaps, but only perhaps, a more prudent or long-sighted man might have thought ahead to the election of a new pope after the death of Alexander, but Machiavelli cannot find it in himself to complain.

Because of the way Machiavelli tells the story, Cesare Borgia comes across as an almost operatic villain; more seriously, he is presented as someone whose wickednesses were directed intelligently and efficiently to the end of making himself master of the Romagna. He was not gratuitously but tactically cruel. One piece of villainy that Machiavelli reports admiringly was Borgia's plot to ensure that the Orsini gave him and his father no trouble. Having persuaded the leading members of the clan that he was genuinely interested in reconciliation, he got them to a conference at Senigallia, seized them, and over the next four weeks had them strangled. Machiavelli treats the behavior of the Orsini and their friends as shockingly naïve; modern readers are likely to think that Borgia's behavior is repulsive, but it could be said on his side that the men he murdered were no strangers to the acquisition of power by murdering friends and relatives, let alone to disposing of sworn enemies.[14]

Borgia's most impressive coup de théâtre was the killing of the unfortunate Messer Remirro de Orco, an event that Machiavelli commented on admiringly in his dispatches and discusses in *The Prince*. The tale and the moral are simple. The Romagna was part of the papal patrimony, but had fallen into the hands of assorted small-time rulers who would today be called kleptocrats, whose only aim was to extract whatever they could from their wretched subjects. Borgia saw that any government that could keep the peace would be accepted, if it provided justice according to law and avoided outright banditry. The first step was to secure the peace. For this purpose, he installed Remirro de Orco, to whom he gave full power to suppress dissent and restore order. His chosen agent was effective, but his methods aroused resentment. Borgia took two steps to ensure that the resentment did not reach back to himself. The first was to establish a regular court, to which lawyers could take grievances. The second was to have Remirro de Orco arrested, "cut in two pieces," and placed in the main square at Cesena the day after Christmas together with an executioner's block and a knife. "This terrible spectacle left the people both satisfied and amazed."[15]

Understanding Machiavelli's project, which was not that of shocking the sensibilities of later ages, but reflecting on the difficulties of instituting political order, whether princely or republican, allows us to move onto terrain where a great deal of ink has been spilled. Machiavelli rounds off the discussion of the establishment of new principalities with a brief chapter on "ecclesiastical principalities." There is something unnerving about Machiavelli's account of the peculiarities of the Papal States. They are "sustained by ancient religious institutions, which have been sufficiently strong to maintain their rulers in office however they live and act. Only they have states and do not defend them, and subjects whom they do not trouble to govern. . . ."[16] That is to say, under successive popes the Papal States fell into the hands of the warring families who monopolized the College of Cardinals, and everything went to rack and ruin. "And their subjects, though not properly governed, do not worry about it; they cannot get rid of these rulers, nor even think about doing so. Only these principalities, then, are secure and successful."[17] To rub in the insult, Machiavelli then observes that since these states are governed by a higher power, there is nothing he can say about them.

Of course, there is, because he goes on to say that the model of a successful ruler is Alexander VI, Cesare's father. By guile and brute force, and the agency of his son, Alexander reestablished the papacy as a secular power to reckon with; this, thought Machiavelli, left his successor Julius II in a strong position to make the church the arbiter of the fate of Italy. Machiavelli was wrong; the monarchies of France and Spain were in a different league from the Italian states in their ability to assemble armies and keep them in the field for long campaigns. Julius II also suffered from Machiavelli's real vice, which was not a taste for wickedness for its own sake, but the belief that a deft operator could outsmart all his enemies all the time.

The second part of *The Prince* then turns into an ironic commentary on the traditional mirror of princes. Machiavelli's obsession was with military effectiveness on the one hand and the ability to form absolutely clear policy on the other. The doctrine that only the armed prophet succeeds is reinforced by reflecting on the failure of the Sforza family to keep itself in power by paying sufficient attention to military matters. "A ruler should have no other objective and no other concern, nor occupy himself with anything else except war and its methods and practices, for this pertains only to those who rule."[18] The injunction spills over into a departure from the usual advice to princes; handbooks for princes praised humane learning and taught the prince to interest himself in the social graces. Machiavelli says the only recreation the prince might usefully take up is hunting because it is a good way of learning how to read the lay of the land, and this is a valuable skill in a general. Humane letters are neither here nor there except for the acquisition of genuine historical knowledge; history provides a storehouse of great achievements to imitate, and a gallery of great men to emulate.

As to princely virtue, princes, says Machiavelli, are blamed only for shortcomings that bring about the destruction of the state. It is good to be loyal, generous, kindly, and the like, just as it is bad to be mean, lascivious, frivolous, and an unbeliever. All the same, the prince should not give much heed to his personal characteristics, save insofar as they lead him astray in matters of policy. This is a dig at Cicero's *De officiis*, though worse is to come. It may seem also to be a rejection of Aristotle's injunction that the ruler should practice self-control in the areas of sex and money. In fact, this is a topic on which Aristotle and Machiavelli are at one: concerned with the political consequences of unchastity, not unchastity as such. Seducing upper-class women creates enmities that undermine the ruler's position. It is worth remembering, however, how far Machiavelli shares the orthodox Christian pessimism about human nature. He is closer to Augustine than to Pico della Mirandola and his conviction that we might make ourselves cherubim. It is not obvious that his grim view of human nature is Christian in origin, but he believes in a version of original sin: "all men are by nature bad and will do all the evil they can." They must be disciplined by good laws, and if law has broken down, then by any means possible. Machiavelli did not have a surprising moral theory; he had a surprising readiness to confront head-on the fact that politics requires the willingness to get your hands dirty.

Then comes the advice that has so upset Machiavelli's readers, when Machiavelli analyzes the prince's *virtù*. The Machiavellian concept of *virtù* has been analyzed to death. That it does not mean "virtue" in the sense of the Christian virtues is obvious; what it does mean, less obvious. Usually, it means ability or almost any quality that makes for political success. These are reflections not on virtuous princes, as one would find in any number of pious writers, but on the qualities that make for effectiveness. *The Prince* is a reflection on the *virtù* of one man, the prince; the *Discourses* is a reflection on the *virtù* of a whole people—the Romans in particular, but also the Swiss and other citizens of successful states. The citizens of Athens and Sparta displayed *virtù*, though their obsession with confining the citizenship to the natives of their cities prevented them from achieving the glory that Rome did. Whether *virtù* is the same property in a prince and a whole people is much debated, but a plausible view is that it is formally the same property, but different in content. It is always defined in terms of the qualities that bring political success, and political success is closely linked to the achievement of glory. Whether it is the Roman people or the hoped-for savior of Italian independence in the early 1500s, political success is the goal; the polity to be established and maintained is not the same, but the enterprise is. Because the Roman people had to create and maintain a free government and did so *collectively*, the qualities they required were different from those a new prince needs. To take an obvious instance, Machiavelli never had a high opinion of the ordinary man's courage in the abstract.[19] Without good leadership and good training, the ordinary man is cowardly and incompetent, though with good leadership and training, he can display great courage and endurance. The prince, on the other hand, is ex hypothesi bold, ambitious, and ready to get himself killed in the attempt to seize power.

The sharpest contrast occurs with virtues such as honesty and loyalty. The people cannot act as an effective collectivity unless everyone treats everyone else with a high degree of honesty and mutual loyalty; these must be proper character traits and not easily turned on and turned off pragmatically. The new prince, in contrast, must be ready to change his colors at a moment's notice. He cannot afford to be so honest that he does not know how to deceive his rivals and murder them when he has the chance. Even those who are generally honest must be ready to be brutal. Machiavelli describes Hannibal's extreme cruelty, his *terribilità*, as part of his *virtù*. Given that most of us dislike behaving brutally or dishonestly, we might wonder whether political success is worth having at this price; indeed, we might wonder what constitutes political success in the first place. Can it really be defined in terms of wading in blood to a tyrant's throne?

Machiavelli leaves the reader to make up his own mind, but some of what he thinks is obvious enough, and the rest must be conjectural. The reward for successfully constructing a republic is freedom; citizens can live a civil life, a *vivere civile*, and enjoy their possessions and their liberties in peace. They will not be victimized by the rich, or invaded by foreigners, or ill treated without recourse to the law. It is possible that this is not wholly different from the ordinary person's rewards for a prince's success in securing and holding a principality. Sheldon Wolin's elegant description of Machiavelli as dealing in "an economy of violence"[20] catches the point nicely; the successful prince may get into power by unpleasant means, may maintain himself in power by unpleasant means, and may be a person whose moral character we do not care for. But he diminishes the amount of random, unpredictable, pointless violence and cruelty that we have to suffer. The prince's political reward is power. The attractions of power are not something Machiavelli troubles to analyze; true to his classical masters, he assumes that we want to exercise power and want not to have it exercised over us.

The thought that violence and treachery are a currency that politicians employ intelligently to avert their excessive and uncontrolled use catches something of Machiavelli's aims. However, his ultimate goal is one the modern world is less happy to avow as he does, other than in sporting contexts. This is the attainment of glory. If one asks why anyone would seek power in the way Machiavelli takes for granted—it is a question Machiavelli asks only in the context of observing that the unpredictability of fortune might make one wonder whether it is worth trying—the answer is that men seek glory. They want to leave a great name. Here there is a real difference in the achievements of a prince and a republic. In a principality glory is obtained by the prince; this is one reason why the romantic idea that the Renaissance saw the state as a work of art is not an inappropriate metaphor for the work of the prince. But the ordinary people are passive; they are the raw material of princely glory. In a republic the people themselves are the heroes and the achievers of glory. If *virtù* is the quality that achieves glory, it is thus both the same and different in the prince and the people; it is the same in being essentially instrumental, that is, the qualities that make for success and enable the possessors of these qualities to achieve glory through that success, and different inasmuch as different sorts of people under very different circumstances achieve glory in principalities and republics. Nor is it merely a matter of success; some highly successful rulers were mere tyrants. Agathocles, the tyrant of Syracuse, illuminates Machiavelli's view. He not only held power for a long period but drove the Carthaginians out of Sicily. But he had been freely elected by the citizens of Syracuse, and then made himself a tyrant, holding by force and treachery what he had been freely given. Needless cruelty and treachery are unforgivable.

Having laid the ground with his discussion of warfare and his scorn for the attainments of the courtier, Machiavelli launches into the characteristics of the successful prince. The most famous moment in the discussion comes in chapter 18, ominously entitled "How Rulers Should Keep Their Promises." The reader has by now been told that the prince should not *be* generous, though he should try to *appear* so, and has been reminded that it is better to be feared than to be loved—since people do not much mind revolting against the good-natured, but think twice about rebelling against the lethally severe—so it comes as no surprise that Machiavelli's advice is to keep faith only as and when it serves our ends. Honesty is a virtue and men are rightly praised for it, but a prince who is honest when he should not be makes himself a prey to his enemies. It is in this context that Machiavelli turns Cicero's advice on its head.

Lions and Foxes and Political Ethics

For Cicero the fact that even animals obey law in a certain sense—they are endowed by nature with habits useful to their survival—does not blur the distinction between man and beast. Men must obey a specifically human law; it teaches rational beings how to act for the common good. Human courage is not the lion's savagery; human intelligence is not the fox's cunning. To which Machiavelli replies, "Since a ruler, then, must know how to act like a beast, he should imitate both the fox and the lion, for the lion is liable to be trapped, whereas the fox cannot ward off wolves. One needs, then, to be a fox to recognise traps and a lion to frighten away wolves." Once more, the ruthless Alexander VI is praised for his duplicity: he "was concerned only with deceiving men; and he always found them gullible."[21]

One question must occur to the reader who reads Machiavelli in a friendly spirit. Setting aside the wickedness of rulers who follow his advice, can anyone act with quite the amoral verve and flair that Machiavelli advocates? Machiavelli takes the question seriously; but he circles around it, first asking how rulers can avoid being despised—mostly by being ferocious in repressing rivals and opponents—and then what they must do to gain a reputation. The discussion once more displays Machiavelli's taste for the spectacular; his hero is Ferdinand of Aragon, who united the Iberian Peninsula, drove out the Moors from their last strongholds, and, by a mixture of guile and military skill, first seized the Kingdom of Naples from its previous ruler with French assistance and then turned around and evicted the French. But Machiavelli admits that we cannot always be on top of events; often we have to cobble together a strategy in circumstances we would not have chosen. Then caution is better than rashness. The concession seems to be wrung from him. The sole point on which Machiavelli and the advice books coincide is the need to avoid flatterers. Like generations of political scientists after him, Machiavelli observes that princes have a hard time obtaining impartial advice, because people will tell them whatever they think the prince wants to hear. The remedy is to appoint to one's service people who are described in terms that sound very like a description of the former secretary of the Ten of War.

The Prince ends with a double peroration. The true peroration is, of course, the exhortation to liberate Italy from the barbarians. The pre-peroration is the engaging chapter on the role of fortune in human affairs. Short though *The Prince* is, one could be forgiven for thinking after a quick reading that being a Machiavellian hero is an exhausting and unprofitable activity; when there is peace, we must be active in making preparations for war; we should befriend the ordinary people, but not be too familiar with them, lest we become despised; we must watch out for our enemies and strike before they do, but we must not attend too carefully to the dangers of assassination, because only the incompetent or the oppressive run much risk. Steering a delicate path between an excess of caution and an overdose of rashness promises to be hard work, too.

Is the task hopeless? Machiavelli observes that it is a common view that "the affairs of the world are so much ruled by fortune and by God that the ability of men cannot control them." It is a view by which he is tempted, especially in view of the chaos that has gripped Italy for the previous two decades. Nonetheless, he refuses to agree that human freedom is of no account, and is "disposed to hold that fortune is the arbiter of half our actions, but that it lets us control roughly the other half."[22] It is interestingly unclear just what Machiavelli thinks. He sometimes suggests that all fortune amounts to is forces that we are commonly bad at controlling: "I compare fortune to one of those dangerous rivers that, when they become enraged flood the plains, destroy trees and buildings, move earth from one place and deposit it in another. . . . But this does not mean that when the river is not in flood, men are unable to take precautions, by means of dykes and dams, so that when it rises next time, it will either not overflow its banks, or if it does, its force will not be so uncontrolled or damaging."[23] That suggests the usual Machiavellian moral: men are chronically idle about taking precautions while things are going well. They are lulled into thinking that all will be well, because things are going well at present, and then something happens that they might have prevented but that they have foolishly taken no trouble to prevent. And as a result they are destroyed.

At other times fortune is represented as a real force for good or evil, even if it is not *wholly* outside our control even then. How well we do in a risky political enterprise is very much a matter of whether our style, temperament, characteristic mode of operation suits the conditions; sometimes the schemes of a cautious man will come adrift because the situation demands boldness, and sometimes the cautious man will succeed where the bold one does not. If—but it is very much the if of *per impossibile*—"it were possible to change one's character to suit the times and circumstances, one would always be successful."[24] Machiavelli then embarks on a set-piece on the character of Julius II. The Florentines found him entirely impossible to deal with; they could not deal with his rages, they could not predict his plans, and he himself may not quite have known what he was going to do next. But he was a bold military leader and during a very brief pontificate strikingly successful.

That, says Machiavelli, was because he was bold and impetuous, and the times suited him. Had he lived when a more cautious policy was required, he would have been undone because he could not possibly have acted otherwise than he did. All the same, says Machiavelli, in terms that cause our eyebrows to lift, "it is better to be impetuous than cautious, because fortune is a woman, and if you wish to control her, it is necessary to treat her roughly. And it is clear that she is more inclined to yield to men who are impetuous than to those who are calculating. Since fortune is a woman, she is always well disposed towards young men, because they are less cautious and more aggressive, and treat her more boldly."[25] How much more than a rhetorical flourish this may be, it is impossible to say. Machiavelli never suggested that he held distinctively un-Christian views; on the other hand, he never said anything to suggest deep piety. Since he cared a great deal about his literary skills, it might have been no more than decoration to make a point of some seriousness; on the other hand, it may have been something deeper than lip service to the idea that fate is an active force in the world, bringing us to good and evil on a whim. Polybius, after all, thought a lot about the reality of *tyche*, or fate, chance, fortune.

From *The Prince* to the *Discourses*

The Prince ends with an exhortation to Leo X to unite Italy and render the Medici forever glorious by expelling the barbarians from Italian soil. Machiavelli's hope is for Italy to recover its ancient Roman glory, and this theme connects *The Prince* and the *Discourses*. The *Discourses* purports to be, and often really is, a commentary on Livy's *History of Rome*. It is broken into three books, of which the first is a sustained discussion of the principles underlying the creation and sustaining of a successful republic; the second focuses on the expansion of Rome, and the third on the importance of great leaders in the life of the Roman Republic. Writers on Machiavelli have some difficulty deciding whether it is astonishing that the *Discourses* is very different from *The Prince*, or whether it is the similarities in the two works that are really astonishing. Part of the answer is that the principles of statecraft that underlie both works are very much the same. Examples of useful ruthlessness often appear briefly in *The Prince* and are discussed at length in the *Discourses*; Cesare Borgia's exploits reinforce the lessons of the Romans; Julius II's impetuousness is praised; and the view of human nature in *The Prince* underpins his complaint in the *Discourses* that even men of the vilest character do not know how to be thoroughgoing in their wickedness and flinch just when they ought to go to extremes.[26]

Although the principles of statecraft and the underlying view of human nature are the same, the occasion and the purpose of the discussion are very different. Republics are not principalities—here thought of as states ruled as if they are the personal possession of a prince—and the focus of the *Discourses* is the creation of a self-sustaining constitutional order in a republic. The model is Polybius. Machiavelli held many views that readers of Polybius would find familiar, and he confronted the same puzzle about Rome's success in reforming its constitutional arrangements by trial and error. The body politic is rightly thought of as like the human body. It is usually essential to be born healthy, since just as a sickly child may, with luck and care, survive a long time, but never do much, so an ill-constructed state will never amount to much on the world stage. But Rome interests Machiavelli in the sixteenth century as it had Polybius and Cicero long before, because it violates that maxim. It went through several constitutional upheavals in its early years when it threw out its kings and adopted a republican constitution, and again when the secession of the plebs forced the ruling elite to open public offices to the lower classes. If it is harder to rebuild one's boat in midocean than to make it watertight before leaving shore, the Romans show that some people have the talent, energy, and good luck to get away with rebuilding on the voyage.

Writers on Machiavelli have debated at length what he thought he was claiming for himself when he claimed that in writing the *Discourses* he was traveling "a new route."[27] He says that he is using historical evidence properly, a thing that "the proud indolence" of these Christian states prevents Italian rulers from doing. It is not clear who these indolent princes are, nor what he thinks distinguishes his use of history from that of previous writers. To the extent that he commits himself to any principle more profound than a contempt for anyone who confuses analysis with moralizing, he echoes Thucydides. Human nature is the same at all times and places, so whatever has happened in the past can be emulated if worth emulating or avoided if it should be avoided. He comments on the absurdity of contemporary aristocrats and rich men who dig up antique statues and have modern copies made of them, but who do not see how much more valuable it would be to understand the actions and ideas of great political and military leaders of the ancient world and learn how to copy them. Indeed, his great complaint appears to be that the majority of those who read history "take pleasure in the variety of events which history relates, without ever thinking of imitating the noble actions, deeming that not only difficult but impossible, as though heaven, the sun, the elements, and men had changed their motions and power, and were different from what they were in ancient times."[28] Machiavelli is not a writer who excites the desire to carp, but his reliance on the uniformity of human nature to underpin what one might describe as the method of "look, analyze, copy" seems on its face to consort badly with his recognition that circumstances change and that we had better change with them. The one thing for which we ought not to reproach him is a failure to appreciate that the cultural, religious, and social *milieu* of the ancient world was too unlike that of Renaissance Italy for "look, analyze, copy" to work. Social thinkers in the nineteenth century ascribed many of the disasters of the French Revolution to the sheer impossibility that eighteenth-century Parisians should be like Romans of the third century BCE. It is not obvious that the complaint has the same force in an Italian city-state three centuries earlier.

Machiavelli's detachment from conventional moralizing has tempted commentators to think that the novelty is that Machiavelli set out to practice what later ages would recognize as political science, an inductively based comparative inquiry into what methods work where, when, and how. This is wholly implausible. Apart from Machiavelli's toleration of internal contradiction, as when he says at one point that Rome was poor and at another that Rome was rich, there is nothing to suggest he had such a conception of science. It would have been surprising if he had, since it would have antedated the scientific self-consciousness of natural scientists themselves by two centuries. Other commentators have made much of his seeming endorsement of the cyclical theory of history that appears in Plato's *Republic* and was borrowed for his own purposes by Polybius.

The *Discourses* is certainly Polybian at the level of style and intellectual concerns, even though Polybius was reflecting on events in his own lifetime whereas Machiavelli is commenting on Livy's account of the foundation and growth of the early republic. Polybius's historical style, and the pleasure he takes in men's securing their ends by deft acts of deceit is very like Machiavelli's; nonetheless, the so-called cyclical theory of history is neither a theory nor very cyclical. What it offers Machiavelli is reinforcement for his conviction that the wheel of fate turns unpredictably. Princes of sufficient flair and republics with good laws allied to good arms can master necessity for a time, but the historical judgment to which Machiavelli is most attached is that success breeds failure, because in the end the imperial republic is corrupted by wealth. And like Polybius, Machiavelli leaves the reader unsure whether chance, *tyche*, or *fortuna* is an active force in history.

Machiavelli does what he does in *The Prince*, which is offer prudential maxims illustrated and defended by appeal to historical events. Machiavelli's reputation as a "teacher of evil" rested on *The Prince*, but his insistence that when the means accuse, the end must excuse is every bit as prominent in the *Discourses*, which is indeed where the aphorism comes from. Machiavelli adopts what would be an uncompromisingly republican standpoint, except that it is *either* republics *or* kingdoms that men are praised for founding; what is indefensible is the institution of a tyranny. How far that conflicts with *The Prince* is an open question; there Machiavelli seems almost to take the view that Hobbes later made famous, that tyranny is but "monarchy misliked." It seems that he thought it perfectly proper to adopt dictatorial methods in emergency as the Romans did, but perfectly intolerable to establish an enduring tyranny. That, after all, is the moral of his defense of Romulus's actions in slaying Remus; one must do whatever it takes to get a political society up and running, but the tyrant is the enemy of his people, is rightly killed by whoever can do it, and is the polar opposite of the lawful ruler. Machiavelli's views on tyranny are conventional in the classical tradition, but decidedly non-Pauline.

For all that, he is committed to the view that only autocrats can institute or restore a state. There must be a founding moment when the new order is laid down, just as there must be a similar moment if a state is rescued by being returned to its first principles in a revolutionary reconstitution. Moses, Romulus, and Theseus are the heroes of both *The Prince* and the *Discourses*. But the emphasis in the *Discourses* falls on what Machiavelli describes as *ordini*, which is not rendered absolutely faithfully as "laws"; much as Rousseau does later, when he appears to distinguish between the fundamental laws of a political system and "decrees," so Machiavelli seems to have in mind something very like the laws that define the constitutional order. It is an idea with which states with written constitutions are wholly familiar, and indeed the constitution of

Germany today is called the "Basic Law." Beginnings are very different from sustainings; the irregular, often violent, and improvised actions of the founder hero must be succeeded by the regular election of leaders according to law.

The element that is hardly touched on in *The Prince* but is very prominent in the *Discourses* is religion. The Romans are praised for taking religion both seriously and unseriously. They took religion seriously in the sense that they understood the importance of religion as social cement. It is a useful aid to public morality; it urges courage in battle; it reinforces the respect for ancestors and affection for children on which solidarity across generations depends. Christianity is on the whole ill suited for such purposes; being other-worldly, it takes people's minds off their political and military duties and makes them attend only to their own salvation. It is a milk and water religion, urging its adherents to turn the other cheek. The Romans were not known for turning the other cheek. Educated Romans did not take religion seriously as a matter of metaphysics; metaphysics was for philosophers, not for the man in the street, let alone for the legionary. A relaxed view of the truth of religion allowed the leaders of Roman society to manipulate the practices and rituals of Roman religious observance as they needed. It was wise to ensure that the auguries before battle predicted success, and a competent commander would know how to do it. However, it was also essential that common soldiers treated the auguries with respect and that anyone who insulted them was promptly executed.

Machiavelli's animus is directed at the institution of the papacy rather than at Christianity or at other nonpagan religions. Chapter 12 of the *Discourses* is entitled "The Importance of Giving Religion a Prominent Influence in a State; and How Italy Was Ruined Because She Failed in This Respect through the Influence of the Church of Rome."[29] Early Christianity could have provided the basis for social cohesion, loyalty, good morals, and public spirit; but early sixteenth-century Italy shows what happens if there is an institution in the midst of society that is both corrupt considered as a religious institution—which sickens all of what passes for religion, and makes them irreligious—and inept as a political institution—one that has lost its grip on its possessions and has invited foreign powers into Italy, to the detriment both of its own subjects and those of all the other Italian states. It is observations such as these that got Machiavelli's works onto the Index.

Three further doctrines of the *Discourses* bear examination, since they had a considerable impact on republican thought and are by no means a reworking of commonplaces. One is Machiavelli's claim that a certain amount of uproar in a republic is conducive to liberty. There seems to be no prior defense of this proposition, and it is at odds with the entire tendency of Christian thinking, with its emphasis on harmony; it is at odds also with the utopian tradition running back to Plato's *Republic* and with all previous republican thinking. It must certainly be true that all defenders of mixed constitutions rely on the common people, or whatever proportion of them they include in "the people" to stand up for their own political rights; if they did not do so, they could not fulfill their role in the system of checks and balances. All classical writers— Aristotle, Polybius, and Cicero among them—took it for granted that they would do so, and were less afraid that they might be too passive than that they would get out of hand. Machiavelli's doctrine is perfectly clear, and offered as a novelty. The secession of the plebeians forced the ruling elite to take seriously the fact that the lower classes fed the city and kept the elite clothed and housed; it encouraged the lower classes to insist on their rights and privileges in the Roman state. It therefore gave notice to those who might oppress them that they would not stand for it, and so preserved liberty.[30] Indeed, continued class conflict and the permanent tension between the upper and lower classes made Rome both powerful and free. We need not accept this rosy view of the freedom available to the Roman lower classes to see the point; it was made by Edmund Burke and many others long afterward. It was shocking to Machiavelli's contemporaries, who thought that endorsing the usefulness of uproar was, in the conditions of early sixteenth-century Italy, much like pouring oil on a raging fire; had they looked north to Reformation Germany, they might have taken an equally cool view about the virtues of disputatiousness.

A second idea that makes a reappearance in republican writers thereafter is Machiavelli's defense of the popular republic against the aristocratic republic. The argument is intricately wound in with another about the merits of a republic designed for longevity as against one designed for increase. The Roman Republic was an expansive republic, and Machiavelli admired it for that reason. Even though Venice had acquired a maritime empire in the Adriatic and beyond, and substantial territories in the terra firma, it was a republic designed for longevity. Machiavelli's passion for a state that cut a great figure on the stage of world events led him to side with Rome against Venice. The defense of a popular rather than an aristocratic republic is not really an argument about the virtues of Rome in particular, but a defense of Florentine populism against Venetian narrowness. The argument runs thus: republics are endangered by "gentlemen"—there are many synonyms, such as *nobili* or *grandi*—who are defined by Machiavelli not simply as men who are rich or wellborn but as those with the vices of feudal landowners. These vices, as in More's *Utopia*, center on their keeping large numbers of retainers who are a threat to the peace both when they are employed to further the political ambitions of their masters and when they have been dismissed from his service and know no way to make a living save banditry. It is the ability of the *grandi* and *nobili* to raise private armies and subvert the state that alarms him; on this matter he and Cicero would speak with one voice.

Venice seemed to be a puzzle because it was aristocratic but had not been ruined by the ruling aristocracy. Venice practiced *guberno stretto*, a "narrow" regime in which eligibility for office was confined to the descendants of those who had been eligible when the Great Council was "closed" in 1297, at the end of a long series of earlier reforms; it was an aristocratic republic, managed by a narrow oligarchy. Florence had adopted *guberno largo*, a "wide" regime, to keep the aristocrats in check and ensure that decisions on taxation and other important matters were made by a wider rather than a smaller body of citizens. In abolishing the Great Council on their return in 1512 and physically destroying the hall in which it met, the Medici were announcing that they would govern as de facto princes behind a republican screen, and that the screen would be an aristocratic rather than a popular republic. Machiavelli's puzzle was to explain why Venice had not been ruined by its gentlemen. His answer was that they were not gentlemen except in name. They were rich merchants whose wealth was in money and goods. As long as traders remain traders, they pose no threat to the republic. They cannot prosper by reducing their fellow citizens to servitude, and they have no interest in maintaining private armies on the landed estates that ex hypothesi they do not have. Later political sociologists agreed.

Finally, then, the fatal question and the third of Machiavelli's surprising thoughts. Like Polybius, Machiavelli thinks that success cannot endure indefinitely, and like Hume after him, he thinks the works of man are destined to decay, no matter what. Within a dozen pages of the end of the *Discourses*, Machiavelli is still insisting that if "on the decision to be taken wholly depends the safety of one's country, no attention should be paid either to justice or to injustice, to kindness or to cruelty, or to its being praiseworthy or ignominious. On the contrary, every other consideration being set aside, that alternative should be wholeheartedly adopted which will save the life and preserve the freedom of one's country."[31] Over and over, he insists that half measures always lead to ruin, that boldness often achieves what caution cannot, as though the cultivation of Roman dash and vigor will carry everything before it. Yet he also says that success is self-defeating, that no republic can last forever, that corruption will always attend the achievement of great things.

A successful republic will acquire more territory, incorporate more citizens, become prosperous. When it becomes prosperous, people will begin to turn in on themselves and think about their own wealth rather than the good of the republic. The martial virtues will decline, and taste for soft living will creep in. Mercenaries will be hired to replace citizen-soldiers. The very rich will think how they can turn their wealth into power, and so subvert the republic. The ordinary people will remain uncorrupted longer than their betters, but they, too, can be suborned and turned into willing accomplices of the men who offer them a share of the loot or an exemption from the demands of the republic. Then there will be the decline and fall that the Roman Republic went through. A strong man lives longer than an unhealthy one, but both die in the end; and so it is with states. Readers' reactions to Machiavelli depend heavily on their reactions to such banal, but important, truths about human existence. It is clear that Machiavelli thought that life was for the living and that death was its inevitable companion; and by the same token that the world of politics had its own raison d'être, which only the fainthearted or slow-footed would fail to be moved by. Those who were neither fainthearted nor slow-footed but who marched to a different drummer could always retire to a monastery and contemplate eternal verities. It does not seem that Machiavelli would have condemned them for so doing; but he had nothing to say to them.

NOTES TO BOOK ONE

CHAPTER 1: WHY HERODOTUS?

1. Aristotle, *The Politics* (I.7), p. 19.
2. Herodotus, *The Histories*, pp. 449–50.
3. Thucydides, *Peloponnesian War*, p. 107.
4. Cartledge, *Thermopylae*, passim.
5. Thucydides, *Peloponnesian War*, p. 92.
6. Ibid.
7. Ibid., p. 97.
8. Ibid., p. 295.
9. Madison, Hamilton, and Jay, *The Federalist Papers*, pp. 122, 152, 292.
10. Plato, *Apology*, in *The Last Days of Socrates*, pp. 56–57, 64–65; Xenophon, *Socrates's Defence*, in *Conversations of Socrates*, pp. 41–49.
11. Plato, *Crito*, in *The Last Days of Socrates*, pp. 94–96; Xenophon, *Conversations of Socrates*, p. 195.

CHAPTER 2: PLATO AND ANTIPOLITICS

1. Wolin, *Politics and Vision*, pp. 27ff.
2. Marx and Engels, *The Communist Manifesto*, p. 244.
3. Aristotle, *The Politics* (2.2), p. 31.
4. Ibid. (2.6), pp. 39–43.
5. Xenophon, *Conversations of Socrates*, passim.

6. The story is told in Plato's *Seventh Letter*, p. 113; Xenophon, *Conversations of Socrates*, p. 195.

7. Xenophon, *Socrates's Defence*, in *Conversations of Socrates*, pp. 47–48.

8. Aristophanes, *Clouds*, p. 23.

9. Plato, *Gorgias*, pp. 32–33.

10. Ibid., p. 76.

11. Plato, *The Republic*, p. 50.

12. Nietzsche, *On the Genealogy of Morality*, pp. 28–29.

13. For instance, Frank, *Passions within Reason*; and for other primates, Frans de Waal, *Good Natured*.

14. Huxley, *Brave New World*, pp. 35–36.

15. Hobbes, *Leviathan*, pp. 86–87.

CHAPTER 3: ARISTOTLE: POLITICS IS NOT PHILOSOPHY

1. Aristotle, *The Politics* (1.4–7, slaves; 12–13, women), pp. 12–15, 27–30.

2. Ibid. (1.12), p. 27.

3. Ibid. (1.7), p. 19.

4. Ibid. (1.2), p. 13.

5. Though some commentators think the conventional ordering of *Politics* is anyway not what Aristotle originally intended.

6. Aristotle, *Politics* (7.2), pp. 168–69.

7. Ibid. (1.2), p. 8.

8. Locke, *Second Treatise* (sections 89–90), in *Two Treatises of Government*, pp. 325–26.

9. Aristotle, *Politics* (1.5), p. 17.

10. Ibid. (7.2), p. 181.

11. Ibid. (1.4), p. 15.

12. Ibid. (7.7), p. 175.

13. Ibid. (1.10), p. 25.

14. Ibid. (4.6), p. 100.

15. Ibid. (7.10), pp. 180–81.

16. Ibid. (3.13), pp. 80–83.

17. Ibid. (3.1), p. 62.

18. Thucydides, *The Peloponnesian War*, pp. 164–72.

19. Aristotle, *Politics* (3.7), p. 71.

20. Ibid. (4.9), pp. 104–5.

21. Lipset, *Political Man*, foreword, pp. 7–10.

22. Hobbes, *Leviathan*, p. 119.

CHAPTER 4: ROMAN INSIGHTS: POLYBIUS AND CICERO

1. Seneca, *De brevitate vitae*, 5.I.
2. *De legibus*, too, is set in his country villa at Tusculum.
3. Polybius, *The Rise of the Roman Empire*, p. 342.
4. Plato, *Gorgias*, p. 140.
5. Aristotle, *The Politics* (4.6), pp. I00–I0I.
6. *The Ethics of Aristotle* (1.3), p. 28.
7. Polybius, *Rise of the Roman Empire* (bk. 6), pp. 302–52.
8. Aristotle, *Politics* (2.6), p. 42.
9. Ibid. (4.8–9), pp. I02–5.
10. Machiavelli, *Discourses on Livy* (1.1–6), pp. 19–38.
11. Polybius, *Rise of the Roman Empire*, p. 342.
12. Ibid., pp. 342–44.
13. Cicero, *On the Commonwealth*, p. 32.
14. Berlin, "Two Concepts of Liberty," in *Four Essays on Liberty*, for the distinction.
15. Wood, *Empire of Liberty*, p. 20.
16. Cicero, *On Duties*, pp. 142–44.
17. Ibid., p. 19.
18. Machiavelli, *The Prince*, pp. 61, 68–69.

CHAPTER 5: AUGUSTINE'S TWO CITIES

1. Romans 13:1–7.
2. Augustine, *The City of God* (21.14), p. 1072.
3. Brown, *Augustine of Hippo*, p. 39.
4. Ibid., pp. 151ff.
5. Herrin, *The Formation of Christendom*.
6. Dewey, *A Common Faith*, in *Later Works*, 9:3–20 ("Religion versus the Religious").
7. Lane Fox, *Pagans and Christians*, emphasizes the point throughout.
8. Brown, *Augustine of Hippo*, pp. 35ff.
9. Augustine, *Confessions* (5.5–10), pp. 76–85.
10. Ibid. (1.10), p. 9.
11. Ibid. (7.9–13), pp. 121–26.
12. By Peter Brown, quoted in the introduction to *City of God*, p. xiv.
13. Augustine, *City of God* (5.24), pp. 231–32.
14. Lane Fox, *Pagans and Christians*, pp. 37ff.
15. Cicero, *On the Commonwealth*, pp. 59–60.
16. Augustine, *City of God* (1.9), pp. 13ff.

17. Augustine, *Confessions* (2.9–17), pp. 28–34.
18. Augustine, *City of God* (14.26), pp. 628–29.
19. Ibid. (5.17), p. 217.
20. Augustine, *Confessions* (1.7), p. 9.
21. Hobbes, *Leviathan*, chaps. 30 et seq.
22. Augustine, *City of God* (5.26), p. 235.
23. Ibid.
24. Ibid. (14.23–24), pp. 623–27.
25. Ibid. (1.19–20), pp. 29–33.
26. Ibid.
27. Ibid. (2.21), p. 80.
28. Ibid. (19.21), pp. 950–52.
29. Ibid. (4.15), p. 161.
30. Ibid. (19.6), p. 928.
31. Ibid. (19.16), pp. 944–45.
32. Ibid. (19.6), pp. 926–28.

PREFACE TO PART II

1. Hume, "The Independency of Parliament," in *Political Essays*, p. 24.
2. Russell, *Autobiography*, pp. 333–35.
3. Augustine, *City of God* (5.17), p. 218.

CHAPTER 6: BETWEEN AUGUSTINE AND AQUINAS

1. Most famously articulated in Ullman, *A History of Political Thought in the Middle Ages*, pp. 12ff.
2. As always, Romans 13 is the key text.
3. Augustine, *City of God* (19.17), pp. 945–46.
4. Ibid.
5. Ibid. (1.17–20), pp. 26–33.
6. Lane Fox, *Pagans and Christians*, pp. 418–27.
7. See John of Salisbury, *Policraticus*, below, pp. 219–23.
8. The Declaration of Right, February 1689.
9. Locke, *Second Treatise* (sec. 242), in *Two Treatises of Government*, p. 427.
10. Matthew 16:19.
11. Augustine, *City of God* (5.23), p. 235.
12. Matthew 22:21.
13. Aristotle, *Ethics* (5.7), p. 158.

14. *History of Sir Charles Napier's Administration of the Province of Scinde*, p. 35.

15. I Timothy 6:10.

16. Locke, *First Treatise* (sec. 42), in *Two Treatises of Government*, p. 170; Hume, *Enquiries concerning Human Understanding and concerning the Principles of Morals*, pp. 186–87.

17. Garnsey, *Thinking about Property*, pp. 217–18.

18. Gibbon, *Decline and Fall of the Roman Empire*, 6:16.

19. Ibn Khaldun, *The Muqadimmah*.

20. Burns, ed., *Cambridge History of Medieval Political Thought*, pp. 605–6.

21. Quoted ibid., pp. 288–89.

22. Haskins, *The Renaissance of the Twelfth Century*.

23. E.g., John of Salisbury, *Policraticus* (8.17), pp. 190ff.

24. Fortescue, *On the Laws and Governance of England*, p. xxxii.

25. John of Salisbury, *Policraticus* (4.1), pp. 27–30.

26. Ibid. (8.19–20), pp. 210–13.

27. Ibid. (4.1), pp. 27–30.

CHAPTER 7: AQUINAS AND SYNTHESIS

1. Aquinas, *Political Writings*, pp. xviii–xxii.

2. *Aquinas on Politics and Ethics*, p. xvi.

3. Ibid., p. xix. The phrase comes from *Commentary on the Sentences of Peter Lombard*, II.

4. Aquinas, *Political Writings*, pp. xxiv–xxv.

5. Brian Tierney, *The Crisis of Church and State*, pp. 139–49.

6. Ibid., pp. 139–41; Ernst Kantorowicz, *Frederick the Second*.

7. Aristotle, *Politics* (1.4–7), pp. 16–19.

8. Aquinas, *Political Writings*, p. 207.

9. Ibid., pp. 5–6, 43–44.

10. Ibid., p. 9.

11. Ibid., pp. 4–6 et seq.

12. Ibid., p. 54.

13. Ibid., p. 3, quoting *City of God* (19.15), pp. 942–43.

14. Ibid., pp. 83ff.

15. Ibid., pp. 91–92.

16. Ibid., pp. 96–97, 126ff.

17. Ibid., pp. 220–34.

18. Ibid., p. 127.

19. Ibid., p. 208.

20. Ibid., pp. 216–17.

21. Locke, *First Treatise* (sec. 42), in *Two Treatises of Government*, p. 170.

22. Aquinas, *Political Writings*, p. 207.

23. Ibid., p. 240.

24. Ibid., p. 241.

25. Ibid., p. 244.

26. Ibid., pp. 277–78.

27. Ibid., p. 271.

28. Ibid., p. 270.

29. Ibid., pp. 267–69.

30. Ibid., pp. 276–77.

31. Ibid., p. 273.

32. Ibid., pp. 233ff.

CHAPTER 8: THE FOURTEENTH-CENTURY INTERREGNUM

1. Marsilius of Padua, *Defensor pacis*, pp. 72–73.

2. *The Inferno of Dante*, canto 3, line 60.

3. Tierney, *The Crisis of Church and State*, pp. 185–86.

4. Ibid., p. 187.

5. But Antony Black describes it as a "masterpiece" in *Political Thought in Europe*, p. 60.

6. Dante, *Monarchy* (1.4), pp. 8–9.

7. Ibid. (1.3), p. 7.

8. Ibid. (2.9), pp. 53–58.

9. Ibid. (3.10), pp. 80–81.

10. Ibid. (3.8), p. 75.

11. Marsilius of Padua, *Defensor pacis* (1.1.3), pp. 4–5.

12. Ibid. (1.2.1), p. 8.

13. Ibid. (1.13.3), p. 51.

14. Dahl, *A Preface to Democratic Theory*, pp. 63ff.

15. Marsilius of Padua, *Defensor pacis* (2.3.2ff.), pp. 109ff.

16. William of Ockham, *A Short Discourse on the Tyrannical Government*.

17. Nicholas of Cusa, *The Catholic Concordance*.

CHAPTER 9: HUMANISM

1. Baron, *In Search of Florentine Civic Humanism*; Grafton in Burns and Goldie, eds., *Cambridge History of Political Thought, 1450–1700*, pp. 15ff.

2. Machiavelli, "Exhortation," in *The Prince*, pp. 87–91.

3. E.g., Erasmus, *The Education of a Christian Prince*, below, pp. 302–6.

4. Christine de Pizan, *The City of Ladies*, pp. 1–2, 237–40.

5. Plato, *The Republic* (bk. 8), pp. 266ff.

6. Christine de Pizan, *The Book of the Body Politic* (3.1), p. 90.

7. Ibid. (3.4), p. 95.

8. Ibid. (1.1), p. 4.

9. Ibid. (1.7), pp. 12–14.

10. Ibid. (3.10), p. 107.

11. Plato, *Gorgias, Menexenus, Protagoras*, pp. 156–57.

12. Erasmus, *Education of a Christian Prince*, p. 1.

13. Ibid., p. 2.

14. Ibid., p. 15.

15. Ibid., p. 65.

16. Ibid., p. 83.

17. Ibid., p. 107.

18. Ibid., pp. 107–8.

19. Erasmus, *The Praise of Folly*, p. 8.

20. Ibid., pp 80–87.

21. Erasmus, *Education*, p. 15.

22. More, *Utopia*, pp. 106–7.

23. Edward Bellamy, *Looking Backward*, pp. 66ff.

24. More, *Utopia*, p. 94.

25. Ibid.

26. Ibid., pp. 79–81.

27. Michel de Montaigne, *Complete Essays*.

CHAPTER 10: THE REFORMATION

1. See above, p. 312, for Henry's defense of the sacraments against Luther.

2. Locke, *Letter concerning Toleration*, in *Selected Political Writings*, pp. 129–32.

3. Ibid., p. 135.

4. Romans 13:8.

5. Luther, "Freedom of a Christian," in *Selected Political Writings*, pp. 27ff.

6. John Man, *The Gutenberg Revolution*; Marshall McLuhan, *The Gutenberg Galaxy*.

7. Luther, "Freedom of a Christian," pp. 29–30.

8. Luther, "To the Christian Nobility," in *Selected Political Writings*, pp. 39–49.

9. *Luther and Calvin on Secular Authority*, p. 5.

10. Ibid.

11. Ibid., p. 4.

12. Ibid., p. 9.

13. Ibid., p. 15.

14. Luther, *Selected Political Writings*, p. 30.

15. Ibid., p. 29.

16. Ibid., p. 88.

17. Ibid., pp. 97–98.

18. Locke, *Second Treatise* (paragraphs 241–42), in *Two Treatises of Government*, p. 427.

19. *Luther and Calvin on Secular Authority*, p. 49.

20. Ibid., p. 82.

21. Norman Cohn, *The Pursuit of the Millennium*.

CHAPTER 11: MACHIAVELLI

1. Machiavelli, letter to Francesco Vettori, December 10, 1513, in *The Prince*, p. 93.

2. Burns and Goldie, eds., *Cambridge History of Political Thought, 1450–1700*, pp. 55–56.

3. Machiavelli, *Discourses on Livy* (I.9), pp. 138–39.

4. Machiavelli, "Dedicatory Letter," in *The Prince*, pp. 3–4.

5. Machiavelli, *The Prince*, p. 88.

6. Ibid., p. 5.

7. Ibid., pp. 6–14.

8. Ibid., p. 13.

9. Ibid., p. 9.

10. Comparing ibid., pp. 8 and 16.

11. Ibid., p. 21.

12. Who makes a cameo appearance in Max Beerbohm's wonderful spoof "'Savonarola' Brown" in *Seven Men*.

13. Machiavelli, *Discourses* (I.12), p. 152.

14. Machiavelli, *The Prince*, p. 25.

15. Ibid., p. 26.

16. Ibid., pp. 39–40.

17. Ibid., p. 40.

18. Ibid., pp. 51–52.

19. Machiavelli, *Discourses* (I.57), pp. 258ff.

20. Wolin, *Politics and Vision*, pp. 197–99.

21. Machiavelli, *The Prince*, pp. 61–62.

22. Ibid., pp. 84–85.

23. Ibid., p. 85.

24. Ibid., p. 86.
25. Ibid., p. 87.
26. Machiavelli, *Discourses* (I.27), pp. 185–86.
27. Ibid., introduction, pp. 103–5.
28. Ibid., p. 105.
29. Ibid., pp. 149–53.
30. Ibid. (1.4), pp. 118–20.
31. Ibid. (3.41), p. 528.

BOOK TWO

HOBBES TO THE PRESENT

Preface to Book Two

❧

A THEME OF THIS BOOK is that the essential elements both of modern political institutions themselves and of our attitudes toward them emerged gradually and fitfully. Our understanding of them generally followed their creation and emerged equally gradually and fitfully, but by no means always. Hegel argued that philosophy is essentially retrospective, but it is impossible not to be struck by insights that seem to have emerged from nowhere and illuminated not only their own time but ours as well. Thomas Hobbes, with whom this volume begins, was a considerable producer of such flashes of illumination. The impact of these insights on our ways of thinking is obviously greater than on political practice, and we must be careful not to exaggerate the role of political thinkers in the rise of the modern state. Not only that, but, as I argued earlier, many features of the state as we now understand it owed more to the papacy than to any secular state; the development of the secular state in medieval Europe was at least in part a reaction to developments in the administration of the church.

The institutional essence of the papacy was less geographical than legal; its identity was that of a corporate person, not physical. Its lifeblood was the canon law that set out the rules governing the conduct of everyone who acknowledged the authority of the church; the papal curia was an early model for modern bureaucracies. Although the papacy was, apart from the "Babylonian Captivity" of the Avignon papacy, located in Rome, and the Papal States were until their dissolution in 1871 governed directly or indirectly by the pope's agents, the fact that between 1871 and 1929 the papacy continued to exist and to exercise its traditional authority over members of the Roman Catholic Church, without possessing any sovereign territory of its own, suggests that a legal and administrative identity is at least as essential as a territorial one. The Latin description of the church as a *corpus mysticum* is misleading, insofar as it suggests to a modern reader something magical or supernatural about its identity; but a *corpus mysticum* is simply a corporation. In the crucial sense, the Ford Motor Company is a *corpus mysticum*, and so is every modern state. It is defined by a combination of a locus of authority, an account of the persons over whom that authority is exercised, and an account of what the purposes are of the combination of persons related to one another as members of the one corporate body.

Yet, of course, the modern state is not only a corporate entity; it is the corporate entity that uniquely claims a monopoly of coercive authority over everyone resident within its territory and commonly over its own citizens even when they are not physically present. Its territorial identity is essential to it. As long as there have been governments, one of their central tasks has been to maintain the territorial integrity of the state they ruled. It took all Pericles's powers of persuasion to unite the Athenians behind a strategy for the war against Sparta that abandoned the territory of Attica to the invaders. Machiavelli's despair at the inability of the disunited Italians of his day to prevent Spanish and French armies from traversing Italian territory at will is well known. It does not follow that the authority of the government has always been tied to the nationality or territorial origin of those who claim that authority; today it is almost unthinkable that a head of government could be other than a citizen of the country whose affairs he or she controls. When the early modern period opened, however, this was far from true. The dynastic principle that set Bourbon rulers against Habsburg rulers visualized authority as something close to a family possession, rather than in the modern fashion as something generated by the "nation" itself.

I refer to "the modern state" and to "modern understandings" of politics and government. It is impossible not to do so, but all periodization is in a high degree arbitrary. We might think that "the modern world" was born in October 1492 when Columbus arrived at the islands off the American coast that he misidentified as part of the Indies; we might think that it was when Luther nailed his ninety-five theses to the cathedral door in Wittenberg in October 1517; we might think it was when Galileo said *eppur si muove* (nonetheless, it moves) when forced to recant his Copernican heresy in 1633; we might think modernity had begun much earlier, perhaps in 1439, when Gutenberg invented movable type and set in train a publishing explosion that in due course led to an explosion of new ideas in religion, science, literature, and politics. Among thought-provoking suggestions about the birth of modernity, one is that the invention of reliable clocks created a new sense of time, allowed more effective coordination of activity, and in a roundabout fashion paved the way for the industrial revolution and the economic disciplines of the modern world. In a work on the history of political thought, it would be out of place to embark on a long dispute over the merits of contending claims of this sort, however much entertainment such arguments can yield. Nonetheless, some sense of the importance of the contributions of a changed geographical consciousness, the rise of a new science, religious upheaval, increased literacy, economic growth, improved military technology, and a great deal more to what we call the rise of the modern world is necessary, not least as a corrective to the temptation to see the history of political thinking as an encounter between texts, propelled by logic rather than passion.

For our purposes, modern ways of thinking about politics can without undue exaggeration be said to begin with Hobbes. It would be intellectual cowardice to shelter behind Hegel's claim that political science begins with Hobbes, let alone to accept at face value Hobbes's own boast that political science was no older than his *Leviathan*. After all, Machiavelli claimed to have invented a new method of political analysis, and if we were to scrutinize every thinker's claims of novelty, we would have a lengthy catalog to explore. The case for thinking that with Hobbes and his contemporaries modern political thinking really begins rests on several distinct bases, none sufficient on its own, but cumulatively persuasive.

The concept of the state of nature is one base. It was a novelty to suppose that the way to become clear about what a state is—what its legitimacy rests on, what the scope of its authority is, and what the rights and duties of its subjects are—is to imagine a world without a state. Or more exactly, perhaps, it was a novelty to employ the idea as a thought experiment, not as a fantasy about a lost golden age of innocence and spontaneous sociability. Not everyone thought that it was a fruitful innovation, and not everyone who appealed to the idea of a "natural" prepolitical condition agreed on what that condition was like; the most famous of such thinkers, Hobbes, Locke, and Rousseau, notoriously did not agree among themselves. Nonetheless, the thought that the state is importantly and interestingly artificial rather than natural takes the discussion of its purposes and its powers and their limits in new directions. Many reasons have been suggested to explain why the contrast between natural and artificial forms of organization should have become salient in this way; most are suggestive rather than compelling. One is that the almost incessant religious and other wars from the early 1500s onward had given everyone a strong sense of the role of sheer accident in politics. Who our rulers were, what faith they proposed we should profess, where the physical boundaries were drawn between one political entity and another—all seemed arbitrary.

The importance of European interactions with societies at a much lower level of technical, political, and military development as a result of the voyages of discovery that took explorers and merchants down the African coast and into the Indian Ocean to India and modern Indonesia and then across the Atlantic to the West Indies and America itself is equally obvious. The impact of a modern, well-armed, and technically increasingly competent civilization with peoples whose technology was that of the European stone age did appalling damage to populations who were enslaved, dispossessed of their lands, dispossessed of their culture, and subjected to the ravages of unfamiliar diseases against which they had no protection; it also gave some, if rather limited, empirical support to conjectures about the natural condition of mankind. The prepolitical condition was not a golden age of innocence, but at best one of hand-to-mouth existence, short lives, and ignorance. Viewed with our modern sensibilities, none of this entitled Europeans to behave toward simple societies as they did; nor did every writer from the sixteenth century to the nineteenth think that less technologically advanced societies were morally inferior to their more sophisticated oppressors.

The new scientific understanding of the world is an element whose role is not easy to pin down. Aristotle's universe was hierarchical through and through. Galileo's universe was in important ways "flat." God might have created the universe on rational lines, and man might be at the summit of creation because man shared in God's rationality. Nonetheless, social hierarchy was not built into the nature of the universe as it had been for Aristotle, say. The universality of the laws of physics was of a wholly different order from the near-universality of many social conventions. From none of this did it follow that nobody could give credence to, for instance, the divine right of kings. It is something of an intellectual puzzle that divine right absolute monarchy was such a prominent feature of seventeenth-century political life and political thought, but the fact itself is undeniable. It is tempting to think that the combination owed something to the suspicion that in the absence of an Aristotelian natural hierarchy of being, all order was a matter of fiat. God ordered the world; absolute monarchs ordered their subjects' lives.

What one might think of as the great tradition of European political thought begins with Hobbes ends with Marx. Everything that can be said about the impossibility of setting wholly defensible starting points to any sort of periodization can be said about the impossibility of setting wholly defensible end points. The thought that animates what follows is simple. In the writings of the theorists of the social contract, Hobbes, Locke, and Rousseau among them, the state is essentially the unifying element in a society; it is artificial, is legal, sustains the top-down authority that is implicit in the notion of legislation, and so on. This rather narrow conception of the nature of political order is evidently very different from what is implicit in classical political thought. The contrast between classical republican theorizing and the modern focus on the nature and origin of legal authority was clear enough to political thinkers in the seventeenth century to the nineteenth. Some of them tried to recover the older way of thinking about politics, some did their best to discredit any such thing; but others began to ask more historically nuanced questions about the conditions under which different forms of legal and political authority could be sustained. This was, in shorthand terms, the rise of political sociology, or sociology *tout court*. One effect was to make politics seem less autonomous than before.

Once attention was turned to the underlying social forces that at a minimum constrained and perhaps simply determined what political leaders could and did do, the thought, familiar since Aristotle, that "man is a political animal," however it was to be construed, became less compelling. Man was perhaps *homo faber*, a generally creative being whose creativity extended far beyond politics in any ordinary sense of the term. Less happily, he might be simply a productive animal, whose essence was the reproduction of the species. What one might term the rise of the social had other implications. Aristotle took it for granted that men, or at any rate the Greeks whom he knew, would be eager to take part in whatever activities citizenship in a polis implied. The rise of what one might term bourgeois comfort made that assumption less plausible. If private values, not selfish values, but family life, cultural activities of all sorts, activities that we can engage in without the assistance of the state and its agents, become unequivocally the most important aspects of our lives, and if our lives as workers and consumers come to seem obviously more central to existence than our lives as citizens and subjects, the way is open to imagine the eventual withering away of the state. The failure of that aspiration is only one of the political tragedies that will occupy the final part of this book.

PART I

❧

MODERNITY

CHAPTER 12

Thomas Hobbes

Modernity

WHEN VIRGINIA WOOLF WROTE that "on or about December 1910, human nature changed," she was being playful and provocative. When historians of ideas and political theorists debate whether it is Hobbes or Machiavelli, or neither, who is to be counted as the first "modern" political thinker, they are usually being wholly serious. This is not to say that any particular candidate is universally accepted as the first modern thinker or that the question is universally thought to make a great deal of sense; the grounds for proposing one or another writer as the first modern thinker necessarily implies a debatable view of what constitutes "modernity." It is unfair to both Machiavelli and Hobbes to attempt an evenhanded resolution of such a debate; Machiavelli praised himself for bringing a "new method" to the discussion of politics, and Hobbes declared that political science was no older than *Leviathan*. The view that animates this part of the book is that to the extent that the question makes sense, modernity begins with Hobbes. The grounds for skepticism about the question are many, not least among them the hankering after the political practices of the ancient world that persists to this day.

The thought that modernity begins with Hobbes is this. Machiavelli was essentially a backward-looking figure. His ideal of a successful political regime was the Roman Republic. His ideas about what made Rome the success it was were much the same as Polybius's and would not have surprised Pericles. Rome was stable, law-abiding, the military superior of any power on earth; its citizens were loyal, public-spirited, courageous, and self-disciplined. Machiavelli says nothing about the intellectual, literary, artistic, or architectural glories of Rome, other than to complain that his contemporaries copied statues but did not copy great men. Although his *Discourses* is a commentary on Livy's *History of Rome*, Machiavelli does not have the modern sense of history as an irreversible process in which our forebears become increasingly remote from us and decreasingly intelligible to us. History is a storehouse of *exempla*, and the underlying thought is that what has worked in one time and place will work everywhere.

Although Hobbes does not appeal to the idea of progress as later writers did, and does not write the panegyrics to the value of science in easing man's estate that his former employer Francis Bacon did, he has a clear sense that the difference between the civilized and the uncivilized worlds—between seventeenth-century England and the world of contemporary Native Americans, for instance—was political, intellectual, and in a broad sense technological. Machiavelli was skeptical about the value of gunpowder because the Romans had not known of it. Hobbes had no doubt that seventeenth-century men knew a great deal more than their forebears.

The thought that it is not Hobbes but Machiavelli who marks the arrival of modern ways of thinking about politics is by no means foolish. At least two ways of defending it make very good sense. The first is to see Machiavelli as announcing the autonomy of politics as a human activity with its own rules and its own standards of success, standards not drawn from natural law or from an overarching Christian cosmology. On this view, what the classical and the medieval worlds have in common, at least in the works of political philosophers, is a moral and metaphysical framework, within which politics is to be judged by transcendental standards, not by worldly success alone. What Machiavelli insists on is that the political realm is all about acquiring, holding, and using power.

Success is a matter of technique, and political analysis is the analysis of these techniques. The second essentially elaborates on this thought, paying less attention to the idea of the autonomy of the political realm, and more to the breach with older notions of mankind's being subject to a natural law that set standards of legitimacy for private as well as public conduct. These ideas have some force, even if it is hard to think of any piece of wickedness that Machiavelli condones when it is necessitated by the demands of either the safety of the state as a whole, or the security of the ruler in particular, that is not also condoned by older writers. The natural law that the Athenians appealed to in answering the Melians was not an overarching moral law in the Christian or the Stoic sense; it was the rule of brutal *raison d'état* that Machiavelli is often credited with having invented. If we should think of Hobbes as marking the birth of modern ways of thinking about politics, and we think that a new view of natural law is part of that, then Hobbes's highly articulate account of the laws of nature and their philosophical status is in a wholly different category from Machiavelli's silent ignoring of such arguments.

Life and Times

Thomas Hobbes is the greatest of British political thinkers, and the boldest, most exciting, and most compelling writer on politics in the English language. He is not the best loved or the most sensible; but even his enemies, of whom he had many, acknowledged that he wrote better than all his virtuous opponents put together. It was neither the first nor the last time the devil had the best tunes. Whether Hobbes was surprised by their hostility is anyone's guess. He claimed that anyone who read his work with an unprejudiced mind would be compelled to believe it; the fact that they did not was dismissed with the observation that "when reason is against a man, he will be against reason," which was not calculated to make friends. He was born prematurely on Good Friday, 1588; his mother was frightened by the rumor—unfounded then but true in September—that the Spanish Armada had been sighted in the Channel, and went into labor. "And hereupon my Mother dear, did bring forth twins, both me and fear" was Hobbes's later comment on this beginning, and "feare is the motive to rely on" the watchword of his masterpiece, *Leviathan*, published in 1651.[1]

He was born in Malmesbury, Wiltshire, where his father was a country clergyman, of few intellectual attainments. He had a violent temper; one day he struck a parishioner at the church door, fled his parish, and died "beyond London."[2] An uncle sent Thomas to the local grammar school and then to Oxford. It was the route for a bright boy with no money. He might become a clergyman or lawyer or the confidential secretary of an aristocrat, or tutor to an aristocrat's son. Of Hobbes's undergraduate career nothing is known, save that he had a taste for snaring birds with pieces of cheese attached to limed string.[3] Later relations with Oxford were bad. He engaged in unedifying debates with Robert Boyle over the possibility of a vacuum, and with John Wallis over the possibility of squaring the circle. The chancellor of the university, the earl of Clarendon, wrote a large volume attacking *Leviathan*, and after Hobbes's death the university condemned his writings and burned them in the quadrangle of the Bodleian Library.[4]

After Oxford he became tutor and chaperone to the son of the earl of Devonshire and, with a break during the civil war, remained with the Cavendish family for the rest of his life. He taught the young man Latin, Greek, mathematics, and history, the accomplishments of a gentleman. He also spent an unconscionable time borrowing money on his master's behalf during their tour of Europe in the 1630s; the downside was waiting in the rain for his money, the upside, spending long hours in other men's libraries, in one of which he read Euclid and fell in love with geometry.[5] Hobbes's first political work was a gift to his employer: a translation of Thucydides's *History of the Peloponnesian War*. He thought it highly relevant to his own times. Thucydides was an effective critic of Athenian democracy, and Hobbes never shed his antipathy to popular government.

Soon afterward, Hobbes changed his mind about the route to political wisdom. Thucydides taught the lessons of history. Hobbes now sought an ahistorical science that would demonstrate from first principles the essence of political authority and what rulers and subjects must do to avoid war and secure peace and prosperity. In 1642, as the civil war was breaking out, a work entitled *The Elements of Law*, which he had written in the previous year, was published without his consent. The book implied that Parliament had no case against the king; Hobbes was terrified that Parliament would imprison or kill him. He fled to France and attached himself to the court of the Prince of Wales, the future Charles II, whose (rather unsuccessful) tutor he was for a time.

The fortunes of the royal and parliamentarian sides ebbed and flowed during the war, and the parliamentarians emerged victorious in 1647. After Charles escaped captivity and tried to recover his throne, he was definitively defeated, tried for treason, and executed on January 30, 1650. To many royalists, this was martyrdom, the blasphemous murder of the Lord's anointed. Hobbes concluded that the royalist game was up and that sensible people must make their peace with the government of Oliver Cromwell. It was then that Hobbes wrote *Leviathan*, which many readers today read as a defense of absolute monarchy, but which was a defense not of *monarchy* but of absolute *authority* in whatever person or persons it was vested. Hobbes certainly thought that monarchy was the best form of government, but he did not think that it was possible to demonstrate it. What he thought he had demonstrated was that political authority must be absolute. The moral of *Leviathan* was that subjects had a duty to obey and assist any regime that would guarantee peace and would allow them to prosper by their own efforts. If Cromwell's protectorate would make peace with him, he would make peace with it. Hobbes had been desperately ill in Paris; he was in his sixties and felt very old; he wanted to go home. When the protectorate offered amnesty and the restoration of property to anyone who would "engage," that is, swear allegiance to the new government, Hobbes went home.

Charles II did not bear him a grudge. At the Restoration in 1660, he invited Hobbes to court and made a pet of his old teacher, who was widely acknowledged to be a considerable wit. But after a few years, Hobbes fell afoul of the church; he was a sharp critic of the pretensions of the clergy, while they thought he corrupted the morals of the court and its hangers-on. His unorthodox opinions made him an easy target, and there was a move to have him tried for heresy. It was an open question whether the medieval statute *De heretico comburendo*—"Of the burning of heretics"—was valid law, but Hobbes, who prided himself on his timidity, did not want to test it. He retired to the country, where he was sheltered by the Devonshires at Chatsworth; he died there in 1679, at the age of ninety. It was unkind of the University of Oxford to burn his works as a second best to burning their author, because Hobbes ends *Leviathan* with the hope that his doctrines would be ordered to be taught in the universities "from whence the Preachers, and the Gentry, drawing such water as they find, use to sprinkle the same (both from the Pulpit and in their Conversation) upon the People."[6] Three centuries later, Hobbes is remembered and the time-serving reactionaries who burned his books are not.

The First Political Scientist?

Hobbes claimed that the science of politics was no older than himself. Before him, historians and rhetoricians—Cicero, Machiavelli, or Erasmus—gave advice based on historical evidence, engaged in simple moral exhortation, or showed off their rhetorical skills. Hobbes claimed to be the first to put the understanding of politics on a scientific basis. He thought that the chief obstacle to the creation of a genuine science of politics was the self-interest of Scholastic philosophers, priests and professors, rhetoricians, and obscurantists. His particular bugbears were those who wanted to revive the ancient republics and Roman *libertas* and those who wanted to derive political authority from religion, whether bishops of the Church of England, the pope, or the assorted self-proclaimed prophets who had sprung up during the civil war. To understand Hobbes as he would have wished, we must explore this claim.

Hobbes's life was deeply affected by two revolutions, one the civil war of the 1640s, the other the intellectual revolution associated with Galileo, Descartes, and English scientists such as Robert Hooke, William Harvey, and Robert Boyle. The first led him to think that any society in which there was doubt over the location of authority and its extent was doomed to civil war; if it avoided it, it was only by good luck. *Leviathan* spelled out Hobbes's argument that the unity of a state consisted in the location of an absolute and arbitrary legislative and executive authority in one person or body of persons; the sovereign (who might be one person, several persons, or the entire political community) possessed unlimited legal authority, and subjects were obliged to obey it in everything that did not threaten their lives or require them to deny Christ. Even if they were required to deny Christ, they should do so, trusting God to know what was in their hearts.[7] We should first place *Leviathan* in the context of Hobbes's intellectual allegiances, then very briefly explore Hobbes's idea of "science." The modern reader is apt to be puzzled that Hobbes thought geometry was a science and to wonder what sort of science Hobbes's theory of politics is. Then we can analyze the central argument of *Leviathan*, which takes the reader from a contentious account of human nature through a contentious picture of the state of nature and on to a still more contentious claim about the need to establish a sovereign authority with absolute and arbitrary power to determine and enforce law. Finally, we should notice how Hobbes makes his claims a lot less alarming by reminding us that a prudent government will do much that it is not legally obliged to do, and will not do much that it is legally entitled to do.

Hobbes's intellectual history and allegiances were complex. As a young man he hoped to make his name as a man of letters; his translation of Thucydides's *History of the Peloponnesian War* and his numerous later Latin poems, including a Latin *Autobiography*, are accomplished and vigorous. After his famous encounter with geometry, and his discovery of the new physical science, he became passionate about optics, but also got into academic scrapes and quarrels in which he came out badly, particularly in controversy with Wallis over the squaring of the circle and with Boyle over the possibility of the vacuum.[8] For our purposes, Hobbes's literary achievements and the deficiencies of his understanding of the new physics matter only insofar as they suggest that Hobbes was pitched into becoming a political theorist by events, and that he was telling the truth when he said that he would rather have lived in quiet times and studied optics.

Leviathan is one of the greatest works of political theory ever penned, but it gives a misleading impression of Hobbes's intellectual attachments. *Leviathan* praises political *science* at the expense of what Hobbes calls "prudence."[9] "Prudence" was Hobbes's term for classical statecraft, the attempt to derive maxims of sound political conduct from the analysis of history and the observation of how people behave in difficult situations. It is what Aristotle sometimes, and Thucydides, Polybius, and Machiavelli always, engaged in. Classical statecraft was defended against Hobbes by his contemporary Sir James Harrington, and afterward by David Hume and others. Hobbes was not an unequivocal critic of a politics based on historical analysis and empirical observation. He not only translated Thucydides in 1629 but engaged in some Thucydidean history of his own after the civil war. To *Leviathan* he added *Behemoth*, a little-read volume, to provide what he called "an historical narration" of the civil wars. It is there that he complains that careless readers of the classics have acquired views on tyrannicide that threaten the peace.[10]

Hobbes's ambivalent reactions to historical writing for political purposes had a simple basis. He thought that Thucydides was "the most politic historiographer that ever writ," and agreed with him that democracy was an intrinsically unsound form of government, not least because democracies got into self-destructive wars and were prone to faction and dissension. But history was put to dangerous uses in seventeenth-century England. Republican writers were moved by their reading of history to advocate tyrannicide; others claimed that the lesson of history was that political freedom existed only in popular republics. Most writers other than himself, he thought, were not thinkers; they decorated their political prejudices with historical allusions to show how well-read they were. They allowed rhetoric to substitute for thought. The attack seems paradoxical: *Leviathan* is itself a masterpiece of well-turned rhetoric. That was no accident; rhetoric was acceptable as the servant of reason. If his discovery of the principles of political science was as original as he thought, rhetoric would make his new science more digestible. What made it science, however, was logical cogency, not literary attractiveness.

Hobbes's first political work in his mature style was *The Elements of Law*. He had imagined a longer work, in three portions, inspired by his encounter with Descartes and his circle in Paris during the 1630s when he and his young master were touring Europe. It was to be in Latin and consist of sections on the nature of physical objects (*De corpore*), on man (*De homine*), and on the citizen (*De cive*); in the end, the third section appeared in 1642 in English as *The Elements of Law*, the first and second only in 1655 and 1658. The work that was published as *De cive* in 1642 and 1647 is more nearly a first draft of *Leviathan*. Hobbes feared that his hostility to the pretensions of Parliament might endanger his life, but his skeptical and secular defense of absolute monarchy was as unwelcome to those who believed that Charles I was king by divine right as his assaults on Parliament were to the friends of popular government. His assault on the idea that a state aims at "liberty" for its citizens implied that subjection to law, like all other forms of subjection, including slavery, is simply inconsistent with liberty. Nobody except its author could be happy with that conclusion. *De cive* was written in Latin in 1642, while he was in exile in Paris; an unauthorized English translation appeared in 1647 and caused Hobbes great anxiety. But the one thing Hobbes could not or would not do to protect himself was to keep quiet.

Whether *Leviathan* was written to ease Hobbes's return to England is moot. Whatever Hobbes's motives, it remains astonishing. Every page contains philosophical insights—or assertions—that repay scrutiny 350 years afterward. Philosophically, the contentious and difficult view that human beings are *no more than* complicated mechanical systems is argued with a mixture of deftness and clumsiness that remains engaging when computer analogies have been commonplace for decades. Hobbes's insistence that sovereignty must be absolute, omnicompetent, indivisible, and ultimate is still fiercely debated, though rarely with reference to Hobbes. His views on the nature of law, the connections of church and state, religious toleration, and much else repay any amount of analysis. Before we engage in it, we should ask what Hobbes's contemporaries made of it.

They understood that *Leviathan* justified Hobbes's submission to the protectorate established by Cromwell. In 1651 Cromwell required subjects who wished to keep their property to "engage" with the new regime, that is, swear allegiance. Only the better-off and politically active had to decide whether or not to swear allegiance, but for them it was a controversial question. Many felt that since they had pledged their allegiance to Charles I they could not go back on their word. Charles was dead and could neither hold them to their allegiance nor release them, but many felt bound to him and his heirs. The question when a man was free to take on new allegiances if not explicitly released by the person to whom he had sworn allegiance before was not easy, but Hobbes provided a clear answer. Once we have pledged allegiance to a government, be it monarchy, aristocracy, or democracy, we are obliged to obey it and help sustain its authority.[11] A sovereign political entity exists to secure the safety of its subjects, and it can do so only if everyone upholds its authority. If in spite of our efforts, the sovereign disintegrates—if the regime is defeated in war or dissolves in civil strife—we may submit to a new sovereign. No sovereign is truly a sovereign who cannot preserve the lives of his subjects. Everyone understood the implication: once Charles I had been defeated in the civil war and could not protect his subjects, they were free to pledge allegiance to whoever could protect them. Others said something similar; Hobbes was unusual in embedding the thought in a complex and comprehensive account of *all* our political rights and obligations.

Many contemporaries fell back on Saint Paul's injunction to "obey the powers that be, for the powers that be are ordained of God," or on the thought that Oliver Cromwell's forces had been victors in a just war, or on an appeal to the right of conquest by which English lawyers had always justified William the Conqueror's right to rule, and the title of his successors. Most people acquiesced in the government of whoever could keep order, were grateful the war was over, and had no need of philosophical assistance. Hobbes wrote for an audience that was used to thinking about its obligations and whose support made a difference to whether the government of the day could govern. They were startled, for instance, by his claim that a man who submits to the conqueror with his sword at his throat submits freely.[12] This was not founding sovereignty on the right of conquest, a familiar move, but founding it on consent, and describing the nature of that consent in highly counterintuitive ways.

Leviathan and Science

What Hobbes thought science, and therefore *political* science, was is surprisingly hard to say. What it is not, is easy. It is not Aristotelian. It is not teleological; and it looks behind appearances for the mechanisms that explain appearances. It is decisively post-Galilean. Hobbes draws an analogy with understanding a watch; someone who knows how a watch works can take it to pieces and put it together again. We are to take the state apart *in thought*. The last thing he wanted was that anyone should take the state apart in fact. One might complain that the *mere* ability to take a watch to pieces and reassemble it is no proof of understanding: a good memory might suffice. But Hobbes was interested in the fact that a watchmaker must understand what he dismantles if he is to see what is broken and repair it; a knowledgeable but clumsy horologist might be a poor watch repairer but able to instruct a deft assistant. When Hobbes talks of the "art" by which God creates nature and we create the state, the presumption is that just as geometry tells us how to construct *perfect* circles and rectangles, so the science of state building is the science of the construction of a perfect state. Actual states will deviate from perfection, just as a drawn straight line will deviate from perfect straightness.

Hobbes's science of politics begins with an account of human nature, and Hobbes tells us where we must go for knowledge of it: *"nosce teipsum; read thyself,"* he says.[13] Hobbes goes on to say that once we have read his account of our passions and opinions in *Leviathan*, "the pains left another, will only be to consider, if he find not the same in himself. For this kind of doctrine, admitteth no other demonstration."[14] Hobbes distinguishes very sharply between the *nature* of our desires and aversions and their *objects*. What we desire and avoid varies from one person to another and within one person from one time to another, but the nature of our passions is common to us all.

Modern readers, for whom "science" means the empirical, physical sciences find it hard to know whether Hobbes believes that we have *scientific* knowledge of the physical world. We know that it is God's creation, and that he has the maker's knowledge of it that we have of geometry. What about us? There are three familiar views, none of them easy to identify as Hobbes's own. The first is that our knowledge of the natural world is well-founded opinion. Physics provides natural histories of the physical world; the laws of physics summarize what we know about the world, and provide recipes for making future discoveries. Geometry is different, because it is knowledge of our own constructions, and Hobbes insists that geometry is the only science with which the Creator has seen fit to bless humanity—until Hobbes's science of politics. But when Hobbes lists the various branches of science, he lists knowledge of the natural world among them.[15]

A second possibility is that our knowledge of the natural world is ideally like our knowledge of geometry. There are principles that nature *must* obey. The universe operates according to self-evident principles; the purpose of thought experiments of the kind Galileo recommended was to uncover those principles. Galileo's demonstration that a body in motion would continue in motion forever, contrary to Aristotle's view, involved asking us to imagine a ball rolled down inside a wineglass. It would travel up the other side of the glass to the height it had been released at. If we now imagine the side of the wineglass lowered until it becomes a flat plane, we can see that barring friction, the ball would travel forever, because it would never reach the height from which it had started. QED. Physics shows how the world must work *if* it conforms to the model drawn by the scientist. The model has the irrefutability of geometry; but whether the world *really* conforms to the model is unanswerable.[16]

A third position is one that Hobbes should have liked, but he contradicts it. The difficulty with the first view is that it implies that the universe *might* have operated according to principles quite different from those on which it actually operates. Hobbes agrees. It is God's universe, built as he chose; if he had chosen to build a universe on different principles, nobody could gainsay him. It is not easy to make sense of that view, because we cannot imagine *what* these principles might be. The difficulty with the second view is that one person finds self-evident what another finds counterintuitive; Hobbes's problems with the idea of a vacuum are evidence of that.[17] The third possibility is to argue that there can be only one physics, just as there can be only one geometry; God could not have designed a different universe, any more than Euclid could have drawn up a different geometry. We now know that different geometries are possible; Hobbes did not.

The reason this matters, to Hobbes or his modern readers, is that many of the difficulties of *Leviathan* have their roots in Hobbes's methodological convictions. It is not surprising that his readers found his ideas hard to swallow. *Leviathan* seems to lay down principles for constructing a commonwealth, but these principles are not advice for founders of republics, or for statesmen or insurgents, such as Machiavelli offered in *The Prince* or the *Discourses*. Hobbes rejects Aristotle's claim that politics is the realm of rules of thumb, and we must be content with only as much certainty as the subject matter allows; but Hobbes has also changed the subject. If he were giving practical advice, he would have to be content with "usually," but he rarely offers advice. Perhaps the most overt practical advice is that *Leviathan* should be taught in the universities.[18]

True science is founded, says Hobbes, on "definitions," or "the imposition of names" and the reckoning of the consequences of names. Hobbes makes life harder for himself and the reader by insisting that naming is in one sense arbitrary, but that in a more important sense it is far from arbitrary. *Blau*, *bleu*, and *azzurro* are synonyms of "blue," and as names of a color none is better or worse than the others, if it names the same visual experience. The definitions of "law," "justice," "authority," and so on can be in Latin, Greek, or English, but if well-chosen, certainty will be achieved, and if ill-chosen, confusion and contradiction will result.

His purpose is to get us to understand the nature of sovereign authority, and the nature of law, and the nature of justice, and he says firmly, "The skill of making and maintaining Commonwealths, consisteth in certain rules as doth Arithmetic and Geometry; not as in Tennis-play on practice only."[19] And this appears to be what he has in mind when he says in the afterword to *Leviathan* that "the matters in question, are not of fact, but of right."[20] If we talk about the state as Hobbes thinks reason requires, we may not manage everyday life much better, but we shall not plunge into war because we are talking nonsense. If *Leviathan* has an ancestor, it is Plato's search in *Republic* and elsewhere for definitions of justice, knowledge, piety, or courage. Its intellectual successor is modern economics. Like geometry, economics works from definitions to conclusions, and abstracts away from most of human life to illuminate what perfectly rational agents will do in their market interactions; it is not a merely empirical account of what most people happen to do but an account of what we rationally *must* do, supposing our ends to be as the theory supposes and ourselves to be fully informed and rational. In the same way, Hobbes offers a theory of what human beings *must* do if they are the rational, well-informed, and fearful creatures he draws for us.

Hobbes on Human Nature

So *Leviathan* begins with a highly persuasive account of human nature and of the role of reason in human life. It begins with an account of human nature for both official and unofficial reasons. The official reason is that since a body politic is constructed from individuals, we must know the nature of the parts to know the nature of the "artificial man" that we shall build.[21] The unofficial reason is rhetorical; Hobbes paints a picture of the capacities that human beings possess in virtue of being self-maintaining physical systems that perceive both things outside them and their own bodily states, that feel desires and aversions, and, above all, that think; then he provides an account of the basic emotions that drive such creatures and the more complex emotions that experience and reason create out of these basic ingredients; by imagining many such creatures placed in an environment with no rules, no laws, nobody in authority who is able to make them act in one way rather than another—the so-called state of nature—he gives a striking account of the problem to which government possessing absolute authority is the solution. It is still known to political theorists and sociologists as "the Hobbesian problem of order."

Hobbes begins from the premise that human beings are complex physical systems—natural automata—endowed with sense, reason, and passions. Much of his account of our intellectual capacities is an exasperated commentary on the nonsense of the Schoolmen, the Scholastic philosophers of his own and the previous two centuries. These are old battles, but Hobbes's uncompromising materialism and nominalism is still exciting. Reason is not a divinely implanted source of illumination; it is the capacity to calculate consequences. Its task is to calculate the consequences of names or, in modern terms, to draw logical inferences. Words get their meaning because human beings impose "names" upon experiences they wish to record. The term "red," for instance, gets its meaning by being imposed upon the experience of seeing a red thing to remind us that the experience was like seeing another red thing. This is not a persuasive theory of meaning in general—it is particularly bad on the meaning of words such as "if" or "and"—but it yields results that Hobbes needs. If everything is body, the world contains only particular entities; but late medieval philosophy invented all manner of terms referring to properties of a more or less occult sort. Where names refer to a suspect entity, Hobbes sometimes declares them "unmeaning"; frequently, he makes the very modern move of analyzing them as the name of something else—the name of a name, for instance.[22]

So Hobbes asserts that almost nothing we say about God is really *about God*. To call God "infinitely good" says nothing about how good God is; it says only that human beings cannot say *how* good God is. Calling God infinitely wise and infinitely powerful is acceptable because the term names the intention to honor God. "Infinite" is the name of our inability to set limits; confessing our inability to limit the attributes of God is to honor him or it.[23] This is more skeptical than anything in Aquinas; Hobbes rejects the idea even of analogical talk. What lies beyond all experience is literally inconceivable. This leads to interesting claims: we cannot know whether God wishes us to honor him by praying with our heads covered—as the Jews suppose—or uncovered—as Christians suppose. But we should worship in a way we all recognize as giving honor: bareheaded or with covered heads, however *we* express honor. This has implications for religious liberty and the separation of church and state; on the one hand, it suggests that uniformity of worship is a good thing, on the other, that this is not for "religious" reasons.

Everything in the world is *particular*, and everything universal is verbal; Hobbes is firmly on the materialist, nominalist, and anti-Platonist side in matters of logic. Traditional philosophy must reduce its ambitions; it cannot see into the essences of things, as Plato hoped. There are no essences. For reason to operate effectively, it must not be dazzled by verbal confusion, whence the need for meticulous definitions, and an end to the unmeaning speech of the Schoolmen. But reasoning is social as well as individual; our opinions can be corrected by other people, and the use of reason implies a willingness to defer to other people. If everyone tries to impose his own ideas on others or to define words as he wants, reasoning is as impossible as playing cards would be if everyone "declared that suit to be trumps of which he had most in his hand." Hobbes is not Humpty Dumpty; words do not mean whatever we want them to mean.[24]

We reason for the sake of successful living. We are moved to do so because we are self-preserving creatures and wish to know how to preserve our lives and how to live well. Hobbes despised Aristotle's ethics and politics. He also despised his physics but conceded some merit to his biology. *Leviathan* was intended to drive Aristotle from the terrain of political debate, but Hobbes silently appropriates his views on many occasions, and our motives for reasoning about the world and ourselves may be one. There is nothing un-Aristotelian about the thought that we are so made that we have a standing desire for self-preservation, and a desire to live well, and that practical reason is the employment of our reason in deciding what to do to secure the good life. If Aristotle's observations are acceptable, the system in which he places them is not. It is absurd and the fount of absurdity. Hobbes's system operates on a mechanical, not a teleological, conception of desire and aversion: something within us drives us to, or away from, what we want or wish to avoid. Our desires are explained by how we are constructed, not by ends inscribed in nature to which we are naturally drawn; the final end of action is set by our desires, not by natural impulsion toward the good. Aristotle's teleological conception of human nature is rejected, and with it any suggestion that we have "proper" or "natural" ends. Aristotle saw values inscribed in nature; Hobbes saw values inscribed on nature by ourselves in the light of our desires and aversions.[25]

Good and Evil

Hobbes gives a strikingly subjective account of the nature of good and evil and of a vexed subject, the existence of an ultimate good, the summum bonum. He famously observed that "whatsoever every man desireth, that for his part he calleth good." *Good* is not the name of a quality of things or states of affairs; it is the name of our desiring whatever it is. What we dislike, we call evil; and what we are indifferent about, we call, in Hobbes's seventeenth-century terminology, "contemnible." The reality is our wishes and fears; "calling good" is prior to "being good." The things we want, we call good, and happiness consists in getting what we want. This holds only for the most part; many things are wanted as the means to something else, and if they turn out to be wrong or to have bad side effects, so that we are mistaken to want them, we shall not be happy getting what we want. Success consists of satisfying one desire after another; and greater happiness rather than less is the result of satisfying more desires rather than fewer, discounting for side effects. This is a strikingly anti-Aristotelian conclusion, reinforced by another. Aristotle's conception of the ultimate good was associated with the idea that once achieved, it leaves us no further longings. It is ultimate in all ways, embracing all partial goods and leaving the desiring soul in a state of rest. Hobbes was cautious enough about giving offense to the pious to refrain from mocking the thought too savagely. Nonetheless, he dismissed it instantly as a thought without any application to the world we actually live in.[26]

The reason is that we are physical systems. The human body is in incessant motion; our desires are constantly changing, and with them the standard by which we judge our happiness and misery. What Hobbes is careful to call "the felicity of this life"—leaving it unspoken but implicit throughout that we can form no clear idea of what the felicity of any other life may be like—consists in satisfying as many of these changeable desires as we can, one by one. There are "second order" desires—the desire that other desires should be satisfied, and the desire that other people's desires should be satisfied: that is what benevolence is. Among these second-order desires, the desire for security is especially powerful. The traditional doctrine of the common good is silently demolished, although a nontraditional account of a very different common good replaces it. We do not naturally converge on any particular goal: there is nothing that pleases everyone, and nothing satisfies any individual forever. Once a desire is satisfied, another takes its place, and we begin the search to satisfy it. This is not to be deplored; nobody thinks it gluttony to eat lunch as well as breakfast. The felicity of the angels makes no sense to us, though we may hanker after whatever we suppose it to be.

The mutability of desire launches two powerful thoughts. The first is Hobbes's analysis of pride. In the modern vernacular, pride is an extreme version of "keeping up with the Joneses." The changeability of our desires means that the standard of how well we are doing comes from within us; but it cannot answer the question whether we get what we should. What we habitually do is look at how other people are doing. If they do better than we, we envy them; and they envy us if we do better than they. We come to desire their envy, their admiration, and their acknowledgment that we are doing better than they. We move from wanting things "naturally," in the familiar sense of that term, to wanting them because other people want them. We want a bicycle, move on to wanting a car, and end by wanting a car to make the neighbors jealous. "Vainglory" is the most important emotion in Hobbes's political theory; in the Book of Job, Leviathan is "ruler over the children of pride," and Job provides both the title and the moral of Hobbes's masterpiece. *Non est potestas super terram quae comparetur ei*: "there is no power on earth that compares with him." Unsurprisingly, one of Hobbes's innumerable critics entitled his attack on Hobbes *Leviathan Drawn Out with an Hook*. It was nonetheless an unfortunate title, since the implication of God's invocation of the great whale was that Job could not draw it out with a hook. Hobbes regarded pride as a peculiarly antisocial emotion; political arrangements had to subdue it, if there was to be peace.

Pride must yield to its opposite; men must consider their most important, long-term interests and concerns. They must understand that they are fragile creatures for whom self-preservation is the overriding imperative, and think about what behavior promotes self-preservation, not what would impress others. Among consequences disagreeable to traditionally minded aristocrats, two are striking. The first is an insistence on the natural equality of all mankind. There are no natural aristocrats; Aristotle thought exactly the opposite—just as there are slaves by nature, so the "best men" are best by nature. Hobbes insists that what it means to be an aristocrat is a matter of what the sovereign authority determines. The crown is the "fount of honor" in the conventional sense, and in a logically more stringent sense: "honor" is what the sovereign confers. Once the two thoughts are put together, we can see that there is no room in Hobbes's theory for any social group to claim to have a natural right to rule in virtue of birth and upbringing. Hobbes was not hostile to the aristocracy. The Cavendish family employed him for almost six decades, he admired the "aristocratic" virtues, such as generosity, and he had little time for merchants or commercial life. He was hostile not to aristocrats but to the idea that there were any "natural" aristocrats.

The second powerful thought is Hobbes's inversion of Aristotle's search for the summum bonum. There can be no consensus on the highest good for mankind, but there is a worst evil, and that is death. *Everyone* has good reason to avoid "sudden and violent death" at all costs; in the absence of a summum bonum we can agree on the existence of a *summum malum*.[27] That death is the worst of all evils is almost a physical truth for Hobbes; as self-maintaining automata, we are "hard-wired" to reject anything that will bring us to a halt. Hobbes says over and over that we may rationally agree to anything except to get killed. A promise or covenant to kill myself or to let myself be killed is void. This has the curious consequence that the coroner's verdict of suicide while of unsound mind is a pleonasm. To kill oneself appears to be insane by definition. It also has some interestingly liberal results; one is that we cannot say to our rulers, "If I do thus and such, kill me." The most we can say is "If I do thus and such, you may *try to* kill me," with the implication that we do no wrong if we try to ensure they do not. Having established sudden and violent death as the ultimate evil, Hobbes inverts much else of Aristotle's view of politics. We come together to establish a political community not out of a sociable impulse to pursue the good life in common but out of an unsociable fear of one another, and for the sake of avoiding the greatest of all evils, death. Without a state, we have no pleasure but much grief in keeping company.[28]

This is not to say that *once a state is established*, its purpose is exhausted by the protection of life and limb; Hobbes is insistent that the state exists to promote what he calls "commodious living," and commodious living includes all the pleasures and benefits of civilized life, certainly starting with law and order but continuing through economic prosperity and on to the benefits of learning and the pleasures of friendship and sociability. Many of the goods that Aristotle assumes as the *point* of the state's existence reappear as *products* of its creation; but the distinctively political good of ruling and being ruled in turn is not one of them. Hobbes despises the suggestion that the state exists because human beings are naturally sociable, or *political animals*, in the Aristotelian sense. As he says (misrepresenting Aristotle), men are not political creatures as bees or cattle are, coming together by natural impulse; states exist artificially, set up by agreement among individuals with strong views about their own rights and the terms of association. Aristotle pointed out precisely this, but whereas Aristotle thought man was a political animal intended by nature to live in a polis, Hobbes was a thoroughly modern thinker who repudiated the idea that nature had any purposes for us whatever, and emphasized that we were driven into political society. The consequence is that for Hobbes it is no loss if we live wholly private lives and take no interest in politics, while for Aristotle it would be a truncated existence suited to women and slaves but not to citizens.

The State of Nature: The Warre of All against All

With this apparatus, and these glimpses of where the argument will go, we can follow Hobbes as he first plunges mankind into the miseries of the state of nature, shows them the way out of those miseries, and elaborates the consequences for a well-constructed and well-conducted state. Men are rational, self-preserving, in touch with the physical world through the medium of the senses. Their language names experiences and allows them to record and anticipate past and future experiences. On these premises Hobbes erects a wholly secular and arm's-length account of religion. The *natural* basis of religion, as distinct from revelation, is that men come to a belief in God through anxiety about causes. We constantly try to discover the cause of events that concern us—the preceding events on which they follow; knowing causes allows us to control events. Following the chain of causes backward, we reach the thought of a cause from which all later events follow, the first cause. This first cause we call God. Belief in God so defined is almost devoid of content, save that it is impossible that we should think any being is capable of creating the universe without also thinking that it is exceedingly—"infinitely"— powerful and has our fate in its hand.[29] Two notable features of Hobbes's discussion are his insistence that religion is a matter of law—"doctrine allowed"—and his constant animadversions against the self-interested overreaching of the priests of the Catholic Church "and even in that church that hath presumed most of reformation."[30]

What of those who disbelieve in the existence of God? Hobbes says they are fools, but not sinners; sin is rebellion against divine law, but those who do not believe in the lawgiver cannot be bound by his laws. God may destroy them as enemies, but he cannot punish them as disobedient subjects. We are "fools" to disbelieve, because it is imprudent to take risks with omnipotence. Hobbes's view that "fear is the motive to rely on" is not only the observation that a government must be able to frighten the recalcitrant into obedience; it is also the thought that to turn ourselves into law-abiding citizens and morally decent individuals we must look to the roots of law and ethics in our need for security. We are encouraged to see the good sense of being on the safe side in the matter of belief in God.

Mankind in the state of nature has the intellectual capacities of civilized men and is deprived only of government. The state of nature is not a primitive or historical condition; it is a theoretical construct. Among the qualities of natural man, the most important is the desire for *power*. This is not specifically political power. Power in Hobbes's understanding is a label for the capacity to control future events. Our present resources for controlling the future constitute our power. Anxious creatures like ourselves *must* want power; once we have eaten, we wonder where the next meal will come from; we need "power" over the food we shall need in future. I may gather food from the bushes, but only if I can be sure of coming back and not finding them stripped by others can I be sure of my next meal. I need to control the bushes' fate. Hobbes thinks that we move swiftly from power over inanimate things to power over people; what happens depends on what other people do, so controlling them is the key to all control. Control over other people is the core of any account of power.

Hobbes insists that *all* of us have a restless desire for "power upon power that ceaseth only in death." This is not because we are power hungry, or full of immoderate appetites, but because we are driven to acquire power to protect ourselves. It was essential that Hobbes could argue that most individuals were ready to live modestly and have moderate aims in life, and yet that under the wrong conditions they would have to behave *as if* they were power hungry, aggressive, and immoderate. If everyone was power hungry by nature, there would be no hope of establishing government; if nobody cared about his own safety, politics would be unintelligible. Secure people will not seek to dominate others, but insecure people will be forced to try for the sake of survival. And power is essentially comparative; if we both want to exercise control over some part of nature, the one who can make the other yield has the real power. So we are forced to try to acquire more power than others; they are forced to try to acquire more power than us. We are in an arms race, even though we may all wish to escape it. The implications for modern nation-states engaged in literal arms races are very obvious. The sources of power are innumerable: strength, obviously, but riches, wisdom, and honor are all power for Hobbes: whatever allows us to bend other men's wills to our own.

Warre

In the state of nature, this leads to no good. Hobbes provides a wonderfully mordant account of what he describes as "the natural condition of mankind as touching their felicity," otherwise, "the miseries of life without government," in which he spells out the effect of living in an environment where there are no rules, and no means of enforcement. The problem is not only that there is no authority that can make us behave in one way rather than another; there is also no common judge of right and wrong. Under government we know who owns what, and who can dictate what happens to this money or these goods or this field. Absent that, none of us has any reason to think that he has less right to anything than anyone else has. As Hobbes bleakly says, in these conditions we all have a right to everything, even to the use of one another's bodies. It is a right that nobody can make use of. What we lack is a mechanism for allocating determinate rights that we can make use of. Recall that Hobbes said, "Whatsoever each man desires, that for his part he calleth good." My own survival is a good to me, but perhaps not to you; your paying your debt to me is a good to me, but not to you. We can all understand that *if* there were a common judge who could decide on our rights and duties, we would be better off, inasmuch as we would all be in less danger of sudden and violent death. To get us to fully appreciate that point, Hobbes spells out what we are logically forced to do in the absence of that common judge.

Hobbes says that there are three causes of quarrel—causes of the war of all against all. They are competition, diffidence, and vainglory. Competition is self-explanatory. If we are all anxious about securing the resources on which our survival depends, and there is no mechanism to provide that security, we have to grab what we can, and that can only be at one another's expense. It is equally easy to see how government cures the problem. Under government clear rules about ownership mean we know how lawfully to acquire the means of life. Only in extreme conditions may we be driven to seize what belongs to another lest we starve.

Diffidence or mutual fear is hardly more complicated, but it leads directly into the reasons why twentieth-century international relations theorists "rediscovered" Hobbes after World War II. Hobbes's claim was that the *logic* of interaction between self-interested individuals who can kill one another tends to violence. The argument was reformulated in the twentieth century by mathematically minded strategic theorists.

Hobbes's premise is that each individual possesses the ability to injure and, in the last resort, to kill any other human being. The strongest man is vulnerable to the weakest when asleep. Since we all know this, we all have a reason to fear everyone else; the only conditions under which we are safe from another person is if he is disabled from killing us. The most effective way of disabling him is to kill him. Since we are rational, we can calculate that all other persons have a reason to kill us and, in the absence of a deterrent, may do so. That they have a reason to kill us stems from the combination of fear and rationality and the absence of a deterrent. *If* they fear we may kill them, their only recourse is to strike first; there is no government to deter us by threatening us with punishment, nor to deter them. We may have no desire to strike, but we may be forced to do it.

This was the situation in the international sphere when the United States and the Soviet Union possessed enough nuclear weapons to "take out" the other side's weapons, but not enough to survive a first strike with enough weapons to retaliate. Each side had a strong incentive to attack first, however little it might want to in the abstract. "Mutual assured destruction," the alarming name given to the policy of acquiring enough weapons and protecting enough from attack to maintain "second-strike capacity," made both sides safe. Once each side could retaliate, neither had an incentive to launch a first strike. Since each knew that about the other, the motives tending to peace were reinforced. What makes the story relevant is that individuals cannot develop a "private" second-strike capacity. To put it another way, a state with second-strike capacity is not "killed" if it is attacked, because it can retaliate. The individual who is killed cannot retaliate. We need the state to provide us with a second-strike capacity. States do not need a supranational state in the same way, though small states may well form alliances with more powerful states to provide it.

The emphatic rationalism implied by Hobbes's view of science makes all the difference to his argument. If the question whether human beings can survive without government is a simple empirical question, the answer is that in many parts of the world they do, as Hobbes well knew. Rules are accepted and observed by everyone in the absence of formal mechanisms for announcing them and enforcing them. Families and tribes live in hunter-gatherer communities with little formal authority; they do not live very peacefully, but they rarely fall into terminal fratricidal conflict. But no member of such groups would think his life worth a moment's purchase if he found himself among strangers—precisely because they would not acknowledge the rules of forbearance toward him that his family and neighbors would. In essence, members of primitive societies are safe where family-level sanctions work, and unsafe where they do not. Hobbes wants to show us the implications of removing government from our own society, which is to say the kind of society that had experienced the English Civil War of the 1640s. It was not a society where the family-level forbearances and sanctions of a primitive society would suffice.

The final reason for conflict is not on all fours with competition and diffidence. Competition can be assuaged by prosperity when we can earn a living by hard work and intelligence. And our willingness to seek our living that way rather than by violence is much increased by the existence of law and its enforcement. Fear may be reduced almost to nothing when we all know that everyone else has every reason *not* to assault us. Pride is different. We have seen how pride results from the combination of the instability of our desires with the ability to compare our successes with those of others; it is the source of an unremitting urge to "come top," no matter what the competition is about. In any competition there is only one top place, and competition for it cannot be diluted by prosperity. Pride makes men overestimate their capacities and take foolish risks; it leads men to be obstinate when they would preserve the peace by being willing to give in gracefully. It leads them to seek occasions to increase the resentment felt by their competitors, when peace suggests we should soothe their feelings. The cures for pride are twofold. The first is that the sovereign is understood to be the fount of honor, and that all understand their social status to be in the sovereign's gift. The other is simply to repress its expression as far as possible. *Leviathan* is king over the children of pride.

The Laws of Nature

When competition, diffidence, and vainglory drive us into conflict, it is
no wonder that Hobbes supposed that life in the state of nature would be
"poore, solitary, nasty, brutish, and short." This does not impugn human
nature, and our actions are not sinful. Unlike Machiavelli, who says
bleakly that men are evil and will do all the evil they can, Hobbes thinks
they are essentially innocent. They are frightened of sudden and violent
death and must do whatever they can to avoid it. In the wrong conditions,
that makes things worse rather than better. The sense in which Hobbes
is an Augustinian about politics does not extend to sharing Augustine's
obsession with original sin. The same emotions and intelligence that lead
to the war of all against all can secure peace and prosperity under stable
and orderly government. We reach that conclusion in two steps. First, we
must ask what will bring about peace. Hobbes has no doubt that everyone
will agree that we need rules to make us keep the peace and fulfill our
agreements with one another. The answer to the question "What rules
would we do well to follow?" is the "laws of nature."

Unlike his predecessors, Hobbes says that they are not strictly *laws*.
Strictly speaking, laws are commands issued by an authority entitled to
issue such commands: "the word of him that by right hath command
over others."[31] The laws of nature are "theorems" about what "conduces
to the safety of them all." As theorems, they are not rules but conclusions
about rules within a piece of hypothetical reasoning—"*if* we all followed
the injunction to keep our covenants, peace and prosperity would ensue,"
and so on. A command is an imperative: "keep faith, practice justice,
eschew cruelty," and the like. Hobbes thinks of the rules of morality,
which is what the laws of nature are, as imperatives we address to ourselves. We may choose to think of them as the laws of God, in which
case they are properly laws, divine laws. They are always binding on the
conscience, which is to say we should always *wish* to act on them and be
willing to do so when it is safe, but we are not bound to act on them

unless it is safe to do so. Hobbes marks the distinction as between being obliged *in foro interno* and *in foro externo.*

The basis of the laws of nature is the preservation of mankind. It was an old thought that God created the world with a view to its preservation; his laws were intended to preserve the creatures whom he had created. Hobbes does not diverge very far from that perspective in spite of his methodological originality. The first law of nature commands us to seek peace; the corollary is that where peace is not to be had we may use all the helps and advantages of war. The first clause is the first law; the second clause, the first right. Hobbes is unclear about how the laws of nature achieve their end. He begins by saying they are precepts found out by reason whereby a man is forbidden to do what is destructive of his life. This is plausible in the sense that *if* everyone else obeys the rules, we shall do well to obey them. But if others do *not* follow the rules, following them is dangerous since others will take advantage of us. The rules are good for us collectively if we all obey them; for an individual thinking selfishly, what matters is whether others obey them. Selfishly, I need others to keep the peace, keep promises, and behave decently. Purely selfishly, I do best if they keep the rules and I do what I choose. The literary expression of that thought goes back to Callicles and Thrasymachus, and more credibly to Glaucon.

Hobbes never raises this anxiety, what is today known as the free-rider problem. The explanation is probably that he did not think that we are selfish *in that sense.* We are *"self*-ish" in the sense that if any of us has an aim it must be *ours;* I can take your pain seriously only if your pain distresses *me,* just as I can take seriously the fact that you are relying on my promise only if honesty matters to *me.* This thought is easily confused with the view that I take my promise seriously only instrumentally—that I keep my promise only to get something on a later occasion from you or from others who notice my honesty. They are not the same thought. Hobbes did not think that we are all selfish in the derogatory sense; some of us are and some of us are not. All of us are self-centered in a physical or physiological sense that is wholly consistent with being benevolent, honest, and just. Our desires are the psychological manifestation of a physical system that attempts (implausibly as a matter of physiology) to maximize the flow of vital motions about the heart (equally implausibly described as being what we feel as happiness). It is a necessary truth that we do what leads to our happiness. It is not a truth at all that we cannot be made happy by being honest, honorable, and benevolent.

Obligation

Like many previous thinkers, Hobbes explains earthly authority, which is to say the sovereign's right to command, in terms that imply both an ascending and a descending view of authority. God's authority is another matter entirely; God can command us because he created us and does not need our assent to be able to make us act as he wishes. Earthly sovereigns are created by the consents of their subjects. What distinguishes Hobbes from his predecessors is his obsessive attention to the individual subject. Where Justinian claimed that "the people" conferred absolute authority on him, Hobbes is concerned with our obligation to obey the sovereign's commands, and he finds that obligation in our individual consent.[32] The question is one not of the pedigree of an existing sovereign but of the moral obligation of each individual. The politically central laws of nature are the second and third. The second tells one to be willing to lay down the right to all things "and to be contented with so much liberty against other men as he would allow other men against himself." The means of laying down our rights is to contract or covenant with others for the purpose; the third law of nature therefore dictates "that men perform their covenants made." Justice consists in fulfilling our obligations; obligations are imposed by us on ourselves when we make a contract or covenant.

Hobbes thought that injustice was literally illogical. One can see why he might have done so: to say, "I promise that I will do such and such, but I have no intention of doing so," comes very close to saying, "I shall and I shall not do it." Hobbes's argument does not achieve what is wanted; *saying* "I promise" while having no intention to do it is not self-contradictory but wicked. The contradiction between what I say and what I know I shall do is, as with lying, the essence of deceit but not a defect of logic. It certainly undermines the possibility of good order; *pacta servanda sunt*—"promises must be kept"—is as important as everyone from Cicero onward has maintained. And it is certainly true that just as communication would be impossible unless most of us most of the time said what we thought to be true, so the institution of promising would simply not exist unless most of us most of the time took the obligations we assumed as seriously as we should. The greater problem for Hobbes's system is this. Hobbes intends that in the state of nature we make a covenant "of all with all" to establish government, that is, to create the artificial body we call the sovereign. But, say many of his critics, he tells us that covenants in the state of nature do not oblige, so the covenant cannot oblige.

This is wrong. Hobbes held two views that are in tension but not at odds. Covenants always oblige *in foro interno*, which is to say that we must be willing to do what we have promised, if it is safe to do it. In the state of nature we are thrown back on our own judgment about what we must do to preserve ourselves; this is the effect of the absence of government. It might seem that we can always find a reason to weasel out of what we have promised. Once there is government, obeying the rules is safe, and there is agreement on what excuses will or will not hold water; so finding excuses not to perform becomes impossible. But Hobbes never says that in the state of nature the laws of nature do not oblige; he claims they do "not always" oblige *in foro externo*. That implies that they sometimes, perhaps often, do oblige. The first law of nature obliges always; it demands only that we seek peace, and no matter what the difficulties, we can always do that. The second law of nature, which requires us to be willing to give up our rights on condition that others give up theirs on equal terms, is equally easy to obey. It is not difficult to be *willing* to consent on equal terms to the creation of government; the difficulty lies in actually laying down my right if that exposes me to attack by others.

The laws of nature, then, oblige always in intention; they bind us to promote peace. They are not *conditional*; they do not invite us to observe them if we wish, or when we think they are to our advantage. We need not observe them *in foro externo* if it is too dangerous; but we are not at liberty to ignore them as we choose. This is essential for the next step of the escape from the state of war. The escape depends on our contracting with one another; Hobbes's account of contract or covenant is the key to everything that follows. Hobbes claimed that although we are obliged to obey the laws of nature *as laws* if they are thought of as the laws of God, the obligation to obey human law rests on our prior agreement to obey a human lawgiver. Nobody is under an earthly obligation that he has not placed himself under; *injustice* consists of a breach of such obligation. Two powerful consequences are that nothing the sovereign does can be unjust, in Hobbes's sense; and that our obligations to the governments we live under have been freely undertaken by ourselves.[33] It is worth recalling yet again that this is not a historical story about the genesis of government; Hobbes says that was a matter of families becoming clans and clans becoming kingdoms. *Leviathan* is an account of right, not fact.

Sovereignty

The covenant that takes us out of the state of nature is a covenant of every man with every man to transfer all their rights to "this man or this body of men," and to take his or their word as *law*. This *institutes* a sovereign. The sovereign is an artificial body—recall the frontispiece of *Leviathan*—and as an artificial person it represents us all, and we are the authors of its acts. Hobbes devotes a lot of detailed explanation to this point, as he needs to do in order to bring off a claim that looks very like squaring the circle. Previous writers who defended absolute monarchy agreed that in extremis kings who were excessively unjust and had therefore become tyrants might be desposed. Hobbes claimed that the sovereign could not commit injustice, because its acts are literally ours. This was not to say that whoever bears the sovereignty cannot behave badly; he might perpetrate *iniquity* and violate the laws of nature and of God. Strictly speaking, however, he could not act unjustly, a point Hobbes reinforces by insisting that it should be unlawful to talk about tyranny at all, no doubt thinking that from discussing the nature of tyranny it would be a short step to advocating tyrannicide. Hobbes's attention to the institution of the sovereign is justified. Although almost all sovereigns in fact acquire authority over their subjects by *acquisition*, institution underlies the existence of all sovereigns. Hobbes understood this and acknowledged that there is a sense in which democracy underpins even absolute monarchy, that sense is that there is no legal system unless all (or the vast majority) accept its requirements as obligatory.

The details of Hobbes's account of the sovereign's institution excite curiosity and skepticism. Critics have wondered why Hobbes said that covenants without the sword are but words and of no power to hold a man at all, and yet relied on a covenant without the sword to create the sovereign who was to wield the sword. *Once* the covenant establishing the sovereign has been entered into, it is maintained by the sword of the sovereign; the difficulty is reaching that point. It is crucial to Hobbes that the sword does not create the obligation imposed by the covenant; I create the obligation that binds me when I covenant. The role of the sword—that is, the sovereign's power to compel me—is to remove any excuse for nonperformance. *I* am bound by my agreement; *you* are bound by your agreement. You may wonder whether I will meet my obligations if no external power can make me do so; I may wonder the same about you. If we are each ready to meet our obligations, the knowledge that there is a sword to ensure that the *other* party performs removes the excuse to not do what we are willing to do. The sword can remain in its sheath; its bare existence achieves what is needed. Second, what sustains government is the readiness of the citizenry to support it—so long as it is not too dangerous. That is a moral, not a legal, commitment. And that is what the covenant of all with all amounts to.

Hobbes was preoccupied with the thought that *one* person or body of persons must be sovereign, that is, to be the unique source of law in a political community. If there is to be obedience to law, we must know what the law is; someone must have the last word on that. Hobbes regarded theories of divided sovereignty as disastrous, and this was a popular refrain among defenders of absolute monarchy. The thought that we might settle on a person or group as the focus of obedience and obey them because everyone else obeys them is not implausible, nor is the argument that if it is to be the source of ultimate authority here on earth, it must be absolute at least in the sense of owning no superior and having no *legal* constraints on what it can do. It opens the door to a thought common in writers of a republican persuasion, but entirely alien to Hobbes. In the republican tradition, the founders of states play a special role. How a state *begins* is decisive for its future health and longevity, and the founding father or fathers correspondingly important. Hobbes has no time for such questions. He is explaining what a state is, and what underpins the claim of a sovereign to absolute authority; its longevity hinges not on its origins but on everyone who matters understanding what a commonwealth is, and what that means for his obligation to support it. The thought that underlying our "vertical" allegiance to this or that ruler—Charles I or Cromwell—there must be a horizontal allegiance to our fellow citizens is a decidedly modern and egalitarian thought. *Perhaps* it is true in fact that creating a state depends on finding a charismatic founder; but what is true in logic is that unless we have some one source of authority entitled to lay down the law and enforce it, we have no state at all, only anarchy.[34]

Hobbes envisaged two sorts of sovereign, although the attention he bestowed on them was in inverse proportion to their occurrence in the world. The *sovereign by institution* is the sovereign authority created out of the state of nature, while the *sovereign by acquisition* is an existent sovereign acquiring new subjects. The second case covers the silent, continuous acquisition of new subjects that takes place as young people become old enough for their allegiance to concern an existing government. It also covers—more importantly for Hobbes—the case where persons defeated in war are spared on condition of subjecting themselves to a new ruler. Making the leap from the state of nature into the political condition is the more intellectually demanding matter; but Hobbes lavished equal ingenuity on both.

The sovereign by acquisition offers the person who may or may not become a subject a simple choice: "obedience or death." Hobbes argued that in this case a promise extorted by force is valid; what normally invalidates the promise to pay a substantial sum the next day to the highwayman who offers you "your money or your life" is the fact that his activity is legally prohibited, and the justified fear that he will kill you if you turn up. The sovereign can spare your life very easily; when he has done, he has fulfilled his side of the bargain, leaving you no excuse not to fulfill yours. Hobbes insisted that the bargain is made "freely." His argument that a promise made out of fear is binding is not wholly unpersuasive. We do not think that a customer who buys bread from a baker need not pay his bill just because he was afraid of going hungry. Why should we think a defeated enemy is excused from obeying his captor just because he was anxious not to be killed? Fear of privation and fear of death are equally fear of coming to a nasty end. In fact, Hobbes tries to be too clever. Many conditions make bargains more or less coercive and therefore less or more binding. The situation when there is one baker in town, famine threatens, and the baker offers to feed us only if we become his slaves is very different from the usual situation where there are many bakers, and the worst that happens if we do not like his bread or his prices is a walk to another baker. The sovereign by acquisition is in the first situation rather than the second.

The claim to which all this is preamble is that the *sovereign* is not bound by any promise to his or their subjects. Hobbes had nothing but contempt for theories of mixed government, and for those who thought that a king's coronation oath constituted the sort of promise that someone else might legitimately try to enforce. It is essential to Hobbes's theory that we give up *all* the rights we can transfer to the sovereign. We cannot give up the right to save our own lives in extremis, so there is no point in trying. All other rights are transferred. The sovereign by institution is not bound by this covenant, because we covenant with one another and not with the sovereign. The sovereign by acquisition is not under an obligation to us, because he fulfilled his side of the bargain when he spared our lives, and has no further obligation to us. Hobbes took a strikingly individualistic view about obligation. We are under an obligation to obey our rulers because we have put ourselves under that obligation. Unlike traditionalists and conservatives, Hobbes did not think we are born into obedience. Most people assent silently to the government in power in the society into which they are born, but in logic the sovereign might legitimately treat them as "enemies" until they explicitly engage to obey him. The sovereign's forbearance is to be understood as the terms for obedience.

Having elaborated the nature of sovereignty and its intellectual origins, Hobbes went on to give an account of the powers and duties of sovereigns and of the nature of life under law. That account has many peculiarities, but its main feature is not a peculiarity but central to accounts of sovereignty for the next several centuries. The point of the sovereign's existence is to settle the question of what the law is in some particular jurisdiction. What the sovereign commands as law is law. The sovereign's laws may be well judged or ill judged, but what makes them laws is not their goodness but their being commanded as rules to guide those subject to them. This is a "pedigree" theory of law, because it claims that the way to discover whether a purported law is really a law is to see whether it has been laid down in the right way by the appropriate authority. For this to be possible, Hobbes thought, the sovereign must be one, indivisible, and absolute. The reason is obvious enough; a decisive answer to the question of what the law is requires an authority able to answer that question. There can be only one such authority, since if there were more than one they might give conflicting answers. The existence of the United States of America suggests other possibilities: one of which is that a sovereign is not what Hobbes says—since the United States possesses a multiplicity of legal systems and no single final arbiter of conflict; or, that the possession of an identifiable sovereign is not a necessary condition of being a single state—since the United States is a single political system, but different bodies have the last word on different issues.

Hobbes had no doubt that divided sovereignty was disastrous. But once he had defended absolute authority as essential to a state's existence, he gave an account of how a state should in fact be governed that made so many concessions to constitutionalist ideas that many commentators have described Hobbes as a "protoliberal," if not a liberal. The awkwardness is that most liberals think citizens have rights against their governments; such as a right to free speech, to the free practice of whatever religion seems compelling to them, to the immunities against arbitrary arrest and ill-treatment we see enshrined in bills of rights. Hobbes, how-ever, insisted that subjects have no such rights. The natural rights we are born with are useless in the state of nature; we give them all up—except the right to save our lives in extremis—to create the government that will protect us.

We have no right to free speech; there is no "right to private judg-ment," such as Protestant dissenters claimed; there is no right to be repre-sented. The king's ministers are counselors; they do not share sovereignty and have no right to have their advice accepted. Hobbes agreed that politi-cal bodies should act by majority decision, but had no enthusiasm for democracy as a political system. A body must speak with one voice, and how else to determine that one voice but by majority decision? Hobbes was unequivocally unliberal if liberalism is a matter of individual rights. His hostility to "free institutions" was unflinching. The city of Lucca wrote the word "Libertas" in great letters on its walls. But nobody could claim that a citizen of Lucca was freer—that is, had more immunity from the service of the commonwealth—than an Ottoman in Constanti-nople.[35] Freedom under government consists "in the silence of the laws";[36] a relaxed absolutism left the citizenry freer than an austere republicanism.

Hobbes's employment of this conception of freedom opens the door to another, non-rights-based form of liberalism. It rests on a negative conception of liberty; freedom is *not* being made to act in one way rather than another. The protoliberal element in Hobbes was his conviction that although governments are *entitled* to legislate on anything whatever, they should actually enact as few laws as possible. The reasoning is what one might expect. What constitutionalists demand from government as a matter of *right* are generally good things in themselves. Governments that consult widely legislate more intelligently; governments that avoid legislating over the minute details of life have happier, and therefore more loyal, subjects; if religion is not likely to cause dissension if left to individual discretion, governments should allow everyone to choose her or his own religious allegiance, at any rate within much the limits that Locke later set out. But peace trumps everything. Where religion is contentious, a compelled uniformity of worship and public doctrine is necessary. The liberal who talks of rights might agree to abrogate the *right to free exercise of religion* in emergency; Hobbes would regret that "independency" was impossible.

Hobbes argues that rulers should behave as if a liberal, constitutional order were in place on instrumental grounds. It is not necessary for the government to legislate us into work and trade; we want to be prosperous and do not need governments to make us do it. What we need is two forms of assistance: first, protection against force and fraud, so that we are not hesitant to take risks because we fear to be robbed or deceived; second, helpful commercial laws. Force and fraud aside, the great handicap to prosperity is unclear laws about ownership and contract. Hobbes advocated an English land register in 1651; it was created only when Parliament finally passed the Real Property Act of 1925. Laws about ownership and contract are minimally coercive; they do not oblige anyone to own anything or make a contract with anyone. They offer individuals the assistance of the state's coercive powers when certain conditions are fulfilled; if you and I make a valid agreement, we can each have it enforced against the other. If we make invalid agreements, we are mugs. Hobbes was not, in fact, an enthusiast for trade, employment, or commercial life in general. He had an intellectual's tastes, not a merchant's. But he believed very firmly that government exists first to keep the peace and then to promote all the arts of civilization, commercial and intellectual.

The small touches that display Hobbes's concern to avoid misery above all else include his advocacy of a (minimal) welfare state. The old, the poor, and the unemployed needed help, and a prosperous society should provide it. This is further evidence that Hobbes's view of human selfishness was not the view that we are doomed to think only of ourselves and to promote only our own interests; if we were so doomed, no society would be possible. There is no difficulty in Hobbes's suggestion that we should provide for the poor, the old, and the sick; we are not so selfish that benevolence toward them is impossible. John Aubrey tells a nice story to make the point that the fact that our feelings of sympathy must be *ours* does not mean they are not feelings of sympathy. "One time I remember going in the Strand, a poor and infirme old man craved his alms. He, beholding him with eyes of pity and compassion, put his hand in his pocket and gave him sixpence. Said a Divine that stood

by, 'Would you have done this if it had not been Christ's command?'"
Hobbes's answer was spot-on: "I was in pain to apprehend the miserable
condition of the old man, and now my alms giving him some relief doth
also relieve me."[37] The same concern to avoid pointless misery animates
Hobbes's discussion of religious toleration. Almost half of *Leviathan* is
devoted to the topic of a "Christian Commonwealth"; after Hobbes had
taken his readers from human nature through the state of nature, thence
through the principles of all government whatever, he had to tackle the
subject that passionately animated his contemporaries—the politics of
a Christian society.

The Christian Commonwealth

From the point of view both of modern commentators and Hobbes's historical legacy, there is a certain awkwardness in the lengthy discussion of
"The Christian Commonwealth." In Western societies, churches go out
of their way to disavow secular political ambitions, so Hobbes's modern
readers are not as interested in the subject as his contemporaries were.
They were used to religious zealots arguing that the classical doctrine of
tyrannicide justified the assassination of a heretical monarch, and to other
enthusiasts advocating the institution of the kingdom of God on earth at
the first opportunity. The argumentative Hobbes also felt honor bound
to fight off many current theological views and to defend some unorthodox views of his own. He was, for instance, a "mortalist," which is to
say that he believed that at death we perish entirely, without continuing
to exist as an immortal soul; at the Last Judgment, we shall be created
anew and judged; the righteous will be granted eternal, bodily existence,
and the unrighteous will be annihilated. Hell as the resting place for the
damned vanishes from the story. Mortalism was not uncommon, though
disapproved of. Today it is a historical curiosity. What presents even
more difficulty is the fact that if one imagines Hobbes posing the question what difference it makes to a commonwealth that it is a Christian
commonwealth, his reply is that it makes none. This is not as astonishing as it might seem, but it has an interesting consequence.

Hobbes argued that religion grew out of anxiety.[38] The human mind is driven to search for the causes of the things that affect our lives; reaching backward along the chain of causes, we finally think that there *must* be some uncaused cause of the sequence, and that we call God. We saw, too, that Hobbes held that "natural theology" was all but a contradiction in terms; unaided reason could tell us nothing about the nature of God, save that he exists and is more powerful than we can set limits to. That skepticism allowed Hobbes to insist that religion is more important as social practice than as intellectual speculation, and must be regulated in the way any other social practice must be regulated—with a view to preserving the peace and physical and psychological security.

Among obvious threats to the peace are self-proclaimed prophets claiming to have a new revelation of God's intentions. Hobbes maintained that prophets ceased when God ceased to provide them with miraculous powers; nowadays, the proper view is that when a man says that God spoke to him in a dream, we should understand that he dreamed that God spoke to him. Hobbes did not deny that Jehovah revealed himself to his chosen people; he merely argued that that fact put the Israelites in a unique situation, which was that until they chose kings for themselves, God was their earthly sovereign. Once he allowed them to choose an earthly sovereign for themselves, God continued to rule the earth in the sense that all believers were obliged to obey his commands, but he was not an earthly sovereign. Anyone attempting to set up a godly kingdom on English soil would rightly be jailed.

As to doctrine, orthodoxy was for the sovereign to define. A sensible sovereign would avoid causing his people anxiety by requiring them to profess beliefs that stretched credulity or came into conflict with their other beliefs; that was asking a man to play at cross and pile for his salvation and frustrated the purpose of government. In any case, men can and may dissimulate in such matters, and a wise sovereign contents himself with outward conformity. Toleration within limits enters through the back door. As to the sacred books of the Christian tradition, the Bible receives its authority from the sovereign. Hobbes had mixed views about the translation of the Bible into English; it gave anyone who could read a compendious account of their duties to man and God, but it also encouraged people to publish strange interpretations of God's word. They must remember that it is an essential attribute of sovereignty that the sovereign alone may decide what doctrines may lawfully be taught.

A Christian commonwealth thus turns out to be one in which the sovereign's authority over doctrine extends to authority over Christian churches. Hobbes's aim was to secure the priority of state over church and to ensure not merely that wild men from the countryside did not set up as prophets but that bishops did not arrogate secular authority to themselves. The bishops would have burned Hobbes as a heretic if the chance had come their way, so mutual animosity was not surprising. There was one area where Hobbes was unsure of his step. This was the ancient problem of the duty of a Christian subject to obey an infidel sovereign. Hobbes insisted that no subject had the right to challenge the legitimacy of a sovereign on religious grounds, and it was easy to see that Christians must in general obey infidel rulers to the point where they demand that we deny Christ. In *De cive*, Hobbes held that at this point the devout must refuse and "go to Christ" by martyrdom. He changed his mind in *Leviathan* and argued that we could deny Christ to save our lives. God enjoined us to preserve ourselves and would not regard the denial as a mortal sin. What a man says and what is in his heart are two different things, and God is concerned with what is in our hearts. His concern, evident in the immensely long chapter 42 ("Ecclesiastical Power"), is to insist that there is no "spiritual power" independent of, separate from, and differently founded from the secular power. There are not two swords, but one. The sovereign wields both sword and scepter.

Conclusion

We therefore find Hobbes arguing consistently for a state whose authority is unlimited, but which exercises that authority discreetly. Since religion was the great source of contention in the seventeenth century, it was the authority of the state over the church that he was particularly anxious to defend, but in the hope that it will be exercised with a light touch. Arguing against Bishop Bramhall over free will and necessity,

Hobbes insisted that religion is a question of law, not truth, which is what he consistently argues in *Leviathan*. Philosophical speculation is one thing, the expressive and moral functions of religion another. How far this was religious skepticism is impossible to say. The range of religious opinion in the sixteenth and seventeenth centuries was wide; none of Hobbes's far-fetched interpretations of the Bible were unique to him, and mortalism in particular was a common view of the afterlife. We may think it casts a curious light on the Last Judgment that dead persons are re-created to be judged for sins that an earlier version of themselves committed in the distant past; but that may well have seemed easier to believe than that disembodied souls existed. We may wonder whether Hobbes's materialism allows room for God, at all; his critics insisted that it did not and that he was an atheist, but Hobbes does not appear to have thought it a problem.

That leaves us with one last riddle. Hobbes thought he had rendered it only "probable" that absolute monarchy was the best of all forms of government; but he was sure that he had proved beyond question that government must have absolute authority, that a constitution could not be sovereign, and that divided authority was disastrous. Later critics were unkind. Locke asked why men who feared to be attacked by polecats should think themselves safer to be the potential prey of lions. Hobbes believed that a rational monarch would see that his interests were identical with those of his subjects. If they were happy and prosperous, they would obey his government and support it conscientiously. Hobbes insisted that we are obliged to support that power by which our safety is secured, which implies the possibility of a "virtuous" (as distinct from a vicious) spiral, where successful government breeds loyalty, which breeds successful government, which breeds . . . The rational sovereign will read *Leviathan* and understand that a temperate government that secures the livelihoods of the citizenry, does not encroach upon their privacy, and encourages initiative, imagination, art, and science will create a loyal, intelligent, and adventurous population.

The difficulty comes with a less intelligent or less competent sovereign, whether this is one man carried away by whim, pride, or ambition or an assembly riven by discord. What can we do? Hobbes had no answer. So much did he fear that his fellow subjects were looking for every least excuse to avoid their duty that he weighted the scales against self-help to an absurd degree. He agrees that we may resist the sovereign *on our own behalf alone* if we are directly threatened; since self-protection is hard-wired into the human organism, nothing we do can commit us to allowing the sovereign to kill us without resisting. Hobbes thought this implied that the sovereign should not add to the penalties of the criminal law further penalties for evading detection or trying to escape the agents of the law. But Hobbes's difficulty is that by insisting that we may resist only to save our own lives and only on our own behalf, he contradicts his own account of human nature and renders resistance too difficult. Anxious creatures gathering evidence about what danger they may be in can hardly help taking the way the sovereign treats others as evidence about how he might treat us. If we see that the sovereign seems bent on folly or misrule, we can scarcely avoid thinking it might be better to hang together than to hang separately, and form an alliance to resist the irrational sovereign while we can. Luther had in essence faced the issue and evaded it by acknowledging that a ruler who behaved badly enough would find that his subjects ignored the Pauline injunction to obey the powers that be and overthrew him, rightly or wrongly. The subjects of a Hobbesian sovereign cannot help asking whether the sovereign may turn from protecting them to attacking them. If the latter, the sovereign and they are back in the state of nature, and they may use all the helps and advantages of war. Hobbes's only recourse is to urge us to give the sovereign the benefit of the doubt, and to urge the sovereign to recall that his or their glory rests on the prosperity and happiness of their subjects.

Nonetheless, the only *authority* over the sovereign is that of conscience and God. It is not difficult to see that, faced with so few resources of our own to oppose to those of the sovereign, subjects might reasonably feel either that they do not care whether it is technically an error to describe the sovereign as unjust—"iniquitous" is the proper term—so long as they can say they are justified in rebellion when the sovereign gets out of hand, or that they are happy to run the risk that divided government will collapse in chaos, seeing that as between a regime of checks and balances on the one hand and the Hobbesian sovereign on the other, it is a question of which presents the lesser evil. To none of this does Hobbes have a conclusive response. It is unfair to suggest that he should have had one. His achievement was to draw a more compelling picture of the political predicament than anyone before him, and one that has never been bettered. The considerations that tell for and against confiding more or less authority to government, and drawing the bands of obedience tighter or looser about the subject, have never been better set out. That his readers, and we ourselves, must make up their own minds about where the balance should finally be struck is a fact of political life, not a failure in Hobbes.

CHAPTER 13

John Locke and Revolution

The Glorious Revolution

BY THE STANDARDS OF the seventeenth century, John Locke's life was long, and by any standards eventful. He was born in 1632, the son of a Puritan lawyer; his father was not quite a gentleman, but he was prosperous and had seen military service on the parliamentary side during the civil war. He was friendly with the local MP, who had been the commander of his cavalry regiment during that war, which enabled him to send his son to Westminster School and thence to Christ Church, Oxford. Locke was an undergraduate and a junior fellow of his college during the ascendancy of Cromwell; at the Restoration, there was a purge of fellows who had been too eager to support the Commonwealth; Locke escaped ejection, although his loyalty to the crown and the Church of England was suspect. In fact, Locke's early views about both religion and political authority were decidedly authoritarian and should have been entirely acceptable to the powers that be. They changed after a visit to the Continent showed him the benign effects of religious toleration and persuaded him that religious liberty would be good for England.

College fellowships required their holders to take holy orders or to study for an advanced degree in law or medicine; Locke decided on medicine. This had important consequences. At an intellectual level, it gave him a respect for careful observation and the application of past experience to new cases that was lacking in Thomas Hobbes. This outlook permeates the *Essay concerning Human Understanding*, on which his philosophical fame rests. It is an "antirationalist" view. Human understanding is bounded by experience; there is no possibility of understanding the world from first principles detached from experience. Human reason is described as "the candle of the Lord," the instrument that enables us to know as much about the workings of the world as we need to live sensibly and virtuously, with a proper regard to our duties to God and man.

Medicine brought Locke into contact with the earl of Shaftesbury, the radical peer who did his best to frighten Charles II into abdication. Locke was recommended to Shaftesbury as the man who could save him from a painful and potentially fatal abscess on the liver. Locke performed a piece of surgery that might well have killed his patient on the operating table or from infection afterward, but which was astonishingly successful. Later he inserted a silver drainage tube in case an abscess opened up again. Although it was not needed and would anyway have done no good, it became famous as Shaftesbury's "tap" and the object of mocking commentary in Dryden's royalist poem *Absalom and Achitophel*.

Shaftesbury converted Locke into the liberal figure we know. Locke initially subscribed to the view that political power was by nature absolute and that a ruler was entitled to make whatever religious dispositions he chose in "things indifferent," that is, outside the essentials of the Christian faith. This was *cuius regio, eius religio* and Hobbes's view. Shaftesbury was a confirmed believer in toleration in the familiar sense of the recognition of a right to religious liberty, and he rejected the suggestion that toleration was a matter of royal concession. He believed what Hobbes denied. Charles II was not a devout believer even in the Catholicism he secretly embraced; he was ready to tolerate Protestant Dissenters, on condition that Catholics were tolerated, too. But he insisted that it was by royal concession that his subjects would enjoy toleration. The Dissenters rejected toleration on those terms. Their view was that Catholics must *not* be tolerated and that Protestants *must be*, by right, not concession. Their intransigence postponed the removal of the legal disabilities of Dissenters, such as the inability to sit in Parliament or to gain a degree from Oxford or Cambridge, for a century and a half.

Locke became Shaftesbury's confidential secretary and followed him into government when Shaftesbury briefly became lord chancellor, and Locke became secretary to the Board of Trade. He followed him into opposition; and as the conflict between Charles and his opponents became fiercer during the 1670s and early 1680s, Shaftesbury drew on Locke for advice on political strategy. The chief object of Charles II's opponents was to prevent him from cementing an alliance with Louis XIV and Catholic France. They rightly suspected that Charles was trying to betray his kingdom to a foreign power. The Treaty of Dover of 1672—a desperately secret treaty—provided that when the time was ripe, Charles would return his country to the Catholic faith; Louis's armies would enter the country to reestablish Catholicism. Shaftesbury and his allies were determined that Charles's brother and heir, the duke of York, a declared and practicing Catholic, should not succeed him. They promoted an exclusion bill in 1679, and a full-scale crisis ensued. For the last five years of his reign, Charles governed without calling a parliament. Locke was under surveillance from royalist spies in Oxford. He was given to extreme suspicion of other people's motives; but he had every reason to fear for his safety. Charles might hesitate to strike at Shaftesbury; but he would have no qualms about the judicial murder of an adviser to teach Shaftesbury a lesson. Oxford was a royalist city where a jury could be paid to bring in a verdict of treason against anyone the crown wished to be rid of; one unfortunate opponent of the government, Stephen College, was acquitted by a London jury, taken to Oxford, tried, and hanged.

Locke ensured that incriminating documents were destroyed, and did nothing that would get him killed if reported to Charles's agents, and it is unclear just what he wrote during these years. It has been suggested that *Two Treatises of Civil Government* was written as a sort of vast memorandum of advice to Shaftesbury during the exclusion crisis and is therefore an "exclusion tract." If so, it was wasted labor; the House of Lords rejected the exclusion bill, Shaftesbury's support unraveled, and

Charles was emboldened to deal more harshly with his critics. Shaftesbury fled to Holland in November 1682 and died the following February. Later in 1683, the scheme to assassinate Charles II known as the
Rye House Plot was discovered, and those suspected of involvement
were executed, the most important of whom was Algernon Sidney, with
whom Locke had often corresponded. Locke slipped away to Holland
and stayed there until the eviction of James II. Whether he was involved
in the Monmouth Rebellion, which followed the accession of James II in
1685, nobody knows; he was certainly suspected of it by the royal agents
who lurked in Holland and would have abducted and murdered him if
they had had the chance.[1]

During his reign of only three years, James II tried to establish the
conditions for a French invasion of his country; he removed Protestant
officers from the militia and attempted to insert Catholics in positions
of authority throughout the country. This created mounting opposition,
and the country headed for civil war. In December 1688, as his army
hesitated in the face of William of Orange's army of invasion, and the
country was racked with anti-Catholic rioting, James realized that he
had come to the end of the road, and tried to flee to France, dropping
(or throwing) the symbol of his authority, the great seal of the kingdom,
into the Thames as he fled. Whether this was spite, or a way of saying
that nothing anyone now did had any legitimacy, it is hard to say. He
was captured en route, entered into desultory negotiations with William
and Mary, was encouraged to leave London and live close to the Thames
estuary, and finally slipped away to France, unpursued.

Locke could now return, and did. He led a quiet, but useful existence
until his death in 1704. He was again made secretary of the Board of
Trade, in recognition of his abilities as an economist; his greater fame
was as a philosopher, the interpreter of Newton to the wider world, and
the defender of a view of religious toleration that no British government
adopted until the abolition of the Test Acts in 1872 removed the last
legal disabilities of Catholics and Dissenters. It was left to the drafters
of the U.S. Constitution in 1787 to establish Locke's principles as the
guiding principles of a legal and political system and especially of the
relations of church and state. In Locke's own day, the American colonies

by no means accepted his ideas about toleration. Puritan New England pleased Charles II by executing more Dissenters than he ever tried to do. Nor did Locke campaign for wider toleration in Britain; his writings said all that intelligent readers needed.

For much of the past two centuries, John Locke epitomized the virtues on which English liberals prided themselves. He was thought to be cautious, commonsensical, matter-of-fact, given neither to the overpassionate enthusiasm for freedom that might lead to upheaval and civil war, nor to the overwillingness to accept authority that might allow dictatorship and despotism to flourish unchecked. This picture has recently been replaced with a more interesting and ambiguous one. Locke has been characterized as a supporter of a capitalist revolution, as a covert disciple of Hobbes, and as a conspirator against Charles II who thought that assassination was the only way to rid the country of a tyrant and whose decision to take refuge in Holland in the last days of Charles II and the short reign of James II was entirely justified.

The Political Writings

Locke's political thinking is difficult to reconstruct because he wrote much that is hard to reconcile with his overtly political writings, of which the two treatises on government are the most important, not least his constitutional proposals for the slave-owning American colony of Carolina. The two treatises are themselves ill assorted. The first is a long drawn-out, blow-by-blow demolition of the political views of Sir Robert Filmer, the author of *Patriarcha*. Filmer's is not a name to conjure with today, and even in Locke's time, he was an oddity. He was a country knight, who wrote *Patriarcha* some time before his death in 1647; it languished in obscurity and unpublished until the defenders of Charles II exhumed it as a propaganda weapon during the exclusion crisis and published it in 1680. *Patriarcha* argued that the authority of kings is the authority of fathers, handed down from Adam, the father of us all. Where it is not restricted by positive law, itself the will of a monarch, it is absolute, arbitrary, and bequeathable. It may seem odd that Locke spent several hundred pages assaulting such a rebarbative view, but Algernon Sidney's *Discourses concerning Government* did exactly that, at the same time, and the book's relevance to the politics of the day got its author killed.

Even so, the contrast with the *Second Treatise* is striking; that is a work that presents its own difficulties, but it is clear, consecutive, and advances from premises about the human condition that many of us take for granted to conclusions about the nature of legitimate government that almost all of us take for granted. The *Second Treatise* is so disarmingly written that it seems to need no commentary, which may be why commentators have strained to find something more surprising to say than that the *Second Treatise* means what it says. Nonetheless, it is hard to see why commentators have felt the urge to represent Locke as a friend to untrammeled capitalism or a friend to dictatorship or a friend to anything other than the moderate, constitutional government that the text defends.

It is all the harder when anyone seeking excitement has no need to look far beyond the text itself. To find Locke's *Second Treatise* astonishing and dangerous, we need only imagine the frame of mind of a conservative royalist of the late seventeenth century. If the *Second Treatise* does not incite the citizens to stretch out their hands against the Lord's anointed, it certainly tells them that in extremis they may have to. Anyone who thinks that kings reign *jure divino* must find Locke's account of the purposes and limits of legitimate government deeply offensive. In a climate where the opponents of Charles II recalled that his father had been beheaded, and were themselves thinking that tyrannicide was the only way to rid the country of a king who proposed to betray it, Locke's little treatise was incendiary. What follows is therefore a brief commentary on the *Second Treatise*, with some asides directed to the *First Treatise*; it ends with Locke's views on toleration, beginning with Locke's first antitoleration-ist thoughts and turning to the better-known and immensely influential *Letter concerning Toleration*, written in 1685 during Locke's exile in Holland and published after his return.

Locke was evasive about his authorship of the *Treatises*; as late as 1703, the year before his death, and many years after James II's abdication, he wrote to a correspondent to praise the account of property offered in the *Second Treatise*, as if he had no idea who had written it.[2] This was not true of his *Essay concerning Human Understanding*, where he was very happy to be known as its author. Locke may have thought that his work would not be wholly to the liking of his new employers after the Glorious Revolution and the installation of William III. Locke published the work in 1690 and said that the point of publishing it—not, as commentators have noted, the point of writing it in the first place—was to establish the throne of the nation's protector William III in the consent of the people.[3] This seems beyond criticism. The new monarch was not regarded as legitimate by a majority of his subjects, but Locke maintained that he was the most legitimate ruler in Christendom. It was an uphill argument. Many who did not care for James II nonetheless believed that the House of Stuart was the legitimate line and the House of Orange not, which was one reason why William reigned jointly with his queen, James II's daughter Mary, and why her sister, Anne, became heir to the throne ahead of any sons the then childless William might have from a later marriage. For Locke to publish something whose purpose was to establish William's throne more firmly was surely acceptable.

However, Locke's emphasis on consent implied that the English, or at least their Parliament, had *chosen* William III. This was less attractive; it opened the perennial question whether a people that had *given* sovereign authority to a monarch could take back what they had given. The Convention Parliament of 1689 offered William the crown on terms, which suggested that Parliament had chosen, elected, or appointed the king; but it was not clear that Parliament had the authority to do so, and Parliament had refused to set itself up as a constituent assembly and arrogate to itself constitution-making powers that had fallen into disrepute after the republican experiment of forty years earlier. It was the Convention Parliament, because it met without being summoned by a reigning monarch—James II having been allowed to slip away to France to avoid the danger of civil war. However, it was not interested in writing an English constitution in the way the Americans set out to construct a constitution for the United States a century later. James II was condemned for having attacked the "ancient liberties" of the English people, and William was asked not to remodel the country's political arrangements but to restore them.

Nor had Parliament thought itself entitled to offer the crown to just anybody; William of Orange was James II's nephew and Mary was one of James's two Protestant daughters. The more conservative members of Parliament thought they were entitled to appoint William as regent only, which was unacceptable to him, while others thought Mary might reign as queen with William as prince regent. The point was moot. William landed at Torbay in response to an invitation, but he arrived with an army, as if to say that what Parliament might not give, he would take. Nor was his army merely decorative; it fought several skirmishes with the royalist forces on the way to London. On the other hand, he had little appetite for war; when the leaders of Parliament dithered about exactly what should happen, William threatened to go back to Holland and leave them to shift as best they could. The outcome owed much to the good sense of James II's daughters, Princesses Anne and Mary. Locke's position was more radical than that of Parliament, and it issued in the views of the American revolutionaries and the radical dissenters that Edmund Burke so hated a century later. If the English people chose their rulers, they might decide on reflection that their rulers were inept or wicked, and assert their right to "cashier them for misconduct," as Richard Price put it a century later, and choose others in their place.[4] Burke argued that the correct view prevailed: the English had reluctantly engaged in a defensive revolutionary restoration of the ancient constitution; it required a monarch, and after James II's de facto abdication, the country was fortunate that his (Protestant) heir was at hand.[5]

The *Second Treatise*

The argument of the *Second Treatise* is justly famous. Locke begins from the premise that men are born free and equal, neither possessing authority over anyone else nor owing allegiance to anyone else. We are so used to this claim that we rarely notice that taken as a statement about how we come into the world, it is glaringly false. We are born helpless and dependent, and most people believe that they acquire their political identity and allegiances in virtue of their birth, along with a host of obligations to parents and other relatives. This gave Filmer's *Patriarcha* a considerable degree of plausibility. If we ask whom we first accept as authorities over our lives and fates, it is our parents; and if we ask how we come to be British subjects or American citizens, the usual answer is a matter of where we were born. Processes such as naturalization confer on us by an artificial act what otherwise comes to us by birth, and many countries are exceedingly reluctant to employ it, as witness Athens two and a half thousand years ago and Germany today. So we must ask what Locke intended this claim to achieve.

It was not Locke's purpose to deny the ordinary facts of life but to make his readers think about them in a new light. To say that we are born free and equal is shorthand for the claim that political arrangements are artifices constructed by human beings for human purposes, and that the rights and duties they bring with them must be justified by those purposes. Since Locke was a devout (if unorthodox) Christian, he thought that there were relationships about which we had no choice, where there was no reciprocity of rights and duties; God's relationship to his creatures is entirely unlike that of a ruler to his subjects or a father to his children. God (and he alone) possesses absolute and arbitrary power over his creation. As God pointed out to Job, he made the world, and it is permeated with the qualities with which he endowed it. As part of God's creation, we are under his absolute power, endowed with the abilities he has given us, and "sent into the world by his order and about his business."[6] An insight into the hatred with which Locke viewed the claim of absolute authority made by Charles II and other monarchs of his day is provided by imagining the contrast in Locke's mind between the rightful authority of God and that of these other claimants. To claim absolute authority for an earthly government, monarchical or other, was blasphemy. It is easy to think that with monarchs and their propagandists on their behalf, claiming to rule *jure divino*, their opponents must have been deeply secular in their thinking, and that we should discount their religious views; in fact, we may have religious reasons for taking a fiercely secularist and antiabsolutist line about politics. Locke did.

To say that men are born free and equal is therefore to say that although many morally important relationships do not depend on agreement or convention, political relationships do. This underlies his doctrine of government by consent of the people. Since Locke is giving an account of what political arrangements rational and morally serious persons would agree to, he begins by giving an account of the purpose and nature of the political society that can legitimately be established. "*Political power* then I take to be a *Right* of making laws with penalties of death, and consequently all less penalties, for the regulating and preserving of property, and employing the force of the community, in the execution of such laws, and in the defence of the Commonwealth from foreign injury, and all this only for the public good."[7] It exists, he says, to secure men's "property," by which he means their "lives, liberties and estates." While "property" today has a much narrower meaning than "lives, liberties and estates," Locke habitually uses the term in both the modern, narrow sense and in an older, wider sense embracing all the "external goods" that governments exist to protect. Governments exist to protect and secure the rights of their subjects; a person with rights has something of his own for the government to secure, and in that sense has "a property" to protect. A person without rights has nothing of his own and is a slave, not a member of political society; this thought has a long lineage and is at least as old as Cicero. It follows, as Locke is at pains to say, that absolute and arbitrary authority is not the essence of political authority, as Hobbes and Filmer said, but inconsistent with it. Like Aristotle confronting Plato, Locke carefully distinguishes the authority of parents over children, masters over slaves, and lawful governments over their subjects.

Locke has one more thing in mind when arguing that the task of government is to secure the citizens' property. In *A Letter concerning Toleration* he gives a similar account of the purpose of government, but sums up its concerns as our *bona civilia*, which is to say the goods that depend on the outward protection of our rights.[8] Negatively, Locke's purpose there, and very plausibly in the *Second Treatise*, too, is to deny that government has any concern with spiritual matters; "property" is the shorthand term for our "external" goods—security against attack, the ability to make a living, freedom of movement, and the like—and sharply distinguished from a concern with our immortal souls. The latter is more important than the former, but Locke wants to protect our inner lives and our spiritual allegiances from the coercive interference of the state just because they are the most important parts of our lives. Positively, we can be free to lead our spiritual lives as we ought, only if our external liberty is secure. Certainly, this extends to protecting the property rights of a congregation that builds a church, for instance; but the protection owes nothing to whatever doctrine the congregation professes, only to its ownership. Locke thought that we required the state's protection of our right to form voluntary associations with like-minded coreligionists to meet and worship according to our own best judgment. No more than that; and in the case of Catholics, who owed allegiance to a foreign sovereign with designs on England and were therefore not entitled to toleration, not even that.

If government exists to protect "property," and the authority of rulers is bounded by that purpose, we have the resources for an account of limited, constitutional government. Since Locke was contending against those who thought there were no limits to monarchical rule, he needed an argument to show that there were limits, and what they were. He sets them by framing political authority within natural law. We are, he claims, born into a world already under law; this law is natural law. Locke does not go into detail about what makes natural law law, but he does tell us briefly how we know what its dictates are; reason tell us that we are made by one almighty creator, sent into the world about his business, and we can infer from that premise and what we know of our natures what our natural rights and duties are. Years earlier he had written lectures on natural law as part of his duties at Christ Church. They are among the texts that seem at odds with the *Two Treatises*, since they were much more anxious about the existence of natural law and how we can know its requirements than the brisk discussion in the *Second Treatise*. The lectures suggest that mankind is not of one mind about the dictates of natural law, and that in any event the opinions of mankind are of little evidential value about the nature of the moral virtues. That there *is* a universal law binding on all mankind, he does not deny; that we can infer it from the opinions of mankind, he does. "Men are everywhere met with, not only a select few and those in a private station but whole nations, in whom no sense of law, no moral rectitude, can be observed. . . . Hence, among these nations, thefts are lawful and commendable, and the greedy hands of robbers are not debarred from violence and injury by any shackles of conscience. For others there is no disgrace in debauchery; and while in one place there are no temples or altars of the gods, in another they are found spattered with human blood."[9]

This was to deny that there is a jus gentium, in the sense of rules accepted by everyone in practice, and to cast doubt on the evidential connection between the jus gentium and the jus naturae or the *lex divina.* Locke was keenly aware that almost nothing that one society counted as a virtue was not by some other society counted as a vice, and conversely. It is possible that he changed his mind about the knowability of natural law; it is also possible that he thought that politics is not concerned about matters where dramatic disagreement is visible. It is also possible that he drew a sharp line between the moral sentiments of civilized and uncivilized peoples and thought that the English had the sensibilities of civilized people. He may also have come to hold the liberal belief that political cooperation is possible between people with different convictions about many moral, religious, and metaphysical issues. It is in the intimate areas of life, especially sexuality, that the greatest diversity of moral views is visible, while the need for honesty, keeping agreements, the duty to care for children, and similar principles are universally accepted. *Honeste vivere, neminem laedere, suum cuique tribuere*—honesty, nonaggression, and giving everyone his due—are, as Cicero said, the basis of social and political life. But one thing that emphasizes how thoroughly his own religious convictions permeated Locke's work was that Locke did not distinguish, as Hobbes had done, between "theorems" about what will conduce to our safety that can be worked out by pure reason and laws strictly speaking that require a lawgiver to promulgate them *as* laws. Locke invokes God as creator and legislator from the outset.

Natural Law

Reason teaches us that there is a natural law and what it is; the argument employs a crucial theological step absent in Hobbes's account. Anyone who consults his reason will see that we are all the workmanship of one almighty and benevolent maker, sent into the world about his business, and made to last during his, not one another's, pleasure. Like Hobbes, Locke believed that law was law because it was the command of a superior; to believe that natural law was strictly law required a belief in God as lawgiver. It did not require a belief in any particular religion or in a deity with any particular qualities, or the illumination of any particular revelation. Natural theology grounded natural law. To the usual conundrums about how we know what God's purposes are, and why we should imagine that he wishes us to thrive, given the seventeenth century's mortality rates, and the horrors of the wars of religion earlier in the century, Locke offers no answer. If God has made us, it is absurd to suppose that he endowed us with a desire to stay alive, appetites for food and drink, pressing needs for shelter and human companionship, and an urge to beget and rear children, only to frustrate the use of these endowments. Constructed as we are, we are evidently intended to use our gifts and satisfy our lawful appetites and flourish. We are sent into the world to secure our own long-term good, and because God has created all of us on the same terms, he must intend that all of us promote the good of everyone to the extent that we do not excessively undermine our own. This hangs on a teleological understanding of human nature more akin to Aristotle's than Hobbes's.

We may wonder what might happen if people held views about the nature of the world different from those Locke took for granted. For Locke, morality implies a lawgiver who lays down rules to bind the conduct of his subjects; this implies that a man who does not believe in God cannot regard himself as *morally* obliged to behave in any particular way. He might behave decently because he felt impelled to do so, but on this view he could not see himself as *obliged* or *bound* to behave decently. This

sets the limits of toleration; atheists could not be trusted to follow the
dictates of morality and had no claim to the toleration extended to all
deists.[10] Locke did not confront the problem that besets many secular
moralities; in many systems of ethics, morality is construed as a set of
rules for promoting the common good or the general welfare. Some of
them, such as utilitarianism, start from the premise that each of us by
nature wants to promote his or her own well-being, and imply a permanent tension between the demands of morality and the promptings
of self-interest. In Locke's universe, there is no such tension; we are the
handiwork of an almighty and benevolent maker, and pursue our well-
being on his terms. He has made us sociable, moral, and reasonable, and
our long-term welfare includes doing our duty according to the rules by
which God governs us. We are entitled to prefer our own safety to that of
others where they come into such severe competition that we would suffer greatly by not doing so; but anyone who is tempted to exploit other
people for his own benefit is wicked and selfish. Thrasymachus must be
suppressed as a danger to the rest of us.

Skeptics often complain that moral theories based on a religious
intuition offer a bribe for good behavior: God repays our sacrifices in
this life with immortal life and endless happiness hereafter. This is not
wholly fair. Locke certainly thought that we should consider more than
our earthly lives. Nonetheless, he did not divide our existence into future
eternal bliss and an earthly life in which we sacrifice ourselves in the
hope of having our losses made up hereafter. He had an Aristotelian
rather than an Augustinian view of the way morality and self-interest
are conjoined. We are social creatures, designed to flourish in open and
friendly relations with others; generally we flourish when other people's
well-being is an important part of our own. The differences between
Locke and Aristotle are not negligible. Locke was a moral individualist with a strong sense that we all have our own road to travel; and he
did not believe that what *all men think* was the best proof of ethical truth.
It mattered, too, that Locke took work infinitely more seriously than
Aristotle. For Aristotle, the mark of a gentleman was his knowledge
of how to employ his leisure; work was for slaves and the lower classes.
Locke subscribed to the work ethic. God has equipped us with skills

and talents and given us a world of resources on which to employ them, in gratitude to God and for the improvement of the human condition. A person who has found a calling and followed it has done what God required, what morality required, and is fulfilled.

One question raised by this account of natural law is how far it loses credibility with "the death of God." Nobody knows. Many writers have feared that modern liberal democracies are living on the borrowed capital of a Lockean religious ethic, and that as it erodes, the foundations of liberal democracy will be eroded, too.[11] Optimists think that Locke's conclusions are persuasive where his premises are not, and that that will suffice. If human beings are happiest when they live in nonviolent, law-abiding societies where work is encouraged and rewarded, liberal democracy will flourish. The latter part of the twentieth century saw the rise of an international consensus that we all possess so-called human rights, which closely resemble the rights that a Lockean system of natural law entails; where these are protected by human rights legislation, as they are by the American Constitution and by the European Convention on Human Rights, they are also part of positive law. Their ultimate metaphysical foundation is another matter entirely. It is at least likely that people who share Locke's view of human nature even if they do not share his religious convictions will do a better job of maintaining a liberal democracy than people who hold very different views about themselves, whether the racist views of the Nazis or the utopian communist views of Lenin and his successors, or the many other nonliberal and nondemocratic alternatives.

The Peaceful State of Nature

For Locke the question was settled: the law of nature set the boundaries of political legitimacy. It also provided rules of conduct by which mankind could under favorable conditions live at peace in the absence of political authority. This is where Locke was at odds with Hobbes. For Hobbes the misery of the state of nature stemmed from the fact that although we knew what rules it would be good to follow, we could not

follow them safely. Locke thought that we could employ them to regulate our conduct with others until life became either too complicated for
them to regulate our conduct in the absence of conventional written law,
or misbehavior was so rife that we could no longer trust one another.
Locke summed up the requirements of the law of nature in the requirement that we should not harm another in his life, liberty, or possessions
unless our very existence depended on it; this is not very different from
Hobbes, but Locke did not think that our lives depend on it very often.
It is vital to Locke that this should be so; if the choice was "despotism
or chaos," we might well hesitate to evict our tyrannical rulers. If the
choice is "despotism or behaving according to unofficial but universally
accepted rules while we find a new government," we would not. The
American colonists drew the right inference in 1776.

Locke imported into the argument something that caused Hobbes
difficulty, and himself almost as much. Locke argued that when a state
is created, rulers acquire no rights that do not already exist in the law
of nature. A ruler is legitimate only when authorized, either directly or
according to rules that have themselves been authorized, by the whole
people. The people cannot grant a ruler powers they did not formerly
possess themselves. The old Latin tag *nemo dat quod non habet*, or "nobody
can give what he does not have," was a principle of Roman law; someone whose title to property was defective could not pass a valid title to
someone else. If it was not his to give, he could not give it. Applied to the
contract that creates government ("authorizes the sovereign," in Hobbesian terms), the principle implies that we cannot give our rulers powers
we do not possess under the law of nature. Since the law of nature gives
nobody an absolute and arbitrary power over his own life and liberty,
let alone anyone else's, no government possesses absolute and arbitrary
power over its subjects. Whatever Charles II or Sir Robert Filmer might
think, absolute monarchy is a moral impossibility. This claim might
have got Locke executed in the last days of Charles II, but it was often
made in the Middle Ages and is persuasive.

The difficulty it poses centers on the right to punish. Governments
lay down positive law and uphold it by punishing the recalcitrant; Locke
took the right to inflict the death penalty "and consequently all lesser

penalties" as the central right of all governments.[12] If men in the state of nature had no right to punish others, governments could not have acquired the right; so Locke duly insisted that we had a right to punish breaches of the law of nature. Hobbes had vacillated; sometimes he said that the right to punish was part of the "right to all things" that we possess by nature, and that the sovereign had simply retained this natural right when the rest of us had given up our rights; sometimes he said that it was a new right, because punishment according to law was very different from the right of self-defense we all possess in the state of nature. Locke refused to see a problem, even though he admitted that some readers would think his view "strange."[13] The state of nature is a juridical state, and each person has a judicial authority, which is both instituted and bounded by law.

We have not only a natural right but a natural duty to punish offenders against the law of nature. We are not intended to act only in self-defense. We should punish offenders for their violations of the rights of others, especially those who are in no position to defend themselves. If you take food from a hungry child who is too weak to prevent your doing so, I ought, if I can, to force you to return it and punish you for the theft. The idea presents many problems; among the most obvious is motivation: shan't we be overeager to punish offenders against ourselves, but slow to defend anyone else? Another is judgment: shan't we be too strict in judging offenses against ourselves, and too lenient when it comes to offenses against others; and sometimes we may simply be uncertain what the law of nature requires. Organizing punishment looks problematic: if nobody in particular is required to punish an offender but anybody who can is entitled to, criminals will either escape punishment because we shall all wait for someone else to act, or they will find themselves punished many times for one offense. Locke acknowledges these problems. Government is the device that solves exactly these difficulties. It provides for a known and settled law, with impartial judges.

He did not anticipate critics who thought that punishment was by definition something inflicted only by government, and that whatever individuals not licensed by government did could not be punishment. He had no reason to. Locke's account of the law of nature makes sense of the thought that each of us can be judge, police, perhaps even a dependent legislature. Locke draws the usual distinction between revenge and punishment—my motive must be to uphold the law and not merely to strike at you, and the punishment must be only as much as will deter others and retribute your wrong. It is doubtful that we shall *in fact* act so dispassionately, but Locke accepts that as an argument for government. So it is not absurd to imagine mankind endowed with a moral right to punish one another and transferring that right to a conventionally recognized authority.

It is far from plain sailing. Consider traffic signals. Governments have the right to regulate traffic, but it is hard to believe that they acquired it when individuals transferred a prior natural right to install traffic signals. A view that is close to Locke's is that we possess a right to do what is necessary to enforce the law of nature, within the limits that the law of nature itself has set. Making traffic regulations prevents people from endangering the lives of others; it regulates our rights in appropriate ways. It implements the natural law injunction to flourish, and it fits neatly with what Locke says about the role of government in remedying the "inconveniences" of the state of nature. Punishment according to law may come into the world with government, but its legitimacy rests on the rights we transfer to our rulers when we establish government. At all events, Locke defines government's purpose as the protection of the "property" of each of us, and insists that we each have a property in ourselves that excludes others from using us for their own purposes. The right to punish is the right to prevent the exploitation of one individual by another. The final step in assembling the ingredients from which Locke constructs his account of legitimate political authority is to give an account of what property in our own persons amounts to and how it generates property in the usual sense.

Property

We must begin with two distinctions. The first is between what we nowadays call property and what Locke, and perhaps most of his contemporaries, called property. We distinguish between rights of ownership and other rights. Most legal systems allow us to transfer our property (in the narrow sense of objects we own) to other persons who then acquire the rights we once had. By contrast, none allow us to transfer such things as our religious liberty or our immunity to physical abuse. If I tell you that you may require me to pray when and where you choose, and then I do not do so, no court will assist you. If I tell you that you may have my "property" in my life and may kill me when you choose, you had better not take me up on the offer, because any court will convict you of murder. But if I sell you my bicycle and then try to take it back, I will be convicted of theft. Locke bundled together all those rights that attach to what one might call our legal and political personality as constituting our "propriety," that which gives us a stake in the world and in the political and legal system. Young children or slaves have only a limited "propriety" because their decisions do not determine what other people must do when dealing with them. This brings us to the second distinction, between what we think the idea of property embraces and what Locke thought. We distinguish property from other rights because we—most of us—think of property as under the absolute control of its owner, but most of us do not think that we can do with our bodies exactly what we like. Libertarians think such laws are illegitimate, but in most societies laws against suicide or prostitution restrict what we may do with our bodies. Locke, on the other hand, called all our rights property, but restricted what we could do with our property. He says we possess "a property in" our own persons that excludes any other human being from claiming ownership of us.[14] We are born free and equal; we could not be born free and equal if someone else could claim to own us.

Nonetheless, we are not absolute and outright owners of ourselves; the only being who owns us in that way is God. No human owns us like that, not ourselves, and certainly not our rulers. Indeed, Locke thinks of our rights less as giving us absolute discretion in what we do with what we "have a property" in than as the powers we must be able to exercise if we are to do what it is our duty to do as God's creatures. We have something like a lease in ourselves; we are entitled only to make of ourselves the creatures that God intends. We have no right to misuse or abuse what God has given us. We cannot commit suicide, since we are "made to last" during God's pleasure not one another's; and it is clear, though Locke never discusses the subject, that using our bodies for the purpose of prostitution would not be a legitimate use of the resources given to us.

Filmer

Locke provides an account of our relationship to the world, and therefore to ourselves, that limits our proprietorship by reminding us that we are the stewards of God's donation and accountable for our employment of it. It is an interesting and important question how this view can be sustained independently of the theological backing it receives in Locke; many of us *feel* constrained in the way Locke suggests, but some of us do not. Before turning to Locke's account of the institution of government, its powers and their limits, and the lawfulness of revolutionary change, we should allow Locke to finish settling accounts with Sir Robert Filmer, since he himself puts the finishing touches to his argument in the *Second Treatise*. Filmer understood the Book of Genesis as recording God's donation to Adam of absolute and arbitrary power over every living thing, just that power which Locke held that God alone possessed and gave to nobody.

Filmer's defense of absolute monarchy rested on the thought that this power descended by inheritance from father to son, so that on his father's death the oldest son moved from subjection to his father's absolute and arbitrary power to exercising that power himself. This power was proprietary and patriarchal; God gave the earth and everything in it to Adam. Adam owned his children; Adam's heirs had the same possessory rights over their children and so onward by descent. There are hints in *Patriarcha* that Filmer was prepared to dispense with the divine origin of the power and rely on a more anthropological account. He argued that the multiplicity of tiny independent kingdoms in the ancient world showed that they must have begun as independent family groups that had pooled their power to create these kingdoms.[15] Locke, indeed, was willing to concede that point in part, but not that the power so pooled was absolute and arbitrary. Filmer claimed that it was, which involved some difficult Old Testament exegesis, but he was helped by the existence in Roman law of the *patria potestas*, the father's absolute and arbitrary authority over his household. Technically, a Roman father could sell his children into slavery, which implies his ownership of them. The defenders of Charles II's right to name his brother as his heir drew on Filmer to support his claim to absolute authority. We, like Locke, find it hard to believe that any rational being could give Filmer's claims houseroom, but *Patriarcha* had two features that gave it purchase on its audience's imagination, besides the obvious attractiveness to conservatives of the running assault on the inconstancy and incompetence of popular governments. Even if Charles II was not Adam's heir, better Charles II than "the people."

Filmer's arguments fit everyday experience; his readers were used to patriarchal authority, they heard it defended from the pulpit, it marked the hierarchies of rural life, and it was bolstered by monarchical propaganda. Alternatives such as Locke offered were difficult to square with that experience; it was obvious that men were not born free and equal but into subjection; it was easy to imagine families turning into tribes and tribes turning into states, but impossible to imagine persons in a state of nature deciding one fine morning that it was time to establish government. One might think that once a monarch had granted his subjects their property on terms, his successors should not interfere with settled expectations; but the idea that men could own property in the absence of government seemed absurd. Ownership implies agreed rules whose existence postdates government. Filmer's reliance on a mixture of biblical authority and selective history is implausible to later readers; but an age that happily conflated biblical with secular history and narratives of origin with principles of justification would not have been so critical.

If God gave the world to Adam, not on terms but outright, and if most ancient societies seemed to be both clan-based and to give heads of families absolute power over the lives and liberties of their children, it was plausible that political authority was by nature absolute and arbitrary, passed by kings to their heirs, and inherited by kings from their fathers.

Locke's *First Treatise* is overkill, but its target was not wholly negligible, and the arguments employed against Filmer do the work of demolition that allows Locke to build constructively in the *Second Treatise*. To us, the proposition that Charles II is not the heir of Adam is blindingly obvious and therefore uninteresting. Locke's claim that Adam received from God only limited powers of stewardship looks plausible on the evidence of the text of Genesis, but hardly something we would go to the stake for. The two claims together give Locke what he needed: English kings did not inherit from Adam the powers they claimed, both because they did not inherit from Adam at all and because the powers they claimed were powers he had not had. Adam's authority over his children was limited, as is all authority by the purpose for which it was granted, namely, to allow him to bring them up to maturity. Adam's ownership of the world was limited, as all property rights are, by his using the world for the benefit of life.

Constructing Legitimate Government

Locke supposes that in the absence of government, men are in a state of nature. As with Hobbes, the state of nature need not have been a historical fact—in the sense that men may never have lived without government—and yet it can be said to still exist today—in the sense that any persons or states interacting without a common superior are, according to this definition, in a state of nature with respect to one another. The state of nature is defined relationally: men are in the state of nature with respect to one another when they have no common government, so sovereign states are always in a state of nature with respect to one another, and individuals are so if they encounter one another where there is no common government. A Swiss and an Indian bartering for trade in "the woods of America" are in the state of nature, says Locke. Not all of America was a pregovernmental state of nature (there were established governments in the early colonies by the time that Locke wrote), but in "inland America" no government has jurisdiction over the parties.[16] Once we know what a state of nature is, Locke can make some far-reaching claims. First, it is a social state. This seems to be a criticism of Hobbes's insistence that in the state of nature we would have no social relations with one another, because of mutual fear. Rousseau subsequently used a very different understanding of the state of nature to attack the idea that it could have been a social state; Locke's thought is only that we can imagine most human relationships working well enough in the absence of government, and it is hard to deny that. Second, the state of nature is a condition governed by its own laws, the laws of nature. In less theocentric terms, these two claims amount to the claim that human beings could in principle live together under generally accepted and morally binding rules without a government to enforce them. To which, as Locke knew, the necessary qualification is "and sometimes it would work well, and sometimes not."

Ownership

The third thing Locke argues is that in the state of nature it would have been possible to acquire legitimate property rights over external objects useful to the life of man, property in the ordinary modern sense. God gave the world to mankind in common for the sustenance and enhancement of human life. If the good things thus given to us are to be used for the purpose they are given for, individuals must have some legitimate way of taking their share from the common stock. This is Locke's reworking of the Scholastic deduction of the lawfulness of ownership, and may well have been inspired by Aquinas or later Thomist writers. If we have property in what we take, then once we have taken it, it is *ours*, and not only de facto no longer part of the common stock, but de jure too. The objection to this line of thought was always that a claim to ownership requires recognition by other people; in the absence of government, would we not have to ask the whole world for permission to take from the common stock? If we had to do this each time we wanted a drink of water, we would die of thirst before we took our first lawful drink. Locke rehearses this argument, knowing that he has the resources to defeat it.

The first move is to analyze the idea of holding the world in common; traditionally, there was a distinction between positive and negative community; positive community is the form of joint ownership under which each owner must give consent for any part of the property to be alienated. Where a village owns land "in common," the terms on which the village can consent to a change of use may range from a simple majority to unanimity. Negative community exists when nobody owns any particular portion of the world, and any (unowned) part of it may be used without infringing anyone's rights. Locke steered between these two poles, though he steers closer to the second than the first. God's donation of the whole world to mankind in common means that it is available for use for all; nobody has been given any particular portion of it. But mankind has a collective interest in its being properly used, and misuse is a violation of everyone else's property in the world. In the same way as our property in our own persons, our property in the world is a claim to use the resources available to us for the purposes for which they are rightly used. How that claim can be effective is one of the questions to which the answer is, "by creating a legitimate government that will enable the rational and industrious to flourish."

Before we can create a government, however, we need to understand what rights we acquire by taking from the common stock. Locke argues that we *must* be able to acquire such rights by simple appropriation, because otherwise the creator's gifts would go to waste, which can be no part of his plans. Still, there is a problem. It is one thing to say that we must be able to appropriate and consume what we need to stay alive, to drink from the stream and gather fruit from the trees; it is another to say that when we drink from the stream we *own* the water we drink. Locke both illuminates and confuses the issue by relying on a labor theory of acquisition that has been inconclusively analyzed for the past three centuries. Locke argued that we can individually and without permission from others acquire what is then our property by "mixing" with it what is already and inescapably ours, that is, our labor.[17]

Locke's conception of what our labor consists in is elastic, embracing any activity by which we make a productive difference to the world, from picking an acorn from a tree at one end of the spectrum to setting up a limited liability company to take settlers to the American colonies at the other. It must be a *productive* or useful difference, because spoiling or wrecking the world is making a difference to it that is forbidden ab initio. The argument is compelling. God grants humanity an abundant world to use and enjoy. It cannot be used and enjoyed unless individuals consume its fruits; since they must be able to do so lawfully, there must be a moment at which things pass from the common stock and into private hands and after which it would be wrong for others to deprive the new possessor. I put a gourd into the stream and carry the dipper of water to my child; is this "my" water? The answer is yes, at any rate prima facie. Where we hesitate, it is because of two further considerations that Locke put into place. The first is whether I have left "as much and as good" for others; if there is a shortage of water, taking a dipper of it may exceed my share, and I may have "a property" in somewhat less. The second is whether I am going to use it for a legitimate purpose; in the case of a dipper of water for my child, that also is taken care of. The three tests for legitimate ownership are that it is acquired by labor, that "enough and as good" is left for everyone else, and that what we take is used and not wasted. "Acquired by labor" is, however, essential only for first appropriation; my child does not have to labor to receive the water from me.[18]

A modern reader will already want to know how far our property rights extend. Locke explains them initially—and always when they embrace our political rights—in negative terms; property is what we cannot be deprived of without our own consent. Arbitrary taxation, as the American colonists complained seventy years later, is a paradigm case of being deprived of our property without our consent. What I get is the right not to have that water taken from me. But an account of property rights must also explain our ability to transfer property to other people and how the rights that we transfer "stick" with the new owner. We normally think of what we own as what we can sell, give, lend, and so on; we also think of it as what can be bequeathed. Locke may well have seen little point in debating how many of the more elaborate features of a developed legal regime would be visible in a world governed only by the law of nature. In a simple society, few possessions would be durable

enough to raise questions about inheritance, and many different arrangements about whatever was durable enough to outlast one owner would be
consistent with the law of nature. He was precise about what he needed
to be precise about: that we acquire individual property rights without
consent from others, and by a route other than donation from a superior.
In the *First Treatise* Locke discusses the question of the rights over other
people's property conferred by sheer necessity. He takes Aquinas's view
that if we have the resources to secure some persons from starving and we
do not use them, our superfluity is really *theirs.* That is, we cannot stand
fast on our property rights and say that although it would be a kindly act
for us to help them, it is our bread or grain or whatever, so they have no
right to it; Locke's view is that if their need is urgent enough, they have
such a right, and that it is *theirs.*[19] It is impossible to guess what Locke
would have said under the circumstances of a twenty-first-century industrial economy, but on the face of it, any wealthy person who complains
about his or her taxes going to the poor has made a mistake about the
ownership of their income above the level at which his welfare would be
severely under threat. Conversely, nobody who can labor but is unwilling
to do so has any claim to assistance from anyone else. Locke's views on
property make the sort of socialism that regards *all* private property as
illicit illegitimate from the outset, but they do not exclude the creation
of a welfare state.

Locke's insistence that we could be governed entirely by the law of
nature raises the awkward question why we should wish to leave the
state of nature. It is less like a Hobbesian war of all against all than the
philosophers' golden age. If we could manage all our relations with one
another by simple moral rules—as we manage the great bulk of our
relations in any society—there seems no need of government. Locke
painted a skeletal picture of a natural growth of complication, including an account of the development of inequality and the invention of
money that suggests that the needs of a developed economy, on the one
hand, and the unsatisfactoriness of a system of regulation so vulnerable
to uncertainty and insecurity, on the other, make government necessary.
A world where we gather what we need for immediate consumption is a
world of equal poverty; there is little room for envy or greed, but life will

be basic. Like others, Locke sometimes suggested that this might none-theless have been the golden age of the poets, before our social vices took hold. The obvious thought, however, is that rational people would move from hunting and gathering to agriculture and commerce; agriculture requires landownership, and the paradigm case of property that outlasts its immediate owners.

Locke employs an argument about productivity in defending the lawfulness of landed property. A man who makes a tree bear more by pruning and fertilizing it acquires the tree as well as its fruit, and in the same way a man who cultivates a field acquires the field as well as its crop. The argument *seems* to depend on the analogy with the simpler cases of mixing our labor with what we own; Locke says of the acquisi-tion of land, "I think it is plain, that property in that too is acquired as in the former."[20] A crucial thought is that in making land fruitful by my efforts, I do not diminish the common stock but add to it: "And there-fore he that incloses land, and has a greater plenty of the conveniences of life from ten acres, than he could have from an hundred left to nature, may truly be said to give ninety acres to mankind."[21] Locke points out that most of what we consume embodies a lot of human labor: we eat bread rather than grains picked from the wild, and so on. Absent the ownership of land, it would be impossible. The difficulty comes when all the readily cultivated land has been acquired and there are landless persons without access to uncultivated land. Locke's answer is that land-owners must employ them as laborers on decent terms. His theory of acquisition now faces the awkward fact that the persons thus employed do not become owners of the fields on which they labor, even though they are on any reckoning mixing much more labor with the earth than the owners of it. The landowners' acquisition does *not* leave "enough and as good" *land* for others, and it seems that the landlord owns without working while his laborers work without owning.

This simple thought formed the basis of agrarian radicalism for the next three centuries, and Locke's resistance to it has led critics to claim that Locke was the advocate of an agrarian capitalist revolution, and an enemy to the just claims of the landless laboring class. The radical view was that the landless laborer had been deprived of his right to the land.

Only periodic redistribution could spread the enjoyment of that right more widely, or a supersession of private rights by common ownership was required. Rousseau says something very like it; the executed French revolutionary radical Gracchus Babeuf demanded it; innumerable early nineteenth-century agrarian reformers said it. Locke disagreed. What we have a right to acquire by labor is not material things, in this case land, but "a living." God wishes us to flourish, not to be attached to a piece of ground; our rights are rights to employ our abilities on the world's resources in order to yield a good living. Nonexploited laborers get what they have a right to. One might, as Locke did, put the matter another way. The best-off member of a hunter-gatherer society lives less well than a laborer in a developed society; he lives less comfortably and eats less well: "A King of a large and fruitful territory there ['inland America'] feeds, lodges, and is clad worse than a day labourer in England."[22] Since the person who benefits least from the transformation benefits so much, the transformation is legitimate. The argument resolves one anxiety, but fails entirely to meet another; it answers the question whether the private ownership of land is justified, by pointing out that even the least benefited is benefited by the change. It does nothing to explain why the particular people who are the least well-off occupy the positions in society that they do. As radicals have always insisted, the worst-off do most of the work; as they only occasionally add, throughout human history 90 percent of the world's work has been done by women.

The final step in the events that make government necessary is the creation of money. It is possible to live a simple life on the basis of barter; but exchange is impeded by the absence of money. There will be a tendency for durable things to be used as protomoney; if I have several nut trees, I can exchange long-lasting nuts for shorter-lasting fruit or meat, and when you exchange meat with me, you will take more nuts than you want to consume, thinking to use them in a further exchange with someone else. Locke defines money functionally; anything will serve as money if it is a store of value and a means of circulation of commodities. The ultimate step is to use as money things that have a "fancy value," do not perish, and are valuable only because they will exchange for what is useful. "Fancy" is an odd word in the context, but necessary to Locke's purposes.

Locke thought that some people had simply liked shiny metals such as gold or bright shells like cowrie shells; someone who acquired them would find that others would exchange genuinely useful things for them, and a price system would emerge. Locke also uses the word "fancy" to indicate that money is accepted by convention, not instituted by nature, and he sometimes suggests that money really isn't valuable at all. With money a developed economy is possible; people can buy land, hire laborers, invest in new projects, and accumulate more money. Readers of Locke wonder whether he really believed that a market economy could have existed in the state of nature; the best guess is that he thought it impossible in fact and possible conceptually. If all accepted the rules that allowed them to know who owned what, who owed what to whom, and what anything was worth in cash terms, they could run a market economy without government; in practice, the complexities would defeat them.

One further implication of Locke's account of property is worth dwelling on. The deep antipathy in Locke's work is to the claim of any human being to exercise an authority that amounts to the ownership of another human being. Nonetheless, he says there can be legitimate forms of slavery. Captives taken in a just war may be held as slaves, since they could lawfully have been killed and are given the lesser of two evils. Unlike Aristotle, Locke does not suggest that "man-hunting" is a lawful form of economic activity, though the slave traders of the seventeenth century were a party to it. The thought that Africans taken to America had been captured in a just war stretches credulity too far. Locke's concern was no doubt to insist that the subjects of Charles II were not captives taken in a just war and were not his property. But a less deeply principled reason for rejecting Filmerian ideas is this: God gave us the world to use productively. Kings are prone to give estates to aristocrats who use them for hunting and other forms of warlike recreation. This is so far from using them productively that one may doubt that aristocrats who use their estates thus have the same entitlement to the unhindered use of their property as the ordinary farmer or, indeed, the kind of careful semicapitalist farmer who was coming on the scene in the seventeenth century. If the original inhabitants of America had no property in the territory they hunted over, one might wonder whether Locke thought royal favorites had more rights over their lands. "God gave it [the world] to the use of the industrious and rational (and labour was to be his title to it) not to the fancy or covetousness of the quarrelsome and contentious."[23]

Setting Up the State

So we come to the creation of government. Its role is obvious: to provide a known and settled law, administered by impartial judges. The brevity of the list is deliberate. It is no part of government's tasks to save our souls, to establish a church, or to take sides in moral controversy. Its authority is limited by the needs of its subjects; they are the protection of their rights and the clarification of their duties to each other. The argument is overdetermined. God grants us only the powers we need to fulfill his purposes; if he requires government to attend only to our earthly needs, no government has absolute and arbitrary authority. It is a contradiction of the very idea of government. Contra Filmer, who had derived absolute monarchy from the rights of fathers, Locke argued that parents' rights over children were neither absolute nor arbitrary, but bounded by the needs of the children; they were parental, not patriarchal, held by both parents, not fathers alone, and naturally dropped away as children reached the age of reason. Even where authority must be absolute to be effective, it is not arbitrary, because it is always bounded by the purpose it served. An officer has the right to shoot a soldier for cowardice in the face of the enemy, and may shoot him on the spot. Nonetheless, he may not touch sixpence of his pay.[24] In any event, because nobody in his right mind would grant another an absolute and arbitrary right over himself, no group of us can grant such a power to a government. Locke relies throughout on two thoughts: one that any persons or institution may claim only the rights needed to fulfill their or its functions, the other that the sanctity of the individual person bars governments from invading his or her rights unless the defense of others absolutely requires it. If the two are put together, the theory of limited government is safe.

As to how government is created, Locke offers an account that critics have cut their teeth on for three centuries. In contrast to Hobbes, Locke imagines the institution of government as a two-stage process. The first is the step by which a people constituted itself a people, which was the prelude to instituting a *political society*; this was genuinely a contract of all with all. Medieval lawyers described it as the *pactum communis*; the second was traditionally known as the *pactum subjectionis*, or the step by which the people put themselves under a government of a specified form. What makes Locke's view modern is what he does with the imagined mechanism. The old vision, as it descended from the Roman lawyers, imagined the people generating political authority in becoming a political society and then giving that authority to their rulers. This is Justinian again, and in republican guise it is Bartolus. Locke's account suggests something closer to the relationship of employer and employee; the people never wholly relinquishes its authority. We the people employ our rulers on whatever terms we rationally choose; if they fail to do their job, we can dismiss them. We do not contract with our rulers; we "trust" them with the powers they need to serve the functions they are to serve.

Government must rest on consent. Conventions operate only because people agree to operate them, and governments are a skein of conventions. It hardly needs saying that our dealings with governments are not paradigms of consent-based relationships, though critics seem to delight in saying it over and over. Our duties to the governments we live under are not voluntarily undertaken; I did not choose to live under the government I find myself obeying, and I cannot revise the terms on which I live under it. Its laws bind me whether or not I consent to what they demand; the government of the day may or may not be one I voted for or would have voted for, but it is there regardless. The consent involved in the authority that government has over me is not the sort of consent involved in commerce or marriage. It really does require my consent for me to be married or be bound by a commercial contract; it really does not require my consent for me be a subject of the government of the United Kingdom. This may not be decisive against Locke. Just as it requires my consent if I am to become the naturalized citizen of another country, Locke may well have thought that because we are all born free and equal, which is to say citizens or subjects of nowhere, giving our allegiance to any particular government required our consent in the same way. In terms familiar to Americans, we might think that we are by nature resident aliens until the question arises of whether we are fully members of the political community in which we happen to be living.

Locke needed an account of the role of consent as the basis of government; the *Two Treatises* founded the throne of William III in the consent of his people. He could have given a minimalist account of what he meant by noting, as antiabsolutist writers had always done, that English monarchs pledged themselves to uphold the laws and liberties of the realm, which implied that if they failed to do it, consent could be withdrawn, perhaps through the agency of Parliament. Parliament had taken this view when demanding that Charles I should promise to observe the familiar constitutional conventions. Locke went further. Like Hobbes, he wanted to found our obligation to obey our rulers on our having consented to do so. Unlike Hobbes, he wanted that consent to be given on terms, and to constrain what governments, including the legislative branch of government, could rightfully do. For ordinary purposes, that consent could be given by our representatives, but our lives and liberties, and our property in the usual sense, are our own and not to be touched or taxed, except with the consent of ourselves or our representatives, and if our representatives violate their trust, then not by them.

Locke makes several different claims about consent. The first is a historical claim about the origin of government. By the time Locke wrote, the modern idea of the state was well entrenched. States were territorial entities; governments claim the allegiance of a people in a geographical area; the government of the United States is entirely unlike General Motors, which operates in many countries. The Holy Roman Empire was by this time an oddity, a multiethnic dynastic entity centered on Austria, and even its authority was substantially territorial. Locke had to explain how mankind could form into the groups that we call "peoples" and each acquire a separate government. Filmer had done it: families became tribes and tribes became peoples. Locke thought preliterate people had often come together and become a political unit by mutual agreement; the nonexistence of written agreements did not mean that no agreements had been made. Historically, it may well have been that families associated with one another, then formed clan societies, and finally acknowledged some person or group as entitled to lay down the rules of association and everyday living. But contra Filmer, when they acquired a government, a new sort of authority, authority by consent, came into the world.

Locke also had in mind something we have been assuming. "Natural" rules of the sort laid down by the law of nature have to be supplemented by conventional rules of the sort we are all familiar with. Double yellow lines on the road "mean" that we must not park there; to say that they exist by consent is an awkward way of expressing the important point that they mark out a no-parking area by a convention that exists because we accept it. The oddity of talking about consent in such cases is partly that we rarely wonder how such conventions are kept alive, and partly that no single individual can do much to bring about the downfall of the institution. Consider money, which Locke also says exists by consent; nobody is in a position to destroy the pound sterling or the U.S. dollar by refusing to agree to its existence. But if all of us became convinced that a currency will lose its value through hyperinflation, we might all refuse to use it, and it would cease to be a currency.

Locke wished to tie consent to obligation, not merely to emphasize the conventional nature of institutions. The question then arises of *who* has consented to *what*. To distinguish between different degrees of obligation that someone living under a government owed to it, Locke drew a distinction between "express" and "tacit" consent that is less famous than notorious. The distinction is useful in everyday life—if you send me a note to say that you presume you will meet me at seven o'-clock unless I say I shan't be there, and I say nothing but do not show up, you will feel that I had tacitly agreed to be there and should have shown up. Locke suggests that if we are never asked to swear allegiance to the current government but accept its benefits without demur, we give tacit consent. Enjoying the benefits of government, including the protection of our lives and liberties, and inheriting property from our parents, permits the presumption that we agree to obey the present government on the terms they did. Express consent is better in the sense that if we are asked for our consent and give it in proper form, we will be thought to have put our-

selves under the obligation to do what we have consented to. That is why
Cromwell's government required the more important members of English
society to "engage." The view that tacit consent is inferior to express consent is reflected in the American habit of having children recite the Pledge
of Allegiance in elementary school. Children thereby give *express consent*
to their government, though they do so at an age when their consents
cannot be binding on an installment plan purchase, let alone in the matter of choosing a system of government. Curiously enough, most school
districts abandon the practice when children attain the age of reason and
might be thought to be bound by what they say.

Complaints against the idea of consent have focused both on the
idea that consent of any kind is involved in political obligation and on
the difficulty of knowing what the distinction between express and tacit
consent was meant to mark. All critics make the simple but devastating
objection that "consent" is binding only when the person giving it has a
fair choice of alternatives; nobody has been impressed by Hobbes's insistence that the man who swears obedience when the conqueror's sword is
at his throat has a choice of alternatives. Even with Locke's milder version of the argument, the objection is the same; the choice we have about
what government to live under varies, but few of us have the luxury of
being able to migrate elsewhere entirely painlessly and whenever we wish.
Those who "engaged" with Cromwell could, perhaps, have remained in
exile without undue difficulty; few modern citizens could simply pick up
and live elsewhere. The complaint against "tacit" consent, on the other
hand, is that it is no consent at all. What can we do but accept the benefits of orderly government? As Hume later observed, the plowman with
barely fourpence in his pocket is in no position to withdraw his consent,
and so cannot be said to have given it. Locke himself made the same
point in the *First Treatise*.[25]

It is not obvious what the distinction between tacit and express was
intended to mark. Locke may have had in mind the difference between
obligations that attach to us because of our location and those that
attach to us in virtue of our nationality, though the difference is not best
marked by talking of consent. An Englishman who lives in the United
States is both legally and morally obliged to obey (most of) the laws of

the United States; he must follow the local legal rules not because he is a citizen, since he is not, but as a matter of moral duty to other people. Anyone who thought that because he was not an American citizen he was not obliged to drive carefully, pay his taxes, and look out for the welfare of those he lived among would be wicked. Yet behaving decently does not make him an American. The unanswerable question is whether Locke held the radical view that there is no difference between the obligations of foreigners and the obligations of the native born, but a difference between the obligations attaching to anyone who accepts the benefits of government and those attaching to those who have sworn allegiance. The first are morally obliged to be law-abiding members of a society; only the latter owe a distinctively political allegiance. It is a view defended in our own day by John Rawls, and a view that I hold.[26] Whether Locke held it is another matter.

There is a personally relevant point that Locke may have had in mind. His view implies that unless we have explicitly sworn allegiance, our former rulers have no authority over us once we leave the country. On that view Locke could not, as a matter of logic, commit treason once he was in Holland. In leaving England, he had abandoned his allegiance to the English crown. For someone who feared that he might be kidnapped and judicially murdered as a traitor, this was not a small consideration. If it was Locke's view, it is at odds with the practices of most countries. The United States regarded citizens who fled during the Vietnam War as draft dodgers, not as persons who had lost the obligation to fight for their country when they left it. Only when they took another country's citizenship did they lose their unfulfilled obligation to perform military service along with their citizenship.

Locke was strangely casual about forms of government and their virtues; he endorsed the views of "the judicious Hooker" about constitutionality, but unlike Thomas Hooker he did not meticulously lay out the case for mixed and balanced government. He was equally casual about just how a political society, once formed, is to create the constitution under which its members will live. He takes majority decision making for granted, with the bare observation that it is necessary that a body moves whichever way the greater force directs it, which hardly justifies majority rule or explains its legitimacy and problems. The point, perhaps, is that what he was doing was resurrecting in a modern form the view of a writer such as Marsilius that "the people" possessed all the legitimate authority that can exist, and that it is up to them to delegate its employment as they choose. Any number of institutionalizations of the process might be imagined. Locke certainly thought that the legislative function of government was overwhelmingly the most important, which suggested an acceptance in general terms of the sovereignty of Parliament, but thought a variety of systems of representation and a variety of legislative bodies were acceptable. He distinguished between the legislative, executive, and "federative" powers of government, rather than what became traditional, and he did not explore the problems posed by theories of the separation of powers and checks and balances. Constitutional details are a matter of prudence. That nonconstitutional governments are not governments at all is the principle to be established. All the regimes of modern Western Europe and North America would pass his tests for legitimacy. A written or an unwritten constitution would be equally acceptable, so long as there were enforceable guarantees of fair trial, equal and impartial laws, and the restriction of law to the regulation of our earthly concerns. Under any constitution, a written constitution, if we have one, must rely on the unwritten understandings that we employ to interpret it. The best we can do is write down our understandings as we go, so that we are guided by precedent. When precedent runs out, we must act as best we can in the light of natural law.

Revolution

We must consider the doctrine that would have cost Locke his life if the agents of Charles II or James II had found the manuscript of the *Second Treatise* and its author. Locke was far from the first writer to discuss revolution. Aristotle considered it in the context of the breakdown of politics; Machiavelli considered it in the context of the renovation of a polity and the revival of its citizens' virtue. Locke's position was not, as theirs was, sociological but moral. It was squarely in the tradition of Augustine, though framed in terms very different from the Pauline tradition, and designed to repudiate it. So far from being "ordained by God," the powers that be are instituted by a social contract; they hold their power as a trust from the people. Locke's understanding of revolution shares with Machiavelli's the idea that the point of a revolution is a renovation of the constitution, and to that extent it is old-fashioned. It is not the modern understanding of a revolution as part of a process of progressive social change; but that conception had to await the French Revolution. Locke's question was whether a citizen had the right to revolt against his government. Like Luther and Calvin, Hobbes firmly said no; like them, he recognized that as a matter of fact we will fight in self-defense if we have to, and that men who fear they may be forced to fight in self-defense may do it sooner rather than later. But Hobbes insisted that each should look to his own welfare; he denied that we have a right, let alone a duty, to attack our sovereign on behalf of others or in the name of principle. Locke's view was exactly the reverse.

Government possesses authority only within constitutional bounds. If it exceeds those bounds, it has declared war on its citizens, and they may resist. Not only may they resist; they have every right to reconstitute the government as they choose to secure constitutional government in future. That is surely an expression of Locke's belief that the Parliament that met after the abandonment of his duties by James II was a constitutional convention, and that William III ruled on the terms established by that Parliament. This radical thought was of a piece with his view of revolution. Morally speaking, justified revolutions are defensive responses to the declaration of war by a corrupt ruling elite. The familiar question "Who started it?" was the right question. Locke's answer was that almost always government starts it. His contemporaries were fearful of disorder and hated anything that smacked of an incitement to rebellion. Locke thought his countrymen were too willing to sit quietly under injustice and that they should be urged to stand up for their rights. He thought that only James II's impetuosity had saved them from a descent into tyranny.

As to what we can say when the supporters of the crown and the supporters of the revolutionaries both claim that right is on their side, Locke replies that we can only appeal to heaven with swords in our hands. The shockingness of all this can only be appreciated in the light of the horror that swept over Europe at the trial and execution of Charles I. To kill a king was to stretch out one's hand against the Lord's anointed, and here was Locke insisting that whatever ceremonies attended a coronation were beside the point; kings who attacked their subjects were criminals, and that was the end of it. He takes on a noted defender of monarchical absolutism and divine right, William Barclay, a Scots Catholic who had spent most of his life in France and was much admired by James I. Barclay was a useful foil, because he admitted that a king may behave so unjustly that in effect he has abdicated. The question then arises whether he can be made to abdicate; this is the old question about the right of resistance. Barclay says that the people may resist, but "with reverence," and Locke uncharacteristically allows him an extended paragraph of mockery, culminating with the observation "He that can reconcile blows with reverence may for aught I know look to receive a civil, respectful cudgelling wherever he may find it."[27]

Locke's point is simple. If resistance is permissible under any circumstances, those who resist must be ready to use force, because force will certainly be used against them. Locke must surely have intended to unnerve his opponents when, in response to the thought that revolution was unlawful, he responded with Cicero's *salus populi suprema lex est.* He had said earlier that when men enter civil society, the bounds of natural law are drawn tighter, in effect that behind positive law there must stand the law of nature. The extraconstitutional defense of constitutional principle is not unlawful; but Locke would have known very well that Cicero uttered those famous words in defense of the summary execution of Catiline's coconspirators. It does not follow that Locke would have approved of the execution of Louis XVI or any of the excesses of the French Revolution that broke out a hundred years later. What does follow is that Locke could not have felt the pious horror of English conservatives. It must also be remembered how important it is that Locke did not think that a revolution overturned the political community; it was precisely because he was attached to the two-stage account of the social contract that he could envisage the political community, so to speak, evicting the government it had installed and installing another. The identity of the underlying political nation was not threatened by such a process. The thought made its way if not into the Declaration of Independence at any rate into the minds of those who wrote it and acted on it.

Locke's radicalism was not complete; unlike Jefferson, who thought that a revolution every thirty years would stir a sluggish nation to recover its sense of purpose, Locke believed in stability and thought that revisiting the system of representation as infrequently as once a century would be enough. He wished to see settled law established in place of arbitrary royal whim, not the permanent revolution of later Marxist imaginings. Nonetheless, in an age when many theorists thought that kings were literally appointed by God, and that absolute authority on the one side must meet absolute obedience on the other, Locke imagined revolution as a measured, controlled but nevertheless violent act that disposed of a tyrannical government yet left intact the bonds of everyday life. The idea that we can evict our rulers without undermining the common understandings that not only make us one people but make us governable was one of the most important ingredients of American radicalism.

Toleration

The other area in which Locke was at odds with his contemporaries, but not with his successors, was religious toleration. Locke began as a firm believer in the crown's right to establish forms of worship. The crown could not command its subjects to disbelieve the basic tenets of the Christian faith, but "things indifferent" were squarely within its power and might be regulated as the crown chose. This was the burden of his *Two Tracts on Government*, written in the early 1660s. At that stage, he held much the same view as Hobbes; in all societies, there must be some absolute and arbitrary power, lodged in the person of a king or an assembly, since otherwise there was no end to disputes about the law. This in essence meant that the government of the day could refuse to allow dissenting sects to practice their religion publicly, and could legitimately do what British governments in fact did for over a century longer and require its citizens to worship in the churches of the established church on several occasions a year. Locke appears to have changed his mind as the result of a visit to the Continent, where he saw the benefits that the Dutch gained from toleration. His *Essay on Toleration* of 1667 marked the change to the view that governments exist only to perform the tasks set out in the *Second Treatise*. The doctrine is nicely stated in an essay entitled *Civil and Ecclesiastical Power* (1674); "There is a twofold society, of which almost all men in the world are members, and that from the twofold concernment they have to attain a twofold happiness; viz. that of this world and that of the other."[28] He also came to think that the royal prerogative was less extensive than he had believed and sided with the Dissenters who refused to accept toleration as a royal concession rather than the acknowledgment of a right. Locke became a confirmed believer in the widest possible toleration, but it was toleration as an acknowledgment of the subject's right to practice his religion as he conscientiously believed he should, not a good-natured concession.

His argument for toleration is circular, but none the worse for it. Its persuasiveness depends on the acceptance of a view of religion that not everyone will accept, but it is an argument in favor of his view of religion that it leads to toleration. In the *Letter concerning Toleration* Locke distinguishes a church from a state: a church is a voluntary association of like-minded persons who wish to give a common, public expression to their desire to honor God and thank him for his blessings. Its only sanction against members who violate the majority conception of what the church is committed to stems from the purpose for which it exists—that is, the majority can separate dissident members. They can excommunicate dissidents, but they cannot levy financial or physical penalties against them. At this time Massachusetts was executing its own dissenters, while Catholic Spain and Italy suffered the terrors of the Inquisition and the French authorities exacted disgusting penalties for blasphemy. The massacre of the Huguenots in France after the revocation of the Edict of Nantes in 1685 was also on Locke's mind. Locke thought that peace could be kept only on the principle of *curat Deus injuria Dei*, which is to say that it is up to God to punish us for offenses against him.

Once we know what a church is, it is easy to see that the state is a compulsory organization, using physical and financial penalties to secure our earthly peace and prosperity. The world is neatly divided between two forms of authority, neither of which has any reason to interfere with the other. Anyone may join whatever church he or she chooses, and may worship God however seems best; the state needs to take no interest in these decisions. There are qualifications to make to this before coming to the largest of Locke's own qualifications. Separation of church and state does not mean that the state will not protect the earthly interests of a church as a corporate body. A person who burns down a church is guilty of arson just as if he burned down a house or a shop; the physical plant of a church is earthly property like any earthly property and receives the same protection. Conversely, there are restrictions on what we can do in our worship; if the law forbids cruelty to animals, I may not flay a cat on the altar as part of my religious practices. A fortiori I cannot claim the right to commit infant sacrifice or ritual mutilation. Locke might have had his doubts about the circumcision of Jewish baby boys; so-called female circumcision would have been prevented as simple assault. Locke's argument is that if there is a good secular reason to prevent something, there can be no good religious reason to permit it.

American Indians wishing to use peyote in their ceremonies would not have got far in courts that adopted Locke's principles. They could not have claimed that their religion rightly required what the secular law rightly forbade. Locke's view would have been that they must find a way of worshipping within the law. However, a law that prevented anyone from consuming peyote might be hard to sustain. Given the intoxicants that are not forbidden, there must be a suspicion that the law forbids the consumption of peyote *because* it is part of Indian religious ritual, and that is a breach of the principle of toleration. Locke's own example is clear enough; if cows may be slaughtered at all, they may be slaughtered ceremonially; if there is a famine and we are forbidden to slaughter cattle, they may not be slaughtered as part of a ceremony.

Locke's readers often overlook the contrast between his view of toleration and the practice of most liberal countries today—which exempts religious practices in such areas as the ritual slaughter of animals from much of the secular law on animal cruelty—because they are so struck by Locke's two exceptions to his claim that "absolute liberty is what we stand in need of." The first exception is atheism; atheists are beyond toleration. His reasons are plausible if we accept Locke's account of morality, and otherwise not. Locke thought that atheists had no reason to keep their promises, or accept the other principles of morality on which society depends, and were therefore not to be trusted. This is at all levels nonsense, however, since the nontoleration of atheists simply gives people Locke deems untrustworthy an added incentive to dissimulate. As to the premises of the argument, Locke's knowledge of the history of philosophy would have shown him innumerable examples of writers and thinkers who were atheists but entirely honest.

The second exception is that of the Roman Catholic Church. Here Locke relied on a wholly different argument, where Hobbes had come to more liberal conclusions from identical premises. Locke did not write his *Two Treatises* and his *Letter concerning Toleration* in criticism of Hobbes, but the contrast is inescapable. Like Hobbes, Locke thought that the Roman Catholic Church was a secular state allied to other secular states and that a good Catholic must have divided loyalties. The pope had excommunicated kings and told their subjects that they were not obliged to obey them; to subscribe to a religion that required us to betray our country is to be a traitor. Hobbes was unwilling to pursue his fellow subjects into the recesses of their beliefs and happy that Catholics should worship in private; this was genuine toleration. The reason for Locke's greater fierceness may partly be that Charles II had tried to betray his own country in the name of Catholicism. It must also have mattered that Locke thought men rightly wanted exactly what Hobbes was not ready to give them—the right to worship *in public*. To give them that would be to acknowledge the legitimacy of the organization, not merely to accept the harmlessness of a personal religious taste. It is because Locke took religion *as religion* more seriously than Hobbes that he was less willing to make any concessions at all.

Locke is a deceptive writer. With him the modern cast of mind has arrived. We read him and argue with him as though he were a contemporary. Of course, it requires a knowledge of seventeenth-century history to know what was happening when he wrote, and a knowledge of his biography to know who his associates were and what he might have hoped and feared at any particular moment. Nonetheless, his arguments for limited and constitutional government, economic freedom, and religious liberty can be read as if they were made yesterday. However, this very transparency may paradoxically blind us to the vitality of other ways of writing about politics in which an older tradition of statecraft was remodeled for the seventeenth and eighteenth centuries. To neglect these would be to neglect a strand of political thinking that has been at least as influential in determining the institutions we live under as the Lockean concern that government should respect our natural rights and the requirements of natural law. To put the issue much too briskly, one strand of thinking focuses on the rights of individuals and the constraints they do (or do not) impose on government, while the other focuses on the capacity of a people collectively to act as citizens rather than subjects. Liberals from the time of Rousseau on have complained that the second tradition has had too little concern for the rights of individuals *against* their governments. The French Revolution gave added force to their fears. The attempt to turn modern Frenchmen into ancient Romans reproduced the entire history of the Roman Republic in fifteen years—from monarchy to republic to tyranny by way of mass murder and warfare on all borders.

Critics were not surprised; the democratic Athenian republic executed Socrates; the concept of a private life that should be immune to public or government scrutiny was unknown to the Romans. Freedom *to* take part in the affairs of your city-state was no compensation for an absence of freedom *from* the state's coercion. Hobbes insisted that if it was freedom that we wanted, under government freedom consisted in the silence of the law, no more and no less. Forms of government were irrelevant to the question of how much liberty we had. Republicans have retorted that there was all the difference in the world between being a slave with a benign master and being a free citizen. We might think, living as we do in modern, constitutional, liberal democratic republics that we have pulled off the trick of achieving both kinds of freedom, the liberty of citizens and the liberty of subjects. Skeptics may respond that we are deceiving ourselves, that *real* citizens were once upon a time directly engaged in the affairs of their republics in ways we are not; given the scale of modern states, they may say, we simply cannot be. The American founders as well as the French revolutionaries hoped to prove the skeptics wrong. Before we see how they set about doing it, we should see what the republican writers on whom they drew thought about republican liberty.

CHAPTER 14

Republicanism

Constitutions and Constitutionalism

HOBBES ASSAULTED THE TWO most cherished beliefs of traditional republicanism: that there was such a thing as free government, and that central to its achievement was the avoidance of tyranny. Tyranny, he observed, "is but monarchy misliked," while the freedom of the state of nature was what we had to abandon to live in peace. Freedom under government was the same thing in Constantinople as at Lucca—the silence of the law. The only sense in which a state could be "free" was that it was a sovereign state, not subject to another state. As to the republicans' favored recipes—the encouragement of civic virtue in the people and the creation of a mixed or balanced constitution—the civic virtue most needed was the punctilious observance of the law, and the mixed constitution was a dangerous attempt to divide sovereignty. Since the essence of sovereignty was that it was absolute and indivisible, limiting and dividing it was a recipe for anarchy. Unlike Hobbes, Locke was sure that tyranny was more than monarchy misliked; tyranny existed when a government of whatever complexion exceeded its legitimate bounds. Nonetheless, Locke shared the view that we gave up our natural freedom to order our lives as we saw fit under the law of nature when we entered into civil society. Government, on this traditional liberal view, requires us to give up some of our freedom for the sake of security, predictability, prosperity, and a guarantee that the freedom we retain is a usable freedom. Political liberty is the protection of natural rights, not the gift of our political arrangements.

This chapter lays out the republican response: the constitutionalist concern for stable, law-abiding, nontyrannical government, and the concern with the *civic liberty* that is said to be the achievement of republican government. We have already explored some traditional defenses of constitutional rule and republican government. Plato's *Republic* (as distinct from his *Laws*) is not an account of a constitutional regime and, in spite of its title, not an account of a republic in the laudatory sense. It is a tale of virtuous shepherds who manipulate the wishes and beliefs of their flock, not the operation of institutions that allow self-government by free and public-spirited, but otherwise ordinary, citizens. Aristotle's *Politics*, by contrast, is concerned throughout with the distribution of legislative authority and the benefits and burdens of office, taking account of the goals of political life, the qualifications of citizens, and the way in which constitutional arrangements assist in the avoidance of stasis. Aristotle focused on citizen virtue, political justice, and stability; and citizen virtue was defined largely in terms of the qualities citizens required to maintain a just and stable regime. Aristotle is much praised by Sir James Harrington.

Aristotle's insistence that a just constitution secured the government of laws, not of men, survived seventeenth-century absolutism, Hobbes's mockery, and the twentieth century's obsession with charismatic leadership. The political sociology of the *Politics* outlasted Aristotle's beliefs about the merits of Greeks, males, landowners, and aristocratic families. Its enduring good sense is one reason why diverse strands of republican thinking so often converge. Not only Aristotle but Polybius and Cicero and their commentators were endlessly exploited for ideas about mixed constitutions and the way to create a political system that would hold the balance between different groups and avert a tyranny of the one, the few, or the many. The dividing line between narrowly republican theories— theories that repudiate monarchy because civic liberty is incompatible with monarchy—and broadly republican theories that accept monarchy as a constitutional possibility is indistinct. Rousseau argued that any lawful regime pursuing the common good was a "republic," but only one in which the people consistently made the laws themselves attained the civic liberty of the classical republics.[1] Civic liberty was the *libertas* that Lucca inscribed on its walls and that Hobbes refused to consider a form of freedom at all. Rousseau was not eccentric; Aristotle considered monarchy a form of constitutional rule and attached the label *politeia* not only to his favored constitutional form of an enlarged aristocracy (or restricted democracy) but to constitutional regimes generally. As we have seen, Aquinas, Marsilius, Bartolus, and their successors regarded nontyrannical monarchy as not merely a form of republican rule but the best form; we should not allow ourselves to be trapped by twentieth-century usage. In their terms the United Kingdom is as much a republic as the United States.

Harrington, Sidney, and Montesquieu

Seventeenth- and eighteenth-century republicanism was a reaction to early modern absolute monarchy and the rise of the modern nation-state. When medieval forms of kingship collapsed under the pressures of religious war and the erosion of their traditional social base, they were eventually replaced by constitutional, power-sharing regimes in England and Holland, and by absolute monarchies working through bureaucratic administrators in much of Europe. This was true of the major German states, such as Prussia and Saxony. There was no unified German state until the late nineteenth century, by which time the disconnect between national identity and state sovereignty had long been felt as a painful wound. English writers took for granted the national identity of the state in which they were interested, and not the least interesting feature of the work of both Harrington and Sidney is the unabashed quality of their nationalism and imperialism. Sidney was one of Thomas Jefferson's favorite authors.

We begin with James Harrington and *Oceana*, a distinctively English work, even though it draws on ideas about balance and counterpoise avowedly derived from Machiavelli and a historian of Venice, Donato

Gianotti; and we end with Montesquieu's *Spirit of the Laws.* Montesquieu's thoughts about what regimes would thrive in what settings were influential both in Europe and in America; and his account of the obsolescence of the classical democratic republic with its reliance on citizen virtue and his defense of the freedom secured by a moderate, constitutional monarchy began a sociologically sophisticated liberal tradition that runs through Constant, Guizot, and Tocqueville to the present. A more inflammatory influence on the American founders was Algernon Sidney, praised by Jefferson as equal to Locke as a defender of liberty. His *Discourses concerning Government* cost him his life. After a corrupt trial, he was executed in 1683, supposedly for his role in the Rye House Plot to assassinate Charles II and his brother, the future James II. Sidney's account of the virtues of mixed constitutions and the badness of absolute monarchy is argumentatively robust and simple, although in a literary sense *Discourses* is ill written and awkwardly assembled, perhaps because of the circumstances under which it was written. The work merits scrutiny not only because of its impact on Jefferson and the future United States but because it shows how easily ideas borrowed from the theory and practice of the ancient republics can draw strength from a Christian conception of natural law and from ideas about natural rights that have in our own day evolved into a belief in universal human rights.

James Harrington

Little is known about the life of James Harrington. He was born in 1611, into the minor gentry of northern England. He took no part in local or national politics until 1647, when he joined the household of Charles I and remained with the king until his execution. This seems to have been an act of purely personal loyalty, and he was not molested for it under the Commonwealth. He spent several years brooding on the collapse of the monarchy and the intractable task of establishing a stable replacement. *Oceana* was published in 1656 and dedicated to Oliver Cromwell in his role of "Lord Protector of the Commonwealth of England Scotland and Ireland." Given the unsettled state of public opinion and his own uncertain legitimacy as dictator de facto, Cromwell did not want the first principles of republican government becoming a matter of public debate; and other writers on the subject only narrowly escaped being tried for sedition. In the event, Harrington was not harassed by Cromwell's agents, although Cromwell is said to have disliked the book. *Oceana* attracted a lot of attention, almost all of it highly critical. Between 1656 and 1661, Harrington wrote extensively in defense of his plans for a secular popular republic, defending it against those who wanted the rule of the saints, those who wanted dictatorship, and those who wanted to restore the aristocracy. After the Restoration, he was imprisoned on suspicion of plotting against Charles II. He was soon released; but both his physical and his mental health had been destroyed, and he took no further part in political life. He died in 1677.

The Structure of *Oceana*

The Commonwealth of Oceana is set out as "preliminaries" followed by the "model" of Oceana. The preliminaries contain the heart of Harrington's theoretical approach; they divide into two parts, the first dealing with "ancient prudence," by which the author meant the classical statecraft practiced by the Greek and Roman Republics and systematized by Machiavelli, the second dealing with "modern prudence," which is to say the operating principles of the feudal monarchies that came into existence on the ruins of the western Roman Empire. The "model" is a precursor in fantasy of Philadelphia in the summer of 1787, a meticulous account of the "orders" or fundamental laws of the perfect commonwealth, embedded in the deliberations of a fictional constitutional convention.[2]

Like Machiavelli, Harrington wished to have his cake and eat it with regard to the creation of republics; he shared Machiavelli's view that constitutions must be the work of one man, be it Moses or Lycurgus, and in *Oceana* the central figure of Olphaus Megaletor (otherwise Oliver Cromwell) anticipates Rousseau's device of the godlike legislator who brings the republic into being. But like Polybius and Machiavelli, Harrington also held that many heads are wiser than one, and that drawing on the experience of others is cheaper than purchasing wisdom—as the Romans had done—by trial and error. So he imagined that rapporteurs would be asked to examine the political arrangements of Israel, Athens, Sparta, Carthage, Rome, Venice, Switzerland, and the Dutch United Provinces and to report on their strengths and weaknesses. The intricacy of the result is less the fault of its basic components than of the decoration with which Harrington surrounded them. As he observed, the republic of Oceana was based on no more than thirty "orders." The U.S. Constitution is based on seven articles, while the abortive attempt to give the European Union a constitution early in the new millennium produced a much-derided document of some seven hundred pages. One might well think briefer is better.

Harrington defended "ancient prudence," the statecraft that maintains a free republic, not only against the operating principles of the monarchy whose last days he had witnessed but against Hobbes's *Leviathan*, and by implication against any philosophical, nonempirical approach to politics. *Oceana* also defended Machiavelli's view of liberty against that of Hobbes, who said there was no more liberty at Lucca than at Constantinople. Harrington insisted that free government was of all things the sweetest to man, and that the difference between absolute rule and the rule of a free republic was infinite.[3] So he begins with a sharp contrast: "government (to define it *de jure* or according to ancient prudence) is an art whereby a civil society of men is instituted and preserved upon the foundation of common right or interest, or (to follow Aristotle and Livy) it is the empire of laws and not of men." In contrast, "government (to define it *de facto* or according unto modern prudence) is an art whereby some man, or some few men, subject a city or a nation, and rule it according unto his or their private interest; which, because the laws in such cases are made according to the interest of a man or of some few families, may be said to be the empire of men and not of laws."[4] "Modern prudence" is the feudal regime built on the basis of the barbarian conquest of the decaying Roman Empire. It was not the only alternative to "ancient prudence," for Harrington counted the despotic rule of the sultan in Constantinople, where the ruler was lord of the persons and property of his subjects, who were to all intents and purposes his slaves, as a form of monarchy like that of the Roman Empire, and no doubt the Persian Empire before it. Neither Turkey nor the Roman Empire was truly stable, since both were vulnerable to palace coups by janissaries and praetorian guards. The feudal system was not, on Harrington's view and entirely contrary to everyone else's, a form of monarchy at all, because the king had granted his property to his barons and they in turn had granted it to their tenants. But pace Hobbes there was no freedom at Constantinople, no matter how laissez-faire or merely idle the sultan might be.

Harrington was obsessed with "balance"; and his distinctive contribution to republican theory was to link political balance to the balance of landed property. What he meant by a balance demands analysis. We should start with Charles I's defense of English monarchy, contained in his *Answer to the Nineteen Propositions of Parliament* of 1642. This *Answer* was a surprising document. It provides an account of the English constitution as a mixed constitution, entirely contrary to Charles's own conception of the rights of kings. He thought kings ruled *jure divino*; on his theocratic conception of kingship, the king received his authority from God, not the consent of his subjects. The law of the land was the king's law, subject to such enforcement or relaxation as he chose, Parliament was an advisory body that he might summon or not, and the citizens' property was more deeply his than theirs. He should govern according to known and settled law, since God ruled the universe in a predictable, rational way; but the king's authority was absolute, personal to himself, paternal and bequeathable. The French bishop Bossuet provided the most intellectually sophisticated defense of this view in his *Politics Taken from the Very Words of Holy Scripture*; in England, Sir Robert Filmer undertook the task, but *Patriarcha* is more famous in the history of political theory for its systematic demolition by Algernon Sidney and John Locke than for its intellectual merits. Hobbes's defense of absolute monarchy was on grounds of convenience; sovereignty was absolute, but neither personal nor paternal, and although it was best if it was lodged in one man, that had nothing to do with him—or God.

Although Charles subscribed to *jure divino* absolutism, what he justified to Parliament was very different; his *Reply* was a reassertion of the traditional "mixed monarchy" view of the English constitution. Good government was a mixture of one, few, and many. It was a balance. All should play their proper roles, and none should play the role of anyone else. It was not the doctrine of the separation of powers, as understood by Montesquieu and subsequent American borrowers from him. It could not be, because Parliament was a judicial body, the "high court of parliament"; indeed, the House of Lords exercised a judicial function until 2009. Most of the king's ministers and advisers were members of the House of Lords, so the "executive" was far from separate from the legislature or the judiciary; and judges who saw themselves as custodians of the common law were not eager to concede to parliament a sovereignty they denied to kings. Sir Edward Coke not only held in "Dr. Bonham's Case" that there were liberties that even Parliament could not override but asserted the principle that the "common law is such a fellow as will have no sovereign sit beside him."[5] The idea of a balance was less the doctrine of the separation of powers than the Aristotelian doctrine that the one, the few, and the many had their own virtues and made their own contributions: decisiveness, wisdom, and common sense, perhaps. It also evoked medieval ideas about the body politic; the head provided wisdom, the arms valor, and the belly sustenance; it was proper for the commons to vote supply, for the lords to represent military leadership, and for the king and his advisers to determine policy. The implication was that things would fall apart if one element encroached on the sphere of another.

Harrington took over the notion of balance, but not to rescue the monarchy. He drew heavily on Machiavelli, though he did not claim that the idea of the balance was fully developed by Machiavelli—it was not. Indeed, "Machiavel missed it very narrowly and very dangerously."[6] That is, Machiavelli thought that there must always be hostility between the nobility and the commons, while Harrington held that if they were at odds, disaster would follow, but that where they cooperated we had the best of all regimes, where the nobility provided leadership for the good of all. Harrington moved the argument away from discussions about the virtues of the one, the few, and the many, perhaps because he did not have a clear conception of an executive, without which the intuitive plausibility of embodying decisiveness in the one is diminished. He was interested in two sorts of balance, ancient and Gothic. They were based on the ownership of land because land was the basis of raising an army. A freeholder had something to defend and the resources to arm himself; and serving as a soldier to defend his country made a man a virtuous citizen. Machiavelli had met with resistance in recruiting the *contadini* from the Florentine countryside to the Florentine militia just because of the local reluctance to dissociate citizenship from the right (and duty) to bear arms. Beyond the examples of Rome and Sparta, Harrington met with problems in arguing that stable republics rested on the farmer's bearing his own arms. Venice was an (almost) perfect republic, but its economy was based on trade, not landed property; the same was true of Genoa and the United Provinces. He did not explore ways to maintain a balance in countries whose wealth lay in movables. His argument for taking land ownership as the basis of political rights was that land was immovable, while money was "easy come, easy go." True as that might be, and important in explaining both the reluctance of many societies to admit merchants to the ranks of the aristocracy and their reluctance to dispense with a property qualification for the franchise, it made Venice inexplicable.

The intriguing question is not the fate of the ancient balance. The downfall of the Roman Republic was a familiar theme. Harrington focused on the "Gothic" balance. By the time he wrote, it was generally believed that modern kingship had grown out of the arrangements made by the barbarian tribes who had first been invited into the western empire to provide soldiers and had then supplanted their employers. This was the origin of the idea of a Gothic system. Medieval kings were the descendants, systemically speaking, of the leaders of tribes organized as military hierarchies. The tribal system stabilized as feudalism, the system of dependent military tenures. Modern historians see this as the stabilization of "warlordism." The king granted lands to nobles who were obliged to provide soldiers when required; the nobles granted lands to their own tenants, who had to provide their share of the military burden. The *balance* was the proportion of land held by the estates of the realm. Harrington thought that in England, the case in which he was really interested, a four-estate balance had long existed: the king, the lords spiritual, the lords temporal, and the commons. The "commons" were the social stratum between the minor nobility and people too poor to "live of their own," which is to say they were the sort of rural gentry and freeholding farmers whom Jefferson considered the salt of the earth. Modern writers are interested in the fate of the enslaved and semienslaved serfs tied to the soil. Harrington was not. He was interested in the freeholder who could bear his own arms in a militia. This was not an outdated concern. The view that standing armies were a threat to liberty was almost universal. It is reflected in the way the army estimates have to be renewed by the British Parliament every year. *Oceana* was republished in 1697, when William III showed no inclination to disband the army he had raised for war on the Continent. The obsession with the preservation of a class of freeholders able to bear their own arms in a militia was enshrined ninety-four years later in the Second Amendment to the U.S. Constitution.

Harrington thought that the whole country had been able to support 60,000 knights, and since the land that supported them was owned by 250 lords, "it was a government of the few or of the nobility, wherein the people might also assemble, but could have no more than a mere name."[7] To say that "the balance was in the nobility" was Harrington's way of describing a world in which the king governed with the concurrence of his barons. Given their concurrence, the king could defend his realm, because they would raise the militia on which defense depended; so long as the nobles had no common interest hostile to the king's, they would not unite against him, and an uprising against the king by a few nobles who were outnumbered by forces loyal to him would have unpalatable results for those few nobles. Harrington understood the tension between the monarch's wish to get more power into the hands of himself and his handpicked favorites and the desire of the barons to prevent him from weakening their economic, social, and political position. When there was trouble, either king or the nobility might recruit the commons to their cause, which appears to be Harrington's explanation of the rise of the power of the commons.

He thought that the whole edifice had collapsed in the English Civil War, but that the root of its downfall lay in measures taken at the end of the fifteenth century by Henry VII. (Among the decorative touches that makes life difficult for the modern reader, Harrington's adoption of Latin names for English monarchs is the most obvious: Henry VII is "Panurgus.") His statute of population increased the number of small independent farmers; the statute of retainers emancipated small farmers from the service of great lords and forbade those lords to keep militias; the statute of alienation made it easy to sell freehold land, and put the last nail in the coffin of the feudal system. At this point, the nobility "may be computed to have been disarmed." Having been disarmed, the nobles could not resist the encroachments of the commons; neither could the king. The aristocratic balance collapsed because political arrangements were aristocratic, while the pattern of landownership favored the commons. Harrington described this as an equality that made anything other than a popular republic an impossibility. The expression is quaint, but the argument itself has been accepted by Americans for 240 years.

The elaborate mechanisms that Harrington proposed for Oceana created an egalitarian pattern of landholding by eliminating primogeniture and created political stability by instituting a representative system that conformed to the economic base. Reason and political capacity, he thought, were spread unequally among humanity; in any group of twenty men, six would be natural leaders and the others natural followers. Natural leaders attract followers without bribery or force, because they are recognized as better fitted to govern than their fellows. Harrington then constructs the mechanism familiar from the history of Italian city-states; it is modeled on Venice, with a small senate to which alone deliberation is permitted, and a much larger popular assembly in which the power of decision resides. It is a "popular republic" in Machiavelli's sense, because the balance is in the commons; that is, the bulk of the land is owned by ordinary persons of the middling sort, not held on feudal tenures from a small aristocracy. That ensures the existence of a free republic, civic virtue, and a valiant people. Much of the detail is of interest only to historians trying to understand how Harrington supposed the combination of election and sortition that he proposed reflected the condition of seventeenth-century England. Two things are of persisting interest to everyone else.

First, Harrington finesses the distinction drawn by Machiavelli between republics for preservation and republics for increase. Machiavelli had assumed that a republic for increase—his model was the aggressive and expansive Roman Republic—must give a larger political role to the people and will inevitably suffer conflict between the people and the aristocracy. It would be free and glorious, but tumultuous and less long-lived than a state with less ambitious goals. A republic for preservation—such as Venice or Sparta—would diminish the role of the ordinary people and sacrifice citizen liberty for stability. Popular opinion would be filtered through elaborate voting mechanisms to ensure that only the wise and the long-established would exercise influence, and that individual ambition did not disturb the serene republic. The U.S. Constitution adopted some of these devices, with the Senate and the president elected only indirectly, to filter the opinions of the common people through the intelligence and experience of their betters. With Elizabethan imperialism a recent memory, and Ireland a newly conquered acquisition, Harrington took it for granted that Oceana was to be a republic for increase; in his model, institutions largely patterned after the Venetian were compatible with increase. Oceana was to be both everlasting and expansive. It was to be an imperial project, but safeguarded against the corruption that brought down Rome; the egalitarian repartition of property that he thought his agrarian laws would promote would avoid the damage done to Rome by the practice of settling soldiers on captured territory. He thought that the Roman general Lucius Sulla in the early first century BCE had "overbalanced" the people by buying himself a private army and having himself made perpetual dictator; Caesar's subsequent acquisition of unchallenged power was simultaneously necessary to restore order and a disaster for republicanism. It is easy to see why Cromwell feared public discussion of the first principles of republican government, and why American revolutionaries who admired Washington to the point of idolatry were both desperate that he should lead the infant republic and fearful of the consequences.

Second, Harrington employs every intellectual weapon in the armory of a seventeenth-century thinker, for very distinctive purposes. Political theorists have long drawn a distinction between the philosopher seeking ultimate truth and the theorist of statecraft offering recipes for the better conduct of political enterprises as we know them. It is a distinction I have relied on here, arguing that Plato's politics are antipolitical and that the rule of philosophers is, as Aristotle observed, not the culmination but the elimination of politics. The distinction blurs under pressure. Harrington is in many ways a paradigm of the nonphilosophically minded practitioner of statecraft. He has Machiavelli's passion for founding republics, and it is not only the utopian form of *Oceana* that places it in a different universe from that of *Leviathan*. His *System of Politics*, which is devoid of literary artifice, is on its face equally unphilosophical.

Yet the appearance is misleading. Among the historical evidence Harrington imagines his rapporteurs coming back with is the history of Old Testament Israel. His use of Old Testament history is not at all philosophically innocent. To cite the political system of the Jews as a political model while draining it of any theocratic implications implied more than it said about the priority of politics over religion. It is a nice irony that Harrington's counter to the seventeenth-century absolutists' view that kings reign *jure divino* was the claim that the Israelites had, until they foolishly embraced monarchy, operated a mixed republican system of government whose excellence stemmed from the fact that God himself had designed it. Whether a scrutiny of the Old Testament would persuade all readers that Israel had possessed an excellent set of agrarian laws creating the republican freeholders necessary for stability and military effectiveness is another matter. Harrington envisaged Oceana possessing a civil religion requiring only the most noncontentious and politically helpful beliefs; what these are is a political and not a theological question. Most strikingly, this Aristotelian and Machiavellian view of political thinking—the construction of a polity de jure—is frequently interrupted by a Platonic insistence that the order established in Oceana will be marked by reason. It will conform to nature, and nature is orderly because it is rational. With Polybius in the background, Harrington hopes to create a republic that will escape the cycle of decay that Polybius identified, and with both Machiavelli and Polybius to prompt him, he is uncertain just how invulnerable to *fortuna* his republic can be made. The rationalist suggests that it may, if made properly, be immortal. This linking of cosmology to politics, common enough in the Renaissance, is squarely philosophical.

The claim that a political system might aim at immortality has its difficulties. Christianity had a strongly historical view of the world. The world was created in time, it was transitory, and at the end of time God would return to sit in judgment. In the middle of the seventeenth century many people who were not obviously insane were seriously persuaded that they were living in the last days and that Christ's return was imminent. Harrington was unaffected by such beliefs, but in a climate where they were widespread, it is not surprising that he reacted by insisting that his construction could, barring accident, endure as long as the world itself. The ambition was pagan, and smacked of *hubris*. Yet it was not so different from Hobbes's intentions in *Leviathan*, and Harrington even offers a paraphrase of Hobbes's famous observation that the art of framing a commonwealth was to be understood as analogous to God's art in framing the universe. But Harrington insisted that it was the statecraft that Hobbes dismissed as mere *prudence*, not *science*, that would create the immortal republic.

The Unkindness of History

Oceana is written as a utopia and is often treated as a work in the same genre as More's *Utopia*, Bacon's *New Atlantis*, or Campanella's *City of the Sun*. But as other commentators have said, Harrington's analysis of the downfall of the Stuart monarchy was written in homage to Machiavelli's *Discourses* and intended as history, and it has been much discussed by historians in the context of the argument whether the economic fortunes of particular social groups were or were not primarily responsible for the outbreak of the English Civil War. Whether the English gentry was rising or declining, or some elements doing the one and some the other, has preoccupied generations of social and economic historians. For the political theorist, it was not his understanding (or misunderstanding) of early capitalist economics that played Harrington false but the success of the English political system after the Glorious Revolution of 1688. It played him doubly false, as in many ways it did the creators of the American Republic. Harrington's argument was based on a simple idea: the central economic task of government was to find the resources to pay for defense, and the way a government did it determined its fate. Since one cause of the English Civil War was Charles I's attempts to levy taxes for his armed forces without the assent of Parliament, it was a plausible thought that one cause of *in*stability was a mismatch between military needs and the tax base. Harrington resembled Machiavelli, Bacon, and Jefferson in wanting to base his republic on the country gentry and the yeoman farmer, and he claimed that this alone would achieve political stability. It was also the only route to free government. The independent freeholder, keeping and bearing his own arms and ready to serve in a militia, was a modernized and Anglicized version of the ideal citizen of Sparta and republican Rome. Harrington believed that political liberty was possible only in a republic founded on the citizen-soldier; standing armies of conscripts or mercenaries were incompatible with liberty.

Hanoverian England made this view obsolete; professional standing armies did not threaten the modern nation-state in the way mercenaries threatened classical and late medieval city-states. Nor were they hard to pay for; England—Britain after the Act of Union in 1707—could raise funds without creating unrest, possessed an efficient central bank, and could float public debt at low rates of interest. If it had been true that the independent farmer with his own land and his own weapons, serving when needed in a militia and returning to the plow when war was over, was the only recipe for an affordable and efficient military and essential to the political socialization of a virtuous citizenry, Harrington's theory would have been cogent. Once it was clear that an effective army could be had by other means without succumbing to the ambitions of merce-nary leaders, the obsession with the armed freeholder became part of the politics of nostalgia, visible in Rousseau's *Discourse on Political Economy*, and audible in American politics ever since Jefferson. The modern British or U.S. Army is not a "well-regulated militia," but it is not obvious that this explains whatever shortfalls in citizen virtue and civic liberty Britain, the United States, or other modern liberal democracies suffer from.

The other way in which history was unkind to *Oceana* was pointed out by Hume. Harrington argued that the English monarchy as Charles I had understood it was doomed. He thought that a postfeudal but non-absolute—parliamentary and constitutional—monarchy was an impossibility; history offered only one freedom-preserving and constitutional regime, the popular republic whose "model" he drew in *Oceana*. All else was deeply unattractive, especially the regime of general servitude exemplified by the Roman and Ottoman empires. In these, the autocrat had absolute power and could dispose of the revenues of his state at his own whim and pleasure. Autocrats were vulnerable to the praetorian guard in the one case and the janissaries in the other, whose ability to murder one autocrat and install another was an obvious threat to stability. Still, their chief defect was not a lack of durability but the total absence of liberty. Harrington thus posed the question as popular republic or tyranny. The revival of interest in Harrington late in the reign of Charles II and in the early eighteenth century owed much more to the fear that tyranny was a real danger than to the technicalities of his concept of the balance. Far from the English crown's being doomed, it seemed entirely probable that under Charles II or James II, England would become an absolute monarchy on the French model. Whether James II's project had more than a limited prospect of success is an open question, but the practical question turned out to be whether royal tyranny could be averted.

Hume pointed out that the old mixed regime turned out to be far from dead; it had been revived in a postfeudal form. Under the Hanoverians it flourished to the point where the British came to believe they had been given it by a dispensation of providence that defied rational analysis but was not to be questioned by revolutionaries. Its success rested on what Harrington would have described as corruption, focused on a central bank that could manufacture credit for the government's purposes and a system of patronage that ensured that the "king's men" could get their way in Parliament, so that struggles over taxation were resolved in the administration's favor. Harrington could not imagine governments disposing of funds beyond those Parliament grudgingly voted for particular purposes. The idea that just as everyone else "lived of his own," the monarch should do so, too, and that the king's own resources should suffice for everyday administration, died hard. Wars were special events that were financed by taxes; taxes were a temporary grant from Parliament, which was why Parliament insisted on redress of grievances before voting supply. After 1689 the principle was maintained and the reality lost. The king's ministers learned how to cajole, bribe, seduce with sinecures, and persuade the ambitious with promises of office, and found it not too difficult to manage Parliament. Patronage made the system work. Judged against Lycurgus's Sparta, it was stable but immoral; judged against Hume's hopes for a stable, prosperous, easygoing, and unfanatical society, it worked very well.[8] Mandeville's *Fable of the Bees* was an even more devastating attack on the very idea of republican virtue; Mandeville essentially argued that it is our vices that enable the economy to grow and prosper, and that the success of Harrington's disciples, the Country Whigs, would mean universal poverty.

Algernon Sidney

Harrington's ideas were resurrected in the late 1670s when Locke's patron the earl of Shaftesbury launched his attempt to exclude the duke of York, Charles II's brother, and a Catholic, from the succession to the crown. The most famous reassertion of republican principles was Algernon Sidney's *Discourses concerning Government*, which defends free government as ardently as *Oceana*, but puts more faith in the aristocracy than Harrington did. Sidney was born in 1622, the second son of the earl of Leicester. He helped to put down the Irish Rebellion in 1641–43, joined the parliamentary side in the civil war, and was badly wounded at Marston Moor. From 1646 he was a member of Parliament; he was appointed as one of the commissioners to try Charles I, but at some risk to himself refused to act. From 1659 to 1677, he was in self-imposed exile on the Continent; when he returned to England, he took up the fight against the absolutist pretensions of Charles II. His militant antityrannical politics were nicely summed up in an inscription in a visitor's book: "Manus haec inimica tyrannis, Ense petit placidam cum libertate quietam"—"this hand, enemy to tyrants, with the sword seeks a tranquil peace with liberty."[9]Arrested at the time of the Rye House Plot, he was tried before the inimitable Judge Jeffreys, convicted on the word of one corrupt witness and a couple of paragraphs of his own prose, and executed in December 1683. He was posthumously acquitted in 1689. As a literary composition, *Discourses* has rarely received high marks: "rambling" and "unfocused" are common complaints; and many commentators claim that it was Sidney's standing as a republican martyr that made the book's reputation.[10] This is exaggerated. Sidney was certainly a republican martyr, but the energy and outrage that permeate *Discourses* would have secured readers without their author's execution. Its vice is repetitiveness, but for sheer vigor it is hard to beat.

Charles II became increasingly autocratic and unpopular during the 1670s. Sir Robert Filmer's *Patriarcha* was pressed into service. As we saw, Filmer's case was simple, and easy to square with historical evidence in a way that social contract theories such as Hobbes's or Locke's were not. It was written for an audience accustomed to drawing ideas about politics from the pages of the Old Testament. Harrington followed the same path when he insisted that the Israelites were a republic under the indirect rule of God: God had got Moses to construct the political arrangements of his chosen people, with the assistance of Jethro the Midianite. Even Hobbes had devoted much of *Leviathan* to showing that his view of political authority could accommodate the situation in which God ruled the Israelites as an absolute monarch issuing his commands through the prophets.

To start with God's grant of dominion to Adam seemed to many to start in the right place. It supported the descending theory of authority that all *jure divino* theories espoused; authority is in essence absolute, and nonabsolute authority is exercised on the basis of a grant with limitations from those who possess unlimited authority. Judges should be faithful to their commissions and act within the limits they set; but they had no right to refuse to give judgment in accordance with the expressed wishes of the king. The defense of absolutism did not demand punctilious obedience to royal commands no matter how wicked, though Sidney maintained that this was Filmer's view. Even an absolute sovereign could be disobeyed, and perhaps even resisted in extremis. Absolutists agreed, too, that the king was bound by his own laws *until* he chose to suspend them; but they insisted that he had the power to suspend them and was not bound once he had exercised that power.

Like Locke's *First Treatise*, Sidney's *Discourses* were written against *Patriarcha*, but their interest is their positive doctrine. Sidney's demolition of Filmer adds nothing to Locke's, and may have been suggested by Locke. It is agreeably simple. Filmer structured *Patriarcha* around three claims: that there is no natural liberty, that popular government is both unnatural and dangerous, and that kings are the source of positive law and cannot be subject to it. To which Sidney, like Locke, retorted that kings are not fathers and political authority is not paternal but rests on consent, that popular government is the best form of government, that kings possess their authority only as long as they observe the constitutional laws of their polity, and that the natural guardian of those laws is a popular assembly or parliament. Sidney's positive doctrines are clear and tough-minded, and may inspire in the reader the same enthusiasm and anxiety as Jefferson's vision of the "empire of liberty": enthusiasm for our own liberation from arbitrary rule, and anxiety whether we are going to be conscripted for wars of liberation that look suspiciously like imperialist adventures. Sidney was an aggressive defender of Protestantism, a faith that a free man and a good citizen could adopt; he was by modern standards somewhat quick to write off the political potential of other races. Like Aristotle, he thought that despotism was the natural condition of "base, effeminate Asiaticks." Like Harrington, Sidney thought that the measure of good government was a society's ability to wield the sword as effectively as the Romans or our Saxon forefathers. Like Harrington, he thought that the aristocracy had been very much weakened since the days of Henry VII; and like Harrington, thought some form of "popular government" the only alternative to despotism. But Sidney made a reinvigorated aristocracy the centerpiece of republican government and looked to it to play a more active role than Harrington had assigned it. Like Machiavelli, Sidney also insisted that the freest and most invigorating societies lived in constant tumult, which rarely damaged them and was a condition of their retaining their liberty. As he observed, the Greeks in

1680 live peacefully under the sway of the Ottoman Empire in deserted towns, where there are few people and no trade. When Athens and Sparta fought the great king of Persia, Greece was tumultuous, seditious, always on the verge of class warfare, and free. Now "the poor remains of these exhausted nations, sheltering themselves under the ruins of the desolated cities, have neither anything that deserves to be disputed amongst them, nor spirit or force to repel the injuries they daily suffer from a proud and insupportable master."[11]

The same robustness marks Sidney's defense of government by consent. Government exists either by force or by consent. The latter is legitimate and the former is tyranny. Anticipating republicans a century later, Sidney argued that the rights of all magistrates, kings included, were conferred on them by the people, and that what the people gave the people could take away. More boldly than Harrington, who thought the foundations of government in the system of land tenure dictated what can and cannot work, Sidney holds that there is a great deal of room for maneuver, so that a people may set up whatever government it chooses, without dissolving itself as a people. As the section devoted to the issue says, "God leaves to man the choice of forms in government; and those who constitute one form may abrogate it."[12] Sidney insisted, as Locke did, that the right to rebel is confined to the right to reinstitute lawful government; nothing justifies mere rebellion, certainly not the ambition of a would-be tyrant. Tyrannical government is the supreme evil against which we have to guard, and tyrants should be resisted and deposed. Sidney emphasizes the freedom of the people to institute whatever *form* of lawful government they want, but lawful governments are not to be captiously undermined.

Sidney never puts forward a view of the absolutely best form of government. This was not a lapse. *Discourses* argues that there is no absolutely best form of government, though tyranny is the absolutely worst. Good government is a matter of time and place; flexibility is needed because the world is full of unpredictable events that have to be handled in whatever way turns out best. Nonetheless, he had an oft-repeated preference for an aristocratic republic where it could work. Sidney saw aristocracy as the great source of political energy. The difference between him and

Harrington may not in the end be great, since the aristocracy Sidney has in mind looks very like Harrington's senatorial class; it is a meritocracy whose leadership is freely accepted, not the hangers-on and royal favorites whom he denounces on every page. He repeats the Latin tag *detur digniori* to the point of tedium; "let it be given to the more worthy" is the principle on which the allocation of political authority should be based. The Danbys and the Cliffords are not aristocrats but placemen, and corruption is their trade. As was conventional, he said that all good governments are a mixture of government by the one, the few, and the many, but this nod to Aristotle and Polybius was less passionate than his invocation of the heroic Saxon aristocracy. When he pauses from assailing Filmer, it is to insist that Xenophon and other critics of Athenian democracy did not really mean that monarchy was their preferred form of government; what they wanted was a well-ordered aristocracy.[13]

Like other writers of the time, he had no difficulty in invoking God, nature, and experience in defense of the same points. Crucial here was the Lockean premise that God created us free and equal, and that it was an insult to God to suppose that we were to subordinate our reason to rulers claiming absolute authority. In a notable phrase, borrowed by Jefferson and much quoted by radicals, he denied that God had caused "some to be born with crowns upon their heads, and all others with saddles upon their backs."[14] God alone possesses absolute authority, no human being. This remained until the nineteenth century the basis of the argument for government by consent; *not* founding government in the consent of the people was multiply a crime, not only tyrannical in the traditional or classical sense but an insult to humanity conceived in the likeness of God. The freedom we have from God is not Hobbesian: that is, not the lawless freedom, described by Hobbes as "a right to everything even to the use of one another's bodies." Sidney shared Locke's view that a small allowance of reason was sufficient to reveal the basic dictates of natural law, and that the obligation of natural law was not weakened by the institution of government but strengthened. That provided both the basis for a theory of resistance to unlawful authority and an account of the purpose of government and the grounds of obedience.

Good government does not preserve *all* our natural liberty; to put ourselves under the law of a civil society is to limit our freedom of choice. Nonetheless, contra Hobbes, who thought that we must give up all our liberty, and contra Filmer, who thought we had none to begin with, Sidney argued that we should give up as little as possible and that the best governments were those that interfered least with their subjects. If these arguments place Sidney squarely in a liberal tradition, the themes of corruption on the one side and citizen loyalty, courage, and military fortitude on the other place him firmly in the republican tradition. The view, popular some years ago, that these are competing traditions, and that we can either emphasize citizen virtue or the liberty of the person, but that the pursuit of the one rules out the pursuit of the other, is a sophistication Sidney knows nothing of. He would have rejected it if offered it. He has distinguished heirs, and not only Jefferson. When Benjamin Constant wrote his famous essay contrasting the liberty of the ancients and the liberty of the moderns, it was not to argue that we must wholly abandon the ancient conception of the liberty of the active citizen.[15] Like Mill, Constant thought that the liberty of the individual would not long survive the loss of a vigorous sense of citizenship.

Montesquieu

To reach Constant's analytical subtlety, the argument had to pass through Montesquieu's thoughts on freedom as well as Rousseau's despairing claim that men in modern commercial society were unfit to be citizens of the kind that Sparta and Rome had produced. Montesquieu—Charles-Louis de Secondat, baron de La Brède et de Montesquieu—was born in 1689. The Secondat family were provincial nobility in the Bordeaux region, and Montesquieu spent much of his life looking after his substantial landholdings in the area, though he also served for some years as a judge—"Président à Mortier"—in the Bordeaux *parlement*. The *parlement* was a court, part of the provincial administration. Like most such offices, the presidency could be bought and sold; Montesquieu's uncle had bought it, and Montesquieu inherited it. It was far from a sinecure, and Montesquieu's education enabled him to do the work it required efficiently; he went to an academically rigorous college in Paris and then studied law at the Sorbonne for three years. Still, he was bored by the work, although it helped him to accumulate the knowledge of the law so visible in *L'esprit des lois*. His son had no interest in the post, and it was sold out of the family. Keeping his estates within the family was another matter; when it became clear that his son would have no heir, Montesquieu arranged for his daughter to marry a distant cousin and to inherit the family property.

Montesquieu cared most for his rich literary and intellectual life. He became a member of the Académie Française in 1728, just before he undertook the three-year journey to England, Italy, and Germany that provided much of the inspiration for *The Spirit of the Laws*. He was a very visible figure in Parisian literary life for the next two decades, friendly with, and writing for, the editors of the *Encyclopédie*. Of his major works, *Persian Letters* was published anonymously in 1721, *Considerations on the Causes of the Greatness and Decline of the Romans* in 1734, and *The Spirit of the Laws* in 1748. The last was placed on the Index in 1751, a badge of honor to the *lumières* of the Enlightenment; Montesquieu died in Paris in 1755. *The Spirit of the Laws* was immediately recognized as a masterpiece, though not the highly structured work that Montesquieu intended. It has always been plundered for aperçus rather than seen as a work with one defining thesis; but Montesquieu's aperçus illuminate not only his but also many of our own political and moral convictions, even if they are not models of clear exposition. As to its originality, seeking the first work in a genre is rarely enlightening, but *The Spirit of the Laws* is surely the foundational work of modern political sociology.

Its impact was assisted by good fortune. It found appreciative readers in Scotland, where Adam Ferguson and Adam Smith were beginning to work in the same vein. Thence it migrated across the Atlantic to the colleges of America, where Scots moral philosophers were much in demand, among them the Reverend John Witherspoon, the president of the College of New Jersey and the teacher of James Madison. Montesquieu's technique, the analysis of political culture, inspired Alexis de Tocqueville to investigate the *moeurs*—the mores, customs, folkways—of the young American Republic and to create one of the most enlightening accounts ever written of a political system in operation. Tocqueville said that Montesquieu was his constant interlocutor whenever his mind turned to political matters. The work's impact in France was complex. It gave comfort to reformers who hoped that the absolute monarchy could be nudged in the direction of an English form of constitutional monarchy. It was only modest comfort. The reigns of Louis XV and Louis XVI were not hospitable to a free and open discussion of constitutional reform, and Montesquieu was himself not encouraging to anyone who wanted to borrow institutions from elsewhere. History, culture, economics, and foreign entanglements interact in a fashion so peculiar to each country that modest improvements to our own institutions is usually wiser than borrowing from other nations.[16]

The pleasures of reading Montesquieu are those of encountering a really well-stocked mind and imagination. Here we can look only at his contribution to three large subjects. The first is his explanation of the difference between the forms of government—by one, few, or many—and their animating spirit. The second is his explanation of the obsolescence of the classical city-state, for it was partly in an attempt to evade Montesquieu's argument that Jefferson suggested that "ward republics"—tiny units of local self-government—could be combined in a confederation to create a modern nation-state animated by the citizen virtue of the ancient republics. The third is his account of how to achieve modern political freedom without re-creating the classical city-state; this is his famous account of the workings of constitutional monarchy in England, his analysis of the separation of powers, and his account of the way their *non*separation preserved the balance between king and commons on which stability, prosperity, and the peculiarly English form of liberty depended. It is impossible not to glance in passing at what this implies for the differences between despotism, lawful absolute monarchy, and constitutional monarchy, and indeed what it implies for modern liberal democracy, but impossible to do more than that here.

Law and the "Spirit" of Institutions

The Spirit of the Laws begins with some general thoughts about the nature of law. They are so confusing that one may wonder whether Montesquieu meant them as more than a pious grace note. "Laws, taken in the broadest meaning, are the necessary relations deriving from the nature of things; and in this sense, all beings have their laws: the divinity has its laws, the material world has its laws, the intelligences superior to man have their laws, the beasts have their laws, man has his laws."[17] Natural law may or may not guide brute beasts; as to human beings, they have the unique ability to choose whether to guide themselves by divine or natural law or not, and very commonly they do not.[18] Then nature has its revenge because their lives go badly, reminding them that imprudence is its own punishment. To the modern analytical mind, this confuses the law of nature in the sense of the physical laws governing the way the world operates and the law of nature in the sense of the unwritten rules that mankind *ought* to follow. Certainly, ignoring the first is imprudent, as it would be if we "flouted" the law of gravity by stepping out of a high window. Whether ignoring the second brings its own punishment in its train is what everyone disputes when insisting on the need for government. More to the purpose, Montesquieu takes a thoroughly naturalistic view of the origins of government and therefore of positive law. So far as positive law goes, he distinguishes between the law of nations that governs the dealings of autonomous states with one another, political or constitutional law, which governs the dealings of the state and its subjects, and civil law, which governs citizens in their dealings with one another. Any modern writer would draw the same lines.[19]

He then puts aside the familiar tripartite classification of governments as monarchical, aristocratic, and democratic in favor of his own division into republican, monarchical, and despotic. The *nature* of government is distinguished from its *spirit*. The nature of a republic is that sovereignty is located in and exercised by the whole people; in a monarchy one man is the source of law, but he governs through intermediate institutions, by fixed and established laws, while in a despotism one man rules, without law and according to his own caprice. The spirit, or animating principle, is virtue in a republic, honor in a monarchy, and fear in a despotism. This may seem to be the moment when the modern distinction between a monarchy and a republic becomes clear. It is not. The existence of the category of despotic regimes reveals that Montesquieu has something in mind quite other than the common distinction between states with elected heads of state and states with hereditary heads.

He is concerned with the "spirit" of the state. Athens was a democratic republic, Sparta an aristocratic republic, with a pair of hereditary kings; crucially, both were republics. In Britain a relatively independent aristocracy played an important role in politics, but it and France were both monarchies; the Ottoman Empire was a despotism. Montesquieu did not object to the Aristotelian distinction of government by one, the few, and the many, but Aristotle and all other classical authors had been confused about the nature of monarchy, and had confined themselves to discussing the personal strengths and weaknesses that a single ruler brought to the job.[20] This failed to reach into the animating principle of monarchical rule, and merely sketched the accidental qualities of this or that monarch. Aristotle treats Persia and Sparta as monarchies, but the first was a despotism and the second a republic. Greek writers never encountered anything resembling modern monarchy. City-states were often ruled by one man, but that was either a tyrannical interlude or a freely assented-to domination by an unusually able leader—as it might be Pericles at the height of Athens's commitment to democracy.

We must not confuse the animating spirit of a regime with the purposes to which this or that nation is committed. The animating spirit of a republic is virtue, of a monarchy honor, and of a despotism fear. "Virtue" in his context is very like the *virtù* that Machiavelli claimed that the Roman citizenry possessed in the great days of the republic; it is public spirit rather than moral rectitude. The animating spirit of a political system does not dictate its goals, however. Rome was organized for expansion and conquest; Sparta, though organized for war, was not organized for expansion; Athens was organized for trade and colonization. All were republics, though over the centuries Rome turned into something very different. Among modern monarchies, France excels in the pursuit of glory and high culture, and England is an oddity as a monarchy whose purpose is its citizens' liberty. The most natural form of a republic is democratic or, at any rate, popular. The thought is this: in a republic, the people is sovereign. In a sufficiently small and simple republic, the people govern themselves directly without representatives; in any case, a republic is defined by the sovereignty of the people. The rule is the reverse of Justinian's "what pleases the emperor has the force of law," being rather "what pleases the people has the force of law."[21] This is the view that Rousseau and Kant spelled out: any state that is constitutionally governed and aims consistently at the public good is properly called a republic, even if its executive power lies in the hands of a monarch. If a state is so constituted that those—the people—who sustain it by their consent are governed for their own benefit, there is a *res publica*, a public "thing," the good of the whole community.

Montesquieu partially anticipated the founders of the American Republic in perhaps their most important achievement. This was the thought that the democratic virtues of the ancient city-states can be reconciled with the administrative and military effectiveness of unitary governments if a confederation of popular republics can unite when unity is needed. Although Montesquieu discusses the possibility in the context of their military capacity, it is not his only thought. Popular republics, he and many others thought, were vulnerable to factional infighting and therefore to self-destruction. The danger increased as they became larger, so there was a tension between the ability to resist aggression from without and the ability to avert self-destructive factionalism from within. The advantage of an "association" is that not only can the association defend itself more effectively than its members singly, its members can also suppress factional disorder in one of their number. Hamilton and Madison appealed in *The Federalist* to Montesquieu's discussion of the Lykian League, which Montesquieu had praised as the best-constituted federation he knew of; and although Jefferson was critical of the chaotic and undigested character of *The Spirit of the Laws*, his own ideas about a republic based on "ward republics" probably originated there. An essential feature of American federalism, the idea of double sovereignty, could hardly have featured in the Lykian League's conception of its institutions, given the absence in classical thought of the modern idea of sovereignty.[22]

Montesquieu sharply distinguished between moderate governments, where authority depended on the law and was limited by it, and despotisms, where the arbitrary will of the ruler was the only principle of action. He also drew an equally sharp contrast between the way citizens of the ancient republics related to their polity and the way modern citizens related to theirs. Nor did he do this to denounce modern men for not being Spartans; that was Rousseau's style, not Montesquieu's. Montesquieu had too acute a sense of what the world had gained from modernity to want it thrown away. But it is easy to see why *The Spirit of the Laws* might make a royal censor uneasy; when Montesquieu observes that in a well-regulated monarchy "everyone will be almost a good citizen," it is tempting to think that his professed intention to show how well modern monarchies are ruled is ironic or worse. The truth seems to be that he was entirely serious, but that he was also acutely aware of the contrast between the absolute necessity for the Spartan citizen to be ready to lay down his life for Sparta and the relaxed modern view that to be law-abiding, sociable, honest, and cooperative is good enough.[23]

Montesquieu did not advocate democracy. Indeed, he forbade himself to advocate any particular regime by declaring that his purpose was to give people reasons to love the government under which they found themselves; we must assume that when he said so, he did not expect *The Spirit of the Laws* to circulate widely in the Ottoman Empire. Nor did he argue for the reestablishment of republican forms of government in modern Europe; he read Harrington and Sidney, quoted the latter favorably, but thought that Harrington had entirely missed the point: the English had thrashed about for a decade trying to establish a democratic republic, but had finally reconciled themselves to their fate and operated the highly successful, if hard to describe, form of government that their circumstances dictated.[24]

The reasons why ancient political virtue was not an option for modern man vary from the simple to the complicated. At one level, Montesquieu anticipated Constant's observation that the modern world offers more sources of private pleasure than the classical city-states. Our loss in submitting to the discipline they imposed on themselves would be enormous, whereas it was none to our forebears. This claim does not involve taking sides on the question who are the better members of the human race. It does suggest some skepticism about the ideology of the Country Whigs, and Rousseau's complaints against the modern world. To enjoy what the modern world has to offer is not the sign of a corrupt character, even if it makes us less devoted to our fatherland. Whether the contrast between ancient and modern is absolutely solid is another matter. Pericles claimed that Athenians were devoted citizens who also had rich private lives; perhaps Pericles—or Thucydides—had formulated Constant's question in advance and had rejected "either or" in favor of "both." Constant himself says "both."[25] It may not be an accident that Sparta and Rome, rather than Athens, furnish Montesquieu's examples and that Constant subsequently treats Athens as unusual among ancient republics.

More deeply, Montesquieu sees that even on the most optimistic interpretation of Pericles's views, Athens did not practice modern liberalism; it insisted on ideological uniformity. In Athens every citizen was under the eye of every other citizen, and the city tried to inculcate absolute devotion to the polity in every active citizen. We would find it stifling; and in any case, it could succeed for any length of time only in a very small state. Ancient and modern critics alike thought that when the Athenian *ecclesia* behaved at its worst, Athens had ceased to be a moderate regime; a modern critic might think that even when Athens was at its best, we would find it stifling. The argument can be linked to Montesquieu's observations on commerce. Classical republics despised manual labor and suspected commercial activity; but to prevent their inhabitants from becoming interested in making money in trade, they had to fill up their time in activities such as public games and festivals, and enforce the social disapproval that curtailed their moneymaking. As the Greek city-state with the most vigorous economic life, Athens again formed something of an exception.

Montesquieu well understood that "the people" whose lives were thus regulated were a small proportion of the whole adult population. Even a radical democracy was an undertaking for economically independent males. Only men, and only men with sufficient property to have a permanent stake in the republic, are eligible for citizenship. The line between democracy and aristocracy is not altogether sharp. We cannot avoid thinking in terms of the few and the many, but Aristotle's advocacy of a polity where aristocratic standards prevailed, but "more" were citizens even if "the many" were not, suggests there is room for maneuver. Cleisthenes's democratic constitution for Athens enfranchised all four citizen classes, but restricted eligibility for office to the top three classes. The thought that government by consent must entail democracy—representative or parliamentary democracy—is a modern notion. Indeed, one of the many arguments we shall meet for supposing that a Hobbesian and Lockean "negative" liberty is the only form of political freedom modern societies can aspire to is just the thought that *everyone* can be guaranteed freedom from ill-treatment, but not everyone can be given a real say in how she or he is governed.

Montesquieu follows Aristotle in thinking that the citizens of popular republics had a passion for equality; this thought dominates Tocqueville's *Democracy in America*, too, and not accidentally. Its essence in the ancient world was political rather than economic; it is a passion for equal political standing, which may have economic consequences, such as forcing the better-off to bear the burdens of military expenditure, pay for festivals and games, and so on. It was not the modern ideal of equal opportunity or social mobility; the modern ideal is economic and social, not primarily political. Montesquieu believed that the classical city-state and the classically virtuous citizen had disappeared as historical possibilities, but Rome at least had left a legacy that enlightened Europeans could not abandon. This is the demand to be treated as persons with rights under the law, not to be subjected to arbitrary mistreatment, and not to be at the mercy of anyone's whims. We cannot re-create the Roman Republic. We can secure the rule of law.

Montesquieu's intentions in discussing the rule of law are not entirely transparent. It is easy to read his description of despotism, monarchy, and the peculiarities of England as an attack on French absolute monarchy. It is not, although it is a criticism of the monarchy's self-destructive tendencies. Montesquieu thought monarchy and nobility stood or fell together, and he criticizes Aristotle for not understanding that monarchy requires "intermediate, subordinate, and dependent powers," in whose absence it is a simple despotism.[26] The great success of the English monarchy was to govern through "intermediary" institutions; it tied the local aristocrats to the crown and they in turn informed the crown of the condition of the country. The French monarchy had gone too far in stripping the nobility of its functions and compensating its members for the loss with financial and fiscal privileges. This was misguided; a useful aristocracy is not an object of popular hatred, but a useless one is. A useful aristocracy will support the regime it helps to administer, but a useless aristocracy will be disaffected and exercise a subversive rather than a supportive influence. The fact that it will itself suffer if general ruin eventuates—"no monarch, no nobility; no nobility, no monarch"[27]— does not ensure that it will behave with foresight. The problem was not that French monarchs wished to be despots; they did not. What they wanted was to manage the country's affairs without interference. Like Tocqueville, who employed the same analysis a century later in *L'ancien régime et la révolution*, Montesquieu thought the monarchy was animated by the desire to govern well. But benevolent intentions would not save the monarchy if it undermined its own foundations.

The difference of *spirit* between despotism and monarchy separated French absolute monarchy from Ottoman despotism. Although the king's authority was in principle unlimited, he had to exercise it in a society founded on honor, rank, and station. A man who would willingly die on the battlefield, rather than retreat dishonorably, could be moved to revolt by being required to do something dishonorable. All this moderated the authority of the monarch and meant that the authority that was in theory his alone was in practice shared with the nobility. Nor did the French king wish to be served by slaves; he did not want to emulate the Ottoman sultan. Montesquieu's notion of *les moeurs*, the values, aspirations, loyalties, and attachments of a people, explains why. Kings cannot govern moderately unless they share the values of their people; the choice would be between reducing everyone to servitude and facing revolution. The amount of real freedom that such a kingdom possesses is something about which Montesquieu is discreet, but critical. There is an irreducible minimum of liberty, but it exists interstitially rather than as the object of the law; France was large, rich, and full of differences of opinion, local customs varied, so did views on the benefits and defects of a commercial society, and so generally on. Montesquieu was not only a noble landowner; he was a wine merchant and knew the pressures of conflicting interests. Social and economic pluralism preserved liberty, though the political laws themselves—the constitution—did not.

England was the oddity. It was not one of "the monarchies that we know," but a country whose laws aimed at liberty.[28] This could not be the liberty of the classical republics; England was a monarchy, and its animating spirit was honor, not virtue. Nonetheless, its laws secured liberty. The secret lay in the separation of powers, a notion that Montesquieu was the first person to spell out in a modern form. The powers in a state were the executive power to enforce the laws—the modern notion of the executive—the executive power to decide cases—the modern notion of the judiciary—and the legislative power. Locke's distinction between executive, federative, and legislative was not this, and his omission of an independent judiciary is both a lapse and an oddity, seeing how important to his *Second Treatise* is the idea of a known and settled law enforced by impartial judges. Montesquieu no sooner draws the now familiar tripartite distinction than he effaces one-third of it by observing that the judicial power is in a sense "null."[29] Making sense of that observation is not easy, but the thought may be that judges ought—ideally—to have little initiative; a clear law, well-attested evidence, and rational court procedures should produce answers with the obviousness of theorems. The trouble with that thought, however, is that when discussing monarchy, he is emphatic that a "depository" of law is essential, and that seems to mean courts and lawyers.

The English have both the separation of powers and their judicious entanglement. The different powers are accessible to different social groups, so each group can check its rivals, while their entanglement means the executive can influence the conduct of Parliament and vice versa. It is this that secures the "balance," says Montesquieu. It is unfortunate that Montesquieu's travel diaries survive only for his journeys to Germany and Italy. A firsthand report on how England had struck him would be extremely enlightening. He was certainly pleased and startled by the vigor of political controversy. Englishmen took for granted a freedom to criticize the king and his ministers that in Paris would have led to a lettre de cachet and a sojourn in the Bastille. When he visited England, the long domination of Sir Robert Walpole over the House of Commons was well established, and Walpole's extraparliamentary enemies, particularly Viscount Bolingbroke, were denouncing the corrupt methods by which this domination was achieved. Montesquieu appreciated the irony that Walpole was a Whig, and in principle an enemy of kings, while Bolingbroke was a Tory, and in principle a defender of royal prerogative. Yet Walpole managed Parliament to secure the aims of the king's administration, and Bolingbroke denounced him in terms that would have come naturally to the Whig opponents of Charles II.

Montesquieu's view of just how the separation of powers preserved liberty in England is unfathomable. It allows him to criticize Venice in a fashion that few other writers ever did. Venice may be *la serenissima*, "the most serene republic," but liberty in the sense of a well-founded confidence that we are not at the mercy of other citizens is not one of its achievements. It possesses a "frightful" inquisitorial system, and citizens are encouraged to denounce one another by posting accusations into the box with a lion's open jaws on top. Because a republic has no natural unity in the form of a single head of state, and its sovereignty is dispersed among all its members, it must ensure that the republic as a whole can exercise absolute authority over each citizen. A hereditary but constitutional monarchy has the advantage.

The connection with the separation of powers is indirect, but intelligible. Montesquieu's idea of the separation of powers was not primarily institutional. A society where individuals are uniformly subject to the "tyranny of opinion"—an idea that Montesquieu was the first to hit upon—could preserve an institutional separation of powers while losing its liberty, if the same convictions permeated all institutions. Tocqueville, who read Montesquieu with great care, feared that the United States might become such a society; critics of McCarthyism in the 1950s complained that the Supreme Court failed to do its Montesquieuan duty to uphold the rule of law against demagoguery in the legislature and executive. A society that met the fate that Tocqueville feared would not have the liberty that Montesquieu thought England had. Individuals would act not from conviction but because they were brainwashed, or frightened. One could even imagine a society full of "intermediary" groups succumbing to such a fate; there would be administrative hierarchies, a highly differentiated working population, local loyalty, and varied religious attachments. But if there was ideological uniformity and a disposition to subject dissenters to whatever psychological pressure was needed to bring them into line, it would not possess the liberty he praised. What Montesquieu praised was what the United States has always prided itself on: multiple points of access to political institutions for different social groups, and the readiness of those who operate the various institutions to stand up for themselves.

Montesquieu set out the elements of a theory of political pluralism and started an argument that continues to this day. For the separation of powers to have benign effects, it must be backed by the right social structure and a population that is self-reliant and vigorous in using the institutions it has available. Montesquieu affects not to know whether the English are really free, only to know that they have the laws that enable them to be so. It is hard to believe that he meant that literally. He laid out the constitutional system that enabled the English to secure a form of liberty appropriate to the modern world and left his readers to make their own minds up about how the English used those arrangements. As he said, he did not intend to make readers read but to make them think. In essence, he provided a more robust account of a political balance than Harrington had done: not a mechanical extrapolation from landownership, but an account of government by continuous negotiation between individuals who had both institutional and class or local loyalties. It also depended, to a degree that would have unnerved Harrington, on individuals' being willing to change their ideas and allegiances as necessary to avert stasis.

Whatever a modern political system might be, it cannot be a machine that goes of itself. Nor can we create a perfect commonwealth that will endure for several hundred years unaltered. Harrington's hope to achieve a balance and maintain it by laws that would never need rethinking is delusive. But the insight that a political constitution must both accommodate and control the economic activities of different social groupings is anything but antiquated. In the hundred years between Harrington's *Oceana* and Montesquieu's *Spirit of the Laws*, one decisive alteration in European thinking had occurred; it had become clear that the moderns had decisively outstripped the ancients in science and technology. It was less clear that they had outstripped them in morals and politics, but it was certainly clear that mimicking their institutions was not the way forward. Machiavelli's advice to copy Roman military and political practices in the way we copy their statuary no longer made sense. But a mind as well-stocked as Montesquieu's was capable of using history as well as contemporary observation to understand the limits of possibility for the eighteenth century. In that regard, the American founders were truly his followers.

CHAPTER 15

Rousseau

Life and Times

ROUSSEAU'S LIFE WAS NEITHER easy nor happy. He was born in Geneva on June 28, 1712. His mother died days after his birth. It does not require the insights of psychoanalysis to make one wonder whether his curious emotional career was set in train by this loss. He invariably addressed Mme de Warens, his aristocratic lover and bene-factress, as "maman," and treated every woman with whom he had close relations with a mixture of petulance and submissiveness. Rousseau's father was a watchmaker in a small way of business; he was educated and ambitious, but neglectful of his business and downwardly socially mobile. He belonged to an awkwardly placed social stratum. Geneva was a republic. As was common in republican governments, sovereignty was notionally in the hands of a *grand conseil*, whose membership was open to all economically independent male citizens; day-to-day affairs were determined by a *petit conseil*. In practice, the *petit conseil* had become a small, self-perpetuating oligarchy, upper-class and arrogant, and unwilling to share power with citizens from the middle and lower-middle classes. Rousseau's father was antiaristocratic, and many readers took his son's work to be a coded assault on the *petit conseil*. The *petit conseil* read the *Social Contract* and *Émile* as such when they were published in 1762. They had them burned and resolved that if Rousseau set foot in Geneva, he would be arrested.

Rousseau's relationship with Geneva was always fraught. In his teens, he was apprenticed to an engraver, but was bored by the work and resentful of his master's authority. He escaped his master by escaping his city. Apprentices who had been in the countryside for whatever reason were supposed to be within the city at curfew. Rousseau had violated the rule twice and would be in trouble if he did so a third time; when he again found himself outside the walls at curfew, he left Geneva for good. He rarely settled in the same place for long and was always dependent on the kindness of others for a roof over his head. He almost invariably bit the hand that fed him, however, and sorely tried his friends' patience. Rousseau had nothing resembling a career. He began as a servant, became a tutor, a music copier, secretary to the French ambassador to Venice, a successful composer, and a man of letters. He was the lover of aristocratic women such as Mme de Warens; but they thought his petit bourgeois sensitivities ridiculous, and he suffered from a jealousy of their "infidelities" that he could neither suppress nor avow.

Once he reached Paris in 1741, he became friendly with Diderot, for whom he subsequently wrote two articles for the *Encyclopédie*, one on music and the other on economics, and through Diderot met other "enlightened" writers with whom he sustained a cautious and distant relationship. He returned to Paris in 1744, after a short excursion to Venice; he went as the French ambassador's secretary but quarreled with him. In 1745 he met Thérèse Levasseur, a laundress with whom he lived on and off for the rest of his life, finally marrying her in 1766. They had five children, all sent to the Foundling Hospital. To dispose of children in this way was near-infanticide, since the mortality rate in the Foundling Hospital was more than 90 percent. It can be said in Rousseau's favor that he and Thérèse were in no position to bring up a family; everything that can be said against him was said by Voltaire in a short but brutal pamphlet published many years later, and one of the many things that drove Rousseau mad toward the end of his life.

From the publication of the *Social Contract* in 1762 until his death sixteen years later, Rousseau led an uneasy existence. Finding somewhere to live unmolested by the authorities was a problem. The *petit conseil* at Geneva would have imprisoned him; *Émile* was burned at Paris because it denied the doctrine of original sin, and a warrant was issued for his arrest; he suffered persecution from the local curé when he tried to settle on Prussian soil in a small Swiss village near Geneva. England could have been a safe if alien refuge, but when David Hume arranged for Rousseau to live in England, Rousseau got it into his head that Hume was plotting to destroy him.[1] It was a melancholy distinction that he was almost the only person ever to quarrel with Hume. By the end of the 1760s, Rousseau was mentally ill. The French authorities eventually realized that Rousseau was in no position to trouble anyone; and a tacit bargain was struck in 1770 that allowed him and Thérèse to live quietly outside Paris under the protection of the prince de Conti, whose family had long supported him financially. He died in 1778, leaving as one of his legacies the *Confessions*, published in 1782, and as another a permanently altered European sensibility. Loathed by conservatives such as Edmund Burke and Joseph de Maistre, he was distrusted by radicals such as Karl Marx; but ideas that were original with him are now so much part of our intellectual equipment that it is impossible to imagine ourselves without them.

Rousseau and Revolution: Reputation and Reality

Jean-Jacques Rousseau is the star—"hero" is not quite the right word—of one of Thomas Carlyle's better remarks about the role of intellectuals in politics. Speaking of the French Revolution, Carlyle observed that the second edition of Rousseau's *Social Contract* had been bound in the skins of those who had laughed at the first edition. It was not true, but it reflects the widespread view that Rousseau's ideas had brought about the greatest political and social upheaval since the sixteenth- and seventeenth-century wars of religion. Burke and Maistre saw Rousseau in that light. Believing that the lower classes would bring destruction, looting, and murder to the streets if they escaped the control of their betters, Maistre observed that we do not blame the tiger for its murderous impulses, but the keeper who slips its leash. Rousseau, with some assistance from other intellectuals, had let slip the tiger. This thought faces a difficulty. Rousseau was opposed to revolution, indeed to all forms of sudden and unpredictable change. He was hostile to the social, economic, and geographical mobility of the modern world. His political ideals were classical or semiclassical; he admired the republican Machiavelli of the *Discorsi* and thought that the Machiavelli of *The Prince* had been forced to set up as an adviser to usurpers and bandits, but had given such outrageous advice that he must have intended *The Prince* as a warning against the wickedness of princes.[2] Certainly, he disliked contemporary monarchies, but it was the most stable of the ancient republics that he admired. The template for political institutions that Rousseau provides at the end of the *Social Contract* is Roman, and he praised Roman and Spartan ideals of citizenship. He was not, in his own understanding, a democrat, though he has been an inspiration to generations of democrats. Athens impressed him less than Sparta, not least because it was chaotic.

With hindsight, and the assistance of Hegel and Marx, most of us think of the French Revolution as a "modernizing" revolution. It destroyed the ancien régime and its traditional ruling elites, and after great turmoil gave birth to a republic equipped with representative government, built around the idea of the nation and dedicated to liberty, equality, and fraternity. That took almost a hundred years to achieve; the Third Republic was born in the aftermath of the Franco-Prussian War of 1870. Indeed, skeptics have thought that the French Revolution definitively ended only in the 1970s. The nation-state embodied in the Third, Fourth, and Fifth Republics was quite outside the range of Rousseau's imagination; if he had encountered it, he would have disliked it. His patriotism was not the nationalism of the French revolutionary armies and their successors, but that of the Spartan warrior, faithful to the injunction to come back with his shield or on it. The society that bred such men was local, small-scale, agricultural, not commercial, let alone industrial, rural not urban, and deeply conservative. The puzzle Rousseau presents is that although he certainly had no part in determining the outbreak, let alone the course, of the French Revolution, he articulated the ideals that animated social and political radicals from the 1760s to the present day—and remained hostile to the society that his radical successors strove to create.

The range of Rousseau's talents and the impact of his work was far wider than my discussion. He was, for instance, a talented composer. His opera *Le devin du village* was much admired at the time of its creation. His epistolary novel, *La nouvelle Héloïse*, invented the romantic novel and spawned countless imitators; the sensibilities it depicted were embraced, or affected, by countless readers. The impact of his political writings, such as the *Social Contract*, his work on constitutions for Poland and Corsica, his educational masterpiece, *Émile*, and his essays on the origin of inequality and on political economy, is harder to assess. His books were banned in France and Geneva, burned by the public hangman, and not readily available. Inventories of private libraries show few copies of the *Social Contract* in circulation; but, given their illicit nature, they would not appear in catalogs, nor would booksellers advertise them. The ancien régime censorship was not rigid, and was adjusted to the social standing of those who fell under its gaze; upper-class intellectuals could get away with a great deal if they were discreet. Discretion is inimical to publicity, and we can only guess who read Rousseau's political works and in what numbers. At the revolution, many leading figures professed themselves disciples of Rousseau; but that is another matter.

Here we focus narrowly on Rousseau the political theorist, reaching out occasionally to remind ourselves of the "other" Rousseau. But Rousseau's intellectual and emotional untidiness is part of his impact. He sided with the Enlightenment's ideal of rationality and advocated a politics governed by an impersonal and impartial law, but he undermined that ideal by an emphasis on the quirky, individual, unsociable aspects of human nature. Whether the moral law, or the law of nature, is apprehended by reason or inscribed in the heart (or both) is merely one of the puzzles he sets us. He admired the Spartans, who were not given to emotional revelation, but the appalling frankness of his *Confessions* brought sexual unhappiness into politics in ways echoed by twentieth-century writers from Freud to Russell and revisionist Marxists such as

Herbert Marcuse. The 1960s slogan "the personal is the political" might have been coined by Rousseau.

His greatest innovation was to analyze the human condition as an essentially social condition, and in the process to remove the burden of original sin from human nature and place it squarely on the back of society. He argued that what all writers before him, and many after him, see as the imperfections of human nature were the result of social, not natural, causes.[3] This is neither Augustinian nor Machiavellian nor Hobbesian. Christianity saw politics as an imperfect remedy for the violence, disorder, and misery that stemmed from original sin; the skeptical Machiavelli saw human nature as forked: men are naturally bad—duplicitous, greedy, and self-seeking—but can be made brave, public-spirited, and honest; but he never doubted that it was human nature we worked with. Hobbes read back into the state of nature qualities that Rousseau thought were very far from "natural"; that error (as Rousseau saw it) is the target of sustained criticism. Rousseau was the first to see human beings as clay in the hands of society and to accuse society of making us self-destructive, psychically and socially disordered. By thrusting the burden of original sin onto social organization, he paved the way for the utopian optimism of Marxism and other radical political movements of the past two centuries, even though he was himself no optimist. It is, as history attests, a grave error to conclude that because our vices are social rather than natural, they will be easier to cure; but radicals have thought just that for the past two hundred years. One minute's reflection on our success in curing bacterial infections with antibiotics contrasted with our failures to prevent war, both civil and international, let alone to prevent domestic crime and other disruptive behavior, shows that "socially caused" does not mean "easy to prevent." In that light, three works are central: his *Discourse on the Origin of Inequality*, which provides the speculative social history that explains why and how we have made ourselves wretched; the *Social Contract*, which sets out the formal conditions for the existence of legitimate authority and the requirements for a society that can meet those conditions; and *Émile*, which describes the educational processes by which an individual might be made fit to be a citizen of a lawful republic if he was lucky enough to find one, or a politically unengaged, but self-sufficient and morally decent, private individual if not.

Rousseau's Discovery of Human Evolution

The *Social Contract* is our main target, but best approached through the *Discourse on the Origin of Inequality* and *Émile*. Rousseau cared more for the *Social Contract* than for anything else he wrote. He deferred the publication of *Émile* so that it would not steal the other book's thunder, knowing that it was the more likely to be a best seller. As insurance, Émile is also given an account of the political theory of the *Social Contract* in book 5 of *Émile*.[4] But what is most novel about Rousseau's political thought is not conveyed in the *Social Contract* itself. Rousseau was far from the first political theorist to take history seriously. Thucydides wrote didactic history; Machiavelli claimed that Italian politics were in a disastrous state because the "proud indolence" of Christian princes led them to ignore the lessons of history. Rousseau's contemporary David Hume wrote historically charged essays on politics and a multivolume *History of England* whose purpose was to show up the Whig account of English history as political mythology. Rousseau went far beyond this.

He situated modern politics within an evolutionary framework and enormously lengthened the historical time frame within which the vagaries of political life were located. Thucydides and Machiavelli shared a vision of the purpose of historical writing: it provided examples of success and failure, and intelligent statecraft would draw on them. Rousseau came close to claiming that what we call human nature is nothing but the play of light on a surface that we can never see below—that although there must be something primordial and original in the human constitution that allows culture to create the finished objects we call persons, our original nature is thoroughly lost and its character something we can only conjecture because it cannot be directly encountered.[5]

An evolutionary perspective raises deep questions about which possibilities for human progress that once existed are irreparably closed off, and which remain open and might be seized. Those are the subject of the theory of human development in the large. It also raises the question how far we can mold the infants that nature brings into the world into adults who can do good both to themselves and to others, who can be rational, and moral, and happy. That is the subject of Rousseau's theory of education. Whether we control the educational process or not, society will equip us with some character rather than none, and will teach us some things and not others; but if the process is not intelligently controlled or not controlled for some serious moral purpose, it may produce anything—and Rousseau complained that his own society created the vain, other-regarding, self-indulgent creatures who populated eighteenth-century Paris. To create men with the virtues of the Spartans and Romans and without their weaknesses would take a heroic effort.

Rousseau's life was too disorganized and too much at the mercy of events for it to be literally true that the *Discourse on the Origin of Inequality* posed a question to which *Émile* and the *Social Contract* provided answers. Nonetheless, that is the internal logic of Rousseau's political theory. One final prefatory point must be made. Rousseau did not argue, as Hegel and Marx did later, that history sets mankind only such problems as it provides the answers to, however bloody and violent those answers may be. They believed in progress, and he did not. Most writers insist that clouds have silver linings; Rousseau's characteristic thought was that the silver lining highlighted the blackness of the cloud. He did not deny that change could improve the human condition. He never claimed that humanity would have been better-off without the discovery of speech, reason, morality, and even politics; he thought we had failed to reap the benefits of our acquired skills and capacities, and had turned them to our disadvantage. Change was more of a threat than a promise, and his politics reflected an attachment to stability, simplicity, and order.

The *Discourse on the Origin of Inequality among Men*

Rousseau wrote his *Discourse on the Origin of Inequality* as a prize essay for the Academy of Dijon in 1754 and published it in 1755. It was a successor to an essay—*Discourse on the Arts and Sciences*—with which he had won a similar prize four years earlier. The first essay, shorter and less intricate than that on the origin of inequality, was a conventional attack on the effects of the arts and sciences—that is, the growth of knowledge generally—on our morals and characters. Although written with Rousseau's trademark flamboyance, it could be taken for a conventional essay on the ancients versus the moderns. Our unlettered forebears were brave, honest, politically loyal, and public-spirited; their overeducated descendants are feeble, dishonest, treacherous, and selfish. Its importance in Rousseau's career was enormous, however. He claimed that its writing had been provoked by a revelation he experienced on a journey to visit Diderot, then imprisoned in the château of Vincennes. According to his account in the *Confessions*, Rousseau had been seized by a violent agitation and had spent half an hour in a trance. Elsewhere he called it an "illumination."[6] Like Saint Paul on the road to Damascus, Rousseau repented of his earlier frivolities, felt that he now saw the human condition clearly, and realized that he must go and preach his own version of salvation— that he must explain how God made man good and society makes him a monster. The essay was Rousseau's first contribution to social and political affairs; his concerns before were literary and musical.

The *Discourse on the Arts and Sciences* made Rousseau famous, and a target for critics. There were two different criticisms. One came from his friends, or at least from the party of the Enlightenment, who complained that his denigration of knowledge was an assault on human reason and would only assist the forces of reaction. Everyone else thought it was absurd to complain about the decayed state of the modern world without offering advice on its improvement. Rousseau's retort was that when the patient is dead it is too late to send for the doctor. He replied to criticism in what he admitted was a sullen and rebarbative fashion, but claimed it was a matter of principle to do so. It was no way to make friends, but it was not intellectually foolish. If someone has a fatal disease, it is not a kindness to sell him false cures. What set Rousseau's denunciation of the modern world apart from most writing on a familiar subject was an acute sense of the contradictory impulses that our socialization sets up within us. Poets in the ancient world had lamented the fact that after the golden age, mankind had become vain, greedy, and treacherous, but they did not suggest that we are tormented by our wickedness. The Christian sense of guilt came much later. Rousseau drew on that essentially Christian sense of doubleness expressed in the old tag "the good I would, I do not; the evil I would not, I do," and used it for secular purposes.

Viewed as a prize essay, *The Discourse on the Origin of Inequality* was a failure. It was twice as long as the rules of the Academy of Dijon permitted, and the judges refused to read it to the end. Viewed as a contribution to social theory, it was astonishing. Rousseau took an old topic and turned it inside out. What lurks behind the essay is Hobbes's depiction of the state of nature in *Leviathan*. Human beings cannot live with each other unless a force stronger than any of them keeps them under control. Unrestrained, they will threaten one another's lives and possessions; because we are forced to do this by the exigencies of the natural condition of mankind, the state is not a remedy for original sin, as Augustine supposed, but for a situational problem. All the same, Hobbes's politics is Augustinian. Rousseau preserved Hobbes's naturalism; and he shared Hobbes's view that the state exists to suppress a state of civil war that remains latent even after the state has been set up. In a devastating move, however, he overturned the idea that human nature is at the root of the problem. Rousseau acquitted human beings of original sin and accused society instead. He insisted that human nature properly speaking was not the human nature Hobbes described; Hobbes described *socialized* human nature. To understand where the roots of our miseries lie, we must go behind civilized mankind and ask ourselves what humanity *must have been* when first on earth.[7]

Rousseau's account of our true original nature is fascinating for several reasons. The first is that in order not to run afoul of the censors by directly contradicting the biblical account of human creation, Rousseau had to offer a hypothetical account of how we *might* have developed if we had not in fact been created by God in the way described in Genesis. *Écartons donc les faits*, says Rousseau.[8] That left it unclear whether he supposed that human evolution was as he depicted it, and he was paying lip service to conventional religion, or whether he supposed that the picture of human evolution he offered was illuminating but literally false. He says that the facts are irrelevant, but he can hardly have been wholly sincere, since he keeps up a running commentary of speculative anthropology.

It is hard not to believe that Rousseau wished to contradict the Genesis account of humanity's origins, not only as part of his campaign against original sin but as a genuinely novel speculation about the continuity between humanity and the great apes. He had read Lord Monboddo's history of the origins of language and was intrigued by the idea that the orangutan, the so-called Wild Man of Borneo, was the missing link between our animal cousins and ourselves. However Rousseau really meant to be taken, the thought that *truly* natural man would have been more like the orangutan than ourselves allowed him to strike out into untraveled territory. Before following him, we should take one last caution to heart. Rousseau was never clear about how to verify his conjectures. It sometimes appears to be a rational process: we look at the evidence of human society, we consider the development of the individual, we subtract those things we must credit to socialization, and we reach what we can properly ascribe to the work of bare nature.[9] In the alternative, the heart rather than the mind does the work: we look into our own hearts and discover what we feel when not under the influence of vanity, snobbery, or other distorting pressures. These natural feelings establish our kinship with our natural ancestors. Rousseau might have thought both. Both have their problems: the claim that our emotions remain at some level uncolored by socialization is at odds with his insistence on the depth of the transformation from natural man into civilized man, and the thought that we can reason our way back to our natural origins contradicts Rousseau's insistence on the paucity of evidence for the raw material supplied by human nature.

Still, *écartons donc les faits*. Although the discourse ranges far wider than the topic—the origin of inequality—on which it is written, Rousseau needed a baseline of natural equality from which the inequalities of human society deviate. Hobbes established a baseline equality of fear and threat: each was vulnerable to violent death, and each could mete out that death to anyone else. Locke had less interest in physical equality and was concerned with the moral equality that reigned under the natural law laid down by God. Of course, absent the physical vulnerabilities dwelled on by Hobbes, natural law would be unintelligible, since we would not need its protections. Even so, the contrast between Hobbes's concerns and Locke's are striking. But Hobbes endowed natural man with the most important of the human characteristics that Rousseau excludes. This is variously characterized as vainglory, self-love, vanity, or pride, the desire to have more or better than other people have, and not because we need it or because it will do us any good, but because we can believe in our own success only if we excite the envy or fear of others. Rousseau agreed with Hobbes that vainglory was a prominent feature of the character of civilized man; much of the *Discourse* is an extended meditation on the ill effects of amour propre. But amour propre is a feature of civilized man, or rather, seeing that it arises in the huts of the Carib Indians, who were hardly paradigms of the civilized state, *socialized* man. Nature, or nature's God, implants in us only the raw material of what became vanity, what Rousseau calls *amour de soi*, or a wish for our own preservation. Everything is good as it comes from the hand of nature; humanity, living in an unhealthy society, corrupts what it has been given.[10]

So, Rousseau paints a picture of the original, truly natural human being as innocent—not virtuous, since that requires moral conceptions of which natural man is unaware, but innocent. Like other animals, the human animal possesses two powerful instincts, *amour de soi*, or care for oneself, and *pitié*, or an instinctive revulsion at the suffering of other members of its own species.[11] The one capacity that humans have and other animals do not is not a moral one, but it is decisive in setting us apart from the rest of the animal creation. It is what Rousseau called *perfectibilité*, a term that has caused endless confusion. It does not mean "perfectibility"; Rousseau was writing a tract on the impossibility of human perfection, and his guiding thought was that every step forward in human development was matched by a corresponding, and perhaps a worse, stumble. "Educability" or "developability" are the nearest translation, but "unfinishedness" catches part of the idea, too.[12] Rousseau had in mind a simple contrast. Almost all other animals grow to maturity rapidly; what they can do after a few months is what they can do all their lives. Human beings have a long period of immaturity during which they are constantly learning, constantly changing their abilities and their desires. Other animals have a brief period of dependency on their parents; ours is lengthy. The species also is transformed. Every other species remains unchanged for millennia; our cousins the great apes live today as they lived ten thousand years ago. In that time, humanity has invented agriculture, commerce, and industry, has made literacy a condition of survival in the developed world, and has entirely transformed the conditions of human existence. Indeed, we may have created the conditions of our nonexistence. We are not the same species we were. That capacity for transformation and self-transformation is what Rousseau means by *perfectibilité*. In our original state, we are much like all other animals. This means that we live within ourselves; what we want is generally what will do us good, and no more; we follow a natural law of self-preservation. *Amour de soi* literally means "love of self," but it is really the instinct of self-preservation. We eat when hungry and only what nourishes us; we sleep when tired; and, says Rousseau, our sexual needs would drive us to short-lived encounters after which the mother and she alone would rear any resulting offspring.[13] We would harm neither ourselves nor other creatures. Since we would have neither language nor reason, we would have no sense of time. We would be frightened by immediate danger, but not disturbed by the memory of dangers past, and we would not be made anxious by the knowledge of our own mortality. We would have no sense of our own identity, and with no sense of time we could not know that death comes to all of us. Unlike Hobbes, always focusing on anxiety and, above all, on the fear of death, Rousseau emphasizes the absence of these fears. Natural man is not a human ideal, but he offers an enviable image of relief from our own anxieties and sufferings.[14]

By the same token, *pitié* ensures that we shall not gratuitously attack others of our kind. Moreover, we shall not get into fights over food or drink or shelter, since we shall be so few in number that we shall have no reason to do so; it is safer and simpler to back off than compete, and so we shall do it—particularly when victory would itself be distressing because the rival's pain would pain us. We have a picture of the self-contained life. We might well suffer accidents, die painfully, and sometimes go hungry or thirsty; but these hazards will not color our lives any more than they do the lives of wild animals. And unlike them, we are unlikely to be the prey of creatures fiercer, stronger, or faster than ourselves, for even in our primitive state, we shall be cleverer than they and better able to protect ourselves. As to equality, there is nothing for inequality to feed on; we shall be candidates for the same simple pleasures and vulnerable to the same simple dangers, and in the absence of settled possessions, and with no vocabulary in which to couch comparisons between ourselves and others, the inequalities of civilized life are unavailable.

So tranquil is the picture Rousseau paints that one may wonder how we ever left our natural state. Hobbes and Locke put civilized human beings in a situation where there was neither law nor government; it was easy to argue that its "inconveniences" would drive us to devise solutions to them. Rousseau put prehuman man in a situation so stable that it is not obvious what could account for the transition to even the simplest human society. Rousseau sketched only the outline of an answer. If population began to increase and put pressure on resources, humans would need social organization and some form of language with which to organize social and family relationships. The need would generate the appropriate skills and arrangements. Then human history would begin, and with it the creation of human beings as we know them. Rousseau wanted to explain two related things. The first was what would follow from the invention of language; the other, how society would inevitably develop from the simplest savage villages to modern commercial and industrial cities such as Paris.

The origin of language is obscure; Rousseau thought it was inexplicable. Having claimed, as he had done, that truly natural man would have been solitary, he went on to argue that in the absence of any repeated encounters with others of his species, the occasions to attempt communication would have been very few. The same argument undermined even the conventional view that language grew up when mothers communicated with their offspring; in any event, says Rousseau, since it is the child who has the greater need to make its wants known, the burden of creating language would have to fall on the infant.[15] Rousseau makes some shrewd observations about the sheer unlikelihood that anyone could have invented terms for abstract entities without having in their minds thoughts that would themselves depend on their possessing the language in which to express them. As he says, "the power of speech appears to have been quite necessary in order to establish the use of speech."[16] What matters more is that the arrivals of language, reason, and self-consciousness coincide. Reason is also the generalizing capacity that turns our emotions of self-love and pity into moral sentiments. It does so by allowing us to generalize from our own wishes to moral principles. "I want" becomes "I have a right to," and "I don't want to hurt him" becomes "I should not hurt him." The arrival of these "moral" verbs indicates the movement from impulse to principle. It is no longer a matter of *my feeling pained* at the thought of someone else's misery but of my thinking that *nobody* ought to cause such misery and applying that general principle to individual cases. As Kant was later to claim, inspired by reading Rousseau, it is as though I addressed commands to myself and everyone else: "don't cause pain," or "let nobody hurt anybody."[17]

These self-addressed commands are, as Kant said, "categorical"; they are valid, whether or not we feel like obeying them. We cannot say that we do not much care whether another person's rights are violated, and our obligation not to harm another does not depend on whether we feel squeamish. Rousseau tied together the arrival of language properly so called with the ability to generalize across space, time, and individuals; and with the arrival of morality, guilt and shame arrived as well. We acquire new, impersonal standards, and the ability to know we have failed to meet them, and to condemn ourselves for the failure. Here is the cloud behind the silver lining. No more than anyone else did Rousseau deny that the acquisition of reason, morality, and the ability to think abstractly marked progress; what impressed him was the new vulnerability they created. We could live up to moral standards rather than enjoying the innocence of mindless animals, or we could fail to live up to those standards and suffer agonies of guilt and self-condemnation. When others mistreat us, we now suffer not only pain but moral resentment. As always with Rousseau, it is debatable whether it is vulnerability to our own self-destructive capacities that occupies center stage or our vulnerability to the sneers and unkindnesses of others. This is not a complaint; Rousseau was clear that we become vulnerable to ourselves in the process of becoming vulnerable to others, but there is inevitably some tension between the Rousseau who was—as he boasted—uniquely gifted as a painter of the human heart, and the Rousseau who was uniquely gifted as a social theorist and a conjectural historian concerned to explain how the descendants of the orangutan came to live in Paris.

Rousseau's sketch of human history in the *Discourse* is a variation on the "stage" theory of human development. The eighteenth century was familiar with the thought that human society had progressed from a hunter-gatherer stage through a nomadic pastoral stage, into a settled agricultural stage, ending with the commercial society of their own time. Versions of the theory went back to antiquity, as did morals drawn from it. Two differences between the eighteenth-century version and later versions of the same general theory are worth noting. Modern social theory is impressed by the immense productivity gap between industrial and preindustrial societies; before Marx, theorists' interest lay in other stages of the transformation. We concentrate on the division between industrial and preindustrial societies and leave the rest to historians. We have forgotten the eighteenth century's concern, because we no longer hanker for the yeoman farmer and the armed peasant who attended the assembly, weapons to hand, ready to decide for war or peace and stand the consequences; and we regard the survivals of such direct democracy in the Swiss cantons as a picturesque hangover rather than a reproach. We are also less anxious about the psychological effects of living in a society dominated by market relationships than our predecessors were. Almost no farmers in the developed world produce mainly for themselves and their immediate families, and sharecroppers in semideveloped societies are so poor, ground down, and exploited that being at the mercy of the market would be a liberation. In Rousseau's world, it was still possible to contrast the sturdy freeholder who was the foundation of Roman liberty with the servile trader and the ingratiating shopkeeper of the modern town, and with the oppressed peasant bowed under feudal obligations, and to do so without closing one's eyes to reality. The attractions of the picture are evidenced by its hold on so many Americans at the end of the nineteenth century when it fueled the rise of Populism.

Rousseau's genius was to make something very novel out of familiar ingredients. He produced a genetic account of the growth of human society in which new social arrangements and new psychological traits matched one another. To the surprise of his enlightened friends, he argued that savage society, the Carib Indians, for example, represented the springtime of the human race and was the happiest condition in which men had ever been found. It was not perfection. Rousseau's insistence that he was not a utopian was justified. Human beings were for the first time acutely conscious of one another. They could and did make comparisons; envy and sexual jealousy appeared in the world. It was a neat observation that when his imagined Carib Indians began to dance, they began to compete; each wished to be thought more attractive than any other. By the same token, envy and shame arrived, as some realized they were less attractive than others.[18] With the resentment this aroused, cruelty for its own sake arrived as well. But the haunting social anxiety of modern life did not. Unlike contemporaries such as Adam Ferguson,[19] Rousseau did not try to give a step-by-step account of the development of forms of property, authority, and the beginnings of social classes. He painted a picture of savage society that was dependent on and a parody of the simple societies described by Enlightenment critics of the modern world such as Diderot, and left it at that. The main aim of the first part of the *Discourse* was to insist that the simple society of the Carib Indians was not "natural"; even so simple a society demanded a break with the non-social animal that humans had once been.

The second part of the *Discourse*, like the first, can be read as a commentary on Hobbes. Just as the first part claims that men in the state of nature depicted by Hobbes are not in their natural state at all, and then proceeds to describe their natural condition in new ways for Rousseau's own purposes, so the second part takes seriously Hobbes's claim that the purpose of government is to prevent the war of all against all, and provides a novel account of how that war comes to exist—not in the state of nature but inside society—and how it continues—not with weapons but in social relations and in the fantasy life of the frustrated members of civilized societies. The second part of the *Discourse* begins with the striking claim that the creator of private property was the founder of civil society and the begetter of all our ills. When the first person to think of it fenced off a piece of land and announced, "This is mine," everyone should have rushed to uproot the fence and declare in response that the fruits of the earth belonged to man in common and the earth itself to nobody. What crimes would have been prevented if they had done so! Of course, Rousseau did not think that property was invented in quite that way, nor did he suppose that human societies could have developed without eventually creating something like individual private property in land.

The poets thought that gold and silver corrupted us; they and Saint Paul concurred that the love of money is the root of evil. Rousseau argued that the more philosophical view was that it was corn and iron that civilized man and ruined humanity.[20] This was a profound insight. If we are overimpressed by the distinction between the industrial and the preindustrial world, we can miss the fact that the agricultural revolution was far more decisive for human progress; it allowed human beings to exist with relatively secure food supplies and to produce a sufficient surplus to create the art, literature, science, and intellectual capital out of which subsequent breakthroughs could come. Rousseau drew the familiar moral; although agriculture produced great benefits, it trapped mankind in drudgery. The fields of smiling corn were watered with the sweat of the laborers' brows. This was the true curse of Adam.

A new division arose between the people who performed the labor necessary to produce the society's food and other goods and those who owned the land and everything else of value. A subdued civil war began that persists in every society built on private property and, indeed, wherever there is a sharp distinction between those who can control the disposition of resources and those who suffer the consequences, as in most communist societies of the twentieth century. Since Rousseau had no great enthusiasm for the blessings enjoyed by the rich, he was not impressed by what they had achieved by monopolizing the benefits of civilization. Beyond a modest limit, food and drink do us more harm than good. Crucially, the creation of more resources allows new forms of competition to arise, and these create new forms of misery. Man is enabled to "live outside himself," *autrui de lui-même*. Once we are obsessed with comparisons between ourselves and other people, we do not care for what does us good and harm, only for how we look.

Even in primitive societies, we crave admiration and the good opinion of others. Since the good opinion of others rests on appearances, we are tempted to seem what we are not; this is an incentive to duplicity, hypocrisy, and resentment. Duplicity is obvious enough; if what we want is the good opinion of others, we must put up a good appearance no matter the underlying reality. Hypocrisy is almost as obvious; we have to side with public opinion in order to benefit from its approval, but we may well think it mistaken or immoral even while going along with it. Rousseau's "sullen and bear-like" response to criticism made the point that he would not be lured into hypocrisy, but it made him an irresistible target for Voltaire when he discovered the fate of Rousseau's children. What could be more hypocritical than professing a love of country and displaying such unconcern for one's children? Resentment is the most interesting reaction. It is analyzed in an extraordinary appendix—note 9—to the *Discourse*, in which Rousseau paints the inner life of modern man. Modern man wants the approval of everyone else. To secure this, he needs complete control over them. This means that he must fancy himself absolute dictator over all his fellows. But as Plato argued in *Republic*, dictators have created innumerable enemies and are permanently terrified that their enemies will kill them. The only remedy is to kill all one's enemies before they get the chance to kill us. The inner life of modern man thus comes to a crashing conclusion: he must kill off in his imagination all the world save himself, to be left secure on a desert island of his own making with nobody to admire, fear, or envy him at all.[21] In these pages are the ingredients of the insights of Hegel, Freud, and Sartre.

Rousseau had other tasks to fulfill, and one was to continue his subversion of the social contract tradition. A society divided into rich and poor would not be stable. The buried civil war would become actual, and the poor would plunder the rich, and the rich would murder the poor. What prevents this from happening and enforces stability is a sinister social contract. The rich—described as "feeling fear in every part of their possessions"—propose to the poor that they should continue to exploit and cheat them, and that in return the poor should protect their possessions and continue to serve them. Needless to say, Rousseau assumes the bargain was dressed up as the proposal that peace and concord should replace exploitation on the one side and brigandage on the other. "All ran headlong into their chains."[22] This is one of the moments at which Rousseau both anticipates the Marxist tradition (as Engels observed), but with a greater degree of disenchantment and a sharper skepticism about human imperfection than Marx and Engels. The thought that all actual governments are a conspiracy against the propertyless, to which the poor have been recruited, is as old as political discontent itself. It has always been clear that the poor many could dispossess the few rich of their lives and property; and equally been clear that one disincentive to trying to do so is that many of the poor would fight to protect the rich rather than dispossess them. There are innumerable explanations of why, and this is not the moment to embark on them.

Rousseau wishes to tell two seemingly contradictory stories, both true, with one possessing structural, and the other historical, truth. Structurally, the state is built on the sinister contract. This is a time-less truth; states protect property rights and allow the rich to exploit the poor. Historically, the state cannot have originated in a transparent fraud. It must have started off as a more plausible, if implicit, agreement among people of a more nearly equal situation to unite for self-defense. Once the state was established, it would become possible for those with access to its resources to improve their own position, and to use their new resources to cement their hold on power. The implication is that small states protecting simple, nonluxurious societies have greater legitimacy than their competitors. This was not something Rousseau could have said too loudly; the French censorship would have picked up the subver-sive implications and perhaps their author as well.

The attractions of the *Discourse* are not narrowly political. They depend on its broad sweep and on its insights into the human heart. The picture of the alienated individual at odds with himself, his conscience, and the public at large is striking, and dangerously attractive. Rousseau's image of man as the victim of social forces has not always been helpful. It can lead to the thought that we are clay in the hands of politicians, a thought that fuels the utopian aims of dictators and ideologues. Con-versely, it can lead to the milder tyrannies of the therapeutic society, the world in which we are all considered incapable of leading our own lives without the assistance of an army of social workers and therapists. In representing our vulnerability as the central fact about the modern world, Rousseau slights the virtues of modernity—one of which is the acute sense of individuality that his own work expresses so eloquently. By the end of his life Rousseau was certainly mad; but he was not in the least mad most of his life, and no good purpose is served by suggesting that people who can manage the ordinary miseries of life are more unhappy than they are. Like great art, the *Discourse* achieves its purposes by heightening reality, not by depicting it photographically.

Émile and Withdrawal

Can we alleviate or escape the tensions that distressed Rousseau? Rousseau offers several remedies, most of them ignored here because they do not illuminate his politics; they amount to the advice to adopt the life of a hermit. Nonetheless, it might be said that even the most solitary "solutions" bear on politics as an indirect but savage critique. If we can be harmlessly happy only in solitude, the sensible person turns his back on the world and its politics, builds himself a hut on the mountain side, and thinks his own thoughts without concern for their impact on others. Machiavelli suggested that the man who hates the idea of "dirty hands" can enter a monastery, and Thoreau built himself a hut on Walden Pond as a physical critique of nineteenth-century American society. There is nothing "wrong" with such a strategy, though it is vulnerable to the observation that it is easier for an educated man living on his royalties than for a peasant farmer scratching a living on grudging soil, and it relies rather heavily on not too many people's adopting the same course of action.

The thought that what matters most in human life can be only indirectly promoted by politics is plausible. Both liberals and conservatives subscribe to it when they insist that governments should fend off dangers to existence, provide a few devices to assist social cooperation, and largely leave it at that. Individual happiness comes from friends, art, strenuous physical activity, and the consciousness of physical well-being, and many other things to which politics is essentially irrelevant. They are private goods. Only a few people will gain satisfaction from thinking up policy, persuading others to cooperate with their vision of what is to be done, and getting on with its implementation. That is one modern answer to the question of how we should govern ourselves; it implies that neither the institutional forms of government nor the personnel who operate it matter as long as governments perform these modest tasks efficiently. Or, more cautiously, the forms matter to the extent that they reliably produce the personnel to operate efficient governments with these modest ambitions. Rousseau could not subscribe to that commonsensical minimalist view. It is a vision of ourselves as consumers of government services, not as true citizens. He was too intoxicated with the classical republican view that the life of the active citizen was the good life, and at the same time too disgusted with the world of the ancien régime. We could not be satisfied with it, because we think the ancien régime was economically incompetent, appallingly inegalitarian, and religiously and morally oppressive. That even well-off Frenchmen were not citizens as Rome or Sparta understood citizens would not be our first objection.

Émile could be fitted neatly into a minimalist view of politics, if we did not know that Rousseau would have resisted the thought. For Émile is provided with an education that has as one of its goals the elimination of the misery that poisoned life in modern society, by giving him the capacity to be entirely happy while detached from the politics of the society in which he lives. The details of the education that Rousseau, operating in the guise of Émile's tutor, provides to his charge are material for the history of educational theory; but its purposes are squarely relevant here. They are that Émile should learn to conduct himself by the light of nature, and that he should do so so thoroughly that if (but only if) he finds himself in a republic where the local laws are in effect the local interpretations of the laws of nature, he will become an active and committed citizen and will otherwise live happily and harmlessly but disengaged.

Rousseau got into trouble by insisting that human nature, like everything natural, was good as it came from the hand of God, and bad when human meddling corrupted it: so much for original sin and the Augustinian view of politics as necessitated by the need to repress antisocial conduct. What natural goodness implied for Rousseau was that education ought so far as possible to be given by Nature herself—with the tutor operating as her voice or agent—and that the child should be protected from society until he was of an age to face its temptations and corruptions.[23] Some of the implications are bizarre, since Rousseau credits the tutor with a degree of control over his charge that no parents imagine they possess de facto, let alone that they would think a tutor could legitimately have de jure. Nature, on the other hand, determines all that we do, like it or not, so anyone who thinks he is speaking on behalf of Nature might well entertain fantasies of pedagogical omnipotence.

The central thought is that things, not persons, must teach the child. Dependence on things is consistent with freedom; dependence on particular persons is slavery. It is not a reduction of our freedom to accommodate ourselves to the characteristics of things that makes them useful or dangerous to us, but it is servitude to be, say, a valet serving Don Giovanni, or a tailor serving the frivolous tastes of a fashionable client. Rousseau's thought is in the Stoic tradition, as his readers would have known. Émile is led to acquire his moral ideas by experience in the same way he acquires his understanding of the world; a detailed investigation of *Émile* would lead us into deep waters, since every reader is shocked by the contrast between Rousseau's profession of the doctrine that things, not persons, should teach us how to live and the duplicitous manipulation that Émile's tutor engages in to set up the situation that will ensure that things teach Émile what Rousseau wants him to learn. Few readers encounter Rousseau's tale of allowing Émile to plant some beans in the gardener's plot, knowing they will be torn up by the gardener, without thinking that the lesson is not the sanctity of property but the wickedness of Rousseau.[24] The depth of the waters is not always a matter of the doubleness of Rousseau's imagination; teaching is genuinely equivocal: a teacher must be a companion and the pupil's equal and yet the pupil's guide and leader and therefore not.

The educational process is first interrupted in book 4 when Rousseau embarks on Émile's religious instruction. The *Profession de foi du vicaire*

Savoyard is often published as a separate pamphlet; the fact that it lent itself to such treatment may have inflamed the censors against the book. It is not anti-Christian, but it is closer to simple deism than to Christianity, and its hostility to all forms of institutionalized religion would not have recommended it either to Catholic France or to Protestant Geneva. In book 5, Rousseau ends Émile's education with the elements of the *Social Contract*. We should now turn to that equivocal masterpiece, after observing that *Émile* tells us much about how to read the *Social Contract*. One topic that we may decently evade is Rousseau's treatment of women. Rousseau marries off Émile to a young woman, Sophie, whose role is to allow Rousseau to draw some exaggerated antitheses between the role of men and women in society and political society. Man is strength, woman weakness; education should develop their characters in such a way as to emphasize these differences; women should not be given a formal education but taught to please. Characteristically, Rousseau could not quite make up his mind whether women were the weaker sex; they were physically weaker, but men's emotional dependency on them gave them a power hardly to be overestimated. Mary Wollstonecraft's *Vindication of the Rights of Woman* devoted a long chapter called "Animadversions on Some of the Writers Who Have Rendered Women Objects of Pity Bordering on Contempt" to the comprehensive demolition of Rousseau's views.[25] What she argues, and what Rousseau knew in his heart, was that he had produced a recipe for educating women to be duplicitous seductresses. His novella *Émile and Sophie*, which forms a coda to *Émile*, describes the breakdown of their marriage and Émile's abandonment of his wife and children.

Émile is a benevolent outsider. He is prepared, both as a matter of principle and impelled by goodness of heart, to live by the rules of a rational morality; he understands that the observance of these rules makes for individual and general happiness. He is not ascetically self-abnegating, but he knows that happiness is found in sufficiency and not in excess—in the riches of the spirit rather than the body. He can earn a living in an honest trade, and because his wants are not extravagant, he is self-sufficient, not *needy*. He need not be an active citizen of a political community to live a good life. There are echoes of Aristotle's *Politics* as

well as the *Discourse on the Origin of Inequality*. So we must give Émile reasons to belong to a political society as a citizen, and to one rather than
another. If he can live well as a citizen of nowhere, we must explain what
he would gain from finding himself in a republic of which he would
be a good citizen. That raises the question of how we regard our own
political community, whether we are happy to see our local political and
legal arrangements as convenient devices for limited purposes, or lament
that we do not love our countries as the Spartans and Romans loved
theirs. It also raises for a modern reader a question that Rousseau does
not: whether after two centuries of wars fueled by assorted forms of
nationalism we should rather lament that so many people feel even more
intensely about their nation than Athenians and Spartans felt about their
cities. Patriotism has a tendency to get people killed.

The *Social Contract*

Rousseau intended to ask skeptical questions about the arguments that
states, or their philosophical propagandists, put forward in asserting
their legitimacy. The *Social Contract* announces itself as an inquiry into
the conditions under which a polity can rightly demand and its subjects
cannot rightly refuse obedience to its laws. It is a book that every reader
finds difficult at different points, and what follows can only suggest where
difficulties lie and some routes out of the maze. One of the problems that
Rousseau sets is how to connect the general theory of legitimacy offered
in book I with the discussion of Roman Republican institutions in book
4; another is distinguishing between the several sorts of freedom that he
touches on—natural, moral, and civil at least—and deciding whether he
has a coherent theory of freedom and its varieties. There is a tension in
the *Social Contract* like the tension in Montesquieu's *Spirit of the Laws*. Rousseau appears to intend that his readers will love their countries while
providing them with reasons to doubt whether most political systems are
legitimate. Unless he thought all his readers would hail from Geneva, a
polity that would meet his requirements if drastically renovated, we have
a problem. But it is not a light matter to accuse an author of not know-

ing what his own book means, especially when Rousseau was well armed against such complaints. As he said, he had thought about the issues long and hard; if he sometimes seemed confused, it was because he could not say everything at once, and he could not in any event be expected to make himself clear to readers who did not read him carefully.

The opening of the *Social Contract* is justly famous. Man is born free and is everywhere in chains. The next sentences heighten the reader's anxiety. "How did this come about; I do not know. What can make it legitimate; that I think I can say."[26] Rousseau's disclaimer of a view about the origins of states is at odds with the *Discourse on the Origin of Inequality* and his later reflections on the founding of Rome, and can hardly be meant altogether seriously. The thought that we can legitimate *chains* is hard to swallow. A willingness to show that *seeming* chains are not real chains is one thing, and Rousseau does much to show that; the offer to show that they really are chains but legitimately clapped upon us is another matter. Nonetheless, Rousseau's understanding of his task was sophisticated. He was clearer than his predecessors that no story about origins could determine a question about right. It might or might not be true that our ancestors had sworn allegiance to the ancestors of the present monarch; if true, it was a historical fact with no moral hold on us. Americans find it easier to believe this about monarchy than about their own Constitution, but on Rousseau's analysis, "they the people" may have done well or badly in establishing the Constitution; the bearing of their acts on us is for us to decide. Rousseau was particularly savage with Grotius's assimilation of political authority to the power of masters over slaves. Perhaps a man with the power of life and death over a community had given people their lives in exchange for their submission to enslavement. So much the worse for him and them; nothing followed for us. The question we must ask is what gives anyone the right to impose rules upon us, and gives us the obligation to obey them. This is a present-focused question, which can be answered only in the light of the right moral theory.[27]

Before we explore his answer, we should notice a thought Rousseau shared with Hobbes that supplies an answer to Émile. A person who expects to live as a friendly alien in a society has to reckon up the whole account, not one side of it. We may think that someone who lives like a foreigner in his natal society could expect to be treated in the same fashion as a foreigner abroad. An Englishman in France obeys the French traffic rules not because he is French, which he is not, but because they do good, and even where they are not entirely sensible, he does not expect to be exempted from them. He also expects that as long as he behaves properly he will be treated decently. The converse is true for a Frenchman living in Britain, or resident aliens in the United States. What none of them have is the right to a say in the *making* of the rules. For that, they must become citizens. Conversely, the less integrated into the society they are, the more they must expect their hosts to want guarantees of their harmlessness that they will not seek from fellow citizens, exception duly made for such events as the U.S. internment of Japanese Americans during World War II.

In practice, stable societies that are not at war treat foreigners exactly like conationals; we think that foreigners living in our midst will do us no harm, and do not worry about them. But if we suspect they wish to harm us, we are not bound to provide them with the legal protections we afford our own citizens. We can, for instance, detain them without trial or expel them peremptorily, as we cannot our own citizens. Hobbes and Rousseau remind their readers that while entering under the protective umbrella of a state imposes duties that may be onerous, it also guarantees that we shall suffer no more than the laws provide by way of penalties or restrictions of our liberty. The benevolent outsider has something to gain from incorporating himself, just as the rest of us have something to gain from incorporating him.

Right Involves a Pact

Rousseau was deeply hostile to the idea that might makes right. We perhaps were forced to obey someone, but that gave him no right to have us obey him. Legitimacy means that a government has the right to demand obedience and subjects a duty to obey. A slave has no duty to obey his master; he may have to do so as long as his master can force him to obey, but if he can regain his freedom he should. The same argument holds for the relationship between a people and a ruler. Grotius argued that a people might yield itself to an absolute monarch, as Justinian held that the Roman people had done. Rousseau responds that the prior question is how a multitude constituted itself as a people in the first place. To be "a people" is not the gift of nature. It can come only from an agreement to be one people.[28]

Rousseau supposes, as Locke had before him, that "inconveniences" drive us to create a civil society when we can no longer live by natural law alone. The basis of right must be an agreement; political right is conventional. The agreement is subject to very demanding constraints: we seek "a form of association that defends and protects the person and possessions of each associate with all the common strength, and by means of which each person, joining forces with all, nevertheless obeys himself alone and remains as free as before."[29] Setting aside the question whether or in what sense such demanding conditions can be met, many critics have argued that no binding agreement can be made before a system of right is in place to declare what a binding agreement is and how it is to be made. Yet, as we saw with Hobbes, the thought that political obligation must be self-imposed is very attractive. If the basis of a *political* or conventional right to command is an agreement, either actual or hypothetical, that is binding according to *natural law*, we have an argument that translates very readily into the twenty-first-century thought that the *political* authority of a legitimate government must rest on the *moral* conviction of its citizens that they should obey its lawfully issued commands, and that one way of testing the claim that our government does rest on such a basis is to ask whether we *would* have made such a legitimating agreement.

Rousseau holds that a legitimate state is created when we place ourselves and our possessions under its authority, on the same terms for all. The thought that we might have possessions to place under its authority has also seemed odd to some commentators, since it appears to run into the same problem as Locke's account of government: we are asked to imagine a social and economic order preexisting government onto which government is then glued. This is said to be impossible, because elaborate rules would have to be accepted as binding to sustain such a system, and that implies that the state must already exist before we can create it. There are two answers. We may agree that a rough-and-ready system of agreed forbearances and expectations that people treated as normative (a moral order that defended simple sorts of property as well as life, limb, and liberty) would have to preexist the state; the decisive shift is introducing an entity—the sovereign—with the power to set up new sorts of rules—conventional law—which bind us because the sovereign makes them. This would be the route by which so-called stateless societies evolve into genuinely political societies. The second approach is to "demoralize" prior expectations and forbearances. "Possessions" are de facto: they are what I happen to have at my disposal. If we have things we value, and want to guarantee our possession, we have a motive to set up a system of binding rules that will guarantee such control. The difference seems slight, but Rousseau appears to envisage the second, which is to say that he contrasts de facto possession with de jure ownership, whereas Locke contrasted a world governed by a moral code, which is to say the law of nature, with one governed by positive law.

Rousseau envisages a contract in which we give ourselves unreservedly and wholly to the sovereign, creating a "moral body" with absolute authority over all its members. "Each of us puts his person and all his power in common under the supreme control of the general will, and as a body, we receive each member as an indivisible part of the whole."[30] The moral body, or "corporate entity," is, like Hobbes's sovereign, an entity with a will; this will is the general will, and being the will of the whole community, the good it aims at is the good of the community, the common good. The *res publica* is a *res populi*, and a *populus* naturally seeks its own good. Cicero is not, but might as well be, cited in a footnote. Readers are often puzzled by all this, but one need only think of the everyday corporations with which we are familiar to understand what Rousseau has in mind. The Ford Motor Company has a purpose—to make money by producing and selling cars—and this is its will; as the will of an artificial and collective entity, it is a general will from the perspective of its employees and managers; its employees have all sorts of different aims, and these are their private and particular wills. In their role as employees, unless they are unduly disaffected, they identify their private wills with the company's will while at work. The topic of corporate personality is one we may leave to lawyers and the courts, but the French notion of a *personne morale*, like the common law notion of corporate personality, is the lineal descendant of the idea that the state, like the church, was a *corpus mysticum*. The body politic is unlike lesser corporations in being the basis of their possibility and in demanding from its members the renunciation of their private wills in case of conflict between the general and the particular. Like Hobbes, who thought that if anyone held back everyone else would be insecure in her or his allegiance, Rousseau insists that the contract binds anyone only if everyone is bound without reservation. Critics have been dubious. Locke's observation that no rational man would escape the threat of polecats by seeking the protection of a lion suggests that giving the power of us all to an entity that can make enforceable rules about everything and anything is rash. Nor does Rousseau seem to endorse Hobbes's backstop reservation that we need not stand still while the sovereign murders us; Rousseau appears to take Socrates's view that if the law requires us to die, we must die.[31]

In fact, he opens several doors for escape. The widest is provided by his definition of the sovereign in essentially moral terms. The sovereign exists only because it is authorized by us all, and only insofar as it embodies the general will—the *moi commun*—which by definition aims only at the common good. To attack an individual, as distinct from imposing a punishment in accordance with properly made law, is not an act of the sovereign and not endorsed by the general will, but a simple assault by particular persons, even if those particular persons happen to be a king and his helpers or a parliament. In concrete terms, the Russian kulaks who were murdered en masse by Stalin's followers in the 1930s were not obliged to go quietly to their deaths, no matter what decrees were issued by the Soviet authorities. Nor is the backstreet crook who expects to be fitted up for a crime he did not commit obliged to help the police with their inquiries.

A well-constituted state will not behave badly. So long as the general will is discernible, its rulings and their implementation will aim at the good of all members impartially considered, and such a state could no more wish to mistreat its citizens than a rational man would wish to cut off his own hand for no reason. The existence of a body politic, that is, of what one would today call a state, creates a set of novel relationships. The body politic has two aspects; it is the sovereign when actively making law, and the state when implementing the laws once made. Its members are not only men but both citizens and subjects. As citizens they make law; as subjects they obey the laws they have made. They are, moreover, as free as ever, or even freer. They make the laws they obey and thus obey themselves alone and remain as free as before; and since slavery consists in dependence on particular other individuals, when we give ourselves to everyone we give ourselves to nobody.[32] A few pages later, Rousseau claims that we are in fact freer than before: we are governed by rules rather than mere expectations and have been transformed from unthinking animals into moral human beings.[33] We are freer or perhaps differently free. "Impulsion to appetite alone is slavery, but obedience to the law one has prescribed for oneself is liberty." Kant took up this thought and made it the basis of a moral theory that supported an account of constitutional government and international relations that has remained perennially interesting and exercised enormous influence down to the present day.

Rousseau leaves it unclear how law and morality relate. He sometimes suggests, but can hardly have intended to, that the edicts of the general will are identical with the demands of morality. For one thing, the general will is made only by citizens, and they are adult, economically independent men; women, children below voting age, and economically dependent men are all outside the regime Rousseau has in mind. If a necessary condition of being a moral agent and not a dumb animal is being a citizen, too many persons seem to be doomed to be dumb animals. Elsewhere Rousseau is quite clear about the contrast between the moral law and positive law. Morality is a matter of the rules we would want to follow as members of the human race; law, what we must follow as subjects of this particular society. Diderot had argued that we should think of ourselves first and foremost as cosmopolitans, citizens of the human race; Rousseau did not deny the existence of a "general society of the human race," but argued that we had to set up particular political societies because the common interests of humanity as a whole cannot motivate us in the way the common interests of our own political community do.[34] In the *Social Contract* he points out that all groups and organizations that exist for some kind of common purpose may be said to have a general will. The strength of that will is greater the smaller the group; that is why making us think as citizens, rather than as members of special interest groups, is not easy. By the same token, the interests of humanity as a whole, which would be reflected in a universal will for the human common good, cannot be expected to move us to act against our selfish interests or the interests of groups to which we are attached.

Living under law implies more than that we are citizens when we make law and subjects when we obey it. Like all contract theorists, Rousseau thinks that the point of creating a civil society is that right will be backed by sanctions. We can work out for ourselves what the general structure of rules *should* be in any society, by asking ourselves the familiar question of what rules we would be prepared to impose on others if we knew that they could impose the same on us. But we shan't obey such rules unless we have guarantees that others will obey them, too, and not take advantage of us; and the same applies to them. They need guarantees that we shall obey the laws we ask them to obey; that guarantee can be provided only by the threat of punishment for breach of the law. By entering a body politic, we set up arrangements to make laws that embody the principles of right, while endowing them with the strength of the collectivity. Rousseau found it difficult to discuss punishment, even though he ends the *Social Contract* with the claim that persons who resile from their religious commitments may be put to death. His difficulty was not that of Hobbes and Locke, who had problems with conceptualizing punishment; his was emotional. "I feel my heart murmuring," he says, and stops.

Rousseau comes close to the view of Kant and the later idealists that lawful punishment is inflicted on ourselves by ourselves. In willing the existence of a lawful state, we choose to have its laws made binding on everyone, including ourselves. To want everyone else but not ourselves to be compelled to obey the law is not incoherent, since it amounts to wanting the benefits of social cooperation without paying the costs; but it is inconsistent with wanting to be governed by law. In effect, we license others to make us observe the agreement we have made. Rousseau, in a notorious phrase, said that the person who is compelled to observe the terms of the social contract is "forced to be free."[35] None of the innumerable attempts to decide just what he meant have been both persuasive and consistent with everything else Rousseau says. On Rousseau's view of legitimacy, the man who is punished is being forced to live up to commitments he has undertaken; on almost anybody's view, and in a tolerably just society at least, he is only being forced to meet the terms of social life that he wants others to meet. Burglars wish not to be burgled themselves. But to suppose that the man thrown into jail is "freed" from anything stretches credulity. One can construct several versions of what Rousseau may have had in mind—that the threat of punishment helps us meet our duty and makes us rational, self-controlled, morally free persons; or that punishment is consistent with freedom in the sense that the law embodies our own will, so that we have freely said, "Let such and such be the rule, and let me be made to obey it if I backslide." The difficulty that remains is that Rousseau appears to open the door to the unattractive thought that when we violate the law we do so in error, or irrationally, or through weakness of will. His discussion of the state's powers of life and death is no more reassuring, including as it does the proposition that when we accept the social contract, our lives cease to be our own and become a gift from the sovereign, given on terms. From which it follows that "when the prince has said to him 'it is expedient for the state that you should die' he should die."[36] Many twentieth-century horrors were perpetrated in the name of these ideas, and not only by avowedly totalitarian states. Still, Socrates thought something very like it.

Rousseauian Liberty

So we must ask what Rousseau meant by freedom. The argument of the *Social Contract* is that it must be possible to combine freedom and law; contra Hobbes and others, he insisted that if we gave away our freedom, we had given away our humanity. He argued that "obedience to a law we prescribe to ourselves is freedom," but left it less than clear how this prescribing happens, and how many kinds of freedom there are. On the face of it, the view he should have held would have distinguished three sorts of freedom. All would meet the requirement that we are not told what to do by other people, and that we are not subject to other people's arbitrary whims. They also, more contentiously, satisfy the requirement that we are not governed by our own arbitrary whims, and are governed reasonably, if not by Reason, or by reasons if not always by our own reason. Thus natural man is free and happy, and enjoys natural freedom. He is free from domination. He does not prescribe laws to himself, because the idea of prescribing is beyond him. He follows the laws that nature prescribes to him—which are such as he *would* prescribe for a creature like himself, if he had the conceptual apparatus to do so. Because nature prompts him to the pursuit of harmless good and away from self-destruction, he is not governed by whim, even if he enjoys harmless play; in short, he acts reasonably without being rational and follows the dictates of the reason embodied in nature, though he is not conscious of it. His obedience to appetite is *not* slavery, for he has in himself nothing to oppose to appetite; only the person for whom acting on principle is a possibility can be a slave to his appetites.

The man whose character is healthy, and whose moral attachments are correct, enjoys *moral freedom* and may with luck enjoy a lot of natural freedom if the state is unoppressive. He truly prescribes rules to himself, the rules of a rational morality. His will is governed by reason, not whim, and to make that freedom secure he requires—here Rousseau's liking for Stoic ideas appears—the ability to stand up to public opinion, to go his own way rather than behave badly in popularly approved ways, and so on. He need not be a philosopher; it is better for him if he is not. The heart is often a better guide to the dictates of duty than the head, even though a philosopher of sound views can explain why the heart prompts him as it does. Finally, the man who finds himself in a lawful republic can enjoy a third sort of freedom—civic freedom—as well as moral freedom and whatever natural freedom local conditions allow. Rousseau appears to have two kinds of civic freedom in mind, one Montesquieuan, the other more nearly Machiavellian; the first says that a state violates my freedom if it forces me to do what I ought not to do, and political freedom is the negative condition of not being made to do what we ought not. A state that is republican in the sense of pursuing a common good and being governed by law achieves that even if it is monarchical in form. It is the achievement of a popular republic uniquely to provide ample scope for citizens to participate in the making and executing of law, and thus for the exercise of citizen virtue. It alone provides true civic freedom. In any lawful state the individual remains as free as he was before and freer, because giving himself to all, he has given himself to none and is governed by rational, well-made law. The popular republic alone achieves the *libertas* that admirers of the Roman Republic hankered after, "the liberty of the ancients." Whether Rousseau saw things in exactly this light is open to question, but it is a coherent view and consistent with *almost* everything he says.

We have thus far established a sovereign whose task is to pronounce the law; we know that there will be punishments to enforce the law; and we know that the civil association enables us to live together as free individuals. Its laws promote our welfare, the general utility. The practical purpose of political life is not lost on Rousseau, but taken for granted. The fact that we have conflicting interests makes politics necessary, and the fact that we have common interests makes politics possible.[37] It is the neatest possible statement of a central truth. If you and I never coveted each other's property, we would not need policing; if you and I did not want secure property rights even more, we could not set up the policing we need. These thoughts about the political structure raise many questions. The first, perhaps, is what the general will is to pronounce on, and the second how we are to know what it says. The *Social Contract* is inexplicit about which issues the general will is to decide. Most readers suppose that it is the source of all law, whereas Rousseau frequently seems to confine it to the main structural features of a polity, suggesting, for instance, that it is the task of the general will to decide whether there should be private property at all, but not to decide the rules of testamentary disposition. Those can be dealt with in something closer to edicts or by prescription. The general will is not restricted to making constitutional law alone, but the laws that fall within its purview are more fundamental than the routine regulations that occupy legislatures or officials operating under devolved powers. Rousseau was right to assume that it is more likely that there will be a consensus on what is most in the interest of all of us when we are thinking of high-level, structural principles than when thinking of minute details.

What alarms readers are Rousseau's claims about the indivisibility, infallibility, and omnicompetence of the general will. Once we see the limited range of what it rules on, some of these claims are more banal than alarming. For instance, one might say that if there is *one* body politic, there must be some point at which we know that it has reached a consensus on what is to be done. If there is no way of achieving that, there is no body politic. This looks very like the view of sovereignty that unites Hobbes and the utilitarians such as Bentham and John Austin. The United States is always held up as the great challenge to such a view, since the Constitution allocates the power of final decision to different authorities on different issues. However, Rousseau's draft of a federal constitution for Poland is not the work of a man who did not understand federalism, and distinguished American constitutional lawyers in the nineteenth century accepted Austin's account of sovereignty without visible qualms. Indeed, the American Civil War might make one sympathetic to Rousseau's claim. It is a decision for the general will whether one human being may be the property of another, even if it is hard to see how the general will could mandate slavery. At the point where Americans went to war to decide whether the answer was positive or negative, they were de facto two bodies politic, not one. When they reunited, the question was answered; to the extent that the answer was accepted, there was one polity. What makes the United States one federal state and not an alliance of independent states is that a decisive answer exists (even if it may take some effort to discover it) about the terms of the division of authority.

The infallibility of the general will is more difficult. The general will must answer the question whether a proposal is in the long-term interests of the body politic. This looks just like the sort of question on which we can easily make mistakes; individually we make mistakes about our own long-term interests, and a political system can surely throw up errors galore. Now we come to the crux. The general will is an idealization; it is the thought that just as the human body has desires and capacities that keep it alive and flourishing, so the body politic has an urge to live and flourish. The individual body seeks to survive; so does the body politic. Our desires may be at odds with what our body really needs; our political desires may be at odds with what the body politic needs. This is treated by Rousseau as our making mistakes about what the general will really requires. The general will is by definition the bearer of the right answer; we, person by person, may be quite wrong about what it is. This does not quite reduce talk of the infallibility of the general will to banality, though it comes perilously close. Rousseau insists that where there are mistakes, which he freely admits there will be, they are the mistakes we make about what the general will requires, not mistakes made by the general will. To the extent that this is not a verbal maneuver, it reflects his wish to insist that the ordinary people are generally uncorrupt and that ignorance is not blameworthy, whereas corruption certainly is.

There is a further point that Rousseau does not make very clearly, but that is of the first importance. The question whether the general will can be discovered is related to, but not the same as, the question whether a community has a general will at all. Since the general will is a theoretical construction, this question is perhaps better phrased as the question whether a community has a common interest, even if it is difficult to define it, or has no common interest at all. One can imagine Cicero making exasperated comments on the awkwardness of this way of asking whether we have a *res publica* before us, whether there is here a common good that the political system is promoting. The answer for any actual society is likely to be that there will be a common interest in some areas and not in others. Even a hideously inegalitarian and oppressive society has at least *a* common interest in not being invaded by Attila and his horde, inasmuch as it will do *nobody* any good to be slaughtered, raped, and robbed. Rousseau's shrewd observation that politics is about both shared and nonshared interests is crucial; owners and employees will have nonshared interests about the distribution of a firm's profits, since more for the workers means less for the shareholders and conversely. They have a shared interest in the profitability of the firm, since without that, there will not be an income to divide. In a modern, complex, liberal society, it will often be very hard to know what is *most* in the shared interests of all members of the society.

Such a society will have many common interests, but on an issue-by-issue basis, it may be hard to know what policy best promotes the common interest of the whole society. Rousseau thought that a society that was both simple and egalitarian was the only society in which the question of what best served the common interest could be answered with certainty. A society where rich and poor were sharply separated by income and way of life was not one society but two, and had no common interest for the general will to discern. For there to be the common project that living together involved, rough equality was required. All must have enough to give them a stake in the society, and nobody should have too much. All should have enough to ensure they could not be bought, and nobody should have enough to buy anyone else.

The question arises of who is to decide what the general will requires. Here is where Rousseau's reputation as a participatory democrat is ordinarily established; we must begin by drawing some distinctions. Rousseau tackled two questions in the *Social Contract*, not one. The first is the famous question with which the book begins: how any political authority can be legitimate at all. We have seen the answer: so long as the authority is such as we could imagine putting ourselves under by a social contract, and it embodies the general will, we are free, equal citizens of a lawful state. As he goes on, he cannot avoid observing that some social conditions help, and others hinder, the creation of such a state. But he is clear that the legitimacy of a state is consistent with a variety of governmental forms. A law-abiding constitutional monarchy, to take an obvious instance, is a republic for the purposes of the discussion of legitimacy. The second question then is that of the best form of government. The first question is absolute and noncircumstantial. Either a state does have the right to require my obedience as a matter of right, or it does not. The second question is circumstantial, nonabsolute, and a matter of more and less. What form of government will work best is a question of the size of territory and degree of prosperity of the state, and Rousseau has no doubt that history shows that democracies fare badly under most conditions. By allowing everyone to exercise the magistracy, they incite faction and dissolve in chaos. This was the lesson of Athens. The "popular republic" was distinguished from democracy and associated with the Roman Republic, whose government was notably oligarchical, though not (in the eyes of overindulgent commentators) obnoxiously so. Rousseau's preferred form of government was what he called "elective aristocracy," of which the Roman Republic was an instance. Aristocracies of birth were the worst of all governments, for reasons one finds in Hobbes—there is no test of competence to govern, and the aristocracy's numbers mean their rapaciousness is a drain on a country's resources; a monarch may or may not be competent, but is intrinsically cheaper. As to mixed republics, Rousseau had read Montesquieu with great care and knew that *all* governments were mixed in some respects; what he was concerned to argue, against Montesquieu, was that governments had to answer to the people and that it was essential that the people were virtuous.

The question of how we are to discover the general will is therefore not the same question as who is to govern. The answer to that second question is familiar: one, few, or many according to circumstance; the answer to the question of how we are to discover the general will is that everyone whose interests are at stake must have a voice. They must ask the right question, which is: what does the general will require? They must not ask: what do I want? They must have wants, otherwise they would have no raw material to think about; but they must see the process as designed to find rules to accommodate everyone's wants and not only their own. They must either have no debate or wide-open debate; this is a republican commonplace. The one fatal situation is limited debate in which factions develop and conspire against the common good. The decision on what the general will dictates is to be taken by majority vote. Rousseau imagines something like a two-stage process in which the first stage would produce an answer to the question at hand, and the second would answer the question whether the voters were happy with the answer.

He expected, quite rightly, that we can often achieve unanimity at the second stage where it is lacking at the first stage. Anyone who has ever chaired a committee knows that. He also thought that a larger majority meant it was more certain the decision was right. For that to be true, two crucial things must also be true: first, that voters are looking at a question to which there is an objectively right answer and, second, that each voter has a better than even chance of being right. Granted both of those things, basic probability theory implies that if the number of voters is large, the chances of the majority's being right (so long as each person answers independently) rise to surprisingly high levels at little more than a bare majority. This is a very powerful consideration in the case of trial by jury, in which context the argument first arose. Sadly, most political debates do not fall neatly into the same framework. The thought that there is a right answer cannot easily survive our earlier doubts about the concept of the general will. That is, if there were something that the general will required, we might really believe that so long as any given individual had a better than even chance of being right, the majority would get the answer right every time. We would be right to vote for our own view on the first vote, and for the majority view on the second. But if talk of the general will is only a roundabout way of talking about what is in the general interest, we may doubt whether in other than very simple cases there is a right answer, and whether any of us has a better than even chance of knowing what it is. The argument does not migrate from the jury room to the assembly.

Rousseau was at pains to distinguish the general will from the "will of all," the latter being only the result of each person's voting for his own narrow interest. He was also hostile to subordinate allegiances within the polity, groups that had a will that was general with respect to their members but particular with respect to the state.[38] This is contentious territory, where Rousseau stands with Hobbes and Bentham in wanting a strong central authority to deal directly with the citizenry and in thinking that subordinate corporate groupings will be conspiracies against the public interest. American pluralism is the extreme opposite of this view, thinking that politics requires innumerable bargaining units to negotiate with each other and the state, and that the common interest, if there be any such thing, is whatever that bargaining throws up. Taking sides on this amounts to taking sides on the question of which shared interests most need the state to protect them against the fissiparous interests represented by the innumerable pressure groups of a modern society. Europeans typically find Rousseau persuasive, Americans less so.

Rousseau's State

Rousseau's account of the legitimate state has much to be said for it. One might be hostile to the very idea of legitimacy, as the utilitarian tradition is, and think the only serious question is whether a decent person ought to go along with the local political and legal arrangements or rebel, emigrate, or ignore them like Thoreau. That does not answer a question that many people want answered, which is whether the people who make the rules are *entitled* to do so. Or rather, skeptics about legitimacy must treat the question as factual, whether the local rule makers and enforcers have acquired the power to make and enforce law by the local rules for acquiring that power. Then the skeptic can decide the moral or prudential question whether the rules that generate a government with de facto legitimacy are just, whether they produce governments that foster the general happiness, and so on. Rousseau answers the question how anyone is *really* entitled to exercise that power, and answers essentially by saying, as I have just said, that they get it by being entitled to it under the rules of a state that is constitutionally beyond reproach and such as we would wish (as rational, moral, modestly self-interested creatures, concerned with our families but also with humanity at large) to join. He can answer the question the utilitarian tradition refuses to take seriously, and also avail himself of the utilitarian answer, by agreeing that where the standards he sets cannot be met, utilitarian considerations take over. Émile is a good citizen where citizenship is possible and a good utilitarian where it is not.

Impact

Some highly consequential features of Rousseau's work emerge only interstitially. Consider a figure not yet mentioned, the Legislator. Rousseau says that law is law only because it is willed as such by the people; but until there is a state, there is no people. The not yet existent people cannot will into existence a state that is the precondition of their existence as a legal entity. Like Machiavelli, Rousseau turns to the semimythical figure of the Legislator, the Moses, or the Romulus who turns a group into a people by the force of his personality and the irresistibility of his vision. Rousseau himself was far from endorsing the great-man view of politics or opening the door to dictatorship in the modern sense. What legitimates the Legislator's vision is acceptance by the people. This is not Machiavelli's insistence on the need for a superhuman leader when a new state is founded. Rousseau's Legislator fills a logical gap in the theory of legitimation that he had pointed to when attacking Grotius's claim that a people could give itself to an absolute ruler.[39] The Legislator who proposes a fundamental law that *becomes* law only when approved by the people squares the circle. Nonetheless, Rousseau himself opens the door to what has been called "democratic dictatorship." He admits that such a Legislator will need to appeal to divine inspiration or some similar source of authority or, in modern terms, will need to exert a charismatic authority of the kind admirers of Napoleon, Mussolini, Hitler, or Fidel Castro have claimed they possessed. In other hands than Rousseau's, the figure who is both the creator and the servant of the people is full of possibilities that Robespierre and his sinister successors may have understood rather than misunderstood.

Less alarming, but certainly puzzling, is the relationship between Rousseau's reflections on Roman institutions in the latter part of *Social Contract* and his discussion of legitimacy in the first part. They seem almost to belong to entirely different books. Some commentators dismiss the chapters in which Rousseau discusses the institutions of the Roman Republic as mere padding. That seems wrong. Rousseau was at least trying to show that we can square the sovereignty of the whole people with the need to confide government to a relatively small number. The Athenians failed, because the Assembly tried to do everything itself. The Romans succeeded in combining popular sovereignty and government by an elective aristocracy.[40]

Parliamentary government will not do it. The English are free only every five years when they vote for their representatives; then they act as citizens, otherwise they have lost their freedom to this institutional sham. Rousseau suggests we should not mind too much, given the way the English exercise their liberty when they regain it.[41] Commentary on the point would be superfluous. The people can exercise the sovereign's lawmaking capacity only if they do it in person. The institutions he admires are those of republican Rome, understood as Machiavelli understood them: as the framework of a popular republic, allowing the ordinary man (not women, not foreigners, not the economically dependent) a substantial part in the affairs of state. Their part is reactive rather than active: the elected aristocrats lead, debate in the Senate, occupy executive positions; the rest of us ratify or disavow what they propose. One might nonetheless wonder why Rousseau devoted so much attention to the details of Roman republican institutions, and draw the same conclusion as his enemies in Geneva. A country of many million inhabitants could not model itself on the Roman Republic of 146 BCE, but Geneva could. The *petit conseil* might well feel that it had encountered a thinly disguised incitement to the lower middle classes to revolt against hereditary aristocracy and revive the authority of the *grand conseil*.

If this was not Rousseau's purpose, it is hard to know what was. To observe that the Romans and Spartans had a conception of citizenship and its obligations more strenuous than our own did not require a discussion of Roman voting procedures. Even if it was Rousseau's purpose, one last puzzle is Rousseau's discussion of the role of a civic religion in such a polity. It was a familiar doctrine, made canonical by Montesquieu, and one that Rousseau made his own, that a republic was held together by *les moeurs* rather than by law strictly speaking. The possession of a strong collective morality was even more important than the possession of good laws (and here Rousseau was thinking of the old adage that good arms and good laws make the republic); Rousseau was happy with the Roman institution of the *censor morum*, the official who could reprove and punish offenses against good morals even when they were not offences against the criminal law. To make morality effective, religious faith was needed.

On the way to his conclusion that there should be a purely civic profession of faith, he says enough to have the *Social Contract* burned several times over. The profession of faith is unexceptionable, though it is deist rather than Christian; positively, it is belief in "the existence of a powerful, intelligent, beneficent, prescient and provident divinity; the life to come; the happiness of the just; the punishment of the wicked; the sanctity of the social contract and the law," and negatively, that intolerance is not to be tolerated. He provides an alarming coda when he says that anyone who first professes that faith and then behaves as though he does not believe it should be executed as a traitor, but the civic faith itself is very like that of More's Utopians. Before reaching that conclusion, however, he announces that Roman Catholicism is a terrible basis for social cohesion because its adherents owe a divided loyalty, to the Catholic Church and to their own state; the pagan civic cults were superstitious and brutal and set city against city, so that war was incessant; but true Christianity will not do, either. It is a religion of the heart, not of the public square. Far from being a perfect society, a society of true Christians would no longer be a society of men. They would be vulnerable to the first ambitious man who chose to reduce them to servitude, and would, if they were sincere Christians, do nothing to resist, because their concerns would be with the next world rather than this. Odd though Rousseau's approach is, it comes down to something much closer to Locke's vision and that of modern Western societies than appears at first sight. In essence, we may believe what we choose so far as the ultimate truths about the meaning of life are concerned, and we may associate as we choose with those of a like faith. The religion of the heart is essentially private. Modern Americans, more deeply attached to an extraordinary variety of religious beliefs than the citizens of any other Western democracy, behave as if they had internalized Rousseau.

Finally, there is the puzzle of Rousseau's attractions to the modern world. Pace Rousseau's mockery of the English Parliament, his theory of legitimacy is consistent with a modern liberal democratic state built around representative government and a parliamentary regime. Such a state is a form of elective aristocracy. It does not purport to represent the will of the inhabitants other than in the sense that the inhabitants will have elected the members of whatever assemblies such a state possesses, but the law is law on Rousseauian principles. Although a law becomes a law *formally* when the queen or president signs what the elective body has voted, the deeper truth is that the law is law because the people acknowledge it as such. If they do not, it is a dead letter. Rousseau would have liked an annual referendum to reratify the constitution and reelect the government; one might say that doing it formally every few years is enough, and that in a liberal democracy it is done informally and continuously in the interactions of the government and the governed. Rousseau would have been unimpressed by that argument. The modern world did not provide the political commitment that, he thought, the classical city-state had done. He was happy to think that we might throw away what we call civilization—commerce, the arts, sophisticated social life, science, and technology—and recover our virtue; the temptation has always been to think that we can keep what he had dismissed as frivolities and still practice a Rousseauian politics. The French revolutionaries were not wrong to think that some combination of a strong central state and innumerable local political entities might provide an answer. They were wrong to think that the virtues professed by the Romans would make much headway in modern France, and they suffered for the error. But although their American predecessors, who also read Rousseau with interest, were far more successful in instituting the first modern republic, they profited from working under much more propitious social, economic, and political conditions than their French counterparts. Their ambitions were not as different as commentators sometimes suggest—nor was their success inevitable.

CHAPTER 16

The American Founding

An Unlikely Achievement

THE CREATION OF THE United States of America was a striking success, but its surprisingness should not be underestimated. The founders of what has been well described as "the first new nation" knew they were embarking on something unprecedented, where success was less likely than failure. Nor were they alone in their fears. The skeptical reactionary Joseph de Maistre grumbled that there was too much of human contrivance about the enterprise—there might be a republic and it might have a capital, but a republic with a capital called Washington was impossible.[1] This chapter takes Maistre's premises seriously but not his conclusions; the creation of the United States was a human contrivance, and a highly intelligent and well-crafted one. Nonetheless, Polybius and Machiavelli would have agreed that *tyche* or *fortuna* had a role. This chapter prescinds almost entirely from the post-1787 future, to give the founding of the United States its due as an event of *theoretical* interest. Its practical importance needs no commentary. It was a highly self-conscious piece of political construction; its creators were theoretically sophisticated, but their success also depended on the ability to give a narrative of their intentions that would convince their hearers and readers. That narrative had to appeal to a historical and theoretical perspective shared with their audience. They could not appeal to a future two and a quarter centuries hence, when the United States would be the world's sole superpower, a hegemon like Polybius's Rome.

The founders—here limited to Thomas Jefferson and the authors of *The Federalist*—were collectively what Cicero longed to be, the creators of a nontyrannical republic. During these years three possible versions of the United States were canvassed, each plausible: a Hamiltonian United States would have been a modernized but wholehearted version of the commercial and monarchical Britain against which the colonies had rebelled, a centralized state, with a focus on military effectiveness, and unabashedly imperialist; the financial and revenue-raising institutions of the modern state would have been in place from the beginning rather than inserted ad hoc. One Jeffersonian version would occupy the other extreme of the discussable possibilities, the political system of ward republics, agrarian, democratic, ideologically hostile to commerce and industry, and perhaps destined to dissolve into a loose association of republics even smaller than the states of the early republic. Between these poles lay what eventuated, largely the result of Madison's extraordinary powers of invention and persuasion. Jefferson wrote the Declaration of Independence; Madison and Hamilton contributed essays to *The Federalist*; Jefferson and Madison became president. Hamilton's political career was at a standstill when he died in a duel with Aaron Burr, who was Jefferson's vice-president and Hamilton's bitter enemy. Jefferson and Hamilton detested each other, even when their membership of Washington's first administration forced them to cooperate. There are voices missing here whose absence I lament: one is that of John Adams, alternatively the supporter, colleague, rival, and critical good friend of Jefferson, but who might decently have been called on to speak for the conservative wing of republican theory. It is an unkindness to say no more than that his country decided definitively that it wanted a more populist, and less self-consciously elitist or aristocratic, republic when it elected Jefferson in preference to him in the election of 1800. Another absence is that of Benjamin Rush, the astonishing physician who tried to keep the Continental army healthy and wrote movingly and ferociously on the evils of slavery.

The United States is often presented to schoolchildren and foreigners as if a magically successful revolt was succeeded after a little hesitation by a federal state that resembled nothing seen before. It was not only the "first new nation" but also generated ex nihilo. The truth is more interesting. It was a contentious and theory-laden enterprise. The rebellious colonists expressed their grievances and recounted their endangered rights in the language of the radicals who had been squeezed out of English politics in the aftermath of the Glorious Revolution of 1688. Behind them stood the republicans of the Cromwellian Commonwealth. Locke was an inspiration not because colonial militias carried his *Second Treatise* in their knapsacks, although Samuel Adams got the Boston City Council to endorse a statement of the principles of government lifted directly from the *Second Treatise*, but because Locke's views were those of Country Whigs and Cromwellian republicans.[2] The Glorious Revolution put an end to absolute monarchy in Britain and the threat of a Catholic restoration. It did not institute government by consent, disestablishment, or the separation of church and state. The Good Old Cause—the cause of English republicanism—got a second wind in America.

The Declaration and Its Sources: Locke and Sidney

The American Revolution was not only *a* "glorious revolution"; it went *the* Glorious Revolution one better. In the course of attacking the French Revolution, Edmund Burke praised the settlement of 1689; he said the Whigs were right to claim that they had fought a wholly defensive and restorative revolution to protect the ancient constitution against assault, and not to vindicate the right of the people to appoint William and Mary.[3] If "we the people" could make kings, "we the people" could unmake them; and kings would serve at their masters' pleasure. Locke was squarely in the other camp; rulers served at the people's pleasure, and Jefferson said the same. His 1774 statement of *The Rights of British North America* tactlessly told George III as much.[4] Whether Jefferson expected George III to agree that "he is no more than the chief officer of his people, appointed by the laws, and circumscribed with definite powers, to assist in working the great machine of government," is quite another matter.

The Declaration of Independence two years later was equally Lockean, but perhaps indebted even more to Algernon Sidney. Much as in Sidney, appeals to the natural rights of individuals, resting on a very "philosophical" idea of natural law, are interwoven with ideas about collective liberty indebted to republicans such as Harrington and more remotely to Seneca and Cicero, which is to say the liberty of self-governing citizens rather than the "let alone" liberty of subjects. The rhetoric of citizen virtue coexists quite happily with the rhetoric of natural rights, without discomfort to anyone but commentators wanting to know where Jefferson's rhetoric came from. Jefferson seemed not to think the question was worth raising. Asked what the inspiration for the Declaration of Independence had been, he replied that he had drawn upon "the harmonizing sentiments of the day," citing Aristotle, Cicero, Locke, and Sidney.[5] Nor does the Declaration display any anxiety that God was usually invoked on behalf of the divine right of kings rather than the divine right of the American people "to assume among the powers of the earth, the separate and equal station to which the laws of nature and of nature's God entitle them."[6] History and philosophy are invoked without any fear they might yield different results. The immemorial liberties of the English and the virtues of the ancient constitution are cited along with appeals to natural right that to a modern eye appear to belong to a different conceptual universe. If we have a natural right to remake our institutions whenever we choose, the authority of the past *as such* cannot be very great, which was one of Burke's complaints against the British supporters of the French Revolution. We might square the circle by supposing that the primordial constitution of Anglo-Saxon England embodied "the laws of nature and of nature's God." Jefferson sometimes seemed to think so; we find it harder. But Cicero thought Stoic philosophy taught the same lessons as the Roman *mos maiorum*, so Jefferson was in good company; and mention of Cicero reminds us that the demands of political oratory are not those of philosophy in the abstract.

The intellectual ingredients are familiar, then: the Petition of Right of 1629 and the Declaration and Bill of Rights of 1689, Sidney's *Discourses*, Locke's *Two Treatises*, Montesquieu's *Spirit of the Laws*, Blackstone's *Institutes*, a classical literature read in college that included Aristotle, Cicero, and Tacitus and modern Scottish philosophy, including Hume's political essays. Equally important was American religious sentiment. Philadelphia was the one city in the British Empire where Jews and Catholics could worship as freely as their Protestant neighbors, but the American sensibility was in broad terms Calvinist and Augustinian in morals and politics even if Jefferson was probably a deist rather than any sort of more orthodox Christian. Politicians whose education had taught them that revelation reinforced the teachings of nature were not concerned to magnify the differences between Christian and pagan writers on politics but to emphasize what they had in common. In the idiom of a later day, they sought an "overlapping consensus" that allowed political action to proceed on agreed principles that could be sustained by very different ultimate allegiances.[7]

Later writers drew a sharp distinction between the liberal concern with individual freedom from government oppression and the republican concern for the collective freedom that self-governing citizens possessed—the distinction made famous in Benjamin Constant's 1818 essay "La liberté des anciens comparée à celle des modernes." Before Constant the distinction was only half-visible; but an American of the late eighteenth century on whom one pressed the distinction would very likely have insisted that Americans needed both kinds of liberty; the liberty of the ancients without the liberty of the moderns would destroy economic freedom, violate the rights of conscience, and degenerate into the tyranny of the majority, while the liberty of the moderns without the liberty of the ancients would deprive the citizenry of the power of self-government claimed by the words "we the people." This is plainly right. The tension between a "politics of virtue," focusing on the citizens' capacity for collective action, and a "politics of rights," focusing on noninterference with the private projects of individuals, emerges only when either is pressed to an extreme. Madison's view that "politics lies in a mean" expresses a particularly sane unwillingness to press things to an extreme; Jefferson was, at least in his correspondence, more eager to see where the limits of the possible lay, though he was reconciled to the need for common sense in practice.

If Americans could not govern themselves, and descended into anarchy, the rebellion would be a disaster, as it would be if they exploited or tyrannized over one another, as they complained the British government had done over them. The new constitutional order must be both Lockean and republican, protecting individual rights against government excess, while devising institutions that made for limited but effective government. Unresolved tensions remained, visible in the Constitution itself. Slavery was the worst in terms of its long-run capacity to destroy national unity. It was not very demanding intellectually to reconcile the institution of slavery with an insistence that men were created free and equal, so long as one was prepared to swallow the appropriate doctrine about the incapacity of enslaved Negroes for any other existence, or to rest on the thought that God had cursed the sons of Ham or the descendants of Cain. The liberty of *citizens* in pagan antiquity had rested on the existence of slavery, on the exclusion of women from political life, and on the exclusion of a substantial part of the population on the grounds of poverty or moral incapacity. Much of pagan antiquity did not believe we were born free and equal; Christian modernity did, and the Declaration said so. But Locke himself wrote a constitution for an American colony based on slavery, and Christian writers had for centuries found ways of squaring the existence of slavery with Stoic and Christian ideas of natural equality.

In any historical account of the revolution, there is much to say about the motivation of the American Revolution and the American revolutionaries. Viewed unkindly, the revolution occurred because some colonists wanted the protection of the British military and navy without being taxed to pay for it, while others wished to exterminate the native population and appropriate their land without the minimal restraints that the home government had tried to impose. There is no doubt something in that story. In a less unkind perspective, a thriving and self-confident people accustomed to managing their own affairs would not defer forever to the home government's notion of the colonial relationship, especially when the British government was distracted by conflicts with France and Spain, in Europe, on the Indian subcontinent, and in distant waters, and inattentive to the needs of America. American independence could not have been long delayed, no matter what. The growth of American commerce, the demand for new land, and immigration from outside the British Isles would have helped sever the formal political ties. Someone with a taste for so-called counterfactual history might wonder whether a more deft government than that of Lord North could have ensured that the history of British North America ended in a "Canadian" outcome, but it seems implausible.

Jefferson's hopes for his ward republics aside, none of the leading figures in the founding thought direct democracy desirable; nobody, Jefferson included, thought democracy (as then understood) was possible on a national scale; and nobody involved in constructing the new republic was an economic egalitarian. Not even Thomas Paine, as we shall see, believed in economic equality. Equality of opportunity was another matter. If property rights were secure, and all the people could reap the fruits of their labors, differential talents, energy, and luck would lead to different degrees of prosperity. There were voices on the other side. Many Antifederalists were enthusiasts for democracy, and for giving local legislative bodies the omnicompetence of the Athenian *ecclesia*; like the Athenians, they saw this as protecting the interests of the ordinary person against exploitation by the rich. Looked at from the other side of the creditor-debtor relationship, they wanted inflation and the cancellation of debts.

Jefferson was more trusting of the good sense of the common man, a more wholehearted disciple of Algernon Sidney, and less fearful that the poor many would attempt to expropriate the property of their superiors. As things turned out, the "middling sort" who complained bitterly that the Constitution was rigged against them were able to use the electoral system to make their views felt, and to gain office themselves, while many of the agrarian poor were able to exploit the almost boundless resources of territory previously occupied by Native Americans. It emerged that the common man was as keen on the sanctity of property as anyone. When the first party system arose, Jefferson and Madison became "Democratic Republicans." Class conflict of a kind familiar in industrializing Europe arrived many years later, but the political landscape was by then structured around sectional, ethnic, and cultural conflicts of interest, and inhospitable to national, class-based political parties. Here we shall focus only on the creation of the new nation. We begin with Jefferson and the Declaration, proceed to the creation of the Constitution, and finally turn to the Jeffersonian and Hamiltonian roads not taken.

Jefferson and Independence

By the time Jefferson presented a draft of the Declaration of Independence to the Second Continental Congress in June 1776, he had already set out for the benefit of his fellow Virginians the main heads under which the colonists' right to separate themselves from their erstwhile rulers was to be defended, and had justified the resort to arms for the members of the Second Continental Congress. Thomas Jefferson was born in 1743; he died a few hours before his friend John Adams, on July 4, 1826, fifty years to the day after the issuing of the Declaration. He came from a moderately prosperous Virginia family, but his father died when he was only fourteen years old. At the College of William and Mary he studied philosophy with William Small, a Scots immigrant, like James Madison's tutor John Witherspoon at Princeton. From him he absorbed the moral-sense theory espoused by most Scots philosophers. Preparing to become a lawyer, he read Grotius, Samuel von Pufendorf, and Locke alongside the usual legal diet of Coke and Blackstone. At the age of twenty-six he was elected to the Virginia legislature. That legislature was dissolved by the British governor in 1774; it promptly reconstituted itself as an assembly owing allegiance to the people of Virginia. To it Jefferson delivered his *Summary View of the Rights of British America*.[8] It frightened his colleagues, who refused to adopt it for themselves, but not so much that they hesitated to send him to the Second Continental Congress in Philadelphia.

The rest of Jefferson's life was spent in the public eye, though he did his best to retire to Monticello in 1809 at the end of his second term as president of the United States. Unlike his father, he was an incompetent man of business and died deep in debt; a blow late in life was the need to sell his library to Congress to raise money—it became the foundation of the Library of Congress. Jefferson's tomb records three achievements: the authorship of the Declaration; the writing of the Virginia statute on religious freedom, and the founding of the University of Virginia. His two presidencies pass without mention, as does the fact that the Louisiana Purchase of 1803 doubled the size of the United States for an outlay of only $15 million and put an end to any danger that the French (or indeed the Spanish or the British) would block expansion across the Mississippi or navigation along its length. Jefferson wrote the inscription, so we know what mattered to him. He had declared himself against "energetic government" and was perhaps embarrassed by the contrast between his profession and the practice of his presidency.

The Declaration was the last of three pieces of Jefferson's thinking on the need for a decisive break with Britain. *A Summary View*, the first, is interesting because it tells its notional addressee, George III, that his position as king is a matter of popular appointment, and backs this claim by an appeal not to Locke but to Cicero's *De officiis*. The supreme magistrate is an agent of the common good, and his task is to secure the welfare of the people.[9] Running alongside that claim are two very Jeffersonian thoughts about the position of the Americans vis-à-vis the home government. Both invoke the Anglo-Saxons, though for different purposes. The first is the question of the powers of home governments over colonists after the colonists have left home and set up elsewhere, either by conquest, occupying unoccupied territory, or some mixture. When the Saxons left their woods and forests and conquered Britain, they never thought they were governed by whoever had governed them before. Having established themselves in a new country, they set up their own government and governed themselves as they thought fit.

That was equally true of the colonies that Greek cities established around the Mediterranean. The claim raises many questions about the terms on which the American colonists had set out, and how binding those terms could be when applied to their descendants generations down the line. Jefferson does not raise them; he simply says that what held for the Saxons holds for the Americans. The benefits the British government provided for the colonists are like the assistance that one nation might render another to which it is bound by treaty. Assistance confers on the nation providing help no political authority over the nation assisted, although assistance is a ground of friendship. If Britain aids Portugal, it gives Britain no sovereignty over the Portuguese. Jefferson did not deny the existence of the British Empire; but he construed it as a confederation of self-governing communities; a benign and well-intentioned monarch should preside over it with an eye to the welfare of every unit, but no unit could claim sovereignty over any other. It was as absurd for Parliament in London to legislate for Massachusetts as it would have been for the council in Boston to legislate for Britain. Curiously enough, some thirty years later, Jefferson imagined that there might be "an empire of liberty" stretching all the way from Canada to South America, and yet that the states west of the Mississippi might form an independent confederation separate from the United States. His picture of the British Empire suggests one way he might have thought of the relationship of the components.

His argument was at odds with practice, though compelling in its own right; in the "proprietary colonies," the crown granted land and rights of government to whomever it had pleased the Crown to benefit. The rights enjoyed by the colonists were a leasehold that the owner could revoke if the terms of the lease were violated. Jefferson's second invocation of the Saxons takes aim at that argument. The crown had no original proprietary rights in America and could not use them to dispose of land in that fashion; nor could it attach rights of government to grants of land. Only in a feudal environment such as the Normans had established in England were subordinate landowners merely the possessors pro tem of what they were granted by their feudal superiors. This was the doctrine of the Norman yoke much loved by English radicals; the Anglo-Saxons had been freeholders, and only when the Normans had expropriated them had they lost their original rights. In America the Norman yoke had never been fastened on the necks of the people; Americans held their lands "allodially." They were self-governing freeholders, and the British government should recognize the fact. In any event, the

British attempt to dissolve the Virginia legislature was null and void because there was no royal power to dissolve the British Parliament, let alone parliaments in another country.[10]

Jefferson's enthusiasm for Saxon liberty provokes a wry smile today, but his enthusiasm makes it easier to see how far his republicanism was independent of the ideas and practices of the Greeks and Romans and squarely in the tradition of the radicals of the English Civil War. Since many American colonists had returned from Massachusetts to England to fight in the English Civil War, and the Restoration of the Stuart monarchy had then led to a substantial traffic in the other direction, it is hardly surprising. Jefferson was unusual, however, in the extent of his enthusiasm for the Anglo-Saxons and his belief that they could teach us more than Aristotle.[11] He met the rhetorical needs of the moment by blurring the difference between one sort of self-governing community and another. Autocratic and aristocratic tyrannies provided the example of what to avoid; self-governing communities, whether Saxon, Greek, or colonial American, provide the positive example. Subsequently, he was more emphatic that the Greek ignorance of the device of representation had "rendered useless" almost everything written by their philosophers on the subject of politics. As to the government of England, it is virtuous when kings have a proper view of their role and vicious when kings bully Parliament or bribe its members. But Jefferson was fundamentally antimonarchical, and correspondingly hostile to his political opponents' wish to establish a monarchical system in the United States.

A Summary View takes the literary form of a petition to the monarch requesting him to redress his petitioners' grievances, but it is a petition from outraged citizens, not supplicant subjects; it is not kindness they seek, but justice. They are not asking for favors, but demanding their rights. The litany of grievances is that of the Declaration of Independence, and ranges from the political through the commercial to the humanitarian. By the time A Summary View was composed, war was under way in New England, and the colonies were under martial law, itself an outrage and an insult to a people capable of managing their own affairs when not impeded by foreign mercenaries. The next year, Jefferson wrote the Continental Congress's declaration of the necessity of taking up arms. It is a curious document because it repudiates any desire for independence while denying that the colonies are subordinate to the British government. As Jefferson recorded in his *Autobiography* many years later, the middle colonies, New York, "the Jerseys," Pennsylvania, and Maryland, were not ready for a final breach; they hoped a controlled insurrection would induce the British government to restore the status quo of a dozen years earlier. In the event, independence was declared a year later.

The Declaration has today become infinitely more than a list of grievances against the British government and an announcement that the colonies considered themselves to be independent states and their ties to Britain severed. Together with the Gettysburg Address, it encapsulates the political identity that Americans acquire in the course of growing up, and that new citizens acquire when they are naturalized.[12] It is therefore difficult to look at it as an intellectual production, and perhaps a mistake to try too hard. Its purpose was, as Jefferson said, not to announce new principles but to remind its readers what they believed: that government exists to secure the natural rights of individuals, these being life, liberty, and the pursuit of happiness, and that if an existing government fails for long enough and badly enough, the people must remove it and institute another. That is an inelegant summary of a stirring document, and it omits the acknowledgment that "a decent respect for the opinions of mankind" required the American colonies to explain to the rest of the world what their grievances were and what they hoped to achieve. That passage is a deft expression of the colonists' pride in their independence and their sense that if they were to be a new nation, there were standards to be met before they could expect to be recognized by the community of civilized people.[13]

The opening paragraphs of the Declaration had a precursor in the Virginia Declaration of Rights issued in June 1776; and in May of that year, the Virginia legislature had urged the Continental Congress to move to a declaration of independence. The logic of the text is that of the discussion of revolution in Locke's *Second Treatise*. In the same vein is the insistence that mankind are more willing to endure ill-treatment than to rise up to remove its causes, and that the revolution announced in the document is a last resort. Matching the complaints against the tyrannical misbehavior of the crown against the Virginia Declaration's list of the rights that government must protect and the ways in which they must do it is both easy and instructive. Neither Declaration gives a wholly impartial view of the balance of wickedness over the previous dozen years as between a wavering British government and the intransigent inhabitants of Massachusetts; but the logic is impeccable. As a good Lockean document, the Declaration assumes without discussion Locke's argument that the only thing that is dissolved is our ties to the malfunctioning government; political society itself is not dissolved. Its members owe it to one another to re-create a form of government that will secure what government is intended to secure. The Americans are *a people*, and even if dissolving their ties to Britain implies the dissolution of some of their local political institutions, it does not mean they dissolve into a formless multitude. They remain one people.

The litany of complaints was conventional, very like the complaints of English radicals against Stuart kings: they ignore requests for the relief of grievances, they frustrate the meetings of the people's representatives, they interfere with the courts, they levy taxes without the consent of the people's representatives, maintain standing armies, and quarter soldiers in private homes. It is wonderfully well written, but as Jefferson said, it appealed to the commonplaces of the age, and indeed to the commonplaces of a century before. The familiarity of the complaints reflects the familiarity of monarchical misbehavior. Complaints against interference with commerce, against the British government's restrictions on immigration and population growth, and against the importation of foreign mercenaries are more distinctively American, as is the complaint that George III has "endeavoured to bring on the inhabitants of our frontiers the merciless Indian savages, whose known rule of warfare is an undistinguished destruction of all ages, sexes, and conditions."[14] By the time the Declaration was published, the war had been in progress for more than a year. The colonists won the ensuing struggle largely because the British were unwilling to devote the resources needed to secure victory; their military and organizational abilities were unimpressive. They also received French assistance at the crucial moment at Yorktown. Six years before their own revolution, the French had no wish to establish republics in

ON POLITICS

the New World or anywhere else, but were happy to distract the British and revenge themselves for their losses in America and India during the Seven Years' War. Success was not a foregone conclusion: the Continental Congress had great difficulty raising a functioning army and keeping it in the field. Nonetheless, the British were right not to waste resources on securing a Pyrrhic victory. A peace without independence could not hold, and hanging on to the thirteen southernmost colonies of British North America in the teeth of guerrilla warfare was pointless. The interesting intellectual question was answered by the Constitution, not by the 1783–84 Treaty of Paris, which ended the war: finding themselves in a position to create a new constitutional order, what was it to be and why?

From Independence to the First New Nation

The colonies had united for the purpose of removing British control of their affairs, but the individual states, as they now were, had no interest in allowing one another to interfere in their internal affairs. The Articles of Confederation of 1781, under which they fought the war, provided for a common foreign and defense policy and declared the union to be perpetual. They also provided for extradition between states and bound each state to give full faith and credit to the acts of all other states. But they were the terms on which a *confederation* was organized; each state had one vote in a unicameral congress; there was no common executive; there was no supreme court, although there was a national maritime court; members of congress were appointed by state legislatures, which emphasized their role as delegates; and there was no central control over the money supply. Both states and congress had the right to coin money; immediately after the war there was a scarcity of bullion, and the combination of postwar depression and aggressive demands from creditors for the repayment in gold or silver of loans to hard-up farmers in western Massachusetts provoked Shays's Rebellion in late 1786. It was suppressed without difficulty and very little bloodshed as soon as the authorities decided to act. Its effect on opinion was nonetheless dramatic.

It provoked Jefferson, then minister to France, to make some famously incendiary remarks about the health-giving properties of a little rebellion now and then; "the tree of liberty must be refreshed from time to time with the blood of patriots & tyrants. It is it's natural manure."[15] Almost everyone else saw it as a reminder that the Articles of Confederation were inadequate as the basis of a United States of America. Not only were the individual states unable to cooperate with each other; they were unable to keep order within their own boundaries, and chaos in one was all too likely to spread to the rest. It reminded everyone of the need for a stable currency and for some central power to regulate interstate commerce. In short, the country required a "more perfect union," and this the Philadelphia convention of the summer of 1787 produced; it was a mark of the feebleness of the government created by the Articles that the convention was essentially a private initiative, belatedly blessed by the Continental Congress. The Continental Congress voted in fact only for a convention to suggest changes to the Articles, and some of its members were outraged to discover that the changes amounted to the replacement of both the Articles and the Congress.

Whereas the Articles provided a unicameral legislature, the Constitution provided a bicameral one, with a lower house elected on the basis of population and an upper house appointed by the legislatures of each state on the basis of two senators per state regardless of population. The annual terms envisaged in the Articles were replaced by two-year and six-year terms, and the independence of the legislators, or their dependence on their own electors rather than their state, was recognized by representatives having a vote apiece, not one per state. The creation of a permanent executive was a decisive difference, although nobody was sure what tasks fell within its reach or how the president was to relate to his executive officers and the legislature. The other important change was the establishment of the Supreme Court—though its powers were not clear, and its right to declare legislation unconstitutional was essentially seized by Chief Justice John Marshall rather than written in by the founders. Madison and Hamilton had wanted the national government to be able to invalidate state law, but apart from the presidential veto, they did not suggest measures to check the federal legislature. The British doctrine of the "sovereignty of Parliament" meant that statutes could not be challenged in court as being ultra vires; it remains one of the most striking differences between the British and the American political systems. Judges were protected from legislative or executive interference: like English judges after 1689, by holding their office during good behavior, *dum se bene gesserint*. The separation of powers and a system of checks and balances were integral to the Constitution; by now these were traditional and well-understood ideas, adduced by Montesquieu as the explanation of the way the English system of government preserved liberty in spite of its monarchical nature, and regarded by Jefferson as sacrosanct. Nonetheless, Montesquieu had been less than clear about how the executive functioned in a parliamentary system, and the Constitution left almost everything to be worked out in practice.

Federalism

The purpose of the Constitution was to create a more powerful central government, but in a country that had been created by a revolution by thirteen separate states against a heavy-handed centralized state, it was essential that the government could not tyrannize over either the states or their inhabitants. On the other hand, experience had shown that states were very likely to engage in democratically driven misbehavior if there was no countervailing power to rein them in. This was the tyranny of the majority. It was not the tyranny of public opinion that Tocqueville thought was the great danger to American liberty; it was the tyranny of an unchecked "factional" ruler, novel only in that the faction in question was the majority in the local legislature. Tyranny, Madison said, existed when the *whole* of legislative, executive, and judicial power rested in one pair of hands, whether the hands of one person or a state legislature.[16] What was needed was a delicately designed but sturdily engineered system of mutual checks, sacrificing speed of action to the need to secure as wide an assent as possible, but not allowing anyone the *liberum veto* that made the half-federal government of Poland simply impossible. The result was a genuine novelty. The Constitution brought into being a system in which there was a double sovereignty, something that Hobbes would have dismissed as a recipe for chaos, and that legal thinkers such as Bentham and Austin found hard to analyze. Citizens were directly acted on by two separate but coordinate authorities under arrangements designed to ensure that neither was simply the agent of the other and that citizens never found themselves facing contradictory demands from the two authorities to which they owed allegiance. State governors are not agents of the president, and state law cannot be appealed on nonconstitutional grounds in federal courts. A lot of policing is needed to ensure that neither side oversteps the line, but the object is always the same, to protect the sovereignty of each authority and to ensure that the citizen is not faced with contradictory demands. As the world has become more complex, the task has become more complex with it. Bentham's unkind joke that the United States could not be an empire of laws, but might well be an empire of lawyers, was prescient.

Since the federal Constitution struck a balance between a fully centralized modern state in which the authority of state governments would be devolved and subordinate and a wholly decentralized alliance of independent states that licensed central bodies to perform only such tasks as states could not perform for themselves, it could be attacked from both sides at once, and the claim that it had struck a perfect balance was hard to make. It was made easier by the fact that almost all the Antifederalists came from a decentralizing, indeed antigovernmental, direction; they wanted less government altogether, a weak executive, a minimalist state with no military or territorial ambitions, and as little power as possible to flow from localities to the national government. The deficiencies in such a view were not hard to point out. It was harder to make the positive case that the federal government had enough, but not too much, authority because everyone knew that Alexander Hamilton, at least, had wanted what critics described as a "British state," which could engage in grand projects and, in the jargon of a later day, "project power" anywhere in the world. Hamilton did not dislike the British system of government against which the colonies had rebelled; he wanted an American version of that system to be run by and for Americans. It was all too easy for the Antifederalists to hang those ambitions around the necks of the defenders of the Constitution. *The Federalist*, the collection of occasional papers that Alexander Hamilton, John Jay, and James Madison wrote and published anonymously to persuade the waverers to support the Constitution of 1787, shows the strains. It was necessary to represent the new government as sufficiently unified to do its work and yet unable to trample on state autonomy or individual liberties; that sometimes stretched consistency to the breaking point.

The Federalist is not a deductively structured work of political theory as the work of Hobbes or Locke was; it was responding to a variety of none too scrupulous attacks from the Constitution's critics and endeavoring to ensure its ratification. The collection consists of polemical essays published in a variety of New York newspapers. Its practical intentions are perhaps less different than the mode of presentation. Hobbes's *Leviathan* was, inter alia, a tract intended to persuade "many gentlemen to a conscientious obedience" to the Cromwellian Commonwealth; Locke's *Two Treatises* may well have been a justification of the uprising that the enemies of Charles II hoped to launch in 1683. The political theory of *The Federalist*, however, is more nearly that of Machiavelli's *Discourses*, Montesquieu's *Spirit of the Laws*, and, behind them, Cicero's speeches. This is not to say that anyone intended to repudiate Locke's conception of a government constrained, as were its subjects, by the dictates of natural law. It was rather that they had a different task to fulfill, one that required a focus on institutional mechanisms. The authors of *The Federalist* had to explain and defend the claim that the Constitution had created a federal union of popular republics; it was a republic of republics, but also one nation. Hamilton wrote more of the papers than anyone else, but *The Federalist* is doctrinally a tribute to the depth of Madison's understanding of what the Constitution was about.

James Madison

The constitutional machinery that the United States operates to this day owes more to James Madison than to anyone else. Madison was eight years younger than Jefferson. Born in 1751, he came from the same social class of upwardly mobile Virginian landowners; he eschewed the Anglican College of William and Mary for the Calvinist College of New Jersey at Princeton. Princeton was a product of the first Great Awakening, the revival that had swept the American colonies after the preaching tour of John Wesley's ally George Whitefield. So-called New Side Presbyterians were deeply committed to the doctrine of total depravity, the Calvinist view that original sin is the central reality of human life; Madison's tutor, the Reverend John Witherspoon, the president of Princeton, was a notable preacher of the doctrine. He was also a very learned Scot, the only clergyman to sign the Declaration of Independence, and as fearless intellectually as politically. Madison received as good an education as he would have had in the Glasgow of Adam Smith, and very like it. Because he had been well taught, he entered Princeton in his junior year, graduated in two years, and stayed on for what Witherspoon termed "graduate study," probably the first graduate student in American history. Almost at once, he became a member of the Virginia legislature and served on the committee to draft the Virginia Declaration of Rights. He was not reelected—his opponent was a tavern keeper, and Madison refused to bribe the electors with drink. It made no difference; he was appointed to the governor's council and in 1780 sent to the Continental Congress as part of the Virginia delegation.

After the war he served in the Virginia legislature, where he succeeded in getting Jefferson's Statute for Religious Freedom onto the statute books while Jefferson himself was in France as U.S. minister. He was sent to Philadelphia in 1787, notionally as a Virginia delegate to the constitutional convention; in fact, the convention that met under Washington's chairmanship was the result of Madison's painstaking efforts in the previous eighteen months, and its success owed a great deal to his meticulous preparation of the new articles. He was hailed as "the father of the Constitution," not only for his success in getting a constitution through the convention but for his subsequent work to secure its acceptance by the often reluctant states; in Massachusetts it took the promise of a bill of rights, and in Virginia a stand-up confrontation with Patrick Henry, to bring the voters round. He balanced national and local concerns and allegiances with a degree of deftness that is still astonishing; more than most of his contemporaries, he understood the degree to which states had to stand up for their rights without shaking the federal structure while accepting that the central government had to be active and energetic in foreign affairs and in promoting domestic prosperity within the bounds of a fastidious attention to the constitutional proprieties. When Thomas Jefferson first complained to Madison that the Constitution of 1787 lacked a bill of rights,[17] Madison initially thought no such thing was needed; the entire Constitution amounted to one, and if the country was hell-bent on violating rights, "parchment barriers" would be ineffectual. When he saw that public opinion needed to be reassured by an explicit statement of fundamental rights, he drafted and steered through the first session of the new Congress the ten Amendments that make up the Bill of Rights. Equipoise was his principle and his practice. When the defenders of states' rights declared that states could nullify federal legislation, he would have none of it, but he was savagely critical of John Adams's Alien and Sedition Acts of 1798, and uninhibited in urging the Virginia legislature to protest against them by all means short of threats of nullification or secession.

He was a very successful secretary of state under Jefferson, and his eye for detail was essential in bringing the Louisiana Purchase to a successful conclusion. He was on that occasion decisive when decisiveness was needed: Jefferson was unsure whether to seek a constitutional amendment to empower him to finalize the Louisiana Purchase, and Madison urged him to act without raising the issue. As president, himself, he was more hesitant about the powers of the office; he only reluctantly conceded the need for a central bank that could control the money supply and promote economic growth. His record as a war leader was mixed. He tried to avoid a war with Britain for which the country was woefully unprepared, but when there was no avoiding it, he minimized the effect on morale of catastrophes such as the burning of Washington by British forces; and he celebrated the victories of the final weeks of the war so enthusiastically that the War of 1812 has come down to posterity as an American triumph rather than an incompetently fought draw that reflected no credit on anyone other than the Canadians, who effortlessly repelled several attempted invasions from the United States.

Madison's career between the end of his presidency in 1817 and his death in 1836 was quiet and agreeable; he looked after his estate at Montpelier, a twenty-five-mile horseback ride from Jefferson's home at Monticello, enjoyed a strikingly happy domestic life with his wife, Dolley, and kept a cautious eye on his creation. He said more than once that he wished not to rule from the grave and expressed anxiety that anyone who had exceeded his three-score years and ten would be genuinely senile or dismissed as such. Nonetheless, at the age of seventy-eight he was called on to take part in the redrafting of the Virginian constitution. Interestingly, his efforts were devoted to expanding the franchise. He saw that the growth of cities and a general expansion of the economy had created many householders who were respectable, sensible men whose interests were aligned with the long-term interests of their society but who did not meet the requirements of the Virginia freeholder franchise. The Madison of 1787, who wanted to create a republican but not a democratic constitution, could still think in nuances more than forty years later.

The Federalist

Madison's fame rightly rests on his contributions to *The Federalist*. Madison was firmly antiutopian. He had no enthusiasm for the activity of politics in itself; he disliked the rough-and-tumble of the hustings; and the classical quest for glory and a great name held no appeal. This is not because he was a pessimist; he was sure that a well-constructed constitution would bring blessings on his country, while a botched job might result in general poverty, secession, a gradual succumbing to foreign powers, or civil war. Nor did he accept Thomas Paine's view that society stems from our virtues and government from our vices. Government was more than a necessary evil. Nonetheless, he was cautious. He had observed during the American War of Independence that it was no use leaving it up to each state, let alone each individual, to recognize its duty and do it. Having seen Rhode Island almost bring the armed forces of the infant republic to their knees by refusing the necessary financial and material levies, he knew how badly state governments could misbehave. As to individuals, nobody with Madison's Calvinist convictions could be of two minds about the human vulnerability to the temptations of self-interest.

He did not draw a sharp line between the frailty of human nature everywhere and in all contexts and the peculiar wickedness that men are prone to display in political contexts. He did not have James Mill's fear of the pointless cruelty to be expected of monarchs; Mill's view was that aristocrats were expensive but kings more likely to be murderous. Nor did he share Hobbes's or Machiavelli's fear of pure self-aggrandizement. It was rational greed that he feared, though he was insistent enough that diluting the currency or equalizing property was a violation of other people's rights and therefore wicked.[18] The crucial point is less his conviction of the frailty of human nature than that he did not think that trying to extirpate self-interested behavior was possible at a price worth paying, and he was confident in the ability of the right institutions to hold it in check. There would always be factions where there was liberty, just as there will always be fires where there is oxygen. But we cannot breathe without oxygen, and life without liberty is intolerable. Institutions must operate on the basis of setting one self-interest against another.

The Constitution achieved two things. First, it established a genuinely federal government. It created a solid national government with its own sources of taxation and its own powers to raise armies and navies for the defense of the republic, a permanent national executive and judiciary, and a monopoly of the power to issue money and conduct foreign relations. This was on the basis not of powers delegated by the individual states but of powers granted by the whole people, so that the collective national will was behind a central government and its laws. The whole edifice was consistent with a scrupulous respect for individual rights because its responsibilities and authority were confined to the tasks enumerated in the Constitution. The stirring opening "We the people of the United States" was a late insertion in the preamble, which would otherwise have referred to the several states. It was a surprising stroke of genius on the part of Gouverneur Morris, who was in general antipopulist and who described the lower classes as "reptiles." He may have intended it in the way it was taken by the Antifederalists, not as populist rhetoric but as a snub to everyone who thought the central government received its powers by concession from the states. Nonetheless, it catches the essence of the system of double sovereignty. The result was truly a government of rights, inasmuch as its existence reflected the fundamental positive right of citizens to constitute for themselves a government to suit their purposes, and its confined powers reflected their natural right not to be tyrannized over or to be forced to do anything inconsistent with their own or other people's natural rights. That explains why Madison initially saw no need for a separate bill of rights; the whole system was predicated on those rights.

The second thing the Constitution achieved was to do this without demanding extraordinary virtue of anyone, whether the president, the justices of the Supreme Court, the senators and representatives, or the citizens. Madison rested his case on the insights of Montesquieu, who had argued that classical republics required a great deal of political competence, public spirit, and a willingness to sacrifice oneself for the common good; the degree of discipline this required explained why the ancient city-states had been societies of mutual surveillance. Madison wanted a system that demanded no more than ordinary capacities. Certainly, the object of indirect election to the Senate and the presidency was to secure men of virtue and talent and to ensure that they would not succumb to the temptations of office. But the system did not rely on extraordinary men with extraordinary virtues; public-spirited men with the virtues of decent, farsighted Americans would do very well. The processes of "filtration" implied both by the existence of a national legislature and by the powers of appointment vested in the president and Congress meant that the federal government could hope to secure the services of the most talented men in the nation, not merely those whose neighbors happened to like them; nonetheless, they need not be supermen.

This intelligent steering in the middle of the seaway is visible in Madison's contributions to *The Federalist*. Most of the papers were written by Hamilton, the staunchest and least inhibited defender of strong central government. A handful were written by John Jay, and some twenty by Madison. Some important papers were joint productions by Madison and Hamilton. The most famous of Madison's contributions was *Federalist* paper no. 10, his explanation of the value of an extensive republic in controlling faction. This is a fair estimate of its importance, but in nos. 14 to 20 Madison, both on his own and writing with Hamilton, explains in detail why a true federal system is needed, and why a confederacy of the kind that had been tried before will not do. No. 39 provides Madison's most cogent and explicit account of what makes a republican government a republican government, while no. 47 and subsequent papers elaborate on the idea of the separation of powers and checks and balances, culminating in no. 51, which has been ascribed to both Hamilton and Madison. Hamilton wrote the final series of papers dealing with what is now a central part of the Constitution, namely, the federal judiciary.

Madison had to reassure his readers that the new federal government was sufficiently *popular* in the sense familiar from the republican tradition: that it was ultimately answerable to the people. Indeed, it was more emphatically so than its classical ancestors since positions of authority could be filled by persons from any rank in society, even if Madison and Hamilton expected them to be filled in practice by men like themselves and not by the "middling sort" of shopkeepers, merchants, and artisans. At the same time he had to reassure them that, unlike the democracies of ancient Greece and Renaissance Italy, it would be stable, peaceful, and immune to tumult and insurrection; the standard view was that factionalism was the standing weakness of democracies, and Madison's deft distinction between a *republic* and a *democracy* was nicely tailored to its task. The purpose of *The Federalist* was to persuade Antifederalist opinion that no looser government than the one proposed can protect the country from invasion, insurrection, and misery. *Federalist* no. 10 has a specific task within that larger program. It lays the foundations of the argument against conflating a well-ordered republic with a pure democracy, but equally importantly, it subverts Montesquieu's claim that a successful republic must be small in extent. The balanced republic Cicero had defended was an aristocratic or oligarchical state, in which the power of the upper classes was checked by a popular veto on legislation. It was a popular republic in Polybius's and Machiavelli's sense, but not in the American sense. It was not even what Jefferson thirty years later described as a *representative democracy*, distinguishing it carefully from a *pure democracy*, to which Montesquieu's argument applied.[19] The Roman governing class was very narrow—though permeable through the device of adoption—and the highest offices were achievable only by members of the upper classes on their way to joining the senatorial elite. Americans had not emancipated themselves from the hereditary nobility of Britain to hand themselves over to a homegrown aristocracy.

The authority of Montesquieu, however, lay behind the proposition that the survival of republics depended on the existence of unusual virtue among the citizens; and conventional wisdom lay behind the view that the farther a republic moved away from the mixed constitution and toward pure democracy, the more vulnerable it would be to faction fighting and instability. That suggested that only small, egalitarian states in which everyone could police everyone else had much chance of surviving as popular republics. *Faction* was the stumbling block. A persuasive case had to be made for the ability of the United States to do without aristocrats and yet protect itself against faction. Madison and Hamilton reminded their readers that the attempts of the Greek city-states of antiquity to unite for the purposes of fighting the Persians without conceding any diminution of their individual sovereignty had often failed, because factions within almost all the Greek city-states would sooner betray their own community to a foreign despot than submit to rivals in their own state. The Peloponnesian War was characterized by states shifting from the Spartan side to the Athenian side and back, according to which faction was on top.[20] This unhappy history was invoked to make the case for a true federal government as distinct from a headless confederacy. But they needed to show both that the federal government could keep individual states in order and that factions—should they emerge—would not generate a nationwide civil war.

Madison's argument was simple and acute, and resolved Montesquieu's anxieties twice over. Madison argued not only against those who conflated all forms of republicanism with its extreme democratic form but also in favor of the proposition that an extensive republic was so far from impossible that it offered the best security against factionalism. Because an extensive republic set faction against faction without damage to the whole, by allowing the factions to exhaust themselves in struggling against one another, it did not demand extraordinary virtue from the citizens to preserve itself. Whether the proposition that "we must set ambition to check ambition," appealed to explicitly much later in *The Federalist*, was Hamilton's coinage or Madison's, the thought was common to them both. Madison did not suppose that factions were a good thing. He ascribed them to outbreaks of a factious spirit, and a factious spirit was one of the frailties to which human nature is depressingly liable. Human beings like to get their own way, to exercise power over others, to give vent to their pride and vanity. It would be better if we were less vulnerable to such vices, but we need not despair of finding remedies. Madison agrees that factionalism abounds and that it was the most frequent cause of the downfall of popular governments both ancient and modern. Whether this is a rhetorical device to lure his readers into his argument is a question that must occur to many readers, but it is unlikely that it was a conscious one. By the mid-1780s he thought that everyone had made mistakes in the early years of the new republic and that the excesses and follies of one party had often inspired the excesses and follies of another.

Madison was careful in his definition of a faction: "a number of citizens, whether amounting to a majority or minority of the whole, who are united and actuated by some common impulse of passion, or of interest, adverse to the rights of other citizens, or to the permanent and aggregate interests of the community."[21] Many readers are brought up short by the suggestion that a faction can be a majority; we usually think of factions as small groups within larger ones. Madison did not. His definition of a faction is morally loaded, couched in terms of the factional impulse running counter to the *rights* of other citizens or to the permanent and aggregate interests of the whole community. Ordinary competition in the marketplace is not factional, even though my pursuit of my interests as a small-town lawyer may damage your interests as a small-town lawyer if there is insufficient trade for the two of us. To attack your *rights*, I should have to try to manipulate the terms of the competition, to secure my goals in unjust and illicit ways. Ordinary conflicts of interest between different economic groups are not factious; but they may become so, if the groups organize themselves to beat their competitors in illicit ways or to favor themselves in ways that worsen the welfare of the rest of the community. It is not hard to see why a faction in Madison's terms could be a majority. Madison thought in Aristotelian terms of the poor many trying to expropriate the better-off, which would be both violative of rights and adverse to the long-term interests of the whole society. Revolutionaries of a non-Madisonian stamp would see things differently.

Madison had two kinds of faction in mind; one more purely political or ideological, the other economic. The first rested on people's attachments to particular leaders or views about the best form of government, or about the one true church, or nice points of faith. And Madison commented gloomily that the desire to magnify differences and make other people's lives miserable on the strength of them was so deeply rooted in human nature that even where there was no real reason for conflict, people would make up frivolous reasons to behave obnoxiously. This assessment was perhaps provoked by the wild accusations leveled against the framers of the Constitution. The second rested on "the various and unequal distribution of property" and was for Madison the more durable and serious cause of faction. Creditors are opposed to debtors, the moneyed interest to the landed interest, and so generally on. "Faction" in a modern society is almost coterminous with class or special interest. The central task of modern government is to regulate and coordinate the conflicts of economic interest for the benefit of the entire community and to keep conflict from getting out of hand.[22]

Madison takes a coolly rational approach to the issue, critical though he was of those he accused of pursuing factious ends in Congress or state legislatures. There are, he says, two approaches to factions, one controlling its causes, the other controlling its effects. One route to controlling its causes is to take away the freedom of speech and organization that allows factions to form, and the other is to remove the diversity of economic interests and ideological allegiances that are at the heart of factional conflict. The first is self-evidently a cure worse than the disease, on a level, as he observes, with trying to abolish the air we breathe because air also allows fire to burn and cause destruction. The second was simply impracticable. The purpose of government is in large part to ensure that people can engage in economic activity; people have different aptitudes and meet with greater or lesser luck in their enterprises. This must mean that there will be a great diversity in the kinds and amounts of property that exist, and an inevitable division of a society into contending parties and classes built around different and competing economic interests.

Since the causes of faction either cannot or should not be controlled, we must control their consequences. Two things gave America a greater chance of escaping the downfall predicted by enemies of popular rule. One rested on the simple fact that this was to be an *extensive* republic; the other rested on the role of representation in republican government, and the difference that this made in any comparison with popular governments of earlier ages. In the first place, an enormous number of different interests will arise in an extensive republic, so the chances that a majority faction will form around any of them are much reduced. That is, we shall not have farmers opposed to urban manufacturers, but New England farmers opposed to Virginia farmers, who will be opposed to Virginia bankers, but perhaps not to New York merchants, and so on. This doctrine was dignified with the label of "the theory of cross-cutting cleavages" in the twentieth century, and it has been widely drawn on to explain why American politics do not on a national scale exhibit the pattern of nonviolent class warfare that marks the politics of many other modern industrial societies.

Madison thought it possible that a factious majority might get control of an individual state, but anticipated that other states would curb any attempt to bias national legislation in the interests of that state. Later commentators have formalized and sophisticated Madison's observations, and have argued, rightly, that *if* there were a determined nationwide majority faction, it could take over the national government. That is, if the politics of class warfare had become the American experience, a national political party determined to pursue the interests of the unpropertied many could within a few years get control of both houses of Congress and the presidency, and over a somewhat longer run get control of the Supreme Court and the federal judiciary. No constitutional arrangements could prevent a "majority faction" from gaining control if it was sufficiently cohesive, persistent, and determined. It is doubtful whether Madison thought otherwise. His argument is that such a faction is less likely to form in an extensive and therefore diverse republic, and that the various barriers to majority tyranny are not likely to be tested to destruction.[23]

The second argument about the unlikelihood that factions will bring America to ruin is Madison's first statement of the difference between a popular republic and pure democracy on the Athenian model. The latter allows the people to participate directly; if their passions become inflamed, nothing stands between them and disastrous political decisions. The former is a representative system. Madison does not argue that representatives will be men of outstanding virtue, intelligence, or imagination. To bank on being saved by a succession of great men is no way to organize a republic. It was an astonishing piece of good fortune that Washington had been so careful of the sensibilities of Congress throughout the Revolutionary War; he behaved with the fastidiousness of the Roman generals of the early republic and not in the self-aggrandizing fashion of a Caesar or a Pompey, nor as Napoleon was to behave a decade later in France. Generals who save the republic on the battlefield are all too likely to betray it thereafter. Needed is a system in which popular passions have to be diluted, filtered, and mutually checked before they have an impact on legislation.

Madison thought that the modern discovery of representative government marked an epoch in politics, as did Jefferson. They were right, but it is not easy to say what was novel about modern representation. Representatives had existed for as long as there had been governments having dealings with one another; ambassadors and delegates had made peace and forged alliances, presented demands and listened to them; *The Federalist* observes more than once that representation was known to the Greek city-states. Medieval Europe possessed many representative institutions, including the French Estates General and the English Parliament. At the same time as Madison was explaining the salutary effects of representation in diluting factious passions, Edmund Burke was explaining to the voters of Bristol the difference between a representative and a delegate, and how he would best serve their interests by serving them according to his own best judgment of those interests, and not their instructions on how to vote.[24] The American novelty was the thought that representation allowed the people to govern themselves through their representatives, that it was *representative democracy*. That is what the United States contrived, and one reason why it was not only a mixed government on the Polybian model, though it was that among other things. It was a popular republic, but the system of representation marked it out as a novel kind of popular republic. The large question this raises is whether we should prefer Madison's view that representation is a form of self-government by way of our representatives or John Stuart Mill's later view that it is not a system of self-government but a system of taking securities for good government. The second view amounts to saying that representative democracy is, strictly speaking, not democracy.

The representatives were likely to be more politically intelligent than the rest of the population, but they did not need to be men of outstanding virtue. There were almost certainly enough of them to do the work required, and Madison thought it another argument in favor of an extensive republic that it supplied a large enough pool of talent for all the purposes of government: the point of representation was in part to provide a debating chamber that was large enough to provide a fair hearing to all rational points of view, but that was not so large as to be unwieldy. Because *Federalist* no. 10 was devoted so thoroughly to the issue of avoiding factions, the elaboration of Madison's views about the nature of republics and their proper organization was deferred to a series of papers—nos. 37 to 48 (or perhaps 37 to 58)—of which no. 39 sets out what makes a republic genuinely such, and nos. 47 to 51 elaborate the doctrine of the separation of powers and its embodiment in the Constitution. The degree of irritation Madison felt in fending off critics from all points of the political compass comes out very eloquently in no. 38, where he observes that very few of the critics stop to think of the deficiencies of the confederation that is being replaced. So consumed are they by the supposed deficiencies of the proposed constitution that they rarely stop to compare it with what the nation was laboring under for a decade. Madison's own notes on those deficiencies are a valuable adjunct to *The Federalist*.[25]

The measured tone returns when he explains what a republic is: "a government which derives all its powers directly or indirectly from the great body of the people, and is administered by persons holding their offices during pleasure, for a limited period, or during good behavior."[26] Britain is not a republic; the Dutch republic is hardly one, because it has a hereditary ruler; Poland combines the worst excesses of monarchy and aristocracy. If there is no popular control of last resort, whatever there is is not a republic. Madison cheerfully acknowledges that common usage describes Venice and Holland as republics, but so much the worse for common usage. The United States is a mixed republic, not in the Polybian sense but in its mixture of dispersed powers—labeled *federal* by Madison—and centralized powers—labeled *national*.

The Constitution preserves liberty by two sorts of devices, one familiar from English practice, the other supposed to characterize English practice but absent. The first is the refusal to give the executive the power to fund a standing army other than by an annual request to the legislature. The second is the separation of powers, implemented very partially in Britain. The effect of 1688 was to make the crown dependent on Parliament for funding, and to fund the army year by year according to the estimates. The republican fear of a standing army that led the Romans to insist that their armies disbanded on the borders of Rome coincided in the American mind with the English fear that Catholic kings would reduce their Protestant subjects to slavery and popery. The separation of powers was a more difficult matter, since Madison well understood the need for the separation not to be so complete that legislature, executive, and judiciary could exercise no checking power over one another. Madison emphasizes in paper no. 47 that when "the *whole* power of one department is exercised by the same hands which possess the *whole* power of another department, the fundamental principles of a free constitution are subverted." The two questions that an insistence on the separation of powers raises are what evils follow from a failure to achieve it, and how the separation of powers protects liberty. The answer to the first supplies only a part of the answer to the second.

The obvious answer is that if some part of the government can make law, decide whether the law has been infringed, and execute its own legal judgments, there is no barrier to error or arbitrary judgment, or to tyranny. The English objection to the Court of Star Chamber was that it allowed the king to bypass Parliament and the regular courts; the objec-

tion to the absence of a written bill of rights from the British constitution was that with the rise of party organization, the executive controlled
Parliament and the courts had no power to restrain liberticide legislation. The English separation of powers was always very partial: ministers
sit in Parliament, and the upper house was until 2009 a court of law as
well as a legislature. All the same, the proposition that for law to be made
and applied, each branch must concur with the others, holds good to a
limited extent. This is much more true in the American system.

The separation of powers provides, as Madison knew, no absolute
guarantee against tyranny. If all three branches of government concur in
a plan to oppress the population, the only remedy is insurrection. Less
dramatically, the separation of powers provides less of a guarantee than
Madison wished if one branch allows another to dominate, which means
in the modern world, if presidents do not stand up to a Congress that
wishes to pass liberticide legislation, or the Supreme Court fails to control overreach by either the executive or Congress, as it failed during the
anticommunist hysteria of the 1950s. As Montesquieu observed, these
are anxieties almost wholly confined to the overreaching of the executive
or the legislature; the Supreme Court is more likely to threaten civil liberties negatively, by not remedying abuses perpetrated elsewhere. Madison was a century too early to anticipate that the courts might subject
workers to the tyranny of employers by preferring the rights of owners
of property to the rights of self-defense of their employees. Madison put
his finger on a distinctively American anxiety. England had always feared
executive oppression: the king might dismiss judges, refuse to summon
Parliament, dissolve it if it displeased him, and so on. Charles II refused
to summon Parliament for the final five years of his reign. Parliamentary
tyranny would have been a surprising idea. In America the danger was
that the legislature would exercise a minute and daily control over every
act of the executive and arm itself with whatever powers it needed to
bend the executive to its will. This was the drawback of the Lockean
view that the legitimacy of a political system was focused on the legislative capacity of a political society, and that the executive was the agent
of the legislative.

Behind the defense of a separation of powers lay an implicit political sociology that is hard to render explicit. The sociology of the mixed or balanced constitution is simple; the common people should have only a small share of the power of initiation, since they have neither the time nor the knowledge to take an initiating role in the political process. But they have legitimate interests that they must have ways of defending if they are to remain loyal to the regime, and so a veto power should rest with them, as in the Roman constitution. A senatorial class represents stable landed interests and intelligence but may quarrel over honors and status or turn into an aristocracy oppressive to ordinary people, while "kings"—one-man executives—provide decisiveness but run the risk of dictatorial ambitions. A well-built mixed constitution provides multiple veto points without inertia. The different modes of election and appointment to positions in the system also reflect a belief in the old Roman arrangements; the common people have a voice in the House of Representatives, a filtered form of expression in the Senate, and an even more elaborately filtered voice in the election of the president. The assumption, a commonplace in modern electoral psychology, was that each electing body would elect persons who were better-off and better-educated than themselves, so that the wisdom of the nation would gravitate upward to the Senate and the presidency.

On that basis, one might think that the sociology behind a belief in the separation of powers must be the same as the sociology behind the defense of a mixed government. The lower house ought to respond swiftly to the needs of the worse-off, the Senate to hold their overenthusiasm in check, and something like an elected aristocracy to emerge at the higher reaches of government in the Senate, presidency, and Supreme Court. A Senate of twenty-six members is a small body, and the idea that a group of around forty of the most distinguished men in the nation, who had known each other in all sorts of circumstances, would form an intellectual and political aristocracy is not absurd. Forty-five years later, Tocqueville declared himself immensely impressed with the Senate—and immensely unimpressed with the House.[27]

Having devised the most durable constitution in the modern world, Madison's last service to the new regime was to create the Bill of Rights. He was a reluctant convert to the need for one, being, as he said in *The*

Federalist, unimpressed by the efficacy of parchment barriers to human passion. It soon became apparent that public opinion required an explicit statement of the rights that Congress was forbidden to violate: freedom of speech and assembly, the right to bear arms, freedom of religion, including the prohibition of a federally established church, no unreasonable search and seizure, no self-incrimination, trial by jury in one's own locality, no cruel and unusual punishments, an explicit statement that rights not given explicitly to central government remained in the hands of the states and the individual citizens severally. Many of these rights were to be found in the English Declaration of Right of 1689; others stemmed from subsequent legal decisions such as *Entick v. Carrington*, which is the foundation of the Fourth Amendment prohibition of search or seizure without a warrant, and they were uncontentious. It was a very long time before lawyers became adept at creatively interpreting the text.[28] Initially, only Congress and the federal government were bound by the Bill of Rights; not until the Fourteenth Amendment after the Civil War extended its reach to the individual states could citizens use the Bill of Rights to fight local oppression, and only the best part of a century after that was it used as a weapon for extending what we now call civil rights. Madison's skepticism of the good the bill would do may therefore have been justified, but with opinion still not reconciled to the enlargement of the powers of central government, passing the Bill of Rights was politically wise.

Roads Not Taken

Madison's insistence that politics was "in a mean" indicated that he was untroubled by the knowledge that it was possible to argue both for a more thoroughgoing nationalization of American politics and for a more thoroughgoing decentralization. Jefferson was a close friend, and Madison wrote *The Federalist* in close collaboration with Alexander Hamilton. A brief reflection on these other poles is of some interest. Although Jefferson wrote and published voluminous notes on the state of Virginia and kept up a vast correspondence, he never set out a systematic account of what his ideal republic might look like if it were institutionalized. Having been sent to France as American ambassador during the 1780s, he saw the French Revolution at first hand, and his inability to regard the revolution or the Terror with the shock and horror that seized most of those who had been friendly to the early stages of the revolution undermined many friendships.

In spite of his insouciant remarks about the need for a revolution every thirty years or so, Jefferson was not an enthusiast for red terror, nor did he invent the doctrine of the permanent revolution before Trotsky and Rosa Luxemburg. Rather, he held all his life that it was the inalienable right of every generation to imagine its own future and rebuild its institutions as it chose. This was one of Thomas Paine's central ideas, and it may have been an element in an emotional affinity that made Jefferson one of the few Americans not to turn his back on Paine in the late 1790s. If he was not an enthusiast for revolution for its own sake, Jefferson nonetheless had many ideas—perhaps too many and too little digested—about what the United States might have been, and these ideas were more democratic, radical, and impracticable than anything Madison envisaged. It makes him deeply attractive. Although Jefferson agreed that the national government could only be a representative democracy, he hankered for some concessions to "pure democracy." Jefferson proposed what he called "ward republics," an idea he spelled out in letters to numerous correspondents. These would be very small, self-governing, wholly participatory units of government. They would be more than that, too.

Such units would be the basis of the militia bands that he much preferred to a standing army; they would also be the providers of education and a minimal system of social welfare. The proposal was not surprising, given his affection for what he supposed to be the ancient liberty of the Saxons. Unlike Madison, who thought everyone was capable of behaving in a selfish and self-deceiving fashion, Jefferson feared the tyranny of the majority only when factions were tempted to violate the rights of people they did not know, could not see, and had no dealings with. He did not think we would oppress near neighbors. Ward republics, organized on the scale of the areas around which the calling out of the militia was based, would not run the risk of majority tyranny. Jefferson's preferred system of national government would have put ward republics at the base and then built an indirectly elected pyramidical regime upon them. The base was modeled on the New England township, but was more radical and egalitarian in its assumptions about the participation in person of every adult male. It was not so radical that he imagined that women would vote, let alone slaves or Native Americans. The method of indirect election was familiar to anyone who had taken an interest in the Venetian Republic, and was in itself neither conservative nor radical but an obvious way of constructing a series of councils. Hume's somewhat tongue-in-cheek essay "The Idea of a Perfect Republic," which builds on Harrington's *Oceana*, had engaged in the exercise years before.

The scheme of ward republics brings out the impossibility of assigning Jefferson to any of the usual categories. When president from 1800 to 1808, he more than doubled the size of the United States by the Louisiana Purchase and talked frequently of an empire of liberty that would extend through the Americas north and south. Yet he imagined all this founded on small-scale agriculture, as though a hundred million Americans might all be yeoman farmers, attached primarily to their own localities but delegating foreign affairs and national military organization to some more remote government. The two largest worms in this apple were trade and industry on the one side and slavery on the other. Jefferson's views on slavery have nothing to recommend them; it was, he said, an evil and likely to be the ruin of the country, but there was no remedy. His hostility to slavery was undoubtedly genuine; the draft of the Declaration of Independence that he presented to the Continental Congress contains a wonderful passage excoriating George III for maintaining the African slave trade, which, on Jefferson's view, amounted to savage war against innocent Africans. "He has waged cruel war against human nature itself, violating it's most sacred rights of life and liberty in the persons of a distant people who never offended him, captivating & carrying them into slavery in another hemisphere, or to incur miserable death in their transportation thither." It was removed at the instance of the delegates from Georgia and South Carolina, two states that had every intention of continuing to import slaves.[29] He seems never to have thought that manufacturing might bring about its peaceful economic extinction in the southern states, or that planters who disliked slavery could replace unfree labor with free labor assisted by machinery. He clung to the view that Negroes were innately the intellectual inferiors of whites, and thought that even when slavery was abolished, their inferiority meant that they could not live in the same society as whites and had better be sent to Africa. His vision of American Indians was not two-faced but certainly of a double aspect. Like many of his contemporaries, he admired their courage, independence, hardiness, and resilience, and he considered them not intrinsically the inferiors of the white man. Nonetheless, their way of life was impossible to sustain alongside that of the planters and farmers who were encroaching on their territory. Jefferson thought the future offered Native Americans two possibilities, either to turn into docile farmers alongside their white neighbors or to be exterminated; "extermination" was Jefferson's term and often repeated.

Jefferson's antipathy to trade and industry brought him into conflict with Alexander Hamilton. Hamilton was a native not of the American colonies but of Nevis in the West Indies. He was clever, an excellent lawyer, but impulsive and argumentative, and not a very deft politician. On the issues that separated him from Jefferson and Madison, he was almost invariably in the right. Hamilton understood Hume better than most of Hume's contemporaries had done. Hume understood the old republican hatred of a central bank and the sort of person who profited by speculating in the public funds; and Hume knew what the argument was for the virtue of solid, stable, immovable property in land as opposed to wealth founded on holdings of paper that could rise and fall in value in unpredictable ways, and whose value could be manipulated by stockjobbers to the ruin of honest farmers and merchants. But Hume also saw that a society that used public credit to drive trade and expand the economy would be a lively and prosperous society and its ruling elite would be internationally minded and outward looking, not conservative and backward looking. In the case of the United States in particular, Hamilton inferred that the future must lie in developing American manufactures and fostering international trade, and to this end cheap credit was essential, and its only plausible source a national bank.

The history of the chartering of the First National Bank, the attacks on it, its abolition, and the chartering of its successor, the Second Bank of the United States, is not a matter for these pages. Its implications are. Hamilton was less hostile to Britain than Madison and Jefferson were. It seemed to him to be successful and prosperous. Once independence was secured, more was to be gained by reestablishing friendly relations than by sulking; by the same token, revolutionary France was a shambles, and Jefferson's attempts to re-create alliances with the French were expensive and dangerous. The new government should nationalize as many issues as possible, because a rational central administration of commercial law and a sound financial system were the great essentials for the development of trade and industry. Hamilton was killed before it became apparent that he had won the argument, and that the future of the United States lay in exploiting the vast wealth of the hinterland and becoming an industrial powerhouse. His lack of success in his own lifetime was not surprising. His vision of a successful state was quite literally monarchical. Like the Florentines desperate for order after the rise and fall of Savonarola's republic, he envisaged a king at the head of affairs and senators appointed for life. His lack of experience of the affairs of the states that had invented their own institutions before and during the insurrection made him tone-deaf to the American hatred of all things monarchical and aristocratic.

The rhetorical brilliance of his opponents has meant that Hamilton's insights have usually been neglected, or perhaps so taken for granted that we forget that they were his. One exception was the book written by Herbert Croly, an early twentieth-century liberal and nationalist; *The Promise of American Life* argued for a much more self-consciously national politics in the United States, making more use of the powers of the federal government and not treating the central government's capacities as somehow residual. The object of a more determinedly national policy, however, was not to excite nationalist feeling or engage in large projects for their own sake but to modernize the United States for the benefit of all its inhabitants. The purpose of so doing would be to make individual lives freer and more interesting, and to give individuals more scope for real self-government. As Croly put it, what Americans must do to fulfill America's promise was achieve *Jeffersonian ends by Hamiltonian means*, a proposition that the two protagonists would have found wholly incomprehensible, but which, with hindsight, one can understand perfectly well.

CHAPTER 17

The French Revolution and Its Critics

The Living Revolution

WHEN THE DISTINGUISHED FRENCH historian of the revolution François Furet announced on the bicentenary of the storming of the Bastille that we could at last be certain that the revolution was over, his readers flinched. Some thought it was not over yet; others did not want it to be over; others felt that writing finis under that piece of history sold out some indispensable ambitions, summed up as *liberté, égalité, fraternité*, however hard of achievement they might be. The French Revolution was a live issue, at least to the extent that two centuries later, conservatives regarded it as an unmitigated disaster and radicals as a partial, if marred, success. In the earlier twentieth century, the communist and fascist movements were, in the one case, an attempt to complete what the revolution had begun and, in the other, to undo its supposed effects. Throughout the nineteenth century, the historiography of the French Revolution played a crucial role in European thinking about politics: Mill, Tocqueville, and Marx are only three of the thinkers whose ideas were shaped by the revolution. This chapter is not the place for a consideration of the revolution's later effects. It takes up, instead, its immediate refraction in political theory, and even that only in three dimensions: its impact on conservative or squarely reactionary thinkers such as

Edmund Burke and Joseph de Maistre; its impact on reformers such as Thomas Paine, who might have been hanged by the British if they had laid hands on him, but who came much closer to execution by the French revolutionaries when he criticized the execution of Louis XVI; and its impact on early socialist thinkers such as Saint-Simon, who saw, or thought they saw, that what was required was the transformation of society to reflect the demands of its economic underpinnings, a process to which political upheaval was irrelevant.

From the outset, the revolution was intellectually contentious and politically unpredictable. Unlike the Glorious Revolution of 1688, in which the London mob played no role, and unlike the American Revolution, which was a war of national liberation, the French Revolution began with a riot by the Paris mob, and its history was substantially determined by the activities of that mob. Needless to say, very few of the leading figures were members of the lower classes who took to the streets; they were members of the bourgeoisie engaged in the dangerous game of riding a tiger they could hardly control. Unlike the revolutions of 1688 and 1776, which claimed to be restoring threatened liberties, the French Revolution *began* as if the aim was to catch up with the achievements of its English and American precursors, and then set increasingly utopian goals. Its motto of Liberty, Equality, and Fraternity gave little hint that it would generate an astonishing mixture of class warfare, government by police spies, and the guillotine working overtime. In the process, the revolutionaries demonstrated what Madison had feared, that the sovereign people could behave worse than the monarchs they had displaced.

But the French Revolution was innovative in ways that the American Revolution never was, perhaps because it never needed to be. It invented the modern conception of the nation under arms, and perhaps nationalism in its modern form. Whereas the rebellious Americans thought in terms of raising local militias, the French revolutionaries inherited the monarchy's standing army and made it the cutting edge of revolutionary change throughout mainland Europe. Nor was the revolution socially unproductive. Old forms of aristocratic privilege were abolished; peasants no longer performed forced labor; the ownership of property was spread more widely. It was less productive of useful political innovation.

Radical democracy was new to modern Europe, and it was unclear what political institutions it demanded; the revolution provided no answer. Between 1789 and 1831, the year Tocqueville came to the United States, France had experienced absolute monarchy, constitutional monarchy, an increasingly radical republic, the directory, the empire, the restored Bourbon regime, the July Revolution of 1830, and the Orleanist monarchy of Louis-Philippe. Unsurprisingly, one question on Tocqueville's mind was whether France could escape the instability from which it had suffered since 1789, and why the Americans had suffered nothing of the sort.

The revolutionaries failed to institute the novel forms of social and political organization they hankered after; workers would not accept a ten-day week, or state-appointed priests, or rectangular *départements*, or the cult of the Supreme Being. The revolution followed a familiar pattern, ending in military dictatorship, as Rome had done two millennia before, and as the Cromwellian revolution had done two and a half centuries earlier. Ironically, the figure who brought the revolution to an end—Napoleon Bonaparte—was both the antithesis of a revolutionary and the perfect instantiation of the revolutionary ideal of *la carrière ouverte aux talents*. Although his family belonged to the Genoese minor aristocracy, he was a Corsican and a provincial; but his military abilities and political boldness took him from junior artillery officer to emperor by the age of thirty-five. He did more than anyone to spread the revolution's ideals throughout Europe; but he saved the French Revolution by destroying the French Republic, making it an empire and himself an emperor. Almost equally ironically, the revolution's most perspicuous critic, who from early days predicted its future course with uncanny accuracy, had defended the American colonists in their grievances against the British government, and surprised not a few of his former allies by his root-and-branch assault on the revolution, on its principles, on the theorists whom he blamed for inciting it, and on the revolution's English supporters. This, of course, was Edmund Burke.

Burke's Critique of the French Revolution

Burke was a self-made Irishman in an English society where political careers were for those who inherited the means to make an impact, or who acquired a patron whose means they could exploit. Born in Dublin in 1729 to a Protestant father and a Catholic mother, he graduated from Trinity College, Dublin, in 1748 and headed to London to seek his fortune. His forays into literature and philosophy were well received, and he became part of Dr. Johnson's circle. Johnson said of Burke that if one merely met him while sheltering from the rain, one would know one had met a very remarkable man. That was high praise from the acerbic Johnson, because their politics—Burke's Whig and Johnson's High Tory—were chalk and cheese. Burke established himself as the editor of the *National Register*, founded in 1758, but his career flowered when he became private secretary to the Whig politician Lord Rockingham during his first ministry. Rockingham found him a seat in Parliament, and from then on Burke was a prominent figure in the acrimonious politics of the day.

Burke came to public notice as a result of the British government's problems with the increasingly rebellious American colonies. Burke argued that conciliatory policies toward the American colonists were required by both justice and political prudence, and his "Speech on Conciliation with America" is endlessly quoted.[1] Burke did not support American independence; but regardless of the merits of British rule in the abstract, it was clear that if all sides stuck rigidly to conflicting understandings of their rights, war and separation were inevitable. The British needed a policy of conciliation more intelligent than any likely from Lord North's ministry. Burke's picture of the vigor of the colonies strongly suggests that the mother country had bred a large and boisterous adolescent who would want independence sooner rather than later, but it was not a conclusion he drew. The imperial relationship was consistent with a very high degree of independence for the colonies, as Jefferson initially argued. Burke's hope that the connection would not be severed was entirely consistent with his distaste for British rule in India, which he deemed brutal and corrupt, and certain to corrupt English politics as a result of the riches extracted from India and deployed in British politics by the so-called nabobs.

Burke wrote extensively, and not only about the difficulties with the American colonies. He produced two statements of the principles underlying successful parliamentary politics that have given comfort to practicing politicians for over two centuries. *Thoughts on the Cause of the Present Discontents* argued that the machinations of George III and his advisers had upset the balance between legislature and executive on which stable policy making depended. Burke demanded the elimination of the king's ability to purchase parliamentary allies by handing out sinecures. Knowing that opposition to the government of "the king's friends" would be denounced by those who professed to be above party, he defended the existence of political parties as essential to the working of a parliamentary—or congressional—system of government. A party, he claimed optimistically, was a body of men united on a conception of the public interest who concerted their actions to pursue that conception.[2] It was a nicely turned thought: hitherto, parties were identified with factions whose aim was assumed to be to seize power in the hope of sharing the spoils of office. Burke made it harder for anyone thereafter to insist that he was "above party," and also made it unnecessary, since anyone aspiring to run a modern government needed to belong to and be supported by a party, so defined. Whether modern political parties live up to Burke's standards is not a question we must settle here.

His "Speech to the Electors of Bristol" of 1774 gave Burke the chance to spell out the maxims of representative government.[3] A representative was not a delegate; he owed his constituents his intelligence and his judgment, not his obedience to whatever they might think at any given moment. They had no right to mandate him, and he had no obligation to act as they would have mandated. He owed them a clear statement of the principles on which he would make up his mind once in Parliament; if they disliked his principles, they should vote accordingly. Whether most modern politicians could provide such a statement that was more than a string of banalities or the outcome of canvassing so-called focus groups is another question we need not answer. Few members of the eighteenth-century House of Commons could have done it. One particularly important claim was that a representative represents those who voted against him as well as those who voted for him, and represents those who had no vote in the election at all. In the England of 1777 those without a vote included 90 percent of the adult male population and 100 percent of the female population.

Readers with a low tolerance for humbug sometimes express outrage at the expression of these sentiments by a man who represented a pocket borough; others argue that unless something like Burke's views is accepted both by voters and their representatives, it is not obvious why we have deliberative assemblies at all. Moreover, if we represent only our own side, it is far from obvious why the losers should accept the outcome of an election any more willingly than they would accept defeat by brute force. We have to believe that the victors in an election will see themselves entrusted with the duty to consider the public interest according to defensible principles, and to do their best to pursue it. It must be the nation as a whole that a representative represents. Anything else turns majority rule into majority tyranny. Burke's account is an apt companion piece to Madison's explanation of the way representation enables modern republics to break free of the restrictions on size that even such subtle writers as Montesquieu had assumed they must be bound by. The diplomatic world was familiar with delegates from independent states who were mandated to present the views of their own state, but the idea of a national deliberative assembly whose members were responsible to, but not mandated by, their constituents was a novelty.

Burke served in the second Rockingham ministry of 1782–83, and achieved some of the "economical reforms" or abolition of sinecures and pensions he had advocated, but the government's attempt to reform the East India Company was opposed by the king, and the ministry fell. He never held office again. The Tory William Pitt the Younger became prime minister in 1783, and with a three-year interlude from 1801–04, when he quarreled with the king over Catholic emancipation, remained in power until he died in 1806. With Rockingham's death in 1783, Charles James Fox became leader of the Whig opposition, but he and Burke quarreled over Fox's support for the French Revolution, and after 1791 they never spoke. Burke's last years were bitterly unhappy for a more personal reason; he had hoped to become a country gentleman and a landowner in a small way, so that his son, Richard, could become fully part of the social order that Burke had spent his life trying to protect. To this end, he bought an estate on a mortgage he struggled to pay. Richard died in 1794, blighting Burke's hopes; he himself died in 1797, at a point where the French revolutionary armies were victorious almost everywhere in Europe.

Burke is a deeply puzzling figure; and the enormous scholarly effort that has been devoted to him over the past century has done more to obscure than to reveal him. Because he writes wonderfully, he charms the reader as a less fluent writer would not; and because he affects to be writing not as a philosopher but as an outraged Englishman speaking from his heart about what his uncorrupted fellow countrymen know to be the case, he leaves his readers free to project onto him almost any doctrine they like (or dislike). He was an accomplished philosopher, as his *Philosophical Enquiry into the Origin of Our Ideas of the Sublime and Beautiful* reveals; but he was also a politician, and he knew as well as Cicero that in politics rhetorical effectiveness is more important than analytical precision. He was not effective in person. He emptied the House of Commons by delivering speeches that were intended for publication and ill adapted to their audience; they bored his hearers; but he (mostly) wrote like an angel.

Burke's *Reflections*

Burke's attacks on the revolutionaries and all their works were spread over several books, of which the *Reflections* is the best-known and the most formidable. It provoked Paine to write *Rights of Man*, and Mary Wollstonecraft to write *Vindication of the Rights of Man*, several years before she wrote her better-known essay *A Vindication of the Rights of Women*. Burke's reactions grew increasingly unrestrained. Other than in urging the arrest and prosecution of Paine for publishing *Rights of Man*, his *Appeal from the New Whigs to the Old* is relatively calm. Like the *Reflections*, it praises the Old

Whigs who said that James II had not been deposed but had resigned, leaving an empty throne for its rightful occupant; the New Whigs held Richard Price's view that the people had an inalienable right to choose their rulers and to revise their constitutional arrangements as they saw fit. The Convention Parliament of 1689 saw that this opened the door to enthusiasts and insurrectionists and the prospect of endless instability and civil war, and it had the good sense to accept the constitution of their country as they found it. Burke's subsequent writings on the revolution culminated in his *Letters on a Regicide Peace* and *Letter to a Noble Lord*. The former demanded a holy war to wipe out the revolutionary infection from Europe; the violence of the latter reflected the death of his son and the extinction of his hopes for establishing his family as English country gentlemen. It denounced the duke of Bedford and Lord Lauderdale for their continued loyalty to the ideals of the revolution, but it is more powerfully an expression of uncontrollable disgust at the thought that he had devoted his life to serving an aristocratic political system whose grandest figures were working to destroy all that Burke had worked to preserve. The works of Burke's last years make painful reading. They were given a new lease of life when American conservatives employed them to argue for the aggressive prosecution of the Cold War in the late 1940s and 1950s in a crusade to turn back communism in Europe; but they show a mind at the end of its tether.

Reflections on the Revolution in France is an astonishing work, not least because so early in the revolution it accurately predicted the ways in which the revolution was likely to get out of hand, and displayed an insight into the revolutionary mind that was lacking in the revolution's English supporters. It was published in November 1790, the revolution having broken out with the fall of the Bastille on July 14, 1789. It had a double origin; it was an answer to a question from a French correspondent, asking Burke's opinion of the revolution. History does not relate his reaction to the length of the reply; even Burke observed after more than 150 pages of enraged denunciation, "This letter is grown to a great length, though it is indeed short with regard to the infinite extent of the subject."[4] He then continued for nearly 100 pages more. The content was provoked, according to Burke, by a sermon, "A Discourse on the Love

of Our Country," delivered by the Reverend Richard Price at a meeting and dinner of the Revolution Society (strictly "The Society for the
Commemoration of the Revolution"), gathered to celebrate the memory
of the Glorious Revolution. Price was not a target of convenience; he was
a distinguished moral philosopher and had been elected to the Royal
Society for his contributions to the theory of probability; indeed, he
drew up the mortality tables on which life insurance companies have
relied for two centuries. He was a Dissenter and excluded from English
political life in a way he would not have been in the United States, where
he was much admired. His political principles were those of Jefferson
and Madison, and he had supported American independence. His sermon is rarely read, but a modern reader finds it unexceptionable, at least
until the point in his peroration when Price recites the Nunc Dimittis
to express his rapture at having lived to see "thirty millions of people,
indignant and resolute, spurning at slavery, and demanding liberty with
an irresistible voice, their king led in triumph, and an arbitrary monarch surrendering himself to his subjects."[5] One need not share Burke's
passion for the pageantry of monarchy to think this is excessive; mere
hindsight will do.

Today we have no problem agreeing with the positive burden of
Price's sermon, that a rational person proportions his love of his country
to the real excellences of the nation he loves. It may underestimate the
irrationality of nationalist passion and be bad sociology, but hardly bad
morals. Price in any event argued that a rational man would regard all
mankind as his fellow countrymen and would be a cosmopolitan rather
than a nationalist—though neither of these terms had yet acquired their
modern meaning. Nor is the modern reader likely to flinch at Price's
wholly Lockean assertion that governments exist to protect our rights,
and that one of those rights is to hold our rulers accountable and to
cashier them for misconduct. Modern elections are devices for holding
our rulers accountable, allowing us to cashier them for misconduct or
incompetence, without resorting to civil war, the ax, or the guillotine.
That, after all, is the force of the cliché about "ballots not bullets."

Burke's contemporaries were astonished at the vehemence of his
attack on the revolution and its English admirers. Locke was a respect-

able source from which to draw one's opinions, as Price had done, and Burke had a track record as a critic of the governments that lost the American colonies and of the system of royal influence by which those governments were sustained. Even in the *Reflections*, Burke is no defender of divine right and no enthusiast for absolute monarchy; he calls the seventeenth-century defenders of divine right "exploded fanatics of slavery" and even thinks their views impious.[6] A properly balanced constitutional monarchy in which a strong legislature holds an uncorrupt executive in check was Burke's ideal. He defended what he thought of as the ancient constitution of England, and it was sanctified by prescription, not divine ordinance. The hereditary principle in a rational form was an excellent one, but what made it excellent was that it was part of a constitution that provided liberty, security, prosperity, and all the goods that civil society could bestow. One might therefore have expected Burke to be sympathetic to a French attempt to do for France what the Glorious Revolution had done for England; Thomas Jefferson's reflective view was that the French should have settled for precisely that.[7] For the first few months of the revolution, it seemed to be happening, and Burke was sympathetic; but early in 1790 Burke decided that the French were engaged in something novel, outrageous, and contrary to the order of things. Moreover, the rationalist universalism of the revolutionary creed made it a danger beyond its national boundaries. The revolutionaries hoped to export their revolution to England, where their English fellow travelers would help spread the infection.

The pamphlet ran into many editions, but it was not a complete success. It was inaccurate in detail, and viewed as an account of what had happened thus far in France, it was unpersuasive. In particular, Burke's great set piece, the account of the events of October 1789 when the mob went to Versailles, seized Louis XVI and Marie-Antoinette, and brought them back to Paris as prisoners in the Tuileries, opened with a dramatic account of a murder that never took place. So far from being cut down by the mob as he shouted to the queen to save herself, the guard at the door of the royal bedchamber was taking English visitors around Paris a few months later.[8] Nor is it a wholly successful literary production; the argumentative work is done in the first hundred pages, after which Burke goes on at length about the wickedness of the French expropriation of church property and the incompetence of the revolutionaries' new system of taxation. He was in the mainstream in arguing that whatever endangered a general respect for property was both violative of individual rights and dangerous to national prosperity, but the disproportion between the brief and effective assault on the radicals' rationalist, ahistorical cosmopolitanism and the long-drawn-out dissection of unreliable French statistics struck his contemporaries unfavorably. Some critics thought Burke had lost his mind, some that he had been bribed by George III, others that he was trying to reestablish himself as a leading figure in Whig circles, yet others that he was a covert Roman Catholic whose defense of the French church had unmasked his allegiances. Jefferson thought the *Reflections* was silly. In fact, Burke was trying to do what he seems to be trying to do: prevent the English from following in French footsteps. There were many radicals, rationalists, dissenters, and merely unscrupulous persons whose ambitions might be satisfied by upheaval.

Reflections is not easy to summarize, because it belongs to no one genre. Its theoretical claims are in literary terms incidental to an indignant narrative of the crimes and follies of the revolutionaries. It is a debating speech, and its theoretical claims are offered as asides. They are nonetheless very striking. One might have thought that Burke would have contented himself with insisting that society is not founded on a contract made in the state of nature to protect our natural rights, that we are born into a particular time and place and must adapt ourselves to it and its mores. He does, though by saying that society is indeed a contract not between a mythical "people" and its rulers but between the living and the dead, and not for political management alone but for all the goodness and virtue in which we can sustain one another over a long history. "It is a partnership in all science; a partnership in all art; a partnership in every virtue and all perfection. As the ends of such a partnership cannot be obtained in many generations, it becomes a partnership not only between those who are living but also between those who are living, those who are dead, and those who are to be born."[9] Although Burke's savagery was surprising, the intellectual case that the *Reflections* makes against revolution, not only in France in 1789 but in any society where the ruling elite is not actually making war upon the citizenry, is highly plausible, made more calmly by Hume, but irresistible. Essentially, it rests on the thought that societies are held together by inarticulate habits of belief and affection, what Burke called "prejudice," or things we believe before consciously thinking about them. Re-creating society ab initio is beyond the powers of human reason; Burke was very eloquent about fearing "to put men to live and trade each one upon his private stock of reason," because each of us has only a small share of the whole reason of society. We must draw on the bank and capital of ages by attending to the experience of mankind embodied in our laws and traditions.[10] Disrupting our beliefs, expectations, and habits of obedience and cooperation easily gets out of hand and produces disastrous and murderous results. Matters have to be very bad indeed to justify taking that risk. The American Revolution was dangerous, because it was not wholly clear that it would not descend into anarchy, but far from mad, because it was intended as a restoration of old liberties, not as a prelude to wholesale social reconstruction. The French Revolution was a utopian project certain to end in catastrophe.

What the deepest philosophical premises of Burke's argument are has long been a matter of scholarly contention. Burke drew on three kinds of argument, distinguishable, but perhaps not in his own mind wholly distinct. The one he employed most often rests on premises he shared with Hume, and for that matter with the radical Jeremy Bentham, even though Bentham was an archetype of the "sophists, economists, and calculators" whom he decried. That argument is utilitarian: revolutions are exceedingly costly in terms of human happiness. Nor is the calculation of just how costly a simple matter. Human beings seek happiness, but their ideas about what will make them happy and how they can attain the means of happiness are very flexible, influenced by social surroundings, religious beliefs, and features idiosyncratic to themselves. The intellectual may look down from his ivory tower at the peasant plowing the fields below and think that the peasant is leading a miserable existence, living from hand to mouth, working all the hours God sends in the wind and rain, with hardly two articulate thoughts to call his own. The peasant, looking up at the intellectual, may wonder how anyone can waste his time in such pursuits, trapped indoors, and producing nothing except vain speech. Each, considering his own life, may think he is doing well; neither needs liberating by the other, though the intellectual will be tempted to liberate the peasant. Because we invest so much in adapting to our surroundings and creating our own form of happiness, the status quo has a built-in advantage. This is not an argument against reform. "A society without the means of some change is without the means of its conservation."[11] But reform is best done gradually, as it were moving steadily from one status quo to the next and acclimatizing to novelties at a sensible pace. The enemy of good sense is the doctrine of universal natural rights—criticized by Burke because there is no such creature as "Man" to be the bearer of the so-called rights of man; Burke had never met "Man," as distinct from the individual Englishmen or Frenchmen for whom the rights appropriate to particular times and places have to be instituted. Those rights promote their happiness; elaborate and rationalistic schemes just disturb their peace of mind.[12]

Burke strikes a deeper and more frightening—and much more frightened—note than that. A second strand in his thinking is often said to derive from the natural law tradition. This is not natural law understood as it was by opponents such as Thomas Paine; natural law, conceived as the deliverances of reason and reason's God, underpinned just the appeal to natural and universal rights that Burke detested. Burke appealed to the tradition that sees the entire universe governed by divinely ordained natural law, and human beings as intended to be regulated by that law. Widely read, but the disciple of nobody, Burke does not appeal to the authority of philosophers; indeed, given that the *Reflections* rests on the defense of prejudice and is unhesitatingly dismissive of Rousseau in particular but the Enlightenment in general, it would have been rhetorically impossible for Burke to appeal to philosophical authority. It is therefore not easy to say which of the innumerable varieties of natural law thinking he was most attuned to. Writing to allies brought up on Cicero, he described himself as defending the *mos maiorum*, the wisdom of our ancestors reverenced by the Romans, and thought by Cicero to reflect natural law. Cicero is certainly the author from whom Burke quotes most frequently. There is no need to decide whether Burke was an Aristotelian by the light of nature or a Stoic by education. What Burke needed was a thought common to all writers in that tradition, and visible in Montesquieu, whom Burke read with pleasure. This is that there is a fundamental harmony, what Montesquieu called "an essential relation between things," which provides a standard for human beings to aspire to.

What makes it easy to think that Burke subscribed to such a version of natural law theory is not only that he frequently condemns the actions of the revolutionaries as "unnatural" but that his vision of the order to be defended against the revolutionaries by war abroad and repression at home is expressed in an imagery reliant on the contrast between a world where everyone does what is appropriate to his condition, and leads a life that is both virtuous and happy as a result, and a world upended by deranged intellectuals, in which psychic and political disorder is everywhere. But Burke could not say that nature assigned us all a fixed and unalterable place in the world and that all alteration was vicious; he emphatically believed in a degree of social mobility that would allow talent to rise from humble backgrounds, and allow the less able members of the gentry to slide gently into obscurity. Politics should be in the hands of a landed gentry, but membership of the landed gentry should be open to talented parvenus like himself. In economic matters more broadly, he was an energetic disciple of Adam Smith, and his paean of praise to the American whalers in his speech "Conciliation with America" is a wonderfully romantic celebration of boldness, ambition, and endurance.[13] He believed in a flexible order, not a rigid Platonic hierarchy. Burke was a Whig, not the devotee of a caste system. Still, even if nature is flexible, it is also the source of limits, and these are felt as much as understood.

The third strand of argument subsumes the first two, but could hardly be employed as a free-standing support for his politics. This was a strongly felt but not very clearly spelled-out attachment to traditional religious forms. Burke could have argued the case that sociologists have made by drawing on his work for the past two hundred years: that societies are held together by nonrational convictions, that these are what Burke described as *prejudices* in a wholly nonpejorative sense, and that the body of these prejudices constitutes a civic religion. If one puts together Montesquieu's and Tocqueville's ideas about *les moeurs* with Tocqueville's and Burke's conviction that religion is an indispensable support for public morality, we arrive at the sociological claim that societies work more smoothly, suffer less violence, and produce individuals who are happier about themselves and more at ease with their lives only when those societies are based on religious conviction. This is not a claim about the truth of one or other religion; it is a this-worldly claim about the causal impact of religious faith on civic morals. Innumerable thinkers in the nineteenth and twentieth centuries devoted anxious thought to the question whether a modern society could survive the death of God, whether it could find some secular substitute for the religious faith that had hitherto given meaning to life, but that seemed increasingly incredible. Optimists like Marx, who thought that a satisfactory human life would not need the myths that now console us for a miserable life, did not concern themselves with what might happen next; but Auguste Comte invented a whole new "religion of humanity," resembling Catholicism in all but its renunciation of the supernatural, and the substitution of his mistress, Clothilde de Vaux, for the Virgin; and he was but one of many. Burke is not the ancestor of the inventors of substitutes for the real thing. Burke was a deeply religious thinker. He saw the world through religiously colored spectacles. Without religion, we are mere creatures of the passing day; we need religion to sustain our morality, to assuage our fears, to strengthen us in adversity. How it is institutionalized seems to be a secondary consideration; but it must be institutionalized, so that it can both humanize the coercive institutions of the state and effectively discipline our wayward emotions. In the last resort, the revolution was a blasphemous undertaking, because human beings had arrogated to themselves the powers of social construction and destruction that belonged to God alone. This was not the arm's-length observation that things go better when human beings have modest aspirations for social change; it was the expression of an outraged religious sensibility.

Burke and the Modern Idea of Revolution

When it came to characterizing what the revolutionaries had done, all these strands of argument came into play, but if Burke's underlying argument was often a utilitarian one, his rhetoric drew heavily on the religious vein. Burke saw that the revolution had broken dramatically with the previous understanding of revolution. In coming to that view, Burke reconceptualized revolution. He invented the modern idea of revolution and made the classical conception obsolete. The classical view of a revolution was not entirely simple. Setting aside Aristotle's discussion of stasis, there were two distinct ideas about what a revolution was. One was the "good" revolution, the return to first principles; such a revolution was approved by Locke and Machiavelli in their own ways, and it was, one might say, the official version of the American Revolution. Burke could approve of 1688 as a revolution that had restored to England its ancient constitution in the face of usurpation and attempted tyranny from the last Stuart kings, even though he thought its success had depended on its being diguised as a response to an abdication; the installation of William III was, he claimed, a small deviation from the strict hereditary principle that had been necessary to preserve it. The other image of revolution was that of a simple catastrophe, a turn of fortune's wheel by which everything was turned upside down. Machiavelli drew on both images when he hoped that a prince with sufficient skill and daring might profit from chaos if *fortuna* was on his side and restore the Italian city-states to their Roman model.

Both images are premodern. Modern ideas about progress are inimical to the politics of turning back the clock. When we make a new start in politics, we do not begin again from the old starting point. Because we are much more accustomed to the thought that almost every aspect of society is in constant flux, we are also inhospitable to the idea that political arrangements can be fundamentally altered without large changes in social organization; a violent change of personnel is a mere coup d'état. Our modern idea of a revolution is that even if the transfer of power takes place suddenly and swiftly through a coup, the revolution properly speaking is the interconnected train of events, social, economic, intellectual, and political, that has issued in and stemmed from the political upheaval more narrowly understood. This was Burke's understanding of the French Revolution; needless to say, he was wholly at odds with those who promoted such revolutions. Burke was not a political sociologist but a practicing politician; he wrote the *Reflections* to denounce the follies and wickednesses of the French revolutionaries rather than to achieve the conceptual clarity about the phenomenon appropriate to an academic setting. Nonetheless, his understanding of the French Revolution became the canonical understanding of revolution, that a revolution was not merely an unconstitutional change of constitution but a protracted, violent, unpredictable transformation of social and political relationships embracing the whole of society.

Burke confidently expected that the revolution would end with the destruction of the French church, the execution of the king and queen, massacre on a large scale, and the restoration of order by a military dictator. Violence there already was; but the rest was not on the horizon in 1789. Because Burke seems so prescient about what would happen in 1792–94, starting with the execution of the king and queen, and culminating in the Terror, the overthrow of Robespierre, and the institution of the Directory to bring something better than the peace of the graveyard to France, it is easy to credit him with a more complicated view of events than he had. Bearing in mind that he was writing to prevent the French infection from crossing the Channel, one can see the historical analogies on which he drew, and that he was gifted not with second sight but with a well-stocked historical intelligence and a thorough knowledge of Cicero. The seventeenth-century wars of religion that had raged throughout Europe were a live historical memory; an Irishman needed no reminding that massacre was a constant possibility when religious passions—or antireligious passions—erupted in political violence. Much blood had been spilled in France by the time Burke started writing the *Reflections* in early 1790; the Parisian mob's taste for beheadings and disembowelings was a familiar item in the press of the day. Any classically educated person knew what happens when the rule of law breaks down and the lower classes erupt in a mixture of fear, excitement, and thirst for revenge; the nonclassically educated could hear it read out from the newspapers.

The strength of the *Reflections* was that Burke set a positive image of a functioning polity against the negative image of pure destruction. The French ancien régime practiced a politics that Burke did not care for: absolute monarchy governing through a centralized bureaucracy and appeasing a functionless aristocracy by giving it economic privileges to compensate for its powerlessness. Burke sometimes suggested that the ancient French constitution could have been revived by the reforms of the years before 1789; and he complained that the French aristocracy had assisted its own downfall by engaging in low political schemes when it should have assisted the monarchy to create a better political order. How far he believed it is impossible to say. His rhetorical needs caused him intellectual difficulties. If the revolution was wholly the fault of some combination of dissolute aristocrats and wicked philosophers, then the ancien régime must have been well adapted to the needs of the French nation, and in Burkean terms, therefore, good absolutely. The problem is that if the regime had been so good, it would surely have been immune to the mutterings of philosophers and connivings of aristocrats. The fact that it collapsed so easily showed that it had weaknesses—and Burke knew what they were. It was bankrupt and permanently vulnerable to the discontent that welled up when harvests failed and the population went hungry. Its apparent strength masked its slender hold on the loyalty of its citizens. The same was true of the church; individual priests served their flocks and were loved by them. The church as a whole was a device for extracting money and services from an overburdened peasantry while offering little in return. Burke knew, but could hardly admit in print, that half the French clergy had welcomed the state's takeover of the church. Impoverished curés were not going to shed tears over aristocratic bishops. Liberals look at the eighteenth-century French church through Voltairean lenses and condemn its complicity in censorship, the mistreatment of Protestants, and the cruelty of the penalties for alleged blasphemy. Burke did not. It was not his church, and he felt no attachment to it; but it was the established church of the French people, and, like the monarchy, it might have been reformed and certainly ought not to have had its property expropriated.

If the natural condition of society is orderly; if authority is usually accepted as a matter of habit, and the legitimacy of government is most securely founded on prescription, what had gone wrong becomes harder to explain. The morality of revolution is an easy topic; nothing save the direst emergency, as Hume observed, justifies one man sheathing his sword in the belly of another. Since that is obvious, the interesting issue is the causal question: why it is that, given the innumerable reasons people have for discontent and disaffection, disaffection so rarely breaks out in insurrection and that insurrection so rarely turns into revolution? It is not as though the world is so obviously just that the disadvantaged have no reason to wonder whether upheaval would yield dividends; indeed, the speed with which insurrections spread as soon as the authorities appear to have lost control suggests that many of us have no particular attachment to whatever regime we live under. Why do the habits that keep us obedient work so effectively so much of the time and break down so swiftly on the rare occasions when they do? We have not made much progress in answering the question in the two centuries since Burke; he posed the question but had other matters on his mind than answering it in those terms.

Joseph de Maistre

Burke was an enraged liberal more than a conservative. The ideas of the French counterpart to Burke, Joseph de Maistre, suggest the distance that separates Burke's essentially liberal objections to revolutionary violence and upheaval and full-blown, theologically based, absolutist reaction. Maistre was twenty years younger than Burke; born in 1753, he died in 1821. He was, strictly speaking, not French; he was a Savoyard and a subject of the king of Piedmont, whose capital was at Turin, and he spent his life in his diplomatic service. Like Burke, he approved the first steps of reform in France; and like Burke, he thought the attempt to create equal representation by amalgamating the three houses of the Estates General—clergy, nobility, and commons—was a revolutionary step toward disaster. He read and admired Burke's *Reflections*, but in 1797 published his own *Considérations sur la France*, in which he set out a violent and apocalyptic account of what had happened and what it meant. Pushing Burke's view that there was something unnatural about the revolution to an extreme, he claimed that it was an act of divine punishment; to the obvious question—punishment for what?—he responded that it did not much matter what, since mankind was so wicked that God might properly punish us at any time he chose and we would have no grounds for complaint. We should not complain at the carrying out of the death sentence when it is carried out; we should be grateful when it is not. He found Voltaire's poem on the Lisbon earthquake a particular provocation; Voltaire had asked why God struck Lisbon when there was dancing and lechery aplenty in Paris. Maistre's reply was that it would have been no injustice if Paris had been struck as well, and Voltaire should have been grateful for divine forbearance.

The force of Maistre's case does not lie in its intellectual plausibility. It lies in its image of authority. Burke's image of authority is often theatrical: it matters to him that Queen Marie-Antoinette has what the twentieth century called "star quality." Star quality allows authority to work on our habits and affections, in effect to govern us by seduction. Maistre wants authority to work on our will, by breaking the will to resist. His God is an absolute ruler whose decrees are inscrutable and whose operations are terrifying. That is the essence of authority. France needed an absolute monarch supported by an infallible pope. Maistre was a founder of the Counter-Enlightenment, the reactionary movement that aimed to undo the work not only of the authors of the *Encyclopédie* but of their philosophical predecessors such as Locke. It was years after the *Considérations* that Maistre produced the image for which he is best known, that of the executioner as "the horror and the bond of human society," an "incomprehensible agent" on whom everything else is built. But that is the thought that underlies the *Considérations*. Authority must be unchallengeable, and its power must be felt in the bowels rather than elaborated in the head, for man is a creature of passion, and if his passions are unleashed, destruction is the natural consequence. When Maistre indicts Rousseau for his role in the revolution, he is at pains to blame not the mob but the philosopher who gives them the idea that they may act as they wish. It is not the tiger we blame when he disembowels his innocent victims but the man who lets the tiger off the leash.

It was not his providentialism alone that made Maistre a prominent figure in the reaction. Other royalists regarded the revolution as a judgment on the French, and providential explanations were common enough; as we have seen, the Reverend Richard Price thought the revolution was a providential event at the opposite end of the political spectrum. The really striking thought was that the revolution showed that God had suddenly taken a closer interest in human affairs than ordinarily. Maistre was a highly educated man, a high official in the government of his native kingdom, and even at his wildest, decidedly astute, but he started a train of thought, less a tradition than an intellectual undercurrent, that surfaced a century later in the irrationalism of the French right with Maurice Barrès and in that unplaceable figure Georges Sorel and his *Reflections on Violence*. The thought that revolution from the left can be met only with violence from the right passed eventually into fascism, though not into the fascism of Benito Mussolini himself, who thought of himself as a man of the left in his own way.

The critics of the revolution had the best of the argument. Whatever else it achieved, it did not implement what its supporters hoped. It did not produce stable constitutional monarchy in the English manner, or a prosperous democratic republic in the American manner, or the reign of virtue that the Jacobins sought after 1792. Its failure to achieve one stable, uncontested outcome meant that French political institutions were seen as illegitimate by much of the population for the next century and a half, under the First and Second Empires, the Bourbon or Orleanist monarchies, the Second, Third, and Fourth Republics, or the Vichy regime of World War II. But the revolution's defenders did not abandon it. It is easy to wonder why not, given the bloodshed, bankruptcy, and misery to which it had led. One answer can be inferred from the success of the French revolutionary armies; the revolution proved capable not only of defending France against invasion but of exporting the revolution at the point of the bayonet. Whatever the revolution meant for the standard of living of peasants, artisans, and many of the professional middle classes, it meant something for which they were willing to fight with an enthusiasm not seen in the armies of their enemies. The promise that they were to be citizens, not subjects, was irresistibly attractive, however often it was honored in the breach.

Thomas Paine

Thomas Paine provides one answer to the question why its defenders did not desert the cause. Paine was born in Thetford in Norfolk in 1737, and he made little of his life before he arrived in America in 1774 armed with a letter of introduction from Benjamin Franklin and not much else. But his pamphlet *Common Sense*, published in January 1776, was a smashing success, both as a publishing event and more importantly as providing a simple, effective, irresistible argument for independence in the months before Jefferson's Declaration. It sold 150,000 copies at a time when few pamphlets sold 1,000. During the war, he wrote a series of articles called the *American Crisis*, the first of which begins with the famous lines "These are the times that try men's souls. The summer soldier and the sunshine patriot will, in this crisis, shrink from the service of his country; but he that stands it *now*, deserves the love and thanks of man and woman."[14] It was read to Washington's troops before they scored the first victory of the war at Trenton on December 26, 1776.

Paine was, as he said, a citizen of the world and did not settle in America. The revolution was led by gentlemen, and Paine was emphatically not one; it was led by native-born Americans, and Paine was a newly arrived foreigner. In 1787 he returned to England; in 1791 he fled to France when he saw that *Rights of Man* would be made the subject of a prosecution for seditious libel, as Burke had urged in his *Appeal*. He was made a French citizen and given a seat in the National Convention, but fell foul of Marat over the execution of Louis XVI, and spent ten months in prison under the Terror. He survived because the chalk mark that indicated he was to be executed was placed on the wrong door. Surprisingly, he stayed in France and did not return to the United States until 1802. He did not receive a hero's welcome when he did; he was reviled for his anti-Christian (not atheistical) tract, *The Age of Reason*, and lived in poverty and obscurity until his death in 1807. The unwillingness of Americans to acknowledge Paine's role in their revolution has several causes, of which his religious unorthodoxy is the most salient; another, which does them even less credit, is that Paine was looked down on by upper-class Americans such as Gouverneur Morris, and their snobbery molded later views. Jefferson was unusual in standing by him, but Jefferson had a taste for intellectual and political wildness that was unusual. The most reputable reason for keeping him at arm's length was that the founders were practically minded political leaders; Paine was an agitator, a journalist, a natural oppositionist. The founders' aim was to build a new and stable republic with all the compromises that might entail, and compromise was foreign to his nature.

Rights of Man, Part One contains Paine's response to Burke, but an intelligent reader could have known what Paine was going to say on the strength of *Common Sense.* Paine was not in all respects a rationalist, but relying on a few optimistic premises about human nature, he was a rationalist about political institutions and their reform. The starting point of the argument was that men are naturally sociable and will manage their affairs cooperatively and efficiently if they are not deluded by superstition or bullied by their rulers. Society is almost always a blessing; politics, even in its best state, a necessary evil. Hardly any government is really necessary. As he says, society stems from our wants and governments from our wickedness; a minimalist state is required to safeguard commerce and industry, and provide for those who cannot provide for themselves. That function overwhelms the minimalism in *Rights of Man, Part Two*, where Paine sets out a program for the creation of a very extensive welfare state, the provisions of which include pensions for soldiers and sailors who will be thrown out of employment when peace with France allows Britain to scale down its naval and military forces. Paine's economics must be neglected here, though Paine's case for confiscatory levels of taxation on very high incomes in order to pay for a welfare state needs to be made more often than it is today.

What is to our purposes is Paine's defense of the Enlightenment view of revolution; it is not a defense of the French Revolution alone, because Paine defends the French by appealing to the experience of the Americans. That position has been out of fashion for some time. He had told the Americans in *Common Sense* that government mattered much less than our rulers claim; many tasks that governments levied taxes to pay for need not be performed at all, and most of the tasks that need to be performed are ones that people can perform for themselves when they must. The War of Independence confirmed his optimism. When the previous British administration collapsed, ordinary people proved perfectly capable of recruiting, arming, feeding, and training armies that could fight the British army to a draw and sometimes beat it. Paine felt that his confidence in the ability of ordinary people to govern themselves and the redundancy of most political institutions had been fully justified.

What was most clearly in his sights, however, was the wickedness of British government. It was a fabric of corruption and malfeasance hardly to be tolerated. It was also absurd. The absurdity started with the role of heredity as regards the monarchy and aristocracy. Hume had suggested in his dry way that heredity was a good way of selecting our rulers because mankind were moved by imagination, and we readily give our allegiance to a son who reminds us of our earlier allegiance to the father; it was an early recognition of the role of celebrity in politics. Paine treated the hereditary principle with contempt. Intelligent fathers often produced stupid offspring; kings and aristocrats frequently died in early middle age, leaving a country to be run by an adolescent, or a regent acting for an infant. The only rational way to choose a ruling elite was some form of electoral process, not that by which the electors of the Holy Roman Empire produced their feeble superior, but that by which the American colonies had long chosen their representatives in their local legislatures.

Paine had no difficulty with the idea of universal human rights. Like Jefferson, who quoted Sidney's memorably indignant insistence that God had not divided humanity into two classes, one of which was entitled to ride booted and spurred on the back of the other, Paine took human equality as a given, and human rationality as another given, and inferred without hesitation that government must be government by consent; that nobody had a right to govern that had not been given him by the consent of the governed; and that individuals had a right to give or withhold their consent as reason dictated. His attitude to Burke was perhaps genuine distress that Burke had deserted the cause in whose behalf he had labored when the freedom of the American colonists was at stake, and certainly coupled with a vast exasperation at the way Burke tried to hide the deliverances of plain reason behind theatrical draperies and rhetorical flimflam. The sharpest of the many moments in *Rights of Man* where Paine punctures the inflated balloon of Burke's defense of the French ancien régime is the riposte to the most famous passage of the *Reflections*.

Although Burke had no particular affection for the French monarchy, his indignation had been aroused by the actions of the Parisian mob, which on October 5 and 6 of 1789 had marched out to Versailles, burst into the royal bedchamber, and carried the king and queen back to Paris. There was a good deal of disgusting violence in the process. Burke, however, made it the centerpiece of a disquisition on the importance of the draperies in which we decently dress the naked realities of political power and coercion. It is a wonderful piece of rhetoric, but decidedly ambiguous. Having said that Marie-Antoinette was a pure and radiant being, in whose defense he would have expected ten thousand swords to fly from their scabbards, Burke turned to the underlying analytical issue. What, he asks, is a queen? His empiricist self admits without flinching that a queen is just a woman. But his political self explains why this is not a truth whose public acknowledgment is compatible with the conduct of politics. To be a queen is not *just* to be a woman, but a woman starring in a political drama whose whole impact depends on the audience's being appropriately moved by what happens on the stage.

Paine simply refused to look for whatever sense there might be to be extracted from Burke's rhetoric. "He pities the plumage but forgot the dying bird," said Paine. Paine did not engage with Burke's argument; he did not think that Burke had an argument. On Paine's view of the matter, Burke blamed the revolutionaries for what was really the fault of the previous government, slandered the high-minded and high-principled defenders of progress, and obfuscated the reality of exploitation and bamboozlement that constituted the truth about all ancien régime societies. When Paine described himself as a citizen of the world—he was genuinely a citizen of Britain, the United States, and France—he meant to be taken seriously. On the one side there was a rationally organized political community: the bourgeois commercial republic, with a safety net provided by a welfare state to look after those who could not look after themselves, and sharp restrictions on bequest and inheritance to preserve social mobility and encourage the rise of talent; on the other side were "things as they are": superstition, exploitation, warfare, and corruption.

From a distance of more than two centuries, it is hard to understand how the essentially pacific radicals who supported the revolution through thick and thin managed to do so. Not only Paine but also William Godwin, Mary Wollstonecraft, and the members of soon to be banned associations such as the Society for Constitutional Information looked forward to the reign of universal peace. Paine relied on the near-abolition of the British naval and military establishments to provide the revenues for the welfare state he drew in great detail in *Rights of Man, Part Two*. How they averted their gaze from the violence and chaos increasingly evident in France by the end of 1789 has puzzled many commentators. It is not as though they did not know about it. Mary Wollstonecraft lived in Paris, and there were innumerable newspaper reports of events. What seems plausible is that it was initially possible to see the violence of the revolution as the effect of a sudden overcoming of preexistent violent repression, and thereafter as a response to the attempts of foreign governments to suppress the revolution. Reading Tocqueville's reflections on the savagery with which any form of popular discontent was treated under the ancien régime—breaking on the wheel was part of it—it is easy to see that if there was an upheaval, it would not be peaceful. The fault, on this view, lay with the previous regime.

It is not an implausible view that the Parisian mob was more disgustingly murderous than the London mob because the old regime in France was more brutal than its British counterpart. But Paine, writing in 1791, compared the Parisian and London mobs without any suggestion that the Paris mob in 1789–90 *was* worse than the London mob during the Gordon Riots of the early 1780s. Both enjoyed bearbaiting and public executions, as many of us would today. Mobs were everywhere brutal and irrational; but whose fault was it that the lower classes expressed themselves in that fashion when their anger was released? It was the regime under which they had grown up. Not merely had the old regime responded to their grievances in a murderous fashion, but everyday life for the lower classes had been brutal. This did not excuse the behavior of the mob, but its critics should acknowledge that its behavior was the rebounding of the official brutality of the old regime upon its perpetrators. None of this explains the air of carnival that accompanied particular outbreaks of savagery; something close to a hysterical sadism seems often to have seized the mob, as though the breach of old taboos liberated some deep and long-repressed urge to perpetrate violence for its own sake. That, again, is something that characterizes modern rioting as much as it did the riots of the eighteenth century. Plaintive commentators wonder why rioters and looters wreck their own neighborhoods, but fail to acknowledge that submitting to the disciplines of self-restraint is hard work and that violence and cruelty are fun. Saint Augustine and Thomas Hobbes before 1789 and Sigmund Freud afterward would have been less surprised.

Rights of Man does not speak in the ecstatic terms of Price's Nunc Dimittis. Nonetheless, there is a millenarian element in Paine's attachment to the simple dichotomy between reason and ignorance. "Reason and Ignorance, the opposites of each other, influence the great bulk of mankind. If either of these can be rendered sufficiently extensive in a country, the machinery of government goes easily on. Reason obeys itself; and Ignorance submits to whatever is dictated to it."[15] Republics are governed by reason; monarchies, by ignorance. Representative government secures the reign of reason; hereditary monarchy and aristocracy are mired in ignorance and suited only to the ignorant. This largely accounts for Paine's contempt for the theatrical aspects of Burke's *Reflections*. He dismisses Burke's rhetoric by observing, "As [to] the tragic paintings by which Mr Burke has outraged his own imagination, and seeks to work upon that of his readers, they are very well calculated for theatrical representation, where facts are manufactured for the sake of show, and accommodated to produce, through the weakness of sympathy, a weeping effect."[16] It is inconceivable that Paine did not understand that he, too, was engaged in a rhetorical competition, but he was picturing himself as the plain speaker, who grounded his ideas in facts.

The rhetorical power of *Rights of Man* rested not only on the dichotomy between the black night of ignorance and the clear light of reason but on the dichotomy between death and life. Paine's best argument was that every generation has an indefeasible natural right to decide for itself what form of government to live under; Burke's was that the securest political title is prescription. So Paine rewrote Burke's defense of prescription as the principle that the dead were to govern the living. The argument is crisp and swift. Either someone once had the right to institute a form of government, or nobody did. If nobody ever had such a right, all argument is at a stand, and government is inexplicable. Assuming that someone had the right to institute a government once upon a time, it is impossible to understand why that same right does not exist in their heirs. The belief that anyone in the past had the right to institute a despotism upon generations yet unborn defies rational analysis. As the Declaration had said, the rights of man were inalienable.

The same rhetoric sustains Paine's defense of the positive doctrine of the rights of man. Although Paine is a quick and aggressive reasoner, the argument was reputable. If any government in the world is legitimate, it must have a pedigree that traces its institution to the free choice of whoever set it up. Mankind may obey governments out of habit, and this may deceive us about the role played by prescription; nonetheless, even a government based on prescription will always have some argument in its armory to show that it began in a legitimate fashion or is legitimately grounded by now. Paine agrees that many or most governments began in conquest; but he takes it for granted as Rousseau did—and contrary to the de facto-ist tradition—that conquest in itself conveys no title to govern. The subjects of a ruler whose title rests on conquest are like men who have been falsely imprisoned. If they can recover their liberty, they should. Whatever is not a despotism requires a foundation in the rights of the citizens.

Paine's position was not utopian. He did not suggest, as William Godwin did at the same date, that enlightenment would bring about "the euthanasia of government" or, as Godwin also did, that sufficiently enlightened persons would live so sensibly that they would eventually become immortal. Paine agreed that free and equal persons must give up many of their natural rights when governments are set up. The broad principle is that rights which we can exercise by our own unaided efforts are never given up, while those we need the help of others to exercise are regulated and curtailed for the sake of our greater freedom and well-being.[17] There is never reason to curtail our intellectual and religious liberty (save in the obvious cases discussed in Locke's *Letter concerning Toleration*, where our external actions are restricted by the ordinary law of the land to prevent cruel and damaging conduct of whatever kind), because all a man needs in order to speculate about the nature of the universe and the meaning of existence is noninterference. The very idea of an established church is off the agenda; an established church involves taxing nonmembers for something they do not wish to support and get no value from and a violation of the indefeasible right to intellectual liberty.

Most rights fall into a gray area. The right to earn a living seen as the right to offer one's services for hire to whoever may wish to have them comes close to a natural right that can be exercised without assistance; but the ability to rely on contracts of employment, and indeed contracts generally, involves the help of others; this means that property must be regulated by the state. This suggests yet another reason why the hereditary principle is treated so lightly by Paine; during my lifetime, I dispose of my property and my person; for the most part, I need protection against interference and only a little positive help. Upon my death, anything I wish to happen postmortem must be achieved on my behalf by others, and they may impose terms for that assistance. Inherited wealth may therefore be used for public purposes, so long as these are proper purposes. So long as the family persists, states should tread delicately and not interfere unduly with the dictates of natural affection and the wishes of testators; but where substantial sums are involved and gross inequalities are created by unregulated bequests, the state should intervene and ensure that large estates are divided among the needy rather than preserved for the benefit of the wealthy.

On that basis Paine defends the French Declaration of the Rights of Man and the Citizen. However, the defense occupies only some 6 pages out of 150, and 3 of those pages list the seventeen clauses of the Declaration. Paine himself says that the essence of political liberty is to be found in the first three clauses: the first declares, "Men are born and always continue free, and equal in respect of their rights. Civil distinctions, therefore, can be founded only on public utility." Paine could hardly be expected to make the point that Marx made ninety years later, that this is the essence of bourgeois right: we have *equal* rights to *unequal* outcomes determined by our talents, energy, and luck. The second clause says, "The end of all political associations is the preservation of the natural and imprescriptible rights of man; and these rights are liberty, property, security, and resistance of oppression." The third reads, "The Nation is essentially the source of all Sovereignty; nor can any INDIVIDUAL, or ANY BODY OF MEN, be entitled to any authority which is not expressly derived from it."[18] There is something puzzling about Paine's casualness about the rest of the clauses, which he treats as if they did no more than spell out the implications of the opening statement of principles. This hardly does justice to the fourth clause, which sets out the standard liberal understanding of the connection between freedom and equality: "Political Liberty consists in the power of doing whatever does not injure another. The exercise of the natural rights of every man, has no other limits than those which are necessary to secure to every *other* man the free exercise of the same rights; and these limits are determinable only by the law." In some form or other, the principle that my rights are bounded by your similar rights is the basis of most liberal democratic conceptions of the legitimate lawmaking authority of governments.

On one thing Paine and Burke saw eye to eye; as much as Burke, Paine saw that the French Revolution was a real novelty. The American Revolution had been its precursor, but the French Revolution revealed the arrival of something new in the social and political world. Paine complained that Burke could see nothing but chaos and disorder and upheaval, and could only say the revolution was unnatural and astonishing; he had no urge to understand it. Paine seized on what made Burke think the event unnatural, namely, that it was both a political and a social revolution, that it embodied a discernible principle, and that it was committed to an idea of progress, "combining moral with political happiness and national prosperity." Past revolutions had been changes of personnel with little impact on the lives and well-being of the citizenry; they were caused by local grievances and based on no principle. Now there had been two revolutions whose principles were universal, and which would beget more of the same. Those of the American founders who devoutly wanted a political revolution without a social revolution would have been less than pleased to see the two revolutions yoked together in this way.

Like Burke, Paine had his eyes fixed on England while talking about the French and the Americans. The latter had created constitutions; the English talked about the British constitution, but nobody could say what it was. A skeptical observer might suspect there was no such entity to be found. If there was no constitution, what was there? A system of hereditary jobbery, oppression, and superstition. It had been put in place by William the Conqueror, but the Norman Yoke was refastened upon the necks of the English every generation by a host of people with an interest in preserving the existing order. On a clear view of the matter, most of the English population got nothing from preserving the status quo. Paine gave particular offense by yoking the established church to the regime of jobbery and place hunting that passed for parliamentary government. He not only rejected the idea that the state had a role in religious life; he thought it monstrous that the employees of the church should batten on the taxpayer. It was Paine who coined the striking doctrine that toleration was as great a piece of despotism as the denial of toleration: the government had no more right to give permission for the practice of faith than it had the right to deny permission. The French and the Americans got that right in their constitutions; the English had hardly advanced an inch since they drove Quakers and Dissenters across the Atlantic.

The French Revolution did not create a bourgeois republic: the Third Republic was installed only after the collapse of the Second Empire in 1870. The revolution did not usher in the reign of peace among nations, but provoked two decades of war. It did a great many other things; church property, once taken, was not given back; a legislature, once instituted, survived, diminished under both Bonapartes, and attenuated under Louis XVIII; but old-fashioned absolute monarchy was dead beyond resurrection. Something had happened beneath the surface of events whose deepest meaning had remained obscure to the actors of the day. For Marx and later Marxists, the revolution was the paradigm case of a bourgeois revolution, caused when the gradual progress of the bourgeoisie toward a dominant position in the economy and the political sphere met resistance from existing social and political forms and shattered the inflexible structure holding it back. With the aid of a peasantry and proletariat who had every reason to detest the previous regime, but would have little reason to think much better of the bourgeois capitalist, a revolution had occurred, at the end of which the bourgeoisie had achieved emancipation but the proletariat had merely changed masters. That the affair was bloody and messy, and does least for the propertiless masses on whom all revolutions depend, was something Marx took for granted; history is a process in which good is wrung out of evil. There were other, less tightly structured views, among them Tocqueville's, which emphasized the deep continuities in French political culture and explained the destruction of the old order as being the result of a fatal alliance between dissident aristocrats and rationalist intellectuals, and the great historian Jules Michelet's, which saw the revolution in almost religious terms as a series of revelatory moments when the potential of the French people for unity, social harmony, liberation—the full achievement of *liberté, égalité, fraternité*—could be glimpsed.

Saint-Simon

An alternative vision, but one that turned out to be even more pregnant with the future than Marx's, came from a very unlikely source, Claude Henri de Rouvroy, comte de Saint-Simon. Saint-Simon was born in 1760, served in the American War of Independence, made a great deal of money during the French Revolution, and lost most of it afterward. He is best known as the founder of Saint-Simonianism, which under the influence of his followers became a quasi-religious utopian socialist sect. More important for us, he had two ideas that underpin a way of thinking about social change and appropriate political institutions that provided a major challenge to Marxism. As against Marx, who prided himself on his materialism, Saint-Simon believed in the power of ideas, particularly scientific ideas, and whereas Marx emphasized class conflict based on the struggle between the owners of resources and the suppliers of labor, Saint-Simon emphasized the importance of rational management, which is to say the principles of organization according to which a society's productive resources are employed in the most productive fashion. Marx's key thought was that workers were sacrificed to the demands of capital; Saint-Simon's, that latent in modern industrial society were miracles of productivity. It is not surprising that the Suez Canal was the work of a Saint-Simonian disciple, Ferdinand de Lesseps—Saint-Simon himself spent some years in Spain working on a plan to dig a canal from Madrid to the Atlantic Ocean. French railways were developed by Saint-Simonians, as was the first French investment bank, the Crédit Mobilier.

All this is surprising, since Saint-Simon was quite often mentally ill, the victim of a failed suicide attempt, and when he was both wholly sane and very rich, an energetic rake. Nor did he focus his eyes on the revolution until many years after the event, during the restoration, in the last five years of his life, between 1820 and 1825. Durkheim published a long essay called *Socialism and Saint-Simon* in which he seized on Saint-Simon's concern with the moral cohesion of society, while Friedrich Engels took his emphasis on society as a mechanism for the production of the means of life to make him an ancestor of Marxism. Both perspectives play down Saint-Simon's wilder ideas, but those too were influential; he was a notable contributor to the passion for designing utopian communities that swept Europe and America between 1800 and 1840. Since their common characteristic was the brevity of their existence in the forms in which they were created, we must reluctantly bypass them here, full of human interest though many of them were.

Marx and Saint-Simon both analyzed the French Revolution as an upheaval driven by economic change and class conflict; both thought that the people who made the revolution did not understand *why*; they were taken in by their own rhetoric. Saint-Simon agreed with the diagnosis, but from a distinctively non-Marxist standpoint. Saint-Simon was a corporatist of a religious bent; a properly functioning society would be *organic*, which is to say that it would possess a hierarchy of authority that reflected merit properly understood. Merit would no longer be hereditary or military; those who exercised authority would do it because they were appropriately qualified to guide a productive and contented society, not because they were the sons of the people who had previously exercised power or because they were good soldiers. But we cannot reinvent the structures of authority every week, and there will also have to be a framework of belief that will attach us emotionally to our society. Function plus emotion is the recipe for peace, good order, productivity, and happiness.

The relevance of this to the French Revolution is that it had become apparent to everyone that the revolution had marked a decisive break in European history. How sharp that break was was debatable; whether it could be reversed was debatable; how long it had been in the making was debatable; and the stability of the post-Napoleonic world was debatable. That a seismic shift had occurred was the only thing universally agreed. The violent tearing apart of the political institutions by which France had been governed for centuries revealed what was thereafter known as "the social question," the question whether the poor must always be with us, whether they could hope to play a nondestructive role in politics, whether they were destined to be hewers of wood and bearers of water even when the wood became coal and the water was needed for steam engines. It became clear to everyone, even if the fact was not as incontestable as it seemed, that the subject matter of politics had changed; authority was not something freestanding, whether conferred by God or popular election. Authority presupposed forms of social integration that it itself could not supply but that it had to draw on. Political sociology had been born, even if not baptized.

The details of Saint-Simon's understanding of what had happened and what needed to happen next are complex and unstable. This is largely because he was so easily distracted by the details of what would happen when traditional Christianity was replaced by the religion of humanity, *le nouveau Christianisme* of his construction. The core of his doctrine, however, was very clear. Society functions happily only when its organization matches human nature, a thought from which neither Plato nor Aristotle would have dissented. Human beings are not born equal in any but the most trivial sense; they are born with different measures of talent and different kinds of talent. The most important distinctions today lie between the temperaments and intellects that lead people to make things, to speculate, and to engage in poetic work. A rational society will be run by a hierarchical organization of managers and scientists; Saint-Simon, like his follower Auguste Comte, included bankers among this elite. This was the first announcement that the modern world was the product of a managerial revolution. At the time nobody understood this; by the 1950s it was clear that Saint-Simon had invented the modern understanding of industrial society, and its organization. "Organization" is the crucial word. Like Plato a long time before and the Fabian socialists eighty years later, Saint-Simon thought that a person who did the right kind of work for his energies and abilities ("from each according to ability") and received proper recompense, both material and spiritual ("to each according to need"), would be happy, socially and psychically integrated, and ready to follow the direction of properly appointed superiors. Just as we are happy to follow the instruction of a mathematician who sees answers to problems that we cannot, so we shall be happy to follow the instructions of people who see further into the needs of society or into its unfulfilled potentialities than we can. Rational authority will be supplemented by the poetic and affectual. This is not Shelley's doctrine that poets are the unacknowledged legislators of mankind, but a more complicated doctrine about the ways in which we are drawn to authority by emotion as well as by a rational perception of its utility. It also implies the abolition of politics, just as Plato's utopia did. The government of men will give way to the administration of things. Coercive law will become unnecessary because everyone will willingly cooperate for the sake of making society a just and efficient productive mechanism.

On Saint-Simon's analysis, the revolution broke out in large part because the old political system had simply run out of authority. Its authority was medieval, not modern. Hereditary rule, whether the rule of aristocrats or of monarchs, was based on blood and supposed military prowess at a time when the world had turned into one in which scientific intelligence, skill, and productivity were decisive. Unsurprisingly, the journals in which Saint-Simon spelled out his views on the emerging world were called *L'organisateur* and *Le producteur*. The productive classes were not manual workers alone; this was not the Marxian vision of the proletariat inheriting the kingdom of heaven, but a simple contrast between those who combined to create something useful for the support of human life and those who either destroyed it in war or squandered it in ostentation. Unlike the Marxists, who explained revolution as an upheaval from below, Saint-Simon explained the ruin of the nobility and monarchy as a failure of the elite. What he offered, or what can be extracted from his work when sieved by a sympathetic reader, is a more persuasive picture of what a later age called "industrial society" than Marx's picture of capitalism. As management has come to be seen as more important than ownership, Saint-Simon's obsession with organization seems more prescient than Marx's obsession with the proletariat.

Retrospect

The French Revolution remains engrossing as an astonishing series of events whose capacity to surprise participants and spectators is almost unmatched by later events. Its effect on later revolutionaries was in many ways disastrous, because in much the same way that generals habitually fight the last war and their soldiers therefore suffer needlessly in the one they are really engaged in, so revolutionaries subsequently believed that they were reenacting the "Great French Revolution," and suffered accordingly. What few people believed, however, was that the revolution made no difference to French and European life. Still, some later writers were inclined to argue that it made much less difference than the bloodshed and the subsequent warfare might suggest. Tocqueville was one of them. Hegel, we shall now see, was not. But Hegel's contribution to our concerns is decidedly double-edged. His vision of a constitutional modern state emphasizes the rule of law, the rights of conscience, and the importance of well-informed and humane government; but it is bureaucratic, not democratic, and provides the beginnings of an answer to the question whether the Persians might after all have defeated the Athenians.

CHAPTER 18

Hegel: The Modern State as
the Work of Spirit

Hegel's Germany

THE GERMANY INTO WHICH Hegel was born was a political oddity. "Germany" did not exist as a single political entity. Germans—ethnic Germans and German speakers—lived in a multitude of states of very different shapes and sizes; the two dominant states in the German-speaking world were Prussia and Austria, European powers militarily and diplomatically central to European politics. With Russia, they were Europe's most formidable absolutist monarchies. Austria was not only a German state but a multiethnic and multinational imperial power. Austria and Prussia were the two largest German states; the others ranged from the substantial kingdoms of Saxony and Bavaria to feudal enclaves that survived by courtesy of their larger neighbors. During the first two-thirds of the nineteenth century, German unification was brought about by force of arms, not by political logic. Prussia conquered non-Austrian Germany and made it one *Reich*, with disastrous consequences for the twentieth century.

Hegel was born in 1770 in Stuttgart, in the southern German state of Württemberg, and died in Berlin in 1831. His father was a civil servant, a member of the class that Hegel fifty years later made the centerpiece of his political theory in *The Philosophy of Right*. Hegel had a much interrupted career, crowned for the last dozen years of his life by the occupancy of a post at the apex of German intellectual life—the chair of philosophy at the University of Berlin. He entered the Tübingen theological seminary at the age of eighteen, spent eight years after graduation as a private tutor, then took advantage of an inheritance to work as a privatdozent at the University of Jena. From 1801 to 1806 he established himself as a figure to be reckoned with and was promoted to professor in 1805. In October 1806 his world was turned upside down by the comprehensive defeat of the Prussian army by Napoleon's forces at the Battle of Jena. Hegel was enraptured by the idea (and perhaps by the sight) of Napoleon, whom he described as the spirit of the world, crowned and riding on horseback, but it ended employment at the university.

Amid these excitements, he published his masterpiece, *The Phenomenology of Spirit*, but found himself with no job and no university. After a brief and unsuccessful career as a newspaper editor, he became in 1808 rector of a *Gymnasium* in Nuremberg. Today the idea of pursuing a philosophical career while working as the headmaster of a secondary school seems odd; but the head of an academic secondary school in nineteenth-century Europe was no drudge, and in Nuremberg, Hegel wrote his enormous *Science of Logic*, the work that obsessed his nineteenth-century philosophical admirers. In 1816 he was appointed to a chair in philosophy at Heidelberg, and two years later to the chair at the recently founded University of Berlin that had been occupied by Johann Gottlieb Fichte. Fichte had been acutely conscious of his role as Germany's national thinker—an ambiguous role in the absence of a German state—but the Berlin chair was unequivocally a cultural landmark.

This made it a prize to be aimed at, but its occupant was politically exposed. Germany generally, and Prussia particularly, had been greatly affected by the impact of Napoleon, who had terrified European rulers with his military prowess and dazzled their subjects with the magic of a political project that combined the egalitarianism of the French Revolution with the glamour of imperialism. Prussia was doubly vulnerable. To be humiliated militarily was intolerable to a state that had been built on military success, but the efforts of Frederick the Great and some very able ministers meant that Prussia had also been a reforming state, if an autocratic one, so that defeat was more than military. Defeat cast doubt on the credibility of the Prussian state in its entirety: Prussia had failed both on the battlefield and in its efforts to become a modern state. The humiliation of Jena led to a move for further reform. Its ingredients were to include a written constitution, and the opening of the officer corps and the higher civil service to appointment on merit, rather than to the feudal Prussian nobility alone. The king agreed to these changes, and Hegel was appointed to the Berlin chair by a reforming minister. But the defeat of Napoleon had changed the political climate again; Prussia came under pressure from the conservative rulers of Austria, Russia, and the minor German states, and Prussian conservatives regained their confidence. In 1819 the Prussian nobility reclaimed its monopoly of state and military office, and the king withdrew his promise of a written constitution; university censorship was reimposed. Such was the climate in which Hegel lectured on the modern state. We must wait until we have made our way through *The Philosophy of Right* to evaluate the work's conservative and liberal tendencies; but Hegel must have found it difficult to square loyalty to his employers with his belief in the virtues of modernity as represented not by the *events* of the French Revolution but by the assimilation of its *values* into the calmer, more stable, more sensibly managed existence sheltered by the modern liberal and constitutional state.

Reputation

Hegel's reputation has waxed and waned even more dramatically than that of most political thinkers. To those intoxicated by his system, he has seemed to illuminate the universe in ways unparalleled by any other thinker. Those who have thought it all hot air have dismissed him (in Schopenhauer's memorably abusive phrase) as "a nauseating, illiterate, hypocritical, slope-headed scribbler." Some admirers of his metaphysics have thought his political philosophy vastly inferior; J. N. Findlay described it as breathing the stuffy atmosphere of the waiting room of a minor Prussian official.[1] Others have thought his metaphysics unintelligible, but admired his insights into social and political life. Even a reader who wishes not to become embroiled in these arguments can scarcely help wondering what Karl Marx saw in Hegel's work, and why it was that having found Hegel (as he thought) standing on his head, he considered it worth trying to set him on his feet, and why late in life he still wished to defend Hegel against critics who treated him "like a dead dog."

Hegel's metaphysics matters to his social and political theory because that theory is embedded in a vision of humanity's moral and cultural history that makes complete sense only within Hegel's philosophy as a whole. But understanding the connection does not oblige us to believe any, let alone all, of the underlying philosophy. While respecting Hegel's philosophical ambitions, we may nonetheless see his philosophy as an elaborate allegory, the philosophical rendering of a dramatic account of human social, cultural, and political development that can stand on its own feet without any additional support. Marx had one account of this, but there are many ways of defending Hegel's insights that do not imply that he was standing on his head or needed rescuing by Marx. Crucially, Hegel was part of the postrevolutionary intellectual movement to which Saint-Simon belonged, a comparison Marx himself drew. Its crucial tenets were that society must be understood organically and historically; the key to social order and individual happiness lay in understanding the cultural—moral, political, and religious—development of the human race. Any ahistorical social theory was archaic and unbelievable. It follows rather swiftly that state-of-nature theories, theories of natural rights, and theories of the social contract are at best metaphors, and not very illuminating ones.

Hegel wrote only one "philosophical" work on politics, *The Philosophy of Right*, published in 1821. As the title suggests, it is concerned not with the rough-and-tumble of politics but with the orderly and rational administration of public affairs and with the maintenance of a framework within which the individual subjects of a modern constitutional state can pursue their private cultural, intellectual, economic, and familial interests. Hegel wrote several short essays on aspects of German politics, and even on the proposals for electoral change in Britain that culminated in the Reform Bill of 1832, the year after his death; but everyone who reads Hegel is conscious that behind his mature, quietist account of the modern constitutional state, lie the harder-to-assimilate insights of *The Phenomenology of Spirit*, and that his view of the nature and purpose of the modern legal and political order is illuminated by his *Philosophy of History*, the work in which he insists that the goal and purpose of history is to bring it about that all persons should be free and that this goal has been realized in the modern world.[2]

Here I simplify a great deal: an account of the purposes of Hegel's philosophy serves as preface, then I turn to elements of his social and political thinking that have resonated with both critics and admirers. I extract Hegel's schematic account of self-consciousness and freedom from the *Phenomenology*, move to the ideas about human freedom to which he devoted his *Philosophy of History*, and finally tackle his formal account of the constitutional state in *The Philosophy of Right*. The logic is this: the French Revolution made everyone aware of the irreversibility of historical change, and the impossibility of thinking about politics without thinking about its economic, cultural, and religious basis. An implication, which makes Hegel a foil not only to Saint-Simon but also to Benjamin Constant, was the need to reconcile ancient and modern liberty, the liberty of the Roman citizen that Hobbes dismissed as no sort of liberty at all, and the "let alone" liberty of the denizens of the marketplace. It was not enough to jeer at the self-destructive follies of French revolutionaries who had dressed up in togas; modern man needed a political environment in which a rational loyalty to the state as well as autonomy for the individual were possible. For all that, the chapter ends on an anxious note: does *The Philosophy of Right* fail to do justice to the *citizen* as well as the *subject*, and therefore to politics as well as rational administration? Or is this the first statement of the inescapability of the modern, bureaucratically administered state, and Hegel's account of it a reminder that whatever freedom for the moderns may be, it is not that of the Athenians? Is liberal democracy, as we practice it, only a variation on the state that Hegel described, as some of his commentators have thought?[3]

Philosophy, Not Political Activism

Hegel gained a posthumous reputation as the embodiment of "Prussianism," but was not active in politics. Unlike Aristotle, he did not die in exile; unlike Machiavelli, he did not handle affairs of state; unlike Hobbes, he was not part of the household of a future king; unlike Locke, he did not consort with those who plotted treason; and unlike Marx, he was not a professional revolutionary. He was a philosopher, content to sum up his own time in thought. He drew a sharp distinction between the activist and the philosopher. "Philosophy," he wrote in the preface to *The Philosophy of Right*, "comes on the scene too late to tell the world how it ought to be."[4] Philosophy is retrospective, paints in gray on gray, and can understand a form of life only when it has grown old. This sounds more quietist than perhaps it is, for the philosopher tells us not merely how the world *is* but how it *must be*. This is not because the philosopher can tell us things that only empirical inquiry will reveal; the philosopher cannot predict the victories and failures of this or that political leader, cannot say whether there will be a famine or a feast when the harvest is gathered in. The philosopher's task is to uncover the meaning of what we do, to reveal how the desires and beliefs that make up our identities hang together in ways that ordinary empirical observation does not reveal. Philosophy does not compete with empirical political and social science; if anything, it competes with religion, which on Hegel's view, does what philosophy does, but pictorially rather than rationally. To all appearances, Hegel was a conventional Lutheran, but it is easy to see why some of his radical disciples later thought he was a covert atheist.

Hegel was an idealist, which is to say that he thought that the ultimate reality was Mind. Christians who understand the opening sentences of Saint John's Gospel, with its claim "In the beginning was the Word," know what Hegel meant. The *logos* that John claimed was God, the begetter of the world, was the Reason that Hegel thought lay at the heart of all things. But Hegel also believed that Mind came to understand itself only by manifesting itself in the created world, and in working through the history of that world in culture, religion, art, politics, and the other expressions of intelligence. He rejected the notion of a God or *Geist* or Mind independent of, and separate from, its own creation.

To explain what Hegel meant when he argued for the mind dependency of the world is not easy. To say what he hoped to accomplish is simpler. It is astonishing that we can understand the universe at all; the world might have been simply unintelligible. Indeed, some scientists think that there are features of the world that our minds cannot grasp. Not Hegel; like many philosophers and some cosmologists today, Hegel thought that the intelligibility of the world is not accidental. The world is a world of facts, but they are not *brute* facts. This explains his insistence on the ideality of the world. Minds understand the workings of minds, but *mere* matter has no workings to understand. If things follow *principles* or *laws*, they embody something mental or mindlike. Why should this matter? Hegel wished to show, without relying on revelation or mystical intuition, that human beings are at home in the world, that the world is *our* world. We are not thrown into an alien, meaningless place. It is perhaps only against the background of the religious traditions of the West that Hegel's project makes complete sense, even if he conflates Mind and the world in ways the Judeo-Christian tradition does not. Hegel interprets the cultural and intellectual history of mankind as the biography of God—or *Geist*. It is this view of the relationship of God to history and human culture that explains the notorious claim in *The Philosophy of Right* that "the State is the March of God on Earth," or the thought that modern western Europe has reached the end of history.[5] The state shelters the cultures that embody the life of *Geist* in history.

The Phenomenology of Spirit

The *Phenomenology* was a masterpiece Hegel could neither repeat nor improve on. It has an intellectual and emotional sweep that few books match, and none in philosophy. Political theorists have been especially taken with Hegel's account of the development of our understanding of freedom, and particularly with the "master-slave dialectic," which we shall explore. Throughout the *Phenomenology* Hegel insists that mind is not passive; thought does not simply register what is happening in the world. The mind is essentially free, and both thought and action spring from the imaginative freedom that is the essence of the mind. Freedom is the origin of knowledge and the source of value. Knowing is knowing why things are the way they are and not some other way; we make the world valuable when take what there is and change it into something that serves our purposes. We transform the world in thought to make it intelligible, and turn the world to our purposes by working on it. To put it so briskly skates over depths whose existence we should acknowledge. For instance, the idea that much of poetry and art *finds* meaning and beauty in the world is not repudiated by Hegel, even though this activist theory of the mind seems to imply that poetry, art, and science all *impose* meaning on the world.

Hegel supposes that our first reaction to the world is to distance ourselves from it by insisting that *we* (the embodiment of Mind and the bearers of desires) are essential and that *it* (the merely material) is inessential. This thought recurs in the justification of property rights a dozen years later in *The Philosophy of Right*.[6] All human activity shows that *we* are free and all else the raw material of our freedom. Even swinging our arms aimlessly displays the right of a mind to embody itself in and exercise its sway over the matter of a human body. Eating and drinking gain a metaphysical interest they would not have in a less imaginative view; consumables gain value by becoming part of *us*. Some readers of Locke have thought his account of the origins of property was "Hegelian" for just this reason. Hegel insists that the world's reality is a *practical* rather than a *theoretical* issue. When Marx later made the same claim, he meant it as a criticism of Hegel, but the complaint was misplaced. Certainly Hegel builds on these foundations an elaborate metaphysical system of just the kind that Marx detested, but Hegel had no doubt that thought begins in action. This underpins his claim that freedom is the central feature of human life.

It also launches the dialectic of master and slave. The mind, the embodiment of freedom, confronts the material world as something "other," or strange, foreign, and hostile. So far as the owner of that mind is concerned, the material world is not—until it is mastered, used, and understood—his own. What of other human beings? They are physically part of the material environment that we have not yet mastered and made our own. Like any other part of the external world, they limit our freedom of maneuver; but unlike any other part of the world, they pose a threat to our belief that the world is *ours* to use, enjoy, and control, because they are not only physical objects. They have a point of view of their own: they see the world as we do. Their view of the world threatens the belief that our view of the world is *the* view of the world. The instinctive response of the unsophisticated self-consciousness imagined by Hegel is to think that if the world is theirs, it cannot be his.[7]

Hegel now explores the competition of viewpoints. The initial confrontation is dyadic; I try to make you acknowledge that the world is mine, and I am master of it and of you, and you try to make me acknowledge that it is yours and you are master of it and of me. It is obvious, and Hegel tells us that it is obvious, that the only *ultimate* resolution is that we all acknowledge each other as equally free and entitled to use the world on equal terms and to employ each other's abilities in ways that do not threaten our freedom; but the embodiment of that solution in law and economics lies at the far end of human history. Hegel begins with two antagonistic projects; I wish to be acknowledged as master of the world and you acknowledged as wholly inessential, and the same is true for you. I cannot *wholly* reduce you to the status of a mere thing, however. For me to be certain of my own status, you must recognize it. Things cannot do that; nor can you if I kill you. Hegel imagines a fight to the death between two competing wills; to display our superiority, we must show ourselves free from the encumbrance of the merely material world, and to show that we must be unafraid of death. The party to the struggle who is least afraid of death, who conquers his fear of extinction and ends victorious, is destined to be master; the one who sees in death the end of everything he values, and would rather live a slave than die a hero, becomes the slave.

Paradoxically, the slave gains an unobvious victory over the master. The master gains the obvious victory; the slave must acknowledge the master's superiority and accept that he is indeed his lord and master. The master also gains a victory over the material world. With the slave to do his bidding and labor for him, the master can enjoy the fruits of the slave's labor and consume what he wants without having to get his hands dirty. The necessity to *earn* a living is not for him. Hegel accepts that because the world exists for us to use, consume, and control, the master has struck a blow for (one kind of) human freedom by reducing another human being to servitude. However, there is a worm in the apple, and the worm carries the future of human culture. The master cannot have what he wants from slavery. He seeks recognition, but a *slave's* recognition is tainted. Being extorted, it is no recognition at all. One might as well recite one's virtues to a recording device and play it back. Sartre made much of this insight in his novels, and Groucho Marx wrote a comic commentary on the thought when he said that he wouldn't join any club that was willing to have him. The slave's acknowledgment of the master's superiority isn't worth having just because it is a slave's recognition.

As a commentary on slavery, Hegel's discussion is full of holes, as commentators have said. Slave owners spend time not in the company of slaves but in that of other slave owners; the ownership of slaves secures the recognition the slave owner wants from persons of his own standing, other slave owners. It has also been said that as a commentary on a slave-owning society, it is full of insights, in particular that in such a society manual labor is despised and ostentatious consumption the norm, and that such societies are economic and technological dead ends. From Benjamin Rush onward, critics of the slave-owning southern United States said just that about them. It is a common complaint against the heroes of the *Iliad* that they display less self-control than a prekindergarten class and that their cruelty, greed, petulance, and volatility are those of small children unfortunately equipped with the bodies of adults. It was another complaint against the slave-owning South that it produced just such an upper class. It is from that perspective (though not only from that perspective) that Hegel approaches his topic. The question is not whether de facto a society of slave owners and slaves is driven to self-destruction through the frustrated search for recognition. Hegel's vision of human culture and the ascent to freedom of the human spirit is teleological. It does not matter how slave owning societies come to grief; the crucial issue is that the slave owner is a cultural dead end. The freedom he aspires to is that of the indulged child, not that of the man who has been disciplined by the knowledge of mortality and the necessity of labor.

Stoic Freedom

The slave owns the future. The slave is disciplined. To put the matter less vertiginously, one might say that if we are to acquire self-mastery and become rational, autonomous creatures, we must learn how to conduct ourselves prudently and intelligently, how to shape means to ends, and see ourselves living in the world, turning it to our purposes and not resenting the constraints it places upon us. It is the slave who can, in principle, understand what human freedom is. However, nothing in Hegel's philosophy takes a direct line, and Hegel observes, rather acutely, that a first thought about freedom that might occur to an intelligence deformed by the experience of enslavement would be that so long as we could withdraw our desires and concerns from the world, we would become invulnerable and therefore free. The master who threatens the slave with terrible punishment for disobedience is powerless if the slave has such self-control that he is not frightened; indeed, the master's passion for the control of another is the real loss of freedom.[8]

This is the insight of Stoicism, which is often accused, as it is to some degree by Hegel, of mistaking withdrawal for liberation. This is not quite right. Hegel agrees that the Stoic offers a genuine recipe for autonomy; that is, the Stoic gave a coherent account of how it could be true that the slave *was his own master*. There is an obvious paradox in saying that a person whose status was defined as unfree, in virtue of having a master who had absolute authority over him, might nonetheless be his own master and obey himself alone. It can, however, be given sense. The claim is often mistaken for the claim that a slave can be happy. That claim is not in the least paradoxical, even if it is unlikely to be true, no matter how often slave owners in the southern United States said it in the years before the Civil War. Slaves are happy if they enjoy their servitude, or at any rate so long as they do not mind servitude more than they enjoy everything else about their lives. The paradox arises only when persons who are paradigmatically *un*free are said to be free. Recall the Roman notion of the *liber*, or free man; he was defined in contrast to the slave.

The Stoic reaches this thought as follows. Loss of freedom occurs when someone else can arbitrarily make us do what he wants; this is the common coin of all discussion. Most of us cannot face the evils with which we are threatened for noncompliance, and yield to threats. The slave's owner expects to subdue the slave's will by threatening him, but the slave who can choose calmly between obedience and punishment ensures that the choice remains *his*, and to that degree remains autonomous, that is, free. Conversely, the master who cannot control his own reactions loses his autonomy. Hegel sees that this is not a satisfying theory of freedom. He is enigmatic about its defects, but he sees the crucial point. The Stoic slave chooses between evils. It is true that the choice is *his*, and we may be impressed by his ability to rise above the fears and anxieties of his non-Stoic fellows, free or slave; nonetheless, we ordinarily think of free choice as a choice between one good and another. The choice that the Stoic insisted we can keep in our own hands, which amounts to the choice between any course of action whatever on the one side and death on the other, is not a free choice. As we saw, Hobbes had to side with the Stoics when he said that our agreement to obey the sovereign who has his sword at out throat is a free choice. Most people would think both the Stoics and Hobbes are just wrong.

Hegel did not complain that the Stoics had tackled the wrong topic. Their subject really was freedom; and Hegel had no doubt that the essence of freedom is that we obey only ourselves. Hegel was always in search of the conditions of autonomy—self-government—in thought and action, and eventually in ethics and politics. He was the heir to Rousseau and Kant. Hegel criticized Rousseau for his belief that states are founded on contracts and criticized Kant both for that and for concentrating on the isolated individual and explaining autonomy in terms of a nonempirical, noumenal self dictating to the merely empirical self. As much as Kant, however, Hegel held that freedom was not simply a matter of the extent to which we were left to our own devices, as Hobbes and his successors claimed. A child cannot be a free agent, because the child's will is unformed; a lunatic cannot be free, because his will is unformable; an addict cannot be free, because his choices do not lie within his own rational control. Nonetheless, the Stoic vision was a retreat from the world, and freedom consists in mastering the world and enjoying it.

The *Philosophy of History*

Hegel's discussion of Stoicism occurs early in the *Phenomenology*. Matters continue through the rise of the individual conscience, the growth of Christianity, and the final resolution of Mind's search for self-understanding in post-Reformation Europe. It is more fruitful for our purposes to follow Hegel's path when he composed his *Encyclopedia of the Philosophical Sciences* for his own students. We should turn to Hegel's philosophy of history and then his account of the rational modern state; Hegel himself ended *The Philosophy of Right* with a thumbnail sketch of the *Philosophy of History*, geared to explicating the sequence of "world-historical epochs" that embody our deepening understanding of freedom.[9]

The *Philosophy of History* was avowedly a "theodicy"; its object was to justify the ways of God to man, save that, as we have seen, "God" is by no means the God of the Old and New Testaments. The *Philosophy of History* ends with the resounding claim that not merely does history not happen "without God"; it is always and everywhere the work of God. If that sounds reassuring, we should notice that Hegel also describes history as a "slaughter bench," a butcher's chopping block. History is a court of judgment as well, and its sentences are death sentences. As if this were not bleak enough, Hegel also insisted that "world history"—*Weltgeschichte*—is not the story of everyone who happens to have existed on the surface of the globe. Very few lives interest philosophical history, because they yield nothing for philosophy to reflect on. The same is true en masse. Even fewer peoples are world-historical peoples than individuals are world-historical individuals. Africa, said Hegel, dismissing the entire continent, was unhistorical; nothing significant for the history of human freedom had come out of Africa, and nothing was likely to.

Although Hegel had a Eurocentric vision of history, he also wondered whether the course of history might be westward across the Atlantic, and the United States be the bearer of some unpredictable future form of human freedom; it was possible, too, that something surprising might come out of Russia, and the future be shared between the United States and Russia. That thought resonated rather powerfully with his modern readers before the collapse of the Soviet Union in 1992.

The *Philosophy of History* offers a triadic history of freedom: human history is the history of freedom, and the development of the concept of freedom has been from a first understanding of freedom as the idea "that one is free," through the thought that "some are free," and on to the understanding that "all men are free." This is not exactly the claim of the *Phenomenology* but not at odds with it. Put so baldly, the claim is hard to swallow at first reading. When we think of the mixture of civil rights and market freedoms that most of us today associate with the "freedom" that liberal democracies promote, we think of freedom as the fragile achievement of a few highly developed and prosperous societies; and we think of "the liberty of the ancients" as embedded in the civic life of Greek and Roman city-states as irreparably lost rather than as somehow subsumed in the freedoms we enjoy today. Nor do most of us think that the freedom achieved in the modern world is "inscribed in history"; it has required luck as well as hard work to achieve, and its future is uncertain. The belief that human history has always been heading toward the achievement of universal freedom is unpersuasive. Hegel did not hold quite such unpersuasive views; nor did he see history as a record of unequivocal progress. He was less convinced of the virtues of modern societies than he sometimes seems, and never quite threw off the nostalgia for ancient Greece that was a marked feature of German intellectual and literary life.

He certainly thought that there was no way of reviving classical politics, and that one reason the French Revolution had collapsed into the Terror was that it pursued inappropriate and anachronistic ideals of citizen virtue. Nor does he look around for modern substitutes. Still, he could not help praising the politics of what he saw as the beautiful youth of humanity, and his conception of what is progressive in our understanding and realization of freedom was neither simple nor linear. This gives his work an interesting flavor. For instance, Socrates anticipated all that Hegel thought valuable in the teachings of Christ, but because freedom had to be embedded within and embodied in the culture and institutions of a particular society, it was the Christian conception of the inner liberty of the individual that—relying on the legal and political culture of the Roman Empire for external sustenance, so to speak—permeated western Europe and our modern consciousness. That leaves wide open the question whether Socrates was not a greater thinker and a better guide than Christ, a question it would have been rash to raise in Hegel's Prussia.

The thought that animates the *Philosophy of History* is not complicated. The human will is the source of freedom. Our first experience of freedom, echoing the discussion of the master-slave dialectic, is making things happen to the world and to other people. So the thought that under oriental despotism one man only is free reflects the fact that the despot alone can act freely and that all others are his slaves. They are objects of his will, not of their own. What does this say about politics? There is no politics in such an environment; there may be discussions of policy, the despot may be under the thumb of advisers and courtiers, not to mention wives and mistresses, his writ may run imperfectly beyond the immediate areas that his armies can subdue, but what there is not is the systematic, public discussion of what a self-governing people should or must do. We have seen how Plato's vision of a polity ruled by philosophers collapses politics into philosophy (or into rational management) by treating the ruler's decisions as the calculation of the answer to a precisely formulated question. As Aristotle said, an aspect of this is that all (rational) wills become one will, and the plurality of legitimate aspirations that makes politics necessary is lost.

Despotism was inconsistent with politics as the Greeks understood it. This conviction sustained them in their long struggle against the Persian Empire at the beginning of the fifth century BCE. The empirically minded will point out that this tidy conceptual opposition was not reflected on the ground, where many Greek cities lived under the sway of the Persians while conducting their own affairs in reasonable con tentment, as they did under the Roman *imperium* later, and Italian city-states under the notional sway of the Holy Roman Empire later still. But Hegel's history is a history of *conceptualizations*; cultures only approximate to those conceptualizations in their practice—the conceptualization is sometimes a reflection on practice, sometimes an ideal, and usually clear only with hindsight. As Hegel wrote in *The Philosophy of Right*, the owl of Minerva flies only at dusk.[10]

The institutionalization of the thought that "some are free" is the Greek polis. The form of freedom that the polis offered was doubly limited. It was limited insofar as the scope of citizenship was limited. To be a politically active citizen in almost every Greek city-state, it was necessary to be a property-owning, arms-bearing native-born male. At Athens, where the extension of democracy went as far as anywhere before the modern world, a citizen had to be descended from citizens. Aristotle was a resident alien and could never have been admitted to citizenship. It was important that citizens were men of military age and capacity, because the crucial decisions they had to make were decisions for peace or war. A man might appear in the assembly, hear the debate, vote for war, and shortly thereafter stand the consequences. All such societies depended heavily upon the existence of slavery. Freedom for some meant servitude for others. Writers on democracy believed for two millennia that the existence of slaves was the price of the leisure that poor Athenians enjoyed, and that allowed them the time to engage in political activity.

Benjamin Constant's famous discussion of the liberty of the ancients and the moderns was in part designed to undermine unthinking nostalgia for the liberty of the ancients by pointing out that its re-creation would demand the reintroduction of slavery, and in part to remind his cultivated liberal listeners what was sacrificed to the all-consuming political life of the ancient world. Constant, however, was more insistent than Hegel that some elements of ancient liberty were necessary to ensure that modern representative government survived and did not turn into some sort of Napoleonic despotism.[11] Unless there were enough active citizens to preserve the rule of law and keep representative institutions in good heart, there would be a return to despotism.

The Greek conception of freedom was inadequate; it was not the recognition that "man as man is free," that is, the recognition that the essence of humanity was liberty. Because Hegel was so insistent that thought is bounded by its time, there was nothing censorious in this view of Greek freedom. It would be absurdly anachronistic to complain that the Greek world did not see what became clear only with the Reformation and Enlightenment. Hegel was also aware that not all elements of the good life can coexist. In his first, youthful writings, he suggested that the beautiful youth of the human race had been lived in classical Greece and that the modern world was a very pale reflection of it. At the end of his life, he seems to have stopped hankering after Athens. In the *Philosophy of History*, he still thought that Athens had achieved something the modern world cannot achieve but can envy. This was an aesthetic unity of everyday life, in which there was a harmony between individual and society of a sort we cannot now recover. For us Athenian patriotism would be claustrophobic and oppressive; for the Athenians, the identity as Athenians was the condition of freedom. For us, the absence of the respect for the individual conscience, which is the gift of the Reformation, would undermine freedom.

The Inadequacy of Greek Institutions

The unity of individual and polis was fragile. Greek politics was always on the verge of degenerating into civil war, and the Greek city-states could never coalesce as a single Greek state or as a solid enough confederation to resist Philip of Macedon, his son Alexander the Great, or the expanding Roman Republic. However, Hegel saw Socrates as the death knell of Athens. He was more important even than Alexander; Socrates's insistence on obeying his *daemon* even when it led him to his death revealed the shallowness of the unity of individual and polity; it revealed that true individual autonomy lay beyond the political ideal of the self-governing citizen. True autonomy is founded in our ability to govern ourselves by the light of reason. This is the crux of Hegel's account of freedom. Freedom cannot be no more than a matter of acting without coercion from others; that would imply that the madman was free so long as nobody else forced him to do what he did. Yet we all know that the madman cannot be free, because he is incapable of exercising self-control. The absence of coercion by others is a condition of freedom, but freedom itself is autonomy, prescribing to ourselves the rules we follow. Since a coherent system of rules is the only one we can live by, freedom is ultimately a matter of following the rules that reason prescribes. The absence of coercion allows us to follow the promptings of reason, so we are right to think of noncoercion as essential to liberty. It is nonetheless not the whole story.

Socrates shows the inadequacy of the freedom of the Greek city-state, but that is only one of his roles; Socrates also prefigured Christ, and the full implications of his insistence on following his *daemon* had to await the working out of the Christian understanding of the world. The other key figure in the destruction of Greek freedom was Alexander the Great, whose physical impact on the Greek city-states of the fourth century BCE needs no elaboration. Alexander is less important to Hegel's story than Socrates, because Socrates showed the *philosophical* or *conceptual* inadequacy of the world-spirit as manifested in Greek culture; Alexander only—although "only" must be taken with a pinch of salt— showed the inadequacy of Greek political organization. Alexander also illustrates the way in which history is propelled by individuals who are simultaneously important and unimportant. Alexander died at the age of thirty-three, perhaps from malaria, perhaps from liver failure, or perhaps from poison. If it was indeed the first, we might well indulge in some clichéd reflections on the vanity of human affairs as we reflected on the king who sighed because there were no more worlds to conquer, but was undone by an insect. Hegel draws a larger historical and philosophical moral: history used Alexander to write finis under humanity's experiment with the Greek conception of freedom and, having done with him, tossed him aside.

Hegel's notion of the hero in history is thus ironic; he certainly believed in the existence of world-historical individuals, of whom Napoleon was one; thus far, he subscribed to the great-man theory of history, the view that historical progress is driven by the doings of heroes. Yet Hegel is famous for the observation that Truth lies not in the individual but in the Whole. The greatness of great men is not theirs but an element of the role they play in the whole drama. The irony lies in the way Hegel insists both that history needs great individuals to do its work and that, once that work is accomplished, history will toss them aside as spent forces. Whatever brought about Alexander's death was an accident in the scheme of things; that *something* had to get him off the stage of history is, Hegel implies, anything but an accident.

Hegel's *Philosophy of History* is a work that ought to make anyone of an analytical philosophical bent uneasy. There is no simple way of understanding Hegel's insistence that his philosophy is a "theodicy." When Hegel says that history not only does not happen "without God" but is everywhere and always the work of God, it is not at all obvious what that implies. The simplest of the many ways in which we might understand it is that Hegel insists that history makes sense; it is not "one damn thing after another" as Henry Ford supposed, nor "a tale told by an idiot, full of sound and fury, signifying nothing," as Macbeth more thoughtfully claimed. It is certainly a tale of sound and fury; it is, after all, a slaughter bench, and a court before which cultures and nations appear and receive their death sentences; but it is far from signifying nothing. It is also far from being a drama behind which there stands a personal deity, the author whose script we are ordained to act out. The idea of a drama that, so to speak, writes itself is not an easy one to grasp.

Nonetheless, once we appreciate Hegel's affection for the world of the ancient Greeks, and his understanding of its inadequacies, we know the plot. The Christian conception of the infinite value of the individual soul will ground inward freedom, and a legal-rational state will ground outward freedom. In a society where religion is not superstition and the rule of law is not a fig leaf behind which autocracy rules, freedom is actualized. *All* will be free. The sense in which we shall all be free is different from the sense in which the Persian autocrat was free or the Athenian citizen was free. Our freedom will be rational autonomy, neither arbitrary, as was the power of the despot, nor engulfed in loyalty to the polity, as was the freedom of the Athenian citizen. Hegel conducts his readers through a complex journey to just this end result. The Roman contribution to rational freedom—the rule of law and the efficient, if soulless, administration of public affairs—combines with the Christian contribution—the world-renouncing search for freedom in the form of submission to God's will—and provides the resources for an individualism that Hegel finds acceptable. Among the dead ends that Hegel rejects on behalf of History is pure asceticism—the search for freedom in abandoning the ties of the world—another is the overrational attempt to govern ourselves and the world by Kantian ethics. The modern constitutional state is the proper home for our aspirations, as he explains in *The Philosophy of Right*.

The Philosophy of Right

Hegel provides a via media that is more than the commonsensical but commonplace thought that we must balance the competing claims of community and individual, tradition and reason, as best we can. Only the community that can provide a satisfying, morally serious, freedom-enhancing life has claims on us; only the individuality that is consistent with being a dutiful member of a community has a claim to respect. Only the tradition that culminates in a rationally acceptable system of law and conventional morality—*Sittlichkeit*—has any claim on an intelligent being, and only rationally defensible ethical principles that can be embedded in habit and custom have any claim to form the basis of our politics. This is the basis of his claim that Reason embodies itself in the practices of a concrete community, that of post-Reformation Europe. That is why Hegel entitled the volume of his *Encyclopedia of the Philosophical Sciences* that dealt with history and politics "objective mind." He describes this community as "the German World" and has often been misunderstood as defending German nationalism and claiming that only the Germans can create a free politics. He thought nothing of the sort, and his immediate successors in Germany complained with much more reason that he was not a German nationalist at all. "The German World" is Europe west of the Elbe; it is Charlemagne's Europe, the Europe that was fed by the Latin Christian tradition, by memories of the glories of Rome, and by the wilder and less tamed individualism of the German tribes that resisted Romanization. It had learned the importance of individual conscience and of social order, and even if its political organization was far from fully manifesting the principles that legitimated it, it was an instantiation, however imperfect, of concrete freedom and practical reason.

The work that explains these principles is one of the simplest of Hegel's works. *The Philosophy of Right* does not have the narrative flair of the *Philosophy of History* or the extraordinary energy of the *Phenomenology*, but it has a lucid structure, and its purpose and argument are easy to grasp. "Simple" is a relative term in the context of Hegel's work, and *The Philosophy of Right* is complicated enough; Hegel offered a thumbnail sketch of its arguments in the third volume of his *Encyclopedia of Philosophical Sciences*. The social world is the world of "objective mind," which is to say the world in which intelligence is embodied in institutions whose meaning must be elicited by the philosopher, but whose rationality is prereflectively apparent to the participants in those institutional arrangements.

The subject matter of *The Philosophy of Right* is what the title suggests: what the rule of law entails, what rights we have in the modern world, how they are generated, and how the modern state that creates these rights is legitimated. It is a treatise in philosophical jurisprudence rather than a treatise on politics. Politics as the rough-and-tumble of political life is markedly absent, and politics as the negotiation of compromises between conflicting interests fares little better. The subject is the way in which the rational will is expressed in social and political life and embodied in institutions. What this means is best seen by contrast. For Bentham, as for all utilitarians, the subject matter of political theory is how to craft institutions that produce maximum happiness for those they affect. Utility, not reason, drives the argument; or, rather, what reason prescribes is whatever affords the greatest utility to everyone whose interests are under consideration. Hegel thought that happiness was too vague, shifting, and indeterminate a goal to provide a test of the reasonableness of political institutions. Most of us take our ideas about our own happiness from what happens to others, so that success in "keeping up with the Joneses" is the greater part of the happiness of socialized mankind. Hobbes, however—and Hegel declared that political science began with Hobbes—builds politics on the will, which Hegel thought the right place to begin. The authority of Hobbes's sovereign rests on the will of the sovereign's subjects. Each says to each, "I will obey this man or body of men if thou dost likewise," and on that commitment political authority arises. This is not enough for Hegel, for these are particular, individual wills, and the mere say-so of each subject cannot vouch for the rationality of the resulting institutions.

Hegel's theory is based on will, not on the pursuit of happiness. But it is not the empirical will of individuals. For Hegel, we are free only when we follow the dictates of our rational wills. Since that will must be the same for all rational beings, it is a general will, but it is unlike anything envisaged by Rousseau. It is not the will of persons who look for abstract rules of conduct that they propose to impose on themselves but a will that grows out of their social interactions and emerges from the lives that they are taught to lead by education and socialization and whose rationality they come to understand retrospectively and reflectively. Hegel thought that the French Revolution had run amok because the revolutionaries had seen the general will in much the way Rousseau had done. They had imagined the general will as an objective emanation that imposed itself on the human will as if it was a natural force. But such a will was contentless. *What* it demanded could not be deduced from the mere fact that it required the same thing of all rational creatures. Without some way of filling in the content of this will that was itself rationally acceptable, the results would be the caprice of one individual or another—which is to say, in the last resort, the arbitrary choices of a Robespierre. One cannot imagine Edmund Burke reading Hegel with pleasure, but Hegel's argument is Burkean.

Hegel divided *The Philosophy of Right* into several interlinked sections; they form two triadic structures, one conceptual, the other institutional. Conceptually, the sections are "abstract right," "morality," and "ethical life." These labels are not self-explanatory, and not only because the German *Moralität* and *Sittlichkeit* do not have the resonances of their English translations. A German reader who had followed Hegel's philosophical progress from the *Phenomenology* to *The Philosophy of Right* would have known that Hegel had earlier described *Sittlichkeit* as an underdeveloped form of ethical consciousness. In that context, *Sittlichkeit* meant "customary morality" and its inadequacy lay in its failure to allow for rational reflection. But "ethical life" in *The Philosophy of Right* is rational as well as customary; it is the institutionalized moral consciousness of the most rational form of society the world has yet produced, the society of post-Reformation western Europe. *Moralität*—of which the obvious translation is "morality"—is morality in the abstract, ungrounded in our attachments to our families, fellows, and nation. The second triad is easier to describe. This is the division of the realm of ethical life into the family, civil society, and the state; these might be called different facets of the institutionalization of modern moral life. What Hegel discusses under these headings is both narrower and wider than an ordinary understanding might suggest, but the logic is clear enough.

Hegel's discussion of civil society in particular draws on an existing tradition of social and political analysis and does something novel with it. In the final decade of the twentieth century, the concept of civil society was on everyone's mind, because the collapse of the communist autocracies of Eastern Europe and the Soviet Union was thought to demonstrate, among many other things, the deficiencies of regimes with weak civil societies. These countries had poorly developed legal arrangements governing trade and production, and lacked the intermediate associations—trade unions, commercial associations, interest groups, and charitable, social, and sporting societies—that operated independently of government to secure the welfare of their members, provide services to others, and articulate their concerns to those who ran the political system narrowly considered. The civil society that was said to be absent or lacking in vitality was civil society as Hegel had conceived it.

The Philosophy of Right begins with a famous preface in which Hegel announces that the goal of political philosophy is to achieve understanding and not to offer advice. This is not a startling claim, but it may have been the first time it had been made. From Plato to Rousseau, advice was just what philosophers gave. Hegel always differentiated sharply between the practical knowledge embodied in *doing* and the theoretical knowledge that was the province of the philosopher; but it was his turn of phrase that made his preface famous. Philosophy arrives on the scene too late to give advice. It paints its gray on gray only when a form of life has grown old. The owl of Minerva flies at dusk.[12] That claim enraged the young Marx and puzzled others; but Hegel did not mean that philosophy was useless. Becoming reconciled to reality with the assistance of philosophy may not have an immediate payoff, but it is nonetheless important. Hegel harks back both to Aristotle and to Spinoza in claiming that a man who understands the world does not rail against it. Philosophy reconciles us to necessity.

Hegel starts with an introduction that his hearers in the lecture hall may well have found very hard work. But he soon announces the principle that holds the key to all else. "The basis of right is the *realm of spirit* in general and its precise location and point of departure is the *will*; the will is *free*, so that freedom constitutes its substance and destiny and the system of right is the realm of actualized freedom, the world of spirit produced from within itself as a second nature."[13] There could be no system of rights unless there were creatures who had desires and needed rules to control and to license those desires; being a slave to impulse is not freedom, so freedom must consist in *autonomy*, which is to say in being self-governing and in following the path of the rational will. It is from this that a concern for rights flows; rights bearers live in a framework of well-ordered rules that confer rights and duties on them, and allow them to interact as persons. To understand what that implies, we must know what rights we need, and what social arrangements they structure.

Abstract Right

The first section of Hegel's *Philosophy of Right*, called "abstract right," is concerned with the nature of property rights. It seems an odd title for a discussion of property rights. What could be more concrete than property? The answer is that the abstractness of abstract right is not that the *objects* of the right are abstract, in the way that copyrights are abstract and books are not, but that the relationship between person and thing is characterized abstractly. The principle of right is that persons recognize persons as such and recognize their rights as the rights of persons; thus,

I respect your ownership of your car not because you are my sister and I do not wish to distress you by taking your car but because the car is *yours* and *not mine.* Its fate is for your will to determine, and I respect that fact. It does not matter who you happen to be; it matters that you are the person who has ownership of the thing, a relationship that makes the thing something we must respect as belonging to another person. This may sound far-fetched, but it captures what we ordinarily think about property relations. We do not think that your ownership of the bicycle is to be respected because the bike is fabricated from steel and rubber; we respect the fact that it is your property. We respect the legal personality of others by keeping our hands off their things, "things" in this context meaning anything ownable, including such nonphysical things as copyrights.

That raises two large questions: why start with ownership rights, and how does anyone acquires ownership of anything? Rights, for Hegel, are grounded in possession of some sort. This is because property is about control. Property licenses or authorizes possession, and in every legal system possession can "ripen" into ownership. My right to act as a free agent, which seems intuitively prior to property rights, manifests possession, in this case my possession of my physical self. When I swing my hand, I manifest my possession of the physical stuff of which my arm and hand are made; if they were someone else's, I could have no right over them, and from this it follows that my rock-bottom rights over myself are possessory. This is not the banality that if I am to raise my arm, there must be an arm that I can raise. It is the thought that acting on the world affirms my right to act. That means that when I "put my will" into my hand or arm—which is what I do when I voluntarily raise my arm—I have rightful possession of *this* body. They are not rights of ownership, because full ownership involves the right to dispose of things, to destroy them or trade them for other things; and Hegel, conventionally enough, thinks that we cannot destroy our bodies without destroying ourselves, and that we do not therefore *own* ourselves.[14] I am "my own property" inasmuch as *nobody else* can own me, however.

Slavery is therefore absolutely wrong, although Hegel character-istically fudges the issue by saying that slavery once had a place in a world where wrong was partial right.[15] What that perhaps means is this: a utilitarian might argue that slavery was prima facie wrong, because people do not like being enslaved, are usually treated badly, may suffer violence and cruelty, and suffer the sort of indignity that most people deeply resent. But this seems inadequate; it provides only prima facie arguments against slavery, and many people think that, like torture, slavery is wrong in a deep and absolute way. Even if there is no point in reproaching ancient Greece and Rome, we may still want to say that the practice was wrong, and is wrong whenever and wherever it occurs. To confuse the uselessness of complaining at the ancient world with the acceptability of the evil is inept. Moreover, any utilitarian argument is vulnerable to factual evidence; we might find that in some societies the enslaved have no sense of dignity, do not resent being enslaved, do not mind being owned by someone else, and are treated less brutally than the poorer members of the free population. They are the "happy slaves" of the political theorist's imagination, and that of the defenders of slavery in nineteenth-century America. If happy slaves exist, they are a problem for the utilitarian. Finally, it is vulnerable to the thought that the miseries endured by persons at one time are justified by the happiness of others, then or later. Mill observed that "despotism is a legitimate mode of government in dealing with barbarians," and slavery a necessary stage in educating a population into the habits of rational cooperation.[16]

A strictly rights-based condemnation of slavery cuts through all these arguments. It might, however, be thought to be *too* absolute. There are many kinds of slavery, and few of them were as bad as the chattel slavery of the American South; slaves in the ancient world led very different lives; some slaves were slave owners themselves. These arguments pass Hegel by. He was not interested in "trade-offs" between rights on the one hand and utilitarian considerations on the other. He thought that there was an epoch when modern conceptions of human rights did not make the sense they make now. Under those conditions, "wrong" was "right." Hegel was not hostile to utilitarian arguments in their place: utilitarian considerations prompt mankind to devise a system of rights over things and ourselves in the first place. Persons with no interest in using the world would have no incentive to develop a conception of rights.

Nonetheless, for Hegel rights are not utilitarian devices, as they are for Bentham, for instance. Utilitarian considerations provide a springboard from which rights-based relationships are launched. Once launched, they have their own logic. So we may be forced to agree that there was a period when the rule of right was impossible and wrong had a place and a partial claim to be right.

Free labor is quite unlike slavery; we must be able freely to sell *part* of our time to an employer, while remaining essentially free.[17] The claim does two different things, one of them not entirely to Hegel's purpose. On the one side it distinguishes the modern free laborer, who makes a wage contract with an employer from the indentured servant of old who is taken into someone else's household, and is for the duration under their control. Hegel had an acute sense of that contrast; serfdom still existed in parts of Prussia. The American colonists had an equally acute sense of the contrast fifty years before. But on the other side it opens the door for the claim that a modern worker who sells to an employer all the hours during which he can work, and then falls exhausted into bed, is really a slave; his conscious human life is wholly owned by someone else. This was a thought that Marx made much of when he found Hegel standing on his head and set him right side up.

This leaves us in the right place to consider Hegel's account of property rights and their place in moral and political life. Hegel takes as a given the absolute right of the free will to put itself into any unoccupied thing. This is a moral tautology. To be unoccupied is to be an entity that a free will may take over and occupy. This was Hegel's treatment of freedom in the "master-slave" dialectic, where he insisted that the valueless world of things derives its value from human occupancy. Ownership lends things a human quality by infusing them with our wills. This sounds more dramatic, or romantic, than Hegel means; it is not what happens to the object that concerns him so much as the skein of human relationships that our dealings with objects bring into existence. Thus Hegel goes on to obliterate the lawyers' distinction between rights *ad personam*—rights against persons—and rights *in rem*—rights over things; all rights are rights against persons and therefore personal. It is our relations with one another as persons that matter, and the treatment of things is a facet of those relations. Things do not respond to us, have no rights against us or duties to us, and do not feature in the narrative. The question is how we give our purposes to the external world. Hegel's subtlety is well to the fore in the explication. Many writers try to reduce all forms of acquisition to one—Locke tried to make work the basis of ownership and struggled to assimilate to work activities that involved little or nothing of what we usually think of as work. Hegel might have chosen to do something similar, given how far his emphasis on the will stresses the activity of mind and the passivity of things. He does not.

Acquisition

He appeals to another triad. The simplest form of possession is consumption. Even animals achieve this; the right of life over the means of its support is manifested in this humble activity. It is a nice rhetorical trick on Hegel's part; if even a sheep nibbling the grass exemplifies the mastery of mind over matter, the argument is won.[18] Then he moves on to the two decisive elements. Here Hegel gives hostages to fortune whom he rescues, though they do not remain rescued. The second way of taking possession is by working. Consumption annihilates nature; work transforms it. Working takes raw materials and turns them into something useful; the thing now has a history, and has been taken into the world of human activity. This opens the door to all sorts of interesting conjectures about the extent to which different forms of work might give us different degrees of ownership; modern European copyright law has taken up some of them by giving the creators of artistic work continuing rights over the use of their work after they have sold the copyright, even absent specific provisions. Hegel had no intention of licensing the thought that the man who puts wheel nuts on the wheels of the car that moves past him on the assembly line owns the car. He knew that the laborer acquired no ownership rights by his work. Hegel's concern is different, and not clearly articulated. If we think of *prelegal* acquisition, the individual's transformation of nature secures possession. This is the Lockean view. Once there is a legal system and the worker's return for his efforts is his pay rather than part ownership of the objects he works on, the focus moves, and we have the thought that it is human intelligence that is embodied in the world on which humans have worked, and that the property rights at stake are not the individual property rights we are all familiar with but all the rights that are mediated by things.

Different kinds of work attach us to the world our work transforms in different ways. A familiar view is that activities such as agricultural labor really root us in the world as desk work does not. Hegel does nothing with such a contrast here, but when he comes to discuss the way in which different economic activities are represented in politics, he makes much of it, because he sees it bound up with the lifestyle and allegiances of different "estates" or classes and how they should be represented in the state. If work only ambiguously grounds property, the third element in this trio unequivocally does what is needed. The most emphatic mode of taking possession is to *mark* something as *mine*. The obvious complaint against this as an explanation of how we own anything is that it puts the cart before the horse. We are trying to explicate the basis of ownership; to say that what we use, we own, makes a certain sense. It says that one way of fixing a right in something is simply to use it. Equally, to say that when we alter something by working on it we make it ours has a certain sense. Both square with the Roman law notion of the natural modes of acquisition.

To say that we acquire a right by asserting it affronts common sense; but Hegel is right. What he says has its counterpart in the rule of Roman law that someone who takes what belongs to nobody and *intends to be taken as* its owner is the owner. Common law rules of adverse possession reflect a similar assumption that what matters is the intention to be taken as the owner. The appearance of circularity is due to Hegel's genetic method; it is easy to think that his aim is to explain the ways in which a new concept emerges from a background where no such concept exists. He is not doing that; he is rationalizing concepts that we are familiar with. The exigencies of life demand that we consume, work on and with, and organize the distribution of things we need. Unless we can simply mark things as ours, there can be no such things as contracts; but if there were no such things as contracts, we would find ourselves unable not only to acquire things but also to release ourselves from ownership of them.

Once he has proprietorship firmly in place, Hegel can move rapidly. Contract is a novelty; the owner does not abandon his property for another to pick up; the transferred object remains *owned* throughout the transfer. Hegel says, not very plausibly, that the owners remain the owners of something that remains the same throughout the transaction: the value of what is transferred. One can see what he means; I sell you a bicycle for thirty dollars, and although you hand over thirty dollars and I hand over the bicycle, I remain entitled to thirty dollars or its equivalent throughout. To couch it in terms of owning anything is far-fetched. It is also vulnerable to counterexamples. You may know that the open-market value of my bicycle is twenty dollars but pay me thirty because you want it so much. It is not obvious that I really owned thirty dollars of value just because you wanted it more than other people.

Moralität

Hegel's purpose is not to draw interesting patterns on legal textbooks by classifying the forms of contract and the rights they create in the contracting parties—though he does that—but to push the argument forward to the discussion of morality, "ethical life," civil society, and the state. The transition is made via the idea of wrongs and punishment. The expression is opaque, but, as usual, something interesting is at issue. If people equipped with property rights can transfer their rights, we can elucidate the obvious distinction between my giving you my property and your stealing it. When you steal my book, you so to speak pass yourself off as the owner of what is mine; for my ownership to be secure, I must be able to rely on your not doing such things. That implies penalties for breaches of right, and the existence of social pressure to induce people to internalize those penalties in the dictates of conscience. If people did not feel conscientiously obliged to respect each other's rights, we could not rely on that forbearance. To put it pictorially, when I steal what is yours,

I do not merely move an object to a different place; I have committed a wrong and I will, if I have a conscience, feel guilt.

When conscience appears on the scene as an internal lawgiver and judge, we have morality, in the narrow sense in which it is to be contrasted with the realm of what Hegel calls "ethical life."[19] What Hegel is doing is contrasting a purely abstract morality evolved by an isolated individual from first principles with the morality embedded in actual ways of life. He has in his sights morality as analyzed by Immanuel Kant in the *Groundwork of the Metaphysics of Morals*. Kant claimed that as moral beings we are governed by rational maxims, which are valid in virtue of their noncontradictory nature. All mistaken maxims, according to Kant, generated contradictions; for instance, the principle that lying is permissible is self-defeating, because lying itself depends on the acceptance that when we say anything we are supposed to be telling the truth. Absent that presumption, all communication fails. Hegel acknowledges the sublimity of Kant's insistence that the dictates of duty and the demands of reason must coincide; but he denies that we can hold ourselves, let alone our social and political institutions, to the standards Kant claims. He launches both a frontal and a flanking attack.

The frontal attack is the familiar claim that Kant's "noncontradiction" principle cannot generate an ethical system unless it is supplemented by an appeal to consequences. Kant's argument against suicide, for instance, was that if we all commit suicide, nobody is left to follow the injunction to kill ourselves. If we do not care that the human race has come to an end, the argument fails. The flanking attack is more interesting and contentious; Hegel implies that Kant's conception of morality—not, of course, Kant—was responsible for the French Revolution's descent into the Terror. The problem was the combination of an extreme moral individualism with an equally extreme rationalism; figures such as Robespierre believed themselves morally infallible, and therefore believed their opponents to be either mad or evil or both. Finally, Kant's insistence that the individual's reason is the final court of judgment before which institutions, actions, and even the dictates of God himself are to be tried was anathema to Hegel. Hegel's slogan that the truth lies in the whole was not, as it has often been taken to be, a form of state worship but an enigmatic way of saying that the proper balance of individual liberty and state authority requires us to look at the needs and values of an entire social and political order. Unlike most liberals, Hegel did not think that individuals had rights against the state—in the last resort, the whole trumps the part.

Ethical Life: *Sittlichkeit*

Now Hegel can turn to his account of the institutions of the rational modern political community. Once again, we encounter a triadic analysis: the family, civil society, and the state. Once again, the simple analysis is that the family is the realm of subjective affection where the institution is held together by love between particular individuals; civil society is the realm of instrumental, means-end, profit-based relationships whose institutions are sustained by our perception of our long-term self-interest; and the state is the realm of loyalty to country and nation rather than to particular others, noninstrumentally constituted and held together by our readiness to sacrifice our interests for its sake. In fact, that simple thought is a good guide to the way Hegel sets out his triad, though it suggests little of the richness of the insights scattered throughout the argument.

Hegel's contrasts do not fall neatly into the categories of common sense. Hegel does not think of the family anthropologically or historically, as the primordial or originative form of social life; he has the modern nuclear family in mind, and the modern family is constituted and protected by the legal arrangements put in place by the modern constitutional state. Similarly, civil society is not the apolitical society of voluntary exchange imagined in Locke's account of the state of nature; it is permeated by politics and structured by laws, and managed by the institutions of a well-ordered administrative state. It is much more than the system of exchange studied by economists, including as it does the laws, culture, institutions, and attitudes appropriate to modern economic life. Hegel says that his predecessors confused the state with civil society and misidentified the state with what is truly civil society; that is a plausible criticism of Locke. Hegel explains the state in terms of the constitutional arrangements appropriate to a rational modern state and ends with a lightning sketch of what it means for the state to be one state among others at a particular time in history. It is because the state is one state among others that it may have to resort to war to preserve its own identity, and it is in his discussion of the state's right to demand that citizens lay down their lives for its survival that Hegel makes some alarming but plausible claims about the value of warfare in giving everyday life a point that it may otherwise lack.

The Family

The family represents one aspect of the demands of "ethical life." It is a realm of unselfish attachment to particular other people, based on the love of two adults and devoted to the end of bringing up children who will make their own way in the world in due course.[20] It is a realm of subjectivity: we fall in love with particular other people and have no need to justify doing so. We are married to *this* husband or wife, and not to *a* husband or wife. Hegel very much disliked Kant's bleak account of marriage as a contract for the mutual use of the sexual organs (though there are ways of rescuing Kant from the criticism) and insisted that marriage was not a contract.[21] The interest of the family for Hegel, however, is that it is not self-sufficient. This is not quite Aristotle's thought that the good life cannot be lived within a family only, but requires a polis; Hegel's thought is that the point of the family is to launch children into the world as adults; a given family is intended not to endure. Children must leave the altruistic world of family relations within which they are cared for out of love and make their way in the realm of civil society, where they must secure their living by working and where their rights will be based on contracts of one sort and another.

Civil Society

Hegel fights a battle on two fronts in his discussion of the *bürgerliche Gesellschaft*, or "civil society." On the one side, his predecessors had discussed civil society when they purported to be discussing the state; on the other, they had not fully understood civil society, either. Civil society is the realm of contractual relationships; it is nonintimate as against the family, and it is built on individual self-interest, as the state is not. Once more, Kant's conception of the state as based on a hypothetical contract to protect prepolitical individual rights is silently repudiated.

Civil society is the world of work and exchange, where our actions are coordinated not by a rational will to secure the welfare of the whole but by Adam Smith's "invisible hand." A devoted reader of classical economics, Hegel knew what he was explaining and criticizing. The individual promotes the general interest in promoting his own, but he is not motivated by an intention to do so. His motivation is his own economic benefit, which he pursues within the framework of legal rights that make concrete the abstract proprietorship that Hegel had earlier discussed. The interest of Hegel's account lies in three areas. The first is the triadic structure he offers as an analytical guide to his account of civil society; the second, his account of the social structure appropriate to and generated by civil society; and the third, his reflections on the way institutions can be created to "mop up" unwanted side effects of the operations of a market society. The triadic structure of civil society shows what Hegel had in mind when he complained that his predecessors had mistaken civil society for the state. For the three analytical frameworks he provides are "the system of needs; the administration of justice; the police and the corporation."[22] By "police" he means the regulatory system that ancien régime societies commonly operated. Hegel's predecessors had— he thought—conflated what he describes as the administration of justice with the province of the state strictly speaking, which was the realm of constitutional arrangements, and the activities of the state as an actor on a historical stage.

The system of needs is what later writers might describe as a regulated capitalist economy; relations are market relations, and owners are largely free to dispose of their capital as they choose, to buy and sell at will, and to employ or dismiss whomever they choose. The most interesting part of the discussion is Hegel's introduction of a trio of social classes—or "estates" (the German is *Stände*)—that form a hinge between civil society and the representative system by which the needs of civil society enter the institutions of the state proper. Unlike most writers, Hegel did not divide society into owners and nonowners, nor did he divide them into classes according to the sort of property they employed: the classical economists' trio of landlords, capitalists, and laborers. He split them into those who worked on the land and those who worked in the nonlanded economy, so that professionals such as lawyers and doctors belonged with the owners of mercantile and industrial capital; over and above the two productive classes stood what he called "the universal class," which is to say the administrators and officials who formed a class, not in virtue of what they owned, but in view of their vocation as the promoters of the general good, the common interests of society.[23] Unlike Saint-Simon, who thought that the government of men would give way to the administration of things, Hegel is infinitely far from envisaging the withering away of the state. Nonetheless, his emphasis on the "universal class" of administrators is squarely in the line of thought that sees a modern industrial society as something to be managed by experts. Hegel discusses a fourth social element that is not strictly a social class, or group with a stake in the political system, but a social problem; the *Pöbel* is the underclass of the unemployed and unemployables, who form a "rabble of paupers," whose condition "agitates and torments modern societies especially."[24]

"Corporations," by which Hegel means professional guilds, integrate individuals into the economic life of society by giving them a career and allegiances to their professional colleagues. Hegel says somewhat sniffily that young men often find this restrictive when they are young, and see the constraints of their profession as something external and coercive; but they grow out of it and their working lives become part of what secures their identity and their freedom. The more interesting thoughts are those that make Hegel vulnerable to Marx, and vice versa. The first is Hegel's distinction between agricultural and other sorts of work. Hegel assigns the agrarian class the title of the *substantial* class, because its members are attached not to property they can buy and sell but to *this farm*; they represent patience and a willingness to trust in what God sends, while the so-called *formal* class will busily get out of one line of business and into another in search of profit wherever it can be had. Marx initially thought that *all* forms of property in the modern economy had become mere capital, fluid as water, and that the agrarian sector could be discounted because it was simply backward. The events of 1848 taught him better. The second is Hegel's invocation of the administrative class's capacity for disinterested management in the public interest. Marx was savagely critical of Hegel's account of their role and insisted that to the extent they were a class, it was because they owned the state. It is a nice joke, but Hegel was more nearly right than Marx, and capitalism turned out to be more amenable to management by governments that took the task seriously than Marx dreamed it could be.

Hegel agreed with critics of early nineteenth-century capitalism that it produced far too many unwanted side effects. The unpredictability of agricultural markets and food supplies meant that there was always a danger of sudden poverty and in the worst cases famine, and throughout the economy unpredictable booms and slumps threatened people's livelihoods and political stability. It was long after 1850 that old-fashioned famine ceased to threaten European countries, to reappear in the twentieth century as the effect of war throughout Europe and of Stalin's mismanagement in the Soviet Union. Hegel offered a regulatory role to government, understanding that the stability of the economy, the security of government, and the happiness of individuals all depended on it. Marx thought such old-fashioned attempts at stabilization would damage a capitalist economy and would anyway be prevented by capitalists wishing not to see their profits diminished by the taxes they would have to pay to provide help to the indigent. Hegel came very close to providing a justification for the modern welfare state by pointing to the virtues of dispassionate official provision as contrasted with the vagaries of individual charity. He also noticed the dangers of indiscriminate welfare in undermining the self-respect of its recipients, who were, after all, members of a society where everyone was supposed to be self-supporting. Whatever else, the English, and more especially Scottish, decision "to leave the poor to their fate and direct them to beg from the public" will not do. Hegel concludes that it is not clear whether market economies can be wholly tamed, and suggests that emigration and colonization may be necessary to take the burden off European states.[25]

The State

Hegel's confidence in the administrative capacity of the modern state is impressive. His account of the state itself is unexciting. An entirely proper retort is that it is not intended to be exciting; it is meant to be a coherent account of the way the state relates to other institutions and how it can demand our allegiance even when it sends us off to risk death and injury in war. This is quite right, but raises the question whether Hegel allows enough room for men as *citizens* as distinct from the efficiently managed *subjects* of a well-run administrative machine. One response to that would be that Hegel was a realist; the modern state could not be modeled on Periclean Athens or republican Rome, and we must grow out of the nostalgic fantasy that it can be. Certainly, Hegel's attempts to balance modernity and tradition have their own fascination.

One such is his account of the representative system; a rational state must allow for the representation of interests, and the will of the people must be, he says, both respected and despised, which is a somewhat dramatic way of making the point that ordinary people know well enough whether affairs are being handled well or badly, but cannot spontaneously make policy as experts can. This would not have come as news to moderate Athenian democrats, but it suggests limits to genuine self-government and suggests that those limits will be drawn more tightly in a complex modern society, where the need for expertise is so much greater than before. Hegel seeks to represent the public through the *Stände*, thinking that corporate representation is necessary for the representation of the "formal" estate, which, as he says in his discussion of civil society, needs the discipline and organization provided by corporations or guilds to offset its tendency to fragmentation; the substantial or agricultural estate is represented by major landowners, and the universal class by senior officials. For all his talk of the owl of Minerva's flying only at dusk, Hegel cannot escape the temptation to offer advice on how to tinker with the institutional arrangements with which he was familiar.

Once again, Hegel offers us a triadic framework with which to consider the state: the constitution, international relations, and the stage of world history. The excitement occurs in the last two sections, which are very much the shortest. Hegel's account of the constitution contains two surprises. One is the insistence that a modern state must be a constitutional monarchy—which seems to slight the successful examples of absolutist Prussia and republican America; it is at least possible that Hegel would have counted a presidential regime as a form of constitutional monarchy, even though the president of the United States even then did much more than "cross the t's and dot the i's of legislation," the role Hegel assigns the monarch. Hegel's argument is not in the mainstream of discussions of a government balancing the one, the few, and the many. A monarchical element or moment in the structure is more nearly a dictate of logic than of prudence: when we assemble the premises of an argument, the decision to draw the conclusion is a *decision*, and Hegel's vision of dotting the i's and crossing the t's reflects the thought that there must be a final moment when a law becomes law. When the queen or president signs a bill, she or he transforms it from bill to act.

The other interesting element is a long and complicated discussion of the state's role in the religious life of the citizen. Indeed, the commentary to section 270 is the longest of all the passages of explication in *The Philosophy of Right*.[26] Prussia had an established Lutheran Church, but Hegel argues that although the state may need the support of faith and religion, the crucial aspect of the relationship of church and state is the need for separation. No church should exercise coercive power, and no state should inspect the religious beliefs of its citizens. The obvious implication is the need to remove all disabilities stemming from the religious attachments of the citizenry, but Hegel does not go so far. Indeed, Hegel followed Kant in one of his less likable thoughts, which was that

Jewish sabbatarianism and Jewish dietary laws made Jews only dubious members of a modern civil society. After the defeat of Napoleon, Prussia reintroduced legal disabilities aimed at restricting the economic activities of Jews. University censorship would have made it difficult for Hegel to speak out on such issues even if he had been inclined to. The evidence is that he was not. Yet Hegel had elsewhere argued that modern *Sittlichkeit* had a religious as well as a political and cultural aspect, which misled some commentators to think he was deifying the Prussian state. It is more plausible that Hegel was deflating the role of religion; this was the man who said that reading the newspaper was a form of morning prayer.

Hegel accepted the familiar Montesequieuan account of the division of powers into legislative, judicial, and executive, argued for a legislature in which members of the landed nobility have a house of their own and administrators sit in parliament, condemned democracy as an exaggerated and excessive way of allowing ordinary people to participate in government, and offered something not unlike Burke's doctrine of virtual representation to palliate the fact that he feared the effects of any expansion of the franchise. Earlier in his life, he had found himself puzzled to know who in a German context—his native Württemberg—could be trusted to put forward intelligent ideas for political change; neither officials, nor the existing representatives, nor an enlarged democratic legislature appealed to him, and he suggested that citizens form groups themselves to lobby for progressive change. *The Philosophy of Right* makes it clear that enlightened officials are his best hope. Some years later, he criticized the English Reform Bill for its extension of the franchise, thinking that it would destabilize a successful constitutional balance. The subsequent importance of the Hegelian model lies not in these commonplace—though sensible—views, but in what sustains the final two elements of his account of the state: his account of war and international relations and of the state as an actor in world history.

Hegel's hostility to social contract theories rested on his disdain for the idea that there could be a contract between the individual and the state. Contracts outside the imagination of philosophers depend on there being a state to enforce them. In any case, a contract is a bargain between two sides and conditional; we contract to gain a benefit, and if we do not receive it, the contract is void. Kant was clear that the social contract was a purely hypothetical contract, but nonetheless employed the idea of a contract to clarify when allegiance could rightly be withdrawn. When the answer to the question "Could a rational person have contracted into a system that allowed a state to do this?" was obviously no, the state's authority was at an end. Hegel thought that the essence of the state was that it can exact unconditional obedience. Most notably, it has our lives in its hand because it is entitled to send us to war. Hegel knew his Hobbes and where the crux came in contractual arguments.

The essence of the state is the unconditionality of our allegiance. What makes it a modern rational state is the existence of a representative system, even if it is built around the Hegelian system of estates, a constitutional monarch who does no more than "cross the t's and dot the i's of legislation," and a well-educated bureaucracy appointed on merit and unable to purchase places in the civilian bureaucracy, or military commissions. What makes it a state at all is its ability to demand unconditional obedience. This launches the brief but striking thought that a state is most visibly itself in the international sphere, where the ultimate test of its being is war. War preserves the "ethical health" of states. Against the projects for perpetual peace offered by Rousseau and Kant, among others, Hegel retorts that even a "lasting, not to say, perpetual peace among nations" would produce "stagnation."[27] We understand the meaning of life when the danger of death is revealed by the flashing sabers of the hussars.

Commentators on Hegel have got overexcited by what is, after all, something of a throwaway remark. Hegel did not say and did not think that the state was to be constantly at war and to hazard its citizens' lives and prosperity in pointless battles. He was, however, eager to emphasize the normality of war as a method of resolving disputes between states; war was not wholly lawless, and a state's motive for engaging in war was not analogous to the rage that drives an individual to commit murder. States do not commit murder and do not become angry. They employ force in a measured fashion to secure national objectives. Soldiers do not hate one another even when they are trying to kill one another; they are the quasi-professional instruments of policy. Hegel's most famous pupil was the great strategist Clausewitz, best known for the claim that war is the promotion of policy by other means; that was Hegel's thought. Nonetheless, the thought is not without its edge. Just as the individual human life is framed by the fact that it ends in death, politics is framed by the fact that states exist in a world of states whose ultimate raison d'être is their ability to resist the incursions of other states.

As to the ultimate point, organized political societies are actors in world history. Without the Greek polis there could have been no exemplification in the world of the Greek conception of freedom. Without the ancient empires, the will of the individual would never have been given the dramatic expression of willful freedom that is encapsulated in Hegel's notion that they embodied the thought that "one is free." Without modern states, the universality of freedom would have no space in which to express itself. This is not Prussian nationalism— the post-Napoleonic Prussian state repudiated almost every constitutional and modernizing ideal that Hegel put forward; it is not German nationalism—Hegel never suggests that all German speakers should be under one political umbrella. There is no reason to think he would have approved of German unification under the aegis of the Prussian army. It is nationalism, but an ambiguous nationalism, because even though the nation can demand that we sacrifice our lives in its service, it is valued in the Hegelian schema as an instrument of a larger historical process. Like all world-historical individuals, it will be discarded once its time is up.[28] The larger purpose served by the existence of states is the spiritual freedom promoted by the cultures that states shelter, and it finds its expression in religion and art, not in warfare.

Coming to terms with Hegel is not easy. Commentators have tried to label him as a reactionary, a totalitarian, a Prussian nationalist, or, on the other side, a liberal of an unusual stripe. It is right to acknowledge the liberal strain in Hegel: he was glad to see the end of the feudal order in Germany, argued for occupational freedom, disapproved of the existence of an established church. The conservative strain exists, too:

he was no friend to democracy, the conviction that the truth is to be found in the Whole gives the status quo the benefit of the doubt, and a man as friendly as he was to the "substantial" or agrarian way of life could not be a wholehearted modernizer. Like Saint-Simon, he put his trust in rational administration and downplayed the role of politics in the everyday rough-and-tumble sense. The tension is greater in Hegel, because he wants to emphasize the freedom of modern man, not only his need for order. Hegel's preference for administration over politics had to do not with his metaphysics, which could have accommodated a great deal more exuberance, but with his sense that democratic decision making was more likely to produce chaos than the rational pursuit of the public interest. His long and complaining comment on William Pitt's need to court public opinion during the Napoleonic Wars exemplifies his doubts.[29] He would very probably have thought the same today.

We began with the question whether the Persians had—belatedly—conquered the Greeks. Hegel's answer amounts to saying that we should accept that they have, not, of course, in the guise of the armies of Darius and Xerxes, but in the guise of a well-run, professionally staffed, bureaucratic delivery system that provides the services a modern state can provide. Moreover, this is in a very different sense from anything Jefferson had in mind, an empire of liberty. In the Persian Empire of the sixth century BCE, only *one* was free, and there was no rule of law, no security that the despot would not act arbitrarily or brutally. The modern state is constitutional, predictable, its actions nonarbitrary, and it is built on a notion of individual freedom that the ancient world did not possess. Although Hegel says the relations between state and subject are not based on a contract of protection on the one side and obedience on the other, the modern state's legitimacy rests on allowing its subjects a very substantial liberty of thought and action: occupational freedom, religious freedom, access to education. He may insist that we have no *right* in the strictest sense to withdraw our allegiance from a state that we disapprove of, but the state betrays itself if it erodes what we think of as the usual civil liberties of the members of a modern liberal state. The subsequent history of Prussia suggests that Hegel underestimated the ability of a traditional, authoritarian state to manage a nineteenth-century industrial economy, but had a rather clear grasp of the unlikelihood that it would pursue its destiny by peaceful means. One should not complain that he did not wholly foresee the future; he was, on his own account of it, looking back rather than forward. "Where have we got to?" is one question; "Where are we going?" another.

CHAPTER 19

Utilitarianism: Jeremy Bentham and James and John Stuart Mill

Godfather, Father, and Son

MODERN LIBERALISM HAS MANY roots. One of the most important is the ideas of the man described by an American critic as "his satanic free-trade majesty John Stuart Mill" and revered by others. Mill himself was deeply conscious of his debts to two predecessors, one his father, the other Jeremy Bentham. Since Mill inherited the reforming project to which Bentham and James Mill had devoted themselves, and transformed it in interesting ways, some introduction to them is needed. Jeremy Bentham was born in 1748 and died in 1832. He was a lifelong bachelor, the object of vituperative attacks from critics of all political persuasions, but easygoing and genial in private life. Politically, he began as a Tory, but came to think that nondemocratic governments could not be trusted to promote the general welfare, and became an enthusiast for parliamentary reform. He had mixed views about the American Revolution; he thought colonies were a waste of money and had no affection for the British Empire in North America. On the other hand, he thought badly of the American appeal to natural rights. He famously declared, "Natural rights, nonsense; natural and imprescriptible rights, rhetorical nonsense, elevated nonsense, nonsense going on stilts."[1] In 1789, provoked by the French and Virginian declarations of the rights of man, he continued to lament that so rational a cause as American independence should have been placed on so irrational a foundation.

His hostility to natural law and his development of a positivist theory of law made Bentham one of the two or three most important figures in the history of anglophone jurisprudence; he was a savage critic of one of the others, William Blackstone, and in his *Fragment on Government* systematically demolished Blackstone's discussion of contractarian and natural law ideas. Bentham thought the British legal system was a tangle of obscurantist and time-wasting procedures, and devoted himself to explaining at great length—excessive length for most audiences—how the law could be codified, how procedures could be simplified, and how the political system could be reformed so that a government could be elected that would put legal and administrative reform in hand. Bentham did not invent the principle of utility, though he probably did invent the phrase "the greatest happiness principle." But he held that only by asking how a proposed law or a system for managing, say, incarcerated prisoners, or the recipients of public welfare, promoted the happiness or well-being of everyone affected by it, could we know what laws to pass, what penalties to attach to their infraction, and how to administer the institutions on which society depended.[2]

One of Bentham's obsessions was prison reform, and he is famous—or notorious—as the designer of the Panopticon, a prison design that envisaged a warden in a central tower being able to see every cell in a series of radiating corridors. The idea was that every prisoner would know that he might at all times be under the gaze of the authorities, so inducing him to mend his ways and earn early release. He described it as "a mill for grinding rogues honest." Critics loathed the idea that even criminals should be so narrowly supervised; they said that this sort of conditioning treated men as if they were machines. Bentham's robust response was "call them soldiers, call them monks, call them machines; so they were but happy ones, I should not care."[3] The United States was friendlier to his plans than Britain, but the architectural model proved highly adaptable for British asylums and hospitals. The theoretical foundations of the utilitarian system were laid in *The Principles of Morals and*

Legislation, which began with the claim that nature had placed mankind under the rule of two sovereign masters, pain and pleasure, and that they not only dictated what we would do but told us what we should do— secure as much as possible of the latter at a minimum cost in the former. To assist this, Bentham developed what he called the felicific calculus, which set out the way to estimate the amount of pleasure or pain to be expected from a given action or course of action. Its scientific status was more dubious than Bentham supposed, but the ambition to achieve precision in determining the rights and wrongs of policy was plain enough.

Bentham's interest lay in law and administration. When he met James Mill, the father of John Stuart, and took him on as his secretary and general assistant, he found the perfect foil. James Mill was born in 1773 and died in 1836, so was a quarter of a century younger than Bentham. He was a more political animal than Bentham, although he was a highly competent economist and for the final twenty years of his life managed the affairs of India as the examiner of India correspondence of the East India Company, in effect the senior civil servant in the London office of the corporation that governed India. He was a major figure among the "philosophical radicals," reformers determined on the modernization of British government and administration. His most notable contribution to the utilitarian theory of politics was the essay "Government," first published in the *Encyclopaedia Britannica* in 1818.[4] Like Bentham, he began with the simple thought that all of us naturally attempt to pursue our own interests; the need for some system of government to coordinate our activities, make law, and repress crime is obvious, but any group of persons with the power to do good by such means has the power to do harm. The central problem of government is to reconcile the interests of the public with the interests of those who hold power. Neither monarchy nor aristocracy fits the bill; the answer must be a form of democracy, understood not as direct participation in an Athenian assembly but as a system of representation that allows the public to dislodge governments that do not serve their interest.

Mill cut many corners in arguing that because each of us is concerned to promote his own interest, the "public" must collectively be concerned to promote the public interest, and more than one critic mocked him for it. Whether there is any such creature as "the public" still exercises political analysts. The more surprising thing was that once he had apparently established the necessity of universal suffrage, years before the Reform Act of 1832 extended the vote to a mere 14 percent of adult males, he set out to reduce the expense of running a representative system by arguing that the interests of women were included within those of their husbands or fathers, so that women needed no separate voting rights; that men under the age of forty had no interest separate from those of men over forty, so a voting age of forty would not damage the representation of all appropriate interests; and that working men had no interests at odds with those of the middle classes, so they did not need separate voting rights, either. Of Mill's exclusion of women, T. B. Macaulay said all that was needed, "Without taking the trouble to perplex the issue with a single sophism, he calmly dogmatises away the interests of half the human race."[5] Bentham did not do so. Nor did John Stuart Mill.

The importance of Bentham and James Mill is not that they determined the education of John Stuart Mill and, with it, much of the character of British liberal thought. There are three important issues at stake. The first is the relationship between freedom and happiness; Bentham was a libertarian because he thought most people know their own interests, and he had a genuine horror of the misery people suffer when they are bullied and oppressed. He was much ahead of his time in thinking that laws criminalizing homosexual behavior served no purpose and caused extreme misery; but he set no store by freedom as such. It was instrumental to happiness. If we could lose the freedom to behave badly, or the freedom to make ourselves miserable, we should. That explained his incomprehension of complaints against the Panopticon. The second is the relationship between politics and administration. Utilitarianism has often been described as "Government House morality"; it seems to assume the point of view of a benevolent colonial administrator thinking how to make his charges happy. As Aristotle pointed out, politics, as distinct from administration, supposes the existence of citizens with their own views. Whether utilitarianism can take politics entirely seriously is a much debated question. One might think that at best it makes political activity instrumental to the real purpose of government, securing the greatest happiness. It makes accountability for the sake of aligning the interests of the governors and the governed absolutely central, but has nothing to say about the life of the citizen. Lastly, the individualism of utilitarian ethics and politics is ambiguous: at one level, utilitarianism is concerned only with individuals, since only individuals are happy or unhappy; at another, it is not really interested in individuals as such, taken individually. Its goal is maximizing the sum of human happiness. An analogy is the concern of governments with GDP; in one way this is an individualistic goal, since the nation's income is the income of individuals; in another way, the reverse. What matters is the total of pounds, dollars, or euros. The individualism that focuses on individuals' characters, and what kind of life they lead, naturally issues in the thought that they should be autonomous, self-actualizing citizens; the individualism that focuses on their capacity for happiness and misery naturally issues in a concern for rational, benevolent management. The younger Mill had much to say on these matters.

Mill's *Autobiography*

John Stuart Mill was born in London in 1806, and died in Avignon, in the south of France, in 1873. He left to be published after his death an extraordinary *Autobiography*; it provides a detailed account of what he wished the reader to know about his education and his lifework. The book raises more questions than it answers. Mill was brought up by his father, James Mill, with the advice and encouragement of Jeremy Bentham and the Radical politician and publicist Francis Place, to be a leader of advanced political opinion in early nineteenth-century Britain. Mill remarks in his *Autobiography* that his whole education was a course of Benthamism, by which he meant that his father and Bentham had provided him with an utterly rational education, replete with history, philosophy, and political economy, in the hope that he would forward the modernization program they had in mind. It did not necessarily mean he was to enter politics. Until 1911, members of Parliament were unpaid, and Mill came from a humble background.

A career at the bar would have paid well. It would have allowed him to pursue his political ambitions by writing for radical newspapers and journals, and to serve in Parliament while practicing law. But when James Mill became a senior administrator with the East India Company, thought of a legal career was given up, and Mill followed his father into the company's employment. He joined at the age of sixteen and retired thirty-six years later when the British government dissolved the company in the wake of the Indian Mutiny of 1857. Only after he retired from the East India Company did he serve as an MP, from 1865 to 1868.[6] Mill's early years matter in ways the early years of most philosophers do not, and the *Autobiography* makes them central. He was the object of an educational experiment that turned out very well in one dimension and less well in another; his consciousness of that fact and the inferences he drew from it permeated his political theory, not least by making him attach great importance to the education of the steadily democratizing society he lived in. James Mill believed that it was possible to teach children vastly more than most parents or schools attempted, and John had his father's undivided attention as he set out to give him a start of a quarter century over his contemporaries. He learned Greek at three, with the aid of "flash cards," pieces of card with an English word on one side and its Greek equivalent on the other, and went on to learn Latin at six. He read prodigious quantities of both classical and modern history, and at twelve embarked on logic and political economy.[7]

James Mill was a tough teacher; his son was more conscious of his father's disapproval of his failings than his approval of his successes. Nonetheless, it was not an education in rote learning. It was tutorial instruction: James Mill taught his son by asking questions, not by providing answers. Mill was encouraged to ask questions about everything he read, and discouraged from accepting any answer with which he was not satisfied. Such brutalities as his education contained were accidental. One of James Mill's ideas was that his son's progress could be assessed by setting him the task of teaching his sisters and seeing how much they had learned; the drawback was that he rather than they went to bed without supper, and Mill later said it was bad for both teacher and taught.[8]

Nonetheless, Mill was no Saint Augustine saying he would die rather than endure childhood again. Bentham was a friend of Lord Shelburne, a reforming Whig magnate; he spent his summers at Bowood, Shelburne's wonderful house in Wiltshire, and took the Mill family with him. When he was fourteen Mill was sent to France to stay for several months with Bentham's brother, Samuel, where he learned to dance and to speak and write fluent French. He also fell in love with the experience of being out of England and in a livelier, less straitlaced culture. He was never dismissive of French frivolity as his Victorian contemporaries were, and regarded the British as congenitally more boring than their Continental neighbors. At sixteen he began work with his father at the East India Company's offices in London. He soon added to his burdens the task of helping Bentham complete his much delayed project, the *Rationale of Judicial Evidence*. Bentham's self-imposed task was to make English law orderly and intelligible, but his working habits were chaotic. It fell to Mill to assemble Bentham's notes, edit the manuscript, and reduce the whole thing to a publishable condition. It was appallingly hard work.

At the end of this time, he suffered a life-changing experience.[9] Tired and depressed, he asked himself the fateful question whether he would be made happy if all his projects for the happiness of others were realized. It became obvious that the answer was no. His life fell to pieces about him. He had been brought up to be a utilitarian, to measure the virtues of government policy and legal arrangements by their tendency to foster the happiness of those they affected. He had taken for granted that a reformer would wish for the well-being of all his or her fellow citizens, and would be gratfied by their happiness, made happy himself by the success of his benevolent projects. Yet, when Mill asked himself what he would feel upon the success of all the schemes he had been brought up to value, the answer was that he would be unmoved. To a sensitive young man of twenty, this was a personal disaster. To a utilitarian, it was a theoretical disaster as well.

The remedy was not obvious. Mill felt that there was no arguing with his feelings. On his own account of the episode, he fell into a depressed state that lasted some months, perhaps two years. He got out of it by accident, but one fraught with meaning. He was reading the memoirs of the French writer Marmontel, when he came across the passage in which

Marmontel describes the death of his father and his intention to fill the gap left by his father in the life of his family. On reading the passage, Mill burst into tears.[10] The effect was to bring back happiness; he had been terrified that he was incapable of human emotion, and feared that his father had turned him into a calculating machine. Here was proof that he was a sentient creature.

No doubt, what Mill felt was a gush of guilty pleasure at the thought that one day he would escape his father's tutelage and become a grown man in his own right. Being the young man he was, he attached great weight to the event. It demonstrated two things: first that education must attend to the cultivation of the emotions as well as that of the intellect. Whether he was right to think that his education had attended only to his intellect may be doubted; his father had introduced him to a lifetime's worth of poetry, epic historical writing, and novels. Mill made his reaction the basis of a distinction between the frame of mind of the eighteenth century and that of the nineteenth, between rationalism and romanticism, or between a mechanical and a historical approach to politics. In so doing, Mill broadened utilitarianism into a much more persuasive vision of life—in the eyes of friendly critics; his sharper critics said he had abandoned utilitarianism for an unprincipled eclecticism.

The second conclusion Mill drew was the importance of moral and political values that are difficult to make complete sense of in utilitarian terms: autonomy, vitality, the desire to be the author of one's own existence, human dignity. Mill had been oppressed by the sensation that he was the manufactured product of someone else's vision of his life, and not the author of his own fate. What rescued him was the sense that he could become his own master after all. The idea of autonomy became central to the way he thought thereafter. Mill's description of the event as "a crisis in [his] mental life" reached both backward into his classical education and forward into the nineteenth century's favorite thought. The Greeks had thought of a "crisis" as a turning point in a drama and a challenge to act boldly. With the French Revolution a recent memory, the nineteenth century looked for crises as a matter of course. Pre-1789 governments had faced revolts, insurrections, peasant rioting, and urban riots; these were treated as threats to the peace and were put down with extreme savagery. Nonetheless, they were a "police" matter. They were disturbances, not crises.

The Great French Revolution was a different creature entirely. Yet it had come out of an almost clear sky. It was no more likely that the assault on the Bastille would launch the greatest political upheaval that Europe had known since the Reformation than that urban riots in London would result in the overthrow of the British monarchy. The nineteenth century became obsessed with revolution and with trying to detect the moment of crisis in politics, art, religion, and the individual life. To us it is second nature to think in such terms; but it was once a real novelty. Mill's framing of the upheaval in his emotional life in terms appropriate to the political and social revolutions of his day was perfectly self-conscious. Mill, the strict philosophical empiricist, shared Hegel's view that a philosophy for the nineteenth century must be historically minded. Mill read Hegel and thought him impossibly obscure; the project itself was not.

Tutor to the Nation

Mill's mental crisis was invisible to his friends. He continued to work at India House, and throughout the late 1820s and 1830s devoted himself to political journalism, culminating in his ownership and editorship of a radical literary and political quarterly, the *London and Westminster Review*. His life was more dramatically changed by falling in love with Harriet Taylor. She was married, and although she was as much in love with Mill as he with her, they behaved with perfect propriety, assisted by her husband, John Taylor, who made no fuss about the fact that his wife had fallen in love with someone else, but wished the proprieties to be observed for the sake of his self-respect and the welfare of their children. Even so, it was a scandalous relationship, and Mill withdrew from social life, spending all the time he could with Harriet and seeing little of his former friends. His communication with the wider world grew impersonal. He became a one-man educational institution, sharing with his readers the insights of advanced liberal thinking—British, European, and American.

He wrote a devastating account of the shortcomings of Bentham in an essay of that name in 1833, and was the first person outside France to hail Alexis de Tocqueville's *Democracy in America* as a work of genius in 1836, on the publication of the first volume, and in 1840, on the publication of the second.[11] In 1843 he published the first of his substantial books, *A System of Logic*, in which he set out an account of the philosophy of science that has been an empiricist's bible ever since. Its aim was to show that all human knowledge began in experience and that we neither had nor needed a faculty or "intuition" attuned to perceiving the truth of ethical, mathematical, or physical laws. *A System of Logic* is a surprisingly political work. Mill believed that the doctrine of special faculties or intuitive capacities was a powerful support of conservative social, ethical, religious, and political doctrines. Anyone who thought that a sufficiently deep *conviction* guaranteed the truth of his beliefs was incapable of self-criticism.[12] The human race's great weakness is that it is too ready to think that whatever we believe deeply enough must be true. The philosophy of intuitionism reinforced this weakness; a better philosophy would try to correct it.

In addition to the negative aim of undermining his conservative opponents, Mill had two important positive aims. One was to advance the view that there was no reason why the social sciences should not eventually provide results as reliable as the physical sciences. The day was far off when this might be expected, but putting our knowledge of the social world on a scientific basis was essential to a rational politics. Unlike his modern descendants, Mill did not appeal to the example of economics in support of this view, although it was a flourishing discipline. Economics was a hypothetical discipline, explaining how human beings *would* behave in tightly structured situations with perfect knowledge and very limited motives for action. It was more important to understand why economics could *not* be a model for politics than to try to model political science on economics.[13] Mill had settled accounts with his father's *Essay on Government*.

Mill's second purpose was to argue that political practice must rest on a historically sensitive political sociology. Since the success or failure of political institutions depended on the characters of the population who had to operate them, the crucial question was how education turns our infant human nature into our settled adult character. He coined the word "ethology" to describe the desired science, one aspect of which was "the science of national character," and he praised Tocqueville for shedding so much light on the difference that national character made to the prospects for democracy in France and America.[14] Mill thought that *the* problem of the age for Victorian Britain was to establish an appropriate form of liberal democracy on a lasting basis. It was a delicate task, because ordinary people had to be emancipated without being cast utterly adrift; and they had to acquire the confidence to exercise the power that was about to fall into their hands without threatening the liberties of themselves and others. The anxious tones in which Tocqueville described the United States in the second volume of *Democracy in America* suggested that the task might be beyond them. Indeed, we shall see that Mill was insistent that what modern states could practice was *representative government*. There were environments in which literal self-government was possible; the government of a modern industrial nation was not one. We could take sureties for good government by electing our rulers and evicting them if they were unsatisfactory. Literal self-rule was not to be had. In Jefferson's terms, we could have representative democracy but not pure democracy.

In 1848 Mill published *The Principles of Political Economy*. It, too, had political implications, not only in the final book, where he explicitly discussed the operations of government. Mill deplored the deterministic picture of social and political life that economists presented. The problem was not that economics tried to give deterministic explanations of the phenomena with which economics dealt. Every science tries to explain events so as to show how causes determine their effects. Rather, Mill thought that economists of his own day were too quick to think that only one economic system was possible, Victorian capitalism. It appeared to them to be a necessary truth that an efficient economy must rest on private property rights familiar to Victorian England. Mill believed it was possible to build a form of socialism in Britain based on worker-owned cooperatives, and highly desirable to do so, because political democracy was insecure in the absence of economic democracy.[15] In any case autonomy was seamless. The justification of democracy was that free persons could not allow themselves to be ruled by authorities they had not chosen. It had to be equally unacceptable to be ruled at work by managers in whose appointment we had no say. Mill did not propose that people like himself should decide what sort of socialism might suit Britain; the economic and political institutions of the future should be decided by working people once they had the vote.

Ten years later Mill published *On Liberty*. In 1851 Harriet Taylor's husband, John, had died, and after a decorous interval she and Mill married. Their happiness was immediately threatened when Mill discovered that they both had consumption—tuberculosis. The rest of their brief marriage was dominated by illness, expeditions to warm climates to find a cure, and the exchange of gloomy reflections on the low state of British intellectual, cultural, and political life, and plans to leave behind a "mental pemmican" to sustain "thinkers after us, if there should be any." In 1858 she died at Avignon, and Mill bought a house to be near her grave. *On Liberty* was her memorial, but it became one of the most important manifestos of social and political liberalism, and remains one of the liveliest and freshest of Mill's works. Its arguments are no more *believed* than when it was first published; but its capacity to spark enthusiasm and outrage has hardly diminished. It received an unwitting tribute from the czarist censors in 1867, when they allowed the publication of a Russian translation of Karl Marx's *Das Kapital* and refused permission for a translation of *On Liberty*. Nobody would make head or tail of *Das Kapital*, but anyone reading Mill would draw unfortunate conclusions about the conservative and despotic near-theocracy over which Alexander III then ruled.

On Liberty was followed by three works that completed the corpus of Mill's liberal politics. In 1861 he wrote a set of short articles in the *Fortnightly Review*, which were republished as *Utilitarianism*. A year later he published *Considerations on Representative Government*, defending such un-English ideas as proportional representation, plural votes, and female suffrage. Finally, in 1869, he secured his reputation as a dangerous radical by publishing *The Subjection of Women*, a companion essay to *On Liberty*, whose argument might without injustice be summarized as the proposition that if freedom is a good thing, it is a good thing—and not for men alone. After his death came his *Autobiography, Chapters on Socialism,* and *Three Essays on Religion. Chapters on Socialism* expanded on the argument for workers' cooperatives, while *Three Essays on Religion* argued, among other things, that it would not be difficult to attach to a "religion of humanity," such as Auguste Comte had envisaged, the sentiments ordinarily attached to conventional Christian faith.

Mill retired from the East India Company in 1858 when the company was dissolved, intending to live in Avignon, where he could mourn Harriet and engage in botanical expeditions in the mountains. His friends dissuaded him from self-exile, and between 1865 and 1868 he was Liberal MP for the City of Westminster; and in the fifteen years after Harriet's death he remade many old friendships and played an active part in many causes—women's suffrage and land reform among them. During his time in Parliament, he came closer to securing the vote for women than anyone else was to do before the government of the day brought in a measure to give the vote to married women over the age of thirty in 1918. He died in 1873 in Avignon.

Rethinking Utilitarianism

The chronology of Mill's work does not reflect the logic of his politics, so although his full-length discussion of utilitarianism postdated *On Liberty*, we should explore it first, because utilitarianism properly understood was—in Mill's view—the foundation of his political and social thought. Many of Mill's critics thought that his liberalism was a good deal more freestanding than that, and that he glossed over the difficulties of defusing the illiberal implications of utilitarianism. It is certainly true that his version of utilitarianism reflects the need to accommodate convictions that he derived from other sources.

Nonetheless, the official program was clear enough. Mill thought British politics suffered from an absence of systematic thinking by both politicians and intellectuals. Since the fate of freedom in Britain would ultimately be determined by the social, moral, and political ideas of the day, philosophers, poets, and social thinkers had to provide for their society's intellectual needs. In "The Spirit of the Age," written in 1829–30, he wrote eloquently about the age's lack of confident and well thought-out moral and political ideals.[16] The nation lacked a "clerisy," a term coined by Samuel Taylor Coleridge to refer to public intellectuals whose views on society and culture—indeed, on the meaning of life generally—would exercise authority throughout society. The term suggests that this group was to fulfill the spiritual role of the clergy of the established church, a role that Mill, like Coleridge, thought that neither the Church of England nor the existing aristocracy could play in a democratic age.[17]

Mill set out to provide the clerisy with a utilitarian creed. The foundation of utilitarianism is the thought that whatever matters, matters because of its effect on human well-being, and that human well-being is constituted by happiness. There are many alternatives to this thought, such as: some things "just" matter; or they matter because they matter to God; or they fit into a more impersonal universal scheme. Far too many people think that what matters matters because it matters to them, their race, their family, their country. In contrast, utilitarianism is secular and universalist. The claim that any state of affairs is good or bad according to its impact on human welfare explains all forms of goodness and badness, not only moral good and evil.[18] Cancer is bad because it causes misery, but cancer is not wicked. Mill's explanation of moral good and evil relies on the idea that morality is a system of rules of conduct that we collectively impose on ourselves and enforce with psychological sanctions. One sanction is that of conscience. If we ask the factual question what a society's actual morality is, we ask what rules its members do follow; if we ask what its morality should be, we ask what rules they should follow. This is the distinction between positive and critical morality. *Positive* morality is Hegel's *Sittlichkeit*: the ethical rules a society actually follows; the individual who asks himself what rules he *ought* to follow asks a question in *critical* morality. The essence of Mill's utilitarianism was the claim that the true critical morality is the rules that would maximize human well-being if we all followed them.

This is a sociological view of morality, not in the sense that it collapses such moral questions as, "Is private property just?" into sociological questions about what different social groups *think* about the justice of private property, but in the sense that morality is understood as an institution. The reason we have the institution we call morality is that human beings need many forbearances from each other, and some, though less, positive help. Forbearances are the more basic inasmuch as we need other people *not* to attack, rob, or ill-treat us more than we need them to like us, or help us; but it is easy to see why we call kindness a virtue and cruelty a vice. It is equally easy to see why rules prohibiting aggression and ill-treatment are more strictly enforced than rules promoting kindness and helpfulness. It is less obvious, but important for Mill's case for individual liberty, that we owe *duties*, strictly speaking, only to other people. Morality is about our relations with others: the repression of damage and the encouragement of assistance; we do not have moral relations with ourselves; but Mill thought an adequate utilitarianism must also have something to say about our conduct beyond the realm of duty.[19]

Mill sometimes said that morality, strictly speaking, was concerned with the "business" side of life. Bentham provided a thin utilitarianism because he had attended to the business side of life and constructed a clear and rational guide to our relations with others, but offered no inspiration for self-development. Mill claimed that if we take the assessment of our own behavior and character seriously we will separate three different dimensions in which we might behave well or wrongly: we might be imprudent, that is, damage our own interests; we might behave immorally, damaging the legitimate interests of others. The first might be exemplifed by our drinking too much and suffering a hangover, the second by our drinking too much and driving dangerously. That is the realm of morality; endangering others is a violation of duty. The third dimension was the assessment of behavior along the spectrum of noble to base rather than virtuous to wicked. A man who pays his debts grudgingly does his duty by repaying what he owes; but his behavior is nonetheless mean. He should reproach himself for being less of a person than he might be. Mill sometimes said this was the "aesthetic" dimension of appraisal.[20]

Mill complained that Bentham ignored the self-regarding side of ethical life. In the light of Mill's insistence in *On Liberty* that society must not try to coerce us into behaving better in matters that are purely self-regarding, it might seem odd that Mill should complain that Bentham neglected the self-regarding excellences. It is not. Mill's point was that they should be fostered, not imposed; they could not be fostered unless they were understood. Bentham had impeded their understanding because he thought it was almost impudent to hold any view about another person's self-regarding conduct. Mill thought that unconcern with another person's self-regarding conduct represented a failure to take an interest in human excellence. He wanted to show that utilitarianism, properly understood, could supply the premises for the assessment of all aspects of human life, one element of which was the self-regarding side of life. Utilitarianism could be extended from the "business" side of life to all others. There is nothing incoherent in holding that these self-regarding sentiments and values are the most important of all values *and* that they were not to be promoted by coercive, organized action. It is the essence of liberalism.

Mill was fearful of the philistinism of Bentham's utilitarianism, exemplified by his famous remark that "quantities of pleasure being equal, pushpin is as good as poetry," because he thought Bentham encouraged the worse effects of democracy. In several essays in the 1830s, Mill described a tendency in modern society for "masses to predominate over individuals"; he meant that society was increasingly dominated by public opinion rather than single, outstanding individuals, that the genius of the age was to organize large numbers of people into joint activities rather than inspire single individuals to do great deeds. Even before reading Tocqueville, Mill was convinced that an age which thought of itself as the age of the individual, because it believed in the economics of self-interest and because the religious constraints of an earlier age had largely fallen away, was in truth an age of mass opinion and mass action.[21] The individuals of whom society was composed acted as a mass. Tocqueville reinforced Mill's doubts; he described America as a country in which there was less real freedom of thought than anywhere else in the world. Yet it had a Bill of Rights, elaborate legal arrangements to secure individual freedom, and a collective enthusiasm for exploration and taming the frontier. According to Tocqueville, it had neither a taste nor a talent for encouraging individuals to think for themselves.

Mill's critique of the utilitarian creed expanded it and corrected its assumptions about human nature. The danger of utilitarianism was that it represented human nature as essentially passive; if we are consumers of stimuli that produce pleasure or pain, and success is to have many of the first and few of the second, the value of action, self-direction, and striving is hard to explain. Why should we not prefer comfort to danger and, on a political level, prefer any tolerably benign and efficient government to self-government. *Self*-government involves more effort and risk than a utilitarian seems likely to want. It is his concern to fight off such thoughts that gives Mill's final account of utilitarianism its peculiar flavor. *Utilitarianism* is one of the most read and best-hated works in the history of moral philosophy. Many critics find it so flawed that they cannot understand how an intelligent man wrote it; its friends find it an intriguing and persuasive account of a secular ethics.

The layout of *Utilitarianism* is simple. Mill begins by trying to clear away confusion about what "utility" means. Ordinarily, we contrast the utilitarian, the *merely* useful, with the beautiful, right, just, or noble. It was important to Mill that his readers understood that what is useful in the ordinary sense along with the good, the right, the just, and the beautiful were all to be explained in terms of utility, that is, in terms of the promotion of happiness. Mill's argument is often negative; he thought there was a great resistance to utilitarianism by critics who misunderstood it; it had to be made clear what utilitarianism really was. Paradoxically, it is hard for later critics to see what Mill was trying to achieve, because his argumentative goals were so different from theirs. Thus one of his fundamental arguments was that utilitarianism was *practicable*. Modern readers believe that without argument. Mill's readers were more likely than we are to think that morality was a matter of God's will and that a secular ethics was a contradiction in terms. Mill was an agnostic, even if he was inclined toward the end of his life to think there might be a benign intelligence at work in the universe. *Utilitarianism* is agnostic in a different sense: utility provides ethical guidance whether or not there is a God. If there is a God, he will wish us to follow the dictates of utility. If there is not, we should follow them anyway. If there is a God, he will promote utilitarian principles; if there is not, society has good reason to do it anyway. History shows that societies of different religious convictions, or none, have adopted similar ethical codes. To the extent that they were coherent and progressive, it was where their codes reflected utilitarian ideas even if their adherents did not use such terms.[22]

Mill's conception of what *morality* embraces emerges during the discussion. Morality is the set of rules that it would maximize human welfare to establish and enforce by psychologically coercive measures. To show that utilitarianism tells us which rules those are, he had to show that it endorsed what nobody could possibly reject—the rules of justice, for instance—and that it allowed us to raise questions about the revisability of debatable rules—rules of private sexual ethics, for instance. Although we already believe most of what we are ever going to believe about ethics, there is room for progress. The positive morality of a society, what a society currently takes to be the content of morality, will already embody much of what utilitarianism would endorse; but the task of utilitarianism is to provide a critical morality against which the positive morality of any society can be tested.

This would have struck many readers as dangerous. For them, talk of moral progress would have struck at the heart of the idea that morality was revealed and set down by divine command. Mill himself was more anxious to fend off other critics. One criticism leveled at utilitarianism, by Thomas Carlyle among others, was that it was a "pig" philosophy. The idea that human beings not only sought pleasure but should take it as the touchstone of ethics was, they said, the worldview of pigs, not humans. Mill was made very angry by such criticism. It occasioned some of his sharpest writing. In the first place, it was simply insulting to human beings to suggest that their pleasures were the pleasures of pigs; that "the accusation supposes that human beings are capable of no pleasures except those of which swine are capable."[23] It was not utilitarians who insulted the human race but their critics. Utilitarians held that human beings must aspire to the happiness appropriate to human beings, not to that appropriate to pigs. Mill went further. He claimed that there were different kinds of pleasures, different forms of happiness, and that they could be compared for "quality" as well as "quantity." Appealing to a famous distinction, he argued that it was better to be a human being dissatisfied than a pig satisfied, better to be Socrates dissatisfied than a fool satisfied.

This raises two difficulties. The first is that it is hard to know what becomes of the idea of maximizing happiness if we introduce qualities into the calculation. The point of utilitarianism is to introduce order and calculation into ethics; but by introducing quality into an argument about quantities, Mill seems to have overthrown that ambition. The second is that if Mill supposes that we do whatever we do for the sake of the happiness it brings us, it is hard to see what he means by saying that a dissatisfied Socrates is better than a satisfied fool. If the fool is happier than Socrates, he must be doing better than Socrates. This is not Thrasymachus's argument; Thrasymachus thought that happiness consisted in self-aggrandizement and doing down everyone else. This view is agnostic about *what* we should do, holding that success consists in being happy no matter how. Thrasymachus would disapprove of the couch potato, but a crude utilitarianism has no room to disapprove of a happy couch potato.

Mill thought that he could defuse these complaints. He thought we knew that it was better to be a man dissatisfied than a pig satisfied and that anyone faced with the choice would agree. No dissatisfied man wishes he were a contented pig. Nor does Socrates wish he were a happy fool. To Mill this is evidence that there are superior and inferior forms of happiness. To the obvious retort that this requires a yardstick other than happiness, Mill produces his second argument, which is that we come to identify our happiness with much that is initially not part of it. There are many things that we do at first only because they will contribute to our happiness in future, but what was once only a means to happiness ends by becoming part of it. We may begin by telling the truth so that other people will trust us, and not because we want to be honest;

after a time we wish not to be dishonest, no matter what. Someone who says we should pursue virtue for its own sake meets no resistance from Mill; it is obviously in the interests of everyone else that a person should do so, and so far as we ourselves are concerned, it becomes part of what we regard as the life we most wish to live.[24]

Justice

We must ask how this bears on Mill's political theory. His ethical theory is political in its entirety, and not only in the sense that *Utilitarianism* is full of throwaway political comment. Morality is a social institution, and Mill agrees with Plato and Aristotle that the promotion of virtue is a central task for politics; but because he has such a different view of ethics, Mill can draw the liberal distinction between the direct and the indirect promotion of virtue in ways they could not. His account of justice is an instance. Utilitarianism has a problem with justice; justice seems to be concerned very directly with individuals, with the distribution of goods and bads, and with strict obligation, while utility is about maximizing happiness over a range of individuals, and its obligations are "more or less," rather than strict. Mill thought that the demands of justice were fundamentally utilitarian, but that we give them a special label and enforce them more fiercely because of the importance of the *kind* of utility that justice promoted. This is security; and while we can do without most things our neighbors can do for us, we cannot do without their respect for our security.

As an account of justice narrowly speaking, Mill's account leaves much to be desired; we do not usually say murder is unjust, though it undermines security, and we do say that praising one student's work above another student's if it is in fact worse, is unjust, though it hardly undermines security. As an account of the areas of morality that most need enforcement, it does better. The enforcement of good behavior by psychological pressure is society's unofficial self-government; it is how society keeps us under control, cooperative, and sensitive to one another's interests. The absence of such self-policing characterizes societies with high levels of violence and low levels of economic success. The communitarian movement in the United States has been emphasizing this point for some years.[25] The part of morality that Mill calls the realm of justice is the most important and most basic part. There it matters more than anywhere else that every individual should be able to call upon society for aid and assistance against attacks of all sorts. Justice is thus, as it should be, the most political of the virtues. Mill was more sanguine about the ability of a society to discipline its members than we are today. His fear was that modern societies were more likely to err on the side of overdisciplining their members, depriving them of initiative and self-confidence. *On Liberty* was intended as a corrective.

On Liberty

Mill's essay *On Liberty* is written with unusual passion and was meant by Mill to last as long as his own reputation. Nonetheless, it was especially aimed at his mid-Victorian countrymen. By the early 1850s when he and Harriet began to draft the essay, they had become convinced that Britain suffered from a stifling conformism. Mill had learned from *Democracy in America* both that democracy could easily mean "the tyranny of the majority" and that this tyranny might be exercised in novel ways. Like Tocqueville, Mill thought democracy was irresistible. Ordinary people had spent centuries gradually securing themselves against the depredations of kings and aristocrats. They had done it by acquiring what was later called "countervailing power," of the sort their oppressors would otherwise exercise over them. To gain the right to a share in government was the way to defeat an oppressive ruling class.[26] The difficulty that this may lead to, and that Mill and Tocqueville thought it had begun to lead to, was a new form of oppression. Paradoxically, it was a gentler form of oppression than before, but harder to resist. A minority ruling class is always in danger of being overthrown because its opponents outnumber it, so it must keep a tight grip on the machinery of power, and the ideological means of securing its authority. Loyal soldiers and persuasive priests had sustained the monarchies and aristocracies that Mill had in mind. A democracy armed with the power of the state hardly needs to worry about maintaining itself in power. Numbers as well as the institutional means of control are on its side.

Mill's predecessors feared that modern democracy would be the faction-ridden and quarrelsome democracy of the ancient world; Mill feared that it would not. It might be a mass democracy, in which the dead weight of public opinion would bear down on every member of the society. It would be a novel kind of oppression, where all of us collectively oppressed each of us individually. Worse, we might oppress ourselves. The mechanism of this process is easy to imagine. The process of socialization by which children acquire a conscience is one of "internalization." We adopt as our own the attitudes and outlooks of other people and society at large. Mill's idea is much like Freud's account of the development of the superego, though stripped of Freud's concern with sexual desire and its restraint. In all such accounts, the child takes the voice of others as an internal censor; our desires will not be expressed or acted on, and if they are, the action or expression will be accompanied by guilt.

The thought that animates *On Liberty* is that if we are brought up in a conformist democracy, we shall internalize public opinion. It may not be brutal, violent, or even prejudiced in familiar ways; but it will stop us from thinking for ourselves. When tempted to speak up, or to entertain a heretical thought in the privacy of our heads, we shall draw back. The question is whether Mill, following Tocqueville, was right to fear that democracy would be conformist, unless steps were taken to prevent its becoming so. In neither thinker's work is there a simple connection between democratic political arrangements and conformist culture. Both wished for a pluralist liberalism, where no opinion was suppressed; both thought the tendency of modern democracy was toward conformism. No such problem threatened ancient democracies; the small size of city-states and the ethos of emulation and competition for glory ensured that the articulate and energetic tried to be unlike others. In modern democracies, the economic basis of social life places many people in similar conditions; they may have conflicts of economic interest that separate them from one another, but the similarity of condition makes for uniformity of opinion.

This is not an attack on the working class for a lack of commitment to liberal values. Mill was certainly anxious about what democracy might mean if the electorate consisted overwhelmingly of ill-educated manual laborers, but here his target was the mores of the middle class. America, after all, was a country that, he thought, was entirely middle class. He wanted to stop the dead hand of respectability from inhibiting what we are willing to think, feel, and do. Mill's primary target is therefore a social attitude rather than political oppression, but his fears about social oppression imply obvious anxieties about the political consequences of such social attitudes. Like Tocqueville, Mill feared quiet despotism. Dissenters would be unemployable, frozen out of clubs, universities, political parties. They would not be jailed or sent to concentration camps. A society where the vast majority was of one mind had no need of sharper weapons.

As to what could be opposed to these forces, Mill had only one thing to hand, which was the liberal and pluralist political theory that he had fashioned after his nervous collapse in the 1820s. Reading Goethe, Wilhelm von Humboldt, and the English Romantic poets, Mill had come to think that human nature was multifaceted, even internally contradictory. He remained a utilitarian, but deemed "happiness" too vague a label for what we really desired for ourselves, and could pursue as a political goal. Autonomous self-fulfillment is the true goal of modern humanity; we seek, when fully self-conscious and in command of our own lives, to create a kind of harmony in our lives, to live life from the inside, as opposed to taking our standards from other persons.

Whether this is defensible on utilitarian grounds is debatable; it is not Benthamite, at any rate. Once we are committed to becoming fully autonomous beings, we shall certainly be unhappy if we are frustrated in the attempt; but after 140 years there is no unanimity among critics on whether Mill succeeded in explaining the value of freedom in terms of its effect on our happiness. However that may be, the shape of the argument in *On Liberty* is clear enough. Mill sets out a general principle to govern the way society collectively treats its individual members. The principle is intended to govern only the *coercion* of individuals by society; and the line it lays down is that society may coerce its members only in self-defense. Other than to prevent harm to someone other than the agent him- or herself, society may encourage, exhort, complain, and cajole, but not *coerce.* This requires a view of what constitutes coercive interference with our conduct, and Mill never defines it. The drift of his thinking is as follows: coercion involves threats of harm; the harm may be psychological or physical; it must be intended to deter us from whatever thoughts or actions are at issue, and is therefore a form of punishment. The principle is thus that society can punish its members only to protect other people. This is the principle of "antipaternalism."

The kind of harm that society may protect others against is also circumscribed; but Mill circumscribes it by telling the reader what it is *not.* It does not harm us to hear our favorite ideas contradicted; it does not harm us to hear our religious beliefs denounced as nonsense; it does not harm us to know that other persons believe our allegiances are a tissue of superstition. This is the principle of "antimoralism"; we cannot invoke the claim that a piece of behavior is immoral in deciding whether it harms people. We can invoke the fact that it harms people in deciding that it is immoral; this is what the utilitarian does. So Mill sets out to persuade his readers that society can coerce its members by mental or physical sanctions only to prevent incontrovertible kinds of harm, and otherwise to prevent the breach of rights that have been contracted for—such as marriage—or are indispensable to the functioning of society—such as giving evidence in courts of law when asked to do so.[27]

The principle, often referred to as the "harm principle," as meaning that society may coerce individuals only to prevent harm to others, is essentially negative. It establishes the line beyond which social coercion is impermissible. It implies absolute freedom of thought, and near-absolute freedom of speech. The restrictions that Mill envisages are cases of incitement or fraud; if we tell an angry mob outside a corn dealer's house that corn dealers are thieves, that is incitement.[28] We can write it in a textbook of economics; we cannot tell an angry crowd as much, since that would be incitement to riot and murder. Fraud, again, is rightly restricted; what I can write in a work of fiction I cannot write in a contract. Mill sees freedom of action as more difficult, but the fundamental rule remains the same. Even in hard cases, such as that of preventing someone from crossing a dangerous bridge over a chasm, Mill thinks interference should extend only to ensuring that the would-be traveler knows what risks he is running. It follows that for Mill truly voluntary prostitution could not be a criminal offence, and that the consumption of dangerous drugs would be regulated only in the way that all dangerous things are—by ensuring that people knew what they were buying. Given what we know about the effects of alcohol, it is right to punish offenses committed while drunk more severely than ones committed when sober, in order to provide an incentive to stay sober in situations where we are likely to get into fights or to injure other people, as we would be when driving an automobile.[29] Otherwise, we may do what we choose so long as it only ourselves at risk.

That is the negative side of the argument. The positive side, under-discussed by commentators, is Mill's insistence that there is more to life than not doing what we must not do. If you drink to excess, I may not force you to stop; but I can remind you that you have become a boring slob, that nobody will wish to be seen in your company, that you will have no friends, no career prospects, and that you will when sober consider your wasted hours with self-disgust. None of this is coercive on Mill's analysis. We do not say to you, "If you drink, we shall get everyone to ostracize you." Instead we say, "If you drink, nobody will be able to stand your company, however hard they try." We point out the results of everyone's using the freedom you claim for yourself. Mill did not deny that we would dislike being told that our behavior was disgusting, boring, or tasteless; he claimed that we should distinguish between the areas where we were justified in making other people behave as we chose and those where we were not.

This is not the place to explore Mill's vision of the ultimate ends of human life; political institutions shelter our individual pursuit of these ends, but cannot do more than provide us with resources. We cannot become freethinking, imaginative, bold, and interesting to order or under tutelage. The delicate line that any liberal must tread in this field is illustrated by Mill's views on education. Parents must see that their children are educated; not to do so violates two sorts of rights, society's right not to have dumped upon it persons who cannot support themselves, and the child's right not to be thrown into the world by those who begat him or her, unable to cope.[30] The state should neither dictate school curricula nor in general run schools beyond a small number of exemplary institutions to demonstrate what a good school can achieve. Parents without the means to pay for an education should be subsidized. If there are national examinations, they must be factual and scrupulously prescind from requiring any sort of political or religious profession. For all that, there are moments in his work when Mill's contempt for the low level of cultivation of the British public gets the better of him and he suggests that the British government follow a decidedly Prussian course in instituting a system of public education; teachers are better guides to a student's needs than the student, and an intelligent government will have a better idea of the public's needs than the public. The benevolent bureaucrat sometimes wins out over the libertarian.

Representative Government

Having provided a philosophical remedy for the defects of democracy, Mill provided a political and institutional remedy in his *Considerations on Representative Government*. The title of Mill's treatise was carefully chosen. Mill did not wish to write about "democracy," in the sense of a system of simple majority rule, or even in the sense of a system in which a political party sustained by a majority (more probably a plurality) of votes at an election is then able to govern by using its majority in parliament. He wanted to write about what the title of the book said, the representative form of government. Over the years Mill moved away from his youthful belief that majoritarian democracy would secure good and uncorrupt government in Britain. In part, this reflected doubts about his father's treatment of the subject in his *Essay on Government*, but the greater influence was Tocqueville's *Democracy in America* with its message that American democracy was consistent with liberty because of the pluralism and diversity of American society, but that even there the principle that the majority may do whatever it chooses was too much in the ascendant. Following Tocqueville, Mill thought that what was needed was to keep alive "the antagonism of opinions," so that the majority ruled but not unchallenged.[31]

More unequivocally than Tocqueville, Mill believed that what mattered most was to secure "progressive" government. Tocqueville was nostalgic for an aristocratic past in a way Mill was not. They shared the view that democracy was the natural product of increasing social equality. They also shared the view that political democracy might too easily turn into the peaceful management of a flock of contented sheep by their shepherds. Even so, there was a difference. Tocqueville was more directly political in his concerns; as the end of the second part of *Democracy* suggests, he feared that privatized individuals would fail to act as publicly engaged citizens. Mill had a vision of indefinite progress, intellectual, industrial, and moral; he posed the question what form of government could make the best use of the human resources available to it and best foster the advance toward a higher stage of human society. In some contexts this supports arguments that modern readers find disturbing. For instance, Mill had no doubt that slavery had been justified in the ancient world; without it, the intellectual and political energies of ancient Greece could not have been liberated. In the modern world, it was an abomination pure and simple. By the same token, despotism was justified if the ruling group or people was so far in advance of those they ruled that it was the only, or best, way of bringing the subject class or peoples into the mainstream of progress. Mill, like Karl Marx, thought British rule in India could be justified by its effect on the future well-being of the Indian people. Few Indians have been persuaded, though more have been persuaded by Mill's picture of progress itself.

In a modern society such as nineteenth-century Britain, there was no case for despotism; benevolent despotism was the worst of all forms of government. The only tolerable government was one accountable to the governed. The differences in capacities and intelligence between one person and another were insufficient to justify a Platonic despotism; a hereditary ruling elite was no answer; bureaucratic government had much to be said for it, but it too often lacked energy and drive. Representative government allowed the citizens of developed societies to govern themselves so as to bring out their ideals and ambitions and energies. This could happen only if it was properly organized and operated in an appropriate spirit. Mill saw, and said very sharply, that self-government in the modern world could not literally be self-government. Direct democracy worked in classical Athens, and there were areas of a modern society where it would work, but as a recipe for the government of thirty million people, it was not plausible. No more than Hegel did Mill sympathize with the hankering after the withering away of the state that animated Marx and innumerable socialists and anarchists. Modern society needed a great deal of administration, and the job was not for amateurs. The essence of modern government was electoral accountability. What the voter got was not the chance to govern, as in Aristotle's ideal of "ruling and being ruled by turns," but the ability to take sureties for good government.

The details of *Representative Government* have never excited the same passion as the details of *On Liberty* or *Utilitarianism*, but the book makes some unusual claims. Not only did Mill insist that self-government could not literally be self-government, but he demanded a high degree of deference from the voter. We are to vote not for people like ourselves but for people superior to ourselves, who hold views we approve of in our better moments. As for the franchise, Mill put forward three views that his contemporaries had difficulty coming to terms with. The first was that the suffrage should be extended to women. In the early 1860s the British electorate was confined to adult males who owned freehold property, some 14 percent of the adult male population. It was clear that the suffrage had soon to be extended, but the limits of imagination at the time were set by the aim of bringing lower-middle-class and some working-class men "within the pale of the constitution." As a member of Parliament during the debates on the 1867 Reform Bill, Mill put forward a proposal to enfranchise women on the same terms as men and got a surprisingly large number of votes for the proposal on second reading. His 72 votes astonished everyone. Only after the First World War did a government measure give the vote to married women over thirty years of age. Mill did not argue in favor of female suffrage; he simply treated the suggestion that women should not have the vote as on a par with suggesting that redheaded men should not have the vote—transparently irrational.

Mill's second breach with orthodoxy was to abandon the principle of "one man one vote" in favor of "one person at least one vote, and up to three or four votes according to education." He knew the proposal for plural voting would be greeted with incredulity; to make quite sure that it was, he did not offer it as a short-term measure to protect the rights of the propertied classes against newly enfranchised working class voters, but as a permanent feature of a satisfactory franchise. Novelists of the day referred to Mill's "fancy franchises." The ballot box should measure intelligent opinion rather than self-interest, and we should encourage intelligence by awarding extra votes to the better educated. Twentieth-century political scientists, who would be shocked at proposals to reward education in this overt fashion, have often praised the fact that the better educated exercise more influence than their numbers alone suggest, by acting as "opinion leaders," determining the way less-educated and less-attentive voters cast their votes.

The third of Mill's unorthodoxies was his defense of the most equitable, and therefore the most complicated, of proportional representation systems. He saw, like others, that it is possible in a two-party system for a party to form a government with slightly over a quarter of the popular vote behind it—if it wins a bare majority of seats by a bare majority in every seat that it wins, and loses the rest by a landslide. In a multiparty system, with a "first past the post," or plurality system of election, governments with large majorities are frequently formed on 40 percent of the popular vote, which means, given a turnout of hardly more than half the eligible voters, not much more than 20 percent of the adult population. Mill wished to put a stop to that. In fact, he wished to put a stop to it twice over. From the side of the voter, he wanted everyone to have the same chance of voting for a successful candidate. To this end, he advocated the transferable-vote system of Thomas Hare. The technicalities of such systems are complex, and writing for a popular audience, Mill ignored them. Their virtue is that if your candidate does not find favor, your second-choice candidate may do so, and if he or she does not, your third choice, and so on down the line. The drawback is that the system requires multimember electoral districts, and like Americans, the British have always been attached to the idea of a geographical link between voters and members of Parliament. However, the Irish Republic has operated the system with no problems for ninety years, and the British employ the system for elections to the European Assembly.

Mill was not concerned to appease the traditional sentiments of British politicians or their admirers. He thought that party government was a mistake and that the purpose of a parliamentary system of government was chronically misunderstood. Just as the voter is supposed to elect people more able than herself to judge the actions of government, the members of Parliament are supposed to establish a government more able than themselves to conduct the affairs of the nation. Taking on critics who complained that Parliament was a "talking shop," Mill retorted that that was exactly what it should be. His understanding of how a legislature should work is not entirely clear, but he supposed that some form of legislative commission would devise legislation and propose it to Parliament; Parliament would act like a jury and accept it or reject it. He considered the power of amendment a mistake, since it encouraged the incompetent to engage in off-the-cuff legislation. If Parliament had the power to say only yes or no, the legislative commission could take away rejected legislation and bring back something improved. It is easy to see three important influences—Bentham's insistence that lawmaking is a scientific matter, not one for amateurs; his own career as an administrator with a deep distrust of the doings of British party politicians; and the example of ancient Athens where the popular, inexpert assembly responded to what was put before it by debating its merits and deciding for or against. The late medieval Florentine Republic operated a similar system of lawmaking, and both Machiavelli and Rousseau took it for granted that a popular republic would operate in some such way. Behind their views, but not Mill's, lay the Roman Republic. Mill's unconventionality extended to a marked preference for Athenian democracy over Roman oligarchy.

Two final features of Mill's vision of a successful liberal democracy retain a good deal of interest: his thoughts on colonies and their government, and his passion for decentralization and devolution. Mill was not in the ordinary sense an imperialist. He did not think it part of a developed country's mission to invade or conquer other countries or to acquire vast overseas territories. But on the supposition that colonies had been acquired, there was reason to retain them until such time as they were ready for independence and self-government. Not only would this be for the benefit of the colonies themselves—Mill's defense of the East India Company's government of India rested on just that point—but it would enhance the prestige of the colonial power, a rather less predictable thought to come from Mill.

Mill was passionate about decentralization but had no strong sentiments about federal systems. Effective federal systems provided a remedy for the absence of a sentiment of nationality on a sufficient scale to hold a country together. Mill had strong opinions about the importance of a strong sense of national identity in unifying a country and inducing its citizens to make sacrifices for one another's benefit. He was a consequentialist, not a chauvinist. He did not suppose that one nation was intrinsically superior to another; at any given moment in history one might have more to contribute to the development of the human race than another, but that was a contingent fact about the way nations contributed to human history, not something that a particular state could rest on forever. Nor did he think, as Hegel did, that *Geist* was implicated in the process. Moreover, although national identity mattered, the pressing need for liberal democracies was to take decentralization seriously. The danger in democratic societies was that a passive populace would get used to allowing the national government to do everything for it; and that was the death of progress. It also exacerbated the liberticide tendencies of mass society. The remedy was to devolve responsibility as deeply into society as possible; knowledge should be centralized and responsibility decentralized. This would permit local democracy and inculcate self-reliance in the public. How many of Mill's readers, or indeed how many of us today, would really want to be drafted onto the local community's sewerage, lighting, educational, library, and highways committees it is hard to tell. It would be an interesting experiment to conscript citizens for such duties in the same way we draft them for jury service, but the outcome would be hard to predict.

The Subjection of Women

The most passionate of all Mill's works was the last to be published, but Mill's commitment to female equality was lifelong. It may have begun in his childhood, when he certainly thought that the irascible James Mill bullied his wife; it may have begun when he came across the body of an abandoned baby on his way to work, and was provoked to distribute birth control leaflets to working-class homes in the East End of London. He wrote savage newspaper articles denouncing domestic violence and attacking the inadequate sentences handed out to men who assaulted their wives and partners. *Representative Government* treats the opponents of female suffrage with withering contempt. But utilitarianism suffers from some obvious difficulties in handling equality, whether of rights or respect. On the face of it, inequalities that create happiness are good, and those that do not are bad. The standard response to anyone arguing for, say, extending the suffrage to women, opening educational and occupational opportunities to women, giving women the same rights over property as men, giving them the same rights over children if a marriage fails, arguing in short, for all the things Mill argued for, is that women are happy with things as they are. This makes it harder to describe *The Subjection of Women* as a utilitarian tract.

Indeed, only at the very end of *The Subjection of Women* does Mill appeal to the utilitarian consequences of allowing women to enter the same professions as men, and to live their lives on the same terms as men. The essay is very simply structured and argued. Mill inquires whether there is any obvious reason why women should enjoy fewer rights than men in education, employment, politics, property ownership, and marriage. Taking it for granted that the onus is on the defenders of inequality to prove their case, Mill's argument is essentially that there is nothing in the nature of women to suggest that, if they were given the same opportunities and education as men took for granted, they would not flourish as lawyers, doctors, politicians, and the like. To the objection that throughout human history women have failed to produce philosophers, mathematicians, playwrights, and the rest, Mill replies always that we have no idea what women can do under conditions of equality. What we call human nature is human nature as it is manipulated through the educational and familial arrangements of the societies that have so far existed. That women have so far not broken through the innumerable obstacles that society has placed in their way tells us nothing about what they might do in the absence of those obstacles.

The fairness of this argument is something on which critics have spilled much ink. Mill raises the evidential stakes very high. It is hard to know what evidence Mill would accept as showing that women might be naturally less capable than men of writing grand opera, while being naturally more capable of writing novels, or vice versa. On the other hand, Mill is surely right to suspect all arguments drawn from the supposed dictates of "nature." Aristotle's belief in the existence of those who were "slaves by nature" is not one a modern thinker could accept. Mill's argument casts an illuminating light on *On Liberty*. Just as we saw reason to believe that what underlay Mill's utilitarian defense of freedom in that essay was really a passion for individual autonomy, so we have reason to think that *The Subjection of Women* is driven by the same conviction. Mill thought that taking our way of life from the ideas of others is a betrayal of our capacity for freedom; and his passion for the life of a free and self-forming individual makes Mill a persuasive critic of the social habits that result in women's occupying an inferior position in work, art, and politics. His final argument in the book consists of a simple appeal to his male readers: would they sacrifice the freedom they had acquired as adults for any amount of the comfort they had enjoyed as children? If the answer was obviously no, they had no business refusing to women the freedom they so passionately wanted for themselves.[32] Since *The Subjection of Women* was the last book Mill published in his lifetime, it offered a significant final commentary on his father's educational experiment.

Mill acquired many of his anxieties regarding the dangers of mass society from the writer to whom we next turn, Alexis de Tocqueville. Before we do so, two more retrospective thoughts may detain us. The first is the importance of Mill's skepticism about the idea of human nature. We saw Rousseau undermine the older view that we could happily talk about human nature and man in the state of nature; what we saw before us was socialized human nature, human nature marked by the workings of a long historical evolution. Mill was seized of that skepticism; it was, he thought, the standing weakness of all forms of conservative thinking to mistake custom for nature. Custom was "second nature," and we must beware of mistaking it for first nature. The point is salutary; when politicians, priests, and polemicists denounce some practice as "unnatural" or attack a proposed reform as "unnatural," it is always worth substituting "not customary" for "unnatural" and seeing what, if anything, is lost. It is not a thought that would distress Hegel, since he had his own reasons for being skeptical about the naturalness of nature. A second point does draw a sharp line between Mill and Hegel and sets up some tension between Mill and Tocqueville. Hegel was comfortable with the way the modern world socialized us into an acceptance of the local social and political norms. Mill was not. Like modern communitarians, Hegel thought society formed us as rational individuals and exercised a continued tutelary discipline on us; in essence, society always gets the benefits of the doubt against an individual who complains that some institution or attitude is irrational or unduly restrictive of his liberty. Mill was as convinced as anyone that selfish infants are turned into dutiful adults only by the socialization process known as child rearing. But he thought society was in danger of overdoing the disciplinary process; for Mill it is the dissident individual who gets the benefit of the doubt. The argument continues, and one of the ways in which Tocqueville has a claim on our attention is that he thought that *political* liberalism had to rest on a more conservative social basis than anything Mill was comfortable with. And unlike Hegel, but entirely like Mill, he could not rest in the confidence that *Geist* was in command of history.

CHAPTER 20

Tocqueville and Democracy

The Unlikely Author of *Democracy in America*

AMERICAN READERS KNOW ALEXIS de Tocqueville as the author of *Democracy in America*. French readers know him better as the author of *L'ancien régime et la révolution*. Historians of the nineteenth-century imperialist ambitions of Britain and France know him as an enthusiast for the French conquest of Algeria and a writer whose ready acceptance of the cruelties suffered by the Berbers at the hands of the French army contrasts surprisingly with his sympathy for the sufferings of Native Americans at the hands of the Anglo-Americans.[1] I begin with Tocqueville's analysis of the successes and failures of American democracy, move on to a very brief discussion of his defense of French imperialism, and end with his account of why (and when) revolutions happen, and in particular why the French Revolution made both a great deal of difference to France and almost none. First, the author himself.

It is, on the face of it, unlikely that the most significant account of American democracy should have been written by a French aristocrat, especially one who was just twenty-five years old when he began his nine-month travels through the United States in 1831–32, and only thirty when he published the first volume of *Democracy in America*. What makes it even more unlikely is that Alexis de Tocqueville came from a strongly legitimist family, who were devoted to the restored Bourbon monarchy of Louis XVIII and Charles X. He went to the United States as a result of the fall of the Bourbon monarchy in the revolution of July 1830. After the installation of the "bourgeois monarch," Louis-Philippe, the duke of Orléans, Tocqueville suffered agonies of conscience when asked to swear allegiance to the new government as a condition of continuing in his career in the national administration. Both he and his superiors thought a period of absence would reduce tensions.[2] It did not; his friend and travelling companion, Gustave de Beaumont, was suspended from his post soon after their return, and both resigned. They had both been junior magistrates at Versailles, and the purpose of the visit was to study the American penal system: *Du système pénitentiaire aux États-Unis* appeared the year after their return and was widely used as a source book on prison reform long after its authors had left the legal service. They took their ostensible reason for the journey entirely seriously. So did their American hosts, and Tocqueville complained that they tried to show him not only every prison in the country but every institution in which Americans might be involuntarily detained.

Tocqueville came from an ancient and distinguished family, whose estates were in Normandy. His parents narrowly escaped death during the Terror; one of his grandparents met his end on the scaffold, as did his great-grandfather M. de Malesherbes, the liberal-minded censor under the old regime, executed because he had defended Louis XVI at his trial. Alexis was the youngest of his father's three sons, born a decade after these terrifying events, in July 1805. Tocqueville's extended family embraced every possible attitude toward the revolution and its aftermath; distant cousins had been Jacobins, and another distant cousin adopted the children of the executed Gracchus Babeuf; some served Napoleon, as others later served Louis-Philippe and Louis Bonaparte. Tocqueville's father, Hervé, was a constitutionally minded aristocrat of the kind his son discussed in *L'ancien régime*; events turned him into a monarchist and legitimist, happy to serve the heirs of Louis XVI and unwilling to serve anyone else. He rose to be *préfet* of several departments, including finally Seine-et-Oise, the summit of prefectorial ambitions. Its headquarters were in Versailles, where Hervé enjoyed the life of a courtier-administrator. His public life came to an end with the July Revolution, in 1830. He retired, and lived till 1856, dying at the age of eighty-four, only three years before Alexis.

Brought up in a pious, conservative household, in a family for whom public service at the highest level was both a duty and a right, Tocqueville was confided to the care of the abbé Leseur, who had been tutor to his father and his two older brothers, Hippolyte and Édouard. The abbé was a religious conservative and energetically contemptuous of liberals and liberalism, but a benign and encouraging tutor who took pains to develop his pupil's intellect. The teenage Tocqueville had a distinguished academic career at the lycée in Metz, went on to study law in Paris, and graduated in 1826. He joined the government legal service as a second best to the military career he was not healthy enough to contemplate. His writings reflect his sense of what he had missed when they praise both the humdrum, everyday, cheerful prosperity that the Americans achieved as rational law-abiding creatures and the glory that the French might achieve through their imperial exploits in Algeria.

In 1827 he was appointed *juge auditeur*. Before he could become bored with life as a bureaucrat, the revolution of 1830 put an end to the Bourbon monarchy and installed Louis-Philippe. Tocqueville gritted his teeth and swore allegiance, alienating his most fiercely legitimist relatives in the process. Soon afterward he and his friend and colleague Gustave de Beaumont devised their plan to visit the United States to examine its penal system. Since they would go at their own expense, their superiors saw no reason to refuse their request for leave, even though they kept them waiting six months for permission. On May 9, 1831, they arrived in New York.

Democracy in America has held an honored place in the canon of political analysis for almost two centuries. Its author wanted literary fame rather than an afterlife in political science syllabuses and a career at the summit of French politics. *Democracy* was written for the audience that had the first in its gift, and he hoped literary fame would launch him on the path to the second. The publication of the first volume of *Democracy*, in 1835, made him famous; the publication of the second volume, in 1840, led to his election to the Académie Française a year later. Fame liberated him in other ways. Throughout his youth he had fallen in love with unsuitable women—unsuitable as a matter of social standing. At the age of thirty, with a position in the world, and his mother dead, he could do as he chose, and he married Mary Mottley, a very ordinary middle-class Englishwoman whose exact age was uncertain, but who was at least six years older than he. It was an oddly successful marriage, though far from easy. They were ill-assorted, but devoted. She became a devout Catholic; he lost his faith in his teens and never got it back. He became a somewhat dilute deist, interested in mysticism, unhappy that he could not confide in his wife, and aware of the jealousy she felt for his confidante in these matters, Mme Swetchine.[3]

Tocqueville's ultimate ambitions were political; in 1837 he failed to be elected to the National Assembly, but succeeded two years after. He was a significant but not a successful figure; he was too visibly contemptuous of the bourgeois politicians whom he had to cultivate for success. In any case, he was opposed to the ministries of the 1840s and seemed destined to permanent opposition. The upheavals that began with the revolution of February 1848 that evicted Louis-Philippe and ended with Louis Bonaparte's coup d'état of December 1851 did not show him at his best. He mocked his sister-in-law for panicking in the face of the revolution, but came close to panic himself. This was intellectual, not physical, panic. His coolness in the face of physical danger was impressive; but his incomprehension of the causes of the revolution was surprising, and his reaction to the misery of the poor ungenerous. Nonetheless, his memoirs of the revolution are engrossing.[4] The underlying cause of the discontent that toppled Louis-Philippe was economic: a string of bad harvests brought ruin and near-famine to the countryside and raised the price of necessities in the cities. The way to preserve political stability was to relieve economic distress by any means possible. Mistakes would be corrigible once there was a decent harvest, social peace, and revived economic activity. Tocqueville's economics was that of the conservative wing of the Manchester school, and he saw measures of relief as steps toward expropriation and the guillotine. Like the British in the face of famine in Ireland, the interim government installed by the revolution responded to falling revenues with retrenchment, exacerbating the problem. When the Parisian workers rose in revolt in June 1848, Tocqueville's allies shot them down.

Things did not turn out as he expected. General Cavaignac, who had suppressed the uprising during the June Days, was defeated in the presidential elections of December 1848 by Louis Bonaparte. Tocqueville detested Bonaparte, but accepted the post of foreign minister in the Barrot government of 1849; when the government fell, he lost office and made it clear that he did not wish to serve again. He remained a member of the National Assembly, and served on the committee appointed to devise a new constitution for the Second Republic; his fame as an expert on the American Constitution gave him credibility, but his enthusiasm for American institutions alienated his fellow members. His political life came to an end with Louis Bonaparte's coup d'état of December 1851; it is possible that Tocqueville's one success in promoting American ideas about constitutions provoked the event: he persuaded the assembly to put term limits on the presidency. Faced with enforced retirement, Bonaparte took the obvious next step. Tocqueville was already very ill with tuberculosis, and until his death, in 1859, he led the life of a retired scholar. During his last years, he wrote the first part of a long-projected history of the French Revolution, *L'ancien régime et la révolution*. When John Stuart Mill wrote to thank Tocqueville for the gift of a copy of the book, he observed that few men had written three distinct masterpieces: the two volumes of *Democracy*, so different from one another, and *L'ancien régime*. Mill's praise was not excessive.[5] One modern critic thinks *Souvenirs*, his account of the 1848 revolution, is even better.[6]

Democracy in America and Democracy in America: Motivation

Tocqueville's ideas have been exploited by left and right; modern conservatives praise his strictures on big government and his enthusiasm for decentralization, many American liberals praise his concern with association and community, and everyone praises his devotion to political liberty. American politicians bask in his praise of their political system and overlook his contempt for the "coarse appearance" of the members of the House of Representatives.[7] Few readers notice his enthusiasm for the brutal methods of punishment he found in American prisons, and not many notice the repressiveness of his views on family life.

Tocqueville is elusive, but not unplaceable. French interest in the United States sprang from the French failure to bring the revolution of 1789 to a successful conclusion. French assistance to the rebellious colonies after 1776 had nothing to do with an enthusiasm for republican government, but was part of a French strategy to recover the ground the country had lost to Britain during the Seven Years' War—the war that ended with the British seizure of French India and much of French North America. Americans saw their revolution as the inspiration for an age of political renovation: free republics would everywhere replace hereditary monarchies and aristocracies. This was not the purpose to which Louis XVI's government committed its navy and seconded army commanders. The leaders of the American Revolution were not deceived; they understood that Spain and France helped them evict the British to protect their position to the south, west, and northwest of the thirteen liberated colonies, and they were unapologetic about making a quick and separate peace with the British to avert future trouble with their allies. Nonetheless, a liberal-minded Frenchman would feel a degree of paternal pride in the United States, and a patriotic Frenchman would see the United States as an ally in cutting Britain down to size.

America posed a deeply interesting question to any Frenchman with the political curiosity to ask it. How had Americans launched a revolution that aimed at establishing a free, stable, and constitutional government and made a success of it, while the French had in forty-one years lurched from absolute monarchy to constitutional monarchy, to the declaration of the republic, to mob rule, the Terror, and mass murder, and thence to a conservative republic, Napoleonic autocracy, the Bourbon restoration, further revolution, and the installation of an Orleanist constitutional monarchy? Up to a point, the answer was obvious; the Americans claimed—not wholly plausibly—that they were reluctant revolutionaries; they wanted to regain the English liberties they had exercised until the tyrannical Parliament of George III and his ministers tried to destroy them. Self-government was a long-established reality in colonial America; the collapse of British rule was followed not by anarchy but by the citizens governing themselves much as before. The democratization of institutions during the American Revolution was to some extent rolled back afterward; but independence was not a leap into the unknown. It was more nearly a leap into the past of the English Civil War, when the New Model Army learned to govern itself and the country by committees answerable to the rank and file. If Washington had been Cromwell, the American Revolution might have ended in military dictatorship; but if Washington had been Cromwell, he would not have been accepted as commander in chief of the Continental army.

That history raised the question of what the social and political attitudes were that meant that in one society individuals could cooperate and make self-government possible, while in another they could not, why the inhabitants of one country were active and ambitious and able to pursue "self-interest rightly understood," and those of another country were not. A stable political order that was both democratic and liberal required distinctive social, moral, and economic attachments; their analysis was an urgent task. These attachments constituted what social scientists later called "political culture," and what Montesquieu had studied as *les moeurs*; they were the product of the distinctive geographical setting of the American experiment and a colonial history of some duration. The United States came into existence as an independent nation-state almost two centuries after the first British colonists had arrived; many things, from the open frontier to the absence of feudalism, to the religious allegiances of the first colonists, shaped the attitudes and created the abilities that allowed Americans to make their revolution without descending into anarchy.

The new republic then reinforced the culture that reinforced it. There was a virtuous circle: the political system gave the citizens an intense attachment to the political system; their attachment helped it to function effectively, and its effectiveness made the citizens still more attached to it. Equally interesting were the indirect supports that enabled the political system to combine popular sovereignty and individual liberty. Tocqueville was particularly impressed by the role of women; although they had almost complete freedom as girls, they became the guardians of respectability once they were married. They exercised a psychological and moral discipline that was badly needed in a raw new country. The benign moral tutelage exerted by American women ensured that enough men were sufficiently public-spirited and law-abiding to govern themselves without anarchy, and that in a highly decentralized country communities could be efficiently self-policing.[8]

Tocqueville's Influences: Rousseau

Tocqueville was sometimes criticized for having gone to America full of preconceptions. "He had thought too much before he had seen anything" was one comment. Whether or not he had thought *too* much before he looked, he certainly went with a mind well stocked with ideas about the prospects of popular government in the nineteenth century. Three sources should be acknowledged. The first is Rousseau, one of the two thinkers whom Tocqueville said he thought about every day. The claim is surprising because Rousseau was a philosopher. Even though he was a composer, a novelist, and a speculative historian as well, he was the philosopher who inspired Kant's moral and political philosophy. Tocqueville was not a philosopher, but a political sociologist, even though he had strong opinions about the meaning of human existence. Rousseau analyzed natural right, individual interest, and the common good, in ways that Kant and later writers took up and extended, and academic philosophers still do; Tocqueville did not. He had the sensibilities of a sociologist and a historian and the political intuitions of a national statesman; he thought the spectacle of American democracy astonishing and wished to know whence it had sprung, how it worked, and what its prospects were. Rousseau's inquest into the legitimacy of the state and his location of that legitimacy in the moral authority of the general will were not Tocqueville's concerns.

Rousseau's impact is nonetheless easily explained. Not only America but the whole Western world were imbued with the spirit of equality that Rousseau had articulated in the *Social Contract* and *Discourse on the Origin of Inequality*. What equality entailed in social, economic, and political contexts was disputable; the compatibility of equality in one realm with equality in another was uncertain; it was essential to discover what kinds of equality sustained liberty and what kinds of equality threatened it. *Democracy* and *L'ancien régime* were eloquent on these points. The new belief in human equality was part of the rise of individualism. Rousseau was as eloquent as Tocqueville on good and bad forms of individuality; Tocqueville was sharper in his analysis, but not at odds with Rousseau. Bad individualism—which Tocqueville tended to call "individualism" without qualification—was a form of self-centeredness quite different from a strong sense of ourselves as moral beings with duties to perform and rights to protect. That was good individualism or individuality. Bad individualism was driven by envy and fear; and its psychological impact on political life was potentially disastrous. Its conception of equality would inspire us to drag others down to our own level rather than inspiring us to cooperate with them to elevate the moral and intellectual level of us all. The egalitarianism that feared all difference and resented all superiority was inimical to variety and change. It was from Tocqueville's plangent discussion in the second volume of *Democracy* that Mill learned the fear that animates *On Liberty*. Although equality and sameness are logically distinct, a democratic—more exactly a "mass"—society would confound them.[9] Nonetheless, in the right conditions, emphasized in the first part of *Democracy*, equality of condition promoted liberty, by promoting self-reliance and ambition. Rousseau's emphasis on the moral equality that a rights-respecting regime is committed to was not alien to Tocqueville, even if he was not disposed to rehearse issues in moral philosophy.

Montesquieu

Rousseau raised difficult questions about the possibility of sustaining republican institutions in the modern world; Montesquieu had raised others forty years before, and his doubts were Tocqueville's companions. Montesquieu had raised many of the same anxieties as Rousseau about the incompatibility of classical ideals of political virtue and classical standards of patriotic self-sacrifice with the comfortable, commercial, self-interested values of the modern world. Montesquieu's style was closer to Tocqueville's own; he was a sociologically minded political analyst, less inclined than Rousseau to complain about the world he was analyzing. He wanted to understand the impact of climate and geography and domestic life and what we have for a century called "political socialization"—the process of bringing up children to understand the political arrangements of their society and induce a sufficient loyalty to them (or perhaps a sufficient loyalty to other features of our society to induce a thoroughgoing disgust with the political arrangements under which they live).

Montesquieu was thoroughly, and rightly, frightened of both the despotism of one man and the damage that religious and ideological passion could do. This prompted him to explain the virtues of French absolute monarchy and its difference from Ottoman despotism in terms of its "moderation." Unlike despotism, it was not a regime of fear. A substantially independent legal system administered legal justice that was not the arbitrary whim of the monarch; individuals owned their own property as something other than the revocable gift of their ruler; French subjects were not the slaves of their sovereign; they might not be Spartan citizens, let alone Athenians, but they were not Persian slaves. Like any regime that depended on a balance of forces, French monarchy was vulnerable to pressures that might render it much less defensible; this was why *les moeurs* were so important. The extrapolitical attitudes, allegiances, habits, and beliefs that maintained a consensus on what was and was not tolerable within the existing political order provided the shock-absorbing mechanisms that allowed the political system to operate, and to secure the attachment of the French people to the regime.

Guizot

Tocqueville spent his life as an intellectual brooding—as volume 2 of *Democracy* and *L'ancien régime* attest—on the strengths and weaknesses of the prerevolutionary monarchy and on the nature of despotism. It was not only his eighteenth-century predecessors whom he listened to. Before he went to the United States, he spent two years listening to François Guizot's lectures called "The History of Civilization in Europe." The critics who said that Tocqueville had thought too much before he saw the United States meant that he went imbued with Guizot's vision of the causes of social change, and with many of Guizot's political attachments; the first was true, the second not. Guizot was eighteen years older than Tocqueville, but long outlived him; he was a Huguenot bourgeois from Nîmes, where his father had been a victim of the revolution. He was educated in Geneva and then in Paris, became a literary figure in his twenties, but even when appointed as a professor by Napoleon I kept his distance from the imperial regime. As a Protestant and a believer in constitutional monarchy, he was persona non grata to the conservative supporters of the restored Bourbon monarchy, but a good servant to more liberal ministries.

When he was appointed professor of modern history at the Sorbonne in 1828, he delivered his famous course of lectures on European history, with their emphasis on the irresistible rise of the middle classes. The British had become the most successful modern nation because they had absorbed this rising class into a stable political system; the English constitutional monarchy had diverted into useful channels the populist energies that exploded in the French Revolution because they had not been made use of earlier. The principle of antagonism and especially the need to maintain and find room for the expression of an antagonism of opinions in order to sustain an open, lively, and progressive society had been usefully embodied in English institutions. The moral was that democracy—in a loose and unpolitical sense that embraced an egalitarian social climate and social and economic mobility rather than universal suffrage and institutions to give effect to the popular will— was irresistible, but had to be directed by a wise political elite. When Tocqueville said in *Democracy* that a new political science was required for a new world, he was agreeing with Guizot.

In their politics, narrowly speaking, Tocqueville and Guizot were not at one. Guizot was a willing Orleanist and Tocqueville not; Guizot saw his political role as that of a barrier to the left, and before 1848 Tocqueville thought safety lay in giving the left a larger role in French politics. As foreign minister and prime minister, Guizot promoted a foreign policy that would conciliate the British and avoid the diversion of French energies into the pursuit of ephemeral glory, while Tocqueville was a less cautious imperialist and colonialist. Guizot's influence was on Tocqueville's analytical approach, and on his preconceptions about what he would find in America, the country that, as Mill said after reading both Guizot and Tocqueville, epitomized the rise of an essentially provincial middle class.[10]

The Frenchness of *Democracy in America*

Rousseau, Montesquieu, and Guizot gave Tocqueville his intellectual bearings and taught him how to frame his questions. America gave him his inspiration, but it was France that he thought about. *Democracy in America* is a book about America; but it is also a very French book about France. It could not have been written by an Englishman or even by an American. This is not only because English visitors who went to the United States wrote snobbish little books about the appalling table manners of the American middle classes; the French did that as well, and Tocqueville's reactions to his hosts' manners were equally sharp; but he knew it did not matter, and he left his observations in his private letters. No English writer could have begun volume 2 of *Democracy* as Tocqueville did, by observing that the Americans are an unphilosophical people, among whom the ideas of Descartes can make no headway, but who nonetheless behave as practical Cartesians: "America is thus one of the countries of the world where the precepts of Descartes are least studied and most widely applied. We need not be surprised by that."[11]

The genius of Americans for starting from scratch and inventing what they needed was a commonplace; the usual and wholly plausible view was that it was born of the fact that they were building a new civilization in the wilderness. It took a Frenchman to draw a philosophical moral and describe it as practical Cartesianism; it may well have taken a Frenchman who had lost his own Catholic faith, but who thought that religion was a vital ingredient in *les moeurs* that sustained American democracy. Analyzing the idea of America was not unintelligible to English observers in the 1830s; if it had been, they could not have read Tocqueville as they did. Nonetheless, the contrasts Tocqueville had in mind were overwhelmingly between American attitudes and beliefs and those of his countrymen; when he says "we," as he often does, it is "we French." English readers found him puzzling, and even Mill admitted that his writing was "abstruse" and suffered from a lack of illustrations to enable his readers to see what he meant. The greater difficulty was that he was drawing contrasts between the mores of Americans and the mores of Frenchmen for French readers.

There are simpler ways in which *Democracy* is very French. Where Tocqueville has a chance to praise the French temperament and dispraise the Anglo-Saxon, he takes it. The nationalist politician of the later 1830s and 1840s was present on his younger self's American journey. The suggestion that Tocqueville went to the United States to see France more clearly might be thought fanciful; but we reach the same point if we begin entirely unfancifully. The Americans had created a republic, and, as Benjamin Franklin had said at the time, the question was whether they could keep it. They had. One did not have to believe that they had created utopia to believe that they had done something astonishing; moreover, they had done what the French could not. The British were not relevant; on one view of British history, the British had rightly not tried again to create another republic after making such a bad job of it in 1649; on another, they had reduced the monarch to a hereditary president for life and dressed up a de facto parliamentary republic in the costume of a de jure constitutional monarchy. Tocqueville could not know that he would live to see the short-lived Second Republic and the early years of the Second Empire, but he knew that in America he must discover what was possible in France.

Tocqueville was not a republican. He thought France would be better off with a constitutional monarchy; but he knew history was not on his side. Montesquieu's recipe for a moderate modern monarchy required a social order in which political power rested in the hands of intermediate social groups; it needed not a small and exclusive nobility but a large and permeable gentry and a self-confident and responsible bourgeoisie.

The lesson was drawn from England, but made sense of America. Tocqueville's view, expressed in *L'ancien régime* but already in place in *Democracy*, was that Louis XIV and his successors had undermined their own position by hollowing out the social hierarchy. The French nobility was bribed with financial privileges to accept the loss of political power; as a result there was no shock absorber between the monarchy and the populace. This analysis rested on a familiar view of the connection between political legitimacy and social function. Deference to our superiors comes easily when they are doing something useful; if they bear more than their share of military service, staff the local system of justice, and represent the district in parliament, we may think they are richer and more privileged than they absolutely deserve, but not that they are parasites. Functionless privilege can only rest on sullen acquiescence or fear.

So Tocqueville looked at America and saw France, talked to Americans and thought of his fellow Frenchmen. *Democracy in America* is an insightful account of the egalitarian United States of 1831, and an eerily prescient analysis of liberal democracy almost two centuries later, written for a French audience. Thanks to John Stuart Mill as much as anyone, it came to be understood as a tract on what was later called "mass society" and a book *for* Americans as well as about them; it also came to be understood as a tract for the English. *On Liberty* would have been a different book, and perhaps not written at all, if Mill had not read *Democracy in America*, and more especially the second volume with its reflections on the quiet despotism to which a mass society might succumb.

Equality as a Providential Force

If *Democracy* generated morals that Tocqueville expected his readers to find universally applicable, the reason was that what was unmissable in America was becoming visible in Europe. Tocqueville's central claim was that increasing social equality was an unstoppable force transforming Western society. How long this had been happening was less clear; sometimes Tocqueville suggested that what was visible in nineteenth-century Europe was the culmination of processes at work since the eleventh century, and sometimes he relied on the more familiar contrast between inegalitarian, aristocratic societies and their egalitarian bourgeois successors that suggested that recent changes mattered more.[12] The claim that there was an irresistible movement toward the "equalization of conditions" underpinned one of Tocqueville's methodological claims. He said that the new world required a new political science for its analysis, but did not say whether he thought he had devised it or what it was.

Tocqueville's comments on equality sometimes sound more providential than scientific. The implacable progress of equality, described as a river that may be channeled but cannot be stopped in its course, suggests to Tocqueville that the process is of divine origin; it is not only the outcome of one thing after another, economic change, intellectual change, moral change, and so on.[13] His readiness to see the hand of God in the process was not just a figure of speech; Tocqueville emphasized the contrast between the viewpoint of the human observer forced to look at a small slice of the historical process and extrapolate as best he can, and that of God, who grasps the whole process in one intellectual moment, needing no generalizations or extrapolations. There is little point in speculating about how far Tocqueville might have pressed the point, since he eschewed methodological commentary on his own work. Mill gave a down-to-earth account of Tocqueville's achievement. Tocqueville had demonstrated the method of a true social science; he had founded his insights into political change upon both a knowledge of fundamental human nature and a knowledge of historical trends. Tocqueville was happy to be praised as a genius but not explicit about how far he accepted Mill's account of what his genius consisted in.

Democracy in America: Volume 1 versus Volume 2

The two volumes of *Democracy* are very different in tone, the first strikingly optimistic about the prospects for the United States and democracy, the second much more uncertain; they are also laid out very differently. The change of approach and expectations between the two volumes is more than enough to justify Mill's observation that they were two masterpieces rather than two halves of one masterpiece. The first volume is not unphilosophical or unreflective, but it hews closer than the second to the task of giving an account of how the United States came into existence, what its salient features are, politically, socially, and intellectually, how relations are conducted between the various social classes—Tocqueville was one of the first visitors to be struck by the way in which almost all issues in the United States were turned into legal issues—and how the religious and moral outlook of Americans sustains their "experiment in liberty."

The first volume was far more than a report to his countrymen by a very clever young man who had taken a close look at the United States; but Tocqueville's introduction suggests that it is at least that. The organization of the book—eighteen chapters in two sections, each chapter broken into very short discussions of particular points—matches the briskness of the style. The first eight chapters introduce the country, its history and its Constitution, and the next ten show the political system in operation. The first volume is firmly focused on democratic political institutions and on the federal system within which the Americans had embedded them. There is a great deal of commentary on the social, economic, and moral conditions that enabled the Americans to make such a success of democracy; the final chapter contains Tocqueville's famously anxious discussion under the title "The Present State and Probable Future of the Three Races That Inhabit America"; but the book is essentially an answer to the question of how the Americans maintain with such success a stable but lively democracy.

The second volume, in contrast, is organized as four distinct sections, focused on the intellectual life of the United States, on the "sentiments" of the American people, on the "morals"—essentially *les moeurs*—of a democracy, and finally on how they come together in affecting the political outlook of Americans. Quite apart from the more pessimistic tone of the whole volume, there is a change of focus from the success of a lively, if chaotic, political system to the cultural failings of mass society. The explanation of the change did not owe much to Tocqueville's reassessment of the American evidence; the nine months he spent there were all he saw of America at first hand, though he kept up a correspondence with the friends he had made for the rest of his life.[14] French political life cast a shadow over his memory of America. The question to which the first volume had offered an optimistic answer was whether equality and liberty are compatible with each other, and the answer was that in the United States they are. The natural conclusion, and the burden of Tocqueville's argument, is that *les moeurs* are favorable to liberty in the United States and that in France they are not. The political culture of the United States had not changed dramatically, but Tocqueville had thought further about the less attractive aspects of Jacksonian America, and his characteristic melancholy reasserted itself when the vivacity of everyday American life had faded from memory and French political life was a daily irritant.

Democracy One

Tocqueville began by saying that a wholly new world needs a new political science to interpret it. What he provided was what Max Weber later described as an "ideal type" analysis. He wanted to reveal the essence of democracy by heightening some empirical phenomena and neglecting others, in order to achieve a sharper picture of the forces sweeping modern societies toward a more egalitarian future. The reader who looks for definitions of Tocqueville's key terms looks in vain; we get a portrait of America, not a photograph. Better, it is a film rather than a photograph: there is a narrative of the movement that generated democracy; it is a narrative of increasing equality of "conditions." *Equality of condition* is the crucial phenomenon under discussion—what creates it, and what its political consequences are. When Mill reviewed volume I of *Democracy*, he complained mildly that Tocqueville talked of democracy—which is essentially a political notion and means, as it says, the rule of the people—but wrote about equality. Mill wished to distinguish sharply between the radical demand for universal suffrage on the one hand and social and economic equality on the other. When he wrote *On Liberty*, he himself conflated the two, much as Tocqueville had done. Equality of condition was not equality of income, education, or anything in particular; it consisted in the absence of social obstacles to whatever ambitions an American entertained. Critics complain that Tocqueville underestimated the extent of economic inequality in the United States, which may well be true; but he was looking at the contrast between his own country and the United States, and was struck by what observers are still struck by—that almost all Americans believed they belonged to the middle class. Some 90 percent of Americans in the early twenty-first century report themselves as "middle class," with more than 50 percent declaring themselves as "middle middle class."

The first volume of *Democracy* is a long argument with historical illustrations. The argument is that in the United States *the people* truly rule, and that there—perhaps there alone—they rule without the danger of a relapse into anarchy or tyranny. Not everything in the United States is admirable; but their example poses to the French the question why the Americans can do what "we" cannot. So we can pursue Tocqueville along the two tracks of his argument: first, that the American people truly rule, nontyrannically, nonchaotically, and preserving the civil liberties of all save slaves and Native Americans, and, second, what enables them to do it.

That the people truly rule is the theme of one of Tocqueville's characteristically brief chapters; it opens part 2 of the first volume and recites the obvious fact that in the United States almost every position of authority is not only elective but requires reelection every year or two; not only legislators but judges in most jurisdictions, and the executive everywhere, answer almost continuously to the people. The surprisingness of this to a Frenchmen used to a hereditary king, senators for life, a very restricted electorate, and a judiciary that was part of the royal bureaucracy can hardly be exaggerated. Tocqueville immediately observes that when we talk of the people governing, we must recall that "it is the majority that governs in the name of the people," bringing to the fore the question raised by Madison and Jefferson of the conditions under which the rule of the people degenerates into the tyranny of the majority. Here he deflates the anxiety by observing that the majority consists for the most part of peaceful citizens who sincerely desire the good of their country, but the anxiety is only momentarily set on one side. Although the majority is composed of peaceful citizens wanting the good of their country, the majority is omnipotent, and defenses against it nonexistent.[15]

Tocqueville's discussion of the tyranny of the majority rests on more than one thought. He assumes that sovereignty, in the Hobbesian sense, must reside somewhere. Like many political philosophers, he thought that in every political and legal system there must somewhere be an absolute and unconstrained power. Critics of the Hobbesian view, a view held not only by Bentham and his followers but by Blackstone as well, point to the United States as a legal and political system where there is no Hobbesian sovereign; it is one system, but does not receive its unity from a sovereign. Tocqueville ignores this line of reasoning. The majority is the sovereign, and absolute; and because there is no appeal against the majority, it is strictly speaking despotic. This is not an absurd thought. Mill held that the government of India by the East India Company was a despotism. It was a benign despotism; and the company was itself regulated by the British government. Nonetheless, it was not answerable to its Indian subjects and was therefore a despotism.

The majority in a democracy is not answerable to the minority, and is strictly in the position of any other despot; but the argument claims too much. It is a logical truth that in all regimes there must be a point at which appeals against legal and political decisions or legislation come to an end, and the losers must either acquiesce or take up arms. It is not a truth at all that any person or group has despotic authority. The U.S. Constitution puts innumerable obstacles in the way of anyone trying to exercise tyrannical power; the president cannot dissolve Congress, but must wait for elections to provide him with a more compliant Congress, if he is lucky. Congress cannot remove the president in the way the English Parliament can remove ministers and governments. Long before Tocqueville went to the United States, the Supreme Court had arrogated to itself the authority to declare legislation unconstitutional, even if passed by Congress and signed by the president. If an enraged majority wants to do something that is at present unconstitutional, and presses for changes in the constitution, it must endure whatever delays it takes for Congress and the individual states to pass the amendment by a sufficient majority. It can be done; during World War I, the Eighteenth Amendment to the Constitution was passed over the veto of President Wilson, and ratified in 1919. It prohibited the sale of alcoholic beverages and had mixed results; it saved many Americans from alcohol-related diseases and opened up a profitable trade for gangsters and bootleggers; and it was repealed by the Twenty-First Amendment in 1933. Whether the fact that it took three years to pass into law and less than one to repeal is a sad commentary on human nature, or a reassuring one, is not at issue. The point is that it takes a long and sustained campaign to pass a constitutional amendment, which makes it very difficult for an enraged majority to rewrite the fundamental rules to suit itself.

Tocqueville knew this. The first part of volume I of *Democracy* gives a long account of the history and geography of the country and its constitutional arrangements. Like other observers, he pointed out that America was to an extraordinary degree a country ruled by lawyers. He thought this was one of its virtues, which may have owed something to pride in his own profession. However that may be, he understood that the constitutional arrangements of the United States were intended to do two things at once, to establish an effective national government and to prevent any faction, even what Madison called the "majority faction," from exercising untrammeled power. He also understood the effects of the way the Constitution gave large and small states identical representation in the Senate, and how it was part of the effort to take the issue of slavery off the agenda. In thinking about Tocqueville's anxieties about the tyranny of the majority, we should recall that the barriers to majority tyranny protected slave owners more effectively than religious minorities and eccentrics.

It is puzzling that Tocqueville supposed that the majority was omnipotent; to an English observer, familiar with the sovereignty of Parliament, it seemed then, as now, that majorities faced innumerable obstacles in getting their own way, and that the most impressive feature of American politics is the ability of well-placed interest groups to extract benefits from the political system that the majority cannot. But like Madison, Tocqueville thought that laws were "parchment barriers." The omnipotence of the majority was a deep fact about American life, and ran deeper than the Constitution. To understand how deep, we must briefly explore Tocqueville's explanation of why the English succeeded in settling America and the French did not. The paradox is that the French did everything needed for success and failed, while the English gave hardly a thought to the matter and succeeded. That had immense consequences for the way Americans—Anglo-Americans—thought of themselves. The French government intended there to be properly organized colonies up and down the Mississippi valley, took pains to understand the geography, climate, soil, and anything else about which information could be had, and placed military settlements in sensible places; it supplied them with efficient government on the French model. They did not thrive; they did not grow, but shrank. When the British found them an obstacle, they brushed them aside.

Conversely, the eastern shores of America were settled by Englishmen who as often as not were fleeing their home government or their creditors. Although the British government claimed sovereignty over their affairs and sent out royal governors, the governments of the colonies were contrived by the emigrants on a self-help basis. Some colonists disliked the governments they had set up as much as they disliked the one they had escaped, and set off to find somewhere where they could establish a community more to their liking. These unorganized and spontaneous communities thrived. It does not follow that Englishmen and Frenchmen are members of wholly different races, although Tocqueville sometimes suggests they might be. Tocqueville's account of the different behavior of the French and English governments of the seventeenth and eighteenth centuries is the key to the underlying claim. French governmental tutelage could do much, but it enervated the individual Frenchman; English neglect liberated the energies of the colonists. That greatly affected *les moeurs* of Anglo-Americans.

There are many problems in Tocqueville's account of his fellow countrymen. He sometimes suggests that the French were essentially stay-at-homes, and sometimes the opposite: the French sought glory while the English did not. To add a final complexity he also observed, as others had, that the English were rarely tempted to slip out of white society and turn themselves into Native Americans. They did not intermarry with

Native Americans, and English trappers and hunters did not merge with the other inhabitants of the wilderness, as their French counterparts did. It is initially difficult to discern what Tocqueville is up to. It is very hard to see the pursuit of glory, the search for domestic tranquility, and a happy return to the life of the noble savage as the major influences on a group of people; the different passions seem too much at odds with one another.

One can rescue Tocqueville, and when we see how, we have the clue to the tyranny of the majority. Tocqueville asks why the English ended up settling America and colonizing the country in ways the French could not. The shortest answer would be "Puritanism," not so much Calvinist Protestantism as the mind-set invoked by Max Weber in *The Protestant Ethic and the Spirit of Capitalism*. Compared with the French in their stay-at-home moods, the Englishman will not live under a government to which he has not consented, and will not accept the boundaries of his present world as those he must accept. Compared with the Frenchman in search of glory, the Englishman will stick patiently to the task he has set himself and beat the wilderness into fertile farmland and pasture. Unlike the Frenchman ready to succumb to the charms of the wilderness, he thinks the wilderness is to be tamed and made useful. His character has drawbacks; it can be hard, narrow, and unimaginative. It is unthinking about the losses suffered by those who get in the way: Native Americans, black slaves, and the perceivedly idle and ignorant of all races.

The United States exists because Englishmen of this kind created the new republic. Imbued with a strong sense of their own rectitude, they set up political institutions that amplified the authority of the majority. Tocqueville knew that the common European view of America was that the government was feeble; observers envied the freedom of American citizens, but were struck by how little authority the federal government wielded and how few levers of power were at its disposal. Tocqueville turns the thought around. What is impressive is not how much freedom Americans possess but how little. He was impressed by how little protection they had against its loss and how far the political system reinforced the authority of the majority. A nontyrannical government requires the possibility of an appeal from the decisions of one authority to another authority that can exercise a check. In America, says Tocqueville, no such check exists. The reason is the omnipresence and omnipotence of public opinion. Every institution is an instrument of public opinion; the legislature reflects public opinion, so the laws it passes reflect public opinion; judges are elected by the people and hold their posts only so long as they implement the law in ways that reflect public opinion. To say that the majority is omnipotent is to say that public opinion is omnipresent and omnipotent. The institutional checks and balances that a legalistic view of the American Constitution emphasizes impressed him less than the ability of public opinion to bypass them.

Nonetheless, America remains free because in practical matters Americans are self-reliant, uninclined to exert their power over one another to the limits of what is possible, and able to organize their lives with little assistance from, or control by, government. Tocqueville writes wryly about the contrast between France and America as regards the invisibility of central government; Americans respond to the absence of the tutelage that the French state aspires to provide by organizing themselves to provide what they need for themselves. Everything hangs together: tasks like jury service force Americans to play a part in public affairs and provide a form of political education. Vast numbers of local newspapers reinforce this political education, and their varied allegiances ensure that the uniformity of opinion to which democracy is vulnerable is constantly broken up and has to reform against opposition.

Tocqueville's recipe for the survival of liberty within a democratic society is not *only* a matter of preserving the "antagonism of opinions," but that antagonism is vital. It does not rest on nothing, as though American society was a debating society. Tocqueville acknowledges the foundations of political debate in economic life. America was the paradigmatic land of opportunity. He was writing before the great period of westward expansion, and before the trading and industrial cities of the east coast and the Mississippi took in Catholic migrants from southern and central Europe, Jews from eastern Europe, radical German and Austro-Hungarian exiles after 1848, and so on. Still, by European standards, the thrust westward was already astonishing. The American economy was agricultural—in the broad sense that included the tobacco, cotton, and sugar produced for distant markets by slave labor—and mercantile, with cities springing up in the interior to service small-scale industry and the processing of agricultural products. The textile industry of New England was growing fast, but the industrialization built on Pennsylvania coal and iron was still thirty years away. America was nonetheless much more prosperous than European societies at the same level of development; the emigrant looked around him and contrasted his situation in America with his situation in Europe, and was content.

Different regions had different interests, saw the world differently; this diversity of economic interests kept political debate bubbling. It nonetheless stayed within bounds. American religion in particular kept American citizens self-disciplined, respectable; it was also important in making them take worldly success seriously as a badge of respectability. Tocqueville's interest in religion was implicit in his Montesequieuan assumptions: physical causes made a difference to the success of a non-tyrannical republic, since some climates fostered despotism and others self-reliance, and bred citizens who would not brook tyranny; the laws made much more difference; and *les moeurs* made the greatest difference. Religion, both in the sense of belief and more importantly in the sense of social practice, was a central part of *les moeurs*. The Americans had contrived a surprising device for making religion a powerful social force. They had written the complete separation of church and state into the Constitution. Unlike ancien régime France, America had no alliance of wealthy and useless clergy with wealthy and useless aristocrats. Whatever reasons Americans might have for disliking their government could not turn into anti-clericalism; conversely, if they were disaffected from whatever church they belonged to, they could move to another or set one up from scratch. The prerevolutionary French union of church and state implicated each in the unpopularity of the other. It was a familiar observation that anticlericalism is more common in Catholic countries than in Protestant ones; Tocqueville was less interested in that fact than in the prospects for the survival of religion in a bustling, progressive, and modernizing society. He thought American democracy needed the support of religion more than more traditional and hierarchical societies. The restlessness of an egalitarian people and the economic uncertainty—

for both the prosperous and the less successful——that permeated such a society demanded an antidote. Religion created the "habits of the heart" that provided consolation in the midst of misfortune and steadiness in the midst of uncertainty.

Tocqueville ends the first volume of *Democracy* with some somber reflections on the relations between "the three races" that coexist in the United States. They are the white Europeans, the American Indians, and the Negro slaves. Tocqueville had no doubt that the Indians were doomed and that their extinction was a moral disaster. The bleakness of this assessment was characteristic of Tocqueville; he had a strong sense of the difference between what was inevitable and what was admirable. The extinction of the Native Americans is a moral disaster not only because the cruelty with which they are treated is disgusting, nor only because the white government has violated every treaty it has signed and respects its own agreements merely as long as it is convenient——though these are actions of which any decent person should be ashamed. It is also a disaster because it is the destruction of an essentially aristocratic way of life. Set against the humdrum, self-centered placidity of ordinary American life, the Indians' cultivation of honor, courage, and the virtues familiar from military aristocracies in Europe exemplified for Tocqueville everything that democracies are in danger of losing. Nonetheless, there was no way of preventing it; to live alongside Europeans has everywhere been disastrous for native peoples. Even if the Europeans were determined to prevent the disaster, they would not know how.[16]

As to the black inhabitants of the United States, Tocqueville was equally bleak. The situation of Negro slaves was obviously intolerable. Tocqueville's concern, however, was with the damage that the institution of slavery did to the white inhabitants of America. His bleakness reflected his sense of the impossibility of achieving any happy outcome, with or without emancipation. His argument about the demoralizing effect of slavery on the slave-owning society was not novel; but his exposition of it was much enlivened by the fact that he had, at great peril, traveled down the Ohio and could see the achievements of slavery on one bank of the river and those of free labor on the other. It was clear to him that the states where slavery was dominant were doomed to backwardness; in absolute terms, they might be more prosperous than most European countries, but they would not feel so, because their northern neighbors would be so much more prosperous than they.[17]

Tocqueville has been rightly admired by sociologists for his insistence that it is not absolute but comparative levels of well-being that determine whether a population is happy or resentful. Just as American patriotism is enhanced by the fact that immigrants compare their American present with their European past, southerners will increasingly resent the superior standard of living of northerners. The danger was that the white population in the slave states would be concerned only to preserve its superiority to its Negro serfs and would acquire all the bad habits of a decadent aristocracy. Meanwhile, the states where free labor was the rule would thrive and prosper; manufacturing cities would spring up, and their banks and trading companies would profit not only from the efforts of the free states but from those of the slave states, too. Such a state of affairs could not continue indefinitely, and whether it would spell the end of the United States was anyone's guess. The misery for the black slaves was that emancipation would do them little good. Northerners were opposed to slavery but no more willing than their southern counterparts to live alongside and intermarry with freed Negro slaves. Second-class citizenship and social apartheid would be the lot of freed slaves.

Tocqueville did not foresee the Civil War, although his letters to American correspondents after 1840 become increasingly unhappy as tensions between the northern and the southern states increased.[18] Nor was slavery the only cause of potential disunion that he mentioned, either in *Democracy* or in his letters. It is often said that he paid too little attention to the impact of Andrew Jackson's presidency and the arrival in the United States of the ethos of *enrichissez-vous* that Louis-Philippe brought to France. This is not quite just. In the middle of the discussion of the impact of slavery on American political cohesion, Tocqueville breaks off to observe that the center of gravity of the United States is inexorably shifting to the Mississippi basin. What concerns him about that fact is the character of the men who are thrusting westward from the eastern states. They are brash, impatient, headstrong, uninterested in the politics of the states from which they have emerged or have been expelled; a few years earlier, they had inspired American commentators to wonder whether civilized Americans tended to degenerate in the wilderness. The frontier is a double-edged feature of American life; it aids cohesion because it offers a safety valve for restless spirits, and the possibility of redemption for individuals whose first gambles have failed; on the other hand, it removes the restless, the ill disciplined, the impatient, and the reckless from the disciplining effects of a settled environment. If such people form the majority of the American population in forty years' time, chaos may be the young democracy's lot. But those fears came to haunt Tocqueville in the 1850s, not in the 1830s.

Democracy Two

After reading the first volume of *Democracy*, one might wonder what was left to say about America. Tocqueville was sure there was much. The division of intellectual labor between the two volumes is not obvious, but four topics have been salient in the minds of commentators for the past half century. The first is Tocqueville's ambivalence about individualism and individuality, a subject that reappeared in American sociology after World War II in David Riesman's *The Lonely Crowd* and two decades later in Richard Sennett's *The Fall of Public Man*. The second is Tocqueville's discussion of the American genius for association, the third his thoughts on the family, and the fourth his vision of "soft despotism."

Tocqueville did not mince his words about American cultural life. He thought democracies unsuited to the production of high culture, and regarded American life as both frenetic and monotonous, a view held by most European visitors. He did not think much of the rhetorical abilities of American statesmen, and although the Americans were practical Cartesians, he did not think they could produce great American philosophers—as, of course, they did, with Peirce, James, and Dewey at the end of the century. American readers do not flinch at this unkindness. What unnerves them is the discussion of individualism. Tocqueville believed that the effect of equality was to make Americans more enthusiastic for equality than for freedom. This is the underlying theme of the second volume of *Democracy*, and its implications are everywhere.

Individualism and Retreat

Tocqueville was one the first writers to use the word "individualism"; he gave it a very particular meaning. It is the polar opposite of "individuality," understood as a strong sense of our own identity and the confidence to make something of ourselves that Mill praises in *On Liberty*. Tocqueville is diagnosing the feeling that leads Americans to turn away from the public realm and inward on themselves. It "is a reflective and peaceable sentiment that disposes each citizen to isolate himself from the mass of those like him, and to withdraw to one side with his family and friends, so that after having thus created a little society for his own use, he willingly abandons society at large to itself."[19] By the end of the short chapter in which this account appears, the world that the citizen, a citizen only in name, has retreated to has shrunk yet further. The process of retreat threatens to "confine him wholly in the solitude of his own heart." This is the image of the lonely crowd, of which so much was later made. Tocqueville does not draw on elaborate psychological theories to explain this retreat from the outside world. It is a retreat from the public world into the domestic world; it is not a manifestation of selfishness but a retreat from engagement.

This incapacity to engage with public affairs and politics is what Tocqueville fears almost more than anything else. These anxieties are more directly political than they became when Mill took them up and made them the foundation of *On Liberty*. Mill wanted individuals to make of themselves everything they could: to think for themselves and each to live her or his life through and through as their own project. Tocqueville's concern was political; he wanted to see fully engaged citizens, not docile breadwinners, but he was more accepting than Mill of the ordinary disciplines of social life. Admirers of Tocqueville emphasize that he thought a considerable degree of social conservatism was required for political liberalism to be possible. Mill did not. So eloquent was Tocqueville in depicting what *might* be the fate of American democracy that readers often fail to notice that he did not suggest that America had already succumbed to individualism. He set out both the dangers if the pressure to retreat into our domestic surroundings was not resisted, and the forces that provided such resistance. The first of these was the American capacity for association; and its analysis rested on another of Tocqueville's legacies to the sociology of democratic societies, the concept of "self-interest rightly understood."[20]

Association and "Self-interest Rightly Understood."

Tocqueville was amazed by the way Americans set up societies and clubs and associations to accomplish almost anything one could think of; by the time he wrote volume 2 of *Democracy*, he had visited Britain, but although America drew its laws and traditions from Britain, there was nothing in British life to match the American enthusiasm for setting up associations. It was not associations with a directly political object such as political parties that impressed him, but those that existed for nonpolitical purposes. Indeed, one frequent complaint against *Democracy* is that it ignores political parties, as indeed it does apart from a brief history of the Federalist and Republican parties. Establishing a school or college, building churches, sending missionaries all over the globe, and creating hospitals and prisons were all the object of associations large and small. Their existence was vital to American democracy: in a society where there were no aristocrats and therefore no natural leaders, and individuals had to cooperate with one another to achieve almost anything, associations were the cradle of democratic self-reliance. Tocqueville's habit of arguing by antithesis is very much in evidence. Following Montesquieu, he saw the natural political condition of a society of equals as a tyranny, where a single despot ruled a state that controlled individuals who lacked the power to resist and had no way of organizing themselves to do so. America was the reverse of such a society. Nonpolitical associations fostered the skills of government, so that America was a genuinely self-governing republic. But if the state were to intervene to take over what was done by voluntary association, the spark that kept freedom alive might be extinguished. Tocqueville's antipathy to measures of relief in 1848, such as the national workshops proposed by Louis Blanc, rested largely on bad economics, but it also rested on a better, if not wholly persuasive, sociology.

Much of the impetus behind the creation of associations to achieve the diverse ends they aimed at came from a form of self-interest that Tocqueville approved of. This was "self-interest rightly understood." Tocqueville thought of this as a force that counteracted individualism. It seems odd to suggest that self-interest counteracts individualism, but once we see what is involved in "rightly understood," it is not. Tocqueville thought that Americans understood that in the absence of an interfering and omnicompetent state, they must manage their own affairs. If they wished their children to have an education, for instance, they must get together with like-minded people and build a school. This is self-interest with an eye to long-run, shared interests. The danger was that individuals would eventually give in to the temptation to have the state do everything for them; it was the natural path of a democracy to look for uniform solutions and centralize power for the purpose, but thus far Americans had resisted. The implications for the French, who had no such tradition of self-help, needed no spelling out.

So we have what became the canonical view of the dangers confronting democracy, and the raw materials for the continuing American anxiety about preserving the delicate balance between the private and the public realms. That anxiety was not drawn from a reading of Tocqueville alone, but he articulated it as eloquently as anyone. It is a platitude that if everyone withdraws into the pursuit of a privatized well-being, there will be no energy to fuel voluntary associations or to inspire the active membership of political parties—which are voluntary associations even if their purpose is to lay hold of the coercive mechanisms of the state. The nonplatitudinous element is partly moral—a question of how hard we should press the citizenry to participate—and partly factual—whether we are threatened by a decline in association. It may be that we blame a lack of civic engagement for things that have no connection to it. Behind these questions lies a normative vision of the engaged citizen that is taken for granted by political theorists such as Tocqueville and modern commentators, but that other writers have disputed. Burke would have thought that ordinary people should get on with their lives untroubled by politics; Plato would have gone much further to make sure they remained unengaged. Tocqueville thought Plato and Burke had been worsted by history. The world had fallen into the hands of the ordinary man and woman; the question was whether they could meet its challenges.

The Family

He therefore turned to the way in which the American family socialized the next generation of citizens. Tocqueville was tougher and bleaker than his modern admirers. With the French Revolution a near memory rather than old history, he emphasized the need for social discipline. He thought the modern world was gentler and more humane than the society of the ancien régime, where arbitrary and disgusting brutalities were perpetrated on political and religious dissenters, let alone on thieves and forgers.[21] The gentleness of the legal regime meant that self-discipline was all the more important, and it could be inculcated only in the family. Tocqueville's concern with the way the next generation was socialized into membership of a democratic society and polity led him to focus intensely on the role of women in American life: "There have never been free societies without *moeurs* . . . and it is woman who makes *moeurs*."[22] But women were located within the family, so Tocqueville's first move was to sketch the democratic family, and then the place of women in the family and the wider society.

The democratic family is contrasted with the aristocratic family. The latter is extended, the former nuclear; the idea of a lineage is un-American. Beyond a child's earliest years, relations within the family are based on friendship rather than authority. This is most vividly true of relationships between fathers and sons, but also of relations between siblings. In an aristocratic family, every person has a rank in the family hierarchy, which is perhaps a youngest son's observation. In a democratic family, children are friendly equals. But it is on American women that the preservation of good morals depends. This thought echoes Pericles and Polybius almost as loudly as Montesquieu. The remarkable feature of the upbringing of American girls was that they had absolute liberty until marriage, but liberty within a strict moral framework. One might glimpse between the lines Tocqueville's liking for young women who knew how to flirt without luring him into dangerous entanglements. Their political role stems from the most remarkable feature of American marriage: absolute freedom before marriage was succeeded within marriage by a strict, self-imposed subordination to its duties and the welfare of the family. The hectic quality of American life demanded a stabilizing force, and it was provided by American women. They held families together in misfortune, and kept their husbands on the path of steady self-reliance. One healthy result was that Americans rated women at their true value as rational creatures and cooperative helpmates, while Europeans exaggerated the seductive power of women, but treated them as incapable of rational reflection.

Soft Despotism

America's success at balancing liberty and equality raised the question whether the mores of the Americans could protect them forever from the dangers of democratic tyranny. This is the topic about which Tocqueville wrote most anxiously in both parts of *Democracy*. In the second volume he spelled out an idea that became part of a permanent legacy of deep philosophical anxieties about the fate of liberal democracies in the twentieth century. He feared, he said, a form of despotism unlike anything that had preceded it. Democracies were capable of cruelty and brutality for short periods; violence was not foreign to them; but brutality and violence were not part of their nature. Their morality was mild, and their *moeurs* softer than those of an aristocratic or monarchical society. They were not likely to fall into the hands of tyrants in the traditional sense. What they had to fear was that their leaders would be schoolmasters, not despots, and this thought took Tocqueville back to his fears about "individualism" in the sense in which he had earlier defined it. Each individual would shrink, his boundaries confined to his family and a few friends. Above this mass of tiny individuals "an immense tutelary power is elevated."[23]

Paradoxically, this tutelary power is the collective power of all the tiny individuals in the aggregate; for this is majority tyranny in a social rather than a narrowly political context. Tocqueville relies on the contrast with what one might call standard tyranny. Here a sole ruler, violent, brutal, selfish, and careless of legality, exercises power by the application of brute force and physical terror. Before the rise of the modern totalitarian state, such rulers were terrifying if one was within range, ineffective if one was not. Traditional tyrants were like cannon firing high explosive into the countryside; if the shell landed where you were standing, you were dead, if not, life went on undisturbed. Democratic despotism is "soft" or "mild," but it is uniform, omnipresent, and inescapable. In a memorable and much quoted phrase, Tocqueville says of it, "It does not tyrannize, it hinders, compromises, enervates, dazes, and finally reduces each nation to being nothing more than a herd of timid and industrious animals of which the government is the shepherd."[24] This is the fear that Mill expressed in his *On Liberty*, and to which Aldous Huxley gave a dramatic twist in *Brave New World*. In contemporary American politics, it looms large in the imagination of the enemies of "big government," and strikes others as absurdly exaggerated.

Whether there is any long-term remedy is a large question. Tocqueville tells us what can certainly delay the process, perhaps forever; it is the pluralism that represents the mirror image of the French centralization that plays a prominent role in *L'ancien régime*. Tocqueville believed that democracy had an inbuilt tendency toward centralization. Aristocracies in contrast were innately and multiply pluralistic: along intellectual, geographical, social, economic dimensions. Critics might think the diversity of status and function in aristocratic societies came at too high a price; the difference of lifestyle between starving peasant and overfed bishop was genuine but not worth preserving. Tocqueville does not demur; but he insists that aristocratic societies can preserve kinds of freedom that more egalitarian societies would struggle to protect. This tenderness toward the old aristocratic order led Mill to remark, "You are much more drawn to the past than I am."[25] How far Tocqueville's anxieties were justified is contentious. In many respects, American society became more pluralistic as the nineteenth century wore on. White America was no longer Anglo-American, but embraced innumerable other European immigrants, including Catholics from Ireland, Italy, and southern and eastern Europe, followed by Jews fleeing Russian pogroms and oppression elsewhere; the opening of the Far West brought in Asian laborers, and the country picked up a substantial Mexican population by conquest, and drew in more by migration. The United States continued, as it still continues, to strike some Europeans as conformist and inhospitable to intellectual independence. Other observers are as impressed as ever by the country's astonishing inventiveness, scientific, technical, and cultural. What the aristocratic Tocqueville would have made of it is another matter, but he ought to have been reassured that democracies can generate a plurality of tastes, ambitions, and allegiances as diverse as anything visible under the ancien régime. In any case, Tocqueville's fears were for France rather than America; the tutelary state was a not implausible extrapolation from an ancien régime state in nineteenth-century conditions. It was a very unlikely extrapolation from the American state of the 1830s.

France and Empire

Tocqueville never wrote anything on French imperialism to match his investigation of what British imperialism had achieved in North America, but throughout *Democracy* he raises the question of why the French failed to match the British in establishing themselves overseas. The interest of his ideas, which are scattered in articles he wrote during his time in the National Assembly and two reports on a visit to Algeria in the early 1840s, is how different a liberal he was from most English liberals, Mill among them. Mill worked for the East India Company, which then ruled British India. He thought the British presence was justified by the good it could do to India; a progressive colonial power could accelerate economic, cultural, and political development as the native inhabitants could not. The question on which Mill was mostly silent was what the benefit to the imperial power was. Colonization, in the sense of settling Britons in Australia, New Zealand, and British North America, had an obvious purpose; Mill's economics depicted overpopulation as a constant danger for developed countries, and emigration was the safety valve. Imperialism as such did not stir his blood. Glory was not something he cared for; he admitted that a colonial empire conferred prestige on Britain, but in a less than enthusiastic tone.[26]

Tocqueville held very different views. He thought the French needed a grand national project to bring the country together, and the conquest and settlement of Algeria could be it. No more than Machiavelli did he think it was worth debating the morality of the matter. Tocqueville's brutal approach to the destruction of Kabyle and Arab villages, which amounted to the deliberate massacre of women and children in order to terrorize their menfolk into abandoning guerrilla war against the French, has shocked later readers. Shock is not the right reaction. Tocqueville was an educated man. He knew how harsh the establishment of imperial rule by Greeks, Romans, Ottomans, and the Spanish had been, and he did not flinch. Politics could not be constrained by squeamishness. Unlike Mill (and Marx), Tocqueville did not invoke a vision of the benefits of progress to justify the methods used to bring it about. Indeed, just as in the case of the American Indians, he was much more sensitive to what was lost than either Mill or Marx. What France would get from success in Algeria was national glory, an increase in self-confidence, and solidarity. This outlook underlay some incidental remarks in *Democracy*, where Tocqueville hopes that a growing American navy will ally itself with the French to check British supremacy. Tocqueville did not imagine that Britain and France would or should go to war again, but it was not good for French self-confidence to lag so spectacularly behind that neighbor.

The Ancien Régime

This chapter has focused on Tocqueville's anxieties about the future of liberal democracy, and what democracy in America suggested about

its prospects in France. Like all commentators, Tocqueville emphasized that the Americans had not had to contend with the class hatreds
left over from the ancien régime or with the unfinished business of the
French Revolution, or even with the less obtrusive social hierarchies of
Britain. The French Revolution had not only made it hard to establish a
constitution—whether republican or monarchical—that would be
widely accepted as legitimate but had made it almost impossible to reach
a consensus on what a legitimate regime might look like. Between the
undesired extremes of anarchy and a theocratic monarchy, there was
much room for dissension and little hope of agreement. Like every reflective Frenchman, Tocqueville was fascinated by the revolution and its
descent from a cautious movement for constitutional change into the
madness of the Terror. For many years he thought of writing a history of
the revolution itself; then he decided that to make sense of the events of
the revolution, it was necessary to go back to the regime that the revolution had destroyed, and wrote his "third masterpiece," L'ancien régime. It is,
like Democracy, a work of great richness, in which it is easy to lose oneself.
Here I touch only on the aspects of the book that are directly reflected
from Democracy.

Tocqueville's account of the French Revolution is justly famous for
its refutation of the claim that it broke out because of the intolerable
misery of the French people. Tocqueville employed what social scientists
later called "reference group theory," the simple idea that whether we are
content or unhappy depends on whom we compare ourselves with. The
real work of the theory is done by answering the question of whom we
take as the appropriate people with whom to compare ourselves. When
this thought was applied to the United States, it suggested that immigrants who compared themselves with their poorer and more confined
European selves felt happier than their objective conditions warranted,
because they took their standards from their old lives and felt better-off
as a result. It is frequently said today that many American who are objectively hard-up continue to think of themselves as "middle-class" because
they compare themselves with their near neighbors rather than with Wall
Street bankers. The theory suggests two things: first, that synchronically
we compare ourselves with those with whom we come into contact, and

accept or resent differences between them and us to the extent that we think there is some justice to those differences, or at least, no injustice; second, that diachronically we become very unhappy if we first begin to become prosperous and then find our path blocked, unhappier than if we had never started on the upward path.

In Tocqueville's view this second factor was the crucial one. The theory is summarized in a chapter heading: "How Efforts to Help the Masses Radicalized Them."[27] The situation an old-fashioned absolute monarchy had to avoid was provoking the bourgeoisie to side with the laboring classes; to do so when the aristocracy had too little loyalty to the regime to defend it with real vigor would be disastrous. The French monarchy had done it. It did it slowly and over a long period, and many other things had made the regime vulnerable, too. In the short term, the revolution spread rapidly because there had been successive failed harvests; but it was not the rural peasantry that stormed the Bastille. It was the Paris mob. It was led by artisans, but behind them lay the political interests of their social superiors. The leaders who emerged during the revolution were mostly members of the professional middle classes. It was not absurd for Marxists to claim that the French Revolution was a bourgeois revolution.

Looking for antithetical examples as always, Tocqueville pointed to Britain. Political power was in the hands of an elite, composed of the gentry, and frequently the sons of the nobility; but nobody expected revolution in Britain. Perhaps the English got the revolutionary virus out of their system by killing one king and driving another into exile, but that was hardly the explanation. Many English writers and political leaders were initially committed to the principles of the French Revolution, which was scarcely surprising when they were to all appearances the principles of 1688. Among them were republicans, rationalists, and democrats, as well as many Dissenters shut out of regular political life by the Test and Corporation Acts. They had no chance of creating in England anything resembling the upheavals in Paris; when the British government took repressive measures against domestic radicalism in the early 1790s, the public was firmly on the government's side. The government did not fear that the army might not obey orders, and had no doubt the courts would find its critics guilty of sedition when they were prosecuted. The French came within a whisper of executing Thomas Paine, but he would probably have been sentenced to death for sedition by a British court, if ministers had been able to prosecute him.

Tocqueville asked two large questions. Why was the French state so vulnerable, and why did the revolution simultaneously change everything and nothing? The vulnerabilities of the French state were innumerable, and by the time Tocqueville has finished explaining the ways in which it was a glittering sham, it is less of a surprise that it fell than that it survived so long. The central theme can be inferred from the reflections on democracy and despotism in the second volume of *Democracy*. In France the aristocracy had become useless; for the sake of increasing royal authority, the monarchy had over centuries reduced the aristocracy to political impotence. In compensation it had allowed it to retain and increase its financial privileges and to exercise an increasingly oppressive power over the peasantry. There were areas of France in which the peasantry was no better off in 1789 than in 1289. The political consequence was that the aristocracy was hated worse in France than elsewhere; feudal institutions not only seemed to have, but actually had, no function but to extract resources from the poor and transfer them to the rich. Since the aristocracy was functionless, its privileges were not a legitimate reward for the social tasks it performed. They were merely privileges. The common people were therefore ready whenever the chance might occur to overthrow the aristocratic regime.

One might think that in any society the worse-off would always be ready to help themselves to the possessions of the better-off; in urban riots there is always a lot of opportunistic looting, as there is in the countryside when villagers have the opportunity to loot a great house. Nonetheless, order only rarely breaks down, and in some societies, of which Tocqueville thought Britain was one, it is never in danger of wholly doing so. The defense against disorder and pillage is not armed force but giving enough people a stake in law and order and the protection of property. In a stable society where the hollowing out that the French state had suffered has not taken place, there is a steady gradation of prosperity from the better-off to the worse-off. The alluring prospect for the middle classes is that they or their children can make their way into the gentry and higher. This was not true in France. Tocqueville provided an interesting variation on the old theme that the aristocracy of Britain was ready to accept into its ranks those who made money from trade. It was not that one could not buy nobility in France; the purchase of an office achieved it. It was rather than the social boundaries of the English nobility were indistinct, which made "In or out?" a less painful question. In contrast, the aristocracy of France was a caste. The whole point of membership was social exclusiveness. The natural allies of an aristocratic regime became its bitterest enemies.[28]

Nonetheless, it astonished observers that an urban riot—the storming of the Bastille—could bring down the most powerful state in Europe. Tocqueville thought it not astonishing at all. The aristocracy had become parasitic, attached to its privileges and serving no social or political function. Unlike the English aristocracy, which lived on its estates and ran the legal and political machinery of the countryside, the French aristocracy was called to court to serve a decorative function. France became a centralized administrative despotism. If anyone wanted redress for a problem, no matter where he might live, it was to the agents of the royal administration that he had to address himself. Although London was disproportionately the largest and most vital city in England, it did not monopolize political authority, energy, and administrative capacity as Paris did. Much as the American colonies practiced their own familiar forms of self-government during the American Revolution, the British could have governed themselves, if London had been overwhelmed by some disaster. Not so the French. This explained the ease with which the revolution overthrew the ancien régime as well as the ease with which the revolutionaries maintained their power and the ease with which they lost it. Tocqueville quoted Burke's astonishment that during the revolution people were arrested for the most contradictory reasons and their neighbors never lifted a finger to help. Tocqueville thought this demonstrated Burke's failure to understand how completely the monarchy had dissolved the ties of affection, self-help, and initiative that Burke took for granted. The Americans had their habits of association and the principle of self-interest rightly understood to protect themselves against the atomization of an egalitarian society; the French did not.

Tocqueville and Burke are at one in their view of the disastrous consequence of French irreligion and the catastrophic rise of the deracinated intellectual that was the other face of increasing skepticism. Tocqueville thought it was a self-inflicted disaster on the part of the aristocracy. If aristocrats had understood the extent to which their position depended on the religious convictions of the rest of society, they would have refrained from sponsoring the intellectuals who mocked religion. The institutional church was no help; indeed, it was its own worst enemy. The senior clergy were aristocrats and attracted the same opprobrium as the rest of the aristocracy; the humble curé had no affection for the church hierarchy, and when the revolution came, the lowest ranks in the church were not sorry to see the hierarchy overthrown.

In Tocqueville's view, the weaknesses of the old regime also explain why everything and nothing was changed by the revolution. Before the revolution, administrative centralization had taken hold; the French had become uniform in their tastes, habits, and allegiances; they had come to expect the state to provide for the whole of life. This did not mean that they had no energy; smallholding peasants worked desperately hard and had great powers of endurance. What they did not have were the habits of association, the capacity to generate "bottom-up" loyalties rather than loyalty to the state, "top-down" allegiance. Because a passion for equality had taken hold before the revolution, all hereditary privileges were destined to be swept away; for a brief period a passion for freedom, self-rule, nondomination by the powers that be was strong. The violence and fury of the revolution reflected the fact that once the common people were liberated, they had no reason to respect the boundaries their erstwhile rulers took for granted. The increasing mildness of manners in the eighteenth century was consistent with the utter savagery of the revolution as it moved toward its explosive climax. But as soon as desire for tranquility overtook the urge to liberate themselves, postrevolutionary France returned to the political passivity of the ancien régime. It became what

America had to ensure it did not become, an easy prey to despotic rulers such as Napoleon III.

Hegel, Mill, and Tocqueville are not usually yoked together; Hegel's reputation is for metaphysical inscrutability, Mill's for a lucidity of expression that fails to hide some deep uncertainties, and Tocqueville is more admired for what he is thought to have written about America in the 1830s than read with care. It would strain the reader's credulity to deny their differences. Nonetheless, they mark a turning point in political thinking and in what are thought to be the crucial questions. This is the moment where liberals begin to ask how a socially egalitarian society can avoid being dominated by public opinion and the dead weight of the "mass," whether middle-class or lower-class, whether resentful and sullen or comfortably oppressive. The age-old question arises in a new form: whether the members of modern society can be citizens as well as subjects, practicing genuine self-government as well as enjoying the benefits of rational administration and the securities for a reasonable level of welfare that an efficient bureaucracy can provide. We know that the modern world is decisively different from the world of the ancients; we do not know which of their ideals and ambitions we must renounce with regret, and which we can recapture in modern forms, not least because we do not know how much effort we would be prepared to devote to the task, let alone how hard it would be. The new sense of how different the modern world had become from what went before also induced a deep uncertainty about how different it might become. Hegel, Mill, and Tocqueville refused to prophesy the future; and as to the means of social change, all were close enough to the French Revolution to think that violent insurrection was the method of last resort in effecting social change. Marx was another matter.

CHAPTER 21

Karl Marx

Marx's Reputation

IF THE GERMAN GOVERNMENT had not sent Lenin across its territory and back to Russia in a sealed train in early 1917, we might today regard Marx as a not very important nineteenth-century philosopher, sociologist, economist, and political theorist. If he had not had the good (or bad) luck to be treated as the source of near-divine wisdom by the ideologists of the Communist Party of the Soviet Union, we might treat his economics as an interesting offshoot of the Ricardian system, and his historical theories as an interesting variation on themes first sketched by Hegel, Saint-Simon, Guizot, and Comte. Political theorists would complain, as I shall, that his political theory is sketchy and unfinished. They might explain his lurchings between cynicism and utopianism as a reaction to the vagaries of his fellow radicals, or a consequence of the fact that Marx was a frustrated academic with a professor's incapacity to finish anything properly, a man of many deep insights who was unable to complete any project before being distracted by the next.

This chapter will pretend, so far as possible, not to know that the revolution of November 1917 ever happened. A later chapter will pick up the twentieth-century fate of Marxism and some socialist alternatives that were overshadowed by the role of Marxism as the official ideology of the Soviet Union and post-1949 China. For the sake of such clarity as Marx's ambitions permit, the chapter begins—after a little biography—with an account of Marx's youthful philosophical allegiances and his theory of alienation; continues with an account of the materialist conception of history; and goes on to explain Marx's accounts of class conflict, revolution, and the nature of the state, with special attention to the dictatorship of the proletariat and the eventual withering away of the state.

It will be a very brief account. Marx wrote voluminously, but not at length on issues in political theory. He has no theory of political authority, although he has interesting ideas about how rulers bamboozle the ruled; less forgivably, he never gives an account of decision-making procedures under socialism. Because the state was to "wither away," he did not need a theory of citizenship; and because law was to wither away along with the state, he had nothing to say about the rule of law. His most striking claim about politics was that in a fully socialized economy there would be no politics. He was not unique; Plato's *Republic* and More's *Utopia* paint elaborate pictures of life in utopia, but share with Marx the presumption that in the absence of conflicts of material interest, *administration* will be necessary, but *politics* will not. Much more sober, entirely matter-of-fact thinkers in the mid-twentieth century thought that political cleavages would vanish, leaving only technical discussions about the efficient management of a modern industrial society. Politicians themselves often profess a distaste for "politicizing" what they present as matters of administrative technique, the assumption being that all reasonable people agree on the goals to be pursued. Nor are they always insincere. Marx's most passionately pursued intellectual goal was uncovering the exploitative mechanisms of a capitalist economy—the mechanisms whose operation he spelled out in the three volumes of *Das Kapital* and the two associated volumes of *Theories of Surplus Value*; in the sphere of politics, he concentrated his analytical energies on the interaction between economic and political transformations, past and present. His account of all this is engrossing, but his reply to our question how we are to govern ourselves is that after the revolution the question will answer itself.

Life and Times

Marx was born in Trier, on the Moselle River, in 1818. His family was
Jewish, and as the family name of Levi suggests, he came from a long
line of rabbis. His father was born Herschel Levi, but after the Napoleonic Wars became Heinrich Marx and a nominal Lutheran, in order to
practice law under the restrictive anti-Semitic legislation of the restored
Prussian monarchy. The region was much influenced by French radicalism and occupied by the French for long periods during the wars of
1792–1815. It was an area hostile both to the monarchical absolutism
of Prussia and to the fragmented condition of early nineteenth-century
Germany, and a natural home to liberal nationalism. Marx's father was
a radical of Voltairean but not insurrectionary inclinations. He enjoyed
the freedom Jews received under the French occupation, but does not
seem to have resented abandoning nominal Judaism for nominal Lutheranism. Karl had no religious leanings, and seems never to have thought
his family's renunciation of their Judaism mattered one way or another.
He was casually anti-Semitic—"Yid" was one of the insults he threw
at his rivals for the leadership of the socialist movement in Germany;
but his murderous feelings toward his rivals, like the abuse he hurled
at them, were political, not racial. Marx studied law and philosophy at
Bonn and Berlin, and if Frederick William IV, the pious but unintelli-
gent king of Prussia from 1840, had not dismissed the philosophers and
theologians who engaged in the "historical criticism" of the Bible, Marx
would have been a successful professor of philosophy.

Instead, he became a professional revolutionary. He began by editing
a liberal journal, the *Rheinische Zeitung* based in Cologne, until it was closed
down. Forced to leave Germany to escape the Prussian police, he went
to Paris, Brussels, and finally London, where he lived, aside from a few
months in 1848, until his death in 1883. He became a member of several
small revolutionary groups, including the Communist League, for which
he wrote the *Communist Manifesto*, with help from Friedrich Engels, his

friend, fellow revolutionary, and financial support. Engels was the rebellious son of a thread manufacturer, but in due course became part-owner
of Engels and Ermen of Barmen and Manchester. He reluctantly worked
in the family business to support the Marx family rather than himself;
when the chance came to sell up and live as a rentier, he took it. He
survived Marx by a dozen years, living in the same part of London, and
dying in 1895. Engels's role in Marx's thinking is complex, but the outline of their division of labor is not. Engels was a more uncomplicated
materialist than Marx, and an enthusiast for philosophical systems that
left Marx cold. Those qualities fitted him to occupy the role he filled
after Marx's death, which was like that of Saint Paul, the expositor of a
complete and clear-cut system whose relationship to the incomplete and
elusive thought of the master has always been contentious.

Engels was interested in religion in a way Marx was not, but both
came to philosophy and thence to radical politics and economics by
way of the religious critique of the Young Hegelian movement. The
Young Hegelians were radical disciples and interpreters of Hegel, who
employed his philosophical methods to rethink the nature of Christianity and religion more generally. Hegel had done so in a cautious fashion, but the more radical implications of his ideas were left for others
to explore. Marx's interest in religion was fleeting; he thought religion
provided consolation for a miserable world, and that when the need for
consoling stories was over, religion would vanish. Engels's interest was
more long-lasting. He came from a pietist family and had a strong sense
that mankind would always require *a* story about the meaning of existence, so that some form of *Lebensphilosophie* would always be required, even
though a scientifically credible one would have to be built on materialist
and atheistic foundations. Engels thus did, and Marx did not, take an
interest in the materialist syntheses intended by their authors to replace
Christianity; and Engels was responsible for turning Marxism into a
philosophical system. Nonetheless, because he worked in Manchester
and encountered the millworkers of the city on a daily basis, Engels
became interested in the actual lives of working people before Marx did.
His *Condition of the English Working Class* of 1844 turned Marx's attention

away from the philosophical exploration of the alienating effect of private property and toward the economics of exploitation and the real lives of the proletariat.

Engels was a physically energetic man who fought with considerable courage in the 1848 revolution in Saxony and relieved the tedium of managing his family's thread mill by riding to hounds. His experience of armed conflict in 1848 and his interest in the practicalities of warfare allowed him in the 1860s to write for the *New York Tribune* commentaries on the American Civil War that appeared under Marx's name. Although he was prosperous and Marx was invariably hard up, Engels was less attached to bourgeois respectability than Marx. Marx led, as best he could without an income, the life of a Victorian paterfamilias; Engels lived with an Irish mistress, Lizzy Burns, whom he married on her deathbed as an act of kindness; he then lived with her sister Mary. It was characteristic of Engels that he wrote in Eleanor Marx's autograph book that his vision of happiness was Chateau Margaux 1848 and that his motto was "take it aisy."[1]

With the failure of the 1848 revolutions, Marx led the life of an impoverished émigré in London. He spent his time in two activities, theoretical and practical; the first was concentrated on explaining the origins, nature, and inevitable downfall of capitalism, and led to the three volumes of *Das Kapital* and an enormous fragmentary output on the history of economics, the politics of the nineteenth century, and much else, while the second involved constant attempts to assemble a revolutionary socialist movement under his and Engels's leadership. He was never employed; when poverty led him to apply for a post as a ticket clerk on the North London Railway, he was turned down because his handwriting was illegible. Engels kept him and his family alive—Marx married an upper-class neighbor, Jenny von Westphalen, who bore five children, of whom three daughters, Laura, Eleanor, and Jenny, survived into adult life. For the last dozen years of his life, Marx was comfortably off; when Engels sold the family firm he handed over some of the capital, which Marx duly invested. Marx also inherited some money from various relatives and lived in a small terraced house in North London, traveling each day to the British Museum to read and write under its great rotunda. He was also active in the organization of the German social democrats and the First International. He was not a deft politician, and being a foreigner in Victorian England did not help; the environment tolerated him, but he did not understand the English working class, and its members did not like him or Engels. He was outflanked on the left by anarchists who owed such allegiances as they owed anyone to the Russian Mikhail Bakunin, himself no politician but a shrewd critic of Marx's political ideas and much his superior as a rabble-rouser. When Marx died in 1883, it would have been a rash observer who predicted that the "specter of revolution" he and Engels conjured up in *The Communist Manifesto* in 1848 would become one of the main driving forces of world history in the twentieth century.

The Philosophy of Alienation

Marx began his intellectual and insurrectionary life as a philosopher. He remained one, even though he himself claimed that he had settled his scores with philosophy in the mid-1840s and had moved on to the study of "real individuals . . . and their material conditions of life."[2] What Marx meant by philosophy was Hegelianism and the ideas of its critics. When Marx first read Hegel, he disliked his work. Then he was briefly converted by what he called his "grotesque and rocky melody."[3] Marx read voraciously in the work of the Young Hegelians, but found his own voice in the *Economic-Philosophical Manuscripts* of 1842–44; there he sketched the theory of alienation that some critics see as the key to his mature work, and that others claim he rejected before he wrote the *Manifesto*. The grounds of this divergence are simple: the idea of alienation is Hegelian; what Marx does with it is un-Hegelian. What follows takes it for granted that the core ideas of the theory of alienation persist in Marx's later work and make it very different from the Marxism that Engels constructed for the benefit of the Second International. The theory of alienation starts with the two thoughts that the world as we immediately encounter it is alien to us, or foreign, and that our estrangement from it, and our feeling that the world is hostile to us, must be overcome. We have seen Hegel's account of this estrangement and its overcoming in the *Phenomenology of Spirit*. For Hegel the world is experienced as alien because we do not understand it as the expression of *Geist*, or spirit. When we understand the world as a construction of mind, we can see reality as *ours*. The fact that Hegel equated understanding with a form of intellectual *ownership* is significant for what Marx does with the concept of alienation.

Alienation is much more than a matter of epistemology. Political and social arrangements receive the same analysis; what appears to be brute force exercised over us by an alien power becomes when rightly understood—and it can be rightly understood only if it is really the product of reason—as the law of a state whose authority stems from spirit and therefore from ourselves. The connection between intelligibility and autonomy is at the heart of Hegel's account, as it is of Marx's. A world whose social arrangements are intelligible because they are what reason dictates to rational creatures for the conduct of their lives is a world whose arrangements *give* us autonomy, rather than restricting it. The idea that *freedom is the consciousness of necessity* is central to Hegel and persists in Marx: a rational person does freely what he *must* do, because the "must" is not an arbitrary imposition but a reflection of the logic of his situation and of his own mind and purposes when he is thinking clearly. Hegel gives both the natural and the social world the benefit of the doubt; we overcome alienation by understanding the inner logic of the way things are, and see that they are what we would rationally legislate. Marx thinks the present actuality is both oppressive and irrational; not reconciliation, but revolution, is needed. But the end of the process is the creation of a world that is genuinely rational and transparent to us.

Hegel was aware that the political world did not always live up to its own implicit standards, but he was wary of individuals using their individual judgment about the shortcomings of the state. Marx turns all this upside down or, in his view, the right way up. Marx claimed that he had found Hegel standing on his head and had set him on his feet. He also claimed, quite implausibly, that the analysis of alienation he offered in his critique of Hegel was a "completely empirical analysis founded on a conscientious and critical study of political economy."[14] Given his contempt for British empiricism and his ignorance of economics at this stage of his life, the imagination with which Marx transformed Hegel's conservative, or accommodationist, philosophy into radical social theory is astonishing. Almost all Marx's later ideas except the technical analysis of surplus value are present in embryo. Methodologically, he argued that Hegel saw history as the history of thought, and its resolution as a matter of learning to think the right thoughts—more exactly the right Thought. This was conservative, no matter what Hegel's own politics were, because it required individuals to adjust their ideas and wishes to the world; the radical holds that the task is to adjust the world to our rational desires. Marx did not offer an elaborate theory of the way in which economic and political life is reflected in thought, but he certainly held that the driving force of historical change was what people *did* to the world rather than what they thought about it. He never denied that what we think makes a difference, but the difference is the difference it makes to how we act, what we do. We are not to write better philosophy but to transcend philosophical ways of thinking to become more effective agents of social and economic change.

Marx always thought that Hegel was a great thinker; late in life he deplored the tendency of less talented thinkers to treat him "as a dead dog." His insights could and should be taken over for radical purposes. So Marx reinterpreted alienation as a phenomenon implicated in all human life, not to be overcome in thought but by action. Alienation is estrangement from our human nature; the essence of human nature is our character as social and productive creatures who create social relations as well as material objects, relationships that under the right conditions are fruitful and life enhancing, and under the wrong conditions oppressive and destructive. The concept of alienation is an all-purpose critical tool to illuminate the ways in which developed modern societies, such as contemporary Prussia, set us at odds with one another, with our work, and with our own deepest natures. The institution on which the weight of criticism fell at this point in Marx's intellectual development was private property, though it was a proxy for all the relationships into which property rights entered. A society built around private property was a society in which the wrong sort of exchange was salient. If we perform mutually beneficial services for one another out of affection, we engage in an exchange that is not alienating; but under the pressure of private property, we overwhelmingly engage in instrumental transactions in which we treat others as means to our ends, never as ends in themselves. This is a variation on Carlyle's claim that "the callous cash nexus" was the only bond between man and man, a phrase that Marx seized on for the *Manifesto*.

What attracted commentators in the 1960s to Marx's theory of alienation was the analysis of alienation at work and in the marketplace. We are, he said, estranged from the products of our work, from the process of working, from one another, and from ourselves.[5] At one level, is is an obvious truth that we are divorced from what we make; in an exchange economy built on private ownership, we make things for the market and not for the pleasure of creation or our own consumption. Marx thinks that producing things to make money is estranging, even if we are self-employed. The worker who works for an employer is more deeply estranged, because he takes part in his own oppression. Workers collectively create the factories in which they work, keep the financial system going whereby banks lend money, capitalists invest it, and workers work to make money for their employers. The more efficient the worker is, the more he adds to his employer's power over him by making his employer richer and increasing his bargaining power. That is the financial aspect of private property. The more the system advances, the greater the estrangement of the worker from what he produces; that is, the more he engages in forced labor. Construed thus, this is not an argument about the quality of working life; it is an argument about the effect on workers of a monetarized economy in which some people own all the capital and others provide all the labor, attached to a view of market relations that disapproves of their instrumental quality and would do so even if they were more egalitarian than they actually are. Marxists have never been attracted to "market socialism," because even if the workers own the capital they manage, they are still at the mercy of the impersonal forces of the market, and engaged in purely instrumental relationships with anonymous others.

Marx thought workers were estranged from the *process* of work. Instead of working to create something they want to create, they are turned into adjuncts of machinery, given mind-numbingly dull and repetitive tasks to perform; they become machines, while machines embody all the intelligence that goes into production. Marx later began to think that a worker who worked with machinery that he understood might in fact acquire a new kind of productive freedom. Although this was not a simple contradiction of his earlier view, it revealed the existence of two distinct currents in Marx's thought. What dominates his early writings is the idea that work is a central characteristic of the human species, and satisfaction in our work the centerpiece of human satisfaction outside intimate relationships. The paradigm of fulfilling work would seem to be the work of the artist; and Marx often seems to endorse that implication. We are unalienated when what we do and what we create express our inner selves and when our inner selves are as they should be. The concept is not wholly subjective: an employer who found great satisfaction in screwing every last ounce of effort out of his exhausted workers would not be unalienated, or expressing his "species-being," because his work is wholly wrong and his nature distorted.

The second strand, more dominant in Marx's later writings, is less concerned with the fulfillment of the individual than with the rationality of the economic and productive system as a whole. The work of particular individuals is satisfying when it is also the work of the species. This thought is deeply indebted to Hegel. Marx takes over Hegel's collectivist assumptions and insists that in a properly functioning society every individual would be fulfilled in the fulfillment of the species. One difficulty in understanding just what Marx thought a society based on rational cooperation might look like is his insistence that there would be no sacrifice of individuality when we all contributed as we should to the productive efforts of us all. The thought seems to be that we so internalize the desire to do what we rationally must do for the benefit of the whole community that we feel no tension between our desires and the community's needs. This is either implausible or alarming; it is at least very hard to believe that work as the free expression of our creative natures will always coincide with work as our optimal contribution to the rationally organized productive mechanism that underpins our society.

However that may be, the gap between what I want for me and what I would happily do for the sake of all of us cannot be closed in a competitive world. Under the rule of private property, says Marx, we are alienated from what he calls our "species-being." Competition sets us at odds with one another when we should be cooperating, makes us treat one another as means when we should be treating one another as ends, and makes us treat our own abilities as a means to bare survival when their proper exercise is the purpose of existence, not a condition of it.[6] The argument is straightforward; in a marketplace where the object of sellers is to get the highest price for what they are selling and the object of the buyer to part with as little as possible, there is enmity between them. It is not a human relationship. If the buyer did not need what she was buying, she would not buy it; but the seller is not interested in what she needs, how much she needs it, and whether what he sells her will meet that need. For him, her need is simply a means to acquiring some of her money. Similarly, she cannot see the seller as someone who is intent on satisfying her needs, because he is not; for her, he is the grudging source of what she needs, and he extracts from her money she would rather not part with.

This lends commodities in the marketplace a communicative quality that Marx notices only very briefly; but anyone who wishes to see the first glimpses of Marx's later doctrine that commodities are the embodiment of social relations, can certainly see them. The idea is best understood by starting from the communicative aspects of satisfactory exchange relations. In those we are motivated by our desire to satisfy the need of the other, and that is clear to the person with whom we are interacting. I want to satisfy your need, and in your satisfaction my own wish is realized; conversely, you receive not only the satisfaction inherent in whatever it is I create for you—an efficient saucepan, a warm sweater, a piano score—but also the satisfaction of knowing that I value you. The objects involved in the exchange carry a symbolic and communicative load as important as their causal properties. When we are all laboring to satisfy the needs of the market, everything is reversed; the commodities in the marketplace tell us that they are extorted from their creators—who would die of starvation if they could not find employment—and that their creators regard their employers and more remotely the ultimate purchasers as the source of their misfortunes.

The diagnosis extends the indictment. Work ceases to be an expression of our individuality—that is, our individuality as one member of the talented and productive species we call humanity—and is just hard labor. Our colleagues, with whom we must cooperate if we are to produce anything, are seen not as collaborators in work we wish to do but as enemies, competitors; they can undercut me by doing the same work for lower wages, or by doing better work than I can do. If they are unemployed, they can compete for my job at any wage that will keep body and soul together. We are therefore at odds with the rest of our own species, at odds with the species' most characteristic activity, and so far from our expressing our ownership of the world through the institutions of private property—as Hegel had claimed—we are owned by it. All this survives in Marx's later work in very different formulations.

Such attacks on property and the market are familiar. They are usually seen as a moral or spiritual denunciation of the greed and selfishness that the marketplace is supposed to foster. But Marx was deeply hostile to the idea that socialism is an ethical or moral imperative. Socialism is not something human beings *ought* to create; it is something they *must* create. The question is why. Some answers are straightforward; in the *Manifesto*, Marx says that capitalism is incompetent even to feed the workers it needs, so the proletarian seems to face a choice between overthrowing capitalism and starvation.[7] This was a rhetorical exaggeration, and nothing in Marx's analysis justified it. What more usually drove his insistence that capitalism must be overthrown was the thought that capitalism was simply irrational and therefore doomed. Before Marx focused on *capital*, it was the system of private property that was declared too irrational to survive. Economic life would be rational if production and consumption were smoothly adjusted to each other, without booms or slumps, and without the grotesque coincidence of some perishing of hunger while others ate themselves to death. Production is intrinsically cooperative, whereas the market is intrinsically competitive and built on mutual hostility. To the suggestion that the market is an elegant coordinating mechanism, Marx would have replied with a snort of disbelief. It was more nearly a disorganizing mechanism, and to the degree that it was a coordinating mechanism, it was insultingly stupid. It worked only on average and by fits and starts, and that was not productive or distributive rationality. Things ruled men, and nobody ruled history.

Alienation and Politics

We must explore the consequences of these philosophical predilections for Marx's politics. Under private property, things rule men. Hegel argued that individual ownership provides the basis of a legal, civic, and political system that permits the rational control of human affairs. The cleverness of Hegel's account is that the state is not excessively dominant—what can be left to the invisible hand of the marketplace is; individuals make most of the choices that affect their lives, the state providing the legal and social framework within which those choices can be given effect. Nonetheless, the existence of the state is essential to the social and economic system. It is more than a night watchman state, and not only because it is the bearer of the nation's role in world history. It controls the operations of the market in the interests of social stability and promotes the welfare of those who would suffer in an uncontrolled competitive environment. We may complain that the actuality of Prussia in the 1820s belies Hegel's picture of a state that provides the liberalism of the rule of law, the conservatism of carefully maintained cultural allegiances, the nationalism of a state taking its place in history, and the benefits of a nascent welfare state. Skeptics see it as a fantasy, just as Marx's picture of a state wholly at the mercy of the market and existing only to secure the property rights of those fortunate enough to own property was. Such complaints are irrelevant here. What is relevant is Hegel's picture of a constitutional monarchy bolstered by an effective bureaucracy managing a modern economy so as to secure the welfare of all the country's inhabitants.

Marx's retort was multidimensional and intriguing.[8] First, the modern state could not be the monarchy depicted by Hegel; a modern state must be a democratic republic. Second, a democratic republic could not satisfy the aspirations for self-rule that the modern state attempted to embody, because of its social foundations. Third, the essence of the state was democracy, but the essence of democracy was the abolition of the state; our needs for coordination would be met noncoercively by a transfigured civil society. The underlying thought is that the modern world is committed to equal legal status and political rights. We are to be *citizens*, not mere *subjects*. Reality betrays that aspiration; what is treated equally is equal amounts of property, and political standing is determined by what property we possess; propertyless workers are politically null. Hegel was multiply and interestingly wrong. Equal citizenship implies a republic. Worse yet, Hegel held that the modern state served the general interest because a "universal class" of bureaucrats had the general interest as *its* interest. Marx thought Hegel had unwittingly revealed something else, which was that the state itself had become an object of ownership; the bureaucrats and their masters controlled the state as a piece of property. The theory of alienation is doing more work; if commodities are the alien objectification of our productive powers, the state is another alien objectification, of our powers of collective and cooperative decision making.[9]

To recover our control over what we create and exchange with each other, we must abolish private property and the market—at this stage of his career, Marx says nothing about how, or about the basis of a new productive order—and we must establish true democracy. True democracy will transcend the liberal republic. The republic rests, as Rousseau saw, on a sharp divide between *homme* and *citoyen*. The individual man is self-centered, moved by private interests, and an egotist in his essence; in adopting the persona of the citizen, the individual becomes an aspect of the collective entity, the sovereign, and thinks of himself as a member of that collective; he thinks only of the general interest and the good of the whole community, and his loyalty is to it, not to himself. In Marx's eyes, this is a fantasy; its appeal to the morality of republican Rome cannot paper over the conflict between individual and public interests. The deeper thought is that the republic *imposes* political unity on economic disunity; the disunity is the internecine strife of competing property owners, and any political order built on that basis can serve only the interests of owners against nonowners. Rousseau said that the law defends those who have something against those who would like to take it, so we must ensure that everyone has something, and nobody too much. Marx does not argue that it is too late to follow that recipe, but that is the implication. The *modern* republic attempts to impose political equality upon an economic inequality it has no way of alleviating.

What implies the withering away of the state is that a deeper unity already exists, implicit in our productive existences. Production is collective and cooperative, but it is a *forced* cooperation. The cooperative unity implicit in the modern economy is waiting to emerge from the conflictual institutions in which it is encased. So the argument ends with the thought that the form of the modern state must be a democratic republic, but that a democratic republic cannot live up to its own aspirations, because it is a *political* state. It must be folded back into civil society, understood in another reversal of Hegel as the self-governing realm of our productive lives. Neither then nor later did Marx explain quite *how* spontaneous, rational, nonconflictual, and apolitical self-government was to emerge. He was always clearer about what the future would *not* hold than what it *would*.

This is a political theory driven by a philosophical vision, and in many ways not a political theory at all, because it already contains the thought that the full realization of our political ambitions—the collective overcoming of conflicts of interest—is achievable only when we transcend politics and institute arrangements that directly express our rational and cooperative natures. This is not a Platonic transcendence of politics that places the state's coercive powers in the service of the philosopher's infallible intuitions. It is genuinely and unforcedly egalitarian. It is Aristotelian in assuming that the nature of human beings is to live fully socialized lives, but wholly un-Aristotelian in its assumption of the universality of human possibility and its nonhierarchical view of our capacities. Forcing Marx's vision into the framework of everyday politics is never easy, and at this early stage almost impossible. Nonetheless, he seems to have thought that if there was universal suffrage—the radicals' demand—it would lead to the creation of an egalitarian republic, initially on the basis of private property but more equally distributed, and finally, with the arrival of socialism, to the abolition of the conflicts of economic interest that make the state necessary. The starting point must be a revolution, and it would have to start in France, the launching pad of every European revolution since 1789.

The Theory of Exploitation; Marx's Politics in the *Manifesto* and After

Marx grew impatient with his philosophical allies and eager to develop what he and Engels later termed "scientific" as opposed to "utopian" socialism. The label "utopian" covered far too many different enterprises; some were genuinely utopian, such as Charles Fourier's project for the phalanstery, a community where every variety of human nature would find itself satisfied, and whose coming would usher in an epoch when the lion would eat grass and the sea be turned into lemonade; others were not. Their common characteristic was that they held that the creation of socialism was a *moral* imperative, whereas Marx held that it was enshrined in historical necessity, based not on a moral decision but on a rational imperative. We must turn to Marx's mature view of the determinants of historical change, then to his views on revolution, the state, and its withering away.

Marx was a highly sophisticated thinker whose views about the nature of science were philosophically subtle and pregnant with implications for the analysis of the economic workings of capitalism. Science uncovers the hidden workings of the social world, just as it does those of the natural world, and the best-hidden secret of capitalism is the origin of capitalist profit. Uncovering the secret is the purpose of Marx's account of exploitation. *Exploitation* allows Marx to provide what he considered a scientific analysis of the generation of profit. Most readers would think it had dramatic moral implications, but Marx defended it as science. Whether he also thought it had moral implications is much disputed. Certainly the capitalist does not obtain his profit by means of a fair exchange; what is disputable is how far Marx thought this was morally objectionable.

The puzzle of profit was this: in a perfect market, the capitalist buys his factors of production, including the time of his workforce, for their full value in the marketplace, and when the process of production is done and the results are sold, he cannot sell them for more than their value in the marketplace—and yet, the capitalist walks away with a profit. The puzzle is how the process of production creates this profit. Modern economists would not start from Marx's starting point; some would discuss the entrepreneur's role in seeing ways in which factors of production that formerly yield a utility of x could be combined differently to yield a utility of $x + y$; this theory would represent profit as something that was always being eroded as competitors come in behind the first person to spot an opportunity, and always being re-created as new opportunities are spotted by the inventive, the imaginative, or the fortunate. Marx ignores all that because he wants to explain the "normal" rate of profit, the average return on capital.

To do this, he drew a distinction between *labor* and *labor power*. Labor is what the worker actually *does* in the productive process; labor has *no* value but creates *all* value; in this it differs from labor power, which is the worker's ability to work for however long the labor contract is for. Labor *power* has a value; its value is what it costs to feed, house, clothe, and get ready a worker able to work. It is what the subsistence wage embodies. The rest of the story is simple; the capitalist buys the worker's labor power at its full market value, the price that represents what it costs to produce the worker's *capacity* to work. What the capitalist gets is the worker's actual labor, which is to say the hours of value-creating effort that the contract requires the worker to give the capitalist. Part of the worker's time is required to replace the value of his labor power, and to cover the cost of raw materials, depreciation and so on; the rest of the working day creates the surplus value that emerges as profit. It is unpaid labor, taken by the owner of capital, who gives nothing in return.

All profit is thus created by the worker; the capitalist contributes nothing. *If* some part of the capitalist's return is explained as the "wages of superintendence," those wages are distinguished from genuine profit; profit is not managerial wages but a return on capital, and is what is left when the wages of the managers have been deducted along with the wages of the laborers, the cost of raw materials, and the depreciation of whatever machinery is involved. The capitalist's share of the proceeds of production is *unearned*; it is deducted from the total and represents unpaid labor. The process does not involve the visible coercion of slavery or the ideological and political apparatus of feudalism, but at the point where he creates surplus value, the proletarian works for nothing, just as slaves and peasants performing unpaid labor services do.

The analysis demonstrates Marx's obsession with the *hiddenness* of the workings of capitalism. What is visible is the exchange of money for services; at that level the bourgeois notion of justice is satisfied. Capitalists pay workers what they are worth, and they do not cheat the workers. Wicked individuals may do, but capitalists as a class have an interest in ensuring that there is no cheating, because cheating will bring down capitalism; Marx says over and over again that profit does not come from visible robbery and fraud; at the level of the wage contract, bourgeois justice prevails. Bourgeois justice is the justice of exchange relations between self-interested individuals, and the rule of justice is that "equals exchange for equals." The market enforces that standard of justice. If an employer pays less than the going rate, other employers will take away his workers; if he pays more, his goods will be too expensive to sell at a profit.

The purpose of science is to show what happens beneath the surface in a way that explains the surface appearances. If reality and appearance coincided, said Marx, there would be no need for science. It is because the sun does not rise in the way that common sense supposes that we need astronomy. So, here. Social processes are doubly deceptive: there is the natural divergence of appearance and reality, and a specifically social deceptiveness rooted in the fact that many social arrangements would break down if they were fully understood. This latter idea is at the heart of Marx's dismissal of much economic theory as mere ideology, and his belief that an intellectual like himself could play an indispensable role in the revolutionary movement. Nothing else could explain his willingness to spend endless days in the reading room of the British Museum writing drafts of *Das Kapital*.

Marx's theory of exploitation is the claim that profit is produced by the unpaid labor of the worker. This is unjust inasmuch as equals have not exchanged for equals. The subtlety of Marx's claim is that the visible surface of market relationships is just according to bourgeois standards of justice, while beneath the surface a process occurs that is unjust according to those bourgeois standards, the extraction of surplus value by the appropriation of the unpaid-for efforts of the worker. When we return to the question of life after the revolution, we can ask whether the postcapitalist regime will be more just, or better in some other, nonmoral way. For the moment, it is enough to see that Marx relied on the scientific quality of his analysis to show that the extraction of surplus value drove capitalism, and on orthodox assumptions about the effects of competition to argue that the ferocity of that extraction would increase. There is endless room for argument about the view that labor is the source of all value. All we need notice is that it seems to be the scientific shadow of the philosophical convictions about work that lay at the heart of Marx's early writings. Capital, which is dead labor, needs constant supplies of living labor; *le mort saisit le vif*, said Marx, describing capital as a vampire.

Class Struggle

The Communist Manifesto announces that history is the history of class struggle; its illustrations of that proposition show how opaque the claim is.[10] Marx was not the first writer to say that class conflict was the central propulsive force in history; Guizot had lectured on the subject in the 1820s. Class conflicts in the sense of conflicts between social groups whose political actions were based on their economic interests were well-known to every writer on politics; Aristotle sketched out a class theory of revolution, while Machiavelli argued that tensions between social classes could preserve freedom as well as threaten chaos. It was the search for a historical theory of social change that was the eighteenth-century novelty. Engels said Rousseau's *Discourse on the Origins of Inequality* was the first work of historical materialism because it tied social change and the origins of political institutions to the growth of new forms of property and to class conflict centered on those new forms, but this was to oversophisticate Rousseau and ignore the claims of Scottish historical sociologists such as Adam Ferguson, William Robertson, and John Millar.

The thought that politics is largely about the resolution or suppression of class conflict is intuitively plausible, although the thought that it is *only* about such conflicts is less so. It requires complicated footwork to show that ethnic, racial, and religious conflicts are invariably, at root, class conflicts. The thought that class conflicts are conflicts of interests tied to our place in the productive process and our ownership or non-ownership of the means of production is equally persuasive. Employers driven by rational self-interest will want workers to work as long as possible for as little as possible, and employees driven by the same motivation will want to be paid as much as possible for as little work as possible; each side would like the legal system to favor its interests. Conflict is intrinsic to all economic systems. Slaves would rather own slaves than be slaves, and so would their owners. Feudal lords want their inferiors to perform their labor services on time and well, and their inferiors want an end to forced labor. The existence of such conflicts is not news. Whether they are the most, let alone the only, important basis of political conflict is another matter.

Marx's official view is that the basis of all class conflict is conflict between owners and workers. But he offers as one of his first examples in the *Manifesto* the conflict of "slave and free," and this shows the difficulty of pinning everything on our place in the productive process.[11] Indeed, his first paraphrase of class conflict is oppressor and oppressed. The distinction of slave and free is not the same as slave and slave owner; a poor freeman was often less well-off than a slave—Roman slaves could go into business on their own account and own slaves themselves—and a poor freeman would not own a slave. Moreover, the distinction of slave and free is one of legal status rather than position in the productive process. Marx was not foolish even when writing under pressure of time, as he and Engels were when trying to put out the *Manifesto* in time to influence the 1848 revolution in Germany. The underlying thought is this: the crucial question in any society is where resources beyond those required for subsistence are generated and how they get into the hands of the social class(es) that dispose of them for their own purposes. Ancient societies depended on unfree labor to generate that surplus; the emphasis on slavery is quite right. Peasants tied to the land generate the surplus under feudalism. The modern proletarian does it under capitalism. Just how the resulting conflicts line up on any given occasion is highly circumstantial, but the essence of politics is that states exist to handle the conflicts of interest generated by coercive measures of surplus extraction.

A conflict-driven model of historical change and political activity has many attractions. The "materialist conception of history," which is Marx's chief claim to analytical originality, relies on his famous but contentious distinction between forces of production and relations of production. There have been some strikingly ingenious interpretations of what Marx had, might have had, or must have had in mind, but the basic thought is, as usual, simple. Forces of production are resources that, when used appropriately, create what we make, use, and consume. A stream is just a stream until somebody invents a waterwheel to harness its power: then the stream becomes a force of production. The crucial force of production is human labor, with or without technological assistance; and not all forces of production are material. Marx counts technological imagination and scientific discovery as forces of production in virtue of their role in allowing us to put together productively natural elements that would otherwise yield nothing.

The materiality of good ideas is not obvious, but Marx was making a sensible point. History did not, pace Hegel, instantiate the self-development of the Idea, but ideas are not powerless, when they are the ideas of particular individuals and lead to action. Ideas have effects by inspiring action, whether by motivating us or enabling us to do what we wish. Only when ideas are embodied in behavior and in what we do with material objects do they have an impact on history. Wishing for a cannon will win no battles; but a battery of field guns will secure victory against less well-armed opponents; ideas matter on the battlefield for the further reason that guns are of no use without the ability to use them. *Whether* forces of production will be productively used depends upon the relations of production into which they are inserted. The concept of the relations of production needs some disentangling. Again, the basic idea is simple. The plow is a force of production and so is the plowman's skill. The fact that I own the plow, the field, and the seed we plant when the plowman has ploughed the field, and that I employ the plowman for wages, is a fact about the relations of production within which these forces are deployed. The field might have been owned by the plowman, or a collective farm, as might his plow and the seed. The point is that in the absence of the right relations of production, potential forces of production are never exploited. A simple steam engine was invented in Alexandria during the Hellenistic period, but the abundance of slave labor meant there was no incentive to economize on human effort and develop the steam engine into more than a toy.

Marx's materialism consisted in the claim that the forces of production dictate the relations of production; progress occurs because the forces of production become increasingly productive and induce changes in relations of production that enhance their productivity. Marx's account of all this is none too clear. He seems at times to suggests that the causation is all one way, as if forces develop autonomously and drag relations along with them; at others, he rightly says that relations help or hinder the development of the forces of production and that whatever brings new relations into existence is less important than that the new relations will "take" only if they improve productivity. He certainly thought the latter. Nor does he underestimate the way in which what starts as an innovation ends as a clog on the progress. This will be the case with capitalism. Hitherto, capitalist relations of production have produced vast gains in productivity, at a fearful price in chaos and insecurity. Sooner rather than later, the division of industrial society into the owners of capital and the suppliers of labor will become a drag on productivity. His theory of revolution culminates in the dramatic claim that when the relations of production that constitute capitalism become a "fetter" on the forces of production, the "integument is burst asunder. The knell of capitalist private property sounds. The expropriators are expropriated." The last revolution will ensue.[12]

There is a plausible construal of what Marx meant: there is always some pressure to develop the productivity of our work, and therefore some pressure toward improving the forces of production. They do not develop by their own volition, but we always have some incentive to improve our productive capacities. Some improvements involve the physical qualities of the forces, such as more efficient steam engines, but others involve changes in the terms on which things are owned, and workers are managed and paid. This takes us back to classes and the claim that large changes occur through revolutionary upheaval. Marx sees the essence of property rights as the ability to dictate access to the means of production; and he treats control over access to the means of production as forms of property, no matter what their legal basis. Officials in a state bureaucracy who in law own nothing may be in charge of the funds that launch production, and be able to dictate production and distribution throughout an entire command economy. It is tempting to think this is quasi-ownership and that the bureaucracy is a class in the full Marxist sense. This was the conclusion drawn by some Trotskyites when they denounced the Soviet Union for practicing "state capitalism."

Under capitalism Marx's schema is persuasive. Owners of productive resources hire laborers and purchase resources, organize production, and sell their products on the open market. It is a ferociously competitive market, so no manufacturer will survive who does not cheapen production and distribution and try to maximize his output so as to gain economies of scale and to create the resources to survive slumps. Capitalists have every incentive to drive down wages; they will ruthlessly fire workers when they do not need their services, replace men with women and children to get the work done more cheaply, and so on. Marx was not the only economist of the day to think this was the logic of capitalist production, and not the only one to think that "immiseration"—steady downward pressure on the standard of living—was the lot of the working class. The capacity of workers to resist in the marketplace was minimal. Not only are those in work threatened by the "reserve army of the unemployed"; competition is increased as increasing numbers fall out of the class of owners and employers and into the class of those with nothing to sell but their labor. We have the ingredients that the *Manifesto* says will bring about the revolution, which is an ever larger and more desperate working class facing an ever smaller class of owners. It is, as we have seen, one of the situations that Aristotle noted as likely to bring about stasis.

The Ultimate Revolution

Importantly for Marx, the fact that this process went along with steadily improving productivity allowed him to imagine what he predicted to be the last revolution. Latent in capitalist society are the resources for a noncoercive society of genuine abundance, such that no future class conflicts need disturb it and therefore no future revolution erupt. Given that history has turned out rather differently, we should retrace our steps to consider how classes form, and why their conflicts erupt in revolution. Marx was a good critic of his own views; he might wriggle and twist in his attempts to make sense of the world, but he was deeply respectful of the facts. "Stupidity never helped the working class" was the insult he hurled at the utopian socialist Wilhelm Weitling in 1847, but it was Marx's motto. Not only did capitalism not destroy itself as predicted, but his analysis had to accommodate too many exceptions for comfort.

One exception was the issue embodied in what came to be known as the theory of the "Asiatic mode of production," but the problem it poses is central to the credibility of Marxism. The standard Marxian view of historical progress envisaged a prehistorical stage, where there was no property, no social classes, no political organization, and no forward momentum. Marx was not interested in drawing distinctions within the prehistorical stage of human history; he wanted to contrast the lack of momentum in the absence of property and class conflict with the momentum they imparted to history. The intellectually omnivorous Marx knew that before settled agricultural communities with private landownership, there were nomadic tribes whose possessions amounted to their furs and weapons and flocks. European colonization in America and southern Africa had also introduced Europe to stone age peoples who lived the lives of hunter-gatherers. To Marx these were unhistorical phenomena, but they provided a rhetorical bookend to his picture of human history. History began when we left the nonpropertied, non-class-divided state of primitive communism, and it will end when we regain a nonpropertied and non-class-divided condition of developed communism.

He sometimes describes the history we have experienced as "prehuman" history inasmuch as what happens is not under our conscious control; truly human history has yet to occur. Marx's account focused on the progression from ancient societies based on slavery, through feudalism and capitalism, to the revolutionary end of the process. His attention was fixed on the origins of bourgeois society and the end of the ancien régime, and he sought in the French Revolution of 1789 clues to the socialist revolution.

The anxiety induced by the phenomenon of the "Asiatic mode of production" is that there was no internal dynamic in the Indian or Chinese economies. India and China had once been more intellectually advanced than Europe; they had possessed but not developed many of the technologies around which the Western industrial revolution had occurred. "Asiatic" relations of production fostered not the development of the forces of production but stagnation; Asiatic political arrangements did not sharpen class conflict, and patterns of ownership did not put competitive pressure on those who owned the means of production. Nothing analogous to the medieval European town with its guilds of artisans made an appearance. Skilled craftsmen were drafted into the palaces of the local rulers when their services were needed, but they remained workers and never became independent entrepreneurs serving a market. No competitive pressures, no classes formed around the antagonism of owners and laborers, no change.

Marx might have thought only that this was an interesting anomaly and gotten on with the task of bringing about a socialist revolution in Europe. To some degree, he did. He praised European incursions into Asia because they would drag India and China into the flow of European world history and set them on the road to socialism. However, it raised a question that could not be ducked, which was whether a form of government and economic system might emerge in Europe that would defuse class conflict, produce economic stagnation, and derail the revolution. In Europe the question was whether the bureaucratic absolutism of Prussia or the imperial France of Napoleon III could defuse class conflict, appease the workers by making their lives less miserable than pure capitalism did, and comfort the capitalists by smoothing out booms and slumps, so that the absence of spectacular economic growth would be made up for by guaranteed security. It turned out that Prussian economic growth and technological innovation swiftly surpassed that of Britain, while the American version of uninhibited capitalism never generated the class-based politics of Europe.

Class Formation

Marx's picture of class conflict in the *Manifesto* was binary: owners versus nonowners, slave versus free. But classes had two aspects; one was their generation in the productive process, the other their role in the political process. If politics is class struggle, we need a clear account of the way the social divisions generated by the productive life of the society emerge in political life. When Marx discussed actual political events, he abandoned the binary model and appealed to the interaction of more than two classes. His expectations for 1848 were disappointed; most of the revolutionary energy was nationalist and liberal, not socialist; none of the revolutions succeeded. In Germany the old elites reestablished themselves, and German unification took place not as a result of a liberal-nationalist consensus but under the aegis of the absolutist Prussian monarchy and its ablest servant, Prince von Bismarck. In France the July Monarchy of Louis-Philippe was overthrown, but the Second Republic was unsustainable, and Louis Napoleon was first elected as president and after a coup d'état turned himself into a self-proclaimed emperor under the label of Napoleon III.[13]

Late in life, Marx came to see that the *Manifesto* mistook the birth pangs of the capitalist economic system in Europe for its death throes. What he thought was an uprising of a socialist proletariat was in part traditional discontent with bad harvests and high food prices and depression, and in part the reaction of workers swept into urban environments where they felt ill at ease and resentful at the loss of past certainties. The 1848 revolutions were as much backward- as forward-looking. Marx had little intuitive feeling for the nationalist sentiments that drove revolution in much of central and eastern Europe and less sympathy; since the workingman has no country, he is, or should be, universal in his aspirations. The fact that he is not has always plagued social democratic movements, and some of Marx's and Engels's most savage denunciations were leveled at such phenomena as Scandinavian nationalism, dismissed as "Old Norse piracy."

Soon after Louis Napoleon's coup, Marx wrote an account of events, later revised to take account of the fact that the coup had been much more than the temporary success he predicted at the time. There he provided an account of why events had not followed the "right" scenario and an account of the way in which a state could be something other than the committee for managing the common interests of the bourgeoisie that he had described in the *Manifesto*.[14] In France in 1848 there were more actors than a large, solid proletariat facing a capitalist bourgeoisie. There was a large peasant population, divided between the owners of large holdings, the owners of small holdings, and those who worked as agricultural laborers with no land of their own; Marx and Engels had earlier dismissed the peasantry as "a bag of potatoes," not a class at all; when the peasants' votes brought Louis Napoleon to power, they had to change their minds. Nor was there a single bourgeoisie; its upper echelons were divided between those who lived on state bonds and formed a kind of financial aristocracy and those who were captains of industry. Below them, and again divided among themselves, was the radical petty bourgeoisie consisting of all sorts of disparate characters, ranging from newspaper writers to radical artisans such as watchmakers. The revolution was—to the extent that one group made it—the work of the radical petty bourgeoisie. That explained why the republic could not be secured.

We have two pictures of class conflict, one a very simple dichotomy between owners and suppliers of labor, the other an analysis of what groupings *in fact* played a decisive role in important political upheavals. These two pictures generate two accounts of the state. The first sees the state as the instrument of the ruling class, which is the dominant economic class, and the state manages its common interests. This is not an unattractive view of the politics of mid-nineteenth-century Britain. It can deal with some obvious difficulties, such as the fact that although the dominant economic class was the bourgeoisie, politicians were overwhelmingly drawn from the landowning gentry and their relatives. The gentry politicians can be analyzed as the hired help of men busy making large fortunes. The theory can also cope with the fact that most of the working population was still employed on the land or as domestic servants by insisting that the issue is the conflict of interests that drives political change, not occupational demography. Many things Marx thought a state seen as a committee for managing the common affairs of the bourgeoisie would do, happened as they ought. The Victorian state became uncorrupt, rooted out sinecures and jobbery, and set up meritocratic systems of recruitment; property law was made simpler and more transparent, and restrictions on the sale of land were abolished, reflecting a shift away from preserving land within a family and toward allowing all assets to be made into liquid capital.

The Victorian state fit the theory because the theory was drawn from it. Indeed, one way in which it frustrated Marx's expectations was by doing such a good job of managing the interests of the bourgeoisie. It averted revolution, incorporated the urban working class into the political system, then seduced the workers with the spectacle of empire; it forced the owners of industry to behave in their own best interests by regulating factory conditions and hours of work, and protected the wages of male heads of families by restricting the employment of women and children. Far from suffering "immiseration," the English workingman had half a century of rising real wages. This was destructive of Marx's hopes of revolution, but it does not wholly subvert his political theory. If Marx had thought through his own account of the "common interests" of the owning classes, he would have seen that they included not only the things he did mention, such as the enforcement of laws against theft and fraud—in the interests of everyone on average, if not the thief or fraudster on particular occasions—but also things he did not, such as regulations that stopped firms from competing in ways that would provoke political unrest. The price of arguing in this way is to give up the claim that revolution is inevitable. Revolution was inevitable only if the government botched the job of securing the common interests of the bourgeoisie.

Two escape routes are worth mentioning. One is to dismiss everything an intelligent government might do as short-term palliatives, doomed to fail in the long run; for example, when worldwide competition began to threaten British economic supremacy and British firms could not compete with firms in other countries paying lower wages, British firms would have to drive down wages, and the *Manifesto* scenario of immiseration leading to revolution would come into operation. The other is to abandon the idea that is encapsulated in the slogan that social evolution proceeds by means of political revolution.[15] Revolutions have been the rule because the excluded classes have lacked peaceful ways of representing their interests and pressing for change. The incumbent ruling class has seen the issue as a zero-sum game. If the lower classes gained in power and wealth, the incumbent upper classes would lose what the lower classes gained. In a more prosperous world with rapidly growing productivity, a gradual improvement in the lot of the workers, and a closing of the differences in income, power, aspirations, and culture between classes, could see a peaceful transition from full-blooded, old-fashioned capitalism to democratic socialism or capitalist welfare state democracy. Late in life, Marx thought that Britain, Holland, and the United States might take that route. Marx's acknowledgment of this possibility suggested some disillusionment with his youthful view that revolution alone would slough off the muck of ages.

Marx's second theory of the state was adapted to France, Germany, and Russia rather than to Britain or the United States. After the revolution of 1848 Louis Napoleon found it easy to rally support from enthusiasts for the army and the military glories of his uncle Napoleon I. There were also many people with a vested interest in the continued existence of the military-bureaucratic state as such. Not only the bondholders and stockjobbers who made their livelihood lending money to the state and selling the state's bonds to other people, but a substantial bureaucratic apparatus had a stake in the preservation of the French state. Since the revolution had not destroyed it, it could put down insurrection in the streets of Paris and Lyons, and turf out parliamentarians opposed to Louis Napoleon. Under those conditions the state ceases to be a committee hired and fired at the will of the bourgeoisie and turns into an independent actor.

Its nature is hard to explain in terms of a simple theory of class conflict. If any state that regulates a capitalist economy is a bourgeois state, its two salient properties should be cheapness and a focus on the common interests of the bourgeoisie. The French state engaged in the pursuit of national glory, which is not cheap and not obviously in the interests of the capitalist; it employed a swollen class of officials who did not come cheap; and it issued a lot of government debt whose interest payments required taxes that many of the bourgeoisie did not want to pay, even though others wanted the income they provided. The explanation of its existence lies in the answer to the question of just what the common interests of the bourgeoisie are. Marx thought that the French bourgeoisie had never established its position as a ruling class. The division of economic interest between the financial and the industrial bourgeoisies was one element; the vigor of the radical bourgeoisie and petty bourgeoisie was another. The state had never been captured by the bourgeoisie; the state's personnel could therefore pursue their own parasitic interests as a social class living off the state. Marx also claimed that a divided bourgeoisie needed a stronger state than an undivided bourgeoisie would have done. The class as a whole needed a strong state to enforce the common interests of all property owners against the separate interests of the holders of particular forms of property. It is not a foolish argument; one could imagine representatives of the different bourgeois interests sitting down to devise a state to which they would all be loyal and coming up with the military-bureaucratic regime that Marx described in France. If they were sufficiently cynical, they might also devise its propensity for military adventures that distracted attention from domestic affairs, but they would have been ill-advised to devise anything that culminated in the disaster of the Franco-Prussian War.

When he first analyzed the peculiarities of Louis Napoleon's coup, Marx said his success would be short-lived. He assumed that the bourgeois state of the *Manifesto* was the normal form of a bourgeois state. The expense of a military-bureaucratic state would be intolerable to an industrial and commercial bourgeoisie. He later saw that the deviant form of state had more staying power. One effect was to lead him to think that there might be more routes from capitalism to socialism than he had anticipated, and that revolution in the literal sense was not the only possible precursor to socialism. So let us turn to the last elements in this account of Marx's politics, the theory of revolution, the withering away of the state, and social organization thereafter. Marx was a tremendous nonfinisher of work that he had projected. This was not idleness or intellectual disorganization. It was the inevitable outcome of his ambition to create an intellectual system that would do full justice to all the phenomena in which he was interested. Since he proposed to tackle the nature of the state at the end of a sequence of investigations of which the three volumes of *Das Kapital* would have formed only the first quarter—only volume one of *Das Kapital* was published in his lifetime—it is easy to see why we have mere fragments of the project.

Revolution

Revolution is the way in which major changes occur because they occur when the old ruling class cannot make enough concessions to secure the acquiescence of the insurgent classes and the insurgent classes have demands that the old regime cannot meet. Not all revolutions are necessary; some occur because of ruling class incompetence. The revolutions in which Marx is interested mark decisive transitions from one mode of production to another, and these seem to be inescapable. Marx did not provide a fully developed theory of revolution, and it is no injustice to suggest that he really offers an account of social tectonics; as emerging economic and social forms slide into the old political carapace, it is more likely that there will be earthquakes than that the stresses will gently distribute themselves all over the landscape. But stresses may dissipate, and when an earthquake will strike may be impossible to predict.

In nineteenth-century Europe, there are two distinct possibilities, one of them even more plausible as a scenario for the United States than for Europe. The first is insurrection and revolution. A state that prevents political participation not only by the growing industrial working class but by their radical bourgeois allies and almost everyone else will create disaffection and eventual rebellion. Whether it can hold that disaffection in check or repress that rebellion is difficult to predict, but under many conditions revolution is likely to succeed. Bismarck's handling of the political pressures on the Prussian monarchy, on the other hand, was a model of deftness. With a more intelligent monarch and intelligent successors to Bismarck the *Reich* might have lasted indefinitely. The conditions under which states such as the Second Empire, the czarist regime in Russia and the Wilhelmine regime in Germany most often end are those in which they in fact did end. Defeat in war leaves a military-bureaucratic state vulnerable because it has lost both its repressive capacity and the legitimacy that came from military success.

Marx's guess that revolution threatened the states that were most resistant to the incorporation of their excluded classes was a good guess. He allowed too little for the astuteness of authoritarian leaders such as Bismarck, who understood Marx's views as well as Marx himself, and bought off working-class discontent by creating an early welfare state while blocking the revolutionary route by ensuring that the armed forces were overwhelmingly powerful and loyal. Marx also paid too little attention to the increasing disparity in simple firepower between the military forces of the state and an untrained and ill-equipped insurrection. Even then, Trotsky's observation that rifles need a human being to fire them always has to be borne in mind; the recent past is full of examples of armies that could, but did not, overwhelm protesters who went on to make a successful revolution. Ayatollah Khomeini's 1979 revolution in Iran is a good example, and the 2011 Arab Spring another.

The other route was the parliamentary road to socialism. The "normal" bourgeois state was in its nature, if not its formal institutions, a democratic republic—Britain was a monarchy in name only. It soon had to accept universal suffrage, and that opened the parliamentary road to socialism. The logic of Marx's case is not foolish, but it is not wholly persuasive, either. He would have had to be right both about the development of the economy and about the class structure of such countries as Britain. If the conditions of all members of the working class had become both uniform and miserable, he would have had good grounds for thinking that the working class would vote solidly as a class. Britain came as close as any state to fulfilling his two-class vision of politics, but there were many divisions within the working class, not simply a cleavage between a homogenous working class and a capitalist exploiting class. Skilled workers were conscious of their differences with unskilled workers; foremen were lower-level managers rather than upper-level laborers. Until the late twentieth century, British voters voted along class lines to a degree unequaled almost anywhere else, but even unskilled workers were far from reliable Labour Party voters, and among skilled workers Labour could count on a bare majority at best. In any case, there was no "immiseration," and it was far from obvious that socialism, in whatever form, would be a better bet than the reformed capitalism that was on offer from intelligent conservatives.

Marx thought that a working-class party armed with the secret ballot and universal suffrage would vote in socialism. It had to be prepared for violent counterrevolution, and there was no assurance that the parliamentary road to socialism would be peaceful. Nonetheless, the familiar scenario of barricades, street fighting, storming of barracks, and looting of weapons need not happen. Some commentators have interpreted Marx to mean that capitalism might dissolve into socialism piecemeal, less the bursting asunder of integuments than quiet euthanasia. Two obvious questions follow: What interim state will exist before there is no state at all, and what happens after that?

Proletarian Democracy

Whichever route to the overthrow of the bourgeois-capitalist form of society is taken, what will occur after the change is the dictatorship of the proletariat. This concept has acquired an unhappy association with the dictatorship that Lenin established in the Soviet Union after 1917, but in principle it is unalarming. The long-run vision is a stateless, self-managing society. Proletarian dictatorship is the intermediate form of democratic government that Marx imagines filling the intervening period. Since all forms of government are, in Marx's analysis, class dictatorships, a democracy with a substantial working-class majority is by definition the dictatorship of the proletariat; liberal democracy is the dictatorship of the bourgeoisie, and few people fear a knock on the door in the middle of the night in liberal democracies. Proletarian democracy should be less repressive than previous regimes because it is not a minority ruling a majority but a majority ruling over itself and a declining bourgeoisie. Unlike earlier regimes where a newly installed ruling class rules a subordinate class or classes, the proletariat is about to abolish classes altogether. This it will do by installing socialism or, in other words, abolishing the private ownership of the means of production and instituting social ownership. Doing that abolishes classes, and whatever is left by way of social organization will not, strictly, be a state.

It is an obvious and easy complaint against Marx's account that everything hangs on definitions and that Marx makes it sound much too simple, smooth, and painless. Defanging the coercive overtones of "dictatorship" by pointing out that all class governments are dictatorships is a fudge; bourgeois republics have a good record in reducing state violence to a minimum, and socialist dictatorships have a terrible record. Similarly, the elimination of the bourgeoisie is one thing when accomplished quietly by taxation over a century, or by nationalization with compensation more rapidly, and quite another when accomplished by the mass murder of the kulaks under Stalin. Marx implies, but never argues, that there will be such an overwhelming majority in favor of the new order that voting will suffice, with coercion only held in reserve in case of last-ditch holdouts. That things will be bloodier in military-bureaucratic despotisms needs no emphasis; losing power after an insurrection leaves the losers in no mood to submit quietly and the winners in no mood to respect parliamentary niceties.

Much can be said about the argument, but one point must suffice. If socialism is to arrive when capitalism has paved the way to abundance, the revolution or "revolution" must not damage the productive capacity of the society in which it occurs. Building socialism among the ruins has been the lot of all socialist regimes, and that task is, in Marxist terms, strictly hopeless. Now we see Marx's picture of the future emerging on the photographic paper. After the change of political regime, there will be a highly democratic state, dominated by the proletariat; it will establish socialism and abolish the private ownership of the means of production. As it does, citizens learn the habits of self-government and—in a way that Marx never spelled out and nobody has ever spelled out for him—learn to organize an economic system in such a way that there is no domination and no exploitation, one that is coordinated without markets and money to perform the signaling functions they perform in most economies. If tastes never changed and techniques were static, we could imagine solving once and for all the equations that represented the answer to the question of how most efficiently to produce and distribute what we need, taking as our *minimand* the quantity of undesired toil. It will not do, however: the liberated creatures Marx thinks we shall become under socialism will change their tastes, invent new enjoyments, and think of new ways of making what we need.

Marx's *Critique of the Gotha Program* at least spells out what happens when there are no capitalists taking off an unearned profit. Marx looks forward to a society where the narrow horizons of bourgeois right are transcended and the motto is "From each according to his ability, to each according to his needs!"[16] The slogan was Saint-Simon's. There is no agreement on what that means. Thinking back to Marx's account of the genesis of profit in the capitalist's unpaid-for taking of the surplus value produced by the worker, it certainly means that no such taking occurs. Marx is quite clear that it does not mean that the worker receives, on the spot and without further ado, the value of everything he creates; resources are needed for those who can no longer work because of old age, for those who cannot yet work because they are infants or are currently sick, to provide education, and to invest. In the first stage of socialism, when we are still thinking in bourgeois terms, a worker will get back all that he produces over a whole lifetime—on average, of course. Stronger, cleverer, more effective workers will produce more and receive more, so there will not be equality between one worker and another, but the equality implied by nonexploitation. The motto is "To each according to his contribution." Only in the second stage of socialism, when we have given up thinking in terms of being rewarded for what we contribute, can we subscribe to "From each according to his ability, to each according to his needs!"

Then we shall have achieved full-fledged socialism. We shall have transcended justice in its usual senses, because nobody thinks in terms of entitlements or rights. Compared with bourgeois society, it is more just, but that is not the point. Citizens contribute because they wish to contribute to the collective project in which they are all engaged, and what they receive is theirs because the only rational purpose of production is to satisfy human needs, and the only rational principle of distribution is "according to need." The last question this leaves us with is whether it is imaginable that there could be a complex but stateless society of this sort. Innumerable writers have observed that particular people would become managers or administrators or whatever in these conditions, and their expertise would secure them the deference of others, and bit by bit they would turn back into a ruling class. Whether we imagine them as Plato's guardians or as Hegel's universal class, they would begin to hold the society's organization as their property, and a new class would emerge and a new but probably no more attractive set of inequalities of power and wealth. This claim often rests on a rather simple appeal to the frailties of human nature and the temptations of authority, combined with some more sophisticated skepticism about the concept of "abundance." If Hobbes and contemporary marketing managers are right, and we are inexorably drawn to wanting more than anyone else has, rather than wanting only as much as is good for us, the achievement of abundance is impossible. Conceptually, there is no such thing.

Marx is both vulnerable and invulnerable to this argument. He is invulnerable because he subscribes to a rationalism that resembles Plato's. If we become rational enough to understand ourselves and our needs, we shall feel that we have all we need, and the critics who believe that we will always wish to do better than our neighbor will be wrong. By the same token, if administrators see the positions they occupy as positions of service, not authority, in which they do what is needed to keep the social and economic order in good heart, they would feel no desire to exploit their authority. Bakunin understood what Marx was looking to, and sneered that it was an aristocracy of professors of economics. Marx sneered back that Bakunin had not understood that under socialism, management superseded the government of men, and administration lost its political character.[17]

The great unsolved questions are whether it can lose its political character, and whether, if it did, we would be happy. We can defer to a later chapter Max Weber's insistence that if there is not to be stagnation and a loss of human aspiration, rational administration is not enough, and that charismatic leaders who can startle us into wanting something new and different will always be needed. We can end this discussion by observing that many worse things have happened to human beings than living in the kind of timeless utopia envisaged by Marx, where the dictates of reason and our best productive natures so happily coincide—and that many less utopian projects have been imagined than this example of what its author believed to be "scientific socialism," but that was as utopian as anything dreamed up by his rivals.

PART II

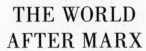

THE WORLD
AFTER MARX

Preface to Part II

ALTHOUGH THE FINAL PART of this book picks up many of the tragedies and anxieties that beset the twentieth century, it is not a jeremiad. Nor is it confined to issues that became important only in the twentieth century, or to ideas that first appeared then. European imperialism and its contribution to the two world wars of the twentieth century cannot be treated as though imperial competition suddenly emerged in the last years of the nineteenth century; much of the politics of the eighteenth and nineteenth centuries was imperial politics, just as the endless conflicts between Britain and Continental powers, including Spain and France, from the sixteenth century onward had their roots in imperial competition. Nonetheless, in the twentieth century the European domination of the globe reached its apogee, and in the latter half of the century the swift, often violent dismantling of the European empires occurred.

Other phenomena had shorter prehistories and brief histories. The totalitarian aspirations of fascism and communism echoed the ambition of religious movements, and perhaps especially the Catholic Church, to regulate every aspect of the believer's life; but their ambitions were secular, the analogy between a church and a political party is at best imperfect, and—allowances made for the uncertain future of Chinese communism—their staying power turned out to be limited. Indeed, as we shall see, there were certainly some unhappy alliances between church and state in Italy and Spain, but understanding them is not much advanced by delving into medieval theology as distinct from nineteenth- and twentieth-century socialist and anarchist movements and conservative reactions to them, and the pressures of abrupt industrialization and political modernization on societies ill adapted to them.

Although this is a history of political ideas, not a work of political history, what follows emphasizes the role of industrialization and the effect of the demographic changes that accompanied it on the way everyone thought about the political and social possibilities of the new world. Anyone reading political writers of the early twentieth century will be struck by their references to the "bigness" of modern society. Whether it was factories, ocean liners, apartment buildings, or bridges across previously impassable rivers, things seemed to have got bigger. The output of these bigger factories was vastly greater than previously; shops had a far wider range of goods than ever before; newspapers had more readers than any previous form of communication.

Reactions were very far from uniform. Conservatives of all stripes complained that modern democracies were impressive on the quantitative dimension and much less so on the qualitative dimension. Anxious liberals wondered how a "big" society might become a "great community." This anxiety took at least three different forms. One was the fear that individuals would feel lost in the crowd, unable to make sense of their lives, feeling that they were insignificant cogs in the industrial machine at work, and a mere number in the polling booth when the time came to elect their leaders. Another was the fear that government would be unable to manage the vast and complex machine that was modern industrial society. Booms and slumps in the economy seemed to be beyond anyone's power to control; when slumps arrived, they brought not only misery but labor unrest and the danger—not, as it turned out, as great as hoped on the left and feared on the right—that an insurrectionary working class would overturn everything, destroy property rights, institute the dictatorship of the proletariat, bring the excesses of the French Revolution back with a vengeance. Its mirror image was the fear that governments would be all too effective in controlling modern industrial societies, perhaps by the sort of brutality associated with fascist or communist regimes, or perhaps by something resembling the Roman recipe of "bread and circuses."

Very few political ideas die so thoroughly that they are beyond hope of resurrection. Even if they did suffer the fate of scientific theories that cease to be part of science and become episodes in the history of science, they would still have the sort of afterlife that heliocentric astronomy and Ptolemaic epicycles do not. There are at least two reasons for this, both of them animating this book. The first is that human beings are historical animals. We mock ourselves for our ignorance of the details of everything from the books of the Old Testament to the names of members of Congress. Nonetheless, we have a strong sense of the pedigree of our institutions, and of the moral and intellectual commitments they embody. For every person who knows what the contents of Magna Carta actually were, there are hundreds who think that the civil liberties of today descend somehow from that document. For every person who knows how Athenians voted in the Assembly, there are hundreds who are aware that it was they who gave a name to what we pride ourselves on as a uniquely legitimate form of government. It is inconceivable that things should be otherwise.

Nor is it a matter only of appealing to the authority of venerable ideas. Often enough, it is a matter of appealing to their badness, whatever form that badness takes. We hope that we know better or have more generous reactions, or at least more squeamish ones than our ancestors. We do not like to dwell on the blood-stained origins of our own political systems or to think in what frame of mind our ancestors committed the brutalities of which we are the remote beneficiaries. Even where the ideas with which we try to make sense of ourselves and the situations in which we find ourselves are distinctively modern, such as Freud's psychoanalytic theories, we find their remote ancestors interesting, not merely as vague prefigurings of what we now possess as science but as insights into ourselves newly understood in a different light. Freud himself agreed that poets and playwrights had always known what he had tried to make newly clear as science.

If the first reason is that we are historical animals, the second is almost the reverse. While we live in societies that are in all sorts of ways vastly different from any that have gone before, we face entirely familiar dilemmas, even if they are on a different scale and our resources for dealing with them are, at least in material terms, very much greater. Viewed as institutional devices for securing ourselves against both external and internal enemies, ensuring that we have enough to live on, that the next generation is brought up as good citizens and loyal members of the political community, and that our ethical and spiritual culture is adequately sustained, states, or political systems more broadly, have performed the tasks that Aristotle identified, save where "failed states" have failed to perform them either comprehensively or in part. Distributive questions about which members of the citizen body should contribute what to their performance rack societies today as they have done throughout history, and the competing conceptions of justice in terms of which they are debated would not have surprised Aristotle in the same way the size of modern states would certainly have done, let alone modern technology in all its aspects.

Indeed, the counterpoint of technological discontinuity and ideological, philosophical, and political continuity runs through all these final chapters. Even where we may hope that we can draw a line under failed experiments such as Stalinism and Nazism, or think, as I do, that we have discovered that any form of socialism that requires a command economy of the Stalinist kind is a dead end, we have certainly not thought our last thoughts or said the last word on how to reconcile the vigor of a free-market economy with a concern for the welfare of those whom it predictably leaves behind, or on how to find a role for strong executive leadership without opening the door to dictatorship, or on how to promote peace while being equipped to make war if we must. In a world with seven billion inhabitants, it is easy to think that modern problems must be unparalleled; we, after all, have enough weaponry to destroy all human life; we may render the planet uninhabitable; we may so deplete resources that wars over oil, water, or arable land return us to a new dark age. But if the scale on which we can damage the planet and with it ourselves is very different from anything imagined before 1900, the damage itself for the individuals in its path is not. Being in the path of a Mongol invasion was no less appalling than being in the target zone of a B-52 strike; earlier societies suffered the consequences of overgrazing, soil erosion, fishing out their resources. If the state exists, among its other purposes, to take care of the side effects of our behavior in ways individuals and smaller groupings cannot, the question we began with remains. How can we govern ourselves? How can we act collectively to resolve the problems that our collective life creates?

CHAPTER 22

The Twentieth Century and Beyond

Moving On

HISTORICAL ACCOUNTS OF POLITICAL thinking usually draw to a conclusion at the end of the nineteenth century; there is much to be said for this practice. Time lends perspective, and the risk of saying something that will immediately look silly in the light of events is much reduced. The next several chapters are written from a different perspective. Long-dead writers often speak to us with greater freshness and immediacy than our contemporaries. The argument between the friends of the tumultuous Athenian democracy and the admirers of Roman stability continues unabated: we—modern Western "we"—want, if possible, to split the difference. We want to give ordinary citizens as much say as possible in the political arrangements of their society and to enhance their control over those who govern them; but we share the fears of the observers of Athenian factionalism, the Reformation, the French Revolution, and the disasters of the twentieth century about what ordinary citizens can do when inflamed by ideological or religious passion, bamboozled by demagogues, or beset by hysterical fears. Not for nothing did a best-selling account of the Nazi attempt to exterminate the Jews bear the subtitle *Ordinary Germans and the Holocaust*.[1] Under the wrong conditions, ordinary Britons and ordinary Americans might have been recruited to behave as atrociously. Indeed, many of them have behaved atrociously towards the subjects of the British Empire and the Native American victims of the westward expansion of the United States.

We share the ancient and medieval world's sense of the fragility of political order. We have in the past century lived through two world wars, innumerable regional conflicts, dashed hopes for freedom and prosperity in the decolonized world, genocide perpetrated by civilized nations— and more recently by struggling and dysfunctional states. We have also become aware that a desire for order can pose its own dangers. Interwar Europe provided an object lesson in the dangers of an alliance between those who were driven by fear and anger and those who were driven by a desire for a quiet life. After 1918 recently democratized European countries repudiated democracy: Italy turned to Mussolini's Fascists, Germany voted Hitler into power in 1933, Hungary, Austria, Romania, Spain, and Portugal became dictatorships of one sort and another; and even the republican French were tempted. Since World War II stable liberal democracies have seen their civil liberties eroded by governments fearful of espionage or terrorism. In Latin America what would always have been a slow emancipation from military dictatorship has periodi- cally been aborted when authoritarian governments stepped in to avert actual or pretended threats of insurrection. In Africa military govern- ments intervene to prevent politicians from looting the public treasury on behalf of their families and friends, and loot the public treasury in turn.

We are also unsure whether we care for politics at all. Politicians are not widely liked and are often suspected with good reason of being more interested in lining their pockets by doing favors for the well-placed and well-off than in disinterestedly pursuing the common good. What many of us want is benign, competent management, not politics. We think, not without reason, that over the past century we have explored the limits of the politically possible and that sober, consensual policy making is what we now need. This view was given canonical expression not long after the Second World War in Daniel Bell's *The End of Ideology*.[2] The thesis of Bell's book was what he called the exhaustion of political ideas, by which he mostly meant radical and revolutionary ideas. It was not a wholly optimistic view of the political culture of countries such as Britain and the United States. The loss of utopian aspirations was really a *loss*. Still, the implication seemed to be that the increasingly prosperous postwar societies of the Western world had come to an unshakable consensus that the political, or semipolitical, task of the day was the intelligent management of a capitalist welfare state; politics was a matter of nudging policy a little one way or a little the other. Deep and intractable differences between political parties were not to be expected and their absence not to be deplored. Politicians had an essential role, but not an exciting one, in connecting the public with the government that managed their welfare.

Because we are so aware that neither progress nor peace can be taken for granted, and two world wars have reminded us how atrociously we can behave in the wrong conditions, our distant predecessors are not very distant. Plato's picture of the psyche in *Phaedrus* is not so different from Freud's in *Civilization and Its Discontents*, and Plato's remedy for chaos in *Republic* not so different from Huxley's ironic nightmare of *Brave New World*. Hobbes's analysis of the state of nature, the *warre of all against all*, is a frighteningly apt rendering of a world where nuclear powers faced each other with the power to "win" a war only if they struck first, incinerating millions. Locke's anxieties about toleration have hardly lost their urgency, even if the country for which he was writing risks nothing worse than bigotry or foolishness. In much of the world, toleration is regarded with contempt. Every writer on just and unjust wars, from Augustine on, speaks to our anxieties, but few speak more plainly than he. Even in less high-stakes settings, our predecessors talk to us still. Aristotle is not a resource for insight into the darker recesses of the soul, but his ideas about the way a society can moderate class warfare seemed newly minted when rediscovered by American political sociologists in the 1960s.[3]

This and the five following chapters are thematic rather than chronological. The remainder of this chapter explores the impact of the idea of a mass society, and the idea that politics consists of so many variations on the mobilization—or tranquilization—of masses by elites; the next chapter takes up the same theme in the context of twentieth-century imperialism and decolonization, phenomena that raise questions about the mass appeal of nationalism. Imperialism was a twentieth-century phenomenon with roots in earlier centuries, and one strikingly relevant long-dead thinker is the sixteenth-century Spanish Dominican Francisco de Vitoria. Then I turn to the successes and failures of the Marxist and non-Marxist socialist projects, whose internationalism and egalitarianism turned out to be less attractive than nationalism for whole countries, and less attractive than individual economic advancement for the individual. Nonetheless, a much diluted semisocialism has been the salvation of capitalism. The twentieth century was a century of revolution, but its revolutions were all too often the prelude to dictatorial and totalitarian regimes, so the third of the following chapters considers revolution and totalitarianism in their own right, and revisits the contrast between the understanding of revolution before and after 1789.

The dissolution of Soviet communism during the 1980s and early 1990s left the world with little ideological competition to liberal democracy as a form of government and (much modified) capitalism as a form of economy; but the most passionate thinkers of the twentieth century were enemies of both. Nonetheless, serious political thinkers have defended the politics of liberal democracy and welfare capitalism as its necessary underpinnings, and the penultimate chapter considers those defenses. The book ends where it began; Athenian political thinkers were provoked to thinking about politics by internal instability, international conflict, and the difficulty of constructing an overarching order that would keep the peace between different polities. They did not ask whether this could be done on a global scale, but we can hardly escape doing so; nor can we avoid asking whether threats other than war are today more menacing and whether they are politically manageable.

Theories of Mass Society

In the twentieth century "democracy" ceased to be a term with dubious political connotations. But as it became universally acceptable, it lost much of its content. By the time it had been qualified to embrace "people's democracies" (communist dictatorships), "guided democracy" (military dictatorships), and "Islamic democracy" (theocratic dictatorships), there seemed almost no sort of regime that could not call itself a democracy. As long as the ruling elite claimed to be endorsed by the bulk of the population and ruling in its interests, it could claim the title. Here we will follow convention and refer to liberal democracies as "democracies" without qualification, observing only occasionally that in strictness they are *popular mixed republics*, representative democracies, and not what Jefferson called "pure" democracies. The point is not pedantic; a major twentieth-century anxiety was how liberal democracy could be preserved, and many writers argued that stability required that ordinary people play a limited and reactive role in politics; that hankerings after purer forms of democracy were likely to be self-destructive.[4] To put it slightly differently, the fear was that the hankering for "pure" democracy would be met not by Jeffersonian ward republics, where neighbors discussed the affairs of their community, but by Nuremberg rallies where dictators whipped crowds into frenzies of hatred for whatever enemies were salient in the dictator's mind.

This is the most acute, though far from the only, form of the fear of "mass society." The concept of mass society is not well defined, and the anxieties it expressed came from all directions, politically speaking, but they all rely on the thought that the ordinary person always had been, or had recently become, or would soon become, not an independent, knowledgeable, self-motivated citizen, with a real stake in his society and its political system, but an element in a mere "mass." If "the people" became a mere mass, many things might follow, but government of the people, by the people, and for the people would not. A mass society might be politically inert, but live contentedly while a political and economic elite got on with the job of managing its affairs; if the institutions of representative democracy remained in place, the elite would understand that the deference of the mass depended on the maintenance of peace and prosperity, and would attend to their welfare, as the governments of liberal democracies by and large do. If things went badly, the masses might become prey to the wiles of demagogues of left or right and be recruited for insurrection or repression at home or for imperialist adventures abroad.

There never was one theory of mass society and its politics in spite of heroic efforts by postwar American sociologists to provide one.[5] Talk of the masses and "mass society" lends itself to simple dichotomies: "mass" versus "elite" or "mass" versus "individual." These are the most popular dichotomies, and very different. When Machiavelli observes that the mass of mankind are driven by fantasies and illusions, so that a political entrepreneur who knows his business will never be short of dupes on whom to practice his wiles, the contrast is between incompetent masses and deft elites or, in a more high-flown vein, between the political virtuoso and his raw material. The masses do not threaten the existence of elites, since they are incapable of independent action, and cannot act without the leadership the political virtuoso can provide. Nevertheless, the virtuoso is riding a tiger. If he loses his touch, he may find himself rent limb from limb by the mob, or in Savonarola's case, burned at the stake. Mussolini's undignified end, his corpse swinging upside down from a lamppost in Milan, epitomizes the fate of a master manipulator who ended as the mob's prey.

The second dichotomy emphasizes the contrast between the mass and the individual. What matters is that the individual is outnumbered, lost in the crowd. When Mill set out in the 1830s to explain to his English readers what his French friends had discovered about the nature of social change, he seized on the idea that the modern world was different from the world of the Renaissance and perhaps that of the ancien régime in that "power passes more and more from individuals, and small knots of individuals, to masses; that the importance of the masses becomes constantly greater, that of individuals less."[6] This is the contrast not between a formless mass and the political elite that gives the mass a shape but between the power of political majorities and the public opinion they represent and the powerlessness of individuals to affect a society's moral, cultural, or political attitudes and institutions. Mill learned from Tocqueville to fear the tyranny of public opinion, and like him feared that stagnation, "Chinese immobility," would be the result.[7]

The description of the prosperous societies of the present-day Western world as "mass" societies may have no pejorative connotations. A mass transit system moves large numbers of people from one place to another; and the mass media aim at large audiences, just as "mass production" is the production of large numbers of items. It is not even true today that what is mass-produced must be uniform; the mass media aim at segmented audiences, and "customized" production is the order of the day everywhere. Discussion of mass society has so often started from an unexamined prejudice against the tastes and ambitions of ordinary people that we must distinguish sharply between the uncontentious fact that something appeals to a large audience and whatever contentious views we entertain about that audience's tastes. In general, however, writers who have talked of mass society have been critics of the way modern society has developed, culturally and politically. Nobody writes a book called *The Revolt of the Masses* to praise the masses for their discriminating tastes and to suggest that they are in revolt against mediocrity and in favor of excellence.[8]

There are many forms of anxiety about mass society, but three matter for our purposes. The first is the fear that modern society is inimical to individuality. The thought has its origins in Tocqueville's *Democracy in America*. Tocqueville thought democratic man might become lost in the crowd; he would take his moral and political cues from all the people around him, just as they would take theirs from those around them. The disaster to be anticipated was cultural, political, spiritual, and psychological in a broad sense of those terms. Although Tocqueville was fearful that a military despotism might arise even in the United States—France having paved the way for these fears under the first Napoleon—he was more afraid of "quiet despotism," the situation in which individuals would have turned inward and away from the public sphere, leaving the affairs of their society to be administered by an unanswerable government.[9] It would be the government of a shepherd over sheep, not self-government by active citizens. Writers after Tocqueville up to the present day have elaborated on the anxiety; for the quiet form of despotism is consistent with a punctilious if soulless preservation of the forms of parliamentary or congressional democracy. All it requires is that the citizens sacrifice their independence to their desire for comfort and a quiet life. This, Tocqueville feared, they might do. They would allow their horizons to shrink and their ambitions to reduce to the prosperity of themselves and their families; they would lose the capacity for independent moral judgment, and the competence to act on a public stage. It is worth noticing that the lonely crowd is a middle-class crowd, not a proletarian mob.

The second sort of anxiety is the unhappiness of Marxists who had thought that the industrial proletariat was the bearer of historical progress, but discovered that the average proletarian had no wish to play the part assigned by history. One aspect was the discovery—if it was one—that the common man's attachment to the socialist project was easily bought off by prosperity; worse was the discovery that he did not need buying off, because he turned out to be intrinsically conservative; worst of all, was the discovery that the common man was easily recruited to distracting adventures at odds with his best interests—nationalism, imperialism, fascist dictatorship. Distinctive about this view of the failings of mass society is the sharp contrast between two different collective actors—on the one side, the wide-awake, courageous, revolutionary proletariat dreamed of by Marx and Lenin and, on the other, the gullible, shortsighted mass manipulated by the yellow press.

The third anxiety was extravagantly on display in Ortega y Gasset's *Revolt of the Masses*, and was a commonplace of twentieth-century cultural criticism. The aristocratic critique of modern society runs thus: in a healthy society, the cultural—and therefore the political—tone is set by an elite whose title to act as an elite stems from tradition as well as a consensus that they know what excellence is. Those in the nonelite are not cut off from the elite, but they defer to the elite's leadership and expect to be educated into its standards. An unhealthy society has substituted mass tastes and inclinations for aristocratic standards. Other versions of this sharp contrast between the civilized elite and the uncivilizable mass are less plangent, but no more friendly to the nonelite. They are less plangent because they hold that the masses cannot substitute their tastes and beliefs for those of the elite; the appearance that they have done is an artifact of their numbers. Millions watch soap operas, but they know that real opera is a different and a better thing entirely, even if they do not enjoy it. We must take these anxieties in turn, and then return to the more narrowly political question of the ways in which elites and masses relate to each other. We shall discover more grounds for cheerfulness about the masses than many critics have done, though we may also be more skeptical about the capacities of political elites.

Tocquevillian Fears: The Liberal Anxiety

American observers have been of several minds about whether Tocqueville's fears have come true. On the face of it, they have not. There are few countries where people are quicker to express their own views, or more convinced that the world should give them a hearing. The United States is a nation of loudmouths, not shrinking violets. Nor does it seem that Americans are incapable of choosing what they consume and how they spend their leisure; almost every item of consumption can be had in infinite varieties, and "choice" is the mantra by which the simplest items are sold. This does not appease the critics, because the critics are looking at voters and consumers not from their own perspective but in the light of a moral and political ideal that few people have lived up to in any society. The critics begin from an ideal of the rational, autonomous, self-critical but self-confident individual, capable of thinking for herself or himself and able to cooperate with others without being swamped by them or trying to dominate them. Such an individual really *thinks*. The creature who expresses her or his *opinions* on the airwaves is not thinking, but parroting. "Public opinion," to which politicians supposedly defer, but spend their time manipulating, is a loud noise made by a flock of parrots, not the speech of citizens.

What matters is not whether we consume things that are marginally different from what everyone around us is consuming, but whether we exercise taste and judgment of our own. The number of slightly different but equally inauthentic and nonautonomous persons a society produces is not the issue; what is missing is the individual who has both a private and a public life, pursuing private concerns chosen for good reasons, which can be fulfilled without constant assistance or reassurance from other people; and public in the sense of pursuing the interests of a citizen who cares about the welfare of the community and nation and knows how to act to promote it. Variations on the theme can be found in authors as different as Walter Lippmann, writing about public opinion, and Hannah Arendt, deploring the absence of real political life in the modern welfare state.[10] The ideal against whom we measure up so poorly is the citizen whom Benjamin Constant, Tocqueville, and Mill wanted liberal democracies to foster, and who they feared might be undermined, so far as Mill was concerned, by the dead weight of a conformist public opinion and, so far as Tocqueville was concerned, by a family-centered "individualism" that turned its back on the public realm. This latter theme has been much emphasized recently.[11]

We inevitably associate the idea of mass society with twentieth-century industrial societies, but what Tocqueville saw in America was not a world of subways and high-rise buildings, commuters and interstate highways, nor of factory production as we know it. The modern world is a very recent creation; demographically, the world's population has risen from one billion to seven billion since 1900; industrially, we have produced more since 1945 than in the whole of previous human history. Tocqueville is relevant because what made America a "mass society" was not population density or industrialization; we do not need to live cheek by jowl with our fellows to be lost in the crowd. The villain of the piece is the unchallengeability of public opinion. Some skepticism is in order. It is not obvious that there was a high degree of unchallengeability then, and it seems even less plausible today, where a cacophony of competing opinions is uttered at a very high volume. *Some* aspects of the "antagonism of opinion" that Tocqueville sought as a remedy for a despotic public opinion are more than adequately catered for. The ignorance and incoherence of much public discourse is indeed striking, but uniformity is not the first word that comes to mind. The societies where there is one voice and one view are those where a dictatorial government controls the media, not those where hucksters compete for attention. The politics of modern liberal democracies is very often "lowest common denominator" politics; and outcomes are too often determined by the deep pockets of those who can buy access to the media and the political hired help, but that is a function of large electorates and short attention spans, not the tyranny of opinion. A plutocracy is not a Tocquevillian "soft despotism."

We are in the dangerous territory of ideal types: social scientists have long created idealized models of social and political arrangements to illuminate striking features of their own or some other society. Even if they are indispensable, as they plainly are in economics at least, they leave out and exaggerate a good deal in picking out what is salient. When David Riesman wrote *The Lonely Crowd* in 1950 to bring Tocqueville up to date with his discussion of the "other-directed" individual, it was easy to overlook the fact that his "inner-directed," "other-directed," and "autonomous" character types were *types* rather than persons one would meet in the street. It is not strictly impossible that the citizens of the United States might universally have turned out to be autonomous citizens of a stable, but lively liberal democracy: rational, flexible, self-confident, well-educated, and highly cultivated; cheerfully cooperating to pursue both their individual interests and the common interest; and operating political arrangements that created intelligently made law and enforced it honestly and economically. But no actual society has ever attained that utopian state, nor is any likely to. Riesman thought the ideal-type American had formerly been an inner-directed Puritan, a slave to conscience, and had become an other-directed conformist, a slave to public opinion. The autonomous American was yet to be achieved. This was a good deal less cheerful than Tocqueville, but in one respect picked up exactly the anxiety that Tocqueville's discussion of "individualism" expressed, perhaps best characterized as a fear of privatization. We would turn away from the public realm, focus all our energies and emotions on our domestic concerns, never raise our eyes from the needs of our families and a very few friends. That is why we might simultaneously be members of a crowd and yet lonely.

Mill's fear that mid-Victorian man would possess as much autonomy as a sheep was increased by his reading Tocqueville; like Tocqueville, Mill thought that a search for psychological comfort would be at the root of the urge to think like everyone else. It was not the only view one could hold. Marx expected the uniformity of working conditions to give the proletariat a sense of its common interests and the need for united action to further them. Like Mill and Tocqueville, he was carried away by a theory, though a different one. Outside the textile industry, mining, iron smelting, and shipbuilding, few enterprises employed more than a dozen people in any one place until the late nineteenth century. Nor did the working class become more homogenous; as fast as one set of jobs were "deskilled," new jobs were created that required new skills. The fact that the factory, mill, and shipyard were both novel and dramatic suggested that they possessed the power to change not only working habits but human nature itself; but few hypotheses about how this happened were clear enough to be tested against the evidence.

The fear persisted through the twentieth century that the uniformity of working conditions, the uniformity of the press, and the uniformity of public education would create the mass-produced man. This was often presented as a cultural disaster rather than a political problem: the "mass man" was more depressing than frightening, a shadow of a human being, uninteresting to contemplate, and devoid of internal motion. The moral ideal implicit in the description of the shortcomings of the mass-produced individual is not complex, but it may be unrealistically demanding. It would be good if everyone was deeply committed to sustaining a well-organized, uncorrupt, and politically intelligent liberal democracy, as well as imbued with the virtues that underpin such a political system—economic self-reliance, cooperativeness, attachment to family and neighborhood, readiness to perform small informal tasks for the preservation of their communities. These are the qualities that Tocqueville thought enough Americans possessed but too few Frenchmen.

The ideal of individuality found in *On Liberty* is less political and makes greater demands. Mill's portrait of the autonomous individual drew on both the Puritan conviction that we must account to the Almighty for what we have done with our lives and an Athenian ideal of a fully lived life. The latter was more obviously political, but a good Calvinist might well think that when we account for ourselves, the Almighty will ask what we did to foster the welfare of our fellows in the social and political setting in which we found ourselves. Nonetheless, one may doubt that either God or Pericles would insist like Mill that we constantly rethink our commitments and take absolutely nothing for granted; even Mill might not have done so if he had been less frightened of the uniformity of Victorian society.

Marxism and Mass Society: The Depoliticized Proletariat

The Marxist, or marxisant, strain of thinking about mass society is not, at least officially, driven by a moral or political ideal, even if Marxism's glorification of the revolutionary proletariat looks very like the expression of a heroic ideal. But it is committed to some debatable sociological ideas. Marxism does not think of "the masses" in pejorative terms, but many Marxists have thought that mass society undermines the revolutionary potential of the masses, that is, the industrial proletariat. To lament the failure of the proletariat to act as it "ought" presupposes some contestable beliefs about the driving forces of history and the revolutionary mission of the proletariat. Marx and Engels sometimes talked of the proletariat's "disgracing" itself, but their theory of history emphasized the demands of the situations in which the workers found themselves and not the workers' moral or psychic shortcomings. Marx did not think the proletariat was wicked when it disgraced itself, just as he was fastidious about seeing capitalists as "bearers of social relations," and not as wicked individuals. In this respect Marx was a good Hegelian. Hegel's philosophy of history was equally un-individualist, though he found more room than Marx for the work of world-historical individuals. History has a shape and a direction because it is the history of cultures, the peoples who embody them, and the institutions that express them, and it is also the history of *Geist*, or spirit, an idea working itself out through its chosen agents.

Marx threw out Hegel's metaphysics but retained his anti-individualist theory of history. History was not the work of *Geist*, but it had an inner logic, it used us without our knowledge, and it had a destination that it would attain after innumerable dead ends and errors but that it would certainly attain, and that destination is freedom. The task of the socialist intellectual was to reveal the process to the working classes, not to harangue them, not to moralize at them, but to show them what they *were* and therefore *must do*. Marx was fully aware that we exist in the world as separate individuals. We are members of collectivities of many kinds, and our membership determines what we think and feel, but to talk about what a collectivity *must do* is to talk about what an indeterminate number of individuals must do. Trying to retain the attractions of Hegel's *Geist*-driven theory of history alongside a down-to-earth insistence on the fact that "individuals make their own history but in circumstances not of their choosing" produces a very unstable structure. The proletarian revolution is inevitable, but only if the workers understand their own interests and pursue them with vigor. What if they do not, if they lack understanding or vigor or both?

Marx left much room for maneuver, both to the working class and to governments that would be undermined by working-class demands if Marx's predictions were right. In 1906 Werner Sombart wrote a striking little book, *Warum gibt es in den Vereinigten Staaten keinen Sozialismus?*[12] He explained the absence of socialism in the United States with a famous quip: the socialist ideal had been shipwrecked on reefs of roast beef and apple pie. The American worker was generally much better-off than his European counterpart. In an immigrant society, workers were conscious of that contrast. Luck was essential, but with luck, effort paid off; European immigrants benefited from geographical and social mobility as they would not have at home. They were not plausible recruits for the socialist revolution. As a good Marxist at the time, Sombart thought that socialism would eventually come to the United States, but European governments took the point that Sombart made. They could not re-create conditions unique to America, such as the absence of a feudal past; they could, however, undermine Marx's claim that socialism on the back of a proletarian revolution was the only cure for "immiseration." They could provide decent public housing, health care, old-age pensions, and unemployment benefits; public education would allow children from humble backgrounds to make their way up the educational and occupational ladder. In Germany such measures were sometimes introduced locally by Marxist social democratic city governments that claimed that the revolution their reforms were making unlikely was nonetheless still on its way, as well as nationally by conservative governments that saw that reform could halt the revolutionary locomotive. It was sensible not to provoke mass revolt if it could be bought off by reform. Stupid conservatives incite revolution; intelligent conservatives defuse it.

This does not yet reach far into the ways in which the proletariat may become a "mass" in the pejorative sense. What became a Marxist obsession was a double problem, the first why working-class political activism was so often conservative or reactionary, the second why the working class is less politically active than it "ought" to be, not that it follows the wrong revolutionary leaders but that it is uninterested in politics altogether. Answers to the first question often emphasize that the urban proletariat of the nineteenth and twentieth centuries was created when workers were wrenched out of traditional rural communities and found themselves in large impersonal cities. They lost the comfort of tight-knit villages and became part of an impersonal urban mass. They lost familiar social supports and found nothing to replace them. It is plausible that anyone seeking the lost comfort of the familiar will find reactionary movements attractive; much of the appeal of socialism has always lain in its reactionary aspects.

Even enthusiastic supporters of ethnic nationalism, anti-Semitism, and the rest of the fascist and Nazi creed may have only half believed the absurdities they were fed. But without intellectual and moral self-discipline, and help from the intellectual discipline supplied by others, all of us can half believe whatever rationalizes our misfortunes and promises something better. This is as true of the wilder reaches of religion as of directly political creeds, and as true today as in sixteenth-century Münster. Nor is it only the working class or the uneducated who are vulnerable; a deracinated middle class is equally susceptible to the attractions of whatever will identify scapegoats for their unhappinesses, and propose simple, dramatic measures to relieve them. In prosperous countries, the second and later generations of urban workers have invariably settled into reformist politics, untempted by insurrection either left or right. Reformist parties have often been undermined by communists to their left, but one of the most interesting twentieth-century Marxist writers, Antonio Gramsci, argued that without a long and determined effort to build a proletarian political culture, unfocused energies may go in any number of dangerous and destructive directions.[13] Gramsci spent eight years in Fascist prisons, which led to his premature death in 1937, after he was released on grounds of ill health. His explanation of how a capitalist regime maintains itself in power without resorting to constant violence appeals to the idea of a "hegemonic" political culture that shapes and constrains what the working class takes to be politically possible. This is the manufacture of consent, a notion that anyone who tries to run any organization whatever does well to take seriously. The cultural task of a radical or revolutionary party is to build its own counterculture.

The fact that the proletariat's politics may be utterly reactionary if it loses its bearings does not explain why the mass is more often *inert* or, if not exactly inert, at any rate depoliticized and interested only in being entertained. Readers of *Brave New World* will remember that the peace is kept in Huxley's hideous utopia by two nonviolent devices. One is the spraying of the wonder drug "soma," a drug whose desirability had been signaled by Bertrand Russell when he complained that science had so far failed to create a drug that produced the agreeable effects of drunkenness without a hangover.[14] Huxley coined a wonderfully appropriate word for the drug. "A gram is better than a damn," say the inhabitants of Brave New World, living without a care, let alone a thought of their own. Huxley's other great narcotic is the "feelies," an invention that combines the sound and pictures of the cinema with the tactile sensations appropriate to the scene on the screen. Needless to say, pornography is the art form most in demand.

The proletarian "many" become a "mass" when they are distracted, lulled into acquiescence in the existing order, kept happy on a diet of trash. In Huxley's world the process is consciously directed; a society has been created in which everyone is happy, in ways that would have appalled Mill. They are too happy to imagine change, let alone rebellion; the thought that "it is better to be Socrates dissatisfied than a fool satisfied" is not one the inhabitants of this utopia could understand.[15] Critics of mass culture and its narcotizing effects concede that the process of depoliticizing the masses is not consciously engineered; there may be entertainment executives who congratulate themselves on staving off revolution by feeding the masses addictive rubbish, but if they exist, they are very few and far between, and are unlikely to reveal themselves. In general, the taste of the producers is that of the consumers; their sincerity explains their success. One of the processes that Marx saw operating behind our backs here becomes a bad joke against his ambitions. The entertainment industry turns out distracting fluff, and an ill-educated public laps it up, because it is easier to enjoy than more demanding, more thought-provoking, and discontent-arousing forms of art. The process is automatic and self-sustaining, and cuts off just that process of increasing discontent that Marx relied on. Such, at least, is the story.

If entertainment was so efficacious, this view would have much to commend it; and *if* popular art was as narcotizing, the theory would be plausible. Sadly, it is not. Much popular culture is deeply subversive, though not in ways that Marxist theorists of the 1920s would have wished. But the idea that mass entertainment is a political narcotic is the right *kind* of theory for Marxian purposes. It unites the idea of a mass with uniform tastes and habits with the idea of a mass that is politically incompetent and incapable of self-directed action. The Frankfurt school—the group of scholars led by Max Horkheimer and Theodor Adorno at the Institut für Sozialforschung in Frankfurt until they had to flee the Nazis in 1934—saw mass culture as such a narcotic. They were not only disappointed Marxists; their analysis of the miseries of modern society drew on Freud as well as Marx, and they condemned a narcotizing culture because it helped us to avoid facing the miseries and irrationalities of the modern world in all their forms, not only because it took the workers into the cinema rather than to political rallies. Critics have always objected that there was too much cultural snobbery in the critique. An equally apt objection is that if consolations are needed, we should make the most of them. It was a philosopher who said that the unexamined life is not worth living, and nobody other than philosophers has ever found the claim wholly compelling.[16]

The final thought borrows for Marxist purposes the ideas of Tocqueville and Mill about the enervating effect of social conformity. If *individuals* have lost the power of action, and cannot do anything by and for themselves, they are *collectively* unable to act in a radical way. From a Marxist perspective, the explanation of their passivity lies less in the cul-

ture than in the routine of the working life; work offers no outlet for creative energy, imagination, or self-government. Even when it is not living
from hand to mouth, it is a life of taking orders and following routines.
Bertrand Russell was appalled that ordinary people welcomed the First
World War; he followed Freud in thinking they welcomed the break
from routine and the liberation it allowed of the destructive—and self-
destructive—instincts they ordinarily repressed. Ordinarily, they are so
disciplined that they have no psychic energy left over for political activity,
neither the ability to imagine a world worth fighting for nor the energy
to organize to create utopia. Years later, in the affluent but boring 1950s,
Herbert Marcuse coined the thought that modern capitalism imposed
"surplus repression," not only the minimal amount required to prevent
Hobbes's war of all against all from breaking loose—the thought that
animates Freud's *Civilization and Its Discontents*—but sufficient to prevent us
from rising up and destroying a system that was psychically unfulfilling
and hideously dangerous as a result of the threat of nuclear destruction.[17]
Yet this was the longest sustained period of economic growth that the
Western world had ever seen, with full employment and the wages of
ordinary working people rising faster than ever before or since. To see its
beneficiaries as inert or repressed required a willingness to subordinate
the evidence of one's own eyes to the implications of a theory, and perhaps a life spent in the study rather than in a bar or a football stadium.

The Revolt of the Masses

We shall return to the thought that politics is inevitably and always
an affair managed by elites. Before we do, we should take up what is
sometimes called the aristocratic critique of mass culture; its political
implications are not easy to spell out, and require a second step of argument. The thought is that mass politics is essentially plebeian and crowd
pleasing, flashy and not serious. Left and right populisms resemble each
other, as when Stalin embarked on his postwar anti-Semitic campaign
or Mussolini told his captors that he had always been a Marxist. The
aristocratic complaint is that mass values swamp elite values. It is such

a simple complaint that it is surprising that so much has been written on it, but people often feel passionately that an area of human life they hold sacred has been ruined because it has been trampled on by the hordes, and the writing of jeremiads is a favorite activity with intellectuals. The argument is wonderfully set out in Ortega y Gasset's polemic *The Revolt of the Masses*. Ortega was not a conservative but a liberal, and one of the intellectual leaders of the Spanish republic destroyed by the Fascist—strictly, Falangist—insurrection led by General Franco. He was, nonetheless, a firm believer in the distinction between mass and elite; he looked back to the Roman proletariat as the first historical example of an insurgent mass, and reacted to the rise of the industrial working class much as the Roman aristocracy reacted to Rome's underclass.

Ortega did not offer a theory of the rise of the masses; rather, he gave a despairing account of their rise as a historical phenomenon and ascribed to it most of what he disliked about the first three decades of the twentieth century. The book appeared in 1930, but the looseness of its construction betrays its origins as a series of essays in a quarterly review. The causative phenomenon is "agglomeration." There are too many people, crowded too closely together, traveling too often and in excessive numbers to too many places by forms of transportation that wrecked the places they had come from and those to which they went. This was not an ecological point but an aesthetic one; nobody has bettered Ruskin's polemic against a new railway line in the Peak District seventy years earlier: "and now, every fool in Buxton can be at Bakewell in half-an-hour, and every fool in Bakewell at Buxton; which you think a lucrative process of exchange—you Fools everywhere."[18] Their numbers and their geographical proximity give the masses a weight in determining the public culture that the intrinsic merits of what they thought and hankered after certainly would not have given them.

What Ortega adds to the anxieties of Mill and Tocqueville is the notion that the masses want to remake society in their own image. Reconciling this claim with the thought that the mass is essentially inert is not easy, but the argument is this: there is a distinction between natural leaders and natural followers, people to whom the strenuous life of constant intellectual and moral challenge comes readily and people to whom it does not. This does not line up exactly with the class structure, but there will be more of the first in the upper classes and more of the second in the lower classes. A well-managed liberal democracy is a version of what Weber described as a *Führerdemokratie* and what we shall see Schumpeter explaining at greater length. The mass has motion imparted to it in ways that mean its behavior is controlled. What threatened post-1918 Europe was the irruption of the masses into violent, direct action.[19]

On Ortega's analysis, the masses are not stupefied as in Huxley's imagined utopia and in the social theory of Horkheimer and Adorno. They are resentful, they actively dislike excellence, and they try to ensure that it has no place in mass society. They have prospered because the capitalist economy is technically efficient and has been well managed by the leaders of liberal democracies, but the effect of their new prosperity is that they want much more and they want it at once. Their irruption into politics will be by way of violent direct action. Written in the late 1920s, *The Revolt of the Masses* had the example of Italian fascism to draw on; Nazism's success was some years off. Ortega did not anticipate full-fledged totalitarianism. He was equally afraid of creeping Americanization and often seems animated mostly by nostalgia for an epoch when European high culture set the standard for the whole world. The horror of at least one form of mass politics was beyond Ortega's imagination.

Elites and Masses

One inspiration of modern discussions of the politics of mass society was Machiavelli's insistence that the mass of mankind is so gullible that a skilled operator is never short of dupes to do his bidding. Sixteenth-century Florence was not a "mass society" in the sense in which the thinkers we have been discussing thought modern Western societies are. Yet Machiavelli's use of the distinction between the mass of mankind and the politically adept was very like Ortega's distinction between natural followers and natural leaders. What of the argument, then, that even in the most stable and modern of liberal democracies, politics is an affair of masses and elites just as Machiavelli said, either in the sense that the politically adept *in fact* run matters or in the sense that they *should be allowed* to run matters unimpeded?

There are three famous views of the matter. The most matter-of-fact is Max Weber's. Weber was a thinker of great delicacy, who never uttered a claim that he did not qualify; but he set out some stark views. The modern world is doomed to have its affairs managed by large impersonal bureaucracies, the political direction of which would inevitably fall to the small number of people with a particular talent and taste for politics. The leaders at the top of this group would have to secure their authority by possessing "charisma"—a term he introduced into modern political analysis and whose overuse a century later he would have deplored. Charisma, literally, is an authority bestowed by God. The Chinese emperor, who was vulnerable to deposition if he was thought to have lost the mandate of heaven, relied on charismatic authority in a literal, technical sense.[20] For Weber almost everything in the modern world had been routinized and rationalized, and the interesting question was where the vital spark was to come from that would provide a culture's goals, values, the ends for which we could be called on to sacrifice our time, our wealth, and, in the last resort, our lives. It could not come from the political and administrative machinery itself, which provided the means but did not set the ends. The question was how goals could be authoritatively set for a whole political society. The answer was that they had to be set by a leader with charismatic authority, a nontechnical, suprarational authority akin to "the mandate of heaven."

Weber thought that democracy was the natural political form of a modern industrial society, but that the only version that could succeed was *Führerdemokratie*, or "leadership democracy." The existence of Hitler makes modern non-German readers uneasy with talk of a *Führer*, but the term is no more alarming than "leader" in English. In a modern democracy, leaders are indispensable; they, not the rank and file, provide initiative, and we need institutions that make it more likely that good leaders will arise. That has been the common sense of political scientists for half a century, and it provides a useful benchmark against which to assess the effectiveness of party systems and electoral processes. Two sorts of theorist dislike it nonetheless. One is disturbed by Weber's insis-

tence on the nonrationality of ultimate moral values. He emphasized
the role of charismatic leaders because he drew the sharpest possible
distinction between technical evaluation and ultimate values. Questions
of efficiency—how well a policy will achieve a given end—are technical
and best answered by experts; once the answer is known, appropriate
policies are best implemented by experts. Questions of ultimate value—
what it is worth doing with one's life, what the place of Germany in the
world is supposed to be, whether our nation is worth fighting for—have
no rational answer. They are matters for decision. No amount of argument can resolve them. Decisionism is deplored by anyone who thinks
that politics should be modeled on an ideally conducted argument; Herbert Marcuse accused Weber of laying the ground for Nazism.

   The other sort of theorist who finds Weber uncomfortably bleak is
the participatory democrat. Whether Weber set much value on political
participation as such is hard to tell. He had strong political views and
was thought of as a potential president of the German republic when it
was set up after World War I, but although he was in his early sixties,
he was already too ill for this to be plausible. He never wrote with much
enthusiasm about politics, being more concerned to draw a very sharp
line between the allegiances of the scholar and the politician and to insist
on their being kept separate.[21] There were many reasons for this. He was
a defender, though not an unqualified one, of the modern nation-state,
and such states are not hospitable to participatory ideals. They demand
centralized authority, they cannot work without a continuous attention
to technical efficiency, and much of their behavior is dictated by the need
to protect their citizens against the predatory behavior of other nation-
states. Weber coined the definition of the state as the entity that claims
a monopoly of legitimate violence, and he would have thought that the
good-natured enthusiasm of late twentieth century participatory democrats reflected credit on their hearts but not their heads.

   This did not mean that democracy was impossible, but only a very
particular sort of democracy was practicable in large modern states. It
is the kind we in fact see, where political parties organize a mass electorate to support teams of leaders professing allegiance to the party's
manifesto. So long as there is free speech, no restriction on organiz-

ing, universal suffrage, and elections whose results are respected, we have democracy as practiced; the important contrast is not with systems in which there is a great deal of popular participation—dictatorial regimes are good at getting the public into the streets—but with systems where elections are rigged, the citizens are threatened by the secret police, and the leaders are indifferent to what the citizens would vote for if they were free to vote as they wished.

There are many variations on this theme. One of the most interesting was the idea of the circulation of elites that was a particular contribution of the late nineteenth-century Italian thinkers Vilfredo Pareto and Gaetano Mosca. They were "elite theorists" in the sense that both took it for granted that only a small minority of people ever exercised real power in a society. Being part of an elite was not for either of them a matter of any particular moral or other virtue; the elites in any field were simply those who were best at whatever might be at stake. Behind this thought was Machiavelli's analysis in *The Prince*. Nobody suggested that Cesare Borgia was a good person, but he was very good at seizing power and destroying his enemies. Machiavelli's contribution to the idea of a circulation of elites is his insistence that a good leader must emulate the lion and the fox. The later view was that what one might call foxlike elites come to grief because they can be destroyed by counterelites with a talent for violence, and lionlike elites come to grief by being undermined by an intelligent counterelite. A way of looking at modern democracies is that they are devices for circulating elites without insurrections or coups d'état.

The Iron Law of Oligarchy

Weber's picture of leadership democracy was transformed by Joseph Schumpeter into what became the orthodoxy among political scientists and other commentators until the present day. So transformed, it served as the basis of the optimistic view that modern Western societies practiced a highly successful form of democracy in which an elite—professional politicians—secured legitimation from the public to take

the decisions that matter, supervising a second elite of civil servants who
implemented them, answering at intervals to a mass electorate that had
the good sense to let them get on with the job between elections.[22] We
shall look more closely at this version of the "elite theory of democracy" when we make a final reckoning with the question whether liberal
democracy is democracy at all. We should look more immediately at
two variations on the less optimistic understanding of the politics of
mass society. The first is provided by Robert Michels. He was a pupil of
Weber and a distinguished political sociologist, usually seen as the third
of the trio of elite theorists who included Pareto and Mosca. Before the
First World War, he was a member of the German Social Democratic
Party (SDP) and later a supporter of Mussolini. He is best known for
his book *Political Parties*, the purpose of which is to explain and justify the
organizational theory embodied in what Michels called the "iron law
of oligarchy."[23] The argument is simple, though the evidence Michels
adduced was substantial and fascinating.

His question was this: why were the German Social Democrats officially a revolutionary party but in practice reformist? Michels's answer had
several twists and turns in it, but the fundamental thought was that to be
a political party at all the SDP had to be an organization, and organization is intrinsically oligarchical. This was not a new point; Lenin pressed
it on the Russian social democrats against a great deal of resistance. The
fact that Lenin insisted on oligarchy to preserve the revolutionary vigor
of the party while Michels pointed to oligarchy as the cause of the loss of
revolutionary vigor is more startling, but the contrast is less damaging to
Michels's case than it looks. They both argued that the spontaneous and
unorganized energy of a mass movement cannot be relied on over a long
period. *Whatever* one's goals, organization is required; and an organization
can be held together only by leaders. Failing firm leadership, the members
will head off in innumerable directions and incoherence will result, never
more certainly than among radicals. Michels saw what Lenin failed to
see and what Lenin's successors discovered by experience: once there is an
organization, its preservation and the preservation of the privileges of the
apparatchiks readily supplant the party's official aims as its de facto goals.
Unless someone takes measures to prevent it, a political party such as the

Communist Party of the Soviet Union will become conservative; it may profess whatever ideology it chooses, but institutional sclerosis will set in. The periodic purges by which Stalin and Mao tried to revive the revolutionary fervor of their respective parties may have been morally repulsive, but they had a certain rationality.

What connects that argument with the theory of mass society is that it takes for granted that the specialized skills and knowledge an organization requires will belong to the elite and not to the many. Needing to be led, the many cannot create organizational forms that evade the need for a managing elite; they are capable of moments of enthusiasm and sudden irruptions into politics, but continuous political activity is an elite function. Critics of Michels pointed out that the iron law of oligarchy was more rubbery than ferrous; Michels knew that elites often maintain their power by making concessions to the rank and file, and that adept elites do it before tensions build up. The "law of anticipated reactions" describes what happens when the elite modifies its views and actions to avoid conflict with the rank and file. It is less clear than Michels suggests whether elite controls mass or vice versa. Less often noticed is Michels's own reaction to his argument. He renounced the liberal or social democratic political party as the means of political change and turned to Mussolini's fascism. *Direct* engagement between a charismatic leader and an enthusiastic rank and file would avoid the lethargy and conservatism of the German SPD.[24]

Finally, we should consider the view made famous in the late 1950s by C. Wright Mills's *Power Elite*: elites rule behind the backs of the masses, in ways that are hardly visible as politics at all. Marxists who loathed both Soviet communism and Western capitalism were attracted to theories of mass society because they felt that the working class had failed the task that history had set it. *The Power Elite* reflected its author's belief that it was the elite that had failed the task history set it. Mills argued that all the important decisions in American life were taken by small numbers of interconnected persons at the head of both political and nonpolitical organizations—celebrities, CEOs, generals, and so on—but his real complaint was that although they alone had the power to take the "historic decisions," they had ducked them.[25] America was neither a dictatorship nor ruled by a junta. Ordinary men and women were not tyrannized over, exploited in hideous ways, sent to labor camps, or murdered in cellars; but their needs were not addressed, and the resources of society were not brought to bear to satisfy them. Mills was not a Marxist, but a distinguished sociologist and an American populist of a kind more common in the early twentieth century than today. He was born in Texas in 1916 and died in 1961, at the early age of forty-five. Like many of his generation, he was appalled at the prospect that miscalculation by an unanswerable elite might bring human history to a sudden end in a nuclear exchange between the Soviet Union and the United States; he died a few months before the Cuban Missile Crisis showed how right he was to be frightened. The largest historic decision the power elite had ducked was deciding how to save us from the nuclear monster we had inadvertently created.

The Power Elite was both wildly popular and savagely criticized. Its importance lies less in the solidity of its arguments—it was a fair complaint that Mills did little to demonstrate that *all* the elites of the United States formed a clandestine, cohesive conspiracy to take power away from ordinary people—than in how well it expressed the widespread sense that mass society rests on a fraud. The fraud is the pretense that the welfare of ordinary people matters to the elite, when the reality is that it does not. The ordinary person in Mills's vision of America was trapped in routine occupations, managed, directed, and fed predigested, pro–status quo information by newspapers, and radio and television stations eager to keep in with advertisers and governments. The last thing that politicians, newspaper companies, industrialists, or the heads of large organizations wanted was a freethinking and wide-awake public and electorate. The anxieties of writers such as Walter Lippmann who thought that public opinion was fickle, ill informed, and incapable of directing public policy received the reply that Lippmann himself might have given as a young radical: the masses were fed pictures, not arguments, fictions, not facts. How could they hold elites accountable?

The Power Elite offered a particularly plangent analysis of mass society and its politics because it suggested that the comfortable and prosperous mass society of midcentury America was sleepwalking toward disaster. The power elite had what nobody else had: celebrity, more money than it knew what to do with, positions on governing boards, control of the enterprises that made up the American economy. A few of the elite, including the president and a few military advisers, had the power to incinerate much of the human race. Oddly enough, and although Mills never quite worked out how to put the point as he wanted, the power elite had little capacity for serious action. Nobody *else* could make a difference to the human future, but outside their own sphere, neither could the elite. John Wain's views on the Vietnam War had no more impact on its conduct than Richard Nixon's taste in movies had on the decisions of Hollywood producers. Far from concentrating power in the hands of an elite, the political system fragmented it so thoroughly that a president who could incinerate humanity could not establish national health care. The masses were powerless, but the elite had not acquired what the masses had lost. When political scientists in the early 1960s looked carefully for answers to the question "Who's in charge around here?" the answer was neither the (nonexistent) insurgent masses nor the (nonexistent) manipulating elite, but sometimes some folks, sometimes different folks, frequently nobody, and surprisingly often—depending on the issue—a person or group to whom the political system had assigned the task of making those decisions under those circumstances.

This may be mildly reassuring about the conduct of everyday democratic politics in prosperous liberal democracies. It can be no more than mildly reassuring because one thing that Mills was right about was that members of "the elite" in the sense of celebrities, the rich, the owners of mass media, bankers, major industrialists, politicians, and top military personnel spend their time in one another's company and are not likely to encourage one another to think radical or transformative thoughts about the society in which they have done so well. Aristotle's "poor many" have good reason to think they live in a plutocracy, even if they are vastly better-off than the poor many of previous centuries. Nor does the fact that the power elite is *elites* in the plural in modern liberal democracies offer any assurance that democracy will emerge in countries where power really is exercised by military dictators, kleptocrats, apparatchiks, ayatollahs, or fundamentalists armed with everything but common sense. Nor does it offer any assurance that if such societies ever achieve the orderly circulation of elites that the prosperous Western world takes for granted, they will not first pass through their own version of the violence of the French Revolution and other populist insurgencies. It offers only the reassurance that there is no Wizard of Oz pulling the strings behind the scenes. How reassuring that is varies from case to case; to know that nobody is in charge is not always reassuring, the point that Mills himself was making in the context of the American nuclear arsenal.

CHAPTER 23

Empire and Imperialism

Empires and the Idea of Empire

THE RISE AND FALL of the great modern empires was one of the most striking political phenomena of the late nineteenth century and the twentieth. It also transformed the idea of empire. Political events often remodel the concepts we use to understand them; the French Revolution changed our idea of what a revolution was and might achieve; what had long been understood either as simple chaos or a conservative return to first principles now came to be seen as the beginning of something wholly new and unpredictable and as being a "real" revolution only if it led to social and economic transformation. The gradual incorporation of women and the unpropertied within the system of political representation in the United States, Britain, and France gave a new meaning to the concept of democracy. What Aristotle defined as the unconstrained rule of the many was redefined as the rule of professional politicians drawn from and answerable to all ranks of society.

In the same way, the imperial projects of the nineteenth and twentieth centuries made us think differently about the nature of empire. Imperialism in its developed modern form was short-lived. Only late in the nineteenth century did "the scramble for Africa" became intense; the British colonial empire was at its largest after the First World War and shrank to nearly nothing soon after the Second World War. The antecedents of twentieth-century imperialism were much older. Between the sixteenth century and the nineteenth, modern empires established themselves and it became clear in retrospect how they differed from their ancient predecessors. Typically, a metropolitan power exercised military and political control over distant overseas territories. The motives for empire building were unsurprising. States sought territorial control for traditional reasons: sometimes for economic and military security, sometimes for economic exploitation, and sometimes for simple aggrandizement. What was distinctive was that the conglomerate did not form a single, unitary state, as the Roman Empire had done. The underlying reason for the difference was that these were maritime empires, and of their predecessors only the Athenian "empire" of the fifth century BCE and the Venetian empire in the Adriatic and Aegean were.

As the Spanish, Portuguese, Dutch, French, and British established colonies and trading posts and claimed ownership of territory at the other side of the globe, new ideas about the right of developed countries to rule the peoples of undeveloped countries also came into existence. Some of these hardened into doctrines of "scientific" racism in the nineteenth century, some remained no more elaborate than the assumption of ethnic superiority enunciated two and a half millennia ago in the explanations of differential aptness of different ethnic groups for politics or for slave status offered in Aristotle's *Politics*.[1] Some of the justifications for empire couched in racial terms or in terms of a "civilizing mission" retained the religious overtones of the Spanish justification of rule over pagan Indians, while some were wholly secular. In the late nineteenth century, racial assumptions became more salient; what had been seen as an attempt to bring Christianity to far-off savages was now described as "the white man's burden." The thought was commonplace, the label itself provided by Rudyard Kipling's poem of 1899, written to celebrate the American acquisition of the Spanish Empire in the Caribbean and the Pacific.[2]

There are striking differences between the empires of different periods. The Roman Empire at its height was a unitary state, and its provinces were provinces. Among modern imperial powers, only the French tried to assimilate overseas territories to *départements*. Nineteenth-century Russia and the United States followed the classical model: they expanded overland east and west, respectively, incorporating new territories and their native inhabitants into a unitary and a federal state, respectively. Neither America nor Russia saw itself as an empire in the same sense as the French, Spanish, and British empires. The American "empire" was decisively different from the Russian in that it gave substance to the idea that it was an "empire of liberty." The U.S. Land Ordinances predated the Constitution of 1787 and stipulated that new territory must be incorporated as separate, individual states with the rights and status of the original thirteen states. Colonists from the eastern states lost none of their rights by migrating westward. Not until the Spanish-American War did the United States acquire extraterritorial colonial possessions in the Philippines, Hawaii, and Puerto Rico; their subsequent history was varied—the Philippines became independent, Hawaii is a state of the union, and the "Commonwealth" of Puerto Rico is an odd hybrid, enjoying many of the rights of a state, but technically a dependency, without representation in Congress.

The Athenian empire by contrast was a confederation of nominally independent states that preserved more than the bare appearance of self-government, and whose subordination to Athens consisted in the payment of tribute in return for the organization of a common system of defense. The Byzantine Empire was the Roman Empire in the East, and inherited its structure. Empires from the Babylonian to the Seleucid fit a similar pattern: the acquisition of neighboring territories by conquest and the installation of provincial governors. The Ottoman Empire, growing to take in the islands of Cyprus and Crete, was not a genuine exception; having secured the lands around the eastern Mediterranean, it took control of islands in a land-locked sea and never sought overseas outlets, either for trade or to provide security for military and commercial fleets at a distance from their home ports. The Ottomans' last attempts at expansion were directed northward through the Balkans and beyond the Black Sea. The empires whose rise and fall provoked two world wars and endless lesser violence in the twentieth century were the product of global seaborne trade and of the emergence of Europeans with large amounts of capital and a great desire to turn a profit. Early modern trading was quintessentially high-risk, high-return; it was accompanied and fueled by the systematic extraction of precious metals from the Americas, itself a high-risk, high-return undertaking. The process was self-reinforcing as liquid capital accumulated in European hands and its owners sought new outlets. This was the beginning of modern capitalism and modern imperialism, in the form of pelagic empires.

This chapter briefly recapitulates older notions of empire, turns to the arguments about when and where colonization is legitimate that were provoked by the first European expansion, and then focuses on three topics. The first follows on from natural law arguments about colonization, and is the idea that developed societies are entitled to subdue less developed or undeveloped societies in pursuit of a "civilizing mission." This idea was (somewhat awkwardly) associated with views about the existence of a hierarchy of races that have fallen so thoroughly out of favor that it is hard to credit not only how easily and widely they were accepted but how roundly they had already been condemned by Enlightenment writers in the eighteenth century. The second is the famous thesis of V. I. Lenin—the argument was borrowed without acknowledgment from the English liberal economist J. A. Hobson—that imperialism was a natural and inevitable part of the economics and politics of advanced industrial countries, even though its consequences were predictably disastrous. The third is the idea, associated with the writings of Franz Fanon, that colonial empires represent a particularly horrific form of oppression and that revolt against them is a decisive act of self-formation. The discussion of this thought provides the opportunity to consider the extraordinary strength of the idea of nationhood and the role that nationalism has played in the politics of the post-1945 world, and to look very briefly at the conjunction of nationalism and religion in the work of Sayyad Qutb. Whether we today live in a postimperial, postcolonial world or a neocolonial, neoimperial world is left for the reader to decide.

The Ancient Concept of Empire

The ancient world took it for granted that states extended their power as best they could, and perhaps the oldest thought about empires is just that. If the twenty-first-century United States is an imperialist power, as many critics maintain, it is not because Americans remain eager to shoulder the white man's burden, or to follow Theodore Roosevelt in wanting to see the world neatly divided into the spheres of influence of a few coexisting nations. It is because the logic of commercial and military competition is, as Hobbes observed, "a perpetual and restless striving for power after power." If Thucydides reported the Athenian view of these matters accurately, the strong do what they wish and the weak do what they must. This is a law of nature, and we must live with it. The idea that a state's boundaries were sacrosanct was not a Greek or a Roman notion. It had to await the rise of the nation-state after the Reformation and, above all, after the Treaty of Westphalia of 1648 put an end to the Thirty Years' War on the basis that a sovereign state was not answerable to any other for its treatment of its own subjects and that the only legitimate ground for military action was self-defense. Colonization, which has been an important feature of modern empires and a factor in making the end of empire bloody and protracted, did not provoke moral unease in the ancient world. Nor were colonies the basis of empire. Unlike their modern counterparts, they did not preserve close political relationships with the mother city, but were new, freestanding enterprises and behaved as such.

What writers of the sixth to the fourth century BCE thought on the subject of empire is mysterious. Conventionally, the Persian monarchy was described in terms always translated as "empire," but writers at the time did not distinguish, as we might, between empires and, say, multiethnic kingdoms, federations, or loose and temporary associations of tribes. The contrast that Greek observers had in mind was between small, self-governing poleis of the Greek sort and vast, sprawling kingdoms ruled by kings who were regarded by their subjects as semidivine. Greeks thought it absurd or blasphemous to accord their rulers divine status, and even Alexander was resisted when he tried to force the Persian custom of prostration upon his Greek troops. Persia was a classic multiethnic kingdom, but to the modern eye it satisfies the requirements for being properly described as an empire; there was a central government at Sardis, and local rulers were substantially the agents of that government. Nonetheless, many of the entities under Persian rule had considerable autonomy in their domestic affairs. Persia fascinated Greek observers, because it posed a standing military threat, was vast in extent, despotically ruled by the agents of the great king, and in many respects efficient. Its fiscal effectiveness was paradoxically fatal, when Philip of Macedon and his son Alexander realized that a successful military assault could be funded from the Persian treasury.

The English word "empire" derives from the Latin *imperium*, and that initially meant little more than "command." Because the Roman expulsion of their early kings held such a symbolic significance in Roman politics, Roman emperors called themselves emperors, not to boast, as the kings of Assyria and Persia had done, that they were greater and mightier than the other kings of the earth—though they would have been entitled to do so—but to avoid the title of *rex*. Like the Greeks, the Romans thought that kingship was a feature of a more primitive politics. The fastidiousness was an affectation like the preservation of a powerless Senate, and consistent with emperors' adopting the eastern habit of having themselves worshipped as divinities. Rome had become, and was universally recognized as, an empire when it was still a republic and had no emperor. What Polybius described and explained was properly translated as *The Rise of the Roman Empire*, but it was an empire created by the Roman Republic. Although local political entities existed under Roman overlordship, their fate lay in the hands of Rome.

Empires are more easily recognized than defined by necessary and sufficient conditions; broadly speaking, they must be larger than most states with which they come into contact, must be multiethnic or multinational, and must acknowledge allegiance to a center of political authority that either licenses local rulers or governs by agents or deputies. Judged by these criteria, the Holy Roman Empire was what it was famously mocked as being: neither holy, nor Roman, nor an empire. A loose confederation, in which the authority and legitimacy of local rulers was often more secure and more effective on the ground than that of the elected emperor, stretches the notion of an empire to its limits, allowance made for unusually effective rulers such as Maximilian and Charles V. In the High Middle Ages, the kings of smaller, but more coherent, states might well refer to themselves as emperors, *imperator sibi*, in order to emphasize that they owed no allegiance to the so-called emperor; city-states might do so, too.

Neither holy, nor Roman, nor imperial, it served the purpose that Pope Leo III had in mind when he crowned Charlemagne on Christmas Day, 800, and that remained in writers' minds thereafter. The emperor was to coordinate the defense of Christendom. Christendom was not a political entity but confessional; its members were the *populi Christiani*, and Christendom meant Latin Christendom. Its enemy was the Moors in 800 and the Ottoman Empire later, although Pope Sylvester's immediate problem was the Lombards. In his plangent essays pleading for Christian rulers to seek peace rather than engage in incessant war, Erasmus says that if they must fight, they should turn their military energies against the Turks.[3] In fairness to Erasmus, it must be said that he much preferred that nobody went to war at all; like the Hohenstaufen emperor Frederick II, who secured the Holy Places in 1229 not by crusade but by purchase, he thought diplomacy and financial inducements would do what brute force could not.

The Americas and the Morality of Conquest and Colonization

The possibility of a new form of empire was created by the discovery of the West Indies and the American mainland and the opening of sea routes around the Cape of Good Hope to Asia. Unlike most imperial adventures in the ancient world, these involved encounters between peoples at very different levels of economic, technological, and political development and raised questions about relations between European powers and the distant peoples they encountered for which there were only partial precedents. In particular, the encounters raised new ques-

tions about the legitimacy of settlers and colonizers claiming ownership of territory over which the indigenous population were hunting and
gathering, but which was not held as private property as understood in
Europe. Since, ex hypothesi, no shared system of positive law bound the
indigenous population and the Western arrivals, the question of how the
civilized new arrivals should treat the less civilized indigenes could be
answered only on natural law or jus gentium principles. These had some,
though only partially relevant, resources for dealing with the problem.
Two of the oldest questions in the tradition were who had jurisdiction
over pirates and other malefactors captured outside a fixed legal jurisdiction and what the nature of the obligation to succor strangers was. If the
indigenes were in violation of natural law, as pirates were, they could be
subjected to punishment, including the forfeiture of their property such
as it was, and even if they were not, they had no right to refuse assistance
to strangers in need, if that was what the colonizers were.

The discussion of these issues began among the Spanish. As always,
there was a gap between the official morality preached in the metropolitan country and the behavior of conquerors and colonizers far from
home. In principle, the Spanish royal government wished its Amerin-
dian subjects to be treated much as peasants were treated in Spain; that
is, allotted to a patron to whom they might owe tribute, or for whom
they were to perform labor services, but not to be slaves. The patron
was supposed in return to see that they were instructed in the Christian faith and to protect them from theft and assault. It was assumed
without argument that the royal government could, as it had with the
inhabitants of the reconquered lands of the Moors in Spain, grant these
jurisdictional and economic privileges to whomever it chose, generally
Spanish soldiers but sometimes Amerindians, including the daughters of
Montezuma. The so-called encomienda system survived in Mexico until
Mexican independence in the early nineteenth century. In practice, it was
strictly a one-way bargain; the Amerindians died in large numbers from
ill-treatment and from novel diseases to which they had no resistance.

Among the writers who thought about the morality of colonization, the most distinguished was the early sixteenth-century legal theorist Francisco de Vitoria, whose learning was deep and of extraordinary

range. He taught at Paris from 1509 to 1523 and at Salamanca from 1526 to his death in 1546. He was a Dominican, a Thomist, deeply hostile to the Reformation and to humanists such as Erasmus who hoped for the enlightened Catholicism that the Counter-Reformation put an end to. He was frequently consulted by the emperor Charles V, especially over the Amerindians, but also over such issues as Henry VIII's intention to divorce Catherine of Aragon, Charles V's aunt. He did not always tell Charles V what he wished to hear; he was an uncompromising defender of absolutism, but would not bend the dictates of rational jurisprudence to the needs of the powerful. He denied that the Spanish had dominion over the Indians of America by reason of the donation of Pope Alexander VI, because the pope had no temporal dominion, let alone the universal dominion on which such a donation must rest. The pope's temporal authority extended only to the protection of the faith. He might declare a heretic king deposed and encourage his subjects to rise up against him, but he could not substitute his own authority for the temporal power.[4] Nor did Vitoria agree that the emperor had universal temporal jurisdiction so that all other earthly rulers were merely his agents. Nonetheless, he made a more than adequate case for the Spanish seizure of the newly discovered territory and the subjection of its inhabitants, though its respectability as an argument meant that it fell short of giving carte blanche to Spanish conquest.

Its Scholastic expository techniques and its reliance on Thomist theology give his work a somewhat contorted appearance to the modern reader. Perhaps even more to the point, the rise of Holland and England as imperial powers was accompanied by new ways of thinking about law and international law that were less dependent on Roman law and ideas about the jus gentium. Nonetheless, discussions of humanitarian intervention are today conducted in terms to be found in Vitoria. He held that there was no general right to punish transgressors against the law of nature *as such*, but there was a duty to protect the innocent when possible. We have a duty to intervene not only when the innocent do not ask for help, but even if they repudiate our assistance. Most of us take that view in the case of domestic violence; doubts about Vitoria's argument are about the facts of the case rather than the principle. Vitoria, as a good Dominican, also insisted that Christians had a *ius predicandi*, the right to preach the gospel to whomever they could, as the Dominicans had been founded to do. Anyone who obstructed them put himself in a state of war. Moreover, the Spanish in the Indies were ambassadors and entitled to be treated as such. The ingenuity of the case was enhanced by a further twist. A punitive incursion would achieve its goal only if there was no risk of additional harm to the innocent, and no risk to converts. Of the two possibilities raised by that proviso—the expulsion of the malefactors and the taking of jurisdiction over their territory—the first was impracticable, so the second was lawful. Conquest and colonization were thus justified by extending Aquinas's view of just war into novel realms; not everyone was persuaded, but it became the orthodox Thomist position.

The more extreme view was that the infidels are, as such, in a state of war with Christian civilization and may rightly be conquered and enslaved. This all-inclusive justification was exactly what Vitoria resisted, with the authority of Aquinas behind him. Aquinas had held that infidel rulers were legitimate, and that war against them, merely because they were infidels, was impermissible. That implied that Caribbean and South American rulers should be left undisturbed. Claiming that Caribbean Indians were natural slaves who should be returned to their proper condition by enslavement following war was plausible only on the basis of Aristotle's scattered remarks about "man-hunting." Nonetheless, Juan Ginés de Sepúlveda did indeed rely on Aristotle to claim that a legitimate goal of war was to reduce unwilling natural slaves to their proper enslaved condition. The argument found some favor, but was not uncontested. Bartolomé de Las Casas wrote a heartbreaking account of the destruction of the Caribbean Indians as early as 1542, emphasizing the innocence and gentleness of the Indians and the rapacity and savagery of their Spanish conquerors. He made little headway; greed is notoriously likely to make us accept bad arguments and reject good ones.

Astonishingly enough, Emperor Charles V arranged the so-called Valladolid controversy in 1550–51 to hear the opposing views of Sepúlveda and Las Casas debated. Once Spain had established colonies in the New World, it needed to establish the legitimacy of military action undertaken other than in self-defense. Charles wanted legal backing for the conquest, since the French, English, and Dutch would not respect Spanish possessions in the New World without it, not that they were likely to respect Spanish acquisitions no matter what their legal cover was. The papal donation of half the New World to Spain did not meet Spain's needs, especially when even Catholic writers like Vitoria thought the donation was invalid. It was in any event an unsatisfactory gift, since it shut Spain out of the Pacific, and there was no prospect that Protestant states such as England would take the donation seriously.

Jurisdiction and Ownership

From the mid-sixteenth century, writers were exercised by the twin questions of jurisdiction and ownership. The rise of maritime empires raised questions both about the rights of states and individuals over the open sea and, by extension, about the rights of foreigners and foreign states in places that were by European standards "unoccupied" or waste. Some jurisdictional rights that states exercised on the open sea were immemorial; the ancient world took it for granted that any state that protected its vessels from pirates acted lawfully. If anyone was an enemy to humanity, the pirate was, and he could be killed wherever he was found. But criminal jurisdiction over pirates did not mean that a state could claim ownership of the open sea. The open sea could not be enclosed; trespassers could not be evicted. The open sea was fundamentally different from rivers and lakes; in the case of enclosed waters, the accepted rule was that riparian owners possessed the river or lake up to some midpoint between their properties. The principle that what was lawful was limited by practicalities was well understood. The Romans could claim ownership of inshore waters and perhaps of the Straits of Gibraltar, seeing that they were in full possession of the land on either side. The open sea was essentially vacant; fishermen were like hunters chasing their prey over unowned land, or land held in negative community, belonging as a collective possession to the people who hunted over it, but none of it belonging to anyone in particular. Since it was impossible to occupy the open sea, as distinct from sailing across it, no one had proprietary rights in it, though all might sail across it and fish in it.

The colonization of the American mainland north and south would have occurred no matter what justification was offered. Nonetheless, colonization by settlers raised a persistent question about the lawfulness of taking possession of land that was hunted over, if not farmed, by an indigenous population. One view was that the native inhabitants were the owners of the territory and that settlers were morally obliged to purchase land from them; the other, that they had no title to the land they lived on, and that it was legitimate to take as much land as would leave them sufficient for their purposes, without asking their leave. A prior question was why the native population should enter into any dealings whatever with the European colonizers. To this there was no persuasive answer. A very old Stoic doctrine was that the law of nature tells us to allow strangers to use our superfluities, if our own existence is not threatened by it. Such a doctrine hardly met the case, however, since the "strangers" in Stoic theory were imagined to be necessitous and at the mercy of the possessors of the resources. Colonizers were neither in intention nor in fact shipwrecked mariners or benighted travelers. The principle was stretched to meet the case. It was argued that settlers had a natural right to live on land surplus to the requirements of the existing inhabitants; if a savage people tries to evict the settlers, they are rightly subdued in war.

Hugo Grotius, who was almost exactly a hundred years younger than Vitoria, and is invariably coupled with him in histories of international law, reasserted the Stoic view that Vitoria had relied on, as well as the doctrine promulgated in the mid-thirteenth century by Innocent IV, that civilized peoples had a natural right of jurisdiction over barbarians, which Vitoria had not accepted. However, Grotius's first concern was with the negative case against claims of dominion over the sea. *Mare liberum*, published in 1609, made the familiar case that the open sea was a highway for all comers; no nation could claim dominion over it. Although the view is plausible enough, his motive was to deny Portuguese claims in the East Indies. The English at this time resisted the principle of *mare liberum*; their view was that the seas that enclosed the

British Isles were British, and the British and the Dutch spent much of the seventeenth century fighting one another in the North Sea. In the early eighteenth century the de facto and the de jure were neatly reconciled when everyone agreed that territorial jurisdiction extended as far as a cannon ball could be fired, the basis of the "three-mile limit," universally accepted until after World War II. There were conflicts over its replacement, including the semicomic "cod wars" when Iceland extended its territorial waters and the British refused to recognize the extension. The United Nations Law of the Sea Conference established in 1958 has over the years produced a series of new conventions that acknowledge the realities of different states' economic interests in adjacent waters up to two hundred miles.

Grotius's full-fledged doctrine of what rights we have over what is not or cannot be owned is offered in the enormous *De jure belli ac pacis*, published in 1625.[5] As to the acquisition of property rights in land settled by newcomers, Grotius provided the basis for Hobbes's and Locke's answers. Using the land, by farming it, established a natural title to ownership that the law should recognize. Hobbes and Locke had very different views about rights in civil society, but their views were alike unfavorable to the rights of native peoples and friendly to the rights of colonizers. How far they foresaw this is debatable, though many commentators have thought they were fully seized of the implications. Hobbes regarded the American Indians as living in the state of nature and described their condition as miserable. It was arguable that the American Indians would be better off if they were conquered with as little brutality as possible and given stable government; resistance would be irrational, a case of mistaking a dangerous anarchy for "liberty." Hobbes believed as firmly as Locke that stable property rights, enforced by an uncorrupt and effective government, were essential to civilized life.

As to Locke, who believed that in the beginning all the world was America, the implication was that, as he argued in the fifth chapter of his *Second Treatise*, the development of property rights in simple consumption goods, then in land, and finally in some equivalent to money, was essential to progress. If labor was the first title to ownership, American Indians who roamed over trackless wastes, hunting and gathering and scratching a very bare living, had no title to the land, even though they had a title to the deer they killed and the acorns they gathered. Losing access to the land occupied by settler farmers would be no loss, seeing that an English day laborer lived, lodged, and was clothed better than "the king of a large and populous country" in inland America.[6] Locke's argument served two purposes at once: against the native Indians, it implied that they did not really own the land from which they were being evicted, and against the English government it implied that the property rights of the colonists were sturdier than those of English gentry who hunted over land they could hardly be said to labor on. Some American colonists, more sympathetic to Indian claims than their fellows, employed the argument to claim that if the gentry's titles were good in law so were the Indians' titles.

The Valladolid controversy had hinged on the question whether the Caribbean Indians were capable of self-government or were natural slaves. Sepúlveda claimed they were natural slaves, standing to the civilized Spanish as women to men, infants to adults, and the fierce to the mild.[7] The classical division of the world into Greeks and barbarians, or Romans and barbarians, began to turn into the modern view of the different duties in international law owed by the civilized to the civilized and the uncivilized. The initial use of the distinction was to provide a new answer to the old question about the obligation to keep faith with infidels. Medieval writers had divided; several had drawn on Cicero's argument in *De officiis* that we need not keep faith with pirates to maintain that we need not keep faith with the infidel. Just as pirates put themselves beyond the natural law, so did the infidel who had no moral principles and lacked the motive of a believer to keep faith. The uncivilized had few rights against the civilized beyond the barest humanitarian constraints. However, the Swiss theorist Emerich Vattel, whose *Droit des nations* of 1758 was immensely influential, employed the contrast between the civilized and the uncivilized, not to defend but to condemn the Spanish conquest of Central America.[8] Vattel held that there was a genuine civilization in Central America, pagan though it might be; for that reason, their conquest was simply unlawful. Grotius's notion that the conquest might be justified as an act of punishment for the Amerindians' violations of natural law was dismissed by Vattel on the simple but persuasive ground that too many people can play that game: the prophet Muhammad conquered swaths of Asia to enforce his view of religious rectitude. In the absence of an international consensus on the details of the law of nature, there was no difference between Grotius's view and a general license to the strong to conquer the weak behind a screen of high principle. Of course, Vitoria and Sepúlveda would have thought that there was a consensus, at least among the enlightened—which raises the question whether there is a consensus on who is enlightened.

Vattel approved of the British colonization of North America, because there was no civilization already in place. Put simply, the savages of North America had failed to meet the natural law obligation to cultivate the earth and make it productive. They had possession but not ownership of their lands under natural law, and no right to prevent settlement if it "was done within just limits." Nonetheless, he approved of the fact that both the New England Puritans and the Quakers in Pennsylvania had gone out of their way to purchase land from the native inhabitants and had not simply seized it. "Just limits" were capable of definition in ways extremely unfavorable to the native occupants. Vattel was a popular resource for American legal theorists, but Jefferson invariably argued that the Indians had to choose between becoming freeholding farmers and being driven into the wilderness to starve. Indeed, he sometimes anticipated driving them into Canada and seizing Canada to ensure that they starved, although Jefferson's most intemperate thoughts were provoked not by pure racial hatred but by such success as the British had in using Indians as auxiliaries during the revolution and the War of 1812.[9] Vattel's arguments that favored native people were undermined by a feature that is one of the intellectual strengths of his work: he was fastidious in distinguishing the law of nature, *lex naturae*, from the law of nations, *jus gentium*, and then distinguishing the different elements of international customary law. The effect was to sharpen the contrast between the dealings of complex developed states with one another and their dealings with people living in simple, prepolitical societies. The latter were not "civilized," could not keep treaties, and could be dealt with as seemed right to the more developed societies that came into contact with them; the civilized were morally obliged to behave decently, but nothing more. John Stuart Mill relied very heavily on just that thought in contrasting the freedom to which civilized peoples were entitled with the benevolent despotism that suited "barbarians."[10]

The *Mission Civilisatrice*

The distinction between the civilized and the uncivilized came to serve a particular purpose in legitimating colonization. The oldest version of the idea, readily derived from Aristotle, was simple: a sufficient difference in the capacity for rational self-government between rulers and ruled allowed despotic authority to the rulers. Aristotle used that argument to lay out the conditions for a *panbasileus* to rule within a polis. The modern use of the distinction was the idea that imperial powers had the right and perhaps the duty to bring uncivilized peoples the blessings of civilization. These blessings came in tiers: minimally, Christian countries should spread knowledge of the Christian faith; less minimally, they should govern their native subjects according to civilized standards of humanity and lawfulness; maximally, they should turn their native subjects into dark-skinned Europeans, appreciative of European culture and European political ideals. When the idea that empires were justified as a means of civilizing native peoples arose is hard to say, but it became a commonplace of imperialist thought in the late nineteenth century. Its popularity seems to have been the result of the scramble for Africa, when its racial aspects were front and center of the argument.

In the eighteenth century, it was more often the object of attack by critics than an idea defended by serious thinkers; but it was common enough in the rhetoric of the defenders of vast enterprises like the East India Company, and of ordinary colonial settlers, to provoke a response. After Montesquieu it was a cliché that the civilizations developed slowly, that it was appallingly difficult to transplant institutions from one society to another, and absurd to expect a society to operate alien institutions as if it had grown them itself. Burke's *Reflections on the Revolution in France* has been read as an implicitly anti-imperialist tract, and Burke himself spent years attacking the East India Company's creation of an Indian empire. The underlying thought was simple: we cannot remodel our own society on a simple rational plan, and a fortiori we cannot interfere in the workings of another, wholly alien society without having unpredictable and uncontrollable effects on it. These are more likely to be malign than benign. In any case, brutality and rapacity more often feature in the behavior of colonists than a self-sacrificing concern for the welfare of native peoples. Kant's comments in *Perpetual Peace* suggest the gap between professions of concern and mistreatment in practice.[11]

These practical objections do not undermine the contrast between the more and the less civilized peoples, although Burke's description of the behavior of the East India Company certainly suggested that looting and pillaging on a Roman scale was closer to its heart than trading. The French *philosophe* Denis Diderot set out to mock the contrast itself, directly undermining the argument for the civilizing mission. He denied flat-out that the contrast between civilized Europe and uncivilized elsewhere told in favor of Europe. No reader of his *Supplément au voyage de Bougainville*, written in the 1770s but published only in 1796, has been able to talk of a *mission civilisatrice* with a straight face; Diderot's comic rendering of the encounter between a repressed Jesuit priest and the benign, sexually liberated Tahitians is a sharp reminder that the question of which society is more civilized than which may defy a rational answer.[12] Most of the *Supplément* is far from comic, and amounts to an outraged assault on the European capacity for murdering, corrupting, and infecting the innocent inhabitants of distant places who live perfectly happily without most of our own vices.

The role of imperialism in bringing about progress, and progress of what sort, was thus deeply contestable. Nor were critics necessarily skeptical about the very idea of progress; the skeptical Diderot was animated by humanitarian distaste for the follies and cruelties of his own society, but others focused on the question whether a more civilized state had the right to force progress on another people. Immanuel Kant was a principled anti-imperialist, although he accepted the fact of human progress, had emphatic views about its nature, and developed a coherent theory of the role of the state in promoting it. His essay *Idea for a Universal History with a Cosmopolitan Purpose* argues that the point of history is to perfect the qualities of humanity; this cannot be done in any one person, but only in the human race as a whole. It is up to each person to make the most of what his or her own abilities are, and it is morally obnoxious to try to make someone else happy according to our ideas about their happiness, or for one people to do the same to another. For a people to make progress, they must form a political community, but it is up to them to form it. He wholly repudiated the tradition that links Pericles, Machiavelli, and Algernon Sidney in the conviction that a healthy republic expands its power wherever it can; his *Perpetual Peace*, written in 1795, looked for a system of international peace promoted by a league of nations.[13] A civilizing mission was the hidden purpose of history, not something the more favored imposed on the less favored. As so often, John Stuart Mill reveals the tensions in a simultaneous commitment to utilitarian values and to liberalism. The utilitarian, after all, should agree that if the uncivilized or less civilized *can* be made civilized by an imperial power, they should be, assuming that it was not the waste of resources that Bentham claimed it always was. This was the nineteenth-century precursor of the twentieth-century urge to export democracy so prominent in American foreign policy. The liberal, on the other hand, is likely to side with Kant and maintain it is not the business of outsiders to impose their ideas about civilization on people who have not asked for their help.

In 1853 Mill appeared before a House of Lords committee to defend the East India Company's government of India. It had, he said, been a government of "improvement"; many of these improvements were exactly what one would expect: widening literacy, paving roads, introducing the railroad, modernizing docks. However, the chief improvement he had in mind was that the company was beginning the long process of teaching the Indian population the arts of rational and uncorrupt self-government. How much *cultural* transformation this required, Mill did not say; but since he accepted his father's description of Indian society as riddled with superstition, servility, and corruption, he no doubt thought it would take some time. Mill's account of the demands of self-government in *Representative Government* suggests that Indian political culture would have to become more Athenian, energetic, and self-improving before the work was done. His noble interlocutors were much more startled by his insistence that the British should leave once the task was completed; if India could be self-governing, the British should leave. If their role was to provide political education, they had no place once their pupils were ready for self-government. The uncomprehending response he received from the House of Lords committee when he presented his account of the self-liquidating imperial mission suggests that British politicians found it easier to think about empires in the traditional terms of commercial and military advantage to the metropolitan country than as an arrangement to assist the native population to become rational, self-governing liberal democrats.

Mill never suggested that Britain had, either alone or with a handful of other European nations, a civilizing mission that entitled it to acquire and control an empire. He was hostile to the idea that one people could civilize another against its will, and unenthusiastic about conquest. The defense of taking empire seriously was that if a more advanced political and economic regime found itself responsible for an underdeveloped one, it was obliged to work for the improvement of the underdeveloped society, rather than exploit it in the Greek or Roman fashion. Mill was unusual in linking improvement so firmly to the acquisition of the skills and tastes that were needed for self-government. He was also perhaps overoptimistic in thinking that the high moral standards he set for a colonial administration would be met by any known government.

Mill's stance was highly moralistic; its mirror image was the deliberate brutality of Marx's views. Marx was even more convinced than Mill that imperialism was a progressive force, but he despised such moralizing. Imperialists were motivated by greed. The truth about the East India Company was not Mill's defense but the Opium Wars fought to ensure that the company could profit from poisoning the Chinese. Marx's contempt for pointless moralizing about matters that would be resolved by force, whether cloaked in fine words or not, underpinned the claim that from the point of view of the human race as a whole, it was a good thing that Britain was a colonial and imperial power. Being "more civilized" gave Britain the right to dictate social, economic, and political change in India and China only in the very arm's-length sense that because Britain was farther along the path of historical development, progress toward worldwide socialism would be accelerated by Britain's dragging backward nations into the developed world. This was far from a defense of empire in general, and anything but admiring of Europe's superior civilization. Capitalism was not a civilized economic system; and only empires that served historical progress had even this limited acceptability. The Russian Empire, for instance, made revolution in Germany less likely; it was a drag on progress throughout Europe and could not be destroyed too soon.

Of major political theorists, Tocqueville articulated the characteristically French ideal of the civilizing mission in his writings on Algeria.[14] Tocqueville thought the British were hypocritical in pretending to have no imperial ambitions; the British legitimating myth—that the empire was acquired "in a fit of absence of mind"—was belied by reality. Wherever British interests were at stake, the British intervened to evict previous colonial powers, among them the French in North America and India, and ensured that British interests were served with no regard to the interests of the local inhabitants. France could become a first-rate power only by taking its rivalry with Britain seriously and extending its own power, in Algeria and the Near East, and elsewhere in Africa. Tocqueville's defense of the French treatment of the native population casts a disturbing light on the author of *Democracy in America* and its moving reflections on the fate of the American Indians. Compared with John Stuart Mill, however, Tocqueville had a strong sense of the costs of social and political change. Mill thought that the inhabitants of India lost nothing by being governed by the East India Company; Tocqueville was quite clear that colonized peoples lost a great deal. Historical progress could not be costless, and France could not conquer Algeria painlessly. It was justified not only by the legitimate French desire for "glory" but by the mission to spread the ideal of French civilization throughout the world. This was the true doctrine of the *mission civilisatrice*. Forty years later Jules Ferry took up the same theme; it sustained French colonialism until the decolonization of the 1950s, and perhaps underpins France's relations with its former African colonies still.

There are many difficulties with the concept of a *mission civilisatrice*.

The first is that it is ambiguous between "civilization" and "civilizations." There is nothing specifically French, American, German, or British about a railroad or a set of port installations, what Mill described as "improvements." They are the infrastructure of economic modernization; but a taste for Racine or Goethe rather than Milton or Henry James is another matter. That is French, German, British, or American culture. There is no room for complacency in the fact that we nowadays distinguish between "modernization" and "civilization," if only because so much of the literature of modernization still conflates modernization in the narrow sense of economic and technical updating and modernization in the sense of acquiring European liberal and democratic attachments. It is obvious that any amount of technical sophistication can be acquired without a taste for liberal democracy and that high culture itself has no connection with liberal democracy; but confusion in this area is a besetting sin of political analysts. The other great problem is that the idea hovers on the edge of self-contradiction. If we have a civilizing mission, the people on whom it is exercised ought to be capable of becoming civilized fairly swiftly; but peoples who can be swiftly civilized are not plausible candidates for colonization, since they are presumably capable of seeing the benefits of civilization and acquiring them voluntarily. Conversely, if the thought is that those whom it is proposed to civilize are so far behind the civilized West that they cannot organize their own social and political affairs, and are condemned to backwardness and anarchy by ethnic, cultural, or racial original sin, forcibly civilizing them makes no more sense than trying to beat advanced calculus into four-year-olds.

Racism: Classical and "Scientific"

An outgrowth of nineteenth-century imperialism and a natural offshoot of thinking in terms of a civilizing mission was "scientific racism." Racial arguments and arguments for a civilizing mission should in principle, but do not in practice, belong to different universes of discourse. That is, a serious racial theory explains why inferior races will *always* be lower in the hierarchy of civilized peoples, or why they do not belong to that hierarchy

at all. One might think of Aristotle as the father of scientific racism, save
that he did not distinguish, as modern racists do, between a genetic incapacity, to which climate and environment are irrelevant, and a contingent
incapacity produced by an unfavorable environment. Both allow for uninhibited exploitation, but the first rules out compulsory civilization. Greeks
alone are fit for political life strictly speaking, but there is no suggestion
that the Scythians and the Persians might be forcibly recruited for Greek
civilization. It is in the same fashion that Algernon Sidney refers to the
"base effeminate Asiaticks and Africans, who for being careless of their
liberty, or unable to govern themselves, were by Aristotle and other wise
men called *slaves by nature*, and looked upon as little better than beasts."[15]
Race as understood within "scientific racism" seems not to enter into
the matter, and the question whether the base effeminate Asiaticks and
Africans might eventually become "just like us" is not raised. A civilizing
mission presupposes that inferiority and hierarchy are temporary, not permanent, otherwise its educational hopes are doomed. They may be doomed
anyway. Distinguished African poets and thinkers have themselves been
ambivalent about the fact that they have become black Frenchmen, with
an understanding of French culture unmatched by most white Frenchmen,
and have questioned whether they should repudiate French culture in the
name of negritude, or repudiate only the cruelty and injustice of spreading
by violence a culture that at its best is not French but human.

The origins of scientific racism are obscure, although casual racism
and ethnic insult are as old as recorded history. Recognizably modern
forms of racism go back at least to the eighteenth century, when the
great naturalist Linnaeus turned his hand to classifying human races
as well as nonhuman organisms. In the nineteenth century they were
given new life by Lamarckian and Darwinian evolutionary theory, and
took on an almost metaphysical flavor as they were invoked to explain
more and more of human history. One curiosity is that although racism
often underpinned the belief that white Europeans should manage the
affairs and colonize the territories of nonwhites and non-Europeans,
the intellectual founder of nineteenth-century scientific racism thought
the opposite. He was the comte de Gobineau, a French aristocrat who
served in the French diplomatic service in Iran and elsewhere and for a

time was Tocqueville's secretary; he wrote novels and short stories and a book with an alarming later life, the *Essai sur l'inégalité des races humaines*, published in 1855. Gobineau was an anti-Semite in the strict sense: he disliked Arabs and Jews alike. He was a bitter critic of democracy and of emergent mass politics; the thought that imperialist adventures might be a way of gratifying the tastes of the masses would have disgusted him. Nonetheless, the book was much admired by Richard Wagner and by Houston Stewart Chamberlain, who was an effective popularizer of the doctrine of Aryan supremacy taken up by Hitler and the Nazis.[16] Gobineau was no enthusiast for a new racial order; he was a quietist and a pessimist and a deep reactionary.

Gobineau thought entirely in racial categories and disliked empires because they inevitably led to miscegenation and thus to a deterioration of the higher race. Why he was so perturbed is not easy to see; he thought that modern Frenchmen were much inferior to their pure Frankish forebears, and had few grounds for fearing further deterioration. Like most racial theorists, he wavered in his views about the source of racial decay; sometimes he seemed committed to the view that even a diluted Aryan stock was superior to all others; at other times, that purity was what counted and that all mongrel peoples were inferior to all pure stocks. Detailed analysis of his views would gratify an antiquarian curiosity, but he serves as a warning against the assumption that all forms of racism must issue in triumphalist forms of imperialism and are inevitably employed in the service of economic exploitation and political tyranny. They can also lead to isolationism.

Lenin and the Marxist View of Empire

Before turning to the ideological revolt against empire, and the success of nationalist anticolonialism, we should recapitulate one of the great debates of the twentieth century. This was the argument between defenders and critics of the Marxian account of why modern imperialism came about, why it was a feature of late capitalism, and why, however disgusting it might be in itself, it was an essential step in the international revolution that would overthrow capitalism once and for all. This is, viewed in a certain light, an account of the civilizing mission that places the idea of a civilizing mission within heavily ironic brackets. Marx's contrast between the progressive results he expected from the Asian empire established by the British and the merely retrograde Russian Empire was matched by the contrast between progressive and reactionary nationalisms. His best-known view was that the working man has no country. Capital has no country, flowing wherever profit is to be found, and the proletariat could not afford to have a country. Since its condition was defined by its members' absence of property, the proletariat had all too literally no stake in any country.

This view led to disaster for socialist parties in both Europe and the United States in 1914, when their expectation that the workers of one country would not fight the workers of another was dashed. Most socialists supported their own country's war effort. Nationalism has defeated socialist internationalism on every occasion on which the question has arisen. Marx and Engels themselves gave qualified approval to some nationalisms; peoples whose aspirations for a national identity and a national government would promote the long-term interests of working people were progressive, and those whose aspirations would hold them back were reactionary. The liberal nationalists of the 1848 revolutions in Germany were on the side of progress, while the Danes and Holsteiners who resisted incorporation within Germany were reactionary. Progressive nationalisms frustrated czarist Russia's attempts to preserve autocracy throughout Europe, and reactionary forms fostered localism and impeded economic transformation. In the twentieth century the most powerful forces supporting decolonization were nationalist rather than socialist, so the distinction between progressive and reactionary forms of nationalism would be of great importance if it could be sustained and the progressive forms alone encouraged. The task is difficult, however, and Marxists have for the most part attacked all forms of nationalism as inimical to socialism and stuck to promoting proletarian internationalism.

The fully developed Marxist theory of imperialism came two decades after Marx's death. It was an offshoot of the interest that Marxists, like others, took in the simultaneous rise of major monopolies within modern industry and the scramble for Africa and Asia. Marx's account of capitalist competition implied that monopolies would be prominent in the modern economic landscape. The savagery of competition assumed in his theory implied that only the most robust firms with the largest resources would survive slumps and benefit from booms. An alliance between finance capital and industrial capital was expected in which banks would take a controlling interest in industry through supplying the loans on which industrial firms depended. Marxists regarded the rise of monopolies as proof of the Marxian theory of the increasing concentration of capital. To subsequent economic theorists, it was a temporary phase in the development of capitalism; monopolies inadvertently create the conditions for smaller and more agile competitors to undermine them. Dinosaurs lose to small mammals.

Marxists and non-Marxists alike became obsessed with the idea that underconsumption, or demand deficiency, would be a major feature of developed capitalism. Monopolies deploying ever larger quantities of capital in a desperate search for profit would generate multitudes of ever poorer proletarians, whose purchasing power was inadequate to allow the monopolies to sell their output at a profit. The question was where monopolies could find the markets that would yield the profit they needed. The answer seemed obvious; they had to expand overseas, where the rate of profit was still high. To a Russian observer such as Lenin, the facts appeared to fall out as the theory suggested. The industrial plants established in St. Petersburg and Moscow by overseas investors were larger than the plants in the investors' home countries; more capital was being invested to reap higher profits. Lenin summed up his views in the subtitle of his pamphlet *Imperialism: The Highest Stage of Capitalism*.[17] This was a novel form of imperialism, since it did not imply settler colonization. Had Lenin lived in Pittsburgh, Pennsylvania, he might have thought that the United States was being recolonized by the British, since American steel plants were far larger than British plants and much of the money invested in them came from the City of London. Lenin was, as always, looking for reasons to think that a successful socialist revolution could be made in Russia. It was obvious enough that Russia was more *politically* unstable than the countries of western Europe where Marx had expected the revolution to break out. Lenin concluded that because Russian investments were essential to the success of European capitalism, political upheaval in Russia would "break the weakest link in the capitalist chain," causing a crisis in European capitalism and bringing on the proletarian revolution.

The writer from whom Lenin borrowed the theoretical underpinning of his account, J. A. Hobson, was an English radical, not a Marxist but a left-wing liberal. Although he disliked the impact of imperialism on the colonized peoples who were asked to share the white man's burden, his view of imperialism, theoretically speaking, was not that it was immoral but that it exacerbated the disease it attempted to cure. If imperialism was prompted by a search for profit in the face of a declining rate of return on capital, and the underlying problem in a developed economy like Britain was a shortage of purchasing power in the hands of working people, the profits fell into the hands of the investing classes and did nothing to resolve the developing crisis of underconsumption. There were many other conclusions one might have come to on the same evidence; one is very important in the rhetorical history of imperialism. Employers securing superprofits on their overseas investments could employ their British workers at higher wages than they would otherwise have been able to do. That would alleviate underconsumption and give the workers an economic interest in the continuation of the capitalist status quo. Marxists seeking explanations for the unwillingness of workers in advanced industrial societies to embark on the revolutionary project that history assigned them have often thought the explanation lay in the fact that the workers shared the proceeds of the exploitation of their colonized cousins. One may decently be skeptical. The simplest explanation of western European imperialism is as plausible as any: competition between states for military security and commercial advantage led to the competing pelagic empires of the past four centuries, while the same search for security and profit goes a long way toward explaining the westward and eastward expansion of the United States and Russia.

Decolonization, Nationalism, and Religion

What is stranger than the rise of empire after Columbus's voyage of 1492 is the speed with which imperialism became morally tainted in the middle of the twentieth century. In the 1920s few Britons doubted that the possession of an enormous empire was a legitimate source of pride. Schoolboys were encouraged to admire the vast areas of red on maps of the world, though the Mercator projection gave Canada a disproportionately large share of the map and gave India less than its due. In the 1950s the chief question about the remaining British colonies was how to bring them to independence as painlessly as possible. By the end of the century, "empire" was a term of abuse. When French writers in the 1960s warned their compatriots of the *nouvelle empire américaine*, they did so from the position that exercising imperial authority was self-evidently a bad thing, and that to do in the way the Americans had done after the war, by means of cultural subversion, that is, by way of Hollywood movies and popular music rather than an above-board military invasion, was underhand. The possibility that French perfume, fashion, and cooking are universally admired because of their merits, and American popular entertainment similarly admired for its merits, was rarely entertained. When it was, nobody talked of "cultural imperialism" or "cultural colonization."

Modern imperialism is an enterprise of the nation-state, and its downfall partly a result of the fact that the imperial powers imparted to their subjects a great desire to be citizens of their own nation-states, not colonial subjects. One peculiarity of the rise of national consciousness is that for all the importance of the nation-state in both the practice and the theory of international relations, there is little consensus on what constitutes a nation, or the nature of the connection between a group of people constituting a nation and their right to form an independent, sovereign state. There is an evident overlap between the idea of being "a people" and constituting "a nation," as the King James Version of the Old Testament reminds us. The Israelites are a chosen people and a favored nation. What constitutes that kind of nation is lineage:

descent from Abraham, to whom the first covenant was delivered. The modern nation-state is commonly said to have originated with the rulers of European monarchies in the sixteenth and seventeenth centuries, who centralized power in their own hands and administered their state's affairs through a well-organized bureaucracy. But when the ideological defenders of these monarchies mentioned nationhood, they had God's creation of the people of Israel in mind, and saw in absolute monarchy a reflection of God's dominion over mankind.[18]

They were wise not to look for linguistic or cultural identity as the basis of political unity, since many monarchs spoke a different language from most of their subjects, as did the first two Hanoverian kings of England. Where the dynastic principle holds sway, as with the Austrian empire, national identity, whatever it may be, cannot be the primary basis of authority; indeed, the rise of nationalism undid Austria-Hungary. Looking for the essence of national identity is an ungrateful task, but the importance of a *felt* sense of national identity, and especially a felt sense of frustrated national identity, is undeniable. If one truth dominates post-1945 decolonization and the end of empire, it is that nationalism trumps socialism; when the colonial powers left, they almost always left behind governments committed to some sort of socialism, whether Marxist or indigenous. Many governments were inept, and many ex-colonial states are failed states; but they have invariably set the preservation of their nationhood ahead of the fulfillment of their socialist ambitions. In the African context, arbitrary national boundaries, tribal loyalties, and the absence of any source of national unity beyond the memory of previous colonization have posed immense problems; since the one unequivocally national institution is usually the army, the unhappy connection between national identity and the rise of military strongmen is obvious enough. Elsewhere, the end of the Soviet Union and the Soviet Empire in Eastern Europe and south-central Asia revealed again that ethnic nationalism had been repressed but not overcome. The dissolution of the Yugoslav federal and socialist republic into half a dozen independent republics—all speaking the same language, although some use Latin script and others Cyrillic—provided depressing evidence of the same phenomenon.

The tone of these paragraphs may appear to imply that nationalism is to be deplored. It is not clear that it is. Modern states rest on complicated economic foundations; they need some unifying principle to provide cohesion and dissuade individuals from picking and choosing which laws they will and will not observe. The unifying principle also needs to be political, not familial; family loyalty enables families more effectively to protect their members, but equally allows one family to exploit another and the larger society. The Italian Mafia plays up the idea that members of the Mafia are members of a family, and the corrosive effect of the Mafia on Italian life needs no emphasis. To the degree that nationalism provides suprafamilial or supertribal attachments, it has valuable consequences. This view underlay the nineteenth-century liberal nationalism espoused by Lord Acton, J. S. Mill, and more radical nationalists such as Garibaldi. A society could advance toward modernity only under the umbrella of political unity; the liberal political regime required for progress needed a unified and efficient legal system, which implied control of a national territory; that in turn implied a national consciousness.

Radical Anti-imperialism

Decolonization has largely been driven by the wish of colonized peoples for national independence, to live in a state that is part of a world of nation-states. This is far from the whole story. We habitually qualify nationalist movements or movements built around nationalist ideas with terms that refer not to states but to peoples who live in many states. "Arab nationalism" is one such. But there have been more radical ambitions for a postimperial world, and even if they have mostly done more to frighten governments and commentators than to influence politics more positively, they are intellectually powerful. Two not very representative, but certainly influential, reflections on these themes were Frantz Fanon's *The Wretched of the Earth* and Sayyad Qutb's *Milestones* and his earlier *Social Justice in Islam*. Neither Fanon nor Qutb is representative of extreme anti-imperialism precisely because each is so strikingly individual. On the other hand, each is representative of the way in which the colonial powers contrived to teach their most intelligent and energetic subjects lessons they did not intend. In Qutb's case, the effect was to throw him back on a fiercely anti-Western form of Islam, so that he articulated the sense of outrage, humiliation, and betrayal that many colonial intellectuals—including Fanon—expressed very differently. They took the offer of membership in the advanced world seriously and then saw that it was not intended seriously. They would always be excluded.

Fanon was born in Martinique in 1925 and as a teenager during World War II joined the resistance. After the war he went to France and studied psychiatry. Almost at once, he drew on his psychiatric training to develop an assault on white racism that owed much to Sartre's existentialism and to Marxist socialism. *Black Skins, White Masks*,[19] published in 1952, was one of the defining works in the postwar anticolonial and antiracist movements. It undermined both the *mission civilisatrice* vision of French colonialism and the idea of a distinctively black worldview and culture that Aimé Césaire had defended under the label of negritude. Drawing on the mixture of Hegelian and Heideggerian ideas that Sartre's *Being and Nothingness* had already employed, Fanon had no difficulty with the thought that a dominant white culture took whiteness as the badge of virtue, blackness as the badge of evil, and imposed on those who were born black an image of themselves as stigmatized from birth. These thoughts became commonplace in the 1960s among black American radicals in particular; but they had an origin, and Fanon seems to have been the first to articulate them in their modern form. He understood the tension between the skin and the mask as a reaction to colonialism and empire in their familiar forms, but it was a short step for black American intellectuals to see their own society as suffering from a form of internal imperialism and to see African Americans as victims of an internal colonialism.

Fanon's career was short, and his life dangerous. He worked as a psychiatrist in Algeria in the early 1950s, but abandoned his profession in 1957 and joined the Algerian national liberation movement. Severely injured in 1959, he died of leukemia in 1961. He died too soon to see Algeria liberated, but it is hard to believe that he would not have been killed in one of the internal struggles that subsequently racked the Algerian revolution. Before he died, he produced two further extraordinary books; in 1959 he published *Year Five of the Algerian Revolution* and in 1961 *The Wretched of the Earth*. The latter came with an introductory essay by Sartre that might make a reader dismiss it as a piece of 1960s revolutionary chic; but its enduring intellectual interest is its sharply analytical account of the task of the revolutionary party and the place of nationalism in decolonization.

Nationalism was a dangerous gift that the colonizers inadvertently gave the colonized. Anticolonial insurrectionary movements were invariably described as movements of national liberation. Fanon understood the problem this posed. As a Marxist, he did not wish to rescue the peasantry and urban workers of Algeria from oppression at the hands of the French and the *colons* only to hand them over to oppression at the hands of a local capitalist elite—what he termed a national bourgeoisie. He was also aware that if there was to be a revolution at all, it would be a movement of national liberation; it was Algerian Arabs against white Frenchmen and *pieds noirs*, a race war and a national war. What struck readers was Fanon's unflinching endorsement of violence. The claim that a colonial subject who killed one of his oppressors had liberated himself in the act of murdering his oppressor was Sartre's overblown summary, but Fanon's views were alarming enough. From a theoretical point of view, it is the pathos of Fanon's position that is truly striking. His anxiety was that the decolonizing revolution would be taken over by a national bourgeoisie; but other and worse fates were always more likely. One of them befell the Algerian revolution: the institution of a military dictatorship, and years of civil war between insurgents wishing to institute an Islamist regime and a secular military government determined to prevent it. Most Algerians would have welcomed the fate Fanon wished to avert, a capitalist liberal democracy in which the working population suffered only the exploitation common to all workers under capitalism.

It would be wrong to end any discussion of the theoretical underpinnings of decolonization without mentioning what no critic of empire anticipated. This is the rise of what is unfortunately termed Islamic fundamentalism; the label is unfortunate because the status of the Koran within Islam is not that of the Bible within Christianity and arguments about its "inerrancy" have played no comparable role in the history of

Islam, even though innumerable arguments about just how to read the Koran have and do. The historical irony is that the rise was utterly unexpected. Twentieth-century radical critics of empire and their imperialist enemies were almost invariably secularists to the core. Whatever deficiencies there are in Marx's account of capitalism and adaptations of that account to explain imperialism, nobody doubts the desire of imperialists and colonizers to exploit the resources—including the physical labor of the inhabitants—of the countries they have colonized. Whatever deficiencies there are in the liberal imperialist ideal of "improving" colonized countries, the progress it implies is secular, individualist, and economically rationalist.

The Marxist view of progress has more in common with the liberal view than either side usually acknowledges. Nationalism is not on all fours with the liberal or Marxian view of politics, because it does not share their universalism. Its one universal value is a demand that the welfare of each nation be treated as an absolute value, not by the inhabitants of other nations but certainly by the inhabitants of each nation with regard to their own nation. Unaggressive nationalism is a doctrine of "to each people its own polity," with no implications about what sort of polity they should establish, only that they, and not outsiders, should establish it. Aggressive nationalism—the nationalism that implies that a nation's historical destiny is discovered in wars of conquest—is another matter; but aggressiveness of this sort is detachable from the emphasis on the importance of national identity and national independence, even though most peoples have developed a national consciousness in war, and aggressive rather than mutually disinterested nationalism has tended to predominate.

The relationship between nationalism and progress is indeterminate; economic growth can be a source of national pride and backwardness a source of national humiliation; the constant is an insistence on the specialness of a nation and its people. That opens the door to Islamic self-assertion. The key figure in the theoretical development of the idea that the Muslim world could regain its self-respect only by purifying itself and separating from the corrupt world of the infidel was Sayyid Qutb, although he himself was inspired by the radical Muslim Maulana Mawdudi, an Indian whose writings in the 1930s and 1940s underpin Pakistani radicalism to this day. Britain was frequently more successful in creating in its Indian subjects a desire for national self-determination than a wish to live happily under British rule, and Mawdudi was no exception. The effect of living under British rule in Egypt was to persuade Qutb that the liberal secular West was either mendacious or self-deceived; it offered its subject peoples educational and economic opportunities that were purportedly cosmopolitan, and notionally did not require their beneficiaries to abandon their own culture for that of their colonizers, but what they offered in reality was cultural death. Qutb was born in 1906 in a poor rural area of Egypt, but he was a clever and studious child, and his family were well-off enough to give him an excellent education. As a teenager he received a religious training, but in his twenties qualified as a teacher and worked for the Egyptian Ministry of Education for more than a decade. In his early years he wrote on literature rather than politics, and his later political career was tragically short, since he spent most of his final ten years in prison under the regime of Colonel Nasser; he was released in 1964, rearrested almost at once, tried, and executed in 1966.

He was always devout, but he became prominent only after World War II, in two distinct steps. In 1949 he published the work usually translated as *Social Justice in Islam*, a book on which he worked in the United States while getting a master's degree in education and working for the Egyptian Ministry of Education studying American educational institutions. Qutb found his firsthand encounter with the Western world so deeply repulsive that he came close to inventing out of whole cloth an alternative Islamist vision of a world governed as the Prophet would have governed it. It is always said that he was shocked by what he saw as the loose behavior of young Americans, especially young women, and this shock made him turn to extreme forms of Islam. It is equally plausible that he simply turned against what he perceived as the false promise of "modernization," in ways that much of the non-Western world has done. Many Western critics have similarly reacted against modernity, even in the United States. The most powerful of such "inside" critics have been conservatives distressed at the loss of religious conviction, hostile to the ugliness of industrial life, and morally at odds with the liberalism and individualism that believers in progress espoused. From "outside," the falsity of the promises made to colonized peoples by advocates of modernization is more glaring. The Western world had developed a way of life whose existence depended on there being only a few nations able to share it, and in the eyes of many critics had been able to develop it only because previously prosperous countries such as India and China were exploited. From the perspective of impoverished and economically deprived societies, the Western dream can very easily look like something offered only on condition that few people take up the offer. Whatever the impulse, Qutb turned to a particularly intransigent form of Islam.

The interest of *Social Justice in Islam*, and even more of *Milestones* (also translated as *Signposts*, which is perhaps a better indication of its purpose as a guide for young Muslims), is the way in which they show many of the features common to secular nationalism. They are full of hostility to the non-Islamic world, but ambivalent as between the view that the task is to protect an Islamic society in its own homeland or homelands and the view that the task is to ensure that there are no non-Islamic societies. From the point of view of the imperialist or formerly imperialist Western world, it is a novelty to be the object of the contempt for feebleness, effeminacy, and decadence so prominent in the European contempt for the "Asiaticks." The question is what is supposed to follow. For Qutb himself, it seems clear enough, the main object of concern was his native Egypt. The terms of the discussion in *Social Justice in Islam*, however, suggest a universalizing ambition for Islam like that which animated the missionary efforts of Christianity during the Middle Ages and after. If there is a God, there is one God only, and there is one law only; to be a good Muslim is to follow that law and no other. It is not surprising that Qutb's support for Colonel Nasser's military-nationalist regime was highly conditional; the Muslim Brotherhood supported the movement for independence from Britain, but wanted an Islamic republic, not a military dictatorship. Qutb's friendship with the new regime lasted for no more than a year or two, and he rejected it in disgust when it would not introduce the sharia as the law of Egypt for Muslims.

The argument that has led to Qutb's being described as the intellectual father of Islamic militancy was developed in *Milestones*. Published in 1964, after Qutb had endured years of imprisonment and ill-treatment in Nasser's prisons, *Milestones* argued the case that was latent in Qutb's earlier work, but which on his own view he had been unable to articulate because he had not freed himself from the colonialist mentality. This was that Islam was the only true civilization. Previously, he had argued as conservative internal critics of the liberal West had argued: in effect saying that if this was civilization, they did not want civilization. Now he said firmly that it was not civilization. Islam was the only civilization, and all *jahili* societies were of their nature backward. This was an elegant, if not wholly persuasive, way of turning the 1950s and 1960s debate about modernization against the "Westernizers" and at the same time condemning all who accepted aid from the Soviet Union in order to preserve their independence from the West. Socialist materialism was no alternative to liberal individualism. Both were equally "backward." The world was divided into two mutually hostile camps, Islam and *jahili* society; all societies that do not follow sharia law are *jahili* societies. The liberal view that freedom of worship is all that different faiths can legitimately ask for is rejected. A society in which Muslims attend the mosque, go on hajj, fast, and pray as they are required to do is still a *jahili* society if Muslims are not governed by the sharia. Since the Koran says quite clearly that Islam is at war with *jahili* societies, this raises large issues for professedly Muslim countries that do not implement sharia, as well as any non-Muslim country that contains a substantial Muslim minority. Christian nations with the power to do so have for centuries insisted that non-Christian states should permit freedom of worship to their Christian subjects, and have sometimes gone further in insisting that Christian minorities be allowed to regulate their own affairs in a Christian fashion. Qutb's views seem to imply that any non-Muslim state that does not accord legal and institutional independence to its Muslim population is at war with Islam; this puts the Christian West in a position interestingly, but alarmingly, like that of Caribbean Indians in the eyes of their Spanish conquerors. They had argued that a native ruler who made it hard for Christians to live as Christians could rightly be deposed. It is easy to see why some critics of Qutb have been very alarmed.

Since this is a history of political ideas and not a political history in the larger sense, it would be out of order to speculate about the eventual impact of "political Islam" on international relations. Concentrating on ideas rather than their impact, we can nonetheless observe that although many commentators have said that Islam never experienced a Reformation or Enlightenment as European Christianity did, Qutb's ideas come close to a search for the rule of the saints of just the kind that animated radical Protestants in the sixteenth and seventeenth centuries. Just as those ideas sparked some extraordinary attempts to institute a religiously based utopia, so have the ideas of Qutb. What is different, obviously, is that the Protestant utopias of Reformation Europe did not reflect a history of colonization and humiliation of the kind that Qutb's ideas and those of radical Islam more generally do today. Whereas a century ago, a critic of empire might have concentrated on the danger—realized in 1914—that imperial rivalries would plunge Europe into a disastrous war between rival imperial states, today the critic must focus on the psychological and cultural animosities and deformations brought about by three centuries of European imperialism. That alone would justify continuing to take Fanon and Qutb seriously.

CHAPTER 24

Socialisms

The Impossibility of Socialism

THE TRIUMPH OF NATIONALISM over proletarian internationalism is not surprising. It is more surprising that the religious attachments that socialism was to eliminate have so effectively resisted the secularizing pressures of industrialization and urbanization. Not only national and ethnic but also confessional solidarity is more visible than proletarian solidarity. There remains a paradox. It is universally agreed that proletarian democracy and the withering away of the state are no longer live options; capitalist liberal democracy is the only game in town.[1] Yet successful modern states are expected to ensure the welfare of their citizens from cradle to grave in ways that nineteenth-century observers would unhesitatingly have described as socialist. Today the publicly funded social insurance system that constitutes the welfare state is seen as a step toward full-blown socialism only by particularly unbalanced conservative critics. The right to vote has been vastly expanded, equality of opportunity is an unchallengeable ideal, barriers of race, class, and gender to participation in politics at the highest level have been abolished; but whatever else modern liberal democracies are, they are not the dictatorship of the proletariat or heading toward the abolition of the coercive state as both Marx and the "utopian socialists" hoped.

The misuse of Marx's ideas and the role of Marxism in underpinning Soviet totalitarianism are discussed elsewhere. Here we explore what Marx and Engels dismissed as "utopian socialism" and everyone else thinks of simply as "socialism." This provides a framework within which to examine some of the varieties of reformist or welfare state socialism that were part of the advanced industrial societies' post–World War II settlement. The argument here is that "full socialism" is a practical and perhaps even a logical impossibility, but that a "pick and mix" welfare state is inescapable, even in countries that resist the idea and make a worse job of running a welfare state than they could. Full socialism imagines a form of collective economic rationality that makes sense only with an omniscient and omnipotent directing intelligence at the heart of the economy, and imagines that intelligence replacing the coercive apparatus of law and government; that comes close to self-contradiction, and if it did not, it would still presuppose an unlikely degree of spontaneous consensus on the merits of a central plan. Pick and mix welfarism resists labeling. In the absence of key socialist ambitions such as workers' self-management, the abolition of private ownership of major industrial enterprises, the replacement of "the anarchy of the market" by central planning, and so on, it is hard to think of it as socialism at all; nonetheless, it is a form of social-ism, in the sense of assigning collective responsibility for individual welfare to society and its agent the government of the day.

Failed Utopias

Almost everyone discussed in this chapter was (up to a point) a failure: Robert Owen did not create a national exchange for the products of labor, Charles Fourier did not find a backer for the phalansteries in which every type of human character would find fulfillment, Mikhail Bakunin did not succeed in abolishing the state by an act of insurrectionary violence, and Peter Kropotkin did not succeed in helping the state to wither away in favor of self-managing and noncoercively governed communities where agriculture and industry happily coexisted. Edward Bellamy would have found Boston in the year 2000 a bustling but unabashedly capitalist city, not the hierarchically organized utopia depicted in *Looking Backward*, while William Morris, who loathed Bellamy's vision of utopia and wrote *News from Nowhere* to counter it, would have found the British Parliament still meeting, and the site of the Houses of Parliament not occupied by a dunghill in a garden city.[2] The most wholly sober socialists, such as J. S. Mill, would be disappointed that self-governing cooperatives have not replaced hierarchically managed firms, and the Fabians would be distressed to find the ethos of public service not diffused throughout British society. In the United States, Eugene Debs would be affronted by the survival of capitalist enterprises, and Samuel Gompers disappointed to see that noninsurrectionary unionism had not enabled the workers to secure as big a slice of the capitalist cake as he anticipated, and that union membership was declining. The post-1945 defenders of the welfare state, some of whom thought what had been achieved by 1950 was the limit of aspiration, would be distressed by how little support there is for the ideal of a society that makes collective provision for common needs and by how far unbridled individualism still thrives.

As that list suggests, *what* non-Marxian socialists have wanted is varied, as are the routes by which they thought it could be obtained. Any reader of a history of socialism is bound to wonder what socialists have had in common and in what sense they were part of one movement. The persuasiveness of any answer depends on the illustrations that support it, so my first answer is brief and only suggestive. Socialism was born in revolt against the horrors of early industrialization. It had precursors in agrarian revolts in which a recurring theme was the equalization of landholdings, the abolition of money, and the abolition of landlords. It had distant ancestors in classical thinking. The ideal states that Aristotle considered in his *Politics* have in common a strong streak of collectivism and an antipathy to moneymaking. Plato's *Republic* offers a more mixed vision than many readers think—the guardians live in austere, propertyless communism, holding everything in common, but the remainder of the population appears to get on with the life of the farmer or the shoemaker or the boatbuilder unhampered; still, the life of the ordinary man is governed by the belly, not the mind, and is tolerated, not praised.

Those who matter hold wives and property in common. Antipathy to money is the common coin of many utopias, including More's *Utopia*, where gold is used for chamber pots and the chains of slaves; the same contempt for gold recurs in a similar form in Morris's *News from Nowhere*. These precursors are important not because they anticipate modern socialism but because they suggest that although socialists looked to the future for the realization of their ideal, and most believed in social progress, there has always been a large element of nostalgia for a vanished golden age within the socialist ideal.

The Varieties of Socialism

As a matter of history, socialism sprang out of the dislocations and unhappinesses created by early industrialization. It is not surprising that socialism appealed to the first generations of industrial workers, who had been swept off the land and into the disgusting conditions of the first industrial towns. Objectively, as regards nutrition and health, they were on average no worse off than they had been; the hideous impression the early industrial towns made on observers owed much to the fact that they crammed so many poor people together. Subjectively, the new working class was angry, disoriented, and readier to be recruited for revolution than it later became. Marx and many others believed the reverse of the truth: they thought that the developed and self-conscious proletariat would make a socialist revolution, but only the uprooted first generation has ever been ready to attempt it. Moreover, the social stratum that supplied revolutionary recruits was skilled artisans such as clockmakers who were threatened economically and psychologically by changes that made their skills obsolete and their old social ties harder to sustain. They were in a nonabusive sense reactionary, reacting against loss. The leading thinkers, as distinct from the insurrectionists themselves, were mostly writers who, by the time that they put pen to paper, were intellectuals or engaged in work of a highly intellectual kind—in Mill's case, the administration of India. Exception must be made for Marx, who was supported by Engels's reluctant employment in his family's thread mill.

The outrage caused by the squalor and brutality of early industrialization was not felt only by socialists. In *The Communist Manifesto*, Marx described what he called "feudal socialism"; and thinkers such as Thomas Carlyle and John Ruskin are often thought to be socialists. They were opponents of Victorian laissez-faire, admirers of cohesive and coherent societies, disdainful of moneymaking, and preachers of the gospel of work. Nonetheless, it is stretching the envelope to call them socialists: Carlyle admired Frederick the Great of Prussia, and Ruskin described himself as "a violent Tory of the old type," in the same breath as he described himself as a communist of the reddest stripe. One reason to exclude them is that they believed in hierarchy, and their social models were avowedly backward looking. The first reason is not quite conclusive: Saint-Simon and Edward Bellamy believed in a hierarchical system of administration. The second is more nearly so. Ruskin loathed industrialization; Carlyle's image of a morally acceptable economic order was drawn from Abbot Samson's thirteenth-century abbey of Bury St. Edmund. Most socialist theorists wanted economic progress; they saw industrialization as the key to emancipating working people from backbreaking toil and wanted technological advance harnessed to something other than the exploitation of the poor and the indulgences of the rich. Many skilled workers, on the other hand, viewed technological change with well-justified fear. Because almost the only unequivocal element in socialism is its emphasis on the idea of production for *social* purposes, little is essential to socialism beyond hostility to the unbridled reign of profit-seeking private property; but for most socialists the remedy lies in heightened industrialization, not in its repudiation.

Marx backed up his attack on capitalism with the extraordinary image of capital as a vampire sucking the lifeblood out of the worker; but all socialists thought that a world where people were allowed to accumulate all they could legally contrive, dispose of it however they wished, and were entitled to manage the labor of others, not in virtue of skill or public spirit but merely in virtue of their ownership of capital, needed reform. Not everyone was as concerned as Marx with what he called the anarchy of production: the unpredictable cycle of boom and slump. Mill deplored the division of producers into workers and managers, as did later writers in the guild socialist tradition and cooperativists generally; Morris wanted men to have fulfilling work. It was not until the last quarter of the twentieth century that the deep intractability of central planning for a complex modern economy was universally understood. Early socialists took it for granted that, what would be produced, distributed, and consumed would be everything people needed, consistent with their being able to produce it under decent conditions. The most obsessively detailed account of how this was to be done appeared in Edward Bellamy's *Looking Backward*. With hindsight, we can see that all such schemes suffered from what all forms of planning suffer from, an inability to handle unpredictable advances in technique and changes in tastes.

Marx denounced his rivals as utopian socialists. What he meant was that they believed that people could be argued into creating a better society by moral exhortation, and were squeamish about revolutionary violence. It is true that many non-Marxist socialists thought that capitalism—though the term was not used before Marx—was bad for everyone's character and that violence would make matters worse. The view of what damage capitalism did differed from one thinker to another. Marx insisted that capitalists might be perfectly decent human individuals; their misfortune was to be the agents of an inhumane system. The utopian socialists were more inclined to moralize, or psychologize; Robert Owen spoke for most in thinking that any system in which inequalities of reward were unrelated to social function was bad for those who received more than their due as well as for those who received less. The thought that we all need work, not drudgery, and to be rewarded fairly in proportion to our usefulness to everyone else unites many besides socialists; but it unites all socialists.

The Politics and Antipolitics of Socialism

To the two vexed questions of how a socialist society will be governed, and by what route socialism will be achieved, there are no agreed answers. Almost all socialists have disliked the state, especially as manifested in bureaucracies, police forces, armies, and the coercive apparatus of the state generally. This is not an observation about socialism as practiced, let alone about the Marxian dictatorship that ruled the Soviet Union for seventy-three years and has ruled China for more than six decades thus far. It is an observation about the inherent logic of the theory. The underlying thought is simple. As Rousseau said, states exist because there are conflicting interests and common interests. There are deep conflicts of interest over outcomes; the rich wish to enslave the poor and exploit them; the poor wish to expropriate the rich and live by their own efforts without paying the rich for the privilege. Nonetheless, these opposed classes share many interests, for instance, in not falling prey to invasion by their neighbours, and not suffering domestic violence and robbery. Even if class antagonisms are as sharp and irreconcilable as revolutionary socialists assert, the contending parties have shared interests. When Marx asserted that the modern state was nothing but a committee for managing the common interests of the bourgeoisie, he left unstated, though he did not always ignore, the fact that the proletariat's interests overlapped with bourgeois interests.[3]

As Rousseau, and more surprisingly Bentham, pointed out, without the state, the rich would be at the mercy of the poor; the defense of property is by its nature the defense of the haves against the have-nots. In theory the law is equally friendly to the small and the large property owner; in practice the law defends the "have a lots" against the "have very littles." The poor would certainly benefit in the short run, but probably not in the long run if they expropriated the rich; the rich would lose out in both the short and the long term. For anyone who thinks that the existence of the rich is offensive, any state that protects the rich in their possessions is a class state in the pejorative sense and should be reformed. Reform will not happen unless power is given to the less fortunate members of society, so the democratization of aristocratic or monarchical regimes is a political precondition of socialism in the eyes of anyone who does not wish to see socialism instituted by revolution. The better-off understood the argument well enough to be frightened of universal suffrage until they discovered that it led to a more reformist and gradualist working-class politics than anyone expected. In Britain, Disraeli was credited with having seen the Conservative-voting workingman "as the sculptor saw the angel in marble." It is not, with hindsight, surprising. The thought that the better-off should be willing to pay a fair price for the protection of their property is uncontentious; what the fair price is is another matter, but since the better-off want to avoid expropriation and the worse-off stand to lose from civil war, everyone has an interest in compromise. This may well mean the use of the tax system to achieve more equality than an unregulated free market would generate, but where the liberal, or the farsighted conservative, would stop there, socialists would think that this halfway house is *only* a halfway house.

The Utopian Socialists

Modern socialism begins, both in fact and in every historical account, with the trio of Robert Owen, Henri de Saint-Simon, and Charles Fourier. Saint-Simon we have seen something of in the context of the French Revolution. Owen was the first British socialist. Born in 1771, he started "adult" life as a shop assistant at the age of nine but advanced swiftly in the commercial world, until he became manager and then part owner of a cotton mill at New Lanark, in Scotland. There he put into action the "one idea" that Jeremy Bentham reckoned was all he possessed. (Bentham's low regard for Owen's theoretical capacities did not prevent him from helping to fund Owen when Owen wanted to buy out his partners.) Owen's one idea was that human nature was infinitely malleable; anyone might be given any character from the best to the worst by a suitable upbringing.[4] This might have led him to the advocacy of a society in which some benevolent force exercised total control over the inhabitants in the manner of the superintendent of Bentham's Panopticon. In fact, it led him to the creation of a community where his millworkers lived in decent cottages with good sanitation and gardens in which to grow fresh food and, when they were at work, experienced a simple monitoring system that consisted of a triangular piece of wood painted different colors on its three faces to indicate the quality of the work they were doing. Owen's emphasis was on character rather than on belief or intellectual training; different people had different inclinations—their natural bent—and different degrees of intellectual capacity. It was the creation of cooperative, dutiful, public-spirited characters that he aimed at.

The mill was highly successful while Owen paid it attention. Its success made him famous; but it also made him intellectually and politically ambitious, and he began to think of setting up a system of cooperation to embrace the entire national economy. He was distracted, too, by his increasing distaste for Christianity. The Christian insistence on original sin and its commitment to divine rewards and penalties to be meted out at the Last Judgment were incompatible with Owen's belief in the infinite malleability of character; Christianity was unsuited to modern industrial society. It may seem curious that Owen simultaneously began to think of ways of organizing an entire economy and became increasingly interested in creating small-scale utopian communities such as New Harmony in Indiana and Queenwood in Hampshire. But this was characteristic of almost all early socialists; Edward Bellamy's vision of a future world of identical towns in a classically planned landscape was atypical. Much more typical was the wish to square the circle of large-scale coordination with local autonomy, fueled by the hope that some novel form of economic organization not based on money, markets, and exchange relations—exchange involving competitors who buy cheap and sell dear—will resolve the obvious difficulties of achieving a coherent national economy while dispensing with the fear of starvation or simple coercion.

Owen began by looking for a way to cure the unemployment that struck Britain after the end of the Napoleonic Wars in 1815. He first proposed the creation of model villages where the unemployed could cultivate their own food and become self-supporting—an idea dismissed by an enraged William Cobbett as the creation of "parallelograms of paupers." Although Owen remained convinced that "spade cultivation" could perform miracles of agricultural productivity, he came to think that the new industrial order would produce such abundance that capital would become so cheap that capitalists would charge nothing for its use. In the meantime, there was the question of how to value people's labor other than by seeing what an employer was willing to pay for it. Owen, like many others, imagined a system of labor exchanges where everyone would get a receipt for the labor he or she had done and would use the receipt to secure what he or she needed through an exchange of labor tickets. It was not unlike the system familiar to anyone who has been a member of a babysitting cooperative. Applied in a more complicated setting, it was naturally a complete failure, but that is less interesting than the thought behind it; work is inevitable and can be satisfying. Everything we consume and enjoy depends partly on natural resources but mostly on human effort. The exchange of labor services reflects reality, while exchange mediated by the exchange of labor for money and money for products does not.

Owen inspired many utopian communities in the United States and elsewhere. He was personally a man of the sweetest disposition, but his reputation as a man with none of the vaulting ambitions for world revolution of Marx and his successors is not wholly deserved: at one stage, he hoped to induce the emperor of Mexico to award him two million acres of Texas on which to plant his communitarian experiments. What sets him apart from many socialists, and certainly from Marx on the one hand and Bakunin on the other, is his absolute commitment to nonviolence in bringing the socialist ideal to fruition. This is where his initial insistence on the centrality of his one idea is important. Having convinced himself that our characters "are made for us, not by us," and that society at large must create citizens with characters fit for the "new moral world" that would replace the "old immoral world" on which he had turned his back, he did not think that punishment or violence more generally was either needed or efficacious.

If Owen wanted a world in which everyone would be happier in ways that demand no effort of the imagination to understand, Charles Fourier envisaged socialism's bringing about not only a change in human nature but a change in human nature that would liberate kinds of happiness hitherto unknown and unimaginable. Fourier was slightly younger than Saint-Simon, born in 1772 and dying in 1837. He spent much of his later life waiting in a cafe, where he hoped that anyone who wished to invest in his "phalansteries" would meet him. Fourier's designs for utopian communities are in some respects not very socialist—he proposed to reward investors with 35 percent of the community's income, which is a lot more than they would make under capitalism; and he was not concerned to abolish inequality so much as to abolish poverty and especially emotional poverty. The theory underlying his design is striking. It was set out in the book he published in 1808, *The Theory of the Four Movements*. Fourier was an antimoralist; he thought traditional morality cut against the grain of human nature and was at odds with our deepest needs. Duty was a human invention, not based on the promptings of nature or the true word of God. God (a very etiolated, non-Judeo-Christian God) had imbued us with desires which, in the right social conditions, would make us wholly happy both as individuals and as members of a larger social whole. It is this that made Fourier a socialist, that is, a social-ist; at present our passions damage us, because we live in self-centered and competitive settings, in which the satisfaction of one person's desires is at odds with the satisfaction of another's. Morality, understood as a system of self-restraint, is a device for limiting the war between one person's satisfaction and another's.

The remedy was to establish associations large enough to satisfy all the emotions he had identified; at that point our passions would cease to be fissiparous, centrifugal forces and become cohesive, centripetal forces. These were the "phalansteries." He insisted that they contain 1,620 adults, to accommodate all of the 810 distinct kinds of temperament that he had identified, one man and one woman of each. Although Fourier is a pleasure to read, and conveys in a poetic fashion a strong sense of the pleasures of harmonious collective enterprise, it cannot be said that he gave a very exact account of just how harmony would replace disorder when the right number of persons of appropriately matched temperaments were assembled in the right place. His recipes for constructing the famous phalansteries were strong on the detail of where they were to be created—he was hostile to flat regions such as Belgium or Saxony, and thought the first phalansteries would need the favorable climate of southern Europe rather than the cold and rainy north—but less strong on just how the inhabitants were to cooperate. In his view of the truly progressive world, the question falls by the wayside because what is liberated in each of us is desires and energies that dovetail without calculation and self-restraint. Nineteenth-century America saw the creation of many utopian communities inspired by Fourier and his contemporaries;

some survived long enough to evolve into less utopian but economically viable communities that eventually merged into the social landscape of conventional America.

So obviously absurd were Fourier's fantastic visions of the final 8,000 years of human history that it is hard to see why his ideas appealed strongly to sober thinkers such as John Stuart Mill and had to be handled with some care even by Marx—who needed to provide his own more plausible account of how work was to be humanly satisfying in the communist future. They ignored Fourier's claim that the sea would turn into lemonade, six moons would rotate around the earth, lions become vegetarian, and more in the same vein. They seized on one central idea. This was his notion of *travail attractif*. Fourier had worked as a commercial traveler and very much disliked commerce; it is not true, but it is tempting to imagine, that he wove his psychological theories for the purpose of making work the opposite of what it was in a commercial, competitive society. It is not true, since the thrust of his argument for the phalanstery is that there is such variety in human nature that we can push the division of labor to the uttermost lengths, and instead of stupefying individuals, as Adam Smith feared they would be stupefied by being set to perform one simple repetitive task such as putting the heads on pins, we can liberate them to express their passionate natures in productive activity.

The possibly depressing implications of that thought were wonderfully counteracted by Fourier's discussion of what he called the "butterfly" passion, the passion for *papillonage*. This was the desire for variety, change of pace, change of circumstance, change of occupation. It implied that nobody should perform any task for more than an hour and a half or two hours; a fourteen-hour day was an affront to human nature and its need for variation. Set up a phalanstery where people performed associative labor in ways that met the needs of *papillonage*, and we would see the members of the phalanstery pour out into the fields and to their other tasks like men set on conquering new worlds; their productivity would be immense, and their standard of living indescribably luxurious. Marx became very grumpy in the face of all this, complaining that *real work* such as composing a symphony or writing a poem was a serious business and that Fourier had a grisette-like idea of *travail attractif*. Among the many ways in which Fourier is not the heir of Sir Thomas More, one of the most obvious is his enthusiasm for the pleasures of the flesh, both sexual and gastronomic. Indeed, one of the new sciences that the progressive world will develop will be that of gastrosophy; like their Spartan forebears, the members of the phalanx will eat in common, but there will be nothing Spartan about their diet.

Throughout this book, I have been cautious about ascribing influence. Nonetheless, Fourier had avowed followers, not only among nineteenth-century utopians in the United States but among thinkers and writers on the anarchist fringe of postwar socialism, including André Breton. He influenced the so-called *situationistes* of the late 1960s, and the famous slogan from the Paris *événements* of 1968, "l'imagination au pouvoir," is more Fourierist than Marxist. Like the reaction of the students of 1968 to hi-tech France, Fourier's reaction to the newly industrializing world was ambivalent in ways Marx's was not. His enthusiasm was for manual labor, and usually quite simple manual labor. Work is not the curse of Adam, but done in moderation, and as a form of self-expression, a pleasure to even the grandest of mankind. As he observed, the Sun King, Louis XIV himself, had enjoyed mending shoes. If he was not passionate for modern industry, he was, in his own words, a fanatic for feats of productivity, leaving it to readers today who are seduced by his vision to think how we might reconcile hi-tech and self-expression.

Fourier could not know what the arrival of the machine age would mean. Until late in the nineteenth century, few people worked in enterprises employing more than a dozen or two workers; factories in the modern sense were a late development. The mass workplaces were coal mines or spinning mills and weaving sheds, not engineering works; it has often been said that if Engels had worked in Birmingham—full of engineering workshops where a handful of skilled workers plied their craft—rather than Manchester—where women and children worked in the cotton mills—he and Marx would have given a very different account of industrial capitalism. Engels, better than Marx, understood that their hopes for *travail attractif* had to be revisited in the light of the productivity that modern industry afforded. "Abandon autonomy all you who enter here," so Engels said, was the motto above the door of the automated factory. Freedom from the backbreaking toil of the peasant was the gift of the machine; but that freedom implied submission to the managerial and organizational needs of factory production. The liberation we can expect *in* work is a diminution of "necessary labor"; "free time" is the increased leisure we would enjoy in consequence. In prosperous Western countries, we have achieved it; but we have not created a world of *travail attractif*. Freedom *from* work is not the same thing as freedom *in* work.

Among the less likely admirers of Fourier's work was John Stuart Mill. His enthusiasm was cautious, but it rested on something solid. Mill thought that socialism in some shape was necessary to develop the capacity of the working classes for free and equal citizenship; and he assumed that as they became more educated, they would demand it. His argument was carefully spelled out, because he wanted to gain a hearing for socialism in the 1870s, when socialism was associated with the anticlericalism and violence of the Paris Commune, and with Bakunin's short-lived insurrection in Lyons. He also wanted to argue that the historical moment was ripe for new forms of social, economic, and political organization, summed up as socialism. He had defended the view that slavery was an appropriate institution in the ancient world and instrumental in propelling the human race on a progressive course, but quite intolerable now; and he defended the rule of the British in India as a temporary despotism whose aim was to bring the Indian people to a level of political development where intelligent self-government became possible. The question was whether Victorian England was mature enough to experiment with socialism. His answer was cautious; socialism as he understood it could be achieved in a piecemeal manner, but there was a great deal that could be done in the interim to reform the present system of private ownership.

Mill's account of socialism gave it a political rather than an economic flavor. He wanted self-government in the workplace, not an economic rationality that the market could not provide. He did not share Marx's hatred of the anarchy of production. He described himself as having become less of a democrat and more of a socialist as he grew older, but this is misleading. What he meant was that simple majority rule is a bad basis for modern politics, but that self-government in the workplace will help create an intelligent electorate. He did not deceive himself about the likelihood that the British would move rapidly toward the system of producer cooperatives that he wanted to see at the heart of modern industry. Nor did he envisage the abolition of private property; he argued for the introduction of inheritance taxes as a way of spreading ownership and alleviating inequality, and for something like land nationalization in Ireland, to achieve equity between landlord and tenant, but the cooperatives that he envisaged replacing existing capitalist enterprises would be owned by the workers and compete in the marketplace. Orthodox Marxists dismiss the idea as "worker capitalism," not socialism.

The logic was simple and consistent. Mankind was capable of self-sacrifice and cooperation for violent and destructive action in war; but a more enlightened humanity could bring the same moral commitment to production rather than destruction. This was one of the durable insights of Auguste Comte, who was otherwise an enemy to freedom and individuality. Once morality enters the sphere of production, issues besides productivity come to the fore. One is the relationship of owner and worker. For Mill it was an affront to human dignity always to be in the position of taking orders and never in the position of deciding one's own fate by free and rational discussion. A well-paid wage slave is a slave. A hard-up cooperator is a free man, even if poor. Mill, in essence, argued that the crucial distinction between being a taker of orders and sometimes at least giving the orders to oneself was a distinction that permeated not only political arrangements but economic ones. If modern men and women are to be citizens, not subjects, they can hardly leave their liberty at the factory gate.

He was too realistic to see most work as pure, free self-expression, even potentially, and too much of an empiricist to see the results of industrial cooperation as the free self-expression of the human race. He was never going to be the poet of production that Marx was. Nonetheless, he had a strong sense of the difference between spending one's life as a taker of orders and spending one's life deciding with other free agents what paths to follow. Cooperators would be better able to implement the complex form of democracy that he envisaged as the political future suited to a developed human race, operating a state that would not wither away as Marx and Engels hoped, but that would become a facilitating state rather than a commanding one.

Anarchism

Socialists must be at best ambivalent about the state; they admire cooperation and dislike coercion, and think that most states have excessively favored the well-off and the state's own agents. Reformist socialism accepts the existence of a welfare state; and revolutionary socialism wants to seize the state apparatus to implement its vision. Pure "state hatred," goes further than that; it is the essence of the anarchist strain within socialism. Even here, one must be cautious; the sweetness of character that Prince Peter Kropotkin displayed under all circumstances makes it misleading to describe him as a state hater *tout court*, since he was hardly capable of hating anyone or anything. And there are many anarchists besides socialist anarchists; in the late twentieth century, anarcho-capitalism was more common in academic circles than anarcho-socialism; in 1974 Robert Nozick's *Anarchy, State, and Utopia* defended anarcho-capitalism with great verve, to the dismay of critics at all points on the conventional political spectrum. Here we can content ourselves with anarcho-socialists alone.

The connection between anarchism and socialism is, at a rudimentary level, obvious. The state exists to protect the haves against the have-nots; if there were no haves on the one side or have-nots on the other, there would be no need for a state. One might object, as every critic of the anarchist view of the world has done, that the state exists not only to protect the property of owners from the depredations of nonowners but to protect the physically weaker from the physically stronger, and to prevent sexual predation as well as simple assault and battery. At that point the real argument commences, because any anarchist who wishes to imagine a stateless world must go on to explain how her preferred form of social organization will eliminate the interpersonal violence that states must, as a bare minimum, control.

Michael Bakunin was perhaps the most prominent modern anarchist; he was a Russian aristocrat, born in 1814, who rebelled against the stifling piety and brutality of the czarist regime under Nicholas I. Although he read Fichte and Hegel, he was less of a philosopher than Marx, whom he knew well and thoroughly disliked, thinking him an authoritarian to his fingertips. He admired the French mutualist Pierre-Joseph Proudhon and was not a natural economist like Marx. He was, rather, a poet of revolt, not literally like Heinrich Heine, but in the sense that his allegiances were to continuous movement. Unlike Marx, he did not think that the revolutionary must first strengthen the state to create a rational society that will function without the aid of the state; instead, he must destroy the state at once, to liberate the energies that will create a new society for free individuals. Bakunin is best remembered for the aphorism "destruction is also a creative act," and he was bravely, or recklessly, unflinching about trying to destroy the old order to leave room for a new order to flourish. As a result, he spent many years in jail. This ruined his health long before his death in 1876.

The ultimate goal was that of Marx and his followers, a society in which freely associated workers would manage their own productive activities, unexploited by capitalists and uncoerced by governments; and although Bakunin was himself too much of an individualist to submit to the demands of any organization, his ethics and aspirations were collectivist. Although this was his own characterization, it does not do complete justice to the distance between his ideas and those of Marx. For Bakunin was also influenced by Proudhon's mutualist ethics, and mutualism is not collectivist, except by contrast with the individualist anarchism of Max Stirner or the anarcho-capitalism of modern American writers. Underlying mutualism was the thought that what we need is justice; and justice is inextricably tied to the idea of a fair exchange. The injustice of capitalism is that workers are coerced into arrangements in which they will be robbed, forced to contribute more than they receive in exchange; hence Proudon's answer to his question "What is property?" was "Property is theft." There is a hard-to-describe distinction between socialists who seek justice between individuals and those who emphasize the rational allocation of work and reward and are not interested in rights and justice. So far as Marx's views can be given a clear interpretation, he belongs to the second side of this division and Proudhon to the first. Bakunin belonged to the first while thinking he belonged to the second. In any event, Bakunin's talent was not for analytical work of the sort that Marx excelled at; it was for unmasking every last sign of authoritarianism and encouraging the spirit of revolt in the working class, for whose allegiance he and Marx—along with many others— were competing. One tribute to his persuasiveness as an insurrectionist was that Marx moved the headquarters of the First International from London to The Hague, and then to New York, to frustrate the attempts of Bakunin's followers to gain control of it.

The best-known of Bakunin's successors was Peter Kropotkin. "The anarchist prince" began his political education as a member of the Corps of Pages to Czar Alexander III and spent most of his life in exile in western Europe. Kropotkin gave intellectual substance to Bakunin's rebelliousness, and he remains the most attractive figure in the anarchist pantheon. He wrote at a time when the Russian populists had resorted to so-called propaganda by the deed, which is to say a campaign of assassination directed at the czar's police and ultimately at the czar himself. Kropotkin was not a pacifist; he thought that in Russian conditions violence against state authority was justified in self-defense against the repression of all reformist, let alone revolutionary, ideas. Outside such conditions he considered violence self-defeating. What he brought to anarchism was the intelligence of a trained scientist, and in *Mutual Aid* he systematically demolished the pretensions of social Darwinism. So far from underpinning capitalist competition and a social policy of "devil take the hindmost," Darwinian evolutionary theory revealed the naturalness of cooperation and mutual assistance throughout the animal kingdom. If such cooperation was natural, it followed that the aggression and competition that states claimed to prevent was a perversion and would wither away once mankind took charge of its own life and began to live in a naturally cooperative fashion. This did not require an overarching state or whatever entity Marx supposed might organize production. Rather, loose federations of communities could evolve whatever systems they need to facilitate the exchange of the means of existence. Like many socialists, Kropotkin looked backward more readily than he looked forward. He optimistically expected that skilled workers could survive the competition from factory production and that—much as in Fourier's utopian vision—we could all change occupations as we felt inclined, and could simultaneously engage in agriculture and craftwork. When the Russian Revolution of 1917 allowed him to return to his native Russia, Kropotkin was horribly disappointed by the tyranny that Lenin's Bolsheviks had established, a tyranny that was particularly hostile to all forms of anarchism.

Bellamy and Morris

Although many socialists have thought that the state, and the activity of politics, would wither away in favor of rational self-management, there is a strain in socialist theory, to say nothing of socialist practice, that emphasizes the importance of centralized economic control, even where this is not conventionally *political*. One instance in the realm of theory is one of the least likable utopias ever composed, Edward Bellamy's *Looking Backward*. Bellamy was a Massachusetts journalist who in the early 1880s was deeply depressed by the horrors of industrial life in New England, both by the conditions of work and by the social and economic inequality of the new industrial system. He opens *Looking Backward* by comparing nineteenth-century America to an overcrowded coach being hauled over a rutted and dangerous road, not by horses but by men.[5] People would fall off the coach and be set to pulling the remaining passengers on their way; a few would scramble back on and displace others. Those on board were terrified of falling off, and those below were exhausted, dispirited, and angry.

The remedy was strict egalitarianism, and his utopian novel of 1887, *Looking Backward*, gave an account of such an egalitarian society. It is a variation on the theme of Rip van Winkle; the book's title encapsulates the plot: a man goes to sleep in Boston in 1887 and wakes in the year 2000; he is then taken around utopia by Dr. Leete, the doctor who has awakened him from his coma. Interestingly, the egalitarian utopia is not very egalitarian at all. There is a leader, who is simultaneously commander in chief and managing director; he has the omniscience of a Platonic guardian and is a precursor of "engine Charlie Wilson," who thought that running General Motors and running the United States were much the same thing. The society is not uniform: there are differences in tastes and education, and in the work everyone does. The equality to which the society is committed is equality of purchasing power, though "purchasing" is something of a misnomer. Everyone has a card that is annually charged with the same number of credits for everyone; and there are stores—identical throughout the whole of the United States and in every city—where goods are displayed, priced in so many credits; shop assistants may elucidate the character of the goods on display, but must not attempt to influence the buyers. Bellamy loathed shops, advertising, and competition.

The truly clever thought is that there is a free market in labor. Since everyone receives the same number of credits, wages or the "credit per hour of labor" rate, are adjusted to attract the numbers needed to work in a given occupation. Disagreeable manual occupations would receive few takers unless the hours worked were few; agreeable professions take their toll in longer hours. Goods whose production requires people to do jobs that human beings ought not to do are not produced at all. That thought is morally compelling: we ought not to demand what we would not be prepared to make for ourselves, a point that vegetarians rely on when rebuking their carnivorous friends for eating animals they would be too squeamish to kill. Whether this is really a socialist vision is debatable; Bellamy called it *nationalism* because, he said, Americans believed that persons who called themselves socialists were bearded atheists, given to adultery and worse; but the crucial elements in most socialisms are in place: cooperation replaces competition, the economy is demonetarized, and labor becomes the direct measure of value. Although the manager in chief seems very like a general, there is universal peace because the causes of war have been abolished. Nor is the socialist slogan "He who does not work, neither shall he eat" neglected; the idle go to jail and live on bread and water until they repent.

This vision of tidy, rational, mechanical good order enraged William Morris, who wrote *News from Nowhere* in just three weeks to oppose

Bellamy. *Looking Backward* was enormously successful, second only to *Uncle Tom's Cabin* among nineteenth-century best sellers. Bellamy Societies sprang up to discuss the book and to promote its message. One particular oddity of the book, however, was that, for a socialist tract, it painted a picture of an astonishingly privatized, middle-class world. The inhabitants of Boston in the year 2000 pride themselves on the fact the need for public concerts had been obviated by something very like a cable audio system; Bellamy had an impressive ability to imagine twentieth-century inventions. In the same way, the community restaurants that have made kitchens in individual houses obsolete serve their guests in private rooms; the thought that an important aspect of socialism is that we shall better enjoy each other's company passed Bellamy by. Morris reacted by painting a rural idyll; his characters walk slowly up the Thames from London, observing in the distance the ruins of the old Parliament. As they walk, they are passed by barges propelled by a mysterious "Force" that leaves neither odor nor exhaust; the barges carry claret from Bordeaux, since one achievement of socialism in Morris's eyes will be that the workers will have been weaned off beer. They see a small boy bowling a golden hoop, since, as in More's *Utopia*, gold and jewelry are regarded as children's trinkets rather than objects of value. At the end of their journey, the walkers arrive at a harvest supper at Morris's own house at Kelmscott. Again, the socialist ambition to leapfrog over capitalism and create abundance without capitalists, lawyers, politicians, and police draws its emotional strength from a bucolic, backward-looking image of the good life. Morris understood everything that Marx had to offer; he read *Capital* from end to end and on occasion professed to subscribe to Marx's economics. He was not unhappy with the thought that a violent, but short-lived and on the whole good-natured, revolution would be needed to bring about socialism in Britain. But if one asks what fuels the socialist imagination, it is the attractive features of the old world that capitalist industrialization was destroying.

Fabianism and the Welfare State

The practically minded persons who founded the Fabian Society in Britain in the 1880s hardly fit the category of "utopian," other than in Marx's abusive sense of the term. Indeed, even making allowances for such of their number as H. G. Wells, they were hardheaded, nonutopian, and initially not socialist either. Nonetheless, they provided the intellectual backing for a labor movement and a political party dedicated to the common ownership of the means of production, distribution, and exchange, and they represent one important strand of European socialism, whose absence from American politics is one of the most striking differences between the opposite shores of the Atlantic. The label "Fabian" refers to the tactics of the Roman general Fabius, nicknamed "cunctator," or "delayer," for his refusal to engage in pitched battle until Hannibal's forces were weakened by fighting so far from home; his methods were disliked by the Romans, but they defeated Hannibal and earned Fabius an honored place in history. The Fabians were believers in national efficiency and social justice rather than in the Marxian or Fourierist dream that work could turn into self-expression, but their view of social justice was squarely anticapitalist and at odds with the view that whatever the market decides is right. They wanted people to be rewarded according to their social usefulness, and to avoid both useless toil and needless unemployment. The key figures in the Fabian Society were Sidney and Beatrice Webb, who gained a real ascendancy over reformist opinion in early twentieth-century Britain by marshaling research on the living conditions of the worst-off British and offering careful recipes for improving them. Beatrice's description of herself and her husband as "bourgeois, bureaucratic, and benevolent" epitomizes the moral basis of Fabianism.

Its natural offspring is the welfare state, though many others contributed to its creation, conservatives among them. But the creation of the welfare state was important in underappreciated ways. The most obvious, well-understood way was that successful welfare programs reduce the threats to the legitimacy of a state that directs a capitalist industrial society; in effect, all know they are insured against the hazards of everyday life such as ill health, unemployment, and, in due course, old age. Welfare programs may also expose the state to discontent and delegitimation in the very circumstances that the welfare state is intended to deal with, since expenditure on unemployment pay, health care, and the like increases when the economy is in trouble and tax revenues are lower; nobody likes an insurance scheme that cannot pay its claims. A welfare state is distinctively different from its liberal and conservative predecessors. The legitimating theory of the liberal state in prewelfare state times was that the state secures us against aggression at the hands of foreigners and fellow nationals; it defines and enforces property rights and facilitates exchange, including the exchange of labor for wages; it imposes on the citizens only as many duties and only as large a tax burden as strictly necessary to sustain such a state. More conservative views of the state's functions included the maintenance of religious institutions that might or might not save our souls but that would socialize us into obedience to the powers that be. Montesquieu, Guizot, and Tocqueville saw how many tasks civil society might perform unobtrusively and without coercion, allowing the state to take minimal responsibility for the welfare of its citizens; citizens should secure their own welfare, not be nursed, employed, or, for the most part, educated by the state. Voluntary organizations should attend to such tasks.

Nonetheless, the provision of relief in time of famine or pestilence has always been inescapable. Whatever ideological commitments a state professed, the need to provide a bare subsistence overrode them. The reluctance (or inability) of the British state to help its famine-stricken Irish subjects in the 1840s has haunted it for almost two centuries, and the lesson was not lost on other governments. What was novel from the late nineteenth century onward was the widespread sense that national governments had a general, and not merely a residual, obligation to ensure the welfare of their citizens "from cradle to grave." Whether this was so theorized in the first instance is doubtful; Bismarck's introduction of health, unemployment, and old-age insurance in Prussia in the 1880s was the carrot that accompanied the stick of the "exceptional laws" that outlawed socialist political organizing and the political activities of trade unions. In the absence of social insurance the German state might have faced the direct assault of the organized working class; the provision of such benefits diminished discontent and allowed the state to get away with political repression that might otherwise have been impossible.

In other contexts, what emerged was a view of the state as the only entity that could provide social insurance to people who could not obtain it on the open market. The terminology of the British and American systems suggests what is at issue: on the one side of the Atlantic, "national insurance"; on the other, "social security." The first describes the mechanism and the second describes the purpose. It is important to appreciate both what a break it marks with the older liberal view of the state and how small a step toward socialism. It secures a bridgehead, but the bridgehead has everywhere turned out to mark the limit of the advance. To revert briefly to the Fabians, their conception of national efficiency was bound up with the thought that a national economy is just that— national; this is very far from the liberal view that an economy is the sum of the interactions of individuals connected by market relations. The liberal accepts the need for a state and, in the modern world, a nation-state. Nonetheless, individual welfare is not part of a national project; making it one is, to borrow the title of F. A. von Hayek's jeremiad, taking a long stride down "the road to serfdom."

Few thinkers have defended the welfare state with the flair with which left- and right-wing opponents have attacked it, but two defenses are worth noting. The first insists that the welfare state must be more than an insurance arrangement if it is to work. We all see the point of belonging to an insurance scheme large enough to spread risks and reap economies of scale; and we all accept the drawbacks of a uniform scheme that is not tailored exactly to our individual needs for the sake of simplicity. From life insurance to motor insurance, the same logic applies. However, people who know they are very unlikely to be ill and unemployed or can easily afford to pay for their children's education will think that the welfare state is a bad bargain if it is nothing more than an insurance policy. They do not need all the health, unemployment, and medical insurance the state insists on providing. Because they are good risks, they could insure themselves as individuals more cheaply than the state can do it for them; and they will resent paying the state's taxes on top of the premiums they pay to the private providers of other benefits. If we are self-centered and self-interested, and look only at our own pay-off, the welfare state will lose its legitimacy. We must be moved by at least a certain amount of altruism and be happy to make contributions that have a low chance of doing us, individually, very much good. Richard Titmuss, a postwar British sociologist, argued that the welfare state needed not only generalized benevolence to sustain it but an expanded sense of social justice, so that we could come to see such things as unemployment pay as more than statutory entitlements; we should see them as dictates of justice.

Unemployment benefits are not only insurance but the recognition of a right; workers run the risk of being unemployed. If they did not, the economy would function less efficiently, so running that risk is part of their contribution to the economy, for which unemployment benefit is payment. It is not charity, not only insurance, but something owed. This does not mean that there is no place for giving to others out of the goodness of our hearts. The relationship between donors and beneficiaries, what Titmuss called "the gift relationship," is exemplified by giving blood in blood donation drives. Donors make a gift to anonymous recipients, and do it it out of benevolence. Public institutions, if not a full-fledged welfare state, are needed to make this altruistic motivation effective; but only when we see the state as an intermediary that allows us to meet the needs of strangers is a welfare state wholly legitimate.[6] The ideal-typical liberal state was a night watchman state that protected person and property, enforced contracts, and facilitated economic activity, but respected its citizens' freedom by otherwise leaving them to care for themselves; it rested on an ethos of self-reliance and individuality that a liberal civil society fostered. The similarly idealized model of a conservative state added the tasks of paternalistically caring for the physical and spiritual welfare of its subjects, and saw the enforcement of the morality on which its legitimacy rested as a proper task of the political state. The welfare state has always been vulnerable to the charge that it was reinstating the paternalist conservative state or, in the alternative, that because it was extending the liberal state beyond its proper boundaries, it would undermine its own social foundations. We need only recall how hostile Tocqueville was to the most minimal programs of poor relief during the 1848 revolution.

One response to these anxieties is to argue that modern citizenship exists in more than one dimension. A running theme of this book has been that the image of the active citizen has always been in competition with that of the well-conducted, well-managed but essentially obedient subject. If the modern welfare state creates a new sort of citizenship, we might hope that the new sort of citizen will support it, by more than their taxes. In the 1950s T. H. Marshall provided a three-stage account of citizenship to make the point.[7] The first claim for full membership of society was the demand for equality before the law; a man might have no vote, and no guarantee of employment, but he would not be a legal nullity. The next two steps are the claim to the vote and thus political citizenship, and lastly the claim to the various social rights that the welfare state confers and thus to social citizenship. The logical order was not invariably the chronological order; before full universal suffrage was universal in western Europe, there was a growing consensus that everyone should have access to education, health care, decent housing, and a basic income when unemployed and in retirement. The state is the only instrumentality capable of securing these, and taxation the only way to secure resources that can be taken from us in small amounts over a working life and redistributed to the needy in childhood, ill health, old age, or whatever. Many variants on state and private provision have been visible; but in most countries private provision depends heavily on the public sector for support.

Nonetheless, the welfare state marks no great advance in the direction of socialism, for several reasons. Its egalitarian elements are more minimal than either its defenders or its critics think; it does not set out to make the poor richer and the rich poorer, which is a central element in socialism, but to help people to provide for themselves in sickness while they enjoy good health, to put money aside to cover unemployment while they are in work, and to have adults provide for the education of their own and other people's children, expecting those children's future taxes to pay in due course for the pensions of their parents' generation.

These are devices for shifting income across different stages in life, not for shifting income across classes. Another distinct difference is that social insurance does not aim to transform work and working relations; employers and employees pay taxes at a level they would not have done in the nineteenth century, but owners are not expropriated, profits are not illegitimate, cooperativism does not replace hierarchical management.

It is easy to lurch too far in either of two opposite directions: either to insist that nothing has changed, because welfare state capitalist economies are capitalist economies, or to insist that the modern world has utterly changed, because modern governments spend upward of a third of their countries' national income, and tax their citizens to an extent that would have been thought confiscatory 150 years ago, committing themselves in return to the "cradle to grave" security of their citizens. Certainly, the *politics* of welfare state capitalism raises different questions from the politics of previous economic and social systems. Similarities must be conceded, too: Athenian democracy provided assistance to the widows and children of Athenians fallen in battle, and modern states have often begun their welfare activities by looking after war widows, and reaching out from that starting point. Still, the capacity of the state to dispose of so much of a country's income and the capacity of the economy to generate so many resources over and above the subsistence requirements of the population make a profound difference. If "welfarism" is so diluted a form of socialism that it is not socialist at all, it has proved a durable solution to the threat of violent class war that both Europe and the United States faced from the 1880s to the 1940s.

Humanist Marxism and the Rediscovery of Civil Society

"Welfarism" poses two interesting questions. These were raised by the humanist Marxist movement of the 1950s and 1960s, as well as by radical liberals and neoconservative or neoliberal critics of the postwar welfare state. They were also raised by political thinkers influenced by Hannah Arendt, and as hard to place on the political spectrum as she. The first question is whether the welfare state has taken the politics out of politics; the second, whether new forms of political association might revive political life or reinvigorate communal life in ways that amount to new forms of political life.

These questions coincide in a focus on the idea of civil society. Marx, as we saw, borrowed from Hegel the thought that the state—the coercive, lawmaking, rule-setting mechanism—could be contrasted with civil society—the economic and social relationships that gave society its vitality. The young Marx imagined the state being absorbed by civil society in such a way that social and economic relationships would be spontaneously and noncoercively self-governing. Nothing is more obvious or more painful to an admirer of the young Marx than the extent to which the Communist parties of the Soviet bloc were bureaucratic, corrupt, conservative, and a joke in execrable taste against Marx's youthful dreams. The "humanist" strain in Marx's early writings was known to scholars in the 1920s and 1930s when his unpublished and partly published writings were edited by David Riazanov in Moscow. This Hegelian, philosophical, and speculative work was hard enough to square with Marx's own later writings, but it was quite impossible to square with the Stalinist view that Marx had produced a historical science—historical materialism—and a methodological system valid in all realms of thought—dialectical materialism. Marx would have thought this pretentious nonsense; Stalin would have murdered Marx.

In the 1960s, and in the West, it was the sense that "things drive men" that was uppermost in the minds of critics who despised the state socialism of the communist bloc but despised capitalism too. It also attracted writers who had moved away from Marx's concern with the irrationality of the economic system as a whole to the particular miseries of everyday working life: the tedium of white-collar work and the mind-sapping boredom of work on an assembly line. Philosophically adept critics such as Herbert Marcuse held on to Marx's central insight, and taught a generation of student radicals to denounce the System. We were governed by It.

The difficulty was the absence of a plausible politics to go with the social analysis. Marcuse briefly imagined an alliance of students, intellectuals, ethnic minorities, and Third World revolutionaries leading us into transcendence, but this was only an intoxicating image; it bore no relation to Marx's view that capitalism itself would create its own gravediggers by building up an industrial proletariat able and willing to build socialism. What ended wishful thinking and abortive attempts to bring imagination to power was not a serious argument against such hankerings but two decades of high inflation, industrial unrest, and a widespread resentment of the levels of taxation required to sustain the modern welfare state. The return of low inflation and a period of economic growth did much to take discontent off the boil, but nothing to build a better understanding of the social contract on which the welfare state was based, and nothing to revive the old hankerings after new forms of social cooperation and industrial management.

Two things ensured that the socialist dream remains just that. The first is the implosion of the Soviet bloc during the late 1980s. The critics who had said for many years that a failure to build the institutions of civil society within the communist carapace would bring about the collapse of the communist regimes of Eastern Europe turned out to be right. Attempts to build socialism with a human face were suppressed by Soviet tanks in 1956 and 1968; and regimes that had depended for their legitimacy on the memory of liberation by the Red Army at the end of World War II found their legitimacy eroded as official corruption disillusioned everyone who encountered it, while West Germany emerged as a byword for prosperity and good government. The Marxian ideal of bottom-up self-government was more obviously at home in the American Midwest than in the exploitative top-down bureaucracy of a failed state such as Ceaușescu's Romania. The extraordinary thing was that the final implosion of "actually existing socialism" was virtually bloodless. It was less surprising that there was no sudden surge of prosperity, no sudden leap into pluralist democracy. The theorists of civil society who had said that democracy required a social infrastructure that would inculcate the habits—Tocqueville's *moeurs*—that sustained cooperative relations, the rule of law, and the like were right. Conversely, skeptics who thought the theorists of civil society underestimated the need for an effective state to make those habits worth acquiring could point to the way in which the collapse of socialist states too often led to kleptocracy and cronyism rather than capitalist liberal democracy. True though it is that efficient and accountable government respectful of its citizens' rights and a heavily regulated market economy are the only basis of a secure twenty-first-century future, not everyone understands this, and not everyone's short-term self-interest is neatly aligned with the long-term welfare of her or his society. A banker who knows full well that his bank will go under in eighteen months' time may know equally well that he can extract many millions of dollars from it before it does. In states such as Russia, seventy-five years of a combination of state terrorism and individual selfishness led naturally enough to the rise of a kleptocracy. One may believe devoutly in the truth of *après moi le deluge*, but the crucial words are "after me."

The second aspect of the demise of the socialist ideal has been less often commented on; Sombart was right about why there was no socialism in early twentieth-century America, and wrong in thinking there ever would be. Most of what socialists wanted could be had within a capitalist framework, not only because welfare state capitalism provided a level of prosperity and security that nobody in the nineteenth century and few before 1950 believed possible, but new forms of occupational freedom emerged that nobody had predicted. Late twentieth-century industrial society turned into something very unlike its nineteenth-century self. It "ran on thin air." Gone were the production lines satirized in Charlie Chaplin's *Modern Times*; good ideas counted more than organization, and start-up firms could form, dissolve, reform, and evaporate in months. Of course, they eventually created something more tangible than their ideas; many trucks and automobiles came off assembly lines, and much "low-value-added heavy metal bashing" went on out of sight in the Third World, as did a lot of drudgery in areas of the United States far away from the commentators on the two coasts. Nonetheless, socialism's hankering for *travail attractif*, work that is almost indistinguishable from play, has to some extent been met within capitalism, and the people best able to take advantage of it are highly educated young people who would have been the radical social critics in other times.

What Marx thought of as "unproductive labor," which did not directly result in the production of usable objects, which has always played a prominent role in the economy, now plays a more prominent role than directly productive labor. Marx could not imagine that capitalists and their political helpers would decide that it was in their own interests to reduce the amount of grinding toil that workers endured. He focused on the grinding toil. The most moving pages of *Capital* describe the horrors of overwork across the board, from seamstresses in sweatshops to signalmen working dangerously long shifts on the railroads. Such work is not repulsive if it is not excessive in amount and allows those who do it a degree of autonomy in determining how and at what pace to do it; Marx assumed that neither condition could be met under capitalism. There is plenty of drudgery still, but it is not universal and is a lot less repulsive in a white-collar setting. Working in a call center is no fun, but much office work is interesting in itself and provides social interaction; conversely, long-distance truck driving removes those who dislike too much social interaction from its burdens, but the work is interesting and affords more autonomy than many grander occupations. In short, the idea that *travail attractif* is a utopian aspiration in the abusive sense of the term is false, but so is the idea that a change in the ownership of the means of production is essential to its achievement. Technological change, the leeway allowed by improvements in productivity, the success of trade unions in making management behave more or less humanely, and the varied tastes prevalent in different societies and sections of society make more difference than the ownership of capital.

We should end on a cautious note. Human beings are historical creatures, moved by reminiscence as much as by hopes for a far future. To announce as aggressively as this chapter has done that one of those hopes must be abandoned invites refutation in much the way that commentators invited refutation when they wrote about the inevitability of secularization immediately before large parts of the world embarked on the desecularization of politics. Still, one set of socialist aspirations has run its course: the belief that public ownership of the means of production and distribution was indispensable to prosperity, and the first step toward making the workplace humane and interesting, is no longer tenable. This does not mean that capitalism in its present-day European, Chinese, or American form constitutes the end of history; we should hope devoutly that it does not.

CHAPTER 25

Marxism, Fascism, Dictatorship

Totalitarianism, Stalinism, Fascism, and Irrationalism

THIS CHAPTER BEGINS BY recapitulating some of the anxieties about mass irrationalism that we touched on in chapter 23, and their invocation to explain the dictatorships that disfigured European politics in the middle of the last century. It then moves on to the distortion of Marx's ideas that underpinned the rule of Stalin and the Communist Party of the Soviet Union before turning to fascism, in its German and Italian forms. To do justice to some interesting thinkers, we should distinguish sharply between *supporting* irrationalist politics and *analyzing* the place of irrational attachments in our political lives. Taking the wickedness and irrationality of Nazism for granted, I try to do some justice to the intelligence of Georges Sorel, who might be thought to have paved the way for irrationalism, left and right. Finally, we return for the last time to the issue of soft despotism and the fear that if we avoid the horrors of Stalinism and Nazism, we may succumb to the kind of total social control envisaged by Aldous Huxley in *Brave New World*. Many critics have thought that Orwell's *1984* turned out to be less prophetic than *Brave New World*.[1] Indeed, Huxley was himself surprised that reality was so swiftly emulating his novel.

"Totalitarianism" must always be read here as if encumbered with

quotation marks and understood as shorthand for "a set of political phenomena that includes dictatorship; one-party rule; systematic violence
against enemies, including but not confined to political dissidents; the
use of state terror as an everyday instrument of government; the destruction or politicization of all institutions save those created or run by the
ruling party; and the systematic blurring of the line between the public
and the private; all this in the interests of securing the total control of a
political elite over every aspect of life." The quotation marks also indicate
skepticism both about the idea that the concept of totalitarianism picks
out something common to and distinctive of the Soviet and Nazi regimes
of the last century and about the overuse of the term in other contexts.

Irrationalism

After World War II it was sometimes said that political theory had
died; one reason for saying so was that would-be reasonable politicians
had been powerless before the waves of irrationality that had swept over
the world. There was no point asking how we should govern ourselves;
nobody would listen. The masses would always prefer the rabble-rousing
of the demagogue. The twentieth century was the century of the cult
of leadership, the cult of the party, government by terror and the concentration camp, the misuse of modern technology for primitive purposes—conquest and mass murder prominent among them. Discussing
political morality in the face of these forces was as useless as discussing
meteorological ethics in the face of a tidal wave. The paradox is that
two of the three paradigms of totalitarianism—Russian Stalinism, German Nazism, and Italian Fascism—that have been analyzed as expressions of mass irrationality were deeply attractive to intellectuals. Even
Nazism had its intellectual defenders, including, briefly, the philosopher
Martin Heidegger and, for much longer, the legal theorist Carl Schmitt.
Marxism, even in its most debased Stalinist form, was an intricate social,
economic, and political theory. Nazism was for the most part untheo-
retical and anti-intellectual; but Italian Fascism drew on some far from
negligible analyses of the nature of mass society, the fragility of capital-

ist economies, the failures of democracy, and the disappointments of modernity in general. Because "fascist" became a term of abuse rather than analysis, the strengths of the political sociology and political psychology on which fascist movements drew have become obscured.

While political theory was said to have died, the century was also said to be the century of ideology, "ideology" in this context meaning a set of ideas whose logic is their capacity to incite their hearers to action, rather than provoke them to thought. The connection to the supposed irrationality of the masses is plain. Walter Lippmann maintained that public opinion was pictorial rather than intellectual, and action-inspiring systems of ideas operate in the realm of painting vivid pictures.[2] This action may be in defense of the status quo, in pursuit of a mythical past, or of a utopian future; ideologies may be more or less secular, more or less chiliastic and millenarian; they *must* be action oriented. The context in which arguments about the nature of ideology occurred was the rise and fall of totalitarian regimes, and the role of intellectuals in creating the ideologies that helped sustain them. Intellectuals seemed not merely to fall for nonsense as uncritically as anyone but to be especially prone to create new forms of it. The explanation of totalitarianism that appealed to many sociologists was that it was one of those irruptions of the irrational into political life that have periodically been unleashed by rapid social change, in this case the disorientation of the masses by swift and chaotic industrialization, by the horrors of the First World War, and by the redrawing of national boundaries and the creation of new states that followed.

The most striking feature of the Nazi regime that ruled Germany from 1933 to 1945 was the industrialized murder of six million Jews in pursuit of the elimination of Judaism from the face of the earth, and it might be thought that anti-Semitism or racism is a defining characteristic of fascist totalitarianism, if not its Marxist counterpart. The division of the world into friends and enemies was a defining characteristic of fascism, but the depth and virulence of racism varied from one country to another, as did its targets; Mussolini's regime was brutal and dictatorial, but not anti-Semitic until Italy allied with Nazi Germany in 1938. Italian Jews escaped the Holocaust until the German army occupied

Italy after the armistice of September 1943 between Italy and the Allies. Nonetheless, racism is a natural accompaniment of any ideology that rests on ultranationalism and is fueled by a belief in the need to fight powerful internal and external enemies. The most frequently invoked enemy in interwar Europe was not racial, however, but "international Bolshevism." This explains the attraction of Italian, German, Spanish, and other fascisms to conservatives in Europe and the United States. The linkage between racism and anticommunism was the Nazi claim that Bolshevism was a Jewish plot; Nazi radicals saw Bolshevism as the socialist version of the Jewish plot against the Aryan race; its capitalist version was the depredations of banking and international finance. Among Stalin's many borrowings from the right was his assault on "rootless cosmopolitans," otherwise Jews.

The role of mass irrationalism in Soviet totalitarianism is a difficult matter. Marxism was never anti-intellectual, and it never invited its adherents to think with their blood. Anyone who has ever debated what kind of materialism Marx espoused, or the question that racked Trotsky's followers—whether the Soviet Union was a state capitalist society or a deformed workers' state—is likely to conclude that Marxism is hyperintellectual, that Marxists overestimate the role of ideas in social and political life, and that they are overly concerned with intellectual correctness. The first generation of Russian social democrats, such as Georgi Plekhanov, Julius Martov, and Lenin himself, were genuinely learned, thoughtful, and theoretically sophisticated; and Marxism was the basis on which the Soviet Union professed to conduct its affairs, until its collapse in 1991.

The contrast with fascism is obvious. Fascism was overtly totalitarian in demanding total loyalty to one's country and in being deeply hostile to the liberal separation of private and public attachments. "Todos por la patria" was inscribed on public buildings throughout Franco's Spain, and Mussolini claimed to be instituting total control of Italian society through his Fascist followers. The practice of fascism was chaotic and corrupt, but the aspiration to total control can hardly be gainsaid. On the face of it, Marx's followers were hostile to every aspect of fascism. Marx was casually anti-Semitic, but only by way of insulting those he disagreed with; Marxism is a universalist and not a racist doctrine. Marxism, like Christianity, imagines a world where there will be neither Jew nor Gentile, Greek nor Barbarian, slave nor free. Nor does the idea of an aroused mass ecstatically sacrificing itself for the nation make any sense to a Marxist. The proletariat has no country. The postrevolutionary society will have no state; what leadership it will have is hard to tell, but the idea of a *postrevolutionary* charismatic leader makes no sense. Rationally organized, self-managing associations of workers will arrange their affairs in whatever way the exigencies of their lives dictate, but there will be no leaders and no followers. George Orwell's dystopian novel *Animal Farm* is a satire on the corruption of this ideal by Stalinism and by Stalin's followers elsewhere, and a rebuke to the hopes of non-Marxists who find Marx's picture of the communist utopia attractive. As Orwell observed elsewhere, there is no such thing as a proletarian government; at most, there are governments staffed by former proletarians.

Accounts of totalitarianism, however, emphasize the features that the professedly Marxist Soviet Union, Nazi Germany, and Fascist Italy had in common: mass mobilization through a political party that held a monopoly of power, the cult of leadership, the destruction of all intermediate and nonstate organizations, such as trade unions, and their replacement by politicized parodies, the abolition of privacy so that the family provided no safe haven against the state, and the replacement of the rule of law by arbitrary violence and a regime based on terror. We saw that Ortega y Gasset's first thought about the natural political expression of the "mass" was that it would be by a violent irruption into matters it did not know how to control other than by brute force. Theorists of totalitarianism emphasize the second phase of the process; mass irruption may break up a liberal or democratic regime, or be a reaction to simple breakdown of all forms of authority as the result of war, but in a totalitarian regime the masses are wholly under the control of elites. Totalitarianism is a phenomenon of mass society; but the masses have no autonomous role in totalitarian states. In all accounts other than Giovanni Gentile's philosophical defense of Italian Fascism, ordinary people are the raw material of the elites. They are to be welded into a fighting force by individual leaders, or by the party.

Although the term "totalitarian" was used approvingly by Fascist theorists in Mussolini's Italy, its main employment was by political commentators during the Cold War, and it was rightly criticized then and later for imputing to the Nazi and Stalinist regimes a degree of efficiency in their control over society that neither achieved, and for importing into political analysis a covert moral judgment to the effect that Marxism and Nazism were indistinguishably disgusting. If what was important about Marxism and Nazism was that they sustained regimes that were dreadful in identical ways, they need not be examined as doctrines, only combated as political dangers; since Nazi Germany had been defeated in 1945, Stalin's Russia was the sole enemy. It was not surprising that when talk of totalitarianism was at its height, there was a renewed interest in Burke's attacks on the French Revolution. Burke, too, had moved swiftly from treating the political rationalism of Price, Paine, and their allies as a serious but mistaken view of politics to regarding it as an infection that would bring chaos and bloodshed to England unless it was stamped out by criminal prosecution. However, the idea that Hannah Arendt, whose *Totalitarianism* is a key document of this moment in political thought, intended to blur the differences between Marxist and fascist worldviews for narrowly political reasons is utterly implausible. She was certainly concerned with the similarities between Soviet Russia and Nazi Germany, but her perspective was not Cold War hostility to the Soviet Union but the desire to defend a distinctively political form of freedom against the threats she thought were inherent in the growth of a mass society. Persons lost in the lonely crowd would be all too easy to recruit for totalitarian projects of left and right, and liberal democracy had few defenses because it had forgotten what freedom really was.

For the moment we may bracket these arguments. Here we can treat the ideological underpinnings and the political actuality of Soviet Russia, Nazi Germany, and Fascist Italy as brute historical facts, and investigate their roots. Fascism presents a seeming difficulty. First, there is in most fascisms a strong anti-intellectualist streak. This is no barrier to its examination; psychoanalysis claims to uncover deep irrationalities in our behavior, but the explanation of what these are and why we are unaware of them is itself a model of rational explanation. Sexual happiness has little to do with reason, but the explanation of why we so often fail to achieve it, and of how we might do better, is a task for reason. By the same token, one can distinguish between the irrational elements of fascism and the rational account of what they are and why they are important; more to the point, fascist thinkers themselves could draw on impeccably rational accounts of why politics at some levels at least must be conducted irrationally.

Second, there is little by way of a core doctrine in fascism, and that does present difficulties for the analyst; a Marxist who did not believe in the class struggle, proletarian democracy, and the withering away of the state would not be a Marxist at all. It is hard to say what would be analogous for a fascist; certainly nobody who disbelieved in leadership or regarded the nation as undeserving of our allegiance could be a fascist, but vast numbers of people are devoted to their own nation, and think its leadership is exceedingly important, without a fascist bone in their bodies. A third difficulty is that most fascisms are ultranationalist, but anyone who subscribes to ultranationalism is devoted to his or her particular nation. As a good fascist, an Italian must think better of Italy and the Italians than of Germany and the Germans, or England and the English; if he is to be a fascist *thinker*, he must at least step outside his attachments to Italy to explain why it is only to be expected, and not to be complained of, that the German and the Englishman so passionately prefer their nations to his. Ultranationalism makes cooperation between fascist states problematic both in theory and in practice, and makes the idea of a fascist international dubious; but it is not in principle more incoherent than parents' loving their own children more than any others, while understanding that other parents feel equally deeply about their own children.

Lastly, "fascist" has become such a term of abuse that describing someone as a fascist is tantamount to declining to reason with them at all. Without denying that much in fascism warrants such a reaction, there were writers—Georges Sorel, Robert Michels, Giovanni Gentile, and Carl Schmitt among them—who gave coherent accounts of something close to fascism or fascism *tout court*. Many people who were not fascists found much to sympathize with in their work—it is an irony of the history of political ideas that both Mussolini and Lenin wished to erect a monument to Sorel after his death in 1922—and they deserve a hearing. So we begin with the way in which Lenin laid the foundations of Soviet totalitarianism, or more exactly of Stalinist autocracy, and then turn to fascism.

From Marxism to Stalinism

That Marxism became the creed of a totalitarian state was not inevitable. To say that the Stalinist state was created by Lenin with contributions in both theory and practice from Trotsky is not to say that they wished to create it but that they laid its foundations in ways that were neither wholly within nor wholly outside the Marxist tradition. Vladimir Ilyich Ulanov, always known as V. I. Lenin, was the second son of a minor official; he was born in 1870 and died prematurely in 1924—he had been wounded two years earlier by a would-be assassin and never regained his health. His great achievement was the invention of the revolutionary party, something Marx had never fully conceptualized. He became a revolutionary when his older brother, implicated in a plot to assassinate Alexander III, was executed in 1887. Russian revolutionaries were at the time not much influenced by Marxism; they were more often populists than socialists, and aimed to achieve their goals by acts of terror against the government, in the belief that an unsettled government would be replaced by a populist government on the back of an uprising by peasants and urban workers.

Lenin was not an insurrectionist, though he became a professional revolutionary. By 1895 he was a fluent Marxist, and became visible enough to the czarist government to be exiled; he left Russia in 1902, returned during the 1905 revolution, and went into exile again when the Second Duma was dissolved in 1907. It was not until 1917 that he returned to Russia, allowed safe passage across Germany by the German military authorities who rightly thought that he would undermine the Russian war effort. His intransigent insistence that a socialist revolution could be launched against the centrist government of Alexander Kerensky was decisive in bringing about the revolution; and after a humiliating peace treaty with Germany, civil war, famine, and innumerable economic missteps, his unflinching leadership established the Soviet Union as it remained until its collapse at the end of the 1980s. He died shortly after the Soviet Union was formally instituted; he was, for good and ill, one of the great nation builders of history; one wonders what Machiavelli would have made of him.

Lenin's great invention was the idea of the revolutionary party. This needs explanation, and the explanation involves two other crucial elements in Lenin's Marxism. The first we have seen already: Lenin's insistence on locating what happened in Russia in the context of global capitalism. Lenin's analysis in *Imperialism, the Highest Stage of Capitalism* allowed him to imagine that Russia might take the lead in overthrowing world capitalism by "breaking the weakest link in the capitalist chain." Events showed how dangerous the thought was. It was also heretical. By the 1890s orthodox Marxism was dictated by Engels and Karl Kautsky; they shared a house in London and were the custodians of Marx's papers and reputation, as well as the organization of the Second International. They held rigid views about what Marx had discovered, and one of the most rigid was the view that the most developed country would make the socialist revolution first. If England, Holland, and the United States grasped their opportunity, they might make an almost bloodless, perhaps even an almost silent, revolution as the workers used parliamentary means to seize real power. Things would be different in Germany, where liberalism and parliamentary democracy had made less headway. The German autocracy would almost certainly meet its end in a less tranquil takeover from below. They were certain that there would be a *revolution*; how violent was another matter. The reformism of Eduard Bernstein, who saw that the German socialist party had become a reformist party interested in promoting workers' rights and a welfare state, and was prospering because of it, was anathema to Kautsky. Bernstein's "gradualism" was indistinguishable from the reformism of the New Liberals in Britain and was treated with contempt by orthodox Marxists. Lenin sided with Kautsky against the revisionists, but took his own line on the prospects of revolution in Russia.

Because capitalism was global, the health of capitalism in the West depended on its profitability in foreign ventures. A successful revolution in Russia would ripple backward through Europe. As to why Russia was a plausible place to launch a revolution, Lenin was politically perceptive but economically naïve: the Russian state lacked legitimacy; the population was kept obedient by fear, not by affection for the czar or belief in the authority of his regime. Lenin also thought that because Russia came late to industrialization, and its workers worked in more modern conditions—in larger plants and with more modern machinery—they were more likely to be class-conscious and ripe for revolution. The implausibility of this view was that worker discontent is always greatest in the early days of capitalism. Lenin was right about the revolutionary potential of the Russian workers, and wrong about the cause; it was the sudden shift into an urban workplace that rendered them discontented, not the technology they encountered. American labor relations at the same period were strikingly violent for much the same reasons.

Lenin thought he saw an advanced revolutionary consciousness, but he probably saw a conservative dislike of change. Even so, the political point was valid; he could make a Russian revolution that *might* lead to something global. It would be a narrowly political revolution, it would be impossible to institute a socialist society in Russia by the unaided efforts of the Russian revolutionaries, and Lenin had no thought of creating "socialism in one country." An orthodox Marxist thought such a project made no sense. What was possible was to make a political revolution whose economic ramifications would bring about revolutions elsewhere, which would ensure that socialism was made not in one country but as an international enterprise.

If looking for the weakest link in the capitalist chain was one innovation, the doctrine of permanent revolution was a second. Running parallel to his thoughts about the possibility of starting the fire in Russia and benefiting from the European conflagration that must follow, Lenin envisaged the possibility that the revolution in Russia would begin as a "bourgeois revolution" whose goal would be the creation of a constitutional republic, and that it would be transformed by pressure from the left into a socialist revolution. The model was the increasing radicalism of the French Revolution of 1789. The crucial question was timescale. On the analysis of revolution offered by Marx, it was impossible to set a simple timetable for the development of a society to the point where it could make a socialist revolution. One might expect the process of development to be lengthy; if the paradigm was the development of Britain as a capitalist economy with bourgeois political institutions after 1688, or the development of the United States after 1776, the period of bourgeois ascendancy and capitalist development would be measured in centuries. This was not what Lenin had in mind.

Enthusiasts for the Soviet Union argued that the March Revolution of 1917, which overthrew the czar, was the Russian bourgeois revolution and that the November Revolution, which overthrew Alexander Kerensky's government, was the socialist revolution. Other than to save the theory, the view has no merits; in the intervening eight months, economic development was negative. The Russian economy was collapsing as the war effort itself was collapsing, and hungry, ill-equipped soldiers were fleeing the battlefield in the hope of getting home to seize some land. After 1917 Lenin was enigmatic about what he had thought ten years earlier; when the czar had granted demands for a parliament, Lenin had argued that the Bolsheviks should assist the liberals to gain power and use their inadequacies to radicalize the population and make a socialist revolution. "We shall support them as the rope supports the hanged man." When he acquired power in 1917, Lenin got his socialist revolution, in the wrong country and in the wrong conditions.

He ended by accepting the possibility of creating socialism in one country because he had no alternative; he had gained and kept power where everyone else had failed, and the only intellectual framework in which he could explain his success made it inexplicable. Something must give, and what gave was the doctrine that socialism must be international. The question is why Lenin was successful, and what he bequeathed by being so. The doctrine of the party is central. Lenin wrote a pamphlet in 1903 that had an enormous influence on party organization all over the world. This was *What Is to Be Done?* The answer to the question was that a cadre of revolutionary activists had to form a revolutionary party capable of uniting the workers and peasants; it became the canonical recipe for national liberation movements in colonial settings, and for all Communist parties, whether overt or clandestine. The party had to adopt the policy of democratic centralism, whereby leaders of the party at every level were democratically elected, but policy was devised at the center, and all members were instructed in it and followed it. The cell structure of Bolshevism was common to all clandestine organizations then and now, but democratic centralism is a distinctively Bolshevik doctrine.

It presupposed what Marx had accepted but others had flinched from, the division of the working class into the revolutionary vanguard and the rest. The party was to be the vanguard, agitating and propagandizing among the masses, and waiting for the moment to lead an actual revolution. This view was anathema to many democratic socialists, who wanted a broad-based party that would embark on a long educative process until there was an overwhelming mass base. Although he eventually accepted Lenin's vanguardist vision, Trotsky was initially deeply hostile. He thought it threatened what he called "substitutism," in which the party substituted for a missing working class, and he accurately predicted what would happen if democratic centralism came to power: the central committee would substitute for the party, and the first secretary would eventually substitute for the central committee. In short, Stalin.

Our concern is not with the tangled history of Stalin's success in allying himself, first with the radicals and then with the conservatives within the politburo, until he was unchallengeably dictator over the Soviet Union; we focus on three questions. The first whether Marxism contains within itself the seeds of the totalitarian outcome; the second whether Lenin's version of Marxism did so; and the last what features of totalitarianism remain of interest to a Marxist—setting aside the objection that most Marxists dislike the concept in the first place. All utopian creeds contain a totalitarian germ; this thought animated Karl Popper's epic work, *The Open Society and Its Enemies*, the first volume of which emphasized the dangers of Plato and the second the dangers of Hegel and Marx. Popper was not the only thinker to hold this view; Isaiah Berlin's liberalism was based on a repudiation of the utopian hopes of Russian Marxism, and Bertrand Russell's short essays of the 1930s on his reasons for being neither a fascist nor a Marxist contain the same message.

Norman Cohn's study of the Münster rebellion of John of Leiden, *The Pursuit of the Millennium*, was both a history of the events it described, and by implication a warning against trying to put chiliastic and millenarian hopes into a political program.

To treat Marxism as a doctrine in the same intellectual category as the creeds of religious radicals like John of Leiden need not be an unfriendly act. Russell's treatment of Marxism in *German Social Democracy* is admiring; but as early as 1896, when he published the book, he took Marx to be more impressive as a prophet than as an economist, and Marxism to be closer to religion than to science. It is more than plausible to link utopia and totalitarianism. Utopias are total solutions; their allure is the opportunity they present for planning in every detail perfect lives for their inhabitants. They are not totalitarian in the sense in which political commentators used the term after World War II; they see order as the natural outcome of everyone's doing what he or she really wants to do, requiring no violence for its maintenance. As part of a practical project, utopian ideals present dangers. One is that people in possession of a total solution will be unwilling to see their designs modified, or to tolerate dissent about the plausibility of the utopian vision. Their attitude to dissenters may turn savage; dissenters are sinning against the light and are therefore either preternaturally wicked or deeply mad, and in either case subhuman. "Shoot the mad dogs" was the injunction of the prosecutors at the Moscow show trials of the 1930s. The purges had an obvious and much remarked precursor in Robespierre's Republic of Virtue.

A second way in which Marxism might be said to embody within itself the seeds of totalitarian politics bears more directly on Lenin's Marxism. Marxism is a doctrine in tension with itself; because it offers itself as science but a science of revolution, it simultaneously demands a deep respect for the intransigence of things as they really are and a deep confidence in the ability of the radicalized working class to change them. Marx emphasized the latter when young and the former later in life. His caution about the likely outcome of the Paris Commune, expressed in *The Civil War in France* and even more in the letters he wrote before the actual uprising, was exemplary. There is no virtue in the workers' sacrificing themselves when they have no prospects of making a successful revolution. Whether Marx in his later life would ever have thought the time was ripe for revolution is hard to guess; he would certainly have thought Lenin's gamble doomed to fail.

This is a delicate topic; Lenin reacted swiftly and intelligently to circumstances, and a summary is bound to be unjust. Lenin's modifications of Marx's original ideas were all in the direction of emphasizing the role of the will and the need to force history to move at a faster pace than history would do unforced. Russia was overwhelmingly an agrarian society, and many peasants were ex-serfs emancipated only in 1862. Literacy levels were the lowest in Europe, and the peasantry had no tradition of commercial farming. Marx himself thought bourgeois society educated the workers in self-management and self-government, and he saw Russia as a peasant society living under an autocracy: violent, illiterate, and superstitious. In a famous letter to Vera Zasulich, Marx suggested the possibility that Russia might bypass capitalism and move from the precapitalist peasant commune to postcapitalist cooperative socialism in one leap; but that, too, would depend on Europe's aiding the process, not on Russia's doing it in isolation, let alone in the teeth of universal hostility.[3] A vanguardist party, an emphasis on the will, and a determination to achieve in a backward, semiliterate country what Marx had envisaged happening in the most developed countries in the world is a recipe for a head-on conflict between an aggressive leadership and a reluctant rank and file.

It was not Marxism that justified and organized Lenin's secret police, the Cheka, nor was it Marxism that inspired summary executions, the establishment of the gulag, and the horrors of Stalin's Russia. The secret police was an inheritance from czarist Russia; it became much nastier, more efficient, and more pervasive in its effect. The resort to terror and the use of secret police armed with the authority to murder on a whim had one intellectual source and one contingent one. The contingent source was the fact that the Bolshevik Revolution was followed by a civil war that the Bolsheviks won with great difficulty. If the White, anti-Bolshevik leaders had had the sense to buy the goodwill of the peasantry with a program of land reform they would have won the war. As it was, the brutal behavior of the White Armies left the Red Army and the

Bolsheviks in possession of such moral high ground as there was. The intellectual defense of employing as much violence as it took to succeed was Marxist only because it was the common inheritance of the revolutionary left, which had come to terms with the French revolutionary terror, and shared a view about how much violence and of what kind was permissible.

Whatever might happen in the long run, the immediate task was to establish the revolution itself. The morality of violence was obvious. The forces opposed to revolution had no qualms about using terror against the revolution, and revolutionaries could have none about employing drastic terror to preserve it. Trotsky drew a famous distinction between "Red" and "White" terror: the former was progressive and justified as the shortest of short-term tactics; the latter was mere brutality. The danger is that if one holds the view, shared by Lenin and Trotsky, that the revolution is permanent, enemies will be created by the pace of change, and terror will itself create more enemies. Then terror as a political weapon begins to feed on itself. The violent history of Russia, the absence of a tradition of parliamentary representation, and the existence of external threats to the Soviet Union all played their part; but if the question is whether there is something in the Marxist tradition that inclines a regime in a direction so flatly contrary to the aspirations of Marxism, it is the passion for revolutionary change, not a romantic enthusiasm for violence for its own sake.

Any Marxist would have thought that the disaster was that means became ends; an ideologically monolithic party backed by a secret police monopolized politics, then that party fell into the hands of Stalin, whose capacity for mastering the details of what was happening in his vast empire was astonishing, and whose lack of inhibition in securing his position by murder both retail and wholesale was equally astonishing. The details of his crimes against the Russian people are not our subject, but if anyone wanted total control over every detail of his subjects' lives, he did; and if anyone regarded everyone else as expendable, he did. There have been many rulers with similar ambitions; our interest is in whether Marxism lent itself to misuse by Stalin. Utopianism, a lack of scruple, a tendency to think only in terms of class struggle, which led to the bizarre situation in which the party made war against its own supporters, all played their part. There was one other feature of the Stalinist autocracy that distinguished it from older autocracies, and also from the autocracies of the right that came to power in interwar Europe. This was its curiously theological quality. Autocracies of the right were interested in holding power, and cared less for doctrinal unity than for unity behind the leader of the day. Whether it was Stalin's early training as a seminarian or simply his obsession with detail, it is impossible to say, but his obsession with laying down a correct party line on matters remote from practical politics seems in retrospect bizarre. Stalin's role was papal; once he had pronounced, the matter was closed, and although he never declared himself infallible, he was treated as if he were. Nor was it merely a matter of establishing that, for instance, reformist social democrats were social fascists in the early 1930s, then allies in a popular front in the later 1930s; doctrinal correctness extended to the making of films and the writing of operas, as Eisenstein and Shostakovich discovered.

Lenin had sown the seed. He had no time for dissent; he held not only the reasonable view that a revolutionary party must preserve a high degree of unity to be effective but also the much less reasonable view that because Marxism was a science, there was no more room for freedom of speech in Marxism than in chemistry. It goes without saying that there is a great deal of freedom of speech in chemistry and that scientific theories are not protected from criticism by putting a bullet in the back of dissenters' heads. The difficulty in saying more than this lies in two obvious facts. The first is that Lenin's success in November 1917 was astonishing and gave his ideas a standing among Marxists everywhere that made them hard to challenge. Marxists might find novel ways of being Leninist, but not ways of being a non-Leninist. Forms of discipline appropriate to clandestine, revolutionary parties were imposed on Communist parties everywhere, along with the attendant machinery of purges, instant changes in party lines that adherents were supposed to accept *de fide*, and a cult of the leader. Once Stalin's dictatorship was firmly established, Stalinist models of leadership became canonical in all parties affiliated to the Comintern. Patterns of control varied, as did the level of violence, the degree of cruelty, and the prevalence of general gangsterism; but the combination of Soviet "imperial" influence and the quasi-theology of "Marxism-Leninism-Stalinism" gave all communist regimes, other than Tito's Yugoslav breakaway regime, a distinctive and all but totalitarian character—not that Tito's regime could have been mistaken for a liberal democracy.

Fascism

We have said that the concept of totalitarianism has been attacked as an ideological device for blurring the difference between communist and fascist regimes, and in particular for blurring the difference between Stalinism and Nazism. We must, therefore, tackle the distinctive ingredients of fascist totalitarianism before turning to "soft" totalitarianism. The origins of fascism are disputed. The irrationalist authoritarian Joseph de Maistre has been offered as an ancestor, if not a progenitor. Johann Gottfried von Herder's insistence on the role of distinct, mutually almost unintelligible cultures in creating human identity has been seen as the foundation of irrationalist nationalism. The more plausible thought is that several decisive elements came together in the late nineteenth and early twentieth centuries; they affected one another in ways that make distinguishing them a matter of intellectual convenience rather than one of clear causality. They are racism, nationalism, irrationalism, and antiliberalism.

Many commentators have rightly said that these ingredients can feature in other political visions. Imperialism can be both racist and liberal, in the sense that it can be genuinely concerned with the best interests of the lesser races whose affairs are to be managed by their betters, and can envisage teaching the lesser races how to manage their own affairs in liberal ways. Liberal nationalism is not merely common but during the nineteenth century the most prominent, if not the most passionate, form of nationalism in the Austro-Hungarian Empire. Conversely, most forms of socialist nationalism have not in the least resembled National Socialism. Antiliberalism poses more conceptual difficulty. The fact that antiliberalism is an element in fascism has always complicated the analysis of fascism for the obvious reason that socialism was antiliberal and anticapitalist, in ways that are sometimes hard to distinguish from the ways in which fascism was; and the fact that twentieth-century liberalism came to terms with the corporate state has inspired at least one writer to take seriously the thought that the New Deal was an instance of "liberal fascism."[4]

Violence

The ingredients acquire their fascist quality when they are united in a movement animated by a taste for violence. This is often linked to the irrationalism of fascist or protofascist writers. Caution is needed. The "discovery" of deep irrationalities within the human psyche need not lead to the conclusion that they are best channeled into violence against our enemies. A sense that the veneer of civilization was alarmingly thin often led to a chastened defense of liberal values. There is much of that in Weber's discussion of the legitimacy of the "rational-legal" state, there is more in Freud's *Civilization and Its Discontents*, and there is some in the political sociology of Vilfredo Pareto. The liberal whose aspirations have been chastened by reading Freud sees the achievement of a degree of rationality in politics as painful and difficult; many immediate satisfactions must be forgone in the interests of not resorting to violence and self-destruction; deferred gratification does not come easily. It does not follow that self-control and deferred gratification are unimportant. The stronger our sense of how violent are the emotions that lie so close to the surface, the more determined we may be to find ways of keeping them under control.

During the 1930s many commentators analyzed the appeal of fascism precisely in terms of the way it offered a relief from self-control and an outlet for what many thinkers had diagnosed as the innate aggression of mankind. When Russell and Dewey in the 1930s wrote the short essays that became famous as *Why I Am Not a Communist*, the essays were initially entitled *Why I Am Not a Communist or a Fascist*, and both Russell and Dewey took it for granted that the common appeal of insurrectionary Marxism and insurrectionary fascism was their violent nature. It was the appeal of violence that they seized on and urged their readers to shun. What these responses acknowledged that is harder to remember is the rational attraction that communism and fascism presented in the 1930s. Since 1950 and 1940, respectively, Western Europe and the United States have by historical standards been astonishingly well ordered and prosperous. Almost nobody today thinks the existing social and economic order is so broken that orthodox political means cannot fix it. In the 1930s, when unemployment in the United States was running at 25 percent, the economic system seemed broken beyond repair; in central and eastern Europe things were worse. Not only was there economic misery; many of the states created after the First World War lacked legitimacy and were torn by battles between left and right, while many of their citizens regarded liberal democracy as a fraud perpetrated on them by the victorious Allies at Versailles. Even if smashing everything and starting again was not a plausible policy prescription, the social and political system targeted for smashing was often one to which a rational person would feel little loyalty. The ease with which Mussolini destroyed Italian parliamentary democracy was a lesson in the inability of corrupt and remote political leaders to secure the loyalty of the citizenry, as well as a lesson in the destabilizing effect of rapid industrialization and an unsuccessful war.

Racism, Nationalism, Antiliberalism

Racism in the modern sense became a serious concern of intellectuals—or quasi-intellectuals—during the latter part of the nineteenth century, but in some form it is one of the standing infirmities of the human mind. Aristotle's conviction that barbarians were by nature unfitted for political life and might properly be enslaved by Greeks is in a long tradition. The Israelites of the Old Testament were instructed by Yahweh to engage in ethnic cleansing, but not for what we should today describe as "ethnicity-based" reasons; God's intention was that His chosen people should settle in areas currently occupied by tribes who worshipped other gods than Him, and these tribes were casualties of the divine plan. Thomas Paine's *The Age of Reason* was quite sharp about Yahweh's genocidal proclivities, but essentially on rationalist and humanitarian grounds; it was, in Paine's view, pointless cruelty. However, Yahweh's motivation was religious rather than racial, and, in any event, the feuds of desert tribes offer few insights into the politics of industrialized European societies two millennia later.

The racism that played a large part in interwar fascism had two sources, one the encounter with preindustrial societies that had been going on since the European expansion overseas, the other a much older tradition of anti-Semitism. Although the racism of the Nazis was anti-Semitic first and generally racist secondarily, the priorities were reversed in scientific racism. In the United States interest focused on the supposed deficiencies of black Africans, since the "peculiar institution" of slavery dominated American politics for forty years either side of the Civil War of 1861–65. Late twentieth-century scientific racism was so far removed from anti-Semitic prejudice that it placed Jews and East Asians on the cultural, intellectual, and economic pinnacle occupied during the nineteenth century by the Anglo-Saxons; American immigration policy eighty years earlier had been energetically anti-Chinese and anti-Jewish.[5] Hitler got his racial theory, as distinct from his anti-Semitic prejudices, from Houston Stewart Chamberlain, the disciple of Gobineau and the son-in-law of Wagner. The pure Aryan peoples stood at the peak of a racial hierarchy; intermarriage was fatal to a race, and only the expulsion of the Jews from Europe could save European world dominance. German anti-Semitism had a very long history, going back to pogroms and mass murder at the time of the First Crusade; it was both sui generis and affected by the incursion into Germany of distinctively Russian forms of anti-Semitism at the end of the nineteenth century. "Exterminism" was Russian rather than German and infected all levels of society. Even the last and relatively liberal czar of all the Russias, Nicholas II, ruminated sadly but unembarrassedly that he supposed one couldn't just kill all the Jews. During the Napoleonic period, it briefly looked as though the legal disabilities under which Jews had labored in the German states would be swept away, but with the defeat of Napoleon, they were reimposed.

Marx's father converted to Lutheranism when Prussia reimposed the rules that barred Jews from practicing law. Russian politics made things worse in western Europe in the late nineteenth century as pogroms drove Russian and eastern European Jews into Austria and Germany, and populist politicians found an easy route to power by stirring up working-class anti-Semitism. Nonetheless, fascism could sustain itself doctrinally with few or no racial components; and as we have already said, Mussolini was not interested in fantasies of Aryan purity, and adopted anti-Semitic policies only in the late 1930s as a concession to pressure from Hitler.

A second strand of thought might have become important without any racial overtones, but invariably acquired them. This was the "blood and soil" movement of the 1880s onward, in its own right an important component of French and German nationalism. The most articulate writers in this tradition were Frenchmen: Charles Maurras and Maurice Barrès; and insofar as there was a fascist political theory worthy of the name, it was almost wholly French, Gentile's thoughts on the matter excepted. Barrès was a novelist and a politician, and a member of the Académie Française; it was he who coined the idea of the *déraciné*, the individual who had left his natural, patrial surroundings and was therefore fickle, self-centered, and a threat to the integrity of the state and the nation. The Jews were paradigmatically deracinated and paradigmatically a danger to the French nation. One might wonder why nobody who complained, as Barrès and Stalin did, of the "rootless cosmopolitanism" of the Jews ever paused to wonder how a people so desperate to live in their own promised land had become deracinated in the first place; but they did not. Barrès began his political career as a revisionist socialist but moved sharply to the right during the Dreyfus Affair, and for the rest of his life represented a Paris constituency as a nationalist.

The origins of French nationalism lay in the radical French Revolution, but Barrès was responsible for its redefinition as a conservative anti-revolutionary ideal—militarist, antiforeigner, anti-Semitic, hostile to the tradition of the rights of man. Barrès, born in 1862, died soon after the First World War, in 1923, but his slightly younger contemporary Charles Maurras, born only six years later, lived through the conflicts of the 1930s, was a propagandist for Pétain during the period of the

Vichy government, and was jailed for life at the liberation. The differences between him and Barrès suggest the difficulty of pinning labels on their ideas; Barrès was antiroyalist, whereas Maurras wanted a revived, nonparliamentary, but decentralized monarchy. Unlike Barrès, who was a staunch Catholic, Maurras's nationalism took him in an anti-Catholic direction. So did his devotion to classical Greece; in the argument between Athens and Jerusalem, he was unabashedly for Athens. Christianity itself was for Maurras stigmatized by its Jewish origins. Maurras's career illustrates one problem faced by fascist ultranationalists. He could not maintain his ferocious hostility to the French liberals and socialists of his day without siding with France's enemies. Yet he was violently anti-German and contemptuous of modern Italy. Faute de mieux he advocated an alliance with Mussolini, and in 1940 was a defeatist; in 1945 he was jailed for supporting a military occupation imposed by people he loathed.

The "blood and soil" movement was broadly nationalist. Most accounts of fascism rightly make nationalism central. Still, as the career of Maurras suggests, there was always room for doubt in the minds of fascists how far the nation *as fact* and the nation *as ideal* coincided. British fascists of the 1930s were often so carried away by their anti-Semitism and their hostility to the lukewarm liberalism of the British political system that they came to regard Nazi Germany as their nation and not the British nation to which they happened to belong. Nor did devotion to the principles of "blood and soil" always lead directly to nationalism. It could lead to something much more localist; this partly explains Maurras's desire for a decentralized monarchy. A sufficient passion for one's own patch of earth might easily lead to the thought that the political leadership based in some remote capital city was not only corrupt and self-serving but unlikely to protect one's own locality. It is not impossible, though it is unusual, for a nationalist to be hospitable to the idea that the nation is a patchwork quilt of localities and ways of life; more common is the view that local allegiances endanger the integrity of the nation, one and indivisible.

That fascism was fueled by powerful negative emotions is hardly surprising. Nor is it surprising that it could appear to be a movement of the left or the right according to circumstance. Its enemy was parliamentary liberal democracy, and it is easy to see how vulnerable parliamentary liberal democracy is to assault from socialists on one side and conservatives on the other, and from radicals and revolutionaries impatient with government by debate. Georges Sorel's *Reflections on Violence* suggests one reason for the surge of negative emotions, and Robert Michels's transformation from a member of the German Social Democratic Party into an admirer of Mussolini suggests another. Fascists and nationalists had a clear target: the liberalism of the nineteenth century, which had subordinated the state to the individual. That is, the liberal state derived its legitimacy from the fact that it protected the rights of the individuals who were its citizens; their rights to its protection were prior to its right to their allegiance. Hegel had tried to finesse this opposition by insisting that although the modern state had to be a liberal, constitutional state, the individual and his rights were the creation of the state. This was an unstable balancing of individualism and statism, and Hegel's critics said so. Ultranationalists and their colleagues were not tempted; they knew that liberalism was a mistake. When they borrowed from Hegel, they borrowed his corporatism along with the thought that war is the health of the state.

If it is often not obvious whether a critic belongs on the left or the right. Sorel is a case in point. His *Reflections on Violence* has even been read as a warning against trusting reason too far. If we are keenly aware of the weakness of human reason, we can guard against that weakness. If we understand the extent to which we are governed by mythical forms of thinking, we can assist reason to exercise a proper control over our conduct. Friendly commentators regard Sorel as an ally of Freud: seeing human beings as vulnerable to irrational promptings, and avoiding rationalist optimism in the hope of securing a limited control of our irrationalities by reason. Much as Freud disclaimed any intention to make us happy, but hoped to replace neurotic misery by "ordinary unhappiness," we could see Sorel as hoping to replace wholesale irrationality by ordinary failures of common sense.

Irrationalism

This is kinder to Sorel than is plausible, and also less kind, because what makes him interesting is his strangeness. Sorel is unplaceable; he was born in 1847 and died in 1922; he attended the École Polytechnique in Perpignan and spent his working life in the Ponts et Chausées, the French public works authority. He became a political theorist in retirement, beginning as an orthodox Marxist, but embracing a variety of antibourgeois and antidemocratic creeds, stretching from Maurras's monarchism to Lenin's insurrectionary communism. His range of interests was enormous, and he wrote interestingly on the trial of Socrates, on the nature of historical materialism, and on the history of Marxism. The identity of the enemy was the one clear element in his thinking: capitalism and liberal democracy. Sorel wrote *Reflections on Violence* in 1908 when he was attracted to the French anarcho-syndicalists, a left-wing socialist movement that—as the name suggests—wanted to abolish capitalism and replace the state by self-governing associations of workers. The change was to occur on the back of the proletarian general strike; the "myth" of the proletarian general strike was the centerpiece of *Reflections*, but Sorel was essentially a reactionary thinker, looking back to classical Greece for his inspiration.

His hatred of modern capitalism was less a hatred of the inequalities of wealth and welfare than of the destruction of the instinct of craftsmanship in a world of industrial mass production. The question was whether there was any way of restoring the craft ideal in the modern world. His answer was that the workers' movement must commit itself to a *myth*. This was the myth of the sudden, violent, and comprehensive overthrow of the existing capitalist order. Among the curiosities of Sorel's conception of this myth was his insistence that the universal overthrow of capitalism must happen in times of prosperity. Only if the workers and the capitalists were confident and full of fight could there be the conclusive struggle that he deemed essential. It had to be war without ill feeling; the capitalist order must appear to the workers as a gigantic obstacle to be smashed, but the owners of capital must not be seen as wicked individuals or be individually ill-treated. There are traces of this view in Marx's account of the capitalist as a "bearer" of the relations of production, but nothing to match Sorel's desire that the struggle of labor and capital should be epic but impersonal.

The sense in which Sorel's mythmaking was reactionary needs explanation. On the face of it, an assault on the existing capitalist order for the sake of replacing it by a worker-cooperative anarchy is a progressive ideal. Sorel's deeper interest lay in the restoration of the ethics of craftsmanship; and this was far from a mere footnote to Marx's concern with happiness, leisure, and the rational minimization of toil. Characteristically, Sorel called Marxism "social poetry," and meant it as praise. He did not think of Marx as a rationalist. Insisting that Marx's sketch of the socialist utopia was not a fully drawn blueprint, he praised Marx's ability to inspire emotional longings and a passion for action. Sorel, too, set out to inspire action. In this frame of mind he praised American capitalism for the aggressive high spirits of its captains of industry. They were Homeric heroes, natural disciples of Friedrich Nietzsche.[6] He did not want conciliation, a welfare state, or a role for trade unions in increasing take-home pay and reducing hours of work. He wanted a terminal conflict.

Why might this vision appeal—as it did—to Mussolini? The one coherent feature of fascist political theory was its account of a corporate state, a state where the system of political representation was constructed around everyone's diverse roles in the economy. It seemed obvious to many early twentieth-century critics that capitalism could not bring about prosperity, and that no system in which individuals just tried to make money for themselves without coordination between one enterprise and another could. Nonsocialists were unhappy at the thought of abolishing private property, and many socialists agreed that trying to run an entire economy as if it were one enterprise was chimerical. On left and right alike, various forms of functional representation were thought up, both to integrate the workers into the political decision making and to coordinate economic activity in ways the market could not. Workers' syndicates were one version. In fascist practice, they became a mechanism whereby governments kept the workers in check and ensured that they worked on whatever terms seemed best to the government. One slightly mad but perfectly sincere experiment with corporatism took place in Fiume—later Rijeka—after the First World War. During the short-lived dictatorship of the poet and fascist intellectual Gabriele D'Annunzio, a corporatist government was set up in the city, composed of nine corporations representing workers, managers, professionals, and the like, with a tenth added on the inspiration of D'Annunzio to represent poets, visionaries, and superior spirits in general. The experiment was stopped by outside force before it could collapse of itself. Mussolini admired D'Annunzio and made him a prince, but the intellectual influence of D'Annunzio on fascist politics—as distinct from Italian fascist aesthetics—was slight.

The two major theorists of Italian fascism were Alfredo Rocco and Giovanni Gentile. The extent to which fascism was an amalgam of ideas culled from Hegel, Saint-Simon, Marx, Nietzsche, and Sorel was apparent to both, and not a source of embarrassment. Rocco was the more influential inasmuch as he was part of the inner circle of Italian fascism, while Gentile was a vastly better philosopher but not part of Mussolini's everyday reading. The essence of fascist doctrine was a series of mirror-images of the nineteenth-century liberalism that fascism was intended to replace, but the culmination of the theory was an assertion that might strike us as unlikely. Gentile claimed that what fascism offered modern man was true freedom, a higher and more vital freedom than liberalism offered, but freedom nonetheless. One might have thought that the obvious argument for fascism would have been a conservative one: freedom within limits is excellent, but the first priority is order. Gentile did not argue this; he argued that fascism could achieve liberty in ways that nineteenth-century laissez-faire liberalism could not.

His thought was this. Liberalism had set everyone adrift; liberal individualism frustrated the deep human desire to be at one with our fellows in collective undertakings to which we can give wholehearted moral allegiance. This criticism was leveled against liberalism by innumerable Catholic thinkers, and one way in which Italian fascism was well adapted to its time and place was that it could keep on good ideological terms with the Vatican. Parliamentary democracy was an error:

liberalism espoused a false conception of political equality and allowed everyone to think she or he was as fit to lead society as the truly talented. The effect was that political pygmies ran a corrupt, self-serving, and nontransparent political system, and the citizens were alienated from it. The same complaint could be leveled at unbridled capitalism—as it is today. Workers worked to scrape together a living, and owners ran their enterprises to make as much money for themselves as they could; but neither side was animated by a sense of social obligation. Needed were the institutions that would restore social cohesion, turn self-seeking into public service, and ensure that only a heroic leader was head of state and that the leading figures in society were genuinely an elite. As to the totalitarian quality of fascism, Gentile boasted of it. Fascism was a spiritual doctrine embracing the totality of social life.[7]

Corporatism

The question this raises is how to distinguish liberal corporatism from fascism. Many observers said that the economic institutions hastily cobbled together by President Roosevelt to further his New Deal in the mid-1930s were not unlike those of Italian fascism. Boards and "administrations" proliferated, with the intention of putting production on a more organized basis and diminishing unemployment. The fascist attachment to autarchy—trying to achieve self-sufficiency to make the national economy immune to the shocks of the global economy—was differently grounded from American protectionism, but no more passionate. Behind the fascist enthusiasm for national self-sufficiency, however, lay ultranationalism and the thought that the economy must always be on a war footing, whereas American protectionism was based on bad economics and the urge to do *something* when nobody had much of an idea what. The idea that the nineteenth-century liberal economy lacked the organizing and integrating mechanisms that must in the twentieth century be provided by the state distinguished nineteenth-century laissez-faire liberalism from the liberalism of the New Deal, but liberal corporatism was very different from its fascist cousin.

It is not at the level of accepting the need for a "corporate state" that the cleavage is to be found; nor at the level of the wish that the managerial elite of the modern state be chosen by meritocratic means. Neither in the United States nor in Italy was this wish wholly sincere; in both countries the leadership appointed its friends, who were sacked only if wholly incompetent. The thought that a managerial revolution was taking place in all modern societies, from the Soviet Union to the United States, was a 1930s commonplace and possessed a modicum of truth; the claim that it was a more important consideration than whether a society recognized the private ownership of the means of production was not true, nor was the thought that it mattered more than whether a society was a one-party Soviet dictatorship or an American multiparty democracy. But the thought that the growth of large-scale industry had brought about a degree of convergence in management methods and relations with government was true within limits; that insight might plausibly be credited to Saint-Simon as the first theorist of "industrial society." We live in a corporate state; it is another word for regulated capitalism.

Crucially, what Soviet and Fascist totalitarianisms shared, and the corporate liberal state does not, was the one-party state. There is and was all the difference in the world between the politics of a competitive two-party or multiparty state and the politics of an avowedly one-party state. In the one-party state, there is no room for individuals to set up independent political structures, and no forum in which they can argue for changes in the existing structure. Fascism is not a creed looking for an interesting debate with its rivals. So we must recur to the paradox that Gentile argued that Italian fascism made the individual free in a way that liberalism could not. He did it by drawing two distinctions that were not unknown, but had not been used in this way before. The first was to detach fascism—Mussolini's fascism—from nationalism; fascism took the idea of the nation with the utmost seriousness, but was not itself a form of Nationalism. Nationalism in the sense that Gentile criticized saw the nation as an entity that preexisted the individual, and in its "blood and soil" manifestation insisted on its presence as a brute fact confronting the individual. Barrès and Maurras would, on this view, be nationalists but not good fascists. In fascism, the nation emerged in a process of constant re-creation by the individuals who constituted the nation. Gentile was a good Hegelian and referred unembarrassedly to the fascist state as the "ethical state."

The second distinction flowed from this insight. The misguided nationalist conception of authority was top-down. Just as the nation confronted the individual as a fact about the world, so the authority embodied in national leaders was set above the individual, who was faced with a simple hierarchical fact. Under fascism, authority flowed upward from the individual and then down again from the state; it was a cyclical process, misunderstood both by liberalism and by old forms of conservatism. Gentile quoted Mussolini's response to a questioner who had asked whether the basis of the fascist state was force or consent; they are inseparable, he replied. This, too, could be read as good Hegelian doctrine; the state does not float free of individual consent to it, and is what it is only because of that consent; but its demands on the individual are backed by force, and unless individuals understood it as a coercive entity, they would have nothing on which to focus their consents. Whence Gentile's belief that fascism gave the individual genuine freedom; only in the right sort of state was freedom possible, and only there were the individual's rights secure.

The unpersuasiveness of this is obvious enough, although what mattered most was the divergence of the theory from fascist practice. The neo-Hegelian theory of the authoritarian nation-state presupposes an unforced consensus on the values embodied in the state. This in turn rested on the Hegelian belief that history unfolds itself in increasingly rational social and political institutions, so that individuals would find their existences more and more satisfactory even if it took a philosopher to give a coherent retrospective account of why. It was a view that allowed room for the wide variation that was visible in the political allegiances of neo-Hegelian political theorists between 1875 and 1930. Although there were among them no laissez-faire liberals, there were more liberals of a moderate corporatist persuasion than simple conservatives. The practice of fascism was a more acerbic commentary on Gentile's philosophical defense than anything one might write from a philosophical point of view. Critics were beaten up or murdered by the *squadristi*, and once the regime was in power, critics were jailed for long periods. Nor was the strutting and posturing of Il Duce himself much of an argument for fascism's claim to have transcended right and left in embodying a wholly new form of nationalism.

Nazism

Nonetheless, it would be a mistake to conflate Italian fascism, German Nazism, and Stalinist communism in the way the "totalitarian" label tends to do. Nazism was an almost wholly unintellectual enterprise, and anti-Semitism was an essential component of Nazism in a way that was true neither of Stalinism nor of fascism. What all three had in common was what the German jurist Carl Schmitt identified as the essence of the political, namely, the division of the world into friends and enemies.[8] Schmitt, who was born in 1888 and died only in 1985, was, along with Heidegger, one of the few serious intellectual figures to side with the Nazis. Unlike Heidegger, whose brief flirtation with the actual regime as opposed to his fantasy of it began and ended with his ten months as rector of the University of Freiburg, Schmitt worked for the duration of the Third Reich in the Nazi legal administration and, among other things, wrote to defend the "night of the long knives," when Hitler's supporters murdered their more radical opponents in the Nazi movement. After the war, he was banned from teaching and writing for five years, but before he died became a cult figure with American conservatives.

What Schmitt's support for the Nazis revealed was not the allure that brutal regimes may hold for intellectuals who would themselves not hurt a fly. It was rather that the Nazis put into practice ideas that Schmitt had held since the end of the First World War, in common with innumerable German critics of socialism, parliamentary government, and constitutionalism. These included the thought that in every regime there must be a dictatorial element, that a charismatic leader was a truer representative of the people than any parliamentary regime can be, and that all authority has an element of the transcendental.[9] Before we decide that these ideas were intrinsically foolish because of the disasters to which they led, it is worth remembering that at the end of the First World War, Lenin and Trotsky were capable of misidentifying the Bolshevik coup d'état of 1917 as a genuinely proletarian socialist revolution, and that the otherwise sober economist Joseph Schumpeter toyed with the notion that absolute monarchy could be restored in Austria and the old, dead, aristocratic Austro-Hungarian regime resurrected. Speculation about the wholesale reconstruction of the ruined states of Central Europe was common currency, and the feasibility of regulated capitalism allied to liberal democracy much less obvious. The danger of doctrines that emphasize the centrality of dictatorship and the need for someone ready to exercise ruthless extralegal power standing behind the everyday legal order hardly needs elaboration; but one ought not to exaggerate their strangeness. Nor, just as in the case of Gentile, should we exaggerate either the extent to which the doctrines reflected a reality that mostly came into existence after the ideas were formulated, or the extent to which they influenced the actions of opportunistic power-seeking politicians. All we should acknowledge is that just as Stalin's autocracy built on a Marxism that Lenin had already distorted, so the fascist autocracies took advantage of ideas that had a good deal of intrinsic credibility.

Soft Totalitarianism?

The Second World War was hailed by the Allied powers as a war on behalf of liberal democracy and against fascism. To believe that the war was waged by genuine democracies against fully paid-up totalitarian dictatorships is doubly implausible. Stalin's regime was no less brutal than Hitler's and had used genocide as an instrument of policy even earlier. Soviet internationalism was wholly notional, as the postwar sacrifice of the satellite states of Eastern Europe to the interests of the Soviet Union demonstrated. The Soviet Union was no less dictatorial than Nazi Germany, and it was a more genuine one-party state inasmuch as the Communist Party of the Soviet Union was part of the administrative mechanism of the state and economy in ways the Nazi party was not. This is not to deny that the Soviet Union bore much the greatest burden in the war, losing colossal numbers both of military personnel and of civilians; the war on the eastern front pitted two dictatorial regimes against each other, to the benefit of the Western democratic powers. The Soviet leadership and ordinary Russians, too, have always seen the war in this light, and still complain that the Western powers were happy to see their enemies engage in mutual bloodletting on a vast scale.

Nonetheless, the self-image of the Western Allies, especially once the Cold War had begun in 1946 was that the United States, the British Commonwealth, and France at least were the defenders of liberal democracy against "totalitarianism." By this time, "totalitarianism" had ceased to mean the creed of fascists who insisted on the unlimited scope of a dictatorial state authority, and had come to be a catch-all for the most dislikable features of Soviet communism and those regimes modeled on it or installed by it. The polemical employment of the term spawned some theoretically ambitious uses, such as Karl Popper's not very credible accusation that Plato had been a totalitarian. Against which Popper's critics insisted that totalitarianism was unintelligible except in the context of a modern, technically competent society with mass communications and the means of exercising detailed control over its subjects in ways that no ancient state could. Critics also insisted that totalitarian movements—and the social theory of fascism—had to be understood as attempts to roll back liberalism. There was no liberalism to roll back in the classical world, no private world to trample on.

One of the most intriguing pieces of post-1945 thinking about totalitarianism was the revival of interest in what we might call "soft" totalitarianism, a variant on Tocqueville's fear of soft depotism. The raw materials were provided much earlier. The first great dystopian novel of the twentieth century was Evgeny Zamyatin's *We*, published in 1924, though not in its author's native Russian. For our purposes, its totalitarianism is not quite "soft" enough, because although the all-powerful dictator is called the "Benefactor," the state he rules—OneState—relies on coercion almost as much as George Orwell's *1984*, even though propaganda does most of the work. There are no gulags, but there is violence. As a work imagining total control without the mass murder to which Stalin resorted, *We* goes further than *1984* in supposing that OneState has almost extinguished individuality and induced all its subjects to think as one: "we." As in *1984* the danger that threatens OneState is sexual attraction, which notoriously gives whomever it afflicts a strong sense of individual identity. Anyone with the ability to say "I" with some conviction is all too likely to question authority. Aldous Huxley's *Brave New World* goes OneState one better. The management of this world full of genetically manipulated and antenatally conditioned individuals holds off revolt by narcotizing the population with a combination of consumer goods, easy sex, the "feelies," and doses of soma, a happiness-inducing drug.

Brave New World is the defining image of really soft totalitarianism. All do what they wish, but what all wish is what they have been conditioned to wish. This is not the utopia imagined by Trotsky in which humanity has reached the point where every intelligent person is as clever as Aristotle, and the best are cleverer than we can imagine. It is a utopia in which the tormenting questions asked by the great novelists and playwrights have been suppressed for the sake of instant gratification; the romantic agony of unrequited love has been removed by constantly available sex; even death has no terrors when euthanasia comes at just the moment we are bored with life. And if we get unhappy and restless, as children must sometimes do, a quick puff of soma blown over us will restore us to good humor. One of the work's antiheroes, the controller for Europe, Mustapha Mond, knows that we have given up things that are worth having and that he is rumored not have given up himself—such as Shakespeare and the Bible, and "Ford knows what." Like Bertrand Russell in some moods, he thinks it a good bargain for everyone else.

The anxiety of the 1950s and 1960s was that the affluent Western liberal democracies had begun to turn into variations on *Brave New World*. There was no controller behind the scenes, no Wizard in Oz; but liberal democracies, or more exactly the affluent societies where liberal democracy was practiced, were accused of having contrived by inadvertence what the controller did of set purpose. The most interesting claims about how it happened rested on the thought that affluence had led to "normalization"; we had collectively created a consensus on what any normal, rational, sensible person might be, do, and want, more by commercial advertising than by indoctrination. If one monument to the sentiment was David Riesman's *Lonely Crowd,* the more dramatic assault on the undermining of real political choice in affluent democratic societies was launched by Herbert Marcuse, who arrived in the United States as a middle-aged refugee from Germany and had a late career as a guru to students less than one-third his age.

Combining the psychoanalytic insights of Freud with the economic analysis of Marx, he lamented that American society had contrived to subvert the imperatives of history, not by making life in American society really satisfying (according to the standards of Marx and Freud accepted by the radical wing of the Frankfurt school) but by diverting the psychic energy that should have resulted in a rebellion against the modern world into acquiescence in an irrational and antihuman social and political order—one whose foreign politics was built on nuclear deterrence, and whose economy was sustained by manufacturing rubbish to satisfy the "false needs" that advertisers created in us. *One-Dimensional Man* combined a plangent unhappiness at the diversion of human history from the path it ought to have taken with a wonderfully optimistic account of what might happen if all the disaffected should somehow manage to unite.

The appeal of this and similar works was its picture of a society that exercises total control without a one-party state, a secret police, a leadership cult, terror, or the obliteration of the distinction between the private and the public. Critics mocked students and their elderly radical comrades who denounced "the system"; but the vocabulary made a well-taken point. Conventional, *bien-pensant* sociology of the day was as attached as the radicals to the concept of a social system that operated behind the backs of the participants, the great difference being that it wrote approvingly of it. Thus Talcott Parsons's structural-functional analysis was intended to show how habits of child rearing, education, political socialization, and the like fit together neatly to produce psychologically well-integrated, socially adept, and politically loyal citizens.[10] It did not take much imagination to see how such an account could be turned inside out by the skeptic, although nobody without Marcuse's intellectual resources could have turned it inside out with such verve.

But when it was turned inside out the idea of a soft totalitarian society revealed itself as deeply flawed. The absence of an all-powerful leader, a one-party state, a secret police, and the systematic use of terror makes all the difference; the horror of Nazi Germany and Stalinist Russia was precisely the absence of political choice and the reality of dictatorship, violence, political murder on a vast scale, and the omnipresent secret police. Take those away, and what is left is the complaint that most of us are not very interesting—interesting to whoever the author happens to be. It may be true, and perhaps deplorable, that most of us are creatures of habit with conventional tastes and careers, that we attach our hopes and fears to our children, vote for the usual political parties, and do not imagine the earthly paradise as imminent; but the fact that we can choose to do something different without fearing a knock on the door from the secret police is not to be slighted. Assimilating the daily round of an affluent society to the sheer nastiness of Nazi Germany and the Soviet Union is a mistake.

CHAPTER 26

Democracy in the Modern World

Ancient and Modern

THE STRUCTURE OF THIS chapter is simple. It begins with some reminders of the difference between democracy in the ancient world and democracy today, and distinguishes between theorists of democracy who think of democracy as a matter of the character of a whole society, extending far beyond its political machinery, and those who see democracy as a set of arrangements for answering the question "Who is to rule?" It takes John Dewey and Joseph Schumpeter as representative of the broad and the narrow conceptions of democracy, respectively. Behind Schumpeter's account stands Max Weber's vision of the politics of a modern industrial society and his idea of *Führerdemokratie*. Behind Dewey's stands the political experience of the United States and a theory about the nature of modernity.

Dewey and Schumpeter wrote during the first half of the twentieth century, when democracies faced a world dominated by dictatorships. After World War II everything changed, and most of the world took the desirability of democracy for granted. This provoked two different kinds of theoretical reflection. One extended Schumpeter's "realistic" theory of democracy in the interests of making it more realistic; the best short account of this remains Robert Dahl's *Preface to Democratic Theory* of 1956,

not least because it is unblinkingly honest about the problems of pluralist democracy. The other was a running critique of the inadequacies of
the liberal state in its own terms. Defenders of participatory democracy
sometimes drew on Marxist ideas to condemn the inegalitarian features
of late twentieth-century democracies, but more often complained that
liberal democracies provided too few opportunities for citizens to participate in running their own lives. The most significant work of political theory in the English-speaking world at the end of the century was
John Rawls's *A Theory of Justice*. It and its successor *Political Liberalism* made
liberal principles a necessary component of democracy; this would have
astonished the Athenians, some of whom might have regretted sentencing Socrates to death, but would have taken a lot of persuading that they
had no right to do it; and it would have surprised Tocqueville and Mill,
who feared that democracy might trump liberalism. They would not
easily have been persuaded that democracy was liberalism's natural ally,
let alone that "illiberal democracy" was a contradiction in terms. The
chapter ends with the work of John Rawls, but begins with a familiar
contrast: ancient and modern.

Writers as varied as Polybius, Machiavelli, Rousseau, and Madison would not have described modern liberal democracies, of which the
archetype is the United States, as democracies without qualification.
Madison accepted Jefferson's distinction between "pure" and "representative" democracy; as the suffrage was expanded, an extensive republic
became a representative democracy. It is not a defect of liberal democracies that they are less "pure" than ancient democracies. Pure democracies were prone to factionalism and inconstancy as assemblies were
bamboozled by demagogues; they were unable to make full use of the
wisdom possessed in any society by only a few; and they undermined
leaders who needed to take decisive action without being second-guessed
by an ignorant assembly. Liberal democracies are—though nobody is
going to call them this—*nontyrannical and liberal popular mixed republics*. They
are nontyrannical because the power of the majority is not absolute, but
constitutionally constrained; they are popular because governments are
answerable to the public at large; and they are mixed regimes because
they combine the rule of the one, the few, and the many with execu-

tives led by a president or prime minister, legislatures of a few hundred members, and little initiative confided to the electorate, whose power is its power to evict its rulers, and the influence that stems from its rulers' knowledge of the electorate's powers of eviction. Whether the head of state is a president or a constitutional monarch is immaterial; that the head of the functional executive is answerable to the people is very material. They are liberal because they give the ordinary person a degree of intellectual, spiritual, and occupational freedom the ancient world never dreamed of. Their existence in the numbers that exist today would have been thought a triumph by most political thinkers in the past two and a half millennia. They would no doubt have disagreed over the parts played by intelligent statecraft and by sheer good luck in their creation.

They do not implement the ancient democratic ideal of political equality so much as the idea that every subject of a modern state is entitled to have his or her interests given equal weight.[1] Athenian democracy was built on the ideal of political equality: every qualified citizen should have an equal share of political power. There is a great difference between the idea that the demos should literally rule, so that the citizens collectively and in person can make the decisions that determine the fate of the polis, and the idea that each person's interests should be given equal consideration. The second is certainly an egalitarian ideal, and it is very plausible that the best way to ensure that everyone's interests are considered is to give everyone a say in the decisions that affect her or him. The Athenians did not overlook that argument; they wanted to protect the interests of the poor many and to prevent the wellborn or the families of tyrants from reducing them to servitude; but considering everyone's interests equally and sharing the exercise of power equally are not the same. A benevolent despot would consider everyone's interests equally; but benevolent despotism is not democracy. The Athenians wanted an equal share in decision making; they wanted that even more than they wanted everyone's interests to be equally considered.

The Athenians used selection by lottery and rapid turnover in office to achieve equality of power. It is often said that democracy in the Athenian sense is a simple impossibility in the modern world. This is false; it would be complicated to institute, but not impossible, and the shade of Thomas Jefferson would enjoy watching us make the attempt. The American conservative William F. Buckley once observed that he would rather be governed by the first 300 people in the Boston phone book than by the faculty of Harvard. That was not a very radical thought. One might well prefer to be governed by 500 people chosen by lot than by the 535 professional politicians who make up the Congress of the United States or the 635 professional politicians who make up the British House of Commons. That would implement the Athenian view of political equality. No individual citizen would have much chance of exercising real power, but each would have the same chance as anyone else. Nor need we stop with Congress or the House of Commons; any body that *oversees* and *approves* the work of legislation and administration as distinct from *devising* legislation and *implementing* it in administration could be chosen in the same way. To the objection that absolutely anybody might end up voting on complicated legislation, one obvious retort is that absolutely anybody might decide on your incarceration for the rest of your life by serving on the jury that tries your case. The complications arise elsewhere, and anyone who works his way through them will begin to see that the problem is not the ignorance of the demos—which is little worse than that of elected legislators—but that just as juries are reliant on judges and counsel, so a modern *ecclesia* would have to be so reliant on the guidance of an expert civil service that de jure democracy might easily turn into a de facto bureaucratic tyranny or a dictatorship of experts. Similarly, just as juries are often swayed by one articulate and well-informed member, a modern *ecclesia* might become what Thucydides said Athens was under Pericles, in theory a democracy and in practice a monarchy.

If modern democracies do not share Athens's commitment to equality in the exercise of power, they are committed to forms of equality the Athenians would have scoffed at. Not the least of them is the enfranchisement of women. What the nineteenth and twentieth centuries thought of as the growth of democracy was the extension of the franchise, first to nonpropertied men and much more slowly to women. In France women obtained the vote only in 1944, in Switzerland only in 1971; non-Athenian as modern democracies are, they inherited the tradition that the right to vote reflected a man's role as breadwinner in peace and soldier in war, and that women's place was in the home. Universal suffrage is no small matter. If modern democracy amounts to rule by professional politicians, universal suffrage makes them accountable, if not to "the many" at least to whoever they think is likely to vote against them if their interests are not attended to. This does not equalize the power of individual voters, since it gives much influence to swing voters and little to those who are reliably in the majority or minority, but if they care to use their collective power, it gives "the many" more power over "the few" than they would have in its absence. One person one vote literally implements Bentham's principle that "each is to count for one and nobody for more than one."

Having distinguished between securing the equal representation of interests, which universal suffrage can achieve, and securing everyone an equal chance of making large decisions, which it does not, it is important to recognize that even the first aim will be achieved only if many other conditions are in place. It is all too obvious that democracy as practiced can easily be the equal representation of the interests of those who form the majority and the complete neglect of those who form the minority. Until public opinion changed in the 1950s, the legal, social, and economic disabilities under which black Americans labored in the American South would not have been removed by ensuring that black Americans could vote. A compact white majority would have voted to neglect the interests of the black population, much as a compact Protestant majority voted for decades to neglect the interests of the Catholic minority in Ulster. Absent the right social conditions, we end up with the tyranny of the majority.

The other striking contrast between the ancient and the modern ideas of democracy is that the intense involvement in public affairs that Pericles said was the outstanding trait of the Athenians of his day is not a feature of large affluent societies. This is felt to be a loss by many commentators, if not by ordinary citizens. The upsurge of interest in creating a more participatory democracy during the 1960s stemmed from the sense that the citizenry had abdicated its political responsibilities. In allowing professional politicians to monopolize political activity, the citizenry had lost "ownership" of public affairs. There are arguments on the other side. The old saying "Happy is the nation that has no history" might suggest that a nation whose population can safely pay attention to more rewarding things than politics is in a happy state. We may nonetheless think that this blessed condition will persist only if there is universal suffrage so that the citizenry can remind the professional politicians who it is that they are supposed to serve, and only if enough of the citizens take a continuous interest in the activities of the political class and can awaken their fellow citizens when they must.

John Dewey and "Social" Democracy

By the end of the nineteenth century, democracy had attained some potency as a moral ideal. Although some critics still talked of "the democracy" as a synonym for the unwashed many, the idea that everyone entered the world with an equal right to a decent life and a modicum of respect for his or her individuality had become a commonplace, while the slow extension of the franchise in Britain and its more rapid expansion in the United States had proved that democracy would not degenerate into mob rule. It had many unlooked-for features, such as machine politics and the boss system of many American cities, but what Mr. Dooley christened "honest graft" is not a precursor to the tumbrels and the guillotine. Democracy gained further support before the First World War, as the contrast between militaristic autocracies and liberal democracies became part of the everyday currency of political controversy. One impressive articulation of the democratic ideal that relies heavily on the contrast between democratic modernity and premodern autocracy and aristocracy was provided by John Dewey. Dewey was born in Vermont in 1859, just before the Civil War, and died in New York ninety-two years later, in 1952. Insofar as anyone could be described as America's national philosopher, it was he. On his death the *New York Times* observed, "America does not know what it thinks until Professor Dewey has spoken." That hardly reflected his own sense of having spent a lifetime battling enemies to left and right with very modest success. He lived through the transformation of the United States from being a society of farms and small towns to being the greatest industrial and military power on earth. He was unimpressed by the brute fact of industrial and military progress, but immensely impressed by the possibilities of the modern world. Bringing them to fruition in the "great community" was what he labeled in a broad-brush fashion "democracy."[2]

Although Dewey was a liberal, it was only late in life that he said anything explicit about the "liberal" element in liberal democracy. He was a liberal in the American sense, a believer in an active state, not the night watchman state praised by Herbert Spencer and the American conservatives whom he influenced. The conception of liberty Dewey employed in *Liberalism and Social Action*[3] was a "positive" view of liberty as self-actualization, not the negative "let-alone" sense of liberty that he associated with old-fashioned laissez-faire and a misguided belief in rugged individualism. He took for granted, and toward the end of his life confessed that he had taken too much for granted, that well-entrenched and meticulously protected civil liberties were intrinsic to anything one could properly call a democracy. Non-Americans, not to say Americans who remember Senator Joseph McCarthy, may flinch at such optimism. It did, however, mean that the key concept in Dewey's political vocabulary was democracy rather than liberty; the idea that one could have too much democracy makes no sense on Dewey's understanding of democracy. This sets him at odds with Mill and Tocqueville, who were eager to restrain democracy for the sake of individual liberty, and with the American founders, who initially thought they were erecting barriers to democracy when they built their new republic.

Dewey was also at odds with the view of democracy that sees its essence in the voters' ability to throw out their masters, and thereby exercise some control over them. His peers, intellectually and politically, were English contemporaries such as T. H. Green and L. T. Hobhouse, who also thought of democracy as the political aspect of a rationally governed society that met the aspirations of its members by making all of them full participants in a rich communal life. Like Hobhouse, Dewey was likely in his optimistic moments to think that individuals did not need protecting *against* society, but enabling to become full members of it; only in his less optimistic moments did he emphasize that they might also need defenses against the bigotries, enthusiasms, and simple errors of their fellows. Dewey did not dwell on *antagonisms*. Although he was uninhibited in criticizing the greed, corruption, and incompetence of the owners of big business and the bankrollers of American politicians, he did not see democratic politics as domesticated class warfare. He had an exaggerated sense of the differences between Europe and the United States, did not think that the United States was a class-divided society, and therefore thought that a labor party in the sense in which the British Labour Party and European Social Democratic parties were such was not only impracticable, but unsuitable for the United States. This did not reflect any enthusiasm for the politicians of his day, whom he dismissed as "bag-carriers for business."

As that suggests, Dewey did not see democracy as a matter of political machinery or even politics in the ordinary sense. The concept of democracy had been extended into realms beyond politics. Writers who would place more emphasis on institutions than Dewey would readily acknowledge that democratic politics must be built on a democratic culture if they are to last, and that democratic political institutions do not exist for their own sake but to have an effect on the whole of social and economic life. Many would, however, argue that the subject matter of modern politics is economic advantage, and that the point of democracy is to close the gap between the fates of the better-off and the worse-off. Dewey, on the other hand, as *The Public and Its Problems* makes clear, thought of democracy in intellectual terms as a problem-solving mechanism, not as an instrument of peaceful class conflict.[4] The political system is supposed to look after "the public" in the sense of meeting needs that other associations do not meet, and mopping up the unwanted effects of what other associations do.

This was squarely in the tradition that equates democracy with "the American way," though for Dewey it was not the American way as it was but the American way as it might be if Americans lived up their ideals. Nor was the ideal American in a narrowly national sense; rather, the United States represented modernity and its possibilities less inhibitedly than other societies. Dewey sometimes pressed the argument to extraordinary lengths. In his very early essay "Democracy and Christianity," he made the striking suggestion that as society evolved, the insights of Christianity would be so incorporated into social attitudes that the church would dissolve into the community and religion would cease to be a distinct activity and would become one aspect of the fully democratic life. Needless to say, the contrast between the legislatures of the Gilded Age and the kingdom of God on earth was extreme enough to make anyone avert their gaze from institutions as they are, and contemplate what Dewey later called "the Great Community" as it might be.[5]

If democracy so broadly conceived was a religious ideal, it was in a wholly secular sense. Brought up by a fiercely Congregationalist mother, Dewey was hostile to institutionalized religion; it separated the ideal from the actual, divided our good selves from our bad selves, and unhelpfully contrasted the bliss of the hereafter with the present vale of tears. Dewey was deeply un-Augustinian. In the 1930s he argued that a democrat would have what he described as a religious outlook, but "the religious" as a cultural outlook must be rescued from "religion," thought of as something confined to and managed by churches. In practical terms, he was a fierce defender of the separation of church and state mandated by the U.S. Constitution, and an intransigent opponent of allowing the teachers of particular faiths into the classrooms of public schools. His theory did not entail such fierceness as a matter of logic. As a matter of logic, Dewey thought that the essence of human existence was life in a community of equals. This was not an identity of abilities, tastes, talents, or resources but a spiritual equality; it was the secular version of equality in the eyes of God, and its short name was democracy.

Just as Dewey did not think of politics as class warfare without bullets, he did not think of voters as calculating economic agents. Hardheaded analysts have for a long time tried to explain political behavior in terms of rational choice models much like the model of "rational economic man." Dewey was part of the revolt against what critics called "atomistic individualism," the precursor of modern rational choice theory. Atomistic individualism saw citizens, like consumers, as rational utility maximizers. Dewey was a communitarian, and thought of individuals as social through and through. This was typical of early twentieth-century social and political thinking. New sociological insights had made "atomistic" individualism seem old-fashioned. It was conceded that writers like Mill were more sophisticated about politics than the psychological theories to which they were officially committed strictly allowed; but the idea that social and political theory might model itself on the abstractions of economics was not popular. Even in economics this was the heyday of institutional and historical economics. Though the emphasis on the sociality of the individual was commonplace, its basis varied from one thinker to another. Dewey began as a philosopher in a Hegelian mold; he thought that the individual becomes truly human and genuinely an individual only by sharing in and drawing on the moral, spiritual, and intellectual resources of the society of which he is part, and from which he can separate himself even in imagination only by an effort. We are separate biological individuals, but our biological identity is not our human identity. We come into the world ready to turn into human individuals, but we are not yet such. Experience works on the raw materials, and as we learn to distinguish ourselves from others and from our environment, we learn to take the responsibility for our thinking and acting implicit in saying, "I think." There could be no "I" without a "we."

The road from that starting point to the conclusion that democracy is the essence of life in a modern community is long, but surprisingly direct. Communities exist to attend to common concerns; as we become better able to manage those common concerns, we can deepen and enrich our communal ties. There are bad communities, such as bands of robbers; their badness lies in their being at odds with other communities and the larger community. Good communities foster cooperative relationships. In practice we belong to many communities, and our membership of each will be more or less salient according to our different concerns. These communal ties become more extensive and deeper as life becomes richer and more varied; in one of Dewey's formulations, democracy is "the great community" or the "community of communities." We give the name of "the state" to the institutions that take care of the interests that are either not met or adversely affected by our pursuit of our interests as members of the other communities to which we belong.[6] Dewey was not unique in holding that view; indeed, it can even be glossed in the hardheaded terms of interest-group theory, as it was by political scientists such as David Truman.[7] Dewey was more nearly unique in linking it to a distinctive account of the nature of the world within which democracy was to operate. He was not interested in elections or voting construed as mechanisms for giving decision makers power and holding them accountable. He saw democracy solving practical problems by something analogous to the procedures of science. A community needed to know what to do, and like the individuals of whom it was composed, it had to deliberate on its needs and resources and find the path of "growth." Dewey was not merely a communitarian but also the begetter of what has recently been termed "deliberative democracy." The practice of democracy is a community working out what its needs are and how to satisfy them.[8]

Dewey eschewed the role of philosopher-king. He did not think that it was his business as a philosopher to tell his fellow citizens what course to pursue. He had no inhibitions about writing polemical essays to tell them what to think about particular issues, but only as a citizen talking to other citizens, as any citizen might. Kings were outmoded and autocracy of any kind was inimical to human development, while philosophy was a form of cultural criticism that philosophers should engage in at one remove from the immediate decisions of the day. Philosophers were not experts and had no standing to provide expert advice. Cars need mechanics, not philosophers, when they go wrong, just as drains need plumbers. What philosophers can usefully do is help the public think by articulating the opportunities and dilemmas confronting modern man. Dewey's task was therefore to lay out the logic—in a rather extended sense of the term—of moral and political deliberation for his fellow citizens, not to preempt their deliberations. There is nothing odd about Dewey's view that philosophers had no particular standing in a democratic society, but he was very unusual in behaving as though he really believed it.

If democracy is not a set of political arrangements centering on voting and the installation and ejection of governments, but rather the name of an ideal of community life in the modern world, sustained by rationality and a scientific view of the world, more detail is needed about how democracy works. The most important aspect is the role of education. Dewey himself said that the best guide to his philosophy was *Democracy and Education*.[9] The way he arranged the book as a dialogue between Plato and Rousseau, with himself as arbiter and conciliator—closer to the thinker that Rousseau would have been if less easily carried away by "nature"—tells us all we need. Plato wants to educate an elite who will think *for* the ordinary person; that is no good, because it is at odds with modern ideals of self-reliance and because elites that are not answerable become corrupted. Conversely, Rousseau believes that every idea we need is latent within us and needs only to be released. On the contrary, says Dewey, as the world becomes more complicated and economic life is based less and less within the natural unit of the family, children need a more elaborate, more articulate education that allows them to function as members of an "arm's length" but cooperative community. Teachers must draw interest and understanding from the child's own self, but children require teachers, and teachers are the builders of the democratic society. We must think for ourselves as Rousseau wanted and Plato did not; but thinking is a skill that must be taught.

Dewey always insisted that human beings are problem-solving creatures; that was what his pragmatism meant. They solve problems, their solutions create more problems, and these in turn need resolution. Readers of Dewey were misled when he called this process "adjustment," a term that seems to suggest a passive adaptation to a fixed environment. Nothing was further from his mind; the environment was as unfixed as our goals, whence his insistence that the only general term for what he sought was "growth." He irritated critics for half a century by refusing to say what "growth" entailed; he thought that a gardener knows whether a plant is thriving without committing himself to a fixed goal, and each of us knows well enough whether a change in our beliefs and attitudes, or in how our lives go, is "growth." In the same way, he misled readers by talking of democracy as "experimental." The easily misled thought that this was a defense of technocracy, the dictatorship of the scientist. But where most of us contrast science and art, or the technical and the aesthetic, Dewey resisted such dichotomies. He came to think that the role of philosophy was less to seek truth than to enhance experience; science does this by allowing us to control the world for utilitarian purposes and by enhancing our appreciation of the world. Art equally illuminates and enhances experience, not in competition with or as a respite from the scientific understanding but as one more way of engaging with experience. The idea that the world is, so to speak, waiting for us to experience it as richly as possible underpins Dewey's idea of modernity. Democracy is what happens when old, superstitious, tradition-bound, and cramped understandings of sociability have been transcended; more positively, it is what a society practices when its citizens are understood to be entitled to equal access to the world and its riches—emotional, intellectual, and spiritual rather than purely material. Dewey was once asked whether he was an optimist or a pessimist; he replied that he was a great optimist about things in general but a terrible pessimist about everything in particular. Democracy is a summary of that outlook; it is the modern ideal of life, one that is everywhere realized in extremely inadequate ways.

To say that Dewey did not carry conviction with all his readers understates the case. Walter Lippmann thought Dewey put far too much faith in the ordinary citizen's capacities; Lippmann had begun as a radical, even working for the socialist mayor of Poughkeepsie after the elections of 1912; but in the 1920s he became increasingly conservative. *Public Opinion* and *The Phantom Public* were implicit critiques of Dewey's views, although both predated *The Public and Its Problems*, which grapples none too successfully with *The Phantom Public*'s critique of "the public." Insofar as Lippmann put his faith in any institutional arrangements, it was in the possibility of councils of expert advisers, insulated from public and political pressure. In the 1930s Lippmann turned to traditional natural law theory in his search for a stable, transcendental source of political truth, far removed from anything Dewey could sympathize with. Reinhold Niebuhr was more directly critical of Dewey; his *Moral Man and Immoral Society* and a string of articles in the 1930s criticized Dewey from the standpoint of a more Augustinian standpoint. Dewey's optimistic picture of a public coming to understand and act on its common interests as the result of reiterated discussion struck Niebuhr as naïve. Conflicts of interests went deep; they were more often exacerbated than diminished by discussion. Since discussion would not lead to agreement, we must face the fact that politics involves the exercise of power, which usually means one group's interests being forcibly subordinated to another group's. Coercion is a fact of life. We must decide which group has justice on its side and fight for it.[10]

Joseph Schumpeter

It was not Dewey's direct critics but Joseph Schumpeter who did the most effective job of demolition in the wonderfully brisk, irritated, and ingenious discussion in *Capitalism, Socialism, and Democracy*.[11] It was the more effective because it never mentioned Dewey and lumped all moral defenses of democracy into one bag labeled "the classical theory," and contrasted them to their disadvantage with his own "realistic" theory. It was extremely unfair, but it drew the line between moralists and realists in a plausible way. Schumpeter was an upper-class Viennese who came to the United States in 1932, when he was not quite fifty. He was the leading economist of his generation at Harvard, and the teacher of many of the next generation of world-class economists. Having had all too intimate an experience of government as the Austrian minister of finance immediately after the end of the First World War, he wrote about democracy in a dry, skeptical fashion that could hardly have been more different from Dewey's. He was the begetter of what was subsequently baptized "the elite theory of democracy," though he himself described it simply as "realistic."

Schumpeter's purpose was not to give an analytical account of democracy. *Capitalism, Socialism, and Democracy* was a riposte to Marx's *Capital*. It explained the nature of capitalism, explained why capitalism would probably evolve into some form of socialism, and why the forms of government appropriate to a nonrevolutionary, noninsurrectionary, nontotalitarian socialism were much the same as those appropriate to liberal capitalism. Published in 1942, the book displays a reasonable anxiety that sentimentalism and superstition may undermine the liberal democracies at a difficult time, and this gives an added urgency to an argument that in any case was marked by Schumpeter's trademark clarity, deftness, and sharpness. His account of what makes democracies democratic has been to all intents and purposes the common sense of political science for the subsequent seventy years, though sadly shorn of many of his more distinctive thoughts. Here, I restore them, although they undermine Schumpeter's self-ascribed "realism."

To set off his "realistic" account, Schumpeter discusses what he called the "classical" account of democracy. Nobody ever subscribed to all the elements of the classical account, and Schumpeter himself was casual about attaching it to anyone in particular. However, one could without injustice argue that Dewey subscribed to enough elements in the classical account to make Schumpeter's criticism something that an admirer of Dewey should take account of. The classical theory of democracy is described as the view that democracy is a method for achieving the common good by means of public discussion and the popular vote. The thought is that the public will come to a view on what the common good is and delegate its representatives to turn that view into policy. This is sufficiently reminiscent of Rousseau's account of the search for the general will to suggest that it was Rousseau that Schumpeter had in mind; fastidious critics who point out that Rousseau was discussing the conditions of the legitimacy of law under any system of government whatever miss the point. Schumpeter aimed at several targets, some of them alternative to one another.[12]

Thus one objection to the classical theory is that the common good is not transparently visible as it needs to be for the Rousseauian method to work. It is not clear from Schumpeter's account whether he thinks that there is *no* common good, as he might well have done, since this was a period of skepticism among moral philosophers about the reality of any ethical standards at all, and among political scientists about the reality of the public interest or common good. It might have been nothing more than the objection that whatever the common good was, it would not be agreed on by all observers. Rousseau himself thought there were societies, of which any modern industrial society would surely be one, in which there could be few common interests, because the antagonism of individuals and classes was so great that it would be like seeking a common interest between the leopard and the goat. Another of Schumpeter's objections, however, is that a single person armed with plenipotentiary power can often bring about a result that is universally agreed to be desirable, but which no group of decision makers, let alone the whole population, would vote for. Schumpeter's example is the concordat between the French state and the papacy that Napoleon contrived when nobody else could have done it. This presupposes that there is a discernible common good, but that it is unachievable by democratic procedures.[13]

The larger objection to the classical theory takes us back to the skepticism about the ordinary man's political capacity that was a central component of theories of mass society. To have a clear, intelligent view about political outcomes is beyond the lay voter. Neither his beliefs nor his wants are fixed, nor can they be clearly articulated by him or anyone else. The classical theory places the initiative in the wrong place. It represents political decision making as a matter of the electorate, or a majority of voters, coming to a view that they then instruct their delegates to put into action. This runs contrary to the way things work. Like the good economist he was, Schumpeter asks us to consider the analogous case of a consumer product. We do not sit at home elaborating the specification of something as complex as an automobile, and then go and find a manufacturer to build it. Entrepreneurs dream up products that they think advertisers can persuade us to want; they assemble the capital and the workforce to create these products, and then offer them to us at a price. If they have guessed right about what we can be persuaded to want, they prosper; if not, they go broke. Schumpeter's economics put entrepreneurial imagination, the source of his famous "gales of creative destruction," at the heart of the explanation of economic growth. It is not surprising to find it at the heart of his account of democracy.

The classical theory cannot give a plausible account of democracy as practiced, or a coherent account of how it might be practiced. It demands unrealistic amounts of knowledge and self-reliance from the voter, and in asking the voter to aim at the common good asks him to aim at what may not be there, and is anyway often not easy to see. This sets the scene for the realistic theory, but it is worth making one preliminary observation. Schumpeter never suggests it is worth discussing the degree of popular suffrage required in order for a polity to be a democracy, nor how much time can elapse between elections before we conclude that a system is not a democracy. Schumpeter puts up a straw man image of democracy as a system that envisaged "the people" forming a view of their common good and sending their delegates off to implement that view. Realism replaces the straw man with its contradictory.

The classical definition of democracy contained an implicit moral assessment: democracy was the method of decision making that secured the common good. It was therefore uniquely legitimate. The realistic definition eschews ethics. It says that the democratic method is the method whereby an elite obtains the power to decide by means of a competitive struggle for the people's vote.[14] Schumpeter adds to the ethical bleakness by insisting that if democracy is only a *method*, then it can have no value in itself, any more than a steam locomotive can. This is not persuasive. Hard work and bank robbery are both methods of acquiring money, but that hardly shows that hard work is no more admirable than bank robbery. Schumpeter did not really resist the point. Democratic competition is one way of acquiring the power to decide, and so is assassination; the virtues of the former and the drawbacks of the latter are obvious enough. Schumpeter's realism required no more than his insistence, first, that it is inevitable that elites exercise power and, second, that what distinguishes elites in democracies is that they are professional politicians who must compete for power by appealing for the votes of the electorate. That is so plausible that his definition of democracy as a competitive struggle for the people's votes became canonical in American political analysis.

The "realistic" theory is more complex than it looks. Schumpeter's amoralism is the insistence that "democratic" means not "good" but "installed by election." A politician may acquire power in a fair election, but be a terrible prime minister, president, or whatever. Being democratically elected is no guarantee of ability; American and British voters habitually despise their politicians, even though they often make an exception of those they have voted for, much as they do for their local schools and their own doctors when denouncing standards of education and health care. Schumpeter diverges from many elite theorists in not suggesting that election is a guarantee of *in*competence; he is not a gloomy aristocrat like Ortega y Gasset but a realist. There are good, bad, and indifferent democratic politicians, and they are good, bad, and indifferent in different ways and at different things. Some are geniuses at wooing the voter and inept at balancing a budget, others mediocre on the campaign trail but excellent managers of government departments. Schumpeter drew on the analogy with economic activity to point up what he had in mind in distinguishing so sharply between the power-seeking elite and the vote-conferring rank and file. Consumers do not design cars and hire manufacturers; they respond to the sales pitches of the manufacturers. So in politics, initiative comes from above, and voters respond to the politicians' sales pitches.

This is all to the good. It provides a coherence in the workings of a political system that would otherwise be unavailable. Having set out to shock the reader, Schumpeter keeps up the good work by limiting the defining features of democracy in a fashion that tells the careful reader much that Schumpeter does not spell out. For Schumpeter, democracy exists if the elites who hold power received their title to it by reference to the electorate, not to a monarch. The model is Britain. Prior to sometime around 1834, a reigning monarch could dismiss a prime minister who enjoyed the confidence of Parliament and not suffer ill consequences. After that, it was assumed that the monarch must appoint the man who commanded the confidence of Parliament and that the monarch must not try to make policy on her or his own. At the time, the British electorate was 14 percent of the adult male population, 7 percent of the adult population as a whole. Schumpeter knew this. The issue was not how many people voted, but whether their votes determined who held power. Because Schumpeter was an economist and enjoyed drawing parallels between politicians and businessmen—"I deal in votes just like they deal in oil" was one of the quotations with which he scandalized his readers—it is easy to think that Schumpeter must have thought of the political system as being wholly like the economic system, and many readers have thought so. He did not. The electorate *legitimates* the rulers. This is not an economic concept. The theory of divine right held that God placed the crown on the ruler's head; the theory of democratic right is that vox populi, not vox Dei, is decisive; the job of the people is not to rule but to place the crown on one set of heads rather than another. So long as it is "the people's vote" that does the crowning, the question of how *many* people the people consists of may safely be ducked.

Schumpeter appreciated that the compatibility of democracy with liberal values depends on the existence of social, religious, and cultural understandings that democracy itself may not be able to create. These understandings impose constitutional constraints on the use of political power, whether they are embodied in a written constitution, as in the United States, or not, as in Britain. Among the most important are provisions that protect religious and ethnic minorities. Schumpeter softened up readers inclined to identify democratically arrived-at decisions with the realization of the ideal by reminding them that often it had been unaccountable ruling elites who protected unpopular religious and ethnic minorities against a widespread and enthusiastic desire to do them harm, which majority rule would have facilitated.[15] To reach an agreement on such constitutional provisions in a confessionally or ethnically divided state may be impossible, but once an agreement is in place and confessional conflict is off-limits as a subject for everyday politics, everyday politics becomes possible. Even then, constitutional provisions may prove to be only parchment barriers. The good sense of this view has been demonstrated in societies as far apart as Northern Ireland, Rwanda, and much of the Middle East.

Democracy as practiced implies the existence of conflicts of interest and conflicts over policy within a consensus on the way to resolve those conflicts; if there were no competing teams of would-be leaders, there would be no politics, and if they secured power other than at the ballot box, it would not be democracy. By the same token, if the politicians who acquire power through the competitive struggle for the popular vote are mere figureheads, or systematically ignored and frustrated by the holders of unofficial and unaccountable power, there is no democracy. Contemporary Russia comes to mind. On the assumption that the elected government really governs, it remains essential to running a successful democracy that there are clear limits to what is subject to the competitive process. The American Constitution, for example, puts many things off-limits, particularly religion and, after the Civil War, the legitimacy of slavery, and as the result of a more recent and very slow change in the moral climate, many forms of racial and sexual discrimination. Constitutional constraints, narrowly construed, can only do so much. Collective opinion or, more grandly, public political morality does more. Governor George Wallace's infamous battle cry of the 1950s "Ain't nobody going to out-nigger me," after he had suffered defeat at the hands of someone even more racist than he, would today instantly terminate a political career.

Other items in Schumpeter's list of prerequisites are more nearly recipes for perfection than prerequisites for any tolerable regime; they affect how well a political system would function, rather than the constraints that protect its legitimacy. He argued, for example, that democracy needs a political class whose members are socially and psychologically capable of enduring political failure with good humor and no resentment. Men whose entire lives are focused on politics find it harder to lose office than men whose lives contain much else. Politics is best conducted by people imbued with a spirit of noblesse oblige, who regard the hurly-burly of campaigning and the strain of governing as a duty that they undertake for the sake of the public good. This is an idealization of the English governing classes of the late nineteenth century and overlooks their actual passion for public office and the misery its loss caused them. It is certainly at odds with the desperation with which most British and American elected politicians cling to their seats, and it squares awkwardly with Schumpeter's nice observation, following Weber, that democracy is the rule of the professional politician.

Schumpeter demands an impartial public service that exists to serve politicians of different parties and is not committed to one political creed or another. Here again, the positive model is late nineteenth-century Britain, and the negative model is the Weimar Republic, many of whose bureaucrats not only were unenthusiastic about the newly minted republic but went to some lengths to betray it. What is contentious in Schumpeter's claims is not the thought that modern states need competent bureaucracies to supply their citizens with the services that modern states commit themselves to supplying, but the insistence on one particular model of such a bureaucracy. European observers thought the U.S. federal bureaucracy before World War II a very amateur and provincial enterprise; but this was partly a failure to understand how much was done by the states and how little by the federal government. When the demands of the New Deal and World War II required a senior civil service of highly skilled managers, it was possible to recruit them very quickly.

Schumpeter was not, for all that, primarily interested in efficiency. His concern was with legitimacy, and that leads to one element in his account that breaks with all subsequent American discussion. Since it was central, deeply felt, and intrinsic to what Schumpeter was trying to do, we should pay it some attention. He insisted, wholly against the grain of American political practice, that once voters had elected a government, their task was to let it govern. At this point all analogies with economics break down. The temptation into which Schumpeter led later writers was to think that casting a vote is like making a purchase; voters buy policies with their votes, and politicians sell policies—more exactly promises about policies—in return for votes. A few moments' thought reveals holes in the analogy. No consumer would buy five years' worth of food, clothing, household supplies, and the rest in one go; nor would a consumer submit to the obligation to make a choice between only two or three bundles of such goods—but in a two- or three-party electoral system that is what the voter does. To this there are two replies. One is to observe that responsive political parties restore flexibility by allowing voters *between elections* to pressure the parties to move more or less aggressively on policies, to steal their opponents' clothes, and so on. In effect, the bundle of policies is constantly reconstructed in response to pressure. The other response is to acknowledge that voting for a party and its policies is not best thought of as purchasing anything. The first implies that if Schumpeter's realism is supposed to be realism about the workings of American politics, it fails. The second makes complete sense of Schumpeter's hostility to pressure groups. He really meant voters to understand that their role in democratic politics is to put the crown firmly on their rulers' heads, and not to put pressure on their rulers in between times. From a realist, it was unrealistic advice. It is unrealistic to suppose that voters will behave in that way, and in the most unequivocally democratic of modern states, the United States, it is particularly unrealistic. Unsurprisingly, postwar American theorists were eager to reintegrate pressure groups into the justification of democracy, though not to distance themselves from Schumpeter's realist and institutional definition of democracy.

Robert Dahl and Polyarchy

The most elegant such account was given by Robert Dahl in 1956 in a small classic called *A Preface to Democratic Theory*. One of his concessions to the desire for "realism" was to recast the idea of democracy; it was not "rule by the people," or *demo*cracy, but "rule by a lot of people," or *polyarchy*. Taking for granted that only small numbers of people do any actual governing, Dahl argued three points that Schumpeter's obsession with legitimacy had hidden from view. The first was that it was a virtue in a political system to be responsive both to numbers and to intensity of feeling, as American polyarchy was. Simple majority rule was neither practiced nor desirable; if majorities made no concessions to minorities there would be civil war. In themselves neither numbers nor intensity were morally admirable: people may be intensely attached to old habits of racial discrimination, to choose Dahl's own example and particularly relevant at the time. Nonetheless, there would be an Aristotelian stasis if they were not taken seriously. The second point was that although politics consisted of a continuous process of accommodating the conflicting demands of a large and varied population, it mattered greatly that a discontinuous electoral process lay behind it; without elected politicians to control the process whereby officials and the representatives of organized groups negotiated with one another, there would be no accepted way of dictating the terms on which negotiations were conducted. The third was that modern societies are pluralist, consisting of great numbers of social groups with different economic interests, cultural attachments, and ethnic, racial, or religious identities. It is not the poor many on the one side and would-be oligarchs on the other. If these differences are "cross-cutting" in the sense that different ethnic or religious groupings contain both rich and poor, radical and conservative members, their members will not press one set of interests beyond reason. The negative examples

make the case. Where, as in Northern Ireland for much of the twentieth century, an economically advantaged Protestant majority formed a
united block against the economically disadvantaged Catholic minority,
accommodation was unlikely and oppression more likely, and civil war,
not democracy, a probable outcome. One virtue of the concept of polyarchy is that it allows us to ask whether disadvantaged groups have adequate
access to different parts of the political system. It was a shortcoming of
Preface that it took too optimistic a view of the answer in the case of black
Americans, but it was a considerable virtue that the book set the standards by which its own shortcomings could be measured.[16]

The great merit of polyarchy as Dahl describes it is its ability to
accommodate many divergent interests, but it was acknowledged by
Dahl himself that this came at the price of slowness and a tendency to
reward those who for whatever reason occupied strategic positions in the
system. Persons or groups who occupy a "veto point" have a disproportionate ability to stop anything from happening, and can demand and
receive unreasonable and disproportionate concessions for their acquiescence in greatly needed change. That so much legislation requires the
government of the day to buy the acquiescence of unscrupulous senators
and congressmen, whose main asset is their ability to engage in what
amounts to the systematic robbery of badly placed voters, is one of many
things that enrages the electorate. Nonetheless, not all veto points are
morally obnoxious; constitutional protection against religious discrimination provides its beneficiaries with a veto over hostile legislation that
few of us object to.

The Farther Shores of Democratic Theory

Liberal democracy seemed all the more attractive after 1945 by contrast
with its wartime and postwar competitors. Fascism was wholly discredited, Nazism was wholly discredited, and although Communist parties
were strong in France and Italy, they posed no real challenge to liberal
democracy. France was more vulnerable to disgruntled army officers who

resented the loss of Indochina and the impending loss of Algeria. But two sentiments became increasingly powerful in the 1960s and early 1970s. The first was the sense that affluence had not given life the meaning that an increasingly well-educated and increasingly leisured society looked for. The other was a sense that society was, in some deep way that was hard to analyze but easy to feel, simply irrational. These discontents in their mildest forms fueled the wish for a more participatory society, where women had more say over the conditions of domestic life, children had more say over the conditions under which they were educated, and workers had more say about the way their workplaces functioned and what they and their employers produced. At their most inflammatory, they fueled a demand for the total transformation of society with a view to ending war and imperialism, profit making and exploitation, sexual frustration, and the alienating tedium of everyday life.

The aspiration for a more participatory society was partly the restatement of a central democratic ideal, and partly instrumental. The ideal is that we should all take ownership of our society, that it should not be divided into haves and have-nots or, more importantly, into the deciders and the decided-fors. Algernon Sidney's insistence that God did not create men to be bridled and saddled so that their privileged fellows could ride was an old statement of an egalitarian truism. It underlay Dewey's vision of a democratic society, and it is what the bleaker disciples of Weber dismiss as impossible. For them, society will always divide into mass and elite, order givers and order takers, even if the possession of power does not bring, as it usually does, excessive inequalities of wealth and status. The anti-Weberians asked a simple question: "Whose world is it?" "Whose school?" invites the answer "It belongs to the pupils as well as the teachers and the local education authority." "Whose workplace?" invites the answer "It belongs to the workers as well as the owners and the managers." Matters get interestingly complicated when we ask "Whose home?" and move beyond "not just father's." The thought is that we should have a right to decide what happens in all these different areas, and we should take responsibility for those decisions. It is an old complaint that workers put up with the consequences of bad decisions made by management, and wives and children with the consequences of bad decisions made by husbands and fathers. If power without responsibility is bad, vulnerability without power is worse.

The morality of the participatory case condenses to the claim that an adult must be self-governing; where "pupil power" is involved, the thought is that growing up involves learning how to be self-governing; literal self-government on a national scale may be unobtainable, but it can be had in institutions such as the home, the workplace, and the school. The instrumental case for participation is very simple. Even the most benign wielder of authority takes more seriously the needs and wishes of those over whom that authority is exercised when they can make trouble if their views are neglected. This is a central element in the case for universal suffrage, but here imagined to imply a more direct democracy because the scale is smaller. Whether Jefferson might have wished to extend the argument for ward republics from Charlottesville to handing his beloved University of Virginia over to student power is an unanswerable question.

Workplaces where the workers habitually share in decision making should operate smoothly and consensually; German industry seemed to bear out this hope. This liberal argument for workplace democracy is not the Marxist argument for the socialization of the means of production. The Marxist ambition was that an entire society should operate *rationally* as a totality. Marx thought this would happen only when society was rationally organized to produce fully human lives for its members, and how that would be done he never spelled out. It is not obvious that global rationality is consistent with workplace democracy, let alone that it entails it; when Engels said that the motto over the door of the automated factory was "Abandon autonomy all ye who enter here," he did not speak lightly. The liberal desire for participation in local institutions and the workplace puts the rationality of society conceived as a productive engine in second place at best. Mill's defense of worker cooperatives in his *Chapters on Socialism* focuses on the workers' control of the enterprises in which they work, and ignores coordination between different enterprises other than through the market. The most influential post-1945 declaration in favor of participatory democracy in the English-speaking world was not in the least Marxist; the *Port Huron Statement*[17] of 1962 was the catechism of the Students for a Democratic Society, a grouping that grew out of the League for Industrial Democracy, an organization that John Dewey chaired for many years.

The pamphlet's argument was simple. The division of the world into the givers of orders and the takers of orders was morally intolerable. Ordinary people were deprived of control of the arrangements within which they worked and were educated. New, more local forms of democratic control were needed. The workers' cooperative was a model for most institutions—schools and universities prominent among them. The argument struck a chord among readers, and far beyond those who read the pamphlet. Indeed, the impact went farther than that, in the sense that it induced many Marxists, too, to look for arguments in favor of local and piecemeal democracy within Marx's own writings. The European attempt to reconcile Catholicism and Marxism in Europe depended on finding the points where Catholic pluralism and Marxist pluralism met, and workplace democracy was one. A graduate student pamphlet would not have had such an impact if other intellectual currents had not helped.

The fortunes of Students for a Democratic Society and the anti–Vietnam War movement that it spawned belong to political history rather than the history of political ideas. Still, the upsurge of demands for greater democracy and the concomitant assault on most existing forms of authority have some theoretical interest. Even friendly critics of participatory democracy reluctantly noted that it was utopian in the pejorative sense of the term. Robert Dahl's *After the Revolution?* pointed out that in New York the mayor could have personal contact with each of the inhabitants for no more than eight seconds a year if he neither ate, drank, nor slept—there being somewhat over thirty-one million seconds in a year and around four million adults in New York.[18] This was not meant dismissively, only as a demand for some serious thought about institutional design. Little emerged, because it turned out that there was no enthusiasm for workplace democracy either among the workers who were supposed to be its beneficiaries or elsewhere. Students and workers might willingly occupy the offices of presidents and managers to ensure their voices were heard; but continuous engagement with the process of managing their universities or places of employment was another matter.

The movement from a liberal defense of participatory democracy to a hankering after an all-encompassing revolution reminded observers of Europe in 1848 when students battled police on the streets of Paris in the spring and summer of 1968. The analogy was not exact. The 1960s were prosperous years, while 1848 was a time of poor harvests and genuine hunger. The 1960s desire for greater democracy came in countries that already had universal suffrage, uncorrupt elections, and a free press, while much of the upheaval of 1848 took the form of nationalist rebellion against alien autocracies. The only place in Europe where a version of 1848 took place was Czechoslovakia, in the form of an attempt by a reformist communist government to practice "socialism with a human face," an attempt the Soviet armies suppressed. The significance of these momentary insurrections in Western Europe and the United States was that they showed that the legitimacy of the modern state was shakier than most people had thought. There was no alternative to liberal democracy, but liberal democracy aroused no enthusiasm. If we take seriously the thought that vox populi may not be *vox Dei*, but is still the only source of legitimacy, the reluctance of the ordinary person to give a more wholehearted assent to the modern state is problematic. It may not threaten revolution or dictatorship, but it undermines the ability of contemporary governments to govern confidently and competently.

Political Liberalism: John Rawls

We must turn to the most philosophically impressive attempt of recent years to give an all-encompassing account of legitimate social, political, and economic arrangements in the modern world. John Rawls's masterpiece, *A Theory of Justice*, provided an account of "justice as fairness" built around one compelling idea. If we were asked to design a social and economic system from behind a "veil of ignorance"—knowing nothing about the place we would occupy in such a system—we would choose the one in which the worst-off person did as well as possible. A just society is therefore one where the worst-off person does as well as possible. It was a powerful and a controversial thought; most people's first thought is that a just society is one where the *average* person does as well as possible, as Rousseau says in the *Social Contract*. Their second thought is to wonder what would happen if they did worse than the average—which Rousseau deals with by demanding that there be very little inequality, so that almost nobody is either much better-off or much worse-off than the average. Rawls answers the question by saying that the society will be fair if the worst-off person does as well as possible.

Critics of Rousseau complain that he was so concerned with the corrosive effects of inequality that he sacrificed too much to avoid them. A more unequal society might be more prosperous, lively, easygoing, and agreeable to live in than the Spartan societies he argued for. If we can provide the talented and energetic with incentives to use their talents, and find ways of distributing some of the benefits to children, the elderly, the infirm, and the disadvantaged generally, the worst-off will do better out of something other than strict equality. A well-designed, democratically governed welfare state could protect the least advantaged while affording scope to the advantaged. *A Theory of Justice* formalizes that thought, without losing sight of the appeal of equality. Rawls argued that a rational person who did not know what position she or he would occupy would agree that inequality is legitimate to the extent that it enables us to make the worst-off person as well-off as possible.[19] It is a dramatic doctrine. As in Rousseau, equality is the starting point. Contrary to Rousseau, Rawls argues that if the worst-off can be made better-off by allowing the better-off to make themselves better-off still, we should allow as much inequality as will make the worst-off person as well-off as possible.

The implications of these arguments for theories of economic justice are beyond the scope of this discussion. Their implications for liberal democracy are our subject. Rawls defined "better-off" and "worse-off" in terms of access to the means of a self-respecting existence. It is easy to frame an economic argument to the effect that the worst-off will get more if we allow the better-off to thrive; Locke's argument for private property in land did it, and Jefferson borrowed Locke's argument when negotiating with Native Americans. There is no comparable consideration in the matter of civil and political rights. The closest parallel is the nineteenth-century argument, familiar in Britain and the United States, for extending the franchise a step at a time, rather than all at once. *Temporarily* allowing some people more political rights than others would protect those others from an upheaval that might cost all people their rights. The argument runs in the opposite direction to the economic argument; in that, we imagine departing from equality for the sake of the prosperity of the worst-off. In the political case, we imagine reaching an absolute equality of political rights by steps that allow for temporary inequality. Political rights embody a fundamental equality whose expression is that everyone has the same rights as everyone else.

The protection of political rights, and civil rights more generally, takes priority over economic welfare. Rawls writes of individuals possessing an inviolability reflected in the rights that a society institutionalizes. Put the other way around, liberal democracy must institutionalize what we can rather awkwardly call "no-rights." Rawls never spelled out just what he thought government entailed, but wrote as though he saw it as the coercive mechanism that Max Weber defined; it does immense good by protecting us from aggression and ill-treatment and by enforcing the arrangements that allow social cooperation to yield its benefits. But in the hands of ideologically or religiously inflamed leaders, whether backed by a majority or a minority, it can do appalling evil. A theory of rights is a theory of when we can make claims on other persons to have them do what they might not do otherwise; when I borrow your car, you have a right to have it back when I agreed, whether or not I want to go on driving it. Conversely, there are many things that we have *no right* to have other people do, however much we would like them to, and no matter how happy they would make us. They include voting and praying as we would have them do.

This begins to resolve the old problem of the tyranny of the majority. Most liberals have defined democracy as rule by majority vote and sought ways to constrain what a majority can do. For Rawls, and more especially his followers, a rights-violating vote is no vote at all.[20] We are not balancing the rights of majorities against the rights of minorities, as older thinkers suggested, but protecting rights, full stop. A vote that violates rights is not a democratic vote. The only form of democracy entitled to the label is *liberal* democracy, because a vote is entitled to respect only if it is cast on terms that respect the equal liberty of everyone, and *democracy* because everyone's vote counts. Voting for racial segregation or for the persecution of a Jewish minority cannot be called "democratic." Even if 90 percent of the population votes to persecute the Jewish 10 percent, it is not a democratic vote. Critics complain that this defines democracy in terms that owe too much to American constitutional arrangements and too little to the populist traditions of Athens onward. It is a complaint I would make, but it picks up an important thought. Justifying majority rule is not easy. If you are accosted by two muggers bent on taking your wallet, it does not diminish the offense if they first take a vote, even if they allow you to vote against their proposal to relieve you of your wallet. You have lost by a two-to-one majority, but what matters are the guns in their hands. One may think that the state is in the same position when it takes one's income in the form of taxes. To argue that it is not, there has to be an elaborate story about what entitles a state, no matter how constituted, to engage in such coercive activities. A democratically sensitive story will make reference to what other people have a right to expect of you and you of them. The introduction of the idea of citizens with equal rights against each other brings us close to the thought that the only morally acceptable form of democracy is liberal democracy.

It is a contentious view that liberal democracy alone can be called democracy. The difficulty is not that the underlying thought is simply wrong—it is obvious that if 90 percent of the people decide to behave wickedly, they have no right to do so, and we have no duty to go along with them. Rather, this way of making the point neglects both the Athenian view that democracy means what it says—the authority of the demos—and the modern view that representative democracy matters because it allows us to "throw the rascals out," and use the threat of eviction to make our rulers behave, as well as the view that the *point* of democracy is to allow the less advantaged to use their numbers to offset the advantages of the well-heeled and well-connected. Schumpeter's definition of democracy implies that a government that institutes racist legislation does so "democratically" so long as those who do it acquired the power to do it by winning a competition for the people's vote. It does not imply that we should go along with it. Modern democracies have in fact been more respectful of individual liberties and less given to religious or racial persecution than any government yet known, but there is a loss of intellectual clarity in sweeping all virtues together and labeling them "democracy." Nineteenth-century liberals feared the illiberal tendencies of the majority and were not always hospitable to democracy. Liberals wish to preserve the distinction between majority rule and sensitivity to human rights; so do the antiliberals who justify the erosion of civil liberties for whatever reason by insisting that they have "the public" on their side.

Let us return to the peculiarities of the modern Western world. Our life expectancy at birth is four times that of an Athenian; we are safer, healthier, and better fed and clothed. An Athenian ran no risk of perishing in a thermonuclear war, the one risk that we face that our forebears did not. Otherwise, we are physically far safer and less likely to perish in war or from disease; we are much freer in the modern, liberal sense— less locked into a social position, unlikely to be persecuted if we change our religious allegiances or behave in ways that strike others as odd or immoral. We may suffer disapproval; but we shall not be required to drink hemlock. Not all of these features of our world owe anything to the democratic quality of our politics. Some are a matter of individual rights that have been in place much longer than modern democratic institutions; others are the result of technological advances that sometimes came about under liberal governments, and sometimes under authoritarian regimes such as that of nineteenth-century Germany.

Democracy is a good thing; but it is not the only good thing. And *political* democracy is not the only thing, and perhaps not the main thing, that people mean by "democracy." Enthusiasts for participatory democracy rightly claimed that a society where more of us participate in a whole host of organizations devoted to the public good will be a happier society in which, inter alia, there will be less crime, better education, and a more attractive environment. They often did not appreciate how much informal, nonpolitical participation already exists in areas ranging from parent-teacher associations to volunteer groups that deliver lunches for meals on wheels. All these require political skills and intelligence; they require us to make decisions, allocate tasks, share burdens fairly, and take responsibility for things going wrong when they do. Nor did they always appreciate the participatory quality of everyday life—from the way in which a cinema queue can turn into a spontaneous seminar on the merits of particular directors and actors, to the activities of good-natured crowds at sports events. "Belonging" is engendered in all sorts of ways, and most of them are unpolitical. There are choices to be made, as Oscar Wilde pointed out when he said—entirely unfrivolously—that socialism would be hard work because it would so severely eat into our evenings. We could say the same in spades about participatory democracy, let alone the liberty of the ancients and Athenian democracy.

The answer to the question whether the Persians turn out to have defeated the Athenians is therefore mixed. We have, perhaps wisely, settled for a less participatory and less generally politicized society than that of Athens. We have, certainly wisely, secured more guarantees of individual liberty and checks on the arbitrary whims of our rulers than the Persians had any inkling of. We are less attached to the ideal of equalizing political power than the Athenians but largely, if not entirely, hostile to the idea of a hereditary ruling class. Class warfare is in most places almost invisible; if the rich secure an unfair share of the economic cake, they do not do it by enslaving prisoners of war, or by slave hunting in Africa, or even by hiring the Pinkerton detective agency to shoot strikers. For anyone with egalitarian leanings, the persistence of extreme inequalities of education, welfare, and income alongside the formal political equality of democratic electoral systems is both puzzling and depressing. For those who do relatively badly out of it, it seems less of a problem than observers find it. There remain many large questions about whether we can hang on to the combination of the liberty of the ancients and the liberty of the moderns that the liberal, nontyrannical, extensive popular republic shelters.

CHAPTER 27

Global Peace and the Human Future

THE SCOPE OF THIS book is wide. Nonetheless, its focus has been on how western Europe and the countries founded by western European nations have thought about the problems of governing themselves. Its organizing paradox has been that we—modern Western "we"—talk about politics in a language bequeathed us by the ancient Greek and Roman world, and apply it to societies utterly unlike those that produced it. The preceding four chapters have widened the geographical range of the discussion beyond the "North Atlantic littoral." This final chapter questions our ability to govern a shrinking world. We began with the politics of Greek city-states; it is often (though not entirely fairly) said that they fell to Philip of Macedon and his son Alexander because they could not develop political arrangements on a larger scale than the polis. It is often said today that we need a new, global political order to deal with problems larger than the nation-state can handle. This final chapter raises the question of how dangerous these problems are and whether they can be met only by a new supranational political order. The discussion is the barest introduction to issues that deserve and have received innumerable longer and more detailed discussions—as well as brief and terrifyingly uninformed and opinionated ones in the mass media. These last pages ask how great the danger is that religious conflict, economic conflict, or the uncontrolled spread of nuclear weapons will result in international violence on a large scale, how great the danger is that the world will end "not with a bang but a whimper" as we fail to halt environmental degradation, and whether the effective control of these dangers requires us to govern ourselves globally rather than nationally and internationally. The thought is simple: if states exist to handle what cannot be handled by families and informal groups, must we create a world state or a world government to handle the problems that individual states cannot?

The Failure of Secularization

A surprising number of writers fear that we are threatened by global wars of religion.[1] To the astonishment of sociologists and political theorists, religion has resisted the forces that were expected to destroy it: industrialization, affluence, democracy, and cultural pluralism. Secularization has not taken place; or more guardedly, it has happened in most of Western Europe and not very widely elsewhere. Secularization means several things; most broadly, that with the rise of science, traditional religious belief will lose its hold. Until recently, few writers would have suggested that religious passions, rather than the secular ideologies of nationalism, fascism, or communism, would threaten world peace. The following pages explore two views of secularization: the first holds that with the death of traditional belief, a surrogate will be needed, often thought of as a "religion of humanity"; the second, that no surrogate will be needed, that traditional belief will simply fade away. The failure of attempts to provide a surrogate and the refusal of religion to fade away quietly, together with the rise of fundamentalism, raise the question how dangerous fundamentalism is.

Before the French Revolution it was neither respectable nor safe to say publicly that a society could prosper if its citizens were not Christians. Public agnosticism invited at best ostracism and at worst the attention of the criminal law and a painful death. Skeptics such as Machiavelli were not secularists; he thought a successful regime required a *civic* religion, as did Rousseau, who followed him in this and much else.[2] Rousseau thought the other-worldliness of Christianity disabled it as a civic religion, but in Machiavelli's eyes it was not Christian doctrine but the corruption of the curia that was the issue. Conversely, and contrary to Rousseau, Machiavelli seems not to have thought that belief in a deity who looked after human affairs was essential to human existence; a meaningful life needed no transcendental guarantees. Nonetheless, the Romans were right to insist that soldiers did not mock the auguries and that citizens acknowledged the claims of the household gods and exhibited piety. A successful political system required a civic religion. This was a view that any pagan author could have endorsed. It was an argument less for *belief* than for the value of collective rituals. These rituals no doubt rested on a belief in the existence of forces that transcended everyday reality, but in Christian terms, these beliefs were pagan superstitions, and in the eyes of many philosophers in the ancient world, they were myths that might or might not contain a deeper truth. Pagan ritual practices either tried to divine the attitude of unseen forces to our projects or tried to induce them to be friendly, but invited no deep theological analysis. Still, they are a form of religion. In that sense Machiavelli was no secularist.

Secularization emerged as a practical issue during the French Revolution. The revolutionaries tried to abolish institutionalized Christianity and replace it with a rationalist civil religion; but nothing shook Catholicism's hold on popular imagination or secured the same hold for itself. The most striking failure was Robespierre's Festival of the Supreme Being, wonderfully mocked by Thomas Carlyle as the cult of "Mumbo-Jumbo."[3] Carlyle presented the festival as low comedy, but he understood that the enemy of most revolutionaries was not Christianity but the French Catholic Church: it was a prop to social hierarchy and political absolutism, helping the well-off to exploit the poor with an easy conscience, and keeping the poor in the mental chains that allowed the rich and powerful to keep them in legal and physical chains. This was traditional anticlericalism and had no antireligious implications. Its target was the parasitism of the senior clergy and the union of a parasitical church and a parasitical state. Anticlericals wanted a reformed church staffed by a purified pastorate that would live simply in the fashion of the early Christian church; many poor parish priests agreed. Such an anticlericalism had been a force in the Protestant Reformation three centuries before, and in the Albigensian heresy three centuries before that. When rationalism and a contempt for superstition were added to the mix, they led to hostility to all forms of revealed religion, though not to all forms of deism. Paine's *Age of Reason* is an English variant on a common theme.

The political consequences were described in Tocqueville's *Ancien régime et la révolution*: many aristocrats and intellectuals despised superstition; they were genuine skeptics, and their skepticism inspired the radicals who hated the church because it was rich. Tocqueville held the traditional view that the monarchy, church, and nobility stood or fell together, and blamed the aristocracy for spreading a hatred of religion fatal to their own social standing; they had sharpened the guillotine for their own necks.[4] He exaggerated. Most skeptics were deists, believing that the universe was governed by an impersonal and noninterventionist, but nonetheless benign, divinity; and their impact on the revolution was less than Tocqueville thought. Money mattered more than ideas; the church's income and wealth became state property in the winter of 1789, and priests became salaried employees of the state. Convents and monasteries were suppressed in August 1792. Only when the revolution grew more radical did the target change; in the autumn of 1793 Christian worship was outlawed, and the French state was secularized. Even then, it was secularized only up to a point: Reason was to be worshipped. Two months before his downfall, Robespierre realized that the French needed something more than Reason alone, and instituted the cult of the Supreme Being. It did not work.

The Religion of Humanity

Robespierre's failure did not stop French thinkers in the nineteenth century from devoting a great deal of effort to imagining a "religion of humanity" and its institutionalization. Its intellectual history began with Saint-Simon's *New Christianity* and came to a florid development in

Auguste Comte's positivism. The underlying thought is easy to accept. Unlike other animals, human beings ask about the meaning of existence. They do not do it continuously; they get by by tackling one task at a time and doing whatever they do out of habit, affection, to get paid, or for amusement. But when they ask what life is about, they want an answer. Religion and its surrogates provide answers. In this sense the Marxism elaborated under Stalin was a surrogate religion and filled a religious function. The question was what would provide answers when traditional Christian or providential answers became unpersuasive. Today we are more agitated by the question that agitated Reformation Europe: how violent disagreement on religious issues can be prevented from spilling over into civil and international war. Nineteenth-century thinkers did not anticipate a revival of religious conflict; they were more concerned to find a surrogate faith than to calm those who believe too passionately.

Auguste Comte's positivism was the most complete version of a religion of humanity. It was a religion of progress: its tenet was that we are participants in the historical and social project to make the human race all it can be, intellectually, spiritually, morally, and productively. If we commit ourselves to this project, we shall find fulfillment in a project that transcends our individual lives and fates in just the way the traditional Christian project did. The extravagant suppression of self-interest implied by Comte's slogan of *vivre pour autrui* ("live for others") was peculiar to himself; but the idea that individuals would find fulfillment in living for the cause of human progress was embraced not only by J. S. Mill, who was avowedly an admirer of French intellectual life, but by Victorian thinkers such as Charles Kingsley and Frederic Harrison. Harrison spent a very long life unsuccessfully promoting positivism in England.[5]

Positivism developed the trappings of a church, but never looked likely to supplant Christianity as a personal or political creed. Mill observed acidly that Comte's prescriptions for the new cult could only have been written by a man who had never laughed. Nonetheless, for sixty years, positivism appealed to intelligent middle-class people who fretted that modern society was fragmented, individualistic, materialistic, and unjust, but who could not embrace Marx's insurrectionary remedies. Although positivism was a French creed, one of its most interesting and persuasive political products was American. Herbert Croly wrote *The Promise of American Life* in 1908 to tell his compatriots that individual rights needed to be sustained by a sense of collective purpose, and that if the United States was to be a genuine nation, it must see the task of uniting efficiency with justice as its defining national project.[6] This was a (largely) demilitarized version of the American belief in Manifest Destiny, itself a form of civic religion; but with a very different flavor. There were many grounds on which Croly might have encouraged Americans to take nationhood seriously; it was a positivist trope to tell them that they would be truly happy only when they played the part that justice demanded in the collective endeavors of their society. Economic activities, thought Croly, must be organized to emphasize their collective and cooperative nature. Providing a spiritual argument (rather than a simple economic one) for nationalizing the American railroads of the early twentieth century was a very Comtean thing to do, but not wholly surprising. The Saint-Simonians had been instrumental in creating the French railroads, and Ferdinand de Lesseps, the creator of the Suez Canal, began his career as a Saint-Simonian missionary. Saint-Simon himself had projected a Panama canal.

The intellectual high point of the French tradition was the political sociology of Émile Durkheim. For Durkheim the essence of religion lay in the individual's sense of being confronted by a spiritual force greater than himself. Sociologically analyzed, this force was society itself, and religious myths from the most simple to most intricate were expressions of our sense of the spiritual power of the social whole. The essence of society was its *moral* quality, not its existence as a collection of individuals. Consider the way members of teams find themselves moved almost against their will by the team's aspirations; or consider Herodotus's Spartan hero Demeratus who told Xerxes that the Spartans were more in awe of their society's *nomoi* than Xerxes's slaves of Xerxes. The implications for modern politics that Durkheim himself drew were not very dramatic; he hoped that a form of market socialism—or moralized capitalism— could give spiritual depth to economic and political life.[7] The religious basis of modern society is the sanctity of the individual; respect for the individual underpins respect for contractual relations and thus for the market. The market must nonetheless be controlled by a political framework that brings it into line with its spiritual nature by ensuring that its outcomes are just, rather than arbitrary. Durkheim speculated that a guildlike organization of workers and employers could ensure that work is seen as a matter of moral duty, not bare survival; moderate socialism (or welfare state capitalism) has a spiritual rather than a merely welfarist purpose. Contemporary communitarians with strong religious sympathies sound very like Durkheim a century ago.[8] Their politics, in spite of complaints against contemporary liberalism and the loss of social values, turn out to be no more dramatic than his. This is not a complaint; undramatic politics meets social needs, and is unlikely to lead citizens to take up arms against one another.

Religious Attachment Redundant

The view that these were groundless anxieties and that we would not miss traditional religious belief and its institutions was equally common, although it was one of the rare topics on which Marx and Engels held different views. Engels came from a pietist family and thought mankind needed a philosophy of existence of some kind. Marx, the son of a Jewish agnostic who had converted to Christianity for pragmatic reasons, was religiously tone-deaf. Organized religion would be redundant once society was rationally organized; no surrogate was needed. Religion existed to console us for the miseries of the world. Absent the miseries, it would lose its grip and not be missed. Marx's immersion in Hegel left no yearning for the Absolute. This may seem surprising. Hegel's account of spirit's coming to full self-consciousness in human history is often said to share the structure of the Judeo-Christian myth of an Edenic beginning, a Fall, a long travail, and eventual redemption; and it is even more often observed that Marx also offered a four-stage myth: primitive communism, a fall with the invention of private property, followed by the history of propertied unhappiness, ending with mature communism. Marx seems neither to have noticed nor cared.

Rather than considering alternative interpretations of Marx's confidence that happy human beings needed neither religious faith nor its philosophical surrogates, we should turn to the really surprising fact. In most of the world, secularization has not happened. The explosion of scientific knowledge and the technological sophistication that draws on that knowledge have not undermined religious belief. The most modern and most powerful of liberal democracies is entirely unsecularized. The United States puts the motto In God We Trust on its currency and takes that affirmation seriously in its public life. The separation of church and state is instituted in the Constitution, and meticulously policed by the Supreme Court; but the Cold War of the 1950s and 1960s was fought against "godless communism," and Christianity (or the "Judeo-Christian tradition" or more broadly "faith") was understood to favor the social and political order of the United States of America. Nobody who declared himself an atheist could get elected to Congress, and politicians running for president declare with a straight face that they would pray for divine guidance when devising policies on health care, the infrastructure, and all else. This flowering of faith is a less surprising result of the institutional separation of church and state than one might think; it was anticipated by eighteenth-century advocates of disestablishment and emphasized by Tocqueville. Anticlericalism flourishes where an authoritarian church and an authoritarian state are allies, as in much of Europe after the Counter-Reformation. In the United States the remedy for religious quarrels has been the same as the remedy for other quarrels, and much the same as the remedy for failure in business—move somewhere else, and set up a new church to attract new worshippers.

The United States is highly religious in the sociologist's, not the theologian's, sense. Not only is there a substantial minority of Jews, Muslims, Hindus, Buddhists, and animists among the population, there is a striking variety of Christian churches, including the hard-to-place Mormons, who belong to the Church of Jesus Christ of Latter Day Saints but hold unorthodox views about the Old Testament and much else. Few Americans care for theological discussion. They believe that the universe is on their side, as Saint-Simon and Comte hoped they would; but they believe it on the strength of what Saint-Simon and Comte did not expect to survive, a widespread faith in the supernatural.

Many non-European religions are so unlike traditional Christianity that the concept of secularization hardly seems applicable in the first place; absent a religion with an elaborate account of the supernatural, it is harder to identify the beliefs that are supposed to wither away under the impulsion of science. From the late nineteenth century onward, Japan modernized its economy and industry, modeled its education system on that of Prussia, and acquired a parliament much like the pre-1914 Reichstag, without undermining popular belief in the divinity of the emperor. One reason was that the divinity of the emperor resembles the divinity of a pagan Roman emperor, not the divinity of Christ. "Secularizing" such a society is not like secularizing Catholic Europe.

Surprise at the coexistence of high technology and religious faith is misplaced: philosophers and sociologists have too readily thought that our beliefs and our economics, politics, and technologies must form a logical unity. The facts are against them. Japanese kamikaze pilots at the end of World War II held a view of their emperor different from that of the sailors and pilots of the U.S. Navy they were fighting, but the competence of the sides did not vary with their religious or quasi-religious convictions. During the long drawn-out war between the Iran of Ayatollah Khomeini and the Iraq of Saddam Hussein, the religious enthusiasm of the Iranian forces led them to be wasteful of human life, but they were no more wasteful than the atheistic Red Army in the Second World War or their secular Baathist opponents in the Iraqi army; nor was the competence of the army or air force on either side traceable to their religious commitments or lack of them.

In short, in societies such as the United Kingdom where the hold of established churches has been weak for two centuries and has weakened further, no institutionalized substitute for traditional faith has made headway, but it has not been missed: the citizens have not become more or less susceptible to demagogues, easier or harder to rally behind dangerous projects, notably more or less at ease with themselves. The thought that once cast adrift from traditional religious belief, citizens would instantly fall for fascist or similar ideologies is wrong; religious faith does not guarantee that citizens will not fall for such creeds, or indeed for any amount of nonsense; nor does the absence of widespread religious conviction guarantee the reign of political common sense. The crucial point is that modernization has had much less impact on religious conviction than we might expect; the conflict between scientific and religious belief does not strike adherents of most faiths as the problem that philosophers assumed it would be. Where religious faith comes with minimal metaphysical commitments, conflict between science and religion is unlikely. This is only moderately good news, for the optimistic view that modernization would result in the abandonment of the more ferocious aspects of religious faith also turns out to be false. Sectarian strife is alive and well.

Fundamentalism

Here we enter on the vexed topic of fundamentalism. It is vexed because "fundamentalist" is commonly a term of abuse with little content. It initially had a relatively clear application to Protestant Christians who believed in the inerrancy of scripture and the priesthood of all believers: an individual and a Bible made a church. Applied to Muslims, it refers to a wholly different phenomenon: to those who have adopted an antimodernizing and anti-Western form of Islamist politics for nationalist and ethnic reasons. If we abandon the term, our question can be rephrased: whether we are in danger of slipping into endless war as the result of religious or—to use the term that Samuel Huntington made famous—"civilizational" conflict.

One alarming feature of recent politics, the rise of terrorism, is illuminated by attending to the peculiarities of religiously based conflict, beginning perhaps with religious conflict in Europe at the time of the Reformation. This is not true of most terrorism. The terrorism of the two decades prior to the First World War had no religious roots and no religious aims; anarchists, socialists, and enraged nationalists saw terror as their best, or only, weapon against a wide range of targets, ranging from Russian czars to American industrialists, or "bourgeois society" generally.[9] In most political contexts, conflict is amenable to the analysis that Hobbes taught us: rational agents will use violence to secure their goals; they will be deterred by the threat of retaliation, and pacified by the offer of benefits they can secure without risking their lives. It was a view from which the anarchists of the late nineteenth and early twentieth centuries would not have demurred. Rational men reduce violence by mutual threat, governments do not alienate their subjects, for fear of violent reactions, and subjects obey their governments for the same reason. Internationally, "mutually assured destruction" was the basis on which the United States and the Soviet Union kept the peace with each other; each side was convinced the other would retaliate with all-out war against a nuclear first strike, so neither was tempted to strike. The acronym MAD reflected the fact that it was a suicide pact; but its logic was impeccable, and its effect benign. Beneath an umbrella of mutual deterrence, individuals and states can cooperate. But everything depends on the rationality of the parties involved. They must calculate consequences, if mutual deterrence is to work. It is assumed that terrorists will be deterred if they run too great a risk of death or incarceration. We should not avert our eyes from the nastiness implicit in the idea of deterrence, however. Among the worst effects of terrorist and antiterrorist campaigns is the collateral damage to innocents: governments are tempted to take hostages or murder the families of terrorists, and terrorists to do the same to government officials and their families.

The Reformation taught Europe that deterrence often does not work. Two features of the religious violence of the time cast light on the present. First, the deeply convinced were happy to give up their lives in the cause; martyrdom was embraced as it had been by the Christians who faced Roman persecution. Second, the true believer saw the destruction of the infidel and the heretic as a good in its own right. Infidels and heretics are not *threatened* with destruction as part of a negotiation; their destruction is the object. Persons happy to embrace martyrdom are not amenable to threats; and persons who wish to extirpate their enemies are not amenable to bargaining about alternatives. Suicide bombers have nonnegotiable aims and are not deterred by threats. They are very different from the IRA bombers who waged a campaign against the British government between 1969 and 1998. It is not surprising that they arouse memories of the sixteenth- and seventeenth-century wars of religion, which killed 30 percent of the population of Germany.

Nonetheless, religiously based terrorism does not threaten world war. Terrorism has caused widespread fear and inconvenience, and in countries without effective police forces, massacres are commonplace. It is not a war between civilizations. The surface attraction of the idea of a conflict of civilizations, or religions, is that the twentieth century was racked with violent conflicts between intransigent enemies whose differences were deeply ideological, as was the conflict between Nazi Germany and Communist Russia, and the Cold War between the United States and its allies and the Soviet Union and its allies. Many contemporary conflicts have religious roots, though they invariably have others as well; the Arab-Israeli conflict is self-evidently ethnic and religious, though equally a conflict over land and resources. The breakup of Yugoslavia was marked by ethnic conflict between Christians and Muslims, and a disgusting civil war. Still, the view that ethnic and religious confrontations are not only intractable but threaten a new world war is not persuasive. The observer in London, New York, or Paris has the Middle East in the center of his or her visual field and looks from there to other countries where Islamist terrorism is an issue. This distorts our vision. Religious conflict is as savage between sects as between faiths. Orthodox and Catholic Christians in the Balkans treated each other as badly as they treated Muslims. Sunni and Shia are more hostile to each other than Christians are to either. Northern Ireland experienced thirty years of low-level civil war on the purported basis of confessional allegiances. None are civilizational cleavages. Nor do they threaten to result in wars between major powers.

This is only partially reassuring, but some numerical considerations are in order. Nobody knows exactly how many people World War II killed, but certainly more than 30 million Russians and 8 million Germans. In the area between the Baltic and the Ukraine, some 14 million people were murdered, upward of a third of them Jews. A war fought across modern Europe *without* nuclear weapons would kill at least 20 percent of a population of 440 million. The proposition that major wars are not likely is reassuring to the extent that we need not fear casualties on that scale. It does not mean that the world is a safe place; where travel is easy, and the means of killing large numbers—several hundred or several thousand—are readily available, nowhere is wholly safe, although everywhere the danger of death from a terrorist attack is much lower than that of death in an accident, or indeed from common or garden-variety murder. The attraction of crowded places to anyone who wants to cause chaos and anxiety makes major cities, airplanes, and mass transit obvious targets; and religious fanaticism breeds determined terrorists. Nonetheless, mass murder by fanatics is nasty enough without our mistaking it for war. The Thirty Years' War was appallingly destructive because organized armies were assembled by rulers who fought one another for religious, dynastic, and territorial reasons; the civilian population died of famine and disease as armies that lived off the land destroyed everything in their path. Contemporary religious fanaticism is nasty, but it would become globally dangerous only if a suicidally minded fanatic takes control of a fully armed state. The only two states with enough weapons of mass destruction to make this truly terrifying are Russia and the United States, neither of which is likely to fall into such hands.

Globalization

We will return to the reality that we live in a dangerous world. First, we should consider another postmillennial anxiety, the political tensions caused by globalization. Socialism, both Marxist and other, was a reaction to the upheaval of industrialization in western Europe and the United States. Analogies between what happens within one country and what happens globally must be drawn with caution, but it is not surprising that reactions to globalization have often been as hostile as reactions to early industrialization, especially because many countries are in the throes of early industrialization. Economists emphasize the benefits of change rather than the injustices and unhappinesses that change brings with it; but even when populations have rising incomes, longer lives, and higher educational standards in total and on average, many individuals within them may be suffering. Critics who emphasize the miseries of dislocation see matters differently from those who emphasize rising GNP.

Even those who prosper may be unhappy if they think they should have done even better. What sociologists call "revolutions of rising expectations" make political thinkers uneasy; the French Revolution is often explained as such a revolution.[10] The communications revolution of recent years makes us much more visible to one another, and the dominant role of America in world popular culture means that even in countries with rapid economic growth, many people can compare themselves with their prosperous contemporaries in the West rather than their worse-off former selves. Being less well-off than contemporary Americans may arouse a sense of injustice that is not assuaged by being better-off than grandparents and parents. "Reference group theory" alerts us to the importance to our subjective happiness and unhappiness of whom we compare ourselves with. Readers of this book do not reflect on how much better-off they are than a Mongolian herdsman or an untouchable sweeping a village street in India, but may well wonder why they are paid so much less than the not very bright lawyer they knew in high school. Conversely, they may be encouraged to reflect on those who are worse-off than they are by someone who hopes to assuage their resentment. Any politician worth his salt knows how to trade on this simple fact.

The fear is that globalization will cause both national and global political instability, and that each will exacerbate the other. It is often said that the world's poor constitute an "international proletariat" in the sense in which Marx and his followers used the term. If they are not industrial workers uniting across the boundaries of the industrialized societies of the Europe of Karl Marx, they may fulfill the proletariat's revolutionary role, the victims of a global system of exploitation, potentially ready to rise in revolt against their exploiters. This was one of the thoughts that animated Fanon's *The Wretched of the Earth*. Its attractions are obvious. But extrapolating from Marx's picture of proletarian insurrection within one country to the global stage is problematic.

Even if the Marxist theory of what would happen within one state

were more credible than it is, extrapolating to a global context is dangerous. It is essential to the Marxist story that there is a state to be captured
and that its capture is the aim of proletarian insurrection; but the world
is a literal anarchy—there is no state to capture. Again, it is essential
to the Marxian story that the numbers of the proletariat increase as
the forces of production develop. Machine production intensifies, and
the proportion of people engaged in industrial production grows. No
such process operates on the global stage. It is difficult even to begin to
describe the global economy, but if some factories are all too like those of
Manchester in 1840, most are not, and the financial arrangements that
underpin the modern global economy are utterly unlike anything imagined by Marx. What excites the anger of protesters against globalization
in developed countries is labor conditions in developing countries: child
labor and female labor in primitive factories, ruthless employers who
take no responsibility for the health, education, or welfare of their workers, political systems that repress workers' attempts to organize themselves and get a better bargain from their employers. There is certainly
far too much of that, but it is not typical, let alone universal. Much is
wholly unlike Britain in the 1840s, and involves high-value production
in technically advanced assembly plants, while "outsourced" services
employ well-spoken urban graduates, not children sold into near-slavery
by desperate rural parents.

Nor does the classical antagonism between the workers and an
owner who both owns and manages the factory in which they are laboring exist in a globalized world. The owners of a modern factory may
live ten thousand miles away; the classical weapon of the proletariat, the
withdrawal of labor, is less effective against a multinational corporation
when production can so readily be moved elsewhere. The world that
Hegel imagined, where the capitalist is defined by the "easy come, easy
go" of his fluid funds, is our world. Marx assumed that worker solidarity
was all but inevitable: workers who worked together would find it easy to
organize—helped by physical proximity, memories of battles fought and
won, local knowledge of who can and cannot be relied on. This vision was
old-fashioned even before his death and is now wholly implausible. Marx

also thought that the new means of communication, whether physical like the railway, or intellectual like the newspaper, would allow workers to understand and unite around their common interests. Critics have always observed that these resources are equally useful to capitalists and governments; capitalists can combine with one another; governments can move their armed forces around more easily; the mass media can deploy propaganda to mislead, discourage, and disorganize the workers. Governments may certainly fail in this, and the rise of new media such as the internet and mobile phones makes possible the very rapid mobilization of large numbers of people for anything from urban rioting to real insurrection. Whether they will facilitate anything resembling the revolution Marx expected is another matter.

These considerations do not answer the question whether the hard-pressed workers of the developing world form a global proletariat. They do suggest that even if they were one, they could not make a global revolution. That leaves two questions hanging. The first is whether they form a proletariat at all; the second, whether they have other possibilities than those imagined by Marx. The answer to the first is no and to the second yes. The classical proletariat was defined by its relationship to the means of production; in its classical form this was a relationship between an unskilled nonowning worker and a nonworking capitalist owner. Between a skilled worker in Taiwan and a twelve-year-old child in a carpet factory in Pakistan, there is nothing in common; they relate in such different ways to their own employers, and through them to the world market, that the antagonism that drives the Marxian drama has little to feed on. There are powerful antagonisms to be exploited, country by country, and not every country will be as successful as those East Asian countries where prosperity has thus far kept a few steps ahead of aspiration; but the worst-off inhabitants of the developing world do not form a global proletariat. There are other possibilities for violent conflict, both within developing countries and, at worst, between substantial nation-states. But they seem likely to resemble the Iran–Iraq war, or the United States' recent wars, not a global proletarian uprising.

Nationalism

Intermittent violence is not war, however horrible it is for those affected. Even when groups of terrorists conduct what they and their targets *call* war, it is not. War, properly speaking, is the systematic and organized use of violent measures by one state against another. Civil war is by analogy the use of systematic and organized violence by sectional groupings that wish to control or reconfigure the state. In failed states, the line between civil war and simple banditry may be impossible to draw. The greatest contemporary danger to peace is presented by failed states, but not because they can wield against other states the violent instruments that ex hypothesi they are too disorganized to make effective use of. The threat they pose is that they collapse in chaos, and suffer humanitarian disasters that the developed world feels impelled to intervene to halt; intervention risks inciting opportunistic intervention by other states or nonstate terrorists, escalating the misery and bloodshed. Again, it poses no risk of war on a large scale. Two decades ago, intervention by one superpower risked inviting counterintervention by another; now that there is only one superpower with any inclination to intervention, that danger is much diminished.

In the absence of superpower rivalry, we may not fear nuclear war between great powers but that civil wars, or subcivil wars, will spill over into neighboring states and destabilize them. This may infect a substantial part of a continent, as conflicts in the Congo and Angola have done in the past, and as conflict in Somalia threatens to do. In such situations there is a head-on conflict between the realist and humanitarian approaches to international affairs; the realist wants the governments of the developed world to ask only whether the vital interests of their own societies are at stake; the humanitarian finds it intolerable that millions may be at risk of massacre merely because they have the bad luck to live where they do. The realist can seem repulsively callous when emphasizing that rape, starvation, and murder suffered in southern Sudan pose little risk to Britain or the United States; but realists can decently retort that ill-judged intervention will leave even more people raped, starved, and murdered. The political question humanitarian disaster poses is tackled briefly below: are there political institutions, perhaps some form of world government, that could produce peace and prosperity where local governments cannot?

The greatest risk of wider conflicts comes from old-fashioned nationalism. One danger arises when an ultranationalist government seeks to embrace conationals beyond its existing borders; another, when a nationalist movement tries to undermine or dismember a transnational regime that blocks its ambitions. The first supplied the pretext for Hitler's attacks on his Czech neighbors. The decomposition of the Soviet Union left the door open to both problems: viewed from different perspectives, the Russian presence in Chechnya is either an instance of Russian ultranationalism trying to crush the legitimate ambitions of Chechens or an attempt by Chechen nationalists to dismember Russia. Both have been elements in Middle East politics since the end of the Second World War. Setting aside the impact of the foundation of the state of Israel, the attempt of one state after another to take a leading role in promoting "Arab nationalism" or "Islamic nationalism," in opposition to the imperialist powers of Britain, France, and the United States, has been central to the region's politics; and it has been uniquely dangerous because the region's position as the leading source of world oil supplies has made its politics global. Readers who can imagine the Middle East without oil can also imagine it tearing itself to pieces to the indifference and uninterest of outside powers.

Arab, Iranian, and other Middle Eastern nationalisms will continue to destabilize global politics, but the danger of their provoking war between major powers is minimal. This is not to underestimate the fear and anxiety they may cause, nor is it to belittle the erosion of civil liberties in liberal democracies that may occur when they take steps to keep the violence from spilling over onto their own territory. Al-Qaeda's target has always been Saudi Arabia, but the conviction that only the United States prevents the reestablishment of the caliphate in Mecca puts the United States and its allies in the firing line. Collateral damage can be extensive; not only may people be killed in a cause that has nothing to do with them, but protecting themselves against collateral damage damages their way of life. The history of the last fifty years suggests that nationalist anger is self-limiting when its target is the colonial or neo-colonial power that controls the region in question, and that this is an important difference from the situation when religion and nationalism are inextricably entangled.

There is ordinarily a natural limit to nationalist aspirations. Thus the object of the Mau-Mau insurgency in Kenya in the 1950s was to be rid of the British colonial authority, and preferably most of the white set-tlers; other anticolonial insurgencies similarly try to make the position of the colonial power untenable, and be rid of colonial rule. The fact that the insurgents commonly find themselves in command of a state apparatus that lacks legitimacy, and an economy that is hard-pressed to meet the pressures of rising populations at home and competitive pres-sures abroad, does not mean that the task of national liberation was not accomplished. Alien powers have been expelled, and a national govern-ment installed. Terrorist attacks directed at the United States on the grounds that it is the root of all evil are different; it is not that the ter-rorists have a homeland to liberate; rather, their homeland is in the hands of the wrong people. The sense in which the United States is a "global" colonizing power is that it is the fount of a secular, this-world, material-ist culture; since its power is in this sense more spiritual than military, there is no way of evicting it as real colonial powers were evicted between 1945 and 1975. Oddly enough, the most likely cause of war is the most old-fashioned. If boundaries are unsettled, well-armed powers may get into fights when they try to adjust them. India has unsettled business with both Pakistan and China, to take but one example.

Nuclear Nightmares

Terrorist and nationalist violence is not World War III. It does not threaten the end of civilization. It makes life in prosperous cities less attractive, but it does not make life there less attractive than life in south-ern Sudan or northern Uganda; one has only to think of the direction of refugee flows to grasp that. We should finally turn to two issues where the destruction of human life on a much greater scale is a genuine possibility: that we shall wipe ourselves out in a nuclear holocaust unless we contrive a world government to prevent it and that we may inadvertently poison ourselves, instead. The fear that we are doomed to destroy ourselves has been widespread since the early twentieth century; it did not arrive only with the use of atomic weapons at Hiroshima and Nagasaki. The First World War led large numbers of thoughtful people to conclude that we were destined to destroy ourselves. The conviction reflected the conjunction of two things: industrialized warfare and the fear that our violent instincts are uncontrollable. The horrors of industrialized warfare were prefigured in the American Civil War. It began as a war in which determined infantry could take an entrenched position by charging with fixed bayonets and overrunning the defenders before they could fire more than one volley; breach-loading rifles and effective field artillery made headlong charges against well-entrenched troops suicidal. Soldiers threw away their weapons more willingly than their entrenching tools. The First World War demonstrated the murderous possibilities of high explosives and the machine gun; bombing aircraft came too late to make much difference to the war, but their potential was obvious. Flesh and blood were at the mercy of death-dealing machinery.

Death in battle killed many fewer people than the Spanish influenza epidemic that followed; but it had an overwhelming impact on political thinking. The shock of seeing civilized peoples killing one another with such seeming enthusiasm and in such numbers persuaded Sigmund Freud that human beings were born with a "death instinct."[11] Freud's vision was grimmer than Hobbes's, if perhaps no grimmer than Augustine's, as it placed the self-destructive—or simply destructive—urges deep in the individual psyche, and almost beyond the reach of social control. The desire for death was one of two powerful inbuilt instincts, the other being the desire for sexual fulfillment. A thinker much affected by this vision was Bertrand Russell, who spent his long life campaigning against militarism and war, and in favor of a form of world government that might keep human destructiveness within bounds.

The subject of humanity's innate aggressiveness and its tendency to turn that aggression into self-destruction is fraught with difficulty. Psychoanalytic interpretations of human behavior are contentious, and for every theorist who has looked to psychoanalysis for insights into ways of making mankind less of a threat to its own continued existence, there is another who insists that psychoanalysis is essentially silent about politics. Freud was equivocal. Although *Civilization and Its Discontents*, published in 1930, was an essay on the difficulty of submitting ourselves to the instinctual repression necessary for a civilized existence, its moral is unclear. Freud certainly argued that individuals are, as Hobbes said, *homo homini lupus*, and must be restrained from harming one another; but he insisted more strenuously than Hobbes that they must internalize these restraints and resign themselves to living with the tension between their deepest desires and the needs of social life. Not for nothing is the book's German title *Unbehagen in der Kultur*—"unease" being the crucial thought.

Nobody has founded a political theory on the view that aggression is innate and beyond human mastery, for obvious reasons. But even if we are not doomed to self-destruction, we may be so vulnerable to aggression and so prone to miscalculation when angry that once we have the means to make an end of ourselves, our life expectancy is limited. The discovery of nuclear fission lends urgency to that thought; we now have the resources to destroy the whole of humanity several times over. Much of the discussion of the dangers of nuclear warfare in the 1950s and 1960s reflected a widespread sense that it was only a matter of time before our destructive urges brought down the curtain on human history. Bertrand Russell was more extreme and more eloquent than most writers, but far from unique.[12] Matters are alarming enough even if we do not possess an innate urge for self-destruction, and have nothing worse than an aggressive streak that is liberated in war and easily excited by irrational forces such as national or ethnic pride, or by religious conviction. The moral is not hard to draw. In situations that bring out the fighting instinct, our judgment is impaired; we underestimate the costs of conflict and overestimate the chances of success. We are not doomed to fight, but we are dangerously prone to fight. Prudent politics must try to counteract these weaknesses; far from glorifying war and pursuing nationalist or imperialist policies that heighten tension and lead to bloodshed, prudent politicians must damp down their own people's hostility to other peoples. That invites the bleak retort that unless we can guarantee that other nations will be equally restrained, the prudent politician must arm his people sufficiently to deter aggressors and avoid becoming an easy prey, even if doing so makes the other side think we are minded to attack them. The motto of the U.S. Strategic Air Command (dissolved in 1992) was "Peace is our profession." This may look like a bad joke, but it expresses the logic of deterrence.

Pacifism and World Government

These are the commonplaces of deterrence theory, and we shall return to them after considering some pacifist recipes for keeping the peace. We should distinguish two strands of pacifist thinking, consider the case for world government, and finally turn to the more recent fear that our fate is to die not with a bang but a whimper. Pacifism is usually divided into its absolutist and consequentialist versions. The absolutist strand is wholly committed to nonviolence. This was the position of Tolstoy and Gandhi. Tolstoy drew on a Christian tradition that stemmed from Christ's injunction to turn the other cheek. Gandhi drew on Hindu traditions of passive resistance to evil and made satyagraha a powerful political weapon against the British occupiers of India. Both echoed Socrates's insistence that doing injustice is worse than suffering injustice: acting violently is worse than suffering violence. Deep pacifism is easy to attack; the pacifist who will not fight to defend others must take on the guilt of letting them die or seeing them suffer atrocious ill-treatment at the hands of their enemies. Some pacifists accept this consequence; others imagine methods of passive resistance that would avert it. The obvious difficulty is that passive resistance works best against an enemy that hopes to gain something from us and can be frustrated by noncooperation. The British wished to govern India with the cooperation of the local population; they did not wish the Indian population dead. An

enemy that simply wishes us dead cannot be inhibited by passive noncooperation; it would have done nothing for Jews facing extermination by
the Nazis.

The more common outlook has been labeled "pacificist," the doctrine
that violence is a last resort.[13] Bertrand Russell's usual view was pacificist
as distinct from absolutist, and he was in a long line of liberal thinkers stretching back to Immanuel Kant, Rousseau, and the abbé Reynal.
It, too, raises familiar issues. Most pacificists are consequentialists who
aim to minimize violent death; they face conflicts between pursuing the
short-term and long-term minimization of casualties, and innumerable
problems about the uncertainty of calculation. It seems on its face a
far from pacifist view to advocate pre-emptive war; but we might under
some conditions believe that a preemptive war will minimize the long-
run numbers of violent deaths. To take a spectacular example, it was not
wholly irrational to think, as Bertrand Russell did in 1946, that a short
war against the Soviet Union before it could acquire nuclear weapons
would secure lasting peace in Europe and avert a future nuclear war,
even if the United States had to use nuclear weapons to bring the Soviet
Union to its knees, as Russell supposed would be necessary. Russell
advocated preemptive war. He agreed it would involve a large number of
casualties, but insisted they would be far fewer than if the Soviet Union
and its Western opponents subsequently fought a European nuclear war,
as he believed they certainly would. With the benefit of hindsight, we
know that no such nuclear war was going to occur; if the United States
had been persuaded by these calculations, millions would have died for
no purpose.

This example is not a conclusive argument against all such calculation. We may sympathize with the (possibly fictional) Scots chieftain
Calgacus quoted by Tacitus who claimed that the Romans created a
desert and called it peace, and yet still think that the Romans reduced
the long-term violence in Europe by brutal short-term military means.[14]
One problem with any such view is uncertainty; another is making morally persuasive comparisons between those whose lives we take and those
whose lives we hope to save. Like too many philosophers, Russell was
prone to deal in large numbers and large abstractions: we might kill a

hundred million people but save "civilization." Many people think it is impossible to balance the fate of the human beings in the here and now whose lives will be lost against the fate of hypothetical creatures not yet born. God may scrutinize past, present, and future with the same impartial eye; and the nineteenth-century utilitarian Henry Sidgwick told his readers that morality takes "the point of view of the universe," but even if the universe has a point of view, politics cannot take it.[15] The interests of the living outweigh the interests of the not yet born, save to the extent that the living care about what will happen after they are dead. This is overwhelmingly significant in the politics of protecting the environment; it is not insignificant in the politics of violent death.

Deterrence and Squeamishness

Setting aside these problems, we face the problems of deterrence. The pacificist who wishes to minimize the chances of war and will try everything before fighting as a last resort faces the problem of deterring aggressors who feel none of his hatred of warfare. Reluctant supporters of rearmament in the 1930s confronted just this question: would a better-equipped army, navy, and air force make it more likely that Britain would get into war or would it deter German militarists by demonstrating that they would either lose a prolonged war, or gain their objectives at a price they recognized was not worth paying? A difficulty more evident at the time to politicians than to moral philosophers is that it is hard to persuade people to pay taxes to build weapons that they loathe the thought of using. A pacificist population might be very hard to persuade to rearm until too late.

One further problem the pacificist faces is that his best policy may require considerable duplicity. Deterrence works only if the opponent we are trying to deter believes we shall make good on our threats, or is fearful that we *might*. This suggests that the more unwilling we are to make war, the more militant we must seem. The creation of nuclear weapons made this point newly important. Writers from the 1920s onward were convinced that bombing civilian populations with high explosives would be the death of civilization; they were not right, but a full-fledged nuclear exchange between the United States and the Soviet Union would be very like it. It followed that each must deter the other from launching the attack that would bring on Armageddon. And it followed from that thought that each state must "assure" the other not only that it had the means to destroy the other side but would unhesitatingly use them.

This is the logic of what came to be known as MAD, the system of mutually assured destruction, under which the United States and the Soviet Union preserved a public posture of unflinching willingness to destroy the other side and much of the globe into the bargain, in the event of serious military attack. The logic of MAD is impeccable but unstable; it is plainly worse for the world at large if the country that is attacked retaliates: the victims are dead or dying, and will not be revived by the death of millions more. If the country attacked is rational, it should capitulate, since further death and destruction serves no purpose. But the knowledge that it would behave rationally destroys the value of its deterrent, since the whole point is to assure the enemy that an attack will provoke a response. MAD is thus mad; or, more cautiously, each side must assure the other that it will react *ir*rationally to secure rational deterrence. It is nonetheless disconcerting if we can behave as cautious, prudent politicians only by conveying the impression that under provocation we would behave like irrationally destructive madmen. It is not to be wondered at that many opponents of the nuclear status quo thought that they were dealing with maniacs rather than politicians—though they were wrong. Among the politicians who understood this was Richard Nixon when he said that he hoped that the North Vietnamese could be persuaded that he was "expletive deleted" crazy, which is to say that he would not hesitate to reduce Phnom Penh to rubble in order to get the enemy to the negotiating table.

World Government

Searching for a solution to the danger of the war that would end all wars by ending the human race, many thinkers were tempted by the panacea of world government. The idea is as old as political theory; the Greek thinker Isocrates argued that the only cure for the incessant warfare that plagued the Greek city-states was an umbrella government capable of keeping all of them in order. The concept of a "universal monarch" was rediscovered in the early medieval period by Dante; but the modern form of the argument might plausibly be thought to have begun with Hobbes and to have reached self-consciousness with Kant. Hobbes's argument for the necessity of instituting a sovereign was that in the absence of an overwhelming power to keep them in check, individuals will succumb to the temptation to attack one other, either for gain, out of fear, or merely in order to assert their own superiority. The natural next step is to ask whether nation-states, being themselves in a state of anarchy, need a sovereign to keep them in check, and to think that perhaps they do.

In Hobbesian terms, the answer is that states do not suffer from the same incentives to "kill" one another that individuals in the state of nature do. An individual who kills or disables his opponent need fear no comeback; states are rarely destroyed as completely and suddenly as individuals, so mutual deterrence will suffice. A relatively weak state can inflict enough damage on an invader to make conquest a bad bargain. This is not a thought that could comfort Liechtenstein or Andorra, but it is persuasive in the case of nation-states the size of France and Britain. It also suggests the limits of this reasoning: nation-states driven by ideological passion or governed by rulers who are prone to miscalculation will get into wars that prudent self-interest would keep them out of. More nuanced ideas had to wait until the end of the eighteenth century, and in Immanuel Kant's *Perpetual Peace* there emerged a vision, not of a world government but of a peacekeeping league of nations, that has not been improved on since. The thought that animated Kant was that peoples have a right to self-government, but that, as with many other rights, the uncontrolled exercise of this autonomy offered the prospect of conflict and war without end. World government was not only impracticable—large and dangerous states that most need to be brought within the rule of law will not surrender their sovereignty—but immoral as well, because it violates the right of peoples to govern themselves. On the whole, utilitarians would want world government, or, if it is impossible, a league of nations as a second best. Kant thought, as did John Rawls in his recent rethinking of the rights of peoples, that this is a moral blind spot in the utilitarian approach to international relations. It does not take seriously the truth that free agents can be governed lawfully only if their freedom is respected. Domestically, only a constitutional state is legitimate; by the same token, a league of nations is legitimate, but global despotism is not.

A league of nations unites all lawful states in lawlike relations with one another; each is independent in the government of its own affairs but yoked to the others so that an act of aggression against a member of the league is a crime in international law. That, and that alone, warrants military intervention by the other members of the league. Readers of Kant's essay of two and a quarter centuries ago are astonished to find article 5 of the United Nations Charter so clearly prefigured; but they should not be. The thought that a treaty for the preservation of international peace rests on the presumption that the signatories secure their autonomy in what concerns only themselves, in return for exposing themselves to sanctions if they violate the autonomy of others, is visible in Hobbes's Scholastic near-contemporaries on the continent. The deeper issue is whether the disanalogy between individuals and states makes the very idea of a realm of affairs that concerns only an individual nation-state suspect. A state that is quietly getting on with murdering its Jewish population may not be attacking its neighbors, but it is not doing something that we should allow it to get on with. There are many things a state may legitimately do even if the rest of us think it ill-advised; genocide is not one of them. Kant and Rawls guard against any such possibility, in the one case by insisting that the members of the league are genuinely legitimate republics, and in the other by the analogous requirement that they are "well-ordered."[16] The Charter of the United Nations has no such requirements, and in the eyes of many critics, myself among them, makes too many concessions to the inviolability of national sovereignty.

Humanitarian Intervention

We have reached a crux. The modern world is not threatened with military catastrophe as a result of economic globalization. It is threatened with anxiety and economic loss, but not military catastrophe, because of the conjunction of nationalist and religious fervor in the Middle East and nearer home. War between nuclear powers may occur in some parts of the world: thus far India and Pakistan have engaged in low-level skirmishes without escalation, but North Korea may make a miscalculation over the consequences of putting pressure on South Korea, and India and Pakistan may make a fatal mistake. This does not threaten global disaster, but unspeakable local horrors. Hankerings after world government have abated with the collapse of the Soviet Union and the elimination of the danger that the two states that could annihilate human life might do so. Two issues remain: the first is the pressure toward intervention in the affairs of states that violate the human rights of their citizens or fail to preserve minimal levels of security and well-being; the second, the possibility that the driving force for forms of international government that go beyond a United Nations built around collective security will be environmental degradation. This is a real novelty, undiscussed in the past two millennia of political thinking, although local environmental degradation has been a fact of life throughout human history.

Pressure for humanitarian intervention begins from the deep disanalogy between individuals and states. An individual without dependents relying on him for their subsistence should be allowed to behave imprudently as long as he does not harm his neighbors; but a state cannot behave imprudently within its own private sphere without violating anyone else's rights. It has no private sphere. A state is a set of institutions claiming a territorial jurisdiction and resting its legitimacy, its title to the obedience of its subjects, on what it does for their welfare. In a world of human rights, citizens possess rights against their government: rights to nonmalicious behavior ranging from immunity to torture to the right to a fair trial, and perhaps wider welfare rights, involving education, health, social security. The question of how to secure those rights is not easily answered. Anyone who accepts Kant's claim that a people has a right to self-government, must be tempted by the answer that, except in extremis, assistance to the subjects of a particular state is permitted only when that state asks for it; but anyone who remembers that a state contains a multitude of members, and that not all of them will see the world from the same perspective, must also be tempted by the thought that a state that fails its citizens loses its immunity against unasked-for interference.[17]

Down that track lies a host of anxieties; not fear of nuclear annihilation, but a well-justified fear that incompetent interference will leave everyone worse-off, and that resentment at interference will prove a breeding ground for terrorism and unofficial war. Conversely, failing to act seems too like the behavior of a passerby who sees a child drowning and hesitates to leap into the water for fear of dirtying his clothes. The constraints of article 5 of the United Nations Charter force politicians to advance duplicitous arguments. Since article 5 allows military action only in self-defense, advocates of humanitarian intervention must argue, not always plausibly, that failed states endanger their neighbors as well as their own citizens. Their opponents argue, often equally implausibly, that even if the local population will suffer in the absence of intervention, their suffering threatens no one else and cannot be ameliorated without doing more harm than good. The argument that a state that fails its inhabitants forfeits its sovereign immunity to outside intervention is repudiated by every government in the world. Nor is it easy to keep in being an international force that is universally respected as the impartial arm of the world's conscience, given the financial difficulty of finding rich countries willing to pay for it, the political difficulty of reaching a consensus on whom it is to police, and the seeming impossibility of keeping it from becoming ensnared in the corruption it is supposed to prevent.

Humanitarian intervention will surely continue to be one of the great unresolved issues both in international ethics and in state practice. The duty to save the innocent from ill usage gives the moral upper hand to interventionists, while the difficulty of intervening intelligently gives the prudential upper hand to their opponents. Since the collapse of the Soviet

Union and the end of nuclear nightmares as a central preoccupation, the issue has preoccupied theorists of the international system. Besides simple practicality—whether foreign countries can assemble what is needed and deliver it efficiently—there are anxieties without precursors in the history of political thinking. Fear of cross-cultural ineptitude did not concern our forebears in the way it does us. When the question arose whether the Spanish invaders were violating the rights of the indigenous peoples of the Caribbean and South America, a popular answer was that the indigenous peoples were violating the rights of the innocent. The view that cannibalism (the main charge against the Caribs) might be a local cultural option and not to be interfered with was not a sixteenth- or seventeenth-century notion. Today we tread more warily in areas such as a local culture's treatment of women. Genital mutilation does not receive the treatment General Napier proposed for the practitioners of suttee. Common sense suggests the existence of a substantial middle ground between the claim that everything is a matter of cultural choice and the claim that the law of nature is inscribed in the heart of every rational being. Genocide violates any conceivable moral code, while a nationalized rather than a private health service or a nationalized rather than a private railway system are paradigmatically matters of local choice; making the wrong choice may be costly, but hardly reaches the level of a humanitarian disaster, nor does the everyday incompetence of our rulers and legislators make our countries failed states. We all live in states with many failings; happily, most of us do not live in failed states.

Environmental Degradation

Finally: "not with a bang but a whimper." Having failed to incinerate ourselves in a nuclear firestorm or to starve in the nuclear winter that followed it, we have come to fear that we are rendering the world uninhabitable and perhaps that wars over natural resources may loom larger in our future. This may be the issue that will demand more powerful international institutions than any we have yet created, something closer to world government than we have thus far contemplated. The Persian

Empire was vulnerable to natural catastrophe; Darius's first invasion fleet was destroyed by a storm in the Bosphorus. Nature was vulnerable to human activity; forests were felled and soils depleted. What is unprecedented is the scale on which nature is now vulnerable to human activity, and the extent to which the natural catastrophes we now face will be the result of human action.

When Edmund Burke praised the courage and energy of the American colonists, these were farmers carving their farms out of the trackless forests that hemmed them in, or deep-sea whalers chasing their prey into the Arctic and Antarctic oceans.[18] Less of the world was known and settled than unknown and unsettled. Nature was a threat or an inspiration, but not tamed. The population of the world was between 650 and 900 million persons in 1750, and the world's resources to all intents and purposes inexhaustible. Economists knew that "inexhaustibility" was far from the truth in regard to the resources of settled and civilized countries. In 1776 Adam Smith's *Wealth of Nations* discussed cultivable land as a constraint on economic growth, and the economic consequences of the diminishing marginal productivity of land were well understood. There was no suggestion that the planet as a whole set limits to population and consumption. A shortage of productive land was a problem in political economy because, in a world of separate nation-states, there was no land to be had beyond a nation's borders, except by colonizing "empty" continents overseas.

The world's population is now some seven billion; projections suggest it will peak at nine billion, and many commentators think this is beyond the "carrying capacity" of the planet. The seven billion consume vastly more per capita than the population in 1750 did, and the burden they place on the environment is exponentially greater. Nature is said by some writers to have disappeared; it has certainly been reconceptualized: we no longer see ourselves surrounded by a world that bears the mark of a divine creation within which we are to find our home, and explore God's purposes for us.[19] The word "environment" suggests that we are looking after a garden rather than taming a wilderness. The two obvious questions are whether we are destroying our own life-support system, and whether stopping the process demands new political institutions.

The answers are "yes, but not yet irreparably," and "no." Nobody who looks at the combined effects of population growth and technological change can be optimistic about the damage humanity has done already and will do over the next half century. The depletion of natural resources is doubly frightening. On the one side, there is the danger of famine and disease; on the other, the most plausible scenarios for widespread military conflict are predicated on the effects of heightened competition for diminishing resources. Military conflicts over access to water in the Middle East and in parts of Asia and Africa are easy to imagine. Conflict over oil is even easier to imagine.

The depletion of oil resources is multiply alarming. The loss of a cheap and abundant fuel and feed stock for the chemical industries will require the reorganization of the developed economies that have relied on oil for the past century. The use of oil is environmentally damaging; like other fossil fuels, it creates large amounts of soot and carbon dioxide and contributes to global warming and whatever disasters that may produce. Competition over declining oil supplies may cause large-scale international conflict. Many major world economies have no indigenous oil supplies; few have enough to run even a reduced version of their present economies. Britain and the United States have for a century pursued foreign policies dominated by the need to secure future oil supplies from countries in the Middle East. Japan's attempts to dominate East Asia were driven by the need for oil, while Bertrand Russell enraged Leon Trotsky in the early 1920s by insisting that Trotsky's talk of bringing communism to Georgia was camouflage for an old-fashioned seizure of the Georgian oil fields. If ideology, religious differences, and cultural misunderstandings will not cause major wars, oil may.

Nonetheless, avoiding these disasters does not demand dramatic institutional innovation. The system of collective security embodied in the United Nations Charter would be adequate if taken with sufficient seriousness; and the imminent threat of major conflict might well instill seriousness. There remains the problem of how to diminish the environmental damage done by the human race. It is tempting to think that if the human race is responsible for the problem, a political system embracing the human race must be the solution. All history is against it. The classical Greek poleis were deeply attached to the land on which they stood; but they cut down forests, grew grain that depleted the fertility of the land, and grazed goats that turned hillsides into rubble. This is where "the tragedy of the commons" bites. Collectively owned property is the least well cared for. The best custodians of the countryside are farmers whose long-run interest in their resources leads them to conserve their surroundings, if not to beautify them. Aristotle observed that what belongs to everyone is cared for by nobody, and the environment is vulnerable because nobody has property rights in its most fragile elements.[20] Compare wildlife with domestic animals; there is no shortage of domestic livestock, but wild species become extinct every year.

The protection of unowned, or hard to own, resources—think of the air—requires regulation; there will always be incentives for governments to secure loopholes in international treaties, and for polluters to ignore regulations in countries where government is corrupt or ineffectual. Nonetheless, there are more than enough international regulatory bodies to create the required regulatory mechanisms, and what they are is obvious in outline, however complex in detail. What is lacking is a consensus on an equitable distribution of the burdens of effective regulation, willingness to comply with them, and in some parts of the world capacity to enforce them. The notion that global government would solve such problems, as distinct from better local governance, and a stronger sense of urgency across the globe, is utopian. The ignorance and corruption of local officials will not be remedied by imposing a layer of authority even more remote than a central government that is already failing in its task. Nor would the forcible displacement of that central government by well-intentioned outsiders be a plausible route to environmental health. There is nothing worse for the environment than war. Only the slow implementation of better governance by weeding out corruption and ignorance will save us, if anything can.

If expectations should be realistic, ambitions need not be subdued. Any historical account of political theorizing and political theorists risks making everyday politics look humdrum by contrasting it with the visions of great, atypical thinkers. Few of us see the world through Plato's spectacles; if we are fortunate, we do not brood on the threats to political order that alarmed Hobbes—even though the invention of nuclear weapons has made us uncomfortably aware of his insights into the logic of mutual deterrence; Marx's expectations for the destiny of the industrial proletariat are epic poetry; local parking regulations are not. Yet far more people today take an interest in politics than can ever have done so in the ancient world, where mobility and communication were so restricted; far more people today lead autonomous and empowered lives in the light of ideas of the good life they have worked out for themselves. They are citizens as well as subjects, and even though their citizenship is largely social rather than conventionally political, it is a *political* triumph that this is possible, that so many well-ordered states exist where law is administered impartially and honestly, and citizens are in charge of their own lives. Some of our success rests on technologies our forebears knew nothing of; we are not morally superior to our ancestors or intrinsically more intelligent or perceptive. But in the absence of the right political framework, we could not have achieved the successes of the post-1945 world. The very different fates of "failed states" tells us that.

The art of self-government remains fragile. Self-government can fail by succumbing to violence or to economic or environmental catastrophe; it can also succumb to lassitude and boredom. We might, after all, settle for the domestication of existence and vote for *Brave New World*—we might turn away from the uncertainty of politics and settle for the administration of comfort. However, we are now at the end of a history of political thinking whose aim is to understand what some great, and engrossing, thinkers have thought. Guessing what the future holds for peoples and their states has never been a profitable activity. All we know is that what happens will come as a surprise.

Acknowledgments

Because this book does not engage directly with the second-ary literature on its subject, this is my only opportunity to express my indebtedness to teachers, colleagues, friends, and students. For help-ing to bring the project to a conclusion, I am very grateful to Roby Harrington and Bob Weil of W. W. Norton, and to Donald Lamm of W. W. Norton for provoking it in the first place. Along the way, I have had a lot of help from Sadie Ryan Simonovich, Vicky Payne, Doris Grabovsky, and Sam Evans. The Andrew W. Mellon Foundation enabled me to spend a productive year at the Center for Advanced Study in the Behavioral Sciences at Palo Alto; New College, Oxford, elected me as a Senior Research Fellow for 2009–10, and Princeton University found room for me as a visiting scholar. I am grateful to all of them.

As to my larger debts, Isaiah Berlin's lectures fifty years ago gave me a taste for his way of writing the history of political thought, while con-versation with Herbert Hart at the same time set standards of clarity in thinking about social and legal philosophy I have struggled to meet ever since. Colleagues whose work has been invaluable to me, both generally and in particular contexts, include Julia Annas, Brian Barry, Jerry Cohen, Janet Coleman, Maurice Cranston, John Dunn, Ronald Dworkin, Peter

Euben, Maurice Goldsmith, Iain Hampsher-Monk, Michael Ignatieff, Terry Irwin, Morris Kaplan, Steven Lukes, Pratap Mehta, David Miller, Thomas Nagel, Carole Pateman, Philip Pettit, Mark Philp, Jennifer Pitts, John Plamenatz, John Pocock, Melvin Richter, John Robson, Michael Rosen, Larry Siedentop, Quentin Skinner, John Skorupski, Charles Taylor, Richard Tuck, Maurizio Viroli, Nadia Urbinati, Bernard Williams, Robert Wokler, and Sheldon Wolin. Large numbers of colleagues and students have made the Universities of Essex, Oxford, and Princeton congenial intellectual environments over more than forty years. Other than to the extent that they have persuaded me to see the world as they do, none is responsible for the above, and in particular for whatever errors of fact and interpretation it contains.

NOTES TO BOOK TWO

CHAPTER 12: THOMAS HOBBES

1. Hobbes, "The Verse Life," in *Human Nature and De Corpore Politico*, p. 224.
2. *Aubrey's Brief Lives*, p. 148.
3. Ibid., p. 149.
4. Clarendon, *A Brief View and Survey*; Nicholas Tyacke, "Tory Oxford," in *History of the University of Oxford*, p. 897.
5. *Aubrey's Brief Lives*, p. 150.
6. Hobbes, "A Review and Conclusion," *Leviathan*, p. 707–8.
7. Hobbes, *Leviathan*, p. 344.
8. Shapin and Schaffer, *Leviathan and the Air-Pump*, recounts the argument with Boyle.
9. Hobbes, *Leviathan*, p. 117.
10. Hobbes, *Behemoth*, p. 3.
11. Hobbes, *Leviathan*, p. 718.
12. Ibid., p. 252.
13. Ibid., p. 82.
14. Ibid., p. 83.
15. Ibid., pp. 147–49.
16. Ibid., pp. 147–48.
17. Shapin and Schaeffer, *Leviathan and the Air-Pump*.
18. Hobbes, "Review and Conclusion," p. 727.
19. Ibid.

20. Ibid.

21. Hobbes, *Leviathan*, pp. 80–82.

22. Ibid., p. 107.

23. Ibid., p. 171.

24. Ibid., pp. 111–12.

25. Ibid., p. 120.

26. Ibid., pp. 129–30.

27. Ibid.

28. Ibid., p. 185.

29. Ibid., pp. 168–70.

30. Ibid., p. 183.

31. Ibid., p. 217.

32. Emphasized in "Review and Conclusion," pp. 718–21.

33. Hobbes, *Leviathan*, pp. 251–52.

34. Ibid., pp. 228ff.

35. Ibid., p. 266.

36. Ibid., p. 271.

37. *Aubrey's Brief Lives*, p. 157.

38. Hobbes, *Leviathan*, p. 169.

CHAPTER 13: JOHN LOCKE AND REVOLUTION

1. Ashcraft, *Revolutionary Politics and Locke's Two Treatises of Government*, passim.

2. Peter Laslett, introduction to *Two Treatises of Government*, p. 3.

3. Locke, preface to *Second Treatise*, in *Two Treatises of Government*, p. 137.

4. Price, "Sermon on the Love of Our Country," in *Political Writings*, pp. 189–90.

5. Burke, *Appeal from the New Whigs to the Old Whigs*, in *The Portable Burke*, pp. 146–47.

6. Locke, *Second Treatise* (sec. 6), p. 271.

7. Ibid. (sec. 3), p. 268.

8. Locke, *A Letter concerning Toleration*, in *Selected Political Writings*, pp. 129–30.

9. Locke, *Political Essays*, pp. 120–21.

10. Locke, *Letter concerning Toleration*, p. 158.

11. Notably, Daniel Bell, *The Cultural Contradictions of Capitalism*.

12. Locke, *Second Treatise* (sec. 3), p. 268.

13. Ibid. (sec. 9), p. 272.

14. Ibid. (sec. 27), pp. 287–88.

15. Filmer, *Patriarcha and Other Writings* (sec. 7), p. 9.

16. Locke, *Second Treatise* (sec. 15), p. 277.

17. Ibid. (sec. 27), p. 288.

18. Ibid. (sec. 31), p. 290.

19. Locke, *First Treatise* (sec. 42), p. 170.

20. Locke, *Second Treatise* (sec. 32), p. 290.

21. Ibid. (sec. 37), p. 294.

22. Ibid. (sec. 41), p. 297.

23. Ibid. (sec. 34), p. 291.

24. Ibid. (sec. 139), pp. 361–62.

25. Locke, *First Treatise* (sec. 43), p. 171.

26. John Rawls, *A Theory of Justice*, pp. 68–93.

27. Locke, *Second Treatise* (sec. 235), pp. 421–42.

28. Locke, *Political Essays*, p. 216.

CHAPTER 14: REPUBLICANISM

1. Rousseau, *The Social Contract* (2.6), p. 67.

2. Harrington, *The Commonwealth of Oceana*, pp. 72ff.

3. Ibid., p. 20.

4. Ibid., pp. 8–9.

5. Coke, "Dr. Bonham's Case," in *Selected Writings*, I:264–83.

6. Harrington, *Oceana*, p. 15.

7. Ibid., p. 52.

8. Hume, "Whether the British Government Inclines More to an Absolute Monarchy or a Republic," in *Political Essays*, pp. 28–32.

9. Editor's introduction to Sidney, *Discourses concerning Government*, p. xvi.

10. Though Blair Worden praises it as "a book of great clarity, elegance, and learning," in Burns and Goldie, eds., *Cambridge History of Political Thought, 1450– 1700*, p. 460.

11. Sidney, *Discourses*, p. 259.

12. Ibid., p. 20.

13. Ibid., pp. 174–75.

14. Ibid., p. 511.

15. Constant, "The Liberty of the Ancients Compared with That of the Moderns," in *Political Writings*, pp. 327–28.

16. Montesquieu, *The Spirit of the Laws*, pp. xliii–xlv.

17. Ibid., p. 3.

18. Ibid., p. 4.

19. Ibid., p. 7.

20. Ibid., p. 168.

21. Ibid., pp. 10–11, 21.

22. Ibid., pp. 131–33.

23. Ibid., p. 26.

24. Ibid., p. 22.

25. Constant, "Liberty of the Ancients," pp. 327–28.

26. Montesquieu, *Spirit of the Laws*, pp. 17–18.

27. Ibid., p. 18.

28. Ibid., pp. 156–66.

29. Ibid., p. 160.

CHAPTER 15: ROUSSEAU

1. Rousseau, *Confessions*, bks. 11 and 12, pp. 533–644.

2. Rousseau, *The Social Contract* (3.6), p. 129.

3. Rousseau, *Discourse on the Origin of Inequality among Men*, in *Rousseau's Political Writings*, pp. 12–14.

4. Rousseau, *Émile*, pp. 321–31.

5. Rousseau, preface to *Inequality*, p. 4.

6. Rousseau, *Confessions*, pp. 339–44.

7. Rousseau, *Inequality*, pp. 4–11.

8. Ibid., pp. 9–10.

9. Ibid., p. 4.

10. Ibid., pp. 38–39.

11. Ibid., p. 6.

12. Ibid., p. 16.

13. Ibid., p. 22.

14. Ibid., p. 20.

15. Ibid., p. 22.

16. Ibid., p. 23.

17. Kant, *Groundwork for the Metaphysics of Morals*, pp. 40–41.

18. Rousseau, *Inequality*, pp. 38–39.

19. Ferguson, *An Essay on the History of Civil Society*.

20. Rousseau, *Inequality*, p. 34.

21. Ibid., pp. 16–19.

22. Ibid., p. 44.

23. Rousseau, *Émile*, pp. 5–6.

24. Ibid., pp. 62–64.

25. Wollstonecraft, *A Vindication of the Rights of Men and A Vindication of the Rights of Woman*, pp. 156–73.

26. Rousseau, *Social Contract* (1.1), p. 85.

27. Ibid. (1.3), p. 88.

28. Ibid. (1.5), p. 91.

29. Ibid. (1.6), p. 92.

30. Ibid. (1.6), p. 93.

31. Ibid. (2.5), p. 104.

32. Ibid. (1.6), p. 93.

33. Ibid. (1.7), p. 96.

34. See the so-called Geneva Manuscript, ibid., pp. 153ff.

35. Ibid. (1.7), p. 95.

36. Ibid. (2.5), p. 104.

37. Ibid. (2.1), p. 98.

38. Ibid. (3.2), pp. 122–23.

39. Ibid. (2.7), pp. 107–10.

40. Ibid. (4.4), pp. 154ff.

41. Ibid. (3.17), p. 144.

CHAPTER 16: THE AMERICAN FOUNDING

1. Maistre, *Works*, pp. 84–85.

2. Bailyn, *Ideological Origins of the American Revolution*; Wood, *The Radicalism of the American Revolution*.

3. Burke, *Appeal*, in *The Portable Burke*, pp. 488–89.

4. Jefferson, *Political Writings*, p. 64.

5. Ibid., p. 148.

6. Ibid., p. 102.

7. Rawls, "The Idea of an Overlapping Consensus," in *Political Liberalism*, pp. 133ff.

8. Jefferson, *Political Writings*, pp. 62ff.

9. Ibid., p. 62.

10. Ibid., pp. 64–66.

11. Ibid., pp. 216–17.

12. This may cease to be true if Texas succeeds in disguising Jefferson's role in the revolution.

13. Jefferson, *Political Writings*, pp. 102ff.

14. Ibid., p. 104.

15. Ibid., p. 110.

16. Madison, Hamilton, and Jay, *The Federalist Papers* (no. 47), pp. 303–8.

17. Jefferson, *Political Writings*, pp. 360–61.

18. *Federalist* (no. 10), p. 128.

19. Jefferson, *Political Writings*, p. 217.

20. *Federalist* (no. 18), pp. 160–61.

21. Ibid. (no. 10), p. 123.

22. Ibid., p. 124.

23. Dahl, "Madisonian Democracy," in *A Preface to Democratic Theory*, pp. 4ff.

24. Burke, *Speech to the Electors of Bristol*, in *Portable Burke*, pp. 155–56.

25. Madison, *Vices of the Political System*, in Kurland and Lerner, eds., *The Founders' Constitution*, vol. I, chap. 5, doc. 16.

26. *Federalist* (no. 39), 254–45.

27. Tocqueville, *Democracy in America*, p. 233.

28. The source of the Fourth Amendment's prohibition on unwarranted search and seizure.

29. Jefferson, *Political Writings*, p. 99.

CHAPTER 17: THE FRENCH REVOLUTION AND ITS CRITICS

1. Burke, *Pre-Revolutionary Writings*, pp. 206–69.

2. Ibid., pp. 116–92.

3. Reprinted in Kurland and Lerner, eds., *The Founders' Constitution*, vol. I, chap. 13, doc. 7.

4. Burke, *Reflections on the Revolution in France*, p. 164.

5. Price, *Political Writings*, pp. 176ff.

6. Burke, *Reflections*, p. 26.

7. Jefferson, letter to Lafayette, in *Political Writings*, pp. 197–202.

8. Burke, *Reflections*, p. 77.

9. Ibid., p. 96.

10. Ibid., p. 87.

11. Ibid., p. 21.

12. Ibid., pp. 56ff.

13. Burke, *Pre-Revolutionary Writings*, pp. 218–20.

14. *Thomas Paine Reader*, p. 116.

15. Ibid., p. 256.

16. Ibid., p. 211.

17. Ibid., p. 218.

18. Ibid., p. 260.

CHAPTER 18: HEGEL: THE MODERN STATE
AS THE WORK OF SPIRIT

1. Findlay, *Hegel*, p. 327.

2. Hegel, *The Philosophy of History*, pp. 456–57.

3. Kojève, *Introduction to the Reading of Hegel*; Fukuyama, *The End of History and the Last Man*.

4. Hegel, preface to *Elements of the Philosophy of Right*, p. 23.

5. Ibid. (addition to sec. 258), p. 279.

6. Ibid., pp. 67–116.

7. Hegel, *Phenomenology of Spirit* (sections 78–96), pp. 111–19.

8. Ibid. (sections 197–201), pp. 119–22.

9. Ibid. (sections 354–60), pp. 377–80.

10. Hegel, *Philosophy of Right*, p. 23.

11. Constant, *Political Writings*, pp. 326–27.

12. Hegel, *Philosophy of Right*, p. 23.

13. Ibid., p. 35.

14. Ibid., p. 87.

15. Ibid., p. 88.

16. Mill, *On Liberty*, p. 16.

17. Hegel, *Philosophy of Right* (sec. 67), p. 97.

18. Ibid. (sec. 44, add.), p. 76.

19. Ibid. (sections 105–41), pp. 135–86.

20. Ibid. (sec. 160), p. 200.

21. Ibid. (sec. 161, add.), p. 201.

22. Ibid. (sec. 188), p. 226.

23. Ibid. (sec. 250), p. 270.

24. Ibid. (sec. 244, add.), pp. 266–67.

25. Ibid. (sections 245, 248), pp. 267, 269.

26. Ibid. (sec. 270 and note), pp. 290–304.

27. Ibid. (sec. 324), p. 361.

28. Ibid. (sections 342ff), pp. 372ff.

29. Ibid. (sec. 329, add.), pp. 365–66.

CHAPTER 19: UTILITARIANISM: JEREMY BENTHAM AND JAMES AND JOHN STUART MILL

1. Bentham, *Handbook of Political Fallacies*; Armitage, *The Declaration of Independence*, pp. 79–80.

2. Bentham *An Introduction to the Principles of Morals and Legislation*, chaps. 1–5, in *Utilitarianism and Other Essays*, pp. 65–111.

3. Bentham, quoted by Hart, *Essays on Bentham*, p. 51.

4. J. Mill, *Political Writings*, pp. 3–42.

5. Ibid., p. 291.

6. J. S. Mill, *Autobiography*, pp. 77–80.

7. Ibid., pp. 25–40.

8. Ibid., pp. 30–31.

9. Ibid., pp. 111ff. ("A Crisis in My Mental History").

10. Ibid., pp. 116–17.

11. J. S. Mill, in *Essays on Politics and Culture*, pp. 77–120, 173–213.

12. J. S. Mill, *Autobiography*, pp. 202–4.

13. J. S. Mill, "Of the Geometrical or Abstract Method," in *System of Logic*, bk. 6, chap. 8, in *The Collected Works*, 8:887-894.

14. J. S. Mill, "Of Ethology or the Science of the Formation of Character," bk. 6, chap. 5, in *Collected Works*, 8:861–74.

15. J. S. Mill, "On the Probable Futurity of the Labouring Classes," in *Principles of Political Economy*, bk. 4, chap. 7, in *Collected Works*, 3:759–96; "Chapters on Socialism," ibid., 5:707–53.

16. J. S. Mill, "The Spirit of the Age," in *Essays on Politics and Culture*, pp 1–44.

17. Ibid., pp. 36–40.

18. J. S. Mill, *System of Logic*, bk. 6, chap. 12, sec. 7, in *Utilitarianism and Other Essays*, pp. 139–40.

19. J. S. Mill, "Bentham," in *Utilitarianism*, pp. 171–73.

20. Ibid., pp. 171–72.

21. J. S. Mill, "Civilization," in *Essays on Politics and Culture*, pp. 47ff.

22. Ibid., pp. 274–75.

23. Ibid., p. 278.

24. Ibid., pp. 304–6.

25. Putnam, *Bowling Alone*.

26. J. S. Mill, *On Liberty*, pp. 8–11.

27. Ibid., p. 17.

28. Ibid., pp. 64–65.

29. Ibid., pp. 106–18.

30. Ibid., pp. 117–21.

31. J. S. Mill, *Representative Government*, in *Collected Works*, 19:458–59.

32. J. S. Mill, *The Subjection of Women*, pp. 238–39.

CHAPTER 20: TOCQUEVILLE AND DEMOCRACY

1. Pitts, *A Turn to Empire*, pp. 200ff.

2. Jardin, *Tocqueville*, pp. 88ff.

3. Ibid., pp. 52–53.

4. Translated as *Recollections*.

5. J. S. Mill, *Letters*, in *Collected Works*, 15:517–18.

6. Brogan, *Alexis de Tocqueville*, p. 501.

7. Tocqueville, *Democracy in America*, pt. I, p. 233.

8. Ibid., pt. 2, pp. 684–96.
9. Ibid., pp. 803ff.
10. J. S. Mill, "The State of Society in America," in *Collected Works*, 18:98–100.
11. Tocqueville, *Democracy*, pt. 2, p. 494.
12. Ibid., pt. I, pp. 14ff. ("Author's Introduction").
13. Ibid., p. 14–16.
14. Usefully collected in Craiutu and Jennings, eds., *Tocqueville on America after 1840*.
15. Tocqueville, *Democracy*, pt. I, pp. 201–2, 223–34.
16. Ibid., pp. 391–97.
17. Ibid., pp. 405–6.
18. Craiutu and Jennings, eds., *Tocqueville on America*, pp. 26–39.
19. Tocqueville, *Democracy*, pt. 2, p. 587.
20. Ibid., pp. 591–600.
21. Ibid., p. 684.
22. Ibid.
23. Ibid., p. 805.
24. Ibid., p. 806.
25. J. S. Mill, *Letters*, in *Collected Works*, 15:518.
26. J. S. Mill, *Representative Government*, in *Collected Works*, 19:565.
27. Tocqueville, *The Old Regime and the Revolution*, pp. 225–30.
28. Ibid., pp. 156–60.

CHAPTER 21: KARL MARX

1. Kapp, *The Life of Eleanor Marx*, 1:300.
2. From Marx, *The German Ideology*, in *Early Political Writings*, p. 123.
3. Marx, letter to his father, November 10, 1837, in *Selected Writings*, p. 12.
4. Marx, *Economic-Philosophical Manuscripts*, in *Selected Writings*, p. 84.
5. Ibid., pp. 85–95.
6. Ibid., p. 89.
7. Marx and Engels, *The Communist Manifesto*, p. 233.
8. Marx, *Critique of Hegel's Philosophy of Right*, in *Selected Writings*, pp. 32–40.
9. Ibid., pp. 34–35.
10. Marx and Engels, *Manifesto*, p. 219.
11. Ibid., p. 220.
12. Marx, *Capital*, vol. I, in *Selected Writings*, p. 525.
13. Marx, *The Eighteenth Brumaire of Louis Bonaparte*, in *Selected Writings*, pp. 329ff.
14. Ibid., pp. 346–47; *Manifesto*, p. 221.
15. Marx, *German Ideology*, pp. 123ff.

16.   Marx, *Critique of the Gotha Programme*, in *Selected Writings*, p. 615.

17.   Marx, "Marginal Notes on Bakunin's *Statism and Anarchy*," in *Selected Writings*, p. 608.

CHAPTER 22: THE
TWENTIETH CENTURY AND BEYOND

1.   Goldhagen, *Hitler's Willing Executioners: Ordinary Germans and the Holocaust*.

2.   Bell, *The End of Ideology*.

3.   Lipset, *Political Man*, p. viii.

4.   Schumpeter, *Capitalism, Socialism, and Democracy*, chaps. 21–23.

5.   Most notably, Kornhauser, *The Politics of Mass Society*.

6.   J. S. Mill, "Civilization," in *Essays on Politics and Culture*, p. 47.

7.   J. S. Mill, *On Liberty*, pp. 81–82.

8.   Ortega y Gasset, *The Revolt of the Masses*, is the locus classicus.

9.   Tocqueville, *Democracy in America*, pt. 2, pp. 803ff.; Sennett, *The Fall of Public Man*.

10.   Lippmann, *Public Opinion*, pp. 12–19; Arendt, *The Human Condition*, pp. 320ff.

11.   Notably in Putnam, *Bowling Alone*.

12.   Sombart, *Why Is There No Socialism in the United States?*

13.   Gramsci, *The Modern Prince*.

14.   In Russell, *The Scientific Outlook*; Huxley, *Brave New World*. It is hard not to wonder whether modern communitarians remember the motto of *Brave New World*, "community, identity, stability."

15.   J. S. Mill, *Utilitarianism*, in *John Stuart Mill and Jeremy Bentham*, pp. 280–81.

16.   Plato, *The Apology of Socrates*, in *Last Days of Socrates*, p. 66.

17.   Freud, *Civilization and Its Discontents*; Marcuse, *Eros and Civilization* and *One-Dimensional Man*.

18.   Ruskin, *Fors Clavigera*, May 1871, in *Selected Writings*, 27:86.

19.   Ortega y Gasset, *Revolt*, pp. 76–77, 115ff.

20.   Weber, "The Types of Legitimate Domination," in *The Theory of Social and Economic Organization*, pp. 324ff.

21.   Weber, "Politics as a Vocation" and "Science as a Vocation," in *From Max Weber*, pp. 77–156.

22.   Schumpeter, *Capitalism, Socialism, and Democracy*, pp. 284–302.

23.   Michels, *Political Parties*, pp. 32ff.

24.   Michels, *First Lectures in Political Sociology*.

25.   Mills, *The Power Elite*, pp. 25–27; Dahl, *Who Governs?*

CHAPTER 23: EMPIRE AND IMPERIALISM

1. Aristotle, *The Politics* (I.4–7), pp. 15–19.

2. Kipling, "The White Man's Burden," *McClure's Magazine*, February 1899.

3. Erasmus, *The Complaint of Peace*, cited in *The Education of a Christian Prince*, p. 109.

4. Vitoria, *Political Writings*, pp. 88ff.

5. Translated as *The Rights of War and Peace*.

6. Locke, *Second Treatise* (sec. 41), in *Two Treatises of Government*, pp. 296–97.

7. Relying in part on *The Politics* (I.4–6), pp. 14–19.

8. Vattel, *The Law of Nations* (sec. 208), p. 128.

9. Jefferson, *Political Writings*, pp. 520–25, 539.

10. J. S. Mill, *On Liberty*, p. 16.

11. Kant, *Perpetual Peace*, in *Political Writings*, pp. 102–7.

12. Diderot, *Supplement to the Voyage of Bougainville*, in *Political Writings*, p. 47.

13. Kant, *Perpetual Peace* and *Idea for a Universal History with a Cosmopolitan Purpose*, in *Political Writings*.

14. Tocqueville, *Writings on Empire and Slavery*.

15. Sidney, *Discourses concerning Government*, p. 9.

16. Gobineau, *The Inequality of the Human Races*; Houston Stewart Chamberlain, *Foundations of the Nineteenth Century*.

17. Lenin, *Imperialism: The Highest Stage of Capitalism*, in *Selected Works*, pp. 667–766.

18. Bossuet, *Politics Drawn from the Very Words of Holy Scripture*, pp. 9ff.

19. Fanon, *Black Skins, White Masks*, translation of *Peau noire, masques blancs*.

CHAPTER 24: SOCIALISMS

1. As argued by Fukuyama, *The End of History and the Last Man*.

2. Owen, *A New View of Society*; Bakunin, *Statism and Anarchy*; Bellamy, *Looking Backward*; Morris, *News from Nowhere*; Kropotkin, *The Conquest of Bread*; Fourier, *The Theory of the Four Movements*.

3. Marx and Engels, *The Communist Manifesto*, p. 221.

4. Owen, *A New View of Society* and *Report to the County of Lanark*.

5. Bellamy, *Looking Backward*, pp. 3–6.

6. Ignatieff, *The Needs of Strangers*.

7. Marshall, *Citizenship and Social Class and Other Essays*.

CHAPTER 25: MARXISM, FASCISM, DICTATORSHIP

1. Orwell, *Animal Farm*; *1984*. Huxley, *Brave New World*; Huxley expresses his surprise in *Brave New World Revisited*.
2. Lippmann, *Public Opinion*, pp. 1–32.
3. Marx to Zasulich, in *Selected Writings*, pp. 623–27.
4. Goldberg, *Liberal Fascism*.
5. Herrnstein and Murray, *The Bell Curve*.
6. Sorel, *Reflections on Violence*, pp. 230ff.
7. Gentile, "What Is Fascism," in *Origins and Doctrine of Fascism*, pp. 53–55.
8. Schmitt, *The Concept of the Political*, pp. 20ff.
9. Schmitt, *Political Theology*, pp. 36ff.
10. Parsons, *The Social System*.

CHAPTER 26: DEMOCRACY IN THE MODERN WORLD

1. Dworkin, introduction to *Freedom's Law*, pp. 1–35.
2. Westbrook, *John Dewey and American Democracy*, pp. 319ff.
3. Dewey, *Liberalism and Social Action*, in *Later Works*, 11:1–65.
4. Dewey, *The Public and Its Problems*, in *Later Works*, 2:324–50.
5. Dewey, "Christianity and Democracy," in *Early Works*, 4:3–10.
6. Dewey, *Public and Its Problems*, pp. 282ff.
7. Truman, *The Governmental Process*.
8. Dewey, *Public and Its Problems*, p. 328.
9. Dewey, *Democracy and Education*, in *Middle Works*, vol. 9.
10. Lippmann, *Public Opinion* and *The Phantom Public*; Niebuhr, *Moral Man and Immoral Society*.
11. Schumpeter, *Capitalism, Socialism, and Democracy*, pp. 235–302.
12. Ibid., pp. 252–55
13. Ibid., p. 256.
14. Ibid., pp. 242, 246, 269ff.
15. Ibid., pp. 241–42.
16. Dahl, *A Preface to Democratic Theory*; compare *Who Governs?* and *After the Revolution?*
17. In Hayden, *The Port Huron Statement*, pp. 45ff.
18. Dahl, *After the Revolution?*, pp. 153ff.
19. Rawls, *Theory of Justice*, pp. 194–200.
20. Dworkin, *Freedom's Law*, pp. 1–35.

CHAPTER 27: GLOBAL PEACE
AND THE HUMAN FUTURE

1. The modern locus classicus is Huntington, *The Clash of Civilizations*, but the rise of Islamic terrorism has more recently spawned a very considerable literature.

2. Machiavelli, *Discourses on Livy* (I.II–I5), pp. I45–60; Rousseau, *Social Contract* (4.8), pp. I66–73.

3. Carlyle, *The French Revolution*, p. 79I.

4. Tocqueville, *The Old Regime and the Revolution*, pp. 202–9.

5. J. S. Mill, *Auguste Comte and Positivism*, in *Collected Works*, I0:263ff.

6. Croly, *The Promise of American Life*; Forcey, *The Crossroads of Liberalism*.

7. Durkheim, *Professional Ethics and Civic Morals*.

8. Bellah, *Habits of the Heart*.

9. Goldman, "Anarchism: What It Really Stands For," in *Anarchism and Other Essays*, pp. 33–44.

10. Most famously by Tocqueville, *The Old Regime*, pp. 2I7–24.

11. Freud, *Beyond the Pleasure Principle*.

12. Russell, *Has Man a Future?*

13. Ceadel, *Thinking about Peace and War*.

14. Tacitus, *The Agricola*, p. 98: *solitudinem faciunt et pacem appellant*.

15. Sidgwick, *The Methods of Ethics*, p. 382

16. Rawls, *Law of Peoples*, pp. 4ff, 63.

17. Beitz, *The Idea of Human Rights*, pp. 97–I0I, 20I–I2.

18. Burke, "Conciliation with America," *Pre-Revolutionary Writings*, pp. 2I8–20.

19. Merchant, *Reinventing Eden*, pp. I–8.

20. Aristotle, *The Politics* (2.5), pp. 35–38.

BIBLIOGRAPHY

Aquinas, Thomas. *Political Writings*. Edited by R. W. Dyson. Cambridge: Cambridge University Press, 2002.

———. *St. Thomas Aquinas on Politics and Ethics*. Edited and Translated by Paul Sigmund. New York: Norton, 1988.

Arendt, Hannah. *The Human Condition*. Chicago: University of Chicago Press, 1958.

———. *The Origins of Totalitarianism*. New York: Harcourt, Brace, 1966.

Aristophanes. *Clouds, Wasps, Peace*. Edited by Jeffrey Henderson. Cambridge: Harvard University Press, 1998.

Aristotle. *The Ethics of Aristotle*. Edited by J. A. K. Thomson. Harmondsworth: Penguin, 1959.

———. *The Politics and The Constitution of Athens*. Edited by Stephen Everson. Translated by Jonathan Barnes. Cambridge: Cambridge University Press, 1996.

Armitage, David. *The Declaration of Independence: A Global History*. Cambridge: Harvard University Press, 2007.

Ashcraft, Richard. *Revolutionary Politics and Locke's Two Treatises of Government*. Princeton: Princeton University Press, 1986.

Aubrey, John. *Brief Lives*. Edited by Oliver Lawson Dick. Harmondsworth: Penguin, 1962.

Augustine. *The City of God against the Pagans*. Translated by R. W. Dyson. Cambridge: Cambridge University Press, 2001.

————. *Confessions*. Translated by Henry Chadwick. Oxford: Oxford University Press, 1991.

Bailyn, Bernard. *Ideological Origins of the American Revolution*. Cambridge: Harvard University Press, 1967.

Bakunin, Mikhail. *Statism and Anarchy*. Edited by Marshall Shatz. Cambridge: Cambridge University Press, 1990.

Baron, Hans. *In Search of Florentine Civic Humanism*. Princeton: Princeton University Press, 1988.

Beerbohm, Max. *Seven Men*. Harmondsworth: Penguin, 1954.

Beitz, Charles. *The Idea of Human Rights*. New York: Oxford University Press, 2009.

Bell, Daniel. *The Cultural Contradictions of Capitalism*. New York: Basic Books, 1976.

————. *The End of Ideology*. Glencoe, Ill.: Free Press, 1960.

Bellah, Robert. *Habits of the Heart*. Berkeley: University of California Press, 1996.

Bellamy, Edward. *Looking Backward*. New York: Random House, 1951.

Bentham, Jeremy. *Handbook of Political Fallacies*. Edited by Harold Larrabee. New York: Harper Torchbooks, 1962.

Bentham, Jeremy, and John Stuart Mill. *John Stuart Mill and Jeremy Bentham: Utilitarianism and Other Essays*. Edited by Alan Ryan. Harmondsworth: Penguin, 1987.

Berlin, Isaiah. *Four Essays on Liberty*. Oxford: Oxford University Press, 1969.

Black, Antony. *Political Thought in Europe, 1250–1450*. Cambridge: Cambridge University Press, 1992.

Bloom, Allan. *The Closing of the American Mind*. New York: Simon and Schuster, 1987.

Bossuet, Bernard. *Politics Drawn from the Very Words of Holy Scripture*. Edited by Patrick Riley. Cambridge: Cambridge University Press, 1990.

Brogan, Hugh. *Alexis de Tocqueville: A Life*. New Haven: Yale University Press, 2007.

Brown, Peter. *Augustine of Hippo*. London: Faber & Faber, 1966.

Burke, Edmund. *The Portable Burke*. Edited by Isaac Kramnick. New York: Viking, 1999.

————. *Pre-Revolutionary Writings*. Edited by Ian Harris. Cambridge: Cambridge University Press, 1993.

————. *Reflections on the Revolution in France*. Edited by L. G. Mitchell. World's Classics. Oxford: Oxford University Press, 2009.

Burns, J. H., ed. *Cambridge History of Medieval Political Thought, 350–1450*. Cambridge: Cambridge University Press, 1988.

Burns, J. H., and Mark Goldie, eds. *Cambridge History of Political Thought, 1450–1700*. Cambridge: Cambridge University Press, 1991.

Calvin, Jean, and Martin Luther. *Luther and Calvin on Secular Authority*. Edited and translated by Harro Höpfl. Cambridge: Cambridge University Press, 1991.

Carlyle, R. W., and A. J. Carlyle. *A History of Medieval Political Theory in the West*. 6 vols. Edinburgh: Blackwood, 1950.

Carlyle, Thomas. *The French Revolution*. New York: Modern Library, 1934.

Cartledge, Paul. *Thermopylae: The Battle That Changed the World*. Woodstock: Overlook Press, 2006.

Ceadel, Martin. *Thinking about Peace and War*. Oxford: Oxford University Press, 1987.

Chamberlain, Houston Stewart. *Foundations of the Nineteenth Century*. New York: H. Fertig, 1968.

Cicero, Marcus Tullius. *On Duties*. Edited by M. T. Griffin and E. M. Atkins. Cambridge: Cambridge University Press, 1991.

————. *On the Commonwealth and On the Laws*. Edited by James E. G. Zetzel. Cambridge: Cambridge University Press, 1999.

Clarendon, Henry Hyde, Earl of. *A Brief View and Survey of the Dangerous and Pernicious Errors to Church and State, in Mr Hobbes's Book Entitled Leviathan*. Oxford, 1676.

Cohn, Norman. *The Pursuit of the Millennium*. London: Secker and Warburg, 1957.

Coke, Edward. *The Selected Writings and Speeches of Sir Edward Coke*. Edited by Steve Sheppard. Vol. I. Indianapolis: Liberty Fund, 2003.

Constant, Benjamin. *Political Writings*. Edited by Biancamaria Fontana. Cambridge: Cambridge University Press, 1988.

Craiutu, Aurelian, and Jeremy Jennings, eds. *Tocqueville on America after 1840: Letters and Other Writings*. New York: Cambridge University Press, 2009.

Croly, Herbert. *The Promise of American Life*. Cambridge: Harvard University Press, 1965.

Dahl, Robert. *After the Revolution?* New Haven: Yale University Press, 1970.

————. *A Preface to Democratic Theory*. Chicago: University of Chicago Press, 1956.

————. *Who Governs?* New Haven: Yale University Press, 1961.

Dante. *The Inferno of Dante*. Translated by Robert Pinsky. New York: Farrar, Straus and Giroux, 1994.

————. *Monarchy*. Edited and translated by Prue Shaw. Cambridge: Cambridge University Press, 1996.

Dewey, John. "Christianity and Democracy." In *The Early Works, 1882–1898*. Vol. 4. Carbondale: Southern Illinois University Press, 1971.

————. *A Common Faith*. In *The Later Works, 1925–1953*. Vol. 9. Carbondale: Southern Illinois University Press, 1986.

————. *Democracy and Education*. Vol. 9 of *The Middle Works, 1899–1924*. Carbondale: Southern Illinois University Press, 1980.

————. *Liberalism and Social Action*. In *Later Works, 1925–1953*. Vol. 11. Carbondale: Southern Illinois University Press, 1991.

————. *The Public and Its Problems*. In *The Later Works, 1925–1953*. Vol. 2. Carbondale: Southern Illinois University Press, 1984.

Diderot, Denis. *Political Writings*. Edited by Robert Wokler. Translated by John Hope Mason. Cambridge: Cambridge University Press, 1992.

Durkheim, Émile. *Professional Ethics and Civic Morals*. Translated by Cornelia Brookfield. London: Routledge & Kegan Paul, 1957.

———. *Suicide*. Edited by George Simpson. Translated by John Spaulding. Glencoe, Ill.: Free Press, 1951.

Dworkin, Ronald. *Freedom's Law: The Moral Reading of the American Constitution*. Cambridge: Harvard University Press, 1996.

Erasmus, Desiderius. *The Education of a Christian Prince*. Edited and translated by Lisa Jardine. Cambridge: Cambridge University Press, 1997.

———. *The Praise of Folly*. Edited and translated by Robert Adams. New York: Norton, 1989.

Fanon, Frantz. *Black Skins, White Masks*. New York: Grove Press, 1967.

———. *The Wretched of the Earth*. New York: Grove Press, 1963.

Ferguson, Adam. *An Essay on the History of Civil Society*. Edited by Fania Oz-Salzberger. Cambridge: Cambridge University Press, 1995.

Filmer, Henry. *Patriarcha and Other Writings*. Edited by Johann P. Sommerville. Cambridge: Cambridge University Press, 1991.

Findlay, J. N. *Hegel: A Re-examination*. London: Allen and Unwin, 1958.

Forcey, Charles. *The Crossroads of Liberalism: Croly, Weyl, Lippmann, and the Progressive Era, 1900–1925*. New York: Oxford University Press, 1961.

Fortescue, John. *On the Laws and Governance of England*. Edited by Shelley Lockwood. Cambridge: Cambridge University Press, 1997.

Fourier, Charles. *The Theory of the Four Movements*. Cambridge: Cambridge University Press, 1996.

Frank, Robert H. *Passions within Reason: The Strategic Role of the Emotions*. New York: Norton, 1988.

Freud, Sigmund. *Beyond the Pleasure Principle and Other Writings*. Translated by John Reddick. Introduction by Mark Edmundson. London: Penguin, 2003.

———. *Civilization and Its Discontents*. Translated by James Strachey. New York: Norton, 2010.

Fukuyama, Francis. *The End of History and the Last Man*. New York: Free Press, 1992.

Garnsey, Peter. *Thinking about Property: From Antiquity to the Age of Revolution*. Cambridge: Cambridge University Press, 2007.

Gentile, Giovanni. *Origins and Doctrine of Fascism*. Edited and translated by A. James Gregor. New Brunswick: Transaction Books, 2004.

Gibbon, Edward. *Decline and Fall of the Roman Empire*. Edited by D. M. Womersley. London: Penguin, 2002.

Gobineau, Arthur de. *The Inequality of the Human Races*. New York: H. Fertig, 1967.

Goldberg, Jonah. *Liberal Fascism: The Secret History of the American Left, from Mussolini to the Politics of Meaning*. New York: Doubleday, 2007.

Goldhagen, Daniel. *Hitler's Willing Executioners: Ordinary Germans and the Holocaust.* New York: Knopf, 1996.

Goldman, Emma. *Anarchism and Other Essays.* New York: Dover Books, 1969.

Gramsci, Antonio. *The Modern Prince and Other Essays.* Translated by Louis Marx. New York: International Publishers, 1967.

————. *Pre-prison Writings.* Edited by Richard Bellamy. Translated by Virginia Cox. Cambridge: Cambridge University Press, 1994.

Grotius, Hugo. *The Rights of War and Peace.* Edited by Richard Tuck. 3 vols. Indianapolis: Liberty Fund, 2005.

Harrington, James. *The Commonwealth of Oceana and A System of Politics.* Edited by J. G. A. Pocock. Cambridge: Cambridge University Press, 1992.

Hart, H. L. A. *Essays on Bentham.* Oxford: Oxford University Press, 1982.

Haskins, Charles Homer. *The Renaissance of the Twelfth Century.* New York: Harvard University Press, 1955.

Haydn, Tom. *The Port Huron Statement: The Visionary Call of the 1960s Revolution.* New York: Thunder's Mouth Press, 2005.

Hayek, Friedrich A. von. *The Road to Serfdom.* Chicago: University of Chicago Press, 1944.

Hegel, Georg Wilhelm Friedrich. *Elements of the Philosophy of Right.* Edited by Allen W. Wood. Translated by H. B. Nisbet. Cambridge: Cambridge University Press, 1991.

————. *Hegel's Phenomenology of Spirit.* Translated by A. V. Miller. Oxford: Oxford University Press, 1977.

————. *The Philosophy of History.* Edited by C. J. Friedrich. Translated by J. Sibree. New York: Dover, 1956.

Herodotus. *The Histories.* Translated by Aubrey de Selincourt. Harmondsworth: Penguin, 2005.

Herrin, Judith. *The Formation of Christendom.* Princeton: Princeton University Press, 1987.

Herrnstein, Richard J., and Charles Murray. *The Bell Curve: Intelligence and Class Structure in American Life.* New York: Free Press, 1994.

Hobbes, Thomas. *Behemoth.* Edited by Stephen Holmes. Chicago: University of Chicago Press, 1990.

————. *Human Nature and De Corpore Politico.* Edited by J. C. A. Gaskin. Oxford: Oxford University Press, 2008.

————. *Leviathan.* Edited by Richard Tuck. Cambridge: Cambridge University Press, 1991.

Hogg, James. *The Private Memoirs and Confessions of a Justified Sinner.* London: Oxford University Press, 1969.

Hume, David. *Enquiries concerning Human Understanding and concerning the Principles of Morals.* Edited by Selby-Bigge. 3d ed. Oxford: Oxford University Press, 1975.

————. *Political Essays*. Edited by Knud Haakonssen. Cambridge: Cambridge University Press, 1994.

Huntington, Samuel. *The Clash of Civilizations and the Remaking of World Order*. New York: Simon and Schuster, 1996.

Huxley, Aldous. *Brave New World and Brave New World Revisited*. Foreword by Christopher Hitchens. New York: HarperCollins, 2004.

Ibn Khaldun. *The Muqaddimah: An Introduction to History*. Edited by N. J. Dawood. Translated by Franz Rosenthal. Princeton: Princeton University Press, 2005.

Ignatieff, Michael. *The Needs of Strangers*. London: Chatto & Windus, 1984.

Jardin, André. *Tocqueville: A Biography*. Translated by Lydia Davis, with Robert Hemenway. New York: Farrar Straus Giroux, 1988.

Jefferson, Thomas. *Political Writings*. Edited by Joyce Appleby and Terence Ball. Cambridge: Cambridge University Press, 1999.

John of Salisbury. *Policraticus*. Edited and translated by Cary U. Nederman. Cambridge: Cambridge University Press, 1996.

Kant, Immanuel. *Groundwork for the Metaphysics of Morals*. Edited and translated by Allen W. Wood. New Haven: Yale University Press, 2002.

————. *Political Writings*. Edited by Hans Reiss. Translated by H. B. Nisbet. Cambridge: Cambridge University Press, 1991

Kantorowicz, Ernst. *Frederick the Second, 1194–1250*. Translated by E. O. Lorimer. New York: R. R. Smith, 1931.

Kapp, Yvonne. *The Life of Eleanor Marx*. 2 vols. London: Lawrence & Wishart, 1972.

Kojève, Alexandre. *Introduction to the Reading of Hegel: Lectures on the Phenomenology of Spirit Assembled by Raymond Queneau*. Edited by Allan Bloom. Translated by James J. Nichols Jr. New York: Basic Books, 1969.

Kornhauser, William. *The Politics of Mass Society*. Glencoe, Ill.: Free Press, 1959.

Kropotkin, Peter. *The Conquest of Bread*. Edited by Paul Avrich. London: Allen Lane, 1972.

Kurland, Philip B., and Ralph Lerner, eds. *The Founders' Constitution*. 5 vols. Chicago: University of Chicago Press, 1987.

Lane Fox, Robin. *Pagans and Christians*. New York: Knopf, 1987.

Lenin, V. I. *What Is to Be Done?* Edited by Robert Service. Translated by Joe Fineberg and George Hanna. Harmondsworth: Penguin, 1988.

Lippmann, Walter. *The Phantom Public*. New Brunswick: Transaction, 1993.

————. *Public Opinion*. New York: Harcourt, Brace, 1922.

Lipset, Seymour Martin. *Political Man: The Social Bases of Politics*. Garden City, N.Y.: Doubleday, 1960.

Locke, John. *Political Essays*. Edited by Mark Goldie. Cambridge: Cambridge University Press, 1997.

————. *The Selected Political Writings of John Locke.* Edited by Paul Sigmund. New York: Norton, 2005.

————. *Two Treatises of Government.* Edited by Peter Laslett. Cambridge: Cambridge University Press, 1998.

Luther, Martin. *Selected Political Writings.* Edited by J. M. Porter. Philadelphia: Fortress Press, 1974.

Machiavelli, Niccolo. *Discourses on Livy.* Edited by Max Lerner. New York: Random House, 1950.

————. *The Prince.* Translated by Quentin Skinner and Russell Price. Cambridge: Cambridge University Press, 1988.

Madison, James. *Writings.* Edited by Jack Rakove. New York: Library of America, 1999.

Madison, James, Alexander Hamilton, and John Jay. *The Federalist Papers.* London: Penguin, 1987.

Maistre, Joseph de. *The Works of Joseph de Maistre.* Edited and translated by Jack Lively. London: Allen and Unwin, 1965.

Man, John. *The Gutenberg Revolution: The Story of a Genius and an Invention That Changed the World.* London: Review, 2002.

Marcuse, Herbert. *Eros and Civilization: A Philosophical Inquiry into Freud.* Boston: Beacon, 1966.

————. *One-Dimensional Man: Studies in the Ideology of Advanced Industrial Society.* Boston: Beacon, 1964.

Marshall, T. H. *Citizenship and Social Class and Other Essays.* Cambridge: Cambridge University Press, 1950

Marsilius of Padua. *Defensor Pacis.* Translated by Alan Gewirth. Afterword by Cary J. Nederman. New York: Columbia University Press, 1991.

————. *Writings on the Empire: Defensor Minor and De Translatione Imperii.* Edited by Cary J. Nederman. Cambridge: Cambridge University Press, 1993.

Marx, Karl. *Selected Writings.* Edited by David McLellan. 2nd ed. Oxford: Oxford University Press, 2000.

Marx, Karl, and Friedrich Engels. *The Communist Manifesto.* London: Penguin, 2002.

McLuhan, Marshall. *The Gutenberg Galaxy: The Making of Typographic Man.* Toronto: University of Toronto Press, 1962.

Merchant, Carolyn. *Reinventing Eden: The Fate of Nature in Western Culture.* London: Taylor and Francis, 2003.

Michels, Robert. *First Lectures in Political Sociology.* Translated by Alfred de Grazia. New York: Arno Press, 1974.

————. *Political Parties: A Sociological Study of the Oligarchical Tendencies of Modern Democracy.* Translated by Eden and Cedar Paul. Introduction by Seymour Martin Lipset. New York: Collier, 1962.

Mill, James. *Political Writings*. Edited by Terence Ball. Cambridge: Cambridge University Press, 1992.

Mill, John Stuart. *Autobiography*. Edited by J. M. Robson. Harmondsworth: Penguin, 1989.

———. *The Collected Works of John Stuart Mill*. 32 vols. Toronto: University of Toronto Press, 1963–96.

———. *Considerations on Representative Government*. Edited by A. D. Lindsay. London: Everyman's Library, 1962.

———. *Essays on Economics and Society*. Vols. 4–5 of *Collected Works*. Toronto: University of Toronto Press, 1967.

———. *Essays on Politics and Culture*. Edited by Gertrude Himmelfarb. Garden City, N.Y.: Doubleday, 1963.

———. *On Liberty and The Subjection of Women*. Edited by Alan Ryan. London: Penguin, 2006.

———. *Principles of Political Economy*. Vols. 2–3 of *Collected Works*. Toronto: University of Toronto Press, 1965.

Mills, C. Wright. *The Power Elite*. New York: Oxford University Press, 1956.

Montaigne, Michel de. *Complete Essays*. Edited and translated by M. A. Screech. London: Penguin, 1991.

Montesquieu. *The Spirit of the Laws*. Edited and translated by Anne M. Cohler, Basia Carolyn Miller, and Harold Samuel Stone. Cambridge: Cambridge University Press, 1989.

More, Thomas. *Utopia*. Edited by George M. Logan. Translated by Robert M. Adams. Cambridge: Cambridge University Press, 2006.

Morris, William. *News from Nowhere*. Edited by Kishnan Kumar. Cambridge: Cambridge University Press, 1995.

Napier, William. *History of Sir Charles Napier's Administration of the Province of Scinde*. London: Chapman and Hall, 1851.

Nicholas of Cusa. *The Catholic Concordance*. Edited and translated by Paul E. Sigmund. Cambridge: Cambridge University Press, 1991.

Nicolet, Claude. *The World of the Citizen in Republican Rome*. Berkeley: University of California Press, 1988.

Niebuhr, Reinhold. *Moral Man and Immoral Society*. New York: Scribner, 1932.

Nietzsche, Friedrich. *On the Genealogy of Morality*. Edited by Keith Ansell-Pearson. Translated by Carol Diethe. Cambridge: Cambridge University Press, 1994.

Nozick, Robert. *Anarchy, State, and Utopia*. New York: Basic Books, 1974.

Ockham, William of. *A Short Discourse on the Tyrannical Government over Things Divine and Human*. Edited by Arthur Stephen McGrade. Translated by John Kilcullen. Cambridge: Cambridge University Press, 1992.

Ortega y Gasset, José. *The Revolt of the Masses*. New York: Norton, 1932.

Orwell, George. *Animal Farm; 1984*. Introduction by Christopher Hitchens. Orlando, Fla.: Harcourt, 2003.

Owen, Robert. *A New View of Society and Other Writings*. Edited by Gregory Claeys. London: Penguin, 1991.

Paine, Thomas. *Thomas Paine Reader*. Edited by Michael Foot and Isaac Kramnick. London: Penguin, 1987.

Parsons, Talcott. *The Social System*. Glencoe, Ill.: Free Press, 1951.

Pitts, Jennifer. *A Turn to Empire: The Rise of Imperial Liberalism in Britain and France*. Princeton: Princeton University Press, 2005.

Pizan, Christine de. *The Book of the Body Politic*. Edited and translated by Kate Langdon Forhan. Cambridge: Cambridge University Press, 1994.

———. *The Book of the City of Ladies*. Edited and translated by Rosalind Brown-Grant. Harmondsworth: Penguin, 1999.

Plato. *Gorgias*. Edited by Chris Emlyn-Jones. Translated by Walter Hamilton. Harmondsworth: Penguin, 2004.

———. *Gorgias, Menexenus, Protagoras*. Edited by Malcolm Schofield. Translated by Tom Griffith. Cambridge: Cambridge University Press, 2010.

———. *The Last Days of Socrates*. Edited by Harold Tarrant. Translated by Harold Tarrant and Hugh Tredennick. Harmondsworth: Penguin, 2003.

———. *Phaedrus and Letters VII and VIII*. Translated by Walter Hamilton. Harmondsworth: Penguin, 1973.

———. *The Republic*. Edited by G. R. F. Ferrari. Translated by Tom Griffith. Cambridge: Cambridge University Press, 2000.

Pocock, J. G. A. *The Machiavellian Moment: Florentine Political Thought and the Atlantic Republican Tradition*. Princeton: Princeton University Press, 1976.

Polybius. *The Rise of the Roman Empire*. Edited by F. W. Walbank. Translated by Ian Scott-Kilvert. Harmondsworth: Penguin, 1979.

Popper, Karl. *The Open Society and Its Enemies*. London: Routledge, 1945.

Price, Richard. *Political Writings*. Edited by D. O. Thomas. Cambridge: Cambridge University Press, 1991.

Putnam, Robert D. *Bowling Alone: The Collapse and Revival of American Community*. New York: Simon and Schuster, 2000.

Qutb, Sayyid. *Milestones*. Indianapolis: American Trust Publications, 1990.

———. *Social Justice in Islam*. Translated by John B. Hardie. New York: Octagon Books, 1970.

Rawls, John. *The Law of Peoples, with The Idea of Public Reason Revisited*. Cambridge: Harvard University Press, 1999.

———. *Political Liberalism*. New York: Columbia University Press, 1993.

———. *A Theory of Justice*. Cambridge: Harvard University Press, 1971.

Redhead, Brian. *Political Thought from Plato to NATO*. London: BBC Publications, 1987.

Rousseau, Jean-Jacques. *Confessions*. London: J. M. Dent, 1962.

———. *Émile*. Translated by Barbara Foxley. London: J. M. Dent, 1974.

———. *Rousseau's Political Writings*. Edited by Alan Ritter and Julia Conaway Bondanella. Translated by Julia Conaway Bondanella. New York: Norton, 1988.

———. *The Social Contract and Other Later Political Writings*. Edited and translated by Victor Gourevitch. Cambridge: Cambridge University Press, 1997.

Ruskin, John. *Fors Clavigera: Letters to the Workmen and Labourers of Great Britain*. In *Selected Writings*. Vol. 27. London: George Allen, 1907.

Russell, Bertrand. *Autobiography*. Boston: Little, Brown, 1967.

———. *German Social Democracy*. Nottingham: Spokesman Books, 2000.

———. *Has Man a Future?* London: Allen and Unwin, 1961.

———. *The Scientific Outlook*. New York: Norton, 1931.

Schmitt, Carl. *The Concept of the Political*. Edited and translated by George Schwab. Foreword by Tracy B. Strong. Chicago: University of Chicago Press, 1996.

———. *Political Theology*. Edited and translated by George Schwab. Cambridge: MIT Press, 1985.

Schumpeter, Joseph. *Capitalism, Socialism, and Democracy*. New York: Harper and Row, 1950.

Sennett, Richard. *The Fall of Public Man*. New York: Knopf, 1976.

Shapin, Steven, and Simon Schaffer. *Leviathan and the Air-Pump: Hobbes, Boyle, and the Experimental Life*. Princeton: Princeton University Press, 1989.

Sidgwick, Henry. *The Methods of Ethics*. Indianapolis: Hackett, 2007.

Sidney, Algernon. *Discourses concerning Government*. Edited by Thomas G. West. Indianapolis: Liberty Fund, 1990.

Skinner, Quentin. *The Foundations of Modern Political Thought*. Cambridge: Cambridge University Press, 1978.

Sombart, Werner. *Why Is There No Socialism in the United States?* White Plains, N.Y.: Arts and Sciences Press, 1976.

Sorel, Georges. *Reflections on Violence*. Edited by Jeremy Jennings. Cambridge: Cambridge University Press, 2000.

Tacitus. *The Agricola and the Germania*. Translated Harold Mattingly. Harmondsworth: Penguin, 1970.

Thucydides. *The Peloponnesian War*. Edited and translated by Steven Lattimore. Indianapolis: Hackett, 1998.

Tierney, Brian. *The Crisis of Church and State, 1050–1300*. Toronto: University of Toronto Press, 1988.

Tocqueville, Alexis de. *Democracy in America*. Edited by Isaac Kramnick. Translated by Gerald Bevan. London: Penguin, 2003.

———. *The Old Regime and the Revolution*. Edited by François Furet and Françoise Mélonio. Translated by Alan S. Kahan. 2 vols. Chicago: University of Chicago Press, 2001.

———. *Recollections*. Edited by J. P. Mayer. Translated by George Lawrence. Garden City, N.Y.: Doubleday, 1970.

———. *Writings on Empire and Slavery*. Edited and translated by Jennifer Pitts. Baltimore: Johns Hopkins University Press, 2001.

Truman, David B. *The Governmental Process: Political Interests and Public Opinion*. New York: Knopf, 1958.

Tyacke, Nicholas, ed. *Seventeenth-Century Oxford*. Vol. 4 of *The History of the University of Oxford*. Oxford: Clarendon Press, 1997.

Ullman, Walter. *A History of Political Thought in the Middle Ages*. Harmondsworth: Penguin, 1970.

Vattel, Emmerich de. *The Law of Nations*. Indianapolis: Liberty Fund, 2007.

Vitoria, Francisco de. *Political Writings*. Edited by Anthony Pagden. Translated by Jeremy Lawrence. Cambridge: Cambridge University Press, 1992.

Waal, Frans B. M. de. *Good Natured: The Origins of Right and Wrong in Humans and Other Animals*. Cambridge: Harvard University Press, 1996.

Weber, Max. *From Max Weber*. Edited and Translated by H. H. Gerth and C. Wright Mills. London: Routledge and Kegan Paul, 1948.

———. *The Theory of Social and Economic Organization*. Edited by Talcott Parsons. New York: Free Press, 1969.

Westbrook, Robert. *John Dewey and American Democracy*. Ithaca: Cornell University Press, 1991.

Wolin, Sheldon S. *Politics and Vision: Continuity and Innovation in Western Political Thought*. Princeton: Princeton University Press, 2004.

Wollstonecraft, Mary. *A Vindication of the Rights of Men and A Vindication of the Rights of Woman*. Edited by Sylvana Tomaselli. Cambridge: Cambridge University Press, 1995.

Wood, Gordon S. *Empire of Liberty: A History of the Early Republic, 1789–1815*. Oxford: Oxford University Press, 2009.

———. *The Radicalism of the American Revolution*. New York: Knopf, 1992.

Xenophon. *Conversations of Socrates*. Edited by Robin Waterfield. Translated by Hugh Tredennick and Robin Waterfield. London: Penguin, 1990.

Zamyatin, Evgeny. *We*. Translated by Mirra Ginsburg. New York: Viking, 1972.

FURTHER READING

The Oxford University Press publishes a series of *very short introductions*; each is three or four times as long as the individual chapters of this book, which may be thought of as "very, very short introductions." Some obvious further reading, then, includes these *very short introductions*:

Ancient Greece Paul Cartledge
Herodotus Jennifer Roberts
Socrates Christopher Taylor
Plato Julia Annas
Aristotle Jonathan Barnes
Augustine Henry Chadwick
Martin Luther Scott Hendrix
The Reformation Peter Marshall
Protestantism Mark Noll
Machiavelli Quentin Skinner
Hobbes Richard Tuck
Locke John Dunn
Rousseau Robert Wokler
Hegel Peter Singer
Tocqueville Harvey Mansfield

Marx Peter Singer

Engels Terrell Carver

Aristocracy William Doyle

Anarchism Colin Ward

Empire Stephen Howe

Communism Leslie Holmes

Fundamentalism Malise Ruthven

Fascism Kevin Passmore

Islam Malise Ruthven

Nationalism Steven Grosby

Democracy Bernard Crick

Citizenship Richard Bellamy

There are many excellent text books; selection is a matter of taste, but Sheldon S. Wolin, *Politics and Vision* (2nd ed., Princeton) has been widely admired for half a century; among more recent work, the three-volume *History of Political Thought* by Janet Coleman (vols. 1 and 2) and Iain Hampsher-Monk (vol. 3) (Blackwell) stands out. Beyond these lies the scholarly territory occupied by the multivolume, multiauthored *Cambridge History of Political Thought*, now including the volumes *Greek and Roman Political Thought*, *Medieval Political Thought*, *Political Thought, 1450–1700*, *Eighteenth-Century Political Thought*, and *Twentieth-Century Political Thought*, with the remaining gap soon to be filled. Alongside these are the many volumes of Cambridge Companions, including those on ancient Greek political thought, Socrates, Plato, Aristotle, Augustine, Aquinas, Dante, Machiavelli, Hobbes, Locke, Rousseau, and Mill. Also very valuable are the Companions to particular works: *Hobbes's Leviathan*, ed. Patricia Springborg, and *Plato's Republic*, ed. G. R. F. Ferrari. The *Blackwell Companion to Greek and Roman Political Thought* is a particularly valuable resource.

Chapter 1: Readers will want to turn to the texts; Penguin Classics has for seventy-five years produced scholarly and readable translations of classical philosophy, history, and literature, among them Herodotus, *The Histories*, trans. Aubrey de Selincourt; Thucydides, *The Peloponnesian War*, trans. Rex Warner. The Peloponnesian War obsesses our own age; Donald Kagan's one-volume *The Peloponnesian War* (Penguin, 2004) takes Thucydides's intention to provide a lesson for all time seriously. Athenian democracy has been well served since the midnineteenth century: of older works, A. H. M. Jones, *Athenian Democracy* (Blackwell, 1957), is briskly comprehensive, while Paul Cartledge, *The Spartans: The World of the Warrior-Heroes of Ancient Greece* (Random House, 2004), provides a vivid, but balanced, account of Athens's rival for the allegiances of contemporaries and everyone thereafter. Pre-Platonic political theory is usefully anthologized in *Early Greek Political Thought from Homer to the Sophists* in the Cambridge Texts series. The

Last Days of Socrates (Penguin Classics) contains *Euthyphro, Apology, Crito,* and *Phaedo*; *Conversations of Socrates* (Penguin Classics) contains all Xenophon's "Socratic" writings—those where Socrates is a central protagonist. Of recent accounts of Socrates's trial and execution, Robin Waterfield, *Why Socrates Died* (Norton, 2009), is excellent, but I. F. Stone, *The Trial of Socrates* (Little, Brown, 1986), serves as a reminder that Athenian democrats had reasons for their hostility.

Chapter 2: I have generally used Cambridge Texts in the History of Political Thought, not least because they contain excellent introductions, suggestions for further reading that would, if acted on, turn a new reader into a serious scholar, and informative chronologies. But the Penguin Classics editions of *Gorgias, Laws,* and *Republic* are also excellent, the last reedited with a new introduction by Melissa Lane. The Penguin Classics edition of *Phaedrus and Letters VII and VIII* was for many years almost the only accessible source for the famous "Seventh Letter." *Statesman* is published in the Cambridge Texts series. The secondary literature on Plato is immense and selection difficult, but Julia Annas, *Introduction to Plato's Republic* (Oxford, 1981), has worn very well. The same can be said of Ernest Barker, *Greek Political Theory* (Methuen, 1918), while Karl Popper's assault in *The Open Society and Its Enemies* (Routledge, 1945) is now something of a historical curiosity. Particular topics can be explored in the Companions; Trevor Saunders's essay on Plato's later political theory in the *Companion to Plato* makes a vigorous case for the *Laws*.

Chapter 3: Nicomachean Ethics is in many ways the best introduction to Aristotle's political theory; it exists in innumerable translations, including a recently revised Penguin Classics edition. Among commentaries, Richard Mulgan, *Aristotle's Political Theory* (Oxford, 1977), is notably clear and helpful; Ernest Barker, *The Political Thought of Plato and Aristotle,* wears well after a century, and *The Blackwell Companion to Aristotle's Politics,* ed. David Keyt and Fred Miller (Oxford, 1991), contains illuminating essays on a wide range of topics. Richard Kraut's *Aristotle: Political Philosophy* (Oxford, 2002) is an excellent guide.

Chapter 4: F. W. Walbank was, until his recent death in his late nineties, the keeper of the Polybian flame; he edited *The Rise of the Roman Empire* in Penguin Classics and wrote both an immensely detailed *Commentary* on Polybius's *Histories* and a shorter account in *Polybius* (California, 1972). It is impossible to know where to start (or stop) with Cicero. His letters and speeches have always been regarded as literary models, and read wonderfully; the Penguin Classics *Letters to Atticus and Letters to Friends* is no longer in print, but many letters and speeches are in the Penguin Classics *Selected Works*. There is only one comprehensive account of Cicero's politics, Neal Wood, *Cicero's Social and Political Thought* (California, 1988), but it is widely regarded as unreliable. The background of Cicero's political thinking is vividly brought out in Ronald Syme, *The Roman Revolution* (Oxford, 1939); for the difficult question of what political role ordinary Roman citizens really played, Claude Nicolet, *The World of the Citizen in Republican Rome* (California, 1980), is indispensable.

Chapter 5: Augustine's *Confessions* is not to be missed; there is an excellent translation by Henry Chadwick (Oxford World's Classics). In addition to *The City of God against the Pagans* in the Cambridge Texts series, a volume of *Political Writings* shows Augustine in his daily, practical political interactions with colleagues, parishioners, and the civil authorities. Of biographies, there is no shortage, but Peter Brown, *Augustine of Hippo* (rev. ed., California, 2000) stands out; Garry Wills, *Saint Augustine* (Penguin Lives, 1999), is shorter but passionate; the same writer has written a "biography" of the *Confessions* (Princeton, 2011). Henry Chadwick's *very short introduction* is masterly, although dismissive of the idea that *City of God* contains "Augustine's political theory."

Chapter 6: The Cambridge History of Medieval Political Thought is the great resource. *Policraticus* is in the Cambridge Texts series; Brian Tierney's *Crisis of Church and State, 1050–1350*, an anthology of otherwise obscure texts with introductions, is a great help to navigating tricky waters; his *The Idea of Natural Rights* (Scholars Press, 1997) is invaluable, as is Richard Tuck, *Natural Rights Theories* (Cambridge, 1979). Peter Garnsey, *Thinking about Property: Antiquity to the Age of Revolution* (Cambridge, 2007), is very helpful, as is Francis Oakley, *Natural Law, Laws of Nature, Natural Right* (Continuum, 2005); Walter Ullman, *A History of Political Thought: The Middle Ages* (Penguin, 1965), is the most accessible of his formidable, though controversial, body of work on medieval kingship and theories of authority in church and state.

Chapter 7: The first place to turn is Paul Sigmund, *St. Thomas Aquinas on Politics and Ethics* (Norton Critical Editions, 1988); more than half the volume is devoted to carefully excerpted passages from Aristotle and Augustine to illuminate Aquinas's sources, and to subsequent commentary from the sixteenth century to the present. The Cambridge Texts volume provides more of Aquinas's own writings. Among general works, Anthony Kenny, *Aquinas* (Hill & Wang, 1980), is brisk and illuminating; John Finnis, *Aquinas, Moral, Political and Legal Theory* (Oxford, 1988), is representative of the recent revival of interest in natural law.

Chapter 8: Although it is a work of general history, Barbara Tuchman, *A Distant Mirror: The Calamitous Fourteenth Century* (Random House, 1978), provides a particularly vivid account of the background to the theorists whose work I discuss. Once again, *The Cambridge History* is indispensable. The *Cambridge Companion to Dante* is very helpful on

Dante's politics. A. P. D'Entreves, *Dante as a Political Thinker* (Oxford, 1952), downplays the importance of *De Monarchia*. Antony Black, *Political Thought in Europe, 1250–1450* (Cambridge, 1992), is enthusiastic about the book and helpful for the whole chapter, and Ernst Kantorowicz, *The King's Two Bodies* (Princeton, 1957), is fascinating in itself and central to all discussions of the medieval idea of kingship. *Defensor pacis* exists in a Cambridge Texts edition, as does Marsilius's own summary of its implications, the *Defensor minor*, as well as Ockham's *Short Discourse on Tyrannical Government* and Nicholas of Cusa's *Catholic Concordance*.

Chapter 9: Christine de Pizan's *Book of the Body Politic* is a Cambridge Text; *The Book of the City of Ladies* is a Penguin Classic. More's *Utopia* and a selection of Erasmus's writings, including *The Praise of Folly*, appear in Norton Critical Editions, with excellent introductions and a selection of secondary literature as well as useful bibliographical and chronological assistance. *Utopia* and *The Praise of Folly* are also in Penguin Classics. Cambridge Texts has both *Utopia* and Erasmus's *Education of a Christian Prince*. For the whole period, Quentin Skinner, *Foundations of Modern Political Thought* (Cambridge, 1979), in two volumes covering the Renaissance and Reformation, is exemplary. Montaigne's *Complete Essays*, trans. M. A. Screech, is a much loved and admired Penguin Classic. A recent, very engaging life of Montaigne is Sarah Bakewell, *How to Live* (Chatto & Windus, 2010).

Chapter 10: Luther and Calvin on Secular Authority and *The Radical Reformation* have the expected virtues of Cambridge Texts, but the former is a rather slender selection and can usefully be supplemented with J. M. Porter's *Luther: Selected Political Writings* (Fortress Press, 1974) as well as John Dillenberger, *Martin Luther: Selections from His Writings* (Doubleday, 1961), and *John Calvin: Selections from His Writings* (Doubleday, 1971). Sheldon S. Wolin, *Politics and Vision*, is illuminating on both Luther and Calvin, and Quentin Skinner, *Foundations*, vol. 2, is indispensable. *The Cambridge History of Political Thought, 1450–1700* is, as always, the gateway to a scholarly grasp of the issues.

Chapter 11: The Prince is a Cambridge Text; the Norton Critical Edition of *The Prince* usefully includes extracts from *Discourses on Livy*. *The Prince* and *Discourses* exist separately in the Oxford World Classics and in Penguin Classics and together in a very old Modern Library edition. Commentaries abound; political theorists have been prone to fight twentieth-century battles in Machiavelli's name, but Janet Coleman's account in *A History of Political Thought* is as uncontentious as there is. Quentin Skinner's *very short introduction* is excellent, and his discussion in *Foundations* indispensable. Maurizio Viroli's *Machiavelli* in the Oxford University Press Founders of Social and Political Thought series is excellent, and his *Machiavelli's Smile* (Farrar, Straus, Giroux, 2000) is an engrossing biography of Machiavelli.

Chapter 12: De cive and *Leviathan* are both in the Cambridge Texts; there is an excellent Norton Critical Edition of *Leviathan*. Both the *Cambridge Companion to Hobbes* and the newer Cambridge Companion to *Leviathan* are valuable further sources. There are innumerable commentaries; Quentin Skinner's *Visions of Politics*, vol. 3 (Cambridge, 2003), contains his pathbreaking articles on Hobbes; *Hobbes and Republican Liberty* (Cambridge, 2008) and *Reason and Rhetoric in the Philosophy of Hobbes* (Cambridge, 1996) flesh out the argument, and the implications are also spelled out in *Liberty before Liberalism* (Cambridge, 1998). Richard Tuck's *Hobbes* is a particularly useful *very short introduction*. *Aspects of Hobbes* (Oxford, 2002), by Noel Malcolm, is immensely illuminating. Among older works, Leo Strauss, *The Political Philosophy of Hobbes* (Oxford, 1936), is ingenious and interesting.

Chapter 13: The great edition of Locke's *Two Treatises* by Peter Laslett is worth reading for its introduction as well as the text itself; the whole is reprinted as a Cambridge Text. Paul Sigmund's *Locke's Political Writings* in Norton Critical Editions is very useful for its introduction and additional texts, such as the *Letter on Toleration*. Cambridge Texts includes a volume of *Political Essays*, which is immensely useful for showing the development of Locke's political thinking. David Wootton's selection of Locke's *Political Writings* (Penguin, 1975) contains Locke's *Letter on Toleration* and much else, together with a long introduction very valuable in its own right. There are many excellent commentaries, among them John Dunn, *The Political Thought of John Locke* (Cambridge, 1969), and Richard Ashcraft, *Revolutionary Politics and Locke's Two Treatises of Government*. Locke is the central figure in C. B. Macpherson, *The Political Theory of Possessive Individualism*, a work of immense popularity in its day. Filmer's *Patriarcha* is a Cambridge Text, and his ideas are given careful assessment in James Day, *Sir Robert Filmer and English Political Thought* (Toronto, 1979), and in Gordon Schochet, *Patriarchalism and Political Thought* (Blackwell, 1975).

Chapter 14: J. G. A. Pocock almost single-handedly revived interest in James Harrington as a political thinker; his *Machiavellian Moment: Florentine Political Thought and the Atlantic Republican Tradition* (Princeton, 1975) and his edition of *The Political Writings of James Harrington* (Cambridge, 1977) persuaded readers that there was more to Harrington than the argument over the "decline of the gentry." Pocock says little about Sir Algernon Sidney, but two recent books have done him justice: a two-volume biography by Jonathan Scott (Cambridge, 1988–91) and Alan Houston, *Algernon Sidney and the Republican Heritage in England and America* (Princeton, 1991). Blair Worden's discussion of English republicanism in *Cambridge History of Political Thought, 1450–1700* is invaluable. To Worden is owed the recovery of Sidney's *Court Maxims*, published for the first time in the Cambridge Texts, and a much more compact account of Sidney's republicanism than his *Discourses*. These are available as a Liberty Classic (1990) with a useful foreword by Thomas G. West. Montesquieu's *Spirit of the Laws* is available as a Cambridge Text; his *Persian Letters* is a Penguin Classic. Two interesting accounts of why he matters are Émile Durkheim, *Montesquieu and Rousseau, Pioneers of Sociology* (Michigan, 1961), and Raymond Aron, *Main Currents in Sociological Thought*, vol. I (Penguin, 1989). Judith Shklar, *Montesquieu* (Oxford, 1987), is an excellent brief account, while Robert Shackleton, *Montesquieu* (Oxford, 1961), remains the definitive biography.

Chapter 15: Like Machiavelli, Rousseau is often a stalking horse for political controversies in our own day, featuring variously as the originator of totalitarian democracy, an anticipator of the insights of psychoanalysis, a proto-Marxist, and a hopeless nostalgic. Rousseau's political writings extend well beyond the *Social Contract* and are collected in two volumes in Cambridge Texts, the second including *Social Contract, Discourse on Political Economy*, and *Considerations on Poland*. The Norton Critical Edition of *Rousseau's Political Writings* is very useful, although the editor's conviction that Rousseau was a "participatory democrat" is to be taken with a pinch of salt. Maurice Cranston's three-volume biography, *Early Life, The Noble Savage*, and *The Solitary Self* (Allen Lane, 1983–93), is a model intellectual biography. Among commentaries, Judith Shklar, *Men and Citizens* (Cambridge, 1969), is among the best, the Cambridge Companion is full of good things, and Robert Wokler's *very short introduction* achieves an extraordinary amount in a very brief compass. Marshall Berman, *The Politics of Authenticity* (Verso, 2009), does justice to the Rousseau who praised himself as a painter of men's hearts, and his politics are well handled by James Miller, *Rousseau Dreamer of Democracy* (Hackett, 1995). And, of course, Rousseau's *Confessions* and *La nouvelle Héloïse* are not to be missed.

Chapter 16: Historians and biographers abound, and selection is invidious; there are innumerable editions of *The Federalist*, including a Penguin Classics edition. The Cambridge Texts series offers a very substantial selection of Jefferson's *Political Writings*, including a great many illuminating letters, as does *Writings* in the Library of America. For historical writing that slights neither the intellectual nor the political context, Gordon S. Wood's work stands out both qualitatively and quantitatively: *The American Revolution* (Modern Library, 2002) is a brisk account of its topic, *The Radicalism of the American Revolution* (Knopf, 1992) highlights the intellectual and political disputes that marked the founding, and *Empire of Liberty* (Oxford, 2009) takes the story through to 1815; Robert Middelkauf, *The Glorious Cause* (Oxford, 2006), covers the origins of the revolution and the revolution itself. On Madison, Jack Rakove, *James Madison and the Creation of the American Republic* (Little, Brown, 1990), is indispensable. Madison's own *Notes on the Debates in the Federal Convention of 1787*, which he meticulously did not publish in his own lifetime but took pains to have published on his death, is a pleasure to read (ed. Adrienne Koch; Norton, 1987). The most accessible source of Madison's ideas is *Writings*, selected and edited by Jack Rakove, in the Library of America series.

Chapter 17: Burke's *Reflections on the Revolution in France* exists in innumerable editions, including Penguin, with an introduction by Conor Cruise O'Brien, and Oxford World's Classics, with an introduction by Leslie Mitchell. Both introductions are well worth reading, as is O'Brien's full-length and passionate biography, *The Great Melody: A Thematic Biography of Edmund Burke* (Chicago, 1992). There is an edition of *Pre-Revolutionary Writings* in Cambridge Texts. François Furet's *Penser la révolution Française* was published in English as *Interpreting the French Revolution* (Cambridge, 1985); an excellent narrative history is William Doyle, *The Oxford History of the French Revolution*. Paine is well served by biographers and commentators, including Mark Philp's *Paine* (Oxford, 2007) and, at greater length, Craig Nelson, *Thomas Paine, Enlightenment, Revolution, and the Birth of Modern Nations* (Penguin, 2006). Paine's political writings are in Mark Philp, ed., *Rights of Man, Common Sense, and Other Political Writings* (Oxford, 2008), and Michael Foot and Isaac Kramnick, eds., *Thomas Paine Reader* (Penguin Classics); both have excellent introductions. *The Works of Joseph de Maistre* (Allen and Unwin, 1965) is a selection of Maistre's political writings translated and introduced by Jack Lively, while *Considerations on France* in the Cambridge Texts series contains that work alone, but is much enlivened by Isaiah Berlin's introduction. Both Richard Price's and Joseph Priestley's *Political Writings* are in the Cambridge Texts.

Chapter 18: The Cambridge edition of *The Philosophy of Right* is excellent, though Knox's older translation wears very well. *Political Writings* in the Cambridge Texts series contains Hegel's thoughts on issues ranging from the German Constitution to the English Reform Bill of 1831. Commentaries are innumerable; once again, Karl Popper's *Open Society and Its Enemies* is more interesting as a reflection of the disrepute into which German idealism fell during World War II than as a commentary on Hegel. Alexandre Kojève's *Introduction to the Reading of Hegel* (Basic Books, 1969), on the other hand, is more nearly a reimagining of the Hegelian project in the light of Marx and Heidegger, and has had a prodigious influence; among its offspring is Francis Fukuyama, *The End of History and the Last Man* (Free Press, 1992). For utterly sober commentary focused on politics, Shlomo Avineri, *Hegel's Theory of the Modern State* (Cambridge, 1972) is excellent. Allen Wood, *Hegel's Ethical Thought* (Cambridge, 1998), is a valuable discussion. Charles Taylor's two volumes, *Hegel* (Cambridge, 1972) and *Hegel and Modern Society* (Cambridge, 1975), provide accessible accounts of Hegel's ideas and the author's own interesting and original views on the subjects Hegel investigated, as does Raymond Plant's *Hegel* (Allen & Unwin, 1975). Several of the essays in Fred Beiser, ed., *The Cambridge Companion to Hegel*, are helpful for his political ideas.

Chapter 19: Bentham's *Fragment on Government* is a Cambridge Text, ed. Ross Harrison, whose *Jeremy Bentham* (Routledge, 1983) is an excellent commentary. Bhiku Parekh's *Bentham's Political Thought* (Croom Helm, 1973) is elderly but helpful. Parekh has also edited the four-volume collection *Jeremy Bentham, Critical Assessments* (Routledge, 1993), which brings together critics and admirers from J. S. Mill to H. L. A. Hart onward. James Mill's *Essay on Government* together with T. B. Macaulay's assault on it and other of James Mill's writings are in *Political Writings* in the Cambridge texts. All his work, including the *History of British India*, is available to download at the "online library of liberty" maintained by the Liberty Fund. There are no recent lives of James Mill, but Alexander Bain, *James Mill: A Life* (Routledge, 1992), is very readable. John Stuart Mill has been well served by commentators and biographers, beginning once more with Alexander Bain, *John Stuart Mill*. John Robson, *The Improvement of Mankind* (Toronto, 1968), is excellent, as is *J. S. Mill on Democracy* (Chicago, 2002), by Nadia Urbinati. The best overview of Mill's philosophy is John Skorupski, *John Stuart Mill* (Routledge, 1989); a good intellectual biography is Nicholas Capaldi, *John Stuart Mill* (Cambridge, 2004); Mill's *Autobiography, Utilitarianism, On Liberty*, and *The Subjection of Women* all exist as Penguin Classics; *On Liberty* is paired with *The Subjection of Women* and *Chapters on Socialism* in Cambridge Texts, with an introduction by Stefan Collini; in Norton Critical Editions, it is paired with *The Subjection of Women* and *Spirit of the Age.* Long out of print, but a valuable resource is *Essays on Culture and Society*, ed. Gertrude Himmelfarb. *The Cambridge Companion to Mill*, ed. John Skorupski, contains many valuable essays. Finally, John Skorupski's *Why Read Mill Today?* (Routledge, 2006) provides good reasons for doing so.

Chapter 20: Democracy in America has been much translated; the most recent translation is by James Schleifer (Liberty Fund, 2009), in four volumes with the French and English text on facing pages. The Penguin Classics translation by Gerald Bevan benefits from an excellent introduction by Isaac Kramnick and the inclusion of *Quinze jours au désert* (Two Weeks in the Wilderness), Tocqueville's travel journal of his excursion on the (then) northwestern frontier, as well as his account of his trip to Lake Oneida. The Norton Critical Edition uses the older—the first English—translation by Henry Reeve, but has an excellent introduction by Isaac Kramnick and a helpful selection of contemporary and modern discussions of the book. Arthur Goldhammer's translation in the Library of America stands out as readable but true to the carefully crafted original. Among other editions, the translation by Harvey Mansfield and Delba Winthrop (Chicago, 2000) is excellent, as are the notes and introduction. Among commentaries and biographies, André Jardin's *Life* is indispensable; Hugh Brogan's manages the difficult feat of being strikingly critical of almost all Tocqueville's ideas while making their author seem wonderfully sympathetic; Harvey Mansfield's *very short introduction* covers a lot of ground in a small compass. L. A. Siedentop, *Tocqueville*

(Oxford, 1994), is out of print but is perhaps the best introduction in the round, though given a run for its money by Cheryl Welch, *Tocqueville* (Oxford, 2001); Cheryl Welch has also edited *The Cambridge Companion to Tocqueville*. On Tocqueville's imperialism, Jennifer Pitts, *A Turn to Empire* (Princeton, 2006), is excellent, and her selection of Tocqueville's *Writings on Empire and Slavery* (Johns Hopkins, 2001) invaluable. There is an excellent new translation of *L'ancien régime* by Arthur Goldhammer in the Cambridge Texts; Tocqueville's memoir of 1848, *Souvenirs*, is translated as *Recollections: The French Revolution of 1848* (Transaction Publishers, 1987) by J. P. Mayer and W. P. Ker.

Chapter 21: Of books about Marx there is no end, and it is correspondingly hard to know where to begin. For practical purposes David McLellan's *Karl Marx, Selected Writings* is the best source of Marx's ideas from Hegelian beginnings to last thoughts on the possibilities of revolution in Russia. McLellan's biography, *Karl Marx* (Viking, 1975), is in its fourth edition, and is the standard account; Francis Wheen, *Karl Marx: A Life* (Norton, 2000), is very readable; Isaiah Berlin, *Karl Marx: His Life and Environment* (Oxford, 2002), shows its age, but is highly readable and interesting as a product of its times. The great account of Marxism and its travails is Leszek Kolakowski, *Main Currents of Marxism* (Norton, 2008), a work that takes the reader from Plotinus to Herbert Marcuse. The Penguin Classics edition of *The Communist Manifesto* boasts a wonderful introduction by Gareth Stedman-Jones. Marx's domestic life is heart-achingly described in Yvonne Kapp's two-volume *Life of Eleanor Marx* (Lawrence & Wishart, 1972–76). Engels is excellently handled, both intellectually and biographically, in Tristram Hunt's *Marx's General* (Metropolitan, 2009). Among commentaries Shlomo Avineri, *Social and Political Thought of Karl Marx* (Cambridge, 1968) is evenhanded and generous, G. A. Cohen's *Karl Marx's Theory of History: A Defence* (Oxford, 1980) is ultimately unsuccessful but very well done, while Jon Elster's longer and shorter accounts, *Making Sense of Marx* (Cambridge, 1985) and *An Introduction to Karl Marx* (Cambridge, 1986), are critical but respectful analyses.

Chapter 22: There are many reasons why political discussion in the twentieth and early twenty-first centuries is impossible to summarize; one is a widening gap between writing aimed at a mass audience and the works of professors writing for one another. What follows is only a gesture toward the most accessible landmarks. The founding works of "elite theory" are Gaetano Mosca, *The Ruling Class*, in James Meisel, *The Myth of the Ruling Class* (Ann Arbor, 1962), Vilfredo Pareto, *The Mind and Society* (Dover Books, 1962), and Roberto Michels, *Political Parties* (Transaction, 1999). The discussion of Durkheim, Pareto, and Weber in Raymond Aron, *Main Currents in Sociological Thought*, vol. 2, is immensely helpful. William Kornhauser's *The Politics of Mass Society* (Free Press, 1959) is a good-natured attempt to bring order to an intrinsically messy discussion. Among variants on the theme that twentieth-century man is overwhelmed by the "bigness" of modern society, Graham Wallas's *The Great Society* (Macmillan, 1936) influenced both Dewey and Lippmann. C. Wright Mills, *The Sociological Imagination* (Oxford, 1959), is a nice complement to *The Power Elite*. Lippmann's *Drift and Mastery* and his unillusioned *Public Opinion* and *The Phantom Public* (all republished by Transaction Books) are written with great verve.

Chapter 23: Richard Tuck's *The Rights of War and Peace* (Oxford, 1999) is a brisk and enlightening guide to the topics of this chapter, from Vitoria to Vattel. There is a recent reprint of the English translation of Bartolomé de Las Casas's *De los Indios, A Short Account of the Destruction of the Indians* (Reada Classic, 2009); Vitoria's *Political Writings* are in the Cambridge Texts series, excellently edited and introduced by Anthony Pagden and Jeremy Laurance. Sepúlveda's tract on the justice of the war against the Indians of America exists only in Spanish, but the Valladolid controversy is discussed in Anthony Pagden, *The Fall of Natural Man* (Cambridge, 1982). Vattel's *Law of Nations* is published in paperback by Woodbine Cottage Publications (2011). Skepticism about Western imperialism is well handled in Sankhar Muthu, *Enlightenment against Empire* (Princeton, 2003). The effect of casual brutality toward native peoples in Africa and Asia in paving the way for equal brutality to Europeans is one of the themes of Hannah Arendt's *Origins of Totalitarianism*; Sayyid Qutb has provoked some sound and fury as well as careful scholarship; an example of the latter is Roxanne Euben, *Enemy in the Mirror* (Princeton, 1999), and of the former Paul Berman's *Liberalism and Terror* (Norton, 2003) and its coda *The Flight of the Intellectuals* (Melville House, 2010). This is not to suggest the sound and fury signifies nothing; many of Qutb's ideas are deeply dangerous, and his anti-Semitism deeply nasty.

Chapter 24: Among older works, G. D. H. Cole's *History of Socialist Thought* (Macmillan, 1953–60) in five volumes is both readable and detailed and covers the ground from 1789 in *The Forerunners* until 1939 with *Socialism and Fascism*; Frank E. Manuel, *The Prophets of Paris* (Harvard, 1962), tackles Condorcet, Turgot, Saint-Simon, and Comte; his *Utopian Thought in the Western World* (Harvard, 1979), written with Fritzie Manuel, begins with the Greeks and ends with "Freudo-Marxism." Fourier's *Theory of the Four Movements* is a Cambridge Text; William Morris's *News from Nowhere* is also a Cambridge Text. Owen's *New View of Society and Report to the County of Lanark* is a Penguin Classic. "Freudo-Marxism" is well represented by Eric Fromm, *The Sane Society* (Rinehart, 1955). Richard Titmuss, *Essays on the Welfare State* (Macmillan, 1962) and *The Gift Relationship* (Allen & Unwin, 1970), are the classic defenses of the welfare state. Michael Ignatieff, *The Needs of Strangers* (Chatto & Windus, 1984), is very nicely done. A very short, engaging defense of socialist egalitarianism is G. A. Cohen, *Why Not Socialism?* (Princeton, 2010).

Chapter 25: Arendt's *The Origins of Totalitarianism*, in three volumes, *Anti-Semitism, Imperialism,* and *Totalitarianism* (Harcourt Brace, 1951), is very worth reading; the best political science treatment is Carl Friedrich and Zbigniew Brzezinski, *Totalitarian Dictatorship and Autocracy* (2d ed., Harvard, 1965). The link to Rousseau is forged in J. L. Talmon, *The Origins of Totalitarian Democracy* (Norton, 1970). The recent historiography of Nazi Germany is very impressive: Ian Kershaw's *Hitler: A Biography* (Norton, 2008) is an abridgment of the author's definitive two-volume account of its subject; Richard J. Evans's three-volume history of the Third Reich (Penguin, 2004–9) is rich, detailed, and distressing. Alan Bullock's "parallel lives" of Hitler and Stalin, *Hitler and Stalin* (Knopf, 1992), is illuminating. On Lenin, Trotsky, and Stalin, Bertram Wolfe's *Three Who Made a Revolution* (Dial Press, 1948) is the classic work; Isaac Deutscher's *Stalin* (Oxford, 1967) parallels his three-volume biography of Trotsky, *The Prophet Armed, The Prophet Unarmed,* and *The Prophet Outcast* (Oxford, 1954–63). There is no history of the Soviet Union comparable to Evans's of the Third Reich, but Geoffrey Hosking, *History of the Soviet Union* (Fontana, 1985), and Trotsky's *The Revolution Betrayed* of 1936 (Pathfinder Press, 1972) provide a perspective from the intransigent left.

Chapter 26: Interest in Dewey has grown in the past two decades, but Robert Westbrook, *John Dewey and American Democracy* (Cornell, 1992), is uniquely comprehensive. Its orientation reflects the influence of Christopher Lasch, whose *The Revolt of the Elites and the Betrayal of Democracy* (Norton, 1995) laments the erosion of the "social" ideal of democracy. Robert Dahl has continued to explore the possibilities of democratic institutions in *Democracy and Its Critics* (Yale, 1989), *On Democracy* (Yale, 1998), and *On Political Equality* (Yale, 2006). Among critics of Schumpeter's "elite competition" picture, Carole Pateman, *Participation and Democratic Theory* (Cambridge, 1970), wears well. Defenses of the view that "democracy" must entail liberal rights include R. W. Dworkin's *Freedom's Law* (Harvard, 1996), *Is Democracy Possible Here?* (Princeton, 2006), and the monumental *Justice for Hedgehogs* (Harvard, 2011).

Chapter 27: The speed at which books appear on the topics of the chapter is astonishing, and selection impossible. One good way into arguments about nuclear deterrence and world government is Ronald Clark, *The Life of Bertrand Russell* (Penguin, 1975); philosophers have written at length about John Rawls's *The Law of Peoples*; a good collection is Rex Martin and David Reidy, *Rawls's Law of Peoples: A Realistic Utopia?* (Blackwell, 2006). Benjamin Barber, *Jihad vs. McWorld* (Ballantine 1996), antedates the events of 2001, but is much referenced in discussion of them. Jared Diamond, *Collapse* (Viking, 2006), raises difficult questions about ecological catastrophe, set in the framework of his earlier *Germs, Guns, and Steel* (Norton, 1999).

INDEX

Abraham, 870
Absalom and Achitophel (Dryden), 454
Absolute, 984
absolute obedience, doctrine of, 336
absolutism, 233, 303, 498, 514–15, 851
Academics, 113
Académie Française, 519, 731, 931
Academy, 36, 37, 59, 71, 106
Academy of Dijon, 539, 541
Achilles, 52
acquisition, Hegel on, 679–81
action, freedom of, 251, 718–19
Actium, Battle of, 116
Act of Union (1707), 511
Acton, Lord, 43, 871
Acts of the Apostles, 129
Adam:
    authority and dominion of, 336, 472, 474, 514
    innocence of, 207
    lust and, 173
    transgression and Fall of, 159, 189
Adams, John, 578, 584, 596
    Polybius admired by, 121
Adams, Samuel, 579
addiction, 81

Address to the Christian Nobility of Germany, An
    (Luther), 332–35
Adeimantus, 47, 49, 57–58, 64
Adeodatus, 150
adjustment, 957
administration, politics vs., 771
administrative hierarchies, 530
admiration, 550
Adorno, Theodor, 831, 834
Adriatic Sea, 844
adultery, 347
adverse possession, 680
advertising, xvi
Aegean, 14, 101
Aegean Sea, 844
Aegospotami, 27
Aeneid (Virgil), 124
aesthetic dimension of appraisal, 709–10
affluence, 979
Africa, 664, 816, 862, 864, 1009
    colonial scramble for, 843, 867
    military strongmen in, 870
African Americans, 872, 930, 950, 968
afterlife, 31, 45, 69, 157, 165, 232, 249, 300, 466
After the Revolution? (Dahl), 971

Agathocles, 377
age, tranquillity of, 49
Age of Reason, The (Paine), 637, 930, 981
agglomeration, 833
Agincourt, Battle of, 295, 299
Agnani, 264
agnosticism, 979
agora, 74
agrarian laws, 140, 508, 509
agrarian revolts, 881
agriculture, xix, 108, 479, 544, 547, 549, 793
    see also farmers
Alaric, 152, 164, 184
Albertus Magnus, 226
Albigensians, 227, 981
Albizzi family, 362
Albornoz, Egidio, 285
Alcibiades, 25, 27, 30, 34, 40, 118, 127
alcohol, 719
Alexander III, Czar, 706, 897, 918
Alexander III, Pope, 235
Alexander V, Pope, 289
Alexander VI, Pope, 364, 369, 371, 372,
    373–74, 378, 851
Alexander the Great, 5, 71, 72, 73, 120, 121,
    182, 368, 668, 848, 978
    death of, 670
Alexandria, 791
Algeria, 729, 731, 762, 763, 862, 872–73,
    969
Alien and Sedition Acts (1798), 596
alienation, 771, 774, 775–82
    politics and, 782–85
allegiance, 419–20
Allegory of the Cave, 59, 66, 304, 310
all-in rightness, 79
Al-Qaeda, 995
ambassadors, 605
ambition, 602
Ambrose, Saint, 119, 151, 153, 202
American Crisis (Paine), 637
Americanization, 834
American Revolution, 129, 582–83, 587,
    589–90, 597, 624, 647
    Bentham's views on, 695–96
    British use of Indian auxiliaries in, 857
    Burke's desire for conciliation in, 619, 629
    dangers of, 627
    democracy in, 735, 767

French aid in, 618, 734
    as intended to restore old liberties, 627,
        631
    as precursor to French Revolution, 638,
        639, 645–46
    success of, 734–35
Americas, 406–7
    European colonization of, 749, 750, 793,
        849–54, 862
Amerindians, *see* Native Americans
Amin, Idi, 102
Amorgos, Battle of, 14, 72, 73
amour de soi, 543, 544, 546
amour propre, 543
Amphipolis, 19
Anabaptists, 326, 347, 349–53
anarchism, 190, 894–97, 987, 988
anarchists, 987, 988
anarcho-capitalism, 895
anarcho-socialism, 894
anarcho-syndicalism, 934
anarchy, 497
    of the market, 880, 883–84, 892, 935
    U.S. founding and, 582
Anarchy, State, and Utopia (Nozick), 894
Anastasius, Emperor, 215
ancien régime, 535, 536, 553, 632–33, 641,
    742, 752, 759, 763–69, 820
Ancien régime et la révolution, L' (Tocqueville),
    729, 730, 733, 737, 761, 763–69, 981
ancient prudence, 501
angels, 428
Anglo-Saxons, 195, 585, 586, 587, 611
Angola, 994
Animal Farm (Orwell), 915
animals, 241, 300
    gregarious, 105–6
    laws obeyed by, 378
Anne, Queen of England, 459
Answer to the Nineteen Propositions of Parliament,
    503
antagonism of opinions, 739, 751, 824
antagonisms, societal, 953
anticipated reactions, law of, 839
anticlericalism, 980–81, 985
anticommunism, 914
Antifederalists, 583, 593, 598
antiliberalism, 927–28
antimoralism, 718

antinomianism, 204, 325–26, 330, 345

Antioch, 216

Antipater, 71, 73, 368

antipaternalism, 717–18

anti-Semitism, 91, 340, 829, 865, 930
  Stalin's campaign of, 832

antiterrorist campaigns, 988

anxiety, 315, 431, 451, 480, 544

apatheia, 237–38

apparatchiks, 841

Appeal from the New Whigs to the Old (Burke), 622–23, 637

appearance, reality vs., 304, 318

Arab-Israeli conflict, 989

Arab nationalism, 871, 995

Arabs:
  philosophy's debt to, 213, 230
  Sicily conquered by, 197, 213

Arab Spring, 801

Aragon, 288

Archelaus, king of Macedonia, 42

Arendt, Hannah, 824, 905, 916

Areopagus, 27

Arezzo, 280, 281

Aristides, 18

aristocracy, 96, 104, 124, 126, 194, 238, 420, 508, 708
  Aquinas on, 239
  Aristotle on, 96–97, 98, 103, 526
  in Athens, 9, 10, 35
  in Carthage, 121
  in democracies, 103
  elective, 97, 570, 574
  expanded, 98
  financial, 796
  in France, 368, 767–68
  French hatred of, 766
  in French Revolution, 617
  in Great Britain, 767
  as Greek term, 5
  hereditary, 96
  in mercantile societies, 281, 282
  modern society critiqued by, 822–23, 832–33
  Paine's attack on, 639
  in prerevolutionary France, 633
  in revolutions, 765
  in Rome, 121, 130, 133, 141
  Rousseau's disdain for, 570

Socrates's defense of, 64
  in Sparta, 122
  spirit of, 521
  as turning into oligarchies, 97
  utilitarianism and, 697

Aristophanes, 34, 41, 86

Aristotelian philosophers, 137

Aristotle, 18, 71–110, 117, 119–20, 138, 156, 168, 190, 194, 248, 267, 274, 276, 282, 287, 408, 418, 421, 481, 502, 509, 555–56, 628, 649, 675, 812
  Alexander the Great tutored by, 71
  Aquinas influenced by, 224, 225, 231, 236–37, 238–39, 242–43, 248, 254, 329
  on aristocracy, 96–97, 98, 103, 526
  astronomy and physics of, 77
  biology of, 77
  on citizenship, 82, 92–97, 284
  coinage denounced by, 90
  constitutions studied by, 8, 18, 33–34, 72, 82, 92–93, 95–96, 97–99, 100, 124
  cosmology of, 63
  Declaration of Independence influenced by, 580, 581
  on defenders of mixed constitution, 386
  democracy denounced by, 98, 99, 103, 843
  on economics, 89–91, 103, 104–5
  on education, 82, 109
  as embroiled in politics, 71, 657
  as father of scientific racism, 863–64, 929
  good as conceived by, 427, 429
  on government of one, few, and many, 98, 103, 504, 522
  on happiness, 79, 140
  heresy as foreign to, 248
  hierarchical universe of, 407
  Hobbes's differences with, 106, 423, 426, 429, 430
  humanist rejection of, 293
  on human pursuit of numerous goals, 80–81
  ideal state of, 32, 82, 86, 97, 105–10, 722, 881
  influence of, 33
  on justice, 70, 74, 78–80, 101, 106
  Locke vs., 466
  medieval commentaries on, 226, 229–30

Aristotle (*continued*)
    metaphysics of, 214, 230, 231
    middle way of, 57, 88, 93, 98, 104, 244
    mixed government and, 103–4, 121–23,
      504, 517
    monarchy and, 98, 271, 272, 284, 298,
      499, 527
    on moneymaking, 107
    on morality, 51, 79, 466
    natural equality rejected by, 205
    on natural law, 204, 207
    Plato criticized by, 33–34, 70, 82, 107, 666
    on *politeia*, 98–105, 277, 278, 284
    politics distinguished from
      administrations by, 698
    "poor many" of, 841
    on positive law, 242–43
    on preservation of social position, 109–10
    and promotion of virtue, 78–81, 714
    on property, 212, 245–46
    rediscovery of, 224
    on revolutions, 76, 82, 92, 100, 122, 254,
      488, 631, 788
    on ruler's self-control, 374
    on self-sufficiency of states, 78, 106–7,
      275
    slavery as viewed by, 73–75, 76, 82,
      85–88, 92, 94, 238, 429, 727
    on sociability, 684, 784
    Sparta praised by, 129
    on stasis, 92, 100–105, 169, 498, 631,
      792, 967
    on syllogisms, 268
    teleological reasoning of, 75–78, 238,
      465
    on tragedy of the commons, 1010
    tyrannies advised by, 101–2, 118
    on women, 73–75, 93
arithmetic, 423
Arpinum, 135
art, 37–38, 59–61, 958
    difficulty of, 831
    meaning found by, 659
Arte della guerra, 356
Articles of Confederation, 590–91
artisans, 298, 882
artists, 59, 779
Aryan stock, 865, 914
ascending theory of authority, 195–96, 242,
    350, 438

asceticism, 171
ascetics, 171, 244
Asia, 1009
    European incursions into, 794
Asia Minor, 14–15
Asiatic mode of production, 793, 794
assassination, 379
assembly, freedom of, 610
association, 82, 83–85, 733, 755, 757–59,
    768
astronomy, 228
Atarneus, 72
atheism, 316, 466, 494, 985
Athenian Assembly, 17, 19, 25, 41, 127, 525,
    574, 811
    blasphemy law passed by, 30
    as inexpert, 724
    as key to Athenian democracy, 11
    omnicompetence of, 583
    Pericles's hold over, 12–13
    right to speak and vote in, xiii, 68, 74
    Thucydides's dislike of, 14
Athenian empire, 17, 18, 522, 844, 845
Athens, xxiii, 7–15, 39, 95, 113, 197, 348,
    368, 369, 375, 502, 933
    in Battle of Marathon, 15–16
    citizenship in, xiii, 10, 11, 86, 95, 195
    as city of festivals, 49
    class warfare in, 95, 106
    constitution of, 8, 9, 18, 82
    coups in, 27, 35
    democracy in, xiii, xiv, 9–21, 22, 27–28,
      35, 48, 111, 129, 194, 196, 414, 522,
      526, 570, 600, 667, 688, 697, 722, 815,
      905, 948–49, 975, 977; *see also* Athenian
      Assembly
    demography of, 6, 97
    factionalism in, 815
    freedom in, xiii, xvii, xxiii, 21, 22, 68, 94,
      656, 667–68
    justice in, 23, 24
    as maritime power, 14, 844
    Melos enslaved by, 19–20, 23–25, 44, 93,
      358–59, 413
    navy of, 21, 27
    in Peloponnesian War, *see* Peloponnesian
      War
    plague in, 21
    power in, 847
    revolts against Macedonian rule by, 71, 72

slavery in, 10, 11, 13, 68, 74, 86, 94, 667

social divisions in, 9

state funerals in, 21

trade in, 7, 10, 56, 522

women in, 10, 136

see also Persian War

atomistic individualism, 954–55

Attica, 27, 404

demes of, 11–12

auguries, 980

Augustine, Saint, 137, 148, 149–84, 187, 188, 205, 215, 224, 225, 239, 240, 269, 292, 332, 375, 466, 488–89, 554, 700–701, 997

background of, 149–51

Cicero's influence on, 137, 139, 153, 162, 165, 187

on citizenship of City of God, 169–73

coercion endorsed by, 338

converted to Christianity, 39

on death penalty, 149, 182

Dewey vs., 954, 958

on the Fall, 149, 168, 176, 189–90, 199

on human nature, 189–90, 541

imperialism denounced by, 175, 187

as influenced by Neoplatonism, 151, 153–54, 158, 162–63, 167

influence of, 153

on justice, 139, 149, 174–75, 179–80, 181, 221

just war theory of, 149, 175, 178–79, 247, 308, 817

Luther influenced by, 321

as Manichaean hearer, 151, 153–54, 158–61, 162, 167

mistress of, 150–51

on mixed quality of human societies, 171

on need for government, 345

as opposed to hierarchy, 240

on original sin, 153, 159, 160, 170, 179–80, 293, 436, 537

on passive disobedience, 199–200, 251

pears stolen by, 167–68, 180

on property rights, 174–75

on punishments, 176–78, 184

on reproving sovereigns, 202

on respect for office, 199

on salvation, 328

skepticism of, 231

suicide denounced by, 173–74, 175

on tyrants, 222

on violence, 642

Ausculta fili (letter), 262, 263

Austin, John, 567, 593

Australia, 763

Austria, 484, 652, 816, 870, 931, 959

Austro-Hungarian Empire, 751, 927, 941

autarchy, 937

authoritarianism, 287

authority, 65–66, 204, 429, 481

of Adam, 336, 472, 474, 514

ascending theory of, 195–96, 242, 350, 438, 939

Burke's image of, 635

constitutionally limited, 255

definition of, 423

de Maistre's image of, 635

descending theory of, 195–97, 205, 242, 438, 514–15, 939

division of, 334

in family, 759

God as fount of, 274

Hobbes on, 416–17, 438–40, 673

Luther on, 335–40, 352

Marx's lack of theory of, 771

medieval conceptions of, 195–98

medieval view of, 193

Paul's theory of, 340, 344, 348

in Saint-Simon's organic society, 648–51

of state, 406

as stemming from spirit, 776

Autobiography (Hobbes), 417

Autobiography (Jefferson), 588

Autobiography (J. S. Mill), 699–703, 707

autocracy, 205, 918–27, 941, 956

"autonomous" individuals, 825

autonomy, 663, 668–69

avarice, 287

Averroës, 214, 230

Avicenna, 214, 230

Avignon, removal of papal court to, 198, 260, 264, 287, 404

ayatollahs, 841

Baath party, 986

Babeuf, Gracchus, 480, 730

Babylon, 8, 73

Babylonian Captivity, 260, 287, 404

Babylonian Empire, 845

babysitting cooperative, 888
Bacon, Francis, 412, 510, 511
Bakunin, Mikhail, 775, 805, 880, 888, 892,
        894–95, 896
Balkans, 213, 845
banausic trades, 98
banditry, 247, 994
banking, 281, 361
    in Athens, 10
baptism, 332, 347
barbarians, 129, 155, 365, 505–6, 854, 856,
        929
Barclay, William, 490
Barrès, Maurice, 636, 931–32, 938
Bartolus of Sassoferrato, 257, 258, 279,
        283–87, 357, 483, 499
Basel, Council of, 289, 290
Basil, Saint, 246
Bastille, 529, 616, 623, 703, 765, 767
Bavaria, 652
Beaumont, Gustave de, 730, 731
Beauty, 60
Bedford, Duke of, 623
beggars, 307
Being and Nothingness (Sartre), 872
Belgium, 889
Bell, Daniel, 816–17
Bellamy, Edward, 315, 880–81, 883, 884,
        887, 897–99
belonging, 977
Bendis, temple of, 49
Benedict IX, Pope, 218
Benedictines, 226
benefit of clergy, 334
Bentham, Jeremy, 243, 567, 593, 672, 699,
        701, 860
    on defense of property, 885
    on each person counting for one, 950
    Hobbes's view of sovereignty criticized by,
        747
    intellectual case against revolutions made
        by, 627
    lawmaking considered science by, 724
    Owen funded by, 886
    parliamentary reform desired by, 695
    strong authority desired by, 571
    as thin utilitarianist, 709
    women's rights defended by, 698
Bentham, Samuel, 701

Berbers, 729
Berlin, Isaiah, xx–xxi, 922
Berlin, University of, 653
Bernstein, Eduard, 919
Berry, duc de, 296
Bible, 44, 163, 204, 236, 323, 334, 448–49,
        450, 987
    historical criticism of, 772
    translations of, 324, 330, 448–49
biblical authority, 254
Big Brother, 319
Bill of Rights, U.S., 596, 711
    creation of, 609–10
bills of rights, 445
biology, 426
Birmingham, England, 891
birth control, 726
bishops, 216–17, 248
    Erasmus's criticism of, 309
    misconduct of, 298
Bismarck, Otto von, xiii, 795, 801, 901–2
Black Guelphs, 265
Black Skins, White Masks (Fanon), 872
Blackstone, William, 584, 696, 747
Blanc, Louis, 758
blasphemy, 30, 184, 316, 492, 633
"blood and soil" movement, 931–32, 938
Bloom, Allan, xxi
Board of Trade, 455, 456
Bockelson, Jan, 353
Bodin, Jean, 235
body, 471, 472
    contempt for, 173
body politic, 296–97, 504, 567–68
Bohemia, 257, 289
Bolingbroke, Lord, 529
Bologna, 204
Bologna, University of, 228, 283
Bolsheviks, Bolshevism:
    cell structure of, 922
    international, 914
    in 1917 Russian Revolution, 897, 941
Bonaparte, Louis-Napoléon (Napoleon III),
        646, 730, 732, 733, 769, 794, 795, 796,
        798, 799
bonds, 798, 799
Boniface VIII, Pope, 249, 258, 260, 261–64,
        265, 267
Book of Peace (Christine de Pizan), 296

Book of the Body Politic, The (Christine de Pizan), 220, 295–99

Book of the City of Ladies, The (Christine de Pizan), 295

Book of the Three Virtues, The (Christine de Pizan), 295

Borda count, 290

Borgia, Cesare, 363, 364, 365, 369, 370–78, 381, 837

Borgia, Lucrezia, 371

Bossuet, Bishop, 503

boule, 12, 17

Bourbon monarchy, 636
    end of, 730, 731
        Habsburgs vs, 404–5
    restoration of, 730, 734, 739

bourgeois comfort, 408

bourgeoisie, 797, 798–99
    dictatorship of, 802–3

bourgeois justice, 787–88

bourgeois republics, state violence reduced in, 803

bourgeois revolutions, 646–47, 648, 765, 920

bourgeois society, 796, 987
    origin of, 794

Bowood, 701

Boyle, Robert, 414, 416, 417

Brabant, duchess of, 232, 253

Bramhall, Bishop, 449–50

Brandenburg, Archbishop of, 329

Brave New World (Huxley), 61–62, 63, 70, 318, 761, 817, 830, 834, 911, 943, 1011

bribery, 507

Bristol, England, 605

British empiricism, 776

Brittany, 368

Bruni, Leonardi, 294

Brutus, 221

Buckley, William F., 949

Buddhists, 985

Bullinger, Heinrich, 347

bureaucracy, 965–66

bureaucratic empire, 169

bureaucratic management, xii, 191, 288
    papal curia as model for, 404

Burgundy, 366, 368

Burgundy, Duke of, 295

Burke, Edmund, 460, 534, 605, 759, 1008

ancien régime defended by, 633–34, 640
    Cicero's influence on, 628, 632
    French Revolution attacked by, 579, 580, 618–34, 638, 767–68, 916
    Hegel's similarity to, 673
    modern idea of revolution created by, 630–34
    Montaigne's influence on, 629
    Paine vs., 622, 639–40, 642–43, 645–46
    religion as seen by, 629–30
    virtual representation doctrine of, 690

Burke, Richard, 621, 623

Burns, Lizzie, 774

Burns, Mary, 774

butterfly passion, 890–91

Byzantine Empire, 155, 164, 194, 197, 845
    destruction of, 213

Byzantium, 151

Caesar Augustus, 113, 116
    principate established by, 128, 154, 194

Cain, 336

Calais, 299

Calgacus, 1000

Caligula, Emperor of Rome, 222

Callicles, 38, 39, 44, 45–46, 51, 52, 62, 80, 437

"callous cash nexus," 778

Calvin, Jean, 291, 344–49, 350, 489

Calvinism, 331, 581, 750

Cambrai, Bishop of, 302

Cambridge University, 307, 455

Campanella, Tommaso, 510

Canada, 583, 596, 857, 868

canon law, 203, 228, 254, 282, 332, 403–4
    Protestant contempt for, 341

canon lawyers, 229, 281

Canossa, 218

Cape of Good Hope, 849

Capetian monarchy, 235

capital:
    as having no country, 866
    property as, 687
    rate of return on, 786–87, 868

capitalism, xviii, 32, 457, 458, 479, 481, 511, 686–87, 705, 794, 873
    beginning of, 846

capitalism (*continued*)
  birth pangs of, 795
  fluid funds in, 992
  fragility of, 912–13
  Hegel's version of, 686–88
  late, 865
  Lenin on imperialism as last stage of,
    846, 865–68
  Marx on inevitable downfall of, 651, 774,
    781–82, 785, 793, 867, 874, 883, 907
  relations of production in, 791
  Schumpeter on evolution of, 959
  semisocialism as savior of, 818
  Sorel's critique of, 934
  state, 792
  triumph in 1990s of, 818
  as uncivilized, 862
  welfare state in, 905
  worker, 893
Capitalism, Socialism, and Democracy
  (Schumpeter), 967
capital punishment, *see* death penalty
captains of industry, 796, 935
Capua, 369
Caracalla, Emperor of Rome, 135
cardinals, 334
  College of, 194, 204, 217, 234, 235, 312
Caribbean, 856, 1007
Carib Indians, 543, 548, 877
Carlyle, A. J., xi, 221
Carlyle, Robert W., xi, 221
Carlyle, Thomas, 712, 883, 980
Carolina, colony of, 457
Carolingian kingdom, 188
Carthage, 146–47, 369, 377, 502
  constitution of, 121
  destruction of, 112, 120–21, 124
Carthusians, 314
Castiglione, Baldassare, 365
Castro, Fidel, 573
casus belli, 178
Catherine of Aragon, 322, 324, 851
Catholic emancipation, 621
Catholics:
  lack of toleration for, 454, 463, 494
  in Northern Ireland, 968
  Protestants vs., 291, 341, 968
  toleration of, 456
  in U.S., 762

Catiline, 114–15, 118, 138, 221, 490
Cato the Censor, 61
Cato the Elder, 125
Cato the Younger, 115
Cavaignac, General, 733
Cavendish family, 429
Ceauşescu, Nicolae, 907
celebrity, 639, 841
Celestine V, Pope, 261–62
celibacy, 171, 176
censor morum, 129, 575
censorship, 633
Central America, 856
central banks, 596, 613–14
centralized authority, xii
centurions, 141
Cephalus, 49–50
certainty, 232
Cerularius, Michael, 218–19
Césaire, Aimé, 872
Chaeronea, 14, 71–72
Chalcis, 73
Chaldean theology, 300, 301
Chamberlain, Houston Stewart, 865, 930
chance (*fortuna*), 364, 369, 371, 379–81, 384,
    577, 631
change, government and, 123
Chaplin, Charlie, 908
Chapters on Socialism (J. S. Mill), 707, 970
charisma, 835
charitable societies, 674
charity, 212, 252
Charlemagne, King of the Franks, 155, 188,
    196, 234, 259, 270, 671, 849
Charles I, King of England, 415, 419–20,
    442, 490, 500, 503, 511, 512, 513
Charles II, King of England, 415, 454, 455–
    56, 457, 458, 461, 468, 473, 481, 488,
    494, 500, 501, 512, 513, 529, 594, 608
Charles IV, Emperor, 257, 259
Charles V, Emperor, 302, 307, 308, 322,
    324, 329, 333, 341, 343, 355, 364, 849,
    852
  de Vitoria's advice to, 850
  legitimacy of empire sought by, 852–53
  Lutheranism outlawed by, 343–44
Charles V, King of France, 294–95, 296
Charles VI, King of France, 295
Charles VIII, King of France, 363

Charles X, King of France, 730
Charles Martel, 213
Charmides, 35
Charter of United Nations, 178, 317, 1004, 1009
Chechnya, 995
checks and balances, 18, 99, 103, 142, 386, 451, 488, 607, 750–51
in *Federalist*, 600
Polybius on, 130
Cheka, 924
Childeric, King of Merovingians, 259
children, child rearing, 74, 82, 84–85, 94, 462, 482, 684, 726, 728, 944
in U.S., 760
chiliasm, 326, 913, 923
chiliastic myths, 326
China, 63, 771, 809–10, 876, 885, 996
economy of, 794
emperor of, 835
Opium Wars in, 861
"Chinese immobility," 820
choice, 823
Christian Commonwealth, 447–49
Christianity, 69, 147–48, 236, 287, 320, 537
on equality, 238
fall of Rome blamed on, 164–65, 168, 174
God's gift of laws to, 241
growth of, 664
guilt sensed in, 541
idea of divine ordering in, 63
infinite value of individual soul in, 670
inward freedom grounded in, 670
Islamic tolerance of, 213–14
Maurras's suspicion of, 932
missionary work and, 844
natural equality accepted by, 205
natural law and, 208, 238, 413
as official Roman religion, 148, 150, 155, 156, 158, 190, 197
Owen's distaste for, 887
persecution of, 156–57, 164–65, 197, 200, 988
Plato's influence on, 32
political theology of, 157
replacement of, 649
and sacrifices to local deities, 156
slavery sanctioned by, 582

as unphilosophical, 230–31
usury banned in, 91
Young Hegelians' rethinking of, 773
Christine de Pizan, 220, 294–99, 306
churches, 757
established, 482, 644, 692
Locke on nature of, 279, 324–25, 492
French, 626, 632, 633, 646, 980, 981
as voluntary association, 279, 324–25
Church of England, 311, 322–23, 416, 646, 708, 986
Hobbes's dispute with, 415
Church of Jesus Christ of Latter Day Saints, 985
church-state relationship, 216
Dewey on, 954
eastern vs. western church views on, 198
in fourteenth century, 258–65
Hobbes on, 419
investiture controversy and, 216–19
in Islam, 213
in Italy, 810
Locke on, 493
Luther on, 332–35
medieval view of, 193
separation of, 158–59, 332–33, 345, 752, 954, 985
in Spain, 810
in U.S., 250, 752, 964
Cicero, xxiii, 69, 110, 125, 136–48, 175, 179, 254, 275, 287, 305, 356, 365, 374, 382, 387, 416, 439, 464, 490, 560, 585, 594, 856
as absent from conspiracy against Caesar, 116
assassination of, 116
Augustine influenced by, 137, 139, 153, 162, 165, 187
background of, 111, 112–13
Burke influenced by, 628, 632
Catiline's conspiracy defeated by, 114–15, 118, 138, 490
citizenship as viewed by, 135
Declaration of Independence influenced by, 580, 581
on defenders of mixed constitution, 386
on duties, 144–45
efficient cause of government and, 276
on happiness, 140

Cicero (*continued*)
    impact of, 357
    influence on U.S. government of, 195
    on justice, xxiii, 139, 145–46, 165, 284
    liberty and, xxiii, 580
    literary style of, 116–17, 120
    Machiavelli's mocking of, 137, 378
    on mixed governments, 122, 123, 498
    natural law theory of, 143–44, 206
    pardoning of, 115
    Plato followed by, 39
    as popular with civil lawyers, 233
    on positive law, 242–43
    as praetor, 114
    on republican governments, 137–42, 175,
        180, 187, 190, 196, 220, 284, 568, 600
    rhetoric valued by, 39, 113, 119, 622
    on rights, 462
    Rome's trial-and-error process praised by,
        125, 140–41
    as Sicilian quaestor, 114
    tyrannicide allowed by, 181, 221, 306
    on virtues, 137, 144, 297
Cicero, Marcus (son), 119, 144
circle, squaring of, 414, 417
Circumcellions, 171
citizen militias, 133
citizenship, citizens, 76, 78, 518
    as abdicating responsibility in 1960s,
        950–51
    Aristotle on, 82, 92–97, 284
    Athenian notions of, xiii, 10, 11, 86, 95,
        195
    Augustine on, 169–73
    in France, 553
    in Great Britain, 95
    in Greek city-states, 132, 133, 195, 667
    liberty and, 518
    Marx's lack of a theory of, 771
    property and, 526
    qualifications of, 498
    Roman notions of, xiii, xiv, 10, 122,
        132–36, 195, 553, 574
    Rousseau on need for, 553, 574, 783
    in Sparta, 553, 574
    three-stage account of, 904
    in U.S., 95
City of God, 190, 332
    citizenship in, 169–73

City of God against the Pagans (Augustine), 148,
        150, 152, 153, 154, 161, 163–69, 174,
        176, 181, 269, 323
    Rome criticized in, 162
    writing of, 165
City of the Sun (Campanella), 510
city-states, 520, 522
    democratic virtues of, 523–24, 716
    liberty in, 665
    political commitment in, 576
    privacy lacking in, 525
civic freedom, 565
civic humanism, 291–92
civic liberty, 498–99, 512
civic religions, 574–75, 980
civic virtue, 497
Civil and Ecclesiastical Power (Locke), 492
civilization, 306, 1001
    conflict of, 987
    death of, 1001–2
    modernization vs., 863
    uncivilized worlds vs., 412
Civilization and Its Discontents (Freud), 817, 832,
        928, 998
"civilizing missions," 844, 846
civil law, 208, 228, 282, 283–84
    usefulness of, 244
civil lawyers, 233
civil liberties:
    as descended from Magna Carta, 811
    post–World War II erosion of, 816
civil religions, 156, 629–30
civil rights, 665
civil servants, 838
civil society, 901, 905–10
    Hegel's discussion of, 674, 683, 684,
        685–89
    necessity of, 674
    state vs., 906
civil war, 99, 100, 127–28, 968, 994
Civil War, English, 62, 326, 414–15, 416,
        420, 435, 507, 510, 513, 587, 735, 997
    causes of, 511
    and dispute between Athens and Rome,
        xiii
Civil War, U.S., 21, 28, 87, 567, 610, 754,
        930, 964
    Marx's commentaries on, 774
Civil War in France, The (Marx), 923

Clarendon, Earl of, 414
class, 879
    forming of, 793, 795–800
    individuals vs., 960
    substantial vs. formal, 687, 693
class warfare, 799
    as absent from U.S., 764, 795, 953, 954
    as almost invisible, 977
    Aristotle on, 100–101, 788, 792, 817
    in Athens, 95, 106
    democracy and, 953
    in globalized world, 992
    Machiavelli on, 788, 834
    Marx's account of, 771, 788–92
    in Rome, 125
    Rousseau on, 537, 539–52, 556, 557, 736,
        788
    in Soviet Union, 925–26
    threat of, 905
Clausewitz, Carl von, 692
Cleisthenes, 10, 13, 27, 98, 127, 526
Clement II, Pope, 218
Clement V, Pope, 265
Clement VII, Pope, 288, 359, 364
clergy, 296–97
    French, 633, 634
    misconduct of, 298
    privilege of, 262–63
    taxing of, 260, 262
    in U.S., 752
    warfare fomented by, 309
clerical celibacy, 332
Clericis laicos, 262
clerisy, 708
clientage, 136
Clifford, Lord, 517
climate, 752
clockmakers, 882
clocks, 405
Clodius, 115
Closing of the American Mind, The (Bloom), xxi
Clouds (Aristophanes), 34, 41
coal mines, 891
Cobbett, William, 887
cod wars, 855
coercion, 183–84, 251–53, 271, 278, 302,
    337, 346–47, 669, 719, 942, 959, 974
    self-defense and, 717–18
coercive laws, 243–44

Cohn, Norman, 923
coinage, 90
Coke, Edward, 504, 584
Cold War, 623, 840, 916, 942, 985, 989
    mutually assured destruction in, 434,
        988, 1002
Coleridge, Samuel Taylor, 708
collective guilt, 178
collectives, 99
College, Stephen, 455
College of Cardinals, 194, 204, 217, 234,
    285, 312, 373
College of New Jersey at Princeton, 519, 595
College of William and Mary, 584, 595
colleges, 757
Collingwood, R. G., xx
colonialism, 872
    insurgencies against, 996
colonies, 367, 585
    proprietary, 586
    see also empires, imperialism
colonization, 847
Colonna family, 261, 262, 264
Columbus, Christopher, 405, 869
Comintern, 926
command economies, 812
commerce, 479, 544
commercial associations, 674
commercial life, 446
common good, 736, 960
common interests, 797
common law, 504, 680
Commons, 103, 195, 506
    French, 634
Common Sense (Paine), 637, 638
commonwealths, 139, 175, 442
    Christian, 170
    Hobbes on, 423–24
communal governments, 272
communes, 196, 728
communications revolution, 991
communism, 351, 623
    attraction to, 929
    brutality of, 811
    dictatorships of, xvii–xviii, 818
    discrediting of, 968
    fascism vs., 914–15
    French Revolution and, 616
    primitive, 793, 984

communism (*continued*)
 reformist parties undermined by, 829
 regulation of life desired by, 809
 as secular, 979
 in *Utopia,* 314
 violence used in, 928–29
communist communities, 176
Communist Manifesto (Marx and Engels),
  772–73, 775, 778, 781, 788, 789, 792,
  795, 798, 883
Communist Party, Soviet Union, 770, 839,
  911, 941
communist societies, 32
 early Christians and, 207–8
communist states, xvii–xviii
communitarianism, 954–55
community, 733
 Dewey on, 751–59
 negative, 476
 positive, 476
community of communities, 955
compelle intrare, 251, 338, 347
competition, 433, 435, 436, 780, 788
Complaint of Peace, The (Erasmus), 308
Comtat Venaissin, 260
Comte, Auguste, 630, 650, 707, 770, 893,
  982, 983, 985
conceptualizations, 667
conciliar movement, 256, 257, 258
Concordat of Worms, 218
Condition of the English Working Class (Engels),
  773–74
confession, 321–22
Confessions (Augustine), 150, 151–52, 160,
  167–68, 319, 327
Confessions (Rousseau), 534, 536, 540
conflicts of interests, 958–59
conformity, 338
Congo, 994
Congress, U.S., 608, 949
conquest, 643
conscience, 581, 682, 708
consent, 276–77, 516
 for government, 483–86
 tacit vs. express, 485–87
consequentialism, 1000
conservatives, 443, 552
 French Revolution disdained by, 616–17
 liberalism founded on basis of, 728, 756

Considerations on Representative Government (J. S.
  Mill), 706, 720–28, 860–61
*Considerations on the Causes of the Greatness and
  Decline of the Romans,* 519
Considérations sur la France (de Maistre), 634–36
Constant, Benjamin, xvii, 500, 518, 524–25,
  581, 656, 667, 824
Constantine, Emperor of Rome, 151, 155,
  194, 270
 conversion to Christianity, 148, 156, 158,
  197
Constantinople, 151, 153, 194, 197, 216, 445,
  497, 502, 503
 fall of, 213, 303
 sacking of, 227
Constantinople, emperor of, 216, 502–3
Constantinople, patriarch of, 198, 215, 216
Constitution, U.S., 130, 459, 557, 583, 584,
  590, 603, 606, 964
 achievements of, 598
 amendments to, 747–48
 arguments against, 593–94
 Aristotle's influence on, 85
 balance of centralization and
  decentralization in, 593
 brevity of, 502
 church-state separation in, 752, 964, 985
 convention of, 123, 131
 double sovereignty in, 592–93
 human rights protected by, 467
 liberty preserved by, 607
 Locke's influence on, 85
 mixed government and, 121
 obstacles to tyranny in, 747
 Polybius's influence on, 121, 125
 preamble to, 598
 Second Amendment to, 506
 unresolved tensions in, 582
 writing of, 591
constitutionalism, 221
constitutionalists, 342
constitutional monarchy, 126, 499, 512, 520,
  569, 689, 691, 739, 741, 782
Constitution of Athens, The (attr. Aristotle), 82
constitutions, 76, 100, 488
 authority limited by, 255
 of Carthage, 121
 as conferring legitimacy on states, 1004
 of Corsica, 536

French, 633
of Germany, 384–85
Hegel's formal account of, 656, 689
Hobbes on, 450
of Holy Roman Empire, 343
Locke's writing of, 582
Marsilius's defense of, 257
Polish, 536, 567
Roman, 609
of Rome, III, II4, I26, I30
Rousseau's writing of, 536, 567
of Sparta, 32, I2I–22, I24, I25–26, 346
of Virginia, 597
constitutions, English, 530, 580, 646, 964
as mixed, 503, 504, 520, 625
separation of powers in, 608
constitutions, Greek, 8, 9, 18, 32, 33, 34, 72,
82, 92–93, 95–96, 97–99
constitutions, mixed, I03–4, III, I2I–26,
I28, I30, I38, I4I–42, I95, 254, 348,
366, 386, 487, 497, 498, 50I–2, 5I2,
5I7, 606, 609, 947–48
English as, 503, 504, 520, 625
Hobbes's dislike of, 443
in Israel, 509
consubstantiation, 346
consuls, II3, I30, I3I, 20I, 28I, 297
election of, I30–3I
consumption, 679
contadini, 28I, 282, 355, 505
Conti, prince de, 534
Continental Congress, Second, 584, 587–88,
590, 595
contracts, 56–57, 438, 680–8I, 684
contractualism, 349
Convention Parliament (I689), 459, 623
conversion, torture in, I64
cooperation, 779, 887
as forced in marked economy, 784
cooperatives, 706, 707, 884, 893–94, 905,
970, 97I
Copernicus, 405
copyright law, 679
Corinth, I3, I4, I8, I9
corn, 549
corporal punishment, I77, I84
corporate body, 560–6I
corporations, 686–87, 689
multinational, 992

corporatism, 933, 936, 937–40
Corps of Pages, 896
Corpus (Justinian), 220
Corpus juris civilis (Justinian), 205–6, 207, 283
corpus mysticum, 289
corruption, 98–99, 5I2, 568, 64I, 953
Stoic view of, 237
Corsica, I2I, 536
cosmology, Christian, 4I2
cosmopolitanism, 624
cotton, 75I
Council of Basel, 289, 290
Council of Constance, 289, 290, 329
Council of Lyons, 227
Council of Sutri, 2I8
Council of the Commune, 36I
Council of the People, 36I
Council of Trent, 356
councils, 28I
Counter-Enlightenment, 635
Counter-Reformation, 85I, 985
countervailing power, 7I5
coups d'états, I00, 63I
courage, 63, II9, I45, I47, 269, 287, 299,
375, 376, 378, 424
court, Roman freedom and, xiii
Courtier, The (Castiglione), 365
Court of Star Chamber, 607
Courtrai, 263
courts, Roman, II7
covenants, 439, 44I
craftsmanship, 794, 934
Crassus, II5, I37
Creation, I52, I68, I89, 230
creative destruction, 96I
creativity, 408
Crédit Mobilier, 648
Crete, 845
crime, 307, 697
punishment for, I76–77
criminal courts, 247
criminal justice, 48
crises, 702–3
Critias, 28–29, 35, 49
critical morality, 708–9
Critique of the Gotha Program (Marx), 804
Croly, Herbert, 6I4–I5, 983
Cromwell, Oliver, 4I5, 4I9, 420, 442, 453,
486, 500–50I, 508, 579, 594, 6I8, 735

cronyism, 908
cruelty, 287
Crusades, 213, 232, 235, 253
    Fourth, 227
    Third, 235
Cuban Missile Crisis, 840
cult of leadership, 915
cultural colonization, 869
cultural pluralism, 979
culture, Hegel's account of, 658, 661–62, 668, 703
curat Deus injuria Dei, 492
curia, 980
currency, 262, 598
cursus honorum, 130
custom, 728
cyclical historical process, 48, 124, 126, 127, 383
Cyprus, 845
Cyprus, king of, 232
Cyrillic, 870
Cyrus, 370
Cyzicus, 27
Czechoslovakia, 972, 995

Dahl, Robert, 946–47, 967–68, 971
Dalmatia, 187
damnation, 199, 331
Danby, Lord, 517
dance, 59
D'Annunzio, Gabriele, 936
Dante Alighieri, 104, 261, 262, 265–72, 281
    in exile, 265–66
    universal monarchy advocated by, 257, 258, 266–72, 1003
Darius I, King of Persia, 6, 15, 16, 368, 693, 1008
Dark Ages, 229
Darwin, Charles, 864
Das Kapital (Marx), 706, 771, 787, 899, 909, 959
death, 287, 315
    fear of, 544
death instinct, 997
death penalty, 149, 182, 315, 468–69, 635
    in Rome, 177
debate, 570
Debs, Eugene, 881
debt forgiveness, 115

debts, 583
decentralization, 335, 724–25, 733
De cive (Hobbes), 419, 449
Declaration and Bill of Rights (1689), 581
Declaration of Independence, 491, 578, 584–90, 595, 612, 637, 643
    sources of, 579–84
decolonization, 866, 870, 871, 873
De concordantia catholica (Nicholas of Cusa), 289–90
De corpore (Hobbes), 419
decrees, laws vs., 384
defense, 511, 526, 593, 598
Defensor minor (Marsilius of Padua), 272, 273
Defensor pacis (Marsilius of Padua), 267, 272–79
De heretico comburendo, 415–16
De homine (Hobbes), 419
deism, 981
De jure belli ac pacis (Grotius), 855
delegates, 605
De legibus (Cicero), 117, 136–37, 138, 143, 144
Delian League, 17
deliberative democracy, 956
Della Scala family, 272
Delos, 17
Delphi, oracle at, 34, 36
de Maistre, Joseph, 170, 534–35, 577, 634–36, 927
demand deficiency, 867, 868
Demaratus, King of Sparta, 6–7, 16, 128
demes, 84
    of Attica, 11–12
democracy, 7, 98, 104, 126, 194, 239–40, 256, 348, 420, 893
    in American Revolution, 735, 767
    ancient vs. modern, 949–51
    aristocracy vs., 526
    aristocratic characteristics in, 103
    Aristotle on, 98–99
    in Athens, xiii, xiv, 9–21, 22, 27–28, 35, 48, 111, 129, 194, 196, 414, 522, 526, 570, 600, 667, 688, 697, 722, 815, 905, 948–49, 975, 977; *see also* Athenian Assembly
    classical theory of, 959, 960, 961–62
    conflicts of interest in, 964–65
    as conformist, 716
    degeneration of, 104

deliberative, 956
Dewey's defense of, 951–59, 969
direct, xvi, 583
elections by lottery and, 99
elite theory of, 838, 959
end of dubious connotations of, 818
equality in, 949–50
ethos of, 21
expanding political representation in, 843
as experimental, 957
as faction-ridden, 716
favoring of poor in, 53
Filmer's denunciation of, 515
freedom as principle of, 67–68
Gobineau's criticism of, 865
as great community, 954, 955
greed in, 296
as Greek term, 5
guided, xvii–xviii, 818
Hegel's view of, 693
Herodotus's doubts about, 14
high culture and, 755
Hobbes's hostility to, 62, 418
human rights and, 19–20, 24
Islamic, 818–19
J. S. Mill's defense of, 706, 720–28
justice and, 101
leadership, 835–37
legitimacy of, 962, 966
liberalism vs., 947, 976
liberal values as compatible with, 964
Marx on need for, 782–84
mischaracterizations of, 68
in modern world, 946–77
narrow, 98
as necessary for socialism, 885
oligarchy vs., 100–101, 127
"people's," xvii–xviii, 818
Plato's disapproval of, 35, 42, 67–68, 123
proletarian, 802–6
pure vs. representative, 97, 600, 601, 611, 705, 819, 947
radical, 618
Rawls's definition of, 974–77
realistic theory of, 946–47, 959–68
religion and, 979
republic vs., 600, 601, 605
revolution in, 101, 102–3
Roman attitudes toward, xiii, xiv, 130, 141

Rousseau's disdain for, 569–70
as rule by competing elites, xvi
Schumpeter's definition of, 959–67, 975–76
social, 951–59
Socrates on, 35
in Sparta, 122
spirit of, 521–22
strength of, 123
tendency toward centralization in, 758, 761, 768
Thucydides's views on, 14, 418
in U.S., 734, 741, 744, 745, 768
utilitarianism and, 697, 710, 715–16
varieties of, xxii–xxiii, 6
see also liberal democracies
"Democracy and Christianity" (Dewey), 953–54
Democracy and Education (Dewey), 957
Democracy in America (Tocqueville), 526, 729, 731–32, 737, 739, 821
equality discussed in, 742–43, 745–46
first volume of, 704, 729, 733, 743–44, 745–55, 760
Frenchness of, 740–42
Mill's praise of, 704, 705
second volume of, 704, 705, 733, 737, 740, 743–45, 755–60, 766
democratic centralism, 922
democratic dictatorships, 573
Democratic Republicans, U.S., 583–84
democratic socialism, 798
demographic changes, 810
demographic revolution, xix
De monarchia (Dante), 261, 265–72, 273
demos, 98
Demosthenes, 72, 73, 116
Denmark, 323, 866
De officiis (Cicero), 119, 128, 137, 143, 144, 145–47, 341, 856
Machiavelli's attack on, 374
déraciné, 931
De regimine principum (Aquinas), 227, 232, 239, 254–56
De republica (Cicero), 69, 112, 117, 120, 136–37, 138, 143, 144, 154, 158, 162, 165
Descartes, René, 416, 418, 740, 755
descending theory of authority, 195–97, 205, 242, 438, 514–15

desire, 165
 mutability of, 428
despotism, 126, 520, 522, 524, 526, 643
 climate's fostering of, 752
 fear in, 522
 in Greek politics, 666–67
 Mill's qualified defense of, 677, 721, 747
 quiet, 715–16, 821
 soft, 755, 824
deterrence, 999, 1001–2, 1011
De translatione imperii (Marsilius of Padua), 259, 272, 273
de Vaux, Clothilde, 630
devin du village, Le (Rousseau), 536
devolution, 724
Devonshire, Earl of, 414, 416
Dewey, John, 755, 928–29, 946, 951–59, 969, 971
 Augustine vs., 954, 958
 communitarianism of, 954–55
dialectical materialism, 906
Dialogues (Plato), 36
dictatores, 292
dictators, dictatorships, xvii–xviii, 104, 297, 458
 of bourgeoisie, 802–3
 proletariat, 32, 33, 771, 802–4, 810
 socialist, 803
 strong executive leadership vs., 812
 theocratic, 818–19
Diderot, Denis, 533, 540, 548, 562, 859
Diet of Speyer (1529), 324
diffidence, 433–35, 436
Digest (Justinian), 280, 283
dike, justice vs., 43–44, 64
Diocletian, 150, 197
Dionysius I, tyrant of Syracuse, 37, 117
Dionysius II, tyrant of Syracuse, 37, 117, 304
Directory, 632
Discourse on Political Economy (Rousseau), 511
"Discourse on the Love of Our Country, A" (Price), 623–25
Discourse on the Origin of Inequality (Rousseau), 537, 539–52, 556, 557, 736, 788
Discourses (Machiavelli), 355, 356, 359, 371, 375, 381–89, 412, 423, 535, 594
 exempla in, 297, 365
 philosophy mocked in, 118
Discourses concerning Government (Sidney), 458, 500, 513, 516–17, 581

Discourses on the Arts and Sciences (Rousseau), 539–40
diseases, xix
disobedience, 199–200, 251, 333, 336
Disraeli, Benjamin, 885–86
dissension, 338, 340
Dissenters, 454–55, 456–57, 492, 624, 646, 715, 765
diversity, 105
divina commedia, La (Dante), 265, 266, 270
divine law, 75–76, 143, 342, 431, 436–37
divine order, 65
divine positive law, 241
divine right:
 of kings, 181, 305, 407, 419, 458, 461, 503–4, 509, 963
 of popes, 334
 theory of, 274
division of labor, 58–59, 216, 334, 337
domestic violence, 885
Dominicans, 226, 227–28, 232, 245, 247
Donation of Constantine, 234, 270
Donatists, 164, 170–71, 182–83
Donatus the Great, 170
double council, 281–82
double sovereignty, 523–24, 592–93, 599
Dover, Treaty of, 455
draft dodgers, 487
drama, 59
Dreyfus Affair, 931
Droit des nations (Vattel), 856
drugs, 719
Dryden, John, 454
duplicity, 550
Durkheim, Émile, 648, 983–84
Du système pénitentiaire aux États-Unis (Tocqueville), 730
Dutch empire, 844, 852, 855
Dutch United Provinces, 502, 607
duty, 133, 406, 469, 889
 Cicero on, 144–45
 truth vs., 320
 in utilitarianism, 709

East Asia, 993
Eastern Europe, 907, 930
East India Company, 621, 697, 700, 701, 707, 725, 747, 859, 860, 861, 862
East Indies, 854
ecclecticism, 299

ecclesia, see Athenian Assembly
ecclesiastical principalities, 373
ecclesiastical tyrant, 220
Eckhart, Meister, 331
École Polytechnique, 934
economic activities:
    Aristotle on, 88–90
    justice of, 89–91
economic equality, 101, 115
economic freedom, 495
economic growth, 405, 907
Economic-Philosophical Manuscripts, 775
economics, 55, 424, 704, 825, 955
Eden, 240, 984
    see also Adam
Edict of Nantes, 492
education, 875, 944, 991, 1005
    access to, 693, 726
    Aristotle on, 82, 109
    liberal, 109
    Locke on, 109
    medieval, 228–30
    Mill's views on, 719–20
    in philosophy, 60
    Plato on, 58–63
    of princes, 297–98, 303–4
    public, 720, 828
    Rousseau on, 61, 537–38, 539, 553–54
    utilitarianism and, 109
    vocational vs. nonvocational, 229
    of women, 726
Education of a Christian Prince, The (Erasmus),
    302–8, 311
Edward I, King of England, 236, 262
Edward VI, King of England, 322
egalitarianism, 818
Egidius Colonna (Giles of Rome), 285
Egypt, 8
Egyptian Ministry of Education, 875
Eighteenth Amendment, U.S., 748
Eisenhower, Dwight D., 357–58
Eisenstein, Sergei, 926
elections, 169–70, 274, 325, 508, 624, 966, 972
    by lottery, 99
    see also voting rights
elections, France, of 1848, 733
elections, U.S.:
    of 1800, 578
    primary, xvi
elective aristocracy, 97, 570, 574

electors, 639
Elements of Law, The (Hobbes), 415, 418–19
eleutheria, 68
elite democracy, xvi–xvii
elites:
    in democracies, xiv
    as manipulative, 841–42
    popular opposition to, xiv–xv
    in totalitarian states, xvi
    see also mass-elite opposition
elite theorists, 837
elite theory of democracy, 838, 959
Elizabeth I, Queen of England, 200, 292,
    344, 346
Émile (Rousseau), 532, 536, 537–38, 539,
    552–56, 557, 572
    burning of, 534
Émile and Sophie (Rousseau), 555
empire of liberty, 515, 586, 612, 693, 845
empires, imperialism, 499, 843–78, 999
    ancient concept of, 847–49
    beginning of modern, 846
    cultural, 869
    definition of, 848–49
    as enterprise of nation-state, 869
    intellectual defenses of, 721, 724–25,
    762–63, 860–61
    Lenin on, as last stage of capitalism, 846,
    865–68
    as liberal, 927
    Marx and Marxists on, 866–67, 868
    pelagic, 845–46, 853, 868
    progress and, 859–60
    as racist, 927
    radical opposition to, 871–78
    reason for, 874
    see also colonies
empiricism, 776
employment, 446
Encomium Moriae (Erasmus), 309–11
Encyclopaedia Britannica, 697
Encyclopedia of the Philosophical Sciences (Hegel),
    664, 671
Encyclopédie, 519, 533, 635
"end justifies the means," 358
End of History and the Last Man, The (Fukuyama),
    xxi
End of Ideology, The (Bell), 816–17
Engels, Friedrich, 32, 330, 551, 648, 772–74,
    775, 785, 882, 894, 919, 970

Engels, Friedrich (*continued*)
 as disappointed in proletariat, 827
 nationalism and, 866
 religion as viewed by, 984
 utopian socialism dismissed by, 880
Engels and Ermen, 773, 882
England, 212, 261, 288, 499, 519, 851
 clergy taxed in, 260
 destruction of monasteries in, 323–24
 in Hundred Years' War, 287, 294–95
 land register in, 446
 legal system of, 280–81
 liberty in, 523, 528–29, 530, 580
 property rights and, 210
English Declaration of Right (1689), 610
Enlightenment, 86, 189, 519, 536, 540, 548,
 643, 878
 Greek freedom vs., 668
 racism condemned by, 846
 revolution as viewed in, 638–39
entertainment, 830–31
Entick v. Carrington, 610
environmental degradations, xix, 979, 1005,
 1007–11
Ephialtes, 16
Epicureans, 144–45
equality, 93–94, 254, 460, 483, 545, 601,
 897–98
 in democracies, 949–50
 economic, 101, 115, 583
 and election by lottery, 99
 freedom and, 645, 761–62
 in French Revolution, 535, 616, 617, 647,
 653, 768
 justice and, 314
 liberalism and, 937
 of opportunity, 583
 Paine and, 583, 639
 Rousseau's advocacy of, 537, 539–52,
 556, 557, 569, 736–37, 788
 in Saint-Simon's philosophy, 649–50
 slavery and, 582
 Tocqueville's praise of, 742–43
 universal suffrage and, 784
 in U.S., 742–43, 745–46, 755–56
 in utilitarianism, 726
 see also isegoria
equalization of conditions, 743, 745–46
equites, 112, 114, 116, 133, 134
 as eligible for office, 129

Er, myth of, 69
Erasmus, 119, 294, 301–11, 312, 329, 346,
 355, 416, 851
 Luther's disputes with, 311
 popes and bishops criticized by, 309
 on punishment, 315
 skepticism of, 319
 on war and peace, 302, 306–9, 317, 849
espionage, 816
Essai sur l'inégalité des races humaines (Gobineau),
 865
Essay concerning Human Understanding (Locke),
 454, 492
Essay on Government (James Mill), 704, 720
estates, 686–88, 689, 691
Estates General, 263, 343, 348, 605, 634
estrangement, 659–60, 776, 777
eternal punishment, 300
ethics:
 Aquinas on, 232
 Aristotle on, 77–81
 foundations of, 145
 Greek notion of, 54
 happiness and, 79
 Hegel on, 673, 683–84
 as practical discipline, 77–78
 secular, 711
 utilitarian, 699, 711–12
ethnic identity, xiv
ethnic minorities, 907
ethology, 705
Euboea, 16
Euclid, 414, 423
eudaemonia, 54
eupatridae, 9, 13
Europe, 572
 Americas colonized by, 793
 Asian incursions of, 794
 in contact with less technical civilizations,
 406–7
 possibility of revolution in, 800–801
 threat of class warfare in, 905
European Assembly, transferable votes in,
 724
European Convention on Human Rights,
 467
European Social Democratic parties, 953
European Union, 258
 proposed constitution for, 502
Eve, 168

evil, 45–46, 48, 167, 427–30
    passive resistance to, 999
    problem of, 161
evolution, 105, 538, 541, 896
    fairness programmed by, 57
    racism justified by, 864
    sociability programmed by, 58
exclusion bill (1679), 455
excommunication, 252–53, 279
executive, 39, 103, 130, 504, 505, 528, 592, 690
    checking power of, 607
    strong, vs. dictatorships, 812
exempla, 220, 293, 297, 299, 365, 412
exile, 93
expanded aristocracy, 98
expediency, justice vs., 358
experience, 454
exploitation, 641
    Marx's theory of, 785, 787–89
Exsurge Domine (papal bull), 332
exterminism, 930
extra ecclesia nulla salvatio, 324

Fabian Society, 650, 900, 902
Fabius, 900
Fable of the Bees (Mandeville), 513
Facta et dicta memorabilia (Valerius Maximus), 297, 299
factionalism, 282, 570, 601, 602–5, 620, 748
failed states, 812, 1011
fairness:
    justice as, 977
    as programmed by evolution, 57
fair trial, 488
faith, 251, 324, 331, 338
    reason and, 231
Falangists, 833
Fall, 149, 159, 168, 176, 189–90, 199, 208, 237, 984
Fall of the Public Man, The (Sennett), 755
family, 82, 915, 979
    democratic vs. aristocratic, 759–60
    Hegel on, 683, 684
    Plato's abolition of, 107
    in U.S., 755, 759–60
famine, 210, 246–47, 287
Fanon, Frantz, 846, 871–73, 991
Farabi, al-, 214

farmers, 91–92, 511, 547
    as substantial class, 687, 689, 693
    see also agriculture
fascism, 32, 636, 829, 914–18, 986
    anti-intellectual streak in, 916–17
    attraction of, 914, 929
    authority flowing upward in, 939
    brutality of, 811
    communism vs., 914–15
    core doctrine in, 917
    discrediting of, 968
    emergence of nation in, 938–39
    French Revolution and, 616
    as fueled by negative emotions, 932–33
    irrationalism and, 912–13, 927, 928, 934–37
    liberal, 928
    one-party states in, 938
    regulation of life desired by, 809
    as secular, 979
    Spanish, 833, 914
    as totalitarian, 927–28
    violence used by, 928–29
    in World War II, 941
fascism, Italian, 816, 834, 839, 912–13, 915–16, 937–38
fate *(tyche)*, 381, 384, 577
fathers, 84–85
fear, 414, 443, 542
    in despotism, 522
federalism, 523–24, 567, 592–93
Federalist, 121, 578, 593–94, 597–610
    authorship of, 599
    No. 10, 599–600, 606
    No. 39, 600, 606
    No. 47, 600, 607
Federalist Party, U.S., 757
federal powers, national powers vs., 607
federal state, 28
federal system, 725
felicific calculus, 697
Ferdinand, King of Spain, 355
Ferguson, Adam, 519, 548, 788
Ferry, Jules, 862
Fesitval of the Supreme Being, 980, 981
feudalism, 211, 281, 501, 502, 505, 507, 547, 586, 735, 787, 789, 790, 794
    ascending and descending conceptions combined in, 195
    in Great Britain, 188, 281

feudalism (continued)
  investiture controversy and, 216–18
  land tenure in, 201–2, 210
  property rights under, 209–10
  as transferring resources from poor to
    rich, 766
feudal socialism, 883
Fichte, Johann Gottlieb, 653, 895
Ficino, Marsilio, 303
Fifth Republic, French, 535
Filmer, Robert, 457–58, 462, 468, 472–74,
    481, 482, 484, 485, 503, 515
"filtration," 599
financial aristocracy, 796
financial status, Roman freedom and, xiii
Findlay, J. N., 654
First Empire, French, 636
First International, 775, 896
First National Bank, 614
First Punic War, 120, 146
First Treatise (Locke), 246, 458, 474, 478, 486,
    515
Flanders, 263, 308
flattery, 304
flood, 336
Florence, 265, 268, 291–92, 354, 355, 359,
    360–64, 614, 834
  constitution of, 361–62
  guberno largo adopted by, 387
  lawmaking in, 724
  populism in, 387
  republic in (1527–30), 359
  superstition in, 369
  trade by, 361, 363
  1291 revolt in, 361
florilegia, 220
force, 370–71, 507
Ford, Henry, xi, 670
foreigners, 94, 110
  in Athens, 10, 13
  in Rome, 574
formal class, 687
Forms, 59
Fortescue, John, 220
Fortnightly Review, 706
fortuna (chance), 364, 369, 371, 379–81, 384,
    577, 631
Foundation of Modern Political Thought (Skinner),
    xii

founders, U.S., 28, 496, 577–615, 678
  arbitrary taxation and, 477
  boundaries to democracy erected by, 952
  capitalism and, 511
  Locke's influence on, 460, 579, 580, 581,
    582, 584
  Montesquieu's influence on, 504, 523,
    531, 592
  Rousseau read by, 576
  on separation of powers, 504
  Sidney's influence on, 500, 580, 581
  surprisingness of, 577
  well-ordered republic desired by, 180
Fourier, Charles, 785, 880, 886, 888–92,
    897, 900
Fourteenth Amendment, U.S., 610
Fourth Amendment, U.S., 610
Fourth Crusade, 227
Fourth Republic, French, 535, 636
Fox, Charles James, 621–22
Fragment on Government (Bentham), 696
France, 212, 213, 261, 262, 288, 363–64,
    404, 520, 522, 523, 583, 589–90, 611,
    798, 821
  as absolute monarchy, 323
  Algeria conquered by, 729, 731, 762, 763,
    862, 872–73, 969
  American colonies of, 749
  American Revolution supported by, 618,
    734
  association lacking in, 768
  clergy taxed in, 260
  in Cold War, 942
  communism strong in, 968
  in concordat with papacy, 961
  disgruntled army officers in, 968–69
  in disputes with pope, 262–63
  expanding political representation in, 843
  failure of democracy in, 741, 744, 745,
    767–68
  feudalism in, 281
  in Hundred Years' War, 191, 287,
    294–95
  in imperial competition, 809
  as launchpad of Marx's revolution, 785
  legal system of, 280–81
  Milan conquered by, 364, 366–67
  military-bureaucratic state in, 798, 799
  monarchs in, 305

nationalism in, 931

near-famine in, 732

rapidly changing governments in, 618, 636, 734

revolution of 1830 in, 730, 731, 795

Scotland assisted by, 344

sixteenth-century civil wars in, 319–20, 323

strong central government in, 751, 758

tradition of self-help lacking in, 758

voting rights in, 949

France bourgeoisie in, 798–99

Francis I, King of France, 308, 344

Franciscans, 227, 236, 245, 247, 278

Franco, Francisco, 914

Franco-Prussian War, 535, 799

Frankfurt, 831

Frankfurt school, 944

Franklin, Benjamin, 637, 741

Franks, 155, 196, 259, 865

fraternity, 535, 616, 617, 647

Frederick II, Emperor, 232, 233, 234–35, 236, 252–53, 258, 260, 261, 263, 280, 334, 849

death of, 265

Frederick Barbarossa, 235, 280, 334

Frederick the Great, King of Prussia, 357, 653–54, 883

Frederick the Wise, Elector of Saxony, 329, 330

Frederick William IV, King of Prussia, 772

freedom, 254, 460, 483, 554

of action, 251, 718–19

of assembly, 610

Athenian notions of, xiii, xvii, xxiii, 21, 22, 68, 94, 656, 667–68

as consciousness of necessity, 776

end of history and, 658, 660, 665, 670–71

equality and, 645, 761–62

Greek polis and, 692

happiness and, 698, 715–16

Hegel's account of development of, 658, 661–71, 776

in master-slave dialectic, 661

of mind, 659

Montesquieu on, 518

negative, 565–66

outward vs. inward, 670

of press, 972

reason and, 669

of religion, 444, 446, 610, 646, 693

Roman notions of, xiii, xxiii, 128–29, 169, 663, 670–71

as share in sovereign authority, xvii

of slaves, 87

in Sparta, 7

of speech, xxiii, 251, 444, 445, 610, 718, 926

Stoic version of, 662–64

of thought, 718

Freedom of a Christian, The (Luther), 337–38

free love, 351

free markets, xviii, 812

alienating effect of, 780, 781–82, 783

anarchy of, 880, 883–84, 892, 935

regulations in, 908

free men, xxiv

in Athens, 10

free people, in Roman politics, xiii

free-rider problem, 55, 437–38

free trade, 695

free will, 153, 168, 176, 311, 449–50

French Declaration of the Rights of Man and the Citizen, 644–45, 696

French Empire, 844, 853

assimilation of overseas territories in, 844–45

French Republic, 618

French Revolution, 129, 170, 260, 383, 489, 496, 589, 611, 616–51, 653, 656, 702, 703, 734, 739, 759, 785, 815, 886

American Revolution as precursor of, 638, 639, 645–46

Burke's attack on, 579, 580, 618–34, 638, 767–68, 916

Burke's expectations for, 632

as changing idea of revolution, 843

citizen virtue in, 665

difficulties of establishing constitution after, 764

as divine punishment, 634–36

exportation of, 636

failures of, 636

Fox's support for, 622

historiography of, 616

increasing radicalization of, 920–21

Kant as responsible for, 682

French Revolution (*continued*)
    Marx's study of, 794
    as "modernizing," 535, 654, 656
    nationalism invented by, 617, 931
    as novelty, 645–46
    Paine and, 637, 638
    rising expectations in, 991
    Rousseau's influence on, 534, 535–36, 636
    secularization in, 979, 980
    spread of, 765
    strong central state and numerous local
        polities sought by, 576
    the Terror and violence in, 632, 637, 640,
        641–42, 665, 682, 730, 734, 768, 769,
        810, 842, 925
    as utopian, 627
Freud, Sigmund, 189, 440, 536, 716, 811,
    817, 831, 832, 944
    on violence, 642, 928, 933, 997
friendship, in family, 759
Führerdemokratie, 834, 835
Fukuyama, Francis, xxi
fundamentalism, 841, 979, 987–90
    Islamic, 873–74
Furet, Fançois, 616

Gaetani family, 261, 264
gales of creative destruction, 961
Galileo Galilei, 77, 405, 407, 416, 420
Gandhi, Mohandas, 999
Garden of Eden, 240
Garibaldi, Giuseppe, 871
Gaul, Gauls, 120, 368
Gelasius I, Pope, 215–16, 259, 271, 333, 341
gender, xviii, 879
    see also men; women
General Motors, 898
generals, 297
general will, 560–64, 566–71, 598, 673,
    736, 960
generosity, 146
Genesis, Book of, 159, 472, 474, 541
Geneva, 343, 344, 345, 346, 532–34, 556, 574
genital mutilation, 1007
Genoa, 618
genocide, 816, 1004, 1007
    Stalin's use of, 941, 942–43
Gentile, Giovanni, 915, 917, 931, 936, 937,
    938, 939

gentry, 510–11
geometry, 76–77, 414, 417, 421, 422, 423,
    424
George III, King of England, 125, 579–80,
    585, 589, 612, 626, 734
Georgia, 1009
Germanic kings, 204, 279
Germanic tribes, 201, 212
German knights, 330
German princes, 264–65
Germans, in U.S., 751
German Social Democracy (Russell), 923
German Social Democratic Party (SDP),
    838, 839, 933
German states, 499
"German World," 671–72
Germany, 196, 212, 235, 329, 340, 363–64,
    386, 519, 528, 652–54, 798, 816, 919,
    976, 989
    anti-Semitism in, 930–31
    civil war in, 218
    constitution of, 384–85
    end of Wilhelmine regime in, 801
    feudalism in, 281
    public service in, 965
    Reformation in, xxiii
    states and statelets in, 349
    taxes for churches in, 212
    unification of, 196, 692, 795
    welfare state created in, 801
Gerson, Jean, 257, 289
Gettysburg Address, 21, 588
Ghibellines, 265, 286
Gianotti, Donato, 499–500
Gibbon, Edward, 213
Gibraltar, Straits of, 853
gift relationship, 903
Giles of Rome (Egidius Colonna), 285
Glaucon, 44, 47, 49, 56–58, 64, 69, 437
globalization, 990–93, 1005
Glorious Revolution, 200, 459, 511, 579,
    607, 617, 624, 625, 765
glory, 165
gluttons, 244
Gnosticism, 160–61
Gobineau, comte de, 864–65, 930
God, 8, 31, 75–76, 166, 167, 175, 195, 197,
    204, 212, 215–16, 220, 239, 245, 274,
    425, 436–37, 438, 448, 461, 464, 465,

466–67, 471, 481, 503, 514, 517, 618, 826
  belief in, 431
  death of, 467, 629
  de Maistre's terrifying view of, 635
  donation of, 472, 476
  as eternal, 240–41
  as fount of authority, 274
  freedom as submission to will of, 671
  Hegel's view of, 658, 664, 670, 671
  history as work of, 670
  human culture and, 658
  kings given authority by, 220–21
  laws given by, 240–41
  and progress of equality, 743
  Reason and, 295
  revelation of, 232
  universe governed by, 199, 222
  utilitarianism and, 712
gods, Greek, 29–30
Godwin, William, 641, 643
Goethe, Johann Wolfgang von, 715
gold, 314, 549, 882, 899
Golden Bull of 1356, 259
Golden Bull of 1365, 278
Golden Lie, 59, 61, 62
Golden Rule, 208, 241
Gompers, Samuel, 881
gonfaloniere, 361
good, 45–46, 60, 427–30, 433, 711
  Aristotle's conception of, 427, 429
good life, 78, 243
good works, 293, 331
Gordon Riots, 641
Gorgias, 38–47, 69
Gorgias (Plato), 32, 34, 35, 38–47, 48, 50, 51, 53, 102, 118
gospel, law in, 242
gospel of work, 883
gospels, 202, 330
Gothic balance, 505 558–64, 572,
govern.
  .nt" (James Mill), 697
  .nment of laws not men, 91

governments, world, 979
Gracchus, Caius, 115
Gracchus, Tiberius, 115, 140
grace, 154, 237, 238, 249
  nature and, 231
  salvation and, 325, 328, 331
Gramsci, Antonio, 829–30
grand conseil, 532
Grand Council, 363
grandi, 363, 387
great apes, 544
Great Awakening, 595
Great Britain, 181, 522, 607
  army of, 511–12
  Bentham's prison reform and, 696
  centralized state in, 188
  citizenship in, 95
  in Cold War, 942
  as constitutional monarchy, 323
  economic growth in, 795
  established church in, 66
  expanding political representation in, 843
  feudalism in, 188, 281
  foreign policy of, 1009
  in imperial competition, 809
  imperialism of, 508, 749, 750, 762–63, 809, 816, 843, 845, 853, 854, 859, 860–61, 866, 869
  India ruled by, 620, 721, 762–63, 860–62, 875, 892, 999–1000
  IRA campaign against, 988
  Irish famine and, 732, 901
  nineteenth-century politics of, 796
  parliamentary road to socialism in, 801–2
  politicians des.   720
          e in, 965
     .lization in, 986
  social hierarchies of, 764
  socialist revolution foreseen in, 919
  universal suffrage in, 801
  voting rights in, 951, 963
  worldwide competition with, 798
great chain of being, 215
Great Community, 954, 955
Great Council, 387
Great Depression, 929

greatest happiness principle, 696
great-man theory of history, 664, 669–70, 827
great-man view of politics, 573
greatness of spirit, 145
Great Schism, 298, 321
Greece, xxiv, 5–30, 213, 366, 515–16, 763, 978
    conquering of, 5
    political terminology from, 5
    rhetoric in, 38–39
    under Rome, 5, 366
    tyranny replaced by democracy in, 9
    warfare in, 10, 11, 12
    see also Persian War
greed, 244, 296, 478, 852, 953
Greek Asia Minor, 121
Greek Christianity, 155
Greek city-states, 193, 282, 978
    citizenship in, 132, 133, 195
    civil wars among, 668
    constitutions of, 8, 9, 18, 32, 33, 34, 72, 82, 92–93, 95–96, 97–99
    extinction of independence in, 71
    liberty in, 665
    peace and, 175
    representation in, 605
    umbrella government proposed for, 1003
    uniting of, 601
    see also polis
Greek language, 197, 230, 292, 414
Greek Orthodox church, 197–98
    Catholic dispute with, 989
    church-state relationship viewed by, 198
    duties of subjects and rulers viewed by, 198
    secular and spiritual authorities viewed by, 198
Green, T. H., 952
Gregory VI, Pope, 218
Gregory VII, Pope, 217–18, 252
Gregory IX, Pope, 260
Gregory XI, Pope, 287–88
Grotius, Hugo, 559, 573, 584, 854–55, 856–57
Groundwork of the Metaphysics of Morals (Kant), 682
growth, 957
Guelphs, 265, 286

Guicciardini, Francesco, 359
guided democracies, xvii–xviii, 818
guilds, 196, 689
guild socialism, 884
guillotine, 617
guilt, 541
Guizot, François, 500, 738–40, 770, 788, 901
gulags, 924
gunpowder, 412
Gutenberg, Johannes, 330, 405
Gyges, 56, 57

Habsburg family, 257, 307, 309, 355, 360
hajj, 877
Hamilton, Alexander, 523, 591, 613–14
    commercial and monarchical U.S. desired by, 578, 593
    Jefferson vs., xx, 578, 605, 613, 615
    see also Federalist, The
Hanc sanctam, 289
Hannibal, 113, 121, 376, 900
Hanovers, 511, 512, 870
happiness, 110, 316, 427, 438, 552–53, 588, 860, 933
    afterlife and, 157
    Aristotle on, 79, 80, 140
    Cicero on, 140
    freedom and, 698, 715–16
    justice and, 65, 79, 80
    as possible in slaves, 662–63
    revolutions as costly to, 627–28
    in utilitarianism, 672, 677, 708, 712–14, 715
    virtue and, 304
Hare, Thomas, 723
harm principle, 718
Harrington, James, 498, 499–513, 515, 517, 524, 530–31, 580, 612
    classical statecraft defended by, 418
    Harrison, Frederic, 982
    heaven, 416
    heavenly, 416
Hegel, Georg, 55,
    267, 405, 55.
    728, 770, 872, 8.

background of, 652–53

Burke's similarity to, 673

on capitalism, 992

constitutional monarchy pictured by, 782

contradictions in, 692–93

on development of freedom, 658, 661–69, 776

development of society studied by, 655, 658

estrangement in work of, 659, 776

fascism influenced by, 936

French Revolution as seen by, 535, 654, 656

Geist seen as guiding history by, 657–58, 725, 728, 790, 827

on happiness, 672–73

on hero in history, 664, 669–70, 827

individualism and statism in work of, 933

Kant vs., 663, 682, 683, 684, 689–90, 691

Marx influenced by, 655, 675, 678, 775–77, 779, 781, 782, 783, 784, 827, 906

master-slave dialectic of, 658–62, 666, 678

metaphysics of, 654–55, 657–58, 693, 769, 827, 984

on morality, 673–74, 681–83

Popper's criticism of, 922

on practical vs. theoretical knowledge, 659, 674–75

property rights defended by, 659, 675–82, 781, 782

religious views on, 657–58

on representative systems, 688–89

reputation of, 654–56, 657

as retrospective, 403

on utilitarianism, 677–78

"hegemonic" political culture, 830

Heidegger, Martin, 37, 872, 912, 940

Heine, Heinrich, 895

Hellenistic monarchies, 5, 15, 121, 194, 205

subjected territories of, 15

helots, 7, 24, 67, 88

Henry, Patrick, 595

Henry II, King of France, 344

Henry III, Emperor, 218

Henry IV, Emperor, 217–18, 252, 261

Henry V, King of England, 295

Henry VII, King of England, 507, 515

Henry VIII, King of England, 302, 308, 311, 322, 851

Luther condemned by, 312

made head of Church of England, 311, 323, 324

Henry of Luxemburg, 257, 266, 273, 283

heralds, 207

Herder, Johann Gottfried von, 927

hereditary principalities, 366

hereditary rule, 96, 639, 644, 650

heresy, 158, 229, 248–52, 338

coercive suppression of, 184, 251–53, 302, 416–17

More on, 302

Hermes Trismegistus, 299–300

Hermias, 72, 74, 75, 102

Herodotus, xii, 111, 983

accuracy of, 14

aristocratic sympathies of, 14

hierarchy, 61–62, 238, 240, 407

High Middle Ages, 849

Hindus, 985

Hippo, 151, 152, 163

Hiroshima, 997

historical materialism, 906, 934

Histories (Herodotus), 14

Histories (Polybius), 126

Histories of Rome (Livy), 381, 383, 412

history, 414, 510–13

end of, 658, 660, 665, 670–71, 910

great-man theory of, 664, 669–70, 827

materialist conception of, *see* materialism, historical

myth vs., 8

prehistorical stage in, 793–94

progress in, 793

purpose of, 656

"History of Civilization in Europe, The" (Guizot), 739

History of Mediaeval Political Theory in the West, A (Carlyle and Carlyle), xi

History of Political Theory (Sabine), xi

History of the Peloponnesian War (Thucydides), 414, 417

History of Western Philosophy (Russell), xxi

Hitler, Adolf, 32, 37, 70, 105, 121, 182, 201, 258, 340, 573, 816, 835, 865, 940, 941, 995

racial theories of, 930

Hitler's Willing Executioners: Ordinary Germans and the Holocaust (Goldhagen), 815

Hobbes, Thomas, xx, xxiv, xxv, 56, 62–63, 70, 77, 117–18, 179, 242, 403, 406, 411–52, 457, 462, 464, 478, 594, 997, 1004, 1011
  as adjective, 357
  Aristotle's differences with, 106, 423, 426, 429, 430
  on civilization, 306
  on coercion, 338
  on democracy, 418
  in dispute with Church of England, 415
  as first political scientist, 405, 406, 407, 411–13, 414–15, 416, 672–73
  on human nature, 421, 424–26, 541
  liberty as viewed by, 499, 502, 503, 517, 518, 656, 663–64
  life of, 413–14
  Locke vs., 462, 467, 468, 475, 483, 494, 497
  monarchy defended by, 415, 419, 503
  on need for government, 179
  on obedience to sovereign, 180–81, 416–17, 438–45, 571, 673, 747
  original sin repudiated by, 179, 436, 537
  popular government and, 414
  possibility of abundance denied by, 805
  on power, 431–32, 847
  on property, 433, 855
  on religion, 448–50
  republicanism assaulted by, 497
  rights denied by, 443, 444–46, 855
  right to revolt denied by, 489
  Roman Catholic Church denounced by, 494
  Rousseau vs., 537, 541, 544, 548, 557–58, 559, 560, 561, 563, 564
  self-aggrandizement feared by, 598
  single sovereign required by, 441–42, 444–45, 450, 567, 673, 747
  skepticism of, 231
  on social contract, 407, 691
  on state of nature, 430–32, 436–38, 541, 817, 855
  on tyranny, 384, 497
  on violence, 642, 987–88
  on war of all against all, 432–35, 817
  on will, 168

  world government proposed by, 1003
  see also Leviathan
Hobhouse, L. T., 952
Hobson, J. A., 846, 868
Hoffman, Melchior, 353
Hogg, James, 331
Hohenstaufen emperors, 334, 849
Holland, 499, 607, 798, 851
  socialist revolution predicted for, 919
  toleration in, 492
Holocaust, 815, 913–14, 989, 1000
Holy Places, 849
Holy Roman Emperor, 216, 218
  election of, 290
Holy Roman Empire, 188, 191, 196, 309, 324, 484
  constitution of, 343
  creation of, 233, 234
  electors in, 639
  Italian city-states under, 667
  and meaning of "empire," 848–49
  papacy vs., 232–33, 258–60, 270, 271, 273–79, 288–89
  religious diversity in, 350
  Rome sacked by, 308, 322, 364
Holy Spirit, 198
Homer, 29–30, 44, 51
homicide, 358
homosexuality, 698
honesty, 269, 376
  Machiavelli on, 377–78
honor, in monarchy, 522
Hooke, Robert, 416
Hooker, Thomas, 487
hoplites, 15–16, 23, 60, 134
Horkheimer, Max, 831, 834
Hortensius (Cicero), 162
hospitals, 757
household gods, 980
House of Commons, British, 529, 621, 622, 949
House of Lords, British, 455, 504, 608, 860, 861
House of Representatives, U.S., 609, 734
"How Rulers Should Keep Their Promises" (Machiavelli), 377–78
Hubmaier, Balthasar, 352
humane letters, 292
human fortune, changeability of, 296

humanism, 316, 329
    literary expression of, 293, 309
humanism, humanists, 291–320
    Cicero admired by, 137
    civic, 291–92
    distinctions among, 293
    Scholasticism attacked by, 292, 293, 294,
        304
humanitarianism, 177
    interventions of, 994, 1005–7
    war and, 306
humanity:
    equality of, 429
    religion of, 630, 649, 707, 979, 981–84
    as self-created, 300
human nature, xix, 20, 411, 649
    as contradictory, 717
    factional impulses in, 602
    Hobbes on, 421, 424–26, 541
    immaturity in, 543–44
    as infinitely malleable, 886
    innate aggressiveness in, 997–98
    Locke on, 467
    Machiavelli's pessimism about, 375, 381,
        382–83, 537
    medieval view of, 189–90
    Mill as skeptic of, 727–28
    modern view of, 189
    religion and, 189–90
    Rousseau on, 534, 537, 538, 541, 553–
        54, 727
    secularism and, 189
    socialized, 727–28
    teleological understanding of, 465
    in utilitarianism, 711, 727
human rights, 500
    as absent in antiquity, 193
    democracy and, 19–20, 24
    humanitarian intervention and, 1005–7
    Paine's defense of, 639, 643–45
Humboldt, Wilhelm von, 715
Hume, David, 189, 388, 486, 512, 534, 581,
        612, 613
    classical statecraft defended by, 418
    hereditary rulers defended by, 639
    intellectual case against revolution made
        by, 627, 633–34
    on property rights, 210
Hundred, 361–62

Hundred Years' War, 191, 287, 294–95,
    298
Hungary, 816
hunter-gatherer communities, 435, 479, 547,
    850, 853, 855–56
hunting, 74, 317, 374
Huntington, Samuel, 987
Hus, Jan, 290, 321, 329
husbands, 74, 82, 84–85, 87, 94
Hussein, Saddam, 986
Hussite rebellion, 289, 370
Huxley, Aldous, 61–62, 63, 318, 761, 817,
    830, 834, 911, 943
"hyphenated Americans," 134–35
hypocrisy, social lure of, 550

Ibn Khaldun, 214
Iceland, 855
iconoclasts, 346, 350
Idea for a Universal History with a Cosmopolitan
    Purpose (Kant), 859–60
idealism, 657–58
"Idea of a Perfect Republic, The" (Hume),
    612
Idea of a University, The (Newman), 109
ideas, impact of, 790–91
ideology, 913
Iliad (Homer), 29–30, 44, 661
immigration, 583, 589, 762, 764
immiseration, 792, 797, 802, 828
immortality, 643
imperialism, see empires, imperialism
Imperialism: The Highest Stage of Capitalism
    (Lenin), 867–68, 919
imprudence, 709
Index auctorum et librorum prohibitorum, 266–67,
    519
    Machiavelli on, 356, 386
India, 205, 406, 583, 590, 697, 700, 747,
    869, 876, 991, 1005
    British rule of, 205, 620, 721, 762–63,
        859, 860–62, 875, 892, 999–1000
    economy of, 794
India House, 703
India Mutiny, 700
Indian Ocean, 406
individualism:
    atomistic, 954–55
    in Hegel, 933

individualism (*continued*)
    Tocqueville's ambiguous views of, 710–11, 737, 755–56, 761, 821, 823, 824, 825, 833
    in utilitarianism ethics, 699
individuality, 903
    in free market, 781
    in Marx's ideal society, 779, 827–28
    mass societies vs., 821–22
    Mill's distrust of, 710, 756, 826, 831–32, 833
individuals:
    classes vs., 960
    polis as logically prior to, 78, 107
Indochina, 969
Indonesia, 406
industrial mass production, 934
industrial revolution, xix, 794
    socialism born in, 881, 882, 990
industrial society, 651, 938
industry, 544, 547, 613–14, 810, 997
    globalization and, 992
    religion and, 979
    socialism and, 882–83
    in U.S., 751
inequality, 478
    common interest and, 568
    origin of, 537, 539–42, 545
    race-based, xviii
"Infinite," God as, 425
inflation, 583, 907
"inner-directed" individuals, 825
innocence, 207, 406
Innocent III, Pope, 234, 235, 260, 261, 262, 263
Innocent IV, Pope, 232, 260, 854
In Praise of Folly (Erasmus), 309–11
Inquisition, 492
Institutes of the Christian Religion (Calvin), 345
Institut für Sozialforschung, 831
insurance, 902
    in Athens, 10
insurgencies, 996
intelligence, 300, 378
interest groups, 674, 748
internalization, 716
internationalism, 818
international law, 207, 857
international relations, 433, 689, 869

investiture controversy, 216–19
IRA, 988
Iran, 66, 801, 864, 986, 993
Iraq, 986, 993
Ireland, 508, 762, 893
    famine in, 732, 901
    transferable votes in, 724
Irish Rebellion, 513
iron, 549
iron law of oligarchy, 837–89
iron smelting, 826
irrationalism, 911, 912–18, 927, 928, 934–37
Isabella of Portugal, 307
isegoria, xiii, 68
Isidore, Saint, 229
Isidore of Seville, 243
Islam, Muslims:
    anti-Western form of, 872
    democracy and, 818–19
    fundamentalist, 873–74, 987
    missionaries to, 227
    political, 878
    as resting on revelation, 231
    rise of, 213
    Sunni-Shia split in, 989
    in U.S., 985
Islamic nationalism, 995
Isocrates, 73, 1003
Israel, 66, 502, 509
    in conflict with Arabs, 989
Israelites, 7–8, 869–70, 929–30
Italian city-states, 277, 279–87, 507, 667
    authority of people popular in, 233–34
    authority over, 281
    as republics, 191, 196, 256, 272
Italy, 187, 322, 492, 519, 528, 762, 871
    armistice of, 914
    attempts to unify, 235, 257
    church property in, 324
    church-state alliance in, 810
    city republics of, 257–58
    civil war in, 218
    communism in, 968
    fascism in, 816, 834, 839, 912–13, 915–16, 937–38
    Machiavelli's desire for liberation of, 379, 381, 404
    nineteenth-century nationalism in, 365

Renaissance, xxiii, 363–64, 600
reunification of, 233
unification of, 371–72, 381
ius ad personam, 209
ius civile, 206
ius honorum, 133
ius in rem, 209
ius suffragii, 133

Jackson, Andrew, 745, 754
Jacobins, 636, 730
jahili society, 877
James, William, 755
James I, King of England, 490
James II, King of England, 455, 456, 457, 459, 460, 488, 489, 500, 512, 513, 623
Japan, 986
Japanese Americans, internment in U.S., 558
Jay, John, 594, 599
Jefferson, Thomas, 500, 517, 518, 578, 596, 610–15, 624, 949, 973
  agrarian society desired by, 511, 578
  Burke's *Reflections* denounced by, 626
  Declaration of Independence written by, 578, 580, 581, 584–90, 637
  as Democratic Republican, 583–84
  on empire of liberty, 515, 586, 612, 693, 845
  equality defended by, 639
  on fate of Native Americans, 857
  French Revolution as seen by, 625
  George III assailed by, 579–80, 585
  Hamilton vs., xx, 578, 605, 613, 615
  idealism of, 581–82
  Paine supported by, 638
  on pure vs. representative democracy, 97, 600, 611, 705, 819, 947
  revolutions desired by, 491, 590–91, 611
  Sidney admired by, 499
  tyranny of majority feared by, 611, 746
  on "ward republics," 520, 583, 611, 819, 970
Jehovah, 448
Jena, Battle of, 653, 654
Jena, University of, 653
Jerusalem, 153, 216, 933
Jesuits, 859

Jesus Christ, 157, 160, 163, 197, 202, 204, 241, 276, 417
  in decent into hell, 300
  Hegel's understanding of, 666
  Second Coming of, 207–8, 210, 326, 351, 510
  on "Two Swords," 271
Jews, 7–8, 156, 208, 248, 425, 930
  church's authority over, 249, 253
  dietary laws of, 690
  God's gift of laws to, 241
  Greek philosophy preserved by, 214
  Islamic tolerance of, 213–14
  Luther's denunciation of, 340
  missionaries to, 227
  Nazi attempted extermination of, 815, 913–14
  as perpetual slaves, 253
  persecution of, 156–58, 214, 815, 913–14, 975, 989, 1000
  as "rootless cosmopolitans," 931
  tolerance of, 248–49, 581
  in U.S., 751, 762, 985
Joan of Arc, 295
Job, Book of, 428
John, King of England, 202, 260, 263
John, Saint, 163, 657
John II, King of France, 295
John XXII, Pope, 273, 288
John XXIII, Pope, 289
John of Leiden, 326, 352–53, 923
John of Paris, 271
John of Salisbury, 193, 219–23
John of Saxony, 341, 343
Johnson, Samuel, 619
Judaea, 157
Judaism:
  Fall in, 237
  as resting on revelation, 231
Judeo-Christian tradition, 984, 985
judiciary, 39, 103, 130, 504, 528, 690
  checking power of, 607
Julius Caesar, 115–16, 118, 127, 128, 131, 135, 137, 154, 221, 305, 508, 605
Julius II, Pope, 309, 329, 364, 372, 380, 381
July Revolution, 730, 731, 795
June Days, 733
jurisdiction, 853
jury service, 725, 751, 949

jus gentium, 158, 206, 207, 464, 851
    imperialism and, 850
    law of nature vs., 857
jus naturae, 464
justice, 145, 285, 712, 959
    Aquinas on, 251
    Aristotle on, 70, 74, 79–80, 101, 106
    in Athens, 23, 24
    Augustine on, 139, 149, 174–75, 179–80,
        181, 221
    bourgeois, 787–88
    as cardinal virtue, 63
    Cicero on, xxiii, 139, 145–46, 165, 284
    classical definition of, 50–51
    definition of, 423, 424
    democracy and, 101
    dike vs., 43–44, 64
    of economic activities, 89–91
    efficiency united with, 983
    equality and, 314
    expediency vs., 358
    as fairness, 977
    as fulfilling obligations, 438
    as giving every man his due, 50–51
    happiness and, 65, 79, 80
    natural law theories of, 57
    as necesssary for republic, 139
    in oligarchy, 101
    origins of, 56–57
    Plato on, 38, 39–40, 42–44, 47–48,
        49–65, 70, 79, 119
    policing of, 55
    rights in, 55, 895–96
    as rule of stronger, 49–50, 52–53
    security and, 714
    self-interest vs., 55, 56, 469
    as skill, 51
    in socialism, 895–96
    universal standards of, 165–66
    in utilitarianism, 714–15
    varieties of, xxiii
justification by faith, 331
Justinian, Emperor of Rome, 36, 187, 204,
    205, 220, 274, 280, 283, 303, 343, 438,
    523, 559
just limits, 857
just prices, 90
just war, 149, 175, 178–79, 247–48, 308,
    817, 852
    slavery and, 87, 481

kabbalah, 300, 301
Kabyle, 763
kallipolis, 33, 48, 59
Kant, Immanuel, 69, 267, 268, 523, 546,
    563, 736, 1006
    as anti-imperialist, 859–60
    ethics of, 671
    Hegel vs., 663, 682, 684, 685, 689–90,
        691
    marriage as seen by, 684
    morality analyzed by, 682
    perpetual peace as project of, 691, 859,
        860, 1000, 1003, 1004
    on state as based on contract, 685, 691
    world government proposed by, 1003
Kapital, Das (Marx), 706, 771, 787, 899, 909,
    959
Kautsky, Karl, 919
Kenya, 996
Keramaikos cemetery, 21
Kerensky, Allexander, 918–19
Khomeini, Ayatollah, 801, 986
King James Bible, 330, 869
kings, kingship, 98, 609
    as answerable to lay body, 201
    authority granted by God to, 220–21
    church's moral guidance and, 250
    in feudal societies, 202
    Filmer on, 515
    governed territory owned by, 209–10
    popes vs., 66, 200, 202–4, 222
    of Rome, 131, 141–42, 154, 281
    tyrants vs., 221
Kingsley, Charles, 982
Kipling, Rudyard, 844
kleptocrats, 841, 908
knights, 298–99
Knipperdolling, Bernhard, 352–53
Koran, 213, 873–74, 877
Kropotkin, Peter, 880, 894, 896–97
kulaks, 561, 803

labor, 314, 476–77, 478–80, 686, 796
    alienating effect of, 778–79
    division of, 58–59, 216, 334, 337
    freedom of, 693
    labor power vs., 786
    necessity of, 662
    Owen's idea of receipts for, 886–87
    ownership and, 855

possession taken by, 679
as self-expression, 900
slavery vs., 678
uniformity of conditions of, 826
unproductive, 909
labor as social duty, 315
laborers, skilled vs. unskilled, 802
labor power, 786
Labour Party, U.K., 802, 953
laissez-faire, 503, 883, 937, 939, 952
Lamarck, Jean-Baptiste, 864
Lamentation on the Troubles of France (Christine de
    Pizan), 296
land, private ownership of, 793, 797
landed gentry, 629
landlords, 686, 881
Land Ordinances, U.S., 845
land ownership, pattern of, 507
land reform, 707
land tenure, 201–2, 210, 516
language, 544
    origin of, 542, 545–46
Las Casas, Bartolomé de, 852
lassez-faire, 129
last days, 350, 351, 510
Last Judgment, 450
late capitalism, 865
Lateran Council, 217
latifundia, 85
Latin, 155, 197, 224, 414
Latin America, 816
Latin script, 870
Lauderdale, Lord, 623
law, 7, 236, 566, 671
    as aimed at common good, 254
    Aquinas on, 240–44
    Bentham's positivist theory of, 696
    Blackstone's theory of, 696
    Cicero on, 143, 206
    definition of, 423
    as eternal, 240–44
    God's law and, 158
    Hobbes on, 418–19, 465
    Marx's lack of theory on, 771
    medieval varieties of, 240–44
    medieval view of, 192, 204–7
    positive, 342, 457–58, 467, 468, 515
    Rousseau's approach to, 573–76
    rule of, 64, 119, 276
law of anticipated reactions, 839

law of nature, 143, 158, 536
laws, 488
    animals obedience to, 378
    decrees vs, 384
    see also ordini
Laws (Cicero), 120, 137
Laws (Plato), 33, 38, 106, 143, 498
lawyers, 219, 229, 748
lay investiture, 217, 218–19
leaders, 833–34
leadership, cult of, 915
leadership democracy, 835–37
League for Industrial Democracy, 971
league of nations, utilitarian hope for,
    1003–4
Lebensphilosophie, 773
legal positivism, 283
legal systems, unity of, 241–42
legislature, 39, 103, 130, 498, 504, 528, 573,
    592, 690, 838
    checking power of, 607
Leicester, Earl of, 513
Lenin, Vladimir, 97, 467, 822, 914, 918, 925,
    934, 941
    dictatorship of proletariat established by,
        802
    dissent rejected by, 926
    on imperialism as last stage of capitalism,
        846, 865–68
    international revolution desired by, 920
    Marxism of, 922–24
    in return to Russia, 770
Leo III, Pope, 196, 849
Leo IX, Pope, 217, 218
Leo X, Pope, 309, 329, 359, 364, 371, 381
Leon, Kingdom of, 288
Leonidas, 16
Lesbos, 23
Leseur (abbé), 731
Lesseps, Ferdinand de, 648, 983
Letter Concerning Toleration (Locke), 279, 324–
    25, 462, 492, 494, 644
Letters on a Regicide Peace (Burke), 623
Letters to a Noble Lord (Burke), 623
Levasseur, Thérèse, 533, 534
Leviathan (Hobbes), xx, xxv, 56, 70, 77, 405,
    411, 414, 415, 502, 509, 510, 541, 594
    Christian Commonwealth in, 447–49
    location of authority as unity of state in,
        416–17

Leviathan (Hobbes) (*continued*)
"problem of order" in, 424–26
as pure political philosophy, 117–18
science and, 421–24
Leviathan Drawn Out with a Hook, 428
lex divina, 464
lex naturae, 158, 206, 207
liberal democracies, 48, 841, 947
accountability to public of, xviii
civil rights and market freedoms in, 665
core values of, xviii
culture and, 863
as dictatorship of bourgeoisie, 802–3
erosion of civil liberties in, 816
Florence vs., 360
Hegel's state vs., 656
legitimacy of, 901
Lockean religious ethic and, 467
as lowest-common-denominator politics, 824
Mill's desire for, 705
as nontyrannical, 947–48
as only true form of democracy, 975–76
Protestantism and, 323
technology and, 863
totalitarianism's Cold War battle with, 942
triumph in 1990s of, 818
voting rights in, xiii–xiv, xvii
welfare state of, 903–4
liberal democracy:
Schumpeter's concerns about, 959–60
in World War II, 941
liberal fascism, 928
Liberalism and Social Action (Dewey), 952
liberals, liberalism, 64, 445–46, 552
American sense of, 952
"big" society feared by, 810
conservative basis for, 728, 756
corporatism and, 937
democracy as compatible with, 964
democracy vs., 947, 976
equality and, 937
French church condemned by, 633
of New Deal, 937
patriotism vs., 190
roots of, 695
utilitarianism vs., 860
libertarians, 471

"Liberté des anciens comparée à celle des modernes, La" (Constant), 581
liberticide, 725
liberty, 386, 517–18, 588
ancient vs. modern, 518, 581, 656, 665, 667, 947
citizenship and, 518
duties and, 709
in England, 523, 528–29, 530, 580
in Florence, 360
in French Revolution, 535, 616, 617, 647
Mill's case for, 709
negative, 129–30, 141, 445, 526, 952
positive, 130, 952
Roman, 128, 141, 280, 282, 416, 547, 580, 656
Rousseau on, 564–72
slavery and, 582
of tribes in Gaul, 368
U.S. Constitution's preservation of, 607
varieties of, xxiii
libido, 166–67, 175, 189
Library of Congress, 585
licentium docendi, 228
licentium studendi, 228
Life (Giovanni Francesco Pico della Mirandola), 301
life expectancy, 976
life insurance, 624
Lincoln, Abraham, Gettysburg Address of, 21
Linnaeus, Carolus, 864
Lippmann, Walter, 824, 840, 913, 958
Lipset, Seymour Martin, 104
Lisbon earthquake, 170, 635
literacy, 405, 544
and communications revolution, xix
literature, 293, 309
Livy, 111, 124, 136, 381, 383, 412, 502
Locke, John, 56, 85, 181, 246, 324, 406, 445, 453–96, 500, 503, 513, 515, 517, 542, 559, 575, 594
Aristotle vs., 466
authoritarian views of, 453
colonial constitution written by, 582
as disciple of Aquinas, 255
on education, 109
exile of, 456, 458, 487
Hobbes vs., 462, 467, 468, 475, 483, 494, 497

human nature as viewed by, 467
medicine studied by, 453–54
on morality, 465–66
on natural law, 464, 465–72, 490, 495, 560
on nature of church, 279, 324–25, 492
on passive obedience, 201
property rights defended by, 462–63, 468, 470–72, 475–82, 659, 679, 855–56, 973
religious liberty endorsed by, 453
revolutions justified by, 255, 341, 342, 349, 488–91, 631
Shaftesbury's influence on, 454
on social contract, 407
on state of nature, 683–84
toleration endorsed by, 453, 454–55, 456–57, 458, 466, 491–96, 817
U.S. founders influenced by, 460, 579, 580, 581, 582, 584
Lombard, Peter, 227, 229
Lombards, Lombardy, 197, 217, 279, 849
London, 767, 867
London and Westminster Review, 703
lonely crowd, 755, 756, 822
Lonely Crowd, The (Riesman), 755, 825, 944
Long Walls, 28
Looking Backwards (Bellamy), 315, 881, 884, 897–99
looting, 766–67
Lords, 103
lords spiritual, 506
Lord's Supper, 350
lords temporal, 506
Lorenzetti, Ambrogio, 286–87
Lorenzo, Piero di, 362, 363
Louis XII, King of France, 355, 367
Louis XIV, King of France, xiv, 305, 455, 742, 891
Louis XV, King of France, 305, 520
Louis XVI, King of France, 520, 625, 632, 637, 730, 734
Louis XVIII, King of France, 646, 730
Louisiana Purchase, 596, 612
Louis of Guyenne (dauphin), 296, 297
Louis Philippe I, King of France, 730, 731, 732, 754
love, Augustine on, 166–67
loyalty, 92–93, 376, 385

Lucca, 445, 497, 499, 502
Lucian, 312
luck, European immigrants and, 828
see also chance
Lucretia, 173–74
Ludwig of Bavaria, 257, 272–73, 277, 288–89
Luther, Martin, 119, 291, 344–45, 355
Augustine's influence on, 321
on authority, 335–40, 352
background of, 327–28
biblical translations advocated by, 330
on church-state relations, 332–35
on coercion, 337–38, 346
death of, 343
Erasmus's disputes with, 311
excommunication of, 332
Henry VIII's condemnation of, 312
Münster uprising inspired by, 352
on necessity of law, 326, 336–37
passive obedience defended by, 333, 489
Peasants' War inspired by, 350
resistance theory of, 339, 340–44, 348, 349, 451
on salvation, 328
theses nailed to church door by, 327, 328, 329, 331–32, 405
Lutheran Church, 689
Luxemburg, Rosa, 611
Lyceum, 72
Lycurgus, 60, 73, 108, 121, 123, 124, 125–26, 140, 501
lying, 59, 682
Lykian League, 28, 195, 523
Lysander, 27, 125

Macaulay, T. B., 698
Macbeth (Shakespeare), xi–xii, 670
Macedon, 14, 28, 42, 71, 72, 73, 111–12, 121, 282
Macedonian Wars, 112, 121
Machiavelli, Niccolò, xxiv, 102, 124, 125, 291, 354–89, 416, 418, 423, 499, 501, 505, 509, 510, 511, 515, 552, 565, 574, 577, 860, 919, 947
as adjective, 357
animus toward papacy, 385–86
as anti-Scholastic, 294
arrest and torture of, 356

Machiavelli, Niccolò (*continued*)
  Cicero mocked by, 137, 378
  claims to originality of, 405, 411–13
  on class warfare, 788, 834
  on conquests, 369
  on courage, 147
  democracy disdained by, xiv
  exempla used by, 293, 297, 365, 412
  on honesty, 377–78
  on human gullibility, 834
  impact of, 357
  Italy's liberation as hope of, 379, 381, 404
  lessons in past sought by, xix
  liberty as viewed by, 502
  on loyalty, 92–93
  on need for civic religion, 979–80
  papacy criticized by, 285
  pessimistic view of human nature of, 375, 381, 382–83, 537
  popular image of, 358, 367
  on popular republics, 507
  on power, 376–77
  on revolutions, 488, 489, 631
  on Roman freedom, 129
  Roman Republic's reinstatement desired by, 357, 359, 365, 412, 508, 600
  self-aggrandizement feared by, 598
  Socrates opposed by, xx
  types of republics distinguished by, 508
  tyranny as transition defended by, 286, 357, 573
  as unplaceable, 357–60
  utopian thinking of, 293
  violence and deceit recommended by, 118, 358, 413, 763, 837
  on virtues for princes, 292, 293, 370, 375, 376, 377, 522
  well-ordered Republic urged by, 180, 357, 359, 365
Machiavellian Moment, The (Pocock), xii
Macrobius, 165
Madison, Dolley, 597
Madison, James, 97, 131, 519, 523, 578, 591, 594–97, 624, 947
  as antiutopian, 597
  on checks and balances, 592
  as Democratic Republican, 583–84
  effect on U.S., 578
  factionalism feared by, 602–5, 748
  fears of sovereign people of, 617
  "politics lies in a mean" view of, 581, 610
  republic and democracy distinguished by, 600
  on size of republics, 600, 621
  tyranny of the majority feared by, 746
  see also Federalist, The
Mafia, 871
magistrates, 130, 281
Magna Carta, 202, 811
magna latrocinia, 181
magnanimity, 287
Magnifico, Lorenzo, 360
majority, tyranny of, *see* tyranny of the majority
Malesherbes, M. de, 730
Manchester, 992
Manchester school, 732
mandate of heaven, 835
Mandeville, Bernard, 513
Mandragola, 359
man-hunting, 481, 852
Mani, 159, 162
Manichaeism, 151, 153–54, 158–61, 162, 167
Manifest Destiny, 983
manual labor, 661, 891
manufacture of consent, 830
manufacturing, 612, 613–14
Mao Zedong, purges by, 839
Marat, Jean-Paul, 637
Marathon, Battle of, xii, 15–16
Marcuse, Herbert, 537, 832, 906–7, 944
Mardonius, 16
Mare liberum (Grotius), 854–55
Marie-Antoinette, 625, 632, 635, 640
Mark Antony, 116
market economy, 481
market freedoms, 665
market socialism, 778, 983–84
Marmontel, Jean-François, 701–2
marriage, 318, 684, 726
  alliances secured by, 307
  dissolution of, 271
marriage customs, 204–5
Marseilles, 307
Marshall, John, 591
Marshall, T. H., 904

Marsilius of Padua, 196–97, 257–58, 259, 267, 272–79, 281, 282, 284, 290, 303, 488, 499
  conciliar movement and, 288
  justice and, xxiii
  liberty and, xxiii
  Scholastic views of, 292
Marston Moor, Battle of, 513
Martin V, Pope, 289
Martov, Julius, 914
martyrdom, 199–200, 988
Marx, Eleanor, 774
Marx, Groucho, 661
Marx, Heinrich, 772, 931
Marx, Jenny (daughter), 774
Marx, Jenny von Westphalen (wife), 774
Marx, Karl, xxii, 267, 407, 534, 539, 547, 706, 769, 770–806, 822, 885, 890, 895, 935, 944, 982
  alienation theory of, 771, 774, 775–82
  anti-Semitism of, 914–15
  bourgeois rights disdained by, 645
  British rule in India defended by, 721, 763, 861
  capitalism's downfall predicted by, 651, 774, 781–82, 785, 793, 867, 874, 883, 907
  on determinants of historical change, 785
  as distorted by communist states, 911
  on division of labor, 58
  Engels's support of, 773, 882
  exploitation theory of, 785, 787–88
  fascism influenced by, 936
  four-stage myth of, 984
  on freedom as consciousness of necessity, 776
  French Revolution as seen by, 535, 646–47, 648
  Hegel's influence on, 655, 675, 678, 775–77, 779, 781, 782, 783, 784, 827, 906
  humanist strain in, 906
  on imperialism, 866–67
  nationalism approved as seen by, 866
  on nature of states, 771
  on necessity for democratic republic, 782–83
  Plato vs., 33
  Popper's criticism of, 922
  property seen as capital by, 687
  on reality as practical, 659
  religion seen as myth by, 630, 984
  on revolutions, 100, 101, 651, 771, 775, 776, 785, 788, 791, 793–95, 797–98, 800–802, 921
  as shaped by French Revolution, 616
  surplus value theory of, 777, 787–88
  unity of proletariat expected by, 825–26, 827, 828, 866, 882, 992–93, 1011
  utopian socialism dismissed by, 880, 884
  as vague about communist societies, 32
  on will, 924
  withering away of the state seen by, 32, 722, 771, 783, 784, 785, 802, 879, 894
Marx, Laura, 774
Marxism, xviii, 330, 818
  Catholicism and, 971
  French Revolution seen as bourgeois by, 646–47, 765
  globalization as seen by, 991–92
  mass society and, 827–32, 839
  on middle class, 105
  permanent revolution and, 491
  proletariat as seen by, 650, 651, 822, 825–26, 827, 882
  Saint-Simon as ancestor to, 648
  seeds of totalitarianism in, 922–24
  sexual unhappiness and, 536–37
  as surrogate religion, 982
  twentieth-century fate of, 770–71
Mary II, Queen of England, 456, 459, 460, 579
Maryland, 588
Mary Tudor, Queen of England, 308, 344
Mary Tudor (sister of Henry VIII), 308
Mass, 350
Massachusetts, 492, 595
mass culture, Marxist view of, 831
mass-elite opposition, xiv–xv, xxiv, 219, 894, 969
  in Athens, 9, 95
  in early U.S., 583–84
  in England, 313
  in French Revolution, 648–49
  leaders and followers in, 833–34
  in Marxism, 647–48
  mobilization of masses in, 817
  in modern society, 822–23, 832–37
  property rights and, 885

mass-elite opposition (*continued*)
  in Rome, 120, 130
  in social contract tradition, 550–51
  in stable societies, 766–67
  Tocqueville on, 765
masses, revolt of, 832–34
mass mobilization, 915
mass production, 820–21
mass society, 727, 769, 817, 818–27, 912, 915
  Democracy in America on, 742
  individuality vs., 821–22
  Marxism and, 827–32, 839
  as resting on fraud, 840
  revolution and, 830–34
  totalitarianism as phenomena of, 915
  in U.S., 824
masters, 74, 82, 85, 462
"master-slave dialectic," 658–62, 666, 678
materialism:
  dialectical, 906
  historical, 647, 771, 788, 790–91, 877, 906, 914
  of Hobbes, 425–26
  see also Marxism
mathematics, 214, 228, 414
matter, 76
Matthys, Jan, 353
Mau-Mau insurgency, 996
Maurras, Charles, 931–32, 934, 938
Maximilian, Emperor, 355, 849
McCarthyism, 529–30, 952
means of production, 792, 938, 993
  abolishing private ownership of, 803–4, 970
  property rights as dictating access to, 803
Mecca, 995
Medici, Cosimo de', 362
Medici, Lorenzo the Magnificent, 362, 364, 371
medicine, 213, 214, 228
Medicis, 129, 355–56, 359, 360, 361, 364–66
medieval political theory, xi
  authority in, 66
  usury condemned by, 91
Mediterranean, 845
Melanchthon, Philipp, 119, 326, 327, 341
Melchiorite missionaries, 353

Melos, 19–20, 23–25, 44, 93, 358–59, 413
men, xxiv
  in Athens, 10
  in Roman politics, xiii
Menippus Goes to Hell (Lucian), 312
mercantilism, 281, 282
Mercator projection, 869
mercenaries, 388
merchants, 298
meritocracy, 62, 517, 648–49, 938
  Socrates's defense of, 58
Merovingian kingdom, 188, 259
metaphysics, 32, 33, 65, 76–77, 214, 230, 385, 654–55, 657–58, 693, 769, 827, 984, 987
Mexico, 762, 850, 888
Michelet, Jules, 647
Michels, Robert, 838–89, 917, 933
middle class, 103, 104–5, 715, 740
  in U.S., 715, 746, 764
Middle East, 964, 995, 1009
Milan, 151, 156, 202, 211, 272, 280, 281, 361
  French conquest of, 364, 366–67
Milestones (Qutb), 871–72, 876–77
Miletus, revolt of, 14–15
military dictatorships, xvii–xviii, 618, 818
military service, 351
  in Rome, xiii
military technology, 405
militias, 617
Mill, James, 97, 695, 697, 700, 726, 727
  monarchies feared by, 598
Mill, John Stuart, xx, xxi, 518, 695, 697, 699–728, 769, 824, 830, 882, 890, 947, 955
  British rule in India defended by, 724–25, 762–63, 860–61, 863
  citizenship seen as necessary by, 518
  democracy defended by, 706, 720–28, 952
  depression of, 701–2, 703, 717
  despotism for barbarians defended by, 677, 721, 747
  on education, 719–20
  education of, 699, 700, 702, 727
  on human nature, 727–28
  loss of autonomy feared by, 825, 826
  mass-society theory of, 727, 820

nationalism as seen by, 871
plural votes defended by, 706, 723
progress embraced by, 982
representation as seen by, 606
as shaped by French Revolution, 616
socialist views of, 892–93
Tocqueville's influence on, 704, 705,
    710–11, 715, 716, 720–21, 727, 733,
    737, 740, 741, 743–44, 756, 761, 762,
    825
women's rights supported by, 698, 706,
    707, 722, 726–28
worker cooperatives defended by, 707,
    970
Millar, John, 788
millenarianism, 326, 330, 350, 351, 642,
    913, 923
Mills, C. Wright, 839–42
Mind (Geist), 657–58, 725, 728, 776, 790,
    827
    humans as embodiment of, 659
    search for self-understanding by, 664
mind, freedom of, 659
mining, 825–26
"mirror of princes" tradition, 293, 297, 302
missionaries, 227
mission civilisatrice, 862–63
mobilization, 817
mob rule, 104, 124, 126, 194
mobs, 641–42
Modena, 359
moderation, 145
modernity, 405, 552
    "bigness" of, 810
    Dewey's idea of, 958
    French Revolution and, 535, 654, 656
modernization, 875–77
    civilzation vs., 863
modern state:
    essence of, xii
    Greek polis vs., xiii
Modern Times (film), 908
Mommssen, Theodor, 137
monarchy, 104, 124, 126, 194, 420, 440,
    501, 526–27, 528–29, 587
    Bartolus's defense of, 284–85
    Burke's views on, 625, 632–33
    constitutional, 126, 499, 512, 520, 569,
        689, 691, 739, 741, 782

Filmer's defense of, 457–58, 472–74, 481,
    482
God's government of universe and, 199
as governed by ignorance, 642
Hobbes's secular defense of, 415, 419, 503
in Israel, 509
James Mill's fear of, 598
Leviathan and, 415
medieval view of, 271–72
as morally impossible, 468
Paine's attack on, 639
as popular with medieval writers, 233–34
republicanism vs., 498, 566
in revolution, 765
in Rome, 130, 141
in Sparta, 122
spirit of, 521–22
strength of, 122–23
tyranny and, 348
universal, Dante's advocacy of, 257, 258,
    266–72, 1003
utilitarianism and, 697
monasteries, 217–18, 307, 333, 334, 389
    destruction of, 323–24
monastic communities, 208
Monboddo, Lord, 542
money, 90–91, 107, 374, 478, 480, 485, 596,
    804, 883
    abolition of, 314, 315, 881–82
    love of, 209, 549
    political influence bought by, xiv
money lending, 91
Mongolian herdsmen, 991
Monica, 150, 160
Monmouth Rebellion, 456
monopolies, 867
monstrosities, 284, 285
Montaigne, 294, 301, 319–20
Monte Cassino, 226
Montesquieu, xx, 130, 500, 504, 518–31,
    556, 565, 592, 608
    Burke influenced by, 629
    on civil society, 901
    on classical republics, 599
    on les moeurs, 527, 574, 629, 735
    on natural law, 629
    on separation of powers, 504, 520, 528–
        29, 690
    on small republics, 600, 621

Montesquieu (*continued*)
 Tocqueville influenced by, 737–38, 752, 757
 travel diaries of, 528–29
 on virtue of citizens, 601, 667, 737
Montezuma, 850
Monticello, 584–85
Montpelier, 597
Moors, 849, 850
moral body, 560–61
moral freedom, 565
morality, 436–37, 465–66, 546, 565, 671, 889
 amorality and, 52–53, 57
 Aristotle on, 51, 79
 as artificial, 57
 atheists and, 494
 Christian, 255
 critical, 708–9
 as form of insurance, 56
 Hegel on, 673–74, 681–83
 nature vs., 57
 "noncontradiction" principle in, 682
 Plato on, 51, 52
 practical politics vs., 358–59
 religion and, 575
 Rousseau on need for, 574–75
 sociological view of, 707–8
 in utilitarianism, 711–13
 see also justice
moral law, 143, 536
 Dante on, 267–68
Moral Man and Immoral Society (Niebhur), 958
morals, 385, 531
More, Thomas, 31, 294, 309, 311–19, 891
 murder of, 311, 312, 319
 and punishment of heretics, 302
 skepticism of, 311, 319
 war hated by, 302
mores, 137, 139
Mormons, 985
Morris, Gouverneur, 598–99, 638
Morris, William, 314, 881, 898–99
mortalism, 447, 450
mortality, 662
Mortmain, Statute of, 212
Mosca, Gaetano, 837, 838
Moscow, 867
Moses, 370, 384, 501, 573

mos maiorum, 138, 146, 147, 580, 628
movies, 869
Muhammad, 213, 857
Mühlberg, Battle of, 343
multinational corporations, 992
Münster uprising, 326, 349, 350–51, 829, 923
Müntzer, Thomas, 326, 339–40, 350–51
murder, 336
Murrone, Peter, 261–62
music, 59, 109, 869
Muslim Brotherhood, 876
Muslims, 197
Muslim world, 66
Mussolini, Benito, 32, 573, 636, 816, 838, 913, 916, 918, 933, 935, 936, 940
 capture and death of, 820, 832
Mutual Aid (Kropotkin), 896
mutually assured destruction, 434, 988, 1002
myth, history vs., 8
Mytilene, 23

nabobs, 620
Nagasaki, 997
Napier, Charles, 205, 1007
Naples, Kingdom of, 288, 309, 361, 363, 372
Napoleon I, Emperor of the French, 121, 234, 258, 573, 605, 618, 646, 654, 667, 669, 692, 730, 734, 798, 821
 concordat with papacy made by, 961
 defeat of, 690, 930
Napoleonic Wars, 693, 887
narrow democracy, 98
Nasser, Gamal Abdel, 875, 876, 877
National Assembly, French, 731, 733, 762
national bourgeousie, 873
national consciousness, 869
National Convention, 637
national insurance, 902
nationalism, 309, 499, 555–56, 624, 994–99
 anticolonialism and, 871–78
 in breakup of Soviet Union, 870
 in France, 931
 in *Looking Backward*, 898
 mass appeal of, 817
 progress and, 874–75
 religion and, 996
 Scandinavian, 796
 as secular, 979

socialism defeated by, 866, 879
totalitarianism and, 927
as unifying principle of states, 871
national powers, federal powers vs., 607
National Register, 619
nation-states, 869–70, 978
Native Americans, xxiv, 20, 412, 493, 582, 583, 589, 612, 613, 750
    European colonization and, 793, 849–57
    French intermarriage with, 749–50
    property rights absent among, 850, 855–56, 973
    Spanish rule over, 844
    Tocqueville's sympathy for, 729, 746, 753, 763, 862
natural freedom, 565
natural law, 75–76, 204–7, 233, 241, 243, 412, 419, 439, 500, 559
    Burke's belief in, 629
    change and, 242
    Christiantiy and, 208, 238
    Cicero's theory of, 143–44
    and "death of God," 467
    in Declaration of Independence, 580
    imperialism and, 850
    law of nations vs., 857
    Locke on, 464, 465–72, 490, 495, 560
    Protestant contempt for, 341
    standards of justice in, 165
    Stoics on, 143, 854
natural law arguments, 846
natural law theories, 57
natural liberty, 515
    Filmer's denial of, 515
natural man, 542–52
natural philosophy, 228
natural resources:
    depletion of, 1008–10
    wars over, 812–13
natural rights, 498, 500
    Bentham's dismissal of, 695–96
    in Declaration of Independence, 580
    Hegel's dismissal of, 655
    Rousseau on, 736
natural theology, 448
nature, 75
    grace and, 231
    Hobbes on, 430–32
    morality vs., 57

Rousseau on, 475, 957
slavery and, 86
values in, 426
nature, state of, 406, 430–32, 436–38, 439, 442, 474
    Rousseau on, 475
Navy, U.S., 763, 986
Nazis, 181, 340, 467, 812, 829, 865, 912, 916, 940–41, 945, 989
    discrediting of, 968
    genocide committed by, 815, 913–14
    racism of, 930
    Stalinism vs., 927
Near East, 213, 862
negative community, 476
negative freedom, 565–66
negritude, 872
neocolonialism, 846
neoimperialism, 846
Neoplatonism, 151, 153–54, 158, 162–63, 165, 167, 214, 215, 229–30, 293, 299
    Arab, 301
    Catholicism influenced by, 310
Nero, Emperor of Rome, 164, 222, 251, 295
Netherlands, 323, 352
New Atlantis (Bacon), 510
New Christianity (Sain-Simon), 981
New Deal, 928, 937, 966
New England, 612
New Harmony, 887
New Jersey, 588
New Liberals, 919
Newman, John Henry, 109
New Model Army, 735
News from Nowhere (Morris), 314, 881, 882, 898–99
New Side Presbyterians, 595
New Testament, 271, 331, 664
New York, 588
New York Times, 951
New York Tribune, 774
New Zealand, 763
Nicaea, Council of, 273
Nicholas I, Czar of Russia, 895
Nicholas II, Pope, 217
Nicholas of Cusa, 257, 258, 289–90, 301
Nicomachean Ethics (Aristotle), 78–81, 119, 226, 232

Niebuhr, Reinhold, 958
Nietzsche, Friedrich, 29, 935
    amorality popularized by, 52
night of the long knives, 940
1968, summer of, 972
1984 (Orwell), 319, 911, 942–43
Nixon, Richard, 841, 1002
nobili, 363, 387
nobility, 296, 506, 526–27
    French, 634
noble savage, 750
noble-to-base spectrum, 709–10
Nogaret, Guillaume de, 264
nomadic societies, 547, 793
nominalism, 425–26
nonbelievers, 248–50
nonresistance, 337, 340–44
nonvocational education, 229
no-rights, 974
normalization, 943–44
Norman yoke, 586, 646
North, Lord, 583, 619
North Africa, 121, 151, 152, 187, 213
Northern Ireland, 964, 968, 989
North Korea, 1005
North Vietnam, 1002
notaries, 354
nouvelle Héloïse, La (Rousseau), 536
Nozick, Robert, 894
nuclear weapons, 434, 812, 817, 840, 979,
    990, 996–99, 1001, 1002, 1007, 1010
Numantia, 369
Nunc Dimittis, 624, 642
Nuremberg rallies, 819

obedience, 202
    habits of, 370–71
    see also disobedience; passive obedience
obligations, 92, 438–40
occupational freedom, xxiii, 726
Oceana (Harrington), 499, 500–501, 509,
    512, 513, 531, 612
    structure of, 501–10
ochlocracy, 98
Octavian, *see* Caesar Augustus
oil, 1009
old-age pensions, 828
Old Norse piracy, 796
Old Oligarch (unknown author), 68

Old Testament, 7–8, 167, 169, 184, 221,
    222–23, 331, 473, 509, 664, 869,
    929–30, 985
oligarchy, 98, 118, 124, 126, 194
    aristocracies becoming, 97
    in Athens, 12, 27, 28–29, 35, 60, 95; *see
        also* Thirty Tyrants
    in Carthage, 121
    democracy vs., 100–101, 127
    iron law of, 837–39
    justice in, 101
    petit conseil as, 532
    in Rome, 121, 571, 724
    after Russian Revolution, 838
    in Sparta, 122
Olympus, 31
One-Dimensional Man (Marcuse), 944
one-man rule, 196, 360
one-party rule, 912
On Liberty (J. S. Mill), xx, xxi, 706, 707, 715–
    20, 722, 727, 737, 742, 745, 756, 761
On Secular Authority (Luther), 335–40
On the Dignity of Man (Pico della Mirandola),
    294, 299–301
"Open Letter on the Harsh Book against the
    Peasants, An" (Luther), 339–40
Open Society and Its Enemies, The (Popper), 922
Opium War, 861
oppression, 286, 568, 715–16, 846
optics, 417
optimates, 115
optimo iure, 135
Orange, House of, 459
orangutan, 542, 547
Orco, Remirro de, 372–73
Order of Preachers, 228
ordination, 332
ordines, 133
ordini, 384–85
original sin, 153, 159, 160, 170, 179–80,
    189, 293, 300, 436
    Machiavelli's belief in, 375, 537
    Rousseau's denial of, 534, 537, 541, 542,
        554
Orleanist monarchy, 636, 734, 739
Orsini family, 372
Ortega y Gasset, José, 822, 833, 834, 915,
    962
orthodoxy, 448

Orwell, George, 319, 911, 942–43
ostracism, 18
"other-directed" individuals, 825
Otto I, Emperor, 188, 196
Ottoman Empire, 213, 214, 303, 309, 367,
    445, 512, 516, 522, 524, 527, 738, 845
  as enemy of Christendom, 849
  harshness of, 763
Ottonian empire, 188
outsourcing, 992
overlapping consensus, 581
Owen, Robert, 880, 884, 886–87
ownership, 853
Oxford University, 213, 228, 288, 414, 416,
    453, 455

pacifism, 175, 351, 999–1001
pacts, 558–64
Padua, 277
pagans, 155, 156, 159, 164, 166, 183, 224,
    249, 250
  suicide of, 200
  superstitions of, 980
pain, 697
Paine, Thomas, 597, 611, 622, 637–47, 766,
    916, 930, 981
  Burke vs., 622, 639–40, 642–43,
    645–46
  as citizen of the world, 640
  equality and, 583, 639
  hereditary principle dismissed by, 639,
    644
  inheritance tax advocated by, 640–41,
    644
  toleration opposed by, 646
  universal human rights defended by, 639,
    643–45
Pakistan, 993, 996, 1005
Pamiers, Bishop of, 262
Panaetius, 117
Panama Canal, 983
panbasileus, 96
Panegyric (Erasmus), 302, 355
Panopticon, 696, 698, 886
papacy, 158, 416
  absolutism of, 215–16
  in Avignon, 198, 260, 264, 287, 404
  in concordat with France, 961
  divine right claimed by, 334–35
    election of, 276
    Erasmus's criticism of, 309
    Holy Roman Empire vs., 232–33, 258–
      60, 270, 271, 273–79, 288–89
    in investiture controversy, 216–19
    kings vs., 66, 200, 202–4, 222
    Machiavelli's animus toward, 385–86
    Marsilius's arguments against, 273–79
    political opposition to, 321–22
    popular judgment of, 202
    property owned by, 208
    Roman empire inherited by, 188
papal authority, theory of, 203–4
papal curia, 404
papal edicts, 235–36
papal indulgences, 293, 325, 328, 329, 331
Papal States, 233, 249, 280, 361, 363, 364,
    371, 372, 373
  dissolution of, 404
papal tiara, 217
papal vicars, 372
"parallelograms of paupers," 887
parchment barriers, 748–49, 964
parents, 74, 82, 84, 462, 482, 584
parent-teacher associations, 976
Pareto, Vilfredo, 837, 838, 928
Paris, 170, 232, 296, 529, 539, 545, 767
Paris, Treaty of, 590
Paris, University of, 228, 272
Paris Commune, 892, 923
Parliament, British, 195, 415, 459, 488, 489,
    506, 513, 528, 587, 605, 620, 699, 881,
    963
  Charles I's view of, 503, 511
  Charles II's refusal to call, 608
  crown's dependency on, 607
  development of, 219
  evolution of, 195
  Hobbes's hostility to, 415, 419
  prime ministers removed by, 747
  Rousseau's mockery of, 575
  as "talking shop," 724
Parson, Talcott, 944
parties, political, 620, 724
passive disobedience, 199–200, 251, 255,
    333, 340, 344
passive obedience, 198–202, 255
  Luther's defense of, 333
  tyrannicide and, 201

passive resistance, 999
passports, 93
past, mythical, 913
pastoral societies, 547
Pater, Walter, 300
patria potestas, 136
Patriarcha (Filmer), 457–58, 472–74, 503, 515
patriotism, 190, 269, 556
patronage, 513
Paul, Saint, 153, 161, 163, 167, 209, 540, 549
    on crucifixion, 310
    on God's ordination of powers that be, 149, 198, 333, 336, 340, 344, 348, 384, 420, 451, 489
    love of money denounced by, 209
    as Roman citizen, 129, 132, 135
    on salvation, 325
Pavia, Battle of, 308
peace, 169, 174, 247, 287, 437
    Dante on, 268
    Erasmus on, 302, 306–9
Peace of Nicias, 25
peasantry, 647, , 789–90, 796
Peasants' War, 326, 330, 349–52
Peirce, Charles Sanders, 755
Peisistratids, 9
pelagic empire, 845–46, 853, 868
Peloponnesian War, 6, 12, 13, 14, 18–19, 30, 32, 35, 60, 71, 95, 124, 125, 127, 404, 601, 651
    atrocities in, 19–20, 23–25, 50, 93, 358–59, 412
    causes of, 69
    oligarchs vs. democrats in, 101, 666
    Sicilian disaster in, 25–28
Peloponnesian League, 19, 25, 95
penances, 325
Pennsylvania, 588, 857
pensions, 638, 901, 904
people:
    in *Book of the Body Politic*, 296, 298
    in mixed constitutions, 386
    as source of authority, 233–34, 438
    see also mass-elite opposition
people's democracies, xvii–xviii, 818
Percussina, 356
peregrini, 239
perfectibilité, 543, 544
perfection, 300

Pergamum, 6
Pericles, 12–13, 25, 68, 127, 404, 412, 522, 688, 826, 860, 949, 950
    death of, 19
    funeral oration of, 19, 20–22
Peripatetics, 113
permanent revolution, 491, 920–21, 925
Perpetual Peace (Kant), 859, 860, 1003
perseverance, 299
Persia, Persian Empire, xxiv, 27, 71, 88, 503, 522, 651, 666–67, 847, 977
    in alliance with Sparta, 28
    in Battle of Marathon, 15–16
    Greek polis vs., xii, xiii
    as lacking politics, 6, 88
    Macedonian invasion of, 72
    modern state vs., xiii
    polis vs., 847–48
    public services lacking in, xii
    rulers worshipped in, 194
    as tyranny, xii
    as vulnerable to natural catastrophe, 1008
Persian Letters (Montesquieu), 519
Persian War, xii, 6, 13, 14, 68
    end of, 16–17
    as fight for Greek way of life, xii
    inevitability of, 14–15
Persian War, Second, 17
persuasion, 307
Perugia, 280, 283
Pétain, Henri, 931–32
Peter, Saint, 156, 202, 203–4, 251, 271, 278, 288
petit conseil, 532–33, 534, 574
Petition of Right (1629), 580–81
Petrarch, 293
peyote, 493
Phaedrus (Plato), 817
phalansteries, 785, 880, 888, 889–91
Phantom Public, The (Lippmann), 958
Phenomenology of Spirit, The (Hegel), xxv, 653, 656, 658–62, 665, 673, 776
Philadelphia, 581
Philip, Archduke of Austria, 302
Philip, King of Macedon, 5, 14, 72, 116, 668, 978
Philip II, King of Spain, 307–8
Philip IV, "the Fair," King of France, 235–36, 258, 260, 262, 324

Philip V, King of Macedon, 121

Philip of Hesse, 343, 353

Philippics (Cicero), 116

Philippines, 845

philosophers, 229
    Aristotle on life of, 83
    as politicians, 34, 44–45, 47–48, 64–65,
        66, 68, 124, 301, 303, 666, 784, 805,
        956

*Philosophical Enquiry into the Origin of Our Ideas of
    the Sublime and Beautiful* (Burke), 622

philosophical radicals, 697

philosophy, 40–41, 69
    education in, 60
    Hegel on, 674–75, 689
    as indebted to Arab scholars, 213, 230
    rhetoric vs., 46–47
    statecraft vs., 117–20, 509
    theology and, 229–30, 236
    use of, 674–75

Philosophy of History, The (Hegel), 656, 664–71

Philosophy of Right, The (Hegel), 653, 654, 655,
    656, 657, 664, 667, 671–94
    property rights defended in, 659

Phnom Penh, 1002

physics, 228, 407, 417, 422–23

Physics (Aristotle), 76

Pico della Mirandola, Giovanni, 293–94,
    299–301, 329, 375

Pico della Mirandola, Giovanni (nephew),
    301

piety, 424, 980

Pippin, 155, 259, 270

pirates, 856

Pisa, 280, 281, 283, 289, 355

pitié, 543, 544, 546

Pitt, William, 693

Pittsburgh, Pa., 867

Place, Francis, 699

plague, 19

Plains Indians, 20

Plataea, 15–17, 23, 24

Plato, xxii, xxiv, xxv, 8, 29, 30, 31–70, 71,
    73, 80, 96, 117, 119–20, 138, 194, 295,
    299, 311, 319, 424, 649, 759, 805, 1010
    abolishing private property favored by, 89
    as adjective, 357
    as antipolitical, 31–32, 33–34, 64–65,
        107, 284, 509, 771, 784

and appearance vs. reality, 304, 318

Aristotle's critique of, 33–34, 70, 82, 107,
    666

on arts, 37–38, 59–61

Christianity influenced by, 32, 301

coinage denounced by, 90

cosmology of, 62–63, 69

death of, 72

disapproval of democracy by, 35, 42,
    67–68, 123

on division of labor, 58–59

on education, 58–63, 957

in exile, 36

family life abolished by, 107

humanists' turning to, 293

imperialism denounced by, 175

on justice, 38, 39–40, 42–44, 47–48,
    49–65, 70, 79, 119

Latin translations of, 229

life of, 35–38

Marx vs., 33

mathematical passion of, 34

metaphysics of, 32, 33, 65, 76–77, 214

on morality, 51

mysticism of, 293

natural equality rejected by, 205

Pericles opposed by, 13

on philosophical contemplation as
    ultimate blessedness, 145, 674

Popper's criticism of, 922, 942

promotion of virtue and, 714

psyche in, 817

on rhetoric, 41

writing skills of, 37–38

Platonic philosophers, 137

pleasure, 697, 712–13

plebians, 386

plebiscites, 276

plebs, 382

Pledge of Allegiance, 486

Plekhanov, Georgi, 914

plenitudo potestatis, 203, 271, 276

Plotinus, 151, 153, 162, 167

pluralism, 571–72, 967
    Islamic vs. Western, 213–14

plural votes, 706, 723

Plutarch, 71

plutocracy, 141, 841
    soft despotism vs., 824

Pöbel, 686

Pocock, John, xii

poetry, 69, 293, 715
  meaning found by, 659

poets, 59, 540–41

Poitiers, Battle of, 213, 294–95

Poland, 536, 567, 592
  monarchy and aristocracy in, 607

Polemarchus, 49

Policraticus (John of Salisbury), 193, 219–23

polis, 5, 6, 38, 48, 56, 63, 100, 169, 193,
      684, 978, 1010
  as built on justice, 79
  class warfare in, 95
  as existing by nature, 78, 83
  Greek freedom and, 692
  as logical prior to individual, 78, 107
  order of nature in, 65
  origins of, 8–9
  Persian empire vs., 847–48
  self-sufficiency of, 199

Politcal Parties (Michels), 838

politeia, 98, 99, 110, 122, 124, 239, 254–56,
      277, 278, 499

political Islam, 878

Political Liberalism (Rawls), 947

Political Man (Aristotle), 104

political rights, Roman freedom and, xiii

political science, 420–24
  origins of, 405, 406, 407, 411–13, 414–
      15, 416

political socialization, 738

political theory, xi–xii
  definition of, xx

politicians, philosophers as, 34, 44–45,
      47–48, 64–65, 66, 68, 124, 301, 303,
      666, 784, 805, 956

politics, 7–8
  administration vs., 771
  empirical discipline of, 72, 81–82
  as Greek term, 5
  morality vs., 358–59
  as necessary evil, 638
  as practical discipline, 77–78
  religion and, 156–57
  vocabulary of, 978

Politics (Aristotle), 18, 32, 33, 73, 76, 78, 82,
      83–85, 105–10, 118–19, 190, 230, 232,
      275, 282, 498, 555–56, 844, 881

Politics Taken from the Very Words of Holy Scripture
      (Bossuet), 503

pollsters, xiv

pollution, xix

Polus, 38, 39, 42–43, 44, 80, 102

polyarchy, 967–68

polyarchy, 277

Polybius, 117, 120–26, 136, 140, 169, 175,
      190, 369, 388, 412, 418, 509, 578, 600,
      848, 947
  background of, 111–12
  on checks and balances, 130
  death of, 137
  on defenders of mixed constitution, 386
  on fate, 381, 577
  mixed constitutions praised by, 103, 122,
      123, 130, 138, 195, 254, 498, 501–2,
      517, 606
  as model for Machiavelli, 381–82,
      383–84
  utopias denounced by, 124, 138–39

polytheism, 156, 159

Pompey, 115, 137, 605

poor, poverty, xxiv, 94, 98, 244, 279, 478
  duty of the rich to, 210, 246–47

poor relief, 904

popes, *see* papacy

Popper, Karl, 922, 942

popular culture, 831

populares, 115, 133

popular mixed republics, 819

popular sovereignty, 350, 574

populism, 547
  elites opposed by masses in, xiv–xv,
      832–34

pornography, 830

Porphyry, 162

Port Huron Statement, 971

Portugal, 816, 844

positive community, 476

positive law, 342, 457–58, 467, 468, 515,
      560

positivism, 144, 982–83
  legal, 283

postcolonialism, 846

postimperialism, 846

Post Office, U.S., xii

postrevolutionary leaders, 915

Poughkeepsie, N.Y., 958

power, 42–43, 92
  Hobbes on, 431–32, 847
  Machiavelli on, 376–77
Power Elite, The (Mills), 839–42
powers, federal vs. national, 607
  see also separation of powers
praetors, 113, 131
pragmatism, 957
prayer, 369
predestination, 153
Preface to Democratic Theory, A (Dahl), 946–47,
    967–68
prehistorical stage, 793–94
prejudice, 627, 629
president, U.S., 689
presidential veto, 591
press, freedom of, 972
Price, Richard, 460, 623–25, 636, 642, 916
prices, 90–91
pride, 168
  Hobbes on, 428, 435
priests, 248, 275
  celibacy of, 333
  Luther on, 332
  war and, 317–18
prime ministers, 963
primitive communism, 793
primogeniture, 507
Prince, The (Machiavelli), 137, 355, 359, 371–
    81, 384, 423, 837
  as failed job application, 357
  "mirror of princes" tradition vs., 293, 302
  philosophy mocked in, 118
  Roman freedom praised in, 129
  unification of Italy urged in, 371–72
princes, 296, 385
  in *Book of the Body Politic*, 296
  education of, 297–98, 303–4
  Machiavelli on virtues of, 292, 293, 370,
    375, 376, 377
  tyrants vs., 220
principle of antagonism, 739
Principles of Morals and Legislation, The (Bentham),
    696–97
Principles of Political Economy, The (J. S. Mill),
    705–6
printing press, 330
priors, 361
prisoners of war, 207

prison reform, 696, 730, 734
prisons, 757
privacy, xvii, 109, 495
  abolition of, 915
  modern vs. ancient, 524–25
Private Memoirs and Confessions of a Justified Sinner
    (Hogg), 331
private property, *see* property
privilege of clergy, 262–63
probability, 624
production, 784, 786
  capitalist relations of, 791
  means of, *see* means of production
  pressure for improvement of, 791–92, 793
production lines, 908
productivity, 647–48, 649, 650, 891–92
productivity gap, 547
Profession de foi du vicaire Savoyard (Rousseau),
    554–55
profit, 785–87, 804, 866, 868
progress, 412, 539, 817
  empire and, 859–60
  Mill's belief in, 712, 721
  modern ideas of, 631
  nationalism and, 874–75
  in positivism, 982
progressives, 866
*Project for a Universal History with a Cosmopolitan
    Purpose* (Kant), 268
proletarian democracy, 802–6
proletariat, 647, 790, 795, 796, 866
  dictatorship of, 32, 33, 771, 802–4, 810
  general strike of, 934
  as having no stake in any country, 866,
    915
  Marx's expectation of unity of, 825–26,
    827, 828, 882, 992–93, 1011
  as seen by Marxists, 650, 651, 822, 825–
    26, 827, 828–29, 866, 882
  welfare state and, 901–2
  withdrawal of labor as weapon of, 992
Promise of American Life, The (Croly), 614–15,
    983
promises, 439
  as extorted by force, 442–43
property, 240, 583, 810, 886, 901
  abolition of, 893, 935
  as absent among Native Americans, 850,
    855–56, 973

property (*continued*)
    alienating effect of, 774, 777–78, 780,
        782, 783
    Aquinas on, 244, 475, 478
    Aristotle on, 212, 245–46
    Augustine on, 174–75
    in Britain, 188
    as capital, 687
    Christian view of, 244
    citizenship and, 526
    defense of, 885
    as dictating access to means of
        production, 792
    equal distribution of, 784
    equalizing, 598
    Filmer on, 473–74
    in French Revolution, 617
    Hegel's defense of, 659, 675–82
    Hobbes on, 433, 855
    Locke's defense of, 462–63, 468, 470–72,
        475–82, 659, 679, 855–56
    medieval view of, 193, 204, 205, 206–7,
        208–10, 241, 244–47
    origin of, 984
    Plato's desire to ban, 89
    publicly owned, 211
    rights of disposal and, 210
    Roman Catholic Church's ownership and,
        210–12, 249, 260–61, 323–24, 626,
        646, 981
    Rousseau's criticism of, 548–49, 566, 783
    simplification of laws on, 797
    states' protection of, 551
    Stoic view of, 244
    as theft, 895
    transfer of, 477–78
    virtues of, 244–47
    of women, 726
property owners, xxiv
prophets, 371
proportional representation, 706, 723–24
proprietary colonies, 586
prostitution, 253, 471, 472, 719
Protagoras (Plato), 38, 300
Protestant Ethic and the Spirit of Capitalism, The
    (Weber), 314, 750
Protestants, Protestantism, 191, 311, 322,
    515
    Catholics vs., 291, 341, 968

    emergence of term, 324
    French church's mistreatment of, 633
    fundamentalist, 987
    liberal democracy and, 323
    in Northern Ireland, 968
    toleration in, 183
Proudhon, Pierre-Joseph, 895, 896
prudence, 418
Prussia, 196, 499, 652, 653–54, 657, 666,
    692, 693–94, 782, 986
    as absolutist, 689
    anti-Semitism in, 772, 931
    bureaucratic absolutism in, 794
    economic growth in, 795
    public education in, 720
    serfdom in, 678
prytany, 11
Pseudo-Dionysius the Areopagite, 215, 226,
    229
Ptolemy of Lucca, 232
Public and Its Problems, The (Dewey), 953, 958
public education, 828
public housing, 828
public intellectuals, xxi
public opinion, 751, 823, 824, 913
Public Opinion (Lippmann), 958
public service, xii, 965–66
public spirit, 385
Puerto Rico, 845
Pufendorf, Samuel von, 584
Punic War:
    First, 120, 146
    Second, 121
    Third, 112, 121
punishment, 243, 247, 306–7, 338, 563,
    564
    Augustine on, 176–78, 184
    capital, *see* death penalty
    corporal, 177, 184
    cruel and unusual, 610
    eternal, 300
    Locke on, 468–70
    More on, 315
    in Rome, 177
purgatory, 328
Puritans, Puritanism, 750, 825, 857
purpose, 76
Pursuit of the Millennium, The (Cohn), 923
Pydna, Battle of, 112

quaestors, 113, 131
Quakers, 646, 857
quartering soldiers, 589
Queenwood, 887
querelle des femmes, 295
quiet despotism, 715–16, 821
Qutb, Sayyad, 846, 871–72, 874–78

race, 879
racism, 32, 872
    democracy and, 950
    Enlightenment condemnation of, 846
    evolution as justification for, 864
    history of, 929–30
    "scientific," 844, 863–64, 929
    totalitarianism and, 927
radicals, radicalism:
    French Revolution as seen by, 616
    Locke quoted by, 517
    "philosophical," 697
    in Reformation, 349–53
    in Marx vs. Hegel, 777
    universal suffrage demanded by, 784
railroads, 863, 983
raison d'état, 413
rape, 173–74, 184
rational choice models, 954
rational economic man, 954
Rationale of Judicial Evidence (Bentham), 701
rationalism, Marx's subscription to, 805
rationality, 536, 564
    Paine's assumption of, 639, 642
    republics governed by, 642
"rational-legal" state, 928
ratione peccati, 203, 249, 341
Ravenna, 151, 156, 211
Rawls, John, 487, 947, 972–77, 1004
reality, appearance vs., 304, 318
Real Property Act (1925), 446
reason, 63, 231, 423, 425, 430–31, 507, 544, 546
    Dante on, 267–68
    freedom and, 669
    natural law and, 165
Reason, 657
    embodied in concrete community, 671
    God and, 295
rebellion, 200, 333, 337, 340
reconquista, 213

Red Army, 907, 924–25, 986
redistribution, 480
    see also welfare states
reference group theory, 764–65, 991
Reflections on the Revolution in France (Burke),
    622–34, 642, 645–46
    inaccuracies of, 625–26
Reflections on Violence (Sorel), 636, 933, 934
reform, Burke on pace of, 628
Reformation, xxiii, 190, 200, 227, 258, 290,
    293, 321–53, 703, 815, 847, 851, 878,
    982, 987
    anticlericalism in, 981
    failure of deterrence in, 988
    Greek freedom vs., 668
    Luther's theses and, 328
Reformation Day, 328
Reform Bill (1832), 655, 690, 698
Reform Bill (1867), 722
regime change, 317
regimen regale, 360
Regulus, Marcus Atilius, 146–47
reincarnation, 69
religion, 174, 405, 735
    Burke's attachment to, 629–30
    civil, 156, 629–30
    Dewey on, 954
    and failure of secularization, 979–81
    freedom of, 444, 446, 610, 646, 693
    as growing out of anxiety, 448
    Hobbes on, 448–50
    human nature and, 189–90
    law and, 493–94
    as limit to leader's authority, 275–76
    Machiavelli on, 385–86
    Marx's dismissal of, 630, 984
    morality and, 575
    nationalism and, 996
    natural basis of, 431
    as necessary to society, 629–30
    persecution of, 156–58, 164–65, 170–71,
    197, 200, 214, 347, 633, 815, 913–14,
    975, 988, 989, 1000
    politics and, 156–57, 193
    as redundant, 984–87
    in Rome, 385
    Rousseau on, 554–55
    state support of, 158, 901
    in U.S., 66, 752–53

religion (*continued*)
  in *Utopia*, 316–17
  wars of, *see* wars of religion
religion of humanity, 630, 649, 707, 979,
    981–84
religions, civic, 980
religious identity, xiv
Remus, 358, 384
Renaissance, xxiii, 152, 321, 354, 361, 367,
    377, 383, 510, 600, 820
  state as work of art in, 377
representation, 97
  proportional, 706, 723–24
  virtual, 690
representative government, 96–97, 605–6,
    620
  Hegel on, 688–89, 691
  J. S. Mill's desire for, 705, 706, 720–28
  as marking an epoch, 605
representative will, 254–55
Republic (Plato), xxv, 31, 32, 33, 35, 37, 38, 44,
    45, 46, 47–58, 59–60, 80, 82, 106, 107,
    424, 498, 550, 771
  afterlife in, 165
  antidemocratic ideas of, 35
  Athens's foreign rich disparaged in, 10
  beggars evicted from, 307
  cave allegory in, 59, 66, 304, 310
  cyclical theory of history in, 383
  education in, 58–63
  eugenic views in, 294
  image of body politic in, 296, 297
  moneymaking in, 881–82
  as pure political philosophy, 117–18
  translation of, 303
  Utopia and, 312–13, 316, 318
  work in, 33
republican ideas, xiv
  ascending and descending authority in,
    195–96
republican liberty, 496
Republican Party, U.S., 757
republican virtue, 291–92, 513
Republic of Virtue, 362
republics, 137–42, 220, 284, 497–531, 737
  civil liberties protected in, 498–99
  common interest in, 568–69
  constitutional emphasis of, 137
  democracy vs., 600, 601, 605

expansion of, 860
extensive, 599–600, 604
freedom and liberty in, 368, 376, 566
as governed by reason, 642
heroic emphasis of, 137
Hobbes's assault on, 497
as immortal, 510
for increase, 508
infighting in, 523
Italian city-states as, 191, 196, 256, 272
justice as necessary for, 139
Machiavelli on, 381–89
Madison's definition of, 606–7
Marx on need for, 782–84
mixed, 570, 947–48; *see also* constitutions,
    mixed
monarchy vs., 498, 566
popular vs. aristocratic, 386–87
for preservation, 508
small, 600
ward, 520, 583, 611
resentment, 550
reserve army of the unemployed, 792
resistance, 181
  Calvin's theory of, 344–45
  constitutional theory of, 348–49
res populi, 139–40
Restoration, 415, 453, 501, 587
revelations, 231–32, 431
Revolt of the Masses, The (Ortega y Gasset), 821,
    822, 833
revolution, classical theory of, 76, 82, 92,
    100, 122, 254, 488, 631
revolutions, 76, 82, 92, 100, 122, 254
  bourgeois, 646–47, 648, 765, 920
  Burke's intellectual case against, 626–30
  in democracy, 101, 102–3
  Enlightenment view of, 638–39
  Locke's justification for, 255, 341, 342,
    349, 488–91, 631
  Marx on, 100, 101, 651, 771, 775, 776,
    785, 788, 791, 793–95, 797–98, 800–
    802, 921
  of masses, 832–34
  mass society and, 830–31
  modern idea of, 349, 630–34
  morality of, 633–34
  permanent, 491, 920–21, 925
  science of, 923

Tocqueville on, 729
utilitarian case against, 627–28
Revolution Society, 624
Revolutions of 1848, 687, 732, 733, 758, 774, 789, 795, 866, 904, 972
revolutions of rising expectations, 991
Reynal, abbé, 1000
Rheinische Zeitung, 772
rhetoric, 38–39, 41, 46–47, 113
   Cicero's importance to, 119, 622
   Hobbes's ambiguous views on, 418
Rhode Island, 597
Rhodes, 113
Riazanov, David, 906
Ricardian system, 770
rich, 94
   duty to poor of, 210, 246–47
Riesman, David, 755, 825, 944
right, utility and, 711
rights, xxiii, 92, 406, 433, 445–46, 476, 526, 602, 1005–6
   as against people, 209
   bourgeois, 645, 804
   as grounded in possession, 676
   Hegel on, 673, 675–79
   Hobbes's denial of, 443, 444–46, 855
   in justice, 895–96
   Locke on, 495, 624, 855
   against persons vs. over things, 678
   slavery and, 677–78
   against state, 683
   theories of, 974
   virtues vs., 581
   will as necessary for, 675
   see also human rights
Rights of British North America, The (Jefferson), 579–80
Rights of Man (Paine), 622, 638, 641–47
right to bear arms, 355, 506, 511, 610
ring of Gyges, 56, 57
Rise of the Roman Empire, The (Polybius), 111, 112, 120–21, 848
risorgimento, 365
rituals, secularization vs., 979–81
Road to Serfdom, The (Hayek), 902
robbery, 180, 885
Robertson, William, 788
Robespierre, Maximilien, 573, 632, 673, 682, 980, 981

Rocco, Alfredo, 936
Rockingham, Lord, 619, 621
Romagna, 372–73
Roman Catholic Church, 75–76, 188, 191
   administration of, 188, 403–4
   and ambition to regulate lives, 809
   Aquinas as official philosopher of, 225, 226
   authority in, 288–89
   church-state relationships viewed by, 198
   as corporation, 404
   desire of kings to tax, 259
   duties of subjects and rulers viewed by, 198
   election in, 274
   English dislike for interference of, 200
   geographical reach of, 155–56
   image of state fostered by, 188, 403–4
   as immortal, 211
   legal essence of, 403–4
   Marxism and, 971
   as monarchical, 258
   Neoplatonic influence on, 310
   Orthodox dispute with, 989
   primacy sought for, 218–19
   property owned by, 210–12, 249, 260–61, 323–24, 626, 646, 981
   Protestants vs., 341
   Rousseau's criticism of, 575
   secular and spiritual authorities viewed by, 198
   social cohesion and, 575
   splits of, 164, 170–71, 182–83, 197–98, 298, 321; *see also* Reformation
   taxation and, 211–12, 259
   as Trinitarian, 198
   see also papacy
Roman constitutions, 111
Roman Empire, 147, 187, 190, 199, 250, 367, 503, 512, 844
   Christianity made official religion of, 148, 150, 155, 156, 158, 190, 197
   cult of emperor in, 197
   Dante on necessity of, 268–70
   decline and fall of, 124, 168, 174, 187, 188, 224, 502
   defense of, 152, 155
   Greece under, 5, 366
   Greek polis vs., xiii

Roman Empire (*continued*)
  harshness of, 763
  imperial system in, 155
  legal systems in, 283
  papacy's inheritance of, 188
  subjected territories of, 15
  trade in, 124
  as unitary, 844
  worship of pagan gods banned in, 166
Romania, 816, 907
Roman Republic, 5, 9–10, 113, 138, 147,
    194, 281, 381, 556, 573, 668, 688
  Cicero's praise of, 175, 190
  civic virtue of, 293, 299, 522
  collapse of, 115, 116, 119, 137, 140, 143,
    154, 194, 212, 257, 280, 388
  as expansive, 387
  Machiavelli's desire to reinstate, 357, 359,
    365, 412, 508, 600
  morality of, 783
  oligarchy in, 121, 571, 724
  Polybius's defense of, 121
Romantic poetry, 715
romantics, 300, 377
Rome, xxiii, 39, 272, 329, 356, 382, 502,
    511, 518, 978
  agrarian reform in, 140
  armies of, 130
  Augustine's criticism of, 162
  citizenship in, xiii, xiv, 10, 122, 132–36,
    195, 553, 574
  civil wars in, 113, 115, 116, 154
  class warfare in, 125
  collective monarchy in, 127
  constitutional reforms in, 114
  constitution of, 111, 114, 126, 130, 609
  democracy disdained by, xiii
  discipline in, 129
  1527 sack of, 308, 322, 364
  founding of, 557
  410 sack of, 152, 164, 165
  freedom in, xiii, xxiii, 18–19, 128–29,
    169, 663, 670–71
  legions of, xxii–xxiii
  liberty in, 128, 141, 280, 282, 416, 547,
    580, 656
  Machiavelli's morals drawn from, 369
  men in politics of, xiii
  military service in, 133

  mixed constitution adopted by, 103, 128,
    138, 141–42
  narrow governing class in, 600–601
  patriotism in, 556
  popular assemblies in, 130
  principate established in, 128, 154, 194
  proletariat in, 833
  property rights in, 210
  punishment in, 177
  religion in, 385
  rhetoric in, 38–39
  right to hold office in, 122, 129, 130–31,
    135
  rise of, 120, 126
  slaves in, xiii, 85, 129, 135, 136, 473, 789
  sovereignty of, 130
  taxation in, xiii, 133, 135
  trial and error in politics of, 125–26,
    140–41
  universality of, 156
  voting rights in, xiii, 129, 133, 135, 141
  western Europe's claim to inheritance of,
    197
  women in, 135, 136
Rome, Bishop of, 250
Romulus, 125, 358, 370, 384, 573
Romulus Augustus, 164, 196
Roosevelt, Franklin D., 937
Roosevelt, Theodore, 847
Rousseau, Jean-Jacques, 92–93, 406, 532–
    76, 674, 947
  background of, 532–34
  on common ownership, 480
  on conquest, 643
  on education, 61, 537–38, 539, 553–54,
    957
  elective aristocracies preferred by, 97,
    570
  English Parliament mocked by, 575
  equality urged by, 537, 539–52, 556,
    557, 569, 637, 736–37, 788, 973
  French Revolution influenced by, 534,
    535–36, 635
  on general will, 560–64, 566–71, 673,
    960
  Hegel as heir to, 663
  Hobbes vs., 537, 541, 544, 548–49,
    557–58, 559, 560, 561, 563, 564
  human history sketched by, 545–47

on human nature, 534, 537, 538, 541, 553–54, 727–28

impact of, 573–76

on importance of citizenship, 553, 574, 783

laws vs. decrees in, 384

on legitimate states, 556, 558–64, 572, 573–76, 736

on liberty, 564–72

on necessity of states, 885

on need for civic religions, 574–75, 980

on need for property, 548–49, 566, 783

original sin denied by, 534, 537, 541, 542, 554

pacifism of, 1000

perpetual peace as project of, 691

"republic" defined by, 498–99, 523

on social contract, xiv, 407

Sparta admired by, 524, 535, 536, 539

on state of nature, 475, 957

Tocqueville influenced by, 736–37, 738

well-ordered republic desired by, 180

women as treated by, 555

royal absolutism, 255–56

Rucellai, Cosimo, 356

Rucellai family, 356

Rudolph of Hapsburg, 265

"rule by professional politicians," *see* elite democracy

rule of law, 64, 119, 276, 526, 529–30, 672, 907

Rush, Benjamin, 578, 661

Ruskin, John, 833, 883

Russell, Bertrand, xxi, 61, 536, 830, 922, 923, 928–29, 943, 997, 998, 1000–1001, 1009

Russia, 652, 762, 798, 862, 866, 908, 964, 990

as agrarian, 924

Bolshevik Revolution in, 897, 941

civil war in, 924

czarist regime in, 801

eastward expansion of, 845, 868

exterminism in, 930

Lenin's return to, 770

Marx on, 924

revolution of 1905 in, 918

see also Soviet Union

Rwanda, 964

Rye House Plot, 456, 500

sabbatarianism of, 690

Sabine, George, xi

sacraments, 312, 332

St. Peter's, 328, 329, 334, 335

St. Petersburg, 867

Saint-Simon, Henri de, 32, 647–51, 655, 656, 686, 693, 770, 804, 883, 886, 888, 936, 938, 981, 983, 985

Salamis, Battle of, xii, 16, 18

Salutati, Coluccio, 294

salvation, 153, 293, 329

grace and, 325, 328, 331

inner certainty and, 325–26

Samson, Abbot, 883

Santa Croce, 356

Sardinia, 121

Sartre, Jean-Paul, 550, 661, 872, 873

satraps, 88

Sattler, Michael, 351–52

satyagraha, 999

Saudi Arabia, 995

savage societies, 548

Savonarola, Girolamo, 354, 362, 363, 370, 614, 820

Saxony, 499, 652, 774, 889

Scandinavia, 796

Schleitheim Articles, 351

Schmalkaldic League, 343

Schmitt, Carl, 912, 917, 940

Scholasticism, 225–26, 416, 425, 851, 1004

humanism's hostility to, 292, 293, 294, 304

Locke's reworking of, 475

schoolmen, *see* Scholasticism

Schopenhauer, Arthur, 654

Schumpeter, Joseph, 837, 941, 946, 959–67, 975–76

science, 228, 383, 405, 412, 416, 417, 420–24, 434, 531, 647, 785, 787, 790, 956, 957–58, 979, 985

as imposing meaning on world, 659

Science of Logic (Hegel), 653

scientific revolution, teleological explanations expelled by, 75

scientific socialism, 785, 806

Scipio Africanus, 121, 124, 125, 165

Scipio Africanus the Younger, 112, 137, 138–39, 165

"Scipio's Dream" (Cicero), 69, 158, 165, 175

Scotland, 344

Scythia, 88, 864

search and seizure, 610

Second Amendment, U.S., 134

Second Bank of the United States, 614

Second Coming, 207–8, 210, 326, 351, 510

Second Continental Congress, 584, 587–88

Second Duma, 918

Second Empire, French, 636, 646, 741, 801

Second International, 775, 919

Second Persian War, 17

Second Punic War, 121

Second Republic, French, 636, 733, 741, 795

second-strike capacity, 434

Second Treatise (Locke), 85, 458–64, 472, 474, 488, 492, 528, 581, 588, 855

secret police, xvi

secularism, human nature and, 189

secularizations, 985

failure of, 979–81

security, 428

justice and, 714

Seleucid Empire, 845

self-consciousness, 656

self-creation, 299, 300

self-defense, 95, 178, 181, 247, 341, 489

coercion and, 717–18

as grounds for war, 847

self-destruction, 997–98

self-formation, 846

self-fulfillment, 715

self-government, 663, 668–69, 711, 804, 970, 1003

fragility of, 1011

limits to, 688

self-incrimination, 610

self-interest, 55, 56, 102, 437, 466, 598, 723, 735, 789

in U.S., 757–59, 768

selfishness, 437–38, 446

self-mortification, 369

self-preservation, 426, 428–29, 544

self-reliance, 751, 760–63, 903, 957

climate's fostering of, 752

self-sufficiency, 76, 106–7, 199, 239, 684, 937

of state, 275

semisocialism, 818

Senate, Roman, 112, 114, 117, 118, 201

as aristocratic, 130, 574

College of Cardinals' replication of, 194

powers of, 131–32

Senate, U.S., 131, 609

Seneca, 115, 365, 580

Sennett, Richard, 755

Sentences (Lombard), 227, 229

separation of powers, 103, 130, 142, 488, 504, 520, 528–29, 592

Athens and, 18

in *Federalist*, 600

Hegel's acceptance of, 690

Madison's defense of, 608–9

Montesquieu on, 504, 520, 528–29, 592

tyranny and, 608

Sepúlveda, Juan Ginés de, 852, 856, 857

Servetus, Michael, 346

Seventh Letter (Plato), 35, 37, 304

Seventy, governmental function of, 361–62

Seven Years' War, 590, 734

sewerage, xix

sex, 173–74, 274–75, 318, 536–37, 712, 916–17

sexual abstinence, 161

sexuality, 464

sexual passion, 49–50

Sforza, Lodovico, 363

Sforza family, 374

Shaftesbury, Earl of, 454, 455, 513

Shakespeare, William, 35, 78

sharecroppers, 547

sharia, 877

Shay's Rebellion, 590

Shelburne, Lord, 701

Shelley, Percy Bysshe, 650

Shias, 989

shipbuilding, 826

Shostakovich, Dmitri, 926

Sicily, 37, 86, 121, 187, 213, 377

Athenian expedition to, 25–28

Byzantine occupation of, 197

Kingdom of, 234, 235, 237, 280

Sidgwick, Henry, 1001

Sidney, Algernon, 456, 458, 499, 503, 513–18, 524, 583, 860, 864, 969

U.S. founders influenced by, 500, 580, 581

Sigismund, Emperor, 289

signoria, 361

Signposts (Qutb), *see Milestones* (Qutb)

silver, 549

simony, 217, 218

sin, 179, 249, 338
    see also original sin

sinecures, 620, 621, 797

sine suffragio, 135

Sittlichkeit, 671, 673–74, 683–84, 708

Six Books of the Commonwealth (Bodin), 235

skepticism, 231–32
    of Montaigne, 319–20
    of More, 311, 319

Skinner, Quentin, xii

slavery, slaves, xxiv, 110, 419, 462, 554, 612,
    624, 750, 787, 789, 794
    Aquinas's acceptance of, 254
    Aristotle on, 73–75, 76, 82, 85–88, 92,
        94, 238, 429, 727
    in Athens, 10, 11, 13, 68, 74, 86, 94, 667
    defenders of, 662, 677
    Hegel's condemnation of, 676–78
    liberty and, 582
    man-hunting and, 481
    in master-slave dialectic, 658–62, 666,
        678
    medieval view of, 193, 204, 206–7, 208,
        238
    Mill's qualified defense of, 677, 721
    by nature, 864
    Persians as, 6
    possibility of happiness in, 662–63, 677
    rights and, 677–78
    in Rome, xiii, 85, 129, 135, 136, 473, 789
    Stoicism's sanctioning of, 582, 662–63
    technology kept back by, 791
    in U.S., xxiv, 85, 87, 578, 661, 662, 677,
        746, 753–54, 964
    war captives as, 481

slave trade, 612–13

Slavs, 197

Small, William, 584

Smith, Adam, 519, 595, 629, 685, 890, 1008

snobbery, xviii

sociability, 168

social cohesion, 385

social conformity, 831–32

social contract, 489, 550–51
    Hegel's dismissal of, 655, 690–91
    state as unifying element in, 407

Social Contract (Rousseau), xiv, 532, 533, 536,
    537, 539, 556–58, 563, 564, 566, 569,
    575, 736, 973

social Darwinism, 896

social democracy, xviii, 951–59

Social Democratic Parties, Europe, xviii

social insurance, 879

socialism, 478, 810, 818, 879–910
    absence of bourgeois rights in, 804–5
    as born from industrialization, 881, 882,
        990
    command economies and, 812
    decolonization and, 870
    as defeated by nationalism, 866, 879
    democracy necessary for, 885
    democratic, 798
    fascism and, 927–28
    feudal, 883
    German critics of, 940
    guild, 884
    with a human face, 972
    imperialism and acceleration of, 862
    impossibility of, 879–80
    as international, 920–22
    justice in, 895–96
    liberation of humans under, 804
    market, 778, 983–84
    means of production in, 803–4, 970
    Mill's defense of, 706
    as necessity, 781
    parliamentary road to, 801–2
    Schumpeter on evolution of, 959
    scientific, 785, 806
    state disliked in, 884–85
    utopian, 785, 879–80, 884
    varieties of, 882–84
    violent road to, 800–801
    welfare state and, 894, 904–5

Socialism and Saint-Simon (Durkheim), 648

socialization, 542

social justice, 900

Social Justice in Islam (Qutb), 875–76

social position, 109–10

social security, 902

social societies, 674

Social War of 90, 113

society:
    as blessing, 638
    development of, 655, 658
    discontents' view of, 969
    origins of, 58

Society for Constitutional Information,
    641

Society for the Commemoration of the
Revolution, 624
sociologists, sociology:
"mass society" defined by, 820
on nonrational convictions, 629–30
on topics from Tocqueville (post-1945),
755–62, 825–26, 942–45
totalitarianism explained by, 913
see also specific sociologists
Socrates, xx, 25, 42, 70, 118, 167, 184, 564,
999
Hegel's understanding of, 666, 668, 669
as historical figure, 34–35
on justice, 41–47, 49, 50–58
rhetoric belittled by, 38–39, 41
as showing inadequacies of Greek city-
states, 668–69
trial and execution of, 29–30, 36, 39,
46–47, 495, 934, 947
writing disapproved of by, 35
Soderini, Piero, 356
soft despotism, 755, 824
soft totalitarianism, 927, 941–45
Solon, 9, 27, 127
Somalia, 994
Sombart, Werner, 828, 908
Sophists, 36–37, 41, 49
nature viewed as amoral by, 57
Sophocles, 49, 51
Sorbonne, 519
Sorel, Georges, 636, 911, 917, 918, 933,
934–35
sortition, 508
souls, 61–62, 66–67, 68–69, 296, 482
transmigration of, 165
South America, 1007
South Korea, 1005
Souvenirs (Tocqueville), 733
sovereign, 783
by acquisition, 442
conscience and God as authority over,
451
Hobbes's insistence on single, 441–42,
444–45, 450, 567, 673, 747
by institution, 442
as not bound by promises, 443–45
orthodoxy defined by, 448–49
powers and duties of, 444
resistance of, 451
Rousseau's definition of, 561

sovereignty, 281, 419, 429, 440–47
double, 523–24, 592–93, 599
of Parliament, 591–92
in U.S., 567, 747
Soviet Union, 839, 870, 938, 945, 972
aid from, 877
bloc of, 906
in Cold War, *see* Cold War
collapse of, 665, 674, 818, 914, 995,
1005, 1006–7
Communist Party of, 911
dictatorship of proletariat established in, 802
Marxism in, 770, 771
mismanagement of, 687
nuclear weapons of, 434, 840
as one-party state, 938
proposed preemptive war against, 1000
state capitalism in, 792, 914
in World War II, 941–42
see also Russia
Spain, 121, 152, 187, 363–64, 366, 404,
492, 583, 734, 809, 816, 844
church property in, 324
church-state alliance in, 810
empire of, 844, 845, 850–53, 877
fascism in, 833, 914
Indians ruled by, 844
monarchs in, 305
reconquista in, 213
unification of, 307
Spanish-American War, 845
Spanish Armada, 413
Spanish influenza, 997
Sparta, 6–7, 14, 18, 19, 21, 61, 67, 88–89,
108, 140, 246, 348, 375, 502, 508, 511,
513, 518, 522, 738
in alliance with Persia, 28
Battle of Marathon and, 15, 16
citizenship in, 553, 574
collective monarchy in, 127
constitution of, 32, 121–22, 124, 125–
26, 346
corruption of, 24–25
economic arrangements in, 124
freedom in, 7, 128–29
Machiavelli's morals drawn from, 369
military training in, 60, 89, 104
mixed political system in, 104, 121–22,
124, 125–26
patriotism in, 556

in Peloponnesian War, *see* Peloponnesian War

Plato's principles inspired by, 58, 59

political organization of, 8–9

Rousseau's admiration of, 524, 535, 536, 539

as timocracy, 67

trade by, 88

tyranny replaced by democracy in, 9

species-being, 779, 780

speech, 105

freedom of, xxiii, 251, 444, 445, 610, 718, 926

"Speech on Conciliation with America" (Burke), 619, 629

"Speech to the Electors of Bristol" (Burke), 620

Spencer, Herbert, 952

spheres of influence, 847

spinning mills, 891

Spinoza, Baruch, 675

"Spirit of the Age, The" (J. S. Mill), 708

Spirit of the Law (Montesquieu), 500, 519, 523–24, 531, 556, 594

spiritual law, 338

spontaneous sociability, 406

sporting societies, 674

squadristi, 939–40

stagnation, 820

Stalin, Joseph, 70, 182, 561, 803, 812, 907, 914, 916, 924, 925–27, 940, 941, 945

anti-Semitic campaign of, 832

genocide used as political tool by, 941, 942–43

Marxism as surrogate religion under, 982

on Marx's writing, 906

purges by, 839

Stände, 686, 688–89

standing armies, 617

starvation, 315

stasis, 92, 100–105, 169, 498, 530, 631, 792, 967

state:

administrative capacity of, 688

as artificial, 406

Church's fostering of modern image of, 188, 403–4

civil society vs., 906–7

for commodious living, 430

constitutions of, 76

as corporate entities, 404

as entity with unified authority, 188

as existing naturally, 240

failed, 1011

families vs., 979

Hegel's account of, 656, 670, 683–84, 685–94, 933, 939

humanitarian intervention and, 1005–7

individual as prior to, 78

legitimacy of, 406, 556, 558–64, 569–70, 572, 573–76, 693, 736, 901, 1004

Locke on nature of, 492–93

as March of God on Earth, 658

Marx on, 771

meanings of, 275

origins of, 408, 557

outward freedom grounded in, 670

property protected by, 551

punishment by, 176

push toward disorder in, 182

rights against, 683

Rousseau on necessity of, 885

scope of authority of, 406

self-sufficiency of, 7

setting up, 482–88

socialist view of, 884–85

state of nature before, 406

as work of art, 377

world, 979

see also church-state relationship

state capitalism, 792

statecraft, philosophy vs., 117–20, 509

state-of-nature theories, 655, 727

Statesman (Plato), 38, 118

statute of alienation, 507

Statute of Mortmain (1279), 212

statute of retainers, 507

steam engine, 791

Stirner, Max, 895

Stoicism, Stoics, 94, 119, 120, 137, 138, 165, 287, 565, 628

apatheia doctrine of, 237–38

on corruption, 237

on equality, 238

freedom as viewed by, 662–64

natural equality accepted by, 205

on natural law, 143, 413

on origins of society, 58

on property, 212, 244

slavery sanctioned by, 582, 662–63

on virtues, 144, 297, 304, 358, 554

Straits of Gibraltar, 853
Strategic Air Command, U.S., 999
strategic theorists, 433–34
strategoi, 12
Stuart, House of, 459, 510, 587, 589, 631
students, 906
Students for a Democratic Society, 971
Subjection of Women, The (J. S. Mill), 707, 726–28
subsistence wages, 786
substantial class, 687
substitutism, Trotsky's concept of, 922
Sudan, 994–95, 996
Suez Canal, 648, 983
suffering, 159–60, 162
Suffolk, Duke of, 308
suicide, 161, 214, 429, 682
    Agustine's denunciation of, 173–74, 175
    laws against, 471, 472
suicide bombers, 988
Sulla, Cornelius Lucius, 113–14, 118, 138, 147, 508
Summa contra Gentiles (Aquinas), 227, 232
Summa Theologiae (Aquinas), 225, 227, 232, 239
Summary View of the Rights of British America (Jefferson), 584, 587
Sunnis, 989
superego, 716
superpowers, 994
superstitions, 641, 980
Supplément au voyage de Bougainville (Diderot), 859
Supreme Court, U.S., 529–30, 591, 608, 747, 985
surplus motivation, 280
surplus repression, 832
surplus value, 777, 787–88, 804
surveillance, in Athens, xvii
suttee, 205, 1007
suzerainty, 15, 263, 280, 369
Sweden, 323
Swetchine, Mme, 732
Switzerland, 93, 343, 344, 363–64, 375, 502, 547, 949
syllogisms, 268, 292, 293
Sylvester I, Pope, 270
Sylvester III, Pope, 218, 234
Symposium (Plato), 38

syndicates, 935–36
synoikismos, 8
Syracuse, 20, 68, 86, 377
System of Logic, A (J. S. Mill), 704–5
System of Politics, A (Harrington), 509

Tacitus, 111, 581, 1000
Tahiti, 859
Taiwan, 993
Tarquin, 173
Tarquin monarchy, 140
taxation, 253, 286, 306, 387, 477, 478, 511, 626
    American complaints against, 582, 589
    Christine de Pisan on, 298
    of clergy, 260, 262
    consent for, 195
    equality achieved by, 886
    for established churches, 644
    inheritance, 640–41, 644
    Paine on, 638–39
    passive obedience and, 201
    in poor economies, 901
    Roman Catholic Church's exemption from, 211–12, 259
    in Rome, xiii, 133, 135
    in U.S. Constitution, 598
    wars financed by, 513
Taylor, Harriet, 703, 706, 707, 715
Taylor, John, 703, 706
technocracy, 957
technology, 531, 790, 795, 986
    as indebted to Arab scholars, 213
    military, 405
teleology, 75–78, 276, 420, 426, 465
temperance, 63, 119, 287, 296
temperate rule, 275–76
Ten of War, 354–55, 379
terrorism, 816, 987, 988–89, 994
Test Acts (1872), 456
Test and Corporation Acts, 765
textile industry, 752, 825–26
textual criticism, 292
Thagaste, 151, 163
Thebes, 16, 24, 28, 72, 369
theft, Aquinas on, 246
Themistocles, 16
theocracy, 181, 230
theocratic dictatorships, 818–19

theodicy, 664, 670

Theodosius, Emperor of Rome, 148, 155, 202

theologians, 229

theology, 301
  philosophy and, 229–30, 236

Theories of Surplus Value (Marx), 771

theory of cross-cutting cleavage, 604

Theory of Justice, A (Rawls), 947, 972–77

theory of surplus value, 777, 787–88, 804

theory of the "Asiatic mode of production," 793, 794

Theory of the Four Movements, The (Fourier), 889

Theramenes, 28–29

Thermopylae, 16

Theseus, 370, 384

Thespians, 16

thetes, 10, 27

Third Crusade, 235

Third Punic War, 112, 121

Third Republic, French, 535, 636, 646

Third World revolutionaries, 907

Thirty Tyrants, 28, 35, 49, 95

Thirty Years' War, 344, 847, 990

Thomas à Becket, 219

Thomas à Kempis, 301, 331

Thomas Aquinas, 188, 190, 224, 244, 267, 275, 499, 851
  Aristotle's influence on, 224, 225, 231, 236–37, 238–39, 242–43, 248, 254, 329
  as difficult for modern reader, 225–26
  hierarchy accepted by, 240
  on justice, 251
  just war theory of, 247–48, 852
  Locke as disciple of, 255
  monarchy defended by, 239, 271, 284
  on property rights, 244, 475, 478
  on religious toleration, 248–49
  slavery accepted by, 254
  teleological view of, 238
  Unam Sanctam's drawing on, 263–64

Thoreau, Henry, 552, 573

Thoughts on the Cause of the Present Discontents (Burke), 620

Thrasybulus, 29

Thrasymachus, 39, 44, 49, 52–53, 55, 56–58, 62, 69, 70, 80, 81, 437, 466, 713

Three Essays on Religion (J. S. Mill), 707

three-mile limit, 855

Thucydides, 12–13, 14, 18–20, 63, 95, 111, 126, 382, 414, 417, 418, 949
  aristocratic sympathies of, 14, 414
  on Athens as monarchy, 127
  on enslavement of Melos, 19–20, 23–25
  lessons in past sought by, xix
  Pericles's funeral oration recorded by, 19, 20–22
  on power, 847
  "rule by first man" praised by, 12–13

Timaeus (Plato), 32, 229

time, 152

timocracy, 67

Titmuss, Richard, 903

Tito, Josip Broz, 927

tobacco, 751

Tocqueville, Alexis de, xviii, 500, 519–20, 526, 609, 647, 651, 729–69, 824, 865, 901, 947
  ambiguous views of individualism of, 710–11, 737, 755–56, 761, 821, 823, 824, 825, 831–32, 833
  on freedoms preserved by aritsocratic order, 761–62
  French imperialism defended by, 729, 731, 740, 762–64, 862
  Guizot's influence on, 738–40
  and liberalism as resting on conservative basis, 728
  Mill influenced by, 704, 705, 710–11, 715, 716, 720–21, 727, 733, 737, 740, 741, 743–44, 756, 761, 762, 825
  moeurs seen as important by, 629, 740–41, 744, 745, 749, 752, 759, 760, 907
  Montesquieu's influence on, 737–38, 752, 757
  Native American sympathies of, 729, 746, 753, 763, 862
  religion seen as indispensable by, 629–30, 981, 985
  on revolutions, 729
  Rousseau's influence on, 736–37, 738
  on savagery of ancien régime, 641
  as shaped by French Revolution, 616, 759, 764–66
  in trip to U.S., 618, 729, 736
  welfare state denounced by, 904
  see also Democracy in America

Tocqueville, Édouard, 731
Tocqueville, Hervé, 730–31
Tocqueville, Hippolyte, 731
Tocqueville, Mary Mottley, 732
toleration, 158, 183, 338, 419, 448, 581
    Aquinas on, 248–49
    by Islam, 213–14
    Locke's endorsement of, 453, 454–55,
        456–57, 458, 466, 491–96, 817
    Paine's opposition to, 646
Tolstoy, Leo, 999
torture, 1005
    in conversion, 164
    in Rome, 177
Tory Party, 529, 619, 695, 883
totalitarianism, 32, 318, 834, 911–45
    arbitrary violence in, 915
    cult of leadership in, 915
    liberal democracy's Cold War battle with,
        942
    in Marxism, 922–24
    mass mobilization in, 915
    as phenomenon of mass society, 915
    privacy abolished in, 915
    regulation of life sought by, 809
    soft, 927, 941–45
    trade unions destroyed in, 915
    in utopias, 922–23
Totalitarianism (Arendt), 916
Tours, France, 213
trade, 361, 446, 474, 845–46
    by Athens, 7, 10, 56, 522
    by Florence, 361, 363
    in Rome, 124
    Sparta and, 88
    in U.S., 613, 614, 751
traders, 388
trade unions, xiv, 90, 674, 901–2, 915, 935
traditionalists, 443
traffic regulations, 201, 470
tragedy of the commons, 1010
tranquilization, 817
transferable-vote system, 723–24
transmigration of souls, 165
transubstantiation, 300
travail attractif, 890–92, 908, 909
treachery, 287
Treasury of the City of Ladies, The (Christine de
    Pizan), 295

Treaty of Dover, 455
Treaty of Paris, 590
Treaty of Westphalia, 847
Trenton, Battle of, 637
trial, 36, 490, 500, 730
    by combat, 269–70
    of foreigners, 488
    by jury, 571, 610
    as right, 488, 1005
    in Rome, 132
Trinitarianism, 198
Trinity, 152, 273, 346
triumvirate, 115, 136
Trotsky, Leon, 95, 611, 792, 801, 914, 922,
    925, 941, 943, 1009
True History (Lucian), 312
Truman, David, 956
truth, 59, 60, 66
    as divine, 231
    duty vs., 320
Tuileries, 625
twelfth-century renaissance, 220, 230
"twelve good men," 361
Twenty-First Amendment, U.S., 748
Two Treatises of Civil Government (Locke), 455,
    463, 484, 494, 594
    see also First Treatise (Locke), *Second Treatise*
        (Locke)
tyche (fate), 381, 384, 577
tyrannicide, 200–201, 440
    Cicero's approval of, 181, 221, 306
    classical Roman view of, 201
    of heretical monarchs, 447
    John of Salisbury's approval of, 222–23
tyranny of the majority, 592, 611–12, 621,
    715, 746–47, 750–51, 760–63, 820,
    967, 974–75
tyrants, tyranny, 9, 42, 68, 69, 70, 98, 99,
    124, 125, 126, 141–42, 194, 251, 283,
    284, 287, 360, 516
    Aquinas on, 239–40
    Aristotle's advice to, 101–2, 118
    Bartolus's disdain for, 285, 357
    degeneration into, 104
    employment rights and, 608
    Erasmus's disapproval of, 303, 305–6
    favoring of tyrants in, 53
    as Greek term, 5
    Hobbes on, 384, 497

Justinian on, 283
kings vs., 221
Machiavelli's ambiguous views of, 286, 357, 384, 573
monarchy and, 348
as "monarchy misliked," 384
Plato's disapproval of, 35
prevention of, 281
princes vs., 220
Republican advocacy of, 418
self-reliance and, 752
Sidney on, 516
Socrates's disapproval of, 35
as transition, 286, 357
U.S. founding and, 582
Tyrol, Countess of, 273

Uganda, 996
Ulpian, on jus gentium, 207
ultranationalism, 914, 917, 937, 995
Unam sanctam (papal bull), 262, 263–64
unanimity, 570
underconsumption, 867, 868
unemployment, unemployed, 313, 937
    reserved army of, 792
unemployment benefits, 828, 900, 901, 903
unions, 881
Unitarianism, 316
United Nations, 1005
    Charter of, 178, 317, 1004, 1009
United Nations Law of the Sea Conference, 855
United States, 6, 10, 28, 181, 258, 689, 798
    agricultural economy of, 751–52
    antagonism of opinions in, 751
    army of, 511–12
    association in, 755, 757–59, 768
    Bentham's prison reform and, 696
    bureaucracy in, 965–66
    capitalism, 935
    Ciceronian ideals in, 195
    citizenship in, 95
    class hatred absent from, 764, 795, 953, 954
    in Cold War, *see* Cold War
    communitarian movement in, 715, 889–90
    culture of, 735–36
    and dispute between Athens and Rome, xiii

diversity of American society, 720
division of authority in, 567, 571, 572
English system of representation in, 195
equality in, 742–43, 745–46, 755–56
expanding political representation in, 843
family in, 755, 759–60, 824
foreign policy of, 860, 1009
freedom of opinion in, 711
frontier in, 755
as "global" colonizing power, 996
Hegel on future of, 665
immigrants in, 762, 764, 930
imperialism of, 845, 847, 869
individualism in, 823, 824
Japanese Americans interned by, 558
justice and, xxiii
liberty in, xxiii
lonely crowd in, 755, 756, 822, 825, 916
manufactures in, 613–14
middle class in, 103, 715, 746, 764
as mixed republic, 607
multiplicity of legal systems in, 444
nuclear weapons of, 434, 840, 842, 990
pluralism in, 571–72
politicians despised in, 962
possibility of military despotism in, 821
pressure groups in, 966–67
primary elections in, xvi
protectionism in, 937
racism in, 930, 950
religion in, 66, 752–53, 985
self-interest in, 757–59, 768
self-reliance in, 751, 752, 760–63
separation of powers in, 103
slavery in, xxiv, 85, 87, 578, 661, 662, 746, 753–54, 964
socialist revolution expected in, 919
threat of class warfare in, 905
tyranny of majority in, 750–51, 760–63
voting rights in, 951
wars of, 993
weak central government in, 750–51, 758
wealth distribution in, 103
westward expansion of, 751, 754–55, 816, 845, 868
women in, 735–36, 759, 760
    see also Democracy in America
unity, 247
universal class, 686, 805

universalism, 874
universities, 109, 196, 228
unproductive labor, 909
urban riots, 766, 767
Urban VI, Pope, 288
usury, 91, 253
utilitarianism, 58, 243, 466, 672, 695–728, 1001
  and case against revolutions, 627
  criticism of, 711, 712–13
  education and, 109
  equality under, 726
  God and, 712
  happiness in, 672, 677, 708, 712–14, 715
  human nature in, 711, 727
  justice in, 714–15
  liberalism vs., 860
  Mill's broadening of, 702
  morality and, 711–13
  as opposed to idea of legitimacy, 572
  as practicable, 711
  as secular, 708
  slavery and, 677
  sovereignty viewed by, 567
  thin, 709
  as universalist, 708
  world government desired by, 1003–4
Utilitarianism (J. S. Mill), 706, 711–15, 722
utility, 244, 786
  definition of, 711–12
utility-maximizers, 80
Utopia (More), 31, 294, 301, 303, 311, 312–19, 387, 510, 575
  labor in, 314–15
  money abolished in, 314, 315, 882
  religion in, 316–17
  war in, 317–18
utopian socialism, 785, 879–80, 884
utopias, 913
  Aristotle's dismissal of, 70, 107
  of Dante, 266
  in early nineteenth century, 648, 889–90, 891
  failed, 880–92
  of humanists, 293
  Huxley's parody of, 61–62, 63
  lack of permanence of, 65, 67–70
  Lenin's view of, 467
  in *Looking Backwards*, 315

  loss of aspirations for, 817
  of Machiavelli, 293
  Madison's opposition to, 597
  of Marx, 33, 770, 806
  in Müntzer uprising, 351
  in *Oceania*, 510
  Peasants' Rebellion and, 330
  Pico della Mirandola as precursor of, 301
  of Plato, 33–34, 56, 65, 66–67, 80, 89, 106, 138–39, 303, 386, 650
  Polybius on, 124, 138–39
  Rousseau's opposition to, 548
  Saint-Simonianism, 647
  as totalitarian, 922–23
  travail attractif and, 909

vacuum, 414, 417, 422
vainglory, 433, 435, 436, 543
valentior pars, 277
Valerius Maximus, 297, 299
Valhalla, 31
Valladolid controversy, 852–53, 856
Valois, 355, 360
values (*moeurs*), 527, 574, 629, 740–41, 744, 745, 749, 752, 759, 760, 907
Vandals, 152
Vatican, 936
Vattel, Emerich, 856, 857
vegetarianism, 159, 161
veil of ignorance, 972–73
Venetian empire, 387, 844
Venice, 234, 316, 361, 499, 502, 507, 508, 529, 607
  aristocratic republic of, 387–88
  maritime empire of, 387, 844
Verona, 266, 272
Verres, prosecution of, 114
Versailles, 625, 640
Versailles, Treaty of, 929
Vesta, temple of, 114
veto point, 968
vice-regents, 285, 286
Vichy regime, 636, 933
Vietcong, 317
Vietnam War, 317, 487, 841, 971, 1102
Vincennes, 540
Vindication of the Rights of Man, A
  (Wollstonecraft), 295, 622

Vindication of the Rights of Woman, A
    (Wollstonecraft), 295, 555, 622
violence, 180, 928–29
    Fanon's endorsement of, 873
    Freud on, 642, 928, 933, 997
    Hobbes on, 642, 987–88
Virgil, 124
Virginia, 595
    constitution of, 597
    legislature of, 587
Virginia, University of, 585, 970
Virginia Declaration of Rights, 588–89,
    595, 696
Virginia statute on religious freedom, 585,
    595
virtual representation, 690
virtues, 79, 117, 183, 601, 714, 967
    Christian vs. classical views on, 243, 297
    Cicero on, 137, 144, 297
    happiness and, 304
    Machiavelli on, for princes, 292, 293,
        370, 375, 376, 377, 522
    Montesquieu on, 601, 667, 737
    in republic, 522
    rights vs., 581
    Stoics on, 144, 297, 304, 358, 554
Visconti family, 272
Visigoths, 152, 164, 165
Vitoria, Francisco de, 818, 850–53, 854,
    857
vivere civile, 376
vocational education, 229
Voltaire, 170, 196, 533, 550, 633, 635, 772
volunteer groups, 976
voting rights:
    English Reform Bill and, 655, 690, 698
    James Mill's desire for universality of,
        698
    in liberal democracies, xiii–xiv, xvii
    plural, 706, 723
    in Rome, xiii, 129, 133, 135, 141
    universal, 698, 745, 784, 837, 879, 885–
        86, 947, 949–50, 972
    of women, 94, 706, 707, 722, 843, 949
voyages of discovery, 406

wages, 792
wages of superintendence, 786
Wagner, Richard, 865, 930

Walden Pond, 552
Wallace, George, 965
Wallis, John, 414, 417
Walpole, Robert, 529
war, warfare, 74, 169, 313, 374, 377, 379, 437,
        442, 522, 691–92
    civil, 127–28, 968, 994
    Erasmus's hatred of, 302, 306, 308–9,
        317, 849
    financing of, 513
    glorification of, 998–99
    as health of state, 933
    Hobbes on, 432–35, 817, 832
    humanitarianism and, 306
    just, *see* just war
    More on, 317–18
    over resources, 812–13
    priests and, 317–18
    self-defense as grounds for, 847
    in sixteenth century, 307
ward republics, 520, 583, 611, 819, 970
Warens, Mme de, 532, 533
warfare, 641
warlords, 188, 505–6
war of conquest, 874
War of 1812, 596, 857
wars of religion, 982
    sixteenth and seventeenth century, 183,
        499, 534, 632, 989
Wars of the Roses, 191
*Warum gibt es in den Vereinigten Staaten keinen
        Sozialismus?* (Sombart), 828
Washington, D.C., 577, 596
Washington, George, 125, 508, 578, 595,
        605, 637, 735
water, clean, xix
Wayne, John, 841
We (Zamyatin), 942–43
wealth, lozenge-shaped distribution of, 103,
        104
Wealth of Nations (Smith), 1008
weapons of mass destruction, 990
weaving sheds, 891
Webb, Beatrice, 900
Webb, Sidney, 900
Weber, Max, 314, 745, 750, 806, 835–36,
        837, 928, 946, 965, 969, 974
Weimar Republic, 965
Weitling, Wilhelm, 793

welfare states, 246, 446, 638, 641, 798, 879,
  880, 935, 984
  as accepted by reformist socialists, 894
  Bismarck's creation of, 801
  in capitalist systems, 905
  creation of, 900–901
  defenses of, 902–3
  Hegel's justification for, 687–88
  liberal democracies and, 818, 903–4
  questions raised by, 905–10
  socialism and, 894, 904–5
Wells, H. G., 900
Weltgeschichte ("world history"), 664–65, 689
Wenceslaus, Holy Roman Emperor, 343
Wesley, John, 595
West Germany, 907
West Indies, 406–7, 849
Westphalia, 352
Westphalia, Treaty of, 847
whalers, 629
What Is to Be Done? (Lenin), 921–22
Whigs, 529, 619, 629
  Country, 513, 579
Whitefield, George, 595
White Guelphs, 265
"white man's burden," 844, 847, 868
White Russians, 924–25
Why I Am Not a Communist (Russell), 928–29
Wilde, Oscar, 977
Wild Man of Borneo, 542
will:
  freedom of, 675, 678
  general, 560–64, 566–71, 598, 673, 736
  in Hegel's theory, 673, 675, 676
  Marx on, 924
  as source of freedom, 666
William of Moerbeke, 227, 230
William of Ockham, 257, 288–89, 290
William of Orange (William III), 456, 459,
  460, 489, 506, 579, 631
William Pitt the Younger, 621
William the Conqueror, 188, 420, 646
will of all, general will vs., 571–72
wills, 168
  as irremediably sinful, 329
  punishment and, 176
Wilson, Woodrow, 748
wisdom, 119, 145, 147
Witherspoon, John, 519, 584, 595

Wittenberg, 327, 328, 344, 405
Wittenberg, University of, 328
wives, 74, 82, 84–85, 87
Wolin, Sheldon, 376
Wollstonecraft, Mary, 295, 555, 622, 641
Wolsey, Cardinal, 311
women, xviii, xxiv, 555
  at Academy, 59
  Aristotle on, 73–75, 93, 110
  in Athens, 10, 136
  in Rome, 135, 136, 574
  suffrage of, 94, 706, 707, 722, 843, 949
  in U.S., 735–36, 759, 760
Wood, Gordon, xxi
Woolf, Virginia, 411
wool trade, 313
worker capitalism, 893
workers' cooperatives, see cooperatives
working class, 715, 801–2, 810
world government, 979, 997, 999–1001,
  1002–4, 1010
world history, 664–65, 689
World War I, 213, 809, 832, 838, 843–44,
  845, 866, 878, 929, 997
World War II, 15, 433, 809, 817, 844, 845,
  855, 875, 907, 941–42, 966, 986, 989,
  995, 1001
worship, freedom of, xxiii
Wretched of the Earth, The (Fanon), 871, 873,
  991
writing, invention of, 35
Wyclif, John, 321, 330

Xenocrates, 72
Xenophon, 34, 302, 517
Xerxes, 6–7, 16, 693, 983

Year Five of the Algerian Revolution (Fanon), 873
yellow press, 822
York, Duke of, see James II, King of England
Yorktown, Battle of, 589
Young Hegelian movement, 773, 775
Yugoslavia, 870, 927, 989

Zamyatin, Evgeny, 942–43
Zasulich, Vera, 924
Zoroastrianism, 159
Zurich, 343, 344, 346, 347
Zwingli, Ulrich, 346, 350

ALLEN LANE
an imprint of
PENGUIN BOOKS

Recently Published

Sendhil Mullainathan & Eldar Shafir, *Scarcity: Why Having Too Little Means So Much*

John Drury, *Music at Midnight: The Life and Poetry of George Herbert*

Philip Coggan, *The Last Vote: The Threats to Western Democracy*

Richard Barber, *Edward III and the Triumph of England*

Daniel M Davis, *The Compatibility Gene*

John Bradshaw, *Cat Sense: The Feline Enigma Revealed*

Roger Knight, *Britain Against Napoleon: The Organisation of Victory, 1793-1815*

Thurston Clarke, *JFK's Last Hundred Days: An Intimate Portrait of a Great President*

Jean Drèze and Amartya Sen, *An Uncertain Glory: India and its Contradictions*

Rana Mitter, *China's War with Japan, 1937-1945: The Struggle for Survival*

Tom Burns, *Our Necessary Shadow: The Nature and Meaning of Psychiatry*

Sylvain Tesson, *Consolations of the Forest: Alone in a Cabin in the Middle Taiga*

George Monbiot, *Feral: Searching for Enchantment on the Frontiers of Rewilding*

Ken Robinson and Lou Aronica, *Finding Your Element: How to Discover Your Talents and Passions and Transform Your Life*

David Stuckler and Sanjay Basu, *The Body Economic: Why Austerity Kills*

Suzanne Corkin, *Permanent Present Tense: The Man with No Memory, and What He Taught the World*

Daniel C. Dennett, *Intuition Pumps and Other Tools for Thinking*

Adrian Raine, *The Anatomy of Violence: The Biological Roots of Crime*

Eduardo Galeano, *Children of the Days: A Calendar of Human History*

Lee Smolin, *Time Reborn: From the Crisis of Physics to the Future of the Universe*

Michael Pollan, *Cooked: A Natural History of Transformation*

David Graeber, *The Democracy Project: A History, a Crisis, a Movement*

Brendan Simms, *Europe: The Struggle for Supremacy, 1453 to the Present*

Oliver Bullough, *The Last Man in Russia and the Struggle to Save a Dying Nation*

Diarmaid MacCulloch, *Silence: A Christian History*

Evgeny Morozov, *To Save Everything, Click Here: Technology, Solutionism, and the Urge to Fix Problems that Don't Exist*

David Cannadine, *The Undivided Past: History Beyond Our Differences*

Michael Axworthy, *Revolutionary Iran: A History of the Islamic Republic*

Jaron Lanier, *Who Owns the Future?*

John Gray, *The Silence of Animals: On Progress and Other Modern Myths*

Paul Kildea, *Benjamin Britten: A Life in the Twentieth Century*

Jared Diamond, *The World Until Yesterday: What Can We Learn from Traditional Societies?*

Nassim Nicholas Taleb, *Antifragile: How to Live in a World We Don't Understand*

Alan Ryan, *On Politics: A History of Political Thought from Herodotus to the Present*

Roberto Calasso, *La Folie Baudelaire*

Carolyn Abbate and Roger Parker, *A History of Opera: The Last Four Hundred Years*

Yang Jisheng, *Tombstone: The Untold Story of Mao's Great Famine*

Caleb Scharf, *Gravity's Engines: The Other Side of Black Holes*

Jancis Robinson, Julia Harding and José Vouillamoz, *Wine Grapes: A Complete Guide to 1,368 Vine Varieties, including their Origins and Flavours*

David Bownes, Oliver Green and Sam Mullins, *Underground: How the Tube Shaped London*

Niall Ferguson, *The Great Degeneration: How Institutions Decay and Economies Die*

Chrystia Freeland, *Plutocrats: The Rise of the New Global Super-Rich*

David Thomson, *The Big Screen: The Story of the Movies and What They Did to Us*

Halik Kochanski, *The Eagle Unbowed: Poland and the Poles in the Second World War*

Kofi Annan with Nader Mousavizadeh, *Interventions: A Life in War and Peace*

Mark Mazower, *Governing the World: The History of an Idea*

Anne Applebaum, *Iron Curtain: The Crushing of Eastern Europe 1944-56*

Steven Johnson, *Future Perfect: The Case for Progress in a Networked Age*

Christopher Clark, *The Sleepwalkers: How Europe Went to War in 1914*

Neil MacGregor, *Shakespeare's Restless World*

Nate Silver, *The Signal and the Noise: The Art and Science of Prediction*

Chinua Achebe, *There Was a Country: A Personal History of Biafra*

John Darwin, *Unfinished Empire: The Global Expansion of Britain*

Jerry Brotton, *A History of the World in Twelve Maps*

Patrick Hennessey, *KANDAK: Fighting with Afghans*

Katherine Angel, *Unmastered: A Book on Desire, Most Difficult to Tell*

David Priestland, *Merchant, Soldier, Sage: A New History of Power*

Stephen Alford, *The Watchers: A Secret History of the Reign of Elizabeth I*

Tom Feiling, *Short Walks from Bogotá: Journeys in the New Colombia*

Pankaj Mishra, *From the Ruins of Empire: The Revolt Against the West and the Remaking of Asia*

Geza Vermes, *Christian Beginnings: From Nazareth to Nicaea, AD 30-325*

Steve Coll, *Private Empire: ExxonMobil and American Power*

Joseph Stiglitz, *The Price of Inequality*

Dambisa Moyo, *Winner Take All: China's Race for Resources and What it Means for Us*

Robert Skidelsky and Edward Skidelsky, *How Much is Enough? The Love of Money, and the Case for the Good Life*

Frances Ashcroft, *The Spark of Life: Electricity in the Human Body*

Sebastian Seung, *Connectome: How the Brain's Wiring Makes Us Who We Are*

Callum Roberts, *Ocean of Life*

Orlando Figes, *Just Send Me Word: A True Story of Love and Survival in the Gulag*

Leonard Mlodinow, *Subliminal: The Revolution of the New Unconscious and What it Teaches Us about Ourselves*

John Romer, *A History of Ancient Egypt: From the First Farmers to the Great Pyramid*

Ruchir Sharma, *Breakout Nations: In Pursuit of the Next Economic Miracle*

Michael J. Sandel, *What Money Can't Buy: The Moral Limits of Markets*

Dominic Sandbrook, *Seasons in the Sun: The Battle for Britain, 1974-1979*

Tariq Ramadan, *The Arab Awakening: Islam and the New Middle East*

Jonathan Haidt, *The Righteous Mind: Why Good People are Divided by Politics and Religion*

Ahmed Rashid, *Pakistan on the Brink: The Future of Pakistan, Afghanistan and the West*

Tim Weiner, *Enemies: A History of the FBI*

Mark Pagel, *Wired for Culture: The Natural History of Human Cooperation*

George Dyson, *Turing's Cathedral: The Origins of the Digital Universe*

Cullen Murphy, *God's Jury: The Inquisition and the Making of the Modern World*

Richard Sennett, *Together: The Rituals, Pleasures and Politics of Co-operation*

Faramerz Dabhoiwala, *The Origins of Sex: A History of the First Sexual Revolution*

Roy F. Baumeister and John Tierney, *Willpower: Rediscovering Our Greatest Strength*

Jesse J. Prinz, *Beyond Human Nature: How Culture and Experience Shape Our Lives*

Robert Holland, *Blue-Water Empire: The British in the Mediterranean since 1800*

Jodi Kantor, *The Obamas: A Mission, A Marriage*

Philip Coggan, *Paper Promises: Money, Debt and the New World Order*

Charles Nicholl, *Traces Remain: Essays and Explorations*

Daniel Kahneman, *Thinking, Fast and Slow*

Hunter S. Thompson, *Fear and Loathing at Rolling Stone: The Essential Writing of Hunter S. Thompson*

Duncan Campbell-Smith, *Masters of the Post: The Authorized History of the Royal Mail*

Colin McEvedy, *Cities of the Classical World: An Atlas and Gazetteer of 120 Centres of Ancient Civilization*

Heike B. Görtemaker, *Eva Braun: Life with Hitler*

Brian Cox and Jeff Forshaw, *The Quantum Universe: Everything that Can Happen Does Happen*

Nathan D. Wolfe, *The Viral Storm: The Dawn of a New Pandemic Age*

Norman Davies, *Vanished Kingdoms: The History of Half-Forgotten Europe*

Michael Lewis, *Boomerang: The Meltdown Tour*

Steven Pinker, *The Better Angels of Our Nature: The Decline of Violence in History and Its Causes*

Robert Trivers, *Deceit and Self-Deception: Fooling Yourself the Better to Fool Others*

Thomas Penn, *Winter King: The Dawn of Tudor England*

Daniel Yergin, *The Quest: Energy, Security and the Remaking of the Modern World*

Michael Moore, *Here Comes Trouble: Stories from My Life*

Ali Soufan, *The Black Banners: Inside the Hunt for Al Qaeda*

Jason Burke, *The 9/11 Wars*

Timothy D. Wilson, *Redirect: The Surprising New Science of Psychological Change*

Ian Kershaw, *The End: Hitler's Germany, 1944-45*

T M Devine, *To the Ends of the Earth: Scotland's Global Diaspora, 1750-2010*

Catherine Hakim, *Honey Money: The Power of Erotic Capital*

Douglas Edwards, *I'm Feeling Lucky: The Confessions of Google Employee Number 59*

John Bradshaw, *In Defence of Dogs*

Chris Stringer, *The Origin of Our Species*

Lila Azam Zanganeh, *The Enchanter: Nabokov and Happiness*

David Stevenson, *With Our Backs to the Wall: Victory and Defeat in 1918*

Evelyn Juers, *House of Exile: War, Love and Literature, from Berlin to Los Angeles*

Henry Kissinger, *On China*

Michio Kaku, *Physics of the Future: How Science Will Shape Human Destiny and Our Daily Lives by the Year 2100*

David Abulafia, *The Great Sea: A Human History of the Mediterranean*

John Gribbin, *The Reason Why: The Miracle of Life on Earth*

Anatol Lieven, *Pakistan: A Hard Country*

William Cohen, *Money and Power: How Goldman Sachs Came to Rule the World*

Joshua Foer, *Moonwalking with Einstein: The Art and Science of Remembering Everything*

Simon Baron-Cohen, *Zero Degrees of Empathy: A New Theory of Human Cruelty*

Manning Marable, *Malcolm X: A Life of Reinvention*

David Deutsch, *The Beginning of Infinity: Explanations that Transform the World*

David Edgerton, *Britain's War Machine: Weapons, Resources and Experts in the Second World War*

John Kasarda and Greg Lindsay, *Aerotropolis: The Way We'll Live Next*

David Gilmour, *The Pursuit of Italy: A History of a Land, Its Regions and Their Peoples*

Niall Ferguson, *Civilization: The West and the Rest*

Tim Flannery, *Here on Earth: A New Beginning*

Robert Bickers, *The Scramble for China: Foreign Devils in the Qing Empire, 1832-1914*

Mark Malloch-Brown, *The Unfinished Global Revolution: The Limits of Nations and the Pursuit of a New Politics*

King Abdullah of Jordan, *Our Last Best Chance: The Pursuit of Peace in a Time of Peril*

Eliza Griswold, *The Tenth Parallel: Dispatches from the Faultline between Christianity and Islam*

Brian Greene, *The Hidden Reality: Parallel Universes and the Deep Laws of the Cosmos*

John Gray, *The Immortalization Commission: The Strange Quest to Cheat Death*

Patrick French, *India: A Portrait*

Lizzie Collingham, *The Taste of War: World War Two and the Battle for Food*

Hooman Majd, *The Ayatollahs' Democracy: An Iranian Challenge*

Dambisa Moyo, *How The West Was Lost: Fifty Years of Economic Folly - and the Stark Choices Ahead*

Evgeny Morozov, *The Net Delusion: How Not to Liberate the World*

Ron Chernow, *Washington: A Life*

Nassim Nicholas Taleb, *The Bed of Procrustes: Philosophical and Practical Aphorisms*

Hugh Thomas, *The Golden Age: The Spanish Empire of Charles V*

Amanda Foreman, *A World on Fire: An Epic History of Two Nations Divided*

Nicholas Ostler, *The Last Lingua Franca: English until the Return of Babel*

Richard Miles, *Ancient Worlds: The Search for the Origins of Western Civilization*

Neil MacGregor, *A History of the World in 100 Objects*

Steven Johnson, *Where Good Ideas Come From: The Natural History of Innovation*

Dominic Sandbrook, *State of Emergency: The Way We Were: Britain, 1970-1974*

Jim Al-Khalili, *Pathfinders: The Golden Age of Arabic Science*

Ha-Joon Chang, *23 Things They Don't Tell You About Capitalism*

Robin Fleming, *Britain After Rome: The Fall and Rise, 400 to 1070*

Tariq Ramadan, *The Quest for Meaning: Developing a Philosophy of Pluralism*

Joyce Tyldesley, *The Penguin Book of Myths and Legends of Ancient Egypt*

Nicholas Phillipson, *Adam Smith: An Enlightened Life*

Paul Greenberg, *Four Fish: A Journey from the Ocean to Your Plate*